PAGE 54

ON THE ROAD

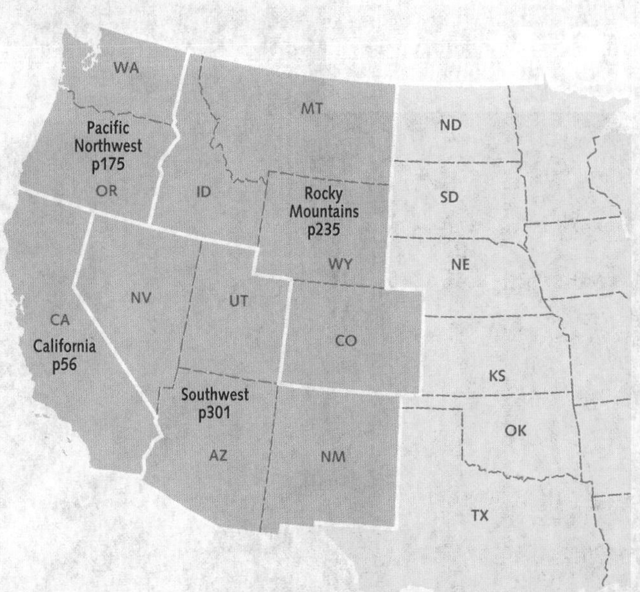

PAGE 439

SURVIVAL GUIDE

VITAL PRACTICAL INFORMATION TO HELP YOU HAVE A SMOOTH TRIP

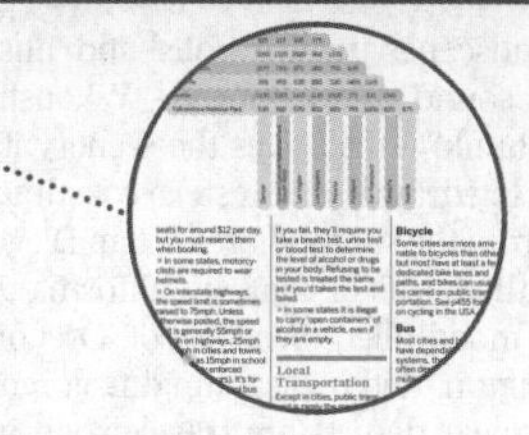

THIS EDITION WRITTEN AND RESEARCHED BY
Amy C Balfour
Michael Benanav, Andrew Bender, Sara Benson, Alison Bing, Nate Cavalieri, Sarah Chandler, Lisa Dunford, Bridget Gleeson, Beth Kohn, Bradley Mayhew, Carolyn B McCarthy, Brendan Sainsbury, Andrea Schulte-Peevers, John A Vlahides

welcome to Western USA

Great Outdoors

Western landscapes inspire 'oohs' and 'ahs,' but it's the sound of adventure – Whoosh! Splash! Kathunk! – that gives the scenery its punch. The big draw is the western coastline, stretching from the sunny shores of San Diego north past the bluffs of central California to the rocky, mood-filled beaches of Oregon and Washington. Red rocks, plunging gorges and prickly-pear deserts are traveler bait in the Southwest where the biggest wonder is the Grand Canyon, a 277-mile stunner that shares its geologic treasures with a healthy dose of fun. In the Rockies, skiing, ice climbing and mountain-biking never looked so pretty. The best of the outdoor west? It's encapsulated in northwest Wyoming, where beauty and adventure were given their due in 1872 with the creation of majestic Yellowstone, America's first national park.

Grapes, Green Chiles & Going Local

Travel in the west isn't *just* about ogling the scenery. It's also about immersing yourself in the culture, which is code for 'digging into the food.' Several dishes are representative of local strengths and traditions: fish tacos in San Diego, Sonoran dogs in Tucson, steak and potatoes in the Rockies, green chile sauces in New Mexico and wild salmon in the Pacific Northwest. Regional specialties are as diverse as the landscapes. But these days there is one commonality –

RALPH HOPKINS / LONELY PLANET IMAGES ©

Landscapes and legends draw adventurers to the West, where a good day includes locavore dining, vineyard wine-sipping, cowboy history and whoa-dude outdoor fun.

(left) Colorado River, Grand Canyon National Park, (p339), Arizona.
(below) Venice Boardwalk, (p71), Venice, Los Angeles.

DAVID PEEVERS / LONELY PLANET IMAGES ©

chefs and consumers alike are focusing on fresh and locally grown, a locavore trend that started in the West. Even better? This eco-consciousness has been embraced by wine producers, who are increasingly implementing organic and biodynamic growing principles. And speaking of winemaking, it's more diverse these days too, with Napa and Sonoma sharing the spotlight with Washington, Oregon, central California and Arizona. All here to play – and stay.

Urban Oases

Very rarely should one dare say, 'Life is good.' But gazing upon twinkling city lights from the rooftop of the Standard Hotel in downtown Los Angeles certainly qualifies as one of those times. Sip that martini, flash that tan and embrace the urban cool. In every region of the West – except the northern Rockies – there's a big-city anchor bursting with museums, malls and restaurants. The differences? In California there's the hey-bro friendliness of San Diego, the Hollywood flash of Los Angeles and the bohemian cool of San Francisco. Further north in Seattle, cutting-edge joins homegrown, often over a cup of joe. Cosmopolitan chic meets plucky frontier spirit in Denver, while patio preening and spa pampering give Phoenix a strangely compelling spoiled-girl vibe. And last there's Las Vegas, a glitzy neon playground where you can get hitched, spend your honeymoon in Paris and then bet the mortgage – all in the very same weekend.

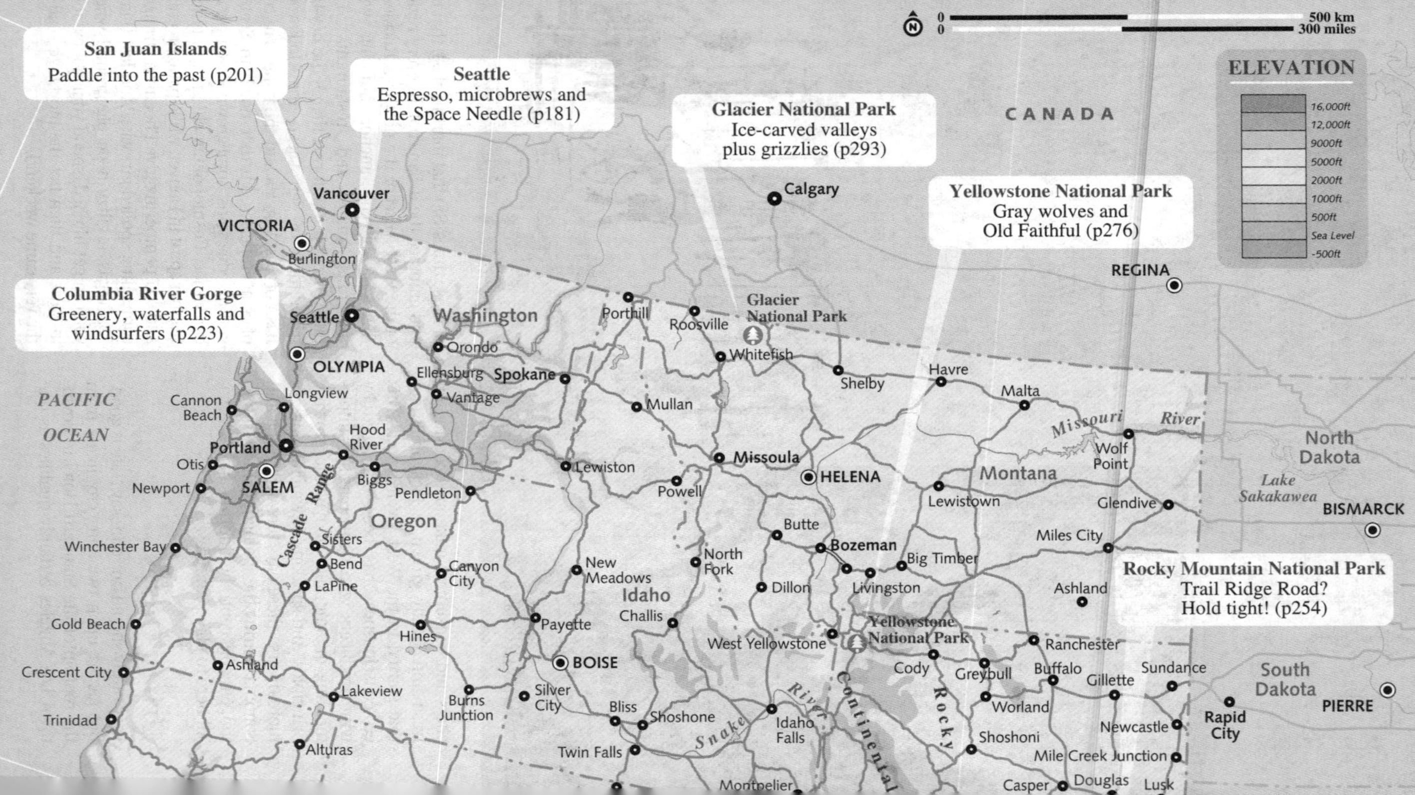

San Juan Islands
Paddle into the past (p201)
Seattle
Espresso, microbrews and the Space Needle (p181)
Glacier National Park
Ice-carved valleys plus grizzlies (p293)
Yellowstone National Park
Gray wolves and Old Faithful (p276)
Columbia River Gorge
Greenery, waterfalls and windsurfers (p223)
Rocky Mountain National Park
Trail Ridge Road? Hold tight! (p254)
0 500 km
0 300 miles
ELEVATION
16,000ft
12,000ft
9000ft
5000ft
2000ft
1000ft
500ft
Sea Level
-500ft
CANADA
PACIFIC OCEAN
Calgary
REGINA
Vancouver
VICTORIA
Burlington
Seattle
OLYMPIA
Washington
Orondo
Ellensburg
Spokane
Vantage
Porthill
Roosville
Glacier National Park
Whitefish
Shelby
Havre
Malta
Missouri River
Wolf Point
Montana
North Dakota
Lake Sakakawea
BISMARCK
Cannon Beach
Longview
Portland
Otis
SALEM
Newport
Hood River
Biggs
Pendleton
Cascade Range
Oregon
Lewiston
Mullan
Missoula
HELENA
Powell
Lewistown
Glendive
Miles City
Winchester Bay
Sisters
Bend
LaPine
Canyon City
New Meadows
Idaho
North Fork
Butte
Bozeman
Big Timber
Livingston
Dillon
Challis
Ashland
Gold Beach
Hines
Payette
BOISE
West Yellowstone
Yellowstone National Park
Ranchester
Cody
Greybull
Buffalo
Gillette
Sundance
South Dakota
PIERRE
Rapid City
Crescent City
Ashland
Lakeview
Burns Junction
Silver City
Bliss
Shoshone
Snake River
Idaho Falls
Continental
Rocky
Worland
Shoshoni
Newcastle
Mile Creek Junction
Trinidad
Alturas
Twin Falls
Montpelier
Casper
Douglas
Lusk

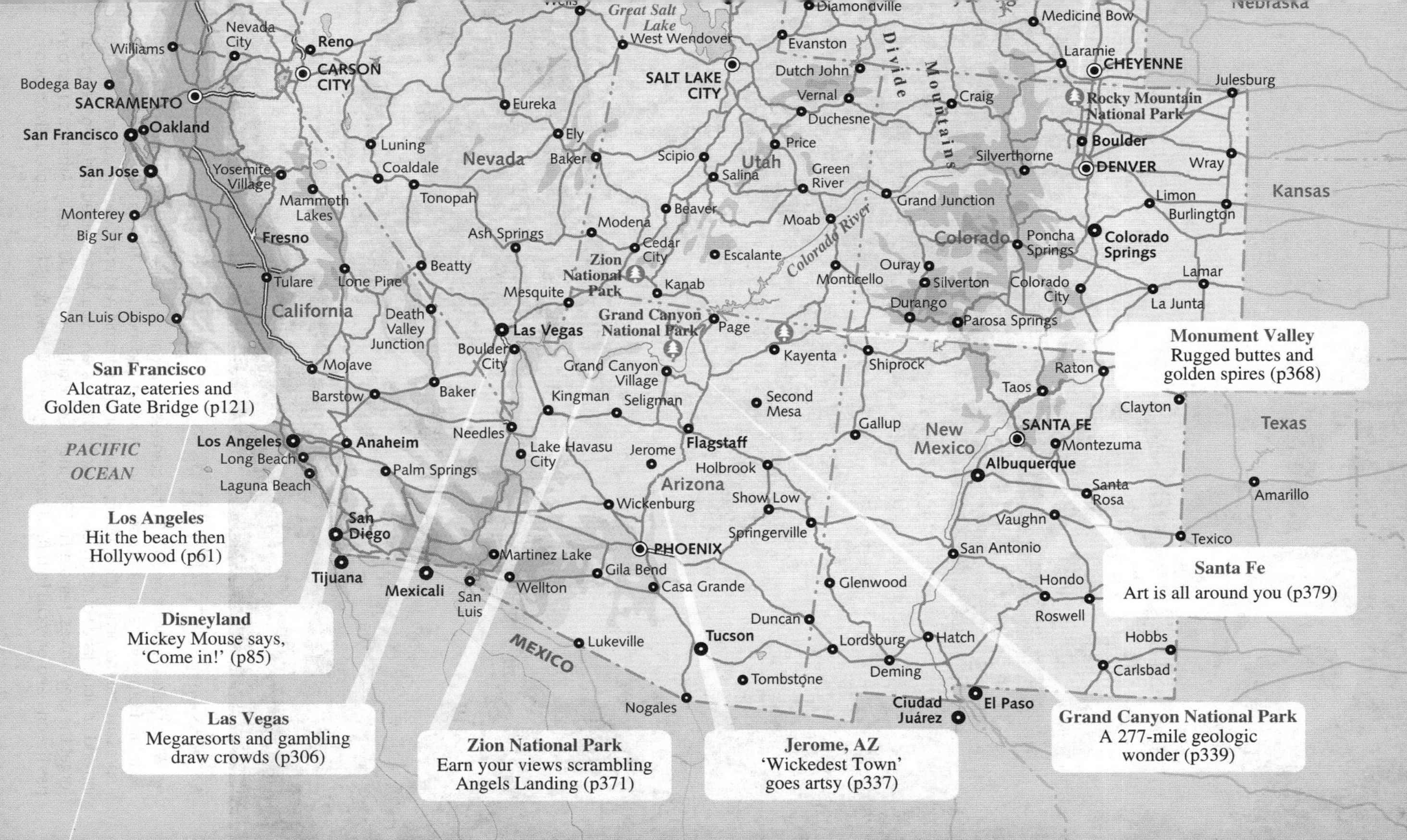
San Francisco
Alcatraz, eateries and Golden Gate Bridge (p121)
Los Angeles
Hit the beach then Hollywood (p61)
Disneyland
Mickey Mouse says, 'Come in!' (p85)
Las Vegas
Megaresorts and gambling draw crowds (p306)
Zion National Park
Earn your views scrambling Angels Landing (p371)
Jerome, AZ
'Wickedest Town' goes artsy (p337)
Grand Canyon National Park
A 277-mile geologic wonder (p339)
Santa Fe
Art is all around you (p379)
Monument Valley
Rugged buttes and golden spires (p368)
PACIFIC OCEAN
MEXICO
California
Nevada
Utah
Arizona
Colorado
New Mexico
Texas
Kansas
Nebraska
Divide
Mountains
Great Salt Lake
Colorado River
Zion National Park
Grand Canyon National Park
Rocky Mountain National Park
SACRAMENTO
CARSON CITY
SALT LAKE CITY
CHEYENNE
DENVER
PHOENIX
SANTA FE
Bodega Bay
Williams
Nevada City
Reno
San Francisco
Oakland
San Jose
Monterey
Big Sur
San Luis Obispo
Yosemite Village
Mammoth Lakes
Fresno
Tulare
Lone Pine
Luning
Coaldale
Tonopah
Eureka
Ely
Baker
Ash Springs
Beatty
Death Valley Junction
Mojave
Barstow
Baker
Los Angeles
Long Beach
Laguna Beach
Anaheim
Palm Springs
San Diego
Tijuana
Mexicali
San Luis
Wellton
Martinez Lake
Needles
Lake Havasu City
Boulder City
Las Vegas
Mesquite
Kingman
Seligman
Grand Canyon Village
Jerome
Flagstaff
Wickenburg
Gila Bend
Casa Grande
Lukeville
Tucson
Nogales
Tombstone
West Wendover
Scipio
Salina
Beaver
Modena
Cedar City
Kanab
Escalante
Page
Kayenta
Second Mesa
Holbrook
Show Low
Springerville
Glenwood
Duncan
Lordsburg
Deming
Hatch
Ciudad Juárez
El Paso
Evanston
Dutch John
Vernal
Duchesne
Price
Green River
Moab
Monticello
Shiprock
Gallup
Grand Junction
Ouray
Silverton
Durango
Parosa Springs
Craig
Silverthorne
Poncha Springs
Colorado City
Colorado Springs
Medicine Bow
Laramie
Boulder
Wray
Limon
Burlington
Lamar
La Junta
Julesburg
Raton
Taos
Clayton
Albuquerque
Montezuma
Santa Rosa
Vaughn
San Antonio
Amarillo
Texico
Hondo
Roswell
Hobbs
Carlsbad
Diamondville

25 TOP EXPERIENCES

Yellowstone National Park

1 What makes Yellowstone (p276) the quintessential national park? Geologic wonders for one thing, from geysers and hot springs to fumaroles and mud pots. There's also Mt Washburn, an impressive central peak with inspiring views from its summit. Add in a towering waterfall, an historic inn and an abundance of bison, elk, moose and bears, and you've described perfection. And don't forget the gray wolves; restored in 1995 they now number about 100. Finally, America's first park has the one-and-only Old Faithful, a beloved geyser still blowing its top for appreciative crowds.

San Francisco

2 Amid the fog and the clatter of old-fashioned trams, San Francisco's (p121) diverse neighborhoods invite long days of wandering, with great indie shops, world-class restaurants and bohemian nightlife. Highlights include peering into the cells at Alcatraz, strolling across the Golden Gate Bridge and dining inside the Ferry Building. And you must take at least one ride on the trolley. How cool is San Francisco? Trust us – turn that first corner to a stunning waterfront view, and you'll be hooked. Tram on Hyde St, with Alcatraz (p134) in the background.

Old West Towns

3 If you judge Old West towns by the quality of their nicknames, then Jerome, Arizona (p337), once known as 'The Wickedest Town in America,' and Tombstone, Arizona (p353), 'The Town Too Tough to Die,' are the most fascinating ex-mining towns in the West. While in New Mexico, Silver City's moniker – 'The Richest Place on Earth' – isn't as snappy, the town (p393) shares key traits with the others: a rough-and-tumble mining past, a remote location at the end of a scenic drive and quirky citizens putting an old-west spin on B&Bs, saloons and museums.

Jerome (p337), Arizona.

Las Vegas

4 Just when you think you've got a handle on the West – majestic, sublime, soul-nourishing – here comes Vegas (p306) shaking her thing like a showgirl looking for trouble. Beneath the neon lights of the Strip, she puts on a dazzling show: dancing fountains, a spewing volcano, the Eiffel Tower. But she saves her most dangerous charms for the gambling dens – seductive lairs where the fresh-pumped air and bright colors share one goal: separating you from your money. Step away if you can for fine restaurants, Cirque du Soleil and a shark-filled reef.

Grand Canyon National Park

5 The sheer immensity of the canyon (p339) is what grabs you at first – it's a two-billion-year-old rip across the landscape that reveals the earth's geologic secrets with commanding authority. But it's Mother Nature's artistic touches, from sun-dappled ridges and crimson buttes to lush oases and a ribbonlike river, that hold your attention and demand your return. As Theodore Roosevelt said, this natural wonder is 'unparalleled throughout the rest of the world.' Or as we might say today, 'Whoa!'

California Wine Country

6 The rolling vineyards of Napa, Sonoma and the Russian River Valley lure travelers north from San Francisco. Sample a world-class cab in chichi Napa (p149), enjoy a picnic in laid-back Sonoma (p151) or cap off an outdoor adventure with a complex Pinot Noir near the Russian River (p152). But wait, there's more. California has more than 100 recognized wine regions, including those east of Santa Barbara (p111), in a bucolic area made famous by the 2004 wine-centric movie *Sideways*. Rutherford, Napa Valley (p149).

Los Angeles

7 A perpetual influx of dreamers, go-getters and hustlers gives this shiny coastal city (p61) an energetic buzz. Learn the tricks of movie-making during a studio tour. Bliss out to acoustically perfect symphony sounds in the Walt Disney Concert Hall. Wander gardens and galleries at the hilltop Getty Museum. And stargazing? Take in the big picture at the revamped Griffith Observatory or look for stylish, earthbound 'stars' at The Grove. Ready for your close-up darling? You will be – an hour on the beach practically guarantees that sun-kissed LA glow. Hollywood Walk of Fame (p67).

Portland

8 It's easy to brag about PDX (Portland; p208), but no one will hassle you for it – after all, everyone loves this city. It's as friendly as a big town and home to a mix of students, artists, cyclists, hipsters, young families, old hippies, ecofreaks and everything in between. There's great food, awesome music and plenty of culture, plus it's as sustainable as you can get. Come and visit, but be careful – like everyone else, you might just want to pack up and move here.

EMILY RIDDELL / LONELY PLANET IMAGES ©

Yosemite National Park

9 Welcome to what conservationist John Muir called his 'high pleasure-ground' and 'great temple' (p163). Meander through wildflower-strewn meadows in valleys carved by glaciers, avalanches and earthquakes. Their hard work makes everything look bigger here, whether you're getting splashed by thunderous waterfalls that tumble over sheer cliffs, staring up at granite domes or walking in ancient groves of giant sequoias, the planet's biggest trees. For the most sublime views, perch at Glacier Point on a full moon night or drive the high country's dizzying Tioga Rd in summer.

RICHARD CUMMINS / LONELY PLANET IMAGES ©

Route 66

10 As you step up to the counter at the Snow-Cap Drive In at Seligman, Arizona (see boxed text, p347), you know a prank is coming – a squirt of fake mustard, ridiculously incorrect change. Though it's all a bit hokey, you'd be disappointed if the owner forgot to 'get you.' It's these kitschy, down-home touches that make The Mother Road – which crosses California, Arizona and New Mexico – so memorable. Begging burros, the Wigwam Motel, the neon signs of Tucumcari – a squirt of fake mustard beats a mass-consumption McBurger every time. Wigwam Motel (p347), Holbrook, Arizona

Coastal Highways

11 Stunning highways track America's western coastline, crossing California, Oregon and Washington. In California, Hwy 1 (also called Pacific Coast Hwy or PCH), Hwy 101 and I-5 pass dizzying sea cliffs, idiosyncratic beach towns and a handful of major cities: laid-back San Diego, rocker LA and beatnik San Francisco. North of the redwoods, Hwy 101 swoops into Oregon for windswept capes, rocky tide pools and – for Twilight fans – Ecola State Park, the stand-in for werewolf haven La Push, Washington. Cross the Columbia River into Washington for wet-and-wild Olympic National Park. Hwy 1, California.

Seattle

12 A cutting-edge Pacific Rim city with an uncanny habit of turning locally hatched ideas into global brands, Seattle (p181) has earned its place in the pantheon of 'great' US metropolises with a world-renowned music scene, a mercurial coffee culture and a penchant for internet-driven innovation. But, while Seattle's trendsetters rush to unearth the next big thing, city traditionalists guard its soul with distinct urban neighborhoods, a home-grown food culture and what is arguably the nation's finest public market, Pike Place.
Space Needle (p185).

Native American History & Culture

13 The Southwest holds a fascinating array of Native American sites. To learn about America's earliest inhabitants, climb into the ancient cliff-top homes of Ancestral Puebloans in Colorado (p272) and New Mexico (p386) or study petroglyphs in Sedona (p336). For living cultures, visit Arizona's Navajo and Hopi nations. Here you'll discover that Native American art is not stuck in the past. While many designs have religious significance, the baskets, rugs and jewelry crafted today often put a fresh spin on the ancient traditions – you may even see pottery emblazoned with a Harry Potter theme!

San Juan Islands

14 Go back in time by hopping on a ferry to the San Juan Islands (p201), a low-key archipelago north of Puget Sound between Washington and Vancouver Island. Out of the more than 450 'islands' (most are only rocky promontories), only about 60 are inhabited and just four are regularly served by ferries. Nature is the main influence here and each island has its own personality, both geographic and cultural. What can you do here? Start with cycling, kayaking and spotting orcas – then just sit back and relax.

Mt Rainier

15 When the skies are clear, Mt Rainier (p205) looms high over Seattle, creating an amazing backdrop to the emerald city. Still very much a live volcano, the 14,411ft peak is the shining centerpiece of the Mt Rainier National Park, which offers a rare inland temperate rainforest, hikes through alpine wildflower meadows and the famous 93-mile Wonderland Trail. If you're fit and adventurous enough, attempt to climb the peak itself; just be ready to traverse some of the largest glaciers outside Alaska.

Disneyland, California Adventure & Orange County

16 Inside Disneyland (p85), Orange County's popular theme park, beloved cartoon characters waltz down Main Street USA, screamalicious Space Mountain rockets through the darkness and fireworks explode over Sleeping Beauty's castle. Next door, California Adventure shows the best of the state with a recreated Hollywood back lot, a coastal boardwalk and a patio perfect for sipping California wines. The Orange County coast (p89) lures travelers with upscale malls, bird-filled nature reserves and a stretch of gorgeous beaches. Laguna Beach (p89).

Boulder, CO

17 Tucked up against its signature Flatirons, Boulder (p250) has a sweet location and a progressive soul, which has attracted a groovy bag of entrepreneurs, hippies and hard-bodies. Packs of cyclists ride the Boulder Creek Bike Path, which links to an abundance of city and county parks purchased through a popular Open Space tax. The pedestrian-only Pearl St Mall (pictured right) is lively, especially at night, when students from the University of Colorado and Naropa University mingle and flirt. In many ways Boulder, not Denver, is the region's tourist hub.

CAROLINE COMMINS / ALAMY ©

TYLER ROEMER / LONELY PLANET IMAGES ©

Columbia River Gorge

18 Carved by the mighty Columbia as the Cascades were uplifted, the Columbia River Gorge (p223) is a geologic marvel. With Washington State on its north side and Oregon on its south, the state-dividing gorge offers countless waterfalls and spectacular hikes, as well as an agricultural bounty of apples, pears and cherries. And if you're into windsurfing or kiteboarding, head straight to the sporty town of Hood River, ground zero for these extreme sports. Whether you're a hiker, apple lover or adrenaline junkie, the gorge delivers.

Monument Valley & Canyon de Chelly

19 Beauty comes in many forms on the Navajos' sprawling reservation, but makes its most famous appearance at Monument Valley (p346), an otherworldly cluster of rugged buttes and stubborn towers rising majestically from the desert. Beauty swoops in on the wings of birds at Canyon de Chelly (p345), a green valley where farmers till the land near age-old cliff dwellings. Elsewhere, beauty is in the connections, from the docent explaining Navajo clans to the cafe waiter offering a welcoming smile. Monument Valley Navajo Tribal Park (p346).

FEARGUS COONEY / LONELY PLANET IMAGES ©

Santa Fe & Taos

20 Santa Fe (p379) may be celebrating her 400th birthday, but she's kicking up her stylish heels like a teenager. On Friday nights, art lovers flock to Canyon Rd to gab with artists, sip wine and explore more than 100 galleries. Art and history partner up within the city's consortium of museums. And, ah, the food and the shopping. With that turquoise sky as a backdrop, the experience is darn near sublime. Artists also converge in gallery-filled Taos (p387) but the vibe is quirkier, with ski bums, Earthshippers and a few celebs keeping things offbeat. Detail of bell tower, New Mexico Museum of Art (p381), Santa Fe.

Rocky Mountain National Park

21 From behind the row of RVs growling along Trail Ridge Rd, Rocky Mountain National Park (p254) can look a bit overexposed. But with hiking boots laced and the trail unfurling before you, the park's majestic, untamed splendor becomes unforgettably personal. From epic outings on the Continental Divide National Scenic Trail to family friendly romps in the Bear Lake area, there's something here for people of every ability and ambition. With just the slightest effort, you'll feel like you have the place to yourself. Maroon Bells (p263), Rocky Mountain National Park.

The Deserts

22 The humanlike saguaro cactus is one of the West's most enduring symbols. A denizen of the Sonoran Desert, it's a hardy survivor in a landscape both harsh and unforgiving, but also strangely beautiful. Four deserts – the Sonoran, Mojave, Chihuahuan and Great Basin – stretch across the Southwest, each with its own distinct climate. Each is also home to an amazing array of well-adapted reptiles, mammals and plants. It's this thriving diversity that makes a stroll through the desert a wondrous, one-of-a-kind experience. Saguaro National Park (p348)

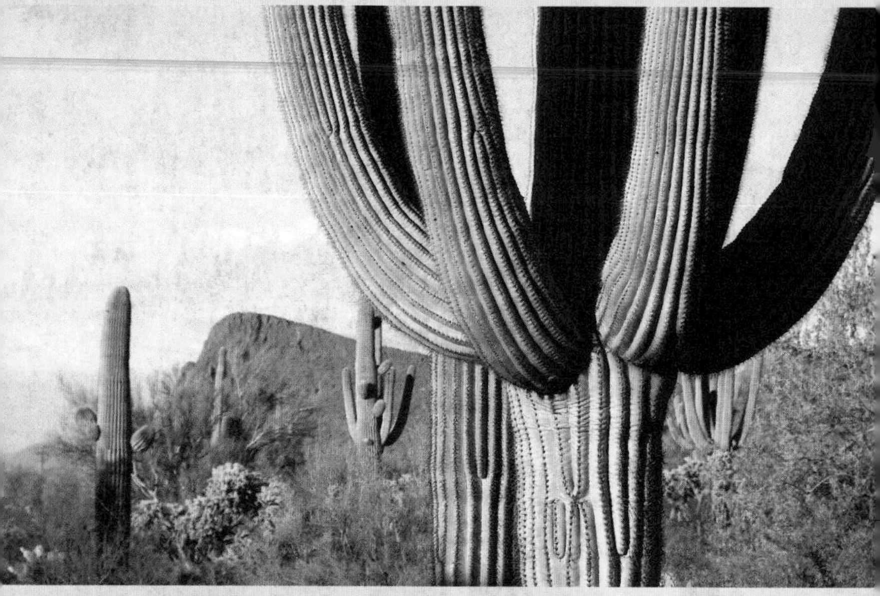

WHIT RICHARDSON / AURORA PHOTOS / CORBIS ©

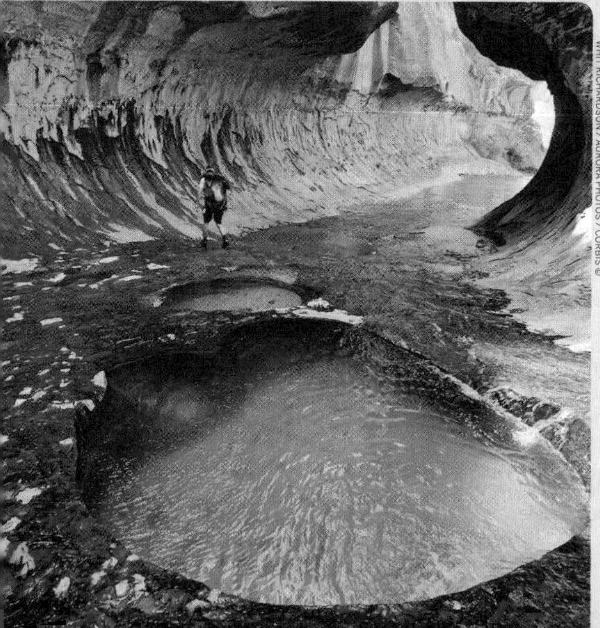

Zion & Bryce Canyon National Parks

23 Towering red rocks hide graceful waterfalls, narrow slot canyons and hanging gardens in Zion National Park (p371). This lush wonderland lies in the shadow of Angels Landing, the terminus of one of the great American day hikes – how can a trail with a section called Walter's Wiggles be anything less than top-notch? Photographers and view hounds should scoot north to Bryce Canyon National Park (p370), where golden-red rock spires shimmer like trees in a magical stone forest – a hypnotic, Tolkienesque place. Zion National Park (p371).

SHANNON NACE / LONELY PLANET IMAGES ©

Glacier National Park

24 Yep, the rumors are true. The namesake attractions at Glacier National Park (p293) are melting away. There were 150 glaciers in the area in 1850; today there are less than 30. But even without the giant ice cubes, Montana's sprawling national park is worthy of an in-depth visit. Road warriors can maneuver the thrilling 50-mile Going-to-the-Sun Road; wildlife-watchers can scan for elk, wolves and grizzly (but hopefully not too close) and hikers have 700 miles of trails, trees and flora – mosses, mushrooms and wildflowers – to explore.

Microbreweries

25 Microbreweries are a specialty of the West, and you'll find at least one in just about every outdoorsy town from Moab to Missoula. Though homegrown, these popular watering holes share a few commonalities: boisterous beer sippers, deep-flavored brews with locally inspired names, and a cavernous drinking room that smells of sweat and adventure. And when it comes to memorable slogans, Wasatch Brew Pub (p362) in Park City, Utah, earns kudos for its Polygamy Porter tagline: Why Have Just One? Hopworks Urban Brewery (p217), Portland, Oregon.

need to know

Currency

» US dollars ($)

Language

» English

When to Go

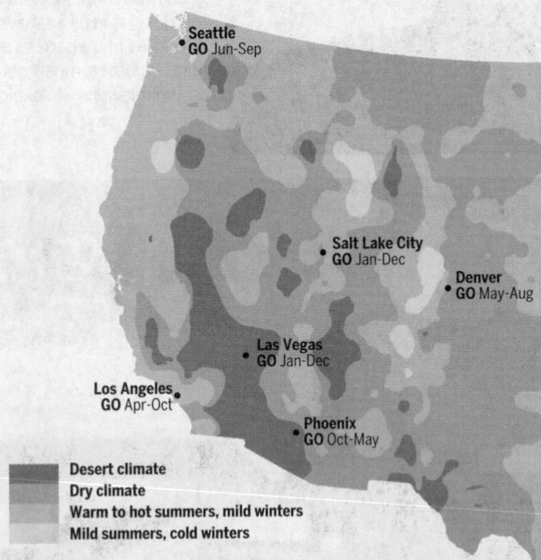

High Season

(Jun–Aug; Sep-Apr)

» Busiest season; sunny days and higher accommodation prices

» Clouds may blanket the southern coast during May and June

» High season in the mountains January to March; in the deserts September to April

Shoulder

(Apr & May; Sep & Oct)

» Crowds and prices drop, especially along the coast and in the mountains

» A good time to visit national parks, with milder temperatures

» Blooming spring flowers; fiery autumn colors

Low Season

(Nov–Mar)

» Accommodation rates drop by the coast

» Dark, wintery days, with snowfall in the north, and heavier rains

Your Daily Budget

budget less than

$100

» Campgrounds and hostel dorms: $18-40

» 'Free admission' days at museums

» Farmers markets, taquerias, sidewalk vendors

Midrange

$100-200

» Mom-and-pop motels, low-priced chains: $60-100

» Car rental from $30 per day, excluding insurance and gas

» Visit museums, theme parks, national and state parks

top end over

$200

» B&Bs, boutique hotels, resorts, lodges

» Three-course meal in top restaurant: $75 plus wine

» Hire an outdoor outfitter; take a guided tour; enjoy top shows

Money
» ATMs are widely available. Credit cards are normally required for hotel reservations and car rentals.

Visas
» Generally not required for citizens of Visa Waiver Program (VWP) countries, but only with ESTA approval (apply online at least 72 hours in advance).

Cell Phones
» The only foreign phones that will work in the USA are GSM multiband models. Cell-phone coverage can be spotty in remote or mountainous areas.

Driving
» Best option for outside major urban areas. Amtrak and Greyhound buses typically do not stop at national parks or small towns. Avoid commuter rush hours.

Websites
» **American Southwest** (www.americansouthwest.net) Site for parks and landscapes.

» **Lonely Planet** (www.lonelyplanet.com/usa) Destination info, hotel bookings and travelers' forums.

» **National Park Service** (www.nps.gov) Information about national parks and monuments.

» **Recreation.gov** (www.recreation.gov) Camping reservations on federally managed lands.

» **Roadside America** (www.roadsideamerica.com) Find 'uniquely odd tourist attractions.'

Exchange Rates

Australia	A$1	$0.99
Canada	C$1	$0.98
Euro zone	€1	$1.36
China	Y10	$1.56
Japan	¥100	$1.31
Mexico	MXN10	$0.75
New Zealand	NZ$1	$0.78
UK	£1	$1.56

For current exchange rates see www.xe.com.

Important Numbers
To call any regular number, dial the area code, followed by the 7-digit number.

USA Country Code	☎1
International Access Code	☎011
Emergency	☎911
National Sexual Assault Hotline	☎800-656-4673
Directory Assistance	☎411
Statewide Road Conditions	☎511

Arriving in the West
» **Denver International Airport** (DEN; p247)
Taxis about $45
Frequent RTD SkyRide buses 3:30am to 1:10am for downtown Denver ($10, 55 minutes) and Boulder ($12, 90 minutes)

» **Los Angeles International Airport** (LAX; p84)
Taxis $30-55, 30-60 minutes
Door-to-door shuttles $16-25, 24 hours
Free Shuttle C to LAX Transit Center; FlyAway bus ($7) to downtown LA

Time Zones in the West
Mountain Standard Time (Denver, Santa Fe, Phoenix) and Pacific Standard Time (Seattle, San Francisco, Las Vegas) cover the 11 states in this guide.

Daylight Savings Time pushes the clocks ahead an hour. It runs from the second Sunday in March to the first Sunday in November.

Arizona does not observe daylight-saving time, so during that period it's one hour behind other Southwestern states. The Navajo Reservation, which lies in Arizona, New Mexico and Utah, *does* use daylight-saving time. The Hopi Reservation, which is surrounded by the Navajo Reservation in Arizona, follows the rest of Arizona.

if you like...

Geology

Red rock deserts, petrified forests, blasting geysers and one massive rip in the ground. In many spots in the West, you might feel like you've stepped into a lab experiment of the gods – one that's not quite done.

Grand Canyon A 277-mile river cuts through two-billion-year-old rocks whose layered geologic secrets are revealed within a mile-high stack (p339)

Yellowstone Massive geysers, rainbow-colored thermal pools and a supervolcano base – this 3472-sq-mile national park puts on a dazzling show (p276)

Chiricahua National Monument A rugged wonderland of rock chiseled by rain and wind into pinnacles, bridges and balanced rocks (p352)

Sand Dunes The white and chalky gypsum dunes at White Sands National Monument are mesmerizing (p394)

Carlsbad Caverns Take a 2-mile walk along a subterranean passage to arrive in the great room – a veritable underground cathedral concealed in the massive cave system (p397)

Old West Sites

The story of the taming of the West has always been America's grandest tale, capturing the imagination of writers, singers, filmmakers and travelers. At atmospheric sites across the region, you can compare the truth to the myth.

Lincoln Billy the Kid's old stomping – and shooting – grounds during the Lincoln County War (p395)

Tombstone Famous for the Gunfight at the OK Corral, this dusty town is also home to Boothill Cemetery and the Bird Cage Theater (p353)

Whiskey Row With sudsy aplomb, a block of Victorian-era saloons in downtown Prescott has survived fires, filmmakers and tourists (p338)

Virginia City Site of the Comstock Lode silver strike, this hard-charging mining town gained notoriety in Mark Twain's semi-autobiographical book *Roughing It* (p322)

Steam Train Channel the Old West on the steam-driven train that's chugged between Durango and Silverton for 125 years (p266)

Film & TV Locations

From glowing red buttes to the twinkling lights of Vegas, the West is a place of refuge, unknown dangers and breathtaking beauty. In other words, its catnip to directors looking to drop their heroes into dramatic settings.

Los Angeles Hollywood was born here, and today you can't throw a director's megaphone without hitting another celluloid site, from Mulholland Drive to Malibu (p61)

Monument Valley Stride John-Wayne tall beneath the iconic red monoliths that starred in seven of the Duke's beloved westerns (p346)

Las Vegas Bad boys and their hi-jinks brought Sin City back to the big screen in *Oceans Eleven* and *The Hangover* (p306)

Moab & Around Directors of *Thelma & Louise* and *127 Hours* shot their most dramatic scenes in nearby parks (p364)

Albuquerque Tax incentives lure production companies. Albuquerque is the backdrop for the TV series *Breaking Bad*. Recent films shot in New Mexico include *Crazy Heart*, *Thor* and the Cohen brothers' *True Grit* (p374)

If you like...
outlandish rock formations
Make the drive to the Bisti Badlands in New Mexico and wander past multicolored hoodoos and balanced rocks (p390)

Fabulous Food

There's a classic dining experience in every region of the West: carving into a steak in the Rockies, slurping green chile stew in Albuquerque, noshing at world-famous restaurants in Los Angeles and San Francisco, and enjoying farm-to-table spots in the Pacific Northwest.

San Francisco An array of temptations awaits food-minded diners: real-deal taquerias and trattorias, top-notch Vietnamese, magnificent farmers markets and acclaimed chefs firing up the best of California cuisine (p121)

Chez Panisse Chef Alice Waters revolutionized California cuisine in the '70s with seasonal Bay Area locavarian cooking (p148)

Food Trucks LA sparked the mobile gourmet revolution (p419), but the food truck craze has also taken hold in **San Francisco** (p140) and **Portland** (p214).

Green Chiles The chiles grown in the town of Hatch are the pride of New Mexico. This spicy accompaniment is slathered over enchiladas, layered onto cheeseburgers and stirred into hearty stews. Try the green chile stew at **Frontier** (p377) in Albuquerque or test the heat at **Horseman's Haven** (p383) in Santa Fe.

Emerging Wine Regions

The American wine industry has grown in leaps and bounds in recent years, to become the world's fourth-largest producer. Visiting wineries isn't just about tasting first-rate drops, but savoring pretty countryside and sampling the enticing farmstands and delectable bistros that often sprout alongside vineyards.

Verde Valley Wine Country Home to an up-and-coming Arizona wine trail that winds past wineries and vineyards in Cottonwood, Jerome and Cornville (boxed text, p338)

Willamette Valley Outside Portland, Oregon this fertile region produces some of the tastiest Pinot Noirs on the planet (p220)

Walla Walla Washington's hot wine-growing region, with its namesake town as a very pretty centerpiece (p207)

Santa Barbara Wine Country Large-scale winemaking has been going on here since the 1980s, and the climate is perfect for Pinots near the coast and further inland (p111)

Hiking

The West is a rambler's paradise, with scenery to satisfy every type of outdoor craving: mountain, coastal, riparian, desert and red rock.

Grand Canyon Rim to Rim Earn bragging rights on this classic 17-mile trek between the Grand Canyon's south and north rims (p339)

Red Rock Country Hike to vortexes in Sedona (p336), hoodoos in Bryce Canyon (p370), and slender spans in Arches (p366) and Canyonlands (p366) National Parks

Rocky Mountain National Park Longs Peak gets all the buzz but there are several loop trails best done in two or three nights; wildlife sightings are the norm here (p254)

Wonderland Trail Circumnavigate Mt Rainier's lofty peak – it's 93 miles of spectacular nature (p206)

Palm Springs & the Deserts Discover hidden palm-tree oases, stroll across salt flats or take a guided walk through Native American canyons (p101)

RAY LASKOWITZ / LONELY PLANET IMAGES ©

» Alien characters, Roswell UFO Festival, Roswell (p396)

Nightlife

You've seen the red carpet rolled out for movie-star premieres. Now it's your turn to step out in style at ultra-chic nightclubs. Or, since this is the West, scruff it up in a few jamming saloons.

Los Angeles From hip-hop to world beats, techno to trance, DJs spin it all in Hollywood's glam club scene, while nearby 'WeHo' is ground zero for LA's gay and lesbian scene (p81)

San Francisco Go beatnik in North Beach, hipster in the Mission or party with the rainbow-flag nation in the Castro (p142)

Tucson Start with a pub crawl on scrappy 4th Ave then head to Congress St downtown for up-close live shows at the historic Hotel Congress (p350)

Las Vegas The Strip's high-powered nightclubs measure up to any fantasy (p315)

Pacific Northwest Portland, Seattle and Vancouver claim some of the hottest new bands on the indie circuit, and the venues – from cozy to quirky to big and loud – to show them off.

National Parks

After camping in Yellowstone, Theodore Roosevelt said, 'It was like lying in a great cathedral, far vaster and more beautiful than any built by the hand of man.' These words could be applied to the great parks of the West: unique in their details, bound by their grandeur.

Yellowstone National Park The nation's first park is a stunner: lakes, waterfalls, mountains, wildlife galore and a cauldron of geysers and springs (p276)

Grand Canyon National Park Two billion years of geologic history? Yeah, yeah, that's cool, but have you seen that view (p339)

Glacier National Park Come for the glaciers, stay for the Going-to-the-Sun Rd, the grand old lodges and the free-range wildlife (p293)

Yosemite National Park Flanked by El Capitan and Half Dome, Yosemite Valley is indeed cathedral-like, but the lush Tuolomne backcountry will have you singing hallelujah too (p163)

Southern Utah Sorry, there's just too much red-rock goodness in Utah to narrow it down to one fave. Arches, Canyonlands, Bryce, Zion and Capitol Reef – got two weeks? See 'em all!

Weird Stuff

There's a lot of empty space in the West, and this emptiness draws out the weird in people. From dinosaur sculptures to two-headed squirrels to festivals that celebrate desert creativity, weird is the way to go. The bumper sticker we saw in Jerome says it best: 'We're all here because we're not all there.'

Route 66 This two-lane ode to Americana is dotted with wacky roadside attractions, especially in western Arizona (boxed text, p347)

Burning Man Festival A temporary city in the Nevada desert attracts 55,000 for a week of self-expression and blowing sand (boxed text, p321)

Roswell Did a UFO crash outside Roswell, New Mexico in 1947? Museums and a UFO festival explore whether the truth is out there (p396)

Seattle's Public Sculptures In Fremont, look for a car-eating troll, a human-faced dog and some folks waiting, and waiting, for the train (p186)

Venice Boardwalk Gawk at the human zoo of chainsaw-jugglers and Speedo-clad snake-charmers (p71)

If you like... spooky stories

The Jerome Grand Hotel in Jerome, Arizona offers guests a ghost tour of the hotel, which is a former hospital for miners (p338)

Museums

Modern art. Native American cultures. Georgia O'Keeffe. Bizarre odds-and-ends. Roswell and UFOs. Nuclear energy. Mining. And Jurassic technology. There seems to be a museum for every taste and interest in the West. Full immersion is easy in the multimillion-dollar art galleries, interactive high-tech science exhibits and out-of-this-world planetariums.

Getty Center & Villa Art museums as beautiful as their ocean views in west LA (p70) and Malibu (p71)

Los Angeles County Museum of Art More than 150,000 works of art spanning the ages and crossing all borders (p69)

California Academy of Sciences SF's natural-history museum breathes 'green' in its eco-certified design, with a four-story rainforest and living roof (p133)

Balboa Park Go all-day museum hopping in San Diego's favorite park where you can dive into top-notch art, history and science exhibitions (p92)

Heard Museum Highlights the history and culture of Southwestern tribes (p325)

Historic Sites

Across the West, dinosaurs left their footprints, ancient peoples left their cliff dwellings and outlaws and sheriffs left behind mythology to fill hundreds of books. Many of these sights have barely changed over the centuries, making it easy to visualize how history unfolded, sometimes just a few steps away.

Dinosaur National Monument OK, it may be a *prehistoric* site, but touching a 150-million-year-old fossil at one of the largest dinosaur fossil beds in North America is too cool to miss (p363)

Mesa Verde Climb up to cliff dwellings that housed Ancestral Puebloans more than 700 years ago (p272)

Manzanar National Historic Site WWII Japanese American internment camp interprets a painful chapter of the USA's collective past (p171)

Little Bighorn Battlefield National Monument Native American battlefields where General George Custer made his famous 'last stand' against the Lakota Sioux (p290)

Spas & Resorts

When it comes to resorts and pampering, the West offers everything from low-frill soaks beside the Rio Grande to pool-centric playgrounds in Vegas to posh retreats in the heart of Scottsdale. And these days, even the kids and Fido can expect some spa lovin' too.

Truth or Consequences Built over hot springs adjacent to the Rio Grande, the bathtubs and pools here bubble with soothing, hydro-healing warmth (p391)

10,000 Waves The soaking tubs at this intimate Japanese spa are tucked on a woodsy hillside (p382)

Phoenix & Scottsdale Honeymooners, families, golfers – there's a resort for every type of traveler within a few miles of Camelback Rd (p329)

Las Vegas Encore, Bellagio, Wynn and other top hotels offer resortlike amenities (p311)

Sheraton Wild Horse Pass Resort & Spa On the Gila Indian Reservation, this resort embraces its Native American heritage with style (p331)

month by month

Top Events

1 **Sundance Film Festival**, January

2 **Cactus League**, March & early April

3 **Aspen Music Festival**, July

4 **Great American Beer Festival**, September

5 **Halloween Carnivals**, October

January

Ski resorts across the region bustle with guests. Palm Springs and southern deserts welcome guests seeking warmer climes and saguaro-dotted landscapes.

Tournament of Roses

This famous New Year's Day parade of flower-festooned floats, marching bands and prancing equestrians draws more than 100,000 spectators to Pasadena, CA, before the Rose Bowl college football game (p75).

Sundance Film Festival

Park City, UT, unfurls the red carpet for indie filmmakers, actors and moviegoers who flock to the mountain town in late January for a week of cutting-edge films (p361).

February

It's the height of ski season, but there are plenty of distractions for those not swooshing down the slopes – low-desert wildflowers bloom, whales migrate off the California coast and dude ranches saddle up in southern Arizona.

Carnival in Colorado

Mardi Gras meets the mountains in Vail, complete with a parade, a king and queen, and plenty of joviality. Breckenridge celebrates with a masquerade ball and a Fat Tuesday parade.

Oregon Shakespeare Festival

In Ashland, tens of thousands of theater fans party with the Bard at this nine-month festival (that's right!) highlighted by world-class plays and Elizabethan drama (p227).

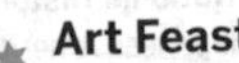

Art Feast

Eat, drink and be merry while gallery hopping in Santa Fe, NM, during this weekend festival in late February that warms up winter with fashion shows and wine tastings.

March

Ah spring, when a young man's fancy turns to thoughts of...beer! jet skis! parties! March is spring break season, when hordes of college students converge on Arizona's lakes. Families ski or visit parks in warmer climes.

Spring Whale-Watching Week

Gray whales migrate along the Pacific Coast. Around Oregon's Depoe Bay, it's semi-organized, with docents and special viewpoints. The northward migration happens through June.

Spring Training

Major league baseball fans head to southern Arizona in March and early April for the preseason Cactus League (see boxed text, p327), when some of the best pro teams play ball in Phoenix and Tucson.

Frozen Dead Guy Days

Celebrate a cryogenically frozen town mascot, 'Grandpa Bredo,' in Nederland, CO, with a snowshoe race, dead guy look-alike contest and copious beer drinking.

April

Migrating birds swoop into nature preserves in southern Arizona while wildflowers bloom in California's high deserts. In the mountains, it's shoulder season, meaning slightly lower room prices (except Easter weekend).

Coachella Music & Arts Festival

Indie rock bands, cult DJs, superstar rappers and pop divas converge outside Palm Springs for a three-day musical extravaganza in mid-April.

Gathering of Nations

More than 3000 Native American dancers and singers from the US and Canada compete in this powwow in late April in Albuquerque, NM (p376). There's also an Indian market with more than 800 artists and craftspeople.

May

Most national parks are ready for the summer crush, but with children still in school the masses don't show until Memorial Day weekend, the last weekend of the month.

Cinco de Mayo

Celebrate the victory of Mexican forces over the French army at the Battle of Puebla on May 5, 1862 with margaritas, music and merriment. Denver, Los Angeles and San Diego do it up in style.

Boulder Creek Festival

Boulder kicks off the summer with food, drink, music and glorious sunshine. It closes with Bolder Boulder, a 10km race celebrated by screaming crowds (p251).

June

High season begins for most of the West. Rugged passes are open, rivers are thick with snowmelt and mountain wildflowers are blooming. There may be gray fog (June gloom) over southern California beaches.

Pride Month

California's LGBTQ pride celebrations occur throughout June, with costumed parades, coming-out parties, live music and more. The biggest, bawdiest celebrations are in San Francisco and Los Angeles.

Bluegrass in the Mountains

In mid-June, join 'Festivarians' for the high lonesome sounds of bluegrass in the mountain-flanked beauty of Telluride, CO (p270).

July

Vacationers descend on beaches, theme parks, mountain resorts, and state and national parks. Broiling desert parks are best avoided.

Independence Day

Across the West, communities celebrate America's birth with rodeos, music festivals, parades and fireworks on July 4.

Aspen Music Festival

Top-tier classical performers put on spectacular shows, while students form orchestras led by sought-after conductors or bring street corners to life with smaller groups (p263).

Oregon Brewers Festival

During this fun beer festival in Portland, more than 50,000 microbrew lovers eat, drink and whoop it up on the banks of the Willamette River (p189).

Comic-Con International

'Nerd Prom' is the alt-nation's biggest annual convention of comic book geeks, sci-fi and animation lovers, and pop-culture memorabilia collectors. Held in San Diego late July.

August

Learn about Native American culture at art fairs, markets and ceremonial gatherings across the Southwest. Rodeos are popular in Colorado and Arizona.

Santa Fe Indian Market

Santa Fe's most famous festival is held the third week of August on the historic plaza where more than 1100 artists from 100 tribes and pueblos exhibit (p382).

Perseids

Peaking in mid-August, these annual meteor showers are the best time to catch shooting stars with your naked eye or a digital camera. For optimal viewing, head into the southern deserts.

September

Summer's last hurrah is the Labor Day holiday weekend. It's a particularly nice time to visit the Pacific Northwest, where nights are cool and the days reliably sunny. Fall colors begin to appear in the Rockies.

Burning Man

Outdoor celebration of self-expression known for elaborate art displays, an easygoing barter system, blowing sand, and the final burning of the man. This temporary city rises in the Nevada desert the week before Labor Day (see boxed text, p321).

Great American Beer Festival

This three-day celebration of beer in Denver is so popular it always sells out in advance, when 400 US breweries get in on the sudsy action (p244).

Bumbershoot

Seattle's biggest arts and cultural event hosts hundreds of musicians, artists, theater troupes and writers on two-dozen stages (p188).

October

Shimmering aspens lure road-trippers to Colorado and northern New Mexico for the annual fall show. Watch for ghouls, ghosts and hard-partying maniacs as Halloween, on October 31, approaches.

International Balloon Fiesta

Look to the skies in early October for the world's biggest gathering of hot-air balloons in Albuquerque, NM (p376).

Halloween Carnivals

Hundreds of thousands of costumed revelers come out to play in LA's West Hollywood LGBTQ neighborhood for all-day partying, dancing, kids' activities and live entertainment.

November

Temperatures drop across the West. Most coastal areas, deserts and parks are less busy, with the exception of the Thanksgiving holiday. Ski season begins.

Día de los Muertos

Mexican communities honor dead ancestors on November 2 with costumed parades, sugar skulls, graveyard picnics, candlelight processions and fabulous altars.

Wine Country Thanksgiving

The Willamette Valley's 150 wineries open their doors to the public for three special days.

Yellowstone Ski Festival

Thanksgiving week celebration at West Yellowstone is a great time for ski buffs and newcomers alike. Highlights include ski clinics and gear demos. Nordic skiing kicks off around this time too.

December

'Tis the season for nativity scenes, holiday light shows and other celebrations of Christmas. The merriment continues through New Year's Eve. Expect crowds and higher prices at ski resorts.

Holiday Light Displays

Communities decorate boats, parks and shopping malls with twinkling lights. In California, watch colorful boat parades in Newport Beach and San Diego, or drive past illuminated icons in LA's Griffith Park. The Desert Botanical Gardens are aglow in Phoenix, as is the Tlaquepaque Arts & Crafts Village in Sedona.

Snow Daze

Vail marks the opening of the mountain with a week-long festival featuring all sorts of competitions and activities and plenty of big-name live performances.

itineraries

Whether you've got six days or 60, these itineraries provide a starting point for the trip of a lifetime. Want more inspiration? Head online to lonelyplanet.com/thorntree to chat with other travelers.

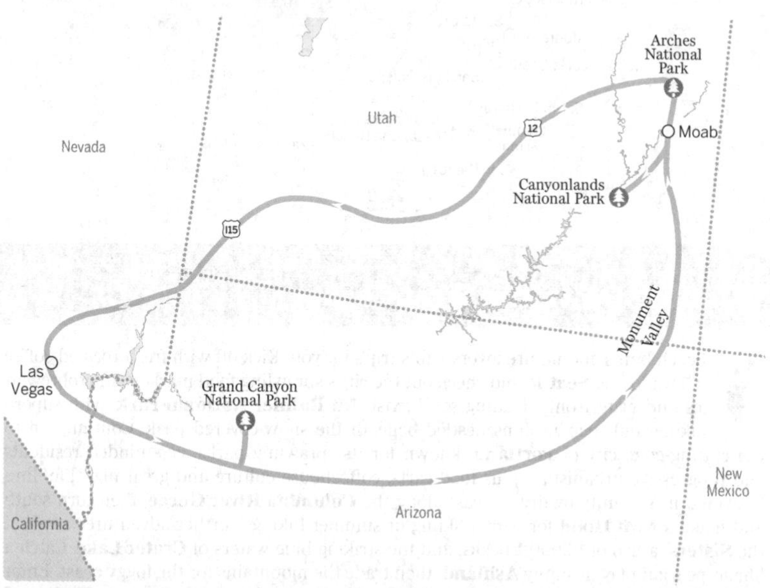

Two Weeks
Best of the Southwest

This tour spotlights the most iconic sites in the Southwest, looping past the region's most famous city, its biggest canyon and its most breathtaking red-rock scenery. Start in **Las Vegas** and spend a few days traveling the world on the Strip. When you've soaked up enough decadence, head east to canyon country – **Grand Canyon** country, that is. You'll want a couple of days to explore America's most famous park. For a once-in-a lifetime experience, descend into the South Rim chasm on the back of a mule and spend the night at Phantom Ranch on the canyon floor.

From the Grand Canyon head northeast to **Monument Valley**, with scenery straight out of a Hollywood Western, to the national parks in Utah's southeast corner – they're some of the most visually stunning in the country. Hike the shape-shifting slot canyons of **Canyonlands National Park**, watch the sunset in **Arches National Park** or mountain bike slickrock outside **Moab**. Drive one of the most spectacular stretches of pavement, **Highway 12**, west until it hooks up with I-15 and takes you back to Las Vegas.

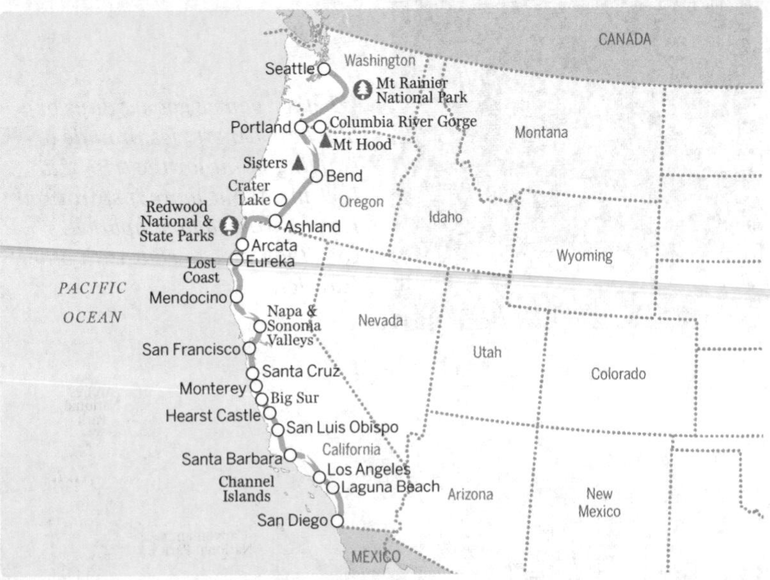

Three Weeks

Winding Down the West Coast

Beach bums and nature lovers – this trip's for you. Kick off with fresh-roasted coffee in java-loving **Seattle** and check out the city's sprawling food markets, microbreweries and waterfront. Heading south, visit **Mt Rainier National Park**, with superb hiking and relaxing inns nestled beneath the snow-covered peak. Continue on to the cutting-edge city of **Portland**, known for its sprawling parks, eco-minded residents and progressive urbanism – plus food carts, coffeehouse culture and great nightlife. Embrace nature's bounty by driving east along the **Columbia River Gorge**, then turn south and make for **Mt Hood** for winter skiing or summer hiking. Further adventures await at the **Sisters**, a trio of 10,000ft peaks, and the striking blue waters of **Crater Lake**. Catch a Shakespearian play in sunny **Ashland**, then trade the mountains for the foggy coast. Enter California via Hwy 199 and stroll through the magnificent old-growth forests in **Redwood National & State Parks**.

Hug the coast as it meanders south through funky **Arcata** and seaside **Eureka**, lose yourself on the **Lost Coast**, and catch Hwy 1 through quaint **Mendocino**, whose scenic headlands and rugged shoreline make for a requisite wander.

For wine tasting with a photogenic backdrop, travel inland to the rolling vineyards of **Napa & Sonoma Valleys**, then continue south to romantically hilly, ever free-spirited **San Francisco**.

Return to scenic Hwy 1 through surf-loving **Santa Cruz**, stately bayfront **Monterey** and beatnik-flavored **Big Sur**, where you can get scruffy again. In no time, you'll reach the surreal **Hearst Castle** and laid-back, collegiate **San Luis Obispo**.

Roll into Mediterranean-esque **Santa Barbara**, and hop aboard a ferry in Ventura to the wildlife-rich **Channel Islands**. The pull from **Los Angeles** is strong. Go ahead – indulge your fantasies of Hollywood then cruise through LA's palm-lined neighborhoods – from Santa Monica to Los Feliz, from Beverly Hills to Long Beach. After racking up a few sins in the City of Angels, move south to wander the bluffs of **Laguna Beach**, then cruise into picture-perfect **San Diego**, visiting the historic Mission, the world-famous zoo and, of course, those enticing beaches.

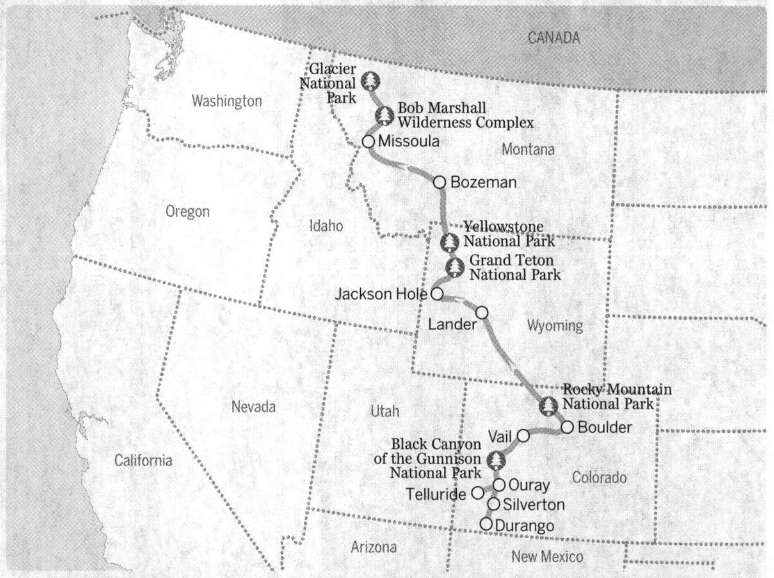

Three Weeks

Rocky Mountain High

Pack your bathing suit, mountain bike and hiking boots for this high-altitude cruise atop the Continental Divide; from here, rivers flow toward the west on one side, toward the east on the other.

Spend your first two days enjoying single-track and microbrews in **Durango**, the quintessential mountain town. From here, take the Million Dollar Hwy (Hwy 550) north through the San Juan Mountain range, sightseeing in **Silverton** and dipping into hot springs in **Ouray**. Take a side trip to **Telluride** for a summer festival – there's one almost every weekend in summer. From Montrose, drive east on Hwy 50, stopping at the **Black Canyon of the Gunnison National Park** to ogle the inky depths of the gorge before continuing to Hwy 24 north. Finish your first week in style with an overnight stay in ritzy **Vail**.

Enjoy kayaking, rock climbing and people-watching in high-energy **Boulder** then twist up to **Rocky Mountain National Park** to hike and horseback ride. While here, drive the thrilling Trail Ridge Rd through alpine vistas. Continue north on I-25. In Wyoming, take I-80 west to Hwy 287; follow this highway to **Lander** for rock climbing.

Continue north to **Jackson Hole**, another fun gateway town. Anchored by a central park surrounded by chic stores and cowboy bars, it's a good place to relax, catch a rodeo or spend the night before rafting on the Snake River. From here, it's an easy glide north into **Grand Teton National Park**, a scenic spot for a lazy lake day and a mountain stroll. Next up is mighty **Yellowstone National Park**, where geysers, bison and hiking are highlights.

Start your last week with a drive on the gorgeous Beartooth Hwy, following it into Montana then hooking onto I-90 west to **Bozeman** and **Missoula**, both good places to stock up before the final push. Serious natue awaits in the **Bob Marshall Wilderness Complex**, while **Glacier National Park** is a place to visit now – there are still some 50 or so glaciers hanging tight, but they may not be there for long. Scan for wildlife on a hike then end with a drive on the stunning Going-to-the-Sun Rd.

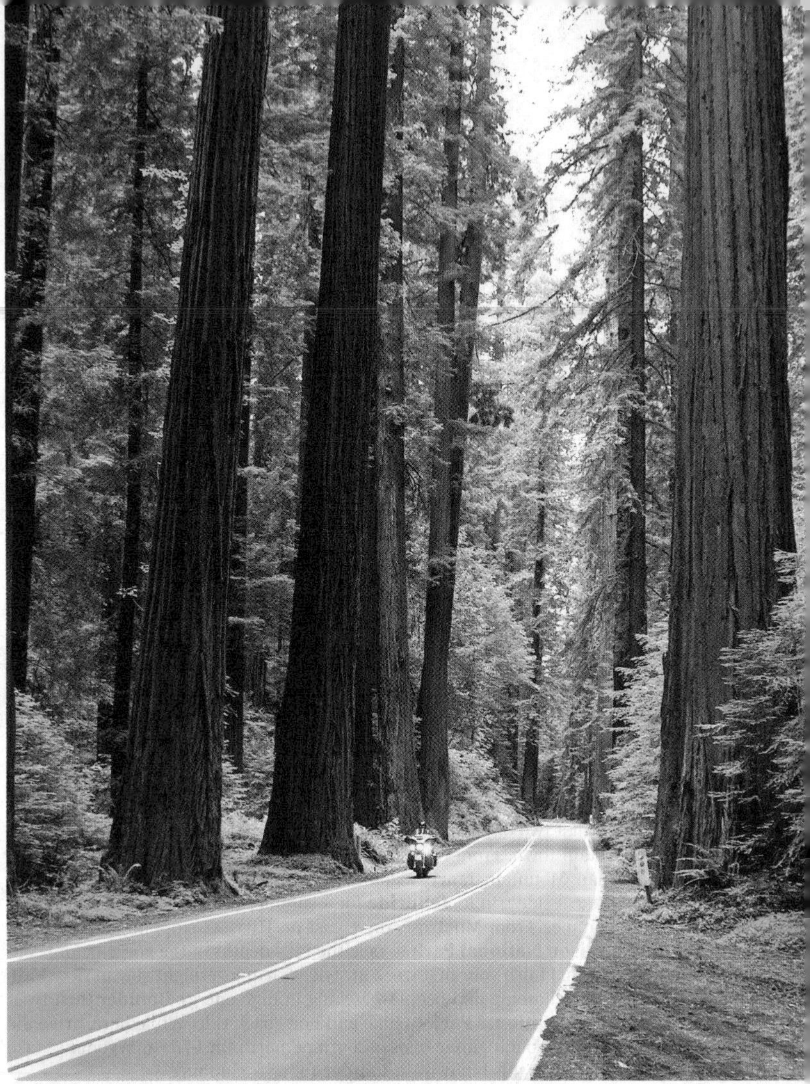

RICHARD CUMMINS / LONELY PLANET IMAGES ©

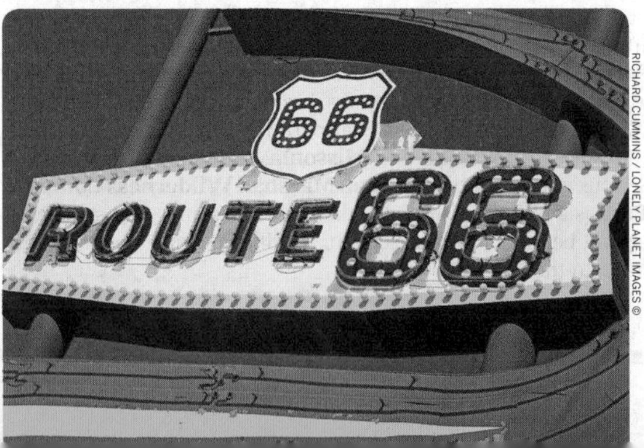

» (above) Avenue of the Giants (p157), Humboldt Redwoods State Park, California.
» (left) Motel sign, Route 66 (p347), Arizona.

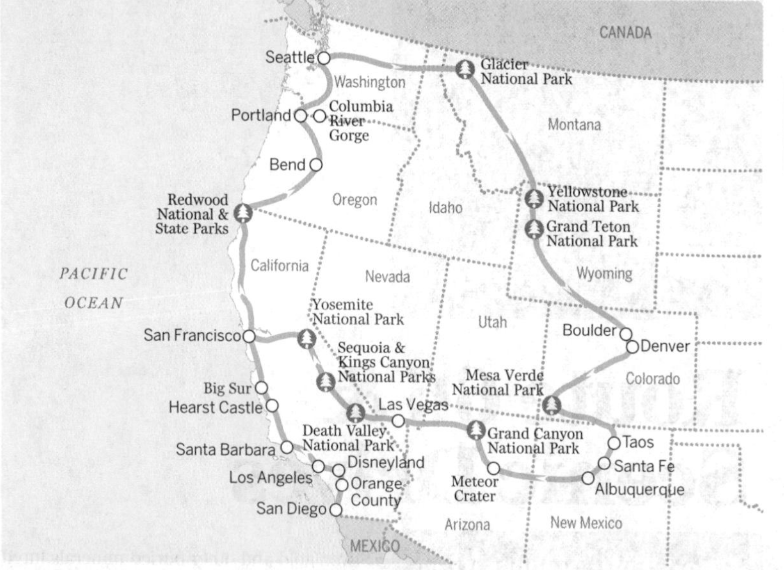

One Month

Western US Grand Tour

This lasso loop takes in the best of the west as it rolls north along the California coast, cruises past the lush landscapes of the Pacific Northwest, the alpine villages of the Rockies and the glowing red-rock beauty of the Southwest, with a final swing back into California for a hits-parade tour of the state's national parks.

From sunny **San Diego**, follow Hwy 1 north through the surf-loving coastal villages of **Orange County**, detouring to **Disneyland** before driving into shiny **Los Angeles**. Continue up the coast on scenic Hwy 1, stopping to shop and sample wine in glossy **Santa Barbara**. Gawk at the gawdy **Hearst Castle** then continue north through woodsy **Big Sur**. Dine, shop and wander through Alcatraz in the bohemian burg of **San Francisco**, then return to Hwy 1 for the quirky towns dotting the northern California coast.

Check out the big trees in **Redwood National & State Parks** and continue into Oregon, taking time for outdoor fun in **Bend**. Soak in the greenery traveling west along the **Columbia River Gorge**, then spend a few days savoring brews and views in **Portland**. Zip up the Space Needle in **Seattle** and drive east into wide-open Montana, heading for the outdoor wonders of **Glacier National Park**. Continue south into **Yellowstone National Park** where Old Faithful still blasts regularly beside its namesake lodge. Swoosh below majestic peaks in **Grand Teton National Park** before swinging southeast through Wyoming's vast cowboy plains.

In Colorado, breathe deep in outdoorsy **Boulder** then embrace the charms of city life in bustling **Denver**. The mining towns of the San Juan Mountains are next on the itinerary followed by the cliff dwellings of **Mesa Verde National Park**. Just south in New Mexico, artist meccas **Taos** and **Santa Fe** are fab stops for one-of-a-kind gifts. Slurp green chile stew in **Albuquerque** and follow Route 66 west into Arizona, stopping at **Meteor Crater** before detouring north for majestic views in **Grand Canyon National Park**. Continue west to roll the dice in **Las Vegas**, then drive into central California for **Death Valley National Park**, and **Kings Canyon** and **Sequoia National Parks**, concluding with a glimpse of the mighty Half Dome in **Yosemite National Park**. Complete the loop with a fine meal and glass of California wine in breezy San Francisco.

Route 66 & Scenic Drives

Road Trip Necessities

A prepared road-tripper is a happy road-tripper, especially in the West with its lonely roads and unpredictable weather. A few things to remember:

» Make sure you have a spare tire and tool kit (eg jack, jumper cables, ice scraper), as well as emergency equipment in your vehicle; if you're renting a car, consider buying a roadside safety kit.

» Bring good maps, especially if you're touring away from highways; don't depend on GPS units as they may not work in remote areas.

» Carry extra water. You may need it if the car breaks down in the desert.

» Fill up the tank regularly; gas stations can be few and far between in the West.

» Always carry your driver's license and proof of insurance.

Best Roadside Dining

The Turquoise Room Rte 66, Winslow, AZ
Cafe Diablo Hwy 12, Torrey, UT
The Asylum Hwy 89A, Jerome, AZ
Frontier Rte 66, Albuquerque, NM
Santa Barbara Shellfish Co PCH, Santa Barbara, CA

Silver, gold and other buried minerals lured prospectors to the West in the 1800s. Today, it's the above-ground asphalt treasures that draw the masses. From desert backroads to coastal highways to mountain-hugging thrill rides, the West is chock-full of picturesque drives.

Route 66

Get your kitsch on Route 66 might be a better slogan for the scrubby stretch of Mother Road running through California, Arizona and New Mexico. A wigwam motel. A meteor crater. Begging burros. And a solar-powered Ferris wheel overlooking the Pacific Ocean. It's a bit off-the-beaten path, but folks along the way will be very glad you're here.

Why Go

History, scenery and the open road. This alluring combination is what makes a Route 66 road trip so enjoyable. In New Mexico, the neon signs of Tucumcari are a fun-loving welcome to the West. They also sets the mood for adventure – the appropriate mood to have before dropping into the scuba-ready Blue Hole in Santa Rosa. Fuel up on lip-smacking green chile stew at Frontier in Albuquerque then grab a snooze at the 1937 El Rancho Motel (John Wayne slept here!) in Gallup.

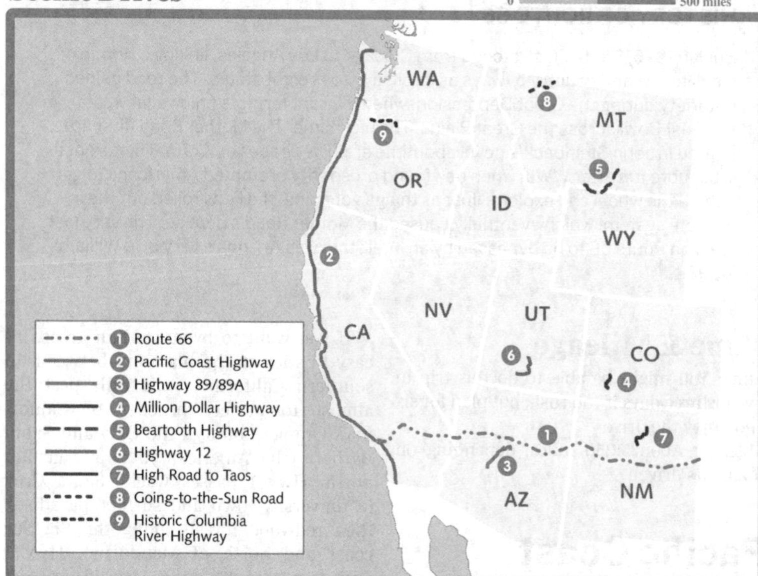

Arizona greets road-trippers with kitschy style in Holbrook, home of the ever-so-retro teepee motel. From here, the next stop is the 'Take It Easy' town of Winslow where there's a girl, my Lord, in a flatbed Ford... Snap a photo of the famous corner then savor a spectacular dinner in the Turquoise Room at La Posada Hotel. Meteor Crater, east of Flagstaff, is a mighty big hole in the ground – and a good place to slow down and catch your breath. From here, Route 66 parallels the train tracks into energetic Flagstaff, passing the wonderful Museum Club, a cabinlike roadhouse where everyone's having fun or about to. Next up is Williams, a railroad town lined with courtyard motels and brimming with small-town charm.

Seligman is a quirky little village that greets travelers with retro motels, a roadkill cafe and a squirt of fake mustard at the Snow-Cap Drive In. Burma Shave signs share funny advice on the way to Grand Canyon Caverns, where you'll be lured 21 stories underground for a tour or possibly an overnight stay. From here, highlights include an eclectic general store in Hackberry, the Route 66 museum in Kingman and snack-loving burros in sun-baked Oatman.

Things stay sun-baked in California as the Mother Road swoops into the Mojave Desert and passes ghost towns heralded by lonesome railroad markers. In Victorville, the Brian Burger comes with a spicy kick at Emma Jean's Holland Burger Café. The vibe kicks up in stylish Pasadena before the road's final push to the Pacific. At the Santa Monica Pier, hop on the solar-powered Ferris wheel and celebrate your journey with a panoramic sunset view.

When to Go

The best time to travel Route 66 is from May to September, when the weather is warm and you'll be able to take advantage of more open-air activities.

The Route

This journey starts in Tucumcari, New Mexico then continues west through Arizona and California, roughly paralleling I-40 all the way to Barstow, CA. After Barstow, Route 66 south passes through San Bernardino on the I-15 before cutting west and heading into Pasadena. Follow I-110 to Santa Monica Blvd west to seaside Santa Monica.

HISTORY OF ROUTE 66

Built in 1926, Route 66 stretched from Chicago to Los Angeles, linking a ribbon of small towns and country byways as it rolled across eight states. The road gained notoriety during the Great Depression, when migrant farmers followed it west from the Dust Bowl across the Great Plains. The nickname 'The Mother Road' first appeared in John Steinbeck's novel about the era, *The Grapes of Wrath*. Things got a little more fun after WWII, when newfound prosperity prompted Americans to get behind the wheel and explore. Just as things got going, the Feds rolled out the interstate system, which eventually caused the Mother Road's demise. The very last town on Route 66 to be bypassed by an interstate was Arizona's very own Williams, in 1984.

Time & Mileage

Time: You might be able to do this trip in two or three days if you rush, but plan for six and enjoy the drive
Mileage: About 1250 miles, depending on segments driven

Pacific Coast Highway

Lovers, ramblers and bohemians, start your engines. The highways connecting Canada to Mexico on the West Coast were made for driving, including the especially scenic Pacific Coast Highway (PCH).

Why Go

This epic West Coast journey, which rolls through California, Oregon and Washington, takes in cosmopolitan cities, surf towns and charming coastal enclaves ripe for exploration. For many travelers, the biggest draw is the magnificent scenery: wild and remote beaches, cliff-top views overlooking crashing waves, rolling hills, and lush forests thick with redwoods and eucalyptus trees. But the route is not loved only for its looks. It's also got personality, offering beside-the-highway adventures for surfers, kayakers, scuba divers and hikers.

Highlights? Let's start with the cities. Coastal highways connect the dots between some of the West Coast's most striking municipalities, starting with surf-loving San Diego in Southern California and moving north through hedonistic Los Angeles and offbeat San Francisco. Way up north, take a worthwhile detour to artsy and alternative-minded Seattle, Washington.

If you want to bypass urban areas, it's easy to stick to the places in between. In southern California, PCH rolls past the almost too-perfect beaches of California's Orange County ('the OC') and Santa Barbara (the 'American Riviera'). Further north, Hwy 1 passes wacky Santa Cruz (a university town and surfers' paradise), then redwood forests along the Big Sur coast and north of Mendocino. Hwy 1 cruises past sand dunes, seaside resorts and fishing villages of coastal Oregon; and finally, the wild lands of Washington's Olympic Peninsula, with its primeval rainforest and bucolic San Juan Islands, served by coastal ferries.

The Route

Highways stretch nearly 1500 miles from border to border – that is, from Tijuana, Mexico to British Columbia, Canada. In California, the coastal route jumps between I-5, Hwy 101 and Hwy 1 (when in doubt, just hug the coast) before committing to Hwy 101 in Oregon and Washington.

When to Go

There's no bad time of year to drive the route, although northern climes will be rainier and snowier during winter. Peak travel season is June through August, which isn't always the best time as many stretches of the coast are socked in by fog during early summer (locals call it 'June Gloom'). The shoulder seasons before Memorial Day (ie April and May) and after Labor Day (ie September and October) can be ideal, with sunny days, crisply cool nights and fewer crowds.

Time & Mileage

Time: No stopping? Give yourself three days because traffic and two-lane roads will slow you down; to fully enjoy the sites, allow 10 to 14 days
Mileage: About 1500 miles

Highway 89/89A: Wickenburg to Oak Creek Canyon

Hwy 89 and its sidekick Hwy 89A are familiar to Arizona road-trippers because they cross some of the most scenic and distinct regions in the state. The route described here travels over the Weaver and Mingus mountains before rolling into Sedona and Oak Creek Canyon.

Why Go

This is our favorite drive in Arizona. It may not be the prettiest or the wildest, but there's a palpable sense of the Old West infusing the trip, like you've slipped through the swinging doors of history. But the route's not stuck in the 19th century. Far from it. Weekend art walks, a burgeoning wine trail, stylish indie-owned shops and restaurants all add some 21st-century sparkle. For those interested in cowboy history, Wickenburg and its dude ranches are a good place to spend some time. Hwy 89 leaves town via Hwy 93 and soon tackles the Weaver Mountains, climbing 2500ft in 4 miles. The road levels out at mountain-topping Yarnell, 'where the desert breeze meets the mountain air,' then swoops easily past grassy buttes and grazing cattle in the Peeples Valley. From here, highlights include Prescott's Whiskey Row, towering Thumb Butte and the unusual boulders at Granite Dells.

Follow Hwy 89A to Jerome and hold on tight. This serpentine section of road brooks no distraction, clinging tight to the side of Mingus Mountain. If you dare, glance east for stunning views of the Verde Valley. The zigzagging reaches epic proportions in Jerome, a former mining town cleaved into the side of Cleopatra Hill. Pull over for art galleries, tasting rooms, quirky inns and an unusually high number of ghosts. Hwy 89A then drops to Clarkdale, Tuzigoot National Monument and Old Town Cottonwood. On the way to Sedona, detour to wineries on Page Springs Rd or loop into town via the Cathedral Rock, passing Red Rock Loop Rd. Sedona is made for rejuvenation, a pretty place to commune with a vortex, dine on a fine meal or shop for art and Navajo rugs. This trip ends with a cannonball into Oak Creek Canyon where the namesake creek sparkles with riparian lushness in the shadows of a towering red rock corridor.

When to Go

This route is best traveled in spring, summer and fall to avoid winter snow – although you might see a few flakes in the mountains in April! In the dead of summer, you won't want to linger in low-lying, toasty Wickenburg.

The Route

From Wickenburg, follow Hwy 93 to Hwy 89 then drive north to Prescott. North of town, pick up Hwy 89A, following it to Sedona.

Time & Mileage

Time: This route can be driven in a half-day, but we recommend two to three days for maximum enjoyment
Mileage: 134 miles

Million Dollar Highway

Stretching between Ouray and Silverton in southern Colorado is one of the most gorgeous alpine drives in the US. Part of the 236-mile San Juan Skyway, this section of US 550 is known as the Million Dollar Hwy because the road, they say, is filled with ore.

Why Go

Twenty-five miles of smooth, buttery pavement twists over three mountain passes, serving up views of Victorian homes, snow-capped peaks, mineshaft headframes and a gorge lined with rock. But the allure isn't just the beauty. Part of the thrill is the driving. Hairpin turns, occasional rock slides and narrow, mountain-hugging pavement flips this route from a Sunday afternoon drive to a Nascar-worthy adventure. Charming Ouray sits at nearly 7800ft, surrounded by lofty peaks. It also fronts the Uncompahgre Gorge, a steep, rocky canyon famous for its ice climbing. While here, take a hike or soak in the town's hot springs. From Ouray, the Million Dollar Hwy – completed in 1884 after three years of construction – hugs the side of the gorge, twisting past old mines that pock the mountainsides. Stay vigilant for the masochistic, spandex-clad cyclists pumping over the passes on the ribbon-thin road. In Silverton, step away from the car and enjoy the aspen-covered mountains or watch the steam-powered Durango & Silverton Narrow Gauge Railroad chug into town.

When to Go

Summer is the best time to visit. In winter, the highest pass sometimes closes and at other times you may need chains. You might even see snow on the ground in summer, though it likely won't be on the road.

Route

From Ouray, follow Hwy 550 south to Silverton.

Detour

The drive between Ouray and Telluride is 50 miles – if you take the paved route. If you're feeling adventurous (and have the right vehicle), consider the 16-mile road over Imogene Pass. On this old mining road you'll cross streams, alpine meadows and one of the state's highest passes. You'll also drive past by an old mine. But we should mention one thing: this 'shortcut' takes three hours. Still game?

Time & Mileage

Time: The drive can be done in a few hours, but give yourself a day to see the sights
Mileage: 25 miles

Beartooth Highway

Depending on who's talking, the sky-high Beartooth Hwy is either the best way to get to Yellowstone, the most exciting motorcycle ride in the West or the most scenic highway in America. We'd say it was all three.

Why Go

Sometimes you just want to find a place so inspirational and beautiful that it'll make you pull over, leave your car, beat your chest (or shake out your hair) and yell 'Yeah!' In the West, that place is the Beartooth Hwy.

From Red Lodge, Montana, this adventurous drive ascends Rock Creek Canyon's glaciated valley via a series of spaghetti-loop switchbacks, gaining an amazing 5000ft in elevation in just a few miles. Pull off at Rock Creek Vista Point Overlook for a short, wheelchair-accessible walk to superb views. The road continues up onto the high plateau, past 'Mae West Curve' and into Wyoming. Twin Lakes has views of the cirque as well as the ski lift that carries the daring to an extreme spring ski run. After a series of switchbacks, look northwest for the Hellroaring Plateau and the jagged Bears Tooth (11,612ft). The route, flanked by alpine tundra, crests at the Beartooth Pass West Summit, the highest point at 10,947ft. Fifteen-foot snowbanks may linger here as late as June (sometimes even July).

After passing more lakes, the road descends past Beartooth Butte, a huge lump of the sedimentary rock that once covered the Beartooths. The highway drops to several excellent fishing areas on the Clarks Fork, then reenters Montana, reaching Cooke City via Colter Pass (8066ft). Yellowstone's northeast entrance is 4 miles from Cooke City.

When to Go

If you'd like to add some hiking to your driving, come in August. That's when the weather's typically the best for outdoor adventure.

Route

From Red Lodge, follow Hwy 212 west – crossing into and out of Wyoming – to Cooke City, MT.

Time & Mileage

Time: It's hard to zip through the twisty Beartooth Highway; allow at least an afternoon or morning to drive it
Mileage: 68 miles

Highway 12

Arguably Utah's most diverse and stunning route, Hwy 12 winds through a remote and rugged canyon land, linking several national and state parks - and a few fantastic restaurants - in the state's red-rock center.

Why Go

With its mesmerizing mix of crimson canyons, sprawling deserts, thick forests and lofty peaks, Hwy 12 in remote southern Utah works well for adventurous explorers. The trip kicks off at Bryce Canyon National Park where the eye-catching gold-and-crimson spires set the stage for the color-infused journey to come. Highlights include Kodachrome Basin State Park, Grand Staircase-Escalante National Monument and the Calf Creek Recreation Area. As you drive, notice how the land quickly and dramatically changes from forested plateau to red-rock canyon and from slickrock desert to alpine forest. Many consider the best section the switchbacks and petrified sand dunes between Torrey and Boulder. The razor-thin Hogback Ridge between Escalante and Boulder is pretty stunning, too.

Take time to stop at the viewpoints and pullouts, especially at Mile 70 where the Aquarius Plateau lords over giant mesas, towering domes, deep canyons and undulating slickrock, all unfurling in an explosion of color. But it's not just about the views. In Boulder, treat your taste buds to a locally sourced meal at Hell's Backbone Grill, followed by homemade cookies and cakes at the Burr Trail Grill & Outpost, or enjoy a flavor-packed Southwestern dish at Café Diablo further north in Torrey.

When to Go

For the best weather and driving conditions – especially over 11,000ft Boulder Mountain – drive Hwy 12 between May and October.

Route

From US Hwy 89 in Utah, follow Hwy 12 east to Bryce Canyon National Park. The road takes a northerly turn at Kodachrome Basin State Park then continues to Torrey.

Time & Mileage

Time: Although the route could be driven in a few hours, two to three days will allow for a bit of exploration
Mileage: 124 miles

High Road to Taos

This picturesque byway in northern New Mexico links Santa Fe to Taos, rippling through a series of adobe villages and mountain-flanked vistas in and around the Truchas Peaks.

Why Go

Santa Fe and Taos are well-known artists' communities, lovely places brimming with galleries, studios and museums. Two cities this stunning should be linked by an aesthetically pleasing byway, and the mountainous High Road to Taos obliges. In Nambe, hike to waterfalls or simply meditate by the namesake lake. From here, the road leads north to picturesque Chimayo where abandoned crutches line the wall in the Santuario de Chimayo, 'The Lourdes of America.' Take some time to wander through the community, to admire the fine weaving and woodcarving in family-run galleries. Near Truchas, a village of galleries and century-old adobes, you'll find the High Road Marketplace. This co-operative on SR 676 sells a variety of artwork by area artists. Original paintings and carvings remain in good condition up Hwy 76 inside the Church of San José de Gracia, considered one of the finest surviving 18th-century churches in the USA. Next is Picuris Pueblo, once one of the most powerful pueblos in the region. This ride ends at Penasco, a gateway to the Pecos Wilderness that's also home to the engagingly experimental Penasco Theatre. From here, follow Hwys 75 and 518 into Taos.

When to Go

The high season is summer, but spring can be a nice time to see blooming flowers. Fall presents a show of colorful leaves. With mountains on the route, winter is not the best time to visit.

Route

From Santa Fe, take 84/285 west to Pojoaque and turn right on Hwy 503, toward Nambe. From Hwy 503, take Hwy 76 to Hwy 75, then drive into Taos on Hwy 518.

Time & Mileage

Time: Without stopping, this drive should take about a half day, but give yourself a full day if you want to shop and explore
Mileage: 85 miles

GOING-TO-THE-SUN ROAD: A LEGEND AND A LANDMARK

Going-to-the-Sun Road was named after Going-to-the-Sun Mountain. According to legend – or a story concocted in the 1880s – a deity of the Blackfeet Tribe once taught tribal members to hunt. After the lesson, he left an image of himself on the mountain as inspiration before he ascended to the sun. Today, the road is a National Historic Landmark and a National Civil Engineering Landmark, the only road in the country to hold both designations.

Going-to-the-Sun-Road

A strong contender for the most spectacular drive in America, the 53-mile Going-to-the-Sun Road is the only paved road through Glacier National Park in Montana.

Why Go

Glaciers! Grizzlies! A mountain-hugging marvel of modern engineering! Yep, the Going-to-the-Sun Road inspires superlatives and exclamation points. But the accolades are deserved. The road, completed in 1933, crosses a ruggedly beautiful alpine landscape, twisting and turning over a lofty Continental Divide that's usually blanketed in snow. From the park's west entrance, the road skirts the shimmering Lake McDonald. Ahead, the looming Garden Wall forms the 9000ft spine of the Continental Divide and separates the west side of the park from the east side. The road crosses the divide at Logan Pass (6880ft). From here, the 18.5-mile Highline Trail traces the park's mountainous backbone, with views of glaciated valleys, sawtooth peaks, wildflowers and wildlife. And oh, the wildlife you might see. Mountain goats. Bighorn sheep. Moose. Maybe even a grizzly bear or an elusive wolverine. But save a few shots on your camera. After Logan Pass, the road passes Jackson Glacier Overlook, where you can bear witness to one of the park's melting monoliths. Experts say that at current global temperatures, all of the park's glaciers will be gone by 2020. So now is the time to visit!

When to Go

This snow-attracting route opens late and closes early, but the full route is typically drivable between mid-June and mid-September. In 2011, due to an unusually heavy snowpack, the road didn't completely open until July 13.

Route

From the west entrance of the park, follow the Going-to-the-Sun Road east to St Mary.

Time & Mileage

Time: It varies depending on conditions, but plan to spend at least a half-day on the drive
Mileage: 53 miles

Historic Columbia River Highway

Lush foliage and trailblazing history are highlights on US 30, a carefully planned byway that ribbons beside the Columbia River Gorge east of Portland, Oregon.

Why Go

Look, there's a waterfall. And another waterfall. And another. Just how many waterfalls can one scenic highway hold? Quite a few if that road is the Historic Columbia River Hwy. The original route – completed in 1922 – connected Portland to The Dalles. The first paved road in the Pacific Northwest, it was carefully planned, built with the pleasure of driving in mind rather than speed. Viewpoints were carefully selected, and the stone walls and arching bridges stylishly complement the gorgeous scenery. Also notable is the history. Lewis and Clark traveled this route as they pushed toward the Pacific Ocean in 1805. Fifty years later, Oregon Trail pioneers ended their cross-country trek with a harrowing final push through the gorge's treacherous waters. Today, although sections of the original byway have been closed, or replaced by US-84, much of US 30 is still open for driving and some closed portions can be traversed by hiking or cycling. One roadside highlight is the Portland Women's Forum Park, which provides one of the best

MORE SCENIC DRIVES

Hungry for more road trips? Check the destination chapters and the list below for a few more good ones.

Turquoise Trail, NM This back route between Tijeras, near Albuquerque and Santa Fe, was a major trade route for several thousand years. Today it rolls past art galleries, shops (with turquoise jewelry), and a mining museum. From I-40, follow Hwy 14 north to I-25. Also see www.turquoisetrail.org,

Apache Trail, AZ This isn't your grandmother's Sunday afternoon drive - unless your grandmother likes 45 miles of rabid road. From Apache Junction east of Phoenix, follow Hwy 88 past a kid-friendly ghost town, the wildflowers of Lost Dutchman State Park and three Salt River lakes. In the middle of it all? A snarling dirt section that drops 1000+ feet in less than three miles. Hold tight!

Eastern Sierra Scenic Byway, CA From Topaz Lake, follow Hwy 395 south along the eastern flank of the mighty Sierra Nevadas, ending at Little Lake. The region holds 14,000ft peaks, ice-blue lakes, pine forests, desert basins and hot springs.

views of the gorge. Nearby, the 1916 Vista House, built to honor the Oregon Trail pioneers, now holds a visitor center. It's perched on Crown Point, a good viewpoint that also marks the western edge of the gorge. And those gushing cascades? For oohs and ahhs, don't miss Multnomah Falls, Oregon's tallest waterfall at 642ft.

When to Go

Waterfalls are at their peak February to May, while summer is great for hiking.

Route

To reach the historic highway, take exit 17 or 35 off I-84 east of Portland and continue east. The western section of the original highway ends at Multnomah Falls. From here hop onto I-84 and continue east to exit 69 at Mosier where you can return to Hwy 30.

Time & Mileage

Time: One day
Mileage: 100 miles

Western USA Outdoors

Ultimate Outdoor Experiences

Rafting Colorado River through the Grand Canyon, AZ
Hiking Summit of Half Dome, Yosemite National Park, CA
Mountain biking Kokopelli's Trail, UT
Rock climbing Joshua Tree National Park, CA
Scrambling Angels Landing, Zion National Park, UT
Splashing Havasu Falls, AZ
Exploring Racetrack Playa, Death Valley National Park, CA
Downhill skiing Vail, CO
Touching a glacier Glacier National Park, MT
Kayaking San Juan Islands, WA

Best Wildlife Watching

Bears Glacier National Park, MT
Elk, bison and gray wolves Yellowstone National Park, WY
Birds Patagonia-Sonoita Creek Preserve and Ramsey Preserve, AZ
Whales and dolphins Monterey Bay, CA
Bighorn sheep and moose Rocky Mountain National Park, CO

Adventure lovers, welcome to paradise. Whether you're a couch potato, a weekend warrior or an Ironman (or maiden), the West has an outdoor activity for you. The best part? Your adventure will likely be accompanied by a stunning backdrop. You can float on an inner tube, scan for hummingbirds, bounce over slickrock trails, swoosh down powdery slopes, surf curling waves or hike into the world's most famous canyon.

Camping

Campers are absolutely spoiled for choice in the West. Pitch a tent beside alpine lakes and streams in Colorado, sleep under saguaro cacti in southern Arizona or snooze on gorgeous strands of California sand.

Campground Types & Amenities

» **Primitive campsites** Usually have fire pits, picnic tables and access to drinking water and vault toilets; most common in national forests (USFS) and on Bureau of Land Management (BLM) land.

» **Developed campgrounds** Typically found in state and national parks, with more amenities, including flush toilets, barbecue grills and occasionally hot showers and coin-op laundry.

» **RV (recreational vehicle) hookups** and **dump stations** Available at many privately owned campgrounds, but only a few public-lands campgrounds.

» **Private campgrounds** Cater mainly to RVers and offer hot showers, swimming pools, wi-fi and family camping cabins; tent sites may be few and uninviting.

» **Walk-in (environmental) sites** Providing more peace and privacy; a few public-lands campgrounds reserve these for long-distance hikers and cyclists.

Rates & Reservations

Many public and private campgrounds accept reservations for all or some of their sites, while a few are strictly first-come, first-served. Overnight rates range from free for the most primitive campsites to $50 or more for pull-through RV sites with full hookups.

These agencies let you search for campground locations and amenities; check availability and reserve campsites online:

Recreation.gov (☎518-885-3639, 877-444-6777; www.recreation.gov) Camping and cabin reservations for national parks, national forests, BLM land etc.

ReserveAmerica (☎916-638-5883, 800-444-7275; www.reserveamerica.com) Reservations for state parks, regional parks and some private campgrounds across North America. See website for phone numbers by state.

Kampgrounds of America (KOA; http://koa.com) National chain of reliable, but more expensive private campgrounds offering full facilities, including for RVs.

Hiking & Trekking

Good hiking trails are abundant in the West. Fitness is a priority throughout the region, and most metropolitan areas have at least

TOP TRAILS IN THE WEST

Ask 10 people for their top trail recommendations and no two answers will be alike. The country is so varied and distances so enormous, there's little consensus. That said, you can't go wrong with the following all-star sampler.

For more details about these trails, check the destination chapters and listed websites, or pick up a trail guide at the appropriate park.

» **South Kaibab/North Kaibab Trail, Grand Canyon, AZ** (p341) A multiday cross-canyon tramp down to the Colorado River and back up to the rim.

» **Longs Peak Trail, Rocky Mountain National Park, CO** (p254) Very popular 15-mile round-trip hike leads to the bouldery summit of Longs Peak (14,259ft) and its views of snow-capped summits.

» **Angels Landing, Zion National Park, UT** (p371) After a heart-pounding scramble over a narrow, precipice-flanked strip of rock, the reward is a sweeping view of Zion Canyon. It's a 5-mile round-trip.

» **Mt Washburn Trail, Yellowstone National Park, WY** (p279) From Dunraven Pass, this wildflower-lined trail climbs 3 miles to expansive views from the summit of Mt Washburn (10,243ft). Look for bighorn sheep.

» **Pacific Crest Trail** (PCT; www.pcta.org) Follows the spines of the Cascades and Sierra Nevada, traipsing 2650 miles from Canada to Mexico, passing through six of North America's seven ecozones.

» **Half Dome in Yosemite National Park, CA** (p166) Scary and strenuous, but the Yosemite Valley views and sense of accomplishment are worth it.

» **Enchanted Valley, Olympic National Park, WA** (p197) Magnificent mountain views, roaming wildlife and lush rainforests – all on a 13-mile out-and-back trail.

» **Great Northern Traverse, Glacier National Park, MT** (p293) A 58-mile haul that cuts through the heart of grizzly country and crosses the Continental Divide.

» **The Big Loop, Chiricahua National Monument, AZ** A 9.5-mile hike along several trails that winds past an 'army' of wondrous rock pillars in southeastern Arizona once used as a hideout by Apache warriors.

» **Tahoe Rim Trail, Lake Tahoe, CA** (p172) This 165-mile all-purpose trail circumnavigates the lake from high above, affording glistening Sierra views.

WESTERN US NATIONAL PARKS

PARK	FEATURES	ACTIVITIES	BEST TIME
Arches (p366)	more than 2500 sandstone arches	scenic drives, day hikes	spring-fall
Bryce Canyon (p370)	brilliantly colored, eroded hoodoos	day & backcountry hikes, horseback riding	spring-fall
Canyonlands (p366)	epic Southwestern canyons, mesas & buttes	scenic viewpoints, backcountry hikes, white-water rafting	spring-fall
Carlsbad Caverns (p397)	extensive underground cave system; free-tail bat colony	cave tours, backcountry hikes	spring-fall
Death Valley (p107)	hot, dramatic desert & unique ecology	scenic drives, day hikes	spring
Glacier (p293)	impressive glaciated landscape; mountain goats	day & backcountry hikes, scenic drives	summer
Grand Canyon (p339)	spectacular 277-mile-long, 1-mile-deep river canyon	day & backcountry hikes, mule trips, river running	spring-fall
Grand Teton (p282)	towering granite peaks; moose, bison, wolves	day & backcountry hikes, rock climbing, fishing	spring-fall
Kings Canyon/Sequoia (p168)	sequoia redwood groves, granite canyon	day & backcountry hikes, cross-country skiing	summer-fall
Mesa Verde (p272)	preserved Ancestral Puebloan cliff dwellings, historic sites, mesas & canyons	short hikes	spring-fall
Olympic (p196)	temperate rainforests, alpine meadows, Mt Olympus	day & backcountry hikes	spring-fall
Petrified Forest (p347)	fossilized trees, petroglyphs, Painted Desert scenery	Day hikes	spring-fall
Redwood (p158)	virgin redwood forest, world's tallest trees; elk	day & backcountry hikes	spring-fall
Rocky Mountain (p254)	stunning peaks, alpine tundra, the Continental Divide; elk, bighorn sheep, moose, beavers	day & backcountry hikes, cross-country skiing	summer-fall
Saguaro (p348)	giant saguaro cactus, desert scenery	day & backcountry hikes	spring-fall
Yellowstone (p276)	geysers & geothermal pools, impressive canyon; prolific wildlife	day & backcountry hikes, cycling, cross-country skiing	year-round
Yosemite (p163)	sheer granite-walled valley, waterfalls, alpine meadows	day & backcountry hikes, rock climbing, skiing	year-round
Zion (p371)	immense red-rock canyon, Virgin River	day & backcountry hikes, canyoneering	spring-fall

one large park with trails. National parks and monuments are ideal for both short and long hikes. If you're hankering for nights in the wilderness beneath star-filled skies, however, plan on securing a backcountry permit in advance, especially in places like the Grand Canyon – spaces are limited, particularly during summer. For information about free dispersed camping on public land beyond the national parks, see the boxed text, p442.

Hiking Resources

» **Survive Outdoors** (www.surviveoutdoors.com) Dispenses safety and first-aid tips, plus helpful photos of dangerous critters.

» **Wilderness Survival**, by Gregory Davenport, is easily the best book on surviving nearly every contingency.

» **American Hiking Society** (www.americanhiking.org) Links to local hiking clubs and 'volunteer vacations' building trails.

» **Backpacker** (www.backpacker.com) Premier national magazine for backpackers, from novices to experts.

» **Rails-to-Trails Conservancy** (www.railstotrails.org) Converts abandoned railroad corridors into hiking and biking trails; publishes free trail reviews at www.traillink.com.

Fees & Wilderness Permits

» State parks typically charge a daily parking fee of $5 to $15; there's often no charge if you walk or bike into these parks.

» National park entry averages $10 to $25 per vehicle for seven consecutive days; some national parks are free.

» For unlimited admission to national parks, national forests and other federal recreation lands for one year, buy an 'America the Beautiful' pass (see p443).

» Often required for overnight backpackers and extended day hikes, wilderness permits are issued at ranger stations and park visitor centers. Daily quotas may be in effect during peak periods, usually late spring through early fall.

» Some wilderness permits may be reserved ahead of time, and very popular trails (eg Half Dome, Mt Whitney) may sell out several months in advance.

» You'll need a National Forest Adventure Pass ($5 per day, $30 per year) to park in some of southern California's national forests. To hike in the forest surrounding Sedona, AZ you'll need to buy a Red Rock Pass (www.redrockcountry.org; $5 per day, $15 per week). Passes can be purchased at USFS ranger stations, kiosks (at some trailheads) and select local vendors.

Cycling

The popularity of cycling is growing by the day in the USA, with cities adding more cycle lanes and becoming more bike-friendly. An increasing number of greenways dot the countryside. You'll find diehard enthusiasts in every town, and numerous outfitters offer guided trips for all levels and durations.

MAD FOR MOUNTAIN BIKING

Mountain-biking enthusiasts will find trail nirvana in Boulder, CO, Moab, UT, Bend, OR, Ketchum, ID and Marin, CA, where Gary Fisher and Co. bunny-hopped the sport forward by careening down the rocky flanks of Mt Tamalpais on home-rigged bikes. Other great destinations include the following:

» **Kokopelli's Trail, UT** One of the premier mountain biking trails in the Southwest stretches 140 miles on mountainous terrain between Loma, CO, and Moab, UT. Other nearby options include the 206-mile, hut-to-hut ride between Telluride, CO, and Moab, UT, and the shorter but very challenging 38-mile ride from Aspen to Crested Butte – an equally stunning ride.

» **Sun Top Loop, WA** A 22-mile ride with challenging climbs and superb views of Mt Rainier and surrounding peaks on the western slopes of Washington's Cascade Mountains.

» **Downieville Downhill, Downieville, CA** Not for the faint of heart, this piney trail, located near its namesake Sierra foothill town in Tahoe National Forest, skirts river-hugging cliffs, passes through old-growth forest and drops 4200ft in under 14 miles.

» **McKenzie River Trail, Willamette National Forest, OR** (www.mckenzierivertrail.com) Twenty-two miles of blissful single-track winding through deep forests and volcanic formations. The town of McKenzie is about 50 miles east of Eugene (p221).

» **Porcupine Rim, Moab, UT** A 30-mile loop from town (p364), this venerable high-desert romp features stunning views and hairy downhills.

Many states offer social multiday rides, such as Ride the Rockies in Colorado. For a modest fee, you can join the peloton on a scenic, well-supported route; your gear is ferried ahead to that night's camping spot. Another standout ride is Arizona's Mt Lemmon, a thigh-zinging 28-mile climb from the Sonoran Desert floor to the 9157ft summit. You can now rent bikes on the South Rim of the Grand Canyon at Grand Canyon National Park. Ride to Hermit's Rest on the park's Hermit Rd and the ever-lengthening Greenway Trail.

Top Cycling Towns

» **San Francisco, CA** A pedal over the Golden Gate Bridge lands you in the stunningly beautiful, and stunningly hilly, Marin Headlands.

» **Boulder, CO** Outdoors-loving town with loads of great biking paths, including the 16-mile Boulder Creek Trail.

» **Portland, OR** A trove of great cycling (on- and off-road) in the Pacific Northwest.

» **Los Angeles, CA** Cycling surface streets isn't great, but the sunny South Bay Trail is a scenic, level bike path, running the length of the coast between Santa Monica and Redondo Beach to the south.

Surfing

The best surf in continental USA breaks off the coast of California. There are loads of options – from the funky and low-key Santa Cruz to San Francisco's Ocean Beach (a tough spot to learn!) or in bohemian Bolinas, 30 miles north. South, you'll find strong swells and Santa Ana winds in San Diego, La Jolla, Malibu and Santa Barbara, all sporting warmer waters, fewer sharks of the great white variety and a saucy SoCal beach scene; the best conditions are from September to November. Along the coast of Oregon and Washington, are miles of crowd-free beaches and pockets of surfing communities.

Top California Surfing Spots

Huntington Beach (aka Surf City, USA) is the quintessential surf capital, with perpetual sun and a 'perfect' break, particularly during winter when the winds are calm.

» **Black's Beach** (p96) This 2-mile sandy strip at the base of 300ft cliffs in La Jolla, San Diego, is known as one of the most powerful beach breaks in SoCal, thanks to an underwater canyon just offshore.

» **Huntington Beach** (p89) Surfer central is a great place to take in the scene – and some lessons.

» **Oceanside Beach, Oceanside** One of SoCal's prettiest beaches boasts one of the world's most consistent surf breaks come summer. It's a family-friendly spot.

» **Rincon, Santa Barbara** Arguably one of the planet's top surfing spots; nearly every major surf champion on the globe has taken Rincon for a ride.

» **Steamer Lane & Pleasure Point, Santa Cruz** There are 11 world-class breaks, including the point breaks over rock bottoms, at these two sweet spots.

» **Swami's, Encinitas** Located below Seacliff Roadside Park, this popular surfing beach has multiple breaks guaranteeing you some fantastic waves.

Rentals & Lessons

You'll find board rentals on just about every patch of sand where surfing is possible. Expect to pay about $20 per half-day for a board, with wetsuit rental another $10.

Two-hour group lessons for beginners start around $75 per person, while private, two-hour instruction costs over $100. If you're ready to jump in the deep end, many surf schools offer pricier weekend surf clinics and week-long 'surfari' camps.

Stand-up paddle surfing (SUP) is easier to learn, and it's skyrocketing in popularity. You'll find similarly priced board-and-paddle rentals and lessons all along the coast, from San Diego to north of San Francisco Bay.

Surfing Resources

» **Surfline** (www.surfline.com) Browse the comprehensive atlas, live webcams and surf reports for the lowdown from San Diego to Santa Barbara.

» **Surfer** (www.surfermag.com) Orange County-based magazine website with travel reports, gear reviews, newsy blogs and videos.

» **Surfrider** (www.surfrider.org) Enlightened surfers can join up with this nonprofit organization that aims to protect the coastal environment.

BEST CALIFORNIA BREAKS FOR BEGINNERS

The best spots to learn to surf are at beach breaks of long, shallow bays where waves are small and rolling, including:

» **San Diego** Mission Beach, Pacific Beach, Oceanside

» **Orange County** Seal Beach, Newport Beach, Dana Point

» **Los Angeles** Santa Monica, Manhattan Beach

» **Central Coast** Santa Cruz, Santa Barbara, Cayucos

White-Water Rafting

There's no shortage of scenic and spectacular rafting in the West. In California, both the Tuolumne and American Rivers surge with moderate-to-extreme rapids, while in Idaho the Middle Fork of the Salmon River has it all: abundant wildlife, thrilling rapids, a rich homesteader history, waterfalls and hot springs. The North Fork of the Owyhee – which snakes from the high plateau of southwest Oregon to the rangelands of Idaho – is rightfully popular and features towering hoodoos. North of Moab, UT, look for wildlife on an easy float on the Colorado River or ramp it up several notches with a thrilling romp through Class V rapids and the red rocks of Canyonlands National Park.

To book a spot on the Colorado River through the Grand Canyon, the quintessential river trip, make reservations at least a year in advance. And if you're not after white-knuckle rapids, fret not – many rivers have sections suitable for peaceful float trips or inner-tube drifts that you can enjoy with a cold beer in hand.

Kayaking & Canoeing

For exploring flatwater (no rapids or surf), opt for a kayak or canoe. For big lakes and the sea coast use a sea kayak. Be aware that kayaks are not always suitable for carrying bulky gear.

For scenic sea kayaking, you can push into the surf just about anywhere off the California coast. Popular spots include La Jolla as well as the coastal state parks just north of Santa Barbara. In the Pacific Northwest, you can enjoy world-class kayaking in the San Juan Islands, the Olympic Peninsula and Puget Sound. There's a full-moon paddle in Sausalito's Richardson Bay, CA. Sea kayak rentals average $40 to $70 per day. Reputable outfitters will make sure you're aware of the tide schedule and wind conditions of your proposed route.

White-water kayaking is also popular in the Pacific Northwest, where water tumbles down from the ice-capped volcanoes. Look for bald eagles on the Upper Sgakit River or slip through remote wilderness canyons on the Klickitat River. Close to Portland, try the Clackamas and the North Santiam. For urban white-water kayaking, you can't beat Colorado where white-water parks are de rigueur. There are relatively new parks in Boulder, Denver and Fort Collins, to name just a few.

Kayaking & Canoeing Resources

» **American Canoe Association** (www.americancanoe.org) Canoeing and kayaking organization publishes *Paddler* magazine (www.paddlermagazine.com), has a water trails database and offers courses.

» **American Whitewater** (www.americanwhitewater.org) Advocacy group for responsible recreation works to preserve America's wild rivers.

» **Canoe & Kayak** (www.canoekayak.com) Special-interest magazine for paddlers.

» **Kayak Online** (www.kayakonline.com) Advice for buying gear and helpful links to kayaking outfitters, schools and associations.

Skiing & Other Winter Sports

There are ski resorts in every western state, including Arizona. Colorado has some of the best skiing in the region, although California and Utah are both top-notch destinations for the alpine experience. The ski season typically runs from mid-December to April, though some resorts have longer seasons. In summer, many resorts offer mountain biking and hiking courtesy of chair lifts. Ski packages (including airfare, hotel and lift tickets) are easy to find through resorts, travel agencies and online travel booking sites; these packages can be a good deal if your main goal is to ski.

Wherever you ski, it won't come cheap. Find the best deals by going midweek, purchasing multiday tickets, heading to lesser-known 'sibling' resorts (like Alpine Meadows near Lake Tahoe) or checking out mountains that cater to locals including Santa Fe Ski Area (p382) and Colorado's Wolf Grade.

Top Ski Resorts

» **For snow, altitude and attitude** Vail, CO (p261), Squaw Valley, CA (p173) and high-glitz Aspen, CO (p263)

» **For an unfussy scene and steep vertical chutes** Alta, UT (p360), Telluride, CO (p270), Jackson, WY (p284) and Taos, NM (p388)

Snowboarding

On powdered slopes across the USA, snowboarding has become as popular as downhill skiing – all thanks to snow-surfing pioneer Jake Burton Carpenter, who set up a workshop in his Vermont garage and began to build snowboards in the mid-1970s. Snowboarders also flock almost everywhere out West, including Sun Valley, Tahoe and Taos. For a fix during the summer months, head to Oregon's Mt Hood area (p224), where several resorts offer snowboard camps.

Cross-country Skiing & Snowshoeing

Most downhill ski resorts have cross-country (Nordic) ski trails. In winter, popular areas of national parks, national forests and city parks often have cross-country ski and snowshoe trails and ice-skating rinks.

You'll find superb trail networks for Nordic skiers and snowshoers in California's Royal Gorge (North America's largest Nordic ski area; p173) and Washington's sublime and crowd-free Methow Valley (p204). Backcountry passionistas will be happily rewarded throughout the Sierra Nevada, with its many ski-in huts. There are more than 60 miles of trails around five ski-in huts in the San Juan Mountains in Colorado (www.sanjuanhuts.com); the 10th Mountain Division Association manages more than two-dozen huts in the Rockies (www.huts.org). The South Rim of the Grand Canyon and the surrounding Kaibab National Forest are also pretty spots for wintery exploring.

Ski & Snowboard Resources

Ski Snowboard America, by Charles Leocha, offers up-to-date overviews of North

WHALE-WATCHING

Gray and humpback whales have the longest migrations of any mammal in the world – more than 5000 miles from the Arctic to Mexico, and back again. In the Pacific Northwest, most pass through from November to February (southbound) and March to June (northbound). Gray whales can be spotted off the California coast from December to April, while blue, humpback and sperm whales pass by in summer and fall. Bring binoculars! Top spots include:

» **Depoe Bay & Newport, OR** Good whale-watching infrastructure; tour boats.

» **Long Beach & Westport, WA** Scan from shore.

» **Puget Sound & San Juan Islands, WA** Resident pods of orcas.

» **Klamath River Overlook, CA** Watch for whales from bluffs.

» **Point Reyes Lighthouse, CA** Gray whales pass by in December and January.

» **Monterey, CA** Whales can be spotted year-round.

» **Channel Islands National Park, CA** Take a cruise or peer through the telescope on the visitor center tower.

» **Point Loma, CA** The best place in San Diego to watch gray whale migration from January to March.

AND LET'S NOT FORGET...

ACTIVITY	WHERE?	WHAT?	MORE INFORMATION PLEASE
Horseback riding	Southern Arizona dude ranches	Old West country; most ranches close in summer due to the heat	www.azdra.com
	Grand Canyon South Rim, AZ	Low-key trips through Kaibab National Forest; campfire ride	www.apachestables.com
	Santa Fe, NM	Themed trail rides; sunsets	www.bishopslodge.com
	Telluride, CO	All-season rides in the hills	www.ridewithroudy.com
	Durango, CO	Day rides and overnight camping in Weminiuche Wilderness	www.vallecitolakeoutfitter.com
	Yosemite National Park, WY	Rides in Yosemite Valley, Tuolumne Meadows and near Wawona	www.yosemiteparks.com
	Florence, OR	Romantic beach rides	www.oregonhorsebackriding.com
Diving	Blue Hole near Santa Rosa, NM	81ft-deep artesian well; blue water leads into a 131ft-long submerged cavern	www.santarosanm.org
	La Jolla Underwater Park, CA	Beginner friendly; snorkelers enjoy nearby La Jolla Cove	www.sandiego.gov/lifeguards/beaches; www.oexcalifornia.com
	Channel Islands National Park, CA	Kelp forests, sea caves off coastal islands	www.nps.gov/chis; www.islandpackers.com/watersport.html
	Point Lobos State Reserve, CA	Fantastic shore diving; shallow reefs, caves, sea lions, seals, otters	www.montereyscubadiving.com
	Puget Sound, WA	Clear water, diverse marine life (giant octopus!)	www.underwatersports.com; www.pugetsounddivecharters.com
Hot-air ballooning	Sedona, AZ	Float above red rock country; champagne picnic	www.northernlightballoon.com
	Napa Wine Country, CA	Colorful balloons float over vineyards	www.balloonrides.com; www.napavalleyballoons.com

America's major resorts. Useful websites include the following:

» **Cross-Country Ski Areas Association** (www.xcski.org) Comprehensive information and gear guides for skiing and snowshoeing across North America.

» **Cross Country Skier** (www.crosscountryskier.com) Magazine with Nordic skiing news articles, online trail reports, and race and events information.

» **Powder** (www.powdermag.com) Online version of *Powder* magazine for skiers.

» **Ski Resorts Guide** (www.skiresortsguide.com) Comprehensive guide to resorts, with downloadable trail maps, lodging info and more.

» **SkiNet** (www.skinet.com) Online versions of *Ski, Skiing* and *Snow* magazines.

» **SnoCountry Mountain Reports** (www.snocountry.com) Snow reports for North America, plus events, news and resort links.

Rock Climbing & Canyoneering

In California, rock hounds test their mettle on world-class climbs on the big walls, granite domes and boulders of Yosemite National Park, where the climbing season lasts from April to October. Climbers also flock to Joshua Tree National Park, an otherworldly shrine in southern California's sun-scorched desert. There, amid craggy monoliths and the country's oldest trees, they make their pilgrimage on more than

8000 routes, tackling sheer vertical, sharp edges and bountiful cracks. For beginners, outdoor outfitters at both parks offer guided climbs and instruction.

In Zion National Park in Utah, multiday canyoneering classes teach the fine art of going *down:* rappelling off sheer sandstone cliffs into glorious, red-rock canyons filled with trees. Some of the sportier pitches are made in dry suits, down the flanks of roaring waterfalls into ice-cold pools.

For ice climbing, try Ouray Ice Park in Ouray, off the Million Dollar Hwy in southwest Colorado. Inside a narrow slot canyon, 200ft walls and waterfalls are frozen in thick sheets.

Other great climbing spots:

» **Grand Teton National Park, WY** (p282) Good for climbers of all levels: beginners can take basic climbing courses and the more experienced can join two-day expeditions up to the top of Grand Teton itself: a 13,770ft peak with majestic views.

» **City of Rocks National Reserve, ID** More than 500 routes up wind-scoured granite and pinnacles 60 stories tall.

» **Bishop, CA** This sleepy town in the Eastern Sierra (p170) is the gateway to excellent climbing in the nearby Owens River Gorge and Buttermilk Hills.

» **Red Rock Canyon, NV** (p318) Ten miles west of Las Vegas is some of the world's finest sandstone climbing.

» **Rocky Mountain National Park, CO** (p254) Offers alpine climbing near Boulder.

» **Flatirons, CO** Also near Boulder, has fine multipitch ascents.

Climbing & Canyoneering Resources

» **American Canyoneering Association** (www.canyoneering.net) An online canyons database and links to courses, local climbing groups and more.

» **Climbing** (www.climbing.com) Cutting-edge rock-climbing news and information since 1970.

» **SuperTopo** (www.supertopo.com) One-stop shop for rock-climbing guidebooks, free topo maps and route descriptions.

Travel with Children

Best Regions for Kids in the West

Grand Canyon & Southern Arizona

Hike the Grand Canyon, splash in Oak Creek and ponder cacti outside Tucson. Water parks, dude ranches and ghost towns will wow kiddies.

Los Angeles & Southern California

See celebrity handprints in Hollywood, take a studio tour in Burbank and hit the beach in Santa Monica. Orange County and San Diego have theme parks galore.

Southern Utah & Wasatch Mountains

National parks in Utah offer hiking, biking and rafting. In the mountains, ski runs and snow tubes are equally fun.

Sierra Nevada

See your kids gawk at waterfalls and granite domes in Yosemite, then giant sequoias. Mammoth Lakes is a all-year family adventure base camp.

Colorado

The whole state is kid-friendly: museums in Denver, outdoor fun in the Rockies, rafting near Buena Vista and Salida, and ski resorts everywhere.

The West is extremely family friendly, and you'll find superb attractions for all ages: amusement parks, aquariums, zoos, science museums, adventurous campsites, hikes in wilderness reserves, boogie-boarding surf at the beach and leisurely bike rides through scenic forests. Most national and state parks gear at least some exhibits, trails and programs (junior ranger activities and the like) toward families with kids.

Western USA for Kids

Child- and family-friendly activities are listed throughout this guide in the On the Road chapters, and major cities have a section devoted specifically to kids. To find family-oriented sights and activities, accommodations, restaurants and entertainment, just look for the child-friendly icon (👪).

Dining with Children

The US restaurant industry seems built on family-style service: children are not just accepted almost everywhere, but are usually encouraged by special children's menus with smaller portions and lower prices. In some restaurants children under a certain age even eat for free. Restaurants usually provide high chairs and booster seats. Some may also offer children crayons and puzzles, and occasionally live performances by cartoonlike characters.

Restaurants without children's menus don't necessarily discourage kids, though higher-end restaurants might; however, even at the nicer places, if you arrive early enough (right at dinner time opening hours), you can usually eat without too much stress – and you'll likely be joined by others with kids. You can ask if the kitchen will make a smaller order of a dish (also ask how much it will cost), or if they will split a normal-size main dish between two plates for the kids. Chinese, Mexican and Italian eateries might be the best bet for finicky young eaters.

Accommodations

Motels and hotels typically have rooms with two beds, which are ideal for families. Some also have roll-away beds or cribs that can be brought into the room for an extra charge (these are usually Pack 'n Plays, which may not work for all children). Some hotels offer 'kids stay free' programs, for children up to 12 or sometimes 18 years old. Many B&Bs don't allow children; ask when reserving. Most resorts are kid friendly and many offer children's programs, but ask when booking, as a few cater only to adults.

Babysitting

Resort hotels may have on-call babysitting services; otherwise, ask the front-desk staff or concierge to help you make arrangements. Always ask if babysitters are licensed and bonded, what they charge per hour per child, whether there's a minimum fee, and if they charge extra for transportation or meals. Most tourist bureaus list local resources for childcare and recreation facilities, medical services and so on.

Necessities, Driving & Flying

Many public toilets have a baby-changing table (sometimes in men's toilets too), and gender-neutral 'family' facilities appear in airports.

Medical services and facilities in America are of a high standard, and items such as baby food, formula and disposable nappies – including organic options – are widely available in supermarkets across the country.

All car-rental agencies should be able to provide an appropriate child seat, since these are required in every state, but you need to request it when booking and expect to pay around $10 more per day.

Domestic airlines don't charge for children under two years. Those two or over must have a seat, and discounts are unlikely. Very rarely, some resort areas (like Disneyland) offer a 'kids fly free' promotion. Amtrak and other train operators occasionally run similar deals (with kids up to age 15 riding free) on various routes.

Discounts for Children

Child concessions often apply for tours, admission fees and transport, with some discounts as high as 50% off the adult rate. However, the definition of 'child' can vary from under 12 to under 16 years. Some popular sights also have discount rates for families. Most sights also give free admission to children under two years.

Planning

Weather and crowds are all-important considerations when planning a US family getaway. The peak travel season across the country is from June to August, when schools are out and the weather is warmest. Expect high prices and abundant crowds – meaning long lines at amusement and water parks, fully booked resort areas and heavy traffic on the roads; you'll need to reserve well in advance for popular destinations. The same holds true for winter resorts (eg the Rockies, Lake Tahoe) during the high season of January to March.

What to Pack

Bring lots of sunscreen, especially if you'll be spending a lot of time outside.

If you plan on hiking, you'll need a front baby carrier (for children under one) or a backpack (for children up to about four years old) with a built-in shade top. These can be purchased or rented from outfitters throughout the region (see listings in regional chapters). Older kids need sturdy shoes and, for playing in streams, water sandals. Other useful items are towels (for playing in water between destinations), rain gear, a snuggly fleece or heavy sweater (even in summer, desert nights can be cold), sunhats (especially if you are camping) and bug repellent. To avoid children's angst at sleeping in new places and to minimize concerns about bed configurations, consider bringing a Pak 'n Play (portable crib) for infants and sleeping bags for older children.

Children's Highlights

Outdoor Adventure

» **Yellowstone National Park** Watch powerful geysers, spy on wildlife and take magnificent hikes

» **Grand Canyon National Park** Gaze across one of the earth's great wonders, followed by a hike, a ranger talk and biking

» **Olympic National Park** Explore the wild and pristine wilderness in one of the world's few temperate rainforests

» **Oak Creek Canyon** Swoosh over red rocks at Slide Rock State Park in Arizona

Theme Parks

» **Disneyland** It's the attention to detail that amazes most at Mickey Mouse's enchantingly imagineered Disneyland, in the middle of Orange County, California

» **SeaWorld** Killer whale shows, fun rides and loads of other amusements in San Diego's aquatic park

» **Universal Studios** Hollywood movie-themed action rides, special effects shows and a working studio back-lot tram tour in Los Angeles

» **Rawhide Western Town & Steakhouse** Relive the rootin' tootin' Old West with gold-panning, burro rides and shoot-outs in Phoenix

Aquariums & Zoos

» **Arizona-Sonora Desert Museum** Coyotes, cacti and docent demonstrations are highlights at this indoor/outdoor repository of flora and fauna in Tucson

» **Monterey Bay Aquarium** Get acquainted with denizens of the deep next door to the California central coast's biggest marine sanctuary

» **San Diego Zoo & Safari Park** Journey around the world and go on safari outdoors at California's best and biggest zoo

» **Aquarium of the Pacific** High-tech aquarium at Long Beach houses critters from balmy Baja California to the chilly north Pacific, plus a shark lagoon

Rainy-Day Activities

» **LA Museums** See stars (the real ones) at LA's Griffith Observatory, dinosaur bones at the Natural History Museum of LA County and at the Page Museum at the La Brea Tar Pits, then get hands-on at the amusing California Science Center

» **SF Museums** San Francisco's Bay Area is a mind-bending classroom for kids, especially at the interactive Exploratorium, multimedia Zeum and eco-friendly California Academy of Sciences

» **Pacific Science Center** Fascinating, hands-on exhibits at this center in Seattle, plus an IMAX theater, planetarium and laser shows

» **Museum of Natural History & Science** Check out the Hall of Jurassic Supergiants here in Albuquerque

» **Arizona Museum of Natural History** Wander past a replicated mining town, explore life-sized displays of Hohokam villages and cower at the base of Dinosaur Mountain.

Offbeat Attractions

» **Route 66 through Arizona** Provides wacky distractions galore: begging burros, kitschy caverns, a fun-loving ice-cream shop, Meteor Crater and a wigwam motel

» **Roswell** The truth is out there in this extraterrestrial-loving city in New Mexico, with a UFO Museum and loads of quirky shops

» **Rattlesnake Museum** Older kids and future herpetologists can gaze at the world's most comprehensive collection of rattlesnake species inside this Albuquerque museum

» **Old Faithful, Yellowstone National Park** The anticipation before she blows might be more fun than the blast

» **Venice Boardwalk** Older kids will get a kick out of the freaky exuberance at LA's famed boardwalk where talented acrobats, flashy roller-bladers and hefty musclemen show off for the crowds

Resources for Families

For all-around information and advice, check out Lonely Planet's *Travel with Children*. For outdoor advice, read *Kids in the Wild: A Family Guide to Outdoor Recreation* by Cindy Ross and Todd Gladfelter, and Alice Cary's *Parents' Guide to Hiking & Camping*.

Family Travel Files (www.thefamilytravelfiles.com) Ready-made vacation ideas, destination profiles and travel tips.

Parents Connect (www.parentsconnect.com/family-travel) A virtual encyclopedia of everything first-time family travelers need to know.

Go City Kids (www.gocitykids.com) Excellent coverage of kid-centric activities and entertainment in over 50 US cities.

Kids.gov (www.kids.gov) Eclectic, enormous national resource; download songs and activities, or even link to the CIA Kids' Page.

regions at a glance

What images come to mind when someone mentions the West? Sunbaked lizards, blowing tumbleweeds or maybe a saguaro cactus? That would be accurate – for southern Arizona. But the West holds so much more. Lush forests in the Pacific Northwest. Sun-kissed beaches in California. Leafy single-track trails in the Rockies. Crimson buttes and hoodoos in Utah. There's a landscape for every mood and adventure.

Cultural travelers can explore Native American sites in Arizona and New Mexico. There's upscale shopping, fine dining and big-city bustle in Los Angeles, San Francisco and Seattle. Are you a history buff? Visit Mormon settlements in Utah, Spanish missions in California or Old West towns just about everywhere. Ready to let loose? Two words: Las Vegas.

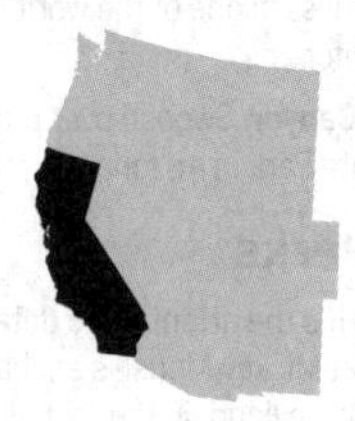

California

Beaches ✓✓✓
Outdoor Adventure ✓✓✓
Food & Wine ✓✓✓

Gorgeous Shores

With more than 1100 miles of coastline, California rules the sands: you'll find rugged, pristine beaches in the north and people-packed beauties in the south, with great surfing, sea kayaking or simply beach-walking all along the coast.

Romping Room

Swoosh down snowy slopes, raft on white-water rivers, kayak beside coastal islands, hike past waterfalls and climb boulders in the desert. The problem isn't choice in California, it's finding enough time to do it all.

King's Table

Fertile fields, talented chefs and an insatiable appetite for the new make California a major culinary destination. Browse local food markets, sample Pinot and Chardonnay at lush vineyards and dine on farm-to-table fare.

p56

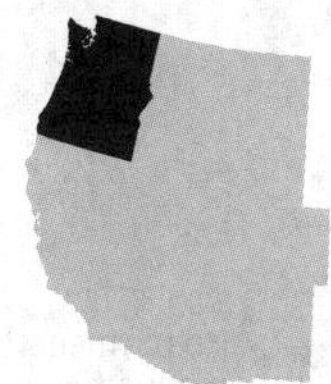

Pacific Northwest

Cycling ✓✓✓
Food & Wine ✓✓
National Parks ✓✓✓

Pedal Power

Cycle rolling paved roads in the tranquil San Juan Islands, cruise the bluff-dotted Oregon coast along Hwy 101 or pedal the streets of Portland, a city that embraces two-wheeled travel with lots of bike lanes, costumed theme rides and handcrafted bike shows.

Locavores & Oenophiles

'Up-and-coming' is the word used for Northwest cities such as Portland and Seattle where chefs blend fish caught in local waters with vegetables harvested in the Eden-like valleys surrounding the Columbia River. Then there is Washington's wine, second only to California's.

Classic Playgrounds

The northwest has four national parks, including three Teddy Roosevelt-era classics – Olympic, Mt Rainier and Crater Lake – each bequeathed with historic lodges; plus a newer, even wilder addition – the North Cascades.

p175

Rocky Mountains

Outdoor Adventure ✓✓✓
Western Culture ✓✓
Landscapes ✓✓✓

Rugged Fun

World-class skiing, hiking and boating make the Rockies a top destination for adrenaline junkies. All are welcome, with hundreds of races and group rides, and an incredible infrastructure of parks, trails and cabins.

Modern Cowboys

Once a land of Stetsons and prairie dresses, today's freedom-loving Rocky folk are more often spotted in lycra, mountain bike nearby, sipping a microbrew or latte at a sunny outdoor cafe. Hard playing and slow living still rule.

Alpine Wonderland

The snow-covered Rocky Mountains are pure majesty. With chiseled peaks, clear rivers and red-rock contours, the Rockies contain some of the world's most famous parks and bucket-loads of clean mountain air.

p235

Southwest

Natural Scenery ✓✓✓
Native Cultures ✓✓✓
Food ✓✓

Red-Rock Country

The Southwest is famous for the jaw-dropping Grand Canyon, the dramatic red buttes of Monument Valley and the vast Carlsbad Caverns – just a few of many regional wonders and spectacular national parks.

Pueblos & Reservations

Visiting the Hopi and Navajo Nations or one of the 19 New Mexico pueblos is a fine introduction to America's first inhabitants.

Good Eats

Try chile-slathered chicken enchiladas in New Mexico, a messy Sonoran hotdog in Tucson or a hearty steak just about anywhere. In Vegas, stretch your fat pants – but not your budget – at one of the ubiquitous buffets or dine like royalty at a chef-driven sanctuary.

p301

Look out for these icons:

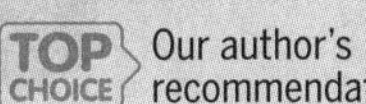

Our author's recommendation

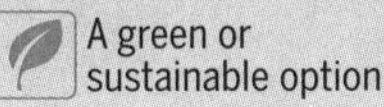

A green or sustainable option

FREE No payment required

See the Index for a full list of destinations covered in this book.

On the Road

California

Includes »

Best Places to Eat

» Benu (p138)
» Chez Panisse (p148)
» Zazu (p153)
» Bazaar (p79)
» Passionfish (p118)

Best Places to Stay

» Beverly Hills Hotel (p76)
» Hotel Del Coronado (p97
» Ahwahnee Hotel (p167)
» Beltane Ranch (p152)
» Mar Vista Cottages (p155)

Why Go?

With bohemian spirit and high-tech savvy, not to mention a die-hard passion for the good life – whether that means cracking open a vintage bottle of Zinfandel, summiting a 14,000ft peak or surfing the Pacific – California soars beyond any expectations sold on Hollywood's silver screens.

More than anything, California is iconic. It was here that the hurly-burly gold rush kicked off in the mid-19th century. Naturalist John Muir rhapsodized about the Sierra Nevada's 'range of light,' and Jack Kerouac and the Beat Generation defined what it really means to hit the road.

California's multicultural melting pot has been cookin' since this bountiful promised land was staked out by Spain and Mexico. Today waves of immigrants still look to find their own American dream on these palm-tree-studded Pacific shores. It's time for you to join them.

When to Go

Los Angeles

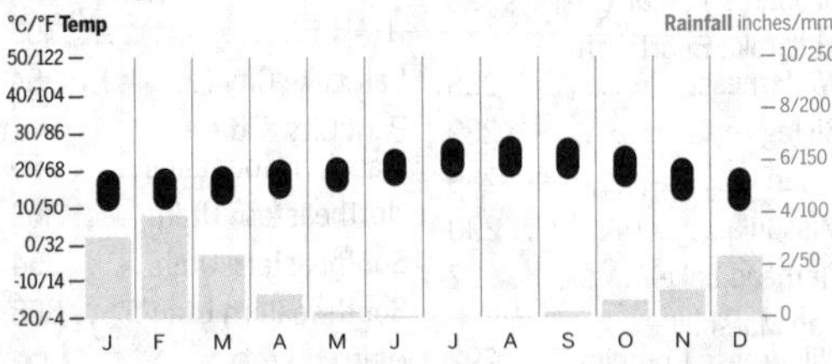

Jun-Aug Mostly sunny weather and crowded with families taking summer vacations.

Apr-May & Sep-Oct Cooler weather, but mostly cloudless days; travel bargains.

Nov-Mar Peak tourism at mountain ski resorts and in SoCal's dry, warm desert regions.

Transportation

Los Angeles (LAX) and San Francisco (SFO) are major international airports. Sacramento, Oakland, San Jose, Burbank, Orange County and San Diego handle primarily domestic flights.

Four main Amtrak routes connect California with the rest of the USA: *California Zephyr* (Chicago–San Francisco Bay Area), *Coast Starlight* (Seattle–Los Angeles), *Southwest Chief* (Chicago–LA) and *Sunset Limited* (New Orleans–LA). Amtrak's intrastate routes include the *Pacific Surfliner* (San Diego–LA–Santa Barbara–San Luis Obispo), *Capitol Corridor* (San Jose–Oakland–Berkeley–Sacramento) and *San Joaquin* (Bakersfield to Oakland or Sacramento, with Yosemite Valley buses from Merced).

Greyhound reaches into many corners of the state. But to really get out and explore, especially away from the coast, you'll need a car.

NATIONAL & STATE PARKS

Yosemite and Sequoia became California's first national parks in 1890, and today there are six more: Kings Canyon, Death Valley, Joshua Tree, Channel Islands, Redwood and Lassen Volcanic. The **National Park Service** (NPS; www.nps.gov) also manages almost 20 other historic sites, monuments, nature preserves and recreational areas statewide.

California's 278 **state parks** (916-653-6995; www.parks.ca.gov) are a diverse bunch: expect everything from marine preserves to redwood forests, protecting nearly a third of the coastline and offering 3000 miles of hiking, biking and equestrian trails.

For camping on federal lands, see p440. Day-use parking fees are $4 to $15; campsites cost $10 to $65 nightly. **ReserveAmerica** (800-444-7275; www.reserveamerica.com) handles state-park camping reservations.

Warning! Check current park closures and reduced opening hours due to state-budget cutbacks – call ahead or check the park website.

Top Five California Beaches

» Coronado (p92) Sun yourself along San Diego's boundless Silver Strand.

» Huntington Beach (p89) Bonfires, beach volleyball and rolling waves in 'Surf City USA.'

» Zuma (p73) Crystal aquamarine waters, frothy surf and tawny sand, just north of Malibu.

» Santa Cruz (p118) Surf's up! And the beach boardwalk's carnival fun never stops.

» Point Reyes (p147) Wild, windy, end-of-the-world beaches, perfect for wildlife watching.

DON'T MISS

You can't leave California without hugging a tree! We suggest coast redwoods, which can live for 2000 years and grow to 379ft tall.

Fast Facts

» Population: Los Angeles (3,792,620), San Francisco (805,235)

» Driving distance: Los Angeles to San Francisco (380 miles)

» Time zone: Pacific Standard

Did You Know?

Just a few of California's inventions: the internet and the iPad, power yoga and reality TV, the space shuttle and Mickey Mouse, the Cobb salad and the fortune cookie.

Resources

» California Travel & Tourism Commission (www.visitcalifornia.com)

» California Highway Information (www.dot.ca.gov/hq/roadinfo)

» Department of Forestry and Fire Protection (www.fire.ca.gov)

» USGS Earthquake Hazards (http://quake.usgs.gov/recenteqs/latest.htm)

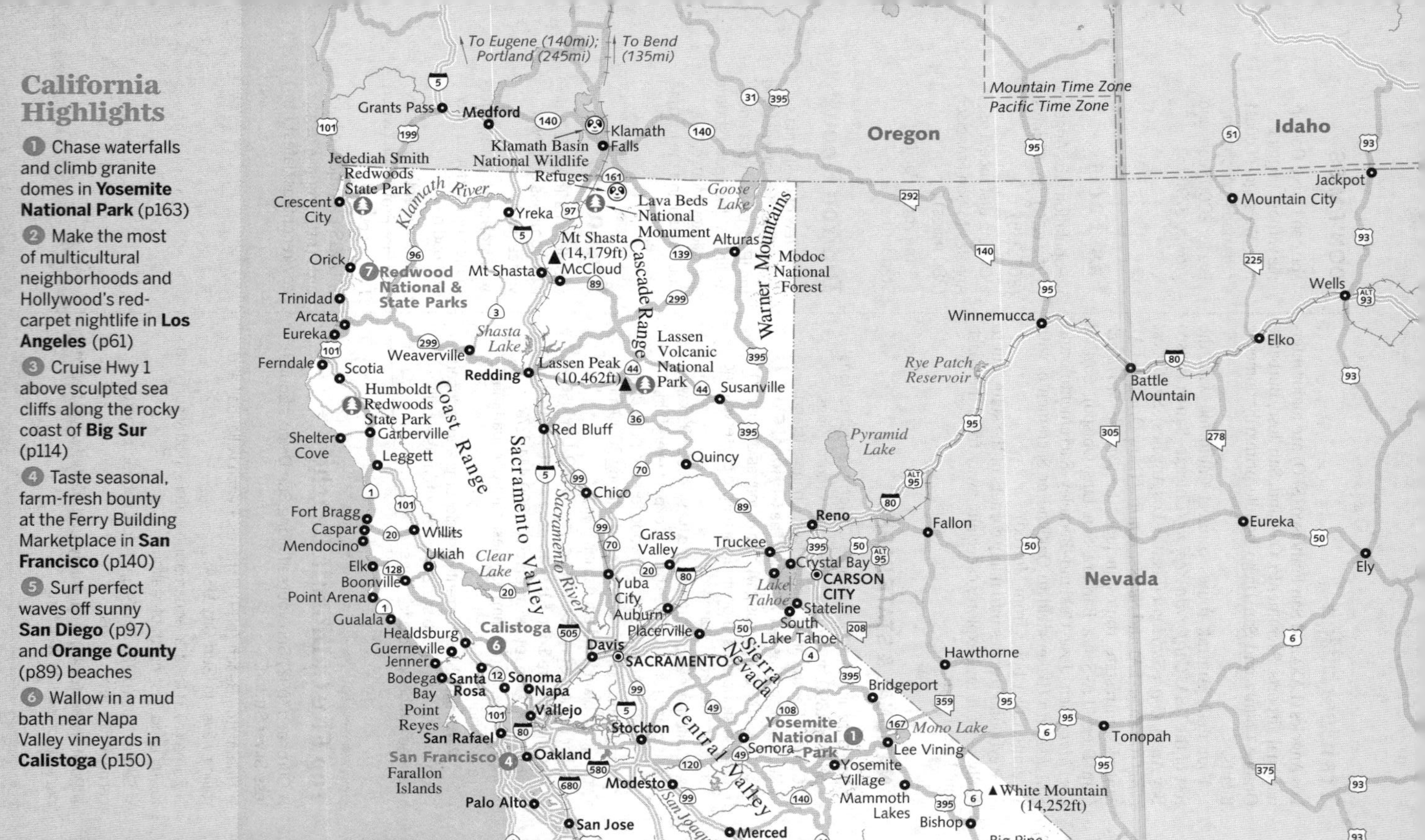

California Highlights

1 Chase waterfalls and climb granite domes in **Yosemite National Park** (p163)

2 Make the most of multicultural neighborhoods and Hollywood's red-carpet nightlife in **Los Angeles** (p61)

3 Cruise Hwy 1 above sculpted sea cliffs along the rocky coast of **Big Sur** (p114)

4 Taste seasonal, farm-fresh bounty at the Ferry Building Marketplace in **San Francisco** (p140)

5 Surf perfect waves off sunny **San Diego** (p97) and **Orange County** (p89) beaches

6 Wallow in a mud bath near Napa Valley vineyards in **Calistoga** (p150)

7 Crane your neck up at the world's tallest trees in **Redwood National & State Parks** (p157)

8 Trek across sand dunes and explore Old West ghost towns in **Death Valley National Park** (p107)

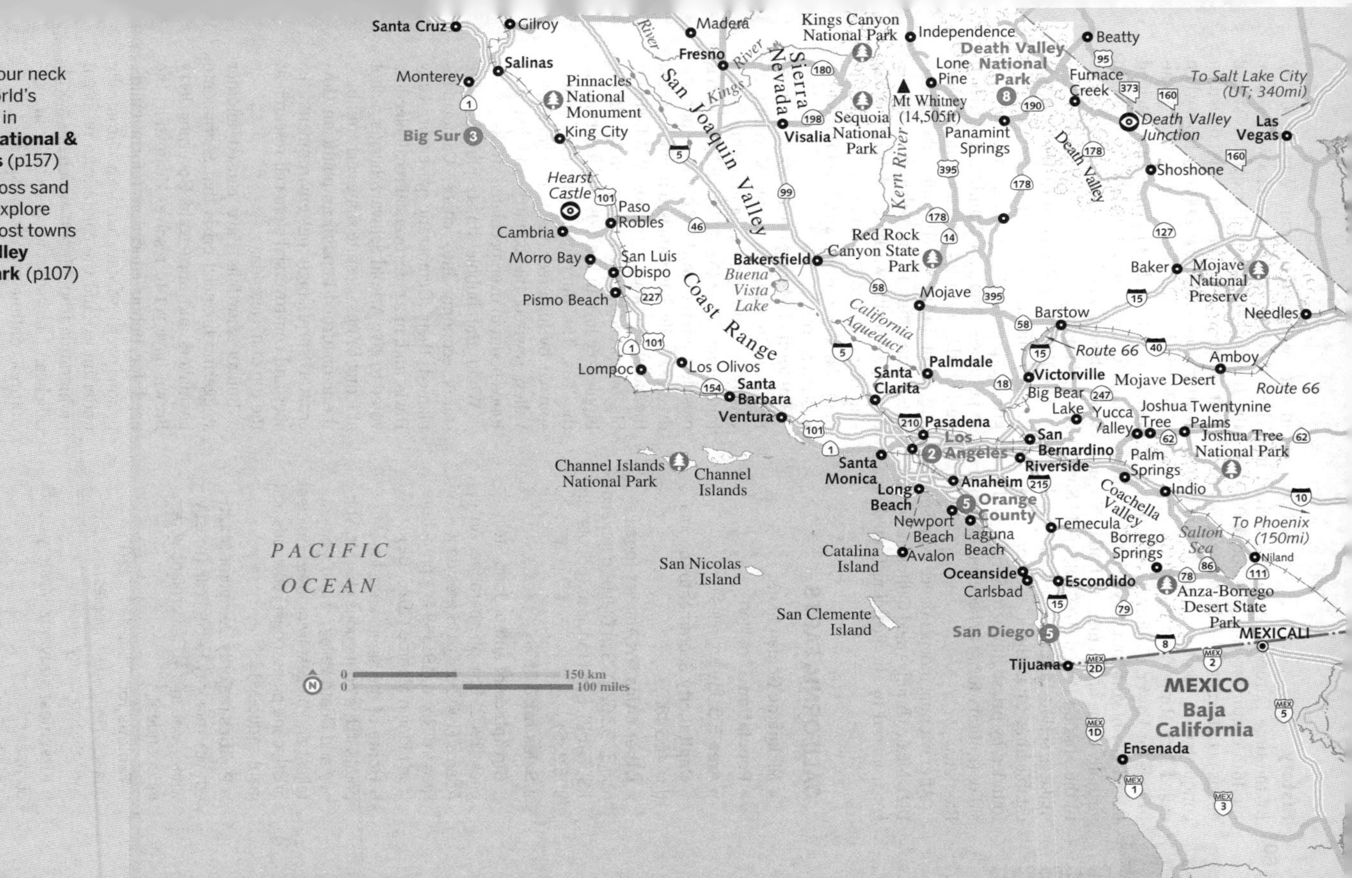

History

By the time European explorers arrived in the 16th century, as many as 300,000 indigenous people called this land home. Spanish conquistadors combed through what they called Alta (Upper) California (as opposed to Baja, or Lower, California) in search of a fabled 'city of gold,' but they left the territory virtually alone after failing to find it. Not until the Mission Period (1769–1833) did Spain make a serious attempt to settle the land, establishing 21 Catholic missions – many founded by priest Junípero Serra – and presidios (military forts) to keep out British and Russians.

After winning independence from Spain in 1821, Mexico briefly ruled California, but then got trounced by the fledgling United States in the Mexican-American War (1846–48). The discovery of gold just over a week before the Treaty of Guadalupe Hidalgo was signed sent the territory's nonindigenous population soaring from 14,000 to 92,000 by 1850, when California became the 31st US state. Thousands of imported Chinese laborers helped complete the transcontinental railroad in 1869, which opened up markets and further spurred migration to the Golden State.

The 1906 San Francisco earthquake was barely a hiccup as California continued to grow exponentially in size, diversity and importance. Mexican immigrants arrived during the 1910–20 Mexican Revolution, and again during WWII, to fill labor shortages. Important military-driven industries developed during wartime, while anti-Asian sentiments led to the unjust internment of many Japanese Americans, including in the Eastern Sierra.

California has long been a social pioneer thanks to its size, confluence of wealth, diversity of immigration and technological innovation. Since the 1930s, Hollywood has mesmerized the world with its cinematic dreams, while San Francisco reacted against the banal complacency of post-WWII suburbia by spreading Beat poetry in the 1950s, hippie free love in the '60s and gay pride in the '70s. The internet revolution, initially spurred by high-tech visionaries in Silicon Valley, rewired the country and led to a 1990s boom in overspeculated stocks.

When the bubble burst, plunging the state's economy into chaos, Californians blamed their Democratic governor, Gray Davis, and, in a controversial recall election, voted to give Arnold Schwarzenegger a shot at fixing things. Despite some early fumbles, the actor-turned-Republican-politician 'Governator' surprisingly put environmental issues and controversial stem-cell research at the top of his agenda.

Budget shortfalls have caused another staggering financial crisis that Sacramento lawmakers and once-again Governor Jerry Brown have yet to resolve. Meanwhile, the need for public education reform builds, prisons overflow, state parks are chronically underfunded and the conundrum of illegal immigration from Mexico, which fills a critical cheap labor shortage (especially in agriculture), continues to vex the state.

CALIFORNIA FACTS

» **Nickname** Golden State

» **Population** 37 million

» **Area** 155,959 sq miles

» **Capital city** Sacramento (population 466,488)

» **Other cities** Los Angeles (population 3,792,620), San Diego (population 1,307,402), San Francisco (population 805,235)

» **Sales tax** 8.25%

» **Birthplace of** author John Steinbeck (1902–68), photographer Ansel Adams (1902–84), US president Richard Nixon (1913–94), pop-culture icon Marilyn Monroe (1926–62)

» **Home of** the highest and lowest points in the contiguous US (Mt Whitney and Death Valley), world's oldest, tallest and biggest living trees (ancient bristlecone pines, coast redwoods and giant sequoias)

» **Politics** majority Democrat (multiethnic), minority Republican (mostly white), one in five Californians votes independent

» **Famous for** Disneyland, earthquakes, Hollywood, hippies, tree huggers, Silicon Valley, surfing

» **Kitschiest souvenir** 'Mystery Spot' bumper sticker

» **Driving distances** Los Angeles to San Francisco 380 miles, San Francisco to Yosemite Valley 190 miles

Local Culture

Currently the world's eighth-largest economy, California is a state of extremes, where

CALIFORNIA IN...

One Week

California in a nutshell. Start in **Los Angeles**, detouring to **Disneyland**. Head up the breathtaking Central Coast, stopping in **Santa Barbara** and **Big Sur**, before soaking up a dose of big-city culture in **San Francisco**. Head inland to **Yosemite National Park**, then zip back to LA.

Two Weeks

Follow the one-week itinerary above, but at a saner pace. Add jaunts to NorCal's **Wine Country**; **Lake Tahoe**, perched high in the Sierra Nevada; the beaches of **Orange County** and laid-back **San Diego**; or **Death Valley** and **Joshua Tree National Park**, near the hip-again desert resort of **Palm Springs** outside LA.

One Month

Do everything described above, and more! From San Francisco, head up the north coast, starting in Marin County at **Point Reyes National Seashore**. Stroll Victorian-era **Mendocino** and **Eureka**, find yourself on the **Lost Coast** and ramble through fern-filled **Redwood National & State Parks**. Inland, snap a postcard-perfect photo of **Mt Shasta**, detour to **Lassen Volcanic National Park** and get dirty in California's historic **Gold Country**. Trace the backbone of the **Eastern Sierra** before winding down into the **Deserts**.

grinding poverty shares urban corridors with fabulous wealth. Waves of immigrants keep arriving, and neighborhoods are often mini-versions of their homelands. Tolerance for others is the social norm, but so is intolerance, which you'll encounter if you smoke or dare to drive on the freeway during rush hour.

Untraditional and unconventional attitudes continue to define California, a trend-setter by nature. Image is an obsession, appearances are stridently youthful and outdoorsy, and self-help all the rage. Whether it's a luxury SUV or Nissan Leaf, a car may define who you are and also how important you consider yourself to be, especially in SoCal.

Think of California as the USA's most futuristic social laboratory. If technology identifies a new useful gadget, Silicon Valley will build it at light speed. If postmodern celebrities, bizarrely famous merely for the fact of being famous, make a fashion statement or get thrown in jail, the nation pays attention. Perhaps no other state's pop culture has as big an effect on how the rest of us work, play, eat, love, consume and, yes, recycle.

LOS ANGELES

While 'All-American' isn't the first thought that comes to mind when thinking of Los Angeles, LA County – America's largest – represents this vast nation in extremes. Its people are among America's richest and poorest, most established and newest arrivals, most refined and roughest, most beautiful and most plain, most erudite and most airheaded. Even the landscape is a microcosm of the USA, from fabled beaches to snowcapped mountains, skyscrapers, suburban sprawl and even wilderness.

The one thing that binds Angelenos is that they are seekers – or descendants of seekers – drawn by a dream, from fame on the silver screen to money to send back to the family. Success can be spectacular and failure equally so. If that's not America, we don't know what is.

If you think you've already got LA figured out – celebrity culture, smog, traffic, Botox babes and wannabes – think again. Although it's the world's entertainment capital, the city's truths aren't delivered on movie screens or reality shows; rather, in small portions of everyday experiences. Chances are, the more you explore, the more you'll enjoy.

Now is an exciting time to visit LA. Hollywood and Downtown are undergoing an urban renaissance, and art, music, fashion and food are all in high gear.

History

The hunter-gatherer existence of the Gabrieleño and Chumash peoples ended with the arrival of Spanish missionaries and pioneers in the late 18th century. Spain's first civilian settlement here (1781), El Pueblo de la Reina de Los Angeles, remained an isolated

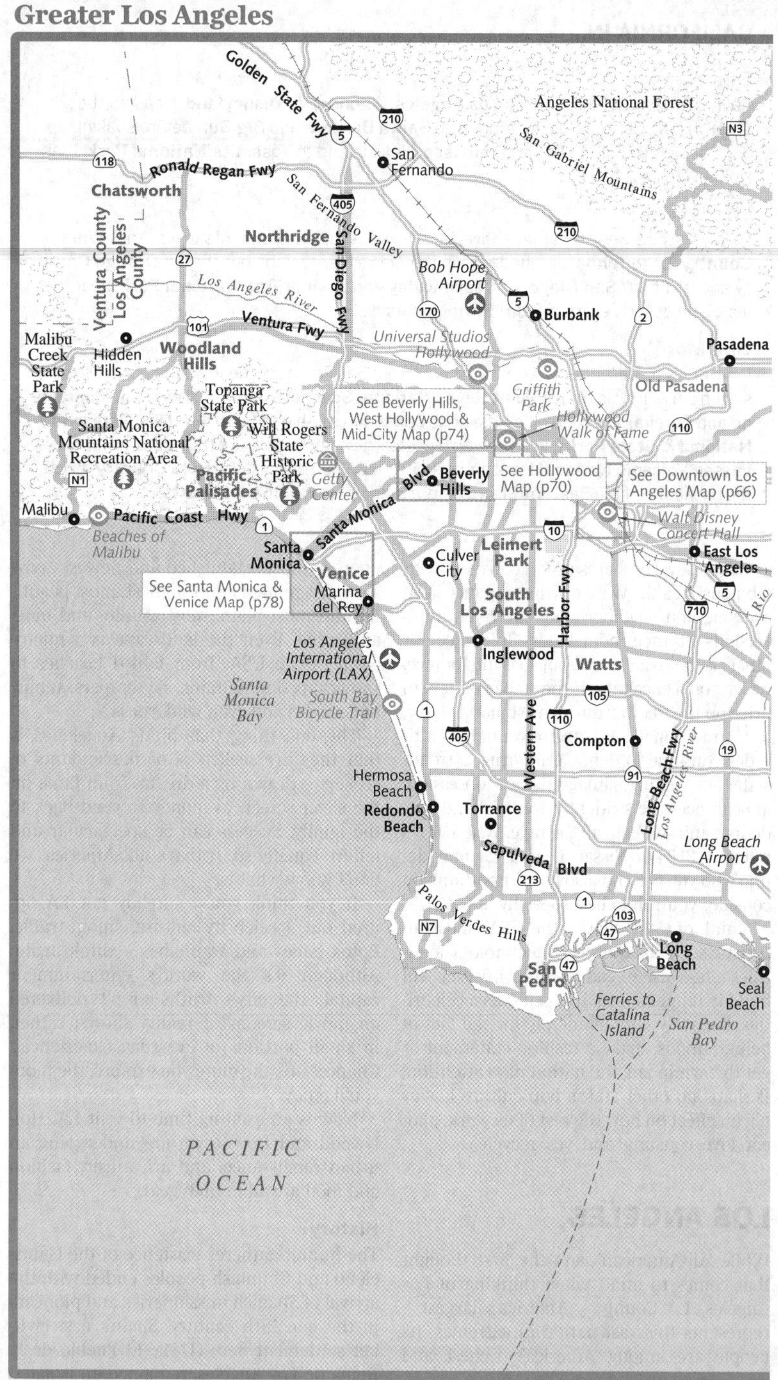
Golden State Fwy
Angeles National Forest
San Gabriel Mountains
San Fernando
Ronald Regan Fwy
Chatsworth
San Fernando Valley
Northridge
San Diego Fwy
Ventura County
Los Angeles County
Los Angeles River
Bob Hope Airport
Burbank
Ventura Fwy
Malibu Creek State Park
Hidden Hills
Woodland Hills
Universal Studios Hollywood
Pasadena
Griffith Park
Old Pasadena
Topanga State Park
See Beverly Hills, West Hollywood & Mid-City Map (p74)
Santa Monica Mountains National Recreation Area
Will Rogers State Historic Park
Hollywood Walk of Fame
Pacific Palisades
Getty Center
Beverly Hills
See Hollywood Map (p70)
See Downtown Los Angeles Map (p66)
Malibu
Pacific Coast Hwy
Santa Monica Blvd
Walt Disney Concert Hall
Beaches of Malibu
Santa Monica
Culver City
Leimert Park
East Los Angeles
See Santa Monica & Venice Map (p78)
Venice
Marina del Rey
South Los Angeles
Harbor Fwy
Los Angeles International Airport (LAX)
Inglewood
Watts
Santa Monica Bay
South Bay Bicycle Trail
Western Ave
Compton
Long Beach Fwy
Los Angeles River
Hermosa Beach
Redondo Beach
Torrance
Long Beach Airport
Sepulveda Blvd
Palos Verdes Hills
Long Beach
San Pedro
Seal Beach
Ferries to Catalina Island
San Pedro Bay
PACIFIC OCEAN

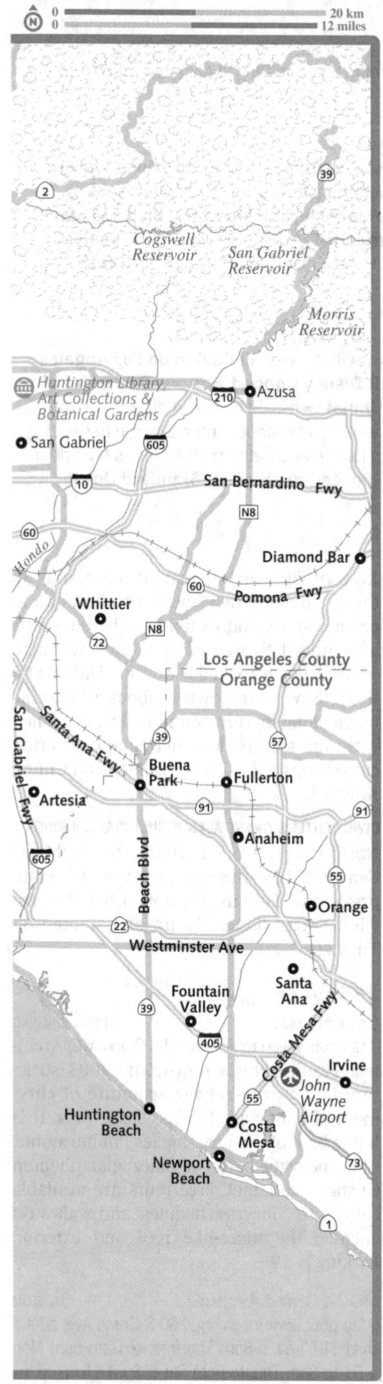

farming outpost for decades. LA was incorporated as a California city in 1850, and by 1830 its population had swollen thanks to the collapse of the Northern California gold rush, the arrival of the transcontinental railroad, the citrus industry, the discovery of oil, the launch of the port of LA, the birth of the movie industry and the opening of the California Aqueduct. The city's population has boomed from some 1.5 million in 1950 to almost four million today.

LA's growth has caused problems, including suburban sprawl and air pollution – though thanks to aggressive enforcement, smog levels have fallen annually since records have been kept. Traffic, a struggling public-education system, a fluctuating real-estate market and the occasional earthquake or forest fire remain nagging concerns, but with a strong and diverse economy and a decreasing crime rate, all things considered, LA's a survivor.

Sights

LA County is vast (88 cities in over 4000 square miles), but the areas of visitor interest are fairly well defined. About 12 miles inland, Downtown combines history, highbrow culture and global-village pizzazz. Hip-again Hollywood is to the northwest, and urban-designer chic and lesbi-gays rule West Hollywood. South of here, Museum Row is Mid-City's main draw, while further west are ritzy Beverly Hills, Westwood and the hilltop Getty Center. Santa Monica is the most tourist-friendly beach town; others include swish but low-key Malibu, boho Venice and hopping Long Beach. Stately Pasadena lies northeast of Downtown.

Getting around is easiest by car, although if you're not in a hurry public transport is usually adequate to most of these neighborhoods.

DOWNTOWN

For decades, Downtown was LA's historic core, and main business and government district – and empty nights and weekends. No more. Crowds fill Downtown's performance and entertainment venues, and young professionals and artists have moved by the thousands into new lofts, bringing bars, restaurants and galleries. Don't expect Manhattan just yet, but for adventurous urbanites, now is an exciting time to be Downtown.

Downtown is easily explored on foot or by subway or DASH minibus. Parking is cheapest (about $6 all day) around Little Tokyo and Chinatown.

LOS ANGELES IN...

Distances are ginormous in LA, so allow for traffic and don't try to pack too much into a day.

One Day

Fuel up for the day at the **Waffle** and then go star-searching on the **Hollywood Walk of Fame** along revitalized Hollywood Blvd. Up your chances of spotting actual celebs by hitting the fashion-forward boutiques on paparazzi-infested **Robertson Blvd** and having lunch at the **Ivy**. Then drive to lofty **Getty Center**, before heading west to the **Venice Boardwalk** to see the seaside sideshow. Watch the sunset over the ocean in **Santa Monica**.

Two Days

Explore rapidly evolving Downtown LA. Start with its roots at **El Pueblo de Los Angeles**, and catapult to the future at the dramatic **Walt Disney Concert Hall** and **Cathedral of our Lady of the Angels**. Dim sum brunch in **Chinatown** is best walked off with a stroll among the nearby art galleries. The new LA Live entertainment center is home to the **Grammy Museum**, and if you're lucky you can join celebs watching the Lakers next door at **Staples Center**. Top it off with cocktails at the rooftop bar of the **Standard Downtown LA**.

EL PUEBLO DE LOS ANGELES & AROUND

Compact, colorful and car-free, this historic district is an immersion in LA's Spanish-Mexican roots. Its spine is **Olvera St**, a festive tack-o-rama where you can chomp on tacos and stock up on handmade candy, folkloric trinkets and bric-a-brac.

FREE **Avila Adobe** HISTORIC BUILDING
(Map p66; ☎213-628-1274; Olvera St; ⊙9am-4pm) This 1818 ranch home claims to be the city's oldest existing building. It's decorated with period furniture, and a video gives history and highlights of the neighborhood.

La Plaza de Cultura y Artes MUSEUM
(Map p66; www.lapca.org; 501 Main St; adult/child $9/5; ⊙noon-7pm Wed-Sun; P) This new museum (opened 2010) chronicles the Mexican-American experience in Los Angeles, in exhibits about city history from the Zoot Suit Riots to the Chicana movement. Calle Principal re-creates Main St in the 1920s.

FREE **Union Station** LANDMARK
(Map p66; 800 N Alameda St; P) This majestic 1939 edifice is the last of America's grand rail stations; its glamorous art-deco interior can be seen in *Blade Runner, Bugsy, Rain Man* and many other movies.

Chinese American Museum MUSEUM
(Map p66; ☎213-485-8567; www.camla.org; 425 N Los Angeles St; adult/child $3/2; ⊙10am-3pm Tue-Sun) This small but smart museum is on the site of an early Chinese apothecary and general store, and exhibits probe questions of identity. LA's original Chinatown was here (moved north to make way for Union Station). 'New' Chinatown is about a half-mile north along Broadway and Hill St, crammed with dim sum parlors, herbal apothecaries, curio shops and edgy art galleries on Chung King Rd.

CIVIC CENTER & GRAND AVENUE CULTURAL CORRIDOR

North Grand Ave is anchored by the Music Center of Los Angeles County, which comprises the famous Dorothy Chandler Pavilion, Mark Taper Forum and Ahmanson Theater.

FREE **Walt Disney Concert Hall** CULTURAL BUILDING
(Map p66; www.laphil.com; 111 S Grand Ave) Architect Frank Gehry's now-iconic 2003 structure is a gravity-defying sculpture of curving and billowing stainless-steel walls. It is home base of the Los Angeles Philharmonic, now under the baton of Venezuelan phenom Gustavo Dudamel. Free tours are available subject to concert schedules, and walkways encircle the maze-like roof and exterior. Parking is $9.

MOCA Grand Avenue MUSEUM
(Map p66; www.moca.org; 250 S Grand Ave; adult/child $10/free, 5-8pm Thu free; ⊙11am-5pm Mon & Fri, to 8pm Thu, to 6pm Sat & Sun) Housed in

a building by Arata Isozaki, which many consider his masterpiece, the Museum of Contemporary Art offers headline-grabbing special exhibits; its permanent collection presents heavy hitters from the 1940s to the present. Parking is $9, at Walt Disney Concert Hall. There are two other branches: the Geffen Contemporary at MOCA (Map p66) in Little Tokyo and at the Pacific Design Center in West Hollywood.

FREE Cathedral of Our Lady of the Angels CHURCH

(Map p66; www.olacathedral.org; 555 W Temple St; 6:30am-6pm Mon-Fri, from 9am Sat, 7am-6pm Sun) Architect José Rafael Moneo mixed Gothic proportions with bold contemporary design for the main church of LA's Catholic Archdiocese. Built in 2002 it teems with art, and soft light through alabaster panes lends serenity. Tours (1pm Monday to Friday) and recitals (12:45pm Wednesday) are both free and popular. Unless you're coming for Mass, weekday parking is expensive – $4 per 15 minutes ($18 maximum) until 4pm, $5 on Saturday.

FREE City Hall LANDMARK

(Map p66; www.lacity.org; 200 N Spring St; 8am-5pm Mon-Fri) Until 1966 no LA building stood taller than City Hall. The 1928 building, with its ziggurat-shaped top, has cameoed in the *Superman* and *Dragnet* TV series and the 1953 sci-fi thriller *War of the Worlds*. There are some cool views of Downtown and the mountains from the observation deck. Tours are available by reservation, seven days in advance.

LITTLE TOKYO

Little Tokyo swirls with shopping malls, Buddhist temples, public art, traditional gardens, authentic sushi bars and *izakaya* (pubs), some of LA's hippest new restaurants and a branch of MOCA, Geffen Contemporary, at 152 N Central Ave.

Japanese American National Museum MUSEUM

(Map p66; www.janm.org; 369 E 1st St; adult/child $9/5; 11am-5pm Tue, Wed & Fri-Sun, to 8pm Thu) Get an in-depth look at the Japanese immigrant experience, including the painful chapter of the WWII internment camps.

SOUTH PARK

The southwestern corner of Downtown, South Park isn't a park but an emerging neighborhood, including Staples Center arena, LA Convention Center, and the dining and entertainment hub **LA Live** (Map p66), which includes a dozen restaurants, live music venues, a 54-story hotel tower and the Nokia Theatre, which is home to the MTV Music Awards and *American Idol* finals.

Parking is in private lots ($8 to $20). South Park is near the Blue Line light-rail.

Grammy Museum MUSEUM

(Map p66; www.grammymuseum.org; 800 W Olympic Blvd; adult/child $12.95/10.95; 11:30am-7:30pm Mon-Fri, from 10am Sat & Sun) Opened in 2008, with mind-expanding interactive displays of the history of American music and plenty of listening opportunities.

EXPOSITION PARK & AROUND

Just south of Downtown LA, this neighborhood has a full day's worth of kid-friendly museums, historic sports facilities and green spaces. Landmarks include the **Rose Garden** (admission free; 9am-dusk mid-Mar–Dec) and the 1923 **Los Angeles Memorial Coliseum**, site of the 1932 and 1984 Summer Olympic Games.

Natural History Museum MUSEUM

(www.nhm.org; 900 Exposition Blvd; adult/child $12/5; 9:30am-5pm) Dinos to diamonds, bears to beetles, hissing roaches to an ultra-rare megamouth shark – the old-school museum will take you around the world and back millions of years in time. Kids love digging for fossils in the Discovery Center and making friends with creepy crawlies in the Insect Zoo.

FREE California Science Center MUSEUM

(www.californiasciencecenter.org; 700 State Dr; 10am-5pm) A simulated earthquake, hatching baby chicks and a giant techno-doll named Tess bring out the kid in all of us at this great hands-on science museum. As we went to press, the museum was preparing to become the permanent home of the Space Shuttle *Endeavour*. The **IMAX** (213-744-7400; adult/child $8.25/5) theater caps off an action-filled day.

FREE California African American Museum MUSEUM

(www.caamuseum.org; 600 State Dr; 10am-5pm Tue-Sat, from 11am Sun) A more grown-up attraction, this museum is a handsome showcase of African American art, culture and history.

Downtown Los Angeles

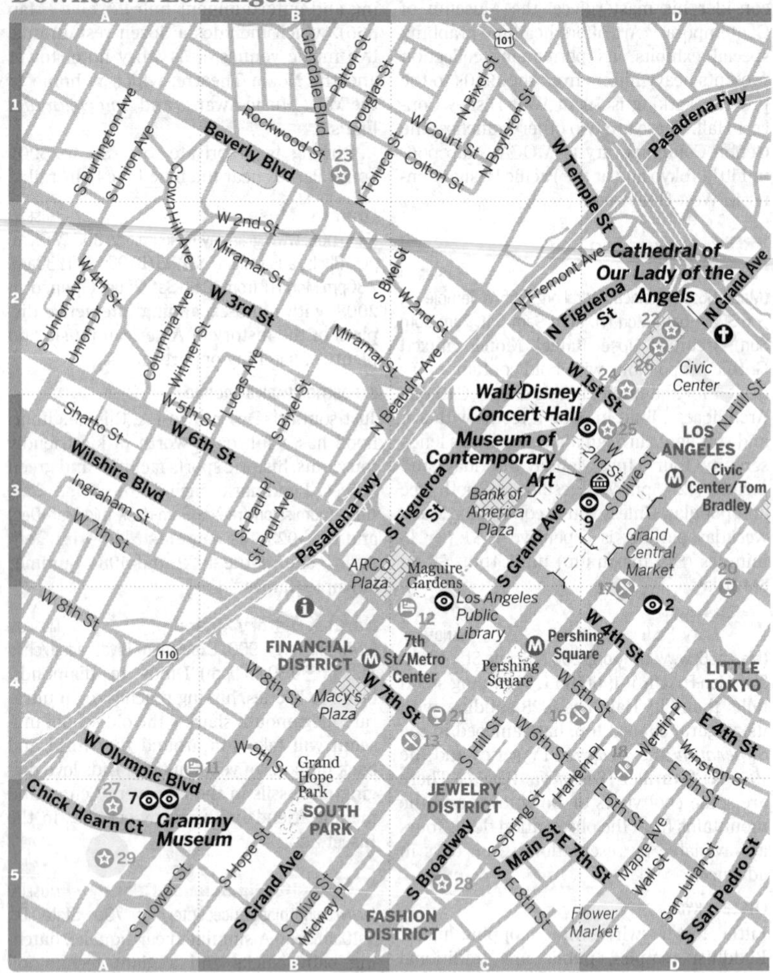

Watts Towers MONUMENT

(www.wattstowers.org; 1727 E 107th St; tours adult/child $7/free; ⏲art center 10am-4pm Wed-Sat, from noon Sun, tours every 30min 11am-3pm Thu & Fri, from 10:30am Sat, from 12:30pm Sun Oct-Jun, from 10:30am Thu-Sat, from 12:30pm Sun Jul-Sep; P) The area south of Exposition Park, known as South Los Angeles, is no stranger to poverty and crime. But one good reason to venture here is the world-famous Watts Towers, a huge and fantastical free-form sculpture cobbled together from found objects – from green 7-Up bottles to seashells and pottery shards – by artist Simon Rodía. Admission is by tour only.

HOLLYWOOD

Just as aging movie stars get the occasional facelift, so has central Hollywood. While it still hasn't recaptured its Golden Age glamour of the 1920s and '40s, much of its late-20th-century seediness is gone.

The Metro Red Line stops beneath Hollywood & Highland, a multistory mall with nicely framed views of the **Hollywood Sign** 2.5 miles away, erected in 1923 as an advertisement for a land development called Hol-

lywoodland. Validated parking here costs $2 for four hours.

Grauman's Chinese Theatre CINEMA
(Map p70; 6925 Hollywood Blvd) Even the most jaded visitor may thrill in the Chinese's famous forecourt, where generations of screen legends have left their imprints in cement: feet, hands, dreadlocks (Whoopi Goldberg), and even magic wands (the young stars of the *Harry Potter* films). Actors dressed as Superman, Marilyn Monroe and the like pose for photos (for tips), and you may be offered free tickets to TV shows.

The theater is on the **Hollywood Walk of Fame**, which honors over 2000 celebrities with stars embedded in the sidewalk. Other historic theaters include the flashy **El Capitan Theater** (Map p70; 6838 Hollywood Blvd) and the 1922 **Egyptian Theater** (Map p70; ☎323-466-3456; www.americancinematheque.com; 6712 Hollywood Blvd), home to American Cinematheque, which presents arty retros and Q&As with directors, writers and actors.

Kodak Theatre THEATER
(Map p70; www.kodaktheatre.com; adult/child $15/10; ⏲10:30am-4pm) Real-life celebs sashay along the Kodak's red carpet for the Academy Awards – columns with names of Oscar-winning films line the entryway. Pricey 30-minute tours take you inside the auditorium, VIP room and past an actual Oscar statuette. Cirque du Soleil presents **Iris** (www.cirquedusoleil.com; tickets $43-253) here, a new film-themed show.

Hollywood Museum MUSEUM
(Map p70; www.thehollywoodmuseum.com; 1660 N Highland Ave; adult/child $15/5; ⏲10am-5pm Wed-Sun) The slightly musty museum is a 35,000-sq-ft shrine to the stars, crammed with kitsch, costumes, knickknacks and props from Charlie Chaplin to *Glee*.

GRIFFITH PARK, SILVER LAKE & LOS FELIZ

FREE **Griffith Park** PARK
(Map p62; www.laparks.org/dos/parks/griffithpk; ⏲6am-10pm, trails close at dusk; P) America's largest urban park is five times the size of New York's Central Park. It embraces an outdoor theater, zoo, observatory, museum, antique trains, golf, tennis, playgrounds, bridle paths, 53 miles of hiking trails, Batman's caves and the Hollywood Sign. The **Ranger Station** (4730 Crystal Springs Dr) has maps.

Griffith Observatory OBSERVATORY, PLANETARIUM
(www.griffithobservatory.org; 2800 Observatory Rd; observatory free, planetarium shows adult/child $7/3; ⏲noon-10pm Tue-Fri, from 10am Sat & Sun, closed occasional Tue; P) Above Los Feliz loom the iconic triple domes of this 1935 observatory, which boasts a super-techie planetarium and films in the Leonard Nimoy Event Horizon Theater. During clear nighttime skies, you can often peer through the telescopes at heavenly bodies.

Los Angeles Zoo ZOO
(www.lazoo.org; 5333 Zoo Dr; adult/child $14/9; ⏲10am-5pm; P) Make friends with 1100

Downtown Los Angeles

Top Sights
- Cathedral of Our Lady of the Angels ... D2
- El Pueblo de Los Angeles ... E2
- Grammy Museum ... A5
- Museum of Contemporary Art ... D3
- Walt Disney Concert Hall ... D3

Sights
- 1 Avila Adobe ... E2
- 2 Bradbury Building ... D4
- 3 Chinese American Museum ... E3
- 4 City Hall ... E3
- 5 Geffen Contemporary at MOCA ... E4
- 6 Japanese American National Museum ... E4
- 7 LA Live ... A5
- 8 La Plaza de Cultura y Artes ... E2
- 9 MOCA Grand Avenue ... D3
- 10 Union Station ... F3

Sleeping
- 11 Figueroa Hotel ... A4
- 12 Standard Downtown LA ... C4

Eating
- 13 Bottega Louie ... C4
- 14 Daikokuya ... E4
- 15 Empress Pavilion ... E1
- 16 Gorbals ... C4
- 17 Grand Central Market ... D4
- 18 Nickel Diner ... D4
- 19 Philippe the Original ... E2

Drinking
- 20 Edison ... D4
- Rooftop Lounge@Standard Downtown LA ... (see 12)
- 21 Seven Grand ... C4

Entertainment
- 22 Ahmanson Theatre ... D2
- 23 Bob Baker Marionette Theater ... B1
- 24 Los Angeles Opera ... D2
- 25 Los Angeles Philharmonic ... D3
- 26 Mark Taper Forum ... D2
- 27 Nokia Theatre ... A5
- 28 Orpheum Theater ... C5
- 29 Staples Center ... A5

Shopping
- 30 Tokyo ... E4

finned, feathered and furry creatures, including in the Campo Gorilla Reserve and the Sea Cliffs, which replicate the California coast complete with harbor seals.

Museum of the American West MUSEUM
(www.autrynationalcenter.org; 4700 Western Heritage Way; adult/child $10/4, free 2nd Tue each month; ⏲10am-4pm Tue-Fri, to 5pm Sat & Sun; P) Exhibits on the good, the bad and the ugly of America's westward expansion rope in even the most reluctant of cowpokes. Star exhibits include an original stagecoach, a Colt firearms collection and a nymph-festooned saloon.

WEST HOLLYWOOD

Rainbow flags fly proudly over Santa Monica Blvd. Celebs keep gossip rags happy by misbehaving at clubs on the fabled Sunset Strip. Welcome to the city of West Hollywood (WeHo), 1.9 sq miles of pure personality.

Boutiques on Robertson Blvd and Melrose Ave purvey the sassy and chic for Hollywood royalty, Santa Monica Blvd is gay central, and Sunset Blvd bursts with clubs, chichi hotels and views across LA. WeHo's also a hotbed of cutting-edge interior design, particularly along the **Avenues of Art and Design** around Beverly Blvd and Melrose Ave.

Pacific Design Center MUSEUM
(PDC; Map p74; www.pacificdesigncenter.com; 8687 Melrose Ave; 9am-5pm Mon-Fri) Some 130 galleries fill the monolithic blue and green 'whales' of the Cesar Pelli–designed Pacific Design Center (a red whale was also under construction as we went to press), including a branch of **MOCA** (www.moca.org; admission free). Visitors are welcome to window-shop, though most sales are to the trade. Parking is $6 per hour.

Schindler House HOUSE
(Map p74; www.makcenter.org; 835 N Kings Rd; adult/child $7/6, 4-6pm Fri free; ⏲11am-6pm Wed-Sun) A point of pilgrimage, pioneering modernist architect Rudolph Schindler (1887–1953) made this building his home. It houses changing exhibits and lectures.

MID-CITY

Some of LA's best museums line Museum Row, a short stretch of Wilshire Blvd just east of Fairfax Ave.

Los Angeles County Museum of Art MUSEUM

(LACMA; Map p74; www.lacma.org; 5905 Wilshire Blvd; adult/child under 17yr $15/free; ⌚noon-8pm Mon, Tue & Thu, to 9pm Fri, 11am-8pm Sat & Sun) One of the country's top art museums and the largest in the western USA. The collection in the Renzo Piano–designed **Broad Contemporary Art Museum** (B-CAM) includes seminal pieces by Jeff Koons, Roy Lichtenstein and Andy Warhol, and two gigantic works in rusted steel by Richard Serra.

Other LACMA pavilions brim with paintings, sculpture and decorative arts: Rembrandt, Cézanne and Magritte; ancient pottery from China, Turkey and Iran; photographs by Ansel Adams and Henri Cartier-Bresson; and a jewel box of a Japanese pavilion. There are often headline-grabbing touring exhibits. Parking is $10.

Petersen Automotive Museum MUSEUM

(Map p74; www.petersen.org; 6060 Wilshire Blvd; adult/child $10/3; ⌚10am-6pm Tue-Sun) A four-story ode to the auto, the museum exhibits shiny vintage cars galore, plus a fun LA streetscape showing how the city's growth has been shaped by the automobile. Parking is $8.

La Brea Tar Pits ARCHAEOLOGICAL SITE

(Map p74) Between 10,000 and 40,000 years ago, tarlike bubbling crude oil trapped saber-toothed cats, mammoths and other extinct ice-age critters, which are still being excavated at the La Brea Tar Pits. Check out their fossilized remains at the **Page Museum** (Map p74; www.tarpits.org; 5801 Wilshire Blvd; adult/child $11/5, 1st Tue each month free; ⌚9:30am-5pm). New fossils are being discovered all the time, and an active staff of archaeologists works behind glass. Parking is $7.

BEVERLY HILLS

The mere mention of Beverly Hills conjures images of Maseratis, manicured mansions and megarich moguls. Stylish and sophisticated, this is a haven for the well-heeled and famous. Stargazers could take a guided bus tour to scout for stars' homes.

No trip to LA would be complete without a saunter along pricey, pretentious **Rodeo Drive**, the famous three-block ribbon of style. Here sample-size fembots browse for fashions from international houses – from Armani to Zegna – in killer-design stores. If the prices make you gasp, Beverly Dr, one block east has more budget-friendly boutiques.

Municipal lots and garages offer two hours of free parking in central Beverly Hills.

Paley Center for Media BROADCASTING MUSEUM

(Map p74; www.paleycenter.org; 465 N Beverly Dr; suggested donation adult/child $10/5; ⌚noon-5pm Wed-Sun) TV and radio addicts can indulge their passion at this mind-boggling archive of TV and radio broadcasts from 1918 through the internet age. Pick your faves, grab a seat at a private console and enjoy. There's an active program of lectures and screenings.

WESTWOOD & AROUND

University of California, Los Angeles UNIVERSITY

Westwood is dominated by the vast campus of the prestigious University of California, Los Angeles (UCLA). The excellent, university-run **Hammer Museum** (www.hammer.ucla.edu; 10899 Wilshire Blvd; adult/child $10/free, Thu free; ⌚11am-7pm Tue, Wed, Fri & Sat, to 9pm Thu, to 5pm Sun) has cutting-edge contemporary art exhibits. Hammer parking is $3.

HIGHLIGHTS OF HISTORIC DOWNTOWN

Pershing Square, the center of Downtown's historic district, was LA's first public park (1866) and has been modernized many times since. Now encircled by high-rises, there's public art and summer concerts.

Nearby, some turn-of-the-last century architecture remains as it once was. Latino-flavored Broadway has the 1893 **Bradbury Building** (Map p66; 304 S Broadway; ⌚9am-6pm Mon-Fri, to 5pm Sat & Sun), whose dazzling galleried atrium featured prominently in *Blade Runner*.

In the early 20th century, Broadway was a glamorous shopping and theater strip, where megastars such as Charlie Chaplin leapt from limos to attend premieres at lavish movie palaces. Some – such as the **Orpheum Theater** (Map p66; 842 Broadway) – have been restored and once again host screenings and parties. The best way to get inside is on tours run by the **Los Angeles Conservancy** (☎213-623-2489; www.laconservancy.org; tours $10).

Hollywood

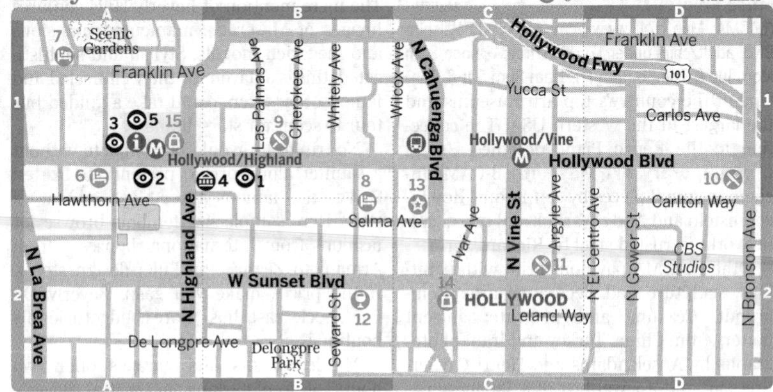

FREE Annenberg Space for Photography MUSEUM
(www.annenbergspaceforphotography.org; 2000 Ave of the Stars, No 10; ⏲11am-6pm Wed-Sun) This fine, camera-shaped museum is just east of Westwood, in the skyscraper village known as Century City. Parking is $3.50 from Wednesday to Friday, $1 on Saturday and Sunday or after 4:30pm daily.

FREE Getty Center MUSEUM
(Map p62; www.getty.edu; 1200 Getty Center Dr; ⏲10am-5:30pm Sun & Tue-Thu, to 9pm Fri & Sat) Triple delights: a stellar art collection, Richard Meier's fabulous architecture and Robert Irwin's ever-changing gardens. On clear days, add breathtaking views of the city and ocean to the list. Visit in the late afternoon after the crowds have thinned. Parking is $15.

Museum of Tolerance MUSEUM
(www.museumoftolerance.com; 9786 W Pico Blvd; adult/child $15/11; ⏲10am-5pm Mon-Thu, to 3:30pm Fri, 11am-5pm Sun; P) This museum uses interactive technology to make visitors confront racism and bigotry. There's a particular focus on the Holocaust, including Nazi-era artifacts and letters by Anne Frank. A history wall celebrates diversity, exposes intolerance and champions rights in America. Reservations recommended.

FREE Westwood Village Memorial Park CEMETERY
(1218 Glendon Ave; ⏲8am-5pm) Tucked among Westwood's high-rises, this postage-stamp-sized park is packed with such famous 6ft-under residents as Marilyn Monroe, Burt Lancaster and Rodney Dangerfield.

MALIBU

Hugging 27 spectacular miles of Pacific Coast Hwy, Malibu has long been synonymous with surfing, stars and a hedonistic lifestyle, but it actually looks far less posh than the glossy mags make it sound. Still, it's been celebrity central since the 1930s. Leo, Brangelina, Streisand and other A-listers have homes here, and can often be spotted shopping at the villagelike **Malibu Country Mart** (3835 Cross Creek Rd; P) and the more utilitarian **Malibu Colony Plaza** (23841 W Malibu Rd; P).

Malibu's twin natural treasures are the Santa Monica Mountains National Recreation Area and its beaches, including the aptly named **Surfrider**.

FREE **Getty Villa** MUSEUM
(www.getty.edu; 17985 Pacific Coast Hwy; ⌚10am-5pm Wed-Mon; P) Malibu's cultural star, a replica Roman villa that's a fantastic showcase of Greek, Roman and Etruscan antiquities. Admission is by timed ticket (no walk-ins). Parking is $15.

SANTA MONICA

Santa Monica is the belle by the beach, mixing urban cool with a laid-back vibe. Tourists, teens and street performers make car-free, chain-store-lined **Third Street Promenade** the most action-packed zone. There's free two-hour parking in public garages on 2nd and 4th Sts ($3 after 6pm).

For more local flavor, shop celeb-favored **Montana Avenue** or down-homey **Main Street**, backbone of the neighborhood once nicknamed 'Dogtown' as the birthplace of skateboard culture.

Santa Monica Pier AMUSEMENT PARK
(Map p78) Kids love the venerable pier, where attractions include a quaint carousel, a solar-powered Ferris wheel and tiny aquarium with touch tanks.

Bergamot Station Arts Center MUSEUM
(2525 Michigan Ave; ⌚10am-6pm Tue-Sat; P) Art fans gravitate inland toward this avant-garde center, a former trolley stop that now houses 35 galleries and the progressive **Santa Monica Museum of Art** (www.smmoa.org; 2525 Michigan Ave; suggested donation $5; ⌚11am-6pm Tue-Sat).

VENICE

The **Venice Boardwalk** (Ocean Front Walk) is a freak show, a human zoo, a wacky carnival and an essential LA experience. This cauldron of counterculture is the place to get your hair braided or a *qi gong* back massage, or pick up cheap sunglasses or a woven bracelet. Encounters with bodybuilders, hoop dreamers, a Speedo-clad snake charmer or a roller-skating Sikh minstrel are pretty much guaranteed, especially on hot summer afternoons. Alas, the vibe gets a bit creepy after dark.

To escape the hubbub, meander inland to the **Venice Canals**, a vestige of Venice's early days when gondoliers poled visitors along quiet man-made waterways. Today ducks preen and locals lollygag in rowboats in this serene, flower-festooned neighborhood.

The hippest Westside strip is funky, sophisticated **Abbot Kinney Boulevard**, a palm-lined mile of restaurants, yoga studios, art galleries and eclectic shops selling mid-century furniture and handmade fashions.

There's street parking around Abbot Kinney, and parking lots ($6 to $15) on the beach.

LONG BEACH

The port of Los Angeles and Long Beach dominate LA County's southern flank, the world's third-busiest container port after Singapore and Hong Kong. But Long Beach's industrial edge has worn smooth in its humming downtown and restyled

TOURING THE STUDIOS

Half the fun of visiting Hollywood is hoping you'll see stars. Up the odds by being part of the studio audience of a sitcom or game show, which usually tape between August and March. For free tickets, contact **Audiences Unlimited** (☎818-260-0041; www.tvtickets.com).

For an authentic behind-the-scenes look, take a small-group tour by open-sided shuttle at **Paramount Pictures** (☎323-956-1777; www.paramount.com; 5555 Melrose Ave, Hollywood; tours $40, minimum age 12yr; ⌚10am-2pm Mon-Fri) or **Warner Bros Studios** (☎818-972-8687; www.wbstudiotour.com; 3400 Riverside Dr, Burbank, San Fernando Valley; tours $45, minimum age 8yr; ⌚8:30am-4pm Mon-Fri; P), or a walking tour of **Sony Pictures Studios** (☎310-244-8687; 10202 W Washington Blvd, Culver City; tours $33, minimum age 12yr; ⌚tours 9:30am, 10:30am, 12:30pm, 1:30pm & 2:30pm Mon-Fri; P). All of these tours show you around sound stages and backlots (outdoor sets), and into such departments as wardrobe and make-up. Reservations are required; bring photo ID.

waterfront. Pine Ave is chockablock with restaurants and clubs popular with everyone from coiffed conventioneers to the testosterone-fuelled frat pack.

The Blue Line (55 minutes) connects Long Beach with Downtown LA, and **Passport** (www.lbtransit.org) minibuses shuttle you around the major sights for free ($1.25 elsewhere in town).

Queen Mary OCEAN LINER

(www.queenmary.com; 1126 Queens Hwy; adult/child from $25/13; ⏲10am-6pm) Long Beach's 'flagship' is the grand (and supposedly haunted!) British ocean liner, which is permanently moored here. Larger and fancier than the *Titanic,* it transported royals, dignitaries, immigrants and troops during its 1001 Atlantic crossings between 1936 and 1964. Parking is $12.

Aquarium of the Pacific AQUARIUM

(www.aquariumofpacific.org; 100 Aquarium Way; adult/child $25/13; ⏲9am-6pm) Children will probably have a better time here, providing a high-tech romp through an underwater world in which sharks dart, jellyfish dance and sea lions frolic. Imagine the thrill of petting a shark! Parking is $8 to $15. *Queen Mary*/Aquarium combination tickets cost adult/child aged three to 11 years $36/20.

Museum of Latin American Art MUSEUM

(www.molaa.org; 628 Alamitos Ave; adult/child $9/free, Sun free; ⏲11am-5pm Wed-Sun; P) One of California's best, as it is the only museum in the western USA specializing in contemporary art from south of the border. The permanent collection highlights spirituality and landscapes, and special exhibits are first-rate.

PASADENA

Resting below the lofty San Gabriel Mountains, this city of 147,000 drips wealth and gentility, and feels a world apart from urban LA. It's famous for art museums, fine arts-and-crafts architecture and the Rose Parade on New Year's Day.

The main fun zone is **Old Town Pasadena** (Map p62), along Colorado Blvd and between Pasadena Ave and Arroyo Pkwy. Metro Gold Line trains connect Pasadena and Downtown LA.

Norton Simon Museum MUSEUM

(www.nortonsimon.org; 411 W Colorado Blvd; adult/child $10/free; ⏲noon-6pm Wed-Thu & Sat-Mon, to 9pm Fri; P) Stroll west and you'll see Rodin's *The Thinker,* a mere overture to the full symphony of European art at this museum. Don't skip the basement, with fabulous Indian and Southeast Asian sculpture.

Gamble House ARCHITECTURE

(www.gamblehouse.org; 4 Westmoreland Pl; adult/child $10/free; ⏲admission by tour only noon-3pm Thu-Sun; P) A masterpiece of California arts-and-crafts architecture, the 1908 Gamble House by Charles and Henry Greene was Doc Brown's home in the movie *Back to the Future.* Admission is by one-hour guided tour.

WORTH A TRIP

UNIVERSAL STUDIOS HOLLYWOOD

Universal Studios (Map p62; www.universalstudioshollywood.com; 100 Universal City Plaza; admission over/under 48in $77/69) first opened to the public in 1915, when studio head Carl Laemmle invited visitors at a quaint 25¢ each (including a boxed lunch) to watch silent films being made. Nearly a century later, Universal remains one of the world's largest movie studios.

Your chances of seeing an actual movie shoot are approximately nil at Universal's current theme park incarnation, yet generations of visitors have had a ball here. Start with the 45-minute narrated studio tour aboard a giant, multicar tram that takes you past working soundstages and outdoor sets like *Desperate Housewives*. Also prepare to survive a shark attack à la *Jaws* and an 8.3-magnitude earthquake. It's hokey but fun.

Among the dozens of other attractions, the **Simpsons Ride** is a motion-simulated romp 'designed' by Krusty the Clown, and you can splash down among the dinos of **Jurassic Park**, while **Special Effects Stages** illuminate the craft of movie-making. **Water World** may have bombed as a movie, but the live action show based on it is a runaway hit, with stunts including giant fireballs and a crash-landing seaplane.

Parking is $12, or arrive via Metro Red Line.

Huntington Library MUSEUM, GARDENS
(Map p62; www.huntington.org; 1151 Oxford Rd; adult/child Tue-Fri $15/6, Sat, Sun & holidays $20/6, 1st Thu each month free; ⌚10:30am-4:30pm Tue-Sun Jun-Aug, Sat & Sun Sep-May, noon-4:30pm Tue-Fri Sep-May; P) LA's biggest understatement does have a library of rare books, including a Gutenberg Bible, but it's the collection of great British and French art and exquisite gardens that make it special. The Rose Garden boasts more than 1200 varieties (and a lovely tearoom; reserve ahead, adult/child $28/15), the Desert Garden has a Seussian quality, and the Chinese garden has a small lake crossed by a stone bridge.

Activities

Bicycling & In-line Skating

Get a scenic exercise kick skating or riding along the paved **South Bay Bicycle Trail** (Map p62), which parallels the beach for most of the 22 miles between Pacific Palisades and Torrance. Rental outfits are plentiful in beach towns. Warning: crowded on weekends.

Hiking

Turn on your celeb radar while strutting it with the hot bods along **Runyon Canyon Park** above Hollywood. **Griffith Park** (Map p62) is also laced with trails. For longer rambles, head to the Santa Monica Mountains, where **Will Rogers State Historic Park**, **Topanga State Park** and **Malibu Creek State Park** (Map p62) are all excellent gateways to beautiful terrain. Parking costs $10 to $12.

Swimming & Surfing

Top beaches for swimming are Malibu's **Zuma**, **Santa Monica State Beach** (Map p78) and **Hermosa Beach** (Map p62). **Surfrider Beach** in Malibu is a legendary surfing spot.

'Endless Summer' is, sorry to report, a myth, so much of the year you'll want to wear a wet suit in the Pacific. Water temperatures become tolerable by June and peak at about 70°F (21°C) in August and September. Water quality varies; check the 'Beach Report Card' at www.healthebay.org.

Los Angeles for Children

Keeping the rug rats happy is child's play in LA. The sprawling Los Angeles Zoo in family-friendly Griffith Park is a sure bet. Dino-fans dig the Page Museum at La Brea Tar Pits and the Natural History Museum, while budding scientists love the California Science Center next door. For live sea creatures, head to the Aquarium of the Pacific; teens might get a kick out of the ghost tours of the *Queen Mary*.

Among LA's amusement parks, Santa Monica Pier is meant for kids of all ages. Activities for younger children are more limited at Universal Studios Hollywood. See also Disneyland and Knott's Berry Farm.

TOP CHOICE **Noah's Ark at Skirball Cultural Center** PLAYGROUND
(☎tickets 877-722-4849; www.skirball.org; 2701 N Sepulveda Blvd; adult/under 12yr $10/5, Thu free; ⌚noon-5pm Tue-Fri, from 10am Sat & Sun; P) This indoor playground of imaginative creatures made from car mats, couch springs, metal strainers and other recycled items is great for those rare days when the weather doesn't cooperate.

Kidspace MUSEUM
(www.kidspacemuseum.org; 480 N Arroyo Blvd, Pasadena; admission $8, ⌚9:30am-5pm Mon-Fri, from 10am Sat & Sun; P) Hands-on exhibits, outdoor learning areas and gardens lure the single-digit set. It's best after 1pm, when the field-trip crowd has left.

Bob Baker Marionette Theater THEATER
(www.bobbakermarionettes.com; 1345 W 1st St; admission $15, reservations required; ⌚10:30am Tue-Fri, 2:30pm Sat & Sun; P) Adorable singing and dancing marionettes have enthralled generations of wee Angelenos.

Tours

Esotouric HISTORY, LITERATURE
(☎323-223-2767; www.esotouric.com; bus tours $58) Hip, offbeat, insightful and entertaining walking and bus tours themed around famous crime sites (Black Dahlia), literary lions (Chandler to Bukowski) and historical neighborhoods.

Los Angeles Conservancy ARCHITECTURE
(☎213-623-2489; www.laconservancy.org; tours $10) Thematic walking tours, mostly of Downtown LA, with an architectural focus. Check the website for self-guided tours.

Melting Pot Tours CULINARY, WALKING
(☎800-979-3370; www.meltingpottours.com; tours from $58; ⌚Wed-Sun) Snack your way through the Original Farmers Market and the aromatic alleyways of Old Town Pasadena.

Beverly Hills, West Hollywood & Mid-City

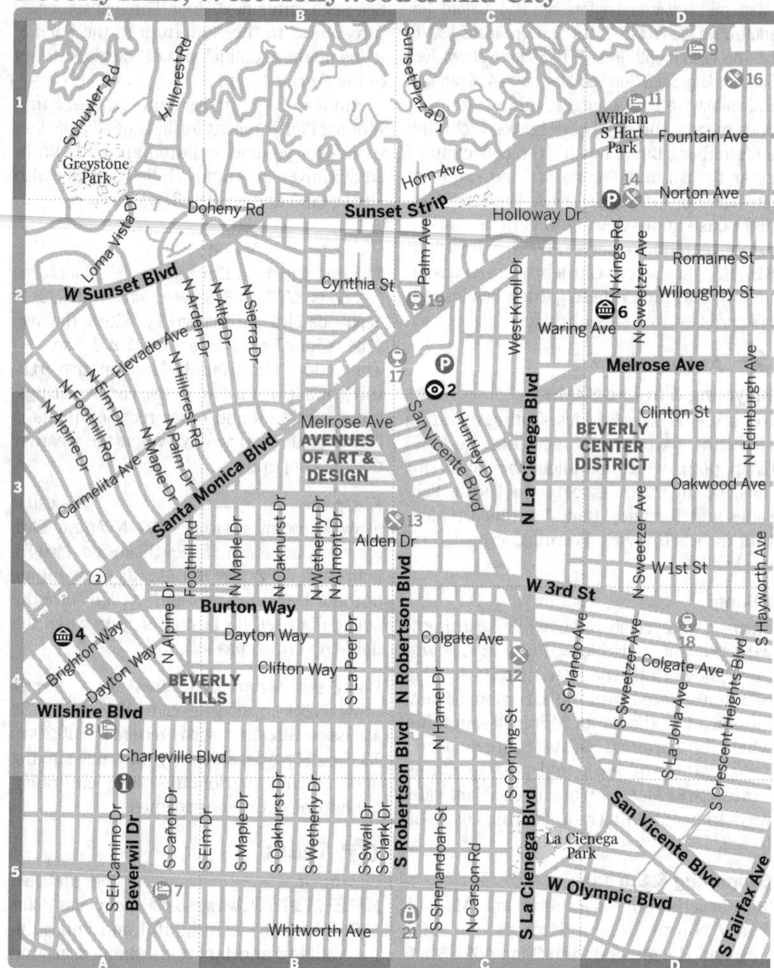

Six Taste CULINARY, WALKING
(☎888-313-0936; www.sixtaste.com; tours $55-65) Walking tours of restaurants in LA neighborhoods including Downtown, Little Tokyo, Chinatown, Thai Town and Santa Monica.

Out & About GAY
(www.outandabout-tours.com; tours $60; ⌚Sat & Sun) Enthusiastic guides show landmarks of LA's gay and lesbian history; there's a lot more than you think!

Red Line Tours WALKING, BUS
(☎323-402-1074; www.redlinetours.com; tours from $25) 'Edutaining' walking tours of Hollywood and Downtown using headsets that cut out traffic noise.

Starline Tours BUS
(☎323-463-333; www.starlinetours.com; tours from $39) Narrated bus tours of the city, stars' homes and theme parks.

Festivals & Events

In addition to the following annual events, monthly street fairs include the gallery and shop open houses and food truck meet-ups of **Downtown LA Art Walk** (www.downtownartwalk.com; ⌚2nd Thu each month) and **First**

Fridays (1st Fri each month) on Abbot Kinney Blvd in Venice.

Tournament of Roses PARADE
(626-449-4100; www.tournamentofroses.com) New Year's Day cavalcade of flower-festooned floats along Pasadena's Colorado Blvd, followed by the Rose Bowl football game.

Toyota Grand Prix of Long Beach AUTO RACE
(888-827-7333; www.longbeachgp.com) Week-long auto-racing spectacle in mid-April drawing world-class drivers.

Fiesta Broadway STREET FAIR
(310-914-0015; www.fiesta broadway.la) Mexican-themed fair along historic Broadway in Downtown, with performances by Latino stars. Last Sunday in April.

Sunset Junction STREET FAIR
(323-661-7771; www.sunsetjunction.org) Silver Lake weekend street party with grub, libations and edgy bands in late August.

West Hollywood Halloween Carnival STREET FAIR
(323-848-6400; www.visitwesthollywood.com) Eccentric, and often NC17-rated, costumes fill Santa Monica Blvd, on October 31.

Sleeping

For seaside life, base yourself in Santa Monica, Venice or Long Beach. Cool-hunters and party people will be happiest in Hollywood or WeHo; culture-vultures, in Downtown. Expect a lodging tax of 12% to 14%; always inquire about discounts.

DOWNTOWN

TOP CHOICE **Standard Downtown LA** HOTEL $$
(Map p66; 213-892-8080; www.standardhotel.com; 550 S Flower St; r from $165;) This 207-room design-savvy hotel in a former office building goes for a young, hip and shag-happy crowd – the rooftop bar fairly pulses – so don't come here with kids or to get a solid night's sleep. Mod, minimalist rooms have platform beds and peek-through showers. Parking is $33.

Figueroa Hotel HISTORIC HOTEL $$
(Map p66; 213-627-8971; www.figueroahotel.com; 939 S Figueroa St; r $148-184, ste $225-265;) A rambling 1920s oasis across from LA Live, the Fig welcomes guests with a richly tiled Spanish-style lobby that segues to a sparkling pool and buzzy outdoor bar. Rooms are furnished in a world-beat mash-up of styles (Morocco, Mexico, Zen…), comfy but varying in size and configuration. Parking is $12.

HOLLYWOOD

Hollywood Roosevelt Hotel HOTEL $$$
(Map p70; 323-466-7000; www.hollywoodroosevelt.com; 7000 Hollywood Blvd; r from $269;) This venerable hotel has hosted elite players since the first Academy Awards were held here in 1929. It pairs a palatial Spanish lobby with sleek Asian contemporary rooms, a busy pool scene and rockin' restos. Parking is $33.

Beverly Hills, West Hollywood & Mid-City

Magic Castle Hotel APARTMENT $$$
(Map p70; ☎323-851-0800; www.magiccastlehotel.com; 7025 Franklin Ave; r $154-304;) Walls are thin, but this renovated former apartment building around a courtyard boasts contemporary furniture, attractive art, comfy bathrobes and fancy bath amenities. Most rooms have a separate living room. For breakfast: freshly baked goods and gourmet coffee on your balcony or poolside. Ask about access to the namesake private club for magicians. Parking is $10.

USA Hostels Hollywood HOSTEL $
(Map p70; ☎323-462-3777; www.usahostels.com; 1624 Schrader Blvd; incl breakfast & tax dm $30-40, r $70-85;) Not for introverts, this energetic hostel puts you within steps of Hollywood's party circuit. Make new friends during staff-organized BBQs, comedy nights and tours, or during free pancake breakfast in the guest kitchen.

WEST HOLLYWOOD & MID-CITY

Standard Hollywood HOTEL $$$
(Map p74; ☎323-650-9090; www.standardhotel.com; 8300 W Sunset Blvd; r $165-250, ste from $350;) This white-on-white property on the Sunset Strip is a scene, with Astroturf-fringed pool with a view across LA and sizable shagadelic rooms with silver beanbag chairs, orange-tiled bathrooms and Warhol poppy-print curtains. Parking is $29.

Farmer's Daughter Hotel MOTEL $$$
(Map p74; ☎323-937-3930; www.farmersdaughterhotel.com; 115 S Fairfax Ave; r $219-269;) Opposite the Original Farmers Market, Grove and CBS Studios, this perennial pleaser gets high marks for its sleek 'urban cowboy' look. Adventurous lovebirds should ask about the No Tell Room… Parking is $18.

Chateau Marmont HISTORIC HOTEL $$$
(Map p74; ☎323-656-1010; www.chateaumarmont.com; 8221 W Sunset Blvd; r $415, ste $500-875;) Its French-flavored indulgence may look dated, but this faux-chateau has long attracted A-listers – Greta Garbo to Bono – with its legendary discretion. The garden cottages are the most romantic. Parking is $28.

BEVERLY HILLS

TOP CHOICE **Beverly Hills Hotel** LUXURY HOTEL $$$
(☎310-276-2251; www.beverlyhillshotel.com; 9641 Sunset Blvd; r from $530;) The legendary Pink Palace from 1912 oozes opulence. The pool deck is classic, the grounds are lush, and the Polo Lounge remains a clubby lunch spot for the well-heeled and well-dressed. Rooms are comparably old-world, with gold accents and marble tile. Parking is $33.

Avalon Hotel HOTEL $$$
(Map p74; ☎310-277-5221; www.avalonbeverlyhills.com; 9400 W Olympic Blvd; r $228-370;) Midcentury modern gets a 21st-century spin at this fashion-crowd fave, Marilyn Monroe's old pad in its days as an apartment building. The beautiful, moneyed and metrosexual now vamp it up in the chic restaurant-bar overlooking a sexy hourglass-shaped pool. Rooms facing the other direction are quieter. Parking is $30.

Beverly Wilshire HOTEL $$$
(Map p74; ☎310-275-5200; www.fourseasons.com/beverlywilshire; 9500 Wilshire Blvd; r $495-545, ste $695-1795;) It has corked Rodeo Dr since 1928, yet amenities are very much up-to-the-minute, both in the original Italian Renaissance wing and in the newer addition. And yes, this is the very hotel from which Julia Roberts first stumbled then strutted in *Pretty Woman*. Parking costs $33.

SANTA MONICA & VENICE

Viceroy HOTEL $$$
(Map p78; ☎310-260-7500; www.viceroysantamonica.com; 1819 Ocean Ave, Santa Monica; r from $370;) Ignore the high-rise eyesore exterior and plunge headlong into *Top Design*'s Kelly Wearstler's campy 'Hollywood Regency' decor and color palette from dolphin gray to mamba green. Look for poolside cabanas, Italian designer linens, and chic bar and restaurant. Parking is $33.

Hotel Erwin HOTEL $$
(☎310-452-1111; www.jdvhotels.com; 1679 Pacific Ave, Venice; r from $169;) A worthy emblem of Venice. Rooms aren't the biggest and in most there's a low traffic hum, but you're steps from the beach and your room features graffiti- or anime-inspired art and an honor bar containing sunglasses and '70s-era soft drinks. The rooftop bar offers spellbinding coastal vistas. Parking is $28.

Embassy Hotel Apartments BOUTIQUE HOTEL $$$
(Map p78; ☎310-394-1279; www.embassyhotelapts.com; 1001 3rd St, Santa Monica; r $169-390;) This hushed 1927 Spanish-Colonial hideaway delivers charm by the bucket. A rickety elevator takes you to units oozing old-world flair and equipped with internet. Kitchens make many rooms well suited to do-it-yourselfers. No air con.

HI Los Angeles-Santa Monica HOSTEL $
(Map p78; ☎310-393-9913; www.lahostels.org; 1436 2nd St, Santa Monica; r $26-30;) Near the beach and Promenade, the location is the envy of much fancier places. Its 200 beds in single-sex dorms and bed-in-a-box doubles with shared bathrooms are clean and safe, and there are plenty of groovy public spaces to lounge and surf; party people are better off in Hollywood.

> **FUN FACT**
>
> At 10.2 million residents, if LA County were a state, it would be the eighth largest in population.

LONG BEACH

Queen Mary Hotel SHIP $$$
(☎562-435-3511; www.queenmary.com; 1126 Queens Hwy, Long Beach; r $110-395;) Take a trip without leaving the dock aboard this grand ocean liner. Staterooms brim with original art-deco details – avoid the cheapest ones that are on the inside. Rates include admission to guided tours. Parking is $12 to $15.

Hotel Varden BOUTIQUE HOTEL $$
(☎562-432-8950; www.thevardenhotel.com; 335 Pacific Ave; r from $109;) The designers clearly had a field day with their modernist renovation of the 35 diminutive rooms in this 1929 hotel: tiny desks, tiny sinks, lots of right angles, cushy beds, white, white and more white. Rates include simple continental breakfast and wine hour. It's a block from Pine Ave's restaurants and night spots. Parking is $10.

Eating

LA's culinary scene is one of the world's most vibrant and eclectic, from celebrity chefs whipping up farmers-market-fab to authentic international cooking.

DOWNTOWN

Downtown's restaurant scene has exploded. Great neighborhoods for browsing include 7th St east of Grand Ave, Little Tokyo (not just for Japanese cuisine anymore), LA Live (Map p66) and the food stalls of the **Grand Central Market** (Map p66; 317 S Broadway; ⊙9am-6pm).

Bottega Louie ITALIAN $$
(Map p66; ☎213-802-1470; www.bottegalouie.com; 700 S Grand Ave; mains $11-18; ⊙10:30am-11pm Mon Fri, Sat & Sun from 9am) The wide marble bar has become a magnet for the artsy loft set and office workers alike. The open-kitchen crew, in chef's whites, grills housemade sausage and wood-fires thin-crust pizzas in the white-on-white, big-as-a-gym dining room. Always busy, always buzzy.

Gorbals JEWISH $$
(Map p66; ☎213-488-3408; www.thegorbals.com; 501 S Spring St; small plates $8-17; ⊙6pm-midnight Mon-Wed, to 2am Thu-Sat) *Top Chef* winner Ilan Hall tweaks traditional Jewish comfort food:

bacon-wrapped matzo balls, potato latkes with smoked applesauce, *gribenes* (fried chicken fat) served BLT style. It's hidden in the back of the Alexandria Hotel lobby.

Nickel Diner DINER $$
(Map p66; ☎213-623-8301; 524 S Main St; mains $8-14; ⏰8am-3:30pm Tue-Sun, 6-11pm Tue-Sat) In Downtown's boho historic district, this red vinyl joint feels like a throwback to the 1920s. Ingredients are 21st century, though: artichokes stuffed with quinoa salad, burgers piled with poblano chilies. Must-try dessert: maple-glazed bacon doughnut.

Santa Monica & Venice

Philippe the Original DINER $
(Map p66; ☎213-628-3781; www.philippes.com; 1001 N Alameda St; sandwiches $6-7.50; ⏰6am-10pm; 🅿) LAPD hunks, stressed-out attorneys and Midwestern vacationers all flock to this legendary 'home of the French dip sandwich,' dating back to 1908 at the edge of Chinatown. Order your choice of meat on a crusty roll dipped in *jus*, and hunker down at the tables on the sawdust-covered floor. Coffee is just 10¢ (no misprint). It accepts cash only.

HOLLYWOOD

Osteria Mozza & Pizzeria Mozza ITALIAN $$$
(☎323-297-0100; www.mozza-la.com; 6602 Melrose Ave, Mid-City; mains Osteria $17-29, Pizzeria $10-18; ⏰lunch & dinner) Reserve weeks ahead at LA's hottest Italian eatery, run by celebrity chefs Mario Batali and Nancy Silverton. Two restaurants share the same building: a wide-ranging menu at the Osteria, and precision-made pizzas baked before your eyes at the **Pizzeria** (☎323-297-0101, 641 N Highland Ave).

Musso & Frank Grill BAR & GRILL $$$
(Map p70; ☎323-467-7788; 6667 Hollywood Blvd; mains $12-35; ⏰11am-11pm Tue-Sat) Hollywood history hangs thickly in the air at the boulevard's oldest eatery. Waiters balance platters of steaks, chops, grilled liver and other dishes harking back to the days when cholesterol wasn't part of our vocabulary. Service is smooth, so are the martinis.

Waffle MODERN AMERICAN $$
(Map p70; ☎323-465-6901; 6255 W Sunset Blvd; mains $9-12; ⏰6:30am-2:30am Sun-Thu,

Santa Monica & Venice

Sights
1 Santa Monica Pier A2

Sleeping
2 Embassy Hotel Apartments B1
3 HI Los Angeles-Santa Monica A2
4 Viceroy A2

Eating
5 3 Square Café & Bakery A5
6 Library Alehouse A4
7 Santa Monica Place B2

Drinking
8 Intelligentsia B5
9 Roosterfish A5

EATING LA: ESSENTIAL ETHNIC NEIGHBORHOODS

Taking nothing away from LA's top-end eateries, some of the city's greatest food treasures are its ethnic restaurants. With some 140 nationalities in LA, we can just scratch the surface, but here are some of the most prominent neighborhoods for authentic cuisine and fun things to do nearby.

Little Tokyo

Daikokuya JAPANESE

(Map p66; ☎213-626-1680; 327 East 1st St; ⏰11am-2:30pm & 5pm-midnight Mon-Sat) In Downtown LA, the essential dish is a steaming bowl of ramen from Daikokuya. While you're there, shop for J-pop culture at **Tokyo** (Map p62; 114 Japanese Village Plaza).

Chinatown

Empress Pavilion CHINESE

(Map p66; ☎213-617-9898; 2nd fl, 988 N Hill St; dim sum per plate $2-6, most mains $10-25; ⏰10am-2:30pm & 5:30-9pm, to 10pm Sat & Sun) In Downtown LA, the essential dish is dim sum. While there, view contemporary art in galleries along Chung King Rd.

Boyle Heights

La Serenata de Garibaldi MEXICAN

(☎323-265-2887; 1842 E 1st St; mains $10-25; ⏰11:30am-10:30pm Mon-Fri, from 9am Sat & Sun) In east LA, the essential dish in this Mexican neighborhood is gourmet tortilla soup. While there, listen to mariachis at Mariachi Plaza.

Koreatown

Chosun Galbee KOREAN

(☎323-734-3330; 3300 Olympic Blvd; mains $12-24; ⏰11am-11pm) West of Downtown LA, the essential dish is barbecue cooked at your table with lots of *banchan* (side dishes). While there, browse the giant Koreatown Galleria mall (Olympic Blvd and Western Ave) for housewares and more food.

Thai Town

Palms Thai THAI

(Map p70; ☎323-462-5073; 5900 Hollywood Blvd; mains $6-19; ⏰11am-midnight Sun-Thu, to 2am Fri & Sat) In East Hollywood, the essential dish is curry with accompaniment by an Elvis impersonator. While there, pick up a flower garland at Thailand Plaza shopping center (5321 Hollywood Blvd).

to 4:30am Fri & Sat) After a night out clubbing, do you really feel like filling yourself with garbage? Us, too. But the Waffle's 21st-century diner food – cornmeal-jalapeño waffles with grilled chicken, carrot cake waffles, mac 'n' cheese, samiches, heaping salads – is organic and locally sourced, so it's (almost) good for you.

WEST HOLLYWOOD, MID-CITY & BEVERLY HILLS

TOP CHOICE **Bazaar** MODERN SPANISH **$$**

(Map p74; ☎310-246-5555; 465 S La Cienega Blvd; dishes $8-18; ⏰6-11pm, brunch 11am-3pm Sat & Sun) In the SLS Hotel, the Bazaar dazzles with over-the-top design by Philippe Starck and 'molecular gastronomic' tapas by José Andrés. Caprese salad pairs cherry tomatoes with mozzarella balls that explode in your mouth, or try cotton-candy foie gras or a Philly cheesesteak on 'air bread.' A word of caution: those small plates add up.

Ivy CALIFORNIAN **$$$**

(Map p74; ☎310-274-8303; 113 N Robertson Blvd; mains $20-38; ⏰11:30am-11pm Mon-Fri, from 11am Sat, from 10am Sun) In the heart of Robertson's fashion frenzy, the Ivy's picket-fenced porch and rustic cottage are *the* power lunch spot. Chances of catching A-lister babes nibbling on a carrot stick or studio execs discussing sequels over the lobster omelet are excellent.

Marix Tex Mex MEXICAN $$
(Map p74; ☎323-656-8800; 1108 N Flores St; mains $9-19; ⊙11:30am-11pm) Many an evening in Boystown has begun flirting on Marix's patios over kick-ass margaritas, followed by fish tacos, fajitas, chipotle chicken sandwiches and all-you-can-eat on Taco Tuesdays.

Veggie Grill VEGETARIAN $
(Map p74; ☎323-822-7575; www.veggiegrill.com; 8000 Sunset Blvd; mains $7-9.50; ⊙11am-11pm; 🖉) If Santa Fe crispy chickin' or a carne asada sandwich don't sound vegetarian, know that this cheery local chain uses seasoned vegetable proteins (mostly tempeh). Try sides of 'sweetheart' sweet potato fries or steamin' kale with miso dressing.

Original Farmers Market MARKET $
(Map p74; cnr 3rd St & Fairfax Ave) The market hosts a dozen worthy, budget-priced eateries, most alfresco. Try the classic diner Dupar's, Cajun-style cooking at the Gumbo Pot, ¡Loteria! Mexican grill or Singapore's Banana Leaf.

SANTA MONICA & VENICE

3 Square Café & Bakery CALIFORNIAN $$
(Map p78; ☎310-399-6504; 1121 Abbot Kinney Blvd; mains $8-20; ⊙cafe 8am-10pm Mon-Thu, to 11pm Fri, 9am-11pm Sat, 9am-10pm Sun, bakery 7am-7pm) Tiny, modernist cafe at which you can devour Hans Röckenwagner's German-inspired pretzel burgers, gourmet sandwiches and apple pancakes. Bakery shelves are piled high with rustic breads and fluffy croissants.

Library Alehouse PUB $$
(Map p78; ☎310-399-7892; www.libraryalehouse.com; 2911 Main St; mains $12-20; ⊙11:30am-midnight) Locals gather as much for the food as the 29 beers on tap, at this wood-paneled gastropub with a cozy outdoor back patio. Angus burgers, fish tacos and hearty salads sate the 30-something regulars.

Santa Monica Place SHOPPING CENTER $$
(Map p78; www.santamonicaplace.com; 3rd fl, cnr 3rd St & Broadway; 👪) We wouldn't normally eat at a mall, but the indoor-outdoor dining deck sets standards: Latin-Asian fusion at Zengo (think Peking duck tacos), sushi at Ozumo, wood-oven-baked pizzas at Antica. Most restaurants have seating with views across adjacent rooftops – some to the ocean. Stalls in the Market do *salumi* to soufflés.

LONG BEACH

Number Nine VIETNAMESE $
(☎562-434-2009; www.numberninenoodles.com; 2118 E 4th St; mains $7-9; ⊙noon-midnight) Maximalist portions of Vietnamese noodles and five-spice chicken with egg roll, in minimalist surrounds on Retro Row. Meats and poultry are sustainably raised.

George's Greek Café GREEK $$
(☎562-437-1184; www.georgesgreekcafe.com; 135 Pine Ave; mains $8-19; ⊙11am-10pm Sun-Thu, to 11pm Fri & Sat) George himself may greet you at the entrance on the generous patio, heart of the Pine Ave restaurant row, both geographically and spiritually. Locals cry *'Opa!'* for the *saganaki* (flaming cheese) and lamb chops.

Drinking

TOP CHOICE Edison BAR
(Map p66; www.edisondowntown.com; 108 W 2nd St, off Harlem Alley, Downtown; ⊙Wed-Sat) *Metropolis* meets *Blade Runner* at this industrial-chic basement boîte, where you'll be sipping *mojitos* surrounded by turbines and other machinery back from its days as a boiler room. Don't worry: it's all tarted up nicely with cocoa leather couches, three cavernous bars and a dress code.

Seven Grand BAR
(Map p66; ☎213-614-0737; 515 W 7th St, Downtown) It's as if hipsters invaded Mummy and Daddy's hunt club, amid the tartan-patterned carpeting and deer heads on the walls. Whiskey is the drink of choice: choose from over 100 from Scotland, Ireland and even Japan.

Cat & Fiddle PUB
(Map p70; www.thecatandfiddle.com; 6530 W Sunset Blvd; ⊙11:30am-2am; P) Morrissey to Frodo, you never know who might be popping by for Boddingtons or Sunday-night jazz. Still, this Brit pub with leafy beer garden is more about friends and conversation than faux-hawks and deal-making.

Dresden RETRO BAR
(1760 N Vermont Ave, Los Feliz) Dresden's answer to Bogey & Bacall is the campy songster duo Marty & Elayne. They're an institution: you saw them crooning 'Stayin' Alive' in *Swingers*.

El Carmen BAR
(Map p74; 8138 W 3rd St; ⊙5pm-2am Mon-Fri, from 7pm Sat & Sun; P) Mounted bull heads and

lucha libre (Mexican wrestling) masks create an over-the-top 'Tijuana North' look and pull in an entertainment-industry-heavy crowd at LA's ultimate tequila and mezcal tavern (over a hundred to choose from).

Intelligentsia CAFE
(Map p78; www.intelligentsiacoffee.com; 1331 Abbot Kinney Blvd, Venice; ⏰6am-8pm Mon-Wed, to 11pm Thu & Fri, 7am-11pm Sat, 7am-8pm Sun; 📶) In this hip, minimalist monument to the coffee gods, skilled baristas never short you on foam or caffeine, and scones and muffins are addictive. Also at 3920 W Sunset Blvd in Silver Lake (open 6am to 8pm Sunday to Wednesday, to 11pm Thursday to Saturday).

☆ Entertainment

LA Weekly (www.laweekly.com) and the *Los Angeles Times* (www.latimes.com/theguide) have extensive entertainment listings. Snag tickets online, at the box office or through **Ticketmaster** (☎213-480-3232; www.ticketmaster.com). For half-price tickets to selected stage shows, visit the visitor centers in Hollywood and Downtown LA; try **Goldstar** (www.goldstar.com) for stage, concerts and events, or **LAStage Alliance** (www.theatrela.org) or **Plays 411** (www.plays411.com) for the theater.

Live Music & Nightclubs

Legendary music venues on the Sunset Strip include Whisky A-Go-Go and House of Blues.

TOP CHOICE **Spaceland** LIVE MUSIC
(www.clubspaceland.com; 1717 Silver Lake Blvd, Silver Lake) Beck played some early gigs at what is still LA's best place for indie and alternasounds. When the ad says 'special guest,' you never know what level of star might show up for quick and dirty impromptu sessions.

Hotel Cafe LIVE MUSIC
(Map p70; www.hotelcafe.com; 1623-1/2 N Cahuenga Blvd; tickets $10-15) The 'it' place for handmade music sometimes features big-timers such as Suzanne Vega, but it's really more of a stepping stone for message-minded newbie balladeers. Get there early and enter from the alley.

McCabe's Guitar Shop LIVE MUSIC
(☎310-828-4403; www.mccabes.com; 3101 Pico Blvd, Santa Monica) This mecca of musicianship sells guitars and other instruments, and the likes of Jackson Browne, Liz Phair and Michelle Shocked have performed live in the postage-stamp-sized back room.

Classical Music & Opera

Los Angeles Philharmonic ORCHESTRA
(Map p66; ☎323-850-2000; www.laphil.org; 111 S Grand Ave, Downtown) The world-class LA Phil performs classics and cutting-edge works at the Walt Disney Concert Hall, under the baton of Venezuelan phenom Gustavo Dudamel.

TOP CHOICE **Hollywood Bowl** AMPHITHEATER
(☎323-850-2000; www.hollywoodbowl.com; 2301 N Highland Ave, Hollywood; ⏰late Jun-Sep) This historic natural amphitheater is the LA Phil's summer home and also a stellar place to catch big-name rock, jazz, blues and pop acts. Come early for a preshow picnic (alcohol is allowed).

Los Angeles Opera OPERA
(Map p66; ☎213-972-8001; www.laopera.com; Dorothy Chandler Pavilion; 135 N Grand Ave, Downtown) Helmed by Plácido Domingo, this renowned opera ensemble plays it pretty safe with crowd-pleasers.

Theater

Centre Theatre Group THEATER
(☎213-628-2772; www.centretheatregroup.org) New and classic plays and musicals, including some Broadway touring companies, are presented in – count 'em – three venues: Ahmanson Theatre (Map p66) and Mark Taper Forum (Map p66) in Downtown LA, and Kirk Douglas Theatre in Culver City. Phone for $20 'Hot Tix' to shows (when available).

Actors' Gang THEATER
(www.theactorsgang.com; 9070 Venice Blvd, Culver City) Cofounded by Tim Robbins, this socially mindful troupe has won many awards for its bold and offbeat interpretations of classics and new works pulled from ensemble workshops.

Will Geer Theatricum Botanicum AMPHITHEATER
(www.theatricum.com; 1419 N Topanga Canyon Blvd, Malibu) Enchanting summer repertory in the woods.

Sports

Dodger Stadium BASEBALL
(www.dodgers.com; 1000 Elysian Park Dr, Downtown) LA's Major League Baseball team plays from April to October in this legendary stadium.

LA: SO GAY

LA is one of America's gayest cities. The *Advocate* magazine, PFLAG (Parents and Friends of Lesbians and Gays), and America's first gay church and synagogue all started here. Gays and lesbians fill every segment of society: entertainment, politics, business and actors/waiters/models.

'Boystown,' Santa Monica Blvd in West Hollywood (WeHo), is gay ground zero. Dozens of high-energy bars, cafes, restaurants, gyms and clubs here are especially busy from Thursday to Sunday; most cater to gay men. Elsewhere, the gay scenes are considerably more laid-back. Silver Lake, LA's original gay enclave, has evolved from largely leather and Levi's to encompass cute multiethnic hipsters. Long Beach also has a significant gay community.

LA's **Gay Pride** (www.lapride.org) celebration in mid-June attracts hundreds of thousands for nonstop partying and a parade down Santa Monica Blvd. Here are some party places to get you started the rest of the year. Freebie listings magazines and www.losangeles.gaycities.com have comprehensive listings.

Weho

Abbey BAR

(Map p74; www.abbeyfoodandbar.com; 692 N Robertson Blvd; mains $9-24; ⏲9am-2am) LA's essential gay bar and restaurant. Take your pick of preening and partying spaces at the Abbey, spanning a leafy patio to slick lounge, and enjoy flavored martinis and *mojitos* and upscale pub grub.

Eleven BAR

(Map p74; www.eleven.la; 8811 Santa Monica Blvd; mains $13-29; ⏲6-10pm Tue-Sun, 11am-3pm Sat & Sun) This glam spot occupies a historic building, serves New American cuisine and offers different theme nights from Musical Mondays to high-energy dance parties; check the website for club nights.

Silver Lake

Akbar BAR

(www.akbarsilverlake.com; 4356 W Sunset Blvd) Best jukebox in town, a Casbah atmosphere, and a crowd that's been known to change from hour to hour – gay, straight or just hip, but not too-hip-for-you. Some nights, the back room's a dancefloor; other nights, you'll find comedy, craft-making or 'Bears in Space.'

MJ's CLUB

(www.mjsbar.com; 2810 Hyperion Ave) Popular contempo hangout for dance nights, 'porn star of the week' and cruising. Young but diverse crowd.

Beach Cities

Roosterfish BAR

(Map p78; www.roosterfishbar.com; 1302 Abbot Kinney Blvd, Venice) The Westside's last remaining gay bar, the 'Fish has been serving the men of Venice for over three decades, but still feels current and chill, with a pool table and back patio. Friday nights are busiest.

Silver Fox BAR

(www.silverfoxlongbeach.com; 411 Redondo Ave, Long Beach) Despite its name, all ages frequent this mainstay of gay Long Beach, especially on karaoke nights. It is a short drive from shopping on Retro Row.

Staples Center SPECTATOR SPORT

(Map p66; www.staplescenter.com; 1111 S Figueroa St, Downtown) All the high-tech trappings fill this flying-saucer-shaped home to the Lakers, Clippers and Sparks basketball teams, and the Kings ice hockey team. Headliners – Britney Spears to Katy Perry – also perform here.

 Shopping

Beverly Hills's **Rodeo Drive** (btwn Wilshire & Santa Monica Blvds) may be the world's most famous shopping street, but LA drips with other options for retail therapy. Fashionistas, and their paparazzi piranhas, flock to **Robertson Boulevard** (btwn Beverly Blvd & 3rd St) and **Montana Avenue** (btwn Lincoln Blvd & 20th St) in Santa Monica. **Melrose Avenue** (btwn San Vicente Blvd & La Brea Ave) in Hollywood and West Hollywood is still a fave of Gen-Y hipsters.

Hollywood is ground zero for groovy tunes at **Amoeba Music** (Map p70; ☎323-245-6400; 6400 W Sunset Blvd). East of here, Silver Lake has cool kitsch, collectibles and emerging LA designers, especially around **Sunset Junction** (Sunset Blvd, btwn Santa Monica & Griffith Park Blvds). Other chain-free strips are Main St in Santa Monica, Abbot Kinney Blvd in Venice and Larchmont Blvd in Hollywood.

In Long Beach, **Retro Row** (E 4th St, btwn Junipero & Cherry Aves) brims with shops selling vintage clothing and mid-century furniture at prices from 'how much?' to '*how* much?'.

Shoppers with couture taste but bargain budgets: head to Downtown's market districts. The 90-block **Fashion District** (Map p66; www.fashiondistrict.org) is a head-spinning selection of samples, knockoffs and original designs at cut-rate prices. The atmosphere is more street market than Rodeo Dr, and haggling is ubiquitous. Gold and diamonds are the main currency in the **Jewelry District** (Map p66) along Hill St, and the **Flower Market** (Map p66; Wall St, btwn 7th & 8th Sts; admission Mon-Fri/Sat $2/1; ⏲8am-noon Mon, Wed & Fri, from 6am Tue, Thu & Sat) is the largest in the country, dating from 1913.

Bookstores include **Book Soup** (☎310-659-3110; www.booksoup.com; 8818 W Sunset Blvd, West Hollywood), with frequent celeb sightings, and **Distant Lands** (www.distantlands.com; ☎626-449-3220; 56 S Raymond Ave, Pasadena), a treasure chest of travel books, guides and gadgets.

Bargains await at two of LA's leading flea markets.

Rose Bowl Flea Market FLEA MARKET
(www.rgcshows.com; 1001 Rose Bowl Dr, Pasadena; admission $8-20; ⏲5am-4:30pm 2nd Sun of the month) The 'mother' of all flea markets, with more than 2500 vendors; monthly.

Melrose Trading Post FLEA MARKET
(Map p74; www.melrosetradingpost.com; Fairfax High School, 7850 Melrose Ave, West Hollywood; admission $2; ⏲9am-5pm Sun) Good weekly flea market which brings out hipsters in search of retro treasure.

Information

Emergency & Medical Services

Cedars-Sinai Medical Center (☎310-423-3277; 8700 Beverly Blvd, West Hollywood; ⏲24hr emergency)

Rite-Aid pharmacies (☎800-748-3243) Call for the nearest branch; some are open 24 hours.

Internet Access

Coffee shops, including the local chain **Coffee Bean & Tea Leaf** (www.cbtl.com), offer wi-fi with a purchase. Libraries offer free access.

Los Angeles Public Library (☎213-228-7000; www.lapl.org; 630 W 5th St, Downtown; wi-fi)

Santa Monica Public Library (☎310-458-8600; www.smpl.org; 601 Santa Monica Blvd; wi-fi)

Media

KCRW 89.9 FM (www.kcrw.org) A Santa Monica–based National Public Radio (NPR) station that plays cutting-edge music and airs well-chosen public affairs programming.

KPCC 89.3 FM (www.kpcc.org) Pasadena-based NPR station with NPR and BBC programming and intelligent local talk shows.

LA Weekly (www.laweekly.com) Free alternative news and listings magazine.

Los Angeles Magazine (www.losangelesmagazine.com) Glossy lifestyle monthly with a useful restaurant guide.

Los Angeles Times (www.latimes.com) The West's leading daily newspaper and winner of dozens of Pulitzer Prizes. Embattled but still useful.

Money

Travelex (☎310-659-6093; US Bank, 8901 Santa Monica Blvd, West Hollywood; ⏲9am-5pm Mon-Thu, to 6pm Fri, to 1pm Sat)

Post

Call ☎800-275-8777 or visit www.usps.com for the nearest branch.

IT'S A WRAP

Dress just like a movie star – in their actual clothes! Packed-to-the-rafters **It's a Wrap** (Map p74; ☎310-246-9727; www.itsawrap.com; 1164 S Robertson Blvd, Mid-City; ⏲11am-8pm Mon-Fri, to 6pm Sat & Sun) sells wardrobe castoffs – tank tops to tuxedos – worn by actors and extras working on TV or movie shoots. Tags are coded, so you'll be able to brag with the knowledge of which person's clothing you are wearing.

Telephone

LA County is covered by 10 area codes. Dial 1+area code before all numbers.

Tourist Information

Beverly Hills (☎310-248-1015; www.lovebeverlyhills.org; 239 S Beverly Dr; ⏰8:30am-5pm Mon-Fri)

Downtown LA (☎213-689-8822; http://discoverlosangeles.com; 685 S Figueroa St; ⏰8:30am-5pm Mon-Fri)

Hollywood (☎323-467-6412; http://discoverlosangeles.com; Hollywood & Highland complex, 6801 Hollywood Blvd; ⏰10am-10pm Mon-Sat, to 7pm Sun)

Long Beach (☎562-628-8850; www.visitlongbeach.com; 3rd fl, One World Trade Center; ⏰11am-7pm Sun-Thu, 11:30am-7:30pm Fri & Sat Jun-Sep, 10am-4pm Fri-Sun Oct-May)

Santa Monica (☎310-393-7593; www.santamonica.com) Visitor center (1920 Main St; ⏰9am-6pm); Information kiosk (☎1400 Ocean Ave; ⏰9am-5pm Jun-Aug, 10am-4pm Sep-May)

Websites

Daily Candy LA (www.dailycandy.com) Little bites of LA style.

Discover Los Angeles (http://discoverlosangeles.com) Official tourist office site.

Gridskipper LA (www.gridskipper.com/travel/los-angeles) Urban travel guide to the offbeat.

LA Observed (www.laobserved.com) News blog that rounds up – and often scoops – other media.

LA.com (www.la.com) Clued-in guide to shopping, dining, nightlife and events.

Getting There & Away

Air

LA's main gateway is **Los Angeles International Airport** (LAX; ☎310-646-5252; www.lawa.org/lax), one of the world's five busiest. The nine terminals are linked by the free shuttle bus A, on the lower (arrival) level. Hotel and car-rental shuttles stop here as well.

Long Beach Airport (LGB) and Burbank's **Bob Hope Airport** (BUR) handle mostly domestic flights.

Bus

The main **Greyhound bus terminal** (☎213-629-8401; 1716 E 7th St) is in an unsavory part of Downtown, so avoid arriving after dark. Some buses go directly to the **Hollywood terminal** (☎323-466-6381; 1715 N Cahuenga Blvd).

Car

The usual international car-rental agencies have branches throughout Los Angeles (see p457 for central reservation numbers and websites).

Train

Amtrak trains roll into Downtown's historic **Union Station** (☎800-872-7245; www.amtrak.com; 800 N Alameda St). The *Pacific Surfliner* travels daily to San Diego ($36, 2¾ hours), Santa Barbara ($29, 2½ hours) and San Luis Obispo ($40, 4¾ hours).

Getting Around

To & From the Airport

At LAX, door-to-door shared-ride vans operated by **Prime Time** (☎800-473-3743; www.primetimeshuttle.com) and **Super Shuttle** (☎310-782-6600; www.supershuttle.com) leave from the lower level of all terminals. Typical fares to Santa Monica, Hollywood or Downtown are $20, $25 and $16, respectively. **Disneyland Express** (☎714-978-8855; www.grayline.com) travels at least hourly between LAX and Disneyland-area hotels for one way/round-trip $22/32.

Curbside dispatchers will summon a taxi for you. There's a flat fare of $46.50 to Downtown LA. Otherwise, metered fares ($2.85 at flag fall plus $2.70 per mile) average $30 to Santa Monica, $42 to Hollywood and up to $90 to Disneyland. There is a $4 surcharge for taxis departing LAX.

LAX Flyaway Buses (☎866-435-9529; www.lawa.org) depart LAX terminals every 30 minutes, from about 5am to midnight, nonstop to both Westwood ($5, 30 minutes) and Union Station ($7, 45 minutes) in Downtown LA.

Other public transportation is slower and less convenient but cheaper. From the lower level outside any terminal, catch a free shuttle bus to parking lot C, next to the LAX Transit Center, the hub for buses serving all of LA. You can also take shuttle bus G to Aviation Station and the Metro Green Line light-rail, from where you can connect to the Blue Line and Downtown LA or Long Beach (40 minutes).

Car & Motorcycle

Unless time is no factor or money is extremely tight, you'll probably find yourself behind the wheel. Driving in LA doesn't need to be a hassle (a GPS device helps), but be prepared for some of the worst traffic in the country during rush hour (roughly 7:30am to 9am and 4pm to 6:30pm).

Parking at motels and cheaper hotels is usually free, while fancier ones charge from $8 to $36. Valet parking at nicer restaurants, hotels and nightspots is commonplace, with rates ranging from $2.50 to $10.

For local parking recommendations, see each of the neighborhoods in the Sights section.

Public Transportation

Tickets cost $1.50 per boarding (get a transfer when boarding if needed). There are no free

ACTUALLY, SOME PEOPLE DO WALK IN LA

'No one walks in LA,' the '80s band Missing Persons famously sang. That was then. Fed up with traffic, smog and high gas prices, the city that defined car culture is developing a foot culture. Angelenos are moving into more densely populated neighborhoods and walking, cycling and taking public transit.

The Metro Red Line subway connects Union Station in Downtown LA to the San Fernando Valley via Koreatown, Hollywood and Universal Studios. Base yourself near one of the arty stations, and you may not need a car at all. Unlimited-ride tickets at $6 a day are a downright bargain; plus, given LA's legendary traffic, it's often faster to travel below ground than above.

While eventual plans call for a 'Subway to the Sea,' for now you'll be busing it to Mid-City, Beverly Hills, Westwood and Santa Monica. The easiest transfer is to the Rapid 720 bus (at Wilshire/Vermont station on the Red Line or Wilshire/Western on the Purple Line), which makes limited stops along Wilshire Blvd. For more information visit www.metro.net.

transfers between trains and buses, but the 'TAP card' unlimited ride passes cost $6/20/75 per day/week/month. Purchase train tickets and TAP cards at vending machines throughout stations, or check out metro.net to search for other vendors.

Local **DASH minibuses** (☎your area code + 808-2273; www.ladottransit.com; fare 35¢) serve Downtown and Hollywood. Santa Monica–based **Big Blue Bus** (☎310-451-5444; www.bigbluebus.com, fare $1) serves much of the western LA area and LAX. Its Line 10 Freeway Express connects Santa Monica with Downtown LA ($2, one hour).

Trip-planning help is available via LA's **Metro** (☎800-266-6883; www.metro.net), which operates about 200 bus lines and six subway and light-rail lines:

Blue Line Downtown (7th St/Metro Center) to Long Beach.

Expo Line Downtown (7th St/Metro Center) to Culver City, via Exposition Park (scheduled opening winter 2011–12).

Gold Line Union Station to Pasadena and east LA.

Green Line Norwalk to Redondo Beach.

Purple Line Downtown to Koreatown.

Red Line Union Station to North Hollywood, via Downtown, Hollywood and Universal Studios.

Taxi

Except for taxis lined up outside airports, train stations, bus stations and major hotels, it's best to phone for a cab. Fares are metered, $2.85 at flag fall plus $2.70 per mile. Taxis serving the airport accept credit cards, though sometimes grudgingly.

Checker (☎800-300-5007)

Independent (☎800-521-8294)

Yellow Cab (☎800-200-1085)

SOUTHERN CALIFORNIA COAST

Disneyland & Anaheim

The mother of all West Coast theme parks, also known as the 'Happiest Place on Earth,' Disneyland is a parallel world that's squeaky-clean, enchanting and wacky all at once. Because it's smaller and somewhat more modest than Florida's Disneyworld, many visitors don't realize that Disneyland was, in fact, Walt Disney's original theme park. He famously dreamt of a 'magical park' where children and their parents could have fun together. For all his visions of waterfalls, castles and gigantic teacups, Disney was a practical businessman, too, choosing to construct his fantastical park within easy reach of the Los Angeles metropolitan area.

The park opened to great fanfare in 1955 and Anaheim grew up around it; today the Disneyland Resort comprises both the original park and the newer California Adventure Park. Though the city of Anaheim doesn't have a strong identity that's independent from Disney – especially after serious revitalization efforts in the 1990s – a few attractions and a large conference center bring in a crowd of visitors who've never posed in front of Sleeping Beauty Castle.

Sights & Activities

You can see either **park** (☎714-781-4565, 714-781-4400; www.disneyland.com; 1313 Harbor Blvd, Anaheim; 1-day pass adult/child 3-9yr $80/74, both parks $105/99) in a day, but going on all the rides requires at least two days (three if

Disneyland Resort

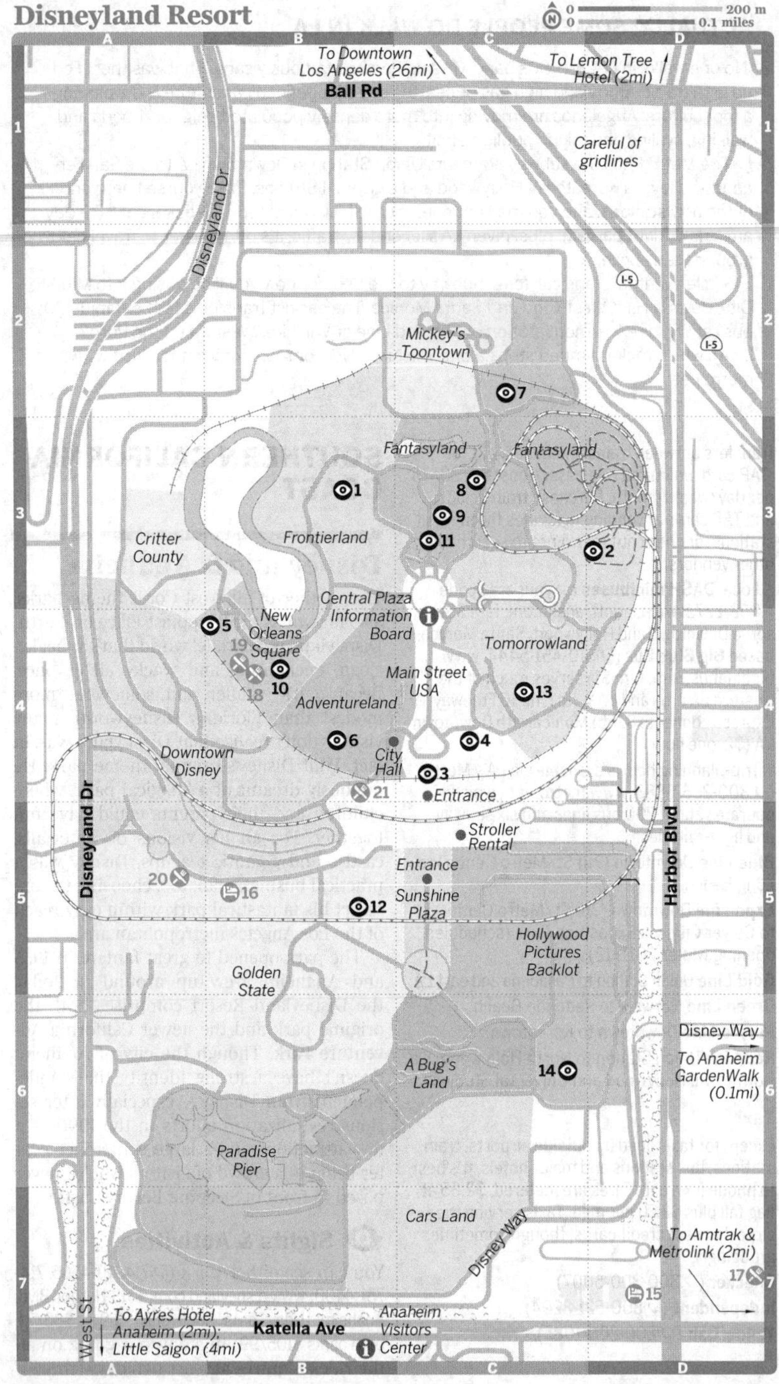

Disneyland Resort

Sights

1 Big Thunder Mountain Railroad B3
2 Disneyland Monorail D3
3 Disneyland Railroad Station C4
4 Disneyland Story: presenting Great Moments with Mr Lincoln C4
5 Haunted Mansion B4
6 Indiana Jones Adventure B4
7 It's a small world C2
8 Mad Tea Party C3
9 Peter Pan's Flight C3
10 Pirates of the Caribbean B4
11 Sleeping Beauty Castle C3
12 Soarin' Over California B5
13 Space Mountain C4
14 Twilight Zone Tower of Terror C6

Sleeping

15 Candy Cane Inn D7
16 Disney's Grand Californian Hotel & Spa B5

Eating

17 Anaheim GardenWalk D7
18 Blue Bayou B4
19 Café Orleans B4
20 Catal Restaurant & Uva Bar A5
Napa Rose .... (see 16)
21 Picnic Area B4

visiting both parks), as waits for top attractions can be an hour or more. To minimize wait times, especially in summer, arrive midweek before the gates open and use the Fastpass system, which assigns boarding times for selected attractions. A variety of multiday passes are available. Check the website for discounts and seasonal park hours. Parking is $15.

Disneyland Park AMUSEMENT PARK
Spotless, wholesome Disneyland is still laid out according to Walt's original plans: **Main Street USA**, a pretty thoroughfare lined with old-fashioned ice-cream parlors and shops, is the gateway into the park. Though kids will make a beeline for the rides, adults will enjoy the antique photos and history exhibit just inside the main park entrance at the **Disneyland Story**: presenting Great Moments with Mr Lincoln.

At the far end of the street is Sleeping Beauty Castle, an obligatory photo op and a central landmark worth noting – its towering blue turrets are visible from many areas of the park. The sections of Disneyland radiate from here like spokes on a wheel. **Fantasyland** is your best bet for meeting princesses and other characters in costume; it's also home to a few notable rides like the famous spinning teacups of Mad Tea Party, Peter Pan's Flight and 'it's a small world.' For something a bit more fast-paced, head to the exhilarating Space Mountain roller coaster in **Tomorrowland** or the popular Indiana Jones Adventure ride in **Adventureland**. Nearby **New Orleans Square** offers several worthwhile attractions, too – the Haunted Mansion (not too scary for older kids) and the otherworldly Pirates of the Caribbean cruise, where cannons shoot across the water, wenches are up for auction and the mechanical Jack Sparrow character is creepily lifelike. Find Big Thunder Mountain Railroad, another popular roller coaster, in the Old West–themed **Frontierland**. If you've got little ones in tow, you'll likely spend time in kid-focused **Critter Country** and **Mickey's Toontown**, too.

Disney's California Adventure AMUSEMENT PARK
Disneyland resort's larger but less crowded park, California Adventure celebrates the natural and cultural glories of the Golden State but lacks the density of attractions and depth of imagination. The best rides are Soarin' Over California, a virtual hang-glide, and the famous Twilight Zone Tower of Terror that drops you 183ft down an elevator chute.

Downtown Disney PLAZA
Disney's open-air pedestrian mall, sandwiched between the two parks, offers plenty of opportunities to drop even more cash in its stores, restaurants and entertainment venues.

Sleeping

Chain hotels are a dime a dozen in the surrounding city of Anaheim.

Disney's Grand Californian Hotel & Spa LUXURY HOTEL $$$
(714-635-2300; http://disneyland.disney.go.com/grand-californian-hotel; 1600 S Disneyland Dr; d $384-445; P ❄ 📶 🏊 👪) Along the promenade of Downtown Disney, you'll see the entrance

to this splurgeworthy arts-and-crafts-style hotel offering family-friendly scavenger hunts, swimming pools bordered by private cabanas and a private entrance to California Adventure. Nonguests can soak up some of the hotel's glamour by stopping for lunch or a glass of wine at Napa Rose, the on-site wine bar and eatery; **Disney Dining** (☎714-781-3463) handles reservations.

Lemon Tree Hotel HOTEL $$

(☎866-311-5595; http://lemon-tree-hotel.com; 1600 E Lincoln Ave; r $89-119, ste $159; P❄📶≋) Disneygoers and road-trippers appreciate the great value and communal BBQ facilities at this Aussie-owned inn. The simple but appealing accommodations include studios with kitchenettes and a two-room, three-bed suite with a kitchen that's ideal for families.

Ayres Hotel Anaheim HOTEL $$

(☎714-634-2106; www.ayreshotels.com/anaheim; 2550 E Katella Ave; r $129-149; P❄@📶≋) For something a bit more upscale but still affordable, try this French country-style hotel where amenities include complimentary evening receptions, large flat-screen TVs and pillow-top beds.

Candy Cane Inn MOTEL $$

(☎714-774-5284; www.candycaneinn.net; 1747 S Harbor Blvd; r $123-144; P❄📶≋👪) At this flowery and family-friendly motel, rates include a fitness center and poolside continental breakfast.

> WORTH A TRIP
>
> **KNOTT'S BERRY FARM**
>
> What, Disney's not enough for you? Find even more thrill rides and cotton candy at the smaller, less commercial **Knott's Berry Farm** (☎714-220-5200; www.knotts.com; 8039 Beach Blvd, Buena Park; adult/child 3-11yr $57/25; ⏲from 10am). The Old West–themed amusement park teems with packs of speed-crazed adolescents testing their mettle on a line-up of rides. Gut-wrenchers include the wooden GhostRider and the '50s-themed Xcelerator, while the single-digit-aged find tamer action at Camp Snoopy. If your stomach's up for it, wrap up a visit with Mrs Knott's classic fried-chicken dinner (mains $12 to $18). Save time and money by printing tickets online. Parking costs $14 (free for restaurant patrons). Closing times vary from 5pm to 1pm; check website.

Eating

There are dozens of dining options inside the theme parks; it's part of the fun to hit the walk-up food stands for treats like huge dill pickles, turkey legs and sugar-dusted churros. If you need to sit down, some of the more memorable eateries include the cafeteria-style **Café Orleans** in New Orleans Square, serving jambalaya and mint juleps (virgin – the park is dry), and the surprisingly romantic **Blue Bayou** restaurant inside the Pirates of the Caribbean complex – whatever the time of day, you'll feel like you're dining outside under the stars as the ride's boats float peacefully by. For reservations or information on these and other Disneyland Resort eating options, including Character Dining, call **Disney Dining** (☎714-781-3463). Budget-conscious visitors and families with kids will also appreciate the picnic area just outside the park's main entrance; there's a nearby set of lockers where you can leave your picnic fixings when you arrive in the morning.

Downtown Disney offers generic but family-friendly chain restaurants; the same is true of the **Anaheim GardenWalk**, an outdoor mall on Katella Ave near the parks.

Catal Restaurant & Uva Bar MEDITERRANEAN $$$

(☎714-774-4442; www.patinagroup.com/catal; 1580 S Disneyland Dr; mains breakfast $9-14, dinner $23-38; ⏲8am-10pm; 👪) Looking for something more sophisticated without having to move the car from the Disneyland parking lot? Your best bet is the Mediterranean-inspired cuisine and cocktail menu at Catal; reserve ahead for balcony seating.

Little Saigon VIETNAMESE $$

If you need to steer totally clear of Mickey Mouse for a few hours, consider driving a few miles southwest to the ethnic community of Little Saigon (near the junction of I-405 and Hwy 22.) In the commercial district around the intersection of Bolsa and Brookhurst Aves, you'll find authentic, no-frills Vietnamese food – many menus aren't in English, so just point at the photo of your chosen dish.

ℹ Information

Stroller Rental

Rent a stroller for $15 per day ($25 for two strollers) outside the main entrance of Disneyland

Park. Rental strollers may be taken into both theme parks.

Tourist Information

Anaheim/Orange County Visitor & Convention Bureau (☎714-765-8888; www.anaheimoc.org; 800 W Katella Ave) Provides maps, tickets and planning tools for the region.

Central Plaza Information Board (☎714-781-4565; Main St USA, Disneyland Park) One of several information centers in the theme parks.

Websites

Mouse Wait (www.mousewait.com) This free iPhone app offers up-to-the-minute updates on ride wait times and what's happening in the parks.

Touring Plans (www.gaslamp.org) The 'unofficial guide to Disneyland' since 1985, this online resource offers no-nonsense advice, a crowd calendar and a 'lines app' for most mobile devices.

ℹ Getting There & Around

The Disneyland Resort is just off I-5 (Santa Ana Fwy), about 30 miles southeast of Downtown LA. As you approach the Disney area, giant easy-to-read overhead signs indicate which ramps you need to take for the theme parks, hotels or Anaheim's streets.

If you're arriving by train, you'll stop at the depot next to Angel Stadium, a quick shuttle or taxi ride east of Disneyland. **Amtrak** (☎714-385-1448; www.amtrak.com; 2150 E Katella Ave) and **Metrolink** (☎800-371-5465; www.metrolinktrains.com) commuter trains connect Anaheim to LA's Union Station ($14, 50 minutes) and San Diego ($27, two hours).

Once you're in the parks, a free tram connects the Disneyland Resort's main parking garage and Downtown Disney, a short walk from the theme parks' main entrance. Trams operate from one hour before Disneyland opens until one hour after the park closes.

Orange County Beaches

If you've seen *The OC* or *Real Housewives,* you *think* you know what to expect from this giant quilt of suburbia connecting LA and San Diego: affluence, aspiration and anxiety. (And if you were a fan of *Arrested Development,* you'll associate the region with frozen bananas, Segways and struggling actors – perhaps a more realistic picture?) But indeed, there is much living large in Orange County: shopping is a pastime, and resorts and restaurants serve its affluent residents. But it's also home to a burgeoning arts community and 42 miles of glorious beaches.

Hummer-driving hunks and Botoxed beauties mix it up with surfers and artists to give Orange County's beach towns their distinct vibe. Just across the LA–OC county-line, **Seal Beach** is refreshingly noncommercial with its pleasantly walkable downtown, while gentrified **Huntington Beach** (aka Surf City, USA) epitomizes the California surfing lifestyle. Fish tacos and happy-hour specials abound along Main St.

Next up is the ritziest of the OC's beach communities: **Newport Beach**, portrayed in *The OC* and nirvana for luxe shoppers. Families should steer toward Balboa Peninsula for its beaches, vintage wooden pier and quaint amusement center. Near the Ferris wheel on the harbor side, the **Balboa Island Ferry** (www.balboaislandferry.com; 410 S Bayfront; car & driver/adult/child $2/1/50¢; ⊙6:30am-midnight) shuttles passengers across the bay to ritzy Balboa Island for ice-cream cones, strolls past historic beach cottages, and the boutiques along Marine Ave.

Laguna Beach is the OC's most cultured and charming seaside town, where secluded beaches, glassy waves and eucalyptus-covered hillsides create a Riviera-like feel. Art galleries dot Pacific Coast Hwy here, and Laguna's summer arts festivals are institutions. To soak up the region's natural beauty right in the center of town, grab your morning café au lait and croissants at **C'est La Vie** (www.cestlavierestaurant.com; 373 S Coast Hwy) and enjoy them on a nearby park bench facing the ocean – there's an incredibly scenic playground right here if you're traveling with kids.

WHAT THE...?

Hey, did that painting just move? Welcome to the **Pageant of the Masters** (☎949-497-6582; www.pageanttickets.com; admission $15-100; ⊙8:30pm Jul & Aug), in which elaborately costumed humans step into painstaking re-creations of famous paintings on an outdoor stage. The pageant began in 1933 as a sideshow to Laguna Beach's **Festival of the Arts** (www.lagunafestivalofarts.org) and has been a prime attraction ever since. Our favorite part: watching the paintings deconstruct.

TOP CHOICE **Mission San Juan Capistrano** (☎949-234-1300; www.missionsjc.com; cnr Ortega Hwy & Camino Capistrano; incl audio tour adult/child $9/5; ⏰8:30am-5pm), about 10 miles south and inland from Laguna, is one of California's most beautiful missions – and the only mission in the OC – featuring lush gardens and the charming Serra Chapel.

San Diego

San Diegans shamelessly yet endearingly promote their hometown as 'America's Finest City.' Smug? Maybe, but it's easy to see why. The weather is practically perfect, with coastal high temperatures hovering around 72°F (22°C) all year. Beaches or forests are rarely more than 10 minutes' drive away. Its population (about 1.3 million) makes it America's eighth-largest city (or about 1.5 times the size of San Francisco), yet we're hard-pressed to think of a more laid-back big city anywhere.

The city languished as a relative backwater until WWII, when the Japanese attack on Pearl Harbor prompted the US Navy to relocate the US Pacific Fleet from Hawaii to San Diego's natural harbor. Growth in the military, tourism, education and research (especially medicine and oceanography), alongside high-tech companies cropping up in the inland valleys, helped to develop the city. It all makes San Diego seem more all-American than its California *compadres*, despite the borderland location.

Sights

San Diego's compact downtown revolves around the historic Gaslamp Quarter, a beehive of restaurants, bars and boutiques with the convention center just to its south. Southwest of here, Coronado is reached via a stunning bridge, while Little Italy and museum-rich Balboa Park (home of the San Diego Zoo) are to the north. The park segues into Hillcrest, the city's lesbi-gay hub. West of here are tourist-oriented Old Town, and the water playground around Mission Bay.

Heading north along the coast, Ocean Beach, Mission Beach and Pacific Beach epitomize the laid-back SoCal lifestyle, while La Jolla sits pretty and privileged. The I-5 Fwy cuts through the region north–south, while the I-8 is the main east–west artery. The CA163 Fwy heads north from downtown through Balboa Park.

DOWNTOWN

In 1867 creative real-estate wrangling by developer Alonzo Horton created the so-called 'New Town' that is today's downtown San Diego. Downtown's main street, 5th Ave, was once a notorious strip of saloons, gambling joints and bordellos known as Stingaree. These days, Stingaree has been beautifully restored as the thumping heart of downtown San Diego and rechristened the **Gaslamp Quarter** (Map p94), a playground of restaurants, bars, clubs, shops and galleries. The commercial focal point of downtown is **Westfield Horton Plaza** (Map p94; Broadway & 4th St; 🅿), a colorful, mazelike shopping mall.

In northern downtown, **Little Italy** (Map p94; www.littleitalysd.com) has evolved into one of the city's hippest places to live, eat and shop. India St is the main drag.

William Heath Davis House HISTORIC BUILDING
(Map p94; ☎619-233-4692; www.gaslampquarter.org; 410 Island Ave; adult/child $5/4; ⏰10am-6pm Tue-Sat, 9am-3pm Sun) For a full historical picture, peruse the exhibits inside this museum; the saltbox house was the onetime home of William Heath Davis, the man credited with starting the development of modern San Diego. Self-guided tours are available and the foundation also offers guided walking tours of the quarter (adult/child $10/8; tours 11am Saturday).

Petco Park STADIUM
(Map p94; ☎619-795-5011; www.padres.com; 100 Park Blvd; tours adult/child $11/7; ⏰tours 10:30am, 12:30pm & 2:30pm Tue-Sun May-Aug, 10:30am & 12:30pm Apr & Sep, subject to game schedule) Just a quick stroll southeast of the Gaslamp Quarter is one of downtown's newer landmarks, home of the San Diego Padres baseball team. Take an 80-minute behind-the-scenes tour; highlights often include the bullpen and press box.

Museum of Contemporary Art MUSEUM
(Map p94; ☎858-454-3541; www.mcasd.org; 1001 & 1100 Kettner Blvd; adult/child $10/free; ⏰11am-5pm Thu-Tue, to 7pm 3rd Thu each month, 5-7pm free) Emphasizes minimalist and pop art, as well as conceptual works and cross-border art. The 1100 Kettner Bldg is at the historic Santa Fe Depot. Another branch is in La Jolla; one ticket admits you to all venues.

USS Midway Museum MUSEUM
(Map p94; ☎619-544-9600; www.midway.org; Navy Pier; adult/child $18/10; ⏰10am-5pm) Step

Greater San Diego

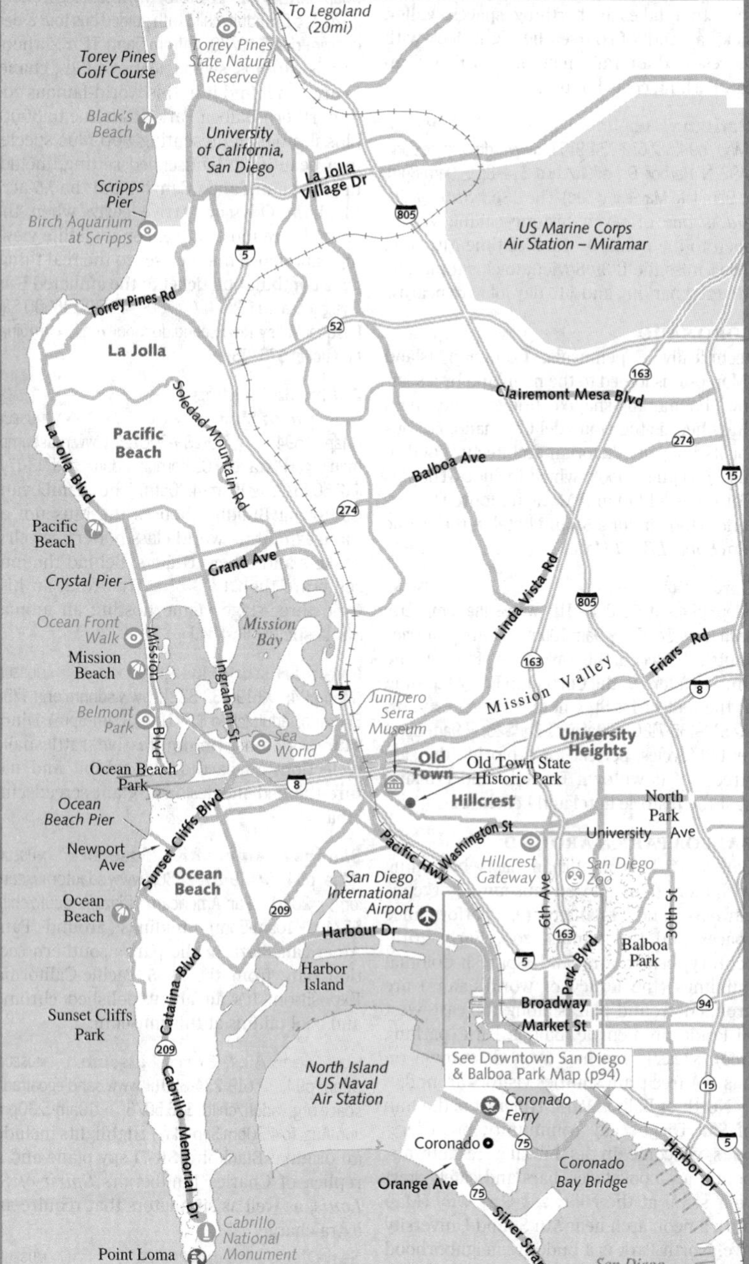

aboard the navy's longest-serving aircraft carrier (1945–91) to take a self-guided audio tour that takes in berthing spaces, galley, sick bay and, of course, the flight deck with its restored aircraft, including an F-14 Tomcat. Parking costs $5 to $7.

Maritime Museum MUSEUM
(Map p94; ☎619-234-9153; www.sdmaritime.com; 1492 N Harbor Dr; adult/child $14/8; ⊙9am-8pm, to 9am late May-early Sep) The 1863 *Star of India* is one of seven historic sailing vessels open to the public at the Maritime Museum. Don't miss the B-39 Soviet attack submarine. Metered parking and $10 day lots are nearby.

CORONADO

Technically a peninsula, Coronado Island (Map p91) is joined to the mainland by a soaring, boomerang-shaped bridge. The main draw here is the Hotel del Coronado, famous for its buoyant Victorian architecture and illustrious guest book, which includes Thomas Edison, Brad Pitt and Marilyn Monroe (its exterior stood in for a Miami hotel in the classic film *Some Like it Hot*).

Coronado ISLAND
(Map p94; ☎619-234-4111; www.sdhe.com; ferry each way $4.25; ⊙9am-10pm) Hourly ferries shuttle between the Broadway Pier on the Embarcadero to the Coronado Ferry Landing at the foot of 1st St, where **Bikes & Beyond** (☎619-435-7180; rental per 1-2hr $25; ⊙9am-8pm) rents bicycles, perfect for exploring the side streets of downtown La Jolla and cruising past the historic hotel and beaches.

BALBOA PARK & AROUND

Balboa Park is an urban oasis brimming with more than a dozen museums, gorgeous gardens and architecture, performance spaces and the famous zoo. Early 20th-century beaux arts and Spanish-Colonial buildings (the legacy of world's fairs) are grouped around plazas along the east–west El Prado promenade. Balboa Park (parking free) is easily reached from downtown on bus 7. A free tram shuttles visitors around.

North of Balboa Park, Hillcrest is the hub of San Diego's gay community, but everyone's welcome in its buzzing restaurants, boutiques, bookstores, bars and cafes. Start your stroll at the **Hillcrest Gateway** (Map p91), a neon arch near 5th St and University Ave. North Park is a budding neighborhood with a youngish, urban vibe and a growing restaurant and nightlife scene around 30th St and University Ave.

TOP CHOICE **San Diego Zoo** ZOO
(Map p91; ☎619-231-1515; www.sandiegozoo.org; 2920 Zoo Dr; adult/child with guided bus tour & aerial tram ride $40/30; ⊙from 9am) If it slithers, crawls, stomps, swims, leaps or flies, chances are you'll find it in this world-famous zoo in northern Balboa Park. It's home to 3000-plus animals representing 800-plus species in a beautifully landscaped setting, including the giant Panda Canyon and the 7.5-acre Elephant Odyssey. Arrive early, when the animals are most active. For a wildlife viewing experience that's closer to the real thing, get a combination ticket to the affiliated **San Diego Safari Park** (☎760-747-8702; 15500 San Pasqual Valley Rd, Escondido; adult/child combination ticket $76/56).

California Building & Museum of Man MUSEUM
(Map p94; ☎619-239-2001; www.museumofman.org; Plaza de California; adult/child/13-17yr $12.50/5/8; ⊙10am-4:30pm) The flamboyant California Building houses the Museum of Man, exhibiting world-class pottery, jewelry, baskets and other artifacts. Behind the museum are the **Old Globe Theaters**, an historic three-stage venue hosting an annual Shakespeare Festival.

Natural History Museum MUSEUM
(Map p94; ☎619-232-3821; www.sdnhm.org; 1788 El Prado; adult/child $17/11; ⊙10am-5pm) Dinosaur skeletons, an impressive rattlesnake collection, an earthquake exhibit and nature-themed movies in a giant-screen cinema.

San Diego Automotive Museum MUSEUM
(Map p94; ☎619-231-2886; www.sdautomuseum.org; 2080 Pan-American Plaza; adult/child $8/4; ⊙10am-5pm) Buildings around Pan-American Plaza in the park's southern section date from the 1935 Pacific-California Exposition. It's all about polished chrome and cool tailfins at this museum.

San Diego Air & Space Museum MUSEUM
(Map p94; ☎619-234-8291; www.sandiegoairandspace.org; adult/child $16.50/6; ⊙10am-5:30pm Jun-Aug, to 4:30pm Sep-May) Highlights include an original Blackbird SR-71 spy plane and a replica of Charles Lindbergh's *Spirit of St Louis,* as well as simulators that require an extra charge.

San Diego Museum of Art MUSEUM
(Map p94; ☎619-232-7931; www.sdmart.org; 1450 El Prado, Plaza de Panama; adult/child $12/4.50;

⏲10am-5pm Tue-Sat, from noon Sun, to 9pm Thu Jun-Sep) Gets accolades for its European old masters and good collections of American and Asian art.

Mingei International Museum MUSEUM
(Map p94; ☎619-239-0003; www.mingei.org; 1439 El Prado, Plaza de Panama; adult/child $7/4; ⏲10am-4pm Tue-Sun) Exhibits folk art from around the globe; don't miss the lovely museum store here.

FREE **Timken Museum of Art** MUSEUM
(Map p94; ☎619-239-5548; www.timkenmuseum.org; 1500 El Prado; ⏲10am-4:30pm Tue-Sat, from 1:30pm Sun) Small but exquisite, the museum showcases European and American heavyweights, from Rembrandt to Cézanne and John Singleton Copley.

Museum of Photographic Arts MUSEUM
(Map p94; ☎619-238-7559; www.mopa.org; 1649 El Prado; adult/child $8/free; ⏲10am-5pm Tue-Sun) Exhibits fine-art photography and hosts an ongoing film series.

San Diego Model Railroad Museum MUSEUM
(Map p94; ☎619-696-0199; www.sdmrm.org; 1649 El Prado; adult/child $7/6; ⏲11am-4pm Tue-Fri, to 5pm Sat & Sun) One of the largest of its kind, with brilliantly 'landscaped' train sets.

Reuben H Fleet Science Center MUSEUM
(Map p94; ☎619-238-1233; www.rhfleet.org; 1875 El Prado; adult/child $10/8.75, incl Imax theater $14:50/11.75; ⏲from 10am) Family-oriented hands-on museum-cum-Imax theater in Plaza de Balboa.

OLD TOWN & MISSION VALLEY

In 1769 a band of missionaries led by the Franciscan friar Junípero Serra founded the first of the 21 California missions on San Diego's Presidio Hill; a small village (pueblo) grew around it. The spot turned out to be less than ideal for a mission, however, and in 1774 the mission was moved about 7 miles upriver, closer to a steady water supply and fertile land.

Mission Basilica San Diego de Alcalá CHURCH
(☎619-281-8449; www.missionsandiego.com; 10818 San Diego Mission Rd; adult/child $3/1; ⏲9am-4:45pm) Secluded in a corner of what's now called Mission Valley, the 'Mother of the Missions' was relocated here in 1774. Come at sunset for glowing views over the valley and the ocean beyond.

Junípero Serra Museum MUSEUM
(Map p91; ☎619-232-6203; www.sandiegohistory.org; 2727 Presidio Dr; adult/child $6/2; ⏲10am-5pm Sat & Sun) On the site of the original mission in Old Town stands this handsome museum, which highlights life during the city's rough-and-tumble early period.

Old Town State Historic Park HISTORIC SITE
(Map p91; ☎619-220-5422; www.parks.ca.gov; San Diego Ave, at Twiggs St; ⏲visitor center 10am-5pm; P) Preserves five original adobe buildings and several re-created structures from the first pueblo, including a schoolhouse and a newspaper office. Most now contain museums, shops or restaurants. The visitor center operates free tours daily at 11am and 2pm.

POINT LOMA

This peninsula wraps around the entrance to crescent-shaped San Diego Bay.

Cabrillo National Monument MONUMENT
(Map p91; ☎619-557-5450; www.nps.gov/cabr; per car/person $5/3; ⏲9am-5pm; P) Enjoy stunning bay panoramas from the monument, which honors the leader of the first Spanish exploration of the West Coast. The nearby 1854 **Old Point Loma Lighthouse** helped guide ships until 1891 and is now a museum.

MISSION BAY & BEACHES

After WWII, coastal engineering turned the mouth of the swampy San Diego River into a 7-sq-mile playground of parks, beaches and bays. Amoeba-shaped Mission Bay sits just inland. Surfing is popular in Ocean Beach and Mission Beach, and all the beaches are naturals for swimming, kite-flying and cycling along miles of paved bike paths.

San Diego's three major beaches are ribbons of hedonism where armies of tanned, taut bodies frolic in the sand and surf. South of Mission Bay, hippie-flavored **Ocean Beach** (OB; Map p91) has a fishing pier, beach volleyball, sunset BBQs and good surf. Newport Ave is chockablock with bohemian bars, eateries and shops selling beachwear, surf gear and antiques.

West of Mission Bay, **Mission Beach** (MB) and its northern neighbor, **Pacific Beach** (PB), are connected by the car-free **Ocean Front Walk**, which swarms with skaters, joggers and cyclists year-round. The small **Belmont Park** amusement park in MB beckons with a historic wooden roller coaster and large indoor pool.

Downtown San Diego & Balboa Park

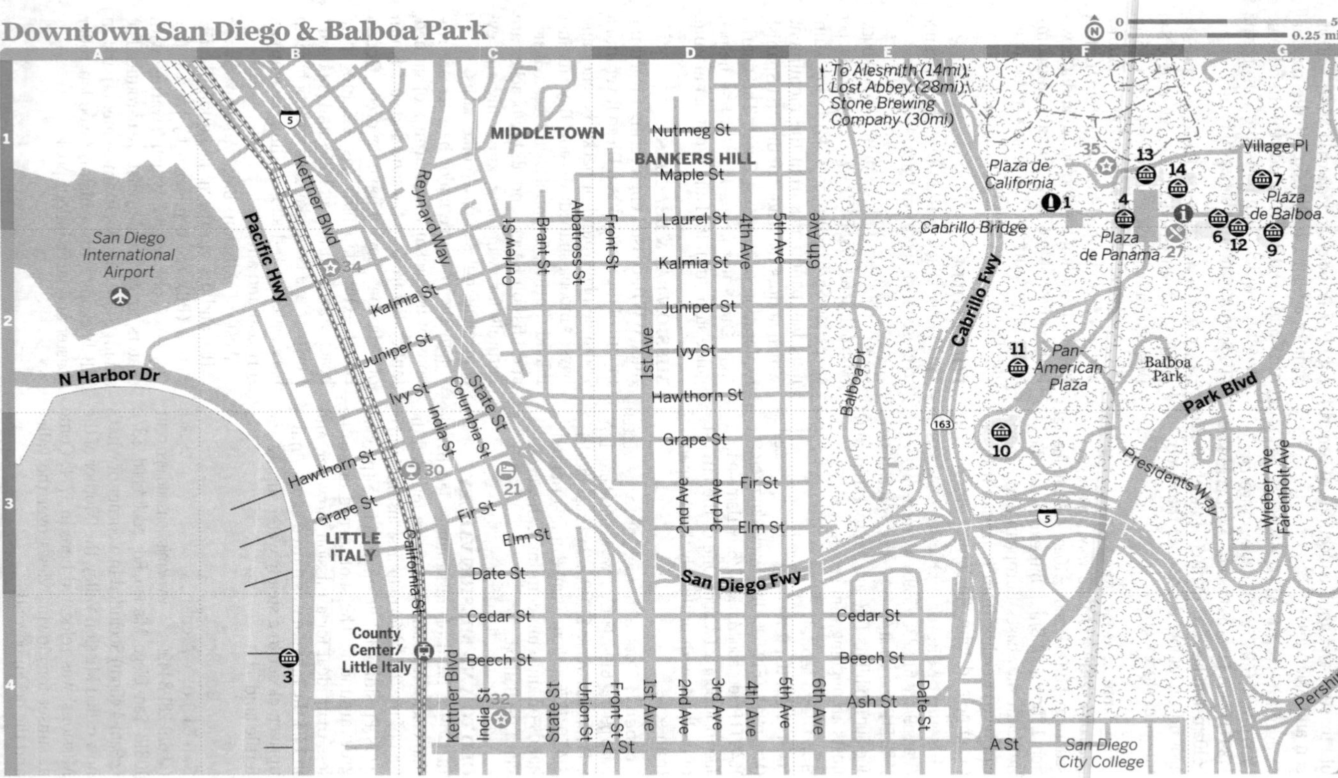

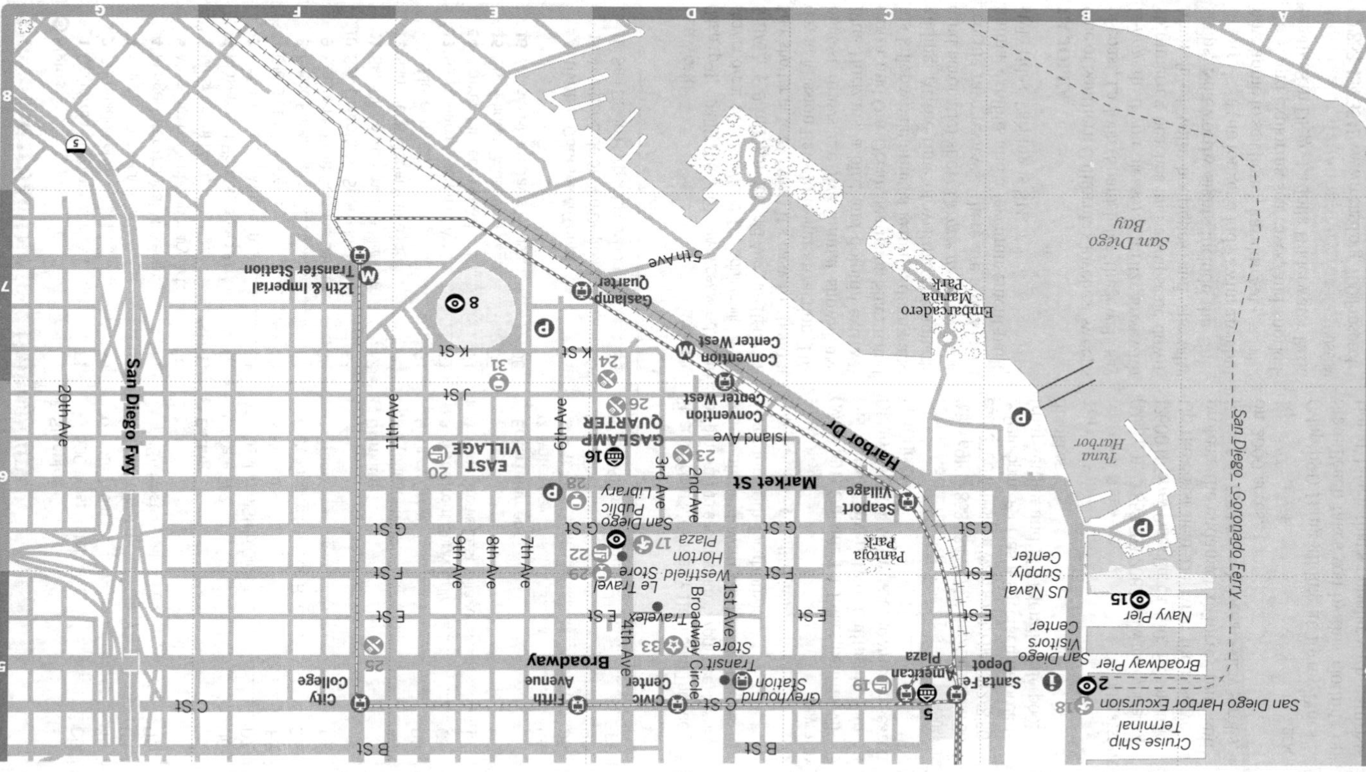
San Diego Fwy
20th Ave
11th Ave
12th & Imperial Transfer Station
City College
25
B St
C St
E St
F St
G St
J St
K St
8
31
EAST VILLAGE
20
9th Ave
8th Ave
7th Ave
6th Ave
Fifth Avenue
Broadway
P
28
GASLAMP QUARTER
16
26
24
Gaslamp Quarter
5th Ave
San Diego Public Library
22
29
Le Travel
Westfield Store
Horton Plaza
17
Travelex
4th Ave
33
Civic Center
3rd Ave
2nd Ave
Broadway Circle
Transit Store
1st Ave
Greyhound Station
23
Island Ave
Convention Center West
Market St
Harbor Dr
Seaport Village
Pantoja Park
19
American Plaza
5
Santa Fe Depot
US Naval Supply Center
San Diego Visitors Center
Embarcadero Marina Park
Tuna Harbor
San Diego Bay
Navy Pier
15
Broadway Pier
2
San Diego Harbor Excursion
18
Cruise Ship Terminal
San Diego - Coronado Ferry
A
B
C
D
E
F
G
5
6
7
8

Downtown San Diego & Balboa Park

Sights

1 California Building ... F1
2 Coronado Ferry ... B5
3 Maritime Museum ... B4
4 Mingei International Museum ... F1
5 Museum of Contemporary Art ... C5
Museum of Man ... (see 1)
6 Museum of Photographic Arts ... G1
7 Natural History Museum ... G1
Old Globe Theaters ... (see 35)
8 Petco Park ... E7
9 Reuben H Fleet Science Center ... G2
10 San Diego Air & Space Museum ... F3
11 San Diego Automotive Museum ... F2
12 San Diego Model Railroad Museum ... G1
13 San Diego Museum of Art ... F1
14 Timken Museum of Art ... F1
15 USS Midway Museum ... B5
16 William Heath Davis House ... D6

Activities, Courses & Tours

17 Another Side of San Diego ... D6
18 San Diego Harbor Excursion ... B5

Sleeping

19 500 West Hotel ... C5
20 Hotel Indigo ... E6
21 Little Italy Inn ... C3
22 USA Hostels San Diego ... D6

Eating

23 Café 222 ... D6
24 Gaslamp Strip Club ... D7
25 Hodad's ... F5
26 Oceanaire Seafood Room ... D6
27 Prado ... F2

Drinking

28 Prohibition ... E6
29 Tipsy Crow ... D5
30 Waterfront Bar & Grill ... C3
31 Wine Steals East Village ... E7

Entertainment

32 Anthology ... C4
33 Arts Tix ... D5
34 Casbah ... B2
35 Old Globe Theaters ... F1

SeaWorld AQUARIUM
(Map p91; ☎619-226-3901; www.seaworld.com/seaworld/ca; 500 SeaWorld Dr; adult/child 3-9yr $70/62; ⊙9am-10pm Jul–mid-Aug, to 11pm Fri-Sun, shorter hr rest of year) It's easy to spend a day at Mission Bay's four-star attraction. The biggest draws are live animal shows, like Blue Horizons, a bird and dolphin extravaganza, and One Ocean, featuring Shamu and his killer whale amigos leaping, diving and gliding. At the time of writing, the aquatic (and acrobatic) show *Cirque de la Mer* was scoring rave reviews. There are also zoolike animal exhibits and a few amusement-park-style rides. Parking is $14.

LA JOLLA

One of Southern California's loveliest sweeps of coast, La Jolla (Spanish for 'the jewel;' say la-*hoy*-ah, if you please) is a ritzy area with shimmering beaches and an upscale downtown filled with boutiques and specialty shops. Noteworthy sights include the **Children's Pool** (no longer a kids' swim area but now home to sea lions), kayaking at **La Jolla Cove** and exploring sea caves, and snorkeling the San Diego-La Jolla Underwater Park.

Museum of Contemporary Art MUSEUM
(☎858-454-3541; www.mcasd.org; 700 Prospect St; adult/child $10/free; ⊙11am-5pm Thu-Tue, to 7pm 3rd Thu each month, 5-7pm free) Sister venue of the downtown branch (same ticket for both locations).

University of California, San Diego UNIVERSITY
(Map p91) Outside La Jolla's central village is the University of California, San Diego (UCSD), with its renowned research facilities.

Birch Aquarium at Scripps AQUARIUM
(Map p91; ☎858-534-3474; http://aquarium.ucsd.edu; 2300 Exhibition Way; adult/child $12/8.50; ⊙9am-5pm; Ⓟ) Has a spectacular oceanfront setting and kid-friendly tide pool displays.

Torrey Pines State Natural Reserve WILDLIFE RESERVE
(Map p91; ☎858-755-2063; www.torreypine.org; 12600 N Torrey Pines Rd; car $10; ⊙8am-dusk) Up the coast near Del Mar, the reserve protects the endangered Torrey pine and is perfect for leisurely ocean-view strolls on 2000 acres.

Black's Beach BEACH
(Map p91) Hang-gliding at Torrey Pines State Beach takes you by this 'clothing optional' beach that's popular with naturists.

Activities

Surfing and windsurfing (for surf reports, call ☎619-221-8824) are both excellent, although in some areas territorial locals are a major irritation.

Pacific Beach Surf School SURFING
(☎858-373-1138; www.pacificbeachsurfschool.com; 4150 Mission Blvd, Suite 161, Pacific Beach; private/semiprivate lessons per person $80/65) Learn to hang 10 at surf school or just rent a board and wetsuit (half-day $25) at San Diego's oldest surf shop.

San Diego-La Jolla Underwater Park SNORKELING, DIVING
Snorkeling and scuba diving here, you'll encounter glowing orange garibaldi flitting around giant kelp forests.

OEX Dive & Kayak DIVING, KAYAKING
(☎858-454-6195; www.oexcalifornia.com; 2243/2132 Avenida de la Playa, La Jolla) For gear or instruction, including spearfishing seminars and stand-up paddleboard lessons, head to this one-stop resource in La Jolla.

Tours

Another Side of San Diego WALKING, BOAT
(Map p94; ☎619-239-2111; www.anothersideofsandiegotours.com; 300 G St) This highly rated tour company does Segway tours of Balboa Park, horseback riding on the beach and Gaslamp Quarter food tours.

Hike, Bike, Kayak San Diego CYCLING, KAYAKING
(☎858-551-9510; www.hikebikekayak.com; 2246 Avenida de la Playa, La Jolla) Just what it says.

Old Town Trolley Tours TROLLEY
(☎619-298-8687; www.trolleytours.com; adult/child $34/17) Hop-on, hop-off loop tour to the main attractions; board at Old Town.

San Diego Harbor Excursion BOAT
(Map p94; ☎619-234-4111; www.sdhe.com; 1050 N Harbor Dr; adult/child from $22/11) A variety of bay and harbor cruises.

Sleeping

Rates quoted here are 'rack' rates; they skyrocket downtown during big conventions and the summer peak, then plummet at other times.

DOWNTOWN

USA Hostels San Diego HOSTEL $
(Map p94; ☎619-232-3100; www.usahostels.com; 726 5th Ave; dm/d incl breakfast from $28/72; ❄@📶) In a former Victorian-era hotel, this convivial Gaslamp hostel has cheerful rooms, a full kitchen and an inviting movie lounge. Rates include a pancake breakfast and laundry facilities; the nightly family-style dinner costs $5.

Little Italy Inn B&B $$
(Map p94; ☎619-230-1600; www.littleitalyhotel.com; 505 W Grape St; r with shared/private bath $89/109, apt from $149; 📶) If you can't get enough of Little Italy's charm, this pretty B&B is an ideal place to hang your hat. The 23-room Victorian-style inn boasts comfortable beds, cozy bathrobes in each room, a casual European-style breakfast and wine socials on weekend evenings.

500 West Hotel HOSTEL $
(Map p94; ☎619-231-4092; www.500westhotelsd.com; 500 W Broadway; s/d with shared bath from $50/62; @📶) Rooms are shoebox-sized and baths are down the hallway in this renovated 1920s YMCA, but hipsters on a budget love the bright decor, flat-screen TVs, communal kitchen and fitness studio.

Hotel Indigo BOUTIQUE HOTEL $$
(Map p94; ☎619-727-4000; www.hotelsandiegodowntown.com; 509 9th Ave; r from $146; P❄@📶≋) The first Leadership in Energy and Environmental Design (LEED) certified hotel in San Diego, Hotel Indigo is smartly designed and ecofriendly. The design is contemporary but colorful; guest rooms feature huge floor-to-ceiling windows, spa-style baths and large flat-screen TVs. Parking is $35.

BEACHES

Inn at Sunset Cliffs HOTEL $$
(☎619-222-7901; www.innatsunsetcliffs.com; 1370 Sunset Cliffs Blvd, Point Loma; r from $175; P❄@📶≋) Hear the surf crashing onto the rocky shore at this breezy charmer wrapped around a flower-bedecked courtyard. Recently renovated rooms are light-filled but on the small side; recent efforts to decrease the hotel's water and plastic consumption have made the place greener.

TOP CHOICE **Hotel del Coronado** LUXURY HOTEL $$$
(☎619-435-6611; www.hoteldel.com; 1500 Orange Ave, Coronado; r from $325; P❄@📶≋) San Diego's iconic hotel, the Del provides more than a century of history, tennis courts, spa, shops, splashy restaurants, manicured grounds and a white-sand beach. Book the original building. Parking is $25.

Ocean Beach Hotel HOTEL $$

(619-223-7191; www.obhotel.com; 5080 Newport Ave, Ocean Beach; d from $129;) This recently remodeled hotel is just across the street from the beach. Spotless guest rooms are on the smaller side; the French provincial look is a bit dated but all feature refrigerators and complimentary wi-fi.

La Valencia LUXURY HOTEL $$$

(858-454-0771; www.lavalencia.com; 1132 Prospect St, La Jolla; r from $285;) This 1926 landmark, the Mediterranean-style 'Pink Lady,' was designed by William Templeton Johnson. Its 116 rooms are rather compact, but it wins for Old Hollywood romance; recent ecofriendly efforts add to the charm. Parking is $32.

Eating

With more than 6000 restaurants, San Diego's dynamic dining scene caters to all tastes. Generally speaking, you'll find fine steakhouses and seafood institutions downtown, casual seafood along the beaches, ethnic food in and around Hillcrest, and tacos and margaritas, well, everywhere.

DOWNTOWN & EMBARCADERO

Café 222 BREAKFAST $

(Map p94; 619-236-9902; www.cafe222.com; 222 Island Ave; mains $7-11; 7am-1:45pm) Downtown's favorite breakfast place for pumpkin waffles, orange-pecan or granola pancakes, and farm-fresh eggs Benedict. The French toast stuffed with peanut butter and bananas was featured on the Food Network.

C Level SEAFOOD $$$

(619-298-6802; www.islandprime.com; 880 Harbor Island Dr; mains $14-30; from 11am) The bay views are stunning from this airy, elegant eatery on Harbor Island, west of downtown; well-prepared seafood dishes include the popular seared Hawaiian 'ahi tuna, lobster truffle mac 'n' cheese and Japanese-style sesame salmon. The Social Hour (3:30pm to 5:30pm Monday to Friday) offers $5 'bites and libations.'

Gaslamp Strip Club STEAKHOUSE $$

(Map p94; 619-231-3140; www.gaslampsteak.com; 340 5th Ave; mains $14-24; 5-10pm Sun-Thu, to midnight Fri & Sat) Pull a bottle from the wine vault and then char your favorite cut of steak, chicken or fish on the open grills in this retro-Vegas dining room.

Oceanaire Seafood Room SEAFOOD $$$

(Map p94; 619-858-2277; www.theoceanaire.com; 400 J St; mains $24-40; 5-10pm Sun-Thu, to 11pm Fri & Sat) The look is art-deco ocean liner and the service is just as refined, with an oyster bar (get them for a buck during happy hour, 5pm to 6pm Monday to Friday) and inventive creations including Maryland blue crab cakes and horseradish-crusted Alaskan halibut.

BALBOA PARK & OLD TOWN

TOP CHOICE **Prado** MEDITERRANEAN $$$

(Map p94; 619-557-9441; www.pradobalboa.com; 1549 El Prado, Balboa Park; mains lunch $10-15, dinner $21-34; 11:30am-3pm Mon-Fri, from 5pm Tue-Sun, 11am-3pm Sat & Sun;) This classic lunch spot in the museum district of Balboa Park serves up fresh Mediterranean cuisine like steamed mussels, shrimp paella and grilled portobello sandwiches. Breezy outdoor seating and the Mexican-tiled interior are equally inviting; happy hour food and drink specials (4pm to 6pm Tuesday to Friday) are a steal.

Old Town Mexican Café MEXICAN $$

(619-297-4330; www.oldtownmexcafe.com; 2489 San Diego Ave, Old Town; mains $4-15; 7am-2am;) Watch the staff turn out fresh tortillas in the window while waiting for a table. Besides breakfast (great *chilaquiles* – soft tortilla chips covered with mole), there's *pozole* (spicy pork stew), avocado tacos and margaritas at the festive central bar.

HILLCREST & NORTH PARK

Bread & Cie BAKERY $

(www.breadandciecatering.com; 350 University Ave, Hillcrest; mains $6-10; 7am-7pm Mon-Fri, to 6pm Sat, 9am-6pm Sun) The fantastic sandwiches and decadent pastries (try the almond croissant or the ridiculously oversized *pain au chocolat*) make this busy bakery a Hillcrest institution.

Alchemy INTERNATIONAL $$$

(619-255-0616; www.alchemysandiego.com; 1503 30th St, North Park; mains $13-25; 4pm-midnight Sun-Thu, to 1am Fri & Sat, 10am-2pm Sat & Sun) It's a spin-the-globe menu of local ingredients from small plates (including charcuterie or Parmesan frites with garlic aioli), and Jidori chicken with bok choy and shiitake dumplings, in an art-filled blond-wood room.

Linkery PUB $$$

(619-255-8778; www.thelinkery.com; 3794 30th St, North Park; mains $10-25; 5-11pm Mon-Thu, noon-midnight Fri, 11am-midnight Sat, 11am-10pm Sun) A daily changing menu of housemade sausages and hand-cured meats from sustainably raised animals is the thing here – on a roll, on a board with cheese or in *choucroute* (French stew).

Saigon on Fifth VIETNAMESE $$
(☎619-220-8828; 3900 5th Ave, Hillcrest; mains $11-16; ⊙11am-late; P) This Vietnamese place tries hard and succeeds, with dishes such as fresh spring rolls, fish of Hue (with garlic, ginger and lemongrass) and rockin' 'spicy noodles.' Elegant but not overbearing.

BEACHES

TOP CHOICE **Cafe 1134** CAFE $
(1134 Orange Ave, Coronado; mains $8-10; ⊙9am-7pm) This cool coffee shop on Coronado's main drag offers more than your morning fix: think delicious Greek-style egg scramblers, grilled panini, spinach salads, high-end teas, and a wine and beer list. Prices are slashed as part of the 'Money Wise Menu' on Sunday, Monday and Tuesday evenings.

George's at the Cove MODERN AMERICAN $$$
(☎858-454-4244; www.georgesatthecove.com; 1250 Prospect St, La Jolla; mains $11-48; ⊙11am-11pm) Chef Trey Foshee's Euro-Cal cuisine is as dramatic as this eatery's oceanfront location. George's has graced just about every list of top restaurants in California. Three venues allow you to enjoy it at different price points: **George's Bar** (mains lunch $9-16), **Ocean Terrace** (mains lunch $11-18) and **George's California Modern** (mains dinner $28-48). Walk-ins welcome at the bar, but reservations are recommended for the latter two.

Hodad's BURGERS $
(www.hodadies.com; 5010 Newport Ave, Ocean Beach; burgers $4-9; ⊙5am-10pm) OB's legendary burger joint serves great shakes, massive baskets of onion rings and succulent hamburgers wrapped in paper. The walls are covered in license plates and your bearded, tattooed server might sidle into your booth to take your order. A second location recently opened **downtown** (Map p94; 945 Broadway Ave).

World Famous SEAFOOD $$$
(☎858-272-3100; www.worldfamous.signonsandiego.com; 711 Pacific Beach Dr, Pacific Beach; mains breakfast & lunch $9-16, dinner $15-25; ⊙7am-11pm) Watch the surf while enjoying 'California coastal cuisine,' an ever-changing menu of inventive dishes from the sea (think banana rum mahi and bacon-and-spinach-wrapped scallops), plus steaks, salads, lunchtime sandwiches and burgers.

Drinking

TOP CHOICE **Wine Steals** WINE BAR
(☎619-295-1188; www.winestealssd.com; 1243 University Ave, Hillcrest) Laid-back wine tastings (go for a flight or choose a bottle off the rack in the back), live music, gourmet pizzas and cheese platters bring in a nightly crowd to this low-lit wine bar. Look for two newer branches in San Diego, **Wine Steals East Village** (Map p94; 793/5 J St, Downtown) and

SAN DIEGO MICROBREWERIES

San Diegans take their craft beers seriously – even at a dive bar, you might overhear local guys talking about hops and cask conditioning. Various microbreweries around the city specialize in India Pale Ale (IPA) and Belgian-style brews. The following venues are beer enthusiast favorites.

Stone Brewing Company BREWERY
(off Map p94; ☎760-471-4999; www.stonebrew.com; 1999 Citracado Pkwy, Escondido; ⊙11am-9pm). Take a free tour before a guided tasting of Oaked Arrogant Bastard Ale and Stone Barley Wine.

Lost Abbey BREWERY
(off Map p94; ☎800-918-6816; www.lostabbey.com; 155 Mata Way, Suite 104, San Marcos; ⊙1-6pm Wed-Thu, 3-9pm Fri, noon-6pm Sat & Sun) More than 20 brews ($1 per taste) are on tap in the tasting room – try Lost and Found Abbey Ale.

AleSmith BREWERY
(off Map p94; ☎858-549-9888; www.alesmith.com; 9368 Cabot Dr; ⊙2-7pm Thu-Fri, noon-6pm Sat, noon-4pm Sun) Wee Heavy and the potent Old Numbskull ($1 per taste) are the stand-out brews.

Lounge-Point Loma (2970 Truxtun Rd, Point Loma).

Tipsy Crow BAR, LOUNGE
(Map p94; www.thetipsycrow.com; 770 5th Ave, Downtown) There are three distinct levels at this historic Gaslamp building that's been turned into an atmospheric watering hole: the main floor with its long mahogany bar, the lounge-like 'Nest' (thought to be the site of a former brothel), and the brick-walled 'Underground' with a dancefloor and live music acts.

Nunu's Cocktail Lounge COCKTAIL BAR
(www.nunuscocktails.com; 3537 5th Ave, Hillcrest) Dark and divey, this hipster haven started pouring when JFK was president and still looks the part with its curvy booths, big bar and lovably kitsch decor.

Bourbon Street GAY
(www.bourbonstreetsd.com; 4612 Park Blvd, North Park) This gay spot's warren of bars, courtyards and dancefloor makes for easy mingling (it's hetero-friendly too.) Look for billiards, guest DJs and wickedly cheap martini happy hours.

Waterfront Bar & Grill BAR
(Map p94; www.waterfrontbarandgrill.com; 2044 Kettner Blvd, Little Italy) Beer and burgers are the orders of choice at this cheerful neighborhood bar, opened in 1933 shortly after Prohibition was outlawed.

☆ Entertainment

Check the *San Diego Reader* (www.sandiegoreader.com) or the Thursday edition of the *San Diego Union-Tribune* (www.signonsandiego.com) for the latest happenings around town. **Arts Tix** (p94; ☎858-381-5595; www.sdartstix.com; 3rd Ave & Broadway, Downtown; ⊙9:30am-5pm Tue-Thu, to 6pm Fri & Sat), in a kiosk on Broadway outside Horton Plaza, has half-price tickets for same-day evening or next-day matinee performances and discounted tickets to all types of other events.

Anthology LIVE MUSIC
(Map p94; ☎619-595-0300; www.anthologysd.com; 1337 India St, Downtown; cover free-$60) Near Little Italy, Anthology presents live jazz, blues and indie music in a swank supper-club setting, from both up-and-comers and big-name performers.

Casbah LIVE MUSIC
(Map p94; ☎619-232-4355; www.casbahmusic.com; 2501 Kettner Blvd, Little Italy; cover free-$20) Liz Phair, Alanis Morissette and the Smashing Pumpkins all rocked the funky Casbah on their way up the charts; catch local acts and headliners like Bon Iver.

Prohibition JAZZ
(Map p91; www.prohibitionsd.com; 548 5th Ave, Downtown; cover free) This sophisticated 1930's-style jazz bar takes music and cocktails (made with gin or rye whiskey) seriously. The house rules aren't a joke either; you have to reserve online, no cell phones are allowed at the bar, and a dress code is enforced.

ℹ Information

Internet Access

For wi-fi hotspot locations, check www.jiwire.com.

San Diego Public Library www.sandiego.gov/public-library; 820 E St, Downtown; 📶) Call or check the website for branch locations.

Media

Gay & Lesbian Times (www.gaylesbiantimes.com) Free weekly.

KPBS 89.5 FM (www.kpbs.org) National public radio.

San Diego Magazine (www.sandiegomagazine.com) Glossy monthly.

San Diego Reader (www.sdreader.com) Free tabloid-sized listings magazine.

San Diego Union-Tribune (www.signonsandiego.com) The city's major daily.

Medical Services

Rite-Aid pharmacies (☎800-748-3243) Call for the nearest branch.

Scripps Mercy Hospital (☎619-294-8111; 4077 5th Ave, Hillcrest) Has a 24-hour emergency room.

Money

Travelex (⊙10:30am-7pm Mon-Fri, 10am-6pm Sat, 11am-4pm Sun) Airport (☎619-295-2501; ⊙8am-5pm); Downtown (☎619-235-0901; Horton Plaza); La Jolla (☎858-457-2412; University Towne Centre mall, 4417 La Jolla Village Dr) Foreign currency exchange services.

Post

Call ☎800-275-8777 or log on to www.usps.com for the nearest branch.

Tourist Information

Balboa Park Visitors Center (☎619-239-0512; www.balboapark.org; 1549 El Prado; ⊙9:30am-4:30pm) In the House of Hospitality, the visitor center sells park maps and the **Passport to Balboa Park** (adult/child $45/24, with zoo admission $77/42), which allows one-time entry to 14 of the park's museums within seven days. Ask about the museums that occasionally have free admission on Tuesday.

San Diego Visitor Information Centers (619-236-1212; www.sandiego.org) Downtown (cnr W Broadway & Harbor Dr; 9am-5pm Jun-Sep, to 4pm Oct-May); La Jolla (7966 Herschel Ave; 11am-5pm) The downtown location is designed for international visitors.

Websites

Accessible San Diego (www.asd.travel) Excellent resource for barrier-free travel around San Diego.

Gaslamp.org (www.gaslamp.org) Everything you need to know about the bustling Gaslamp Quarter, including parking secrets.

San Diego Convention & Visitors Bureau (www.sandiego.org) Search hotels, sights, dining, rental cars and more, and make reservations.

San Diego.com (www.sandiego.com) Comprehensive ad-based portal to all things San Diegan, from fun stuff to serious business.

Getting There & Away

San Diego International Airport (Lindbergh Field; 619-400-2404; www.san.org) sits about 3 miles west of Downtown; plane-spotters will thrill watching jets come in for a landing over Balboa Park.

Greyhound (619-515-1100; 120 W Broadway, Downtown) has hourly direct buses to Los Angeles (one way/round-trip $19/31, two to three hours).

Amtrak (800-872-7245; www.amtrak.com) runs the *Pacific Surfliner* several times daily to Los Angeles ($36, three hours) and Santa Barbara ($41, 5½ hours) from the **Santa Fe Depot** (1055 Kettner Blvd, Downtown).

All major car-rental companies have desks at the airport, or call the national toll-free numbers (p457). **Eagle Rider** (619-546-5066; www.eaglerider.com; 4236 Taylor St, Old Town; 9am-5pm) rents motorcycles and scooters.

Getting Around

Bus 992 ('the Flyer,' $2.25) operates at 10- to 15-minute intervals between the airport and downtown, with stops along Broadway. Airport shuttles such as **Super Shuttle** (800-974-8885; www.supershuttle.com) charge $8 to $10 to downtown. A taxi fare to downtown from the airport is $10 to $15.

Local buses and the San Diego Trolley, which travels south to the Mexican border, are operated by **Metropolitan Transit System** (MTS; www.sdmts.com). The **Transit Store** (619-234-1060; Broadway & 1st Ave; 9am-5pm Mon-Fri) has route maps, tickets and Day Tripper passes for $5/9/12/15 for one/two/three/four days. Single-day passes are available for purchase onboard buses. Taxi fares start at $2.20 for the first 1/10 mile and $2.30 for each additional mile.

Around San Diego

SAN DIEGO ZOO SAFARI PARK

Take a walk on the 'wild' side at this 1800-acre open-range **zoo** (760-747-8702; www.sandiegozoo.org; 15500 San Pasqual Valley Rd, Escondido; general admission incl tram adult/child $40/30, with San Diego Zoo $76/56; from 9am). Giraffes graze, lions lounge and rhinos romp more or less freely on the valley floor. For that instant safari feel, board the Journey to Africa tram ride, which tours you around the second-largest continent in under half an hour.

The park is in Escondido, about 35 miles north of downtown San Diego. Take I-15 Fwy to the Via Rancho Pkwy exit and then follow the signs. Parking is $10.

LEGOLAND

This fun fantasy **park** (760-918-5346; www.california.legoland.com; 1 Legoland Dr, Carlsbad; adult/child $69/59; from 10am) of rides, shows and attractions is mostly suited to the elementary-school set. Tots can dig for dinosaur bones, pilot helicopters and earn their driver's license. From downtown San Diego (about 32 miles), take the I-5 Fwy north to the Cannon Rd E exit. Parking is $12.

PALM SPRINGS & THE DESERTS

From swanky Palm Springs to intriguing Death Valley, the California desert region – swallowing 25% of California – is a land of contradictions: vast yet intimate, searing yet healing. Over time, you may find that what first seemed harrowingly barren will transform in your mind's eye to perfect beauty: weathered volcanic peaks, sensuous sand dunes, purple-tinged mountains, cactus gardens, tiny wildflowers pushing up from hard-baked soil in spring, lizards scurrying beneath colossal boulders, and in the night sky uncountable stars. California's deserts are serenely spiritual, surprisingly chic and ultimately irresistible, whether you're a boho artist, movie star, rock climber or 4WD adventurer.

Palm Springs

The Rat Pack is back, baby – or, at least, its hangout is. In the 1950s and '60s, Palm Springs (population 44,500), some 100 miles east of LA, was the swinging getaway of Sinatra, Elvis and other big stars. Once the Rat Pack packed it in, however, Palm Springs surrendered to retirees in golf clothing. In the 1990s, a new generation rediscovered the city's retro-chic charms: kidney-shaped pools, starchitect bungalows, vintage boutique hotels, and piano bars serving perfect martinis. Today retirees mix comfortably with hipsters and a significant gay and lesbian contingent.

Sights & Activities

Palm Springs is the principal city of the Coachella Valley, a string of desert towns ranging from ho-hum Cathedral City to glamtastic Palm Desert, all linked by Hwy 111. In Palm Springs' compact downtown, Hwy 111 runs one way south as Palm Canyon Dr, paralleled by northbound Indian Canyon Dr.

TOP CHOICE Palm Springs Aerial Tramway CABLE CAR
(☎760-325-1449; www.pstramway.com; 1 Tram Way; adult/child $23.25/16.25; ⏲10am-8pm Mon-Fri, from 8am Sat & Sun, last tram down 9:45pm) Enjoy dizzying views as you're whisked 2.5 miles from sunbaked desert to a pine-scented alpine wonderland atop Mt San Jacinto. It gets chilly up here, so bring a jacket. Hiking trails through the wilderness of **Mt San Jacinto State Park** include a 5.5-mile nontechnical summit trek. In winter, rent snowshoes and cross-country skis at the mountain station's **Adventure Center** (⏲10am-4pm Thu-Mon, last rental 2:30pm).

Indian Canyons CANYON
(☎760-323-6018; www.indian-canyons.com; off S Palm Canyon Dr; adult/child $9/5, 90min guided hike $3/2; ⏲8am-5pm Oct-Jun, Fri-Sun only Jul-Sep) Shaded by fan palms and flanked by soaring cliffs, these ancestral lands of the Cahuilla tribe are a hiker's delight, especially during the spring wildflower bloom.

Tahquitz Canyon CANYON
(☎760-416-7044; www.tahquitzcanyon.com; 500 W Mesquite Ave; adult/child $12.50/6; ⏲7:30am-5pm Oct-Jun, Fri-Sun only Jul-Sep, last entry 3:30pm) Featured in Frank Capra's 1937 movie *Lost Horizon*, this canyon is famous for its seasonal waterfall and ancient rock art. Explore on your own or join a ranger-guided hike.

Palm Springs Art Museum MUSEUM
(☎760-322-4800; www.psmuseum.org; 101 Museum Dr; adult/child $12.50/free, 4-8pm Thu free; ⏲10am-5pm Tue-Wed & Fri-Sun, noon-8pm Thu) This art beacon is a good place for keeping tabs on the evolution of American painting, sculpture, photography and glass art over the past century or so.

Living Desert Zoo & Gardens ZOO
(☎760-346-5694; www.livingdesert.org; 47900 Portola Ave, off Hwy 111, Palm Desert; adult/child $14.25/7.75; ⏲9am-5pm Oct-May, 8am-1:30pm Jun-Sep) At this engaging park you can pet exotic animals, hitch a camel ride or take a spin on the endangered species carousel. It's educational fun and worth the 30-minute drive down-valley.

Knott's Soak City AMUSEMENT PARK
(☎760-327-0499; www.knotts.com/public/park/soakcity; 1500 S Gene Autry Trail, Palm Springs; adult/child $32/22; ⏲mid-Mar–Sep) A great place to keep cool on hot days, Knott's boasts a massive wave pool, towering water slides and tube rides. Parking is $10.

Sleeping

Rates are lower during midweek. High-season winter rates are quoted below; summer savings can be significant. Chain motels are on Hwy 111 south of downtown.

TOP CHOICE El Morocco Inn & Spa BOUTIQUE HOTEL $$$
(☎760-288-2527; www.elmoroccoinn.com; 66814 4th St, Desert Hot Springs; r incl breakfast $169-249; ❄📶🏊) Heed the call of the Kasbah at this exotic adult-only hideaway whose 10 rooms wrap around a pool deck and perks include a spa, DVD library and homemade lemonade. No kids. In Desert Hot Springs, about a 20-minute drive north of Palm Springs.

Ace Hotel & Swim Club HOTEL $$
(☎760-325-9900; www.acehotel.com/palmsprings; 701 E Palm Canyon Dr; r $119-190, ste $200-440; P@📶🏊) Palm Springs goes Hollywood – with all the sass but *sans* attitude – at this hipster hangout. Rooms (many with patio) sport a glorified tent-cabin look and are crammed with lifestyle essentials (big flat-screen TVs, MP3 plugs). Good on-site restaurant and bar to boot.

Orbit In HOTEL $$$
(☎760-323-3585; www.orbitin.com; 562 W Arenas Rd; r incl breakfast $149-259;) Swing back to the '50s at this quintessential mid-century property set around a quiet saline pool. Rooms sport designer furniture (Eames, Noguchi et al), while freebies include cocktail hour, bike rentals, and daytime sodas and snacks.

Palm Springs Travelodge MOTEL $$
(☎760-327-1211; www.palmcanyonhotel.com; 333 E Palm Canyon Dr; r incl breakfast $60-140;) Travelodge 2.0 with a sleek lobby, mod black furniture and a cool pool with barbecue, fire pits and canopied lounge beds.

Caliente Tropics MOTEL $$
(☎760-327-1391; www.calientetropics.com; 411 E Palm Canyon Dr; d $66-111;) This impeccably kept tiki-style motor lodge, where Elvis once frolicked poolside, is a premier budget pick with spacious rooms and comfy beds.

Eating

Note that many restaurants are closed in July and August.

TOP CHOICE **Trio** MODERN AMERICAN $$$
(☎760-864-8746; www.triopalmsprings.com; 707 N Palm Canyon Dr; mains $13-28; 4-10pm) The winning formula in this '60s modernist space: updated American comfort food (awesome Yankee pot roast!), eye-catching artwork and picture windows. The $19 'early bird' three-course dinner (served 4pm to 6pm) is a steal.

Cheeky's MODERN AMERICAN $$
(☎760-327-7595; www.cheekysps.com; 622 N Palm Canyon Dr; mains $6-13; 8am-2pm Wed-Mon) Waits can be long and service only so-so, but the farm-to-table menu dazzles with witty inventiveness. Actual dishes change weekly, but custardy scrambled eggs, arugula pesto frittata and bacon bar 'flights' keep making appearances.

Wang's in the Desert ASIAN $$
(☎760-325-9264; www.wangsinthedesert.com; 424 S Indian Canyon Dr; mains $12-20; 5-9:30pm Sun-Thu, to 10:30 Fri & Sat) This mood-lit gay-fave with indoor koi pond delivers creatively crafted Chinese classics and has a busy daily happy hour.

Sherman's DELI $$
(☎760-325-1199; www.shermansdeli.com; 401 E Tahquitz Canyon Way; sandwiches $9-12; 7am-9pm;) With a breezy sidewalk patio, this 1950s kosher-style deli pulls in an all-ages crowd with its 40 sandwich varieties (great hot pastrami!), finger-lickin' rotisserie chicken and to-die-for pies.

Copley's on Palm Canyon AMERICAN $$$
(☎760-327-9555; www.copleyspalmsprings.com; 621 N Palm Canyon Dr; mains $27-38; 6pm-late Jan-Apr, closed Mon May, Jun & Sep-Dec) Swoon-worthy American fare on the former Cary Grant estate.

Tyler's Burgers BURGERS $
(149 S Indian Canyon Dr; burgers $4.50-9; 11am-4pm Mon-Sat) The best burgers in town. Enough said. Expect a line.

Native Foods VEGAN $
(☎760-416-0070; www.nativefoods.com; Smoke Tree Village, 1775 E Palm Canyon Dr; mains $8-11; 11:30am-9:30pm Mon-Sat;) Organic and meatless without sacrificing a lick to the taste gods.

Drinking & Entertainment

Arenas Rd, east of Indian Canyon Dr, is lesbigay nightlife central.

Birba BAR
(622 N Palm Canyon Dr; 6-11pm Wed-Fri, from 9:30am Sat & Sun) It's cocktails and pizza at this fabulous indoor-outdoor space where floor-to-ceiling sliding glass doors separate the long marble bar from a hedge-fringed patio with sunken fire pits.

Shanghai Red's BAR
(235 S Indian Canyon Dr; 5pm-late) Behind a casual fish restaurant, this joint has a busy courtyard, an intergenerational crowd and live blues on Friday and Saturday nights.

Melvyn's BAR
(200 W Ramon Rd) Join the Bentley pack for stiff martinis and quiet jazz at this former Sinatra haunt at the Ingleside Inn. Shine your shoes.

Shopping

For art galleries and indie boutiques, head 'Uptown' to North Palm Canyon Dr. If you're riding the retro wave, ferret for treasure in thrift shops and consignment boutiques scattered along Hwy 111. For the local version of Rodeo Dr, drive 14 miles down-valley to El Paseo in Palm Desert. For bargain-hunters, there's the huge Desert Hills Premium Outlets, 20 minutes west on the I-10.

WHAT THE...?

West of Palm Springs, you may do a double-take when you see the **World's Biggest Dinosaurs** (951-922-0076; www.cabazondinosaurs.com; 50770 Seminole Dr, off I-10 exit Main St, Cabazon; adult/child $7/6; 10am-6pm). Claude K Bell, a sculptor for Knott's Berry Farm, spent over a decade crafting these concrete behemoths, now owned by Christian creationists who contend that God created the original dinosaurs in one day, along with the other animals. In the gift shop, alongside the sort of dino-swag you might find at science museums, you can read about the alleged hoaxes and fallacies of evolution and Darwinism.

Information

Desert Regional Medical Center (800-491-4990; 1150 N Indian Canyon Dr; 24hr) Emergency room.

Palm Springs Official Visitors Center (760-778-8418; www.visitpalmsprings.com; 2901 N Palm Canyon Dr; 9am-5pm) Inside a 1965 Albert Frey–designed gas station at the tramway turnoff north of downtown.

Post office (333 E Amado Rd; 8am-5pm Mon-Fri, 9am-3pm Sat)

Public library (300 S Sunrise Way; 9am-8pm Tue-Wed, to 6pm Thu-Sat; @)

Getting There & Around

Ten minutes' drive from downtown, **Palm Springs International Airport** (PSP; www.palmspringsairport.com; 3400 E Tahquitz Canyon Way) is served by domestic and Canadian airlines; major car-rental agencies are on-site.

Thrice-weekly Amtrak trains to/from LA ($37, 2¾ hours) stop at the unstaffed, kinda-creepy North Palm Springs Station, 5 miles north of downtown, as do several daily Greyhound buses to/from LA ($32.50, three hours). **SunLine** (www.sunline.org; single ride/day pass $1/3) runs slow-moving local buses throughout the valley.

Joshua Tree National Park

Like figments from a Dr Seuss book, the whimsical Joshua trees (actually tree-sized yuccas) welcome visitors to this 794,000 acre (321,000 hectare) park at the convergence of the Sonora and Mojave Deserts. The park is hemmed in by the I-10 in the south and by Hwy 62 (Twentynine Palms Hwy) in the north, and you'll find most of the attractions, including all of the Joshua trees, in its northern half.

Joshua Tree is popular with rock climbers and day hikers, especially in spring when the trees send up a huge single cream-colored flower. The mystical quality of this stark, boulder-strewn landscape has inspired many artists, most famously the band U2.

There are no park facilities aside from restrooms, but you can gas and stock up in the trio of desert communities linked by Twentynine Palm Hwy (Hwy 62) along its northern boundary. Of these, Yucca Valley has the most facilities and arty Joshua Tree the best eating. Twentynine Palms, home to the country's largest US marine base, is more down-to-earth.

Sights & Activities

The epic **Wonderland of Rocks**, a mecca for climbers, dominates the park's north side. Sunset-worthy **Keys View** overlooks the San Andreas Fault and as far as Mexico. For Western pioneer history, visit **Keys Ranch** (reservations 760-367-5555; 90min walking tour adult/child $5/2.50; 10am & 1pm year-round, plus 7pm Tue, Thu-Sat Oct-May). Hikers can search out native desert fan-palm oases like **49 Palms Oasis** (3-mile round-trip) or **Lost Palms Oasis** (7.2-mile round-trip). Kid-friendly nature trails include **Barker Dam** (1.1-mile loop), which passes Native American petroglyphs; **Skull Rock** (1.7-mile loop); and **Cholla Cactus Garden** (0.25-mile loop). For a scenic 4WD route, tackle the bumpy 18-mile **Geology Tour Road**, also open to mountain bikers.

Sleeping

The national park itself has only camping, but there's plenty of lodging along Hwy 62, as well as the deliciously kooky Pioneertown Motel.

Desert Lily B&B $$
(760-366-4676; www.thedesertlily.com, Joshua Tree Highlands; s/d incl breakfast $140/155; closed Jul & Aug; @) The charming Carrie presides over this three-room adobe retreat and will happily dole out insider tips about the area. Breakfasts are scrumptious.

Spin & Margie's Desert Hide-a-Way CABIN $$
(760-366-9124; www.deserthideaway.com; 64491 Twentynine Palms Hwy; ste $125-175;)

This hacienda-style inn harbors five boldly colored suites with striking design using corrugated tin, old license plates and cartoon art.

29 Palms Inn HOTEL $$$
(760-367-3505; www.29spalmsinn.com; 73950 Inn Ave, Twentynine Palms; r & cottages incl breakfast $95-258;) History oozes from every nook and cranny in these historic adobe-and-wood cabins dotted around a palm oasis.

High Desert Motel MOTEL $
(760-366-1978; www.highdesertmotel.com; 61310 Twentynine Palms Hwy, Joshua Tree; r $50-70;) Near the park entrance, rooms here are plain-Jane plus minifridges and microwaves.

Camping CAMPGROUNDS $
(campsites $10-15) Of the park's eight campgrounds, only Cottonwood and Black Rock have potable water, flush toilets and dump stations. Indian Cove and Black Rock accept **reservations** (877-444-6777; www.recreation.gov); the others are first-come, first-served. None have showers. Backcountry camping (no campfires) is allowed 1 mile from any trailhead or road and 100ft from water sources; free self-registration is required at the park's 13 staging areas. **Joshua Tree Outfitters** (760-366-1848; 61707 Twentynine Palms Hwy, Joshua Tree) rents quality camping gear.

WHAT THE...?

Just north of Yucca Valley, **Pioneertown** (www.pioneertown.com; admission free) was built as a Hollywood Western movie set in 1946, and it hasn't changed much since. On Mane St, witness mock gunfights at 2:30pm on Saturdays and Sundays from April to October. Enjoy BBQ, cheap beer and live music at honky-tonk **Pappy & Harriet's Pioneertown Palace** (760-365-5956; www.pappyandharriets.com; 53688 Pioneertown Rd; burgers $5-12, mains $16-30; 11am-2am Thu-Sun, 5pm-midnight Mon). Then bed down at **Pioneertown Motel** (760-365-7001; www.pioneertown-motel.com; 5040 Curtis Rd; r $50-100;), where yesteryear silver-screen stars once slept and rooms are now crammed with Western-themed memorabilia.

Eating & Drinking

Ricochet Gourmet INTERNATIONAL $$
(www.ricochetjoshuatree.com; 61705 Twentynine Palm Hwy, Joshua Tree; mains $8-15; 7am-5p Mon-Sat, from 8am Sun;) At this much adored cafe-cum-deli, the menu bounces from breakfast frittatas to curry chicken salad and fragrant soups, all of them homemade using organic and seasonal ingredients.

Restaurant at 29 Palms Inn AMERICAN $$
(760-367-3505, www.29spalmsinn.com; 73950 Inn Ave, Twentynine Palms; mains lunch $7.50-10, dinner $9-21;) The well-respected restaurant has its own organic garden and does burgers and salads at lunchtime and grilled meats and yummy pastas for dinner.

Joshua Tree Saloon AMERICAN $$
(http://thejoshuatreesaloon.com; 61835 Twentynine Palms Hwy, Joshua Tree; mains $9-17; 8am-late;) For rib-sticking burgers and steaks, report to this raucous watering hole that also offers nightly entertainment (over 21s only).

Sam's PIZZA, INDIAN $
(760-366-9511; 61380 Twentynine Palms Hwy, Joshua Tree; mains $8-11; 11am-9pm Mon-Sat, 3-8pm Sun;) Sure, there's pizza but clued-in locals flock here for the flavor-packed Indian curries, many of them meatless. Takeout available.

Information

Joshua Tree Outfitters (760-366-1848; 61707 Twentynine Palms Hwy, Joshua Tree) has internet access for $2 per 15 minutes.

Park entry permits ($15 per vehicle) are valid for seven days and come with a map and newspaper guide. Get information at the **visitor centers** (760-367-5500; www.nps.gov/jotr) Cottonwood (north of I-10, Cottonwood Springs; 9am-3pm); Joshua Tree (Park Blvd, off Hwy 62; 8am-5pm); Oasis (Utah Trail & National Park Dr, Twentynine Palms; 8am-5pm).

Anza-Borrego Desert State Park

Shaped by an ancient sea and tectonic forces, Anza-Borrego is the largest state park in the USA outside Alaska. Cradling the park's only commercial hub – tiny Borrego Springs (pop 2535) – are 600,000 acres of mountains, canyons and badlands; a fabulous variety of plants and wildlife; and intriguing relics

WHAT THE...?

East of Anza-Borrego and south of Joshua Tree awaits a most unexpected sight: the **Salton Sea** (www.saltonsea.ca.gov), California's largest lake in the middle of its biggest desert, created in 1905 when the Colorado River breached its banks. Originally a tourist destination, it's reputation has been tainted since the 1980s by the annual fish die-offs caused by chemical runoff from surrounding farmland. It's an environmental nightmare with no easy solutions.

An even stranger sight near the lake's eastern shore is **Salvation Mountain** (www.salvationmountain.us), a 100ft-high hill blanketed in colorful paint and found objects, and inscribed with religious messages. The vision of Leonard Knight, it's become one of the great works of American folk art and has even been recognized as a national treasure in the US Senate. It's in Niland, about 3 miles off Hwy 111, via Main St.

of native tribes, Spanish explorers and gold-rush pioneers. Wildflower season (usually March to May; for updates call ☎760-767-4684) is peak season and right before the Hades-like heat makes exploring dangerous.

Sights

Park highlights include: **Fonts Point** desert lookout; **Clark Dry Lake** for birding; the **Elephant Tree Discovery Trail**; Split Mountain's wind caves; and **Blair Valley**, with its Native American pictographs and *morteros* (seed-grinding stones). Further south, **Agua Caliente County Park** has hot springs.

Sleeping & Eating

Aside from developed **Borrego Palm Canyon** (☎reservations 800-444-7275; www.reserveamerica.com; tent/RV sites $25/35), there are a handful of primitive campgrounds with vault toilets but no water. Free back-country camping is permitted anywhere that's off-road and at least 100ft from water but open ground fires and vegetation gathering are *verboten*.

For country-style B&Bs and famous apple pie, the gold-mining town of **Julian** (www.juliancca.com) is a 45-minute drive southwest of Borrego Springs.

TOP CHOICE **Borrego Valley Inn** BOUTIQUE HOTEL $$$
(☎760-767-0311; www.borregovalleyinn.com; 405 Palm Canyon Dr, Borrego Springs; r incl breakfast $185-275;) This intimate spa-resort inn has 15 adobe-style rooms brimming with Southwestern decor, plus two pools (one clothing-optional) and a hot tub.

Palms at Indian Head BOUTIQUE HOTEL $$$
(☎760-767-7788; www.thepalmsatindianhead.com; 2200 Hoberg Rd, Borrego Springs; r $169-249;) This former haunt of Cary Grant, Marilyn Monroe and other old-time celebs has been reborn as a chic mid-century-modern retreat. Connect with the era over martinis and chicken cordon bleu at the on-site bar and grill while enjoying enchanting desert views.

Carlee's Place AMERICAN $$
(660 Palm Canyon Dr, Borrego Springs; mains lunch $7-14, dinner $12-23; ⊙11am-9pm) Join the locals for casual American fare, karaoke nights and pool.

Information

Borrego Springs has stores, ATMs, gas stations, a post office, supermarket and a public library with free internet access and wi-fi. The park's comprehensive **visitor center** (☎760-767-4205; www.parks.ca.gov; 200 Palm Canyon Dr; ⊙9am-5pm Nov-Apr, Sat & Sun only May-Oct) is 2 miles west. For additional information, see www.california-desert.org. Driving through the park is free, but if you camp, hike or picnic, a day fee of $8 per car applies. You'll need a 4WD to tackle the 500 miles of back-country dirt roads. For hikes or mountain biking along dirt roads, pack extra water and don't go at midday.

Mojave National Preserve

If you're on a quest for the 'middle of nowhere,' you'll find it in the wilderness of the **Mojave National Preserve** (☎760-252-6100; www.nps.gov/moja; admission free), a 1.6-million-acre jumble of sand dunes, Joshua trees, volcanic cinder cones and habitats for desert tortoises, jackrabbits and coyotes. No gas is available here.

Southeast of Baker and the I-15 Fwy, Kelbaker Rd crosses a ghostly landscape of cinder cones before arriving at **Kelso Depot**, a handsome 1920s railroad station in Spanish mission revival style, which now houses the park's **visitor center** (☎760-252-6108; ⊙9am-5pm) with excellent natural and cultural history exhibits and an old-fashioned **lunch counter** (dishes $3.50-8.50). It's another 11 miles southwest to the 'singing' **Kelso Dunes** which, at 600ft high, are the country's third-tallest sand dunes. When conditions are right, they emanate low humming sounds that are caused by shifting sands – running downhill sometimes jump-starts the effect.

From Kelso Depot, Kelso–Cima Rd takes off northeast. After 19 miles, Cima Rd heads back toward I-15 around **Cima Dome**, a 1500ft-high hunk of granite with crusty lava outcroppings. Its slopes are smothered in the world's largest **Joshua tree forest**. For close-ups, summit Teutonia Peak (3 miles round-trip); the trailhead is 6 miles northwest of Cima.

East off the Kelso–Cima Rd, Mojave Rd is the backdoor route to two first-come, first-served **campgrounds** (sites $12) with potable water at Mid Hills (no RVs) and Hole-in-the-Wall. They bookend a rugged 10-mile scenic drive along **Wild Horse Canyon Rd**. Ask at Hole-in-the-Wall's **visitor center** (☎760-252-6104; ⊙9am-4pm Wed-Sun Oct-Apr, Fri-Sun only May-Sep) about the slot-canyon **Rings Loop Trail**. Roads in this area are mostly unpaved but well maintained.

Southwest of Hole-in-the-Wall, the splendid **Mitchell Caverns** (☎760-928-2586) unlock a world of quirky limestone formations but tours were suspended until further notice at press time.

Sleeping & Eating

Free backcountry and roadside **camping** is permitted throughout the preserve in areas already used for this purpose. Check the website for locations or ask at the visitor center. Baker is the nearest town with bare-bones motels.

For more ambience, detour to the **Hotel Nipton** (☎760-856-2335; www.nipton.com; 107355 Nipton Rd, Nipton; d incl breakfast $79; ⊙reception 8am-6pm; 📶) in a century-old adobe villa in a remote railway outpost northeast of the preserve. Check-in is at the well-stocked trading post adjacent to the **cafe-bar** (dishes $7-10; ⊙11am-6pm, dinner by arrangement). There's also a **campground** (per site $25) and **tent cabins** ($65).

Death Valley National Park

The name itself evokes all that is harsh and hellish – a punishing, barren and lifeless place of Old Testament severity. Yet closer inspection reveals that in Death Valley nature is putting on a spectacular show with water-sculpted canyons, singing sand dunes, palm-shaded oases, eroded mountains and plenty of endemic wildlife. It's a land of superlatives, holding the US records for hottest temperature (134°F, or 57°C), lowest point (Badwater, 282ft below sea level) and largest national park outside Alaska (over 5000 sq miles). Peak tourist season is when spring wildflowers bloom. Furnace Creek is the park's commercial hub.

Sights & Activities

Drive up to **Zabriskie Point** at sunrise or sunset for spectacular valley views across golden badlands eroded into waves, pleats and gullies. Some 20 miles further south, at **Dante's View**, you can simultaneously see the highest (Mt Whitney, 14,505ft) and lowest (Badwater) points in the contiguous USA. En route, consider detouring along the bone-rattling scenic one-way loop through **Twenty Mule Team Canyon**.

Badwater itself, a timeless landscape of crinkly salt flats, is a 17-mile drive south of Furnace Creek. Along the way, narrow **Golden Canyon** and **Natural Bridge** are both easily explored on short hikes. On the **Devils Golf Course**, crystallized salt has piled up into saw-tooth mini mountains. A 9-mile detour along **Artists Drive** is best in the late afternoon when eroded hillsides erupt in fireworks of color.

North of Furnace Creek, near Stovepipe Wells, you can scramble along the smooth marble walls of **Mosaic Canyon** or roll down the Saharan-esque **Mesquite Flat sand dunes** – magical during a full moon.

Another 36 miles north is whimsical **Scotty's Castle** (☎760-786-2392; adult/child $11/6; ⊙tours 9am-5pm Nov-Apr, to 4pm May-Oct), where costumed guides bring to life the strange tale of con-man Death Valley Scotty.

In summer, stick to paved roads (dirt roads can quickly overheat vehicles), limit your exertions and visit higher-elevation areas. For example, the scenic drive up **Emigrant Canyon Road**, starting west of Stovepipe Wells, ends 21 miles later at the historic beehive-shaped **Charcoal Kilns**, near the trailhead for the 8.4-mile round-trip hike up

Wildrose Peak (9064ft). At the park's western edge, utterly remote **Panamint Springs** offers volcanic vistas, Joshua tree forests and the scenic Darwin Falls.

Activities back at Furnace Creek Ranch include horseback riding and golf.

Sleeping & Eating

In-park lodging is pricey and often booked solid in springtime when even first-come first-served campgrounds fill by midmorning, especially on weekends. The closest town with cheaper lodging is Beatty in Nevada (44 miles from Furnace Creek), although choices are more plentiful in Las Vegas (120 miles southeast) and Ridgecrest (122 miles west).

Stovepipe Wells Village MOTEL **$$**
(760-786-2387; www.escapetodeathvalley.com; Hwy 190; RV sites $31, r $80-155;) Newly spruced-up rooms feature quality linens beneath cheerful Native American bedspreads as well as coffeemakers. The small pool is cool and the cowboy-style restaurant (mains $5 to $25) delivers three square meals a day.

Furnace Creek Ranch RESORT **$$**
(760-786-2345; www.furnacecreekresort.com; cabins $130-162, r $162-213;) Tailor-made for families, this rambling resort has been subjected to a vigorous facelift resulting in rooms dressed in desert-color decor, updated bathrooms and porches with comfortable patio furniture. The grounds encompass a playground, spring-fed swimming pool, tennis courts and the Forty-Niner Café (mains $12 to $25), which cooks up decent American standards. The next-door Wrangler serves juicy steak dinners (mains $22 to $39) and run-of-the-mill breakfast and lunch buffets ($11.25/14.95).

Furnace Creek Inn HOTEL **$$$**
(760-786-2345; www.furnacecreekresort.com; r $330-460; early Oct-early May;) At this elegant, mission-style hotel you can count the colors of the desert while unwinding by the spring-fed pool with sweeping valley views. The restaurant (dress code) serves upscale American fare (lunch mains $13 to $17, dinner $24 to $38) and an opulent Sunday brunch.

Camping CAMPGROUNDS **$**
(campsites free-$18) Of the park's nine campgrounds, only Furnace Creek accepts **reservations** (877-444-6777; www.recreation.gov) from mid-April to mid-October. In summer, Furnace Creek is first-come, first-served, and the only other campgrounds open are Mesquite Spring, near Scotty's Castle, and those along Emigrant Canyon Rd west of Stovepipe Wells. Some are accessible to high-clearance vehicles only. Other valley-floor campgrounds – like roadside Stovepipe Wells, Sunset and shadier Texas Springs – cater primarily to RVs; they're open October to April.

Backcountry camping (no campfires) is allowed 2 miles off paved roads and away from developed and day-use areas, and 100yd from any water source; pick up free permits at the visitor center.

Furnace Creek Ranch and Stovepipe Wells Village offer public showers ($5, including swimming-pool access).

Information

Entry permits ($20 per vehicle) are valid for seven days and sold at self-service pay stations throughout the park. For a free map and newspaper, show your receipt at the **visitor center** (760-786-3200; www.nps.gov/deva; 8am-5pm) in Furnace Creek, which has a general store, gas station, post office, ATM, internet access, lodging and restaurants. Stovepipe Wells, a 30-minute drive northwest, has a general store, gas station, ATM, motel and cafe. Panamint Springs, on the park's western edge, has gas and snacks. Cell-phone reception is poor to nonexistent in the park.

CENTRAL COAST

No trip to California would be worth its salt without a jaunt along the surreally scenic Central Coast. Hwy 1, one of the USA's most iconic roads, skirts past posh Santa Barbara, retro Pismo Beach, collegiate San Luis Obispo, fantastical Hearst Castle, soul-stirring Big Sur, down-to-earth Monterey Bay and hippie Santa Cruz. Slow down – this idyllic coast deserves to be savored, not gulped. (That same advice goes for locally grown wines.)

Santa Barbara

Life is certainly sweet in Santa Barbara, a coastal Shangri-La where the air is redolent with citrus and jasmine, flowery bougainvillea drapes whitewashed buildings with Spanish-esque red-tiled roofs, and it's all cradled by pearly beaches. Just ignore those pesky oil derricks out to sea. State St, the

WHAT THE...?

Four miles west of Beatty, NV, look for the turnoff to the ghost town of **Rhyolite** (www.rhyolitesite.com; Hwy 374; admission free; ⌚sunrise-sunset), which epitomizes the hurly-burly, boom-and-bust story of so many Western gold-rush mining towns. Don't overlook the 1906 'bottle house' or the skeletal remains of a three-story bank. Next door is the bizarre **Goldwell Open Air Museum** (www.goldwellmuseum.org; admission free; ⌚24hr), a trippy art installation started by Belgian artist Albert Szukalski in 1984.

main drag, abounds with bars, cafes, theaters and boutique shops.

Sights

Mission Santa Barbara CHURCH
(www.sbmission.org; 2201 Laguna St; adult/child $5/1; ⌚9am-4:30pm) Established in 1786, California's hilltop 'Queen of the Missions' was the only one to escape secularization under Mexican rule. Look for Chumash artwork inside the vaulted church and a moody cemetery out back.

Santa Barbara Museum of Art MUSEUM
(www.sbma.net; 1130 State St; adult/child $9/6; ⌚11am-5pm Tue-Sun) These downtown galleries hold an impressive, well-edited collection of contemporary California artists, modern masters like Matisse and Chagall, 20th-century photography and Asian art, with provocative special exhibits. Sundays are pay-what-you-wish.

FREE **County Courthouse** HISTORIC BUILDING
(www.santabarbaracourthouse.org; 1100 Anacapa St; ⌚8am-5pm Mon-Fri, 10am-4:30pm Sat & Sun) Built in Spanish-Moorish-revival style, it's an absurdly beautiful place to stand trial. Marvel at hand-painted ceilings and intricate murals, then climb the *Vertigo*-esque clock tower for panoramic views. Free tours.

Santa Barbara Historical Museum MUSEUM
(www.santabarbaramuseum.com; 136 E De La Guerra St; donations welcome; ⌚10am-5pm Tue-Sat, from noon Sun) By a romantic cloistered adobe courtyard, peruse a fascinating mishmash of local memorabilia, including Chumash woven baskets, and learn about odd historical footnotes like the city's involvement in toppling the last Chinese monarchy.

Santa Barbara Botanic Garden GARDEN
(www.sbbg.org; 1212 Mission Canyon Rd; adult/child 2-12yr/youth 13-17yr $8/4/6; ⌚9am-6pm, to 5pm Nov-Feb) Uphill from the mission, this garden is devoted to California's native flora. Rolling trails meander through cacti and wildflowers past the historic mission dam and aqueduct. Nearby is a natural-history museum for kiddos.

Santa Barbara Maritime Museum MUSEUM
(www.sbmm.org; 113 Harbor Way; adult/child $7/4, 3rd Thu of month free; ⌚10am-5pm Thu-Tue, to 6pm Jun-Aug) At the harbor, this museum celebrates the town's briny history with historical artifacts, hands-on and virtual-reality exhibits, and a small documentary-movie theater.

Activities

On the waterfront and good for a stroll, 1872 **Stearns Wharf** is the West's oldest continuously operating wooden pier, strung with restaurants and touristy shops. Outside town along Hwy 101, look for palm-fringed **state beaches** (www.parks.ca.gov; per car $10; ⌚8am-sunset) at Carpinteria, about 12 miles east, and El Capitan and Refugio, over 20 miles west.

Wheel Fun CYCLING
(www.wheelfunrentals.com; 22 State St & 23 E Cabrillo Blvd; ⌚8am-8pm) Rents bicycles (from $8 per hour) for the paved recreational trail that skirts miles of beautiful city beaches.

Paddle Sports KAYAKING, SURFING
(☎805-899-4925; www.kayaksb.com; 117b Harbor Way; kayak/SUP rentals from $25/40, 2hr SUP lesson from $80) Friendly kayaking and stand-up paddle boarding (SUP) outfitter.

Santa Barbara Adventure Co KAYAKING, SURFING
(☎805-884-9283; www.sbadventureco.com; tours/lessons from $50/99) Guided kayaking tours and traditional board-surfing and SUP lessons.

Santa Barbara Sailing Center KAYAKING, SAILING
(☎805-962-2826; www.sbsail.com; 133 Harbor Way; kayak rental per hr $10-15, cruises/tours from $25/60) Rents kayaks, teaches sailing and offers sunset cocktail cruises and guided paddling tours.

Condor Express WHALE-WATCHING
(☎805-882-0088; www.condorcruises.com; 301 W Cabrillo Blvd; adult/child from $48/25) Narrated year-round whale-watching tours.

Sleeping

Prepare for sticker shock: even basic rooms command over $200 in summer. Search out motel bargains along upper State St, north of downtown. For state-beach campgrounds off Hwy 101, make **reservations** (☎800-444-7275; www.reserveamerica.com; campsites $35-50).

Inn of the Spanish Garden BOUTIQUE HOTEL $$$
(☎805-564-4700; http://spanishgardeninn.com; 915 Garden St; d incl breakfast $259-519;) Elegant Spanish-revival-style downtown hotel has two dozen romantic luxury rooms and suites facing a gracious fountain courtyard. Concierge services are top-notch.

TOP CHOICE **El Capitan Canyon** CABINS, CAMPGROUND $$
(☎805-685-3887; www.elcapitancanyon.com; 11560 Calle Real, off Hwy 101; safari tents $155, cabins $225-350;) Go 'glamping' in this car-free zone near El Capitan State Beach, a 30-minute drive up Hwy 101. Safari tents are rustic, while creekside cedar cabins come with heavenly mattresses, kitchenettes and outdoor fire pits.

Presidio Motel MOTEL $$$
(☎805-963-1355; http://thepresidiomotel.com; 1620 State St; r incl breakfast $119-220;) Like the H&M of motels, this affordable gem has panache and personality thanks to arty flair, dreamy bedding and free loaner bikes. Noise can be an issue. Its sister motel, the nearby Agave Inn, is cheaper.

Brisas del Mar HOTEL $$$
(☎805-966-2219; www.sbhotels.com; 223 Castillo St; r incl breakfast $145-290;) Big kudos for the freebies (DVDs, wine and cheese, milk and cookies) and Mediterranean-style front section, although the motel wing is unlovely. Its sister properties away from the beach are typically lower-priced.

Eating

Olio Pizzeria ITALIAN $$$
(☎805-899-2699; www.oliopizzeria.com; 11 W Victoria St; dishes $3-24; ⏰11:30am-2pm Mon-Sat, 5-10pm Sun-Thu, to 11pm Fri & Sat) Cozy, high-ceilinged pizzeria and enoteca with a happening wine bar proffers a tempting selection of crispy pizzas, imported cheeses and meats, traditional antipasti and *dolci* (desserts).

TOP CHOICE **Santa Barbara Shellfish Company** SEAFOOD $$
(www.sbfishhouse.com; 230 Stearns Wharf; dishes $5-19; ⏰11am-9pm) 'From sea to skillet to plate' best describes this end-of-the-wharf crab shack that's more of a counter joint. Great lobster bisque, ocean views and the same location for 25 years.

Silvergreens CAFE $
(www.silvergreens.com; 791 Chapala St; dishes $4-10; ⏰7:30am-10pm Mon-Fri, from 11am Sun;) Who says fast food can't be fresh and tasty? With the tag line 'Eat smart, live well,' this sun-drenched cafe makes nutritionally sound salads, soups, sandwiches, burgers, breakfast burritos and more.

D'Angelo Pastry & Bread CAFE $
(25 W Gutierrez St; dishes $2-8; ⏰7am-2pm) Retrolicious bakery with shiny-silver sidewalk bistro tables is a perfect quick breakfast or brunch spot, whether for a buttery croissant or Iron Chef Cat Cora's favorite 'Eggs Rose.'

Lilly's Taquería MEXICAN $
(310 Chapala St; items from $1.50; ⏰11am-9pm Mon & Wed-Thu, to 10pm Fri & Sat, to 9:30pm Sun) There's almost always a line, so be snappy with your order – locals fight over *adobada* (marinated pork) tacos.

Drinking & Entertainment

Nightlife revolves around lower State St. Pick up the free alt-weekly *Santa Barbara Independent* (www.independent.com) for an events calendar. You can ramble between a dozen wine-tasting rooms (and a microbrewery, too) along the city's **Urban Wine Trail** (www.urbanwinetrailsb.com).

Soho LIVE MUSIC
(☎805-962-7776; www.sohosb.com; 1221 State St; cover $12-25) Unpretentious brick room located upstairs behind a McDonald's has live bands nightly, from indie rock, funk and folk to jazz and blues.

Brewhouse BREWERY
(www.brewhousesb.com; 229 W Montecito St; ⏰11am-11pm Sun-Thu, to midnight Fri & Sat;) Rowdy dive down by the railroad tracks crafts its own unique small-batch beers and has rockin' live music Wednesday to Saturday nights.

IF YOU HAVE A FEW MORE DAYS

Remote, rugged **Channel Islands National Park** (www.nps.gov/chis) earns the nickname 'California's Galápagos' for its unique wildlife. The islands offering superb snorkeling, scuba diving and sea kayaking too. Spring when wildflowers bloom is a gorgeous time to visit; summer and fall can be bone-dry, and winter stormy.

Anacapa, an hour's boat ride from the mainland, is the best island for day-tripping, with easy hikes and unforgettable views. Santa Cruz, the biggest island, is for overnight excursions, offering camping, hiking and kayaking. Other islands require longer channel crossings and multiday trips: San Miguel is often shrouded in fog; tiny Santa Barbara supports seabird and seal colonies, as does Santa Rosa, which also protects Chumash archaeological sites.

Boats leave from Ventura Harbor, off Hwy 101, where the park's **visitor center** (805-658-5730; 1901 Spinnaker Dr; 8:30am-5pm) has info and maps. The main tour-boat operator is **Island Packers** (805-642-1393; www.islandpackers.com; 1691 Spinnaker Dr; adult/child from $33/24); book ahead. Primitive island **campgrounds** (reservations 877-444-6777; www.recreation.gov; tent sites $15) require reservations; bring food and water.

French Press CAFE
(1101 State St; 6am-7pm Mon-Fri, from 7am Sat, 8am-5pm Sun;) With shiny silver espresso machines from Italy and beans roasted in Santa Cruz, these baristas know how to pull their shots.

Information

Santa Barbara Car Free (www.santabarbaracarfree.org) Helpful website for ecotravel tips and valuable discounts.

Visitor center (805-965-3021; www.santabarbaraca.com; 1 Garden St; 9am-5pm Mon-Sat, from 10am Sun) Near the waterfront, offers maps and self-guided tour brochures.

Getting There & Around

Amtrak (209 State St) Trains run south to LA ($25, three hours) and north to San Luis Obispo ($29, 2¾ hours).

Greyhound (34 W Carrillo St) A few daily buses to LA ($18, three hours), San Luis Obispo ($26, 2¼ hours) or San Francisco ($53, nine hours).

Metropolitan Transit District (805-963-3366; www.sbmtd.gov) Runs city-wide buses (fares $1.75) and electric shuttles (25¢) from State St downtown to Stearns Wharf and along beachfront Cabrillo Blvd.

Santa Barbara to San Luis Obispo

You can speed up to San Luis Obispo in just two hours along Hwy 101, or take all day detouring to wineries, a historical mission and hidden beaches.

A scenic backcountry drive north of Santa Barbara follows Hwy 154, where you can go for the grape in the **Santa Ynez & Santa Maria Valleys** (www.sbcountywines.com). Keep an eye out for *Sideways* (2004) film locations. For ecoconscious vineyard tours, check **Sustainable Vine** (805-698-3911; www.sustainablevine.com; all-day tour $125). Or start DIY explorations at **Los Olivos Cafe & Wine Merchant** (805-688-7265; www.losolivoscafe.com; 2879 Grand Ave, Los Olivos; mains $11-25; 11:30am-8:30pm), a Cal-Mediterranean bistro with a tasting bar, then follow the **Foxen Canyon Wine Trail** (www.foxencanyonwinetrail.com) north to cult winemakers' vineyards.

Further south, the Danish-immigrant village of **Solvang** (www.solvangusa.com) is a kitsch lovers' dream with decorative windmills and fairytale-esque bakeries. For a picnic lunch or BBQ takeout, swing by **El Rancho Marketplace** (www.elranchomarket.com; 2886 Mission Dr/Hwy 246, Solvang; 6am-10pm). Nearer Hwy 101, **Hitching Post II** (805-688-0676; www.hitchingpost2.com; 406 E Hwy 246, Buellton; mains $22-48; 5-9:30pm Mon-Fri, 4-9:30pm Sat & Sun) is an old-guard steakhouse that makes its own Pinot Noir (which is damn good, by the way); reservations are essential.

Follow Hwy 246 about 15 miles west of Hwy 101 to **La Purísima Mission State Historic Park** (www.lapurisimamission.org; 2295 Purisima Rd, Lompoc; per car $6; 9am-5pm). Exquisitely restored, it's one of California's most evocative Spanish-Colonial missions, with flowering gardens, livestock pens and adobe buildings. South of Lompoc off Hwy 1, Jalama Rd travels 14 twisting miles to utterly isolated **Jalama Beach County Park**

(☎805-736-3504; www.sbparks.org; per car $10). Its crazy-popular **campground** (tent/RV sites $25/40, cabins $80-200) only accepts reservations for its newly built cabins – otherwise, look for the 'campground full' sign a half-mile south of Hwy 1.

Heading north on Hwy 1, rough-and-tumble **Guadalupe** is the gateway to North America's largest coastal dunes. Here the **Lost City of DeMille** (www.lostcitydemille.com), the movie set of the 1923 version of *The Ten Commandments,* lies buried beneath the sands. Scenes from *Pirates of the Caribbean: At World's End* (2007) were shot here. The best dunes access is west of town via Hwy 166. Downtown, dig into juicy steaks at genuine Old West–flavored **Far Western Tavern** (☎805-343-2211; www.farwesterntavern.com; 899 Guadalupe St; dinner mains $22-35; ⏰11am-8:30pm Tue-Thu, to 9pm Fri & Sat, 9am-8pm Sun).

Where Hwy 1 rejoins Hwy 101, **Pismo Beach** has a long, lazy stretch of sand and a **butterfly grove** (www.monarchbutterfly.org), where migratory monarchs perch in eucalyptus trees from late October to February. The grove stands south of **Pismo State Beach campground** (☎reservations 800-444-7275; www.reserveamerica.com; Hwy 1; campsites $35; 📶), which offers beach access and hot showers. Pismo Beach has dozens of motels by the beach and off Hwy 101, but rooms fill quickly, especially on weekends. **Pismo Lighthouse Suites** (☎805-773-2411; www.pismolighthousesuites.com; 2411 Price St; ste incl breakfast $149-329; ❄@📶🏊👪) has everything vacationing families need, from kitchenette suites to a life-sized outdoor chessboard.

By Pismo's seaside pier, lines go out the door at scruffy, hole-in-the-wall **Splash Cafe** (www.splashcafe.com; 197 Pomeroy Ave; dishes $4-10; ⏰8am-9pm; 👪), famed for its clam chowder served in homebaked sourdough-bread bowls. Nearby, **Old West Cinnamon Rolls** (www.oldwestcinnamon.com; 861 Dolliver St; snacks $3-5; ⏰6:30am-5:30pm) bakery is sugary goodness. Uphill at the **Cracked Crab** (www.crackedcrab.com; 751 Price St; mains $9-50; ⏰11am-9pm Sun-Thu, to 10pm Fri & Sat), make sure you don a plastic bib before that fresh bucket o' seafood gets dumped on your table.

The nearby town of Avila Beach has a waterfront promenade. Grab a chipotle tri-tip sandwich from **Avila Grocery & Deli** (354 Front St; mains $5-11; ⏰7am-7pm). Nearer Hwy 101, pick berries and feed the goats at **Avila Valley Barn** (http://avilavalleybarn.com; 560 Avila Beach Dr; ⏰9am-6pm, reduced winter hr) farm stand, then do some private stargazing from a redwood hot tub at **Sycamore Mineral Springs** (☎805-595-7302; www.sycamoresprings.com; 1215 Avila Beach Dr; 1hr per person $12.50-17.50; ⏰8am-midnight, last reservation 10:45pm).

San Luis Obispo

Halfway between LA and San Francisco, San Luis Obispo is a low-key place. But CalPoly university students inject a healthy dose of hubbub into the streets, pubs and cafes, especially during the weekly **farmers market** (⏰6-9pm Thu), which turns downtown's Higuera St into a street festival with live music and sidewalk BBQs.

Like many other California towns, SLO grew up around a Spanish Catholic **mission** (☎805-543-6850; www.missionsanluisobispo.org; 751 Palm St; donation $2; ⏰9am-4pm), founded in 1772 by Padre Junípero Serra. These days, SLO is just a grape's throw from thriving **Edna Valley wineries** (www.slowine.com), known for Chardonnays and Pinots.

Sleeping

San Luis Obispo's motel row is north of downtown along Monterey St, with cheaper chains along Hwy 101.

Peach Tree Inn MOTEL **$$**
(☎805-543-3170; www.peachtreeinn.com; 2001 Monterey St; r incl breakfast $79-200; ❄@📶) Folksy, nothing-fancy motel rooms are relaxing, especially those set creekside or with rocking chairs overlooking a rose garden. Hearty breakfasts include homemade breads.

WHAT THE...?

The fabulously campy **Madonna Inn** (☎805-543-3000; www.madonnainn.com; 100 Madonna Rd; r $179-299; ❄📶🏊) is a garish confection visible from Hwy 101. Japanese tourists, vacationing Midwesterners and irony-loving hipsters adore the 110 themed rooms – including Yosemite Rock, Caveman and hot-pink Floral Fantasy (check out photos online). The urinal in the men's room is a bizarre waterfall. But the best reason to stop here? Old-fashioned cookies from the storybook bakery.

HI Hostel Obispo HOSTEL $
(☎805-544-4678; www.hostelobispo.com; 1617 Santa Rosa St; dm $24-27, r from $45; ⊙check-in 8-10am & 4:30-10pm; @☜) Cozy solar-powered ecohostel inhabits a converted Victorian one block from the train station. Amenities include a kitchen and bike rentals (from $10 per day). No credit cards; BYOT (bring your own towel).

Eating & Drinking

Downtown overflows with cafes, restaurants, wine-tasting rooms, brewpubs and the USA's first solar-powered cinema, **Palm Theatre** (☎805-541-5161; www.thepalmtheatre.com; 817 Palm St), showing indie art-house flicks.

Luna Red FUSION $$$
(☎805-540-5243; www.lunaredslo.com; 1009 Monterey St; small plates $4-15, dinner mains $18-26; ⊙11am-9pm Mon-Thu, to 10pm Fri, 4-10pm Sat, 5-9pm Sun) A locally inspired chef spins Californian, Mediterranean and Asian tapas, with a keen eye toward freshness and spice, bounty from the land and sea, and crazily creative cocktails, all with a surprisingly sophisticated ambience.

Big Sky Café CALIFORNIAN $$$
(www.bigskycafe.com; 1121 Broad St; mains $6-22; ⊙7am-9pm Mon-Wed, to 10pm Thu-Fri, 8am-10pm Sat, 8am-9pm Sun; ✍) With the tagline 'analog food for a digital world,' this airy, ecoconscious cafe gets top marks for market-fresh breakfasts (served until 1pm daily), although big-plate dinners trend toward bland.

Firestone Grill BARBECUE $$
(www.firestonegrill.com; 1001 Higuera St; mains $5-12; ⊙11am-10pm Sun-Wed, to 11pm Thu-Sun; 👪) Sink your teeth into an authentic Santa Maria–style tri-tip steak sandwich on a toasted garlic roll, or a rack of succulent pork ribs.

Information

Car-free SLO (http://slocarfree.org) Helpful website for ecotravel tips and valuable discounts.

Visitor center (☎805-781-2777; www.visitslo.com; 1039 Chorro St; ⊙10am-5pm Sun-Wed, to 7pm Thu-Sat) Downtown, off Higuera St.

Getting There & Around

Amtrak (1011 Railroad Ave) Daily Seattle–LA *Coast Starlight* and twice-daily *Pacific Surfliner* trains stop 0.6 miles east of downtown en route to/from Santa Barbara ($29, 2¾ hours) and LA ($34, 5½ hours).

Greyhound (1023 Railroad Ave) Runs a few daily buses to Santa Barbara ($26, 2¼ hours), LA ($38, 5¼ hours) or San Francisco ($48, 6½ hours).

SLO Regional Transit Authority (☎805-541-2228; www.slorta.org; fares $1.50-3, day pass $5) County-wide buses with limited weekend services converge on downtown's **transit center** (cnr Palm & Osos Sts).

Morro Bay to Hearst Castle

A dozen miles northwest of SLO via Hwy 1, **Morro Bay** is home to a commercial fishing fleet and Morro Rock, a volcanic peak jutting up from the ocean floor – your first hint of the coast's upcoming drama. (Too bad about those power-plant smokestacks obscuring the views, though.) Buy boat-tour tickets and rent kayaks along the Embarcadero, where **Giovanni's Fish Market & Galley** (www.giovannisfishmarket.com; 1001 Front St; mains $7-13; ⊙9am-6pm; 👪), a classic California seafood shack, cooks killer garlic fries and fish-and-chips. Midrange motels cluster uphill off Harbor and Main Sts. Downtown's **Shine Café** (www.sunshinehealthfoods-shinecafe.com; 415 Morro Bay Blvd; mains $5-14; ⊙11am-5pm Mon-Fri, from 9am Sat, 10am-4pm Sun; ✍) offers takeout karma-cleansers like tempeh tacos and tofu scrambles.

Nearby are fantastic state parks for coastal hiking and **camping** (☎reservations 800-444-7275; www.reserveamerica.com). South of the Embarcadero, **Morro Bay State Park** (www.parks.ca.gov; tent/RV sites $35/50) has a natural-history museum and heron rookery. Further south in Los Osos, west of Hwy 1, wilder **Montaña de Oro State Park** (www.parks.ca.gov; campsites $20-25) features coastal bluffs, tide pools, sand dunes, peak-hiking and mountain-biking trails, and primitive camping. Its Spanish name ('mountain of gold') comes from native California poppies that blanket the hillsides in spring.

Heading north along Hwy 1, surfers love the Cal-Mexican **Taco Temple** (2680 Main St, Morro Bay; mains $7-13; ⊙11am-8:30pm Sun, to 9pm Mon & Wed-Sat), a cash-only joint, and **Ruddell's Smokehouse** (www.smokerkjim.com; 101 D St, Cayucos; items $5-12; ⊙11am-6pm), serving smoked-fish tacos by the beach in small-town Cayucos. Vintage motels line Cayucos' Ocean Ave, including cutesy, family-run **Seaside Motel** (☎805-995-3809; www.seasidemotel.com; 42 S Ocean Ave, Cayucos; d $80-160; ☜), offering kitchenettes. In a historic sea captain's home, **Cass House Inn** (☎805-995-3669; www.casshouseinn.com; 222 N Ocean Ave, Cayucos; d incl breakfast $165-325; 📶) has plush rooms, some with soaking tubs and antique fireplaces to ward off chilly coastal fog. Downstairs is a creative, seasonally inspired French-Californian **restaurant** (prix-fixe dinner $65; ⏲5-9pm Thu-Mon).

Less than 4 miles north of Hwy 46, which leads east into the vineyards of **Paso Robles wine country** (www.pasowine.com), quaint **Cambria** has lodgings along unearthly pretty Moonstone Beach. The charming, pet-friendly **Blue Dolphin Inn** (☎805-805-927-3300; www.cambriainns.com; 6470 Moonstone Beach Dr; d incl breakfast $159-329; 📶) harbors crisp, modern rooms with romantic fireplaces. Inland, **HI Cambria Bridge Street Inn** (☎805-927-7653; www.bridgestreetinncambria.com; 4314 Bridge St; dm $22-25, r $45-80, all with shared bath; ⏲check-in 5-9pm; 📶) sleeps like a hostel but feels like a grandmotherly B&B. The artisan cheese and wine shop **Indigo Moon** (www.indigomooncafe.com; 1980 Main St; lunch mains $6-13; ⏲10am-4pm Mon-Sat, to 3pm Sun, 5-9pm Wed-Sun) has breezy bistro tables, market-fresh salads and gourmet sandwiches for lunch. With a sunny patio and takeout counter, **Linn's Easy as Pie Cafe** (www.linnsfruitbin.com; 4251 Bridge St; mains $6-9; ⏲10am-7pm; 👪) is famous for its olallieberry pie and preserves.

Another 10 miles north of Cambria, hilltop **Hearst Castle** (☎805-927-2020; www.hearstcastle.org; tours adult/child from $25/12; ⏲tours from 9am) is California's most famous monument to wealth and ambition. William Randolph Hearst, the newspaper magnate, entertained Hollywood stars and royalty at this fantasy estate dripping with European antiques, accented by shimmering pools and surrounded by flowering gardens. Try to make tour reservations in advance, especially for Christmas holiday evening living-history programs. On the opposite side of Hwy 1, historic **Sebastian's Store** (442 San Simeon Rd; mains $7-12; ⏲11am-5pm Tue-Sun) sells cold drinks, Hearst Ranch beef burgers, giant deli sandwiches and salads for beach picnics. Five miles back south off Hwy 1, **San Simeon State Park** (☎reservations 800-444-7275; www.reserveamerica.com; campsites $20-35) has creekside campsites.

Heading north, Point Piedras Blancas is home to an enormous **elephant-seal colony** that breeds, molts, sleeps, frolics and, occasionally, goes aggro on the beach. Keep your distance from these wild animals who move faster on the sand than you can. The main viewpoint, 4.5 miles north of Hearst Castle, has interpretive panels. Seals haul out here year-round, but the exciting birthing and mating season runs January through March, peaking on Valentine's Day. Nearby, the 1875 **Piedras Blancas Lightstation** (☎805-927-7361; www.piedrasblancas.org; tours adult/child $10/5) is an outstandingly scenic spot.

Big Sur

Much ink has been spilled extolling the raw beauty and energy of this 100-mile stretch of craggy coastline shoehorned south of the Monterey Peninsula. More a state of mind than a place you can pinpoint on a map, Big Sur has no traffic lights, banks or strip malls. When the sun goes down, the moon and stars provide the only illumination – if summer fog hasn't extinguished them. Lodging, food and gas are all scarce and pricey. Demand for rooms is high year-round, so book ahead. The free, info-packed newspaper *Big Sur Guide* (www.bigsurcalifornia.org) is available everywhere along the way. The $10 parking fee at Big Sur's state parks is valid for same-day entry to all.

It's about 25 miles from Hearst Castle to blink-and-you-miss-it Gorda, home of **Treebones Resort** (☎877-424-4787; www.treebonesresort.com; 71895 Hwy 1; d with shared bath incl breakfast $169-199; 📶🏊), which offers back-to-nature cliff-top yurts, some with ocean-view decks. Don't expect much privacy though. Basic **USFS campgrounds** (☎877-444-6777; www.campone.com, www.recreation.gov; campsites $22) are just off Hwy 1 at Plaskett Creek and Kirk Creek.

Ten miles north of Lucia is the new-agey **Esalen Institute** (☎831-667-3047; www.esalen.org; 55000 Hwy 1), famous for its esoteric workshops and ocean-view hot-springs baths. With a reservation you can frolic nekkid in the latter from 1am to 3am ($20, credit cards only). It's surreal.

Three miles north, **Julia Pfeiffer Burns State Park** harbors California's only coastal waterfall, 80ft-high McWay Falls, which is reached via a quarter-mile stroll. Two more miles north, a steep dirt trail descends from a hairpin turn on Hwy 1 to **Partington Cove**, a raw and breathtaking spot where crashing surf salts your skin – truly scenic, but swimming isn't safe.

Around 7 miles further north, nestled among redwoods and wisteria, the quaint restaurant at **Deetjen's Inn** (☎831-667-2377; www.deetjens.com; 48865 Hwy 1; mains breakfast $10-12, dinner $24-36; ⏲8-11:30am & 6-9pm) serves country-style comfort food. Just north, the beatnik **Henry Miller Memorial Library** (☎831-667-2574; www.henrymiller.org; Hwy 1; ⏲11am-6pm Wed-Mon; @📶) is the art and soul of Big Sur bohemia, with a jam-packed bookstore, live-music concerts and DJs, open-mic nights and outdoor film screenings. Opposite, food takes a backseat to dramatic ocean views at cliff-top **Nepenthe** (☎831-667-2345; 48510 Hwy 1; mains $14-39; ⏲11:30am-10pm), meaning 'island of no sorrow.' Its Ambrosia burger is mighty famous.

Heading north, USFS rangers at **Big Sur Station** (☎831-667-2315; ⏲8am-4pm Wed-Sun Nov-Mar, daily Apr-Oct) can clue you in about hiking trail conditions and camping options. They also issue overnight parking ($5) and campfire permits (free) for backpacking trips into the Ventana Wilderness, including the popular 10-mile trek to Sykes Hot Springs. Across the road, turn onto obscurely marked Sycamore Canyon Rd, which drops two narrow, twisting miles to crescent-shaped **Pfeiffer Beach** (per car $5; ⏲9am-8pm), with a towering offshore sea arch and strong currents too dangerous for swimming. But dig down into the sand – it's purple!

Next up, **Pfeiffer Big Sur State Park** is crisscrossed by sun-dappled trails through redwood forests, including a 1.4-mile round-trip to seasonal Pfeiffer Falls. Make campground **reservations** (☎800-444-7275; www.reserveamerica.com; campsites $35-50) or stay at the rambling, old-fashioned **Big Sur Lodge** (☎831-667-3100; www.bigsurlodge.com; 47225 Hwy 1; d $199-319; 🏊), which has rustic attached cottages (some with kitchens and wood-burning fireplaces), a well-stocked general store and a simple **restaurant** (mains $9-27; ⏲7:30am-9pm; 👪).

Most of Big Sur's commercial activity is concentrated along the next 2 miles, including a post office, shops, gas stations, private campgrounds, motels and restaurants. At **Glen Oaks Motel** (☎831-667-2105; www.glenoaksbigsur.com; Hwy 1; d $175-350; 📶), a chic, redesigned 1950s redwood-and-adobe motor lodge, snug rooms and woodsy cabins all have gas fireplaces. Pick up a giant burrito or deli sandwich at the Big Sur River Inn's **general store** (http://bigsurdeli.com; 47520 Hwy 1; dishes $1.50-7; ⏲7am-8pm). Nearby, **Maiden Publick House** (☎831-667-2355) has an encyclopedic beer menu and live-music jams.

Heading north, many visitors overlook **Andrew Molera State Park**, a trail-laced pastiche of grassy meadows, waterfalls, ocean bluffs, rugged beaches and wildlife watching. Learn all about endangered California condors at the park's **Discovery Center** (☎831-620-0702; www.ventanaws.org; admission free; ⏲9am-4pm Fri-Sun late May–mid-Sep) and the on-site bird-banding lab. From the parking lot, a half-mile trail leads to a first-come, first-served **campground** (tent sites $25).

Six miles before the famous Bixby Bridge, take a tour of 1889 **Point Sur Lightstation** (☎831-625-4419; www.pointsur.org; tour adult/child from $10/5). Meet your guide at the locked gate a quarter-mile north of Point Sur Naval Facility; arrive early because space is limited (no reservations).

Carmel

Once a bohemian artists' seaside resort, quaint Carmel-by-the-Sea now has the well-manicured feel of a country club. Simply plop down in any cafe and watch the parade of behatted ladies toting fancy-label shopping bags to lunch and dapper gents driving top-down convertibles along Ocean Ave, the village's slow-mo main drag.

👁 Sights & Activities

Not always sunny, Carmel Beach is a gorgeous white-sand crescent, where pampered pups excitedly run off-leash.

Point Lobos State Reserve PARK
(www.pointlobos.org; per car $10; ⏲8am-30min after sunset) They bark, they bray, they bathe and they're fun to watch – sea lions are the stars here, 4 miles south of Carmel, where a dramatically rocky coastline offers excellent tide-pooling. The full perimeter hike is 6 miles, but shorter walks take in Bird Island, Piney Woods and the Whalers Cabin. Arrive early on weekends; parking is limited.

San Carlos Borroméo de Carmelo Mission CHURCH
(www.carmelmission.org; 3080 Rio Rd; adult/child $6.50/2; ⏲9:30am-5pm Mon-Sat, from 10:30am Sun) A mile south of downtown, this gorgeous mission is an oasis of calm and solemnity,

ensconced in flowering gardens. Its stone basilica is filled with original art, while a separate chapel holds the memorial tomb of California missions founder Junípero Serra.

Tor House HISTORIC BUILDING
(☎831-624-1813; www.torhouse.org; 26304 Ocean View Ave; tour adult/child $10/5; ⏰10am-3pm Fri & Sat) Even if you've never heard of 20th-century poet Robinson Jeffers, a pilgrimage to this house, which was built with his own hands, offers fascinating insights into bohemian Old Carmel (reservations required). A porthole in the Celtic-inspired Hawk Tower reputedly came from the wrecked ship that carried Napoleon from Elba.

Eating & Drinking

La Bicyclette FRENCH, ITALIAN $$$
(www.labicycletterestaurant.com; Dolores St, at 7th Ave; lunch mains $7-16, 3-course prix-fixe dinner $28; ⏰11:30am-4pm & 5-10pm) Rustic European comfort food using seasonal local ingredients packs canoodling couples into this bistro, with an open kitchen delivering wood-fired pizzas. Excellent local wines by the glass.

Mundaka TAPAS $$
(www.mundakacarmel.com; San Carlos St, btwn Ocean & 7th Aves; small plates $4-19; ⏰5:30-10pm Sun-Wed, to 11pm Thu-Sat) This courtyard hideaway is a svelte escape from Carmel's stuffy 'newly wed and nearly dead' crowd. Take Spanish tapas plates for a spin and sip housemade sangria while DJs or flamenco guitars play.

Carmel Belle CALIFORNIAN $$
(www.carmelbelle.com; Doud Craft Studios, cnr Ocean Ave & San Carlos St; brunch mains $5-12; ⏰8am-5pm) Fresh, often organic ingredients flow from Carmel Valley farms onto tables at this charcuterie, cheese and wine shop hidden in a mini mall.

Bruno's Market & Deli GROCERY STORE $
(www.brunosmarket.com; cnr 6th & Junípero Aves; sandwiches $5-8; ⏰7am-8pm) Makes a saucy tri-trip beef sandwich and stocks all the accoutrements for a beach picnic.

Monterey

Working-class Monterey is all about the sea. Today it lures visitors with a top-notch aquarium that's a veritable temple to Monterey Bay's underwater universe. A National Marine Sanctuary since 1992, the bay begs for exploration by kayak, boat, scuba or snorkel. Meanwhile, downtown's historic quarter preserves California's Spanish and Mexican roots. Don't waste too much time on the tourist ghettos of Fisherman's Wharf and Cannery Row, the latter immortalized by novelist John Steinbeck back when it was the hectic, smelly epicenter of the sardine-canning industry, Monterey's lifeblood till the 1950s.

Sights

Monterey Bay Aquarium AQUARIUM
(☎831-648-4800, tickets 866-963-9645; www.montereybayaquarium.org; 886 Cannery Row; adult/child $30/20; ⏰10am-5pm Sep-May, 9:30am-6pm Mon-Fri, to 8pm Sat & Sun Jun-Aug) We dare you not to be mesmerized and enriched by this ecoconscious aquarium. Give yourself at least half a day to see sharks and sardines play hide-and-seek in kelp forests, observe the antics of frisky otters, meditate upon ethereal jellyfish and get touchy-feely with sea cucumbers, bat rays and other tide-pool creatures. Feeding times are best, especially for watching penguins. To avoid the worst crowds, get tickets in advance and arrive when the doors open.

Monterey State Historic Park PARK
(☎831-998-9458; www.parks.ca.gov; tours $3-10) Downtown, Old Monterey has a cluster of lovingly restored 19th-century brick-and-adobe buildings, including novelist Robert Louis Stevenson's one-time boarding house and the Cooper-Molera Adobe, a sea captain's house. Admission to the gardens is free, but the buildings' opening hours and tour times vary. Pick up walking-tour maps and check schedules at the **Pacific House Museum** (☎831-649-7118; 20 Custom House Plaza; ⏰10am-4:30pm), which has in-depth period exhibits on California's multinational history.

Monterey History & Maritime Museum MUSEUM
(☎831-372-2608; http://montereyhistory.org; 5 Custom House Plaza; admission $5; ⏰11am-5pm Wed-Sat, 1-4pm Sun) Near the waterfront, this voluminous modern exhibition hall illuminates Monterey's salty past, including the roller-coaster-like rise and fall of the local sardine industry that brought Cannery Row to life. Gems include a ship-in-a-bottle collection and the historic Fresnel lens from Point Sur Lightstation.

Point Pinos Lighthouse LIGHTHOUSE (www.ci.pg.ca.us/lighthouse; adult/child $2/1; ⏲1-4pm Thu-Mon) The West Coast's oldest continuously operating lighthouse has been warning ships off this peninsula's hazardous point since 1855. Inside are exhibits on its history and its failures: local shipwrecks.

FREE **Monarch Grove Sanctuary** PARK (www.ci.pg.ca.us/monarchs; Ridge Rd, Pacific Grove; ⏲dawn-dusk) Between October and February, migratory monarch butterflies cluster in a thicket of eucalyptus trees off Lighthouse Ave.

Activities

Diving and snorkeling reign supreme, although the water is rather frigid, even in summer. Year-round, Fisherman's Wharf is the launch pad for whale-watching trips. Another favorite four-seasons activity is walking or cycling the paved 18-mile **Monterey Peninsula Recreation Trail**, which edges the coast past Cannery Row, ending at Lovers Point in Pacific Grove. The overhyped **17-Mile Drive** (www.pebblebeach.com; per car/bicycle $9.50/free) toll road connects Monterey and Pacific Grove with Carmel-by-the-Sea.

Monterey Bay Kayaks KAYAKING (☎800-649-5357; www.montereybaykayaks.com; 693 Del Monte Ave; rental kayak per day $30-50, tours adult/child from $50/40) Kayak and SUP rentals, lessons and guided tours of Monterey Bay and Elkhorn Slough, including full-moon paddles.

Sanctuary Cruises WHALE-WATCHING (☎831-917-1042; www.sanctuarycruises.com; adult/child under 3yr/child 3-12yr $48/10/38) Departing from Moss Landing, 20 miles north of Monterey, this biodiesel boat runs recommended whale-watching and dolphin-spotting tours (reservations essential).

Monterey Bay Dive Charters SCUBA DIVING (☎831-383-9276; www.mbdcscuba.com; scuba rental $79, shore/boat dive from $49/199) Rent a full scuba kit including wetsuit, book a small-group dive or take the plunge with a three-hour beginners' dive experience ($159, no PADI certification required).

Adventures by the Sea KAYAKING, CYCLING (☎831-372-1807; www.adventuresbythesea.com; 299 Cannery Row & 210 Alvarado St; rental kayak per day $30, bicycle per hr/day $7/25) Also offers sunset kayaking tours at Lovers Point and SUP rentals and lessons.

Bay Bikes CYCLING (☎831-655-2453; www.baybikes.com; 585 Cannery Row; per hr/day from $8/32) Cruiser, tandem, hybrid and mountain-bike rentals near the aquarium.

Sleeping

Skip the frills and save a bunch of dough at chain and indie motels along Munras Ave south of downtown or on N Fremont St, east of Hwy 1.

InterContinental–Clement HOTEL $$$ (☎831-375-4500; www.intercontinental.com; 750 Cannery Row; r $200-455; ❄@📶≋👪) Like an upscale version of a millionaire's seaside clapboard house, this sparkling resort presides over Cannery Row. For utmost luxury, book an ocean-view suite with a balcony and private fireplace, then breakfast in bayfront C Restaurant. Parking $18.

TOP CHOICE **Asilomar Conference Grounds** LODGE $$ (☎831-372-8016; www.visitasilomar.com; 800 Asilomar Ave, Pacific Grove; r incl breakfast $115-175; 📶≋👪) Coastal state-park lodge has buildings designed by architect Julia Morgan, of Hearst Castle fame. Historic rooms are small and thin-walled, but charming nonetheless. The lodge's fireside rec room has ping-pong and pool tables. Bicycle rentals available.

Monterey Hotel HOTEL $$$ (☎831-375-3184; www.montereyhotel.com; 406 Alvarado St; r $70-310; 📶) Right downtown, this quaint 1904 edifice harbors small, somewhat noisy but freshly renovated rooms sporting reproduction Victorian furniture. No elevator. Parking $17.

HI Monterey Hostel HOSTEL $ (☎831-649-0375; www.montereyhostel.org; 778 Hawthorne St; dm $25-28, r $59-75; ⏲check-in 4-10pm; @) Four blocks from Cannery Row, this simple, clean hostel is just the ticket for backpackers on a budget (reservations strongly recommended). No private bathrooms. Take MST bus 1 from downtown's Transit Plaza.

Veterans Memorial Park CAMPGROUND $ (☎831-646-3865; www.monterey.org; campsites $27) Forested hilltop public campground has 40 well-kept, grassy nonreservable sites with hot showers, drinking water and fire pits (three-day maximum stay).

Eating & Drinking

Many more eateries, bars, live-music venues and cinemas line Cannery Row and downtown's Alvarado St.

TOP CHOICE **Passionfish** SEAFOOD $$$
(☎831-655-3311; www.passionfish.net; 701 Lighthouse Ave, Pacific Grove; mains $17-26; ⊙5-10pm) Eureka! Finally, a perfect, chef-owned seafood restaurant where the sustainable fish is dock-fresh, every preparation fully flavored and the wine list more than affordable. Reservations recommended.

First Awakenings DINER $$
(www.firstawakenings.net; American Tin Cannery, 125 Oceanview Blvd, Pacific Grove; mains $5-12; ⊙7am-2pm Mon-Fri, to 2:30pm Sat & Sun; 🚻) Sweet and savory creative breakfasts and lunches, plus bottomless pitchers of coffee, make this hideaway cafe in an outlet mall near the aquarium worth seeking out.

Montrio Bistro CALIFORNIAN $$$
(☎831-648-8880; www.montrio.com; 414 Calle Principal; mains $14-29; ⊙5-10pm Sun-Thu, to 11pm Fri & Sat; 🚻) Inside a 1910 firehouse, this classy restaurant's tables are covered in butcher paper with crayons for kids. Seasonal New American cooking and Monterey County wines satisfy.

East Village Coffee Lounge CAFE $
(www.eastvillagecoffeelounge.com; 498 Washington St; snacks & drinks $3-6; ⊙6am-late Mon-Fri, from 7am Sat & Sun) Sleek coffeehouse with a liquor license and live-music, DJ and open-mic nights.

Crêpes of Brittany SNACKS $
(www.vivalecrepemonterey.com; 6 Old Fisherman's Wharf; snacks $4-9; ⊙8:30am-7pm Sun-Thu, to 8pm Sun) Authentic savory and sweet crepes swirled by a French expat; expect long lines and shorter hours in winter.

Information

Visitor center (☎831-657-6400; www.seemonterey.com; 401 Camino El Estero; ⊙9am-6pm Mon-Sat, to 5pm Sun, closing 1hr earlier Nov-Mar) Ask for a free *Monterey County Film & Literary Map.*

Getting Around

Monterey-Salinas Transit (☎888-678-2871; www.mst.org; fares $1-3, day pass $8) Local buses converge on downtown's Transit Plaza (cnr Pearl and Alvarado Sts), including routes to Pacific Grove, Carmel, Big Sur and Salinas. In summer, a free trolley loops around downtown Monterey and Cannery Row daily from 10am until 7pm or later.

Santa Cruz

SoCal beach culture meets NorCal counterculture in Santa Cruz. The UCSC student population makes this old-school radical town youthful, hip and lefty-political. Some worry that Santa Cruz's weirdness quotient is dropping, but you'll disagree when you witness the freak show (and we say that with love) along Pacific Ave, downtown's main drag. For the beach and boardwalk, head south.

Sights & Activities

In Santa Cruz most of the action takes place at the beach.

Beach Boardwalk AMUSEMENT PARK
(☎831-423-5590; www.beachboardwalk.com; 400 Beach St; rides $3-5, all-day pass $30; ⊙daily May-Sep, off-season hr vary) A short walk from the municipal wharf, this slice of Americana boasts the West Coast's oldest beachfront amusement park, with the 1924 Giant Dipper roller coaster and 1911 Looff carousel. Free Friday-night summer concerts.

Surfing Museum MUSEUM
(www.santacruzsurfingmuseum.org; 701 W Cliff Dr; donations welcome; ⊙noon-4pm Thu-Mon Sep-Jun, 10am-5pm Wed-Mon Jul & Aug) About a mile south along the coast, the old lighthouse is packed with memorabilia, including vintage redwood boards. It overlooks experts-only **Steamers Lane** and beginners' **Cowell's**, both popular surf breaks.

Natural Bridges State Beach BEACH
(www.parks.ca.gov; per car $10; ⊙8am-sunset) Further west, this beach bookends a scenic coastal drive or cycle, about 3 miles from the wharf. There are tide pools for exploring and leafy trees in which monarch butterflies roost from October through February.

Seymour Marine Discovery Center MUSEUM
(www2.ucsc.edu/seymourcenter; end of Delaware Ave; adult/child $6/4; ⊙10am-5pm Tue-Sat, from noon Sun, plus 10am-5pm Mon Jul & Aug) University-run Long Marine Lab has cool interactive science exhibits for kids, including touch tanks, with the world's largest blue-whale skeleton outside.

Santa Cruz State Parks HIKING
(www.santacruzstateparks.org; per car $10; sunrise-sunset) Streamside trails through old-growth redwood forests await at Henry Cowell Redwoods and Big Basin Redwoods, off Hwy 9 north in the Santa Cruz Mountains, and the Forest of Nisene Marks, off Hwy 1 south near Aptos. Mountain bikers ride Wilder Ranch, off Hwy 1 west.

Roaring Camp Railroads TRAIN RIDES
(831-335-4484; www.roaringcamp.com; adult/child from $24/17) For family fun, hop aboard a narrow-gauge steam train up into the redwoods or a standard-gauge train leaving from the beach boardwalk. Check the website or call ahead for seasonal opening hours.

Venture Quest KAYAKING
(831-427-2267; www.kayaksantacruz.com; Municipal Wharf; kayak rentals/tours/lessons from $30/55/85; 10am-7pm Mon-Fri, from 9am Jun-Sep, off-season hr vary) Experience the craggy coastline with sea-cave and whale-watching kayak tours, including to Elkhorn Slough and moonlight paddles.

Santa Cruz Surf School SURFING
(831-426-7072; www.santacruzsurfschool.com; 322 Pacific Ave; 2hr lesson $80-90) Near the wharf, these folks can get you out there, all equipment included.

O'Neill Surf Shop SURFING
(831-475-4151; www.oneill.com; 1115 41st Ave; wetsuit/surfboard rental $10/20; 9am-8pm Mon-Fri, from 8am Sat & Sun) Head east to Capitola to this internationally renowned surfboard maker. Downtown branch is at 110 Cooper St.

Sleeping

For motels, try Ocean St near downtown and Mission St by the UCSC campus. Make **reservations** (800-444-7275; www.reserveamerica.com; campsites $35-65) for state-park campgrounds at nearby beaches and in the Santa Cruz Mountains.

Dream Inn HOTEL $$$
(831-426-4330; www.dreaminnsantacruz.com; 175 W Cliff Dr; r $200-380;) Overlooking the wharf from its hillside perch, this retro-chic boutique-on-the-cheap hotel is as stylish as Santa Cruz gets. Rooms have all mod cons, while the beach is just steps away. Hit happy hour at ocean-view Aquarius restaurant.

Adobe on Green B&B B&B $$
(831-469-9866; www.adobeongreen.com; 103 Green St; r incl breakfast $149-199;) Peace and quiet are the mantras here. The hosts are practically invisible, but their thoughtful touches are everywhere: from boutique-style amenities inside spacious, stylish and solar-powered rooms to breakfast spreads from the organic gardens.

Pacific Blue Inn B&B $$$
(831-600-8880; http://pacificblueinn.com; 636 Pacific Ave; r incl breakfast $170-240;) Downtown courtyard B&B is truly ecoconscious, with water-saving fixtures and renewable and recycled building materials. Clean-lined rooms have pillow-top beds, fireplaces and flat-screen TVs with DVD players. Free loaner bikes.

Pelican Point Inn INN $$
(831-475-3381; www.pelicanpointinn-santacruz.com; 21345 E Cliff Dr; ste $99-199; @) Ideal for families, these roomy apartment-style lodgings near kid-friendly Twin Lakes Beach are equipped with everything you'll need for a lazy beach vacation, including kitchenettes and high-speed internet. Weekly rates available.

HI Santa Cruz Hostel HOSTEL $
(831-423-8304; www.hi-santacruz.org; 321 Main St; dm $25-28, r $55-105; check-in 5-10pm; @) Budget overnighters dig this cute hostel at the Carmelita Cottages in a flowery garden setting, two blocks from the beach. One bummer: the 11pm curfew. Make reservations. Shared bath.

Eating

Downtown, especially Pacific Ave, is chockablock with just-OK cafes. Mission St near the UCSC campus and neighboring Capitola offer cheap takeout and ethnic eats.

Soif BISTRO $$$
(831-423-2020; www.soifwine.com; 105 Walnut Ave; small plates $5-17, mains $19-28; 5-10pm Sun-Thu, to 11pm Fri & Sat) Downtown wine shop where bon vivants flock for a heady selection of 50 international wines by the glass paired with a sophisticated, seasonally driven Euro-Cal menu.

Engfer Pizza Works PIZZERIA $$$
(www.engferpizzaworks.com; 537 Seabright Ave; pizzas $8-23; 4-9:30pm Tue-Sun;) Detour to find this old factory, where wood-fired pizzas

are made from scratch with love – the no-name specialty is almost like a giant salad on roasted bread. Play ping-pong and down draft microbrews while you wait.

Tacos Moreno MEXICAN $
(www.tacosmoreno.com; 1053 Water St; dishes $2-6; ⏲11am-8pm) Who cares how long the line is, especially at lunchtime? Seekers will find taqueria heaven here – from pork, chicken and beef soft tacos and quesadillas to stuffed burritos.

Penny Ice Creamery DESSERT $
(www.thepennyicecreamery.com; 913 Cedar St; items $2-4; ⏲noon-9pm Sun-Wed, to 11pm Thu-Sat) With a cult following, this artisan ice-cream shop makes zany flavors from scratch using wild local ingredients like avocado, roasted barley or cherry balsamic.

Drinking & Entertainment

Pacific Ave downtown is jam-packed with bars, live-music lounges and coffeehouses. Check the free *Santa Cruz Weekly* (www.santacruzweekly.com) tabloid for more venues and events.

Caffe Pergolesi CAFE
(www.theperg.com; 418 Cedar St; ⏲7am-11pm; wi-fi) On a leafy sidewalk verandah, discuss art and conspiracy theories over strong coffee, organic juices or beer.

Santa Cruz Mountain Brewing BREWERY
(www.santacruzmountainbrewing.com; 402 Ingalls St; ⏲noon-10pm) Bold, organic brews west of downtown off Mission St, squeezed between local winery tasting rooms.

Surf City Billiards & Café BAR
(www.surfcitybilliards.com; 931 Pacific Ave; ⏲4-11pm Mon-Thu, to 1am Fri & Sat, 10am-11pm Sun) For shooting stick, dartboards, big-screen TVs and darn good pub grub.

Moe's Alley MUSIC
(☎831-479-1854; www.moesalley.com; 1535 Commercial Way) Tiny venue for jazz, blues, folk, rock, reggae and world beats.

Kuumbwa Jazz Center MUSIC
(☎831-427-2227; www.kuumbwajazz.org; 320 Cedar St) Books big-name jazz sounds.

Information

KPIG (107.5 FM) Plays the classic Santa Cruz soundtrack – think Bob Marley, Janis Joplin and Willie Nelson.

Visitor center (☎831-425-1234; www.santacruzca.org; 303 Water St; ⏲9am-5pm Mon-Fri, 10am-4pm Sat & Sun; @) Free public internet terminal.

Getting There & Away

Greyhound (920 Pacific Ave) A few daily buses to San Francisco ($16, three hours), Santa Barbara ($50, six hours) and Los Angeles ($57, nine hours).

Santa Cruz Metro (☎831-425-8600; www.scmtd.com; single ride/day pass $1.50/4.50) Local and regional buses converge on downtown's Metro Center (920 Pacific Ave).

Santa Cruz to San Francisco

Far more scenic than any freeway, this curvaceous, 70-mile stretch of coastal Hwy 1 is bordered by wild beaches, organic farm stands and sea-salted villages, all scattered like loose diamonds in the rough.

About 20 miles northwest of Santa Cruz, **Año Nuevo State Park** (☎tour reservations 800-444-4445; www.parks.ca.gov; per car $10, tour per person $7; ⏲8:30am-3:30pm Apr-Aug, to 3pm Sep-Nov, tours mid-Dec–Mar) is home base for the world's largest colony of northern elephant seals. Call ahead to reserve space on a 2½-hour, 3-mile guided walking tour, given during the cacophonous winter birthing and mating season. On a quiet windswept coastal perch further north, green-certified **HI Pigeon Point Lighthouse Hostel** (☎650-879-0633; www.norcalhostels.org/pigeon; dm $24-29, r $72-156; ⏲check-in 3:30-10:30pm; @ wi-fi) inhabits historic lightkeepers' quarters. It's popular (especially for its cliff-top hot tub), so book ahead.

Five miles north, **Pescadero State Beach & Marsh Natural Preserve** (www.parks.ca.gov; per car $8; ⏲8am-sunset) attracts beachcombers and birders. Inland Pescadero village is home to famed **Duarte's Tavern** (☎650-879-0464; www.duartestavern.com; 202 Stage Rd; mains $8-35; ⏲7am-9pm), where creamy artichoke soup and homemade pies are crowd-pleasers. For a beach picnic, visit the bakery-deli at **Arcangeli Grocery Co** (287 Stage Rd; ⏲10am-6pm) and family-owned **Harley Farms Cheese Shop** (250 North St; ⏲11am-5pm), which offers weekend goat-dairy farm tours.

Less than 20 miles north, busy Half Moon Bay is defined by pretty **Half Moon Bay State Beach** (www.parks.ca.gov; per car $10, campsites $35-50), offering scenic campsites. To get out on the water, talk to **Half Moon**

Bay Kayak (☎650-773-6101; www.hmbkayak.com; 2 Johnson Dr, Pillar Point Harbor; kayak rentals from $20, tours $65-150). For oceanfront luxury, the pet-friendly **Inn at Mavericks** (☎650-728-1572; www.innatmavericks.com; 364 Princeton Ave; r $199-239; 📶) offers spacious, romantic roosts. It overlooks Pillar Point Harbor, which has a decent brewpub with a sunset-view patio. Back south in Half Moon Bay's quaint downtown, cafes, restaurants and eclectic shops line Main St, just inland from Hwy 1. Nearby, **Flying Fish Grill** (www.flyingfishgrill.net; 211 San Mateo Rd; dishes $5-15; ⏲11am-8pm) is the tastiest seafood shack around.

Six miles north of downtown, follow the signs to **Moss Beach Distillery** (www.mossbeachdistillery.com; 140 Beach Way; appetizers $4-30; ⏲noon-8:30pm Mon-Thu, to 9pm Fri & Sat, 11am-8:30pm Sun), a historic bootleggers' joint with a dog-friendly deck for sunset drinks. Just north, **Fitzgerald Marine Reserve** (http://fitzgeraldreserve.org; California St, off Hwy 1) protects tide pools teeming with colorful sea life. Another mile north, **HI Point Montara Lighthouse Hostel** (☎650-728-7177; www.norcalhostels.org; Hwy 1 & 16th St; dm $26-31, r $70-105; ⏲check-in 3:30-10:30pm; @📶) is an airy, ecofriendly hostel with a small private beach (reservations essential). From there, it's just 20 more miles to San Francisco via Devil's Slide.

SAN FRANCISCO & THE BAY AREA

San Francisco

If you've ever wondered where the envelope goes when it's pushed, here's your answer. Psychedelic drugs, newfangled technology, gay liberation, green ventures, free speech and culinary experimentation all became mainstream long ago in San Francisco. After 160 years of booms and busts, losing your shirt has become a favorite local pastime at the clothing-optional Bay to Breakers race, Pride Parade and hot Sundays on Baker Beach. This is no place to be shy: out here among eccentrics of every stripe, no one's going to notice a few tan lines. So long, inhibitions; hello, San Francisco.

History

Oysters and acorn bread were prime dinner options in the Mexico-run Ohlone settlement of San Francisco c 1848 – but a year and some gold nuggets later, Champagne and chow mein were served by the bucket. Gold found in the nearby Sierra Nevada foothills had turned a waterfront village of 800 into a port city of 100,000 prospectors, con artists, prostitutes and honest folk trying to make an honest living – good luck telling which was which. That friendly bartender might drug your drink, and you'd wake up a mile from shore, shanghaied into service on some ship bound for Argentina.

By 1850 California was nabbed from Mexico and fast-tracked for US statehood, and San Francisco attempted to introduce public order to 200 saloons and untold numbers of brothels and gambling dens. Panic struck when Australia glutted the market with gold in 1854, and ire turned irrationally on SF's Chinese community, who from 1877 to 1945 were restricted to living and working in Chinatown by anti-Chinese laws. The main way out of debt was dangerous work building railroads for the city's robber barons, who dynamited, mined and clear-cut their way across the Golden West, and built grand Nob Hill mansions above Chinatown.

The city's lofty ambitions and 20-plus theaters came crashing down in 1906, when earthquake and fire left 3000 dead, 100,000 homeless and much of the city reduced to rubble – including almost every mansion on Nob Hill. Theater troupes and opera divas performed for free amid smoldering ruins downtown, establishing SF's tradition of free public performances in parks.

Ambitious public works projects continued through the 1930s, when Diego Rivera, Frida Kahlo and federally funded muralists began the tradition of leftist politics in paint visible in some 400 Mission murals.

WWII brought seismic shifts to San Francisco's community as women and African Americans working in San Francisco shipyards created a new economic boom, and President Franklin Delano Roosevelt's Executive Order 9066 mandated the internment of the city's historic Japanese American community. A 40-year court battle ensued, ending in an unprecedented apology from the US government. San Francisco became a testing ground for civil rights and free speech, with Beat poet Lawrence Ferlinghetti and City Lights Bookstore winning a landmark 1957 ruling against book banning over the publication of Allen Ginsberg's splendid, incendiary *Howl and Other Poems*.

San Francisco & the Bay Area

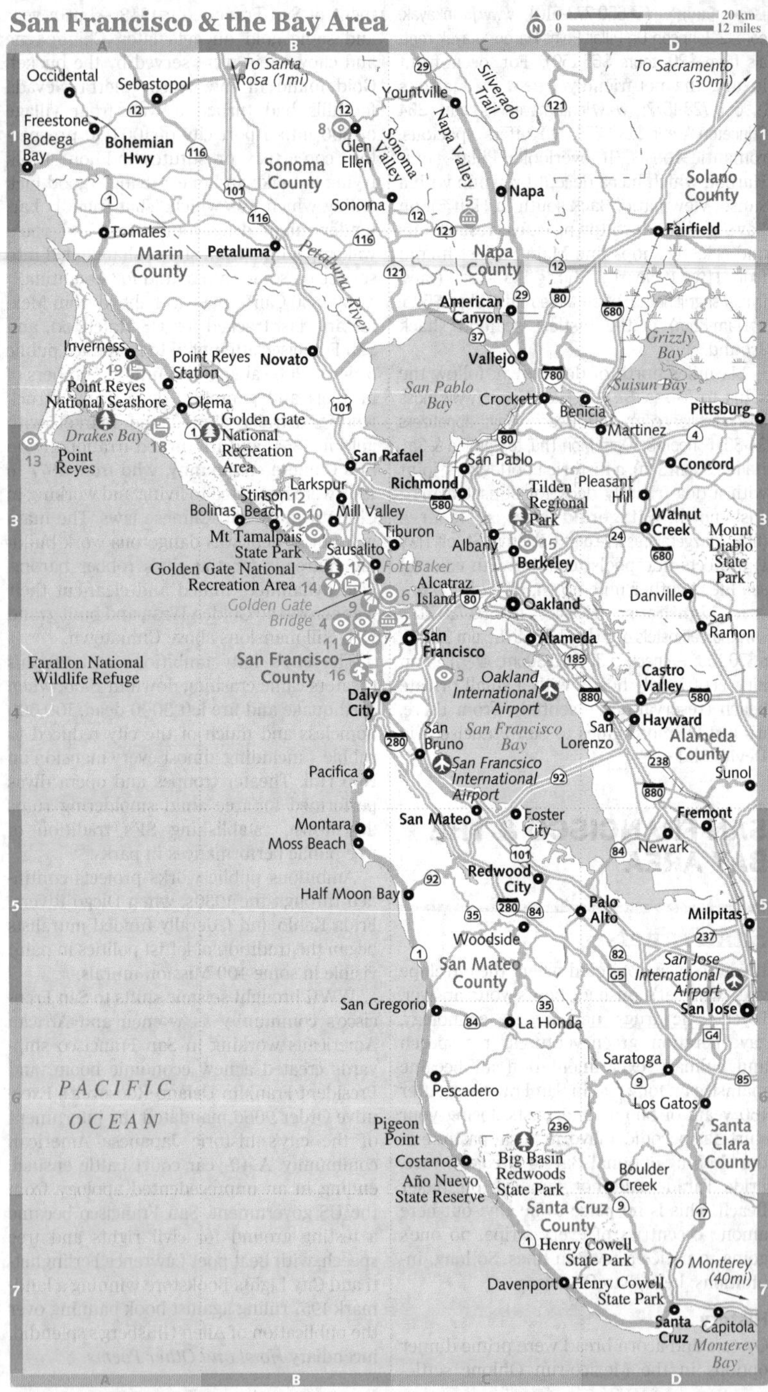

San Francisco & the Bay Area

Sights

1 Baker Beach B3
2 California Palace of the Legion of Honor B4
3 Candlestick Park C4
4 Cliff House B4
5 di Rosa Art + Nature Preserve C1
6 Fort Point C3
7 Golden Gate Park B4
8 Jack London Historic State Park B1
9 Lands End B4
10 Muir Woods National Monument B3
11 Ocean Beach B4
12 Pantoll Station B3
13 Point Reyes Lighthouse A3
14 Rodeo Beach B3
15 University of California, Berkeley C3

Activities, Courses & Tours

16 Aqua Surf Shop B4
Sutro Baths .... (see 4)

Sleeping

17 HI Marin Headlands Hostel B3
18 HI Point Reyes Hostel A3
19 Motel Inverness A2

The Central Intelligence Agency (CIA) hoped an experimental drug called LSD might turn San Francisco test subject Ken Kesey into the ultimate fighting machine, but instead the author of *One Flew Over the Cuckoo's Nest* slipped some into Kool-Aid and kicked off the psychedelic '60s. The Summer of Love meant free food, love and music in the Haight until the '70s, when enterprising gay hippies founded an out-and-proud community in the Castro. San Francisco witnessed devastating losses from AIDS in the 1980s, but the city rallied to become a model for disease treatment and prevention.

Geeks and cyberpunks converged on SF in the mid-1990s, spawning the web and dot-com boom – until the bubble popped in 2000. But risk-taking SF continues to float new ideas, and as recession hits elsewhere, social media, mobile apps and biotech are booming in San Francisco. Congratulations: you're just in time for San Francisco's next wild ride.

Sights

Let San Francisco's 43 hills and more than 80 arts venues stretch your legs and imagination, and take in some (literally) breathtaking views. The 7 x 7-mile city is laid out on a staid grid, but its main street is a diagonal contrarian streak called Market St. Downtown sights are within walking distance of Market St, but keep your city smarts and wits about you, especially around South of Market (SoMa) and the Tenderloin (5th to 9th Sts). SF's most historic landmarks are in the Mission, while exciting new destinations are inside Golden Gate Park.

SOMA

Cartoon Art Museum MUSEUM
(Map p126; ☎415-227-8666; www.cartoonart.org; 655 Mission St; adult/child $7/5; ⏲11am-5pm Tue-Sun) Comics earn serious consideration with shows of original *Watchmen* covers, too-hot-to-print political cartoons and lectures with local Pixar studio heads. Even fanboys will learn something from lectures about 1930s efforts to unionize overworked women animators, and shows on SF underground comics legends like R Crumb, Spain Rodriguez and Trina Robbins.

Contemporary Jewish Museum MUSEUM
(Map p126; ☎415-655-7800; www.jmsf.org; 736 Mission St, at 3rd St; adult/child $10/free; ⏲11am-5:30pm Fri-Tue, 1-8:30pm Thu) In 2008 architect Daniel Liebskind reshaped San Francisco's 1881 power plant with a blue steel extension to form the Hebrew word *l'chaim* ('to life'). Inside this architectural statement are lively shows, ranging from a retrospective of modern art instigator and Bay Area native Gertrude Stein to Linda Ellia's *Our Struggle: Artists Respond to Mein Kampf*, for which 600 artists from 17 countries were invited to alter one page of Hitler's book.

Museum of African Diaspora MUSEUM
(Map p126; ☎415-358-7200; www.moadsf.org; 685 Mission; adult/child $10/5; ⏲11am-6pm Wed-Sat, noon-5pm Sun) An international cast of characters tell the epic story of diaspora, from Ethiopian painter Qes Adamu Tesfaw's three-faced icons to quilts by India's Siddi community, descended from 16th-century African slaves. Themed interactive displays vary in interest and depth, but don't miss

SAN FRANCISCO IN...

One Day

Since the gold rush, great San Francisco adventures have started in **Chinatown**, where you can still find hidden fortunes – in cookies, that is. Beat it to **City Lights Bookstore** to revel in Beat poetry, then pass the **Transamerica Pyramid** en route to dumplings at **City View**. Hit **SFMOMA** and the downtown **gallery scene**, then head over to the **Asian Art Museum**, where art transports you across centuries and oceans within an hour. Toast hearts lost and inspiration found in SF with wine on tap and sensational small plates at **Frances**. End the night with silver-screen revivals at the **Castro Theatre**, or swaying to glam-rock anthems at **Café du Nord**.

Two Days

Start your day amid mural-covered garage doors lining **Balmy Alley**, then window-shop to **826 Valencia** for pirate supplies and ichthyoid antics in the Fish Theater. Break for burritos, then hoof it to the Haight for flashbacks at vintage boutiques and the Summer of Love site: **Golden Gate Park**. Glimpse Golden Gate Bridge views atop the **MH de Young Museum**, take a walk on the wild side inside the **California Academy of Sciences** rainforest dome, then dig into organic Cal-Moroccan feasts at **Aziza**.

the moving video of slave narratives recounted by Maya Angelou.

UNION SQUARE

The paved square is nothing special, but offers front-row seating for downtown drama: bejeweled theater-goers dodging clanging cable cars, trendy teens camped out overnight for limited-edition sneakers, and business travelers heading into the Tenderloin for entertainment too scandalous to include on expense reports. The action begins with shoppers clustered around the Powell St cable-car turnaround, gets dramatic along the Geary St Theater District and switches on the red lights south of Geary.

CIVIC CENTER

Asian Art Museum MUSEUM
(Map p126; ☎415-581-3500; www.asianart.org; 200 Larkin St; adult/child $12/7; ⊙10am-5pm Tue, Wed, Fri-Sun, to 9pm Thu) Imaginations race from ancient Persian miniatures to cutting-edge Japanese fashion through three floors spanning 6000 years of Asian arts. Besides the largest collection outside Asia – 17,000 works – the Asian offers excellent programs for all ages, from shadow-puppet shows and yoga for kids to monthly over-21 Matcha mixers with cross-cultural cocktails and DJ mashups.

City Hall HISTORIC BUILDING
(Map p126; ☎docent tours 415-554-6139; www.sfgsa.org; 400 Van Ness Ave; ⊙8am-8pm Mon-Fri, tours 10am, noon & 2pm Mon-Fri) Rising from the ashes of the 1906 earthquake, this beaux-arts building houses San Francisco's signature mixture of idealism, corruption and opposition politics under a splendid Tennessee pink marble and Colorado limestone rotunda. Historic firsts here include America's first sit-in on the grand staircase in 1960, the 1977 election and 1978 assassination of openly gay Supervisor Harvey Milk, and 4037 same-sex marriages in 2004. Intriguing art shows are in the basement and weekly Board of Supervisors meetings are open to the public (2pm Tuesday).

FINANCIAL DISTRICT

Back in its Barbary Coast heyday, loose change would buy you time with loose women in this neighborhood – now you'd be lucky to see a loose tie during happy hour. But the area still has redeeming quirks: a redwood grove has taken root in the remains of old whaling ships below the rocket-shaped **Transamerica Pyramid** (Map p126; www.thepyramidcenter.com; 600 Montgomery St), and eccentric art collectors descend from hilltop mansions for First Thursday gallery openings at **14 Geary**, **49 Geary** and **77 Geary** (Map p126; www.sfada.com; San Francisco Art Dealers Association; ⊙10:30am-5:30pm Tue-Fri, 11am-5pm Sat).

Ferry Building LANDMARK
(Map p126; ☎415-983-8000, www.ferrybuildingmarketplace.com; ⊙10am-6pm Mon-Fri, from 9am Sat, 11am-5pm Sun) Hedonism is alive and well at this transit hub turned gourmet empor-

ium, where foodies happily miss their ferries slurping local oysters and bubbly. Star chefs are frequently spotted at the **farmers market** (⏲10am-2pm Tue & Thu, from 8am Sat) that wraps around the building year-round.

CHINATOWN

Since 1848 this community has survived riots, earthquakes, bootlegging gangsters and politicians' attempts to relocate it down the coast.

Chinese Historical Society of America Museum MUSEUM
(CHSA; Map p126; ☎415-391-1188; www.chsa.org; 965 Clay St; adult/child $5/2, 1st Tue of month free; ⏲noon-5pm Tue-Fri, 11am-4pm Sat) Picture what it was like to be Chinese in America during the gold rush, transcontinental railroad construction or the Beat heyday at the nation's largest Chinese American historical institute. Rotating exhibits are across the courtyard in CHSA's graceful red-brick, green-tile-roofed landmark building, built as Chinatown's YWCA in 1932 by Julia Morgan, chief architect of Hearst Castle.

Chinese Culture Center GALLERY
(Map p126; ☎415-986-1822; www.c-c-c.org; 3rd fl, Hilton Hotel, 750 Kearny St; donation requested; ⏲10am-4pm Tue-Sat) You can see all the way to China on the 3rd floor of the Hilton inside this cultural center, which hosts exhibits of traditional Chinese arts; Xian Rui (Fresh & Sharp) cutting-edge art installations, such as Stella Zhang's discomfiting toothpick-studded pillows; and Art at Night, showcasing Chinese-inspired art, jazz and food. Check the center's online schedule for concerts, hands-on arts workshops, Mandarin classes, genealogy services and Chinatown arts festivals.

NORTH BEACH

Beat Museum MUSEUM
(Map p126; ☎800-537-6822; www.thebeatmuseum.org; 540 Broadway; admission $5; ⏲10am-7pm Tue-Sun) Beat writers Jack Kerouac, Allen Ginsberg and Lawrence Ferlinghetti made North Beach the proving ground for free spirits and free speech in the 1950s, as shown in this rambling, shambling museum of literary curios and vintage video. Entry to the bookstore and frequent readings are free.

RUSSIAN HILL & NOB HILL

Gardeners, fitness freaks and suckers for sunsets brave the climbs west of North Beach up Russian and Nob Hills. Drivers test themselves on the crooked 1000 block of Lombard St, but many obliviously roll past one of the best sunset vista points over the Golden Gate Bridge at **George Sterling Park** (Map p126) and a Diego Rivera mural at **Art Institute** (Map p126; ☎415-771-7020; www.sfai.edu; 800 Chestnut St; ⏲9am-7:30pm).

Grace Cathedral CHURCH
(Map p126; ☎415-749-6300; www.gracecathedral.com; 1100 California St; suggested donation adult/child $3/2; ⏲7am-6pm Mon-Fri, from 8am Sat, 8am-7pm Sun, services with choir 8:30am & 11am Sun) Take a shortcut to heaven: hop the cable car uphill to SF's progressive Episcopal church, where the AIDS Interfaith Memorial Chapel features a bronze Keith Haring altarpiece; stained-glass 'Human Endeavor' windows illuminate Albert Einstein in a swirl of nuclear particles; and pavement labyrinths offer guided meditation for restless souls.

DON'T MISS

SAN FRANCISCO MUSEUM OF MODERN ART

Bold moves have set the **San Francisco Museum of Modern Art** (SFMOMA; Map p126; ☎415-357-4000; www.sfmoma.org; 151 3rd St; adult/child $18/free, 1st Tue of month free; ⏲11am-6pm Fri-Tue, to 9pm Thu) apart since 1935, with curatorial gambles on then-controversial contemporary painters like Diego Rivera and Frida Kahlo, and history-making works by local photographers Dorothea Lange, Eadweard Muybridge, Ansel Adams and Edward Weston. The museum moved into architect Mario Botta's light-filled brick box just in time for the tech boom in 1995, making room for new media mavericks such as San Franciscan Matthew Barney, who debuted his dazzling Vaseline-smeared videos at SFMOMA. Today installations fill the atrium, sculpture sprouts from the rooftop garden and a $480 million expansion is under way to accommodate 1100 major modern works donated by the Fisher family (local founders of the Gap) alongside emerging niches: conceptual architecture, wall-drawing installations and relational art. Go Thursday nights after 6pm for half-price admission and the most artful flirting in town.

Downtown San Francisco

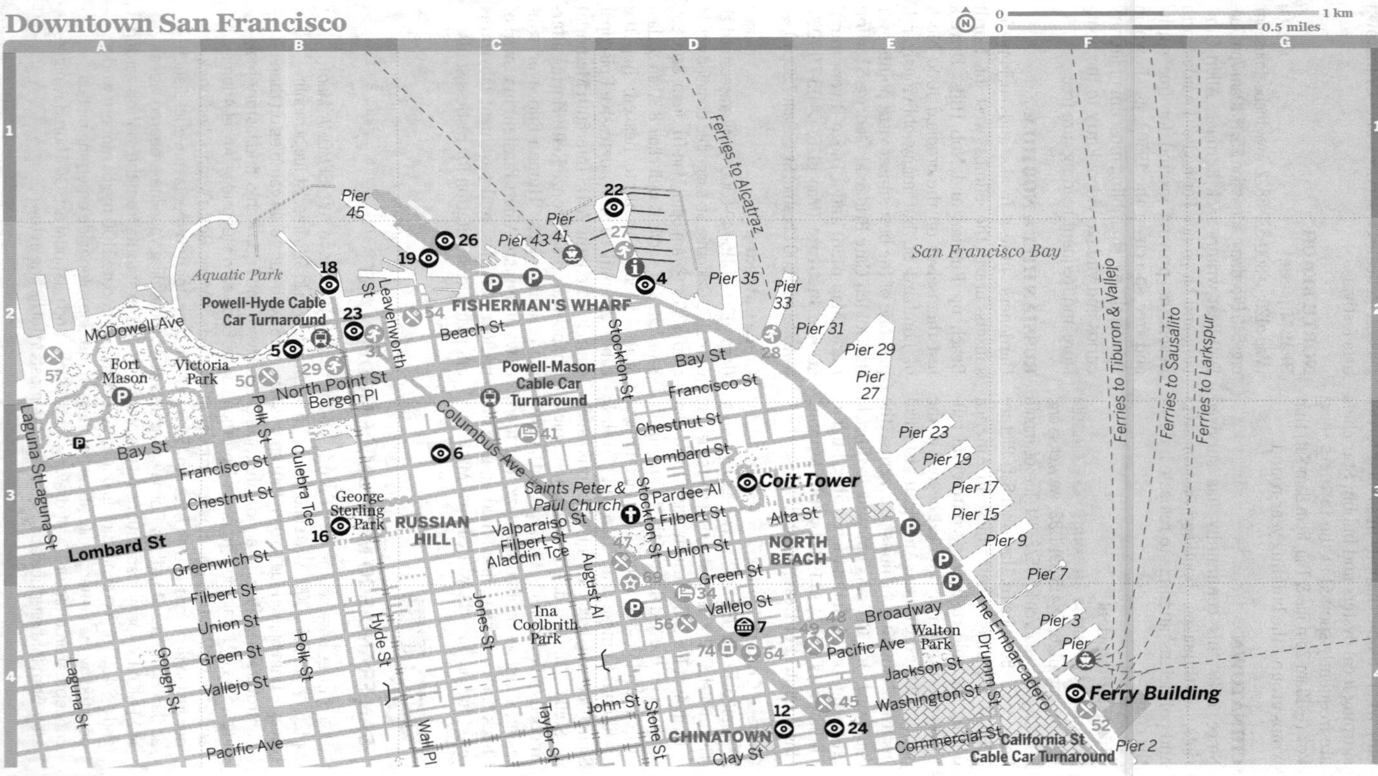

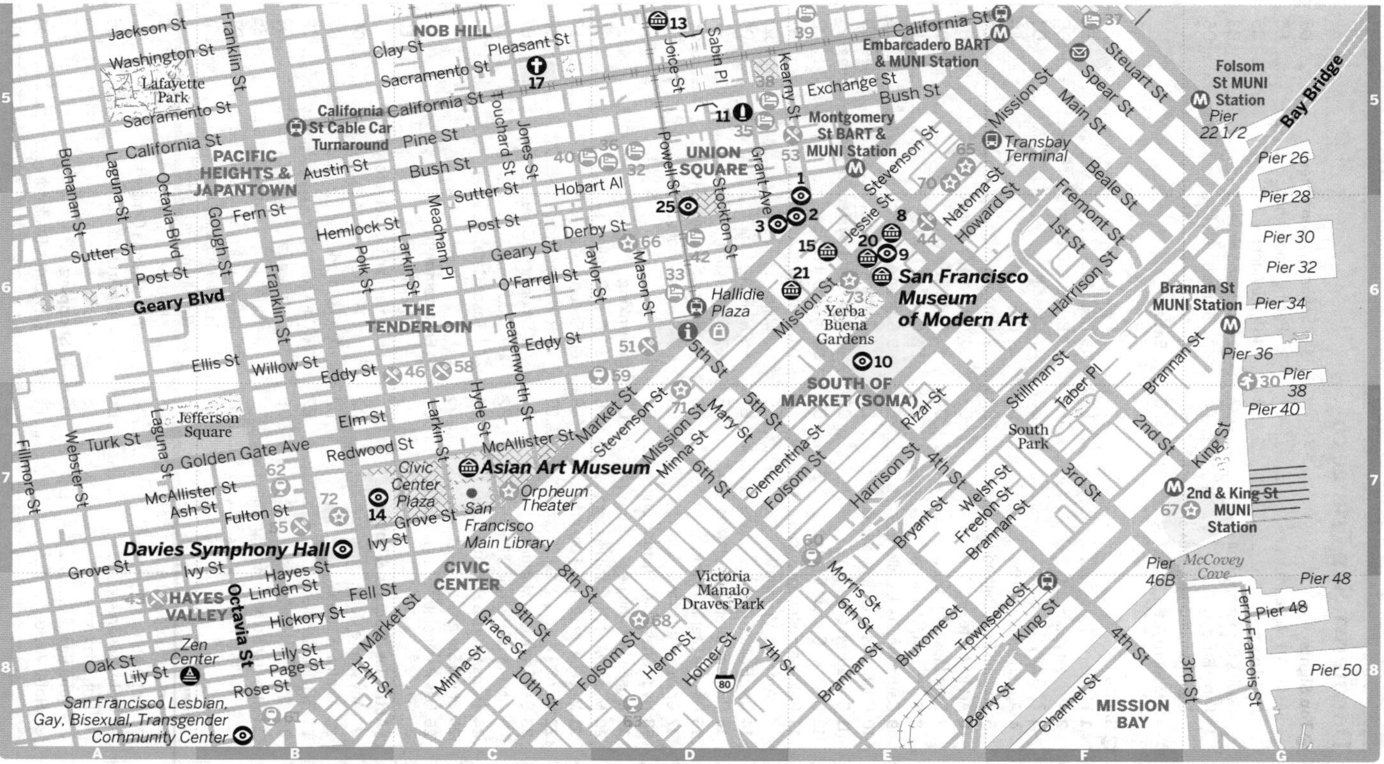
NOB HILL
Lafayette Park
California St Cable Car Turnaround
PACIFIC HEIGHTS & JAPANTOWN
Geary Blvd
THE TENDERLOIN
Jefferson Square
UNION SQUARE
Hallidie Plaza
Embarcadero BART & MUNI Station
Montgomery St BART & MUNI Station
Transbay Terminal
Folsom St MUNI Station
Pier 22 1/2
Bay Bridge
Pier 26
Pier 28
Pier 30
Pier 32
Pier 34
Pier 36
Pier 38
Pier 40
Pier 46B
Pier 48
Pier 50
Brannan St MUNI Station
2nd & King St MUNI Station
McCovey Cove
San Francisco Museum of Modern Art
Yerba Buena Gardens
SOUTH OF MARKET (SOMA)
South Park
Asian Art Museum
Civic Center Plaza
Orpheum Theater
San Francisco Main Library
CIVIC CENTER
Davies Symphony Hall
HAYES VALLEY
Zen Center
Victoria Manalo Draves Park
MISSION BAY
San Francisco Lesbian, Gay, Bisexual, Transgender Community Center
Jackson St
Washington St
Clay St
Sacramento St
California St
Pleasant St
Pine St
Bush St
Sutter St
Post St
Geary St
O'Farrell St
Ellis St
Eddy St
Turk St
Golden Gate Ave
McAllister St
Fulton St
Grove St
Hayes St
Fell St
Oak St
Page St
Market St
Mission St
Howard St
Folsom St
Harrison St
Bryant St
Brannan St
Townsend St
King St
Berry St
Channel St
Terry Francois St
Steuart St
Spear St
Main St
Beale St
Fremont St
1st St
2nd St
3rd St
4th St
5th St
6th St
7th St
8th St
9th St
10th St
12th St
Kearny St
Grant Ave
Stockton St
Powell St
Mason St
Taylor St
Jones St
Leavenworth St
Hyde St
Larkin St
Polk St
Franklin St
Gough St
Octavia Blvd
Octavia St
Laguna St
Buchanan St
Webster St
Fillmore St

Downtown San Francisco

Top Sights
- Asian Art Museum ... C7
- Coit Tower ... D3
- Davies Symphony Hall ... B7
- Ferry Building ... F4
- San Francisco Museum of Modern Art ... E6

Sights
- 1 14 Geary ... E6
- 2 49 Geary ... E6
- 3 77 Geary ... D6
- 4 Aquarium of the Bay ... D2
- 5 Aquatic Park Bathhouse ... B2
- 6 Art Institute ... C3
- 7 Beat Museum ... D4
- 8 Cartoon Art Museum ... E6
- 9 Catharine Clark Gallery ... E6
- 10 Children's Creativity Museum ... E6
- 11 Chinatown Gate ... D5
- 12 Chinese Culture Center ... D4
- 13 Chinese Historical Society of America Museum ... D5
- 14 City Hall ... B7
- 15 Contemporary Jewish Museum ... E6
- 16 George Sterling Park ... B3
- 17 Grace Cathedral ... C5
- 18 Hyde Street Pier Historic Ships ... B2
- 19 Musée Mécanique ... C2
- 20 Museum of African Diaspora ... E6
- 21 Museum of Craft & Folk Arts ... E6
- 22 Pier 39 ... D1
- 23 San Francisco Maritime National Historical Park ... B2
- 24 Transamerica Pyramid ... E4
- 25 Union Square ... D6
- 26 Uss Pampanito ... C2

Activities, Courses & Tours
- 27 Adventure Cat ... D2
- 28 Alcatraz Cruises ... D2
- 29 Blazing Saddles ... B2
- 30 City Kayak ... G6
- 31 Meeting Point for Fire Engine Tours ... B2

Sleeping
- 32 Golden Gate Hotel ... D5
- 33 Hotel Abri ... D6
- 34 Hotel Bohème ... D4
- 35 Hotel des Arts ... D5
- 36 Hotel Rex ... D5
- 37 Hotel Vitale ... F5
- 38 Orchard Garden Hotel ... D5
- 39 Pacific Tradewinds ... E5
- 40 Petite Auberge ... C5
- 41 San Remo Hotel ... C3
- 42 Stratford Hotel ... D6

Eating
- 43 Bar Jules ... A8
- 44 Benu ... E6
- 45 Bocadillos ... E4
- 46 Brenda's French Soul Food ... B6
- 47 Cinecittà ... D3
- 48 Coi ... E4
- 49 Cotogna ... E4
- 50 Crown & Crumpet ... B2
- 51 Farmerbrown ... D6
- 52 Farmers Market ... F4
- 53 Gitane ... E5
- Gott's Roadside ... (see 52)
- Hog Island Oyster Company ... (see 52)
- 54 In-N-Out Burger ... C2
- 55 Jardinière ... B7
- Mijita ... (see 52)
- 56 Molinari ... D4
- 57 Off the Grid ... A2
- 58 Saigon Sandwich Shop ... C6
- Slanted Door ... (see 52)

Drinking
- 59 Aunt Charlie's ... D6
- 60 Endup ... E7
- 61 Rebel Bar ... B8
- 62 Smuggler's Cove ... B7
- 63 Stud ... D8
- 64 Tosca Cafe ... D4

Entertainment
- 65 111 Minna ... E5
- 66 American Conservatory Theater ... D6
- 67 AT&T Park ... G7
- 68 Cat Club ... D8
- 69 Club Fugazi ... D3
- 70 Harlot ... E5
- 71 Mezzanine ... D7
- TIX Bay Area ... (see 25)
- 72 War Memorial Opera House ... B7
- 73 Yerba Buena Center for the Arts ... E6

Shopping
- 74 City Lights Bookstore ... D4

FISHERMAN'S WHARF

FREE **Aquatic Park Bathhouse** HISTORIC BUILDING

(Map p126; ☎415-447-5000; www.nps.gov/safr; 499 Jefferson St, at Hyde St; ⏰10am-4pm) A monumental hint to sailors in need of a scrub, this recently restored, ship-shape 1939 streamline moderne landmark is decked out with Works Progress Administration (WPA) art treasures: playful seal and frog sculptures by Beniamino Bufano, Hilaire Hiler's surreal underwater dreamscape murals and recently uncovered wood reliefs by Richard Ayer. Acclaimed African American artist Sargent Johnson created the stunning carved green slate marquee doorway and the verandah's mesmerizing aquatic mosaics, which he deliberately left unfinished on the east side to protest plans to include a private restaurant in this public facility. Johnson won: the east wing is now a maritime museum office.

Musée Mécanique AMUSEMENT ARCADE

(Map p126; ☎415-346-2000; www.museemecaniquesf.com; Pier 45; ⏰10am-7pm Mon-Fri, to 8pm Sat & Sun) Where else can you guillotine a man for a quarter? Creepy 19th-century arcade games like the macabre French Execution compete for your spare change with the diabolical Ms Pac-Man.

Pier 39 LANDMARK

(Map p126; www.pier39.com) With the notable exception of sea lions gleefully belching after fish dinners at Pier 39, most of Fisherman's Wharf is packed with landlubbers attempting to digest sourdough-bread bowls of gloppy clam chowder (don't bother: can't be done).

USS Pampanito MUSEUM

(Map p126; ☎415-775-1943; www.maritime.org; Pier 45; adult/child $10/4; ⏰9am-5pm) Explore a restored WWII submarine that survived six tours of duty, while listening to submariners' tales of stealth mode and sudden attacks in a riveting audio tour ($2) that makes surfacing afterwards a relief (caution claustrophobes).

Hyde Street Pier Historic Ships HISTORIC SITE

(Map p126; ☎415-447-5000; www.nps.gov/safr; 499 Jefferson St, at Hyde St; adult/child $5/free; ⏰9am-5pm) Tour 19th-century ships moored here as part of the Maritime National Historical Park, including triple-masted 1886 **Balclutha** and 1890 steamboat **Eureka**; summer sailing trips are available aboard elegant 1891 schooner **Alma** (adult/child $40/20; ⏰Jun-Nov).

THE MARINA & PRESIDIO

TOP CHOICE **Exploratorium** MUSEUM

(☎415-561-0360; www.exploratorium.edu; 3601 Lyon St; adult/child $15/10, incl Tactile Dome $10; ⏰10am-5pm Tue-Sun) Budding Nobel Prize winners swarm this hands-on discovery museum, learning the scientific secrets to skateboarding and groping through the Tactile Dome (ages seven+). Mad-scientist cocktails, live performances and scientific experiments draw the over-21 crowd to **After Dark** (⏰6-10pm Thu). With exhibits that won designers a McArthur Genius Grant, the Exploratorium is outgrowing its picturesque Palace of Fine Arts location and moving to the piers in 2013. Meanwhile, ducklings march past the Exploratorium through Bernard Maybeck's faux-Roman 1915 **rotunda**, where friezes depict Art under attack by Materialists, with Idealists leaping to her rescue.

Crissy Field WATERFRONT, BEACH

(☎415-561-7690; www.crissyfield.org) The Presidio's army airstrip has been stripped of asphalt and reinvented as a haven for coastal birds, kite-fliers and windsurfers enjoying sweeping views of Golden Gate Bridge.

Baker Beach BEACH

(Map p122; ⏰sunrise-sunset) Unswimmable waters (except when the tide's coming in) but unbeatable views of the Golden Gate make this former Army beachhead SF's tanning location of choice, especially the

WORTH A TRIP

COIT TOWER

Adding an exclamation mark to San Francisco's landscape, **Coit Tower** (Map p126; ☎415-362-0808; elevator rides $5; ⏰10am-6pm) offers views worth shouting about – especially after you climb the giddy, steep Filbert St steps to get here. Check out 360-degree views of downtown from the viewing platform, and wrap-around 1930s lobby murals glorifying SF workers – once denounced as communist but now a beloved landmark. To see more murals hidden inside Coit Tower's stairwell, take free docent-led tours at 11am Saturdays.

clothing-optional north end – at least until the afternoon fog rolls in.

Fort Mason HISTORIC SITE
(☎415-345-7500; www.fortmason.org) Army sergeants would be scandalized by the frolicking at this former military outpost, including comedy improv workshops, kiddie art classes, and **Off the Grid** (http://offthegridsf.com), where gourmet trucks circle like pioneer wagons.

Fort Point HISTORIC SITE
(Map p122; ☎415-561-4395; www.nps.gov/fopo) Despite its impressive guns, this Civil War fort saw no action – at least until Alfred Hitchcock shot scenes from *Vertigo* here, with stunning views of the Golden Gate Bridge from below.

THE MISSION

Mission Dolores CHURCH
(Map p132; ☎415-621-8203; www.missiondolores.org; cnr Dolores & 16th Sts; adult/child $5/3; ⊙9am-4pm) The city's oldest building and its namesake, the whitewashed adobe Misión San Francisco de Asis was founded in 1776 and rebuilt in 1782 with conscripted Ohlone and Miwok labor – note the ceiling patterned after Native American baskets. In the cemetery beside the adobe mission, a replica Ohlone hut is a memorial to the 5000 Ohlone and Miwok who died in 1814 and 1826 mission measles epidemics. The mission is overshadowed by the adjoining ornate 1913 basilica, where stained-glass windows commemorate the 21 original California missions, from Santa Cruz to San Diego.

Balmy Alley STREET
(Map p132; off 24th St, near Folsom St) Mission activist artists set out in the 1970s to transform the political landscape, one mural-covered garage door at a time. Today, a one-block walk down Balmy Alley leads past three decades of murals, from an early memorial for El Salvador activist Archbishop Óscar Romero to an homage to the golden age of Mexican cinema. Nonprofit Precita Eyes restores these murals, commissions new ones and offers mural tours (see p135).

826 Valencia CULTURAL BUILDING
(Map p132; ☎415-642-5905; www.826valencia.org; 826 Valencia St; ⊙noon-6pm) 'No buccaneers! No geriatrics!' warns the sign above the vat of sand where kids rummage for buried pirates' booty. The eccentric Pirate Supply Store sells eye patches, scoops from an actual tub o' lard, and McSweeney's literary magazines to support a teen writing nonprofit and the Fish Theater, where a puffer fish is immersed in Method acting.

Creativity Explored GALLERY
(Map p132; ☎415-863-2108; www.creativityexplored.org; 3245 16th St; donations welcome; ⊙10am-3pm Mon-Fri, to 7pm Thu, 1-6pm Sat) Fresh perspectives on themes ranging from superheroes to architecture by critically acclaimed, developmentally disabled artists – don't miss joyous openings with the artists, their families and fans.

Dolores Park PARK
(Map p132) Sunshine and politics come with the Mission territory: protests are held almost every weekend, alongside soccer, tennis and hillside tanning.

THE CASTRO

Rainbow flags fly high over **Harvey Milk Plaza** (Map p132) in San Francisco's historic out-and-proud neighborhood, home of the nation's first openly gay official.

GLBT History Museum MUSEUM
(Map p132; ☎415-621-1107; www.glbthistory.org/museum; 4127 18th St; admission $5, 1st Wed of month free; ⊙11am-7pm Tue-Sat, noon-5pm Sun-Mon) America's first gay-history museum captures proud moments and historic challenges: Harvey Milk's campaign literature, interviews with trailblazing bisexual author Gore Vidal, matchbooks from long-gone bathhouses and pages of the 1950s penal code banning homosexuality.

THE HAIGHT

Better known as the hazy hot spot of the Summer of Love, the Haight has hung onto its tie-dyes, ideals and certain habits – hence the Bound Together Anarchist Book Collective, the Haight Ashbury Free Clinic and high density of medical marijuana dispensaries (sorry, dude: prescription required). Fanciful 'Painted Lady' Victorian houses surround **Alamo Square Park** (Hayes & Scott Sts) and the corner of Haight and Ashbury Sts, where Jimi Hendrix, Janis Joplin and the Grateful Dead crashed during the Haight's hippie heyday.

JAPANTOWN & PACIFIC HEIGHTS

Atop every Japantown sushi counter perches a *maneki neko,* the porcelain cat with one paw raised in permanent welcome: this is your cue to unwind with shiatsu massages at Kabuki Hot Springs, eco-entertainment and non-GMO popcorn at Sundance Kabuki Cinema, world-class jazz at Yoshi's or mind-blowing rock at the Fillmore.

GOLDEN GATE PARK & AROUND

San Francisco was way ahead of its time in 1865, when the city voted to turn 1017 acres of sand dunes into the world's largest city stretch of green, Golden Gate Park (Map p122). This ambitious green scheme scared off Frederick Law Olmstead, the celebrated architect of New York's Central Park, and thwarted real estate speculators' plans to turn Golden Gate Park into a theme-park resort. Instead of hotels and casinos, park architect William Hammond Hall insisted on botanical gardens and a Japanese Tea Garden.

GAY/LES/BI/TRANS SAN FRANCISCO

Doesn't matter where you're from, who you love or who's your daddy: if you're here, and queer, welcome home. The intersection of 18th and Castro Sts is the heart of the gay cruising scene, but dancing queens and slutty boys head South of Market (SoMa) for thump-thump clubs. The Mission is the preferred 'hood of alt-chicks, trans FTMs (female-to-males) and flirty femmes. *Bay Area Reporter* (aka BAR; www.ebar.com) covers community news and listings; *San Francisco Bay Times* (www.sfbaytimes.com) also has good resources for transsexuals; and free mag *Gloss Magazine* (www.glossmagazine.net) covers nightlife.

To find out where the party is, check **Honey Soundsystem** (www.honeysoundsystem.com) for roving queer dance parties; **Betty's List** (www.bettyslist.com) for parties, fundraisers and power-lesbian mixers; and **Juanita More** (www.juanitamore.com) for fierce circuit parties thrown by a drag superstar. **Sisters of Perpetual Indulgence** (www.thesisters.org), 'the leading-edge order of queer nuns,' organizes parties, guerrilla street theater and the subversive 'Hunky Jesus Contest' in Dolores Park at Easter.

Other top GLBT venues:

Stud BAR

(Map p126; ☎415-252-7883; www.studsf.com; 399 9th St; admission $5-8; ⊙5pm-3am) Rocking the gay scene since 1966, and branching out beyond leather daddies with rocker-grrrl Mondays, Tuesday drag variety shows, raunchy comedy/karaoke Wednesdays, Friday art-drag dance parties, and performance-art cabaret whenever hostess/DJ Anna Conda gets it together.

Rebel Bar BAR

(Map p126; ☎415-431-4202; 1760 Market St; ⊙5pm-3am Mon-Thu, to 4am Fri, 11am-4am Sat & Sun) Funhouse southern biker disco, complete with antique mirrored walls, Hell's Angel cocktails (Bulleit bourbon, Chartreuse, OJ) and exposed pipes. The crowd is mostly 30-something, gay and tribally tattooed; on a good night, poles get thoroughly worked.

Aunt Charlie's BAR

(Map p126; ☎415-441-2922; www.auntcharlieslounge.com; 133 Turk St; ⊙9am-2am) Total dive, with the city's best classic drag show Fridays and Saturdays at 10pm. Thursday nights, art-school boys freak for bathhouse disco at Tubesteak ($5).

Endup BAR

(Map p126; ☎415-646-0999; www.theendup.com; 401 6th St; admission $5-20; ⊙10pm-4am Mon-Thu, 11pm-11am Fri, 10pm Sat-4am Mon) Home of Sunday 'tea dances' (gay dance parties) since 1973, though technically the party starts Saturday – bring a change of clothes and Endup watching Monday's sunrise over the freeway on-ramp.

Lexington Club LESBIAN

(Map p132; ☎415-863-2052; 3464 19th St; ⊙3pm-2am) The baddest lesbian bar in the West, with pool, pinball and grrrrls galore.

Cafe Flore CAFE

(Map p132; ☎415-621-8579; http://cafeflore.com; 2298 Market St; mains $8-11; ⊙7am-2am; wi-fi) Coffee, wi-fi and hot beefy dishes – and the burgers aren't bad either.

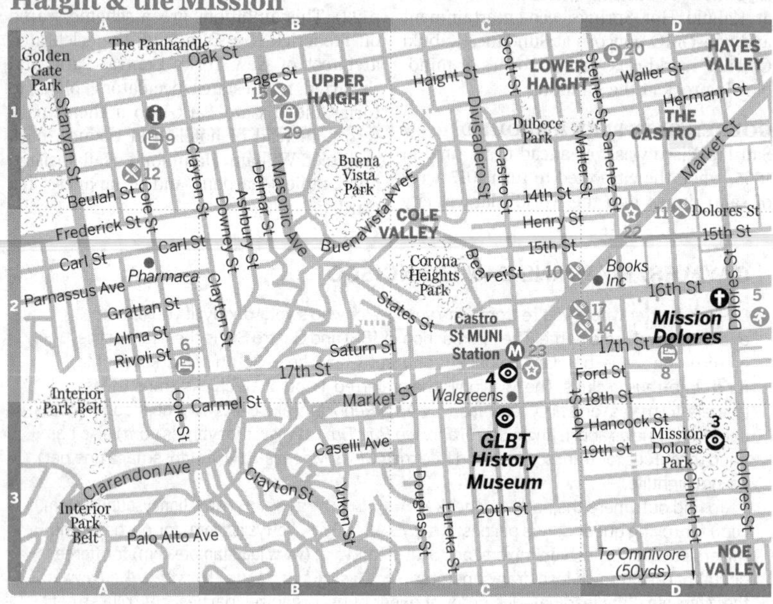

Haight & the Mission

Top Sights
- 826 Valencia E3
- Balmy Alley E2
- GLBT History Museum C3
- Mission Dolores D2

Sights
- 1 Alamo Square Park E1
- 2 Creativity Explored E2
- 3 Dolores Park D3
- 4 Harvey Milk Plaza C2

Activities, Courses & Tours
- 5 18 Reasons D2

Sleeping
- 6 Belvedere House A2
- 7 Inn San Francisco F3
- 8 Parker Guest House D2
- 9 Red Victorian A1

Eating
- 10 Cafe Flore C2
- 11 Chilango D1
- 12 Cole Valley Cafe A1
- 13 Commonwealth E2
- 14 Frances D2
- 15 Magnolia Brewpub B1
- 16 Pizzeria Delfina E2
- Rosamunde Sausage Grill .... (see 20)
- 17 Starbelly C2

Drinking
- 18 Bar Agricole F1
- 19 Lexington Club E3
- 20 Toronado D1
- 21 Zeitgeist E1

Entertainment
- 22 Café du Nord D2
- 23 Castro Theatre C2
- 24 DNA Lounge F1
- 25 Marsh E3
- 26 Roxie Cinema E2
- 27 Slim's F1

Shopping
- 28 Adobe Books E2
- 29 Bound Together Anarchist Book Collective B1

Toward Ocean Beach, the park's scenery turns quixotic, with bison stampeding in their paddock toward windswept windmills. At the north end of Ocean Beach, the recently restored **Cliff House** (Map p122; www.cliffhouse.com) restaurant overlooks the splendid ruin of **Sutro Baths**, where Victorian ladies and dandies once converged by the thousands for bracing baths in rented itchy wool bathing suits. Follow the partly paved hiking trail above Sutro Baths around **Lands End** (Map p122) for end-of-the-world views of Marin and the Golden Gate Bridge.

California Academy of Sciences WILDLIFE RESERVE

(☎415-379-8000; www.calacademy.org; 55 Concourse Dr; adult/child $29.95/24.95, $3 discount with Muni ticket, 6-10pm Thu $10 (age 21+ only); ⏰9:30am-5pm Mon-Sat, from 11am Sun) Architect Renzo Piano's 2008 landmark LEED-certified green building houses 38,000 weird and wonderful animals in a four-story rainforest and split-level aquarium under a 'living roof' of California wildflowers. After the penguins nod off to sleep, the wild rumpus starts at kids'-only Academy Sleepovers and over-21 NightLife Thursdays, when rainforest-themed cocktails encourage strange mating rituals among shy internet daters.

MH de Young Fine Arts Museum MUSEUM

(☎415-750-3600; www.famsf.org/deyoung; 50 Hagiwara Tea Garden Dr; adult/child $10/free, $2 discount with Muni ticket, 1st Tue of month free; ⏰9:30am-5:15pm Tue-Sun, to 8:45pm Fri) Follow sculptor Andy Goldsworthy's artificial fault line in the sidewalk into Herzog & de Meuron's sleek, copper-clad building that's oxidizing green to blend into the park. Don't be fooled by the de Young's camouflaged exterior: shows here boldly broaden artistic horizons from Oceanic ceremonial masks and Balenciaga gowns to sculptor Al Farrow's cathedrals built from bullets.

California Palace of the Legion of Honor MUSEUM

(Map p122; ☎415-750-3600; http://legionofhonor.famsf.org; 100 34th Ave; adult/child $10/6, $2 discount with Muni ticket, 1st Tue of month free; ⏰9:30am-5:15pm Tue-Sun) Never doubt the unwavering resolve of a nude model: sculptor's model and heiress 'Big Alma' de Bretteville Spreckels donated her fortune to build this monumental tribute to Californians killed in France in WWI. Featured artworks range from Monet water lilies to John Cage soundscapes, Iraqi ivories to R Crumb comics – part of the Legion's Achenbach collection of 90,000 graphic artworks.

Ocean Beach BEACH

(Map p122; ☎415-561-4323; www.parksconservancy.org; ⏰sunrise-sunset) The park ends in this blustery beach, too chilly for bikini-clad clambakes but ideal for wet-suited pro surfers braving rip tides (casual swimmers beware). Bonfires are permitted in designated fire pits only; no alcohol allowed.

Conservatory of Flowers GARDEN

(☎415-666-7001; www.conservatoryofflowers.org; Conservatory Dr West; adult/child $7/2; ⏰10am-4pm Tue-Sun) This recently restored 1878 Victorian greenhouse is home to outer-space orchids, contemplative floating lilies and creepy carnivorous plants that reek of insect belches.

Japanese Tea Garden GARDEN

(http://japaneseteagardensf.com; Hagiwara Tea Garden Dr; adult/child $7/5; ⏰9am-6pm) Since 1894, this picturesque 5-acre garden and bonsai grove has blushed with cherry blossoms in spring, turned flaming red with maple leaves in fall, and lost all track of time in the meditative Zen Garden.

WORTH A TRIP

ALCATRAZ

For 150 years, the name has given the innocent chills and the guilty cold sweats. **Alcatraz** (☎Alcatraz Cruises 415-981-7625; www.alcatrazcruises.com, www.nps.gov/alcatraz; adult/child day $26/16, night $33/19.50; ⏰call center 8am-7pm) has been the nation's first military prison, a maximum-security penitentiary housing A-list criminals like Al Capone, and hotly disputed Native American territory. No prisoners escaped Alcatraz alive, but since importing guards and supplies cost more than putting up prisoners at the Ritz, the prison was closed in 1963. Native American leaders occupied the island from 1969 to '71 to protest US occupation of Native lands; their standoff with the FBI is commemorated in a dockside museum and 'This is Indian Land' water-tower graffiti.

Day visits include captivating audio tours, with prisoners and guards recalling life on 'the Rock,' while night tours are led by a park ranger; reserve tickets at least two weeks ahead. Ferries depart Pier 33 every half-hour from 9am to 3:55pm, plus 6:10pm and 6:45pm.

Stow Lake LAKE
(http://sfrecpark.org/StowLake.aspx; per hr paddleboats/canoes/rowboats/tandem bikes/bikes $24/20/19/15/8; ⏰rentals 10am-4pm) Huntington Falls tumble down 400ft Strawberry Hill into the lake, near a romantic Chinese pavilion and a 1946 boathouse offering boat and bike rentals.

SAN FRANCISCO BAY

Golden Gate Bridge BRIDGE
(www.goldengatebridge.org) Imagine a squat concrete bridge striped black and caution yellow spanning the San Francisco Bay – that's what the US Navy initially had in mind. Luckily, engineer Joseph B Strauss and architects Gertrude and Irving Murrow insisted on a soaring art-deco design and International Orange paint of the 1937 Golden Gate Bridge. Cars pay a $6 toll to cross from Marin to San Francisco; pedestrians and cyclists stroll the east sidewalk for free.

Activities

Kabuki Hot Springs SPA
(☎415-922-6000; www.kabukisprings.com; 1750 Geary Blvd; admission $22-25; ⏰10am-9:45pm) Soak muscles worked by SF's 43 hills in Japanese baths. Men and women alternate days, and bathing suits are required on coed Tuesdays.

Oceanic Society Expeditions BOATING
(☎415-474-3385; www.oceanic-society.org; per person $100-120; ⏰office 8:30am-5pm Mon-Fri, trips Sat & Sun) Whale sightings aren't a fluke on naturalist-led, ocean-going weekend boat trips during mid-October through December migrations.

Golden Gate Park Bike & Skate CYCLING, SKATING
(☎415-668-1117; www.goldengateparkbikeandskate.com; 3038 Fulton St; skates per hr/day from $5/20, bikes $3/15, tandem bikes $15/75, discs $6/25; ⏰10am-6pm) To make the most of Golden Gate Park, rent wheels – especially Sundays and summer Saturdays, when JFK Dr is closed to vehicular traffic – or disc golf equipment.

Blazing Saddles CYCLING
(☎415-202-8888; www.blazingsaddles.com; 2715 Hyde St; bikes per hr/day from $8/$32; ⏰8am-7:30pm) From this bike rental shop's Fisherman's Wharf outposts, cyclists can cross the Golden Gate Bridge and take the Sausalito ferry back to SF (weather permitting).

18 Reasons COOKING
(Map p126; ☎415-252-9816; www.18reasons.org; 593 Guerrero St; ⏰6:30am-5pm Mon-Sat, 7am-4:30pm Sun) Go gourmet at this local food community nonprofit offering knife-skills and edible perfume workshops, wine and cheese tastings, and more.

City Kayak KAYAKING
(Map p126; ☎415-357-1010; http://citykayak.com; South Beach Harbor; kayak rentals per hr $35-65, 3hr lesson & rental package $59, tours $65-75) Experienced paddlers hit the choppy waters beneath the Golden Gate Bridge or take a moonlit group tour, while newbies venture calm waters near the Bay Bridge.

Adventure Cat SAILING
(Map p126; ☎415-777-1630; www.adventurecat.com; Pier 39; adult/child $35/15, sunset cruise $50) Three daily catamaran cruises depart

March to October; weekends only November to February.

FREE **Potrero del Sol/La Raza Skatepark** SKATING
(www.sfgov.org; 25th & Utah Sts) Skate the bowl or watch in awe as pro street skaters hit air and padded kindergartners scoot along.

Aqua Surf Shop SURFING
(Map p122; ☎415-876-2782; www.aquasurfshop.com; 1742 Haight St; ⊙11am-7pm; rental per day board/wetsuit $25/15) Even kooks (newbies) become mavericks with Aqua's wetsuit rentals, tide updates and lesson referrals.

Tours

Chinatown Alleyway Tours WALKING
(☎415-984-1478 www.chinatownalleywaytours.org; adult/child $18/5/; ⊙11am Sat & Sun) Neighborhood teens lead two-hour tours for up-close-and-personal peeks into Chinatown's past (weather permitting). Book five days ahead or pay double for Saturday walk-ins; cash only.

Precita Eyes Mission Mural Tours WALKING
(☎415-285-2287; www.precitaeyes.org; adult $12-15, child $5; ⊙11am, noon & 1:30pm Sat & Sun) Muralists lead two-hour tours on foot or bike covering 60 to 70 murals in a six- to 10-block radius of mural-bedecked Balmy Alley; proceeds fund mural upkeep.

FREE **Public Library City Guides** WALKING
(www.sfcityguides.org) Volunteer local historians lead tours by neighborhood and theme: Art Deco Marina, Gold Rush Downtown, Pacific Heights Victorians, North Beach by Night, and more. See website for upcoming tours.

Festivals & Events

Chinese New Year Parade CULTURAL
(www.chineseparade.com) Chase the 200ft dragon, and see lion dancers and toddler kung-fu classes parade through Chinatown in February.

SF International Film Festival FILM
(www.sffs.org) Stars align and directors launch premieres each April at the nation's oldest film festival.

Bay to Breakers RACE
(www.baytobreakers.com; race registration $44-48) Run costumed or naked from Embarcadero to Ocean Beach the third Sunday in May, while joggers dressed as salmon run upstream.

Carnaval CULTURAL
(www.carnavalsf.com) Brazilian, or just faking it with a wax and a tan? Shake your tail feathers in the Mission the last weekend of May.

SF Pride Celebration CULTURAL
A day isn't enough to do SF proud: June begins with **International LGBT Film Festival** (www.frameline.org), and goes out in style

SAN FRANCISCO FOR CHILDREN

Although it has the least kids per capita of any US city – according to recent SFSPCA data, there are about 19,000 more dogs than kids under age 18 in town – San Francisco is packed with attractions for kids, including Golden Gate Park, Exploratorium, California Academy of Sciences, Cartoon Art Museum and Museé Mechanique. For babysitting, **American Child Care** (☎415-285-2300; www.americanchildcare.com; 580 California St, Suite 1600) charges $20 per hour plus gratuity; four-hour minimum.

Children's Creativity Museum MUSEUM
(☎415-820-3320; www.zeum.org; 221 4th St; admission $10; ⊙11am-5pm Tue-Sun) Technology that's too cool for school: robots, live-action video games, DIY music videos and 3D animation workshops with Silicon Valley innovators.

Aquarium of the Bay AQUARIUM
(Map p126; www.aquariumofthebay.com; Pier 39; adult/child $17/8; ⊙9am-8pm summer, 10am-6pm winter) Glide through glass tubes underwater on conveyer belts as sharks circle overhead.

Fire Engine Tours TOUR
(Map p126; ☎415-333-7077; www.fireenginetours.com; Beach St at the Cannery; adult/child $50/30; ⊙tours depart 1pm) Hot stuff: a 75-minute, open-air vintage fire-engine ride over Golden Gate Bridge.

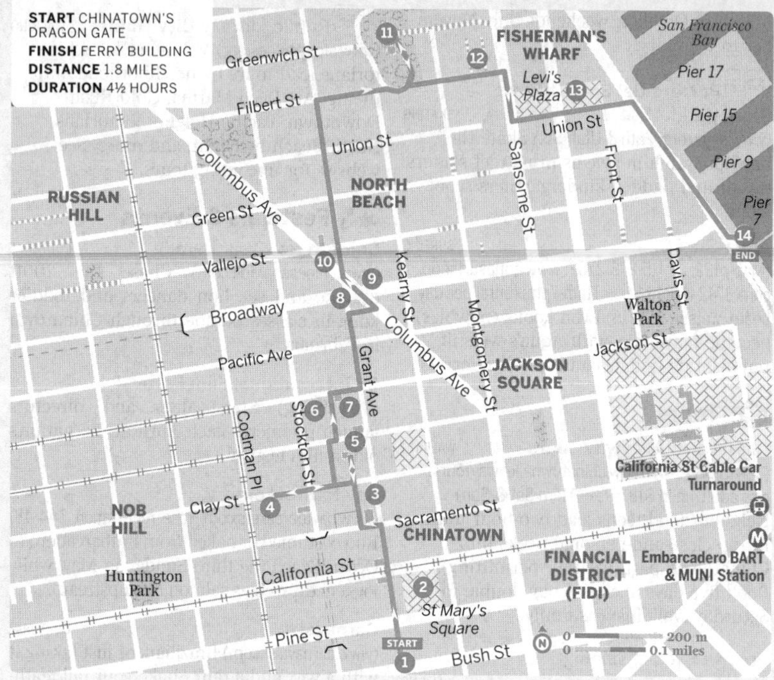

Walking Tour
Chinatown

Limber up and look sharp: on this walk, you'll discover revolutionary plots, find hidden fortunes, see controversial art and go gourmet with Gandhi.

Starting at 1 **Chinatown's Dragon Gate**, head past Grant St's gilded dragon lamps to 2 **Old St Mary's Square**, site of a brothel leveled in the 1906 fire where renegade skateboarders turn a different kind of tricks under the watchful eye of Beniamino Bufano's 1929 statue of Chinese revolutionary Sun Yat-Sen. Walk uphill to spot flag-festooned temple balconies along 3 **Waverly Place**, then head up to the 4 **Chinese Historical Society of America Museum**, in the majestic Chinatown YWCA built by Julia Morgan.

Backtrack past Stockton to 5 **Spofford Alley**, where mahjong tiles click, Chinese orchestras warm up and beauticians gossip indiscreetly over blow-dryers. Once you might have heard Prohibition bootlegger turf wars, or Sun Yat-Sen at No 36 plotting the 1911 overthrow of China's last dynasty. Once packed with brothels, 6 **Ross Alley** was more recently pimped as the picturesque setting for such forgettable sequels as *Karate Kid II* and *Indian Jones and the Temple of Doom.* At No 56, get your fortune while it's hot, folded into warm cookies at 7 **Golden Gate Fortune Cookie Factory**.

Back on Grant, take a shortcut through 8 **Jack Kerouac Alley**, where poetry marks where the binge-prone author sometimes wound up *On the Road*. The light at the end of the alley is 9 **City Lights Bookstore**, champion of Beat poetry and free speech. Savor poetry with espresso at 10 **Caffe Trieste** at 601 Vallejo St, under the Sicilian mural where Francis Ford Coppola legendarily wrote *The Godfather* script.

Climb to 11 **Coit Tower** for viewing-platform panoramas and 1930s lobby murals critics have called communist, courageous, or both. Take 12 **Filbert Steps** downhill past wild parrots and hidden cottages to 13 **Levi's Plaza**, named for San Francisco's denim inventor. Head right on Embarcadero to the 14 **Ferry Building** for lunch Bayside, with a gaunt bronze Gandhi peeking over your shoulder.

the last weekend with Pink Saturday's **Dyke March** (www.dykemarch.org) and the frisky, million-strong **Pride Parade** (www.sfpride.org).

Folsom Street Fair STREET FAIR
(www.folsomstreetfair.com) Work that leather look and enjoy public spankings for local charities the last weekend of September.

Hardly Strictly Bluegrass MUSIC
(www.strictlybluegrass.com) SF celebrates Western roots with three days of free Golden Gate Park concerts and headliners ranging from Elvis Costello to Gillian Welch in early October.

LitQuake CULTURAL
(www.litquake.org) Authors tell stories at the biggest lit fest in the West and spill trade secrets over drinks at the legendary Lit Crawl; second week in October.

SF Jazz Festival MUSIC
(www.sfjazz.org) Old-school greats and breakthrough talents blow horns and minds in late October.

Sleeping

San Francisco is the birthplace of the boutique hotel, offering stylish rooms for a price: $100 to $200 rooms midrange, plus 15.5% hotel tax (hostels exempt) and $35 to $50 for overnight parking. For vacancies and deals, check SF Visitor Information Center's **reservation line** (☎415-391-2000; www.onlyinsanfrancisco.com), **Bed & Breakfast SF** (☎415-899-0060; www.bbsf.com) and **Lonely Planet** (http://hotels.lonelyplanet.com).

UNION SQUARE & CIVIC CENTER

Hotel Rex BOUTIQUE HOTEL $$$
(Map p126; ☎415-433-4434; www.jdvhotels.com; 562 Sutter St; r $169-279; P❄@📶) Noir-novelist chic, with 1920s literary lounge and compact rooms with hand-painted lampshades, local art and sumptuous beds piled with down pillows.

Orchard Garden Hotel BOUTIQUE HOTEL $$$
(Map p126; ☎415-399-9807; www.theorchardgardenhotel.com; 466 Bush St; r $179-249; ❄@📶) SF's first all-green-practices hotel has soothingly quiet rooms with luxe touches, like Egyptian-cotton sheets, plus an organic rooftop garden.

Hotel des Arts HOTEL $$
(Map p126; ☎415-956-3232; www.sfhoteldesarts.com; 447 Bush St; r with bath $139-199, without bath $99-149; 📶) A budget hotel for art freaks, with specialty rooms painted by underground artists – it's like sleeping inside an art installation. Standard rooms are less exciting, but clean and good value; bring earplugs.

Petite Auberge B&B $$$
(Map p126; ☎415-928-6000; www.jdvhotels.com; 863 Bush St; r $169-219; @📶) An urban French-provincial country inn with cheerful rooms, some with gas fireplaces; don't miss chatty fireside wine hour.

Hotel Abri BOUTIQUE HOTEL $$$
(Map p126; ☎415-392-8800; www.hotel-abri.com; 127 Ellis St; r $149-229; ❄@📶) Snazzy boutique hotel with bold black-and-tan motifs and ultramod cons: iPod docking stations, pillow-top beds, flat-screen TVs and rainfall showerheads.

Golden Gate Hotel HOTEL $$
(Map p126; ☎415-392-3702; www.goldengatehotel.com; 775 Bush St; r without/with bath $105/165; @📶) A homey Edwardian hotel with kindly owners, homemade cookies and a cuddly cat, safely uphill from the Tenderloin. Most rooms have private baths, some with claw-foot tubs.

Stratford Hotel HOTEL $$
(Map p126; ☎415-397-7080; hotelstratford.com; 242 Powell St; r incl breakfast $89-149; @📶) Simple, smallish, clean rooms with rainfall showers; request rooms facing away from clanging Powell St cable cars.

FINANCIAL DISTRICT & NORTH BEACH

TOP CHOICE **Hotel Bohème** BOUTIQUE HOTEL $$
(Map p126; ☎415-433-9111; www.hotelboheme.com; 444 Columbus Ave; r $174-194; @📶) A love letter to North Beach's Beat era, with vintage photos, retro orange, black and sage-green color schemes, and Chinese parasols for lampshades; no elevator.

TOP CHOICE **Hotel Vitale** LUXURY HOTEL $$$
(Map p126; ☎415-278-3700; www.hotelvitale.com; 8 Mission St; d $239-379; ❄@📶) The shag-adelic-chic Vitale is SF's sexiest splurge, with roof hot tubs at the on-site spa, silky 450-threadcount linens on sumptuous beds, and some sweeping bay views.

San Remo Hotel HOTEL $
(Map p126; ☎415-776-8688; www.sanremohotel.com; 2237 Mason St; d $65-99; @📶) The 1906

San Remo is long on old-fashioned charm, with mismatched turn-of-the-century furnishings and shared bathrooms. Bargain rooms face the corridor.

Pacific Tradewinds HOSTEL $
(Map p126; ☎415-433-7970; www.sanfranciscohostel.org; 680 Sacramento St; dm $29.50; @📶) SF's smartest-looking hostel has a blue-and-white nautical theme, full kitchen and spotless glass-brick showers. Three flights up; no elevator.

FISHERMAN'S WHARF & THE MARINA

Hotel Del Sol MOTEL $$
(☎415-921-5520; www.thehoteldelsol.com; 3100 Webster St; d $149-199; P❄@📶≋👪) A colorful, revamped 1950s motor lodge, with heated outdoor pool, board games and family suites with trundle beds.

Marina Motel MOTEL $
(☎415-928-1000; www.marinainn.com; 3110 Octavia Blvd; r $79-109; 📶) Bougainvillea-bedecked 1930s motor court, offering some rooms with kitchens ($10 extra) and free parking. Request one of the quiet rooms at the back.

HI San Francisco Fisherman's Wharf HOSTEL $
(☎415-771-7277; www.sfhostels.com; Fort Mason, Bldg 240; dm $25-30, r $65-100; P@📶) Barracks converted to dorms, with unparalleled waterfront park setting, communal showers, limited free parking, no curfew and no daytime heat (dress warmly year-round).

THE MISSION

Inn San Francisco B&B $$$
(Map p132; ☎415-641-0188; www.innsf.com; 943 S Van Ness Ave; r incl breakfast $175-285, with shared bath $120-145, cottage $335; P@📶) Impeccably maintained and packed with antiques, this 1872 Italianate-Victorian mansion contains a redwood hot tub in the English garden, genteel guestrooms with freshly cut flowers and featherbeds, and limited parking.

THE CASTRO

Parker Guest House B&B $$$
(Map p132; ☎415-621-3222; www.parkerguesthouse.com; 520 Church St; r incl breakfast $149-229; P@📶) SF's best gay B&B has cushy rooms in adjoining Edwardian mansions, a steam room and garden.

Belvedere House B&B $$
(Map p132; ☎415-731-6654; www.belvederehouse.com; 598 Belvedere St; r incl breakfast $125-190; @📶) Castro's romantic getaway on a leafy side street, with vintage chandeliers and eclectic art in six cozy rooms.

THE HAIGHT

Red Victorian B&B $$
(Map p132; ☎415-864-1978; www.redvic.net; 1665 Haight St; r incl breakfast $149-229, with shared bath $89-129; 📶) Peace, love and nature worship live on in themed rooms at the tripped-out Red Vic. Four of 18 rooms have baths, but all include organic breakfasts; wi-fi and meditation pillows available in the lobby.

Eating

Hope you're hungry – there are 10 times more restaurants per capita in San Francisco than in any other US city. Graze your way across SF, with stops at the Ferry Building farmers market, Omnivore (p144) for signed cookbooks, knife-skills workshops at non-profit 18 Reasons (p134) and gourmet food trucks at Off the Grid (p140). Most of SF's top restaurants are quite small, so reserve now.

SOMA, UNION SQUARE & CIVIC CENTER

TOP CHOICE **Benu** CALIFORNIAN FUSION $$$
(Map p126; ☎415-685-4860; www.benusf.com; 22 Hawthorne St; mains $25-40; ⏲5:30-10pm Tue-Sat) SF has refined fusion cuisine over 150 years, but no one rocks it quite like chef Corey Lee, who remixes local fine-dining staples and Pacific Rim flavors with a SoMa DJ's finesse. Velvety Sonoma foie gras with tangy, woodsy yuzu-sake glaze makes taste buds bust wild moves, while Dungeness crab and black truffle custard bring such outsize flavor to faux-shark's fin soup, you'll swear there's Jaws in there. The tasting menu is steep ($160) and beverage pairings add $110, but you won't want to miss star-sommelier Yoon Ha's flights of fancy – including a rare 1968 Madeira with your soup.

Jardinière CALIFORNIAN $$$
(Map p126; ☎415-861-5555; www.jardiniere.com; 300 Grove St; mains $19-37; ⏲5-10:30pm Tue-Sat, to 10pm Sun-Mon) Iron Chef and Top Chef Master Traci Des Jardins is better known locally as a mastermind of sustain-

able, salacious California cuisine, lavishing braised oxtail ravioli with summer truffles, and stuffing crispy pork belly with salami and Mission figs. Go on Mondays, when $45 scores three decadent courses with wine pairings.

Saigon Sandwich Shop SANDWICHES $
(Map p126; ☎415-474-5698; 560 Larkin St; ⏰6:30am-5:30pm) Join the line for Vietnamese *banh mi,* baguettes piled with roast meat, pâté, meatballs and/or tofu with pickled carrots, jalapeño, onion and cilantro. Order two now, and spare yourself a return trip.

Brenda's French Soul Food CREOLE $$
(Map p126; ☎415-345-8100; www.frenchsoulfood.com; 652 Polk St; mains $8-12; ⏰8am-3pm Sun-Tue, to 10pm Wed-Sat) Chef-owner Brenda Buenviaje combines Creole cooking with French technique in hangover-curing Hangtown fry (omelet with cured pork and corn-breaded oysters), shrimp-stuffed po'boys, and fried chicken with collard greens and hot-pepper jelly – all worth inevitable waits on a sketchy stretch of sidewalk.

Bar Jules CALIFORNIAN $$$
(Map p126; ☎415-621-5482; www.barjules.com; 609 Hayes St; mains $10-26; ⏰6-10pm Tue, 11:30am-3pm & 6-10pm Wed-Sat, 11am-3pm Sun) Small and succulent is the credo at this corridor-sized neighborhood bistro, where the short daily menu packs a wallop of local flavor – think duck breast with cherries, almonds and arugula. Waits are a given, but so is unfussy, tasty food.

Farmerbrown MODERN AMERICAN $$$
(Map p126; ☎415-409-3276; www.farmerbrownsf.com; 25 Mason St; mains $12-23; ⏰6-10:30pm Tue-Sun, weekend brunch 11am-2pm) A rebel from the wrong side of the block, dishing up seasonal watermelon margaritas with a cayenne-salt rim, ribs that stick to yours and coleslaw with kick. Chef-owner Jay Foster works with local organic and African American farmers to provide food with actual soul, in a shotgun-shack setting with live funk bands.

FINANCIAL DISTRICT, CHINATOWN & NORTH BEACH

TOP CHOICE **Coi** CALIFORNIAN $$$
Map p126; ☎415-393-9000; http://coirestaurant.com; 373 Broadway; set menu per person $145; ⏰6-10pm Tue-Fri, from 5:30pm Fri & Sat;) Chef Daniel Patterson's wild tasting menu featuring foraged morels, wildflowers and Pacific seafood is like licking the California coastline. Black and green noodles are made from clams and Pacific seaweed, and purple ice-plant petals are strewn atop Sonoma duck's tongue, wild-caught abalone and just-picked arugula. Only-in-California flavors and intriguing wine pairings ($95; pours generous enough for two to share) will keep you California dreaming for a while afterwards.

Cotogna ITALIAN $$$
(Map p126; ☎415-775-8508; www.cotognasf.com; 470 Pacific Av; mains $14-24; ⏰noon-3pm & 7-10pm Mon-Sat;) No wonder chef-owner Michael Tusk won the 2011 James Beard Award: his rustic Italian pastas and toothsome pizzas magically balance a few pristine, local flavors. Book ahead; the $24 prix-fixe is among San Francisco's best dining deals.

City View CHINESE $
(Map p126; ☎415-398-2838; 662 Commercial St; small plates $3-5; ⏰11am-2:30pm Mon-Fri, from 10am Sat & Sun) Dim sum aficionados used to cramped quarters and surly service are wowed by impeccable shrimp and leek dumplings, tender black-bean asparagus and crisp Peking duck, all served with a flourish in a spacious, sunny room.

Bocadillos MEDITERRANEAN $$
(Map p126; ☎415-982-2622; www.bocasf.com; 710 Montgomery St; dishes $9-15; ⏰7am-10pm Mon-Fri, 5-10:30pm Sat) Lunchtime fine dining that won't break the bank or pop buttons, with just-right Basque bites of lamb burger, snapper ceviche with Asian pears, Catalan sausages and wines by the glass.

Molinari ITALIAN SANDWICHES $
(Map p126; ☎415-421-2337; 373 Columbus Ave; sandwiches $5-8; ⏰9am-5:30pm Mon-Fri, from 7:30am Sat) Grab an Italian roll and get it stuffed with translucent sheets of Parma prosciutto, milky buffalo mozzarella, marinated artichokes and legendary house-cured salami.

Cinecittà PIZZERIA $$
(Map p126; ☎415-291-8830; 663 Union St; pizzas $9-14; ⏰noon-10pm Sun-Thu, to 11pm Fri & Sat) That aroma you followed into this 18-seat eatery is thin-crust Roman pizza, probably the savory Trastevere (fresh mozzarella, arugula and prosciutto). Drink locally – Anchor

FIVE TASTY REASONS TO MISS THAT FERRY

When it comes to California dining, you'll be missing the boat unless you stop and taste the local treats at the Ferry Building (Map p126).

» Today's catch at **Hog Island Oyster Company** (415-391-7117; www.hogislandoysters.com; half-dozen oysters $15-17; 11:30am-8pm Mon-Fri, 11am-6pm Sat & Sun, happy hour 5-7pm Mon & Thu), including $1 oysters at happy hour.

» Gourmet picnic supplies from the **farmers market** (415-291-3276; www.cuesa.org; 10am-2pm Tue & Thu, from 8am Sat) – especially Andante cheeses, 4505 artisan meats, Donna's tamales and Namu's Korean tacos.

» Chef Traci des Jardins' *nuevo* Mexican street eats at **Mijita** (399-0814; www.mijitasf.com; menu items under $10; 10am-7pm Mon-Wed, to 8pm Thu-Sat, to 4pm Sun;).

» Free-range beef burgers and sweet-potato fries at **Gott's Roadside** (415-318-3423; www.gotts.com; burgers $7-10; 10:30am-10pm).

» Cal-Vietnamese Dungeness crab over cellophane noodles at Charles Phan's family-operated **Slanted Door** (415-861-8032; http://slanteddoor.com; mains $13-36; 11am-10pm).

Steam on tap or Claudia Springs Zin – and save room for housemade tiramisu.

Gitane MEDITERRANEAN $$$

(Map p126; 415-788-6686; www.gitanerestaurant.com; 6 Claude Lane; mains $15-25; 5:30pm-midnight Tue-Sat, bar to 1am;) Slip out of the Financial District and into something more comfortable at this boudoir-styled bistro, featuring Basque- and Moroccan-inspired stuffed squash blossoms, silky pan-seared scallops, herb-spiked lamb tartare and craft cocktails.

FISHERMAN'S WHARF

Crown & Crumpet DESSERTS, SANDWICHES $$

(Map p126; 415-771-4252; www.crownandcrumpet.com; 207 Ghirardelli Sq; dishes $8-12; 10am-9pm Mon-Fri, from 9am Sat, 9am-6pm Sun;) Designer style and rosy cheer usher teatime into the 21st century: dads and daughters clink teacups with crooked pinkies, Lolita goth teens nibble cucumber sandwiches, and girlfriends rehash dates over scones and Champagne. Reservations recommended weekends.

In-N-Out Burger BURGERS $

(Map p126; 800-786-1000; www.in-n-out.com; 333 Jefferson St; meals under $10; 10:30am-1am Sun-Thu, to 1:30am Fri & Sat;) Serving burgers for 60 years the way California likes them: with prime chuck ground on-site, fries and shakes made with pronounceable ingredients, served by employees paid a living wage. Ask for yours 'wild style,' cooked in mustard with grilled onions.

THE MARINA

Off the Grid FOOD TRUCKS $

(Map p126; http://offthegridsf.com; Fort Mason parking lot; dishes under $10; 5-10pm Fri) Some 30 food trucks circle their wagons at SF's largest mobile-gourmet hootenanny (other nights/locations attract less than a dozen trucks; see website). Arrive before 6:30pm or expect 20-minute waits for Chairman Bao's clamshell buns stuffed with duck and mango, Roli Roti's free-range herbed roast chicken, and dessert from the Crème Brûlée Man. Cash only; take dinner to nearby docks for Golden Gate Bridge sunsets.

Greens VEGETARIAN $$

(415-771-6222; www.greensrestaurant.com; Fort Mason Center, Bldg A; mains $7-20; noon-2:30pm Tue-Sat, 5:30-9pm Mon-Sat, 9am-4pm Sun;) Career carnivores won't realize there's no meat in roasted eggplant panini or hearty black bean chili with crème fraîche and pickled jalapeños. Book ahead or enjoy takeout at redwood-stump cafe tables or wharfside benches.

Warming Hut CAFE

(9am-5pm) When the fog rolls into Crissy Field, head here for Fair Trade coffee, organic pastries and hot dogs within walls insulated with recycled denim; all purchases support Crissy Field conservation.

THE MISSION

TOP CHOICE **La Taquería** MEXICAN $

(415-285-7117; 2889 Mission St; burritos $6-8; 11am-9pm Mon-Sat, to 8pm Sun) No debatable tofu, saffron rice, spinach tortilla or mango salsa here: just classic tomatillo or mesquite salsa, marinated, grilled meats and flavorful beans inside a flour tortilla – optional housemade spicy pickles and sour cream highly recommended.

Commonwealth CALIFORNIAN $$
(Map p132; ☎415-355-1500; www.commonwealthsf.com; 2224 Mission St; small plates $5-16; ⏰5:30-10pm Tue-Thu & Sun, to 11pm Fri & Sat; ☑) California's most imaginative farm-to-table dining isn't in some quaint barn, but the converted cinderblock Mission dive where chef Jason Fox serves crispy hen with toybox carrots cooked in hay (yes, hay), and sea urchin floating on a bed of farm egg and organic asparagus that looks like a tide pool and tastes like a dream. Savor the $65 prix-fixe knowing $10 is donated to charity.

Pizzeria Delfina PIZZERIA $$$
(Map p132; ☎415-437-6800; www.delfinasf.com; 3611 18th St; pizzas $11-17; ⏰11:30am-10pm Tue-Thu, to 11pm Fri, noon-11pm Sat & Sun, 5:30-10pm Mon; ☑) One bite explains why SF is so obsessed with pizza lately: Delfina's thin crust supports the weight of fennel sausage and fresh mozzarella without drooping or cracking, while white pizzas let chefs freestyle with Cali-foodie ingredients like maitake mushrooms, broccoli rabe and artisan cheese. No reservations; sign up on the chalkboard and wait with wine at Delfina bar next door.

THE CASTRO

TOP CHOICE **Frances** CALIFORNIAN $$
(Map p132; ☎415-621-3870; www.frances-sf.com; 3870 17th St; mains $14-27; ⏰5-10.30pm Tue-Sun) Chef/owner Melissa Perello earned a Michelin star for fine dining, then ditched downtown to start this market-inspired neighborhood bistro. Daily menus showcase bright, seasonal flavors and luxurious textures: cloud-like sheep's-milk ricotta gnocchi with crunchy breadcrumbs and broccolini, grilled calamari with preserved Meyer lemon, and artisan wine served by the ounce, directly from Wine Country.

Chilango MEXICAN $$
(Map p126; ☎415-552-5700; chilangorestaurantsf.com; 235 Church St; dishes $8-12; ⏰11am-10pm) Upgrade from to-go taquerias to organic, *chilango* (Mexico City native) dishes worthy of a sit-down dinner, including grass-fed filet mignon tacos, sustainable pork *carnitas* and sensational free-range chicken *mole.*

Starbelly CALIFORNIAN $$
(Map p132; ☎415-252-7500; www.starbellysf.com; 3583 16th St; dishes $6-19; ⏰11:30am-11pm, to midnight Fri & Sat) Reclaimed wood decor to match the food: market-fresh salads, scrumptious pâté, roasted mussels with housemade sausage and juicy grass-fed burgers. Reserve ahead to lounge amid flowering herbs on the heated patio, or join the communal table.

THE HAIGHT

Rosamunde Sausage Grill SAUSAGES $
(Map p132; ☎415-437-6851; 545 Haight St; sausages $4-6; ⏰11:30am-10pm) Impress a dinner date for $10: load up classic brats or fig-duck links with complimentary roasted peppers, grilled onions, wholegrain mustard and mango chutney, washed down with microbrews at Toronado next door.

Cole Valley Cafe SANDWICHES $
(Map p132; ☎415-668-5282; www.colevalleycafe.com; 701 Cole St; sandwiches $5-6; ⏰6:30am-8:30pm Mon-Fri, to 8pm Sat & Sun; ☑) Powerful coffee, free wi-fi and hot gourmet sandwiches that are a bargain at any price, let alone $6 for lip-smacking thyme-marinated chicken with lemony avocado spread.

Magnolia Brewpub CALIFORNIAN $$
(Map p132; ☎415-864-7468; www.magnoliapub.com; 1398 Haight St; mains $11-20; ⏰noon-midnight Mon-Thu, to 1am Fri, 10am-1am Sat, 10am-midnight Sun) Organic pub grub and homebrew samplers keep conversation flowing at communal tables, while grass-fed Prather Ranch burgers satisfy stoner appetites in side booths – it's like the Summer of Love is back, only with better food.

JAPANTOWN & PACIFIC HEIGHTS

Tataki SUSHI $$
(☎415-931-1182; www.tatakisushibar.com; 2815 California St; dishes $12-20; ⏰11:30am-2pm & 5:30-10:30pm Mon-Fri, 5-11:30pm Sat, 5-9:30pm Sun) Rescue dinner dates and the oceans with sensational, sustainable sushi: silky Arctic char drizzled with yuzu-citrus and capers replaces dubious farmed salmon, and the Golden State Roll is a local hero with spicy line-caught scallop, Pacific tuna, organic apple slivers and edible gold.

THE RICHMOND

Aziza NORTH AFRICAN $$$
(☎415-752-2222; www.azizasf.com; 5800 Geary Blvd; mains $16-29; ⏲5:30-10:30pm Wed-Mon; 🖉) Mourad Lahlou's inspiration is Moroccan and his produce organic Californian, but his flavors are out of this world: Sonoma duck confit melts into caramelized onion in flaky pastry *basteeya,* while sour cherries rouse slow-cooked local lamb shank from its barley bed.

Namu KOREAN $$
(☎415-386-8332; www.namusf.com; 439 Balboa St; small plates $8-16; ⏲6-10:30pm Sun-Tue, to midnight Wed-Sat, 10:30am-3pm Sat & Sun) Organic ingredients, Silicon Valley inventiveness and Pacific Rim roots are showcased in Namu's Korean-inspired soul food, including house-made kimchee, umami-rich shiitake mushroom dumplings and NorCal's definitive *bibimbap:* organic vegetables, grass-fed local steak and a Sonoma farm egg served sizzling on rice in a stone pot.

Drinking

TOP CHOICE **Smuggler's Cove** THEME BAR
(Map p126; http://smugglerscovesf.com; 650 Gough St; ⏲5pm-2am) Yo-ho-ho and a bottle of rum…or make that 200 at this Barbary Coast shipwreck of a tiki bar. With tasting flights and 70 cocktail recipes gleaned from around the world, you won't be dry-docked.

Zeitgeist BAR
(Map p132; www.zeitgeistsf.com; 199 Valencia St; ⏲9am-2am) When temperatures rise, bikers and hipsters converge on Zeitgeist's huge outdoor beer garden for 40 brews on tap and late-night tamales.

Bar Agricole BAR
(Map p132; ☎415-355-9400; www.baragricole.com; 355 11th St; ⏲6-10pm Sun-Wed, 6pm-late Thu-Sat) Drink your way to a history degree with well-researched cocktails: Bellamy Scotch Sour with egg whites passes the test, but Tequila Fix with lime, pineapple gum and hellfire bitters earns honors.

Toronado PUB
(Map p132; www.toronado.com; 547 Haight St) Glory hallelujah, beer-lovers: 50-plus microbrews, with hundreds more in bottles. Stumble next door to Rosamunde for sausages.

Tosca Cafe COCKTAIL BAR
(Map p126; http://toscacafesf.com; 242 Columbus Ave; ⏲5pm-2am Tue-Sun) With red vinyl booths and a jukebox of opera and Sinatra, Tosca is classic North Beach.

Entertainment

TIX Bay Area (Map p126; ☎415-433-7827; www.tixbayarea.org; ⏲Tue-Sun) sells last-minute theater tickets half-price. More options:

7x7 (www.7x7.com)

SF Bay Guardian (www.sfbg.com)

SF Weekly (www.sfweekly.com)

Squid List (http://squidlist.com/events)

Live Music

Fillmore LIVE MUSIC
(www.thefillmore.com; 1805 Geary Blvd; tickets from $20) Hendrix, Zeppelin, Janis – they all played the Fillmore, where the 1250 capacity means you're close to the stage. Don't miss the psychedelic poster-art gallery upstairs. Nightly shows.

Yoshi's JAZZ
(www.yoshis.com; 1300 Fillmore St; tickets $12-50; ⏲most shows 8pm) San Francisco's definitive jazz club draws the world's top talent, and adjoins a pretty good sushi restaurant.

Slim's LIVE MUSIC
(Map p132; ☎415-255-0333; www.slims-sf.com; 333 11th St; tickets $11-28; ⏲5pm-2am) Guaranteed good times by Gogol Bordello, Tenacious D and AC/DShe (the hard-rocking female tribute band) fill the bill at this mid-sized club, where Prince and Elvis Costello have turned up to play improptu sets unannounced.

Mezzanine LIVE MUSIC
(Map p126; ☎415-625-8880; www.mezzaninesf.com; 444 Jessie St; admission $10-40) The best sound system in SF bounces off the brick walls at breakthrough hip-hop shows by Quest Love, Method Man, Nas and Snoop Dogg, plus throwback alt-classics like the Dandy Warhols and Psychedelic Furs.

Café du Nord LIVE MUSIC
(Map p132; www.cafedunord.com; 2170 Market St) The historic speakeasy in the basement of the Swedish-American Hall with glam-rock, afrobeats, retro-rockabilly and indie-record-release parties almost nightly.

Nightclubs

Cat Club CLUB
(Map p126; www.catclubsf.com; 1190 Folsom St; admission after 10pm $5; ⏲9pm-3am Tue-Sun) Thursday's '1984' is a euphoric bi/straight/

gay party scene from a lost John Hughes movie; other nights vary from Saturday power pop to Bondage-a-Go-Go.

DNA Lounge CLUB

(Map p132; www.dnalounge.com; 375 11th St; admission $3-25; ⌚9:30pm-3am Fri & Sat, other nights vary) SF's mega-club hosts live bands and big-name DJs. Second and fourth Saturdays bring Bootie, the kick-ass original mashup party; Mondays mean Goth Death Guild, with free tea service.

El Rio CLUB

(☎415-282-3325; www.elriosf.com; 3158 Mission St; admission $3-8; ⌚5pm-2am Mon-Thu, from 4pm Fri, from noon Sun) 'Salsa Sundays' are legendary: arrive at 3pm for lessons. Other nights: oyster happy hours, eclectic music, pan-sexual crowd flirting on the patio.

Harlot CLUB

(Map p126; www.harlotsf.com; 46 Minna St; admission $10-20, 5-9pm Wed-Fri free; ⌚5pm-2am Wed-Fri, from 9pm Sat) Aptly named after 10pm, when the bordello-themed lounge cuts loose to house Thursdays, indie-rock Wednesdays and women-only Fem Bar parties.

111 Minna CLUB

(Map p126; www.111minnagallery.com; 111 Minna St) Street-wise art gallery by day, after-work lounge and club after 9pm, when '90s and '80s dance parties take the back room by storm.

Classical Music & Opera

Rivaling City Hall's grandeur is SF's 1932 **War Memorial Opera House** (Map p126; 301 Van Ness Ave), home to **San Francisco Opera** (www.sfopera.com), whose season runs from June to December, and **San Francisco Ballet** (www.sfballet.org), performing January to May. For more, check **SF Classical Voice** (www.sfcv.org).

TOP CHOICE **Davies Symphony Hall** CLASSICAL MUSIC

(Map p126; ☎415-864-6000; www.sfsymphony.org; 201 Van Ness Ave) Home of nine-time Grammy-winning SF Symphony, conducted with verve by Michael Tilson Thomas. The season runs September to July.

Yerba Buena Center for the Arts CONCERT VENUE

(Map p126; ☎415-978-2787; www.ybca.org; 701 Mission St) Hosts concerts and modern dance innovators Liss Fain Dance, Alonzo King's Lines Ballet and Smuin Ballet.

Theater

SF is home to the cutting-edge professional **American Conservatory Theater** (ACT; ☎415-749-2228; www.act-sf.org; 415 Geary St). **SHN** (☎415-512-7770; www.shnsf.com) hosts touring Broadway shows. See also **Theatre Bay Area** (www.theatrebayarea.org).

Club Fugazi COMEDY, CABARET

(Map p126; ☎415-421-4222; www.beachblanketbabylon.com; 678 Green St; seats $25-78) Home of ribald, satirical *Beach Blanket Babylon,* featuring giant hats and belly laughs.

Magic Theater THEATER

(☎415-441-8822; www.magictheatre.org; Fort Mason, Bldg D) Risk-taking original productions from major playwrights, including Sam Shepard, Edna O'Brien and Terrence McNally, starring actors like Ed Harris and Sean Penn.

Marsh THEATER

(Map p132; ☎415-826-5750; www.themarsh.org; 1062 Valencia St; tickets $15-35) Choose your seat wisely: you'll spend the evening on the edge of it, with one-acts, monologues and works-in-progress that involve the audience.

Cinema

TOP CHOICE **Castro Theatre** CINEMA

(Map p132; www.thecastrotheatre.com; 429 Castro St; adult/child $10/7.50) The city's grandest movie place screens vintage, foreign, documentary and new films.

Sundance Kabuki Cinema CINEMA

(www.sundancecinemas.com/kabuki.html; 1881 Post St; admission $10-14) The silver screen gone green, from recycled-fiber reserved seating to local Hangar vodka cocktails at 21+ shows.

Roxie Cinema CINEMA

(Map p132; www.roxie.com; 3117 16th St; adult/child $10/6.50) Documentaries, indie premieres, rare imports.

Sports

San Francisco Giants BASEBALL

(Map p126; http://sanfrancisco.giants.mlb.com; AT&T Park; tickets $5-135) Watch and learn how the World Series is won – bushy beards, women's underwear and all.

San Francisco 49ers FOOTBALL

(☎415-656-4900; www.sf49ers.com) For NFL football, beer and garlic fries, head to Candlestick Park (Map p122).

Shopping

All those rustic-chic dens, well-stocked spice racks and fabulous outfits don't just pull themselves together – San Franciscans scoured their city for it all. Here's where to find what:

Hayes Valley Local and independent designers, home design, sweets, shoes.

Valencia St Bookstores, local design collectives, art galleries, vintage whatever.

Haight St Head shops, music, vintage, skate, snow and surf gear.

Upper Fillmore & Union Sts Date outfits, girly accessories, wine and design.

Powell & Market Sts Department stores, megabrands, discount retail, Apple store.

Grant St From Chinatown souvenirs to eccentric North Beach boutiques.

Ferry Building Local food, wine and kitchenware.

Bookstores

City Lights Bookstore BOOKS
(Map p126; www.citylights.com; 261 Columbus Ave; ⌚10am-midnight) Landmark bookseller, publisher and free-speech champion; browse Muckraking and Stolen Continents sections downstairs and find Nirvana upstairs in Poetry.

Adobe Books BOOKS
(http://adobebooksbackroomgallery.blogspot.com; 3166 16th St; ⌚11am-midnight) Books you never knew you needed used and cheap, hidden among sofas, cats and art installations.

Omnivore BOOKS
(☎415-282-4712; www.omnivorebooks.com; 3885a Cesar Chavez St; ⌚11am-6pm Mon-Sat, noon-5pm Sun) Salivate over books signed by chef-legend Alice Waters and rare Civil War cookbooks; check events calendar for standing-room-only events with star chefs.

Bound Together Anarchist Book Collective BOOKS
(Map p132; www.boundtogetherbooks.com; 1369 Haight St; ⌚11:30am-7:30pm) All-volunteer bookstore featuring conspiracy-theory comics, alternative histories, organic farming manuals and other radical notions.

Green Apple BOOKS
(☎415-387-2272; www.greenapplebooks.com; 506 Clement St; ⌚10am-10:30pm Sun-Thu, to 11:30pm Fri & Sat) Three stories of new releases, remaindered titles and used nonfiction; mags, music and used novels two doors down.

Information

Emergency & Medical Services

American College of Traditional Chinese Medicine (☎415-282-9603; www.actcm.edu; 450 Connecticut St; ⌚8:30am-9pm Mon-Thu, 9am-5:30pm Fri & Sat) Acupuncture and herbal remedies.

Haight Ashbury Free Clinic (☎415-746-1950; www.hafci.org; 558 Clayton St) Free doctor visits by appointment; substance abuse and mental health services.

Pharmaca (☎415-661-1216; www.pharmaca.com; 925 Cole St; ⌚8am-8pm Mon-Fri, from 9am Sat & Sun) Pharmacy and naturopathic remedies.

Police, fire & ambulance (☎911)

San Francisco General Hospital (☎emergency room 415-206-8111, main 415-206-8000; www.sfdph.org; 1001 Potrero Ave) Open 24 hours.

Trauma Recovery & Rape Treatment Center (☎415-437-3000; http://traumarecoverycenter.org) A 24-hour hotline.

Walgreens (☎415-861-3136; www.walgreens.com; 498 Castro ST; ⌚24hr) Pharmacy with locations citywide (see website).

Internet Access

SF has free wi-fi hot spots citywide – locate one nearby with www.openwifispots.com. Connect for free in Union Sq, and most cafes and hotel lobbies.

Apple Store (www.apple.com/retail/sanfrancisco; 1 Stockton St; ⌚9am-9pm Mon-Sat, 10am-8pm Sun; 📶) Free wi-fi and internet terminal usage.

San Francisco Main Library (http://sfpl.org; 100 Larkin St; ⌚10am-6pm Mon & Sat, 9am-8pm Tue-Thu, noon-5pm Fri & Sun; 📶) Free 15-minute internet terminal usage; spotty wi-fi access.

Media

KALW 91.7 FM (www.kalw.org) National Public Radio (NPR) affiliate.

KPFA 94.1 FM (www.kpfa.org) Alternative news and music.

KPOO 89.5 FM (www.kpoo.com) Community radio with jazz, R & B, blues and reggae.

KQED 88.5 FM (www.kqed.org) NPR and Public Broadcasting (PBS) affiliate offering podcasts and streaming video.

San Francisco Bay Guardian (www.sfbg.com) San Francisco's free, alternative weekly covers topics such as politics, theater, music, art and movie listings.

San Francisco Chronicle (www.sfgate.com) Main daily newspaper with news, entertainment and event listings.

Money

Bank of America (www.bankamerica.com; 1 Market Plaza; ⏲9am-6pm Mon-Fri)

Post

Rincon Center post office (www.usps.com; 180 Steuart St; ⏲8am-6pm Mon-Fri, 9am-2pm Sat) Postal services plus historic murals.

Tourist Information

San Francisco's Visitor Information Center (☎415-391-2000; www.onlyinsanfrancisco.com; lower level, Hallidie Plaza; ⏲9am-5pm Mon-Fri, to 3pm Sat & Sun)

Websites

Craigslist (http://sfbay.craigslist.org) SF-based source for jobs, dates, free junk, Buddhist babysitters, the works.

Twitter (www.twitter.com) SF-based social media alerts on SF pop-up shops, food trucks, free shows and weekend recommendations from Lonely Planet authors.

Yelp (www.yelp.com) Locals trade verbal fisticuffs on this San Francisco–based review site that covers shopping, bars, services and restaurants.

Getting There & Away

Air

San Francisco International Airport (SFO; www.flysfo.com) is 14 miles south of downtown off Hwy 101 and accessible by Bay Area Rapid Transit (BART).

Bus

Until the new terminal is complete in 2017, San Francisco's intercity hub remains the **Temporary Transbay Terminal** (Howard & Main Sts), where you can catch buses on **AC Transit** (www.actransit.org) to the East Bay, **Golden Gate Transit** (http://goldengatetransit.org) north to Marin and Sonoma Counties, and **SamTrans** (www.samtrans.com) south to Palo Alto and the Pacific coast. **Greyhound** (☎800-231-2222; www.greyhound.com) buses leave daily for Los Angeles ($56.50, eight to 12 hours), Truckee near Lake Tahoe ($33, 5½ hours) and other destinations.

Train

Amtrak (☎800-872-7245; www.amtrakcalifornia.com) offers low-emissions, leisurely travel to and from San Francisco. *Coast Starlight*'s spectacular 35-hour run from Los Angeles to Seattle stops in Oakland, and the *California Zephyr* takes its sweet time (51 hours) traveling from Chicago through the Rockies to Oakland. Both have sleeping cars and dining/lounge cars with panoramic windows. Amtrak runs free shuttle buses to San Francisco's Ferry Building and CalTrain station.

CalTrain (www.caltrain.com; cnr 4th & King Sts) connects San Francisco with Silicon Valley hubs and San Jose.

Getting Around

For Bay Area transit options, departures and arrivals, check ☎511 or www.511.org.

To/From San Francisco International Airport

BART (www.bart.gov; one way $8.10) Offers a fast, direct ride to downtown San Francisco.

SamTrans (www.samtrans.com; one way $5) Express bus KX gets you to the Temporary Transbay Terminal in about 30 minutes.

SuperShuttle (☎800-258-3826; www.supershuttle.com; one way $17) Door-to-door vans depart from baggage-claim areas, taking 45 minutes to most SF locations.

Taxi To downtown San Francisco costs $35 to $50.

To/From Oakland International Airport

BART is the cheapest way to get to San Francisco from the Oakland airport. AirBART shuttle ($3) operates every 10 to 20 minutes to the Coliseum station to catch BART to downtown SF ($3.80, 25 minutes). Taxis from Oakland airport average $25 to Oakland and around $50 to $60 to San Francisco. **SuperShuttle** (☎800-258-3826; www.supershuttle.com) offers shared van rides to downtown SF for $25 to $30. **Airport Express** (☎800-327-2024; www.airportexpressinc.com) runs a scheduled shuttle every two hours (from 6am to midnight) between Oakland airport and Sonoma ($32) and Marin ($24) counties.

Boat

Blue & Gold Ferries (www.blueandgoldfleet.com) operates the Alameda–Oakland ferry from Pier 41 and the Ferry Building. **Golden Gate Ferry** (www.goldengate.org) runs from the Ferry Building to Sausalito and Larkspur in Marin County.

Car

Avoid driving in San Francisco: street parking is harder to find than true love, and meter readers are ruthless. Downtown parking lots are at Embarcadero Center, 5th and Mission Sts, Union Sq, and Sutter and Stockton Sts. National car-rental agencies have airport and downtown offices.

Public Transportation

MUNI (Municipal Transit Agency; www.sfmuni.com) operates bus, streetcar and cable-car lines. Two cable-car lines leave from Powell and Market Sts; a third leaves from California and Markets Sts. A detailed *MUNI Street & Transit Map* is available free online and at the Powell MUNI kiosk ($3). Standard fare for buses or streetcars is $2; cable-car fare is $6. A **MUNI Passport** (1/3/7 days $14/21/27) allows unlimited travel on all MUNI transport, including cable cars; it's sold at San Francisco's Visitor Information Center and at the TIX Bay Area kiosk at Union Sq. A seven-day **City Pass** (adult/child $69/39) covers Muni and admission to five attractions.

BART links San Francisco with the East Bay and runs beneath Market St, down Mission St and south to SFO and Millbrae, where it connects with CalTrain.

Taxi

Fares run about $2.25 per mile; meters start at $3.50.

DeSoto Cab (☎415-970-1300)

Green Cab (☎415-626-4733; www.626green.com) Fuel-efficient hybrids; worker-owned collective.

Luxor (☎415-282-4141)

Yellow Cab (☎415-333-3333)

Marin County

Majestic redwoods cling to coastal hills just across the Golden Gate Bridge in woodsy, wealthy, laid-back **Marin** (www.visitmarin.org). **Sausalito**, the southernmost town, is a cute, touristy bayside destination for bike trips over the bridge (take the ferry back). At the harbor, the **San Francisco Bay-Delta Model** (☎415-332-3871; www.spn.usace.army.mil/bmvc; 2100 Bridgeway Blvd; admission free; ⏲9am-4pm Tue-Fri, plus 10am-5pm Sat & Sun in summer) is a way-cool 1.5-acre hydraulic re-creation of the entire bay and delta.

MARIN HEADLANDS

The windswept, rugged headlands are laced with hiking trails, providing stunning views of SF and the Golden Gate. To reach the **visitor center** (☎415-331-1540; www.nps.gov/goga/marin-headlands.htm; ⏲9:30am-4:30pm), take the Alexander Ave exit from the Golden Gate Bridge, turn left under the freeway, and then turn right on Conzelman Rd and follow signs. Attractions include the **Point Bonita Lighthouse** (⏲12:30-3:30pm Sat-Mon), climbable Cold War–era bunkers and **Rodeo Beach** (Map p122). At Fort Baker, **Bay Area Discovery Museum** (☎415-339-3900; www.baykidsmuseum.org; 557 McReynolds Rd, Sausalito; adult/child $10/8; ⏲9am-4pm Tue-Fri, 10am-5pm Sat & Sun) is a cool destination for kids.

Near the visitor center, the **HI Marin Headlands Hostel** (Map p122; ☎415-331-2777; www.norcalhostels.org/marin; dm $22-26, r $72-92; @) occupies two historic 1907 buildings on a forested hill. Private rooms in the former officer's house are sweet.

MT TAMALPAIS STATE PARK

Majestic 2571ft 'Mt Tam' is fantastic for mountain biking and hiking. **Mt Tamalpais State Park** (☎415-388-2070; www.mttam.net; parking $8) encompasses 6300 acres of parklands, plus over 200 miles of trails; don't miss the East Peak lookout. Panoramic Hwy climbs from Hwy 1 through the park to **Stinson Beach**, a mellow seaside town with a great 3-mile-long sandy beach. Park headquarters are at **Pantoll Station** (Map p122; 801 Panoramic Hwy; tent sites $25; 📶), the nexus of many trails and location of a wooded first-come, first-served campground. Or hike in food, linen and towels to the rustic, electricity-free **West Point Inn** (☎415-646-0702; www.westpointinn.com; 1000 Panoramic Hwy, Mill Valley; r per adult/child $50/25); reservations required.

Near park headquarters, **Mountain Home Inn** (☎415-381-9000; www.mtnhomeinn.com; 810 Panoramic Hwy; r incl breakfast $195-345, dinner $38, brunch $10-21; ⏲restaurant 11:30am-3pm & 5:30-8pm Wed-Sun, to 9pm Fri & Sat; 📶) sits atop a wooded ridge. Its romantic, woodsy rooms have gorgeous views; the restaurant serves good brunches and prix-fixe dinners.

MUIR WOODS NATIONAL MONUMENT

Wander among an ancient stand of the world's tallest trees in 550-acre **Muir Woods National Monument** (Map p122; ☎415-388-2595; www.nps.gov/muwo; adult/child under 16yr $5/free), 12 miles north of the Golden Gate. The easy 1-mile Main Trail Loop leads past thousand-year-old redwoods at Cathedral Grove and returns via Bohemian Grove. Come midweek to avoid crowds; otherwise arrive early morning or late afternoon. Take Hwy 101 to the Hwy 1 exit, and follow the signs.

The **Muir Woods shuttle** (☎415-455-2000; www.goldengatetransit.org; adult/child $3/1) bus 66 operates weekends and holidays, May to September, and runs about every 30 minutes from Marin City and Mill Valley, with limited connections with the Sausalito ferry terminal.

POINT REYES NATIONAL SEASHORE

The windswept peninsula of Point Reyes National Seashore juts 10 miles out to sea on an entirely different tectonic plate, and covers 110 sq miles of beaches, lagoons and forested hills.

TOP CHOICE **Point Reyes Lighthouse** (Map p122; ⏲10am-4:30pm Thu-Mon), crowns the peninsula's westernmost point and is ideal for whale-watching. To see Tule elk, hike the bluff-top Tomales Point Trail on the peninsula's north tip, reached via Pierce Point Rd. The **Bear Valley Visitors Center** (☎415-464-5100; www.nps.gov/pore) is just past Olema and has trail maps and cool displays. Point Reyes has four hike-in **campgrounds** (☎reservations 415-663-8054; tent sites $15), two near the beach.

The **West Marin Chamber of Commerce** (☎415-663-9232; www.pointreyes.org) has information on cozy inns and cottages. The bayside **Tomales Bay Resort** (☎415-669-1389; www.tomalesbayresort.com; 12938 Sir Francis Drake Blvd, Inverness; r $120-225;) has pleasant motel rooms, with bargain rates from Sunday through Thursday and in winter.

Nature lovers bunk at the only in-park lodging, **HI Point Reyes Hostel** (Map p122; ☎415-663-8811; www.norcalhostels.org/reyes; dm/r $24/68; @), off Limantour Rd, 8 miles from the visitor center. Kayaking scenic Tomales Bay gets you up close to seals, birds and the occasional elk, and **Blue Waters Kayaking** (☎415-669-2600; www.bwkayak.com; guided trips $68-98, 4hr rentals $60-130) has locations in Inverness and Marshall.

TOP CHOICE **Drake's Bay Oyster Company** (☎415-669-1149; 1 dozen oysters to go/on the half shell $15/24; ⏲8:30am-4:30pm), off Sir Francis Drake Blvd in the park, is the place for oyster-lovers. Nearby, cute little Point Reyes Station has excellent restaurants.

Berkeley

Not much has changed since the 1960s heyday of anti–Vietnam War protests – except the bumper stickers: 'No Blood for Oil' has supplanted 'Make Love Not War.' Birkenstocks and pony tails remain perennially in fashion. You can't walk around nude on campus anymore, but 'Berserkeley' remains the Bay Area's radical hub, crawling with university students, scoffing skateboarders and aging hippies. Stroll its wooded university grounds and surrounding streets to soak up the vibe.

Sights & Activities

University of California, Berkeley UNIVERSITY

(Map p122) 'Cal' is one of the country's top universities and home to 35,000 diverse, politically conscious students. The **Visitor Services Center** (☎510-642-5215; http://visitors.berkeley.edu; 101 Sproul Hall; tours 10am Mon-Sat, 1pm Sun) has info and leads free campus tours (reservations required). Cal's landmark is the 1914 Sather Tower (also called the Campanile), with elevator rides ($2) to the top. The Bancroft Library displays the small gold nugget that started the California gold rush in 1848.

Leading to the campus's south gate, **Telegraph Avenue** is as youthful and gritty as San Francisco's Haight St, packed with cafes, cheap eats, record stores and bookstores.

UC Berkeley Art Museum MUSEUM

(☎510-642-0808; www.bampfa.berkeley.edu; 2626 Bancroft Way; adult/child $10/7; ⏲11am-5pm Wed-Sun) A campus highlight with 11 galleries showcasing a wide range of works, from ancient Chinese to cutting-edge contemporary. Across the street, its world-renowned **Pacific Film Archive** (☎510-642-1124; 2575 Bancroft Way; adult/child $9.50/6.50) screens little-known independent and avant-garde films. Both are scheduled to move to a new Oxford St location by 2014.

Tilden Regional Park PARK

(www.ebparks.org/parks/tilden) In the Berkeley hills, this 2079-acre park has hiking, picnicking, swimming at Lake Anza, and fun stuff for kids, including a merry-go-round and steam train.

Sleeping

Basic and midrange motels are clustered west of campus along University Ave.

Hotel Durant BOUTIQUE HOTEL $$

(☎510-845-8981; www.hoteldurant.com; 2600 Durant Ave; r from $134; @) A block from campus, this 1928 hotel cheekily highlights that connection. The lobby's adorned with embarrassing yearbook photos and a ceiling mobile of exam books, and smallish rooms have dictionary-covered shower curtains and bongs repurposed into bedside lamps.

IF YOU HAVE A FEW MORE DAYS

Right across the bay, gritty-urban Oakland's got attitude, the A's baseball team and deep African American roots that shine through in world-celebrated arts and food. It has a lovely historic downtown, saltwater lake for joggers and kids, and some happening clubs and restaurants.

Oakland Museum of California MUSEUM
(☎510-238-2200; www.museumca.org; cnr 10th & Oak Sts; adult/child $12/6; ⊙11am-5pm Wed-Sun, to 9pm Fri) A must-see. Relevant, fascinating rotating exhibits plus permanent galleries dedicated to California's history and ecology.

Heinhold's First & Last Chance Saloon BAR
(48 Webster St) In Jack London Sq, this lopsided quake survivor and National Literary Landmark is open daily for inspirational drinking. Yes, your beer *is* sliding off the counter.

Yoshi's CLUB
(☎510-238-9200; www.yoshis.com; 510 Embarcadero West; admission $12-40) One of the country's major jazz clubs; also a sushi restaurant.

YMCA HOSTEL $
(☎510-848-6800; www.baymca.org/dt/downtown-hotel.aspx; 2001 Allston Way; s/d with shared bath $49/81; @🛜🏊) The recently remodeled 100-year-old downtown Y building is still the best budget option in town. Rates for the austere private rooms include use of the pool, fitness center and kitchen facilities.

Downtown Berkeley Inn MOTEL $$
(☎510-843-4043; www.downtownberkeleyinn.com; 2001 Bancroft Way; r $89-109; ❄🛜) A 27-room budget boutique-style motel with good-sized rooms and correspondingly ample flat-screen TVs.

Eating & Drinking

TOP CHOICE **Chez Panisse** AMERICAN $$$
(☎restaurant 510-548-5525, cafe 510-548-5049; 1517 Shattuck Ave; restaurant $60-95, cafe mains $18-29; ⊙restaurant dinner Mon-Sat) Genuflect at the temple of Alice Waters: the birthplace of California cuisine remains at the pinnacle of Bay Area dining. Book one month ahead for its legendary prix-fixe meals (no substitutions); or book upstairs at the less-expensive, à la carte cafe.

Café Intermezzo CAFETERIA $
(2442 Telegraph Ave; sandwiches & salads $6.50; 🌿) Mammoth salads draw a constant crowd, and we're not talking about delicate little rabbit food plates. Bring a friend, or you might drown while trying to polish one off yourself.

Cheese Board Pizza PIZZERIA $
(1512 Shattuck Ave; pizza slice $2.50; ⊙11:30am-3pm & 4:30-8pm Tue-Sat; 🌿) Sit down for a slice of the fabulously crispy one-option-per-day veggie pizza at this worker-owned collective where there's often live music.

Caffe Strada CAFE $
(2300 College Ave; ⊙6am-midnight; 🛜) University students get wired on caffeine on the giant outdoor patio and study, ardently talk philosophy or make eyes at each other.

Triple Rock Brewery & Ale House BREWERY $
(1920 Shattuck Ave) One of the country's first brewpubs, the house beers and pub grub are quite good, and the antique wooden bar and rooftop sun deck are delightful.

Entertainment

Berkeley Repertory Theatre THEATER
(☎510-647-2949; www.berkeleyrep.org; 2025 Addison St) A highly respected company that has produced bold versions of classical and modern plays since 1968.

Freight & Salvage Coffeehouse LIVE MUSIC
(☎510-644-2020; www.thefreight.org; 2020 Addison St) This legendary club has over 40 years of history and features great traditional folk and world music. All ages; half-price tickets for under 21s.

Getting There & Around

AC Transit (☎510-817-1717, 511; www.actransit.org) runs local buses in Berkeley, as well as between Berkeley and Oakland ($2.10), and Berkeley and San Francisco ($4.20). **BART** (www.bart.gov) trains run from SF to downtown Berkeley ($3.50), which is four blocks from the main campus gate.

NORTHERN CALIFORNIA

The Golden State goes wild in Northern California, with giant redwoods emerging from coastal mists, wallows in volcanic mud amid Wine Country vineyards, and the majestic Sierra Nevada mountains framing Yosemite and Lake Tahoe. Northern California's backwoods are surprisingly forward-thinking, with organic diners, ecoresorts, and the nation's earliest national and state parks. Pack your trash and be mindful of private property – local goatherds and medical-marijuana growers can get touchy about trespassers. Come for the scenery, but stay for superb wine and cheese, the obligatory hot tub, and conversations that begin with 'Hey dude!' and end hours later.

Wine Country

A patchwork of vineyards stretches from sunny inland Napa to chilly coastal Sonoma – America's premier wine-growing region. Napa has art-filled tasting rooms by big-name architects, with prices to match; in down-to-earth Sonoma, you'll drink in sheds and probably meet the vintner's dog. NB: There are three Sonomas: the town, the valley and the county.

NAPA VALLEY

Some 230 wineries crowd 30-mile-long Napa Valley along three main routes. Main Hwy 29 is lined with blockbuster wineries; it jams weekends. Parallel-running Silverado Trail moves faster; it's lined with boutique wineries, bizarre architecture and cult-hit cabs. Hwy 121 (aka Carneros Hwy) runs west toward Sonoma, with landmark wineries specializing in sparkling wines and Pinot Noir.

Traveling south to north, **Downtown Napa** – the valley's workaday hub – lacks rusticity, but has trendy restaurants, tasting rooms and mansions reinvented as B&Bs. Picky picnickers head to Oxbow Public Market; bargain hunters hit **Napa Valley Welcome Center** (☎707-260-0107; www.legendarynapavalley.com; 600 Main St; ⏲9am-5pm) for spa deals, wine-tasting passes and winery maps.

Formerly a stagecoach stop, tiny **Yountville** – home of famous French Laundry – has more Michelin-starred eateries per capita than anywhere else in America.

Charming **St Helena** – the Beverly Hills of Napa – is where traffic jams, but there's great strolling and shopping, if you find parking.

Folksy **Calistoga** – Napa's least-gentrified town – is home to hot-spring spas and mud-bath emporiums that use volcanic ash from adjacent Mt St Helena. To find spas, contact **Calistoga Visitors Center** (☎707-942-6333; www.calistogavisitors.com; 1133 Washington St; ⏲9am-5pm).

Sights & Activities

Most Napa wineries require reservations. Book one appointment, then build your day around it. Plan to see no more than three in one day. The following are in south-to-north order.

di Rosa Art + Nature Preserve GALLERY
(Map p122; ☎707-226-5991; www.dirosapreserve.org; 5200 Carneros Hwy 121; ⏲gallery 9:30am-3pm Wed-Fri, by appointment Sat) When you notice scrap-metal sheep grazing Carneros vineyards, you've spotted di Rosa Art + Nature Preserve, one of the best-anywhere collections of Northern California art. Reservations are highly recommended for tours.

Vintners' Collective TASTING ROOM
(☎707-255-7150; www.vintnerscollective.com; 1245 Main St, Napa; tasting $25; ⏲11am-6pm) Inside a former 19th-century brothel, VC represents 20 high-end boutique wineries too small to have their own tasting rooms.

DON'T MISS

DON'T MISS...

» Dig into farm-to-table cooking at **Zazu** (p153) and **Ad Hoc** (p151)

» Cycle Sonoma's sun-dappled Dry Creek Valley, braking for Zin in a cave at **Bella Vineyards** (p153) and Pinot in a tool shed at **Porter Creek Vineyards** (p153)

» Wander beneath 1000-year-old redwoods at **Armstrong Redwoods State Reserve** (p153)

» Find inspiration among vineyards, peacocks and surreal sculptures at Napa's **di Rosa Art + Nature Preserve**

» Race otters down the lazy **Russian River** in a canoe (p152)

» Wallow in **volcanic-mud baths** at Calistoga's Indian Springs (p150)

Twenty Rows WINERY
(☎707-287-1063; www.vinoce.com; 880 Vallejo St, Napa; tasting $10; ⏲11am-5pm Tue-Sat) Downtown Napa's only working winery crafts light-on-the-palate Cabernet Sauvignon for a mere $20 a bottle.

Hess Collection WINERY, GALLERY
(☎707-255-1144; www.hesscollection.com; 4411 Redwood Rd, Napa; tasting $10; ⏲10am-4pm) Northwest of downtown, Hess pairs monster cabs with blue-chip art by mega-modernists like Francis Bacon and Robert Motherwell. Reservations suggested.

Darioush WINERY
(☎707-257-2345; www.darioush.com; 4240 Silverado Trail, Napa; tasting $18-35; ⏲10:30am-5pm) Stone bulls glower from atop pillars lining the driveway of Darioush, a jaw-dropping Persian-temple winery that crafts monumental Merlots.

Frog's Leap WINERY
(☎707-963-4704; www.frogsleap.com; 8815 Conn Creek Rd, Rutherford; tours with tasting $20; ⏲by appointment) Meandering paths wind through magical gardens surrounding an 1884 barn at this LEED-certified winery, known for Sauvignon Blanc and Cabernet. Reservations required.

Culinary Institute of America at Greystone COOKING SCHOOL
(☎707-967-2320; 2555 Main St, St Helena; mains $25-29, cooking demonstration $20; ⏲restaurant 11:30am-9pm, cooking demonstrations 1:30pm Sat & Sun) An 1889 stone chateau houses a gadget-filled culinary shop, fine restaurant, and weekend cooking demonstrations and wine-tasting classes.

Cade WINERY
(☎707-965-2746; www.cadewinery.com; 360 Howell Mountain Rd, Angwin; tasting $20; ⏲by appointment) Ascend Mt Veeder for drop-dead vistas at Napa's oh-so-swank, first-ever LEED gold-certified winery, which crafts Bordeaux-style Cabernet Sauvignon. Hawks ride thermals at eye level. Reservations required.

Pride Mountain WINERY
(☎707-963-4949; www.pridewines.com; 4026 Spring Mountain Rd, St Helena; tasting $10; ⏲10:30am-3:45pm by appointment) Cult-favorite Pride straddles the Sonoma–Napa border and makes stellar Cabernet, Merlot and Viognier at an unfussy hilltop estate with spectacular picnicking. Reservations required.

Casa Nuestra WINERY
(☎866-844-9463; www.casanuestra.com; 3451 Silverado Trail, St Helena; tasting $10; ⏲10am-4:30 by appointment) A peace flag and portrait of Elvis greet you at this tiny mom-and-pop winery, known for its unusual varietals. Goats frolic beside the picnic area.

Castello di Amorosa WINERY
(☎707-967-6272; www.castellodiamorosa.com; 4045 Hwy 29, Calistoga; tasting $10-15, tour adult/child $32/22; ⏲by appointment) You'll need reservations to tour this near-perfect re-creation of a 12th-century Italian castle, complete with moat and torture chamber. The respectable Italian varietals include a good Merlot blend, great with pizza.

Lava Vine TASTING ROOM
(☎707-942-9500; www.lavavine.com; 965 Silverado Trail, Calistoga; tasting $10; ⏲10am-5pm, appointment suggested) The party kids at Lava Vine take a lighthearted approach to seriously good wine, offering food pairings with tastings. Kids and dogs play outside. Bring a picnic. Reservations recommended.

Indian Springs SPA
(☎707-942-4913; www.indianspringscalistoga.com; 1712 Lincoln Ave, Calistoga; ⏲9am-8pm) Book ahead for a volcanic-mud bath at Calistoga's original 19th-century hot-springs resort; treatments ($85) include access to the hot-springs-fed pool.

Sleeping

Napa's best values are midweek and off-season in Calistoga and at downtown Napa motels and B&Bs – see www.lonelyplanet.com and www.legendarynapavalley.com for more options.

Eurospa Inn MOTEL $$
(☎707-942-6829; www.eurospa.com; 1202 Pine St, Calistoga; r $139-189; ❄📶🏊) Immaculate single-story motel.

El Bonita Motel MOTEL $$
(☎707-963-3216; www.elbonita.com; 195 Main St, St Helena; r $119-179; ❄@📶🏊) Book well ahead for this mid-valley motel; up-to-date rooms, hot tub and sauna.

Chablis Inn MOTEL $$
(☎707-257-1944; www.chablisinn.com; 3360 Solano Ave, Napa; r weekday $89-109, weekend $159-179; ❄@📶🏊) Good-value motel, on Napa's suburban strip.

Calistoga Inn INN $$
(☎707-942-4101; www.calistogainn.com; 1250 Lincoln Ave, Calistoga; r midweek/weekend $69/119) Bargain inn upstairs from a brewery-restaurant (bring earplugs). No TVs, shared bathrooms.

Mountain Home Ranch B&B, RESORT $$
(☎707-942-6616; www.mountainhomeranch.com; 3400 Mountain Home Ranch Rd, Calistoga; r $109-119, cabins $69-144;) Secluded, rustic 1913 guest ranch on 340 acres, with hiking, canoeing and farm animals.

Bothe-Napa Valley State Park CAMPGROUND $
(☎707-942-4575, reservations 800-444-7275; www.parks.ca.gov; campsites $35;) Hillside campsites with hiking beneath moss-covered oaks.

Eating

Wine Country restaurants cut their hours in winter and spring. Plan to eat dinner by 8pm in the off-season.

Oxbow Public Market MARKET $
(☎707-226-6529; www.oxbowpublicmarket.com; 610 & 644 1st St, Napa; 9am-7pm Mon-Sat, 10am-5pm Sun) Oxbow showcases sustainably produced artisanal foods by multiple vendors. Feast on Hog Island oysters (six for $15), Pica Pica's Venezuelan cornbread sandwiches ($8) and Three Twins certified organic ice-cream ($4 cones).

Gott's Roadside/Taylor's Automatic Refresher BURGERS $$
(☎707-963-3486; www.gottsroadside.com; 933 Main St, St Helena; dishes $8-15; 10:30am-9pm;) A 1950s drive-in diner with 21st-century sensibilities: burgers are all-natural Niman Ranch beef or lean 'ahi tuna, with optional sides of chili-dusted sweet-potato fries.

JoLé CALIFORNIAN $$
(☎707-942-5938; www.jolerestaurant.com; 1457 Lincoln Ave, Calistoga; mains $15-20; 5-9pm) Small plates, modest prices and outsize flavor – chef-owned JoLé evolves seasonally and scores high marks for consistency and farm-to-table flavors.

TOP CHOICE **Ad Hoc** AMERICAN $$$
(☎707-944-2487; www.adhocrestaurant.com; 6476 Washington St, Yountville; 5-9pm Wed-Mon, 10:30am-2pm Sun brunch) Don't ask for a menu at Thomas Keller's most innovative restaurant since French Laundry: chef Dave Cruz dreams up his four-course, $48 market menu daily. No substitutions (except for dietary restrictions), but none needed – every dish is comforting, fresh and spot-on.

Ubuntu VEGETARIAN $$$
(☎707-251-5656; www.ubuntunapa.com; 1140 Main St, Napa; dishes $14-18; 11:30am-2:30pm Sat & Sun, 5:30-8:30pm daily;) The Michelin-starred seasonal, vegetarian menu features wonders from the kitchen garden, satisfying hearty eaters with four-to-five inspired small plates, and eco-savvy drinkers with 100-plus sustainably produced wines.

French Laundry CALIFORNIAN $$$
(☎707-944-2380; www.frenchlaundry.com; 6640 Washington St, Yountville; fixed-price menu $270; 11:30am-2:30pm Sat & Sun, 5:30-9pm daily) A high-wattage culinary experience on par with the world's best, French Laundry is ideal for marking lifetime achievements. Book exactly two months ahead: call at 10am (or try OpenTable.com at midnight). If you can't score a table, console yourself at Keller's nearby note-perfect French brasserie Bouchon; or with chocolate cake at Bouchon Bakery.

SONOMA VALLEY

More casual, less commercial than Napa, Sonoma Valley has 70 wineries around Hwy 12 – and unlike Napa, most welcome picnicking.

Sights & Activities

Sonoma Plaza SQUARE
(Napa, Spain & 1st Sts, Sonoma) Downtown Sonoma was once the capital of a rogue nation. Today's plaza – the state's largest town square – looks stately with chic boutiques, historical buildings and stone **visitor center** (☎707-996-1090; www.sonomavalley.com; 453 1st St E; 9am-5pm), but it gets lively during summer evenings and **farmers markets** (9am-noon Fri, 5:30-8pm Tue Apr-Oct).

Gundlach-Bundschu WINERY
(☎707-938-5277; www.gunbun.com; 2000 Denmark St, Sonoma; tasting $10; 11am-4:30pm) West of downtown, Gundlach-Bundschu dates to 1858 and looks like a storybook castle. Winemakers craft legendary Tempranillo and signature Riesling and Gewürztraminer. GunBun also operates nearby **Bartholomew Park Winery** (☎707-939-3026; www.bartpark.com; 1000 Vineyard Lane; tasting $5-10; 11am-4:30pm), a 400-acre preserve with vineyards cultivated in 1857, now

certified organic, yielding citrusy Sauvignon Blanc and smoky Merlot.

Jack London Historic State Park HISTORIC SITE
(Map p122; ☎707-938-5216; www.jacklondonpark.com; 2400 London Ranch Rd, Glen Ellen; per car $8; ⏰10am-5pm Thu-Mon) Up Hwy 12, obey the call of the wild at Jack London State Historic Park, where adventure-novelist Jack London moved in 1910 to build his dream house – which burned on the eve of completion in 1913. His widow built the house that now stands as a museum to London. Miles of **hiking trails** (some open to mountain bikes) weave through 1400 hilltop acres; an easy 2-mile loop meanders to a lake, great for picnicking.

Kaz Winery WINERY
(☎707-833-2536; www.kazwinery.com; 233 Adobe Canyon Rd, Kenwood; tasting $5-10; ⏰11am-5pm Fri-Mon) Veer off Hwy 12 near Kenwood for offbeat, organically grown, cult-favorite wines, poured inside a barn.

FREE **Cornerstone** GARDENS
(☎707-933-9474, 707-933-3010; www.corenerstonegardens.com; 23570 Hwy 121; ⏰10am-5pm) There's nothing traditional about this tapestry of gardens, south of downtown Sonoma, showcasing 25 renowned avant-garde landscape designers.

Sleeping

At the northern end of Sonoma Valley, Santa Rosa has chain hotels near Railroad Sq.

TOP CHOICE **Beltane Ranch** RANCH $$$
(☎707-996-6501; www.beltaneranch.com; 11775 Hwy 12; r incl breakfast $150-240; 📶) Surrounded by pasturelands, Beltane's cheerful 1890s ranch house occupies 100 acres and has double porches lined with swinging chairs and white wicker. Five rooms. No phones or TVs.

Sonoma Hotel HISTORIC HOTEL $$
(☎707-996-2996; www.sonomahotel.com; 110 W Spain St, Sonoma; r incl breakfast midweek/weekend Nov-Mar $140/170, Apr-Oct $170/200) Charming 1880 landmark hotel on happening Sonoma Plaza, with larger/smaller rooms for $30 more/less; two-night minimum weekends. No elevator or parking lot.

Hillside Inn MOTEL $
(☎707-546-9353; www.hillside-inn.com; 2901 4th St, Sonoma; s/d Nov-Mar $70/82, Apr-Oct $74/86; 📶🏊) One of Santa Rosa's best-kept (if dated) motels lies close to wineries; add $4 for kitchens.

Sugarloaf Ridge State Park CAMPGROUND $
(☎707-833-5712, reservations 800-444-7275; www.parks.ca.gov; Adobe Canyon Rd; tent sites $30) Northeast of Kenwood wineries, find 50 sites (no hookups) in two hilltop meadows. Superb hiking.

Eating

Fremont Diner AMERICAN $
(☎707-938-7370; 2698 Fremont Dr/Hwy 121, Sonoma; mains $8-11; ⏰8am-3pm Mon-Fri, 7am-4pm Sat & Sun; 👪) Feast on Southern-inspired, farm-to-table cooking at this order-at-the-counter diner. Arrive early to avoid queues.

Fig Cafe & Winebar CALIFORNIAN $$
(☎707-938-2130; www.thefigcafe.com; 13690 Arnold Dr, Glen Ellen; mains $15-20; ⏰10am-2:30pm Sat & Sun, 5:30-9pm daily) Sonoma's take on comfort food: organic salads, Sonoma duck cassoulet and free corkage on Sonoma wines, in a convivial room with vaulted wooden ceilings.

Cafe La Haye MODERN AMERICAN $$$
(☎707-935-5994; www.cafelahaye.com; 140 E Napa St, Sonoma; mains $19-26; ⏰from 5:30pm Tue-Sat) This tiny bistro, with open kitchen, creates earthy New American dishes from ingredients sourced within 60 miles. Reservations essential.

Red Grape PIZZERIA $$
(☎707-996-4103; www.theredgrape.com; 529 1st St W, Sonoma; pizzas $10-16; ⏰11:30am-10pm; 👪) Thin-crust pizza with local cheeses, plus small-production Sonoma wines.

Sonoma Market DELI $
(☎707-996-3411; 500 W Napa St, Sonoma; ⏰6am-9pm) Superior grocery-store deli with hot-pressed panini and picnic fixings.

RUSSIAN RIVER VALLEY

The West preserves its wild ways in woodsy Russian River, two hours north of San Francisco (via Hwys 101 and 116) in western Sonoma County (aka West County), where redwoods tower over small wineries.

Sebastopol has good shopping, with antique shops lying south of downtown. Find clever crafts at **Renga Arts** (☎707-874-9407; www.rengaarts.com; 2371 Gravenstein Hwy S, Sebastopol; ⏰Thu-Mon) and vintage-thrift at **Aubergine** (☎707-827-3460; auberginea fterdark.com; 755 Petaluma Ave, Sebastopol). Lunch in the beer garden at **Hopmonk Tavern** (☎707-829-9300; www.hopmonk.com; 230 Petaluma Ave, Sebastopol; mains $10-20; ⏲11:30am-9:30pm), or gather picnic supplies at **Pacific Market** (www.fiestamkt.com; 550 Gravenstein Hwy N).

Guerneville is the main river town, with hippie craft galleries and gay-friendly honky-tonks; its **visitor center** (☎707-869-9000; www.russianriver.com; 16209 1st St, Guerneville; ⏲10am-5pm) provides winery maps and lodging info. Explore old-growth redwoods at 805-acre **Armstrong Redwoods State Reserve** (☎707-869-2015; www.parks.ca.gov; 17000 Armstrong Woods Rd; entry per car $8, camping $25; ⏲8am-sunset), which includes the 308ft, 1400-year-old Colonel Armstrong Tree. Paddle downriver, past herons and otters, with **Burke's Canoe Trips** (☎707-887-1222; www.burkescanoetrips.com; 8600 River Rd, Forestville; canoes $60). Or head south to sip bubbly – the label the White House pours – at the outdoor hilltop tasting bar at **Iron Horse Vineyards** (☎707-887-1507; www.ironhorsevineyards.com; 9786 Ross Station Rd, Sebastopol; tasting $10-15; ⏲10am-4:30pm). Find other excellent wineries along rural Westside Rd, which follows the river to Healdsburg.

Guerneville's best eats are at California-smart **Boon Eat + Drink** (☎707-869-0780; www.eatatboon.com; 16248 Main St, Guerneville; lunch mains $9-11, dinner $12-22; ⏲11am-3pm & 5-9pm). Dinner and a movie await at **Rio Theater** (☎707-865-0913; www.riotheater.com; 20396 Bohemian Hwy, Monte Rio; adult/child $8/6; ⏲Wed-Sun), a converted 1940s Quonset hut, featuring Oscar contenders and gourmet hot dogs ($7). For bona fide farm-to-table cooking, detour southeast to roadhouse-restaurant **Zazu** (☎707-523-4814; 3535 Guerneville Rd, Santa Rosa; brunch mains $11-15, dinner $18-26; ⏲5:30-8:30pm Wed-Mon, 9am-2pm Sun), which farms its own pigs and chickens for earthy-delicious Italian-inspired comfort cooking.

South of Guerneville, the 10-mile-long, aptly named **Bohemian Highway** (www.bohemianconnection.com) runs to tiny **Occidental**, great for strolling. For a spectacular scenic drive to the ocean, take Coleman Valley Rd. Meet locals at Occidental's weekly organic **farmers market** (☎707-793-2159; www.occidentalfarmersmarket.com, ⏲4pm-dusk Fri Jun-Oct). **Howard Station Cafe** (☎707-874-2838; www.howardstationcafe.com; 3811 Bohemian Hwy, Occidental; mains $8-11; ⏲7am-2:30pm) serves hearty breakfasts and lunches.

HEALDSBURG TO BOONVILLE

More than 90 wineries dot the Russian River, Dry Creek and Alexander Valleys within a 30-mile radius of **Healdsburg**, where upscale eateries, wine-tasting rooms and stylish inns surround the Spanish-style plaza. For tasting passes and maps, hit the **Healdsburg Visitors Center** (☎707-433-6935; www.healdsburg.org; 217 Healdsburg Ave, Healdsburg; ⏲9am-5pm Mon-Fri, to 3pm Sat, 10am-2pm Sun).

Picture-perfect farmstead wineries await discovery in Dry Creek Valley, across Hwy 101 from downtown Healdsburg. Rent a bike downtown and pedal for Zin tasting in the caves at **Bella Vineyards** (☎707-473-9171; www.bellawinery.com; 9711 West Dry Creek Rd; tasting $5-10; ⏲11am-4:30pm), or drive southwest to certified-biodynamic **Porter Creek Vineyards** (☎707-433-6321; www.portercreekvineyards.com; 8735 Westside Rd; tasting free; ⏲10:30am-4:30pm) for Pinot Noir served on a bar made from a bowling-alley lane.

North of Healdsburg, take Hwy 128 to **Anderson Valley** for organic eats and award-winning beer amid vineyards and orchards. In **Boonville**, brake for disc-golf and beer-tasting at solar-powered **Anderson Valley Brewing Company** (☎707-895-2337; www.avbc.com; 17700 Hwy 253, Boonville; tasting $5; ⏲11am-6pm, tours 1:30pm & 3pm).

Sleeping & Eating

Best Western Dry Creek MOTEL $$$
(☎707-433-0300; www.drycreekinn.com; 198 Dry Creek Rd, Healdsburg; r weekday $59-129, weekend $199-259;) Spiffy motel.

L&M Motel MOTEL $$
(☎707-433-6528; www.landmmotel.com; 70 Healdsburg Ave, Healdsburg; r $100-140;) Old-fashioned motel.

Bovolo ITALIAN $$
(☎707-431-2962; www.bovolorestaurant.com; 106 Matheson St, Healdsburg; lunch mains $8-14; ⏲9am-4pm Mon, Wed & Thu, to 8pm Tue, Fri & Sat, to 6pm Sun) Bovolo puts a Slow Food spin on fast food, with salads, panini and pizza made with house-cured salumi.

Cyrus CALIFORNIAN $$$
(☎707-433-3311; www.cyrusrestaurant.com; 29 North St, Healdsburg; fixed-price menus $102-130; ⏲11:30am-2pm Sat, 6-10pm Thu-Mon) Critics rave about ultra-chic Cyrus, but the local secret is the bar, where mad-scientist cocktails accompany truffle-laced dishes.

Boonville General Store CAFE $$
(☎707-895-9477; 14077 Hwy 128, Boonville; ⊙8am-3pm; 🅘) House-baked pastries and pizza, plus locally grown organic salads.

ℹ Getting There & Around

Wine Country begins 75 minutes north of San Francisco, via Hwy 101 or I-80. For transit information, dial ☎511.

Public Transportation

Slow, but possible. Take **Vallejo Ferry** (www.baylinkferry.com; adult/child $13/6.50) from San Francisco's Ferry Building; weekday boats leave hourly, 6:30am to 7pm, and every two hours weekends, 11am to 7:30pm. In Vallejo, connect with **Napa Valley Vine** (www.napavalleyvine.net; adult/child $2.90/2.15) buses to Napa and Calistoga. Alternatively, take BART to El Cerrito, then transfer to **Vallejo Transit** (www.vallejotransit.com; $5) to Vallejo and connect with Napa buses.

For Sonoma, **Greyhound buses** (www.greyhound.com) connect San Francisco and Santa Rosa ($22). **Golden Gate Transit** (goldengatetransit.org) links San Francisco to Petaluma ($8.80) and Santa Rosa ($9.70), where you connect with **Sonoma County Transit** (www.sctransit.com).

Napa Valley Vine provides public transit within Napa Valley; Golden Gate Transit and Sonoma County Transit provide transit around Sonoma.

Bicycle

Rentals cost about $25 to $45 per day; inquire about wine pick-up.

Calistoga Bike Shop (☎707-942-9687; www.calistogabikeshop.com; 1318 Lincoln Ave, Calistoga) Bike rental.

Getaway Adventures (☎707-568-3040; www.getawayadventures.com) Offers easy 'Sip-n-Cycle' tours around Calistoga ($149, six hours).

Napa River Vélo (☎707-258-8729; www.naparivervelo.com; 680 Main St, Napa) Bike rental; rear of building.

Napa Valley Adventure Tours (☎707-259-1833; www.napavalleyadventuretours.com; Oxbow Public Market, 610 1st St, Napa) Rents bikes and leads wine-tasting bicycle trips with lunch and introductions to winemakers.

Sonoma Valley Cyclery (☎707-935-3377; www.sonomacyclery.com; 20091 Broadway, Sonoma) Bike rental.

Spoke Folk Cyclery (☎707-433-7171; www.spokefolk.com; 201 Center St, Healdsburg) Bike rental.

Train

Napa Valley Wine Train (☎707-253-2111; www.winetrain.com; per person from $89-189) Cushy, touristy three-hour trips with an optional winery stop.

North Coast

Valleys of redwoods amble into the moody crash of the Pacific along the North Coast, home to hippies, hoppy microbrews and flora that famously includes the tallest trees and most potent marijuana in the world.

Road-tripping in this part of California is best if you just keep driving: the winding coastal drive gets more rewarding with every gorgeous, white-knuckled mile of road. Along the jagged edge of the continent, the metropolitan charms of San Francisco, only a few hours behind in the rear view mirror, feel eons away from the frothing, frigid crash of Pacific tide and the two-stoplight towns.

BODEGA BAY TO FORT BRAGG

Compared to the famous Big Sur coast, the serpentine stretch of Hwy 1 up the North Coast is more challenging, more remote and more *real:* it passes farms, fishing towns and hidden beaches. Drivers use roadside pull-outs to scan the hazy Pacific horizon for migrating whales and explore a coastline dotted with rock formations that are relentlessly pounded by the surf. The drive between Bodega Bay and Fort Bragg takes four hours of daylight driving without stops. At night in the fog, it takes steely nerves and much, much longer.

Bodega Bay is the first pearl in a string of sleepy fishing towns and the setting of Hitchcock's terrifying 1963 avian psycho-horror flick *The Birds*. The skies are free from bloodthirsty gulls today (though you best keep an eye on the picnic); it's Bay Area weekenders who descend en masse for extraordinary **Sonoma Coast State Beaches** between here and Jenner, 10 miles north. This system of beaches has arched rocks, wildflower-covered bluffs and tons of coves for lovers to spread a blanket and watch the fog roll in. **Bodega Charters** (www.bodegacharters.com; 1410 Bay Flat Rd, Bodega Bay) and several other one-boat outfits run whale-watching trips ($35 per person, 3½ to four hours). Migrating whales are most active between January and May. **Bodega Bay Surf Shack** (www.bodegabaysurf.com; 1400 N Hwy 1, Bodega Bay; surfboards per day $15, kayaks per 4hr single/double $45/65) rents surfboards, wetsuits and kayaks. Landlubbers can enjoy the views of the coastline and rolling inland hills on horseback with **Chanslor Riding**

Stables (www.chanslorranch.com; 2660 N Hwy 1, Bodega Bay; 1hr rides from $70).

There isn't much to **Jenner**, just a cluster of shops and restaurants dotting the coastal hills where the wide, lazy Russian River meets the Pacific. The main attraction is the resident harbor seal colony. Look for them from Hwy 1 turnouts north of town. Volunteers protect the seals and educate tourists at **Goat Rock State Beach** (Mile 19.15) during pupping season, between March and August.

The salt-weathered structures of **Fort Ross State Historic Park** (707-847-3286; www.fortrossstatepark.org; 19005 Hwy 1; per car $8), 12 winding miles north of Jenner, were an 1812 trading post and Russian Orthodox church. It's a quiet place, but the history is riveting; this was once the southernmost reach of Tsarist Russia's North American trading expeditions. The small, wood-scented museum offers historical exhibits and respite from windswept cliffs. Budget cuts have impacted seasonal hours, but the park is almost always open on weekends.

Salt Point State Park (800-444-7275; www.reserveamerica.com; Mile 39; per car/campsites $8/35) has hiking trails, tide pools and two campgrounds where pink blooms spot the misty green woods in springtime. Cows graze the surrounding rock-strewn fields on the bluffs, which are home to organic dairy cooperatives.

Eight miles north of Elk, **Van Damme State Park** (800-444-7275; www.reserveamerica.com; per car/campsites $8/35) has the popular **Fern Canyon Trail**, which passes through a pygmy forest and a fern- and elderberry-lined canyon. The car-accessible camping is pleasant, but an easy 2-mile hike-in offers a secluded option and the hill-top sites are situated around a grassy clearing and good for families.

The most popular village on this stretch is **Mendocino**, a salt-washed historical gem perched on a gorgeous headland. For 40- and 50-somethings from the Bay Area, the New England saltbox B&Bs and quaint shops make the town seem like a baby step from heaven. A headland walk passes berry bramble and wildflowers, where cypress trees stand guard over dizzying cliffs (ideal for a picnic). Nature's power is evident everywhere: from driftwood littered fields and cave tunnels to the raging surf. The **visitor center** (www.gomendo.com; 735 Main St, Mendocino; 11am-4pm) is in the Ford House and is the place to start.

Medocino's scrappy sister city, **Fort Bragg** is trying to lure some of the well-heeled weekenders a bit further north, but it still has a way to go. You'll find cheap gas, large motels and a mess of fast food, but it's not without its charm. The elegant and well-balanced brews at **North Coast Brewing Co** (www.northcoastbrewing.com; 455 N Main St, Fort Bragg; pint $4, 10-beer sampler $12) are reason enough to pull over. Fort Bragg also boasts the 1885 **Skunk Train** (800-866-1690; www.skunktrain.com; adult/child 3-11yr $49/24), whose diesel and steam engines make half-day trips through the woods to Ukiah.

Sleeping & Eating

Every other building in Mendocino seems to be a B&B; there are dozens to choose from and many are stuffed with frilly decor and return guests.

TOP CHOICE **Mar Vista Cottages** CABIN $$
(707-884-3522; www.marvistamendocino.com; 35101 S Hwy 1, Anchor Bay; cottages from $155;) The elegantly renovated 1930s fishing cabins of Mar Vista are a simple, stylish seaside escape with vanguard commitment to sustainability. The harmonious environment, situated in the sunny 'Banana Belt' of the North Coast, is the result of pitch-perfect details: linens are line-dried over lavender, guests browse the organic vegetable garden to harvest their own dinner, and chickens cluck around the grounds laying the next morning's breakfast. Often requires a two-night stay.

Andiorn CABIN $$
(800-955-6478; www.theandiorn.com; 6051 N Hwy 1, Mendocino; r $99-149;) Styled with hip vintage decor, this cluster of 1950s roadside cottages is a refreshingly playful option amid the stuffy cabbage-rose and lace aesthetic of Mendocino. Each cabin houses two rooms with complementing themes: 'Read' has old books, comfy vintage chairs and hip retro eyeglasses, while the adjoining 'Write' features a huge chalk board and ribbon typewriter. A favorite for travelers? 'Here' and 'There,' themed with old maps, 1960s airline paraphernalia and collectables from North Coast's yesteryear.

Gualala Point Regional Park CAMPGROUND $
(www.sonoma-county.org/parks; 42401 S Highway 1, Gualala; campsites $28) Shaded by a stand of redwoods and fragrant California bay laurel trees, a short trail connects this creekside

campground to the windswept beach. The quality of sites, including several secluded hike-in spots, makes it the best drive-in camping on this part of the coast.

Brewery Gulch Inn B&B **$$$**
(800-578-4454; www.brewerygulchinn.com; 9401 N Hwy 1, Mendocino; r $210-450;) Just south of Mendocino; this place wins with modern fireplace rooms, hosts who pour heavily at the wine hour and sweets for midnight snacking. Breakfast is served in a small dining room overlooking the distant water.

TOP CHOICE **Piaci Pub & Pizzeria** PIZZERIA **$$**
(www.piacipizza.com; 120 W Redwood Ave, Fort Bragg; pizza $8-12; 11am-4pm Mon-Fri, 4-9pm Sun-Thu, to 10pm Fri & Sat) Fort Bragg's must-visit pizzeria is the place to chat up locals while enjoying microbrews and a menu of fantastic wood-fired, brick-oven, 'adult' pizza. The 'Gustoso' – an immaculate selection with chevre, pesto and seasonal pears – speaks to the carefully orchestrated thin-crust pies. It's tiny, loud and fun, but expect to wait at peak times.

Spud Point Crab Company SEAFOOD **$**
(www.spudpointcrab.com; 1860 Bay Flat Rd, Bodega Bay; dishes $4-10; 9am-5pm Thu-Tue;) In the classic tradition of dockside crab shacks, Spud Point serves salty-sweet crab cocktails and *real* clam chowder, served at picnic tables overlooking the marina.

Café Beaujolais CALIFORNIA FUSION **$$$**
(707-937-5614; www.cafebeaujolais.com; 961 Ukiah St, Mendocino; lunch $9-16, mains $24-36; 11:30am-2:30pm Wed-Sun, from 5:30pm daily) Mendocino's iconic, beloved country Cal/French restaurant occupies an 1896 house restyled into a monochromatic urban-chic dining room, perfect for holding hands by candlelight. The refined and inspired cooking draws diners from San Francisco, who make this the centerpiece of their trip. The locally sourced menu changes with the seasons, but the Petaluma duck breast served with crispy skin is a gourmand's delight.

Bones Roadhouse BARBECUE **$$**
(www.bonesroadhouse.com; 39350 S Hwy 1, Gualala; mains $10-20; 11:30am-9pm Sun-Thu, to 10pm Fri & Sat) Savory smoked meats make this Gualala's best lunch. On weekends, a codgerly blues outfit may be growling out 'Mustang Sally.'

Patterson's Pub PUB **$$**
(www.pattersonspub.com; 10485 Lansing St, Mendocino; mains $10-15) If it's late, you'll thank heavens for this pub, which stays open after all the fancier options close to serve big salads and first-class pub fare.

Getting There & Away

Although Hwy 1 is popular with cyclists, a car is nearly a necessity along Hwy 1. Those determined to travel via bus can connect through the **Mendocino Transit Authority** (MTA; 800-696-4682; www.4mta.org), which operates a daily ride from Fort Bragg south to Santa Rosa via Willits and Ukiah ($21, three hours); at Santa Rosa, catch San Francisco-bound bus 80 ($8.80), operated by **Golden Gate Transit** (415-923-2000; www.goldengate.org). Neither Greyhound nor Amtrak serves towns along Hwy 1.

UKIAH TO SCOTIA

If the coastal route along Hwy 1 is ideal for ambling, much of the traffic that heads between Ukia and Scotia on Hwy 101 is rushing toward remote regions beyond the so-called 'Redwood Curtain.' Still, there are a number of worthy diversions, including excellent vineyards around Ukiah, redwood forests north of Leggett and the abandoned wilds of the Lost Coast.

Although **Ukiah** is mostly a place to gas up or get a bite, it boasts the nearby Vichy Springs Resort.

North of tiny **Leggett** on Hwy 101, take a dip at the **Standish-Hickey State Recreation Area** (707-925-6482, 69350 Hwy 101; per car $8). It has river swimming and fishing, as well as 9 miles of hiking trails in virgin and second-growth redwoods (look for the 225ft-tall Miles Standish tree). Fourteen miles further north is **Richardson Grove State Park** (per car/campsites $8/35), for 1400 acres of more virgin redwoods and camping.

The **Lost Coast** tops a serious hiker's itinerary, offering the most rugged coastal camping in California. It became 'lost' when the state's highway bypassed the rugged mountains of the King Range, which rise 4000ft within several miles of the ocean, leaving the region largely undeveloped. The scenery is stunning. From Garberville it's 23 miles along a rough road to Shelter Cove, the main supply point for Lost Coast's adventurers, little more than a seaside subdivision with a deli, restaurant and motels. Heed those 'no trespassing' signs before wandering off trail, lest you encounter farmers who are extremely protective of the region's illicit cash crop.

Along Hwy 101, 80-sq-mile **Humboldt Redwoods State Park** (www.humboldtredwoods.org; campsites $20-35) protects some of the world's oldest redwoods and has three-quarters of the world's tallest 100 trees. Tree huggers take note: these groves rival (and many say surpass) those in Redwood National Park, which is a long drive further north. Even if you don't have time to hike, drive the park's awe-inspiring **Avenue of the Giants**, a 32-mile, two-lane road parallel to Hwy 101. Book ahead for magnificent campsites near the informative **visitor center** (707-946-2409; 9am-5pm).

Sleeping & Eating

The camping options are plentiful and extremely high quality, and every one-horse town guarantees at least a deli, a taqueria and a dog-earned motel. The Avenue of the Giants has *excellent* camping – the best of which is in Humboldt Redwoods State Park – and scads of musty midcentury motels, to be approached with caution.

Vichy Springs Resort RESORT, SPA $$$
(707-462-9515; www.vichysprings.com; 2605 Vichy Springs Rd, Ukiah; lodge s/d $135/195, creekside r $195/245, cottages from $280;) This 700-acre resort has the only warm-water, naturally carbonated mineral baths in North America (two hours/all-day use $30/50). Unlike other nearby hot springs, it requires swimwear – you'll be thankful.

Benbow Inn HISTORIC HOTEL $$
(800-355-3301; www.benbowinn.com; 445 Lake Benbow Dr, Garberville, r $130-200;) Though the English countryside decor has a comically highbrow quality, this Tudor-style manor is a memorable getaway. There's complimentary decanted sherry in each room. The white-tablecloth restaurant and wood-paneled bar are inviting on foggy evenings.

Ukiah Brewing Company BREWERY $$$
(www.ukiahbrewingco.com; 102 S State St, Ukiah; dinner mains $15-25; 11:30am-9pm Sun-Thu, to 9:30pm Fri & Sat,) The brews might outshine the food, but the dancefloor gets a bit rowdy to live music on the weekend. The menu has a strong organic and sustainable bent, with plenty of vegan and raw options.

Getting There & Around

Greyhound (800-231-2222; www.greyhound.com) operates from San Francisco to Ukiah ($40). The **Redwood Transit System** (www.hta.org,) operates buses Monday through Saturday between Scotia and Trinidad ($2.50, 2½ hours).

EUREKA TO CRESCENT CITY

Passing the strip malls that sprawl from the edges, **Eureka** is unlikely to have you shouting the town's name from the hills; however, it does have an Old Town with fine Victorians, inviting shops and restaurants. You can blow right by on Hwy 101 without getting much of a hint of the town's charm though – for the best window-shopping, head to 2nd St between D and G Sts.

The **Eureka visitor center** (www.eurekachamber.com; 2112 Broadway, Eureka; 8:30am-5pm Mon-Fri, 10am-4pm Sat) has maps and information. In Old Town, **Going Places** (328 2nd St, Eureka; 10:30am-5:30pm Mon-Sat, 11am-5pm Sun) is a fabulous travel bookstore with tons of guidebooks and gear.

The best thing going in Eureka is **Blue Ox Millworks** (www.blueoxmill.com; adult/child 6-12yr $7.50/3.50; 9am-4pm Mon-Sat), one of a small handful of mills in the nation that hand-tools Victorian detailing using traditional carpentry and 19th-century equipment. Fascinating self-guided tours let you watch the craftsmen work.

Cruising the harbor aboard the blue-and-white 1910 **Madaket** (707-445-1910; www.humboldtbaymaritimemuseum.com; adult/child 5-12yr $15/7.50; May-Oct) is also fun. It departs from the foot of F St and the $10 sunset cocktail cruise serves from the smallest licensed bar in the state.

Nine miles north of Eureka, **Arcata** is a patchouli-dipped bastion of radical politics set around a quaint square, where trucks run on biodiesel and recycling gets picked up by tandem bicycle. On the northeast side of town lies the pretty campus of **Humboldt State University** (www.humboldt.edu). At the junction of Hwys 299 and 101 is a **California Welcome Center** (www.arcatachamber.com; 9am-5pm;), with area info.

Trinidad, a working fishing town 16 miles north of Arcata, sits on a bluff overlooking a glittering harbor. There are lovely sand beaches and short hikes on Trinidad Head. Nearby Luffenholtz Beach is popular (but unpatrolled) for surfing; north of town, Patrick's Point Rd is dotted with lodging and forested campgrounds. **Patrick's Point State Park** (www.reserveamerica.com; day use/campsites $8/35) has stunning rocky headlands, tide pools and camping.

Highway 101 passes the **Redwood National & State Parks Visitor Center** (www.nps.gov/redw; 9am-5pm). Together, Redwood National Park and three state parks – Prairie Creek, Del Norte and Jedediah Smith – are a designated World Heritage Site containing almost half the remaining old-growth redwood forests in California. The national park is free; the state parks have an $8 day-use fee in some areas and the only developed campsites ($35). Peering out of the tent at the surreal size of the trunks makes this excellent camping. The visitor center has info about the parks and free permits for backcountry camping. At first glance it's a bit confusing to understand this patchwork of state and federally managed land, as the combined park area stretches all the way north to the Oregon border and is interspersed with several towns.

From south to north, you'll first encounter **Redwood National Park**, which is under Federal jurisdiction and includes the Lady Bird Johnson Grove and Tall Trees Grove, home to several of the world's tallest trees. Dispersed backcountry camping along Redwood Creek is free with a permit and idyllic.

Several miles north of tiny Klamath, **Del Norte Coast Redwoods State Park** contains redwood groves and 8 miles of unspoiled coastline. The Damnation Creek Trail is only 4 miles long, but the (1100ft) elevation change and cliff-side redwood makes it the park's best hike. The unmarked trailhead starts from a parking area off Hwy 101 at mile mark 16.

Jedediah Smith Redwoods State Park is the northernmost park in the system, 5 miles northeast of Crescent City. It's less crowded than the other parks but also beautiful. The redwood stands are so dense that there are few trails, but the outstanding 11-mile Howland Hill Scenic Drive is the best way to see the forest if you can't hike.

Sprawling over a crescent-shaped bay, **Crescent City** is a drab little town, but the only sizable coastal settlement north of Arcata. More than half the town was destroyed by a tidal wave in 1964 and rebuilt with ugly utilitarian architecture. When the tide's out, you can check out the 1865 **Battery Point Lighthouse** (admission $3; 10am-4pm Wed-Sun Apr-Oct) at the south end of A St.

Sleeping & Eating

A mixed bag of midcentury motels are scattered throughout every town along Hwy 101. In Eureka, the cheapest options are south of downtown. The best food and widest variety is in Arcata.

Requa Inn B&B $$

(707-482-1425; www.requainn.com; 451 Requa Rd, Klamath; r $85-155;) Built in 1914, this simple historic inn caters to hikers, with a big breakfast and country-style rooms overlooking the river.

Hotel Arcata HISTORIC HOTEL $$

(707-826-0217; www.hotelarcata.com; 708 9th St, Arcata; r $96-156;) On the Arcata town square, the stately 1915 hotel is a bit stuffy but right in the center of town.

Carter House Inns B&B $$$

(707-444-8062; www.carterhouse.com; 301 L St, Eureka; r incl breakfast $185-213;) The cushy option near Old Town Eureka is this complex of several lovingly tended Victorians. French fusion at Restaurant 301 is the most haute dining around.

TOP CHOICE **Six Rivers Brewery** BREWERY $$

(www.sixriversbrewery.com; 1300 Central Ave, McKinleyville; mains $11-18; 11:30am-midnight Tue-Sun, from 4pm Mon) One of the first female-owned breweries in California, the 'brew with a view' kills it in every category: great beer, community vibe, occasional live music and delicious hot wings. The spicy chili pepper ale is amazing.

Getting There & Around

Greyhound (www.greyhound.com) serves Arcata; from San Francisco budget $53 and seven hours. **Redwood Transit** (www.hta.org) buses serve Arcata and Eureka on the Trinidad–Scotia routes ($2.50, 2½ hours), which don't run on Sunday. Though hitchhiking is still fairly rare and safety concerns should be taken seriously, a culture of hippies of all ages and transient marijuana harvesters makes this the easiest region in California to thumb a ride.

Sacramento

Sacramento was the first nonmission European settlement in California, and the state's capital is an anomalous place: the first city to shoot up from gold discovery is flat and fairly bland with shady trees, withering summer heat and jammed highways.

In 1839 eccentric Swiss immigrant John Sutter built a fort, and after gold was discovered nearby in 1848, the town's population exploded. In 1854, after several years of legislative waffling, it became California's capital. Old Sacramento remains the visitor's magnet – a riverside area with raised wooden sidewalks that can feel like a ye olde tourist trap. Better food and culture lie hidden among the grid of streets in midtown, where a fledgling arts scene is quietly defying the city's reputation as a cow town. During **Second Saturday** (www.2nd-sat.com) events, the galleries and shops in midtown draw loads of boozy stumblers.

Sights

TOP CHOICE California Museum MUSEUM
(www.californiamuseum.org; 1020 O St; adult/child 6-13yr $8.50/7; 10am-5pm Mon-Sat, from noon Sun) The attractive, modern California Museum is home to the California Hall Of Fame – perhaps the only place to simultaneously encounter Cesar Chavez, Mark Zuckerburg and Amelia Earhart. The newly opened exhibit *California Indians: Making A Difference* is the state's best view of the traditions and culture of California's first residents, past and present.

State Capitol HISTORIC BUILDING
The 19th-century state capitol at 10th St is the brilliant white jewel rising from the manicured Capitol Mall. The **Capitol Museum** (www.statecapitolmuseum.com; admission free; 9am-5pm) gives tours through period-furnished chambers. The Assembly and Senate rooms are open to the public.

California State Railroad Museum MUSEUM
(www.californiastaterailroadmuseum.org; 125 I St; adult/child 6-17yr $9/4; 10am-5pm) A must-stop for train-lovers, allows visitors to board dozens of meticulously restored beasts of steam and diesel; ride a steam train (adult/child $10/5) at summer weekends. The museum is in Old Sacramento, at the river.

Old Town Sacramento HISTORIC DISTRICT
(www.oldsacramento.com) It's more than a little stagey, where candy-scented streets rumble with baby boomers on Harleys, but this walkable district holds California's largest concentration of historic buildings and a few fine museums.

Sutter's Fort HISTORIC FORT
(cnr 27th & L Sts; adult/child 5 $5/3; 10am-5pm) Restored to its 1850s appearance, the fort has historical actors in summer and some Saturdays throughout the year.

Sleeping & Eating

Sacramento's hotels cater to those doing business at the capitol, so there are serious weekend bargains, especially with last-minute bookings on Priceline. Midtown has a glut of midrange chain hotels. For restaurants, make for J St between 16th and 25th Sts.

TOP CHOICE Citizen Hotel BOUTIQUE HOTEL $$$
(916-492-4460; 926 J St; r $159, ste from $215;) With an elegant, ultrahip upgrade by the Joie de Vivre group, the long-vacant Citizen has suddenly become one of the coolest stays in this part of the state. Rooms are lovely with luxurious linen, bold patterned fabrics and stations for your iPod. The little touches make a big impression too: vintage political cartoons adorning the walls, loaner bikes and a nightly wine reception. There's an upscale farm-to-table restaurant on the ground floor (a daily menu of seasonal mains starts around $25).

HI Sacramento Hostel HOSTEL $
(www.norcalhostels.org/sac; 925 H St; dm/r $28/55.75; P@) This is a *hostel*? Sweet! The public areas in this restored Victorian mansion are nearly B&B quality, the spacious dorms are clean and the staff knows the local nightlife.

TOP CHOICE Andy Nguyen's THAI $$
(www.andynguyenvegetarianrestaurant.com; 2007 Broadway; meals $8-16; 11:30am-9pm Sun-Mon, to 9:30pm Tue-Thu, to 10pm Fri & Sat;) The best vegetarian fare in all of California might be at this tranquil Buddhist Thai diner. Try the steaming curries and artful fake meat dishes (the 'chicken' leg has a little wooden bone).

Mulvaney's B & L CALIFORNIA $$$
(916-441-6022; www.mulvaneysbl.com; 1215 19th St; mains $20-40; 11:30am-2:30pm & 5-10pm Tue-Fri, 5-10pm Sat) The class place in town; an expert French-touched menu changes every day.

Rubicon BREWERY $
(www.rubiconbrewing.com; 2004 Capitol Ave; sandwiches $7-11; 11am-11:30pm Mon-Thu, to 12:30am Fri & Sat, to 10pm Sun) For award-winning IPAs and decent pub grub.

Getting There & Around

Sacramento is 91 miles east of San Francisco via I-80, and 386 miles north of LA via I-5. **Sacramento International Airport** (www.sacairports.org) is a great small airport to access Lake Tahoe, 15 miles north of downtown off I-5.

Sacramento's **Amtrak** (www.capitolcorridor.org; cnr 5th & I Sts) is the best way to travel to the Bay Area, with frequent trains on the Capitol Corridor line. The depot is near downtown. Trains leave daily for Oakland ($26, two hours) and Los Angeles ($57, 14 hours). **Greyhound** (www.greyhound.com; 7th & L Sts) connects to San Francisco ($22, two hours) or Los Angeles ($66, nine hours) and all points beyond. **Sacramento Regional Transit** (www.sacrt.com) runs a bus and light-rail system (fare $2.25).

Gold Country

Hard to believe, but this is where it all began – the quiet hill towns and drowsy oak-lined byways of Gold Country belie the wild, chaotic, often violent establishment of California. Shortly after a glint of gold caught James Marshall's eye in Sutters Creek in 1848, the rush for gold brought a 300,000-stong stampede of 'forty-niners' to the Sierra foothills. By the time the dust settled, several of the first urban areas in the West were booming, immigration routes were traced from Asia and the Americas, and the 31st state was founded. The frenzy for gold paid little heed to the starched moral decorum of the Victorian society but only traces of environmental havoc and lawless boom towns remain. Traveling here might be a thrill ride for history buffs – the fading historical markers tell tales of bloodlust and banditry – but more tactile pleasures await the traveler willing to plunge into a swimming hole or rattle down single-track mountain-bike trails.

Situated along Hwy 49, Gold Country warrants a two-day detour, where tiny towns survive on selling antiques, ice-cream and gold-rush ephemera. For something adventurous, try a white-water trip down the American River; its three forks are inviting for beginners and experts alike.

In the summer when temperatures soar, there's reprieve in the icy currents of the American, Tuolumne, Kings and Stanislaus Rivers. **All-Outdoors California Whitewater Rafting** (www.aorafting.com) is the favorite; the family-run outfitter does single- and two-day wilderness adventures. **Wolf Creek Wilderness** (www.wolfcreekwilderness.com; 595 E Main St, Grass Valley; kayaks per day from $40) has kayak rentals and lessons ($40 to $150).

The **Gold Country Visitors Association** (www.calgold.org) has detailed local tourist information.

NORTHERN MINES

Highway 50 divides the Northern and Southern Mines; the former stretch south from Nevada City to Placerville. Winding Hwy 49, which connects it all, has plenty of pull-outs and vistas of the surrounding hills. If it's sweltering and you see a line of cars parked roadside, it's likely a swimming hole. Don't ask questions; just park, strip and jump. One of the best is where North and South forks of the American River join up, 3 miles south of Auburn on Hwy 49.

Nevada City was known as the 'Queen City of the Northern Mines,' and her streets gleam with lovingly restored buildings, an arty folk scene, organic cafes and boutiques. The **chamber of commerce** (www.nevadacitychamber.com; 132 Main St, Nevada City; ⏲9am-5pm Mon-Fri, 11am-4pm Sat, 11am-3pm Sun) has self-guided walking tours and excellent information. The **Tahoe National Forest Headquarters** (☎530-265-4531; ⏲8am-4:30pm Mon-Fri, plus Sat in summer), on Hwy 49 at the north end of Coyote St, has hiking and backcountry info, including details about mountain-biking trails.

About 5 miles southwest, **Grass Valley** is Nevada City's functional sister, where artists, hippies and ranchers get their oil changed. Two miles east of town, the landscaped **Empire Mine State Historic Park** (www.empiremine.org; adult/child 6-16yr $7/3; ⏲10am-5pm) marks the site of one of the richest mines in California; from 1850 to 1956 it produced 5.8 million ounces of gold – about $5 billion in today's market.

Coloma is where the gold rush started, and the **Marshall Gold Discovery State Historic Park** (☎530-622-3470; per car $8; ⏲8am-dusk) makes an eerily quiet tribute to the riotous discovery, with a replica of Sutter's Mill, restored buildings and short hikes. There's a statue of Sutter himself, who, in one of the many ironic twists of the gold rush, died a ward of the state.

Sleeping & Eating

Cafes, ice-cream parlors and upscale eateries are in nearly every sizable town along Hwy 49. Nevada City has a spread of eating and sleeping options (including *tons* of B&Bs), and is the cutest place to stay.

TOP CHOICE **Broad Street Inn** B&B $$
(☎530-265-2239; www.broadstreetinn.com; 517 E Broad St, Nevada City; r $110-120; ❄📶) It seems as if there are a million bed and breakfasts in town, but this six-room inn is a favorite

because it keeps it simple. (No weird old dolls, no yellowing lace doilies.) The rooms are modern, brightly furnished and elegant, the breakfast is delicious and it's an amazing value.

Outside Inn MOTEL $$
(☎530-265-2233; www.outsideinn.com; 575 E Broad St, Nevada City; r $75-150;) The most fun of the motels just south of town, this has clean, themed rooms, grills for guests to use and is run by exceedingly friendly outdoor enthusiasts.

Holbrooke Hotel HISTORIC HOTEL $$
(☎800-933-7077; www.holbrooke.com; 212 W Main St, Grass Valley; r from $105;) The register of this 1852 hotel boasts Ulysses Grant and Mark Twain. Elegant Victorian rooms have claw-foot tubs. A recommended restaurant is on-site.

TOP CHOICE **Ikedas** BURGERS $
(www.ikedas.com; 13500 Lincoln Way; ⌚8am-7pm, to 8pm Sat & Sun) If you're cruising this part of the state without time to explore, the best pit stop is off I-80 at exit 121. This place feeds Tahoe-bound travelers thick, grass-fed burgers, homemade pies and snacks. The seasonal fresh peach shake is deliriously good.

SOUTHERN MINES

The towns of the Southern Mines – from Placerville to Sonora – receive less traffic and the dusty streets still have a whiff of Wild West, today evident in the motley assortment of Harley cruisers, weed farmers, outsider winemakers and gold prospectors (still!) who populate them. Some, like **Plymouth** (Ole Pokerville) and **Mokelumne Hill** (Moke Hill), are virtual ghost towns, slowly crumbling into photogenic oblivion. Others, like **Jackson**, **Murphys** and **Sutter Creek**, are frilly slices of Americana. Get off the beaten path for family-run vineyards (especially around Plymouth in Amador County, a region that invented Zinfandel) and underground caverns, where geological wonders reward those willing to navigate the touristy gift shops above.

Columbia (www.columbiacalifornia.com) is Gold Country's best historic site, with four square blocks of authentic 1850s buildings and concessionaires in period costumes right in the middle of town. It's crazy with kids panning for gold. The park itself doesn't close, but most businesses are open from 10am to 5pm.

Sleeping & Eating

This area's best-value camping is in the national forests, which is free. Lacy B&Bs are in nearly every town and usually priced over $100 per night. Busy Sonora is a bit drab, but it's just over an hour from Yosemite National Park and has serviceable midrange hotels.

Gunn House Hotel HISTORIC HOTEL $$
(☎209-532-3421; www.gunnhousehotel.com; 286 S Washington St, Sonora; r $79-115;) For a lovable alternative to Gold Country's cookie-cut chains, this historic hotel hits the sweet spot. Rooms feature period decor and guests take to rocking chairs on the wide porches in the evening. Stuffed bears, a nice pool and a big breakfast also make it a hit with families.

City Hotel & Fallon Hotel HISTORIC HOTELS $$
(☎800-532-1479; www.cityhotel.com; r incl breakfast from $90-145;) These co-run hotels have 24 stunning, rooms and common spaces, decked out with museum-quality pieces. The City Hotel has an acclaimed **restaurant** (meals $14-30) frequented by a Twain impersonator. The Fallon hosts a repertory theater.

Volcano Union Inn HISTORIC HOTEL $$
(☎209-296-4458; www.volcanounion.com; 16104 Main St, Volcano; r incl breakfast $109-129;) The preferred of two historic hotels in Volcano, there are four lovingly updated rooms with crooked floors and two have street-facing balconies. The Union Pub has a menu designed by the guys from Taste and will host the occasional old-time fiddler.

TOP CHOICE **Taste** CALIFORNIAN, FRENCH $$$
(☎209-245-3463; www.restauranttaste.com; 9402 Main St, Plymouth; mains $31-50; ⌚5-10pm Thu-Mon, 11:30am-2pm Sat) The antidote to Gold Country's dependence on burgers and chops, Taste plates artful, fresh, seasonal dishes which come well paired with bold Zinfandels from the surrounding hills of Amador County.

Lighthouse Deli & Ice Cream Shop DELI $
(www.thelighthousedeli.com; 28 S Washington, Sonora; sandwiches $7-9; ⌚10am-4pm Mon-Fri, 11am-3pm Sat) The flavors of N'awlins make this unassuming deli an unexpected delight. The muffeletta – a toasted piece of Cajun paradise that's stacked with ham, salami, cheese and olive tapenade – is the best sandwich within 100 miles.

Getting There & Around

About 26 miles northeast of Sacramento, Hwy 49 intersects I-80 in the town of Auburn. Local bus systems include **Gold Country Stage** (☎530-477-0103), which links Nevada City, Grass Valley and Auburn (fare $1.50 to $3), and **Placer County Transit** (☎530-885-2877). No public transit serves the Southern Mines on Hwy 49.

Northern Mountains

Remote, empty and eerily beautiful, the Northern Mountains are some of California's least-visited turf; it's an endless show of geological wonders, alpine lakes, rivers and desert. The major peaks – Lassen, Shasta, Lava Beds National Monument and the Trinity Alps – have virtually zero geological features in common, but all offer isolated backcountry camping under sparkling skies. The towns dotting the regions aren't attractions, but are good enough to supply a launch into the wild.

REDDING TO YREKA

Much of the drive north of Redding is dominated by **Mt Shasta**, a 14,179ft snow-capped goliath that rises out of the Central Valley as dramatically as the anticipation felt by outdoor enthusiasts who seek adventure along its slopes. An extremely helpful pit stop just off I-5 is the **Shasta-Cascade Wonderland Association** (www.shastacascade.com; ⏲9am-10pm Mon-Fri, to 4pm Sat & Sun). It's 10 miles south of Redding in the Shasta Factory Outlets Mall.

Don't believe the tourist brochures; **Redding**, the largest town in the region, is a snooze. The best reason to stop is the **Sundial Bridge**, a glass-deck pedestrian marvel designed by world-class architect Santiago Calatrava. It leads over the Sacramento River and to the **Turtle Bay Exploration Park** (www.turtlebay.org; 840 Auditorium Dr, Redding; adult/child 4-12yr $14/10; ⏲9am-5pm in summer, 9am-4pm Wed-Sat, from 10am Sun in winter), a kid-friendly science center.

Eight miles west of Redding on Hwy 299 (the Trinity Scenic Byway) is the **Whiskeytown National Recreation Area**, home of Whiskeytown Lake, a vast reservoir with hiking, camping and several sandy beaches. The **visitor center** (☎530-246-1225; ⏲9am-6pm summer, 10am-4:30pm winter) has maps, permits and information. **Weaverville**, another 35 miles west, is the launching point for mountains, and a lovely detour from Redding. The **Weaverville Ranger Station** (☎530-623-2121; 210 N Main St, Weaverville; ⏲8am-5pm Mon-Fri, to 4:30pm Sat) issues backcountry permits to surrounding **Trinity Alps**, some of the most pristine wilderness in California.

North of Redding, I-5 crosses deep-blue **Shasta Lake**, California's biggest reservoir, which is surrounded by hiking trails and RV parks. High in the limestone megaliths at the north end of the lake are the prehistoric caves of **Lake Shasta Caverns** (www.lakeshastacaverns.com; adult/child 3-11yr $22/13; ⏲tours 9am-4pm). Tours come with a pontoon ride.

Dunsmuir is a teeny historic railroad town, a bit down on its luck due to the crummy economy, but distinguished with a healthy scene for culture and cuisine. If for no other reason, stop to fill your bottle from the public fountains; Dunsmuir claims it's got the best H_20 on earth.

Gorgeous **Mt Shasta town** lures climbers, burnouts and back-to-nature types, all of whom revere the majestic mountain that looms overhead with varying degrees of mystical and physical engagement. **Mt Shasta visitor center** (☎530-926-4865; www.mtshastachamber.com; 300 Pine St, Mt Shasta; ⏲9am-5:30pm Mon-Thu, to 6pm Fri & Sat, to 4pm Sun) is a useful info hub.

Everitt Memorial Hwy climbs the mountain to 7900ft; to access it, simply head east from town on Lake St and keep going. Ten-thousand-foot-plus climbs require a $20 Summit Pass from the **Mt Shasta Ranger Station** (☎530-926-4511; 204 W Alma St, Mt Shasta; ⏲8am-4:30pm Mon-Sat). Campers note: even in summer, temperatures on the mountain drop below freezing.

Sleeping & Eating

The best option in this part of the state is to camp. Midcentury motels are abundant in all but the remote northeast. Redding has the most chain lodging, but clustered near major thoroughfares, it can be noisy.

Railroad Park Resort BOUTIQUE HOTEL **$$**
(☎800-974-7245; www.rrpark.com; d from $115; ❄📶🏊) The most memorable indoor stay is in a wood-paneled caboose, off I-5 just south of Dunsmuir.

Sengthongs THAI **$$**
(www.sengthongs.com; 5855 Dunsmuir Ave; mains $15-22; ⏲5-9pm Thu-Mon) An excellent Thai restaurant; also hosts live music in an adjoining room.

DON'T MISS

SIERRA NEVADA PARKS

Bodie State Historic Park (p171) A real gold-rush ghost town

Mono Lake (p171) Unearthly, mysterious-looking mineral formations

Ancient Bristlecone Pine Forest (p171) The world's oldest living trees

Manzanar National Historic Site (p171) Uncensored history of WWII-era internment camps

Mammoth Mountain (p170) Lofty winter sports and mountain biking

Getting There & Around

Amtrak (www.amtrak.com) services Redding and Dunsmuir; **Greyhound** (☎800-231-2222; www.greyhound.com) buses serve Redding and Yreka. By car, San Francisco to Redding is 215 miles (four hours). For updated road conditions call **Siskiyou County** (☎530-842-4438).

NORTHEAST CORNER

Site of one of the last major Indian wars and a half-million years of volcanic destruction, **Lava Beds National Monument** is a quiet monument to centuries of turmoil. This park's got it all: lava flows, craters, cinder and spatter cones, and more than 500 lava tubes. It was the site of the Modoc War, and Native Americans maintain a strong presence here today – their ancestors' petroglyphs adorn some cave walls. Info, maps and flashlights (for cave exploring) are available at the **visitor center** (☎530-667-8113; www.nps.gov/labe; 1 Indian Well; ⏲8am-6pm May-Oct, to 5pm Nov-Sep). Nearby is the park's only **campground** (campsites $10). The simple sites (no showers) are suitable for tents and small RVs.

Just north, the **Klamath Basin National Wildlife Refuges** consists of six separate refuges. This is a prime stopover on the Pacific Flyway and an important wintering site for bald eagles. The **visitor center** (http://klamathbasinrefuges.fws.gov; 4009 Hill Rd; ⏲8am-4:30pm Mon-Fri, 10am-4pm Sat & Sun) is along the road to Lava Beds Monument on Hwy 161. Self-guided 10-mile auto tours (free) of the Lower Klamath and Tule Lake reserves provide excellent viewing. For commercial services, go to Klamath Falls, OR, just over the border.

Modoc National Forest blankets over 3000 sq miles of California's northeast. Camping is free and no reservations are accepted, though permits are required for campfires. **Medicine Lake**, 14 miles south of Lava Beds Monument on Hwy 49, is a pristine, gleaming blue crater lake surrounded by pine forest, hulking volcanic formations and cool, secluded campgrounds (also free). Twenty-four miles east of Alturas, on the California–Nevada border, is the high desert of **Surprise Valley**, which is the gateway to the wild **Warner Mountains** – possibly the least visited range in the state.

The impressive **Lassen Volcanic National Park** (per car $10, campsites $10-18) has hydrothermal sulfur pools and cauldrons with names like 'Devil's Kitchen.' At 10,462ft, Lassen Peak is the world's largest plug-dome volcano. The park has two entrances with visitor centers: the smaller on Hwy 44 at Manzanita Lake, and a newly remodeled one off Hwy 89, where **park headquarters** (☎530-595-4444; www.nps.gov/lavo; ⏲8am-4:30pm Jul-Sep, Mon-Fri Oct-Jun) is located. Hwy 89 through the park is open to cars from June to October (and to cross-country skiers in winter).

SIERRA NEVADA

The mighty Sierra Nevada – baptized the 'Range of Light' by naturalist John Muir – is California's backbone. This 400-mile phalanx of craggy peaks, chiseled and gouged by glaciers and erosion, both welcomes and challenges outdoors enthusiasts. Cradling three national parks (Yosemite, Sequoia and Kings Canyon), the Sierra is a magical wonderland of both wilderness and superlatives, embracing the contiguous USA's highest peak (Mt Whitney), North America's tallest waterfall and the world's biggest trees.

Yosemite National Park

There's a reason why everybody's heard of it: the granite-peak heights are dizzying, the mist from thunderous waterfalls drenching, the Technicolor wildflower meadows amazing, and the majestic, hulking silhouettes of El Capitan and Half Dome almost shocking

Yosemite Valley

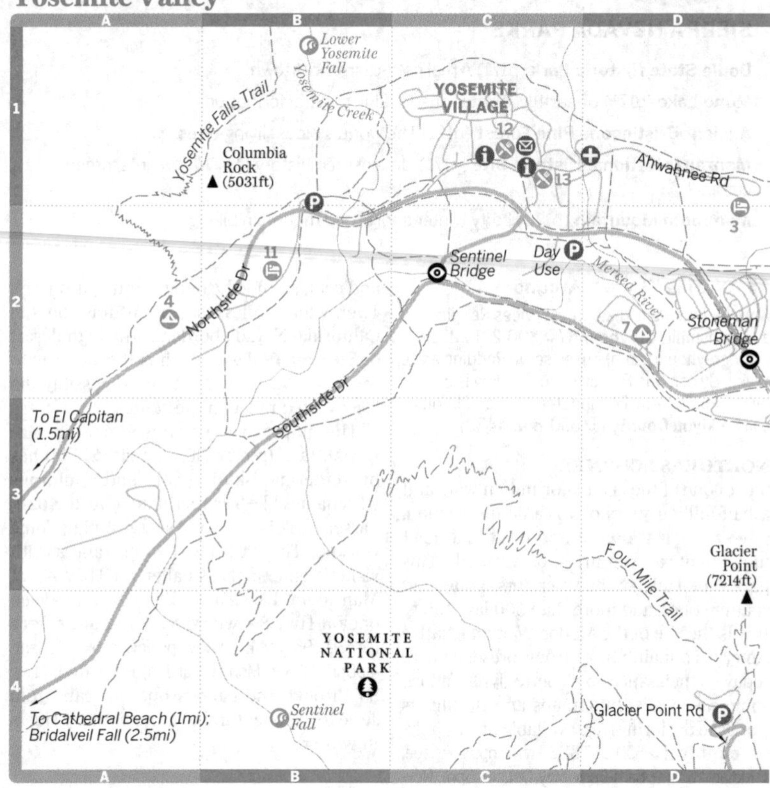

against a crisp blue sky. It's a landscape of dreams, relentlessly surrounding us oh-so-small people on all sides. Then, alas, the hiss and belch of another tour bus, disgorging dozens, rudely breaks the spell. While staggering crowds can't be ignored, these rules will shake most of 'em:

» Avoid summer in the valley. Spring's best, especially when waterfalls gush in May. Autumn is blissfully peaceful, and snowy winter days can be magical too.

» Park your car and leave it – simply by hiking a short distance up almost any trail, you'll lose the car-dependent majority of visitors.

» To hell with jet lag. Get up early, or go for moonlit hikes and do unforgettable stargazing.

Sights

Yosemite's entrance fee ($20 per car, $10 on bicycle, motorcycle or foot) is valid for seven days and includes a free map and helpful newspaper guide. The primary entrances are loctaed at: Arch Rock (Hwy 140), South Entrance (Hwy 41), Big Oak Flat (Hwy 120 west) and Tioga Pass (Hwy 120 east). Open seasonally, Hwy 120 traverses the park as Tioga Rd, connecting Yosemite Valley with Hwy 395 in the Eastern Sierra Nevada.

Overrun, traffic-choked Yosemite Village is home to the park's main visitor center, museum, general store and many other services. Curry Village is another Yosemite Valley hub, offering showers, wi-fi and outdoor equipment rental and sales, including for camping. Along scenic Tioga Rd, high-altitude Tuolumne (pronounced *twol*-uh-mee) Meadows draws hikers, backpackers and climbers to the park's northern region. Wawona, near the southern entrance, has a pioneer history village, golf course and giant sequoias.

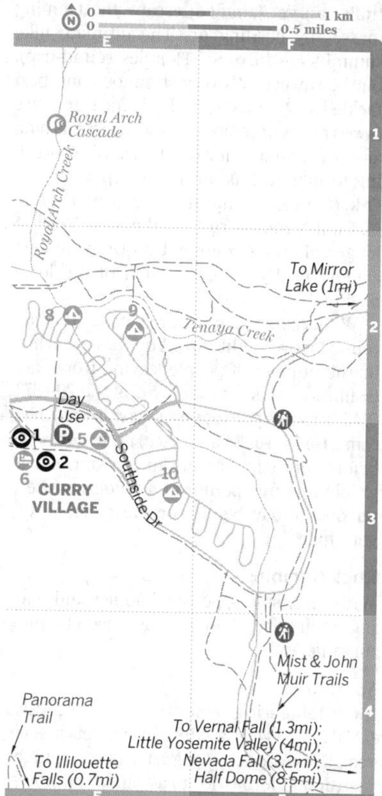

Yosemite Valley

Activities, Courses & Tours

1 Curry Village Ice Rink ... E3
2 Yosemite Mountaineering School ... E3

Sleeping

3 Ahwahnee Hotel ... D2
4 Camp 4 Campground ... A2
5 Campground Reservation Office ... E3
6 Curry Village ... E3
7 Housekeeping Camp ... D2
8 Lower Pines Campground ... E2
9 North Pines Campground ... E2
10 Upper Pines Campground ... E3
11 Yosemite Lodge at the Falls ... B2

Eating

Ahwahnee Dining Room ... (see 3)
Degnan's Deli ... (see 12)
12 Degnan's Loft ... C1
Mountain Room ... (see 11)
13 Village Store ... C1

YOSEMITE VALLEY

From the ground up, this dramatic valley cut by the meandering Merced River is song-inspiring: rippling green meadowgrass; stately pines; cool, impassive pools reflecting looming granite monoliths and cascading, glacier-cold white-water ribbons.

You can't ignore monumental **El Capitan** (7569ft), an El Dorado for rock climbers, while toothed **Half Dome** (8842ft) is Yosemite's spiritual centerpiece. The classic photo-op is up Hwy 41 at **Tunnel View**. Sweat it out and you'll get better views – sans crowds – from the **Inspiration Point Trail** (2.6 miles round-trip), starting near the tunnel. Early or late in the day, head up the 2-mile round-trip trail to **Mirror Lake** to catch the ever-shifting reflection of Half Dome in the still waters, full only in spring and early summer.

Spring snowmelt turns the valley's famous waterfalls into thunderous cataracts; most are reduced to a mere trickle by late summer. **Yosemite Falls** is North America's tallest, dropping 2425ft in three tiers. A wheelchair-accessible trail leads to the bottom of this cascade or, for solitude and different perspectives, you can trek the grueling switchback trail to the top (7.2 miles round-trip). No less impressive are nearby **Bridalveil Fall** and other waterfalls scattered throughout the valley. A strenuous staircase climb beside **Vernal Fall** leads you, gasping, right to the top edge of the falls for a vertical view – look for rainbows in the clouds of mist.

GLACIER POINT & WAWONA

Rising 3200ft above the valley floor, dramatic **Glacier Point** (7214ft) practically puts you at eye level with Half Dome. It's about an hour's drive from Yosemite Valley up Glacier Point Rd (usually open late May to mid-November) off Hwy 41, or a strenuous hike along the **Four Mile Trail** (actually, 4.8 miles one way) or the less-crowded, waterfall-strewn **Panorama Trail** (8.5 miles one way). To avoid backtracking, reserve a seat on the hikers' shuttle bus.

At Wawona, a 45-minute drive south of Yosemite Valley, drop by the **Pioneer Yosemite History Center**, with its covered bridge, pioneer cabins and historic Wells Fargo office. Further south, wander giddily in the

IMPASSABLE TIOGA PASS

Hwy 120 is the only road connecting Yosemite National Park with the Eastern Sierra, climbing through Tioga Pass (9945ft). Most California maps mark this road 'closed in winter,' which, while literally true, is also misleading. Tioga Rd is usually closed from the first heavy snowfall in October or November until May or June. If you are planning a trip through Tioga Pass in spring, you'll likely be out of luck. The earliest date that the road through the pass is plowed is April 15, yet it has only opened in April once since 1980. In 1998 it didn't open until July 1! Call ☎209-372-0200 or check www.nps.gov/yose/planyourvisit/conditions.htm for current road and weather conditions.

Mariposa Grove, home of the 1800-year-old Grizzly Giant and other giant sequoias.

TUOLUMNE MEADOWS

A 90-minute drive from Yosemite Valley, Tuolumne Meadows (8600ft) is the Sierra Nevada's largest subalpine meadow. It's a vivid contrast to the valley, with wildflower fields, azure lakes, ragged granite peaks and domes, and cooler temperatures. Hikers and climbers will find a paradise of options; swimming and picnicking by lakes are also popular. Access is via scenic Tioga Rd (Hwy 120), which follows a 19th-century wagon road and older Native American trading route. West of the meadows and **Tenaya Lake**, stop at **Olmsted Point** for epic vistas of Half Dome.

HETCH HETCHY

It's the site of perhaps the most controversial dam in US history. Despite not existing in its natural state, Hetch Hetchy Valley remains pretty and mostly crowd-free. It's a 40-minute drive northwest of Yosemite Valley. **Wapama Falls**, approached via a 5-mile round-trip hike across the dam and through a tunnel, lets you get thrillingly close to an avalanche of water crashing down into the sparkling reservoir. In spring, you'll get drenched.

Activities

Hiking & Backpacking

With over 800 miles of varied hiking trails, you're spoiled for choice. Easy valley floor trails can get jammed; escape the teeming masses by heading up. The ultimate hike summits **Half Dome** (14 miles round-trip), but be warned: it's very strenuous and best tackled in two days, and advance **permits** (www.nps.gov/yose/planyourvisit/hdpermits.htm) are now required for day hikes. It's rewarding to hike just as far as the top of **Vernal Fall** (3 miles round-trip) or **Nevada Fall** (5.8 miles round-trip) via the **Mist Trail**. A longer, alternate route to Half Dome follows a more gently graded section of the long-distance **John Muir Trail**.

Wilderness permits are required year-round for overnight trips. A quota system limits the number of people leaving from each trailhead. Make **reservations** (☎209-372-0740; www.nps.gov/yose/planyourvisit/wpres.htm; permit fee $5, plus $5 per person) up to 24 weeks before your trip, or you can try your luck at grabbing a free permit at a wilderness center on the day before (or the morning of) your hike.

Rock Climbing

With sheer spires, polished domes and soaring monoliths, Yosemite is rock-climbing nirvana.

Yosemite Mountaineering School ROCK CLIMBING
(☎209-372-8344; www.yosemitemountaineering.com; Curry Village; ⊙Apr-Nov) Offers topflight instruction for novice to advanced climbers, plus guided climbs and equipment rental. During peak summer season, it also operates at Tuolumne Meadows.

Winter Sports

Badger Pass SKIING
(☎209-372-8430; www.badgerpass.com; lift ticket adult/child $42/23; ⊙9am-4pm mid-Dec–late Mar) Gentle slopes are perfect for beginning skiers and snowboarders. Cross-country skiers can schuss along 25 miles of groomed tracks and 90 miles of marked trails, which are also great for snowshoers. Equipment rental and lessons are available.

Curry Village Ice Rink SKATING
(adult/child $8/6, skate rental $3) At Curry Village in Yosemite Valley.

Sleeping & Eating

Concessionaire **Delaware North Companies** (DNC; ☎801-559-4884; www.yosemitepark.com) has a monopoly on park lodging and eating establishments, including mostly forgettable food courts, cafeteria buffets and snack bars. All park accommodations, campgrounds and eateries are shown on the free map and newspaper guide given out to visitors as they enter the park. Lodging reservations (available up to 366 days in advance) are essential from May to September. In summer, DNC sets up simple canvas-tent cabins at riverside **Housekeeping Camp** (cabins $93) in Yosemite Valley, busy **Tuolumne Meadows Lodge** (cabins $107) and serene **White Wolf Lodge** (cabins $99-120) off Tioga Rd. Tuolumne Meadows is about a 90-minute drive northeast of the valley, while White Wolf is an hour away.

Curry Village CABINS $$
(Yosemite Valley; tent cabins $112-120, cabins without/with bath $127/168, cottage r $191;) With a nostalgic summer-camp atmosphere, Curry Village has hundreds of helter-skelter units scattered beneath towering evergreens. Tent cabins resemble Civil War army barracks with scratchy wool blankets; wooden cabins are smaller but cozy.

Yosemite Lodge at the Falls MOTEL $$$
(Yosemite Valley; r $191-218; @) Spacious motel-style rooms have patios or balconies overlooking Yosemite Falls, meadows or the parking lot. Fork into grass-fed steaks, river trout and organic veggies at the lodge's Mountain Room (dinner mains $17 to $35), open nightly (no reservations). The food court has a decent range of cafeteria fare and the casual lounge has a convivial open-pit fireplace.

Wawona Hotel HISTORIC HOTEL $$$
(Wawona; r without/with bath incl breakfast $147/217;) Filled with character, this Victorian-era throwback has wide porches, manicured lawns and a golf course. Half the thin-walled rooms share baths. The romantic dining room with vintage details serves three meals a day (dinner mains $19 to $30). Wawona is about a 45-minute drive south of the valley.

Ahwahnee Hotel HISTORIC HOTEL $$$
(Yosemite Valley; r from $449; @) Sleep where Charlie Chaplin, Eleanor Roosevelt and JFK bedded down at this national historic landmark, built in 1927. Sit a spell by the roaring fireplace beneath soaring sugar-pine timbers. Skip the formal dining room, serving overpriced Californian fare (dinner mains $26 to $46), for the lobby bar with its small plates and inspired cocktails.

Degnan's Deli & Loft DELI, PIZZERIA $
(Yosemite Village; mains $6-10; deli 7am-5pm year-round, restaurant 5-9pm Mon-Fri, to 9pm Sat & Sun Apr-Oct) Grab a custom-made deli sandwich and bag of chips downstairs before hitting the trail. After dark, head upstairs for cold brewskies and crispy pizzas.

Camping

All campgrounds have bearproof lockers and campfire rings; most have potable water.

In summer, most campgrounds are noisy and booked to bulging, especially **North Pines** (tent & RV sites $20; Apr-Sep), **Lower Pines** (tent & RV sites $20; Mar-Oct) and **Upper Pines** (tent & RV sites $20; year-round) in Yosemite Valley; and **Tuolumne Meadows** (tent & RV sites $20; Jul-late Sep) off Tioga Rd, a 90-minute drive northeast of the valley.

Camp 4 (shared tent sites per person $5; year-round), a rock climber's hangout in the valley, and **Bridalveil Creek** (tent & RV sites $14; Jul-early Sep), a 45-minute drive south of the valley off Glacier Point Rd, are first-come, first-served and often full by noon, especially on weekends. Also 45 minutes south is pretty riverside **Wawona** (tent & RV sites $20; year-round).

Looking for a quieter, more rugged experience? Try smaller primitive spots like **Tamarack Flat** (tent sites $10; Jul-Sep), **Yosemite Creek** (tent sites $10; Jul–mid-Sep) and **Porcupine Flat** (tent & RV sites $10; Jul-Sep) off Tioga Rd.

OUTSIDE YOSEMITE NATIONAL PARK

Gateway towns that sometimes have lodgings include Fish Camp, Oakhurst, El Portal, Midpines, Mariposa, Groveland and Lee Vining.

Yosemite Bug Rustic Mountain Resort CABINS, HOSTEL $
(209-966-6666; www.yosemitebug.com; 6979 Hwy 140, Midpines; dm $25, tent cabins $45-75, r $75-155, cabins with shared bath $65-100; @)

YOSEMITE CAMPING RESERVATIONS

In summer, many campgrounds require **reservations** (518-885-3639; www.recreation.gov), which are available starting five months in advance. Campsites routinely sell out online within *minutes*. See www.nps.gov/yose/planyourvisit/camping.htm for sale dates.

Tucked into a forest about 25 miles west of Yosemite Valley, this mountain hostelry hosts globetrotters who dig the clean rooms, yoga studio and gorgeous spa, shared kitchen access and laundry. The cafe's fresh, organic and vegetarian-friendly meals (dinner mains $8.50 to $18) get raves.

TOP CHOICE **Evergreen Lodge** RESORT $$$
(209-379-2606; www.evergreenlodge.com; 33160 Evergreen Rd, Groveland; tents $75-110, cabins $175-350;) Near the entrance to Hetch Hetchy, this classic 90-year-old resort lets roughing-it guests cheat with comfy, prefurnished tents and deluxe mountain cabins. Outdoor recreational activities abound, with equipment rentals available. There's a general store, tavern with a pool table and a restaurant (dinner mains $18 to $28) serving three hearty meals every day.

Narrow Gauge Inn INN $$$
(559-683-7720; www.narrowgaugeinn.com; 48571 Hwy 41, Fish Camp; r incl breakfast $145-220; restaurant 5:30-9pm Wed-Sun Apr-Oct;) Swiss chalet-esque, this small inn has 26 comfy rooms, each with balcony or patio, and the Yosemite Mountain Sugar Pine steam railway next door. The 'buffalo bar' is authentic, and elk, venison and rib-eye appear on the Euro-Cal menu. It's 4 miles south of the park.

Information

Yosemite Village, Curry Village and Wawona stores all have ATMs. Drivers should fill up the tank before entering the park, or buy high-priced gas at Wawona or Crane Flat year-round or at Tuolumne Meadows in summer. Cell phone service is spotty throughout the park; Verizon and AT&T have some coverage. Pay internet kiosks are available adjacent to Degnan's Deli, and at Yosemite Lodge, which also has fee-based wi-fi.

Curry Village Lounge (Curry Village, behind registration office) Free wi-fi.

Mariposa County Public Library Wawona (Chilnualna Falls Rd; 1-6pm Mon-Fri, 10am-3pm Sat); Yosemite Valley (Girls Club Bldg, 58 Cedar Ct, Yosemite Valley; 8:30am-11:30am Mon, 2-5pm Tue, 8:30am-12:30pm Wed, 4-7pm Thu) Free internet terminals available.

Valley Wilderness Center (209-372-0745; Yosemite Village; 7:30am-5pm, shorter winter hr) Backcountry permits and bear-canister rentals; also available seasonally at Wawona, Tuolumne Meadows and Big Oak Flat.

Yosemite Medical Clinic (209-372-4637; Ahwahnee Dr, Yosemite Valley; 9am-7pm, emergencies 24hr) Also runs a dental clinic.

Yosemite Valley Visitor Center (209-372-0299; www.nps.gov/yose; Yosemite Village; 9am-7:30pm, shorter winter hr) Smaller visitor centers at Wawona, Tuolumne Meadows and Big Oak Flat are open seasonally.

Getting There & Around

The nearest Greyhound and Amtrak stations are in Merced. **YARTS** (209-388-9589; www.yarts.com) buses travel from Merced to the park along Hwy 140, stopping at towns along the way. In summer, YARTS buses run from the valley to Mammoth Lakes along Hwy 120. One-way tickets including the park-entry fee cost $13 from Merced, $15 from Mammoth Lakes.

Free shuttle buses loop around Yosemite Valley and, in summer, the Tuolumne Meadows and Wawona areas. DNC runs hikers' buses from the valley to Tuolumne Meadows (one way/round-trip $14.50/23) or Glacier Point (one way/round-trip $25/41). Bike rentals (per hour/day $10/28) are available at Yosemite Lodge and Curry Village, both in the valley. In winter, valley roads are plowed and the highways to the parks are kept open (except Tioga Rd/Hwy 120) – although snow chains may be required – and a free twice-daily shuttle bus connects Yosemite Valley with Badger Pass.

Sequoia & Kings Canyon National Parks

In these neighboring parks, the famous rust-red giant sequoia trees are bigger – up to 30 stories high! – and more numerous than anywhere else in the Sierra Nevada. Tough and fire-charred, they'd easily swallow two freeway lanes each. Giant, too, are the mountains – including Mt Whitney (14,505ft), the tallest peak in the lower 48 states. Finally, there is the giant Kings Canyon, carved out of granite by ancient glaciers and a powerful river. These are what lure the vast majority of 1.6 million annual visitors here; however, for quiet, solitude and close-up sightings of wildlife, including black bears, hit the trail to quickly lose yourself in the epic wilderness.

Sights

Sequoia was designated a national park in 1890; Kings Canyon, in 1940. Though distinct, the two parks operate as one unit with a single admission fee (valid for seven days) of $20 per car, $10 on motorcycle, bicycle or foot. For updates and general info, call 559-565-3341 or check the park website (www.nps.gov/seki).

From the south, Hwy 198 enters Sequoia National Park beyond the town of Three Rivers at Ash Mountain, from where it ascends the zigzagging Generals Hwy. From the west, Hwy 180 leads to the Big Stump entrance near Grant Grove before plunging into Kings Canyon.

SEQUOIA NATIONAL PARK

We dare you to try hugging the trees in **Giant Forest**, a 3-sq-mile grove protecting the park's most gargantuan specimens; the world's biggest is the **General Sherman Tree**. With sore arms and sticky sap fingers, lose the crowds by venturing onto any of the many forested trails (bring a map).

Giant Forest Museum MUSEUM

(559-565-4480; Generals Hwy; 9am-5pm mid-May–late May & mid-Aug–mid-Oct, to 6pm late May–late Jun, to 7pm late Jun–mid-Aug, sometimes to 4pm mid-Oct–mid-May) Four miles south of Lodgepole Village, a number of hiking trails start here, including a wheelchair-accessible route. For 360-degree views of the Great Western Divide, climb the steep quarter-mile staircase up **Moro Rock**.

Crystal Cave CAVE

(559-565-3759; www.sequoiahistory.org; Crystal Cave Rd; tours adult/child from $13/7; mid-May–late Oct) Discovered in 1918, the cave has marble formations estimated to be 10,000 years old. Tickets for the 45-minute basic tour are available at the Lodgepole and Foothills visitor centers, *not* at the cave. Bring a jacket.

Mineral King HISTORIC SITE

Worth a detour is Mineral King, a late-19th-century mining and logging camp ringed by craggy peaks and alpine lakes. The 25-mile one-way scenic drive – navigating almost 700 hair-raising hairpin turns – is usually open from late May to late October.

KINGS CANYON NATIONAL PARK & SCENIC BYWAY

North of Grant Grove Village, **General Grant Grove** brims with majestic giants. Beyond here, Hwy 180 begins its 35-mile descent into **Kings Canyon**, serpentining past chiseled rock walls laced with spring waterfalls. The road meets the Kings River, its roar ricocheting off granite cliffs soaring over 4000ft high, making this one of North America's deepest canyons.

Boyden Cavern CAVE

(559-965-8243; www.boydencavern.com; Hwy 180; 45min tour adult/child $13/8; May–mid-Nov) While smaller and less impressive than Crystal Cave in Sequoia National Park, the beautiful and whimsical formations here require no advance tickets.

Cedar Grove Village LANDMARK

The last outpost of civilization before the rugged grandeur of the Sierra Nevada backcountry. A popular day hike climbs 4 miles one way to roaring **Mist Falls** from Roads End; continue uphill alongside the river 2.5 more miles to **Paradise Valley**. A favorite of birders, an easy 1.5-mile nature trail loops around **Zumwalt Meadow**, just west of Roads End. Watch for rattlesnakes, black bear and mule deer.

Activities

Hiking is why people come here – with over 850 miles of marked trails to prove it. Cedar Grove and Mineral King offer the best backcountry access. Trails usually begin to open by mid-May, though there's hiking year-round in the Foothills area. Overnight backcountry trips require wilderness permits ($15), subject to a quota system in summer; for details, see www.nps.gov/seki/planyourvisit/wilderness.htm.

You can take a naturalist-led field trip with the **Sequoia Natural History Association** (559-565-3759; www.sequoiahistory.org). Horseback riding is offered at **Grant Grove Village** (559-335-9292) and the **Cedar Grove Pack Station** (559-565-3464). In summer,

SUPERSIZED FORESTS

In California you can stand under the world's oldest trees (ancient bristlecone pines) and its tallest (coast redwoods), but the record for biggest in terms of volume belongs to the giant sequoias *(Sequoiadendron giganteum)*. They grow only on the western slope of the Sierra Nevada range and are most abundant in Sequoia, Kings Canyon and Yosemite national parks. John Muir called them 'Nature's forest masterpiece,' and anyone who's ever craned their neck to take in their soaring vastness has probably done so with the same awe. These trees can grow 300ft tall and nearly 60ft in diameter, with bark up to 2ft thick. The Giant Forest Museum in Sequoia National Park has exhibits about the trees' unusual ecology.

cool off by swimming at Hume Lake, on national forest land off Hwy 180, and at riverside swimming holes in both parks. In winter, you can cross-country ski or snowshoe among the snow-draped giant sequoias. Equipment rental is available at Grant Grove Village and Wuksachi Lodge; for the best cross-country skiing and other winter sports, visit old-fashioned Montecito Sequoia Lodge, off the Generals Hwy between the two parks.

Sleeping & Eating

Outside Sequoia's southern entrance, several independent and chain motels line Hwy 198 through unexciting Three Rivers town.

Camping **reservations** (518-885-3639; www.recreation.gov) are accepted only at Lodgepole and Dorst in Sequoia National Park. The parks' dozen other campgrounds are first-come, first-served. Most have flush toilets; sites cost $10 to $20. Lodgepole, Azalea, Potwisha and South Fork are open year-round. Overflow camping is available in the surrounding Sequoia National Forest.

The markets in Grant Grove, Lodgepole and Cedar Grove have limited, pricey groceries; the latter two have snack bars serving burgers and basic meals for under $10, while Grant Grove has a simple restaurant and a cozy pizzeria. The Wuksachi Lodge's upscale **restaurant** (559-565-4070; dinner mains $18-38; 7-10am, 11am-2:30pm & 5-9:45pm) is hit-or-miss.

John Muir Lodge & Grant Grove Cabins LODGE, CABINS **$$**
(559-335-5500; www.sequoia-kingscanyon.com; Hwy 180, Grant Grove Village; d $69-190;) The woodsy lodge has good-sized, if generic, rooms and a cozy lobby with a stone fireplace and board games. Oddly assorted cabin types range from thin-walled canvas tents to nicely furnished historical cottages with private bathrooms.

Cedar Grove Lodge MOTEL **$$**
(559-335-5500; www.sequoia-kingscanyon.com; Hwy 180, Cedar Grove Village; r $119-135; mid-May–mid-Oct;) The 21 motel-style rooms with common porches overlooking Kings River are simple and well worn, but they're still your best option down the canyon.

Montecito Sequoia Lodge RESORT **$$**
(559-565-3388; www.mslodge.com; 63410 Generals Hwy, btwn Sequoia & Kings Canyon national parks; d incl meals $119-169;) Basic, recently renovated rooms include all meals. Family-fun camps keep things raucous all summer long; in winter there's cross-country skiing lessons and 50 miles of groomed trails.

Wuksachi Lodge HOTEL **$$$**
(559-565-4070; www.visitsequoia.com; off Generals Hwy, 4 miles north of Lodgepole Village; r $215-335;) Don't be misled by the grand lobby – because oversized motel-style rooms are nothing to brag about.

Bearpaw High Sierra Camp CABINS **$$**
(www.visitsequoia.com; tent cabin & meals per person $175; mid-Jun–mid-Sep) An 11-mile backcountry hike and unforgettable wilderness adventure.

Information

Lodgepole Village (559-565-4436; mid-Apr–mid-Oct), in Sequoia, and **Grant Grove Village** (559-565-4307; year-round), in Kings Canyon, are the main hubs. Both have visitor centers, post offices, markets, ATMs and public showers (summer only).

Foothills Visitor Center (559-565-3135) at Ash Mountain is open year-round. **Cedar Grove Visitor Center** (559-565-3793) and the **Mineral King Ranger Station** (559-565-3768) are open during summer. Check the free park newspaper for opening hours of visitor centers and other services.

Expensive gas is available at Hume Lake (year-round) and Stony Creek (summer only) outside park boundaries on national forest land.

Getting There & Around

In summer, free shuttle buses cover the Giant Forest and Lodgepole Village areas of Sequoia National Park, while the **Sequoia Shuttle** (877-287-4453; www.sequoiashuttle.com) connects the park with Three Rivers and Visalia (round-trip fare $15), with onward connections to Amtrak; reservations are required. Currently, there is no public transportation into Kings Canyon National Park.

Eastern Sierra

Vast, empty and majestic, here jagged peaks plummet down into the Great Basin desert, a dramatic juxtaposition that creates a potent scenery cocktail. Hwy 395 runs the entire length of the Sierra Nevada range, with turn-offs leading to pine forests, wildflower-strewn meadows, placid lakes, simmering hot springs and glacier-gouged canyons. Hikers, backpackers, mountain bikers, fishers and skiers love to escape here. The main visitor hubs are Mammoth Lakes and Bishop.

At **Bodie State Historic Park** (☎760-647-6445; www.parks.ca.gov; Hwy 270; adult/child $7/5; ⊙9am-6pm Jun-Aug, to 3pm Sep-May), a gold-rush ghost town is preserved in a state of 'arrested decay.' Weathered buildings sit frozen in time on a dusty, windswept plain. To get there, head east for 13 miles (the last three unpaved) on Hwy 270, about 7 miles south of Bridgeport. The access road is often snowed in during winter.

Further south, **Mono Lake** (www.monolake.org) is famous for its unearthly tufa towers, which rise from the alkaline water like drip sand castles. The best photo ops are from the south shore's **South Tufa Reserve** (adult/child $3/free). Off Hwy 395, **Mono Basin Scenic Area Visitor Center** (☎760-647-3044; ⊙8am-5pm mid-Apr–Nov) has excellent exhibits and schedules of guided walks and talks. From the nearby town of Lee Vining, Hwy 120 heads west into Yosemite National Park via the Tioga Pass.

Continuing south on Hwy 395, detour along the scenic 16-mile **June Lake Loop** or push on to **Mammoth Lakes**, a popular four-seasons resort guarded by 11,053ft **Mammoth Mountain** (☎760-934-2571, 24hr snow report 888-766-9778; www.mammothmountain.com; Minaret Rd; lift ticket adult/child $92/46), a top-notch skiing area. The slopes morph into a mountain-bike park in summer, when there's also camping, fishing and day hiking in the Mammoth Lakes Basin and Reds Meadow areas. Nearby are the near-vertical, 60ft-high basalt columns of **Devils Postpile National Monument** (☎760-934-2289; www.nps.gov/depo; shuttle fee adult/child $7/4), formed by volcanic activity. Hot-springs fans can soak in primitive pools off Benton Crossing Rd, 9 miles south of town, or view the geysering water at the **Hot Creek Geological Site** ⊙sunrise-sunset), 3 miles south. The **Mammoth Lakes Welcome Center & Ranger Station** (☎888-466-2666, 760-924-5500; www.visitmammoth.com; Hwy 203; ⊙8am-5pm) has maps and information about all of these places.

Further south, Hwy 395 descends into the Owens Valley, soon arriving in frontier-flavored **Bishop**, whose minor attractions include art galleries and an interesting railroad museum. Bishop provides access to the best fishing and rock climbing in the entire Eastern Sierra, and it's the main gateway for packhorse trips.

To check out some of the earth's oldest living things, budget a half-day for the thrilling trip up to the **Ancient Bristlecone Pine Forest** (☎760-873-2500; per car $5). These gnarled, otherworldly looking trees are found above 10,000ft on the slopes of the parched White Mountains, where you'd think nothing could grow. The oldest tree – called Methuselah – is estimated to be over 4700 years old. The road (usually open May to October) is paved to the visitor center at Schulman Grove, where there are hikes of varying lengths. From Hwy 395 in Big Pine, take Hwy 168 east for 12 miles and then head uphill another 10 miles from the marked turnoff.

Hwy 395 barrels on south to Independence and **Manzanar National Historic Site** (☎760-878-2194; www.nps.gov/manz; admission free; ⊙visitor center 9am-4:30pm, to 5:30pm Apr-Oct), which memorializes the war relocation camp where some 10,000 Japanese Americans were unjustly interned during WWII following the attack on Pearl Harbor. Interpretive exhibits and a short film vividly chronicle life at the camp.

South of here, in Lone Pine, you finally catch a glimpse of 14,505ft **Mt Whitney** (www.fs.usda.gov/inyo), the highest mountain in the lower 48 states. The heart-stopping, 11-mile scenic drive up **Whitney Portal Road** (closed in winter) is spectacular. Climbing the peak is hugely popular, but requires a permit issued on a lottery basis. West of Lone Pine, the bizarrely shaped boulders of the **Alabama Hills** have enchanted filmmakers of such Hollywood Western classics as *How the West Was Won* (1962). Peruse vintage memorabilia and movie posters at the **Museum of Lone Pine Film History** (☎760-876-9909; www.lonepinefilmhistorymuseum.org; 701 S Main St; admission $5; ⊙10am-6pm

SCENIC DRIVES IN THE SIERRA NEVADA

Tioga Road (Hwy 120; p166) Yosemite's rooftop of the world

Generals Highway (Hwy 198; p168) Historic byway past giant sequoias

Kings Canyon Scenic Byway (Hwy 180; p169) Dive into North America's deepest canyon

Eastern Sierra Scenic Byway (US 395; p170) Where snowy mountains overshadow the desert

Mon-Wed, to 7pm Thu-Sat, to 4pm Sun). At the Hwy 395/136 junction, the **Eastern Sierra InterAgency Visitor Center** (☎760-876-6222; www.fs.fed.us/r5/inyo; ⏰8am-5pm, extended summer hr) issues wilderness permits and dispenses information about regional parks, forests and deserts.

Sleeping

The Eastern Sierra is freckled with campgrounds. Backcountry camping requires a wilderness permit, reservable in advance or available at ranger stations. Bishop, Lone Pine and Bridgeport have the most motels. Mammoth Lakes has countless inns, B&Bs and condo and vacation rentals.

Tamarack Lodge & Resort RESORT **$$**
(☎760-934-2442; www.tamaracklodge.com; off Lake Mary Rd, Mammoth Lakes; r $99-169, cabins $169-599; @📶) In business since 1924, this woodsy lakeside resort offers lodge rooms and cabins with kitchens, ranging from very simple to simply deluxe, and some even have wood-burning stoves.

Redwood Motel MOTEL **$**
(☎760-932-7060; www.redwoodmotel.net; 425 Main St, Bridgeport; d from $59-89; ⏰Apr-Nov; ❄📶) Wacky farm animal sculptures give a cheerful welcome to this spotless motel. Your host will shower you with travel tips.

Whitney Portal Hostel HOSTEL **$**
(☎760-876-0030; www.whitneyportalstore.com; 238 S Main St, Lone Pine; dm/q $20/60; ❄@📶) The carpeted bunk-bed rooms are a popular launching pad for Whitney hikes, and public showers are available. Reserve two months ahead for July and August.

Chalfant House B&B **$$**
(☎760-872-1790; www.chalfanthouse.com; 213 Academy, Bishop; d incl breakfast $80-110; ❄📶) Lace curtains and Victorian accents swirl through the six rooms of this restored historic home.

Eating & Drinking

Good Life Café CALIFORNIAN **$**
(126 Old Mammoth Rd, Mammoth Lakes; mains $8-10; ⏰6:30am-3pm) Stomach-stuffing Mexican breakfasts, healthy veggie wraps, brawny burgers and big salad bowls make this place perennially popular.

TOP CHOICE **Whoa Nellie Deli** MODERN AMERICAN **$$**
(Hwys 120 & 395, Lee Vining; mains $8-19; ⏰7am-9pm mid-Apr–Oct) Great food in a gas station? Really, you gotta try this amazing kitchen, where chef Matt 'Tioga' Toomey serves up delicious fish tacos, wild buffalo meatloaf and other tasty morsels.

Raymond's Deli DELI **$**
(206 N Main St, Bishop; sandwiches $7-9; ⏰10am-6pm; 🍸) A sassy den of kitsch, pinball and Pac-Man, it serves heaping sandwiches with names like 'When Pigs Fly,' 'Flaming Farm' and 'Soy U Like Tofu.' Kick back with a Lobotomy Bock.

Mammoth Brewing Company Tasting Room BREWERY
(☎760-934-7141; www.mammothbrewingco.com; 94 Berner St, Mammoth Lakes; ⏰10am-6pm) Free samples anyone? Try some of the dozen brews on tap, then buy some IPA 395 or Double Nut Brown to go.

Lake Tahoe

Shimmering in myriad blues and greens, Lake Tahoe is the nation's second-deepest lake. Driving around its spellbinding 72-mile scenic shoreline gives you quite a workout behind the wheel. The north shore is quiet and upscale; the west shore, rugged and old-timey; the east shore, undeveloped; and the south shore, busy and tacky with aging motels and flashy casinos. The horned peaks surrounding the lake, which straddles the California–Nevada state line, are four-seasons playgrounds.

Tahoe gets packed in summer, on winter weekends and holidays, when reservations are essential. **Lake Tahoe Visitors Authority** (☎800-288-2463; www.tahoesouth.com) and **North Lake Tahoe Visitors' Bureaus** (☎888-434-1262; www.gotahoenorth.com) can help with accommodations and tourist information. There's camping in **state parks** (☎800-444-7275; www.reserveamerica.com) and on **USFS lands** (☎877-444-6777; www.recreation.gov).

SOUTH LAKE TAHOE & WEST SHORE

With retro motels and eateries lining busy Hwy 50, South Lake Tahoe gets crowded. Gambling at Stateline's casino hotels, just across the Nevada border, attracts thousands, as does the world-class ski resort of **Heavenly** (☎775-586-7000; www.skiheavenly.com; 3860 Saddle Rd). In summer, a trip up Heavenly's gondola (adult/child $32/20) guarantees fabulous views of the lake and **Desolation Wilderness** (www.fs.fed.us/r5/ltbmu).

This starkly beautiful landscape of raw granite peaks, glacier-carved valleys and alpine lakes is a favorite with hikers. Get maps, information and overnight **wilderness permits** (per adult $5-10; www.recreation.gov) from the **USFS Taylor Creek Visitor Center** (☎530-543-2674; Hwy 89; ⊙daily May-Oct, winter hr vary). It's 3 miles north of the 'Y' intersection of Hwys 50/89, at **Tallac Historic Site** (tour $5; ⊙10am-4:30pm mid-Jun–Sep, Fri & Sat only late May–mid-Jun), which preserves early-20th-century vacation estates. **Lake Tahoe Cruises** (☎800-238-2463; www.zephyrcove.com; adult/child from $39/15) ply the 'Big Blue' year-round. Back on shore, vegetarian-friendly **Sprouts** (3123 Harrison Ave; mains $6-10; ⊙8am-9pm; ☑) is a delish natural-foods cafe.

Hwy 89 threads northwest along the thickly forested west shore to **Emerald Bay State Park** (www.parks.ca.gov; per car/campsites $8/35; ⊙late May-Sep), where granite cliffs and pine trees frame a fjordlike inlet, truly sparkling green. A steep 1-mile trail leads down to **Vikingsholm Castle** (tours adult/child $5/3; ⊙10:30am-4:30pm). From this 1920s Scandinavian-style mansion, the 4.5-mile **Rubicon Trail** ribbons north along the lakeshore past an old lighthouse and petite coves to **DL Bliss State Park** (www.parks.ca.gov; entry per car $8, campsites $35-45; ⊙late May-Sep), offering sandy beaches. Further north, **Tahoma Meadows B&B Cottages** (☎530-525-1553; www.tahomameadows.com; 6821 W Lake Blvd, Tahoma; d incl breakfast $109-269) rents darling country cabins (pet fee $20).

NORTH & EAST SHORES

The north shore's commercial hub, **Tahoe City** is great for grabbing supplies and renting outdoor gear. It's not far from **Squaw Valley USA** (☎530-583-6985; www.squaw.com; off Hwy 89), a megasized ski resort that hosted the 1960 Winter Olympics. Après-ski crowds gather for beer 'n' burgers at woodsy **Bridgetender Tavern** (www.tahoebridgetender.com; 65 W Lake Blvd; mains $8-12; ⊙11am-11pm Sun-Thu, to midnight Fri & Sat) back in town, or fuel up on French toast and eggs Benedict at down-home **Fire Sign Cafe** (1785 W Lake Blvd; dishes $6-12; ⊙7am-3pm).

In summer, swim or kayak at Tahoe Vista or Kings Beach. Spend a night at **Franciscan Lakeside Lodge** (☎530-546-6300; www.franciscanlodge.com; 6944 N Lake Blvd, Tahoe Vista; d $80-265;) , where simple cabins, cottages and suites have kitchenettes. East of Kings Beach, which has cheap, filling lakeshore eateries, Hwy 28 barrels into Nevada. Try your luck at the gambling tables or catch a live-music show at the **Crystal Bay Club Casino** (☎775-831-0512; www.crystalbaycasino.com; 14 Hwy 28). But for more happening bars and bistros, drive further to **Incline Village**.

With pristine beaches, lakes and miles of multiuse trails, **Lake Tahoe-Nevada State Park** (http://parks.nv.gov/lt.htm; per car $7-12) is the east shore's biggest draw. Summer crowds splash in the turquoise waters of **Sand Harbor**. The 15-mile **Flume Trail** (☎775-749-5349; www.theflumetrail.com; trailhead bike rental $45-65, shuttle $5-10), a mountain biker's holy grail, starts further south at **Spooner Lake**.

TRUCKEE & AROUND

North of Lake Tahoe off I-80, Truckee is not in fact a truck stop but a thriving mountain town, with organic-coffee shops, trendy boutiques and dining in downtown's historical district. Ski bunnies have several area resorts to pick from, including glam **Northstar-at-Tahoe** (☎800-466-6784; www.northstarattahoe.com; off Hwy 267); kid-friendly **Sugar Bowl** (☎530-426-9000; www.sugarbowl.com; off Hwy 40), cofounded by Walt Disney; and **Royal Gorge** (☎530-426-3871; www.royalgorge.com; off I-80), paradise for cross-country skiers.

West of Hwy 89, Donner Summit is where the infamous Donner Party became trapped during the fierce winter of 1846–47. Led astray by their guidebook, less than half survived – by cannibalizing their dead friends. The grisly tale is chronicled at the museum inside **Donner Memorial State Park** (www.parks.ca.gov; Donner Pass Rd; per car/campsites $8/35; ⊙museum 9am-4pm year-round, campground mid-May–mid-Sep), where **Donner Lake** is popular with swimmers and windsurfers.

Ecoconscious **Cedar House Sport Hotel** (☎530-582-5655; www.cedarhousesporthotel.com; 10918 Brockway Rd; r incl breakfast $170-270;) is green building-certified, and has an outdoor hot tub and stylishly modern boutique rooms (pet fee $50). For live jazz and wine, **Moody's Bistro & Lounge** (☎530-587-8688; www.moodysbistro.com; 10007 Bridge St; dinner mains $18-40; ⊙11:30am-9:30pm Sun-Thu, to 10pm Fri & Sat) sources locally ranched meats and seasonal produce. Down pints of 'Donner Party Porter' at **Fifty Fifty Brewing Co** (www.fiftyfiftybrewing.com; 11197 Brockway Rd) across the tracks.

Getting There & Around

South Tahoe Express (☎866-898-2463; www.southtahoeexpress.com) runs frequent shuttles from Nevada's **Reno-Tahoe International Airport** to Stateline (one way adult/child $27/15). **North Lake Tahoe Express** (☎866-216-5222; www.northlaketahoeexpress.com) connects Reno's airport with Truckee, Squaw Valley and north-shore towns (one way/round-trip $40/75).

Truckee's **Amtrak depot** (10065 Donner Pass Rd) has daily trains to Sacramento ($37, 4½ hours) and Reno ($15, 1½ hours), and twice-daily Greyhound buses to Reno ($18, one hour), Sacramento ($42, 2½ hours) and San Francisco ($40, six hours). Amtrak Thruway buses connect Sacramento with South Lake Tahoe ($34, three hours).

Tahoe Area Regional Transit (TART; ☎800-736-6365; www.laketahoetransit.com; single ride/24hr pass $1.75/3.50) runs local buses to Truckee and around the north and west shores. South Lake Tahoe is served by **BlueGO** (☎530-541-7149; www.bluego.org; single ride/day pass $2/6), which operates a summer-only trolley up the west shore to Tahoma, connecting with TART.

If you're driving, tire chains are often required in winter on I-80, US 50, Hwy 89 and Mt Rose Hwy, any or all of which may close during and after snowstorms.

Pacific Northwest

Includes »

Why Go?

As much a state of mind as a geographical region, the US's northwest corner is a land of subcultures and new trends, where evergreen trees frame snow-dusted volcanoes, and inspired ideas scribbled on the back of napkins become tomorrow's business start-ups. You can't peel off the history in layers here, but you *can* gaze wistfully into the future in fast-moving, innovative cities such as Seattle and Portland, sprinkled with food carts, streetcars, microbrews, green belts, coffee connoisseurs and weird urban sculpture.

Ever since the days of the Oregon Trail, the Northwest has had a hypnotic lure for risk-takers and dreamers, and the metaphoric carrot still dangles. There's the air, so clean they ought to bottle it; the trees, older than many of Rome's Renaissance palaces; and the end-of-the-continent coastline, holding back the force of the world's largest ocean. Cowboys take note; it doesn't get much more 'wild' or 'west' than this.

Best Places to Eat

» Seeds Bistro & Bar (p200)
» Allium (p202)
» Paley's Place (p215)
» New Sammy's Cowboy Bistro (p228)

Best Places to Stay

» Sun Mountain Lodge (p204)
» Ace Hotel – Portland (p213)
» McMenamins Old St Francis School (p225)
» Enzian Inn (p203)

When to Go

Seattle

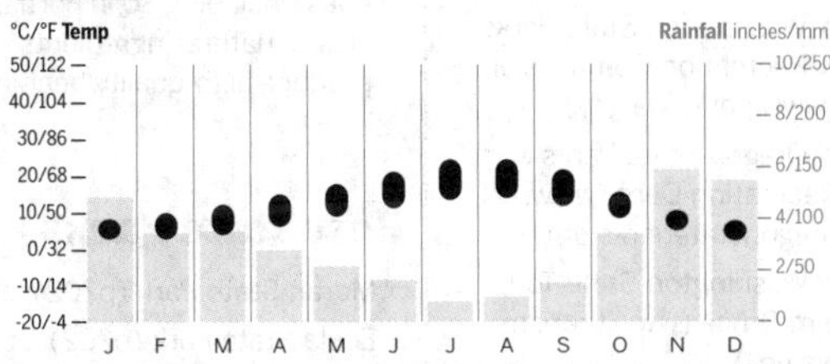

Jan-Mar Most reliable snow cover for skiing in the Cascades and beyond.

May Festival season: Portland Rose, Northwest Folklife, the Seattle International Film Festival.

Jul-Sep The best hiking window in-between the spring snowmelt and the first fall flurries.

DON'T MISS

Between them, the states of Washington and Oregon harbor four of the US's most spectacular national parks: Mt Rainier (established 1899), Crater Lake (1902), Olympic (1938) and North Cascades (1968).

Fast Facts

» Population: Seattle (608,660), Portland (583,770)

» Distances from Seattle: Portland (174 miles), Spokane (280 miles)

» Time zone: Pacific Standard

» States covered in this chapter: Washington, Oregon

Did You Know?

Over the winter of 1998–99, the Mt Baker ski resort in northwest Washington received 1140in of snow in a single season, the largest annual snowfall ever recorded.

Resources

» Washington State Parks & Recreation Commission (www.parks.wa.gov)

» Oregon State Parks & Recreation Dept (www.oregonstateparks.org)

» Washington State Tourism Office (www.tourism.wa.gov)

» Oregon Tourism Commission (www.traveloregon.com)

Grunge & Other Subcultures

Synthesizing Generation X angst with a questionable approach to personal hygiene, grunge first dive-bombed onto Seattle's music scene in the early 1990s like a clap of thunder on an otherwise dry and sunny afternoon. The anger had been fermenting for years. Hardcore punk originated in Portland in the late 1970s, led by resident contrarians the Wipers, whose antifashion followers congregated in legendary dive bars such as Satyricon. Another musical blossoming occurred in Olympia, where DIY-merchants Beat Happening invented 'lo-fi' and coyly mocked the corporate establishment. Scooping up the fallout of a disparate youth culture, Seattle quickly became grunge's pulpit, spawning bands like Pearl Jam, Soundgarden and Alice in Chains. The genre went global in 1991 when Nirvana's *Nevermind* album knocked Michael Jackson off the number-one spot, but the movement was never meant to be successful and the kudos quickly killed it. Since the mid '90s the Pacific Northwest has kept its subcultures largely to itself, though the music's no less potent or relevant.

MICROBREWERIES

'Beer connoisseurship' is a nationwide phenomenon these days, but the campaign to put a dash of flavor back into insipid commercially brewed beer was first ignited in that longstanding bastion of good taste, the Pacific Northwest, in the 1980s.

One of America's first microbreweries was the mercurial, if short-lived, Cartwright Brewing Company, set up in Portland in 1980. The nation's first official brewpub was the now defunct Grant's, which opened in the Washington city of Yakima in 1982. The trend went viral in 1984 with the inauguration of Bridgeport Brewing Company in Portland, followed a year later by Beervana's old-school brewing brothers Mike and Brian McMenamin, whose quirky beer empire still acts as a kind of personification of the craft-brewing business in the region.

Today the Pacific Northwest has over 200 microbreweries (including 30 in Portland alone), all of which take classic natural ingredients – malt, hops and yeast – to produce high-quality beer in small but tasty batches.

Best State Parks

» Moran State Park (p202), on Orcas Island

» Ecola State Park (p232), at Cannon Beach

» Deception Pass State Park (p199), on Whidbey Island

» Fort Worden State Park (p197), in Port Townsend

» Lime Kiln Point State Park (p202), on San Juan Island

» Cape Blanco State Park (p234), near Port Orford

» Smith Rock State Park (p225), near Bend

History

Native American societies, including the Chinook and the Salish, had long-established coastal communities by the time Europeans arrived in the Pacific Northwest in the 18th century. Inland, on the arid plateaus between the Cascades and the Rocky Mountains, the Spokane, Nez Percé and other tribes thrived on seasonal migration between river valleys and temperate uplands.

Three hundred years after Columbus landed in the New World, Spanish and British explorers began probing the northern Pacific coast, seeking the fabled Northwest Passage. In 1792 Capt George Vancouver was the first explorer to sail the waters of Puget Sound, claiming British sovereignty over the entire region. At the same time, an American, Captain Robert Gray, found the mouth of the Columbia River. In 1805 the explorers Lewis and Clark crossed the Rockies and made their way down the Columbia to the Pacific Ocean, extending the US claim on the territory.

In 1824 the British Hudson's Bay Company established Fort Vancouver in Washington as headquarters for the Columbia region. This opened the door to waves of settlers but had a devastating impact on the indigenous cultures, assailed as they were by the double threat of European diseases and alcohol.

In 1843 settlers at Champoeg, on the Willamette River south of Portland, voted to organize a provisional government independent of the Hudson's Bay Company, thereby casting their lot with the USA, which formally acquired the territory from the British by treaty in 1846. Over the next decade, some 53,000 settlers came to the Northwest via the 2000-mile Oregon Trail.

Arrival of the railroads set the region's future. Agriculture and lumber became the pillars of the economy until 1914, when WWI and the opening of the Panama Canal brought increased trade to Pacific ports. Shipyards opened along Puget Sound, and the Boeing aircraft company set up shop near Seattle.

Big dam projects in the 1930s and '40s provided cheap hydroelectricity and irrigation. WWII offered another boost for aircraft manufacturing and shipbuilding, and agriculture continued to thrive. In the postwar period, Washington's population, especially around Puget Sound, grew to twice that of Oregon. But hydroelectricity production and the massive irrigation projects along the Columbia have nearly destroyed the river's ecosystem, and logging has also left its scars, especially in Oregon. The environment remains a contentious issue in the Northwest; flash points are the logging of old-growth forests and the destruction of salmon runs in streams and rivers.

In the 1980s and '90s, the economic emphasis shifted again with the rise of the high-tech industry, embodied by Microsoft in Seattle and Intel in Portland. The region has also reinvigorated its eco credentials,

THE PACIFIC NORTHWEST IN...

Four Days

Hit the ground running in **Seattle** with the main sights, Pike Place Market and the Seattle Center, on days one and two. On day three, take the train down to **Portland** where you can rent a bike and spin around the bars, cafes, food carts and nightlife.

One Week

Add in some extra sights along the I-5 corridor, such as Washington state capital **Olympia**, the pastoral fields of **Whidbey Island** or the magnificent University of Oregon campus in left-field **Eugene**. You may also have time for day sorties to spectacular **Cannon Beach** on the Oregon Coast, or the historic seaport of **Port Townsend** on the Olympic Peninsula.

Two Weeks

It's time to visit some national parks. **Mount Rainier** is doable in a day trip from Seattle, while **Crater Lake** can be combined with a trip to **Ashland** and its Shakespeare Festival. Don't miss the ethereal **San Juan Islands** up near the watery border with Canada, or **Bend**, Oregon, the region's biggest outdoor draw. If time allows, head across the Cascades to the dramatically different east. **Walla Walla** is wine-quaffing heaven, while **Steens Mountain** is a lightly trodden wilderness that feels as remote as parts of Alaska.

Pacific Northwest Highlights

1 Use human-powered bikes and kayaks to get around the quieter corners of the **San Juan Islands** (p201)

2 Admire trees older than Europe's Renaissance castles in Washington's **Olympic National Park** (p196)

3 View one of the greatest pages of American history in the Columbia River's **Lewis & Clark National & State Historical Parks** (p231)

4 Watch the greatest outdoor show in the Pacific Northwest in Seattle's theatrical **Pike Place Market** (p181)

5 Ride a bike around clean, green, serene **Portland** (p208), energized by beer, coffee and food-cart pizza

6 Descend on **Bend** (p225) in Oregon to review the most multifarious list of outdoor activities in the state

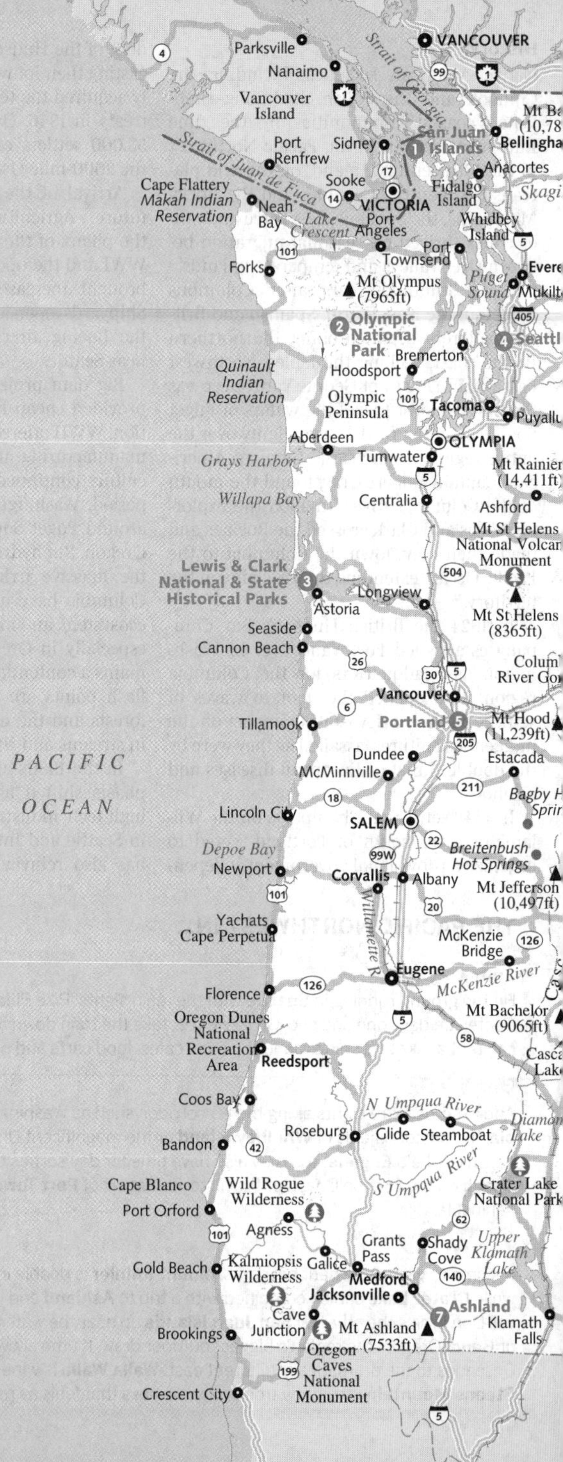

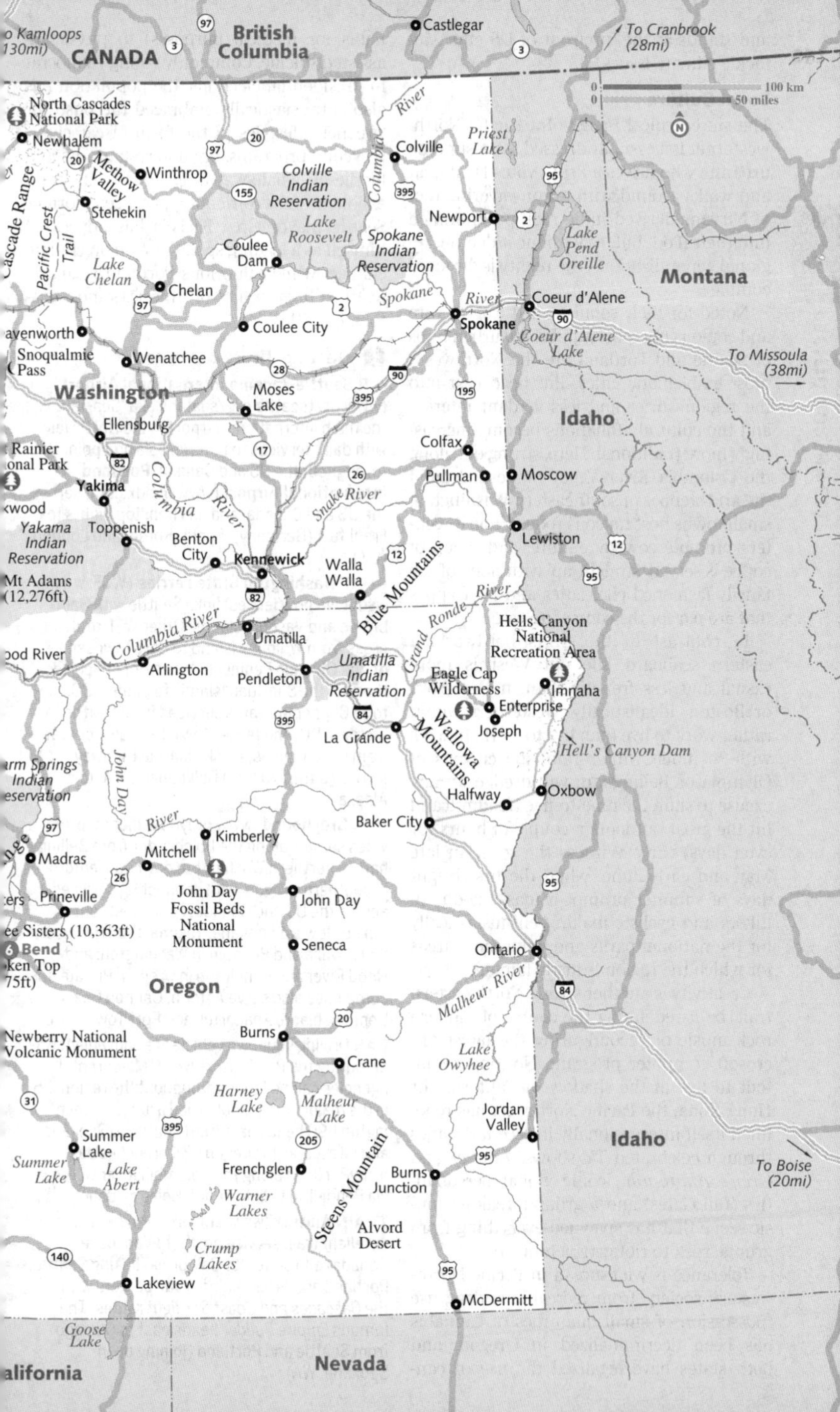

To Kamloops (130mi)
CANADA
British Columbia
Castlegar
To Cranbrook (28mi)
0 100 km
0 50 miles
North Cascades National Park
Newhalem
Methow Valley
Winthrop
Cascade Range
Pacific Crest Trail
Stehekin
Lake Chelan
Chelan
Colville Indian Reservation
Lake Roosevelt
Columbia River
Colville
Priest Lake
Newport
Lake Pend Oreille
Montana
Coulee Dam
Spokane Indian Reservation
Spokane River
Coeur d'Alene
Spokane
Coeur d'Alene Lake
To Missoula (38mi)
Leavenworth
Coulee City
Snoqualmie Pass
Wenatchee
Washington
Moses Lake
Idaho
Ellensburg
Colfax
Pullman
Moscow
Rainier National Park
Yakima
Columbia River
Snake River
Kirkwood
Yakama Indian Reservation
Toppenish
Benton City
Kennewick
Walla Walla
Blue Mountains
Lewiston
Mt Adams (12,276ft)
Grande Ronde River
Hells Canyon National Recreation Area
Columbia River
Umatilla
Hood River
Arlington
Pendleton
Umatilla Indian Reservation
Eagle Cap Wilderness
Imnaha
Enterprise
Joseph
La Grande
Wallowa Mountains
Hell's Canyon Dam
Warm Springs Indian Reservation
John Day River
Halfway
Oxbow
Baker City
Kimberley
Madras
Mitchell
John Day Fossil Beds National Monument
John Day
Prineville
Three Sisters (10,363ft)
Bend
Broken Top (9175ft)
Seneca
Ontario
Oregon
Malheur River
Burns
Newberry National Volcanic Monument
Crane
Lake Owyhee
Harney Lake
Malheur Lake
Jordan Valley
Idaho
Summer Lake
Summer Lake
Lake Abert
Frenchglen
Steens Mountain
Burns Junction
To Boise (20mi)
Warner Lakes
Alvord Desert
Crump Lakes
Lakeview
McDermitt
Goose Lake
California
Nevada

and stands at the forefront of US efforts to tackle climate issues.

Local Culture

The stereotypical image of a Pacific Northwesterner is a casually dressed, latte-supping urbanite who drives a Prius, votes Democrat and walks around with an unwavering diet of Nirvana-derived indie rock programmed into their iPod. But, as with most fleeting regional generalizations, the reality is far more complex.

Noted for their sophisticated cafe culture and copious microbrew pubs, the urban hubs of Seattle and Portland are the Northwest's most emblematic cities. But head east into the region's drier and less verdant interior, and the cultural affiliations become increasingly more traditional. Here, strung out along the Columbia River Valley or nestled amid the arid steppes of southeastern Washington, small towns host raucous rodeos, tourist centers promote cowboy culture, and a cup of coffee is served 'straight up' with none of the fancily fashioned chai lattes and icy frappés that are par for the course in Seattle.

In contrast to the USA's hardworking eastern seaboard, life out West is more casual and less frenetic than in New York or Boston. Idealistically, Westerners would rather work to live than live to work. Indeed, with so much winter rain, the citizens of Olympia or Bellingham will dredge up any excuse to shun the nine-to-five treadmill and hit the great outdoors a couple of hours (or even days) early. Witness the scene in late May and early June, when the first bright days of summer prompt a mass exodus of hikers and cyclists making enthusiastically for the national parks and wilderness areas for which the region is justly famous.

Creativity is another strong Northwestern trait, be it redefining the course of modern rock music or reconfiguring the latest Microsoft computer program. No longer content to live in the shadow of California or Hong Kong, the Pacific Northwest has redefined itself internationally in recent decades through celebrated TV shows (*Frasier* and *Grey's Anatomy*), iconic global personalities (Bill Gates) and a groundbreaking music scene that has spawned everything from grunge rock to riot grrrl feminism.

Tolerance is widespread in Pacific Northwestern society, from recreational drug use (possession of small quantities of cannabis has been decriminalized in Oregon, and both states have legalized the use of cannabis for medical purposes) to physician-assisted suicide. Commonly voting Democrat in presidential elections, the population has also enthusiastically embraced the push for 'greener' lifestyles in the form of car clubs, recycling programs, organic restaurants and biodiesel whale-watching tours. An early exponent of ecofriendly practices, former Seattle mayor Greg Nickels has advocated himself as a leading spokesperson on climate change, while salubrious Portland regularly features high in lists of America's most sustainable cities.

Getting There & Around

AIR **Seattle-Tacoma International Airport** (www.portseattle.org/seatac), aka 'Sea-Tac,' is the main international airport in the Northwest, with daily services to Europe, Asia and points throughout the US and Canada. **Portland International Airport** (www.flypdx.com) serves the US and Canada, and has nonstop flights to Frankfurt (Germany), Seoul (Korea) and London (UK).

BOAT **Washington State Ferries** (WSF; www.wsdot.wa.gov/ferries) links Seattle with Bainbridge and Vashon Islands. Other WSF routes cross from Whidbey Island to Port Townsend on the Olympic Peninsula, and from Anacortes through the San Juan Islands to Sidney, BC. Victoria Clipper operates services from Seattle to Victoria, BC, and ferries to Victoria also operate from Port Angeles. Alaska Marine Highway ferries (p456) go from Bellingham, WA, to Alaska.

BUS **Greyhound** (www.greyhound.com) provides service along the I-5 corridor from Bellingham in northern Washington down to Medford in southern Oregon, with connecting services across the US and Canada. East–west routes fan out toward Spokane, Yakima, the Tri-Cities, Walla Walla and Pullman in Washington, and Hood River and Pendleton in Oregon. Private bus companies also serve Astoria, Cannon Beach, Bend, Ashland, Anacortes and Port Townsend.

CAR Driving your own vehicle is a convenient way of touring the Pacific Northwest. Major rental agencies can be found throughout the region. I-5 is the major north–south road artery. In Washington I-90 heads east from Seattle to Spokane and into Idaho. In Oregon I-84 branches east from Portland along the Columbia River Gorge via Pendleton to link up with Boise in Idaho.

TRAIN **Amtrak** (www.amtrak.com) runs an excellent train service north (to Vancouver, Canada) and south (to California) linking Seattle, Portland and other major urban centers with the *Cascades* and *Coast Starlight* routes. The famous *Empire Builder* heads east to Chicago from Seattle and Portland (joining up in Spokane, WA).

WASHINGTON

Divided in two by the spinal Cascade Mountains, Washington isn't so much a land of contrasts as a land of polar opposites. Centered on Seattle, the western coastal zone is wet, urban, liberal and famous for its fecund evergreen forests; splayed to the east between the less celebrated cities of Spokane and Yakima, the inland plains are arid, rural, conservative and covered by mile after mile of scrublike steppe.

Of the two halves it's the west that harbors most of the quintessential Washington sights, while the more remote east is less heralded, understated and full of surprises.

WASHINGTON FACTS

» **Nickname** Evergreen State

» **Population** 6,724,540

» **Area** 71,342 sq miles

» **Capital city** Olympia (population 46,480)

» **Other cities** Seattle (population 608,660), Spokane (population 208,915), Yakima (population 91,065), Bellingham (population 80,000), Walla Walla (population 31,730)

» **Sales tax** 6.5%

» **Birthplace of** singer and actor Bing Crosby (1903–77), guitarist Jimi Hendrix (1942–70), computer geek Bill Gates (b 1955), political commentator Glen Beck (b 1964), musical icon Kurt Cobain (1967–94)

» **Home of** Mt St Helens, Microsoft, Starbucks, Nordstrom, Evergreen State College

» **Politics** Democrat governor, Democrat senators, Democrat in presidential elections since 1988

» **Famous for** grunge rock, coffee, *Grey's Anatomy*, *Twilight*, volcanoes, apples, wine, precipitation

» **State vegetable** Walla Walla sweet onion

» **Driving distances** Seattle to Portland 174 miles, Spokane to Port Angeles 365 miles

Seattle

Combine the brains of Portland, Oregon, with the beauty of Vancouver, BC, and you'll get something approximating Seattle. It's hard to believe that the Pacific Northwest's largest metropolis was considered a 'secondary' US city until the 1980s, when a combination of bold innovation and unabashed individualism turned it into one of the dot-com era's biggest trendsetters, spearheaded by an unlikely alliance of coffee-supping computer geeks and navel-gazing musicians. Reinvention is the buzzword these days in a city where grunge belongs to the history books and Starbucks is just one in a cavalcade of precocious indie coffee providers eking out their market position.

Surprisingly elegant in places and coolly edgy in others, Seattle is notable for its strong neighborhoods, top-rated university, monstrous traffic jams and proactive city mayors who harbor green credentials. Although it has fermented its own pop culture in recent times, it has yet to create an urban mythology befitting Paris or New York, but it does have 'the Mountain.' Better known as Rainier to its friends, Seattle's unifying symbol is a 14,411ft mass of rock and ice, which acts as a perennial reminder to the city's huddled masses that raw wilderness and potential volcanic catastrophe are never far away.

Sights

DOWNTOWN

TOP CHOICE **Pike Place Market** MARKET

(www.pikeplacemarket.org) Take a bunch of small-time businesses and sprinkle them liberally around a spatially challenged waterside strip amid crowds of bohemians, restaurateurs, tree-huggers, bolshie students, artists, vinyl lovers and artisans. The result: Pike Place Market, a cavalcade of noise, smells, personalities, banter and urban theater that's almost London-like in its cosmopolitanism. In operation since 1907, Pike Place Market is famous for many things, not least its eye-poppingly fresh fruit and vegetables, its anarchistic shops and its loquacious fish-throwing fishmongers. Improbably, it also spawned the world's first Starbucks, which is still there (if you can get past the tourists) knocking out the old 'joe' from under its original brown logo. But, more importantly, Pike Place is Seattle in a bottle, a wonderfully 'local' experience that highlights the city for what it really is: all-embracing, eclectic and proudly singular.

Seattle

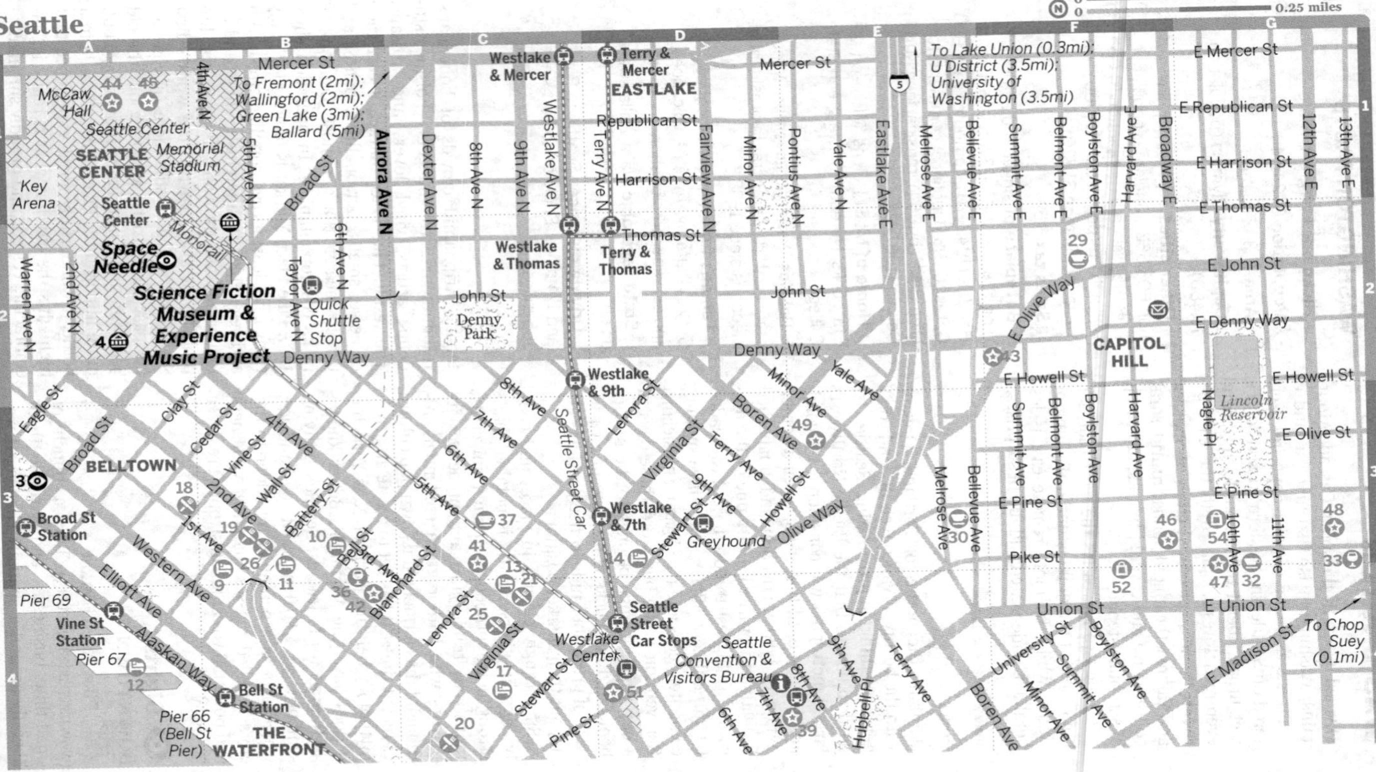
500 m
0.25 miles
Mercer St
To Fremont (2mi); Wallingford (2mi); Green Lake (3mi); Ballard (5mi)
McCaw Hall
Seattle Center
SEATTLE CENTER
Memorial Stadium
Key Arena
Seattle Center
Monorail
Space Needle
Science Fiction Museum & Experience Music Project
Quick Shuttle Stop
Westlake & Mercer
Terry & Mercer
EASTLAKE
Westlake & Thomas
Terry & Thomas
Thomas St
Republican St
Harrison St
John St
Denny Park
Denny Way
Westlake & 9th
Westlake & 7th
Seattle Street Car
Seattle Street Car Stops
Westlake Center
Seattle Convention & Visitors Bureau
Greyhound
To Lake Union (0.3mi); U District (3.5mi); University of Washington (3.5mi)
E Mercer St
E Republican St
E Harrison St
E Thomas St
E John St
E Denny Way
E Olive Way
CAPITOL HILL
E Howell St
Lincoln Reservoir
Nagle Pl
E Olive St
E Pine St
Pike St
Union St
E Union St
E Madison St
To Chop Suey (0.1mi)
BELLTOWN
Broad St Station
Vine St Station
Bell St Station
Pier 69
Pier 67
Pier 66 (Bell St Pier)
THE WATERFRONT
Alaskan Way
Elliott Ave
Western Ave
1st Ave
2nd Ave
3rd Ave
4th Ave
5th Ave
6th Ave
7th Ave
8th Ave
9th Ave
Eagle St
Broad St
Clay St
Cedar St
Vine St
Wall St
Battery St
Bell St
Blanchard St
Lenora St
Virginia St
Stewart St
Pine St
Howell St
Olive Way
Terry Ave
Boren Ave
Minor Ave
Yale Ave
Hubbell Pl
University St
Summit Ave
Boylston Ave
Warren Ave N
2nd Ave N
4th Ave N
5th Ave N
Taylor Ave N
6th Ave N
Aurora Ave N
Dexter Ave N
8th Ave N
9th Ave N
Westlake Ave N
Terry Ave N
Fairview Ave N
Minor Ave N
Pontius Ave N
Yale Ave N
Eastlake Ave E
Melrose Ave E
Bellevue Ave E
Summit Ave E
Belmont Ave E
Boylston Ave E
Harvard Ave E
Broadway E
12th Ave E
13th Ave E
Melrose Ave
Bellevue Ave
Belmont Ave
Harvard Ave
10th Ave
11th Ave
A
B
C
D
E
F
G
1
2
3
4
44
45
4
3
18
19
26
9
11
10
36
42
12
37
41
13
21
25
17
20
14
51
39
49
43
29
30
46
52
54
47
32
48
33

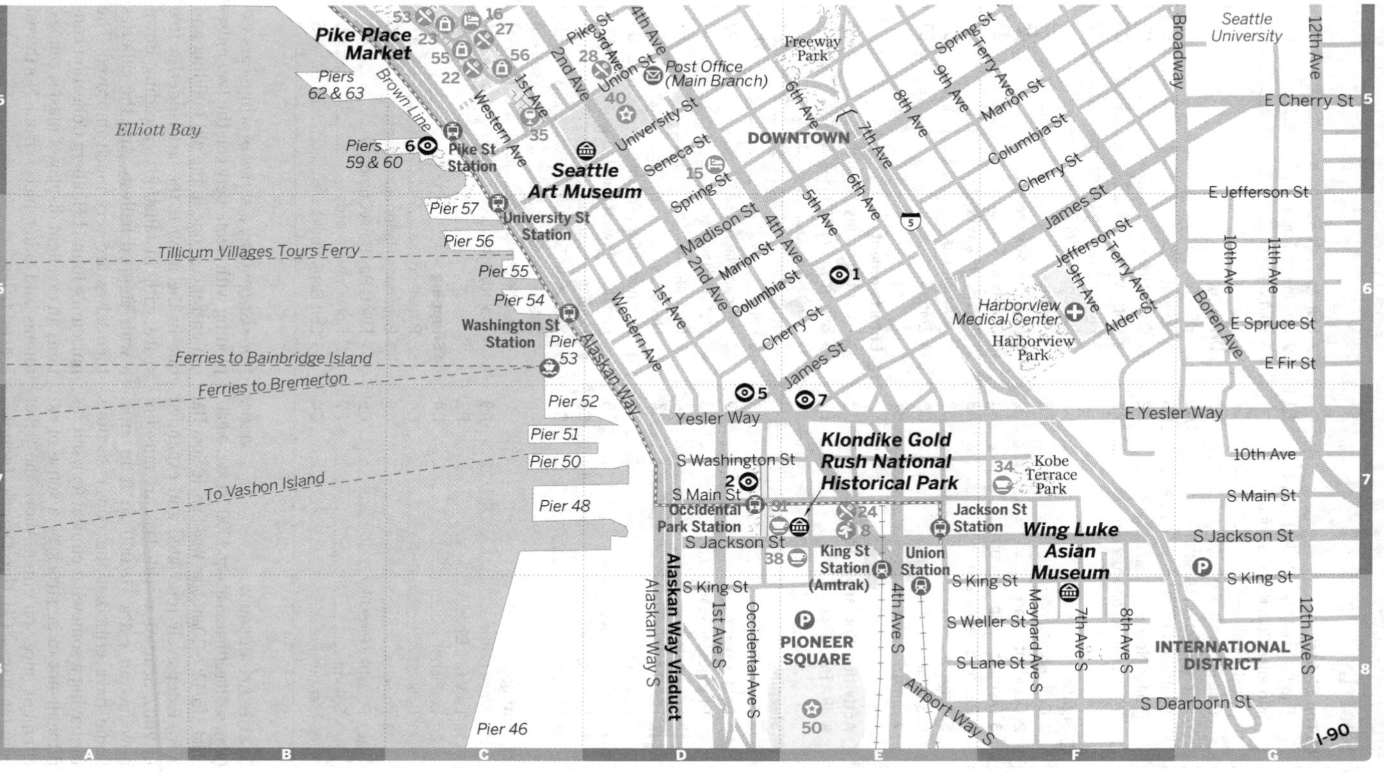
Pike Place Market
Piers 62 & 63
Brown Line
Elliott Bay
Piers 59 & 60
Pike St Station
Western Ave
1st Ave
2nd Ave
3rd Ave
Pike St
Union St
4th Ave
Post Office (Main Branch)
Freeway Park
Seattle Art Museum
University St
Seneca St
Spring St
Madison St
Marion St
Columbia St
Cherry St
James St
DOWNTOWN
6th Ave
7th Ave
8th Ave
9th Ave
Terry Ave
Spring St
Marion St
5th Ave
Jefferson St
Alder St
Harborview Medical Center
Harborview Park
Broadway
Seattle University
12th Ave
E Cherry St
E Jefferson St
10th Ave
11th Ave
Boren Ave
E Spruce St
E Fir St
Pier 57
University St Station
Pier 56
Tillicum Villages Tours Ferry
Pier 55
Pier 54
Washington St Station
Pier 53
Alaskan Way
Ferries to Bainbridge Island
Ferries to Bremerton
Pier 52
Yesler Way
E Yesler Way
Pier 51
Pier 50
To Vashon Island
Pier 48
Pier 46
S Washington St
S Main St
Occidental Park Station
S Jackson St
Klondike Gold Rush National Historical Park
King St Station (Amtrak)
Union Station
Jackson St Station
Kobe Terrace Park
Wing Luke Asian Museum
S King St
Alaskan Way Viaduct
Alaskan Way S
1st Ave S
Occidental Ave S
PIONEER SQUARE
4th Ave S
S Weller St
S Lane St
Maynard Ave S
7th Ave S
8th Ave S
Airport Way S
INTERNATIONAL DISTRICT
S Dearborn St
12th Ave S
10th Ave
S Main St
S Jackson St
S King St
I-90
5
A
B
C
D
E
F
G
5
6
7
8

Seattle

Top Sights
Experience Music Project B1
Klondike Gold Rush National Historical Park E7
Pike Place Market C5
Science Fiction Museum B2
Seattle Art Museum D5
Space Needle A2
Wing Luke Asian Museum F8

Sights
1 Columbia Center E6
2 Occidental Park D7
3 Olympic Sculpture Park A3
4 Pacific Science Center A2
5 Pergola D7
6 Seattle Aquarium C5
7 Smith Tower E7

Activities, Courses & Tours
8 JRA Bike Shop E7

Sleeping
9 Ace Hotel B3
10 Belltown Inn B3
11 City Hostel Seattle B3
12 Edgewater A4
13 Hotel Andra C4
14 Hotel Max D3
15 Hotel Monaco D5
16 Inn at the Market C5
17 Moore Hotel C4

Eating
18 Black Bottle A3
19 La Vita é Bella B3
20 Le Pichet C4
21 Lola C4
22 Lowells C5
23 Piroshky Piroshky C5
24 Salumi E7
25 Serious Pie C4
26 Shiro's Sushi Restaurant B3
27 Steelhead Diner C5
28 Wild Ginger D5

Drinking
29 B&O Espresso F2
30 Bauhaus E3
31 Caffè Umbria D7
32 Caffé Vita G3
33 Elysian Brewing Company G3
34 Panama Hotel Tea & Coffee House F7
35 Pike Pub & Brewery C5
36 Shorty's B3
37 Top Pot Hand-Forged Doughnuts C3
38 Zeitgeist E7

Entertainment
39 A Contemporary Theater D4
40 Benaroya Concert Hall D5
41 Cinerama C3
42 Crocodile B4
43 Elite F2
44 Intiman Playhouse A1
45 McCaw Hall A1
46 Neighbours F3
47 Neumo's G3
48 Northwest Film Forum G3
Pacific Nothwest Ballet ..... (see 45)
49 Re-Bar E3
50 Seahawks Stadium E8
Seattle Opera ..... (see 45)
Seattle Symphony ..... (see 45)
51 TicketMaster D4

Shopping
52 Babeland F4
53 Beecher's Handmade Cheese C5
54 Elliott Bay Book Company G3
55 Holy Cow Records C5
56 Left Bank Books C5

Seattle Art Museum MUSEUM
(www.seattleartmuseum.org; 1300 1st Ave; adult/child $15/12; ⏲10am-5pm Wed-Sun, to 9pm Thu & Fri) Extensively renovated and expanded in 2007, Seattle's world-class art museum now has an extra 118,000 sq ft in area. Some have criticized the newer sections for having a somewhat clinical feel, but it's difficult not to be struck by a sense of excitement once you enter. Above the ticket counter hangs Cai Guo-Qiang's *Inopportune: Stage One,* a series of white cars exploding with neon. Between the two museum entrances (one in the old building and one in the new) is the 'art ladder,' a free space with installations cascading down a wide stepped hallway. And the galleries themselves are very much improved. The museum's John H Hauberg Collection contains an excellent display of masks, canoes, totems and other pieces from Northwest coastal tribes.

Belltown NEIGHBORHOOD

Where industry once fumed, glassy condos now rise in the thin walkable strip of Belltown. The neighborhood gained a reputation for trend-setting nightlife in the 1990s and two of its bar-clubs, the Crocodile and Shorty's, can still claim legendary status. Then there are the restaurants – over 100 of them – and not all are prohibitively expensive.

FREE **Olympic Sculpture Park** PARK

(2901 Western Ave; ⏲sunrise-sunset) After sharing lattes with the upscale condo crowd in Belltown, you can stroll over to the experimental new sculpture park (an outpost of the Seattle Art Museum) overlooking Elliott Bay.

PIONEER SQUARE

Pioneer Sq is Seattle's oldest quarter, which isn't saying much if you're visiting from Rome or London. Most of the buildings here date from just after the 1889 fire (a devastating inferno that destroyed 25 city blocks, including the entire central business district), and are referred to architecturally as Richardson Romanesque, a redbrick revivalist style in vogue at the time. In the early years, the neighborhood's boom-bust fortunes turned its arterial road, Yesler Way, into the original 'skid row' – an allusion to the skidding logs that were pulled downhill to Henry Yesler's pier-side mill. When the timber industry fell on hard times, the road became a haven for the homeless and its name subsequently became a byword for poverty-stricken urban enclaves countrywide.

Thanks to a concerted public effort, the neighborhood avoided being laid to waste by the demolition squads in the 1960s and is now protected in the Pioneer Sq–Skid Rd Historic District.

The quarter today mixes the historic with the seedy, while harboring art galleries, cafes and nightlife. Its most iconic building is the 42-story **Smith Tower** (cnr 2nd Ave S & Yesler Way; observation deck adult/child $7.50/5; ⏲10am-dusk), completed in 1914 and, until 1931, the tallest building west of the Mississippi. Other highlights include the 1909 **Pergola**, a decorative iron shelter reminiscent of a Parisian Metro station, and **Occidental Park**, containing totem poles carved by Chinook artist Duane Pasco.

FREE **Klondike Gold Rush National Historical Park** MUSEUM

(www.nps.gov/klse; 117 S Main St; ⏲9am-5pm) A shockingly good museum with exhibits, photos and news clippings from the years of the 1897 Klondike gold rush, when a Seattle-on-steroids acted as a fueling depot for prospectors bound for the Yukon in Canada. It would cost $10 anywhere else; in Seattle it's free!

INTERNATIONAL DISTRICT

For 'international' read Asian. East of Pioneer Sq, the shops and businesses are primarily Chinese, Vietnamese and Filipino.

Wing Luke Asian Museum MUSEUM

(www.wingluke.org; 719 S King St; adult/child $12.95/8.95; ⏲10am-5pm Tue-Sun) Relocated and refurbished in 2008, the Wing Luke examines Asian and Pacific American culture, focusing on prickly issues such as Chinese settlement in the 1880s and Japanese internment camps in WWII. There are also art exhibits and a preserved immigrant apartment. Guided tours are available and recommended.

SEATTLE CENTER

The remnants of the futuristic 1962 World's Fair hosted by Seattle and subtitled Century 21 Exposition are now into their sixth decade at the Seattle Center. And what remnants! The fair was a major success, attracting 10 million visitors, running a profit (rare for the time) and inspiring a skin-crawlingly kitschy Elvis movie, *It Happened at the World's Fair* (1963).

Space Needle LANDMARK

(www.spaceneedle.com; adult/child $18/11; ⏲9:30am-11pm Sun-Thu, to 11:30pm Fri & Sat) Standing apart from the rest of Seattle's skyscrapers, the needle is the city's undisputed modern symbol. Built for the World's

HIGHER THAN THE SPACE NEEDLE

Everyone makes a rush for the iconic Space Needle, but it's neither the tallest nor the cheapest of Seattle's glittering viewpoints. That honor goes to the sleek, tinted-windowed **Columbia Center** (701 5th Ave), built in 1985, which at 932ft high is the loftiest building in the Pacific Northwest. From the plush **observation deck** (adult/child $5/3; ⏲8:30am-4:30pm Mon-Fri) on the 73rd floor you can look down on ferries, cars, islands, roofs and – ha, ha – the Space Needle!

Fair in 1962, it was the highest structure in Seattle at the time, topping 605ft, though it has since been easily usurped. Visitors make for the 520ft-high observation station with a revolving restaurant.

Monorail TRAIN
(www.seattlemonorail.com; adult/child $4/1.50; ⌚9am-11pm) Floating like a low-flying spaceship through Belltown, this 1.5-mile experiment in mass transit was so ahead of its time that some American cities have still to cotton on to it. The slick raised train runs every 10 minutes daily from downtown's Westlake Center to a station next to the Experience Music Project.

TOP CHOICE **Experience Music Project** MUSEUM
(EMP; www.empmuseum.org; 325 5th Ave N; adult/child $15/12; ⌚10am-5pm Sep-May, to 7pm Jun-Aug) This modern architectural marvel or monstrosity (depending on your view), the brainchild of Microsoft cofounder Paul Allen, is a dream fantasy to anybody who has picked up an electric guitar and plucked the opening notes to 'Stairway to Heaven.' The ultramodern Frank Gehry building houses 80,000 music artifacts, many of which pay homage to Seattle's local music icons. There are handwritten lyrics by Nirvana's Kurt Cobain, a Fender Stratocaster demolished by Jimi Hendrix, Ray Charles' first album and the stage suits worn by power pop duo Heart.

Science Fiction Museum MUSEUM
(www.sfhomeworld.org; 325 5th Ave N; adult/child $15/12; ⌚10am-5pm Sep-May to 8pm Jun-Aug) Attached to the EMP, this is a nerd paradise of costumes, props and models from sci-fi movies and TV shows. Admission is included with your EMP ticket.

CAPITOL HILL

Millionaires mingle with goth musicians in irreverent Capitol Hill, a well-heeled but liberal neighborhood rightly renowned for its fringe theater, alternative music scene, indie coffee bars, and vital gay and lesbian culture. You can take your dog for a herbal bath here, go shopping for ethnic crafts on Broadway, or blend in (or not) with the young punks and the old hippies on the eclectic Pike-Pine Corridor. The junction of Broadway and E John St is the nexus from which to navigate the quarter's various restaurants, brewpubs, boutiques and dingy, but not dirty, dive bars.

Seattle Asian Art Museum MUSEUM
(www.seattleartmuseum.org; 1400 E Prospect St; adult/child $7/5, 1st Thu & Sat of month free; ⌚10am-5pm Wed-Sun, to 9pm Thu; P) In stately Volunteer Park, the museum houses the extensive art collection of Dr Richard Fuller, who donated this severe art-moderne-style gallery to the city in 1932.

Volunteer Park PARK
Seattle's most manicured park merits a wander in its own right. Check out the glass-sided Victorian **conservatory** (admission free), filled with palms, cacti and tropical plants, and don't depart before you've taken in the opulent mansions that embellish the streets immediately to the south.

FREMONT

The humorously coined 'Artist's Republic of Fremont' about 2 miles north of Seattle Center is known for its lefty inclinations, nude solstice cyclists, farmers market and wacky public sculpture.

Fremont Sunday Market MARKET
(www.fremontmarket.com; Stone Way & N 34th St; ⌚10am-5pm Sun) People come from all over town for the market. It features fresh fruit and vegetables, arts and crafts, and all kinds of people getting rid of junk.

Public Sculpture MONUMENTS
Public art has never been as provocative as it is in Fremont. Look out for **Waiting for the Interurban** (cnr N 34th St & Fremont Ave N), a cast-aluminum statue of people awaiting a train that never comes: the Interurban linking Seattle and Everett stopped running in the 1930s (it started up again in 2001 but the line no longer passes this way). Check out the human face on the dog; it's Armen Stepanian, once Fremont's honorary mayor, who made the mistake of objecting to the sculpture. Equally eye-catching is the **Fremont Troll** (cnr N 36th St & Troll Ave), a scary-looking 18ft troll crushing a Volkswagen Beetle in its left hand. The **Fremont Rocket** (cnr Evanston Ave & N 35th St) is a rocket that was found lying around in Belltown in 1993 and that now sticks out of a building – mmm, interesting. Fremont's most controversial art is the **Lenin statue** (cnr Evanston Ave & N 36th) salvaged from Slovakia after it was toppled during the 1989 revolution. Even if you hate the politics, you have to admire the art – and audacity!

THE U DISTRICT

University of Washington UNIVERSITY
(www.washington.edu) Seattle's university (founded 1861) is almost as old as the city itself and is highly ranked worldwide. The beautiful 700-acre campus sits at the edge of Lake Union about 3 miles northeast of downtown and affords views of Mt Rainier. The main streets are University Way, known as 'the Ave,' and NE 45th St, both lined with coffee shops, restaurants and bars. The core of the campus is **Central Plaza**, known as Red Sq because of its brick base. Get information and a campus map at the **visitor center** (4014 University Way; 8am-5pm Mon-Fri).

Burke Museum MUSEUM
(adult/child $9.50/7.50; 10am-5pm) The best museum of natural history in the Northwest is situated near the junction of NE 45th St and 16th Ave. The main collections are of fossils, plus artifacts from 19 different Native American cultures.

Henry Art Gallery MUSEUM
(adult/child $10/6, Thu free; 11am-4pm Wed, Sat & Sun, to 8pm Thu & Fri) At the corner of NE 41st St and 15th Ave is a sophisticated space centered on a remarkable permanent exhibit by light-manipulating sculptor James Turrell, featuring various temporary and touring collections.

BALLARD

Despite its recent veneer of hipness, Ballard still has the feel of an old Scandinavian fishing village – especially around the locks, the marina and the Nordic Heritage Museum. Six miles northwest of downtown, the old town has become a nightlife hot spot, but even in the daytime its historic buildings and cobblestoned streets make it a pleasure to wander through.

Hiram M Chittenden Locks LOCKS
(3015 NW 54th St; 24hr) Here, the waters of Lake Washington and Lake Union flow through the 8-mile-long Lake Washington Ship Canal and into Puget Sound. Construction of the canal began in 1911; today 100,000 boats a year pass through the locks, about a half-mile west of Ballard, off NW Market St. Take bus 17 from downtown at 4th Ave and Union St. On the southern side of the locks you can watch from underwater glass tanks or from above as salmon navigate a **fish ladder** on their way to spawning grounds in the Cascade headwaters of the Sammamish River, which feeds Lake Washington.

Activities

Hiking

There are great hiking trails through old-growth forest at Seward Park, which dominates the Bailey Peninsula that juts into Lake Washington, and longer but flatter hikes in 534-acre Discovery Park northwest of Seattle.

Sierra Club WALKING
(www.sierraclub.org) Leads day-hiking and car-camping trips on weekends; most day trips are free.

Cycling

A cycling favorite, the 16.5-mile **Burke-Gilman Trail** winds from Ballard to Log Boom Park in Kenmore on Seattle's Eastside. There, it connects with the 11-mile **Sammamish River Trail**, which winds past the Chateau Ste Michelle winery in Woodinville before terminating at Redmond's Marymoor Park.

More cyclists pedal the popular loop around **Green Lake**, situated just north of Fremont and 5 miles north of the downtown core. From Belltown, the 2.5-mile **Elliott Bay Trail** runs along the Waterfront to Smith Cove.

Get a copy of the *Seattle Bicycling Guide Map,* published by the City of Seattle's **Transportation Bicycle & Pedestrian Program** (www.cityofseattle.net/transportation/bikemaps.htm) online or at bike shops.

The following are recommended for bicycle rentals and repairs:

Recycled Cycles CYCLING
(www.recycledcycles.com; 1007 NE Boat St; rentals per 6/24hr $20/40; 10am-8pm Mon-Fri, to 6pm Sat & Sun;) A friendly U District shop, this place also rents out chariots and trail-a-bike attachments for kids.

JRA Bike Shop CYCLING
(www.jrabikeshop.com; 311 3rd Ave S; 9am-5pm Mon-Fri) The handiest rental outlet for downtown is JRA, bivouacked close to Pioneer Sq and King Street train station.

Counterbalance Bicycles CYCLING
(www.counterbalancebicycles.com; 2943 NE Blakeley St; 7:30am-7pm Mon-Fri, 10am-6pm Sat & Sun) Counterbalance is handily situated on the Burke-Gilman cycling trail as it cuts its way through the U District.

SEATTLE FOR CHILDREN

Make a beeline for the Seattle Center, preferably on the monorail, where food carts, street entertainers, fountains and green space will make the day fly by. One essential stop is the **Pacific Science Center** (www.pacsci.org; 200 2nd Ave N; adult/child $14/9, plus Imax show $4; ⏲10am-5pm Mon-Fri, to 6pm Sat & Sun), which entertains and educates with virtual-reality exhibits, laser shows, holograms, an Imax theater and a planetarium – parents won't be bored either.

Downtown on Pier 59, **Seattle Aquarium** (www.seattleaquarium.org; 1483 Alaskan Way, at Pier 59; adult/child $19/12; ⏲9:30am-5pm) is a fun way to learn about the natural world of the Pacific Northwest. The centerpiece of the aquarium is a glass-domed room where sharks, octopuses and other deepwater denizens lurk in the shadowy depths.

Water Sports

Seattle is not just on a network of hiking and cycling trails. With Venice-like proportions of downtown water, it is also strafed with kayak-friendly marine trails. The **Lakes to Locks Water Trail** links Lake Sammamish with Lake Washington, Lake Union and – via the Hiram M Chittenden Locks – Puget Sound. For launching sites and maps, check the website of the **Washington Water Trails Association** (www.wwta.org).

Northwest Outdoor Center Inc KAYAKING
(www.nwoc.com; 2100 Westlake Ave N; kayaks per hr $13-20) On Lake Union, rents kayaks and offers tours and instruction in sea and white-water kayaking.

Tours

Argosy Cruises Seattle Harbor Tour CRUISE
(www.argosycruises.com; adult/child $22.50/8.50) Argosy's popular Seattle Harbor Tour is a one-hour narrated tour of Elliott Bay, the Waterfront and the Port of Seattle. It departs from Pier 55.

Coffee Crawl COFFEE
(www.seattlebyfoot.com; tours $22; ⏲10am Thu-Mon) Touring Seattle's coffee bars is a local experience akin to exploring Rome's ruins. This two-hour caffeine-fueled romp starts at Pike Place Market under the famous coffee sign and continues along Post Alley, with explanations on the city's coffee history and culture.

Seattle Food Tours FOOD
(www.seattlefoodtours.com; tours $39) A culinary hike in and around Pike Place Market, this 2½-hour excursion takes in a bakery, chowder house, Vietnamese restaurant and Mexican kitchen. You'll also get some historical and artistic background.

Festivals & Events

Northwest Folklife Festival MUSIC
(www.nwfolklife.org) International music, dance, crafts, food and family activities held at Seattle Center on the Memorial Day weekend in May.

Seafair WATER
(www.seafair.com) Huge crowds attend this festival held on the water in late July/August, with hydroplane races, a torchlight parade, an air show, music and a carnival.

Bumbershoot MUSIC, LITERATURE
(www.bumbershoot.com) A major arts and cultural event at Seattle Center on the Labor Day weekend in September, with live music, author readings and lots of unclassifiable fun.

Seattle International Film Festival FILM
(SIFF; www.siff.net; tickets $13-30) Held in mid-May, the city's biggest film festival uses a half-dozen cinemas but also has its own dedicated cinema, in McCaw Hall's **Nesholm Family Lecture Hall** (321 Mercer St, Seattle Center).

Seattle Lesbian & Gay Film Festival FILM
(www.threedollarbillcinema.org; tickets $6-8) This popular festival in October shows new gay-themed films from directors worldwide at the **Three Dollar Bill Cinema** (1122 E Pine St).

Sleeping

From mid-November through to the end of March, most downtown hotels offer Seattle Super Saver Packages – generally 50% off rack rates, with a coupon book for savings on dining, shopping and attractions. Make reservations online at www.seattlesupersaver.com.

TOP CHOICE **Belltown Inn** HOTEL $$
(☎206-529-3700; www.belltown-inn.com; 2301 3rd Ave; s/d $109/119; P❄@☎) Can it be true? The Belltown is such a bargain and in such a prime location that it's hard not believe it hasn't accidently floated over from a smaller, infinitely cheaper city. But no, clean functional rooms, handy kitchenettes, roof terrace, free bikes and – vitally important – borrow-and-return umbrellas are all yours for the price of a posh dinner.

Hotel Andra BOUTIQUE HOTEL $$
(☎206-448-8600; www.hotelandra.com; 2000 4th Ave; r $189-229; P❄☎) It's in Belltown (so it's trendy), and it's Scandinavian-influenced (so it has lashings of minimalist style), plus the Andra's fine location is complemented by leopard-skin fabrics, color accents, well-stocked bookcases, fluffy bathrobes, Egyptian-cotton bed linen and a complimentary shoe-shine. The Lola restaurant next door does room service. Say no more.

Ace Hotel HOTEL $$
(☎206-448-4721; www.acehotel.com; 2423 1st Ave; r with shared/private bath $99/190; P☎) Emulating (almost) its hip Portland cousin, the Ace sports minimal, futuristic decor (everything's white or stainless steel, even the TV), antique French army blankets, condoms instead of pillow mints and a copy of *Kama Sutra* in place of the Bible. Parking costs $15.

City Hostel Seattle HOSTEL $
(☎206-706-3255; www.hostelseattle.com; 2327 2nd Ave; 6-/4-bed dm $28/32, d $73; @☎) Sleep in an art gallery for peanuts – in Belltown, no less. That's the reality in this new 'art hostel', which will make your parent's hostelling days seem positively spartan by comparison. Aside from arty dorms, expect a common room, hot tub, in-house movie theater (with free DVDs) and all-you-can-eat breakfast.

Mediterranean Inn HOTEL $$
(☎206-428-4700; www.mediterranean-inn.com; 425 Queen Anne Ave N; r from $119; P❄@) There's something about the surprisingly un-Mediterranean Med Inn that just clicks. Maybe it's the handy cusp-of-downtown location, or the genuinely friendly staff, or the kitchenettes in every room, or the small downstairs gym, or the surgical cleanliness in every room. Don't try to define it – just go there and soak it up.

Hotel Max BOUTIQUE HOTEL $$
(☎206-441-4200; www.hotelmaxseattle.com; 620 Stewart St; s/d from $188/219; P@) Original artworks hang in the small but cool guest rooms, and it's tough to get any hipper than the Max's super-saturated color scheme – not to mention package deals such as the Grunge Special or the Gaycation. Rooms feature menus for your choice of pillows and spirituality services.

Edgewater HOTEL $$$
(☎206-728-7000; www.edgewaterhotel.com; Pier 67, 2411 Alaska Way; r 289-349; P❄@☎) Fame and notoriety once stalked the Edgewater. Perched over the water on a pier, it was once the hotel of choice for every rock band that mattered, including the Beatles, the Rolling Stones and, most infamously, Led Zeppelin, who took the 'you can fish from the hotel window' advertising jingle a little too seriously and filled their suite with sharks. These days, the fishing – and Led Zeppelin – is prohibited, but the rooms are still deluxe with a capital 'D.

Hotel Monaco BOUTIQUE HOTEL $$$
(☎206-621-1770; www.monaco-seattle.com; 1101 4th Ave; r $260-400; P@☎) Whimsical, with dashes of European elegance, the downtown Monaco is worthy of all four of its illustrious stars. Bed down amid the stripy wallpaper and heavy drapes.

College Inn HOTEL $
(☎206-633-4441; www.collegeinnseattle.com; 4000 University Way NE; s/d incl breakfast from $65/75; @☎) This pretty, half-timbered building in the U District, left over from the 1909 Alaska-Yukon-Pacific Exposition, has 25 European-style guest rooms with sinks and shared baths. Pub in the basement!

Inn at the Market BOUTIQUE HOTEL $$$
(☎206-443-3600; www.innatthemarket.com; 86 Pine St; r with/without water view $370/255; P❄☎) The only lodging in venerable Pike Place Market, this elegant 70-room boutique hotel has large rooms, many of which enjoy views onto market activity and Puget Sound. Parking costs $20.

Moore Hotel HOTEL $
(☎206-448-4851, www.moorehotel.com; 1926 2nd Ave; s/d with shared bath $59/71, with private bath $74/86; ☎) Old-world and a little moth-eaten, the Moore nonetheless has a friendly front desk and a prime location. If that doesn't swing you, the price should.

Eating

The best budget meals are to be found in Pike Place Market. Take your pick and make your own from fresh produce, baked goods, deli items and take-out ethnic foods.

TOP CHOICE Lola GREEK $$$
(☎206-441-1430; www.tomdouglas.com; 2000 4th Ave; mains $22-32) Seattle's ubiquitous cooking maestro, Tom Douglas, goes Greek in this new Belltown adventure and delivers once again with gusto. Stick in trendy clientele, some juicy kebabs, heavy portions of veg, shared meze dishes and pita with dips, and you'll be singing Socratic verse all the way home.

La Vita é Bella ITALIAN $$
(www.lavitaebella.us; 2411 2nd Ave; pasta $10-14) As any Italian food snob will tell you, it's very hard to find authentic home-spun Italian cuisine this side of Sicily. Thus extra kudos must go to La Vita é Bella for trying and largely succeeding in a difficult field. Judge the pizza margherita as a good yardstick, though the *vongole* (clams), desserts and coffee are also spot on. As in all good Italian restaurants, the owners mingle seamlessly with the clientele with handshakes and good humor.

Serious Pie PIZZERIA $$
(www.tomdouglas.com; 316 Virginia St; pizzas $16-18) Gourmet pizza sounds like an oxymoron until you stumble upon this place in Belltown which adds ingredients no one else would dare use to embellish its crispy Italianate crusts. Bank on truffles, Brussels sprouts, clams, eggs and a variety of herbs and cheeses.

Lowells DINER $
(www.eatatlowells.com; 1519 Pike Pl; mains $6-9) 'Fish-and-chips' is a simple meal often done badly – but not here. Slam down your order for Alaskan cod at the front entry and take it up to the top floor for delicious views over Puget Sound. It also serves corned-beef hash and an excellent clam chowder.

Piroshky Piroshky BAKERY $
(www.piroshkybakery.com; 1908 Pike Pl; snacks $2-7; ⏱8am-6:30pm Oct-Apr, from 7:30am May-Sep) Proof that not all insanely popular Pike Pl holes-in-the-wall go global (à la Starbucks), Piroshky is still knocking out its delectable mix of sweet and savory Russian pies and pastries in a space barely big enough to swing a small kitten. Join the melee and order one 'to go.'

Salumi SANDWICHES $
(www.salumicuredmeats.com; 309 3rd Ave S; sandwiches $7-10, plates $11-15; ⏱11am-4pm Tue-Fri) The queue outside Mario Batali's dad's place has long been part of the sidewalk furniture. It's even formed its own community of chatterers, note comparers, Twitter addicts and gourmet sandwich experts. When you get in, the sandwiches come with any of a dozen types of cured meat and fresh cheese. Great for a picnic!

Paseo CUBAN $
(www.paseoseattle.com; 4225 Fremont Ave N; sandwiches $6-9; ⏱11am-9pm Tue-Fri, to 8pm Sat) Proof that most Seattleites aren't posh (or pretentious) is the local legend known as Paseo, a Cuban hole-in-the-wall that's in a nondescript part of Fremont and which people alter their commute drive to visit. The fuss centers on the sandwiches; in particular the Midnight Cuban Press with pork, ham, cheese and banana peppers, and the Cuban Roast (slow roasted pork in marinade). Grab plenty of napkins.

Peso's Kitchen & Lounge MEXICAN $$
(www.pesoskitchen.com; 605 Queen Anne Ave N; breakfast $7-10, dinner $10-15; ⏱9am-2am) A place that wears many sombreros, Pesos serves fine Mexican food in the evenings amid a cool trendy 'scene' that is anything but Mexican. But the trump card comes the next morning, after the beautiful people have gone home, with an acclaimed egg-biased breakfast.

Shiro's Sushi Restaurant JAPANESE $$$
(www.shiros.com; 2401 2nd Ave; mains $26.75; ⏱5:30-9:45pm) There's barely room for all the awards and kudos that cram the window in this sleek Japanese joint. Grab a pew behind the glass food case and watch the experts concoct delicate and delicious Seattle sushi.

5 Spot BREAKFAST $
(1502 Queen Anne Ave N; brunch $8-10, dinner $13-17; ⏱8:30am-midnight) Top of the hill, top of the morning and top of the pops; the queues outside 5 Spot at 10am on a Sunday testify to a formidable brunch. The crowds mean a great atmosphere and the hearty menu, which has perfected French toast, *huevos rancheros* and plenty more American standards, will shift even the most stubborn of hangovers.

Black Bottle MODERN AMERICAN $
(www.blackbottleseattle.com; 2600 1st Ave; plates $8-12; ⏱4:30pm-2am) This trendy minimalist bar-restaurant showcases the new Belltown of smart condo dwellers and avid wine quaf-

fers. The food is mainly appetizers, but with menu items such as grilled lamb and sumac hummus, and braised artichoke heart and greens, even the nostalgic grunge groupies of yore will find it hard to resist.

Steelhead Diner SEAFOOD **$$**
(☎206-625-0129; www.steelheaddiner.com; 95 Pine St; sandwiches $9-13, mains $15-33; ⊙11am-10pm Tue-Sat, 10am-3pm Sun) Homey favorites such as fish-and-chips, grilled salmon or braised short ribs and grits become fine cuisine when they're made with the best of what Pike Place Market has to offer.

Wild Ginger ASIAN **$$**
(www.wildginger.net; 1401 3rd Ave; mains $15-28) All around the Pacific Rim – via China, Indonesia, Malaysia, Vietnam and Seattle, of course – is the wide-ranging theme at this highly popular downtown fusion restaurant. Try the fragrant duck first.

Le Pichet FRENCH **$$**
(www.lepichetseattle.com; 1933 1st Ave; lunch/mains $9/18; ⊙8am-midnight) Say *bienvenue* to Le Pichet just up from Pike Place Market, a *très français* bistro with pâtés, cheeses, wine, *chocolat* and a refined Parisian feel.

Drinking

You'll find cocktail bars, dance clubs and live music on Capitol Hill. The main drag in Ballard has brick taverns old and new, filled with the hard-drinking older set in daylight hours and indie rockers at night. Belltown has gone from grungy to shabby chic, but has the advantage of many drinking holes neatly lined up in rows.

Coffeehouses

Starbucks is the tip of the iceberg. Seattle has spawned plenty of smaller indie chains, many with their own roasting rooms. Look out for Uptown Espresso, Caffe Ladro and Espresso Vivace.

TOP CHOICE **Bauhaus** CAFE
(www.bauhauscoffee.net; 301 E Pine St; ⊙6am-1am Mon-Fri, from 7am Sat, from 8am Sun) Drink coffee, browse books, nibble pastries, stay awake…until 1am! Bauhaus positively encourages lingering with its mezzanine bookshelves, Space Needle view and lazy people-watching opps. One senses that the next great American novel could be getting drafted here.

Top Pot Hand-Forged Doughnuts CAFE
(www.toppotdoughnuts.com; 2124 5th Ave; ⊙6am-7pm) Top Pot is to doughnuts what champagne is to wine – a different class. And its cafes – this one in an old car showroom with floor-to-ceiling library shelves and art-deco signage – are equally legendary.

B&O Espresso CAFE
(www.b-oespresso.com; 204 Belmont Ave E; ⊙7am-late Mon-Thu, from 8am Fri-Sun) Full of understated swank, this piece of the Capitol Hill furniture (open since 1976) is the place to go for Turkish coffee – if you can get past the pastry case up front.

Caffé Vita CAFE
(www.caffevita.com; 1005 E Pike St; ⊙6am-11pm) The laptop fiend, the date, the radical student, the homeless hobo, the philosopher, the business guy on his way to work: watch the whole neighborhood pass through this Capitol Hill institution (one of four in Seattle) with its own on-site roasting room visible through a glass partition.

Panama Hotel Tea & Coffee House CAFE
(607 S Main St; ⊙8am-7pm Mon-Sat, from 9am Sun) The Panama, a historic 1910 building containing the only remaining Japanese bathhouse in the US, doubles as a memorial to the neighborhood's Japanese residents forced into internment camps during WWII.

Zeitgeist CAFE
(www.zeitgeistcoffee.com; 171 S Jackson St; ⊙6am-7pm Mon-Fri, from 8am Sat & Sun; 📶) Plug into the spirit of the times with the rest of the laptop crew at this lofty, brick-walled cafe near the train station.

Caffè Umbria CAFE
(www.caffeumbria.com; 320 Occidental Ave S; ⊙6am-6pm Mon-Fri, from 7am Sat, 8am-5pm Sun) Premier roasters of blended coffee, the Bizzarri family, from Perugia in Italy, founded this European-flavored outlet in Pioneer Sq in 1986.

Bars

Shorty's BAR
(www.shortydog.com; 2222 2nd Ave) A cross between a pinball arcade and the Korova Milk Bar in the film *A Clockwork Orange,* Shorty's is a Belltown legend where you can procure cheap beer, hot dogs, alcohol slushies and a back room of pinball heaven.

Pike Pub & Brewery BREWERY
(www.pikebrewing.com; 1415 1st Ave) Leading the way in the microbrewery revolution, this

brewpub opened in 1989 underneath Pike Place Market. Today it still serves great burgers and brews in a neo-industrial multilevel space that's a beer nerd's heaven.

Blue Moon BAR
(712 NE 45th St) A legendary counterculture dive that's near the university and first opened in 1934 to celebrate the repeal of the prohibition laws, the Blue Moon has served its mellow beer to the likes of Dylan Thomas, Allen Ginsberg and Tom Robbins. It's lost its luster a bit in recent times, but be prepared for impromptu poetry recitations, jaw-harp performances and inspired rants.

Brouwer's BEER HALL
(400 N 35th St; 11am-2am) This dark cathedral of beer in Fremont has rough-hewn rock walls and a black metal grate in the ceiling. Behind an epic bar are tantalizing glimpses into a massive beer fridge. A replica *Mannequin Pis* statue at the door and the Belgian crest everywhere clue you in to the specialty.

Copper Gate BAR
(6301 24th Ave NW) Formerly one of Seattle's worst dives, the Copper Gate in Ballard is now an upscale bar-restaurant focused on meatballs and naked ladies. A Viking longship forms the bar, with a peepshow pastiche for a sail and a cargo of helmets and gramophones.

Hale's Ales Brewery BREWERY
(www.halesbrewery.com; 4301 Leary Way NW) Hale's makes fantastic beer, notably its ambrosial Cream Ale. Its flagship brewpub in Fremont feels like a business-hotel lobby, but it's worth a stop. There is a self-guided tour near the entrance.

Elysian Brewing Company BREWERY
(www.elysianbrewing.com; 1221 E Pike St) On Capitol Hill, the Elysian's huge windows are great for people-watching – or being watched, if your pool game's good enough.

☆ Entertainment

Consult the *Stranger*, *Seattle Weekly* or the daily papers for listings. Tickets for big events are available at **TicketMaster** (206-628-0888), which operates a **discount ticket booth** (206-233-1111) at Westlake Center.

Live Music

Crocodile LIVE MUSIC
(www.thecrocodile.com; 2200 2nd Ave) Reopened in March 2009 after a year in the doldrums, the sole survivor of Belltown's once influential grunge scene (formerly known as the Crocodile Café) will have to work hard to reclaim an audience who grew up listening to Nirvana, Pearl Jam and REM at this hallowed music venue.

Neumo's LIVE MUSIC
(www.neumos.com; 925 E Pike St) A punk, hip-hop and alternative-music venue that counts Radiohead and Bill Clinton (not together) among its former guests, Neumo's (formerly known as Moe's) fills the big shoes of its original namesake. You can mark the passage of time at 'Sad Bastards Mondays', which offer 'tunes to cry into your beer to.'

Chop Suey LIVE MUSIC
(www.chopsuey.com; 1325 E Madison St) Chop Suey is a dark, high-ceilinged space with a ramshackle faux-Chinese motif and eclectic bookings.

Cinema

Northwest Film Forum CINEMA
(www.nwfilmforum.org; 1515 12th Ave) Impeccable programming, from restored classics to cutting-edge independent and international films. In Capitol Hill, of course!

Cinerama CINEMA
(www.cinerama.com; 2100 4th Ave) One of the very few Cineramas left in the world, it has a fun, sci-fi feel.

Harvard Exit CINEMA
(www.landmarktheatres.com; cnr E Roy St & Harvard Ave) Built in 1925, this is Seattle's first independent theater.

Performing Arts

Seattle Opera CLASSICAL MUSIC
(www.seattleopera.org) At McCaw Hall, features a program of four or five full-scale operas every season, including a Wagner's *Ring* cycle that draws sellout crowds in summer.

Intiman Playhouse THEATER
(www.intiman.org; 201 Mercer St) The Intiman Theatre Company, Seattle's oldest, takes the stage at this playhouse.

Pacific Northwest Ballet BALLET
(www.pnb.org) The foremost dance company in the Northwest puts on more than 100 shows a season from September through June at Seattle Center's McCaw Hall.

Seattle Symphony CLASSICAL MUSIC
(www.seattlesymphony.org) A major regional ensemble. It plays at the Benaroya Concert

Hall, which you'll find downtown at 2nd Ave and University St.

A Contemporary Theatre THEATER
(ACT; www.acttheatre.org; 700 Union St) One of the three big companies in the city, fills its $30-million home at Kreielsheimer Place with performances by Seattle's best thespians and occasional big-name actors.

Gay & Lesbian Venues

Elite BAR
(1520 Olive Way;) An extremely friendly Capitol Hill establishment with darts, pool, not-too-loud music and decent cocktails.

Re-Bar CLUB
(1114 Howell St) Storied dance club, where many of Seattle's defining cultural events happened (such as Nirvana album releases), welcomes gay, straight, bi or undecided revelers to its lively dance floor.

Neighbours CLUB
(1509 Broadway Ave E) Check out the always-packed dance factory for the gay club scene and its attendant glittery straight girls.

Sport

Seattle Mariners BASEBALL
(www.mariners.org; tickets $7-60) The beloved baseball team plays in Safeco Field just south of downtown.

Seattle Seahawks FOOTBALL
(www.seahawks.com; tickets $42-95) The Northwest's only National Football League (NFL) franchise plays in the 72,000-seat Seahawks Stadium.

Shopping

The main big-name shopping area is downtown between 3rd and 6th Aves and University and Stewart Sts. Pike Place Market is a maze of arts-and-crafts stalls, galleries and small shops. Pioneer Sq and Capitol Hill have locally owned gift and thrift shops. The following are some only-in-Seattle shops to seek out.

Elliott Bay Book Company BOOKS
(www.elliottbaybook.com; 1521 10th Ave; 10am-10pm, to 11pm Sat, 11am-9pm Sun) Perish the day when ebooks render bookstores obsolete. What will happen to the Saturday-afternoon joy of Elliott Bay books, where 150,000 titles inspire author readings, discussions, reviews and hours of serendipitous browsing?

Beecher's Handmade Cheese FOOD
(www.beechershandmadecheese.com; 1600 Pike Pl; 9am-6pm) Artisan beer, artisan coffee… next up, Seattle brings you artisan cheese and it's made as you watch in this always-crowded Pike Pl nook, where you can buy all kinds of cheese-related paraphernalia. Don't leave without tasting the wonderful home-made mac 'n' cheese.

Babeland ADULT
(www.babeland.com; 707 E Pike St; 11am-10pm Mon-Sat, noon-7pm Sun) Remember those pink furry handcuffs and that glass dildo you needed? Well, look no further.

Holy Cow Records MUSIC
(1501 Pike Pl, Suite 325; 10am-10pm Mon-Sat, to 7pm Sun) Proceed to Pike Place Market and let your fingers flick through the aging vinyl at this shrine to music geekdom; you might just stumble upon that rare Psychedelic Furs 12-inch that has been eluding you since 1984.

Left Bank Books BOOKS
(www.leftbankbooks.com; 92 Pike St; 10am-7pm Mon-Sat, 11am-6pm Sun) This 35-year-old collective displays 'zines in *español*, revolutionary pamphlets, a 'fuck authority' notice board and plenty of Chomsky. You're in Seattle, just in case you forgot.

Information

Emergency & Medical Services

45th St Community Clinic (206-633-3350; 1629 N 45th St, Wallingford) Medical and dental services.

Harborview Medical Center (206-731-3000; 325 9th Ave) Full medical care, with emergency room.

Seattle Police (206-625-5011)

Seattle Rape Relief (206-632-7273)

Washington State Patrol (425-649-4370)

Internet Access

Seattle is a computer geek's heaven and practically every bar and coffee shop has free wi-fi, as do most hotels.

Cyber-Dogs (909 Pike St; 1st 20min free, then per hr $6; 10am-midnight) A veggie hot-dog stand (dogs $2 to $5), espresso bar, internet cafe and youngster hangout and pick-up joint.

Online Coffee Company (www.onlinecoffeeco.com; 1st 30min free, then per hr $1; 7:30am-midnight) Olive Way (1720 E Olive Way); Pine St (1404 E Pine St) The Olive Way location is in a cozy former residence, while the Pine St shop is more utilitarian-chic. The first hour is free for students.

Internet Resources

Seattle's Convention and Visitors Bureau (www.visitseattle.org)

Seattlest (www.seattlest.com) A blog about various goings-on in and around Seattle.

Media

KEXP 90.3 FM Legendary independent music and community station.

Seattle Times (www.seattletimes.com) The state's largest daily paper.

Seattle Weekly (www.seattleweekly.com) Free weekly with news and entertainment listings.

The Stranger (www.thestranger.com) Irreverent weekly edited by Dan Savage of 'Savage Love' fame.

Money

American Express (Amex; 600 Stewart St; ⏲8:30am-5:30pm Mon-Fri)

Travelex-Thomas Cook Currency Services Airport (⏲6am-8pm); Westlake Center (400 Pine St, Level 3; ⏲9:30am-6pm Mon-Sat, 11am-5pm Sun) The booth at the main airport terminal is behind the Delta Airlines counter.

Post

Post office (301 Union St; ⏲8:30am-5:30pm Mon-Fri)

Tourist Information

Seattle Convention & Visitors Bureau (www.visitseattle.org; cnr 7th Ave & Pike St; ⏲9am-5pm Mon-Fri) Inside the Washington State Convention and Trade Center; it opens weekends June to August.

ℹ Getting There & Away

Air

Seattle-Tacoma International Airport (SEA; www.portseattle.org/seatac), aka 'Sea-Tac,' 13 miles south of Seattle on I-5, has daily services to Europe, Asia, Mexico and points throughout the USA and Canada, with frequent flights to and from Portland, OR, and Vancouver, BC.

Boat

Victoria Clipper (www.victoriaclipper.com) operates several high-speed passenger ferries to Victoria, BC, and to the San Juan Islands. It also organizes package tours that can be booked in advance through the website. Victoria Clipper runs from Seattle to Victoria up to six times daily (round-trip adult/child $147/73).

The **Washington State Ferries** (www.wsdot.wa.gov/ferries) website has maps, prices, schedules, trip planners and weather updates, plus estimated waiting times for popular routes. Fares depend on the route, vehicle size and trip duration, and are collected either for round-trip or one-way travel depending on the departure terminal.

Bus

The **Bellair Airporter Shuttle** (www.airporter.com) has daily buses between Seattle, Sea-Tac Airport, Ellensburg, Yakima, Anacortes and Bellingham. Reserve in advance.

Greyhound (www.greyhound.com; 811 Stewart St; ⏲6am-midnight) connects Seattle with cities all over the country, including Chicago, IL ($206 one way, two days, three daily), Spokane, WA ($74, five to seven hours, three daily), San Francisco, CA ($89, 20 hours, four daily), and Vancouver, BC ($28, three to four hours, six daily).

More comfortable and offering free on-board wi-fi is the super-efficient **Quick Shuttle** (www.quickcoach.com) that runs five times daily along I-5 between Sea-Tac Airport and Central Vancouver (BC), also stopping in downtown Seattle (at the Best Western Executive Inn, 200 Taylor Ave N), Bellingham airport and Vancouver airport.

Train

Amtrak (www.amtrak.com) serves Seattle's **King Street Station** (303 S Jackson St; ⏲6am-10:30pm, ticket counter 6:15am-8pm). Three main routes run through town: the *Amtrak Cascades* (connecting Vancouver, Seattle, Portland and Eugene), the very scenic *Coast Starlight* (connecting Seattle, Oakland and Los Angeles) and the *Empire Builder* (a cross-continental roller coaster to Chicago).

Chicago, IL From $205, 46 hours, daily

Oakland, CA $154, 23 hours, daily

Portland, OR $31, three to four hours, five daily

Vancouver, BC $38, three to four hours, five daily

ℹ Getting Around

To/From the Airport

There are a number of options for making the 13-mile trek from the airport to downtown Seattle. The most efficient is via the new light-rail service run by Sound Transit.

Gray Line's **Airport Express** (www.graylineseattle.com) fetches passengers in the parking lot outside door 00 at the south end of the baggage-claim level. It will drop you at a choice of eight different downtown hotels (one way $11 to $15).

Taxis and limousines (about $35 and $40, respectively) are available at the parking garage on the 3rd floor. Rental-car counters are located in the baggage-claim area.

Car & Motorcycle

Trapped in a narrow corridor between mountains and sea, Seattle is a horrendous traffic bottleneck and its nightmarish jams are famous. I-5 has a high-occupancy vehicle lane for vehicles carrying two or more people. Otherwise, try to work around the elongated rush 'hours.'

Public Transportation

Buses are operated by **Metro Transit** (www.transit.metrokc.gov), part of the King County Department of Transportation. Fares cost $2 to $2.75. Bus travel within the central core demarcated by Bell St, 6th Ave, I-5 and S King St is free.

The recently installed **Seattle Street Car** (www.seattlestreetcar.org) runs from the Westlake Center to Lake Union along a 2.6-mile route. There are 11 stops allowing interconnections with numerous bus routes.

Seattle's brand new light-rail train, **Sound Transit** (www.soundtransit.org), runs between Sea-Tac Airport and downtown (Westlake Center) every 15 minutes between 5am and midnight. The ride takes 36 minutes and costs $2.50. There are additional stops in Pioneer Sq and the International District.

Taxi

All Seattle taxi cabs operate at the same rate, set by King County; at the time of research the rate was $2.50 at meter drop, then $2.50 per mile.

Orange Cab Co (206-444-0409; www.orangecab.net)

Yellow Cab (206-622-6500; www.yellowtaxi.net)

Around Seattle

OLYMPIA

Small in size but big in clout, state capital Olympia is a musical, political and outdoor powerhouse that punches well above its 46,480 population. Look no further than the street-side buskers on 4th Ave belting out acoustic grunge, the smartly attired bureaucrats marching across the lawns of the resplendent state legislature, or the Goretex-clad outdoor fiends overnighting before rugged sorties into the Olympic Mountains. Truth is, despite its classical-Greek-sounding name, creative, out-of-the-box Olympia is anything but ordinary. Progressive Evergreen college has long lent the place an artsy turn (creator of *The Simpsons,* Matt Groening studied here), while the dive bars and secondhand guitar shops of downtown provided an original pulpit for riot grrrl music and grunge.

Sights & Activities

FREE **Washington State Capitol** LANDMARK

(8am-4:30pm) Looking like a huge Grecian temple, the Capitol complex, set in a 30-acre park overlooking Capitol Lake, dominates the town. The campus' crowning glory is the magnificent **Legislative Building** (1927), a dazzling display of craning columns and polished marble, topped by a 287ft dome that is only slightly smaller than its namesake in Washington, DC. Free guided tours are available.

State Capital Museum MUSEUM

(211 W 21st Ave; admission $2; 10am-4pm Tue-Fri, from noon Sat) Preserves the general history of Washington State, from the Nisqually tribe to the present day.

Olympia Farmers Market MARKET

(10am-3pm Thu-Sun Apr-Oct, Sat & Sun Nov-Dec) At the north end of Capitol Way, this is one of the state's best markets, with fresh local produce, crafts and live music.

Sleeping & Eating

Phoenix Inn Suites HOTEL $

(360-570-0555; 415 Capitol Way N; s/d $99/109;) The town's most upmarket accommodations is slick, efficient and well tuned to dealing with demanding state government officials.

Batdorf & Bronson CAFE $

(Capitol Way S; 6am-7pm Mon-Fri, 7am-6pm Sat & Sun) Olympia's most famous java comes from a local roaster offering ethical coffee. Aside from this downtown cafe, you can buy or try the latest blends at its popular **Tasting Room** (200 Market St NE; 9am-4pm Wed-Sun).

TOP CHOICE **Oyster House** SEAFOOD $$

(320 W 4th Ave; seafood dinners $15-20; 11am-11pm, to midnight Fri & Sat) Olympia's most celebrated restaurant also specializes in its most celebrated cuisine, the delicate Olympia oyster, best served pan-fried and topped with a little cheese and spinach.

Spar Bar Café CAFE $

(www.mcmenamins.com; 114 4th Ave E; breakfast $4-5, lunch $5-8; 7am-9pm) A cozy old-school cafe-cum-bar-cum-cigar store run by McMenimans with good brews, classic comfort food and supersonic service.

Drinking

The city's never-static music scene still makes waves on 4th Ave at the retrofitted **4th Avenue Tavern** (210 4th Ave E) or the graffiti-decorated **Le Voyeur** (404 4th Ave E), an anarchistic, vegan-friendly dive bar with a busker invariably guarding the door.

Information

The **State Capitol Visitor Center** (cnr 14th Ave & Capitol Way) offers information on the capitol campus, the Olympia area and Washington State.

Olympic Peninsula

Surrounded on three sides by sea and exhibiting many of the insular characteristics of a full-blown island, the remote Olympic Peninsula is about as 'wild' and 'west' as America gets. What it lacks in cowboys it makes up for in rare, endangered wildlife and dense primeval forest. The peninsula's roadless interior is largely given over to the notoriously wet Olympic National Park, while the margins are the preserve of loggers, Native American reservations and a smattering of small but interesting settlements, most notably Port Townsend. Equally untamed is the western coastline, America's isolated end point, where the tempestuous ocean and misty old-growth Pacific rainforest meet in aqueous harmony.

OLYMPIC NATIONAL PARK

Declared a national monument in 1909 and a national park in 1938, the 1406-sq-mile **Olympic National Park** (www.nps.gov/olym) shelters one of the world's only temperate rainforests and a 57-mile strip of Pacific coastal wilderness that was added in 1953 – it exists as one of North America's last great wilderness areas. Opportunities for independent exploration abound, with visitors enjoying such diverse activities as hiking, fishing, kayaking and skiing.

EASTERN ENTRANCES

The graveled Dosewallips River Rd follows the river from US 101 (turn off approximately 1km north of Dosewallips State Park) for 15 miles to **Dosewallips Ranger Station**, where the trails begin; call ☎360-565-3130 for road conditions. Even hiking smaller portions of the two long-distance paths – with increasingly impressive views of heavily glaciated **Mt Anderson** – is reason enough to visit the valley. Another eastern entry for hikers is the **Staircase Ranger Station** (☎360-877-5569; ⊙May-Sep), just inside the national park boundary, 15 miles from Hoodsport on US 101. Two state parks along the eastern edge of the national park are popular with campers: **Dosewallips State Park** (☎888-226-7688; tent/RV sites $21/28) and **Lake Cushman State Park** (☎888-226-7688; tent/RV sites $22/28). Both have running water, flush toilets and some RV hookups. Reservations are accepted.

NORTHERN ENTRANCES

The park's easiest – and hence most popular – entry point is at **Hurricane Ridge**, 18 miles south of Port Angeles. At the road's end, an interpretive center overlooks a stupendous view of Mt Olympus (7965ft) and dozens of other peaks. The 5200ft altitude can mean inclement weather and the winds here (as the name suggests) can be ferocious. Aside from various summer trekking opportunities, the area maintains one of only two US national-park-based ski runs, operated by the small, family-friendly **Hurricane Ridge Ski & Snowboard Area** (www.hurricaneridge.com).

Popular for boating and fishing is **Lake Crescent**, the site of the park's oldest and most reasonably priced **lodge** (☎360-928-3211; www.olympicnationalparks.com; 416 Lake Crescent Rd; lodge r with shared bath $76, cottages $142-224; ⊙May-Oct; P❄📶). Delicious sustainable food is served in the lodge's ecofriendly restaurant. From **Storm King Information Station** (☎360-928-3380; ⊙May-Sep) on the lake's south shore, a 1-mile hike climbs through old-growth forest to Marymere Falls.

Along the Sol Duc River, the **Sol Duc Hot Springs Resort** (☎360-327-3583; www.northolympic.com/solduc; 12076 Sol Duc Hot Springs Rd, Port Angeles; RV sites $33, r $131-189; ⊙late Mar-Oct; ❄🏊) has lodging, dining, massage and, of course, hot-spring pools (adult/child $10/7.50), as well as great day hikes.

WESTERN ENTRANCES

Isolated by distance and one of the country's rainiest microclimates, the Pacific side of the Olympics remains its wildest. Only US 101 offers access to its noted temperate rainforests and untamed coastline. The **Hoh River Rainforest**, at the end of the 19-mile Hoh River Rd, is a Tolkienesque maze of dripping ferns and moss-draped trees. You can get better acquainted with the area's complex yet delicate natural ecosystems at the **Hoh visitor center and campground** (☎360-374-6925; campsites $12; ⊙9am-6pm Jul & Aug, to 4:30pm Sep-Jun), which has information on guided walks and longer backcountry hikes. There are no hookups or showers; first come first served.

A little to the south lies **Lake Quinault**, a beautiful glacial lake surrounded by forested peaks. It's popular for fishing, boating and swimming, and is punctuated by some of the nation's oldest trees. **Lake Quinault Lodge** (☎360-288-2900; www.visitlakequinault.com; 345 S Shore Rd; lodge r $134-167, cabins $125-243;), a luxury classic of 1920s 'parkitecture,' has a heated pool and sauna, a crackling fireplace and a memorable dining room noted for its sweet-potato breakfast pancakes. For a cheaper sleep nearby, try the ultrafriendly **Quinault River Inn** (☎360-288-2237; www.quinaultriverinn.com; 8 River Dr; r $75-115; P) in Amanda Park, a favorite with anglers.

A number of short hikes begin just outside the Lake Quinault Lodge, or you can try the longer **Enchanted Valley Trail**, a medium-grade 13-miler that begins from the Graves Creek Ranger station at the end of South Shore Rd and climbs up to a large meadow resplendent with wildflowers and copses of alder trees.

Information

The park entry fee is $5/15 per person/vehicle, valid for one week, payable at park entrances. Many park visitor centers double as United States Forestry Service (USFS) ranger stations, where you can pick up permits for wilderness camping ($5 per group, valid up to 14 days, plus $2 per person per night).

Forks Visitor Information Center (1411 S Forks Ave, Forks; 10am-4pm) Suggested itineraries and seasonal information.

Olympic National Park Visitor Center (3002 Mt Angeles Rd, Port Angeles; 9am-5pm) The best overall center is situated at the Hurricane Ridge gateway, a mile off Hwy 101 in Port Angeles.

Wilderness Information Center (3002 Mt Angeles Rd, Port Angeles; 7:30am-6pm Sun-Thu, to 8pm Fri & Sat May-Sep, 8am-4:30pm daily Oct-Apr) Directly behind the visitor center, you'll find maps, permits and trail information.

PORT TOWNSEND

Historical relics are rare in the Pacific Northwest, which makes time-warped Port Townsend all the more fascinating. Small, nostalgic and culturally vibrant, this showcase of 1890s Victorian architecture is the 'New York of the West that never was,' a onetime boomtown that went bust at the turn of the 20th century, only to be rescued 70 years later by a group of far-sighted locals. Port Townsend today is a buoyant blend of inventive eateries, elegant fin de siècle hotels and quirky annual festivals.

Sights

Jefferson County Historical Society Museum MUSEUM
(210 Madison St; adult/12yr & under $4/1; 11am-4pm Mar-Dec) The local historic society runs this well-maintained exhibition area that includes mock-ups of an old courtroom and jail cell, along with the full lowdown on the rise, fall and second coming of this captivating port town.

Fort Worden State Park PARK
(www.parks.wa.gov/fortworden; 200 Battery Way; 6:30am-dusk Apr-Oct, from 8am Nov-Mar) This attractive park located within Port Townsend's city limits is the remains of a large fortification system constructed in the 1890s. The extensive grounds and array of historic buildings have been refurbished in recent years into a lodging, nature and historical park. The **Commanding Officer's Quarters** (admission $4; 10am-5pm Jun-Aug, 1-4pm Sat & Sun Mar-May & Sep-Oct), a 12-bedroom mansion, is open for tours, and part of one of the barracks is now the **Puget Sound Coast Artillery Museum** (admission $2; 11am-4pm Tue-Sun), which tells the story of early Pacific coastal fortifications.

Hikes lead along the headland to **Point Wilson Lighthouse Station** and some wonderful windswept beaches.

Sleeping

Palace Hotel HISTORIC HOTEL $
(☎360-385-0773; www.palacehotelpt.com; 1004 Water St; r $59-109;) Built in 1889, this beautiful Victorian building is a former brothel that was once run by the locally notorious Madame Marie, who managed her dodgy business from the 2nd-floor corner suite. Reincarnated as an attractive period hotel with antique furnishings and old-fashioned claw-foot baths, the Palace's former seediness is now a thing of the past.

Manresa Castle HISTORIC HOTEL $$
(☎360-385-5750; www.manresacastle.com; cnr 7th & Sheridan Sts; d & ste $109-169) This 40-room mansion-castle, built by the town's first mayor, sits high on a bluff above the port and is supposedly haunted. The vintage rooms may be a little spartan for some visitors, but in a setting this grandiose it's the all-pervading sense of history that counts.

Eating

TOP CHOICE **Waterfront Pizza** PIZZERIA $
(951 Water St; large pizzas $11-19) Arguably the best pizza in the state, this buy-by-the-slice

outlet inspires huge local loyalty and will satisfy even the most querulous of Chicago-honed palates with its crisp sourdough crusts and creative toppings.

Salal Café BREAKFAST **$**
(634 Water St; breakfast $7-8, lunch $8-9; ⏲7am-2pm) The Salal specializes in eggs. Scrambled, poached, frittatas, stuffed into a burrito or served up as an omelet – you can ponder all varieties here during a laid-back breakfast or a zippy lunch.

Information

To get the lowdown on the city's roller-coaster boom-bust history, call in at the **visitor center** (www.ptchamber.org; 2437 E Sims Way; ⏲9am-5pm Mon-Fri, to 4pm Sat & Sun).

Getting There & Away

Port Townsend can be reached from Seattle by a ferry-bus connection via Bainbridge Island and Poulsbo (bus 90 followed by bus 7). **Washington State Ferries** (www.wsdot.wa.gov/ferries) goes to and from Keystone on Whidbey Island (car and driver $11.70/foot passenger $2.75, 35 minutes).

PORT ANGELES

Despite the name, there's nothing Spanish or particularly angelic about Port Angeles, propped up by the lumber industry and backed by the steep-sided Olympic Mountains. Rather than visiting to see the town per se, people come here to catch a ferry for Victoria, BC, or plot an outdoor excursion into the nearby Olympic National Park. The **visitor center** (121 E Railroad Ave; ⏲8am-8pm May-Oct, 10am-4pm Nov-Apr) is adjacent to the ferry terminal. For information on the national park, the **Olympic National Park Visitor Center** (3002 Mt Angeles Rd, Port Angeles; ⏲9am-5pm) is just outside town.

The **Olympic Discovery Trail** (www.olympicdiscoverytrail.com) is a 30-mile off-road hiking and cycling trail between Port Angeles and Sequim, starting at the end of **Ediz Hook**, the sand spit that loops around the bay. Bikes can be rented at **Sound Bikes & Kayaks** (www.soundbikekayaks.com; 120 Front St; bike rental per hr/day $9/30).

Port Angeles' most comfortable accommodations, hands down, is the **Olympic Lodge** (☎360-452-2993; www.olympiclodge.com; 140 Del Guzzi Drive; r from $119; ❄@📶🏊), with a swimming pool, on-site bistro, so-clean-they-seem-new rooms and complementary cookies and milk.

Bella Italia (118 E 1st St; mains $12-20; ⏲from 4pm) has been around a lot longer than Bella, the heroine of the *Twilight* saga, but its mention in the book as the place where Bella and Edward Cullen go for their first date has turned an already popular restaurant into an icon. Try the clam linguine, chicken marsala or smoked duck breast washed down with an outstanding wine from a list featuring 500 selections.

THE TWILIGHT ZONE

Forks, a small lumber town on Hwy 101, was little more than a speck on the Washington state map when publishing phenomenon Stephenie Meyer set the first of her now famous *Twilight* vampire novels here in 2003. Ironically, Meyer – America's answer to JK Rowling – had never been to Forks when she resurrected the ghoulish legacy of Bela Lugosi et al with the first of what has become a series of insanely popular 'tweenage' books. Not that this has stopped the town from cashing in on its new-found literary fame. Forks has apparently seen a 600% rise in tourism since the *Twilight* film franchise began in 2008, the bulk of the visitors comprising of gawky, wide-eyed under 15-year-old girls who are more than a little surprised to find out what Forks really is – chillingly ordinary (and wet).

A fresh bit of color was needed and it was provided in November 2008 with the opening of **Dazzled by Twilight** (www.dazzledbytwilight.com; 11 N Forks Ave; ⏲10am-6pm), which runs two *Twilight* merchandise shops in Forks (and another in Port Angeles) as well as the Forks **Twilight Lounge** (81 N Forks Ave). The lounge hosts a downstairs restaurant along with an upstairs music venue that showcases regular live bands and a blood-curdling Saturday-night 'tween' karaoke (5pm to 8pm). The company also runs four daily **Twilight Tours** (adult/child $39/25; ⏲8am, 11:30am, 3pm & 6pm) visiting most of the places mentioned in Meyer's books. Highlights include Forks High School, the Treaty Line at the nearby Rivers Resort and a sortie out to the tiny coastal community of La Push.

The ferry that runs from Port Angeles to Victoria, BC, is called the **Coho Vehicle Ferry** (www.cohoferry.com; passenger/car $15.50/55). The crossing takes 1½ hours. **Olympic Bus Lines** (www.olympicbuslines.com) runs twice daily to Seattle ($39) from the public transit center at the corner of Oak and Front Sts. **Clallam Transit** (www.clallamtransit.com) buses go to Forks and Sequim, where they link up with other transit buses, enabling you to circumnavigate the whole Olympic Peninsula.

NORTHWEST PENINSULA

Several Native American reservations cling to the extreme northwest corner of the continent and welcome interested visitors. Hit hard by the decline in the salmon-fishing industry, the small settlement of Neah Bay on Hwy 112 is characterized by its weather-beaten boats and craning totem poles. It's home to the Makah Indian Reservation, whose **Makah Museum** (www.makah.com; 1880 Bayview Ave; admission $5; ⏲10am-5pm) displays artifacts from one of North America's most significant archaeological finds. Exposed by tidal erosion in 1970, the 500-year-old Makah village of Ozette quickly proved to be a treasure trove of Native American history, unearthing a huge range of materials including whaling weapons, canoes, spears and combs. Seven miles beyond the museum, a short boardwalk trail leads to **Cape Flattery**, a 300ft promontory that marks the most northwesterly point in the lower 48 states.

Convenient to the Hoh River Rainforest and the Olympic coastline is **Forks**, a one-horse lumber town that's now more famous for its *Twilight* paraphernalia. Get cozy in the amiable **Forks Motel** (☎360-374-6243; www.forksmotel.com; 432 S Forks Ave; s/d $65/70; ❄📶🏊) with kitchen suites, a small pool and a very friendly welcome.

Northwest Washington

Wedged between Seattle, the Cascades and Canada, northwest Washington draws influences from three sides. Its urban hub is collegiate Bellingham, while its outdoor highlight is the pastoral San Juan Islands, an extensive archipelago that glimmers like a sepia-toned snapshot from another era. Equally verdant, and simpler to reach, Whidbey Island contains beautiful Deception Pass State Park and the quaint oyster-fishing village of Coupeville. Situated on Fidalgo Island and attached to the mainland via a bridge, the settlement of Anacortes is the main hub for ferries to the San Juan Islands and Victoria, BC. If your boat's delayed you can pass time in expansive Washington Park or sample the local halibut and chips in a couple of classic downtown restaurants.

WHIDBEY ISLAND

Whidbey Island is an idyllic emerald escape beloved of stressed-out Seattleites. While not as detached or nonconformist as the San Juans (there's a bridge connecting it to adjacent Fidalgo Island at its northernmost point), life is certainly slower, quieter and more pastoral here. Having six state parks is a bonus, along with a plethora of B&Bs, two historic fishing villages (Langley and Coupeville), famously good clams and a thriving artist's community.

Deception Pass State Park (☎360-675-2417; 41229 N State Hwy 20) straddles the eponymous steep-sided water chasm that flows between Whidbey and Fidalgo Islands, and incorporates lakes, islands, campsites and 27 miles of hiking trails.

Ebey's Landing National Historical Reserve (www.nps.gov/ebla; admission free; ⏲8am-5pm mid-Oct–Mar, 6:30am-10pm Apr–mid-Oct) comprises 17,400 acres encompassing working farms, sheltered beaches, two state parks and the town of **Coupeville**. This small settlement is one of Washington's oldest towns and has an attractive seafront, antique stores and a number of old inns, including the **Coupville Inn** (☎800-247-6162; www.thecoupevilleinn.com; 200 Coveland St; r with/without balcony $140/105; P❄@📶), which bills itself as a French-style motel (if that's not an oxymoron) with fancy furnishings and a substantial breakfast. For the famous fresh local clams, head to **Christopher's** (www.christophersonwhidbey.com; 103 NW Coveland St; mains $17-26), which offers exciting and creative modern cooking in huge portions.

Washington State Ferries (www.wsdot.wa.gov/ferries) link Clinton to Mukilteo (car and driver $9/foot passenger free, 20 minutes, every 30 minutes) and Keystone to Port Townsend (car and driver $11.70 /foot passenger $2.75, 30 minutes, every 45 minutes). Free **Island Transit buses** (www.islandtransit.org) run the length of Whidbey every hour daily, except Sunday, from the Clinton ferry dock.

BELLINGHAM

Imagine a slightly less eccentric slice of Portland, Oregon, broken off and towed 250 miles to the north. Welcome to laid-back Bellingham, a green, liberal and famously livable settlement that has taken the libertine, nothing-is-too-weird ethos of Oregon's 'City of Roses' and given it a peculiarly Washingtonian twist. Mild in both manners and weather, the 'city of subdued excitement,' as a local mayor once dubbed it, is an unlikely alliance of espresso-supping students, venerable retirees, all-weather triathletes and placard-waving Peaceniks. Publications such as *Outside Magazine* have consistently lauded it for its abundant outdoor opportunities, while adventure organizations such as the American Alpine Institute call it home base.

Activities

Bellingham offers outdoor activities by the truckload. **Whatcom Falls Park** is a natural wild region that bisects Bellingham's eastern suburbs. The change in elevation is marked by four sets of waterfalls, including **Whirlpool Falls**, a popular summer swimming hole. The substantial intra-urban trails extend south as far as Larabee State Park, with a popular 2.5-mile section tracking Bellingham's postindustrial waterfront. **Fairhaven Bike & Mountain Sports** (1103 11th St) rents bikes from $20 a day and has all the info (and maps) on local routes.

Victoria/San Juan Cruises (www.whales.com; 355 Harris Ave) has whale-watching trips to Victoria, BC, via the San Juan Islands. Boats leave from the Bellingham Cruise Terminal in Fairhaven.

Sleeping

TOP CHOICE **Hotel Bellwether** BOUTIQUE HOTEL **$$$**
(☎360-392-3100; www.hotelbellwether.com; 1 Bellwether Way; r $156-272, lighthouse from $473; ❄📶) Bellingham's finest and most charismatic hotel is positioned on a redeveloped part of the waterfront, and offers European-style furnishings in 66 luxury rooms and an adjoining lighthouse condominium.

Guesthouse Inn MOTEL **$**
(☎360-671-9600; www.bellinghamvaluinn.com; 805 Lakeway Dr; s/d $81/91; ❄📶) The secret of a good 'chain' hotel is that it doesn't seem like a chain at all. To put this theory into practice, check out the clean, personable Guesthouse Inn, just off I-5 and an easy 15-minute walk from downtown.

Eating

TOP CHOICE **Pepper Sisters** MODERN AMERICAN **$$**
(www.peppersisters.com; 1055 N State St; mains $9-13; ⏲from 5pm Tue-Sun; 👪) People travel from

WORTH A TRIP

LA CONNER

Celebrated for its tulips, wild turkeys, erudite writer's colony and (among other culinary treats) enormous doorstep-sized cinnamon buns, La Conner's myriad attractions verge on the esoteric. Abstract writer Tom Robbins lives here, if that's any measuring stick, along with about 840 other creative souls.

Aside from three decent museums, the zenith of La Conner's cultural calendar is its annual Tulip Festival, when the surrounding fields are embellished with a colorful carpet of daffodils (March), tulips (April) and irises (May). But they're not the only valuable crops. The flat, fertile Lower Skagit River delta worked by hardworking second-, third- and fourth-generation Dutch farmers also produces copious amounts of vegetables, including 100% of the nation's parsnips and Brussels sprouts.

Many of the products find their way into La Conner's stash of creative restaurants. Situated inside the old Tillinghurst Seed building, **Seeds Bistro & Bar** (www.seedsbistro.com; 623 Morris St; mains $18-25) is the cream of the crop, offering a rare combo of classy food and brunch-cafe-style friendliness. The fresh flavors of the surrounding farmland are mixed with equally fresh fish plucked from the nearby ocean to concoct unparalleled ling cod, off-the-ratings-scale crab cakes, and a raspberry and white chocolate bread pudding you'll still be talking about months later.

The size of the cinnamon buns at **Calico Cupboard** (www.calicocupboardcafe.com; 720 S 1st St; ⏲7:30am-4pm Mon-Fri, to 5pm Sat & Sun) beggar belief, and their quality (there are four specialist flavors) is equally good. Factor in a 10-mile run through the tulip fields before you tackle one and you should manage to stave off instant diabetes.

far and wide to visit this cult restaurant with its bright turquoise booths. The hard-to-categorize food is Southwestern with a Northwest twist. Try the cilantro-and-pesto quesadillas, or blue corn rellenos.

Swan Cafe CAFE $
(www.communityfood.coop; 220 N Forest St; dishes $5-7; 8am-9pm;) A Community Food Co-op with an on-site cafe-deli that offers an insight into Bellingham's organic, fair-trade, community-based mentality.

Colophon Café CAFE $
(1208 11th St; mains $7-10; 9am-10pm) The toast of the Fairhaven district is known for its African peanut soup and chocolate brandy cream pies.

Information

The best downtown tourist information can be procured at the **Visitor Info Station** (www.downtownbellingham.com; 1304 Cornwall St; 9am-6pm).

Getting There & Away

San Juan Islands Shuttle Express (www.orcawhales.com) offers daily summer service to the Orcas and San Juan Islands ($20). Alaska Marine Highway ferries (see p456) go to Juneau (60 hours) and other southeast Alaskan ports (from $363 without car). The **Bellair Airporter Shuttle** (www.airporter.com) runs to Sea-Tac Airport ($34), with connections en route to Anacortes and Whidbey Island.

San Juan Islands

Take the ferry west out of Anacortes and you'll feel like you've dropped off the edge of the continent. A thousand metaphoric miles from the urban inquietude of Puget Sound, the nebulous San Juan archipelago conjures up Proustian flashbacks from another era and often feels about as American as – er – Canada (which surrounds it on two sides). Street crime here barely registers, fast-food franchises are a nasty mainland apparition, and cars – those most essential of US travel accessories – are best left at home.

There are 172 landfalls in this expansive archipelago but unless you're rich enough to charter your own yacht or seaplane, you'll be restricted to seeing the big four – San Juan, Orcas, Shaw and Lopez Islands – all served daily by Washington State Ferries. Communally, the islands are famous for their tranquility, whale-watching opportunities, sea kayaking and seditious nonconformity.

The best way to explore the San Juans is by sea kayak or bicycle. Kayaks are available for rent on Lopez, Orcas and San Juan Islands. Expect a guided half-day trip to cost $45 to $65. Note that most beach access is barred by private property, except at state or county parks. Cycling-wise, Lopez is flat and pastoral and San Juan is worthy of an easy day loop, while Orcas offers the challenge of undulating terrain and a steep 5-mile ride to the top of Mt Constitution.

Information

For good general information about the San Juans, contact the **San Juan Islands Visitor Information Center** (360-468-3663; www.guidetosanjuans.com; 10am-2pm Mon-Fri).

Getting There & Around

Airlines serving the San Juan Islands include **San Juan Airlines** (www.sanjuanairlines.com) and **Kenmore Air** (www.kenmoreair.com).

Washington State Ferries (www.wsdot.wa.gov/ferries) leave Anacortes for the San Juans; some continue to Sidney, BC, near Victoria. Ferries run to Lopez Island (45 minutes), Orcas Landing (60 minutes) and Friday Harbor on San Juan Island (75 minutes). Fares vary by season; the cost of the entire round-trip is collected on westbound journeys only (except those returning from Sidney, BC). To visit all the islands, it's cheapest to go to Friday Harbor first and work your way back through the other islands.

Shuttle buses ply Orcas and San Juan Island in the summer months.

LOPEZ ISLAND

If you're going to Lopez – or 'Slow-pez,' as locals prefer to call it – take a bike. With its undulating terrain and salutation-offering locals (who are famous for their three-fingered 'Lopezian wave'), this is the ideal cycling isle. A leisurely pastoral spin can be tackled in a day with good overnight digs available next to the marina in the **Lopez Islander Resort** (360-468-2233; www.lopezislander.com; 2864 Fisherman Bay Rd; d from $120;), which has a restaurant, gym and pool and offers free parking in Anacortes (another incentive to dump the car). If you arrive bikeless, call up **Lopez Bicycle Works** (www.lopezbicycleworks.com; 2847 Fisherman Bay Rd; 10am-6pm May-Sep), which can deliver a bicycle to the ferry terminal for you.

SAN JUAN ISLAND

San Juan Island is the archipelago's unofficial capital, a harmonious mix of low forested hills and small rural farms that resonate with a dramatic and unusual 19th-century history. The only settlement is Friday Harbor, where the **chamber of commerce** (www.sanjuanisland.org; 135 Spring St; ⏲10am-5pm Mon-Fri, to 4pm Sat & Sun) is bivouacked inside a small mall off the main street.

Sights & Activities

FREE **San Juan Island National Historical Park** HISTORIC SITE
(www.nps.gov/sajh; ⏲8:30am-4pm) San Juan Island hides one of the 19th-century's oddest political confrontations, the so-called 'Pig War' between the USA and Britain. This curious 19th-century cold war stand-off is showcased in two separate historical parks on either end of the island that once housed opposing American and English military encampments. On the southern flank of the island, the **American Camp** hosts a small **visitors center** (admission free; ⏲8:30am-4:30pm Thu-Sun, daily Jun-Sep) with the remnants of an old fort, desolate beaches and a series of interpretive trails. At the opposite end of the island, **English Camp**, 9 miles northwest of Friday Harbor, contains the remains of the British military facilities dating from the 1860s.

Lime Kiln Point State Park PARK
(⏲8am-5pm mid-Oct–Mar, 6:30am-10pm Apr–mid-Oct) Clinging to the island's rocky west coast, this beautiful park overlooks the deep Haro Strait and is, reputedly, one of the best places in the world to view whales from the shoreline.

San Juan Vineyards WINERY
(www.sanjuanvineyards.com; 3136 Roche Harbor Rd; ⏲11am-5pm) Washington's unlikeliest winery has a tasting room next to an old schoolhouse built in 1896. Open-minded tasters should try the Siegerrebe and Madeleine Angevine varieties.

Sleeping & Eating

There are hotels, B&Bs and resorts scattered around the island, but Friday Harbor has the best concentration.

TOP CHOICE **Earthbox Motel & Spa** BOUTIQUE MOTEL $$
(☎360-378-4000; www.earthboxmotel.com; 410 Spring St; r from $197; P 🛜 🏊) Reaching out to retro-lovers, Earthbox styles itself as a 'boutique motel,' a hybrid of simplicity and sophistication that has taken a former motor inn and embellished it with features more commonly associated with a deluxe hotel. The only downside is the prices, which aren't very motel-like.

Market Chef DELI $
(225a St; ⏲10am-6pm) Several hundred locals can't be wrong, can they? The 'Chef's' specialty is deli sandwiches and very original ones at that. Join the queue and watch staff prepare the goods with fresh, local ingredients.

ORCAS ISLAND

Precipitous, unspoiled and ruggedly beautiful, Orcas Island is the San Juans' emerald icon, excellent for hiking and, more recently, gourmet food. The ferry terminal is at Orcas Landing, 8 miles south of the main village, Eastsound. On the island's eastern lobe is **Moran State Park** (⏲6:30am-dusk Apr-Sep, from 8am Oct-Mar), dominated by Mt Constitution (2409ft), with 40 miles of trails and an amazing 360-degree mountaintop view.

Kayaking in the calm island waters is a real joy here. **Shearwater** (www.shearwaterkayaks.com; 138 North Beach Rd, Eastsound) has the equipment and know-how. Three-hour guided trips start at $69.

Sleeping

TOP CHOICE **Rosario Resort & Spa** RESORT $$$
(☎360-376-2222; www.rosario-resort.com; 1400 Rosario Rd, Eastsound; r $188-400; P ❄ 🛜 🏊) A magnificent seafront mansion built by former shipbuilding magnate Robert Moran in 1904 and now converted into an exquisite, upscale resort and spa.

Outlook Inn HOTEL $$
(☎360-376-2200; www.outlookinn.com; 171 Main St, Eastsound; r with shared/private bath $89/119; P ❄ 🛜) Eastsound village's oldest building (1888) is an island institution that has kept up with the times by expanding into a small bayside complex. Also onsite is the rather fancy New Leaf Café.

Eating

Allium INTERNATIONAL $$$
(☎360-376-4904; www.alliumonorcas.com; 310E Main St, Eastsound; dinner mains $30; ⏲10am-2pm Sat & Sun, 5-8pm Thu-Mon) Orcas got a destination restaurant in 2010 with the opening of the illustrious Allium, where the secret is simplicity (local ingredients, limited opening hours and only five mains on the menu). The result: food worth visiting the island for.

Cafe Olga CAFE $
(11 Point Lawrence Rd, Olga; mains $9-11; ⏲9am-6pm Mon-Fri, to 8pm Sat & Sun, closed Wed Mar-Apr) Tucked inside a barn alongside a crafts gallery, 6 miles southeast of Eastsound, Olga specializes in homemade pies and provides a sweet treat for cyclists and hikers who've just conquered lofty Mt Constitution.

North Cascades

Geologically different from their southern counterparts, the North Cascade Mountains are peppered with sharp, jagged peaks, copious glaciers and a preponderance of complex metamorphic rock. Thanks to their virtual impregnability, the North Cascades were an unsolved mystery to humans until relatively recently. The first road was built across the region in 1972 and, even today, it remains one of the Northwest's most isolated outposts.

MT BAKER

Rising like a ghostly sentinel above the sparkling waters of upper Puget Sound, Mt Baker has been mesmerizing visitors to the Northwest for centuries. A dormant volcano that last belched smoke in the 1850s, this haunting 10,781ft peak shelters 12 glaciers and in 1999 registered a record-breaking 95ft of snow in one season.

Well-paved Hwy 542, known as the Mt Baker Scenic Byway, climbs 5100ft to **Artist Point**, 56 miles from Bellingham. Near here you'll find the **Heather Meadows Visitor Center** (Mile 56, Mt Baker Hwy; ⏲8am-4:30pm May-Sep) and a plethora of varied hikes including the 7.5-mile Chain Lakes Loop that leads you around a half-dozen icy lakes surrounded by huckleberry meadows.

Receiving more annual snow than any ski area in North America, the undone **Mt Baker Ski Area** (www.mtbakerskiarea.com) has 38 runs, eight lifts and a vertical rise of 1500ft. Due to its rustic facilities, ungroomed terrain and limited après-ski options, the resort has gained something of a cult status among snowboarders, who have been coming here for the Legendary Baker Banked Slalom every January since 1985.

On the 100 or so days a year when Baker breaks through the clouds, the views from the deck at the **Inn at Mount Baker** (☎360-599-1359; www.theinnatmtbaker.com; 8174 Mt Baker Hwy; r $155-165; P❄@) can divert your attention away from breakfast. Situated 7 miles east of Maple Falls, this six-room B&B is welcoming, private and mindful of its pristine setting.

LEAVENWORTH

Blink hard and rub your eyes. This isn't some strange Germanic hallucination. This is Leavenworth, a former lumber town that underwent a Bavarian makeover back in the 1960s after the rerouting of the cross-continental railway threatened to put it permanently out of business. Swapping wood for tourists, Leavenworth today has successfully reinvented itself as a traditional Romantische Strasse village, right down to the beer and sausages and the lederhosen-loving locals (25% of whom are German). The classic *Sound of Music* mountain setting helps, as does the fact that Leavenworth serves as the main activity center for sorties into the nearby Alpine Lakes Wilderness.

The **Leavenworth Ranger Station** (600 Sherbourne St; ⏲7:30am-4:30pm daily mid-Jun–mid-Oct, from 7:45am Mon-Fri mid-Oct–mid-Jun) can advise on the local outdoor activities. Highlights include the best climbing in the state at **Castle Rock** in Tumwater Canyon, about 3 miles northwest of town off US 2.

The Devil's Gulch is a popular off-road bike trail (25 miles, four to six hours). Local outfitters **Der Sportsmann** (www.dersportsmann.com; 837 Front St) rents bikes from $25 a day.

Sleeping

TOP CHOICE **Enzian Inn** HOTEL $$
(☎509-548-5269; www.enzianinn.com; 590 Hwy 2; d $125-155; ❄📶🏊) Taking the German theme up a notch, the Enzian goes way beyond the call of duty with an 18-hole putting green, a racquetball court, a sunny breakfast room and a lederhosen-clad owner who entertains guests with an early-morning blast on the alphorn.

Bavarian Lodge HOTEL $$
(☎509-548-7878; www.bavarianlodge.com; 810 Hwy 2; d/ste $149/249; P❄📶🏊) This lodge takes the Bavarian theme to luxury levels in a plush, clutter-free establishment with modern – but definably German – rooms complete with gas fires, king beds and funky furnishings. Outside there's a heated pool and hot tub.

Eating

Café Christa GERMAN $$
(www.cafechrista.com; upstairs 801 Front St; mains $14-18) Christa's features quaint

European decor, discreet yet polite service, and a menu that rustles up German classics such as bratwurst, Wiener schnitzel and Jäger schnitzel.

München Haus GERMAN $
(www.munchenhaus.com; 709 Front St; snacks from $6; ⊙11am-11pm May-Oct, closed Mon-Fri Nov-Apr) An alfresco beer garden that serves the best charbroiled Bavarian sausages this side of Bavaria.

LAKE CHELAN

Long, slender Lake Chelan is central Washington's water playground. **Lake Chelan State Park** (☎509-687-3710; S Lakeshore Rd; tent/RV sites $21/28) has 144 campsites; a number of lakeshore campgrounds are accessible only by boat. The town of **Chelan**, at the lake's southeastern tip, is the primary base for accommodations and services, and has a **USFS ranger station** (428 Woodin Ave). **Link Transit** (www.linktransit.com) buses connect Chelan with Wenatchee and Leavenworth ($1).

Beautiful **Stehekin**, on the northern tip of Lake Chelan, is accessible only by **boat** (www.ladyofthelake.com; round-trip from Chelan $39), **seaplane** (www.chelanairways.com; round-trip from Chelan $159) or a long hike across Cascade Pass, 28 miles from the lake. Most facilities are open mid-June to mid-September.

METHOW VALLEY

The Methow's combination of powdery winter snow and abundant summer sunshine has transformed the valley into one of Washington's primary recreation areas. You can bike, hike and fish in the summer, and cross-country ski on the second-biggest snow trail network in the US in the winter.

The 200km of trails are maintained by the nonprofit organization **Methow Valley Sport Trails Association** (MVSTA; www.mvsta.com), which, in the winter, provides the most comprehensive network of hut-to-hut (and hotel-to-hotel) skiing in North America. An extra blessing is that few people seem to know about it. For classic accommodations and easy access to the skiing, hiking and cycling trails, decamp at the exquisite **Sun Mountain Lodge** (☎509-996-2211; www.sunmountainlodge.com; Box 1000, Winthrop, WA 98862; r $170-350, cabins $275-460;), 10 miles west of the town of Winthrop.

NORTH CASCADES NATIONAL PARK

The wildest of all Pacific Northwest wildernesses, the lightly trodden **North Cascades National Park** (www.nps.gov/noca) has no settlements, no overnight accommodations and only one unpaved road. The names of the dramatic mountains pretty much set the tone: Desolation Peak, Jagged Ridge, Mt Despair and Mt Terror. Not surprisingly, the region offers some of the best backcountry adventures outside of Alaska.

The **North Cascades Visitor Center** (502 Newhalem St; ⊙9am-4:30pm mid-Apr–Oct, closed Mon-Fri Nov-Mar), in the small settlement of Newhalem on Hwy 20, is the best orientation point for visitors and is staffed by expert rangers who can enlighten you on the park's highlights.

Built in the 1930s for loggers working in the valley that was soon to be flooded by Ross Dam, the floating cabins at the **Ross Lake Resort** (☎206-386-4437; www.rosslakeresort.com; cabins d $145-169, cabins q $210; ⊙mid-Jun–Oct) on the eponymous lake's west side are the state's most unique accommodations. There's no road in – guests can either hike the 2-mile trail from Hwy 20 or take the resort's tugboat-taxi-and-truck shuttle from the parking area near Diablo Dam.

Northeastern Washington

SPOKANE

Washington's second-biggest population center is one of the state's latent surprises and a welcome break after the treeless monotony of the eastern scablands. Situated at the nexus of the Pacific Northwest's so-called 'Inland Empire,' this understated yet confident city sits clustered on the banks of the Spokane River, close to where British fur traders founded a short-lived trading post in 1810. Though rarely touted in national tourist blurbs, Spokane hosts the world's largest mass participation running event (May's annual Bloomsday), a stunning Gilded Age hotel (the Davenport) and a spectacular waterfall throwing up angry white spray in the middle of its downtown core.

⊙ Sights & Activities

Riverfront Park PARK
(www.spokaneriverfrontpark.com) On the former site of Spokane's 1974 World's Fair, the park provides a welcome slice of urban greenery in the middle of downtown. It has been redeveloped in recent years with a 17-point **sculpture walk**, along with plenty of bridges and trails to satisfy the city's plethora of amateur runners. The park's centerpiece is **Spokane Falls**, a gush-

ing combination of scenic waterfalls and foaming rapids. There are various viewing points over the river, including a short **gondola ride** (adult/child $7.25/4; ⏲11am-6pm Sun-Thu, to 10pm Fri & Sat Apr-Sep) that takes you directly above the falls. Walkers and joggers crowd the interurban **Spokane River Centennial Trail** (www.spokanecentennialtrail.org), which extends for 37 miles to the Idaho border and beyond.

Northwest Museum of Arts & Culture MUSEUM
(www.northwestmuseum.org; 2316 W 1st Ave; adult/child $7/5; ⏲10am-5pm Wed-Sat) Encased in a striking state-of-the-art building in the posh Browne's Addition neighborhood, the museum has – arguably – one of the finest collections of indigenous artifacts in the Northwest.

Sleeping

Davenport Hotel HISTORIC HOTEL $$
(☎509-455-8888; www.thedavenporthotel.com; 10 S Post St; standard/deluxe r $139/159; ❄📶🏊) A historic Spokane landmark (opened in 1914) that is considered one of best hotels in the US. If you can't afford a room, linger in the exquisite lobby.

Montvale Hotel BOUTIQUE HOTEL $$
(☎509-747-1919; www.montvalehotel.com; 1005 W 1st Ave; queen/king r $119/189; ❄📶) The Montvale is situated in a former brothel, but don't be fooled by the small, rather plain lobby. Upstairs a refined inner quadrangle has a distinct European feel.

Hotel Ruby BOUTIQUE MOTEL $
(☎509-747-1041; www.hotelrubyspokane.com; 901 W 1st Ave; d from $69; P❄📶) This new boutique motel has replaced an old Rodeway Inn. Furnished with modern gadgets and funky color accents, it has an unbeatable downtown location opposite the Davenport.

Frank's Diner BREAKFAST $
(www.franksdiners.com; 516 W 2nd Ave; breakfast $5-9) A little west of downtown, but worth the walk, this restored vintage railway car knocks out a classic breakfast including extraordinarily good eggs and no-frills biscuits and gravy. Arrive early to beat the queues.

Rock City Grill INTERNATIONAL $$
(www.rockcitygrill. Com; 505 W Riverside Ave; mains $12-19) An atmospherically lit, youthful bar-restaurant with an expansive menu of old staples prepared in imaginative ways.

Drinking & Entertainment

With a vibrant student population based at Gonzaga University, Spokane has a happening nighttime scene.

Northern Lights Brewing Company BREWERY
(www.northernlightsbrewing.com; 1003 E Trent Ave) You can sample the locally handcrafted ales at Spokane's best microbrewery, near the university campus.

Dempsey's Brass Rail CLUB
(www.dempseysbrassrail.net; 909 W 1st; ⏲9pm-2am) An alternative gay-friendly nighttime establishment.

Bing Crosby Theater THEATER
(www.mettheater.com; 901 W Sprague Ave) The former Met, now named after local hero Bing, presents concerts, plays, film festivals and the Spokane Opera in a fairly intimate setting.

Information

Spokane Area Visitor Information Center (www.visitspokane.com; 201 W Main Ave at Browne St; ⏲8:30am-5pm Mon-Fri, 9am-6pm Sat & Sun) keeps a raft of information.

Getting There & Away

Buses and trains depart from the **Spokane Intermodal Transportation Station** (221 W 1st Ave). **Amtrak** (www.amtrak.com) has a daily service on the esteemed *Empire Builder* to Seattle ($48, 7½ hours), Portland ($48, 9½ hours) and Chicago ($205, 45 hours).

South Cascades

The South Cascades are taller but less clustered than their northern counterparts, extending from Snoqualmie Pass east of Seattle down to the mighty Columbia River on the border with Oregon. The highpoint in more ways than one is 14,411ft Mt Rainier. Equally compelling for different reasons is Mt St Helens (8365ft), still recovering from a devastating 1980 volcanic eruption. Lesser known Mt Adams (12,276ft) is renowned for the huckleberries and wildflowers that fill its grassy alpine meadows during the short but intense summer season.

MT RAINIER NATIONAL PARK

The USA's fourth-highest peak (outside Alaska), Majestic Mt Rainier is also one of its most beguiling. Encased in a 368-sq-mile national park (the world's fifth national park when it was inaugurated in 1899), the mountain's snowcapped summit and forest-covered foothills harbor numerous hiking trails, huge swaths of flower-carpeted meadows and an alluring conical peak that presents a formidable challenge for aspiring climbers.

The park has four entrances. Nisqually, on Hwy 706 via Ashford, near the park's southwest corner, is the busiest and most convenient gate, being close to the park's main nexus points and open year-round. The other entrances are Ohanapecosh, via Hwy 123; White River, off Hwy 410; and Carbon River, the most remote entryway, at the northwest corner. Call ☎800-695-7623 for road conditions. For information on the park, check out the National Park Service (NPS) website at www.nps.gov/mora, which includes downloadable maps and descriptions of 50 park trails.

Park entry is $15 per car or $5 per pedestrian. For overnight trips, get a wilderness camping permit (free) from ranger stations or visitor centers. The six campgrounds in the park have running water and toilets, but no RV hookups. **Reservations** (☎800-365-2267; www.mount.rainier.national-park.com/camping.htm; reserved campsites $12-15) are strongly advised during summer months and can be made up to two months in advance by phone or online.

The park's two main nexus points are Longmire and Paradise. Longmire, 7 miles inside the Nisqually entrance, has a **Museum & Information Center** (admission free; ⏱9am-6pm Jun-Sep, to 5pm Oct-May), a number of important trailheads and the rustic **National Park Inn** (☎360-569-2275; www.guestservices.com/rainier; r with shared/private bath $104/139, units $191; P❄) complete with an excellent restaurant. More hikes and interpretive walks can be found 12 miles further east at loftier Paradise, which is served by the informative **Henry M Jackson Visitor Center** (⏱10am-7pm daily Jun-Oct, to 5pm Sat & Sun Oct-Dec), completely rebuilt and reopened in 2008, and the vintage **Paradise Inn** (☎360-569-2275; www.mtrainierguestservices.com; r with shared/private bath $105/154; ⏱May-Oct; P❄📶), a historic 'parkitecture' inn constructed in 1916 and long part of the national park's fabric. Climbs to the top of Rainier leave from the inn; excellent four-day guided ascents are led by **Rainier Mountaineering Inc** (www.rmiguides.com; 30027 SR706 E, Ashford) for $944.

The **Wonderland Trail** is a 93-mile path that completely circumnavigates Mt Rainier via a well-maintained unbroken route. The hike is normally tackled over 10 to 12 days, with walkers staying at one of 18 registered campsites along the way. Before embarking you'll need to organize a free backcountry permit from the **Wilderness Information Center** (www.nps.gov/mora; 55210 238th Ave E, Ashford, WA 98304-9751); forms are available online.

The remote Carbon River entrance gives access to the park's inland rainforest. The **ranger station** (☎360-829-9639), just inside the entrance, is open daily in summer.

Gray Line (www.graylineseattle.com) runs guided bus tours from Seattle between May and September (one/two days $85/179).

MT ST HELENS NATIONAL VOLCANIC MONUMENT

Thanks to a 1980 eruption that set off an explosion bigger than the combined power of 1500 atomic bombs, Washington's 87th-tallest mountain needs little introduction. What it lacks in height, Mt St Helens makes up for in fiery infamy – 57 people perished on the mountain on that fateful day in May 1980 when an earthquake measuring 5.1 on the Richter scale sparked the biggest landslide in human history and buried 230 sq miles of forest under millions of tons of volcanic rock and ash.

For the carless, Mt St Helens can be seen on a day trip by bus from Portland with **Eco Tours of Oregon** (www.ecotours-of-oregon.com) for $69.50. If traveling independently, your first port of call should be the **Silver Lake Visitor Center** (3029 Spirit Lake Hwy; admission $3; ⏱9am-5pm), 5 miles east of Castle Rock on Hwy 504, which showcases films, exhibits and free information on the mountain.

For a closer view of the destructive power of nature, venture to the **Johnston Ridge Observatory** (⏱10am-6pm May-Oct), situated at the end of Hwy 504 and looking directly into the mouth of the crater. The observatory's exhibits take a more scientific look at the geologic events surrounding the 1980 blast.

A welcome B&B in an accommodations-lite area, the **Blue Heron Inn** (☎360-274-9595; www.blueheroninn.com; Hwy 504; d/ste $175/215; 📶) offers seven rooms including a Jacuzzi suite in a large house opposite the Silver Lake Visitor Center.

Central & Southeastern Washington

While they're rarely the first places visitors to Washington head for, the central and southeastern parts of the state harbor one secret weapon: wine. A Johnny-come-lately to the viticultural world, the fertile land that borders the Nile-like Yakima and Columbia River valleys is awash with enterprising new wineries producing quality grapes that now vie with California for national recognition. Yakima and its smaller and more attractive cousin Ellensburg have traditionally held the edge, but look out too for emerging Walla Walla, where talented restaurateurs and a proactive local council have begun to craft a wine destination par excellence.

YAKIMA & ELLENSBURG

Situated in its eponymous river valley, the city of Yakima is a rather bleak trading center that doesn't really live up to its 'Palm Springs of Washington' tourist label. The main reason to stop here is to visit one of the numerous wineries that lie between Yakima and Benton City; pick up a map at the **Yakima Valley Visitors & Convention Bureau** (www.visityakima.com; 10 N 8th St; ⌚9am-5pm Mon-Sat, 10am-4pm Sun).

A better layover is Ellensburg, a diminutive settlement 36 miles to the northwest that juxtaposes the state's largest rodeo (each Labor Day) with a town center that has more coffee bars per head than anywhere else in the world (allegedly). Grab your latte at local roaster **D&M Coffee** (www.dmcoffee.com; 301 N Pine St), browse the history section in the **Kittitas County Historical Museum** (www.kchm.org; donations accepted; ⌚10am-4pm Mon-Sat Jun-Sep, from noon Tue-Sat Oct-May) opposite, and stay over in **Inn at Goose Creek** (☎509-962-8030; www.innatgoosecreek.com; 1720 Canyon Rd; r from $99; 📶), one of the most imaginative motels in the Pacific Northwest with 10 completely different offbeat rooms, including the Victorian Honeymoon Suite, the Ellensburg Rodeo Room (cowboy memorabilia) and the I Love Christmas Room (with a red-and-green Santa carpet).

WALLA WALLA

Over the last decade, Walla Walla has converted itself from an obscure agricultural backwater, famous for its sweet onions and large state penitentiary, into the hottest wine-growing region outside of California's Napa Valley. While venerable Marcus Whitman College is the town's most obvious cultural attribute, you'll also find zany coffee bars here, along with cool wine-tasting rooms, fine Queen Anne architecture and one of the state's freshest and most vibrant farmers markets.

Sights & Activities

You don't need to be sloshed on wine to appreciate Walla Walla's historical and cultural heritage. Its Main Street has won countless historical awards, and to bring the settlement to life, the local **chamber of commerce** (www.wallawalla.org; 29 E Sumach St; ⌚8:30am-5pm Mon-Fri, 9am-4pm Sat & Sun May-Sep) has concocted some interesting walking tours, complete with leaflets and maps. For information on the region's wine culture, check out **Walla Walla Wine News** (www.wallawallawinenews.com), an excellent online resource.

Fort Walla Walla Museum MUSEUM
(755 Myra Rd; adult/child $7/6; ⌚10am-5pm Apr-Oct) A pioneer village of 17 historic buildings, with the museum housed in the old cavalry stables. There are collections of farm implements, ranching tools and what could be the world's largest plastic replica of a mule team.

Walla Walla Wineworks WINE TASTING
(www.waterbrook.com; 31 E Main St; ⌚10am-6pm Mon-Thu & Sun, to 8pm Fri & Sat) A good starting point for aspiring wine-quaffers in the town center, this new tasting room is affiliated with the local Waterbrook winery. It offers good Cabernet Sauvignons accompanied by cheese, cured meats and live music at weekends.

Sleeping & Eating

Marcus Whitman Hotel HOTEL $$
(☎509-525-2200; www.marcuswhitmanhotel.com; 6 W Rose St; r/ste $139/279; ❄📶) Walla Walla's best known landmark is impossible to miss with its distinctive rooftop turret visible from all around. In keeping with the settlement's well-preserved image, the red-bricked 1928 beauty has been elegantly renovated with ample rooms kitted out in rusts and browns, and embellished with Italian-crafted furniture.

TOP CHOICE **Saffron Mediterranean Kitchen** MEDITERRANEAN $$$
(☎509-525-2112; www.saffronmediterraneankitchen.com; 125 W Alder St; mains $15-27; ⌚2-10pm, to 9pm in winter) This place isn't about cooking,

it's about alchemy; Saffron takes seasonal, local ingredients and turns them into – well – pure gold. The Med-inspired menu lists dishes like pheasant, ricotta gnocchi, amazing flatbreads and weird yogurt-cucumber combo soups that could stand up against anything in Seattle.

Olive Marketplace & Café CAFE $
(21 E Main St; breakfast & sandwiches $7-12; ⏲7am-9pm) Run by local gourmet restaurateurs T Maccerones and set in the historic 1885 Barrett Building, this breezy cafe-market is famous for its breakfast (until 11am) and is a good place to line your stomach for the impending wine-tasting.

OREGON

Spatially larger than Washington but with only half the population, Oregon is the Pacific Northwest's warm, mild-mannered elder cousin (it joined the union 30 years earlier than Washington). Physically, the state shares many characteristics with its northern neighbor, including a rain-lashed coast, a spectacular spinal mountain range and a drier, more conservative interior plateau. But, with better urban planning laws and less sprawl, Oregon retains a more laid-back and tranquil feel.

Portland

If you want to see what the future looks like, come to Portland, Oregon, a city that is 10 years ahead of its time and as definitive of its age as the Rome of Caesar or the Paris of Haussmann. What Portland lacks in Coliseums and baroque opera houses, it makes up for in innovation and ideas that start from the ground up. No thought is too outlandish here, and no behavioral pattern too weird. Urban growth boundaries (which have prevented ugly suburban sprawl) were established in 1973, a light-rail network was instituted in 1986, and the first community bike projects hit the streets in 1994. Prone to becoming daring rather than depressed during economic downturns, Portland's pugnacious DIY attitude has charitably endowed the metro area (and, in some cases, the nation) with food carts, microbreweries, hardcore punk rock, bike culture, indie 'zines and a traffic-calmed downtown that feels more small town than big city. While the results might often look distinctly European, the 'can-do' ethos behind it is 100% American.

OREGON FACTS

» **Nickname** Beaver State

» **Population** 3,831,074

» **Area** 95,997 sq miles

» **Capital city** Salem (population 154,637)

» **Other cities** Portland (population 583,776), Eugene (population 156,185), Bend (population 76,639)

» **Sales tax** Oregon has no sales tax

» **Birthplace of** former US president Herbert Hoover (1874–1964), writer and Merry Prankster Ken Kesey (1935–2001), actress and dancer Ginger Rogers (1911–95), *The Simpsons* creator Matt Groening (b 1954), filmmaker Gus Van Sant (b 1952)

» **Home of** Oregon Shakespeare Festival, tree-sitting, Nike, McMenamins

» **Politics** Democratic governor, Democrat majorities in Congress, Democrat in Presidential elections since 1984

» **Famous for** the Oregon Trail, forests, rain, beer, not being able to pump your own gas

» **State beverage** milk (dairy's big here)

» **Driving distances** Portland to Eugene 110 miles, Pendleton to Astoria 295 miles

Sights

DOWNTOWN

Tom McCall Waterfront Park PARK
In case you hadn't noticed, Portland is famous for its parks. Sinuous, 2-mile-long Tom McCall Waterfront Park flanks the west bank of the Willamette River and is both an unofficial training ground for lunchtime runners and a commuter path for the city's avid army of cyclists.

The east side of the river is embellished by the **Eastbank Esplanade**, a path that tracks below the roaring overpasses that carry traffic north and south. You can loop back over half a dozen bridges.

Steel Bridge BRIDGE
'City of bridges' is one of numerous Portland monikers, and in this case it's justified; there are 11 of these river-spanning edifices across the Willamette. If you've only got time to

traverse one, then walk, cycle, drive or catch the train across the multimodal, vertical-lift Steel Bridge built in 1912, the city's second-oldest.

Pioneer Courthouse Square LANDMARK
Portland's downtown hub is Pioneer Courthouse Sq, a redbricked people-friendly square with minimal traffic interference and where you'll find chess players, sunbathers, lunching office workers, buskers and the odd political activist. Formerly a car park, and before that a posh hotel, the square today hosts concerts, festivals and rallies. Across 6th Ave is the muscular **Pioneer Courthouse** (1875), the oldest federal building in the Pacific Northwest.

Portland Building LANDMARK
(cnr SW 5th Ave & SW Main St) In a downtown devoid of big skyscrapers, the city's signature structure is the emblematic, if architecturally dull, Portland Building, designed in 1980 by Michael Graves. A triumph of postmodernism to some, but a mine of user unfriendliness to others, the 15-story utilitarian block is embellished by the Neptune-like **Portlandia** statue, added above the front door in 1985, representing the Goddess of Commerce.

Oregon Historical Society MUSEUM
(www.ohs.org; 1200 SW Park Ave; adult/child $11/9; ⏲10am-5pm Tue-Sat, from noon Sun) Along the tree-shaded South Park Blocks sits the state's primary history museum, which dedicates most of its space to the story of Oregon and the pioneers who made it. There are interesting sections on Native American tribes and the travails of the Oregon Trail. Temporary exhibits furnish the downstairs space.

Portland Art Museum MUSEUM
(www.portlandartmuseum.org; 1219 SW Park Ave; adult/child under 17yr $10/free; ⏲10am-5pm Tue, Wed & Sat, to 8pm Thu & Fri, noon-5pm Sun) Just across the park, the art museum's excellent exhibits include Native American carvings, Asian and American art, and English silver. The museum also houses the Whitsell Auditorium, a first-rate theater that frequently screens rare or international films.

Aerial Tram CABLE CAR
(www.gobytram.com; 3303 SW Bond Ave; ⏲5:30am-9:30pm Mon-Fri, 9am-5pm Sat) Portland's aerial tram runs from the south Waterfront (there's a streetcar stop) to Marquam Hill. The tram runs along a 3300ft line up a vertical ascent of 500ft. The ride takes three minutes and costs $4 round-trip. The tram opened in 2007, smashing its budget predictions and causing much public controversy.

OLD TOWN & CHINATOWN

The core of rambunctious 1890s Portland, the once-notorious Old Town still exhibits a slightly seedy, if innocuous, underbelly. Among the poster-covered brick buildings and doorways full of down-and-outs lie several of the city's better music clubs and – slightly to the north – the city's main 'gayborhood.'

Shanghai Tunnels HISTORIC SITE
(www.shanghaitunnels.info; adult/child $13/8) Running beneath Old Town's streets is this series of underground corridors through which, in the 1850s, unscrupulous people would kidnap or 'shanghai' drunken men and sell them to sea captains looking for indentured workers. Tours run Fridays and Saturdays at 6:30pm and 8pm. Book online.

Chinatown NEIGHBORHOOD
Don't expect flashbacks of Shanghai in Portland's lackluster Chinese quarter, which begins (and largely ends) at the deceptively impressive pagoda-style **Chinatown Gates** (cnr W Burnside St & NW 4th Ave). Aside from some token chow mein takeouts, the main attraction here is the terribly overpriced **Classical Chinese Garden** (www.portlandchinesegarden.org; cnr NW 3rd Ave & NW Everett St; adult/child $8/7; ⏲10am-5pm), a deliciously tranquil block of reflecting ponds and manicured greenery, but for $8! Thankfully, tours are included with admission.

Saturday Market MARKET
(www.portlandsaturdaymarket.com; ⏲10am-5pm Sat, 11am-4:30pm Sun Mar-Dec) The best time to hit the river walk is on a weekend to catch the famous market, which showcases handicrafts, street entertainers and food carts.

Skidmore Fountain FOUNTAIN
Victorian-era architecture and the attractive Skidmore Fountain give the area beneath the Burnside Bridge some nostalgic flair.

NORTHWEST PORTLAND

Pearl District NEIGHBORHOOD
(www.explorethepearl.com) Slightly to the northwest of downtown, the Pearl District is an old industrial quarter that has transformed its once grotty warehouses into expensive lofts, upscale boutiques and creative restaurants.

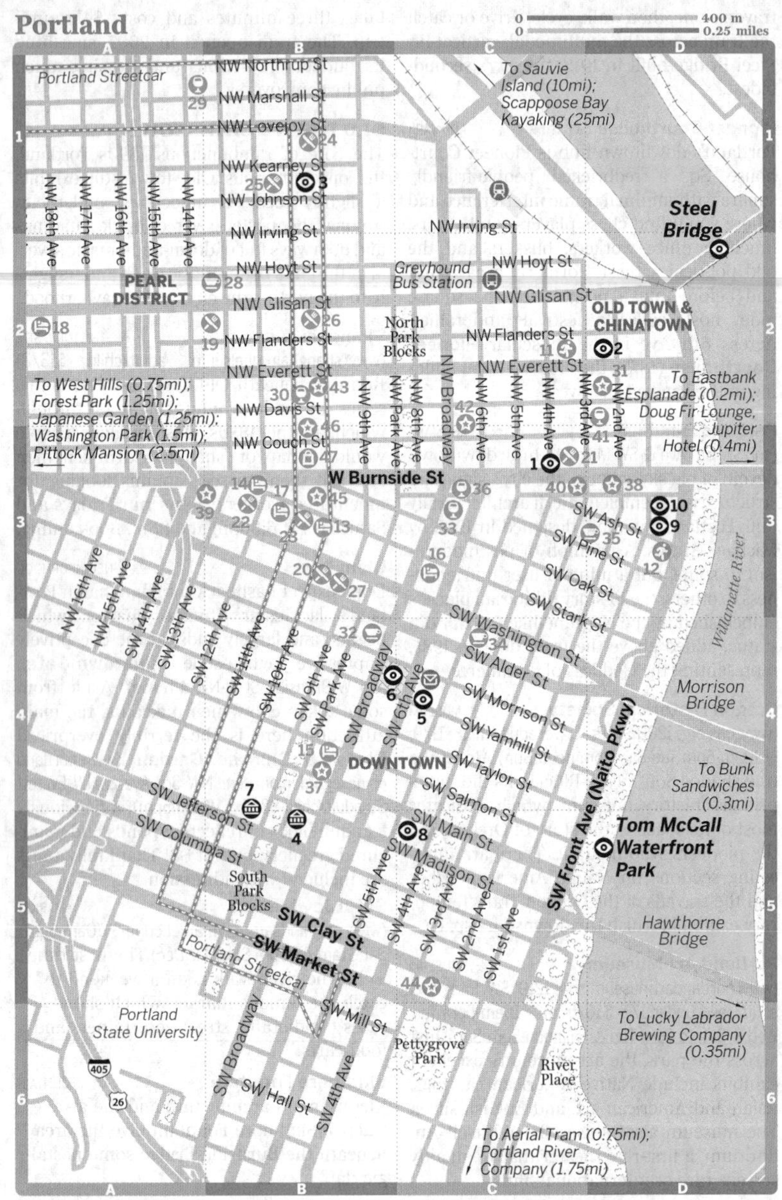

On the first Thursday of every month, the zone's abundant **art galleries** extend their evening hours and the area turns into a fancy street party of sorts. The **Jamison Square Fountain** (cnr NW Johnson St & NW 10th Ave) is one of its prettier urban spaces.

Nob Hill NEIGHBORHOOD

Nob Hill – or 'Snob Hill' to its detractors – has its hub on NW 23rd Ave, a trendy neighborhood thoroughfare that brims with clothing boutiques, home decor shops and cafes. The restaurants – including some of Portland's

Portland

Top Sights
- Steel Bridge ... D2
- Tom McCall Waterfront Park ... D5

Sights
1. Chinatown Gates ... C3
2. Classical Chinese Garden ... D2
3. Jamison Square Fountain ... B1
4. Oregeon Historical Society ... B5
5. Pioneer Courthouse ... C4
6. Pioneer Courthouse Sq ... B4
7. Portland Art Museum ... B4
8. Portland Building ... C5
9. Saturday Market ... D3
10. Skidmore Fountain ... D3

Activities, Courses & Tours
11. Portland Bicycle Tours ... C2
12. Waterfront Bicycles ... D3

Sleeping
13. Ace Hotel ... B3
14. Crystal Hotel ... B3
15. Heathman Hotel ... B4
16. Hotel Lucia ... C3
17. Mark Spencer Hotel ... B3
18. Northwest Portland Hostel ... A2

Eating
19. Andina ... B2
20. El Cubo de Cuba ... B3
21. Gaufre Gourmet ... C3
22. Jake's Famous Crawfish ... B3
23. Kenny & Zuke's ... B3
24. Lovejoy Bakers ... B1
25. Piazza Italia ... B1
26. Silk ... B2
27. Ziba's Pitas ... B3

Drinking
28. Barista ... B2
29. Bridgeport Brewpub ... A1
30. Deschutes Brewery ... B2
31. Hobo's ... D2
32. Public Domain Coffee ... B4
33. Saucebox ... C3
34. Spella Caffè ... C4
35. Stumptown Coffee ... D3
    Stumptown Coffee ... (see 13)
36. Tugboat Brewery ... C3

Entertainment
37. Arlene Schnitzer Concert Hall ... B4
38. Berbati's Pan ... D3
39. Crystal Ballroom ... B3
40. Dante's ... C3
41. Darcelle XV ... D2
42. Embers ... C2
43. Jimmy Mak's ... B2
44. Keller Auditorium ... C5
45. Living Room Theater ... B3
46. Portland Center Stage ... B3

Shopping
47. Powell's City of Books ... B3

finest, lie mostly along NW 21st Ave. This is a perfect neighborhood for strolling, window-shopping and looking at houses you'll never be able to afford.

WEST HILLS

Behind downtown Portland is the West Hills area, known for its exclusive homes, huge parks and – if you're lucky – peek-a-boo views of up to five Cascade volcanoes.

Forest Park PARK

Not many cities have 5100 acres of temperature rainforest within their limits, but then not many cities are like Portland. Abutting the more manicured Washington Park to the west (to which it is linked by various trails) is the far wilder Forest Park, whose dense foliage harbors plants, animals and an avid hiking fraternity. The **Portland Audubon Society** (www.audubonpoerland.com; 5151 NW Cornell Rd; ⌚store 10am-6pm Mon-Sat, to 5pm Sun) maintains a bookstore, wildlife rehabilitation center and 4 miles of trails within its Forest Park sanctuary.

The main sight in the park is the **Pittock Mansion** (www.pittockmansion.com; 3229 NW Pittock Dr; adult/child $7/4; ⌚11am-4pm; P), a grand mansion built in 1914 by Henry Pittock, who revitalized the Portland-based *Oregonian* newspaper. It's worth visiting the (free) grounds just to check out the spectacular views – bring a picnic.

Washington Park PARK

West of Forest Park, the more tamed Washington Park contains a good half-day's worth of attractions within its 400 acres of greenery. **Hoyt Arboretum** (www.hoytarboretum.org; 4000 Fairview Blvd; admission free; ⌚trails 6am-10pm, visitor center 9am-4pm Mon-Fri, to 3pm

Sat) showcases more than 1000 species of native and exotic trees and has 12 miles of walking trails. It's prettiest in the fall. The **International Rose Test Gardens** (www.rosegardenstore.org; admission free; sunrise-sunset) is the centerpiece of Portland's famous rose blooms; there are 400 types on show here, plus great city views. Further uphill is the **Japanese Garden** (www.japanesegarden.com; 611 SW Kingston Ave; adult/child $9.50/6.75; noon-7pm Mon, from 10am Tue-Sun; P), another oasis of tranquility.

NORTHEAST & SOUTHEAST

Across the Willamette River from downtown is the **Lloyd Center** shopping mall (1960), the usual fluorescent amalgamation of fast-food franchises and chain stores, of interest only because it was – apparently – the first of its kind in the US. A few blocks to the southwest is the equally ugly glass-towered **Oregon Convention Center** and the **Rose Garden Arena**, home of local basketball heroes, the Trailblazers.

Further up the Willamette, **N Mississippi Avenue** used to be full of run-down buildings but has undergone a yuppification in recent times. Northeast is artsy **NE Alberta Street**, a ribbon of art galleries, boutiques and cafes. **SE Hawthorne Boulevard** (near SE 39th Ave) is affluent hippy territory; think tie-dye T-shirts, homeopaths and cafes where every menu item can be veganized. One leafy mile to the south, the connecting thoroughfare of **SE Division Street** has in recent years become a kind of SE Delicious Street with an ample quota of excellent new restaurants, bars and pubs.

Activities

Hiking and mountain biking are to Portland what driving is to LA – part of the cultural make-up.

Hiking

The best hiking is found in **Forest Park**, which harbors an unbelievable 70 miles of trails and often feels more like Mt Hood's foothills than Portland's city limits. The park's all-encompassing **Wildwood Trail** starts at the Hoyt Arboretum and winds through 30 miles of forest, with many spur trails that allow for loop hikes. Other trailheads into Forest Park are located at the western ends of NW Thurman and NW Upshur Sts.

Cycling

Coming to Portland and not cycling isn't really playing the game – and you'll get few better opportunities to pedal freely in an urban area in North America.

Two unbroken trails head out from downtown. To the east the **Springwater Corridor** starts near the Oregon Museum of Science & Industry (as an extension of the Eastbank Esplanade) and goes all the way to the suburb of Gresham – 21 miles away. In the northwest the **Leif Erikson Drive** is an old logging road leading 11 miles into Forest Park and offering occasional peeks over the city.

PORTLAND FOR CHILDREN

Fear not, overworked parent. Kids love Portland for multiple reasons, and you might not even need the car seat. **Waterfront Bicycles** (www.waterfrontbikes.com) rents out tandem bikes ($75 per day), trek trailer kid extensions ($30) or chariots ($30) from its SW Ash St store. Throw your kid on the back and discover Portland on two wheels. On the riverside, the **Oregon Museum of Science & Industry** (OMSI; www.omsi.edu; 1945 SE Water Ave; adult/child $12/9; 9:30am-5:30pm Tue-Sun, to 7pm Jun-Aug) has playful science exhibits for the whole age range. There's also an Omnimax theater, planetarium shows and a submarine tour (all separate charge).

Three further kid-orientated sights are located in expansive Washington Park, with its ample tearing-around possibilities. The **Children's Museum** (www.portlandcm.org; 4015 SW Canyon Rd; admission $9; 9am-5pm Mon-Sat, from 11am Sun) is more a play centre than a museum, with numerous opportunities to crawl, climb, paint and create. Nearby, the **World Forestry Center** (www.worldforestry.org; 4033 SW Canyon Rd; adult/child $8/5; 10am-5pm) offers similar experiences but with a woodsy twist.

The default sight for pacifying parents is **Oregon Zoo** (www.oregonzoo.org; 4001 SW Canyon Rd; adult/child $9.75/6.75; 8am-6pm Apr-Sep), connected in summer to Washington Park's rose garden by the Zoo Train. Don't miss 'zoolights' during the holiday season, when the complex is filled with lit-up trees and animal figures.

For scenic farm country, head to **Sauvie Island**, 10 miles northwest of downtown Portland. This island is prime cycling land – it's flat, has relatively little traffic and much of it is wildlife refuge.

For bike rental, try **Waterfront Bicycles** (www.waterfrontbikes.com; 10 SW Ash St), where the ballpark price for day rental is $35. The tourist office gives out an excellent free cycling map.

Kayaking

Situated close to the confluence of the Columbia and Willamette Rivers, Portland has miles of navigable waterways. Kayaking is a popular water-based pursuit. Rentals start at approximately $10 per hour ($50 per day), and you can also sign up for instruction and guided tours.

Portland River Company KAYAKING
(☎503-459-4050; www portlandrivercompany.com.; 6320 SW Macadam Ave) Kayaking rentals and tours including a three-hour circumnavigation of Ross Island on the Willamette River for $45.

Scappoose Bay Kayaking KAYAKING
(☎503-397-2161, www.scappoosebaykayaking.com; 57420 Old Portland Rd) Rentals, instruction and wildlife-biased tours around Sauvie Island.

Tours

Portland Bicycle Tours BICYCLE
(☎503-360-6815; www.intrepidexperience.com; 345 NW Everett St) Bike the 'City of Roses' on a parks, bridges or market tour energized with plenty of Stumptown coffee. Two-hour tours with own/rented bike cost $30/40.

Eco Tours of Oregon NATURE
(☎503-245-1428; www.ecotours-of-oregon.com) Naturalist tours of northwest Oregon and Washington, including the Columbia River Gorge, Mt St Helens and the wine country.

PDX Running Tours RUNNING
(☎503-334-7334; www.pdxruntours.com; tours $30-45) Discover both weird and wild Portland with your own personal trainer-cum-guide on these cross-city running tours for all abilities.

Festivals & Events

Portland International Film Festival FILM
(www.nwfilm.org) Oregon's biggest film event highlights nearly 100 films from over 30 countries. Held mid- to late February.

Portland Rose Festival ROSES
(www.rosefestival.org) Rose-covered floats, dragon-boat races, fireworks, roaming packs of sailors and the crowning of a Rose Queen all make this Portland's biggest celebration. Held late May to early June.

Queer Pride Celebration GAY & LESBIAN
(www.pridenw.org) Keep Portland queer in mid-June: enjoy a kick-off party, take a cruise or join the parade.

Oregon Brewers Festival BEER
(www.oregonbrewfest.com) Quaff microbrews during the summer (late July) in Tom McCall Waterfront Park and during the winter (early December) at Pioneer Courthouse Sq.

Sleeping

Reserve ahead in summer.

TOP CHOICE **Ace Hotel** BOUTIQUE HOTEL $$
(☎503-228-2277; www.acehotel.com; 1022 SW Stark St; d with shared/private bath from $107/147; ❄@📶) A microcosm of the Portland scene, Ace is what the word 'hipster' was invented for. The reception area is a good indication of what's to come: big sofas, retro-industrial decor, the Ramones on the sound system and the comforting aroma of Stumptown coffee wafting in through the connecting door. If you make it upstairs you'll find chic minimalist rooms (some with shared bath) kitted out with wonderfully comfortable beds.

Crystal Hotel HOTEL $$
(☎503-972-2670, www.mcmenamins.com; 303 SW 12th Ave; queen/king r $105/165; 📶) Room furnishings that blend Grateful Dead–inspired psychedelia with the interior of a Victorian boudoir can only mean one thing. Welcome to the latest McMenamins hotel, an action-packed accommodations option, bar, cafe and restaurant that shares a name and ownership with the famous Ballroom across the road.

Jupiter Hotel BOUTIQUE MOTEL $$
(☎503-230-9200; www.jupiterhotel.com; 800 E BurnsideSt; d $114-149; P❄@📶) Take a dull concept – in this case a motel – give it a sleek makeover and behold! The Jupiter has hijacked America's most ubiquitous cheap-sleep idea and personalized it with retro furnishings, chalkboard doors (on which you can write instructions to the room maid) and vivid color accents. No two rooms are

alike (ironic given the motel shell) and the adjacent Doug Fir Lounge is one of the city's coolest live-music venues. Hit the bar with the band roadies and check in after midnight for a discount.

Northwest Portland Hostel HOSTEL **$**
(☎503-241-2783; www.nwportlandhostel.com; 425 NW 18th Ave; dm $20-26, d $42-68; P❄@☜) Perfectly located between the Pearl District and NW 21st and 24th Aves, this highly rated hostel is spread across a couple of quintessential Northwest District houses and features plenty of common areas (including a small deck), good rooms and bike rentals. Non-HI members pay $3 extra.

McMenamins Edgefield HOTEL **$$**
(☎503-669-8610; www.mcmenamins.com; 2126 SW Halsey St, Troutdale; dm $30, d with shared bath $60-80, with private bath $110-145; ❄@☜) This former county poor farm, restored by the McMenamin brothers, is now a one-of-a-kind, 38-acre hotel complex with a dizzying variety of services. Taste wine and homemade beer, play golf, watch movies, shop at the gift store, listen to live music, walk the extensive gardens and eat at one of its restaurants. It's about a 20-minute drive east from downtown.

Kennedy School HOTEL **$$**
(☎503-249-3983, www.mcmenamins.com; 5736 NE 33rd Ave; d $109-130; P@☜) At this Portland institution, a former elementary school, you can relive those halcyon days when you used to fall asleep in biology classes. A few miles from the city center, the school is now home to a hotel (yes, the bedrooms are converted classrooms), a restaurant, several bars, a microbrewery and a movie theater. There's a soaking pool, and the whole school is decorated with mosaics, fantasy paintings and historical photographs.

Mark Spencer Hotel HOTEL **$$**
(☎503-224-3293, www.markspencer.com; 409 SW 11th Ave; d incl breakfast from $129; ❄@☜) If the Ace is just too trendy, head next door to this more refined and down-to-earth (some would say 'boring') choice where spacious, unmemorable rooms, all with kitchens, are economically priced for such a well-placed, comfortable city-center option. There's complimentary tea with cookies during the afternoon.

Hotel Lucia BOUTIQUE HOTEL **$$$**
(☎503-225-1717; www.hotellucia.com; 400 SW Broadway; d $199-299; ❄@☜) A boutique hotel with sleek black-and-white furnishings topped with arty displays of polished (but still edible) apples. Rooms are design-show funky and geek-friendly gadgets include wi-fi, flat-screen TVs and iPod docking stations. The downtown location is handy for everywhere.

DON'T MISS

PORTLAND'S FOOD CARTS

Perhaps one of the best (and cheapest) ways to uncover Portland's cultural pastiche is to explore its diverse **food carts** (www.foodcartsportland.com). Largely a product of the last decade, these semipermanent kitchens-on-wheels inhabit parking lots around town and are usually clustered together in rough groups or 'pods,' often with their own communal tables, ATMs and portaloos. As many of the owners are recent immigrants (who can't afford a hefty restaurant start-up), the carts are akin to an international potluck with colorful kitchen hatches offering soul food from everywhere from Bosnia and Czechoslovakia to Vietnam and Mexico. While prices are low ($5 to $6 for a filling and tasty lunch), standards of hygiene – thanks to tight city regulations – are kept high and the banter between customer and proprietor is a kind of geography lesson meets recipe exchange.

Food-cart locations vary, though the most significant cluster is on the corners of SW Alder St and SW 9th Ave. Some of the newer carts have no fixed abode and announce their daily whereabouts on Facebook and Twitter. Highlights in a highly competitive field:

Ziba's Pitas (SW 9th Ave & SW Alder St) Stuffed flat-breads from Bosnia.

Potato Champion (SE 12th Ave & Hawthorne) Twice-fried *pommes frites* with dips.

El Cubo de Cuba (SW 10th Ave & SW Alder St) *Ropa vieja* (shredded stewed beef) and classic Cuban sandwiches.

Gaufre Gourmet (NW 4th Ave & W Burnside St) Liège-style Belgian waffles with innovative toppings.

Inn at Northrup Station HOTEL $$
(☎503-224-0543, www.northrupstation.com; 2025 NW Northrup St; d incl breakfast from $156; P❄@📶) Almost over the top with its bright color scheme and funky decor, this super-trendy hotel boasts huge artsy suites, many with a patio or balcony. There's a cool roof-top patio with plants.

Heathman Hotel LUXURY HOTEL $$$
(☎503-241-4100, www.heathmanhotel.com; 1001 SW Broadway; d from $200; ❄@📶) Portland's token old-school 'posh' hotel has a door-man dressed as a London beefeater (without the accent) and one of the best restaurants in the city. It also hosts high tea in the afternoons, jazz in the evenings and a library stocked with signed books by authors who have stayed here. Rooms are elegant, stylish and luxurious. Parking costs $30.

Eating

Portland's rapidly evolving food scene tore up the rule book years ago and has branched out into countless genres, subgenres, and subgenres of subgenres. Vegetarianism is well represented, as is brunch, Asian fusion and the rather loose concept known as 'Pacific Northwest.' Then there are the international food carts, cramming the entire cuisine of planet Earth into a single city block.

Paley's Place FRENCH, FUSION $$$
(☎503-243-2403; www.paleysplace.net; 1204 NW 21st Ave; mains $20-32; ⏰5:30-10pm Mon-Thu, to 11pm Fri & Sat, 5-10pm Sun) It takes a special kind of talent to win a Food Network *Iron Chef*, but, truth be told, Vitaly Paley, a recent recipient of the honor, had been serving up top-drawer duck confit, Kobe burger and veal sweetbreads long before reality TV came knocking. Paley's Gallic-leaning Portland restaurant occupies a refined perch above a spa in salubrious Nob Hill. Eating there is a memorable experience.

Andina SOUTH AMERICAN $$$
(☎503-228-9535; www.andinarestaurant.com; 1314 NW Glisan St; mains $25-30) Always the trend-setter, Portland's restaurant-of-the-moment is not French, Italian or Thai but…novo-Peruvian. The hook? Take locally grown ingredients and inject them with flavors reminiscent of the High Andes. The result? Food that's daring, delicious and – above all – different.

Piazza Italia ITALIAN $$
(☎503-478-0619; www.piazzaportland.com; 1129 NW Johnson; pasta $12-18; ⏰11:30am-3pm & from 5pm) Remember that great *ragù* (meat sauce) you last had in Bologna or those memorable *vongole* (clams) you once polished off in Sicily. Well, here they are again courtesy of Piazza Italia, a highly authentic restaurant that succeeds where so many fail: replicating the true essence of Italian food in North America.

Kenny & Zuke's DELI $$
(www.kennyandzukes.com; 1038 SW Stark St; sandwiches $9-13; ⏰7am-8pm Sun-Thu, to 9pm Fri & Sat) Portland takes on New York in this traditional Jewish-style deli next to the Ace Hotel, where the *pièce de résistance* is – surprise, surprise – the hand-sliced pastrami (cured for five days, smoked for 10 and steamed for three). Try the classic pastrami on rye, and leave room for a blintz, latke or formidable dessert.

Silk VIETNAMESE $$
(1012 NW Glisan St; mains $9-14; ⏰11am-3pm & 5-10pm Mon-Sat) An interesting modern take on Vietnamese cuisine, for Silk read Slick. The clean-lined minimalist decor offers sit-down or cocktail-bar options but the atmosphere is laid-back (lots of single diners) and the prices are very reasonable. Highlights include the banana-blossom salad, the prawn and chicken spring rolls and the pho (noodle soups).

Pambiche CUBAN $$
(☎503-233-0511; www.pambiche.com; 2811 NE Glisan St; mains $11-17; ⏰11am-10pm Sun-Thu, to midnight Fri & Sat) Most good Cuban food emigrated with two million others after the revolution in 1959, meaning the best place to find it these days is in Miami, New Jersey or – slightly more serendipitously – this multicolored restaurant in the northeast district of Portland. Open all day, *la hora del amigo* (Cuban happy hour, 2pm to 6pm Monday to Friday, 10pm to midnight Friday and Saturday) is the best time to chow: lashings of *ropa vieja* (shredded beef), snapper in coconut sauce and that rich Cuban coffee. Warning – the place is insanely popular, but tiny. Arrive early!

Jake's Famous Crawfish SEAFOOD $$$
(☎503-226-1419; 401 SW 12th Ave; mains $17-32; ⏰11am-11pm Mon-Thu, to midnight Fri, noon-midnight Sat, 3-11pm Sun) Portland's best seafood lies within this elegant old-time venue, which serves up divine oysters, revelatory crab cakes and a horseradish salmon made in heaven. Come at 3pm and praise the lord for (cheap) happy hour.

Lovejoy Bakers BAKERY, SANDWICHES $
(www.lovejoybakers.com; 939 NW 10th Ave; lunch $7-10; ⏲) Another typically stylish Pearl District abode; this bakery has on-site ovens, creative breads and an inviting streamline dmoderne cafe where you can embellish the home-baked stuff with exotic sandwich fillings.

Bunk Sandwiches SANDWICHES $
(www.bunksandwiches.com; 621 SE Morrison St; light meals $5-7; ⏲8am-3pm) This unfussy hole-in-the-wall brunch-lunch spot necessitates multiple napkins. Choose from a blackboard of po'boys, tuna melts and meatball parmigianas and find out why.

Drinking

Coffeehouses

The Seattle coffee boom is ancient history. Portland grabbed the 'best coffee-making city' baton a decade ago and has been running with it ever since. You ain't seen nothing yet!

TOP CHOICE **Stumptown Coffee** CAFE
(www.stumptowncoffee.com;) Ace Hotel (1022 SW Stark St); Belmont (3356 SE Belmont St); Division (3377 SE Division St); Downtown (128 SW 3rd Ave) The godfather of the micro-roasting revolution still takes some beating. The Ace Hotel location is the coolest nook, where trendy baristas compare asymmetrical haircuts over an Iggy Pop soundtrack. You'll be back multiple times.

Barista CAFE
(www.baristapdx.com) Pearl District (539 NW 13th Ave); Alberta (1725 NE Alberta St) Pro baristas serve made-to-perfection coffee with charm at these two newish locations that showcase different roasts every week and get their fresh pastries from a nearby Pearl district bakery.

Coava Coffee CAFE
(www.coava.myshopify.com; 1300 SE Grand Ave; ⏲7am-5pm Mon-Fri, from 8am Sat & Sun) Despite having no menu and a decor that takes the concept of 'neo-industrial' to ridiculous extremes (think school woodwork classes), Coava delivers where it matters – java that tastes so good you wonder if they've been out hand-picking it bean by bean. Unmissable!

Public Domain Coffee CAFE
(www.publicdomaincoffee.com; 603 SW Broadway, cnr Alder St; 6am-7pm Mon-Fri from 7am Sat & Sun) A swanky new downtown outlet owned by long-time indie roasters Coffee Bean International. Admire the plush wood and shiny high-end espresso machines, and call in for the public cuppings (2pm weekends) and home-brewing classes (first Saturday of the month).

Spella Caffè CAFE
(www.spellacaffe.com; 520 SW 5th; ⏲7:30am-4pm Mon-Fri) A former food-cart coffee specialist now bivouacked in a tiny standing-room-only shop, Andrea Spella roasts his Brazilian beans with the precision of an experienced oenologist and dispatches espresso from a unique hand-operated, piston-style machine.

Bars & Brewpubs

It's enough to make a native Brit jealous. Portland has about 30 brewpubs within its borders – more than any other city on earth. A good way to taste as much as possible without going into liver failure is to order four to eight beer samplers.

TOP CHOICE **Bridgeport Brewpub** BREWERY
(www.bridgeportbrew.com; 1313 NW Marshall St) This huge, relaxing unpretentious bar (which also sells great food) hides a small piece of history. This is where the micro-brewing industry in the US was kick-started in 1984. And yes, it's still here working the magic.

Lucky Labrador Brewing Company BREWERY
(www.luckylab.com) Hawthorne (915 SE Hawthorne Blvd); Pearl District (1945 NW Quimby St) The name's no joke. Dogs are welcome at this mild-mannered and mild-beer-ed pub; there's even a dog-friendly back patio at the Hawthorne branch where movies are shown in summer.

Deschutes Brewery BREWERY
(www.deschutesbrewery.com; 210 NW 11th Ave) Proof that not all good ideas start in Portland is Deschutes, an import from Bend that serves great pub grub and beer from its swanky perch in the Pearl District. The beer is brewed on-site.

Saucebox BAR
(www.saucebox.com; 214 SW Broadway) Trendy downtowners slink into this ubersleek downtown restaurant with pretty bar staff serving upscale Asian-fusion cuisine; but entertainment-seeking out-of-towners are welcome to pop by for a creative cocktail. DJs fire up at 10pm.

Tugboat Brewery BREWERY
(711 SW Ankeny; 5-10pm Mon, 4pm-midnight Tue-Thu, 4pm-1am Fri & Sat) Dive-bar-ish and, well, different, the Tugboat is on the periphery of the shabby Old Town and has an English front parlor feel to its small interior lined with bookshelves and jovial locals.

Horse Brass Pub BAR
(www.horsebrass.com; 4534 SE Belmont St) Portland's most authentic English pub, cherished for its dark-wood atmosphere, excellent fish and chips, and 50 beers on tap. Play some darts, watch soccer on TV or just take it all in.

Crush BAR
(www.crushbar.com; 1400 SE Morrison St) Slip into this sexy lounge with all the pretty people and order one of the exotic cocktails. The menu's gourmet (try brunch) and there's a 'vice' room just for smokers. Great for a girls' night out, straight or lesbian.

LaurelThirst Pub BAR
(2958 NE Glisan St) Crowds sometimes spill onto the sidewalk at this dark, funky neighborhood joint. Regular live music is free in the early evening, but incurs a cover charge after 9pm. Good beer and wine selection (but no liquor), along with fine breakfasts.

Amnesia Brewing BREWERY
(832 N Beech St) Hip N Mississippi Ave's main brewery, with a casual feel and picnic tables out front. Excellent beer – try the Desolation IPA or Wonka Porter. Outdoor grill offers burgers and sausages.

Hopworks Urban Brewery BREWERY
(www.hopworksbeer.com; 2944 SE Powell Blvd) One of the newer kids on the brewpub block has furnished Portland with its first 100% ecobrewery – all organic ales, local ingredients, composting and even a 'bicycle bar.'

Hair of the Dog Brewing BREWERY
(www.hairofthedog.com; 61 SE Yamhill; 2-8pm Wed-Sun) Beer connoisseurship took a leaf out of the wine snob's guidebook when this beer geek's heaven opened in 2010, billing itself as a 'tasting room' as opposed to a pub. Complex 'bottled-conditioned' beer is brewed on the premises with all the precision of a scientific experiment.

☆ Entertainment

That cozy brewpub was just the ice-breaker. Portland has been manifesting a dynamic music scene, ever since hardcore punk merchants the Wipers stood up and yelled 'Is This Real?' in 1979. Then there are the cinemas, wonderfully congenial places where wait staff will bring your food orders into the auditorium *during the movie!*

Check the *Mercury* or *Willamette Week* for entertainment schedules and cover charges.

Live Music

Doug Fir Lounge LIVE MUSIC
(www.dougfirlounge.com; 830 E Burnside St) Since the closing of the legendary Satyricon nightclub in the late 2000s, Portland's musical baton has been passed onto the Doug Fir, a bar-lounge with a personality that's more middle-aged rock star than angry young punk. But, true to form, the Fir still delivers where it matters, luring edgy, hard-to-get talent into a venue that pits tattooed youths against suburban yuppies. Its ascent has enlivened the new trendy neighborhood of South Burnside, recently christened with the acronym SoBu.

Dante's LIVE MUSIC
(www.danteslive.com; 1 SW 3rd Ave) This steamy red bar near Chinatown books vaudeville shows along with national acts such as the Dandy Warhols and Concrete Blonde. Drop in on a Monday night for the ever-popular 'Karaoke from Hell.'

Berbati's Pan LIVE MUSIC
(www.berbati.com; 10 SW 3rd Ave) An established rock club that nabs some of the more interesting acts in town, including big band, swing, acid rock and R & B. Outdoor seating and pool tables are a plus.

Crystal Ballroom LIVE MUSIC
(www.mcmenamins.com; 1332 W Burnside St) Opened in 1914, the Crystal saw it all – jazz, beat poets and psychedelic – until a 1968 closure led to it becoming the city's favorite squat. The McMenamin brothers rescued it from oblivion in 1997 and it's back to its '50s high-water mark, complete with a 'floating' dance floor that bounces at the slightest provocation.

Jimmy Mak's LIVE MUSIC
(www.jimmymaks.com; 221 NW 10th Ave music from 8pm) Stumptown's premier jazz venue serves excellent Mediterranean food in its posh dining room. There's a casual smoking bar-lounge in the basement.

Cinema

Living Room Theater CINEMA
(www.livingroomtheaters.com; 341 SW 10th Ave) Almost too good to be true! These six movie

theaters with cutting-edge digital technology screen art-house, foreign and retro films while the staff bring you drinks and tapas to enjoy in front of the big screen. There's an adjacent bar with wine, wi-fi, coffee and comfy sofas.

Kennedy School CINEMA
(www.mcmenamins.com; 5736 NE 33rd Ave) The McMenamin brothers' premier Portland venue. You can watch movies in the old school gym.

Bagdad Theater CINEMA
(www.mcmenamins.com; 3702 SE Hawthorne Blvd) Another historic McMenamins venue over on the eastside; has bargain flicks.

Cinema 21 CINEMA
(www.cinema21.com; 616 NW 21st Ave) Portland's premier art-house and foreign-film theater.

Performing Arts

Portland Center Stage THEATER
(☎503-445-3700; www.pcs.org; 128 NW 11th Ave) The city's main theater company now performs in the Portland Armory – a newly renovated Pearl District landmark with state-of-the-art features.

Arlene Schnitzer Concert Hall CLASSICAL MUSIC
(☎503-228-1353; www.pcpa.com/events/asch.php; 1037 SW Broadway) The Oregon Symphony performs in this beautiful, if not acoustically brilliant, downtown venue.

Artists Repertory Theatre THEATER
(☎503-241-1278; www.artistsrep.org; 1516 SW Alder St) You can catch some of Portland's best plays, including regional premieres, in this intimate space.

Keller Auditorium THEATER
(☎503-248-4335; www.pcpa.com/events/keller.php; 222 SW Clay St) The Portland Opera, Oregon Ballet Theatre and Oregon Children's Theatre all stage performances here.

Gay & Lesbian Venues

For current listings, see *Just Out,* Portland's free gay biweekly. Or grab a *Gay and Lesbian Community Yellow Pages* (www.pdxgayyellowpages.com) for other services.

Darcelle XV CABARET
(www.darcellexv.com; 208 NW 3rd Ave) Portland's premier drag show, featuring queens in big wigs, fake jewelry and overstuffed bras. Male strippers perform at midnight on weekends.

Embers CLUB
(110 NW Broadway) Regulars come to meet up for the music (from '80s tunes to techno and pop), amateur drag shows, a fun dance floor and friendly camaraderie. Mixed crowd.

Hobo's BAR
(www.hobospdx.com; 120 NW 3rd Ave) Past the old historic storefront is a classy restaurant-piano bar popular with older gay men. It's a quiet, relaxed place for a romantic dinner or drink.

Sports

Portland's only major-league sports team is the **Trail Blazers** (www.nba.com/blazers), which plays basketball at Rose Garden Arena.

PGE Park hosts the Portland's minor-league baseball team, the **Portland Beavers** (www.portlandbeavers.com), along with the A-League soccer team, the **Portland Timbers** (www.portlandtimbers.com). The Timbers, now in their fourth incarnation, were first formed in 1975 and logged some early successes in the erstwhile NASL. They are well known for their vociferous supporters, the *Timbers Army,* and long succession of British coaches.

Shopping

Portland's downtown shopping district extends in a two-block radius from Pioneer Courthouse Sq and displays all of the usual suspects. Pioneer Pl, an upscale mall, is be-

DON'T MISS

POWELL'S CITY OF BOOKS

Remember those satisfying weekend afternoons in the 1980s and '90s, when you could bivouac yourself inside the local bookstore with a takeout coffee and let your eye carry you spontaneously from shelf to shelf? Well, it's not all ancient history – at least, not yet. Like a Proustian flashback from a pre-ebook era, **Powell's City of Books** (www.powells.com; 1005 W Burnside St; ⌚9am-11pm) reacquaints incurable bookworms with dog-eared dust jackets, geeky assistants and unexpected literary epiphanies. Founded in 1971, it claims to be the largest independent bookstore in the world and its labyrinthine interior takes up a whole city block.

tween SW Morrison and SW Yamhill Sts, east of the square. The Pearl District is dotted with high-end galleries, boutiques and home-decor shops. On weekends, you can visit the quintessential Portland Saturday Market by the Skidmore Fountain.

Eastside has lots of trendy shopping streets that also host a few restaurants and cafes. SE Hawthorne Blvd is the biggest, N Mississippi Ave is the most recent and NE Alberta St is the most artsy and funky. Down south, Sellwood is known for its antique shops.

Information

Emergency & Medical Services

Legacy Good Samaritan Hospital & Medical Center (☎503-413-7711; 1015 NW 22nd Ave)

Portland Police (☎503-823-0000)

Walgreens (☎503-238-6053; 940 SE 39th Ave) Has a 24-hour pharmacy in the city's east.

Internet Access

Backspace (www.backspace.bz; 115 NW 5th Ave; ⏲7am-11pm Mon-Wed, to midnight Thu & Fri, 10am-midnight Sat, to 11pm Sun) Youth-oriented hangout with arcade games, coffee and long hours.

Urban Grind Coffeehouse (www.urbangrindcoffee.com) NE Oregon St (2214 NE Oregon St); NW 14th Ave (911 NW 14th Ave; ⏲6am-10:30pm) Slick cafe with computers and free wi-fi.

Internet Resources

City of Portland (www.portlandonline.com) Stumptown's official website.

Gay Oregon (www.gaypdx.com) A resource for Portland's gay and lesbian communities.

PDX Guide (www.pdxguide.com) Fun and spot-on food and drink reviews by a guy who knows, plus other happenings around town.

Portland Independent Media Center (www.portland.indymedia.org) Community news and lefty activism.

Media

Just Out (www.justout.com) Free biweekly serving Portland's gay community.

KBOO 90.7 FM Progressive local station run by volunteers; alternative news and views.

Portland Mercury (www.portlandmercury.com) The local sibling of Seattle's *Stranger*, this free weekly is published on Thursdays.

Willamette Week (www.wweek.com) Free alt-weekly covering local news and culture, published on Wednesdays.

Money

Travelex (⏲5:30am-4:30pm) Downtown (900 SW 6th Ave); Portland International Airport (main ticket lobby) Foreign-currency exchange.

Post

Post office Main branch (715 NW Hoyt St); University Station (1505 SW 6th Ave)

Tourist Information

Portland Oregon Visitors Association (www.travelportland.com; 701 SW 6th Ave; ⏲8:30am-5:30pm Mon-Fri, 10am-4pm Sat, 10am-2pm Sun) Super-friendly volunteers man this office in Pioneer Courthouse Sq. There's a small theater with a 12-minute film about the city, and Tri-Met bus and light-rail offices inside.

Getting There & Away

Air

Portland International Airport (PDX; www.flypdx.com) has daily flights all over the US, as well as to four international destinations. It's situated just east of I-5 on the banks of the Columbia River (20 minutes' drive from downtown). Amenities include money changers, restaurants, bookstores (including three Powell's branches) and business services like free wi-fi.

Bus

Greyhound (www.greyhound.com; 550 NW 6th Ave) connects Portland with cities along I-5 and I-84. Destinations include Chicago, IL (50 hours, $197), Boise, WA (9½ hours, $69), Denver, CO (28 hours, $135), San Francisco, CA (17½ hours, $87), Seattle, WA (four hours, $28) and Vancouver, BC (8½ hours, $55).

Train

Amtrak (www.amtrak.com; cnr NW 6th Ave & NW Irving St) serves Chicago, IL ($267, two days, two daily), Oakland, CA ($122, 18 hours, one daily), Seattle, WA ($31, 3½ hours, four daily) and Vancouver, BC ($58, four hours, two daily).

Getting Around

To/From the Airport

Tri-Met's MAX light-rail train runs between PDX airport and downtown ($2.35, 45 minutes). Taxis from the airport cost about $30.

Bicycle

Portland is regularly touted as the most bike-friendly city in the US and there are miles of dedicated paths. Rentals start at $35. Some hotels (eg Ace Hotel) offer bikes free of charge.

Bus, Light Rail & Streetcar

Another Portland tour de force is its comprehensive public transportation network. The city runs standard local buses, a MAX light-rail system – run by Tri-Met, and with an **information center** (www.trimet.org; ⏲8:30am-5:30pm Mon-Fri) at Pioneer Courthouse Sq – and a streetcar (tram) introduced in 2001, which runs from Portland State University, south of downtown, through the Pearl District to NW 23rd Ave. Within the downtown core, public transportation is free; outside downtown, fares run $2 to $2.35. Services run until 1:30am.

Car

Major car-rental agencies have outlets at Portland International Airport and around town. Oregon law prohibits you from pumping your own gas. Most of downtown is metered parking; a free option is to park along an inner-southeast street and walk across a bridge to the city center.

Taxi

Cabs are available 24 hours by phone. Downtown, you can often just flag them down. Try **Broadway Cab** (503-227-1234) or **Radio Cab** (503-227-1212).

Around Portland

Beer, coffee and wine: Portland excels at all three. For the latter you'll have to venture a little out of town to the wineries that embellish the Willamette Valley, in particular those around the towns of Dundee and McMinnville along Hwy 99W. **Willamette Valley Wineries Association** (www.willamettewines.com) is a good information portal for this alluring region.

For a decent overview of the area's many wineries, visit **Ponzi Vineyards** (14665 SW Winery Lane, Beaverton; 10am-5pm), 30 minutes southwest of downtown Portland, where you can taste current releases and visit the historic cellars and vineyards.

Meandering through plush green hills on winding country roads from one wine-tasting room to another is a delightful way to spend an afternoon (just make sure you designate a driver). Alternatively, Portland-based **Pedal Bike Tours** (http://pedalbiketours.com) runs five-hour spins ($89) from the town of Dundee on Hwy 99W. Wine in Oregon is all about its premier grape variety – Pinot Noir. One of the earliest planters was **Erath Winery** (www.erath.com; 9409 NE Worden Hill Rd, Dundee; 11am-5pm), harvesting grapes since 1969 – there's no better place to start your tasting. For some oenological back-up, contact **Grape Escape** (www.grapeescapetours.com), which specializes in wine-country tours.

For something different (or to sober up), head to McMinnville's **Evergreen Aviation Museum** (www.sprucegoose.org; 500 NE Capt Michael King Smith Way; adult/child $20/18; 9am-5pm) and check out Howard Hughes' **Spruce Goose**, the world's largest wood-framed airplane. There's also a replica of the Wright brothers' Flyer, along with an Imax theater (movie admission separate).

There are several fine restaurants in the area, but for something spectacular consider **Joel Palmer House** (503-864-2995; www.joelpalmerhouse.com; 600 Ferry St, Dayton; mains $29-38; 5-9pm Tue-Sat); its dishes are peppered with wild mushrooms collected by hand from the surrounding woods by the chefs! And if you need an interesting place to stay, consider **McMenamins Hotel Oregon** (503-472-8427; www.mcmenamins.com; 310 NE Evans St, McMinnville; d $60-130;), an older building renovated into a charming hotel. It has a pub (of course) with a wonderful rooftop bar.

Willamette Valley

The Willamette Valley, a fertile 60-mile-wide agricultural basin, was the Holy Grail for Oregon Trail pioneers who headed west more than 150 years ago. Today it's the state's breadbasket, producing more than 100 kinds of crops – including renowned Pinot Noir grapes. Salem, Oregon's capital, is about an hour's drive from Portland at the northern end of the Willamette Valley, and most of the other attractions in the area make easy day trips as well. Toward the south is Eugene, a dynamic college town worth a few days of exploration.

SALEM

Less interesting than Washington's state capital, Olympia, Oregon's legislative center is day-trip fodder, renowned for its cherry trees, art-deco capitol building and Willamette University. You can get orientated at the helpful **Visitors Information Center** (www.travelsalem.com; 181 NE High St; 8:30am-5pm Mon-Fri, 10am-4pm Sat).

Following an Oregon trend, Salem's best museum is housed in the local university. Willamette University's **Hallie Ford Museum of Art** (900 State St; adult/senior $3/2; 10am-5pm Tue-Sat, from 1pm Sun) showcases the state's best collection of Pacific Northwest art, including an impressive Native American gallery.

The **Oregon State Capitol** (900 Court St NE), built in 1938, looks like a background prop from a lavish Cecil B DeMille movie. Free tours run hourly between 9am and 4pm in summer. Rambling 19th-century

WORTH A TRIP

HOT SPRINGS

Oregon trumps its northern neighbor Washington in its abundance of hot springs and there are a couple of good ones within easy striking distance of the state capital, Salem. Two hours' drive east of the city is **Bagby Hot Springs** (www.bagbyhotsprings.org), a revitalizing free hot tub in a rustic forest bathhouse 1.5 miles down a hiking trail. From Estacada, head 26 miles south on Hwy 224 (which becomes Forest Rd 46); turn right onto Forest Rd 63 and go 3 miles to USFS Rd 70. Turn right and drive 6 miles to the parking area ($5 Northwest Forest Pass required).

If the communal bathing doesn't cut it, enjoy more salubrious climes at **Breitenbush Hot Springs** (www.breitenbush.com), a fancier spa with massages, yoga and the like. Day-use prices are $14 to $26. Breitenbush is east of Salem on Hwy 46, just past the settlement of Detroit.

Bush House (600 Mission St SE; adult/child $4/2; ⌚noon-5pm Tue-Sun) is an Italianate mansion now preserved as a museum with historic accents, including original wallpapers and marble fireplaces.

On the main Oregon north–south artery, Salem is served daily by **Greyhound** (450 Church St NE) buses and **Amtrak** (500 13th St SE) trains.

EUGENE

Zany has long passed for 'normal' in countercultural Eugene, a bolshie offshoot of metro Portland that invented tree-sitting as a means of protest, stoked bike friendliness decades before it was trendy, and has long manifested a uniquely West Coast spirit of sedition.

While the downtown's no oil painting, Eugene wins kudos for its academic institution, the magnificently landscaped University of Oregon, which also doubles up as an arboretum. Elsewhere Eugene is an underneath-the-surface kind of place where some gentle prodding reveals running trails, workers coops and the odd aging Merry Prankster. The Prankster's original psychedelic bus, *Further*, remains at the farm of former Eugene resident Ken Kesey in Pleasant Hill, 10 miles away.

Sights & Activities

As the city that gave the world Nike, Eugene (or 'Tracktown' as it likes to call itself) safeguards some of the best running facilities in the nation. Many trails hug the Willamette River and some are floodlit after dark.

Alton Barker Park PARK

Eugene's largest park is renowned for its running trails, most notably the wood-chip **Pre's Trail** named for Eugene's Olympian running icon Steve Prefontaine, who was killed in a car crash in 1975. The **Adidas Oregon Trail** (cnr 24th Ave & Amazon Pkwy) is a 1-mile loop popular with interval runners (it's floodlit at night). The park is divided roughly in half, demarcating wild and manicured areas. Abutting the Willamette River, it connects to the city's wider trail network via three footbridges. **Skinner Butte** (682ft) is a landmark hill on the opposite side of the river replete with lawns, hiking trails and a prime city view.

University of Oregon UNIVERSITY, MUSEUM

(1680 E 15th Ave; adult/child $3/2; ⌚11am-5pm Wed-Sun) What America lacks in cobbled Italianate piazzas it makes up for in beautifully laid-out university campuses, and few are as authentic and salubrious as this one. Showcased on the 295-acre campus you'll find a splendid art museum, a top research library, illustrious Romanesque revival architecture and an arboretum with over 500 species of tree. Previous alumni include Ken Kesey (writer) and Steve Prefontane (athlete). A campus highlight is the **Jordan Schnitzer Museum of Art** (1430 Johnson Lane; adult/child $5/3; ⌚11am-8pm Wed, to 5pm Tue & Thu-Sun), offering a rotating permanent collection of world-class art from Korean scrolls to Rembrandt paintings.

Sleeping

Eugene's accommodations consist of mainly unexciting chain hotels and motels, with the odd B&B thrown in to break the monotony.

C'est La Vie Inn B&B $$

(☎541-302-3014; www.cestlavieinn.com; 1006 Taylor St; d $125-140; ❄@📶) Break the monotony of the utilitarian downtown in this classic turreted Queen Anne B&B that

WHAT THE...?

It stands to reason that the city that invented tree-sitting as a means of environmental protest would be equally expert in the art of tree-*climbing*. Re-creating one of our strongest childhood impulses, the **Pacific Tree Climbing Institute** (☎866-653-8733; www.pacifictreeclimbing.com; 605 Howard Ave) offers day and overnight trips to a nearby forest where you can shin up an old-growth Sitka spruce or Douglas fir with all the exuberance of a 10-year-old. If the primate in you still isn't satisfied, the institute offers the opportunity to spend the night amid the leafy branches in a specially rigged hammock. Climbs start at $200.

dates from the late 19th century but offers comforts more in keeping with the internet age. C'est La Vie is run by a French woman (no surprise there) and La France is evident in everything from the coffee mugs to the furniture.

Campus Inn MOTEL $
(☎541-343-3376; www.campus-inn.com; 390 E Broadway; d from $66; ❄@📶) An independent and comfortable family-run motel perched between the university and downtown with friendly helpful staff, a Jacuzzi and a small gym. Prices depend on the season but are negotiable.

Courtesy Inn MOTEL $
(☎541-345-3391; www.courtesyinneugene.com; 345 W 6th Ave; d from $60; P📶) Friendly nook near the train station that is above average in the motel stakes and offers free wi-fi, HBO and a snack breakfast. The town and parks are within walking distance.

Eating & Drinking

TOP CHOICE **Sweet Life Patisserie** CAFE, BAKERY $
(www.sweetlifedesserts.com; 755 Monroe St; pastries $2-5; ⏲7am-11pm Mon-Fri, from 8am Sat & Sun) You might want to warm up on Track-town's ample trails before you hit this sugarfest situated on a quiet street on the cusp of downtown. Everything is homemade with the emphasis on sweet – pies, cheesecakes, pastries, cup cakes, the works. The coffee's good as well.

McMenamins PUB $
(⏲11am-11pm Sun-Thu, to midnight Fri & Sat) E 19th St (1485 E 19th St); High St (1243 High St); North Bank (22 Club Rd) Gloriously located on the banks of the mighty Willamette, the North Bank pub-restaurant has riverside patio tables. The other two locations lack water views but offer similar fare ('classic pub food with a Northwest kick' – pasta, salads, burgers and steaks).

Morning Glory Café VEGETARIAN $
(450 Willamette St; ⏲7:30am-3:30pm; 🖉) Eugene in a nutshell (or should that be a nut roast?). This sustainable place is good for breakfast, lunch and brunch, and rarely will vegans have a better choice – everything on the menu is either vegan or can be made vegan. Try the biscuits, tofu sandwiches or cookies, and as the in-shop sign says 'make tea not war.'

Beppe & Gianni's Trattoria ITALIAN $$
(☎541-683-6661; www.beppeandgiannis.net; 1646 E 19th Ave; mains $16-20; ⏲5-9pm Sun-Thu, to 10pm Fri & Sat) An insanely popular local Italian place where you can choose from antipasti, *primi* and *secondi* plates, or enjoy all three. The homemade pastas are the best.

Voodoo Doughnuts CAFE, DESSERTS $
(www.voodoodoughnut.com; 20 E Broadway; ⏲24hr) This weird and wonderful Portland import recently introduced Eugene to 24-hour doughnuts with flavors such as 'bacon and maple,' and 'iced fruit-loop' served in a psychedelic downtown cafe.

Information

For more information, visit the **Visitors Association** (www.visitlanecounty.com; 754 Olive St; ⏲8am-5pm Mon-Fri, 10am-4pm Sat & Sun).

Getting There & Around

Eugene's plush **Amtrak station** (www.amtrak.com; cnr E 4th Ave & Willamette St) runs daily trains to Vancouver, BC, and LA, and everywhere in between on its *Cascade* and *Coast Starlight* lines. **Greyhound** (www.greyhound.com; 987 Pearl St) runs north to Salem and Portland, and south to Grants Pass and Medford. **Porter Stage Lines** runs a daily bus from outside the train station to Coos Bay in the west, and Bend and Ontario in the east. Book tickets through Amtrak.

Local bus service is provided by **Lane Transit District** (www.ltd.org). For bike rentals, try **Paul's Bicycle Way of Life** (152 W 5th St; ⏲9am-7pm Mon-Fri, 10am-5pm Sat & Sun) near the train station.

Columbia River Gorge

The fourth-largest river in the US by volume, the mighty Columbia runs 1243 miles from Alberta, Canada, into the Pacific Ocean just west of Astoria. For the final 309 miles of its course, the heavily dammed waterway delineates the border between Washington and Oregon and cuts though the Cascade Mountains via the spectacular Columbia River Gorge. Showcasing numerous ecosystems, waterfalls and magnificent vistas, the land bordering the river is protected as a National Scenic Area and is a popular sporting nexus for windsurfers, cyclists, anglers and hikers.

HOOD RIVER & AROUND

The surrounding apple orchards and wineries are just the wrapping paper. The small town of Hood River, 63 miles east of Portland on I-84, is famous for its legendary windsurfing (on the Columbia River), arguably the best in the world, and – to a lesser extent – its mountain biking south of town off Hwy 35 and Forest Rd 44. A sporting triumvirate is completed by year-round skiing facilities on nearby Mt Hood. For more on the outdoor bounty, call in at the **chamber of commerce** (www.hoodriver.org; 720 E Port Marina Dr; ⌚9am-5pm Mon-Fri, from 10am Sat & Sun).

Sights & Activities

In operation since 1906, the 22-mile **Mount Hood Railroad** (110 Railroad Ave; www.mthoodrr.com; adult/child $27/17) was built to carry lumber to the Columbia River. Today it serves mainly as a tourist train. Spectacular two-hour trips run Wednesdays to Sundays from April through December, starting from the historic rail depot in Hood River on the corner of 1st St and Cascade Ave.

For Hood River's real deal, check in with **Hood River Waterplay** (www.hoodriverwaterplay.com; Port of Hood River Marina), where you can procure windsurfing rentals ($60 per day) and partake in lessons ($199 for a two-day beginners course).

Sleeping & Eating

Columbia River Gorge Hostel HOSTEL $
(☎509-493-3363; www.bingenschool.com; cnr Cedar & Humbolt Sts; dm/r from $19/49; ❄@📶) Across the Columbia in Bingen on the Washington side, this hostel has simple and affordable lodging in an old schoolhouse.

Hood River Hotel HISTORIC HOTEL $$
(☎541-386-1900; www.hoodriverhotel.com; 102 Oak St; d $99-164; ❄📶) A vintage 1913 hotel in the heart of downtown that still scores highly with its old-fashioned four-poster beds and general air of conviviality.

Full Sail Brewery PUB $$
(www.fullsailbrewing.com; 506 Columbia St; mains $9-23; ⌚11:30am-8pm) This cozy tasting-room bar has a small pub menu and good river views. Free 30-minute microbrewery tours end up here.

Getting There & Away

Hood River is connected to Portland by daily **Greyhound** (www.greyhound.com) buses. Alternatively, take the **Amtrak** (www.amtrak.com) *Empire Builder* and disembark at Bingen on the Washington side.

Oregon Cascades

An extension of their Washington cousins, the Oregon Cascades offer plenty of dramatic stand-alone volcanoes that dominate the skyline for miles around. Mt Hood, overlooking the Columbia River Gorge, is the state's highest peak and has year-round skiing plus a relatively straightforward summit ascent. Tracking south you pass Mt Jefferson and the Three Sisters before reaching Crater Lake, the ghost of erstwhile Mt Mazama that collapsed in on itself after blowing its top approximately 7000 years ago.

MT HOOD

If the Cascade Mountains were people, Mt Hood – Oregon's highest peak at 11,239ft – would be the congenial, easy-to-get-to-know one. There are plenty of reasons to admire its ethereal snowcapped beauty. You can ski Hood year-round (unique to the US), ascend it inside a day without Reinhold Messner-like climbing skills, circumnavigate it on a well-trodden 40-mile path known as the Timberline trail, and reach it within a one-hour drive from Portland. But like all people, Hood has its bad days when it walks off and sulks and the sky turns black with ugly, potentially lethal storms. The Native Americans knew the score. They called the mountain Wy'east, after a legendary native chief, and witnessed the dormant stratovolcano's latent anger on more than one occasion, most recently during an eruption in the 1790s.

Hood was named by the 1792 Vancouver expedition after Samuel Hood, a British admiral who somewhat ironically fought patriotically *against* the Americans in the American War of Independence.

Activities

SKIING

Hood is rightly revered for its skiing. There are six ski areas on the mountain, including **Timberline** (www.timberlinelodge.com; lift tickets adult/child $48/30), which lures Canadians and Californians (as well as Oregonians) with the only year-round skiing in the US. Closer to Portland, **Mt Hood SkiBowl** (www.skibowl.com; lift tickets adult/child $44/24) is no slacker either. It's the nation's largest night-ski area and popular with city slickers who ride up for an evening of powder play from the metro zone. The largest ski area on the mountain is **Mt Hood Meadows** (www.skihood.com; lift tickets adult/child $69/39) and the best conditions usually prevail here.

HIKING

The Mt Hood National Forest protects an astounding 1200 miles of trails. A Northwest Forest Pass ($5) is required at most trailheads.

One popular trail loops 7 miles from near the village of Zigzag to beautiful **Ramona Falls**, which tumbles down mossy columnar basalt. Another heads 1.5 miles up from US 26 to **Mirror Lake**, continues a half-mile around the lake, then tracks 2 miles beyond to a ridge.

The 41-mile **Timberline Trail** circumnavigates Mt Hood through scenic wilderness. Noteworthy portions include the hike to McNeil Point and the short climb to Bald Mountain. From Timberline Lodge, Zigzag Canyon Overlook is a 4.5-mile round-trip.

Climbing Mt Hood should be taken seriously, as deaths do occur, though dogs have made it to the summit and the climb can be done in a long day. Contact **Timberline Mountain Guides** (541-312-9242; www.timberlinemtguides.com) for guided climbs.

Sleeping & Eating

Reserve **campsites** (877-444-6777; www.reserveusa.com; campsites $12-18) in summer. On US 26 are streamside campgrounds Tollgate and Camp Creek. Large and popular Trillium Lake has great views of Mt Hood.

TOP CHOICE **Timberline Lodge** LODGE $$
(800-547-1406; www.timberlinelodge.com; d $115-290;) Stanley Kubrick fans will have no trouble recognizing this historic 1937 lodge as the fictional Overlook Hotel from the film *The Shining* (exterior shots only). 'All work and no play makes Jack a dull boy,' typed Jack Nicholson repeatedly in the movie. If only he'd known about the year-round skiing, the hikes, the cozy fires and the hearty restaurant.

Huckleberry Inn INN $
(503-272-3325; www.huckleberry-inn.com; 88611 E Government Camp Loop, Government Camp; d $85-180;) A family-run rustic inn and restaurant with dorm and private rooms, along with a 24-hour restaurant serving up formidable milk shakes and – as the name suggests – huckleberry pie! It's handily located in Government Camp village.

Ice Axe Grill PUB $$
(www.iceaxegrill.com; 87304 E Government Camp Loop, Government Camp; mains $12-18; 11:30am-9pm Tue-Thu, from 7am Fri & Sat, 7am-8pm Sun) Anyone up for fine-dining after a day of skiing and/or wilderness hiking? Thought not. All the more reason to drop into Government Camp's only brewery-restaurant to fill that hole with shepherd's pie, bacon burgers and thick pizzas.

Rendezvous Grill & Tap Room MODERN AMERICAN $$$
(503-622-6837; 67149 E US 26, Welches; mains $20-30; 11:30am-9pm) Outstanding dishes such as porterhouse steak and Dungeness crab linguine are served here. Also great desserts and wine list.

Information

If you're approaching from Hood River, visit the **Hood River Ranger Station** (6780 Hwy 35, Parkdale; 8am-4:30pm Mon-Sat). The **ZigZag Ranger Station** (70220 E Hwy 26, Zigzag; 7:45am-4:30pm Mon-Sat) is more handy for Portland arrivals. There's another helpful office in Government Camp. The weather changes quickly here; carry chains in winter. For road conditions, dial 800-977-6368.

Getting There & Away

The prettiest approach to Hood by car is from Hood River (44 miles) on Hwy 35. Alternatively, you can take Hwy 26 directly from Portland (56 miles). The **Breeze Shuttle** (www.cobreeze.com) between Bend and Portland stops briefly at Government Camp, 6 miles from the Timberline Lodge. There are regular **shuttles** (www.skihood.com) from Portland to the ski areas during the winter.

SISTERS

Named for the trio of eponymous 10,000ft-plus peaks that dominate the skyline, Sisters is the unofficial 'sister' of Bend, 22 miles to the southeast, a town with which it shares a penchant for the gritty outdoors. The main difference between the two is size. Sisters is a one-horse town of Hollywood 'Western' folklore, where cowboy-themed shop-fronts hide modern boutiques and art galleries. There's nothing faux about the surroundings though – raw mountains, roller-coaster single-track bike trails, and wilderness of the highest order.

For local orientation, see the **chamber of commerce** (www.sisterschamber.com; 291 Main St; 9am-5pm). The most accessible bike trail is the recently extended **Peterson Ridge Trail** system, 28 miles of moderate single-track with loop-back possibilities that starts half a mile south of town.

At the southern end of Sisters, the city park has **camping** (sites $10), but no showers. For ultra-comfort, bag a room in the **Five Pine Lodge** (866-974-5900; www.fivepinelodge.com; 1021 Desperado Trail; d $149-219, cottages $199-219;), ridiculously luxurious for a so-called cowboy town, though none of the guests are complaining. On the quieter and cheaper side is **Sisters Motor Lodge** (541-549-2551; www.sistersmotorlodge.com; 511 W Cascade St; d from $89;), offering 11 individually crafted rooms with a nonmotel-like atmosphere.

It's hard to drive past **Bronco Billy's Ranch Grill & Saloon** (www.broncobillysranchgrill.com; 190 E Cascade Ave; mains $10-25; 11:30am-9pm), the town's most obvious Wild West facade, a historic hotel reincarnated as a restaurant with a carnivorous menu anchored by hamburgers and steaks.

Getting There & Away

A daily **Porter Stage Line** bus runs through town on its way between Eugene and Bend. There's no official stop, but you should be able to be dropped off. Bookings are through **Amtrak** (www.amtrak.com).

BEND

Sandwiched in between the east's high desert plateau and the west's snow-choked Cascade Mountains, Bend is where the two radically different halves of Oregon meet. And what a collision! Herein lies the best mountain biking in the state, the best skiing in the state, the best rock climbing in the state…and all of this before you've even got round to examining the town itself, whose lush riverside parks do a good impersonation of a Monet canvas.

Sights

TOP CHOICE **High Desert Museum** MUSEUM
(www.highdesertmuseum.org; 59800 S US 97; adult/child $15/12; 9am-5pm) This extraordinary museum, 6 miles south of Bend, is undoubtedly one of the best in the state. It charts the settlement of the West, along with the region's natural history. The sea-otter exhibit and trout pool are highlights.

Activities

Couch potatoes will be deathly bored in Bend, where most things are orientated around outdoor pursuits.

CYCLING

Within riding distance of the town center lies one of the most comprehensive networks of mountain-biking trails in the nation – 300 miles worth and counting. **Cog Wild** (www.cogwild.com; 255 SW Century Dr) offers bike rental (from $30 per day), along with organized tours and shuttles out to the best trailheads.

CLIMBING

Not 25 miles northeast of Bend lies **Smith Rock State Park** (www.oregonstateparks.org; day use $5), where 800ft ballast cliffs guarding the Crooked River have become the G-spot of sport climbing in the US. The park's 1800-plus routes are, without question, among the best in the nation. Guides for both experienced and inexperienced climbers can be procured with **Smith Rock Climbing Guides Inc** (www.smithrockclimbingguides.com; excursions $90-225).

SKIING

As improbable as it may seem on a hot spring day, Bend hosts Oregon's best skiing, 22 miles southwest of the town at the glorious **Mount Bachelor Ski Resort** (www.mtbachelor.com; lift tickets adult/child 6-12yr $50/29), famous for its 'dry' powdery snow, long season (until late May) and ample terrain (it's the largest ski area in the Pacific Northwest). The mountain has long advocated cross-country skiing in tandem with downhill and maintains 35 miles of groomed trails.

Sleeping & Eating

TOP CHOICE **McMenamins Old St Francis School** HOTEL $$
(541-382-5174; www.mcmenamins.com; 700 NW Bond St; d $145-175, cottages $190-330;) It's the usual McMenamins quandary. How do you tear yourself away from the establishment's fine eating-sleeping-cinema triumvirate and see the town? Old St Francis

School is what it says it is: an old Catholic school remodeled into a classy 19-room hotel complete with saltwater Turkish bath, restaurant-pub, pool tables and a movie theater. It's a destination in itself.

Oxford Hotel BOUTIQUE HOTEL **$$$**
(☎877-440-8436; www.oxfordhotelbend.com; 10 NW Minnesota Ave; d $199-259; P❄☎☒) Central Oregon was crying out for a decent boutique hotel to break the monotony of the usual suspects on its all-too-familiar motel strip. So, along came the Oxford to embellish Bend's already salubrious downtown and blow away most of the opposition with huge luxurious rooms, a gym, a fancy on-site restaurant and free bikes.

Victorian Café BREAKFAST **$**
(1404 NW Galveston Ave; mains $7-12; ⊙7am-2pm) A Bend classic and a must-see for anyone with a hearty morning appetite, the Victorian is a formidable American brunch stop housed in an inviting red chalet in the city's leafy western suburbs. Brave the weekend queues to get in – you won't regret it.

Bourbon Street CAJUN **$$**
(www.bourbonstreetbend.com; 5 NW Minnesota Ave; mains $16-34) Fresh farmed local goods with a Cajun twist are on offer in this remodeled fire station in recently trussed-up Minnesota Ave.

Deschutes Brewery & Public House BREWERY **$$**
(1044 NW Bond St; ⊙11am-11pm Mon-Thu, to midnight Fri & Sat, to 10pm Sun) Bend's first microbrewery, gregariously serving up plenty of food and handcrafted beers.

ℹ Information

Information is available at the **visitor and convention bureau** (www.visitbend.com; 917 NW Harriman St; ⊙9am-5pm Mon-Fri, 10am-4pm Sat).

ℹ Getting There & Away

The **Breeze Shuttle** (www.cobreeze.com) runs once a day between Bend (Sugarloaf Mountain Motel, US 97 62980) and Portland. **Porter Stage Lines** also runs a daily bus east to Ontario and west to Eugene. Book tickets online through **Amtrak** (www.amtrak.com).

NEWBERRY NATIONAL VOLCANIC MONUMENT

Weird landscapes get ever weirder as you head south out of Bend. Case in point is the Newberry National Volcanic Monument (day use $5), which showcases 500,000 years of dramatic seismic activity. Start your visit at the **Lava Lands Visitor Center** (☎541-593-2421; ⊙9am-5pm Jul-Sep, limited hours May, Jun, Sep & Oct, closed Nov-Apr), 13 miles south of Bend. Nearby attractions include **Lava Butte**, a perfect cone rising 500ft, and **Lava River Cave**, Oregon's longest lava tube. Four miles west of the visitor center is **Benham Falls**, a good picnic spot on the Deschutes River.

Newberry Crater was once one of the most active volcanoes in North America, but after a large eruption a caldera was born. Close by are **Paulina Lake** and **East Lake**, deep lakes rich with trout, while looming above is 7985ft **Paulina Peak**.

CRATER LAKE NATIONAL PARK

Get ready for a sharp intake of breath. It may be a cliché but it certainly isn't an exaggeration: the still, deep blue waters of Crater Lake reflect the surrounding cliffs like a giant mirror. The secret lies in the water's purity. No rivers or streams feed the lake, meaning its H_2O content is made up entirely of rain and melted snow. It is also exceptionally deep – indeed at 1949ft (maximum) it's the deepest lake in the US. The classic tour is the 33-mile self-guided rim drive (open approximately June to mid-October), but there are also exceptional hiking and cross-country skiing opportunities. As Oregon's sole national park, there's a $10 vehicle fee to enter the Crater Lake area. It receives some of the highest snowfalls in North America and the rim drive and north entrance are sometimes closed up until early July. Check ahead. For more park information, head to **Steel Visitor Center** (☎541-594-3100; ⊙9am-5pm May-Sep, 10am-4pm Nov-Apr).

You can stay overnight from early June to early October at the **Cabins at Mazama Village** (☎541-830-8700; www.craterlakelodges.com; d $124; P) or the majestic old **Crater Lake Lodge** (☎541-594-2255; www.craterlakelodges.com; d $149-275; P❄), opened in 1915 as a classic example of rustic 'parkitecture.' The updated facilities still retain their rustic elegance. Nearby campgrounds include the large **Mazama Campground** (www.craterlakelodges.com; tent/RV sites $21/27), managed by Crater Lake Lodge.

Southern Oregon

With a warm and sunny climate that belongs in nearby California, southern Oregon is the state's banana belt. Rugged landscapes, scenic rivers and a couple of attractive towns top the highlights list.

ASHLAND

Oregon was unknown territory to the Elizabethan explorers of William Shakespeare's day, so it might seem a little strange to find that the pretty settlement of Ashland in southern Oregon has established itself as the English playwright's second home. The irony probably wouldn't have been lost on Shakespeare himself. 'All the world's a stage,' the great Bard once opined, and fittingly people come from all over the world to see Ashland's famous Shakespeare Festival, which has been held here under various guises since the 1930s.

The 'festival' moniker is misleading; the shows here are a semipermanent fixture occupying nine months of the annual town calendar and attracting up to 400,000 theatergoers per season. Even without them, Ashland is an attractive town, propped up by various wineries, upscale B&Bs and fine restaurants. For information, visit the **chamber of commerce** (www.ashlandchamber.com; 110 E Main St; ⌚9am-5pm Mon-Fri).

Sights & Activities

The Shakespearian attractions contrast sharply with Ashland's other main draw: the outdoors.

Lithia Park PARK

Adjacent to the three splendid theaters (one of which is outdoors) lies what is arguably the loveliest city park in Oregon, whose 93 acres wind along Ashland Creek above the center of town. Unusually, the park is in the National Register of Historic Places and is embellished with fountains, flowers, gazebos and an ice-skating rink (winter only).

Schneider Museum of Art MUSEUM

(www.sou.edu/sma; 1250 Siskiyou Blvd; suggested donation $5; ⌚10am-4pm Mon-Sat) Like all good Oregonian art museums, this one's on the local university campus and displays a kind of global potluck of paintings, sculptures and artifacts.

Jackson Wellsprings SPA

(☎541-482-3776; www.jacksonwellsprings.com; 2253 Hwy 99) For a good soak, try this casual New Age–style place, which maintains an 85°F (29°C) mineral-fed swimming pool ($8) and 103°F (39°C) private Jacuzzi tubs ($25 to $35 for 75 minutes). It's 2 miles north of town.

Mt Ashland Ski Resort SKI AREA

(www.mtashland.com; lift pass adult/child $39/29) Powdery snow is surprisingly abundant here, 18 miles southwest on Mt Ashland (7533ft), which has some excellent advanced terrain.

Siskiyou Cyclery CYCLING

(www.siskiyoucyclery.com; 1729 Siskiyou Blvd; per day $35; ⌚10am-5:30pm Tue-Sat) Pedal-pushers can rent a bike here and explore the countryside on the semicompleted Bear Creek Greenway, a 21-mile bike path between Ashland and the town of Central Point.

Sleeping

Reserve in summer when the thespians descend in their droves.

TOP CHOICE **Columbia Hotel** HOTEL $

(☎541-482-3726, www.columbiahotel.com; 262 1/2 E Main St; d $89-149; ❄@📶) Get in a Shakespearean mood at this quaint European-style hotel with period rooms (some with shared baths), a comfy sitting area, complimentary morning coffee and an ideal theater-side location.

Ashland Springs Hotel HISTORIC HOTEL $$$

(☎541-488-1700; www.ashlandspringshotel.com; 212 E Main St; d $179-269; ❄@📶🏊) An Ashland institution and National Historic Landmark that was painstakingly restored in 2000, the Springs glistens with plenty of Shakespearean splendor, although it actually dates from 1925. Elegant rooms are bedizened with pastel colors and common areas include a grand ballroom, a conservatory, an English garden and Larks Restaurant.

Ashland Hostel HOSTEL $

(☎541-482-9217; www.theashlandhostel.com; 150 N Main St; dm $28, d $59-89; ❄📶) It might sound like an oxymoron, but Ashland's rather 'posh' hostel should quickly banish memories of those youth hostelling free-for-alls of yore with clean dorms and the options to go private in compact doubles with their own bath.

Cowslip's Belle B&B B&B $$

(☎541-488-2901, www.cowslip.com; 159 N Main St; d/ste $170/245; ❄📶) A top-rated B&B with four luxurious rooms in a 1913 bungalow along with a couple of suites in a separate town house. Highlights include a beautiful garden, love seats, rockers, private decks and Jacuzzi tubs.

Manor Motel MOTEL $

(☎541-482-2246; www.manormotel.net; 476 N Main St; d $69-125; ❄📶) Handily located independent hotel on the threshold of the central area with 11 rooms, friendly service and plenty of greenery.

Eating

TOP CHOICE New Sammy's Cowboy Bistro MODERN AMERICAN $$$
(☎541-535-2779; 2210 S Pacific Hwy, Talent; mains $23-36; ⊙5-8:30pm Thu-Sun) Sammy's might sound like a French cowboy restaurant, but there are no such oxymorons at this funky spot, considered by some to be Oregon's best restaurant. It's small, understated and located 3 miles north of Ashland in the village of Talent. Reserve weeks in advance to taste its highly creative cuisine.

Sesame Asian Kitchen ASIAN $$
(www.sesameasiankitchen.com; 21 Winburn Way; mains $11-16; ⊙11:30am-9pm) This is a chic but relatively cheap Asian-fusion restaurant where quick service and hearty but healthy portions make for an ideal pre-Shakespeare dinner. Try the tangerine chicken or the Mongolian beef short ribs as you discuss the merits of *Hamlet* over *The Merchant of Venice.*

Chateaulin FRENCH $$$
(☎503-482-2264; www.chateaulin.com; 50 E Main St; mains $24-36; ⊙5-9pm Wed-Sun) More European fantasies are stirred at this fine-dining French bistro right next to the theaters. The decor and menu are *très* Parisian (dishes include duck, vol-au-vent and *filet mignon)* but the wine list stays patriotically local with some hard-to-find Oregonian vintages. There's a wine shop next door.

JACKSONVILLE

This small but endearing ex-gold-prospecting town is the oldest settlement in southern Oregon and a National Historic Landmark. The main drag is lined with well-preserved buildings dating from the 1880s, now converted into boutiques and galleries. Music-lovers can't miss the September **Britt Festival** (www.brittfest.org), a world-class musical experience with top-name performers. Seek more enlightenment at the **chamber of commerce** (www.jacksonvilleoregon.org; 185 N Oregon St; ⊙10am-5pm Mon-Fri, 11am-4pm Sat & Sun).

Jacksonville is full of fancy B&Bs; for budget motels head 6 miles east to Medford. The **Jacksonville Inn** (☎541-899-1900; www.jacksonvilleinn.com; 175 E California St; d $159-199; ❄📶) is the most pleasant abode, shoehorned downtown in an 1863 building with regal antique-stuffed rooms. There's a restaurant on-site.

WILD ROGUE WILDERNESS

Yes, it's *wild* and it's *rogue*. Situated between the town of Grants Pass on I-5 and Gold Beach on the Oregon coast, the aptly named Wild Rogue Wilderness is anchored by the turbulent Rogue River, which cuts through 40 miles of untamed, roadless canyon. People regularly underestimate the powerful force of nature here and the area is known for challenging white-water rafting (classes III and IV) and long-distance hikes.

Basking in its own warm microclimate, the medium-sized town of **Grants Pass** is the gateway to adventures along the Rogue. The **chamber of commerce** (www.visitgrantspass.org; 1995 NW Vine St; ⊙8am-5pm Mon-Fri) is right off I-5, exit 58. For raft permits and backpacking advice, contact the Bureau of Land Management's **Smullin Visitors Center** (☎541-479-3735; www.blm.gov/or/resources/recreation/rogue/index.php; 14335 Galice Rd; ⊙7am-3pm) in Galice.

Rafting the Rogue is legendary, but not for the faint of heart; a typical trip takes three days and costs upward of $650. A good outfitter is **Rogue Wilderness Adventures** (☎800-336-1647; www.wildrogue.com). Kayaking the river is equally exhilarating; for instruction and guidance (and you'll need it!), contact **Sundance River Center** (☎541-386-1725; www.sundanceriver.com).

Another highlight of the region is the 40-mile **Rogue River Trail**, once a supply route from Gold Beach. The full trek takes four to five days; day hikers might aim for Whiskey Creek Cabin, a 6-mile round-trip from the Grave Creek trailhead. The trail is dotted with rustic lodges ($110 to $140 per person with meals; reservations required) – try **Black Bar** (☎541-479-6507; www.blackbarlodge.net; d $120). There are also primitive campgrounds along the way.

NORTH UMPQUA RIVER

This 'Wild and Scenic' river boasts world-class fly-fishing, fine hiking and serene camping. The 79-mile **North Umpqua Trail** begins near Idleyld Park and passes through Steamboat en route to the Pacific Crest Trail. A popular sideline is pretty **Umpqua Hot Springs**, east of Steamboat near Toketee Lake. Not far away, stunning, two-tiered **Toketee Falls** (113ft) flows over columnar basalt, while **Watson Falls** (272ft) is one of the highest waterfalls in Oregon. For information, stop by Glide's **Colliding Rivers Information Center** (18782 N Umpqua Hwy, Glide; 9am-5pm May-Oct). Adjacent is the **North Umpqua Ranger District** (541-496-3532; 8am-4:30pm Mon-Fri).

Between Idleyld Park and Diamond Lake are dozens of riverside campgrounds; these include lovely **Susan Creek** and primitive **Boulder Flat** (no water). A few area accommodations fill up quickly in summer; try the log-cabin-like rooms at **Dogwood Motel** (541-496-3403; www.dogwoodmotel.com; 28866 N Umpqua Hwy; d $70-75;).

OREGON CAVES NATIONAL MONUMENT

This very popular cave (there's only one) lies 19 miles east of Cave Junction on Hwy 46. Three miles of passages are explored via 90-minute **walking tours** (541-592-2100; www.nps.gov/orca; adult/child $8.50/6; 9am-6pm Jun-Sep, hours vary Oct-May) that include 520 rocky steps and dripping chambers running along the River Styx. Dress warmly, wear shoes with good traction and be prepared to get dripped on.

Cave Junction, 28 miles south of Grants Pass on US 199 (Redwood Hwy), provides the region's services. Here you'll find the decent **Junction Inn** (541-592-3106; 406 Redwood Hwy; d from $70;), along with a few restaurants. For fancy lodgings right at the cave there's the impressive **Oregon Caves Chateau** (541-592-3400, www.oregoncaves chateau.com; d from $90-165; May-Oct); grab a milk shake at the old-fashioned soda fountain here. Campers should head to **Cave Creek Campground** (541-592-2166; campsites $10), 14 miles up Hwy 46, about 4 miles from the cave.

Eastern Oregon

Mirroring Washington, Oregon east of the Cascades bears little resemblance to its wetter western cohort either physically or culturally. Few people live here – the biggest town, Pendleton, numbers only 20,000 – and the region hoards high plateaus, painted hills, alkali lakebeds and the country's deepest river gorge.

JOHN DAY FOSSIL BEDS NATIONAL MONUMENT

Within the soft rocks and crumbly soils of John Day country lies one of the world's greatest fossil collections, laid down between six and 50 million years ago. Roaming the forests at the time were saber-toothed nimravids, pint-sized horses, bear-dogs and other early mammals.

The national monument includes 22 sq miles at three different units: Sheep Rock Unit, Painted Hills Unit and Clarno Unit. Each has hiking trails and interpretive displays. To visit all of the units in one day requires quite a bit of driving, as more than 100 miles separate the fossil beds. See www.nps.gov/joda for more details.

Visit the excellent **Thomas Condon Paleontology Center** (32651 Hwy 19, Kimberly; 9am-5pm), 2 miles north of US 26 at the Sheep Rock Unit. Displays include a three-toed horse and petrified dung-beetle balls, along with many other fossils and geologic history exhibits. If you feel like walking, take the short hike up the **Blue Basin Trail**, which will make you feel like you've just landed on the sunny side of the moon.

The **Painted Hills Unit**, near the town of Mitchell, consists of low-slung, colorfully banded hills formed about 30 million years ago. Ten million years older is the **Clarno Unit**, which exposes mud flows that washed over an Eocene-era forest and eroded into distinctive, sheer white cliffs topped with spires and turrets of stone.

Rafting is popular on the John Day River, the longest free-flowing river in the state. **Oregon River Experiences** (800-827-1358; www.oregonriver.com) offers trips of up to five days. There's also good fishing for smallmouth bass and rainbow trout. Enquire at the **Oregon Department of Fish & Wildlife** (541-575-1167; www.dfw.state.or.us).

Every little town in the area has at least one hotel; these include the clean, economical **Oregon Hotel** (541-462-3027; 104 E Main St; dm $15, d $39-89) in Mitchell and the friendly **Sonshine B&B** (541-575-1827; www.sonshinebedandbreakfast.com; 210 NW Canton St; d $85-95;), in John Day itself, which has four rooms, formidable breakfasts and a warm welcome. There are several public campgrounds in the area including Lone Pine and Big Bend (sites $5) on Hwy 402.

WALLOWA MOUNTAINS

The Wallowa Mountains, with their glacier-hewn peaks and crystalline lakes, are among the most beautiful natural areas in Oregon. The only drawback is the large number of visitors who flock here in summer, especially to the pretty Wallowa Lake area. Escape them all on one of several long hikes into the nearby **Eagle Cap Wilderness** area, such as the 6-mile one-way jaunt to **Aneroid Lake** or the 9-mile trek on the **West Fork Trail**. From the upper Lostine Valley, or from the Sheep Creek Summit of USFS Rd 39, there is easier day-hike access to the Eagle Cap's high country.

Just north of the mountains, in the Wallowa Valley, **Enterprise** is a homely backcountry town with several motels such as the **Ponderosa** (☎541-426-3186; www.ponderosamotel.hotels.officelive.com; 102 E Greenwood St; d $70-80; ❄📶). If you like beer, don't miss the town's microbrewery, **Terminal Gravity** (www.terminalgravitybrewing.com; 803 School St; mains $7-11). Just 6 miles south is Enterprise's fancy cousin, the upscale town of **Joseph**. Expensive bronze galleries and artsy boutiques line the main strip, and accommodations comprise mostly B&Bs.

HELLS CANYON

North America's deepest river gorge (yes – even deeper than the Grand Canyon) provides Oregon with its northeastern border (with Idaho) and visitors with one of the state's wildest and jaw-dropping vistas. The mighty Snake River (a 1000-mile-long tributary of the even mightier Columbia) has taken 13 million years to carve its path through the high plateaus of eastern Oregon to its present depth of 8000ft. The canyon itself is a true wilderness bereft of roads but open to the curious and the brave.

For perspective, drive 30 miles from Joseph to Imnaha, where a 24-mile slow gravel road leads up to the excellent lookout at **Hat Point** (USFS Rd 4240). From here you can see the Wallowa Mountains, Idaho's Seven Devils, the Imnaha River and the wilds of the canyon itself. This road is open from late May until snowfall; give yourself two hours each way for the drive.

For white-water action and spectacular scenery, head down to **Hells Canyon Dam**, 25 miles north of the small community of Oxbow. Just past the dam, the road ends at the **Hells Canyon Visitor Center** (☎541-785-3395; ⌚8am-4pm May-Sep), which has good advice on the area's campgrounds and hiking trails. Beyond here, the Snake River drops 1300ft in elevation through wild rapids accessible only by jet boats and rafts. **Hells Canyon Adventures** (☎541-785-3352; www.hellscanyonadventures.com; 4200 Hells Canyon Dam Rd) is the main operator running raft trips and jet-boat tours from May through September (reservations required).

The area has many campgrounds. Just outside Imnaha is the huntsman-style **Imnaha River Inn** (☎541-577-6002; www.imnahariverinn.com; s/d $70/130), a B&B replete with Hemingway-esque animal trophies, while Oxbow has the good-value **Hells Canyon B&B** (☎541-785-3373; www.hellscanyonb-b.com; 49922 Homestead Rd; d $70; ❄📶). For more services, head to the towns of Enterprise, Joseph and Halfway.

STEENS MOUNTAIN & ALVORD DESERT

Wonderfully remote, Steens Mountain, the highest peak (9670ft) in southeastern Oregon, is like an alpine island towed off the Cascades and plonked in the middle of the stark Alvord Desert, near the Nevada border. On the west slope of the range, ice-age glaciers bulldozed massive U-shaped valleys into the flanks of the mountain. To the east, delicate alpine meadows and lakes flank the Steens, dropping off dizzyingly into the Alvord Desert, 5000ft below.

Beginning in Frenchglen, the 66-mile gravel **Steens Mountain Loop Road** offers access to Steens Mountain Recreation Area; it's open from late June to October (depending on the weather) and requires a high-clearance vehicle in parts. Call the **Bureau of Land Management** (BLM; ☎541-573-4400; www.blm.gov; ⌚7:45am-4:30pm Mon-Fri) for information. If you happen to be in the area outside these months or have a low-clearance vehicle, consider seeing the Steens via the flat eastern gravel road through the scenic Alvord Desert. Take a full gas tank and prepare for weather changes year-round.

There are campgrounds on the Steens Mountain Loop, such as the BLM's pretty Page Springs and fine South Steens Campgrounds (campsites $6 to $8, water available). Free 'dispersed' camping is allowed in the Steens and Alvord Desert (bring water). The historic **Frenchglen Hotel** (☎541-493-2825; fghotel@yahoo.com; 39184 Hwy 205, Frenchglen; d $70-110; ⌚mid-Mar–Oct; ❄) in the eponymous hamlet has small, cute rooms with shared bath, plus five modern rooms with private bath. Dinners are available (reserve ahead).

Oregon Coast

While Washington's coast is speckled with islands and inland seas, Oregon's 362 miles get full exposure to the crashing waves of the Pacific. This magnificent littoral is paralleled by view-hugging US 101, a scenic

LEWIS & CLARK: JOURNEY'S END

In November 1805 William Clark and his fellow explorer Meriwether Lewis of the Corps of Discovery staggered, with three dozen others, into a sheltered cove on the Columbia River, 2 miles west of the present-day Astoria-Megler Bridge, after completing what was indisputably the greatest overland trek in American history. After setting up a temporary camp, the party trekked west to what is now **Cape Disappointment State Park** (Hwy 100; ⌚dawn-dusk) to gaze upon the Pacific and search for a winter bivouac. Located on a high bluff inside the park not far from the Washington town of Ilwaco, the sequentially laid-out **Lewis & Clark Interpretive Center** (Hwy 100; adult/child $5/2.50; ⌚10am-5pm) faithfully recounts the Corps of Discovery's cross-continental journey using a level of detail the journal-writing explorers would have been proud of. A succinct 20-minute film backs up the permanent exhibits.

After the first truly democratic ballot in US history (in which a woman and a black slave both voted), the party elected to make their winter bivouac across the Columbia River in present-day Oregon. A replica of the original **Fort Clatsop** (adult/child $3/free; ⌚9am-6pm Jun-Aug, to 5pm Sep-May), where the Corps spent a miserable winter in 1805–06, lies 5 miles south of Astoria. Also on-site are trails, a visitor's center and historical reenactments (summer only).

There are 10 additional sites in the so-called **Lewis & Clark National & State Historical Parks** (www.nps.gov/lewi), all of them clustered around the mouth of the Columbia River and each relating important facts about the Corps of Discovery and its historic mission to map the American West.

highway that winds its way through towns, resorts, state parks (over 70 of them) and wilderness areas.

ASTORIA

There are three alluring reasons to visit Astoria, Oregon: first, it's the oldest Caucasian-founded settlement west of the Rockies; second, it's awash with poignant Lewis & Clark memorabilia; and third, the historic seaport is speckled with attractive Victorian heritage houses akin to a mini San Francisco.

Sitting at the wide mouth of the Columbia River, Astoria was founded by America's first multimillionaire, John Jacob Astor, in 1811. The town is dominated by the impossible-to-miss 4.1-mile-long **Astoria-Megler Bridge** (1966), which takes US 101 into Washington state and is the world's longest continuous truss bridge.

Sights & Activities

Aside from the not-to-be-missed Lewis and Clark sites, Astoria has a handful of other lures.

Columbia River Maritime Museum MUSEUM
(www.crmm.org; 1792 Marine Dr; adult/child $10/8; ⌚9:30am-5pm) The 150-year-old seafaring and river heritage is well interpreted at this fine museum, with mock-up lifeboats and details of the hundreds of shipwrecks that litter the river mouth.

Heritage Museum MUSEUM
(www.cumtux.org; 1618 Exchange St; adult/child $4/3; ⌚10am-5pm) The decidedly less flashy Heritage Museum contains historical exhibits, which include Ku Klux Klan (KKK) paraphernalia.

Flavel House HISTORIC BUILDING
(www.cumtux.org; 441 8th St; adult/child $5/4; ⌚10am-5pm) Extravagant Flavel House is a Queen Anne Victorian built by Captain George Flavel, one of Astoria's leading citizens during the 1880s.

Astoria Column LOOKOUT
(recommended donation $1) For a fantastic view, head uphill to this 125ft tower painted with scenes from the westward sweep of US exploration and settlement.

Fort Stevens State Park PARK
(tent/RV sites $18/22, yurts $30) Located about 10 miles west of Astoria off US 101, this park commemorates the historic military reservation that once guarded the mouth of the Columbia River. There's beach access, camping and bike trails. Reservations are accepted.

Sleeping & Eating

Astoria has two revitalized historic hotels and a stash of interesting independent bars and coffeehouses.

TOP CHOICE **Hotel Elliott** HISTORIC HOTEL $$
(☎503-325-2222; www.hotelelliott.com; 357 12th St; d $149-169; ❄️📶) Encased in the oldest part of the oldest town in the Pacific Northwest, the elegant Elliott is a period piece that has clawed its way up to boutique standard without losing its historical significance.

Commodore Hotel BOUTIQUE HOTEL $$
(☎503-325-4747; www.commodoreastoria.com; 258 14th St; d with shared/private bath from $69/129; @📶) Even trendier and equally historic is this early-20th-century wonder that reopened in 2009 after 45 years as a pigeon coop. The birds and moths have been replaced by a stylish set of European-style rooms and suites. Don't miss the Portland-esque 14th Street Coffee House next door, with its fine java and neo-industrial decor.

TPaul's Urban Café INTERNATIONAL $$
(1119 Commercial St; mains $9-16; ⏱9am-9pm Mon-Thu, to 10pm Fri & Sat, 11am-4pm Sun) Cooks up formidable lunchtime quesadillas served with nachos and a homemade salsa dip.

Baked Alaska SEAFOOD $$$
(1 12th St; mains $18-24; ⏱11am-10pm) Astoria's finest fine-dining is perched on stilts over the water with great views and equally memorable seafood.

Information

Find information at the **visitor center** (www.oldoregon.com; 111 W Marine Dr; ⏱9am-5pm).

Getting There & Away

A daily bus run by **Northwest Point** (www.northwest-point.com) connects Astoria with Portland's Amtrak station ($18, 2½ hours) via Cannon Beach.

CANNON BEACH

The low-key antidote to gaudy Seaside, 9 miles to the north, Cannon Beach is a sensitively laid-out small resort where upmarket serenity is juxtaposed with thunderous Pacific breakers and fickle weather. Immense basalt promontories and a sweeping sandy beach have given the town its tourist-brochure wrapping paper, but Cannon Beach is uniquely beautiful and far from spoiled. The town itself is replete with small art galleries and esoteric shops.

Sights & Activities

Photogenic **Haystack Rock**, a 295ft sea stack, is the most spectacular landmark on the Oregon coast and accessible from the beach. Birds cling to its ballast cliffs and tide pools ring its base.

The coast to the north, protected inside **Ecola State Park**, is the Oregon you may have already visited in your dreams: sea stacks, crashing surf, hidden beaches and gorgeous pristine forest. The park is 1.5 miles from town and is crisscrossed by paths, including part of the Oregon Coast Trail, which leads over Tillamook Head to the town of Seaside.

The Cannon Beach area is good for surfing – though not the beach itself. The best spots are Indian Beach in Ecola State Park, 3 miles to the north, and Oswald West State Park, 10 miles south. **Cleanline Surf Shop** (www.cleanlinesurf.com; 171 Sunset Blvd) is a friendly local shop that rents out boards and mandatory wetsuits for $35 a day.

Sleeping & Eating

Cannon Beach Hotel HISTORIC HOTEL $$
(☎503-436-1392; www.cannonbeachhotel.com; 1116 S Hemlock St; d $132-242; @📶) A classy joint with small but meticulously turned-out rooms in a historic wooden arts-and-crafts building dating from 1914. A downstairs lounge and cafe-bistro add to the charm.

Blue Gull Inn Motel MOTEL $
(☎800-507-2714; www.haystacklodgings.com; 487 S Hemlock St; d/cottages from $69/125; @📶) Proving that Cannon Beach can still deliver to the budget-conscious is this modest but pleasant arc of motel-style rooms clustered around an outdoor fountain.

Newman's FRENCH, ITALIAN $$$
(☎503-436-1151; www.newmansat988.com; 988 S Hemlock St; mains $19-28; ⏱dinner Tue-Sun) Fuse the world's two greatest cuisines (Italian and French) to create a regionally lauded fine-dining experience in this historic beach house turned restaurant.

Sleepy Monk Coffee CAFE $
(www.sleepymonkcoffee.com; 1235 S Hemlock St; ⏱8am-4pm Fri-Sun) Slide under the skin of this free-and-easy beach town with a pastry and a cup of homemade joe (beans roasted on-site).

Information

For a full Cannon Beach rundown, look in at the **chamber of commerce** (www.cannonbeach.org; 207 N Spruce St; ⏱10am-5pm Mon-Sat, 11am-4pm Sun).

Getting There & Away

NorthWest Point (www.northwest-point.com) runs two comfortable daily buses (with on-board wi-fi) to and from Portland Amtrak station ($17), continuing on to Astoria. The bus stop is at the Beach Store at 1108 S Hemlock St.

NEWPORT

Oregon's second-largest commercial port, Newport is a lively tourist city with several fine beaches and a world-class aquarium. Good restaurants – along with some tacky attractions, gift shops and barking sea lions – abound in the historic Bayfront area, while bohemian Nye Beach offers art galleries and a friendly village atmosphere. The **Newport Seafood & Wine Festival** in late February draws the West's top chefs and literally dozens of wineries from California up to Washington. Get information at the **visitor center** (www.newportchamber.org; 555 SW Coast Hwy; ⌚8am-5pm Mon-Fri, 10am-3pm Sat).

The top-notch **Oregon Coast Aquarium** (www.aquarium.org; 2820 SE Ferry Slip Rd; adult/child $15.95/9.95; ⌚9am-6pm) is well known on the scenic coast, featuring a sea otter pool, surreal jellyfish tanks and Plexiglas tunnels through a shark tank. An alternative is the **Oregon Coast History Center** (www.oregoncoast.history.museum; 545 SW 9th St; suggested donation $2; ⌚10am-5pm Tue-Sun), housed in the turreted Burrows House and adjacent Log Cabin. There's more history at the breezy **Yaquina Head Outstanding Area** (750 Lighthouse Dr; admission $7; ⌚sunrise-sunset), site of the coast's tallest lighthouse and an interesting interpretive center.

Campers can head to **South Beach State Park** (☎541-867-4715; www.oregonstateparks.org; RV sites/yurts $27/40), which is 2 miles south on US 101, and has 227 reservable campsites and 27 yurts. Book-lovers shouldn't miss the **Sylvia Beach Hotel** (☎541-265-5428; www.sylviabeachhotel.com; 267 NW Cliff St; d incl breakfast $100-193), with simple but comfy rooms, each named after a famous author (Steinbeck, JK Rowling, Dr Seuss); reservations are mandatory. For a fancy meal, try **Saffron Salmon** (☎541-265-8921; www.saffronsalmon.com; 859 SW Bay Blvd; mains $22-30; ⌚11:30am-2:30pm & 5-8:30pm Thu-Tue). Once you get past the stellar wall-to-wall view, dig into grilled wild salmon fillet or rack of lamb with sumac. Reserve for dinner.

YACHATS & AROUND

Tiny Yachats (population 675) is what travel magazines describe as 'up-and-coming'; (read: unspoiled and hoping to stay that way). There are some interesting festivals here, including an October Mushroom Festival and a November Celtic Music Festival, but the real beauty is in the setting, in particular lofty **Cape Perpetua**, 3 miles to the south and first sighted by Captain Cook in 1778. Volcanic intrusions have formed a beautifully rugged shoreline, with dramatic features such as the Devil's Churn, where powerful waves crash through a 30ft inlet. Hikes start from the **visitors center** (www.fs.fed.us/r6/siuslaw; ⌚10am-5pm May-Sep, to 4pm Wed-Sun Sep-May), including the 1.2-mile Captain Cook Trail down to Cook's Chasm and tide pools, and the precipitous 1.3-mile St Perpetus Trail through meadows to an astounding viewpoint.

Fifteen miles to the south on US 101 is the almost tourist trap but fun **Sea Lion Caves** (www.sealioncaves.com; adult/child $12/8; ⌚8am-6pm Jul & Aug, 9am-5:30pm Sep-Jun), a noisy grotto filled with groaning sea lions accessed via an elevator.

Camp at **Beachside State Park** (☎541-563-3220; www.oregonstateparks.org.com; tent/RV sites $21/26, yurts $40), 5 miles north on US 101 (reservations accepted). A mile further on is the quirky lesbian-owned **See Vue Motel** (☎541-547-3227; www.seevue.com; 95590 Hwy 101 S; d $95-120; @📶), whose 11 individually crafted rooms are perched high above the Pacific breakers. In town you can bed down at the posher **Overleaf Lodge** (☎541-547-4880; www.overleaflodge.com; 280 Overleaf Lodge Lane; d $190-290; @📶), a highly popular resort-spa where all rooms have ocean views and some also have balconies, Jacuzzis and fireplaces.

OREGON DUNES NATIONAL RECREATION AREA

Stretching for 50 miles between Florence and Coos Bay, the Oregon Dunes form the largest expanse of coastal dunes in the USA. The dunes tower up to 500ft and undulate inland as far as 3 miles to meet coastal forests, harboring curious ecosystems that sustain an abundance of wildlife. Hiking trails, bridle paths, and boating and swimming areas are available, but avoid the stretch south of Reedsport as noisy dune buggies dominate this area. Inform yourself at the Oregon Dunes National Recreation Area's **headquarters** (☎541-271-3495; www.fs.fed/us/r6/sius law; 855 Highway Ave; ⌚8am-4:30pm Mon-Fri, to 4pm Sat & Sun) in Reedsport.

State parks include popular **Jessie M Honeyman** (☎541-997-3641; US 101; tent/RV sites $17/22, yurts $29), 3 miles south of Florence, and pleasant **Umpqua Lighthouse**

(☎541-271-4118; US 101; tent/RV sites/yurts/cabins $16/20/27/35), 6 miles south of Reedsport. USFS campgrounds include **Eel Creek** (☎877-444-6777; US 101; campsites $17), 10 miles south of Reedsport.

PORT ORFORD

Occupying a rare natural harbor and guarding plenty of spectacular views, the hamlet of Port Orford (population 2000) sits on a headland wedged between two magnificent state parks. **Cape Blanco State Park**, 4 miles to the north, is the second most-westerly point in the continental USA, and the trail-crisscrossed promontory is often lashed by fierce 100mph winds. As well as hiking, visitors can tour the **Cape Blanco Lighthouse** (adult/child $2/free; ⏱10am-3:30pm Tue-Sun Apr-Oct), built in 1870, and the oldest and highest operational lighthouse in Oregon.

Six miles south of Port Orford, in **Humbug Mountain State Park**, mountains and sea meet in aqueous disharmony with plenty of angry surf. You can climb the 1750ft peak on a 3-mile trail through old-growth cedar groves.

For an affordable B&B call in at **Home by the Sea** (☎877-332-2855; www.homebythesea.com; 444 Jackson St; d $105-115; @📶), where crashing waves will (hopefully) lull you to sleep and first-class hospitality will wake you up. Food in this fishing village means a visit to the slick, view-embellished confines of newly opened **Redfish** (☎541-336-2200; 517 Jefferson St; mains $15-20; ⏱7am-10pm Wed-Sun) for organic Northwest haute cuisine.

GOLD BEACH

Situated at the mouth of the fabulous Rogue River, Gold Beach attracts anglers and adventurers looking to zip upstream via jet boat into the Wild Rogue Wilderness area. Hikers can appreciate the area's spectacular coastline; visit **Cape Sebastian State Park**, a rocky headland 7 miles south, for a panorama stretching from California to Cape Blanco. Get details at the **visitors center** (www.goldbeach.org; 94080 Shirley Lane; ⏱9am-5pm).

For rustic, modern or beach cabins (along with RV sites), head to **Ireland's Rustic Lodges** (☎541-247-7718; www.irelandsrusticlodges.com; 29346 Ellensburg Ave; d $79-149; 📶). There's a glorious garden area in front and beach views in back. Tasty cheeses, meats, soup and sandwiches can be had at **Patti's Rollin 'n Dough Bistro** (☎541-247-4438; 94257 N Bank Rogue Rd; mains $9-15; ⏱9am-3pm Tue-Sun summer, Wed-Sun winter), one of the coast's best cheap eats (reserve ahead).

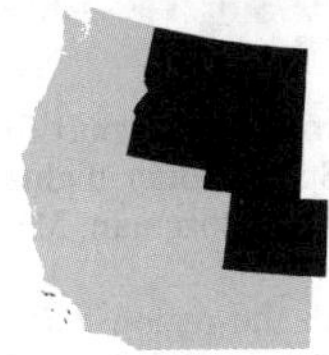

Rocky Mountains

Includes »

Best Places to Eat

» Kitchen (p252)
» Root Down (p245)
» Silk Road (p291)
» Pine Creek Cookhouse (p264)
» Domo (p245)
» Cafe Diva (p259)

Best Places to Stay

» Queen Anne Bed & Breakfast Inn (p244)
» Modern Hotel (p296)
» Chautauqua Lodge (p252)
» Alpine House (p284)
» Old Faithful Inn (p281)

Why Go?

The high backbone of the lower 48, the Rockies are nature on steroids, with rows of snowcapped peaks, rugged canyons and wild rivers running buckshot all over the Western states. With their beauty and vitality, it's no wonder that 100 years ago ailing patients came here with last-ditch hopes to be cured.

The Rocky Mountains' healing powers persist. You can choose between tranquility (try Wyoming, the USA's most under-populated state) and adrenaline (measured in vertical drop). Locals love a good mud-spattered adventure and, with plenty of climbing, skiing and white-water paddling, it's easy to join in. Afterwards, relax by soaking in hot springs under a roof of stars, sipping pints of cold microbrews or feasting on farm-to-table food.

Lastly, don't miss the supersized charms of Yellowstone, Rocky Mountain, Grand Teton and Glacier National Parks, where the big five (grizzly bears, moose, bison, mountain lions and wolves) still roam wild.

When to Go

Denver

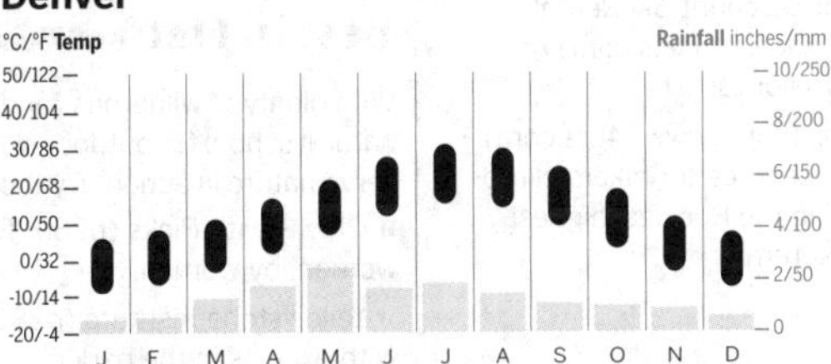

Jun-Aug Long days of sunshine ideal for biking, hiking, farmers markets and summer festivals.

Sep & Oct Fall foliage coincides with terrific lodging deals.

Jan & Feb Snow dusted peaks, powdery slopes, après-ski parties deluxe.

DON'T MISS

Don a Stetson and gallop the sagebrush wilderness of Wyoming or Montana.

Fast Facts

» Hub city: Denver (population 600,000)

» Denver to Yellowstone National Park: 595 miles

» Time zone: Mountain (two hours behind NYC)

» States covered in this chapter: Colorado, Idaho, Montana & Wyoming

Did You Know?

Pitch your tent in Yellowstone National Park and you'll be sleeping atop one of the world's largest supervolcanoes. It's active every 640,000 years: an eruption is due soon – give or take 10,000 years.

Resources

» Denver Post (www.denverpost.com) The region's top newspaper

» 5280 (www.5280.com) Denver's best monthly magazine

» Discount Ski Rental (www.rentskis.com) At major resorts

» 14ers (www.14ers.com) Resource for hikers climbing the Rockies' highest summits

Getting There & Around

Denver (DEN) has the only major international airport in the region. Both Denver and Colorado Springs offer flights on smaller planes to Jackson, WY, Boise, ID, Bozeman, MT, Aspen, CO, and other destinations.

Two Amtrak train routes pass through the region. *California Zephyr,* traveling daily between Emeryville, CA and Chicago, IL, has six stops in Colorado, including Denver, Fraser-Winter Park, Glenwood Springs and Grand Junction. *Empire Builder* runs daily from Seattle, WA, or Portland, OR, to Chicago, IL, with 12 stops in Montana (including Whitefish and East and West Glacier) and one stop in Idaho at Sandpoint.

Greyhound travels some parts of the Rocky Mountains. But to really get out and explore you'll need a car.

NATIONAL PARKS

The region is home to some of the USA's biggest national parks. In Colorado, **Rocky Mountain National Park** offers awesome hiking through alpine forests and tundra. There's also the Sahara-like wonder of **Great Sand Dunes National Park** and **Mesa Verde National Park**, an archaeological preserve with elaborate cliffside dwellings.

Wyoming has **Grand Teton National Park**, with dramatic craggy peaks, and **Yellowstone National Park**, the country's first national park, a true wonderland of volcanic geysers, hot springs and forested mountains. In Montana, **Glacier National Park** features high sedimentary peaks, small glaciers and lots of wildlife, including grizzly bears. Idaho is home to **Hells Canyon National Recreation Area**, where the Snake River carves the deepest canyon in North America. The **National Park Service** (NPS; www.nps.gov) also manages over two dozen other historic sites, monuments, nature preserves and recreational areas statewide.

Best in Outdoor Instruction

With plenty of wilderness and tough terrain, the Rockies are a natural school for outdoor skills, and a perfect place to observe nature in action. Try these:

» Chicks with Picks (p269) Fun ice-climbing clinics for women, by women.

» Yellowstone Institute (p280) Study wolves, ecology or arts with experts in the park.

» Teton Science Schools (p284) Best for kids; both about nature and in it.

» Colorado Mountain School (p256) Climb a peak safely or learn belay skills.

History

Before the late 18th century, when French trappers and Spaniards stepped in, the Rocky Mountain area was a land of many tribes, including the Nez Percé, the Shoshone, the Crow, the Lakota and the Ute.

Meriwether Lewis and William Clark claimed their enduring fame after the USA bought almost all of present-day Montana, Wyoming and eastern Colorado in the Louisiana Purchase in 1803. The two explorers set out to survey the land, covering 8000 miles in three years. Their success urged on other adventurers, and soon the migration was in motion. Wagon trains voyaged to the mountainous lands right into the 20th century, only temporarily slowed by the completion of the Transcontinental Railroad across southern Wyoming in the late 1860s.

To accommodate settlers, the US purged the western frontier of the Spanish, British and, in a truly shameful era, most of the Native American population. The government signed endless treaties to defuse Native American objections to increasing settlement, but always reneged and shunted tribes onto smaller reservations. Gold-miners' incursions into Native American territory in Montana and the building of US Army forts along the Bozeman Trail ignited a series of wars with the Lakota, Cheyenne, Arapaho and others.

Gold and silver mania preceded Colorado's entry to statehood in 1876. Statehood

ROCKY MOUNTAINS IN...

Two Weeks

Start your Rocky Mountain odyssey in the **Denver** area. Go tubing, vintage-clothes shopping or biking in outdoor-mad, totally boho **Boulder**, then soak up the liberal rays eavesdropping at a sidewalk cafe. Enjoy the vistas of the **Rocky Mountain National Park** before heading west on I-70 to play in the mountains around **Breckenridge**, which also has the best beginner slopes in Colorado. Go to ski and mountain bike mecca **Steamboat Springs** before crossing the border into Wyoming.

Your first stop in the state should be **Lander,** rock-climbing destination extraordinaire. Continue north to chic **Jackson** and the majestic **Grand Teton National Park** before hitting iconic **Yellowstone National Park**. Save at least three days for exploring this geyser-packed wonderland.

Cross the state line into 'big sky country' and slowly make your way northwest through Montana, stopping in funky **Bozeman** and lively **Missoula** before visiting **Flathead Lake**. Wind up your trip in Idaho. If it's summer, you can paddle the wild white-water of **Hells Canyon National Recreation Area** before continuing to up-and-coming **Boise**. End your trip with a few days skiing **Sun Valley** and partying in **Ketchum**. The town and ski resort, despite being *the* winter playground du jour for today's Hollywood set, are refreshingly unpretentious and affordable.

One Month

With a month on your hands, you can really delve into the region's off-the-beaten-path treasures. Follow the two-week itinerary, but dip southwest in Colorado – an up-and-coming wine region – before visiting Wyoming. Ride the 4WD trails around **Ouray**. Be sure to visit **Mesa Verde National Park** and its ancient cliff dwellings.

In Montana, you'll want to get lost backpacking in the **Bob Marshall Wilderness Complex** and visit **Glacier National Park** before the glaciers disappear altogether. In Idaho, spend more time playing in **Sun Valley** and be sure to explore the shops, pubs and yummy organic restaurants in delightful little **Ketchum**. With a one-month trip, you also have time to drive along a few of Idaho's fantastically remote scenic byways. Make sure you cruise Hwy 75 from Sun Valley north to **Stanley**. Situated on the wide banks of the Salmon River, this stunning mountain hamlet is completely surrounded by national forest land and wilderness areas. Wild good looks withstanding, Stanley is also blessed with world-class trout fishing and mild to wild rafting. Take Hwy 21 from Stanley to Boise. This scenic drive takes you through miles of dense ponderosa forests, and past some excellent, solitary riverside camping spots – some of which come with their own natural hot-springs pools.

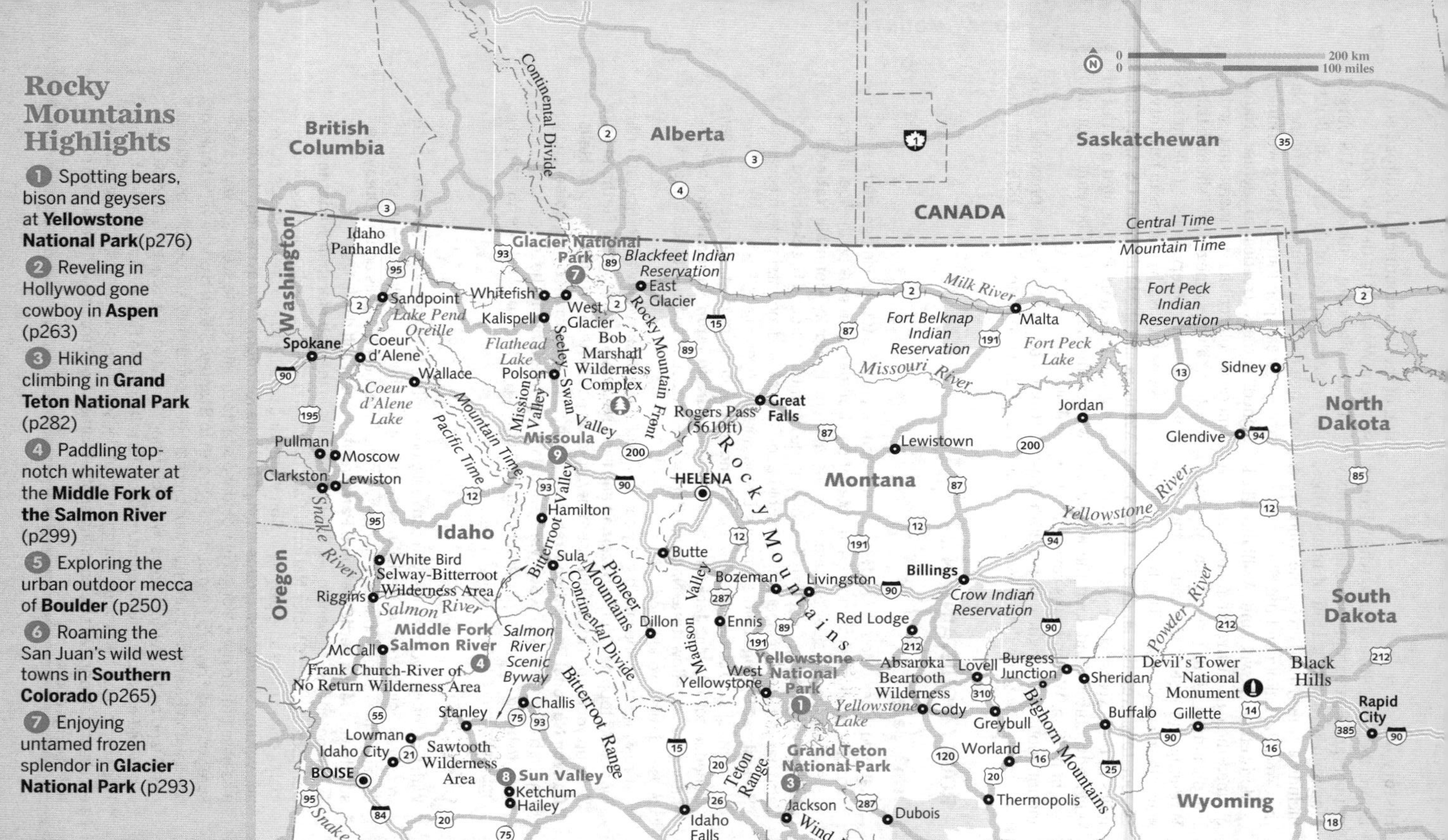
Rocky Mountains Highlights
1 Spotting bears, bison and geysers at Yellowstone National Park(p276)
2 Reveling in Hollywood gone cowboy in Aspen (p263)
3 Hiking and climbing in Grand Teton National Park (p282)
4 Paddling top-notch whitewater at the Middle Fork of the Salmon River (p299)
5 Exploring the urban outdoor mecca of Boulder (p250)
6 Roaming the San Juan's wild west towns in Southern Colorado (p265)
7 Enjoying untamed frozen splendor in Glacier National Park (p293)
0 200 km
0 100 miles
British Columbia
Alberta
Saskatchewan
CANADA
Continental Divide
Central Time
Mountain Time
Washington
Oregon
Idaho
Montana
Wyoming
North Dakota
South Dakota
Idaho Panhandle
Glacier National Park
Blackfeet Indian Reservation
East Glacier
West Glacier
Whitefish
Kalispell
Sandpoint
Lake Pend Oreille
Spokane
Coeur d'Alene
Coeur d'Alene Lake
Wallace
Flathead Lake
Polson
Mission Valley
Seeley-Swan Valley
Bob Marshall Wilderness Complex
Rocky Mountain Front
Rogers Pass (5610ft)
Great Falls
Missoula
Pacific Time
Pullman
Moscow
Clarkston
Lewiston
Snake River
Hamilton
Bitterroot Valley
HELENA
Rocky Mountains
Butte
Sula
Pioneer Mountains
Continental Divide
White Bird
Selway-Bitterroot Wilderness Area
Riggins
Salmon River
Middle Fork Salmon River
Salmon River Scenic Byway
McCall
Frank Church-River of No Return Wilderness Area
Bitterroot Range
Challis
Stanley
Lowman
Idaho City
Sawtooth Wilderness Area
BOISE
Sun Valley
Ketchum
Hailey
Dillon
Madison Valley
Bozeman
Ennis
Livingston
Idaho Falls
Teton Range
Grand Teton National Park
Jackson
Yellowstone National Park
West Yellowstone
Yellowstone Lake
Red Lodge
Absaroka Beartooth Wilderness
Cody
Dubois
Billings
Crow Indian Reservation
Lovell
Burgess Junction
Greybull
Worland
Thermopolis
Bighorn Mountains
Sheridan
Buffalo
Gillette
Devil's Tower National Monument
Black Hills
Rapid City
Powder River
Yellowstone River
Lewistown
Milk River
Fort Belknap Indian Reservation
Missouri River
Malta
Fort Peck Lake
Fort Peck Indian Reservation
Jordan
Glendive
Sidney

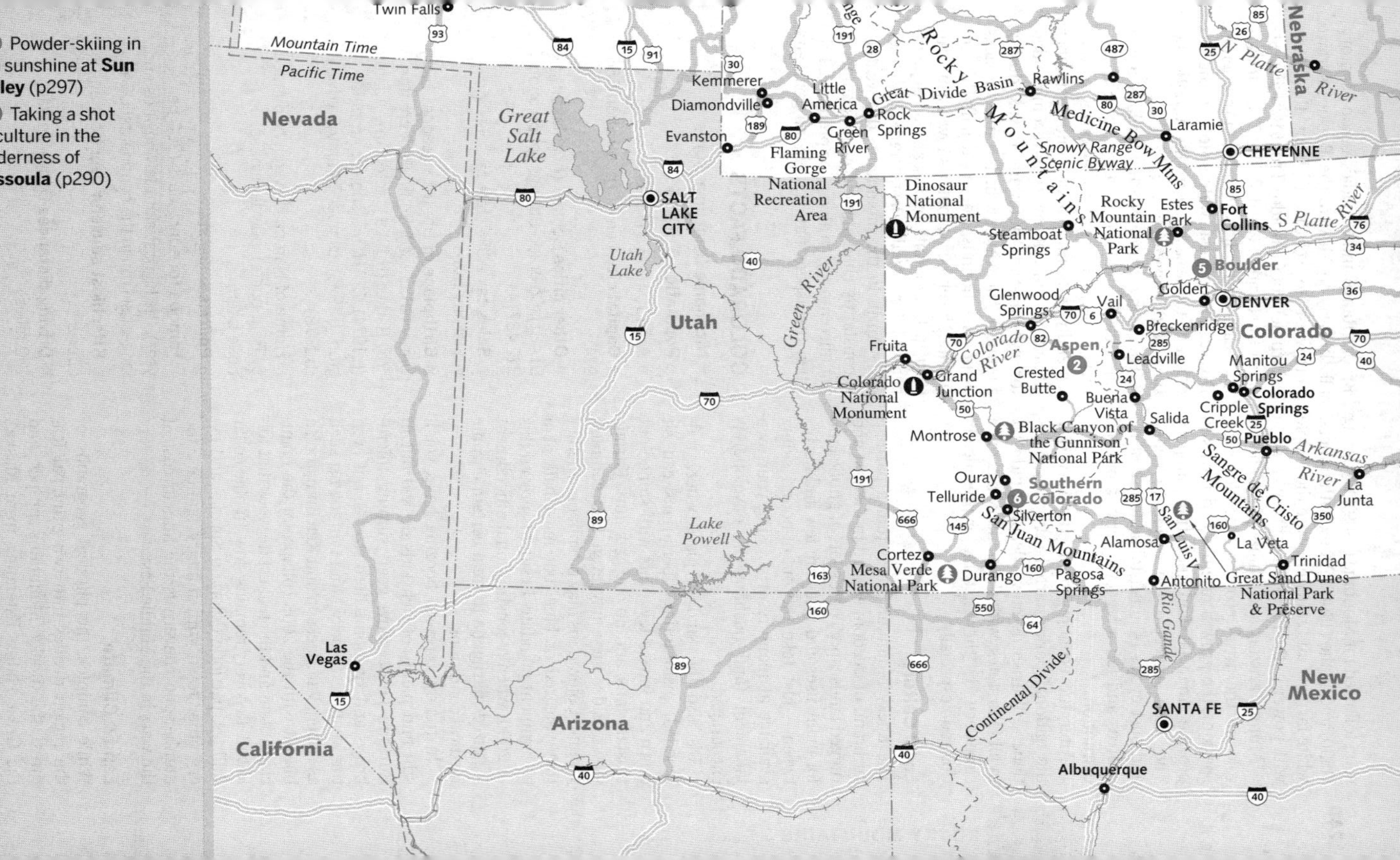

8 Powder-skiing in the sunshine at **Sun Valley** (p297)

9 Taking a shot of culture in the wilderness of **Missoula** (p290)

soon followed for Montana (1889), Wyoming (1890) and Idaho (1890). Along with miners, white farmers and ranchers were the people with power in the late 19th century.

Mining, grazing and timber played major roles in the area's economic development, sparking the growth of cities and towns to provide financial and industrial support. They also subjected the region to boom-and-bust cycles by unsustainable use of resources and left a legacy of environmental disruption.

After the economy boomed post-WWII, the national parks started attracting vacationers. Tourism is now a leading industry in all four states, with the military placing a close second – there is a major presence in Colorado especially.

Local Culture

The Rocky Mountain states tout a particular brand of freedom echoed in the vast and rugged landscape. There's lots of public land for many uses and rules are few and far between – just take the out-of-bound skiing available at many resorts. Using your own judgment (and pushing the envelope) is encouraged.

It's also the kind of place where red-blooded, pistol-toting libertarians can sit down and have a few pints with stoned-out trustafarians, and no one gets hurt. Karmic views aside, they may even find common ground. Coloradans may be split on whether they vote red or blue, but most balk at a government mandate. Residents proved this in 2000, when a constitutional amendment legalized marijuana to treat certain chronic medical conditions.

In trendy après-ski boozing holes you'll still find plenty of rich kids decked out in Burton's latest snow gear, sipping microbrews and swapping hero stories, but even the wealthiest Rocky Mountain towns, such as Aspen, Vail, Jackson and Ketchum, took a big hit with the 2008 collapse of the financial system and the real-estate woes that followed. Recovery remains slow. In blue-collar Billings, patriotic Colorado Springs and every other town with military families, the number-one concern is the human cost of the wars in the Middle East.

Land & Climate

While complex, the physical geography of the region divides into two principal features: the Rocky Mountains proper and the Great Plains. Extending from Alaska's Brooks Range and Canada's Yukon Territory all the way to Mexico, the Rockies sprawl northwest to southeast, from the steep escarpment of Colorado's Front Range westward to Nevada's Great Basin. Their towering peaks and ridges form the Continental Divide: to the west, waters flow to the Pacific, and to the east, toward the Atlantic and the Gulf of Mexico.

For many travelers, the Rockies are a summer destination. It starts to feel summery around June, and the warm weather generally lasts until about mid-September (though warm outerwear is recommended for evenings in mountain towns during summer). The winter, which brings in packs of powder hounds, doesn't usually hit until late November, though snowstorms can start in the mountains as early as September. Winter usually lasts until March or early April. In the mountains, the weather is constantly changing (snow in summer is not uncommon), so always be prepared. Fall, when the aspens flaunt their fall gold, and

COLORADO FACTS

- **Nickname** Centennial State
- **Population** 5 million
- **Area** 104,247 sq miles
- **Capital city** Denver (population 566, 974)
- **Other cities** Boulder (population 91,481), Colorado Springs (population 372,437)
- **Sales tax** 2.9% state tax, plus individual city taxes
- **Birthplace of** Ute tribal leader Chief Ouray (1833–80); South Park creator Trey Parker (b 1969); actor Amy Adams (b 1974); *127 Hours* subject Aron Ralston (b 1975), climber Tommy Caldwell (b 1978)
- **Home of** Naropa University (founded by Beat poets), powder slopes, boutique beers
- **Politics** swing state
- **Famous for** sunny days (300 per year), the highest altitude vineyards and longest ski run in the continental USA
- **Kitschiest souvenir** deer-hoof bottle openers
- **Driving distances** Denver to Vail 100 miles

early summer, when wildflowers bloom, are wonderful times to visit.

Getting There & Around

Travel here takes time. The Rockies are sparsely developed, with attractions spread across long distances and linked by roads that meander between mountains and canyons. With limited public transportation, touring in a private vehicle is best. After all, road-tripping is one of *the* reasons to explore this scenic region.

In rural areas services are few and far between – the I-80 across Wyoming is a notorious offender. It's not unusual to go more than 100 miles between gas stations. When in doubt, fill up.

The main travel hub is **Denver International Airport** (DIA; www.flydenver.com), although if you are coming on a domestic flight, check out **Colorado Springs Airport** (COS; www.springsgov.com/airportindex.aspx) as well: fares are often lower, it's quicker to navigate than DIA and it's nearly as convenient. Both Denver and Colorado Springs offer flights on smaller planes to cities and resort towns around the region – Jackson, WY, Boise, ID, Bozeman, MT, and Aspen, CO, are just a few options. Salt Lake City, UT, also has connections with destinations in all four states.

Greyhound (800-231-2222; www.greyhound.com) has fixed routes throughout the Rockies, and offers the most comprehensive bus service. The following **Amtrak** (800-872-7245; www.amtrak.com) services run to and around the region:

California Zephyr Daily between Emeryville, CA (in San Francisco Bay Area), and Chicago, IL, with six stops in Colorado, including Denver, Fraser-Winter Park, Glenwood Springs and Grand Junction.

Empire Builder Runs daily from Seattle, WA, or Portland, OR, to Chicago, IL, with 12 stops in Montana (including Whitefish and East and West Glacier) and one stop in Idaho at Sandpoint.

COLORADO

Graced with the greatest concentration of high peaks – dubbed 14ers for their height of 14000ft – Colorado is a burly state. From its double-diamond powder runs to the stout microbrews and stiff espresso drinks, all this sunny energy conspires to remind you of this. With universities and hopping high-tech, Coloradans do have a highly industrious side, though more than a few will call in sick to work when snow starts dumping in the high country.

It's no wonder that so many East Coasters, Californians and everyone in between have come to make their homes in this modern Shangri-La, propped up by Latin American workers meeting the endless needs of the hospitality industry. While much of the state is considered conservative, many Coloradans care deeply about environmental issues and have a friendly can-do ethos that is inspiring.

Information

Colorado Road Conditions (877-315-7623; www.state.co.us) Highway advisories.

Colorado State Parks (303-470-1144; www.parks.state.co.us) Tent and RV sites cost from $10 to $24 per night, depending on facilities. Rustic cabins and yurts are also available in some parks and those with wood-burning stoves may be available year-round. Advance reservations for specific campsites are taken, but subject to a $10 nonrefundable booking fee. Reservation changes cost $6.

Colorado Travel & Tourism Authority (800-265-6723; www.colorado.com) State-wide tourism information.

Denver Post (www.denverpost.com) Denver's major daily newspaper.

Denver

Spirited, urbane and self-aware, Denver is the region's cosmopolitan capital. The gleaming skyscrapers of Denver's Downtown and historic LoDo districts sit packed with breweries and the best culinary scene between Chicago and California – not to mention the 40ft blue bear and 60ft dancer sculptures. In the iconic sports arenas of Invesco Field at Mile High and Coors Field, home runs, high fives and mobs of rabid sports fans are nearly a nightly spectacle. Way off in the distance, rising though the high-altitude haze and all that thin air, is the jagged purple line of the Front Range, a gateway to some of the most spectacular wilderness on the continent. There's a whole lot to do in Denver.

The city is compact and friendly. Sitting at exactly 5280ft (1 mile) high – hence the nickname 'Mile High City' – this one-time Wild West railway town is a cool place to acclimatize, with low humidity and lots of Colorado sunshine.

Sights & Activities

16th Street Mall & LoDo NEIGHBORHOOD

The 16th Street Mall, a pedestrian-only strip of downtown, is lined with shops, restaurants and bars. The funkier **LoDo**, around Larimer Sq, is the best place to have a drink or browse the boutiques.

Denver Art Museum MUSEUM
(☎720-865-5000; www.denverartmuseum.org; 100 W 14th Ave; adult/student $13/10; 1st Sat of month free; ⊙10am-5pm Tue-Thu, Sat & Sun, 10am-8pm Fri) The DAM is home to one of the largest Native American art collections in the US and puts on special avant-garde multimedia exhibits. The Western American Art section of the permanent collection is justifiably famous.

Denver

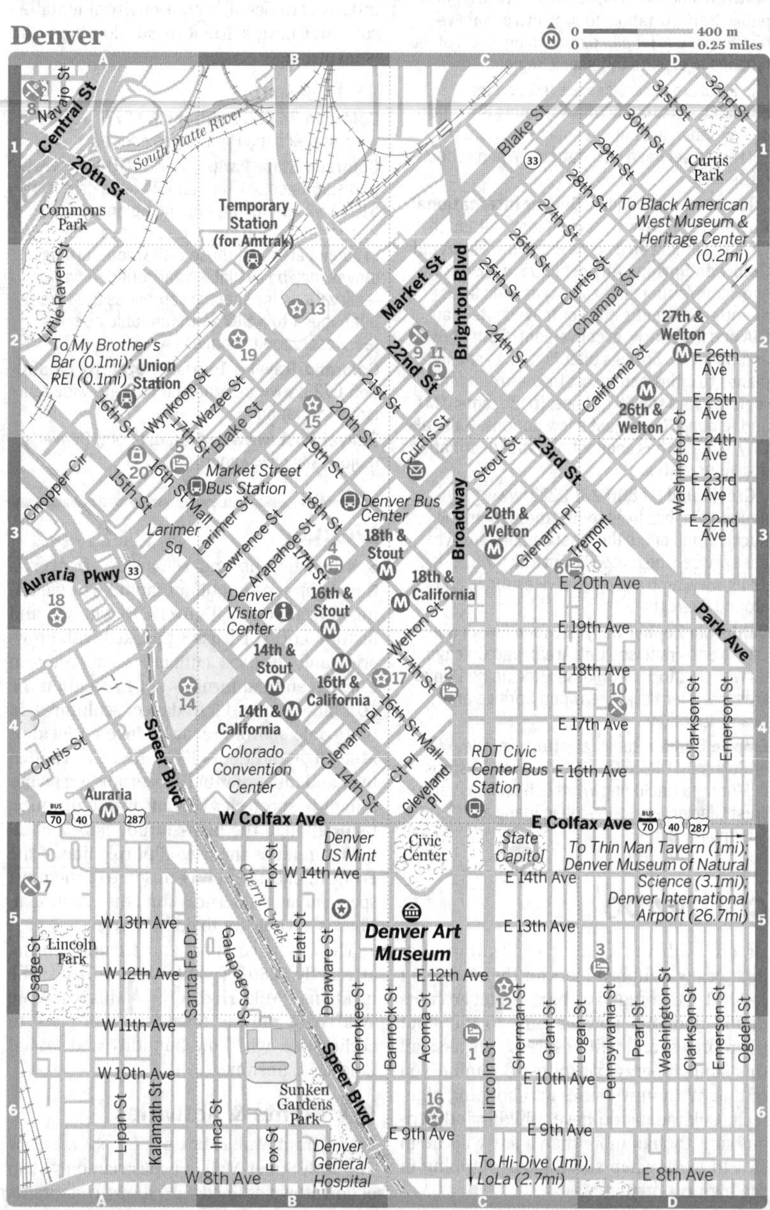

The $110-million Frederic C Hamilton wing, designed by Daniel Libeskind, is a strange, angular, fanlike edifice. It's inspired and mesmerizing. If you think the place looks weird from the outside, look inside: shapes shift with each turn, thanks to a combination of design and uncanny natural-light tricks.

Black American West Museum & Heritage Center MUSEUM

(☎303-482-2242; www.blackamericanwestmuseum.com; 3091 California St; adult/child $8/6; ⏰10am-2pm Tue-Sat) Denver is also home to the excellent Black American West Museum & Heritage Center, dedicated to 'telling history how it was.' It provides an intriguing look at the contributions of African Americans during the pioneer era – according to museum statistics, one in three Colorado cowboys were African American.

Red Rocks Park & Amphitheatre ARTS CENTER

(☎303-640-2637; www.redrocksonline.com; 16352 County Rd 93; park admission free; ⏰5am-11pm) Set between 400ft-high red sandstone rocks 15 miles southwest of Denver, this natural amphitheater was a Ute camping spot. Acoustics are so good, artists record live albums here. The 9000-seat theater offers stunning views and draws big-name bands.

Children's Museum MUSEUM

(☎303-433-7444; www.mychildsmuseum.org; 2121 Children's Museum Dr; admission $8; ⏰9am-4pm Mon-Fri, 10am-5pm Sat & Sun; 👪) If you've got kids, check out the Children's Museum, which is full of excellent interactive exhibits. A particularly well-regarded section is the kid-size grocery store, where your little consumers can push a shopping cart of their very own while learning about food and health. In the 'Arts à la carte' section kids can get creative with crafts that they can take home, using recycled materials.

Denver Museum of Nature & Science MUSEUM

(☎303-322-7009; www.dmns.org; 2001 Colorado Blvd; museum adult/child $12/6, IMAX $10/8; ⏰9am-5pm; 👪) Located 3.5 miles east of downtown, it has an IMAX theater, the Gates Planetarium and absorbing exhibits for all ages.

Festivals & Events

FREE **Cinco de Mayo** CULTURAL

(☎303-534-8342; www.cincodemayodenver.com; Civic Center Park) Enjoy salsa music and margaritas at one of the country's biggest Cinco de Mayo celebrations, held over two days on the first weekend in May. With three stages and more than 350 exhibitors and food vendors, it's huge fun.

Cherry Creek Arts Festival ARTS

(www.cherryarts.org; cnr Clayton St & E 3rd Ave) A sprawling celebration of visual, culinary and performing arts where a quarter of a million visitors browse the giant block party. The three-day event takes place around July 4.

Taste of Colorado FOOD

(☎303-295-6330; www.atasteofcolorado.com; Civic Center Park) Food stalls of over 50

Denver

Top Sights

Denver Art Museum ... C5

Sleeping

1 11th Avenue Hotel ... C6
2 Brown Palace Hotel ... C4
3 Capitol Hill Mansion B&B ... D5
4 Hotel Monaco ... B3
5 Jet Hotel ... A3
6 Queen Anne Bed & Breakfast Inn ... C3

Eating

7 Domo Restaurant ... A5
8 Root Down ... A1
9 Snooze ... C2
10 Steuben's Food Service ... D4

Drinking

11 Great Divide Brewing Company ... C2
Jet Lounge ... (see 5)

Entertainment

12 Church ... C5
13 Coors Field ... B2
14 Denver Center for the Performing Arts ... A4
15 El Chapultepec ... B2
16 La Rumba ... C6
17 Paramount Theatre ... B4
18 Pepsi Center ... A3
19 Sing Sing ... B2

Shopping

20 Tattered Cover Bookstore ... A3

restaurants; there's also booze, live music, and arts-and-crafts vendors at this Labor Day festival.

Great American Beer Festival BEER
(☎303-447-0816, 1888-822-627; www.greatamericanbeerfestival.com; 700 14th St) Colorado has more microbreweries than any other US state, and this hugely popular event in early September sells out in advance. More than 500 breweries are represented, from the big players to the home-brew enthusiasts.

Sleeping

Besides the places mentioned here, there are chain and independent motels throughout the city, with rooms starting at $75. Check out **Lonely Planet Hotels & Hostels** (www.lonelyplanet.com/hotels), with a range of sleeping options in the Denver 'burbs. Those on a budget should consider the very clean International Youth Hostel in nearby Boulder, as Denver's hostels were catering more to transients than backpackers when we dropped by.

TOP CHOICE **Queen Anne Bed & Breakfast Inn** B&B $$
(☎303-296-6666; www.queenannebnb.com; 2147 Tremont Pl; r incl breakfast $135-215; P❄☎) Earthy, cool and modern, this outstanding B&B is also cutting-edge sustainable. That means almost zero waste, a high standard of recycling and composting, locally sourced furnishings and gorgeous edible gardens. But the verve and romance comes mainly from its design. Four Denver artists have remade the suites with stunning results. Highlights include a forest mural that engulfs guests slumbering in organic bed sheets and a playful suite with oversized modern art in black-and-white motifs.

Chef-owner Milan Doshi keeps the kitchen on too. Guests get happy hour with Colorado wines and hors d'oeuvres. Breakfasts vary from waffles with blueberries and lavender to Indian-style potato pancakes. Free townie bikes let you ditch the car to explore Denver like a local

Hotel Monaco BOUTIQUE HOTEL $$$
(☎303-296-1717; www.monaco-denver.com; 1717 Champa St; r from $199; P❄@☎) This ultra-stylish boutique joint is a favorite with the celebrity set. Modern rooms blend French and art deco – think bold colors and fabulous European-style feather beds. Don't miss the evening 'Altitude Adjustment Hour,' when guests enjoy free wine and five-minute massages. The place is 100% pet-friendly; staff will even deliver a named goldfish to your room upon request. Discounts are routinely offered online.

Capitol Hill Mansion B&B B&B $$
(☎303-839-5221; www.capitolhillmansion.com; 1207 Pennsylvania St; r incl breakfast $119-219; P❄@☎) Stained-glass windows, original 1890s woodwork and turrets make this delightful, gay- and family-friendly Romanesque mansion a special place to stay. Rooms are elegant, uniquely decorated and come with different special features – one has a solarium, another boasts Jacuzzi tubs.

Brown Palace Hotel HISTORIC HOTEL $$$
(☎303-297-3111; www.brownpalace.com; 321 17th St; r from $299; P❄) Gaze up to the stained-glass crowned atrium and it's clear why this palace is shortlisted among the country's elite historic hotels. There's deco artwork, a four-star spa, imported marble, and staff who discretely float down the halls. The rooms, which have been hosting presidents since Teddy Roosevelt's days, have the elegance of a distant era.

One of the coolest features is the pianist playing Gershwin and ragtime favorites (we hear rooms on the 4th and 5th floors have an acoustically perfect perch).

If it's beyond your budget, ask a concierge for a free self-guided tour or check out tea time or a cocktail. The martini is predictably perfect and served with a sterling bowl of warm pecans.

Jet Hotel BOUTIQUE HOTEL $$
(☎303-572-3300; www.thejethotel.com; 1612 Wazee St; r $99-169; P❄@☎) Priced for partying, this slick (if slightly pretentious) boutique hotel in the heart of LoDo is all about fun, especially on weekends. That's when Denver's beautiful people come for the slumber-party-with-bottle-service experience – you can dance all night in the swank 1st-floor lounge, then stumble up to your bold lollipop-color quarters, burrow under the thick white comforters and sleep until brunch. Stay on a weekday if you want a posh central hotel room without the boozy party scene and accompanying noise. The healthy Asian fusion menu of the Swing Thai is perfect for kicking last night's hangover.

11th Avenue Hotel HOTEL $
(☎303-894-0529; www.11thavenuehotel.com; 1112 Broadway; dm $20, s/d $43/54, without bath

WHAT THE...?

So you just get into Denver and you have a few microbrews and suddenly your head is swirling. What's going on? Longstanding claims say that a person gets drunk quicker at high altitudes. Recent studies, including some conducted by the FAA, prove this to be untrue. However, don't say 'make mine a double' just yet. While altitude doesn't change how the body metabolizes alcohol, studies show it may exacerbate problems with acclimating, such as headaches and dizziness.

$37/48; ❄📶) Well located in the Golden Triangle district, this bare budget hotel may look vaguely like something from a Jim Jarmusch movie, but it's clean. Part of its MO is to assist people recovering from drug and alcohol problems (staff and residents) with affordable accommodations. It's safe, secure and a decent place for budget travelers.

Eating

Cheap street meals are found on the 16th St Mall. The pedestrian mall and LoDo are full of restaurants catering to all budgets and continents, and many of them have great sidewalk seating in the summer months.

TOP CHOICE Steuben's Food Service AMERICAN $$
(☎303-803-1001; www.steubens.com; 523 E 17th Ave; mains $8-21; ⏰11am-11pm Sun-Thu, 11am-midnight Fri & Sat; 👪) Although styled as a mid-century drive-in, the upscale treatment of comfort food (mac 'n' cheese, fried chicken, lobster rolls) and the solar-powered kitchen demonstrate Steuben's contemporary smarts. In summer, open garage doors lining the street create a breezy atmosphere and bargains come after 10pm with a burger, hand-cut fries and beer for $5.

Follow the restaurant on Facebook or Twitter to get details about Steuben's mobile truck, powered by recycled veggie oil and often seen at Civic Park.

Root Down MODERN AMERICAN $$$
(☎303-993-4200; www.rootdowndenver.com; 1600 W 33rd Ave; small plates $6-15; ⏰5-10pm Sun-Thu, 5-11pm Fri & Sat, brunch 10am-2:30pm Sat & Sun) In a converted gas station, chef Justin Cucci has undertaken one of the city's most ambitious culinary concepts, marrying sustainable 'field-to-fork' practices, high-concept culinary fusions and a low-impact, energy-efficient ethos. The menu changes seasonally, but consider yourself lucky if it includes the sweet-potato falafel or hoisin-duck confit sliders.

Root Down is largely wind-powered and decorated with reused and reclaimed materials, and it recycles *everything*. It's conceptually brilliant and one of Denver's most thrilling dining experiences.

Domo Restaurant JAPANESE $$
(☎303-595-3666; www.domorestaurant.com; 1365 Osage St; mains $10-22) Nestled in a beautiful Japanese garden, Denver's best Japanese restaurant is undeniably a romantic spot. This is Japanese country food and quality sushi too good to be served with heaps of soy. Each main is accompanied by seven traditional side dishes. The spicy *maguro* and *hamachi* combination *donburi* is an explosively flavorful combination of fresh fish, seaweed and chili-soy dressing.

Snooze CAFE $
(☎303-297-0700; www.snoozeeatery.com; 2262 Larimer St; mains $4-12; ⏰6:30am-2:30pm Mon-Fri, 7am-12:30pm Sat & Sun; 👪) Stomachs unite and grumble for this brick cafe's soft breakfast tacos with ranchero sauce, sweet potato pancakes with ginger sauce or salmon benedict. Creative and fresh, it's a strong start to any day. The restaurant also has a strong sustainability focus, which includes using local organic produce.

LoLa MEXICAN $
(☎720-570-8686; www.loladenver.com; 1575 Boulder St; mains $4-12; ⏰5pm-close Mon-Fri, 10am-2pm & 2:30-5pm Sat & Sun) Bringing costal Mexican to a landlocked town, LoLa pleases with fresh, smoky, chili-infused fare, best paired with a fantastic cocktail (try the hibiscus tea with citrus-infused tequila). Everybody loves the guacamole that's handmade at your table. To continue the party, check out the downstairs tequila bar. To get there, take 15th St past Confluence Park.

Drinking

Most bars and nightspots are in LoDo and around Coors Field. The biweekly gay newspaper *Out Front*, found in coffee shops and bars, has entertainment listings. Many of the venues listed in the Eating section of this book are also bars.

Great Divide Brewing Company BREWPUB
(www.greatdivide.com; 2201 Arapahoe St; ⌚2-8pm Mon & Tue, 2-10pm Wed-Sat) An excellent local brewery focused on crafting exquisite beer. Belly up to the bar and try the spectrum of seasonal brews.

Thin Man Tavern BAR
(www.thinmantavern.com; 2015 E 17th Ave) Considered among the best low-key singles' spots in the city, this neighborhood tavern is unexpectedly decked out with old Catholic paintings and ambient vintage lampshades. See free art films in the basement-level Ubisububi Room or classics flicks outside in the parking lot in summer.

Jet Lounge BAR
(www.thejethotel.com; 1612 Wazee St) This place to see and be seen in Denver has a bedroom-meets-house-party vibe: candles, cozy couches and a weekend DJ. Order bottle service, sit back and melt into the party.

My Brother's Bar BAR
(2376 15th St) Classic rock and roll, lacquered booths and tables made from old wood barrels greet you inside Denver's oldest bar. Grab a seat on the leafy patio if it's nice outside. The bar is on a popular cycle path, and has been a local institution since it opened.

☆ Entertainment

To find out what's happening with music, theater and other performing arts, pick up a free copy of *Westword*.

TOP CHOICE **Hi-Dive** LIVE MUSIC
(☎720-570-4500; www.hi-dive.com; 7 S Broadway) Local rock heroes and touring indie bands light up the stage at the Hi-Dive, a venue at the heart of Denver's local music scene. During big shows it gets deafeningly loud, cheek-to-jowl with hipsters and humid as an armpit. In other words, it's perfect.

El Chapultepec LIVE MUSIC
(☎303-295-9126; 1962 Market St; ⌚7am-2am, music from 9pm) This smoky little old-school joint is a dedicated jazz venue attracting a diverse clientele. Since it opened in 1951 Frank Sinatra, Tony Bennett and Ella Fitzgerald have played here, as have Jagger and Richards. Local jazz bands take the tiny stage nightly, but you never know who might drop by.

Grizzly Rose LIVE MUSIC
(www.grizzlyrose.com; 5450 N Valley Hwy; ⌚from 6pm Tue-Sun; 👪) This is one kick-ass honky-tonk – 40,000 sq ft of hot live music – attracting cowboys from as far away as Cheyenne. The Country Music Association called it the best country bar in America. If you've never experienced line dancing, then put on the boots, grab the Stetson and let loose.

Just north of the city limits off I-25 (you'll have to drive or cab it), the Grizzly is famous for bringing in huge industry stars – Willie Nelson, Lee Ann Rimes – for more than reasonable ticket prices.

La Rumba CLUB
(www.larumba-denver.com; 99 W 9th Ave; ⌚9pm-2am Fri-Sun) Though this place wobbles along as a salsa club the rest of the weekend, its Club Lip Gloss on Friday nights is a great party. Indie rock, garage and British pop bring an ultra-hip, gay-friendly vibe to the dance floor.

Church CLUB
(1160 Lincoln St) In a former cathedral, this club draws a large and diverse, though young, crowd. Lit by hundreds of altar candles and flashing blue strobe lights, it has three dance floors, a couple of lounges and even a sushi bar! Arrive before 10pm on weekends to avoid the $10 cover charge.

Sing Sing BAR
(☎303-291-0880; 1735 19th St) Very popular with bachelorette parties, this campy dueling piano bar fills quickly. Arrive around 6:30pm to score a table near the pianos. It's loud and the food is lackluster but the atmosphere is really fun. Song requests are taken (usually accompanied by $5).

Denver Performing Arts Complex PERFORMING ARTS
(☎720-865-4220; www.artscomplex.com; cnr 14th & Champa St) This massive complex – one of the largest of its kind – occupies four city blocks and houses several major theaters, the historic Ellie Caulkins Opera House and the Seawell Grand Ballroom. It's also home to the Colorado Ballet, Denver Center for the Performing Arts, Opera Colorado and the Colorado Symphony Orchestra.

Paramount Theatre CONCERT VENUE
(☎303-534-8336; www.denverparamount.com; 1621 Glenarm Pl) Music venue for national acts.

Invesco Field at Mile High STADIUM
(☎720-258-3000; www.invescofieldatmilehigh.com; 1805 S Bryant St; 👪) The much-lauded Denver Broncos football team and the Colorado Rapids soccer team play here, 1 mile

west of Downtown. It also plays host to big acts, like U2.

Coors Field BASEBALL
(800-388-7625; www.mlb.com/col/ballpark/; 2001 Blake St;) Denver is a city known for manic sports fans, and boasts five pro teams. The Colorado Rockies play baseball at the highly rated Coors Field.

Pepsi Center STADIUM
(303-405-1111; www.pepsicenter.com; 1000 Chopper Circle) The mammoth Pepsi Center hosts the Denver Nuggets basketball team, the Colorado Mammoth of the National Lacrosse League and the Colorado Avalanche hockey team. In off-season it's a mega concert venue.

Shopping

The pedestrian-only 16th St Mall and the boutiques of LoDo are the city's main downtown shopping areas.

TOP CHOICE **Tattered Cover Bookstore** BOOKS
(1628 16th St; 6:30am-9pm Mon-Fri, 9am-9pm Sat, 10am-6pm Sun) Denver's most loved bookstore is in this main shopping area. The armchair-travel section is wonderful – curl into the battered and comfy chairs scattered around the shop.

REI OUTDOOR EQUIPMENT, SPORTS
(Recreational Equipment Incorporated; 303-756-3100; www.rei.com; 1416 Platte St) The flagship store of this outdoor equipment supplier is an essential stop for those using Denver as a springboard into the great outdoors. In addition to top gear for camping, cycling, climbing and skiing, it has a rental department, maps and the Pinnacle, a 47ft indoor structure of simulated red sandstone for climbing and repelling.

There's also a desk of Colorado's Outdoor Recreation Information Center, where you can get information on state and national parks.

Information

In the event of a citywide emergency, radio station KOA (850 AM) is a designated point of information.

5280 Monthly glossy mag, has a comprehensive dining guide.

Denver Post (www.denverpost.com) The mainstream newspaper.

Denver Visitor Center (303-892-1505; www.denver.org; 918 16th St; 9am-5pm Mon-Fri)

ORIC Desk (Outdoor Recreation Information Center; REI main line 303-756-3100; www.oriconline.org; 1416 Platte St;) For outdoor trips, hit this desk inside the REI store, with maps and expert information. Hosts free Discover Colorado classes every Sunday at 3pm.

Police Headquarters (720-913-2000; 1331 Cherokee St)

Post office (951 20th St; 8am-6:30pm Mon-Fri, 9am-6:30pm Sat) Main branch.

University Hospital (303-399-1211; 4200 E 9th Ave; 24hr) Emergency services.

Westword (www.westword.com) This free weekly is the best source for local events.

Getting There & Away

Denver International Airport (DIA; www.flydenver.com; 8500 Peña Blvd) is served by around 20 airlines and offers flights to nearly every major US city. Located 24 miles east of downtown, DIA is connected with I-70 exit 238 by 12-mile-long Peña Blvd. Tourist and airport information is available at a **booth** (303-342-2000) in the terminal's central hall.

Greyhound buses stop at **Denver Bus Center** (303-293-6555; 1055 19th St), which runs services to Boise (from $151, 19 hours), Los Angeles (from $125, 22 hours) and other destinations.

Amtrak's *California Zephyr* runs daily between Chicago and San Francisco via Denver. Trains arrive and depart from a **Temporary Station** (1800 21st St) behind Coors Field until light-rail renovations at Union Station finish in 2014. For recorded information on arrival and departure times, call 303-534-2812. **Amtrak** (800-872-7245; www.amtrak.com) can also provide schedule information and train reservations.

Getting Around

To/From the Airport

All transportation companies have booths near the baggage-claim area. Public **Regional Transit District** (RTD; 303-299-6000; www.rtd-denver.com) runs a SkyRide service to the airport from downtown Denver hourly ($9 to $13, one hour). RTD also goes to Boulder ($13, 1½ hours) from the **Market Street Bus Station** (cnr 16th & Market Sts). **Shuttle King Limo** (303-363-8000; www.shuttlekinglimo.com) charges $20 to $35 for rides from DIA to destinations in and around Denver. **SuperShuttle** (303-370-1300) offers shared van services (from $22) between the Denver area and the airport.

Bicycle

For two-wheel transportation, **Denver B-Cycle** (denver.bcycle.com) is a new, citywide program that has townie bikes available at strategic locations, but riders must sign up online first (24 hours $6).

Car & Motorcycle

Street parking can be a pain, but there are slews of pay garages in downtown and LoDo. Nearly all the major car-rental agencies have counters at DIA, a few have offices in downtown Denver. Before you rent, check rates where you will be staying – it may be considerably cheaper than the airport.

Public Transportation

RTD provides public transportation throughout the Denver and Boulder area. Local buses cost $2.25 for local services, $4 for express services. Useful free shuttle buses run along the 16th St Mall.

RTD also operates a light-rail line serving 16 stations on a 12-mile route through downtown. Fares are the same as for local buses.

Taxi

For 24-hour cab service:

Metro Taxi (☎303-333-3333)

Zone Cab (☎303-444-8888)

Front Range

In addition to Denver, the Front Range is home to Colorado Springs, Boulder and Rocky Mountain National Park. Colorado's most populated region – and still growing – it's the launch pad for most Rocky Mountain adventures. I-25 is the north–south artery along the Front Range (which is just a name for this part of the Rocky Mountains), with Colorado Springs and Denver, 65 miles apart, both sitting on this highway.

COLORADO SPRINGS

The site of one of the country's first destination resorts, Colorado Springs sits at the foot of stunning Pikes Peak. You can summit this 14er by cars or cog railway or just lace up your boots and hike it. The city's craggy, striking red-rock vein that juts and runs for more than 10 miles is best admired at the Garden of the Gods.

Pinned down with four military bases, Colorado Springs is also a strange and sprawling quilt of neighborhoods of old (and new) money in Broadmoor, the evangelized planned community that is Briargate, the hippie stronghold of Manitou Springs, the pioneer sector of Old Colorado City, and finally the downtown district which mixes fine art, Olympic dreams and, yes, a touch of downbeat desperation.

Sights & Activities

TOP CHOICE **Pikes Peak** MOUNTAIN

(☎719-385-7325; www.springsgov.com; Pikes Peak; per adult/child/5-person car $12/5/40, cog railway round-trip adult/child $33/18; ⌚9am-3pm winter, 7:30am-8pm Memorial Day-Labor Day, 9am-5pm Oct 1-Memorial Day) At 14,110ft, Pikes Peak may not be one of the tallest of Colorado's 54 14ers, but it's certainly the most famous. Maybe because it's the only one with a road and a train to the top? That's where you'll find an observation platform and a kitschy gift shop.

FREE **Garden of the Gods** PARK

(☎719-634-6666; www.gardenofgods.com; 1805 N 30th St; ⌚8am-8pm Memorial Day-Labor Day, 9am-5pm Labor Day-Memorial Day) A compound

DON'T MISS

CLIMBING YOUR FIRST 14ER

Known as Colorado's easiest 14er, **Quandary Peak** (www.fs.usda.gov; County Rd 851; 👪), near Breckenridge, is the state's 15th highest peak at 14,265ft. Though you will see plenty of dogs and children, 'easiest' may be misleading – the summit remains three grueling miles from the trailhead. Go between June and September.

The trail ascends to the west; after about 10 minutes of moderate climbing, follow the right fork to a trail junction. Head left, avoiding the road, and almost immediately you will snatch some views of Mt Helen and Quandary (although the real summit is still hidden).

Just below timberline you'll meet the trail from Monte Cristo Gulch – note it so you don't take the wrong fork on your way back down. From here it's a steep haul to the top. Start early and aim to turn around by noon, as afternoon lightning is typical during summer. It's a 6-mile round-trip, taking roughly between seven and eight hours. To get here, take Colorado 9 to County Rd 850. Make a right and turn right again onto 851. Drive 1.1 miles to the unmarked trailhead. Park parallel on the fire road.

of 13 bouldered peaks and soaring red-rock pinnacles accessed by a network of concrete paths and trails. It's a great place for families.

FREE **Barr Trail** HIKING

You can also reach the Pike's Peak summit on foot, via the tough 12.5-mile Barr Trail. From the trailhead, just above the Manitou Springs depot, the path climbs 7300ft. Fit hikers should reach the top in about eight hours, but should leave very early to avoid dangerous afternoon thunderstorms. Many hikers split the trip into two days, stopping to acclimatize overnight at Barr Camp at the halfway point (10,200ft).

Colorado Springs Fine Arts Center MUSEUM

(FAC; ☎719-634-5583; www.csfineartscenter.org; 30 W Dale St; adult/senior & student $10/8.50; ⏲10am-5pm Tue-Sun) A sophisticated collection with terrific Latin American art, Mexican clay figures, Native American basketry and quilts, wood-cut prints from social justice artist Leopold Mendez, and abstract work from local artists. Recently and beautifully redone, it also houses a fine restaurant and cafe.

Festivals & Events

Colorado Balloon Classic BALLOONING

(☎719-471-4833; www.balloonclassic.com; 1605 E Pikes Peak Ave) For 35 years running, hot-air ballooners, both amateur and pro, have been launching Technicolor balloons just after sunrise for three straight days over the Labor Day weekend. You'll have to wake with the roosters to see it all, but it's definitely worth your while.

Emma Crawford Coffin Races RACE

(www.manitousprings.org; Manitou Ave) In 1929 the coffin of Emma Crawford was unearthed by erosion and slid down Red Mountain. Today, coffins are decked out with wheels and run down Manitou Ave for three hours on the Saturday before Halloween (October).

Sleeping

There are cheap 1950s-style independent motels on Nevada Ave about 1 mile north and 1 mile south of the central business district. For the more upscale chains, like Holiday Inn and Best Western, try the Fillmore, Garden of the Gods and Circle Ave exits off I-25.

TOP CHOICE **Broadmoor** RESORT $$$

(☎719-634-7711; www.broadmoor.com; 1 Lake Ave; r from $300; P❄@☎≋) One of the top five-star resorts in the US, the 744-room Broadmoor sits before the blue-green slopes of Cheyenne Mountain. Hollywood stars, A-list pro athletes, and nearly every president since FDR have made it a point to visit (and that includes Obama). Everything here is exquisite: acres of lush grounds and a shimmering lake, pool, world-class golf, ornately decorated public spaces, myriad bars and restaurants, an incredible spa and ubercomfortable European-style guest rooms that invoke Marie Antoinette on a binge. Service is spectacular and dogs are welcome too. Check online for seasonal deals.

Two Sisters Inn B&B $$

(☎719-685-9684; www.twosisinn.com; 10 Otoe Pl; r without bath $79, with bath $135-155; P❄☎) A longtime favorite among B&B aficionados, this place has five rooms (including the honeymoon cottage out back) set in a rose-colored Victorian home, built in 1919 by two sisters. It was originally a boarding house for schoolteachers, and has been an inn since 1990. There's a magnificent stained-glass front door and an 1896 piano in the parlor; it has won awards for its breakfast recipes.

Hyatt Place HOTEL $

(☎719-265-9385; www.coloradosprings.place.hyatt.com; 503 West Garden of the Gods Rd; r $71-99; P❄@☎≋♿) Even with its corporate sheen and IKEA-chic decor, we can dig this place. Okay, it's a chain and a bit close to Hwy 25, but rooms are sizable and super-clean with cushy linens, new beds, massive flat-screens and a comfy sitting area. Factor in the helpful staff and free continental breakfast, and it's a steal.

Barr Camp CAMPGROUND $

(www.barrcamp.com; Barr Trail; tents $12, lean-tos $17, cabin dm $28) At the halfway point on the Barr Trail, about 6.5 miles from the Pikes Peak summit, you can pitch a tent, shelter in a lean-to or reserve a bare-bones cabin. There's drinking water and showers; dinner ($8) is available Wednesday to Sunday. Reservations are essential and must be made online in advance. The camp is open year-round and gets fully booked up, even in winter.

Eating

The Tejon Strip downtown has the most offerings for dining.

La'au's MEXICAN $

(www.laaustacoshop.com; 830 N Tejon St; dishes $6-9; ⏲11am-9pm) Fresh, light and deeply

WORTH A TRIP

CRIPPLE CREEK CASINOS

Just an hour from Colorado Springs yet worlds away, Cripple Creek hurls you back into the Wild West of lore. This once lucky lady produced a staggering $413 million in gold by 1952.

The booze still flows and gambling still thrives, but yesteryear's saloons and brothels are now tasteful casinos.

It's 50 miles southwest of Colorado Springs on Hwy 67. Catch the **Ramblin' Express** (719-590-8687; www.ramblinexpress.com; round-trip tickets $25; departures 7am-10pm) from Colorado Springs' 8th St Depot.

flavorful, this modern taco hut hits the spot. If you've never had Hawaiian tacos before, think peanut chicken topped with fresh mango and Peruvian *ají* (hot peppers). Best for a quickie, it sits in the alley behind Tejon and Cache la Poudre.

Shugas CAFE $

(719-328-1412; www.shugas.com; 702 S Cascade St; dishes $6-9; 11am-midnight Mon-Sat;) If you thought Colorado Springs couldn't be hip, stroll to Shuga's, a southern-style cafe with a knack for knockout espresso drinks and hot cocktails. Cuter than buttons, this little white house is decked out in paper cranes and red vinyl chairs. There's also patio seating. The food – brie BLT on rosemary toast, Brazilian coconut shrimp soup – comforts and delights. Don't miss vintage-movie Saturdays.

Nosh MODERN AMERICAN $$

(719-635-6674; www.nosh121.com; 121 S Tejon St; small plates $9-21; 11am-10pm) Everyone's favorite downtown dining room and patio. Doused in color and artwork, this upscale cafe serves small plates of lentil or bison dumplings, scallop crudo, chili-glazed burgers and all manner of roasted veggies. These are the best downtown eats by far.

Adam's Mountain Cafe MODERN AMERICAN $$

(719-685-1430; www.adamsmountain.com; 934 Manitou Ave; mains $7-16; 8am-3pm & 5-9pm Tue-Sat, to 3pm Sun;) In Manitou Springs, this slow-food cafe makes a lovely stop. Breakfast includes orange-almond French toast and huevos rancheros (eggs and beans on a tortilla). Dinner gets eclectic with offerings such as Moroccan chicken with preserved lemons and Brazilian spiced barramundi. The interior is airy and attractive with marble floors and exposed rafters, and there's patio dining too.

Drinking

The downtown Tejon Strip, between Platte and Colorado Sts, is where most of the after-dark action happens, although it's relatively tame.

TOP CHOICE **Swirl** WINE BAR

(www.swirlwineemporium.com; 717 Manitou Ave; 4-10pm Sun-Thu, to midnight Fri & Sat) Behind a stylish bottle shop in Manitou Springs, this nook bar is intimate and cool. The garden patio has dangling lights and vines while inside there are antique armchairs and a fireplace. It's a superb spot to celebrate life, beauty and love.

Trinity Brewing Co BREWPUB

(www.trinitybrew.com; 1466 Garden of the Gods Rd; 11am-midnight Thu-Sat, 11am-10pm Sun-Wed) Inspired by Belgium's beer cafes, the eco-friendly Trinity Brewing Co serves potent artisanal beers made from rare ingredients. The slow food menu has vegan BBQ sandwiches and 10% discounts are bestowed if you arrive on foot or by bike.

Information

Colorado Springs Visitor Center (719-635-7506; www.visitcos.com; 515 S Cascade Ave; 8:30am-5pm;) Has all the usual tourist information.

Getting There & Around

Colorado Springs Municipal Airport (719-550-1972; www.springsgov.com/airportindex.aspx; 7770 Milton E Proby Parkway) is a viable alternative to Denver. The **Yellow Cab** (719-634-5000) fare from the airport to the city center is $30.

Buses between Cheyenne, WY, and Pueblo, CO, stop daily at **Greyhound** (719-635-1505; 120 S Weber St). **Mountain Metropolitan Transit** (719-385-7433; www.springsgov.com; adult $1.75) offers schedule information and route maps for all local buses; find information online.

BOULDER

Tucked up against its soaring signature Flatirons, this idyllic college town has a sweet location and a palpable ecosophistication that has attracted entrepreneurs, athletes, hippies and hard-bodies like moths to the moonlight.

Boulder's mad love of the outdoors was officially legislated in 1967, when it became the first US city to tax itself specifically to preserve open space. Thanks to such vision, packs of cyclists whip up and down the Boulder Creek corridor, which links city and county parks those taxpayer dollars have purchased. The pedestrian-only Pearl St Mall is lively and perfect for strolling, especially at night, when students from University of Colorado and Naropa University mingle into the wee hours.

In many ways it is Boulder, not Denver, that is the region's tourist hub. The city is about the same distance from Denver International Airport, and staying here puts you closer to local trails in the foothills, as well as the big ski resorts west on I-70 and Rocky Mountain National Park.

Sights & Activities

Boulder's two areas to see and be seen are the downtown Pearl St Mall and the University Hill district (next to campus), both off Broadway. Overlooking the city from the west are the Flatirons, an eye-catching rock formation.

TOP CHOICE Chautauqua Park PARK
(www.chautauqua.com; 900 Baseline Rd) This historic landmark park is the gateway to Boulder's most magnificent slab of open space (we're talking about the Flatirons), which also has a wide, lush lawn that attracts picnickers. It also gets copious hikers, climbers and trail runners. World-class musicians perform each summer at the auditorium.

Boulder Creek Bike Path CYCLING
(24 hr;) The most utilized commuter bike path in town, this fabulously smooth and mostly straight creekside concrete path follows Boulder Creek from Foothill Parkway all the way to the spilt of Boulder Canyon and Four Mile Canyon Rd west of downtown – a total distance of over 5 miles one-way. The path also feeds urban bike lanes that lead all over town.

Boulder Rock Club ROCK CLIMBING
(303-447-2804; www.totalclimbing.com; 2829 Mapleton Ave; day pass adult/child $15/8, private lessons $50, 3 2hr intro classes with gear rental $130; 8am-10pm Mon, 6am-11pm Tue-Thu, 8am-11pm Fri, 10am-8pm Sat & Sun;) Climb indoors at this massive warehouse full of artificial rock faces cragged with ledges and routes. The auto-belay system allows solo climbers an anchor. Staff is a great resource for local climbing routes and tips too.

Eldorado Canyon State Park OUTDOORS
(303-494-3943; visitor center 9am-5pm) One of the country's most favored rock-climbing areas, offering Class 5.5 to 5.12 climbs and some nice hiking trails. The park entrance is on Eldorado Springs Dr, west of Hwy 93. Information is available from Boulder Rock Club.

University Bicycles CYCLING
(www.ubikes.com; 839 Pearl St; 4hr rental $15; 10am-6pm Mon-Sat, 10am-5pm Sun) There are plenty of places to rent bicycles to cruise around town, but this has the widest range of rides and the most helpful staff.

Festivals & Events

FREE Boulder Creek Festival MUSIC, FOOD
(303-449-3137; www.bceproductions.com; Central Park, Canyon Blvd) Billed as the kick-off to summer and capped with the fabulous Bolder Boulder, this massive Memorial Day weekend (May) festival has 10 event areas featuring more than 30 live entertainers and 500 vendors. With food and drink, music and sunshine, what's not to love?

Bolder Boulder ATHLETICS
(303-444-7223; www.bolderboulder.com; adult $44-48) Held in a self-consciously hyper

WORTH A TRIP

SUSTAINABLE BREWS

New Belgium Brewing Co (800-622-4044; www.newbelgium.com; 500 Lined St; admission free; guided tours 10am-6pm, Tue-Sat) satisfies beer connoisseurs with its hearty Fat Tire Amber Ale, and diverse concoctions like 1554, Trippell and Sunshine Wheat. Recognized as one of the world's most environmentally conscious breweries, a 100,000kw turbine keeps it wind-powered. The brewery also sponsors cool events such as bike-in cinema and scavenger hunts on the ski slopes. It's in the college town of Fort Collins (home to Colorado State University), a worthwhile 46-mile drive north of Boulder on I-25 – especially if you're heading to Wyoming. Reserve tickets online – these popular tours include complimentary tasting of the flagship and specialty brews.

athletic town, this is the biggest foot race within the city limits. It doesn't take itself too seriously – spectators scream, there are runners in costume, and live music plays throughout the course. It's held on Memorial Day (May).

Sleeping

Boulder has dozens of options – drive down Broadway or Hwy 36 to take your pick. Booking online usually scores the best discounts.

TOP CHOICE Chautauqua Lodge HISTORIC HOTEL $
(303-442-3282; www.chautauqua.com; 900 Baseline Rd; r from $73, cottages from $139; P❄📶👪) Adjoining beautiful hiking trails to the Flatirons, this leafy neighborhood of cottages is our top pick. It has contemporary rooms and one- to three-bedroom cottages with porches and beds with patchwork quilts. It's perfect for families and pets. All have full kitchens, though the wraparound porch of the Chautauqua Dining Hall is a local favorite for breakfast.

Hotel Boulderado HISTORIC HOTEL $$$
(303-442-4344; www.boulderado.com; 2115 13th St; r from $224; P❄📶) Celebrating a century of service in 2009, the charming Boulderado, full of Victorian elegance and wonderful public spaces, is a National Register landmark and a romantic place to spend the night. Each antique-filled room is uniquely decorated, and the stained-glass atrium and glacial water fountain accent the jazz-washed lobby.

Boulder International Youth Hostel HOSTEL $
(303-442-0522; www.boulderinternationalhostel.com; 1107 12th St; dm $27, s/d without bath $52/62; P📶) A great deal in the raucous university frat-house neighborhood, this hostel has been meeting the needs of travelers since 1961. Single-sex dorms and private rooms are worn but clean. Bring bedding or rent linens for $7 per stay.

Alps B&B $$$
(303-444-5445; www.alpsinn.com; 38619 Boulder Canyon Dr; r $159-279; P❄@📶) Constructed in the 1870s, this inn charms with Mission furnishings, stained-glass windows and antique fireplaces. Many rooms feature a private whirlpool for two with French doors leading to a garden, patio or private porch with views of Boulder Creek and the canyon. The generous spa amenities may appeal to couples looking for a romantic stop.

St Julien Hotel & Spa HOTEL $$$
(720-406-9696, reservations 877-303-0900; www.stjulien.com; 900 Walnut St; r from $289; P❄@📶🏊👪) In the heart of downtown, Boulder's finest four-star is modern and refined, with photographs of local scenery and cork walls that warm the room ambience. With fabulous Flatiron views, the back patio hosts live world music, jazz concerts and wild salsa parties. Rooms are plush, and so are the robes.

Eating

Boulder's dining scene has dozens of great options. Most are centered on the Pearl Street Mall, while bargains are more likely to be found on the Hill. Between 3:30pm and 6:30pm nearly every restaurant in the city features a happy hour with some kind of amazing food and drink special. It's a great way to try fine dining on a budget – check websites for details.

TOP CHOICE Kitchen MODERN AMERICAN $$$
(303-544-5973; www.thekitchencafe.com; 1039 Pearl St; mains $11-25; 11am-9pm Mon, to 10pm Tue-Fri, 9am-2pm & 5:30-10pm Sat, 9:30am-2pm & 5:30-9pm Sun; 📶) Clean lines, stacks of crusty bread, a daily menu and lots of light: Kitchen is one of the finest kitchens in town. Fresh farmers-market ingredients are crafted into rustic tapas: think roasted root vegetables, shaved prosciutto and mussels steamed in wine and cream. The pulled-pork sandwich rocks, but save room for the sticky toffee pudding. Check out community hour (daily 3pm to 5:30pm) – a good way to meet the neighbors. A younger crowd gathers at the more casual upstairs bar.

Boulder Dushanbe Teahouse FUSION $$
(303-442-4993; 1770 13th St; mains $8-20; 8am-10pm) No visit to Boulder is complete without a meal at this incredible Tajik work of art, a gift from Boulder's sister city (Dushanbe, Tajikistan). Incredible craftsmanship and meticulous painting envelop the vibrant multicolored interior. The international fare ranges from Amazonian to Mediterranean to, of course, Tajik. Outside, in the quiet gardens, is a lovely, shaded full-service patio. It's an intimate place to grab cocktails or dinner with friends on a warm summer day.

EATING THE ROCKIES

Start by digging into regional *Edible* (www.edible.com) magazines online – a great resource for farmers markets and innovative eats.

Boulder is worth a stop since it is America's Foodiest Small Town, according to *Bon Appetit*. At **Kitchen** (☎303-544-5973; www.thekitchencafe.com; per person $35) Monday is community night, which means shared tables and a homegrown five-course meal served family-style, with 20% of proceeds going to charity. Go behind the scenes with **Local Table Tours** (☎303-909-5747; www.localtabletours.com; tours $20-70), a tour presenting a smattering of great local cuisine and inside knowledge on food and wine or coffee and pastries. The cocktail crawl is a hit.

For fine dining in a warehouse or an airplane hangar, Denver's **Hush** (www.hushdenver.com) sponsors fun pop-up dinners with top regional chefs, by invitation only – make contact online.

Our favorite farm dinner, **On the Farm** (☎307-413-3203; onthefarminidaho@gmail.com; Victor, ID; 6-course meal $75), in Idaho's Teton Valley, serves sumptuous and sustainable local food with the most spectacular backdrop.

Lucile's CAJUN $
(☎303-442-4743; www.luciles.com; 2142 14th St; mains $7-14; ⏰7am-2pm Mon-Fri, from 8am Sat & Sun; 👪) This New Orleans–style diner has perfected breakfast; the Creole egg dishes (served over creamy spinach alongside cheesy grits or perfectly blackened trout) are the thing to order. Start with a steaming mug of chai or chicory coffee and an order of beignets.

Zoe Ma Ma CHINESE $
(2010 10th St; mains $5-13; ⏰11am-10pm Sun-Thu, 11am-11pm Fri & Sat) At Boulder's hippest noodle bar you can slurp and munch fresh street food at a long outdoor counter. Mama, the Taiwanese matriarch, is on hand, cooking and chatting up customers in her Crocs. Organic noodles are made from scratch, as are the garlicky melt-in-your mouth pot stickers.

Sink PUB $
(www.thesink.com; 1165 13th St; mains $5-10; ⏰11am-2am, kitchen to 10pm) Dim and graffiti-scrawled, the Sink has been a Hill classic since 1923. Colorful characters cover the cavernous space – the scene alone is almost worth a visit. Almost. Once you've washed back the legendary Sink burger with a slug of a local microbrew, you'll be glad you stuck around.

Alfalfa's SELF-CATERING
(www.alfalfas.com; 1651 Broadway St; ⏰7:30am-10pm) A small, community-oriented natural market with a wonderful selection of prepared food and an inviting indoor-outdoor dining area to enjoy it in.

Drinking & Entertainment

Playboy didn't vote CU the best party school for nothing – the blocks around the Pearl St Mall and the Hill churn out fun, with many restaurants doubling as bars or turning into all-out dance clubs come 10pm.

Mountain Sun Pub & Brewery BREWERY
(1535 Pearl St) Boulder's favorite brewery serves a rainbow of brews from chocolaty to fruity, and packs in an eclectic crowd of yuppies, hippies and everyone in between. Walls are lined with tapestries, there are board games to amuse you and the pub grub (especially the burgers) is delicious. There's usually live music of the bluegrass and jam-band variety on Sunday and Monday nights.

Bitter Bar COCKTAIL BAR
(☎303-442-3050; www.happynoodlehouse.com; 835 Walnut St; cocktails $9-15) A chic Boulder speakeasy – think pan-Asian environs and killer cocktails, like the scrumptious lavender-infused Blue Velvet – that make the evening slip happily out of focus.

West End Tavern PUB
(www.thewestendtavern.com; 926 Pearl St) Nothing fancy, just loungy booths, a fantastic roof deck and tasty pub grub.

Boulder Theater CINEMA, MUSIC
(☎303-786-7030; www.bouldertheatre.com; 2032 14th St) This old movie-theater-turned-historic-venue brings in slightly under-the-radar acts like jazz great Charlie Hunter, the madmen rockers of Gogol Bordello and West African divas, Les Nubians. But it also screens classic films and short-film festivals

that can and should be enjoyed with a glass of beer.

Shopping

Boulder has great shopping and galleries. The outdoor 29th St Mall, with a movie theatre, just off 28th St between Canyon and Pearl St, is a recent addition.

Pearl Street Mall MALL

The main feature of downtown Boulder is the Pearl Street Mall, a vibrant pedestrian zone filled with kids' climbing boulders and splash fountains, bars, galleries and restaurants.

Momentum HANDICRAFTS

(www.ourmomentum.com; 1625 Pearl St; 10am-7pm Tue-Sat, 11am-6pm Sun) The kitchen sink of unique global gifts – Zulu wire baskets, fabulous scarves from India, Nepal and Ecuador – all handcrafted and purchased at fair value from disadvantaged artisans. Every item purchased provides a direct economic lifeline to the artists.

Common Threads CLOTHING

(www.commonthreadsboulder.com; 2707 Spruce St; 10am-6pm Mon-Sat, noon-5pm Sun) Vintage shopping at its most haute couture, this fun place is where to go for secondhand Choos and Prada purses. The shop is a pleasure to browse, with clothing organized by color and type on visually aesthetic racks, just like a big-city boutique.

Boulder Bookstore BOOKS

(www.boulderbookstore.indiebound.com; 1107 Pearl St) Boulder's favorite indie bookstore has a huge travel section downstairs and hosts readings and workshops.

Information

Boulder Visitor Center (303-442-2911; www.bouldercoloradousa.com; 2440 Pearl St; 8:30am-5pm Mon-Thu, 8:30am-4pm Fri) Offers information and internet access.

Getting There & Around

Boulder has fabulous public transportation, with services extending as far away as Denver and its airport. Ecofriendly buses are run by **RTD** (303-299-6000; www.rtd-denver.com; per ride $2-4.50). Maps are available at **Boulder Station** (cnr 14th & Walnut Sts). RTD buses (route B) operate between Boulder Station and Denver's Market St Bus Station ($3.50, one hour). RTD's SkyRide bus (route AB) heads to Denver International Airport ($13, 1½ hours, hourly). **SuperShuttle** (303-444-0808) provides hotel ($25) and door-to-door ($32) shuttle service from the airport.

For two-wheel transportation, **Boulder B-Cycle** (boulder.bcycle.com; 24-hr rental $5) is a new citywide program with townie bikes available at strategic locations, but riders must sign up online first.

ROCKY MOUNTAIN NATIONAL PARK

Rocky Mountain National Park showcases classic alpine scenery, with wildflower meadows and serene mountain lakes set under snowcapped peaks. There are over three million visitors annually, but many stay on the beaten path. Hike an extra mile and enjoy the incredible solitude. In winter the park becomes a great place to snowshoe or go backcountry skiing. Elk are the park's signature mammal – you will even see them grazing hotel lawns, but also keep an eye out for bighorn sheep, moose, marmots and black bears.

Activities

Trails OUTDOORS

The bustling Bear Lake Trailhead offers easy **hikes** to several lakes and beyond. Another busy area is Glacier Gorge Junction Trailhead. The free Glacier Basin–Bear Lake shuttle services both.

Forested Fern Lake, 4 miles from the Moraine Park Trailhead, is dominated by craggy Notchtop Peak. You can complete a loop to the Bear Lake shuttle stop in about 8.5 miles for a rewarding day hike. The strenuous **Flattop Mountain Trail** is the only cross-park trail, linking Bear Creek on the east side with either Tonahutu Creek Trail or the North Inlet Trail on the west side.

Families might consider the moderate hikes to **Calypso Cascades** in the Wild Basin or to **Gem Lake** in the Lumpy Ridge area.

Trail Ridge Rd crosses the Continental Divide at Milner Pass (10,759ft), where trails head 4 miles (and up 2000ft!) southeast to Mt Ida, which offers fantastic views.

Trails on the west side of the park are quieter and less trodden than those on the east side. Try the short and easy East Inlet Trail to **Adams Falls** (0.3 miles) or the more moderate 3.7-mile Colorado River Trail to the **Lulu City** site.

Before July, many of the trails are snowbound, and high water runoff makes passage difficult. On the east side, the Bear Lake and Glacier Gorge Junction Trailheads offer good routes for **cross-country skiing** and **snowshoeing**. **Backcountry skiing** is also possible; check with the visitor centers.

Sleeping & Eating

The only overnight accommodations in the park are at campgrounds. Dining options and the majority of motel or hotel accommodations are around Estes Park or Grand Lake, located on the other side of the Trail Ridge Road Pass.

The park's formal campgrounds provide campfire programs, have public telephones and a seven-day limit during summer months; all except Longs Peak take RVs (no hookups). The water supply is turned off during winter.

You will need a backcountry permit to stay outside developed park campgrounds. None of the campgrounds have showers, but they do have flush toilets in summer and outhouse facilities in winter. Sites include a fire ring, picnic table and one parking spot.

Olive Ridge Campground CAMPGROUND $
(☎303-541-2500; campsites $14; ⊙mid-May–Nov) Well-kept United States Forest Service (USFS) campground with access to four trailheads: St Vrain Mountain, Wild Basin, Longs Peak and Twin Sisters.

Moraine Park Campground CAMPGROUND $
(☎877-444-6777; www.recreation.gov; off Bear Lake Rd; summer campsites $20) Has 245 sites. Reserve via the website. Walk-in, tent-only sites in the D Loop are recommended if you want quiet. At night in the summer, there are numerous ranger-led programs in the amphitheater.

The campground is served by the shuttle buses on Bear Lake Rd through the summer.

Aspenglen Campground CAMPGROUND $
(☎877-444-6777; www.recreation.gov; State Hwy 34; campsites summer $20) With only 54 sites, this is the smallest of the park's bookable camping. There are many tent-only sites, including some walk-ins, and a limited number of trailers are allowed. This is the quietest park that's highly accessible (5 miles west of Estes Park on US 34).

Timber Creek Campground CAMPGROUND $
(Trail Ridge Rd, US Hwy 34; campsites $20) This campground has 100 sites and remains open through the winter. No reservations accepted. The only established campground on the west side of the park, it's 7 miles north of Grand Lake.

Glacier Basin Campground CAMPGROUND $
(☎877-444-6777; www.recreation.gov; off Bear Lake Rd; campsites summer $20) This developed campground has a large area for group camping and accommodates RVs. It is served by the shuttle buses on Bear Lake Rd throughout the summer. Reserve through the website.

Information

Entry to the park (vehicles $20, hikers and cyclists $10) is valid for seven days. Backcountry permits ($20) are required for overnight trips.

Alpine Visitor Center (www.nps.gov/romo; Fall River Pass; ⊙10:30am-4:30pm late May–mid-Jun, 9am-5pm late Jun-early Sep, 10:30am-4:30pm early Sep–mid-Oct) Right in the middle of the park at 11,796ft, with views, cafeteria and information.

Beaver Meadows Visitor Center (☎970-586-1206; www.nps.gov/romo; US Hwy 36; ⊙8am-9pm late Jun-late Aug, to 4:30pm or 5pm rest of year) The primary visitor center and best stop for park information, if you're approaching from Estes Park. You can see a film about the park, browse a small gift shop and reserve backcountry camping sites.

Kawuneeche Visitor Center (☎970-627-3471; 16018 US Hwy 34; ⊙8am-6pm last week May-Labor Day, 8am-5pm Labor Day-end of Sep, 8am-4:30pm Oct-end of May) On the west side of the park, with ranger-led walks and discussions, backcountry permits and family activities.

Getting There & Away

Trail Ridge Rd (US 34) is the only east–west route through the park and is closed in winter. The most direct route from Boulder follows US 36 through Lyons to the east entrances.

There are two entrance stations on the east side, Fall River (US 34) and Beaver Meadows (US 36). The Grand Lake Station (also US 34) is the only entry on the west side. Year-round access is available through Kawuneeche Valley along the Colorado River headwaters to Timber Creek Campground. The main centers of visitor activity on the park's east side are the Alpine Visitor Center, high on Trail Ridge Rd and Bear Lake Rd, which leads to campgrounds, trailheads and the Moraine Park Museum.

North of Estes Park, Devils Gulch Rd leads to several hiking trails. Further out on Devils Gulch Rd, you pass through the village of Glen Haven to reach the trailhead entry to the park along the North Fork of the Big Thompson River.

Getting Around

A majority of visitors enter the park in their own cars, using the long and winding Trail Ridge Rd (US 34) to cross the Continental Divide. In summer a free shuttle bus operates from the Estes Park Visitor Center multiple times daily, bringing hikers to a park-and-ride location where you can pick up other shuttles. The year-round option leaves the Glacier Basin parking area toward Bear Lake, in the parks lower elevations. During the summer peak, a second shuttle operates between Moraine Park campground and the Glacier Basin parking area. Shuttles run on weekends only from mid-August through September.

ESTES PARK

It's no small irony that becoming a nature-lovers hub has turned the gateway to one of the most pristine outdoor escapes in the US into the kind of place you'll need to escape from. T-shirt shops and ice-cream parlors, sidewalks jammed with tourists and streets plugged with RVs: welcome to Estes Park, the chaotic outpost at the edge of Rocky Mountain National Park.

Activities

Colorado Mountain School ROCK CLIMBING
(☎303-447-2804; www.totalclimbing.com; 341 Moraine Ave; half-day guided climbs per person from $125) The largest climbing operator in the region has world-class instructors. It's the only organization allowed to operate within Rocky Mountain National Park and offers basic courses such as Intro to Rock Climbing as well as dorm lodging at Total Climbing Lodge.

Sleeping

Estes Park's dozens of hotels fill up fast in summer. There are some passable budget options but the many lovely area campgrounds are the best-value. You can rent camping gear from **Estes Park Mountain Shop** (☎970-586-6548; www.estesparkmountainshop.com; 2050 Big Thompson Ave; 2-person camping set-up $32; ⌚8am-9pm).

Try the **Estes Park Visitor Center** (☎970-577-9900; www.estesparkresortcvb.com; 500 Big Thompson Ave; ⌚9am-8pm Jun-Aug, 8am-5pm Mon-Fri, 9am-5pm Sat, 10am-4pm Sun Sep-May), just east of the US 36 junction, for help with lodging; note that many places close in winter.

TOP CHOICE **Stanley Hotel** HOTEL $$$
(☎970-586-3371; www.stanleyhotel.com; 333 Wonderview Ave; r from $199; P 🛜 ✱ 👪) The inspiration for Stephen King's famous cult novel *The Shining*, this white Georgian Colonial Revival is the grand dame of Rocky Mountain resort hotels. Stately rooms evoke the Old West, with replica antiques and modernized amenities. Vast public spaces with plump leather couches are warmed with stone fireplaces. In addition to mountain views and splendid dining, there are even nighttime ghost hunts (they claim 17 haunted rooms).

YMCA of the Rockies – Estes Park Center RESORT $$
(☎970-586-3341; www.ymcarockies.org; 2515 Tunnel Rd; r & d from $109, cabins from $129; P ✱ 🛜 👪) This very kid-friendly resort sits in a serene and ultra-pristine location in the mountains just outside town. The 860-acre plot is home to cabins and motel rooms along with lots of wide-open spaces dotted with forests and fields of wildflowers. Just a few minutes outside of Estes Park (but definitely away from the hustle of town), it offers a range of activities.

Mary's Lake Lodge LODGE $$$
(☎970-577-9495; www.maryslakelodge.com; 2625 Marys Lake Rd; r & d from $99, cabins from $199; P ✱ 🛜 👪) This old wooden lodge reeks of Wild West ambience, down to the creaky front porch. Rooms and condo cabins are a blend of modern and historic. Both the saloon-style **Tavern** (mains $7-20; ⌚11am-11pm) and fine-dining **Chalet Room** (mains $12 -20; ⌚5pm-10pm) have seating on the heated porch. A big hot tub under the stars, a fire pit and live music five nights per week nicely round out the amenities. Mary's is 3 miles south of Estes Park off Hwy 7.

Total Climbing Lodge HOSTEL $
(☎303-447-2804; www.totalclimbing.com; 341 Moraine Ave; dm $25; P @ 🛜) Lodging at this bustling hub of climbers is the best dorm option in town, with sleeping bags, soap, pillow and towels included in the price. Expect simple pine bunks, a Ping-Pong table and a laid-back vibe.

Eating

Estes Park Brewery BREWPUB
(www.epbrewery.com; 470 Prospect Village Dr; ⌚11am-2am Mon-Sun) The town's brewpub serves pizza, burgers and wings, and at least eight different house beers, in a big, boxy room resembling a cross between a classroom and a country kitchen. Pool tables and outdoor seating keep the place rocking late into the night.

Ed's Cantina & Grill MEXICAN $$
(☎970-586-2919; www.edscantina.com; 390 E Elkhorn Ave; mains $9-15; ⌚11am-late daily, from 8am Sat & Sun) With an outdoor patio right on the river, Ed's is a great place to kick back with a margarita and one of the daily $3

blue-plate specials (think fried, rolled tortillas) with shredded pork and guacamole). Serving Mexican and American staples, the restaurant is in a retro-mod space with leather booth seating and a bold primary color scheme. The bar is in a separate room with light-wood stools featuring comfortable high backs.

Getting There & Away

From Denver International Airport, **Estes Park Shuttle** (970-586-5151; www.estesparkshuttle.com) runs four times daily to Estes Park (one-way/return $45/85).

Central & Northern Mountains

Colorado's central and northern mountains are well known for their plethora of ski resorts – including world-famous Aspen and Vail, family-friendly Breckenridge and never-summer A-Basin.

WINTER PARK

Less than two hours from Denver, unpretentious Winter Park is a favorite ski resort with Front Rangers, who flock here from as far away as Colorado Springs to ski fresh tracks each weekend. Beginners can frolic on miles of powdery groomers while experts test their skills on Mary Jane's world-class bumps. The congenial town is a wonderful base for year-round romping. Most services are along US 40 (the main drag), including the **visitor center** (970-726-4118; www.winterpark-info.com; 78841 Hwy 40; 8am-5pm Mon-Fri, 9am-5pm Sat & Sun).

South of town, **Winter Park Resort** (970-726-5514; www.winterparkresort.com; cnr Hwy 40 & Colorado 81; 2-day lift ticket adult $120-172, child $66-86) covers five mountains and has a vertical drop of more than 2600ft. Experts love it here because more than half of the runs are geared solely for highly skilled skiers. It also has 45 miles of lift-accessible **mountain-biking trails** connecting to a 600-mile trail system running through the valley. Other fine rides in the area include the road up to **Rollins Pass**.

Devil's Thumb Ranch (800-933-4339; www.devilsthumbranch.com; 3530 County Rd 83; r from $93, cabins from $165, trail passes adult/child & senior $18/8, rental packages $20/10, ice skating $10;), with a cowboy chic bunkhouse and cabins alongside a 65-mile network of trails, makes an ultra-romantic getaway for the active-minded. Geothermal heat, reclaimed wood and low-emission fireplaces make it green. Summer guests can go horseback riding ($90 to $170 per person) in the high country. It's north of Fraser.

The best deal around is the friendly **Rocky Mountain Chalet** (970-726-8256, 866-467-8351; www.therockymountainchalet.com; 15 Co Rd 72; dm $36, r $89-179; P), with plush, comfortable doubles, dorm rooms and a sparkling kitchen.

For inspired dining, **Tavern at Tabernash** (970-726-4430; www.tabernashtavern.com; 72287 US Hwy 40; mains $17-32; 5-9pm Tue-Sat;) whets the appetite with barbecued pork chops served with grilled Palisades peaches or venison burgers. There are vegan and gluten-free options too. Reserve ahead. It's just north of Fraser.

STEAMBOAT SPRINGS

With luxuriant tree-skiing, top-notch trails for mountain-biking and a laid back Western feel, Steamboat beats out other ski towns in both real ambience and offerings. Its historic center is cool for rambling, hot springs top off a hard day of play, and locals couldn't be friendlier.

WORTH A TRIP

THE VAGABOND RANCH

Moose outnumber people at the remote **Vagabond Ranch** (303-242-5338; www.vagabondranch.com; per person $45;), a fine backcountry in Colorado's pristine Never Summer Range. By backcountry we mean a 3-mile dirt access road – it can be driven in summer but you'll need to park the car and ski or snowmobile in for winter fun.

Ringed by high peaks and ponderosa forest, this former stagecoach stop features a smattering of comfortable cabins – ranging from rustic to elegant – at 9000ft. Features include chef-worthy cooking facilities, firewood, a hot tub, solar power and composting toilets. Like any ski hut, lodgings may be shared, but couples or groups can book privates (we recommend the retro-gorgeous Parkview for couples). Dedicated trails are groomed in winter for cross-country skiing or snowmobiling and it also hosts yoga and meditation retreats.

It's 22 miles from Granby (near Winter Park).

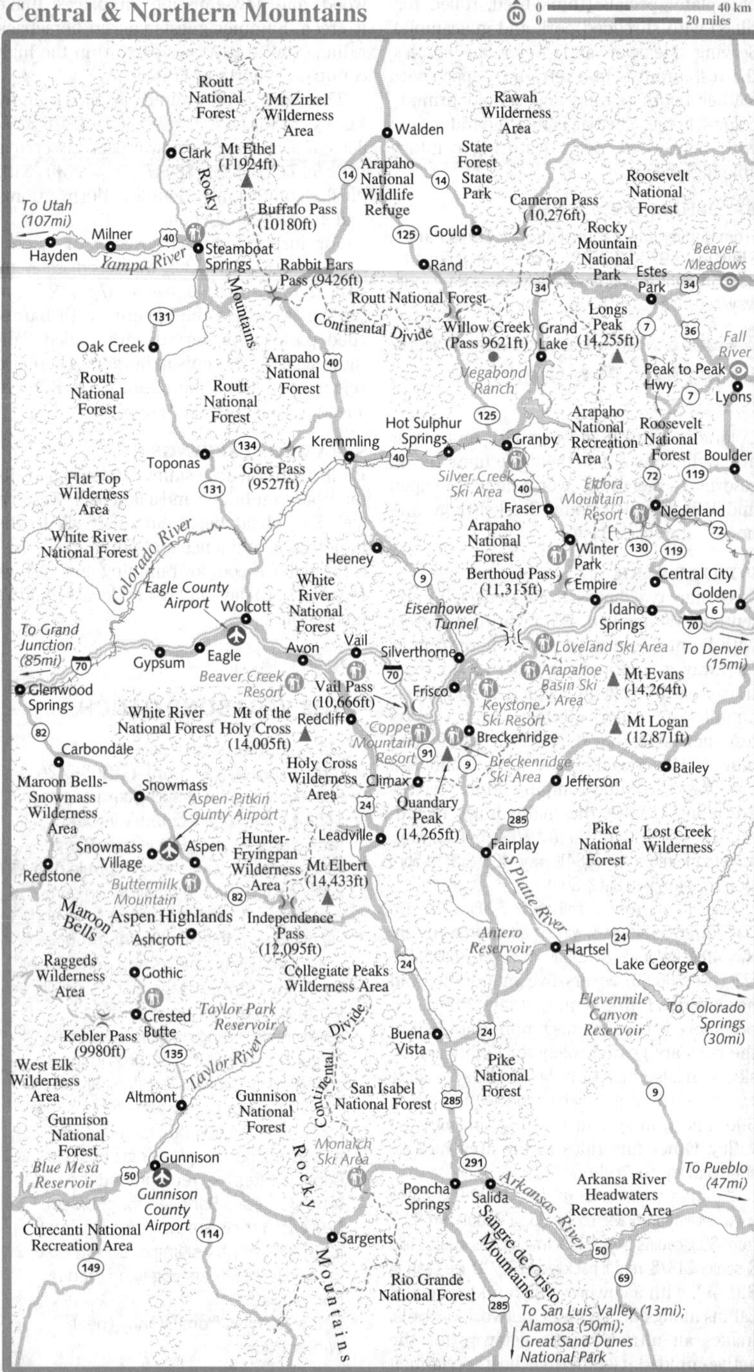
0 40 km
0 20 miles
Routt National Forest
Mt Zirkel Wilderness Area
Walden
Rawah Wilderness Area
State Forest State Park
Clark
Mt Ethel (11924ft)
Arapaho National Wildlife Refuge
Roosevelt National Forest
Cameron Pass (10,276ft)
To Utah (107mi)
Buffalo Pass (10180ft)
Gould
Rocky Mountain National Park
Hayden
Milner
Yampa River
Steamboat Springs
Rabbit Ears Pass (9426ft)
Rand
Beaver Meadows
Estes Park
Routt National Forest
Longs Peak (14,255ft)
Continental Divide
Willow Creek (Pass 9621ft)
Grand Lake
Fall River
Oak Creek
Rocky Mountains
Arapaho National Forest
Peak to Peak Hwy
Routt National Forest
Vegabond Ranch
Lyons
Arapaho National Recreation Area
Roosevelt National Forest
Hot Sulphur Springs
Kremmling
Granby
Boulder
Toponas
Gore Pass (9527ft)
Silver Creek Ski Area
Flat Top Wilderness Area
Eldora Mountain Resort
Fraser
Nederland
Arapaho National Forest
White River National Forest
Colorado River
Winter Park
Heeney
Berthoud Pass (11,315ft)
Central City
White River National Forest
Empire
Golden
Eagle County Airport
Wolcott
Idaho Springs
Eisenhower Tunnel
To Grand Junction (85mi)
Eagle
Avon
Vail
Silverthorne
Loveland Ski Area
To Denver (15mi)
Gypsum
Beaver Creek Resort
Arapahoe Basin Ski Area
Mt Evans (14,264ft)
Glenwood Springs
Vail Pass (10,666ft)
Frisco
Keystone Ski Resort
White River National Forest
Mt of the Holy Cross (14,005ft)
Redcliff
Mt Logan (12,871ft)
Copper Mountain Resort
Breckenridge
Carbondale
Breckenridge Ski Area
Bailey
Maroon Bells-Snowmass Wilderness Area
Holy Cross Wilderness Area
Climax
Jefferson
Snowmass
Aspen-Pitkin County Airport
Quandary Peak (14,265ft)
Pike National Forest
Lost Creek Wilderness
Snowmass Village
Aspen
Hunter-Fryingpan Wilderness Area
Leadville
Fairplay
Redstone
Mt Elbert (14,433ft)
S Platte River
Buttermilk Mountain
Maroon Bells
Aspen Highlands
Independence Pass (12,095ft)
Ashcroft
Antero Reservoir
Hartsel
Lake George
Ragged Wilderness Area
Gothic
Collegiate Peaks Wilderness Area
Elevenmile Canyon Reservoir
Crested Butte
Taylor Park Reservoir
To Colorado Springs (30mi)
Kebler Pass (9980ft)
Divide
Buena Vista
West Elk Wilderness Area
Taylor River
Pike National Forest
Altmont
Gunnison National Forest
Continental
San Isabel National Forest
Gunnison National Forest
Monarch Ski Area
Gunnison
Blue Mesa Reservoir
Gunnison County Airport
To Pueblo (47mi)
Poncha Springs
Salida
Arkansas River
Arkansa River Headwaters Recreation Area
Curecanti National Recreation Area
Rocky Mountains
Sargents
Sangre de Cristo Mountains
Rio Grande National Forest
To San Luis Valley (13mi); Alamosa (50mi); Great Sand Dunes National Park

Sights & Activities

Steamboat Mountain Resort SNOW SPORTS
(Steamboat Mountain Resort; ticket office 970-871-5252; www.steamboat.com; lift ticket adult/child $94/59; ticket office 8am-5pm) Known for a 3600ft vertical drop, excellent powder and trails for all levels, this is the main draw for winter visitors and some of the best skiing in the US. In the ski area there are (overpriced) food and equipment vendors galore.

TOP CHOICE **Strawberry Park Hot Springs** SPRING
(970-879-0342; www.strawberryhotsprings.com; 44200 County Rd; per day adult/child $10/5; 10am-10:30pm Sun-Thu, to midnight Fri & Sat;) Steamboat's favorite hot springs are actually outside the city limits, but offer great back-to-basics relaxation. Water is 104°F in these tasteful stone pools formed by cascading drops. To stay over, choose from covered wagons ($65) with a double mattress on the floor (quite unique) or rustic cabins ($55). There's no electricity (you get gas lanterns) and you'll need your own linens.

Be sure to reserve. Weekend reservations require a two-night stay. Note that the thermal pools are clothing optional after dark.

Old Town Hot Springs SPRING
(970-879-1828; www.steamboathotsprings.org; 136 Lincoln Ave; adult/student & senior/child $15/10/7; 5:30am-9:45pm Mon-Fri, 7am-8:45pm Sat, 8am-8:45pm Sun;) Right in the center of town, the mineral water here is warmer than most in the area. Kids will dig the 230ft-long waterslides and the aquatic climbing wall.

Sleeping & Eating

There are plenty of places to sleep; contact **Steamboat Central Reservations** (970-879-0740, www.steamboat.com; Mt Werner Circle, off Gondola Sq) for condos and other options near the ski area.

Hotel Bristol HOTEL $$
(970-879-3083; www.steamboathotelbristol.com; 917 Lincoln Ave; d $149;) The elegant Hotel Bristol has small, but sophisticated, Western digs, with dark-wood and brass furnishings and Pendleton wool blankets on the beds. There's a ski shuttle, a six-person indoor Jacuzzi and a cozy restaurant.

TOP CHOICE **Cafe Diva** FUSION $$$
(970-871-0508; www.cafediva.com; 1855 Ski Time Square Dr; mains $21-40; 5:30-10pm) Locals love this romantic nook where every dish is worth savoring. Offerings change, but always fuse Asian, Italian and Latin flavors. Think duck tamales with avocado cream, and sweet-pea ravioli with homemade ricotta.

Backcountry Provisions DELI $
(www.backcountryprovisions.com; 635 Lincoln Ave; sandwiches $7-10; 7am-5pm;) Efficient and delicious, this Colorado sandwich chain uses ultra-fresh ingredients. The curried turkey smothered in cranberry hits the spot. Take it to go if you're hiking or skiing for the day.

Slopeside Grill BAR
(www.slopesidegrill.com; 1855 Ski Time Sq; noon-midnight) The uncontested hub of après-ski activity, this ski-up bar also has excellent pizza and cooks a range of food well. In summer, kids can play on the lawn.

Information

Steamboat Springs Visitor Center (970-879-0880, 877-754-2269; www.steamboatchamber.com; 1255 S Lincoln Ave; 8am-5pm Mon-Fri, 10am-3pm Sat)

Getting There & Away

Buses between Denver and Salt Lake City stop at the **Greyhound Terminal** (970-870-0504; 1505 Lincoln Ave), about half a mile west of town. **Steamboat Springs Transit** (970-879-3717, for pick-up in Mountain Area 970-846-1279; http://steamboatsprings.net) runs free buses between Old Town and the ski resort year-round. Steamboat is 166 miles northwest of Denver via US 40.

BRECKENRIDGE & AROUND

Set at 9600ft, at the foot of a marvelous range of treeless peaks, Breck is a sweetly surviving gold-mining town with a lovely national historic district. With down-to-earth grace, the town boasts family-friendly ski runs that don't disappoint and always draw a giddy crowd. If you should happen to grow restless, there are four great ski resorts and outlet shopping less than an hour away.

Activities

Breckenridge Ski Area SNOW SPORTS
(970-453-5000; www.breckenridge.snow.com; 150 Watson Ave; lift ticket adult/child/senior $63/44/53; lifts 8:30am-4pm, gondola 8am-5pm Nov-April;) Spans four mountains and features some of the best beginner and intermediate terrain in the state (the green runs are flatter than most in Colorado), as well as killer steeps and chutes for experts, and a renowned snowboard park.

Arapahoe Basin Ski Area SNOW SPORTS
(☎970-468-0718, 888-272-7246; www.arapahoebasin.com; lift adult/child/15-19yr/senior $54/29/49/51; ⏲9am-4pm Mon-Fri, from 8:30am Sat & Sun) North America's highest resort, about 12 miles from Breck, is smaller, less commercial and usually open until at least mid-June! Full of steeps, walls and backcountry terrain, it's a local favorite because it doesn't draw herds of package tourists. The outdoor bar is a great place to kick back with a cold microbrew, and people are always grilling burgers and socializing at impromptu tailgate parties in the parking lot (known as 'the beach').

Peak 8 Fun Park AMUSEMENT PARK
(☎970-453-5000; www.breckenridge.com/peak-8-fun-park.aspx; Peak 8; half-/full-day pass $50/65; ⏲8:30am-5pm Jun-Aug;) With a laundry list of made-for-thrills activities, including a big-air trampoline ($10), climbing wall ($8), mountain-bike park (adult/child $30/20) with bike rentals (half-/full day $42/52) and the celebrated SuperSlide – a luge-like course taken on a sled at exhilarating speeds.

Festivals & Events

Ullr Fest CULTURAL
(www.gobreck.com) In early to mid-January, the Ullr Fest celebrates the Norse god of winter with a wild parade and four-day festival featuring a twisted version of the Dating Game, an ice-skating party and a bonfire.

FREE **International Snow Sculpture Championship** SNOW
(www.gobreck.com; 150 W Adams Ave; ⏲mid-Jan–early Feb;) Sculptors from around the world descend on Breck to create meltable masterpieces. It starts in mid-January and lasts for three weeks on River walk.

Sleeping

For slope-side rentals, contact **Great Western Lodging** (☎888-333-4535; www.gwlodging.com; 322 N Main St) for mostly upscale options. Campers can look for USFS campgrounds outside of town.

TOP CHOICE **Fireside Inn** B&B, HOSTEL $
(☎970-453-6456; www.firesideinn.com; 114 N French St; dm $39, d $134-168;) The best deal for single travelers, this cozy hostel and B&B is a find. The bunks with extra blankets are probably a better deal than the private rooms, which, though charming, have seen a little wear. All guests can enjoy the chlorine-free barrel hot tub and resident snuggly dog. Niki, the English host, is a delight and very helpful with local information. It's a 10-minute walk to the gondola in ski boots.

Abbet Placer Inn B&B $$
(☎970-453-6489; www.abbettplacer.com; 205 S French St; r Jun-Aug $129-219, Dec-Feb $129-239;) This violet house has five large, themed rooms well decked-out with wood furnishings, iPod docks and fluffy robes. It's very low key. The warm and welcoming hosts cook big breakfasts, and guests can enjoy a lovely outdoor Jacuzzi deck and use of a common kitchenette. Check-in is from 4pm to 7pm.

Eating & Drinking

TOP CHOICE **Hearthstone** MODERN AMERICAN $$$
(☎970-453-1148; www.stormrestaurants.com; 130 S Ridge St; mains $13-38; ⏲4pm-late) One of Breck's favorites, this restored 1886 Victorian churns out creative mountain fare such as house-smoked trout and chile relleno (stuffed chilies) with goat's cheese and honey. Fresh and delicious, it's worth a splurge, or hit happy hour (4pm to 6pm) for $5 plates paired with wine. If the weather cooperates, you can dine out on the three-tiered patios out front. Reservations are highly recommended.

Clint's Bakery & Coffee House SANDWICHES $
(131 S Main St; sandwiches from $5.95, coffee drinks from $2; ⏲7am-9pm Sun-Thu, to 10pm Fri & Sat;) Brainy baristas steam up a chalkboard full of latte and mocha flavors and dozens of loose-leaf teas. If you're hungry, the downstairs bagelry stacks burly sandwiches and tasty breakfast bagels with egg and ham, lox, sausage and cheese. The bagelry closes at 3pm.

Downstairs at Eric's BAR
(www.downstairsaterics.com; 111 S Main St; ⏲11am-midnight;) Downstairs at Eric's is a Breckenridge institution. Locals flock to this electric basement joint with a game room full of vintage pinball machines, for the pitchers, juicy burgers and delicious mashed potatoes (mains from $6). There are more than 120 beers, including several microbrews, to choose from.

THE ROCKIES FOR POWDER HOUNDS

Well worth the five-hour road trip from Denver, **Crested Butte** promises deep powder and lovely open terrain, next to a mining outpost re-tooled to be one of Colorado's coolest small towns.

If you're short on travel time, go directly to Summit County. Use lively **Breckenridge** as your base and conquer four areas on one combo lift ticket, including the mastodon resort of **Vail**, our favorite for remote back bowl terrain, and the ultra-local and laid-back **Arapahoe Basin Ski Area**. A-basin stays open into June, when spring skiing means tailgating with beer and barbecue between slush runs.

From Crested Butte, you can head a little further south and ski the slopes at **Telluride**; from Summit County and Vail, **Aspen** is nearby. Both are true old gold towns. Be sure to devote at least a few hours to exploring Aspen's glitzy shops and Telluride's down-to-earth bars for a real local vibe in a historic Wild West setting.

From Aspen, catch a local flight up to **Jackson Hole Mountain Resort** to do some real vertical powder riding in the Grand Tetons.

Shopping

Outlets at Silverthorne CLOTHING

(www.outletsatsilverthorne.com; Silverthorne; 10am-8pm Mon-Sat, 11am-6pm Sun) Located 15 minutes from Breckenridge, just off I-70, are three shopping villages of designer brand stores with discount prices. Brands include Calvin Klein, Nike, Levi's, Gap and many others.

Information

Visitor center (970-453-6018, 888-251-2417; www.gobreck.com; 309 N Main St; 9am-5pm) Has information on the myriad area activities.

Getting There & Around

Breckenridge is 9 miles south of I-70 on Hwy 9 and about 100 miles from Denver or Colorado Springs.

Colorado Mountain Express (970-926-9800; www.ridecme.com; per person $79) runs shuttles between Breckenridge and Denver International Airport.

For free rides within the city limits, **Free Ride** (Summit County Public Transport; 970-547-3140; www.townofbreckenridge.com) patrols the streets.

To get between Breckenridge, Keystone or Vail, hop on free **Summit Stages buses** (970-668-0999; www.summitstage.com; 150 Watson Ave; 6:25am-1:45am), which run all day.

VAIL

Darling of the rich and sometime famous, Vail resembles an elaborate adult amusement park, with everything man-made from the golf greens down to the indoor waterfalls. It's compact and highly walkable, but the location (a highway runs through it) lacks the natural drama of most Rocky Mountain destinations. That said, no serious skier would dispute its status as the best ski resort in Colorado, with its powdery back bowls, chutes and wickedly fun terrain.

Sights & Activities

Vail Mountain SNOW SPORTS

(970-476-9090; www.vail.com; lift ticket adult/child $99/46; 9am-4pm, longer hours in season;) Vail Mountain is our favorite in the state, with 5289 skiable acres, 193 trails, three terrain parks and some of the highest lift-ticket prices in the country. If you're a Colorado ski virgin, it's worth paying the extra buck to pop your cherry here. Especially on a sunny, blue, fresh-powder day.

For deals, try City Market grocery stores, which often sell reduced-price tickets. The mountaintop Adventure Ridge has child-friendly winter and summer sports.

FREE **Colorado Ski Museum** MUSEUM

(970-476-1876; www.skimuseum.net; 231 S Frontage Rd E; 10am-6pm) Humble but informative, this museum takes you from the invention of skiing to the trials of the Tenth Mountain Division, a decorated WWII alpine unit that trained in these mountains. There are also hilarious fashions from the past, as well as the fledgling Colorado Ski and Snowboard Hall of Fame.

TOP CHOICE **Mount Holy Cross Wilderness** HIKING

(] 970-328-8688; 125 West 5th St, Eagle; 9am-5pm Mon-Fri) Consult rangers for hiking tips. There are six developed campgrounds in the region. The strenuous Notch Mountain Trail affords great views of Mt of the Holy Cross

(14,009ft), or very experienced hikers can climb the mountain itself (a class 2 scramble) via Half Moon Pass Trail.

Vail to Breckenridge Bike Path CYCLING
(www.vail.com; 24hr;) From the West Vail Market you can ride along N Frontage Rd, crossing I-70 at the pedestrian overpass to Lionshead. On the south side of the freeway, a paved bike route extends from W Gore Creek Dr through Cascade Village, Lionshead and Vail Village and continues east on the 10-Mile Canyon Trail through auto-free road-bike heaven over Vail Pass to Frisco.

Sleeping

Vail is expensive, but rates do drop during the off-season.

Sebastian LODGE $$$
(970-888-1540; www.thesebastianvail.com; 16 Vail Rd; r & condos from $450;) Deluxe and modern, this upscale lodging is the latest addition to the Vail scene and its list of amenities is impressive, including a mountainside ski valet, goddess spa and adventure concierge. Room rates dip to affordable in the summer, the perfect time to enjoy the farm-to-table restaurant and a spectacular pool area with hot tubs frothing and spilling over like champagne. Not bad at all.

Austria Haus LODGE $$
(970-754-7850; www.austriahaushotel.com; 242 E Meadow Dr; r incl breakfast $106-559;) With outstanding service, Austria Haus is a great value for Vail. Tasteful rooms are post and beam and a touch retro, while corner suites have gorgeous adobe fireplaces and oversized tubs. Guests can book their preferred tee-off times at the prestigious Red Sky Ranch golf course nearby.

Gore Creek Campground CAMPGROUND $
(970-945-2521; Bighorn Rd; tent sites $13; Memorial Day-Labor Day) With pit toilets at the end of Bighorn Rd, this campground has 25 first-come, first-served tent sites with picnic tables and fire grates nestled in the woods by Gore Creek. Try the Slate Creek or Deluge Lake trails; the latter leads to a fish-packed lake. It's 6 miles east of Vail Village via the East Vail exit off I-70.

Eating & Drinking

TOP CHOICE **Osaki's** JAPANESE $$
(970-476-0977; 100 E Meadow Dr; sushi $8-20; 6pm-late Tue-Sat) A star disciple of Nobu Matsuhisa (yes, *that* Nobu), Osaki opened this low-key hole-in-the-wall temple devoted to all that is sweet, tender and raw. For a splurge, try the $100 seven-course tasting menu. But don't leave without tasting the salmon – it's simply spectacular. In summer it's 30% off. Reserve ahead.

Westside Cafe BREAKFAST $
(970-476-7890; www.westsidecafe.net; 2211 N Frontage Rd; mains $6-14; 7am-10pm;) Set in a West Vail mini-mall off the freeway, this morning beacon sets up skiers and boarders for a long day in the back bowls. Terrific breakfast skillets, large steaming mugs of coffee and Bloody Marys get our thumbs up.

Tap Room SPORTS BAR
(970-479-0500; www.taproomvail.com; 333 Bridge St; 11am-late Mon-Fri, 10am-late Sat & Sun;) A favorite on the Vail bar-hopping circuit, this laid-back sports bar shows ballgames all day and has a giant selection of beers and day-long drink specials. The kitchen churns out middling pub grub, but the chipped-wood bar is a fine place to sip a Native Z draft, plus, it has views of the mountain from the back patio.

Bōl THEME BAR
(970-476-9300; www.bolvail.com; 141 E Meadow Dr; plates $12-24; 5pm-1.30am;) Only in Vail, this high-energy bowling alley (lanes per hour $50, shoe rental $5) has progressive rock pumping, a sleek neon bar and strobe lights on the lanes. It's a magnet for the hip and beautiful. Try the fusion menu featuring pork buns with ponzo sauce and balsamic-tossed arugula. Kids are welcome until 9pm.

Information

Vail Visitor Center (970-479-1385; www.visitvailvalley.com; Transportation Center; 9am-5pm)

Getting There & Around

From December to early April only, **Eagle County Airport** (EGE; 970-524-9490), 35 miles west of Vail, has direct jet services to destinations across the country and rental car counters.

Colorado Mountain Express (970-926-9800; www.cmex.com) shuttles to/from Denver International Airport ($89) and Eagle County Airport ($49). Greyhound buses stop at the **Vail Transportation Center** (970-476-5137; 241 S Frontage Rd) en route to Denver ($34, 2½ hours) or Grand Junction ($30, 3¼ hours).

Vail's **free buses** (☎970-328-8143; http://vailgov.com/transit) stop in West Vail, East Vail and Sandstone; most have bike racks. Regional buses to Avon, Beaver Creek and Edwards charge $4.

Compact Vail Village, filled with upscale restaurants, bars and boutiques, is traffic free. Motorists must park at the Vail Transportation Center & Public Parking garage before entering the pedestrian mall area near the chairlifts. Lionshead is a secondary parking lot about half a mile to the west. It has direct lift access and is usually less crowded.

ASPEN

Immodestly posh Aspen is Colorado's glitziest high-octane resort, playing host to some of the wealthiest skiers in the world. The handsome, historic red-brick downtown is as alluring as the glistening slopes, but Aspen's greatest asset is its magnificent scenery. The stunning alpine environment – especially during late September and October, when the aspen trees put on a spectacular display – just adds extra sugar to an already sweet cake.

Sights & Activities

Aspen Mountain SNOW SPORTS

(☎800-525-6200; www.aspensnowmass.com; E Durant Ave; Aspen Mountain day pass summer $24, Aspen & Snowmass summer $29, Four Mountain 2-day pass $158-192, 1-day pass adult/teen & senior/child $96/87/62; ⊙lift 9am-3.30pm Nov 25-Apr 10;) Forget beginner terrain. Intermediate and advanced skiers do best at this iconic resort. For gentler terrain, check out the nearby sister resorts of Buttermilk and Snowmass, which has the longest vertical drop in the US.

Aspen Highlands SNOW SPORTS

(☎970-925-1220; www.aspensnowmas.com; Prospector Rd; Aspen Mountain day pass summer $24, Aspen & Snowmass Mountain $29, Four Mountain 2-day pass $158-192; ⊙9am-3.30pm) A favorite of expert skiers, with steep, deep, tree runs and bumps.

Ashcroft Ski Touring SNOW SPORTS

(☎970-925-1971; www.pinecreekcookhouse.com/ashcroft.html; 11399 Castle Creek Rd; half-/full-day pass $10/15, child & senior $10;) With 20 miles of groomed trails through 600 acres of subalpine country with a spectacular backdrop. Rent classic cross-country ski equipment (rental packages $20), ski gear or snowshoes. Individual and group lessons ($75), as well as snowshoe and ski tours, are available daily. Shuttles ($35) to and from Aspen are available.

FREE **Hunter-Fryingpan Wilderness Area** HIKING

(☎970-925-3445; www.fs.usda.gov;) From Lone Pine Rd in Aspen, the Hunter Valley Trail (USFS Trail 1992) follows Hunter Creek northeast about 3 miles through wildflower meadows to the Sunnyside and Hunter Creek Trails, which lead into the 82,026-acre Hunter-Fryingpan Wilderness Area. It's less visited than other slices of the Rockies, with stunning campsites and rugged peaks, as well as the headwaters to both Hunter Creek and the Fryingpan River.

Ute City Cycles CYCLING

(☎970-920-3325; www.utecitycycles.com; 231 E Main St; bike rental per 24hr $75; ⊙9am-6pm) A high-end road- and mountain-bike retailer offering limited rentals from its demo fleet. Rentals have a two-day maximum; no reservations. Staff can also point you in the direction of Aspen's best cycling.

Festivals

Aspen Music Festival MUSIC

(☎970-925-3254; www.aspenmusicfestival.com; 2 Music School Rd) Every summer (in July and August) classical musicians from around the world come to play, perform and learn from the masters of their craft. Orchestras and smaller groups are led by world-famous conductors and perform at the Wheeler Opera House, the Benedict Music Tent or on Aspen street corners.

Sleeping

Book through an online consolidator for the best deals. Avoid the week between Christmas and New Year, when prices skyrocket.

DON'T MISS

CYCLING TO MAROON BELLS

According to the Aspen cycling gurus, the most iconic road-bike ride in Aspen is the one to the stunning Maroon Bells. The climb is 11 lung-wrenching miles to the foot of one of the most picturesque wilderness areas in the Rockies. Your other alternative is the bus – the Maroon Bells road is actually closed to incoming car traffic – but if you crave sweet, beautiful pain, let your quads sing.

St Moritz Lodge HOSTEL $

(970-925-3220; www.stmoritzlodge.com; 334 W Hyman Ave; dm $58, r incl breakfast $189;) St Moritz is the best no-frills deal in town. Perks include a heated outdoor pool and grill overlooking Aspen Mountain, and a lobby with games, books and a piano. The European-style lodge offers a wide variety of options, from quiet dorms to two-bedroom condos. The cheapest options share bathrooms.

Annabelle Inn HOTEL $$$

(877-266-2466; www.annabelleinn.com; 232 W Main St; r incl breakfast $159-229;) Personable and unpretentious, the cute and quirky Annabelle Inn resembles an old-school European-style ski lodge in a central location. Rooms are cozy and come with flat-screen TVs and warm duvets. You can also enjoy after-dark ski video screenings from the upper-deck hot tub (one of two on the property).

Little Nell HOTEL $$$

(970-920-4600; www.thelittlenell.com; 675 E Durant Ave; r from $545;) This is a long-time Aspen institution at the foot of Aspen Mountain. Gas-burning fireplaces, high-thread-count linens and rich color schemes make up the elegant modernist decor. An adventure concierge is on hand to help guests get the most from the outdoors. Dining is outstanding and its open air Ajax Tavern is the town hot-spot for some après-ski unwinding.

The **USFS White River National Forest's Aspen Ranger District** (970-925-3445; www.fs.fed.us; 806 W Hallam St; 8am-4:30pm Mon-Fri winter, 8am-4:30pm Mon-Sat summer) operates nine **campgrounds** (campsites $15-20).

Eating & Drinking

Aspen has few deals but après-ski is an institution, and even the better spots have food and drink bargains during happy hour.

TOP CHOICE **Pine Creek Cookhouse** AMERICAN $$$

(970-925-1044; www.pinecreekcookhouse.com; 12700 Castle Creek Rd; mains $16-24; noon-8pm Jun-Sep, sittings at noon, 1:30pm & 6pm Nov-Apr;) The best setting around – a gorgeous cross-country ski-in to a log-cabin restaurant serving outstanding, fresh fusion fare. It's 11 miles up Castle Creek Canyon past the old mining town of Ashcroft. Shrimp tikka masala, grilled quail served over greens and house-smoked trout are all outstanding.

It's closed in October and May, but stays open all summer and winter, when you can get here from Ashcroft skiing or aboard the cookhouse's horse-drawn sleigh, then warm up by the crackling fire.

BB's Kitchen MODERN AMERICAN $$$

(970-429-8284; 525 E Cooper Ave, 2nd fl; mains $11-27; 8am-5pm, 6-10pm) A local darling and winner of the 2011 Diners' Choice award, this 2nd-floor patio is the best spot for a casual lunch or a leisurely gourmet breakfast (think lobster Benedict or wild morel omelet). This isn't show food – the chef-owners are committed to quality, down to curing their own meats. For dinner, slip into a red booth for delicious house sausage pizza or poached halibut served over a gorgeous mint pea puree.

Pitkin County Steakhouse STEAKHOUSE $$$

(970-544-6328; www.pitkincountysteakhouse.com; 305 E Hopkins Ave; mains $26-58; from 6pm) Down-home and the most popular place for prime dry-aged steaks with a great salad bar. Set in the basement of a Hopkins Ave complex, it has an open kitchen scattered with dim-lit tables. In low season the dining room is only open Thursday to Saturday, but its adjacent tavern is always open for business.

Aspen Brewing Co BREWERY

(970-920-2739; www.aspenbrewingcompany.com; 557 N Mill St; pints $2.75; noon-9pm Mon-Sat, noon-6pm Sun) Tibetan prayer flags fly and reggae grooves at this microbrewery with six flavors brewed behind the bar.

J-Bar BAR

(www.hoteljerome.com; 330 E Main St) Once Aspen's premier saloon, back when the word 'saloon' had its own unique meaning, this bar was built into the Hotel Jerome in 1889 and remains full of historic charm and packed with everyone from local shopkeepers to Hollywood stars.

Information

Aspen Visitor Center (970-925-1940; www.aspenchamber.org; 425 Rio Grande Pl; 8am-5pm Mon-Fri) Has all the usual information.

Getting There & Around

Four miles north of Aspen on Hwy 82, **Aspen-Pitkin County Airport** (970-920-5380; www.aspenairport.com; 233 E Airport Rd;) has commuter flights from Denver, and nonstops to Phoenix, Los Angeles, San Francisco, Minneapolis and Memphis. **Colorado Mountain Express** (970-947-0506; www.cmex.com) runs frequent shuttles to/from Denver International Airport ($100, three hours).

Roaring Fork Transit Agency (☎970-920-1905; www.rfta.com) buses connect Aspen with the ski areas and runs free trips to and from Aspen-Pitkin County Airport.

BUENA VISTA & SALIDA

Buena Vista and Salida's small-town charms complement the fun of shooting the Arkansas River's rapids or soaking in hot springs under the stars. There are plenty of cheap motels, campgrounds and public lands suited to camping.

For rafting, stop by **Buffalo Joe's Whitewater Rafting** (☎866-283-3563; www.buffalojoe.com; 113 N Railroad St; day trip adult $64-105, child $45-69, 2-day trip $179/139; ⏰8am-7pm; 👪). You'll want to run Brown's Canyon (Class III to IV), the Narrows (III to IV) or the Numbers (IV to V), and the earlier in the season the better (try for May and June, when the river is bloated with snow runoff and the rapids are much more intense). The company also rents mountain bikes and can recommend some great trails in the area.

After a day on the river, forget the soreness with a soak at **Cottonwood Hot Springs Inn & Spa** (☎719-395-6434; www.cottonwood-hot-springs.com; 18999 Co Rd 306; adult/child 16yr & under Mon-Fri $15/12, Sat & Sun $20/17, towel rental $1; ⏰8am-midnight; 👪). These renovated springs are set on leafy grounds with gushing fountains of hot water, dangling vines and wind chimes. The five pools range in temperature from 94° to 110°F (34° to 43°C). For those staying here, **rooms** (from $102) have floral bedspreads and cheap wood furnishings, but they're super-clean and you can use the natural springs all night.

You'll need a car to get to this area south of Leadville on US 24.

CRESTED BUTTE

Powder-bound Crested Butte has retained its rural character better than most Colorado ski resorts. Remote, and ringed by three wilderness areas, this former mining village is counted among Colorado's best ski resorts (some say it's *the* best). The old town center features beautifully preserved Victorian-era buildings refitted with shops and businesses. Strolling two-wheel traffic matches its laid-back, happy attitude.

Most everything in town is on Elk Ave, including the **visitor center** (☎970-349-6438; www.crestedbuttechamber.com; 601 Elk Ave; ⏰9am-5pm).

Crested Butte Mountain Resort (☎970-349-2222; www.skicb.com; lift ticket adult/child $87/44) sits 2 miles north of the town at the base of the impressive mountain of the same name, surrounded by forests, rugged mountain peaks and the West Elk, Raggeds and Maroon Bells-Snowmass Wilderness Areas. The scenery is breathtakingly beautiful. It caters mostly to intermediate and expert riders.

Crested Butte is also a **mountain-biking** mecca, full of excellent high-altitude singletrack trails. For maps, information and mountain-bike rentals, visit the **Alpineer** (☎970-349-5210; www.alpineer.com; 419 6th St).

Crested Butte International Hostel (☎970-349-0588; www.crestedbuttehostel.com; 615 Tonally Ave; dm $25-31, r $65-110; @) is one of Colorado's nicest hostels. The best private rooms have their own baths. Dorm bunks come with reading lamps and lockable drawers. The communal area is mountain rustic with a stone fireplace and comfortable couches. Rates vary dramatically by season, with fall being cheapest.

With phenomenal food, the funky-casual **Secret Stash** (☎970-349-6245; www.thesecretstash.com; 21 Elk Ave; mains $8-20; ⏰5-10pm; 🍸👪) is adored by locals, who also like the original cocktails. The house specialty is pizza; its Notorious Fig (with prosciutto, fresh figs and truffle oil) won the 2007 World Pizza Championship.

Crested Butte has an interesting music scene year-round. Check out the lively **Eldo Brewpub** (☎970-349-6125; 215 Elk Ave), one of the town's most popular microbreweries, which doubles as the club where most out-of-town bands play. Check out the great outdoor deck.

Crested Butte's air link to the outside world is **Gunnison County Airport** (☎970-641-2304), 28 miles south of the town. Shuttle **Alpine Express** (☎970-641-5074; www.alpineexpressshuttle.com; per person $34) goes to Crested Butte; reserve ahead in summer.

The free **Mountain Express** (☎970-349-7318; www.mtnexp.org) connects Crested Butte with Mt Crested Butte every 15 minutes in winter, less often in other seasons; check times at bus stops.

Southern Colorado

Home to the dramatic San Juan and Sangre de Cristo mountain ranges, Colorado's bottom half is just as pretty as its top, has fewer people and is filled with stuff to see and do.

GREAT SAND DUNES NATIONAL PARK

Landscapes collide in a shifting sea of sand at **Great Sand Dunes National Park** (☎719-378-2312; www.nps.gov/grsa; 11999 Hwy 150; admission $3; ⊙visitor center 9am-5pm, longer hours in summer), making you wonder whether a spaceship has whisked you to another planet. The 55-sq-mile dune park – the tallest sand peak rises 700ft above the valley floor – is squeezed between the jagged 14,000ft peaks of the Sangre de Cristo and San Juan Mountains and flat, arid scrub-brush of the San Luis Valley.

Plan a visit to this excellent-value national park (at just $3, admission is a steal) around a full moon. Stock up on supplies, stop by the visitor center for your free backcountry camping permit and hike into the surreal landscape to set up camp in the middle of nowhere (bring plenty of water). You won't be disappointed.

There are numerous **hiking trails**, or the more adventuresome can try **sandboarding** (where you ride a snowboard down the dunes) or sledding. You can rent a sled or sandboard for some of the world's greatest dune riding from Great Sand Dunes Oasis just outside the park. Don't bother to bring a bike – they are useless in these conditions. Spring, when the dunes are at their most moist, is the best time for boarding. For the slickest boarding, arrive a few hours after it rains, when the dunes are wet underneath, but dry on top. Try riding down Star Dune, roughly 750ft high. It's a strenuous 3-mile hike from the Dunes parking lot. The High Dune, about 650ft tall, is another option. Be sure to bring lots of water. Walking in loose sand is difficult, and summer temperatures on the dunes can exceed 130°F (54°C).

Owned and operated by the Nature Conservancy, **Inn at Zapata Ranch** (☎719-378-2356; www.zranch.org; 5303 Hwy 150; d with full board $250; 👪) is a working cattle and bison ranch set amid groves of cottonwood trees. Peaceful, it features historic buildings, including the main inn, a refurbished 19th-century log structure, with distant views of the sand dunes. Horseback riding, mountain-bike rentals and massage therapy are also on offer.

In the national park, **Pinyon Flats Campground** (www.recreation.gov; Great Sand Dunes National Park; campsites $14; ⊙year-round) has 88 sites and year-round water. The less appealing **Great Sand Dunes Oasis** (☎719-378-2222; www.greatdunes.com; 5400 Hwy 150; tent/RV sites $18/28, cabins $40) has spartan cabins, showers and a laundry service.

The national park is about 35 miles northeast of Alamosa and 250 miles south of Denver. From Denver, take I-25 south to Hwy 160 west and turn onto Hwy 150 north. There is no public transportation.

DURANGO

An archetypal old Colorado mining-town, Durango is a regional darling that is nothing short of delightful. Its graceful hotels, Victorian-era saloons and tree-lined streets of sleepy bungalows invite you to pedal around soaking up all the good vibes. There is plenty to do outdoors. Style-wise, Durango is torn between its ragtime past and a cool, cutting-edge future where townie bikes, caffeine and farmers markets rule.

The town's historic central precinct is home to boutiques, bars, restaurants and theater halls. Foodies will revel in the innovative organic and locavore fare that is making it the best place to eat in the state. But the interesting galleries and live music, combined with a relaxed and congenial local populace, also make it a great place to visit.

Sights & Activities

TOP CHOICE **Durango & Silverton Narrow Gauge Railroad** TRAIN TOUR

(☎970-247-2733, www.durangotrain.com; 479 Main Ave; adult/child return from $83/49; ⊙departures 8am, 8:30am, 9:15am & 10am) Riding the Durango & Silverton Narrow Gauge Railroad is a Durango must. These vintage steam locomotives have been making the scenic 45-mile trip north to Silverton (3½ hours each way) for over 125 years. The dazzling journey allows two hours for exploring Silverton. This trip operates only from May through October. Check online for different winter options.

Mountain Biking CYCLING

From steep single-track to scenic road rides, Durango is a national hub for mountain biking. The easy **Old Railroad Grade Trail** is a 12.2-mile loop that uses both US Hwy 160 and a dirt road following the old railway tracks. From Durango take Hwy 160 west through the town of Hesperus. Turn right into the Cherry Creek Picnic Area, where the trail starts.

For something a bit more technical, try **Dry Fork Loop**, accessible from Lightner Creek just west of town. It has some great drops, blind corners and vegetation. Cycling shops on Main or Second Ave rent out mountain bikes.

Durango Mountain Resort SNOW SPORTS

(970-247-9000; www.durangomountainresort.com; 1 Skier Pl; lift tickets adult/child from $65/36; mid-Nov–Mar;) Also known as Purgatory, this resort, 25 miles north on US 550, offers 1200 skiable acres of varying difficulty and boasts 260in of snow per year. Two terrain parks offer plenty of opportunities for snowboarders to catch big air. Check local grocery stores and newspapers for promotions and two-for-one lift tickets.

Sleeping

TOP CHOICE Strater Hotel HOTEL $$

(970-247-4431; www.strater.com; 699 Main Ave; d $169-189;) The past lives large in this historical Durango hotel with walnut antiques, hand-stenciled wallpapers and relics ranging from a Stradivarius violin to a gold-plated Winchester. But we can boast about the friendly staff, who go out of their way to resolve guests' quiries. Rooms lean toward the romantic, with comfortable beds amid antiques, crystal and lace. The hot tub is a romantic plus (reserved by the hour) as is the summertime melodrama (theater) the hotel runs. In winter, rates drop by more than 50%, making it a virtual steal. Look online.

Rochester House HOTEL $$

(970-385-1920; www.rochesterhotel.com; 721 E 2nd Ave; d $169-219;) Influenced by old Westerns (movie posters and marquee lights adorn the hallways), the Rochester is a little bit of old Hollywood in the new West. It's linked to smaller accommodations, Leland House, across the street, where all guests check in. Rooms in both are spacious but slightly worn, some with kitchenettes. Still, you can't beat the cool townie bikes, available for guests to take spins around town. Pet rooms come with direct access outside.

Hometown Hostel HOSTEL $

(970-385-4115; www.durangohometownhostel.com; 736 Goeglein Gulch Rd; dm $30; reception 3:30-8pm;) The bee's knees of hostels, this suburban-style house sits on the winding road up to the college, next to a convenient bike path. A better class of backpackers, it's all-inclusive, with linen, towels, lockers and wi-fi. There are two single-sex dorms and a larger mixed dorm, and a great common kitchen and lounge area. Room rates fall with extended stays.

Day's End MOTEL $

(970-259-3311; www.daysenddurango.com; 2202 N Main Ave; r from $55;) The best budget motel bet is on a small creek just north of town. Rooms are well maintained and many have king-size beds. Skiers get discounts at Durango Mountain Resort. There's an indoor hot tub and BBQ grill by the creek. Pets are welcome.

Eating & Drinking

Durango has a fantastic dining scene, especially strong on organic and locally sourced foods. Get a local dining guide for all the options. It's also home to a slew of breweries.

TOP CHOICE East by Southwest ASIAN $$

(970-247-5533; http://eastbysouthwest.com; 160 E College Dr; sushi $4-13, mains $12-24; 11:30am-3pm Mon-Sat, 5-10pm daily;) Low-lit but vibrant, this is a worthy local favorite. Skip the standards for goosebump-good house favorites like sashimi with jalapeño and rolls with mango and wasabi honey. Fish is fresh and they don't serve endangered species. An extensive fusion menu also offers Thai, Vietnamese and Indonesian, well matched with creative martinis and sake cocktails. For a deal, check out the happy hour food specials (5pm to 6:30pm) for around $6.

Randy's STEAK, SEAFOOD $$$

(970-247-9083; www.randysrestaurant.com; 152 E College Dr; mains $20-25; 5-10pm) A popular seafood and steak spot, with refreshing lighter fare and specialties such as garlic polenta fries. Between 5pm and 6pm earlybirds score the same menu for $12 to $14. Happy hour runs from 5pm to 7pm.

Durango Diner DINER $

(970-247-9889; www.durangodiner.com; 957 Main Ave; mains $7-18; 6am-2pm Mon-Sat, 6am-1pm Sun;) Enjoy the open view of the griddle at this lovable greasy spoon with button-cute waitresses and monstrous plates of eggs, smothered burritos or French toast. It's a local institution.

Jean Pierre Bakery SANDWICHES, BAKERY $$

(970-247-7700; www.jeanpierrebakery.com; 601 Main Ave; mains $5-16; 8am-9pm;) This French patisserie has tempting delicacies made from scratch. Prices are dear, but at $15 the soup-and-sandwich lunch special, with a sumptuous French pastry (we recommend the sticky pecan roll), is a deal.

Steamworks Brewing BREWERY
(☎970-259-9200; www.steamworksbrewing.com; 801 E 2nd Ave; mains $10-15; ⏰1pm-midnight Mon-Fri, 11am-2am Sat & Sun) DJs and live music pump up the volume at this industrial microbrewery with high sloping rafters and metal pipes. College kids fill the large bar area, but there's also a separate dining room with a Cajun-influenced menu.

Diamond Belle Saloon BAR
(☎970-376-7150; www.strater.com; 699 Main Ave) A rowdy corner of the historic Strater Hotel, this elegant old-time bar has waitresses dressed in vintage Victorian garb and flashing fishnets, and live ragtime that keeps out-of-town visitors packed in, standing room only, at happy hour. Half-price appetizers and drink specials run from 4pm to 6pm.

ℹ Information

Visitor center (☎800-525-8855; www.durango.org; 111 S Camino del Rio) South of town at the Santa Rita exit from US 550.

ℹ Getting There & Around

Durango-La Plata County Airport (DRO; ☎970-247-8143; www.flydurango.com; 1000 Airport Rd) is 18 miles southwest of Durango via US 160 and Hwy 172. Greyhound buses run daily from the **Durango Bus Center** (☎970-259-2755; 275 E 8th Ave), north to Grand Junction and south to Albuquerque, NM.

Check **Durango Transit** (☎970-259-5438; www.getarounddurango.com) for local travel information. Durango buses are fitted with bicycle racks. It's free to ride the red T shuttle bus that circulates Main St.

Durango is at the junction of US 160 and US 550, 42 miles east of Cortez, 49 miles west of Pagosa Springs and 190 miles north of Albuquerque.

SILVERTON

Ringed by snowy peaks and steeped in sooty tales of a tawdry mining town, Silverton seems more at home in Alaska than the lower 48. But here it is. Whether you're into snowmobiling, powder skiing, fly-fishing, beer on tap or just basking in some very high-altitude sunshine, Silverton delivers.

It's a two-street town, but only one is paved. The main drag, Greene St, is where you'll find most businesses. Notorious Blair St, still unpaved, runs parallel to Greene and is a blast from the past. During the silver rush, Blair St was home to thriving brothels and boozing establishments.

In summer, Silverton has some of the west's best 4WD trails. Traveling in modified Chevy Suburbans without the top, **San Juan Backcountry** (☎970-387-5565; www.sanjuanbackcountry.com; 1119 Greene St; 2hr tours adult/child $60/40; ⏰May-Oct; 👪) offers both tours and rental jeeps.

Campers can try **Red Mountain Motel & RV Park** (☎970-382-5512; www.redmtmotelrvpk.com; 664 Greene St; motel r from $78, cabins from $70, tent/RV sites $20/38; P📶👪), a pet-friendly place that stays open year-round. Or splurge for romance at **Inn of the Rockies at the Historic Alma House** (☎970-387-5336; www.innoftherockies.com; 220 E 10th St; r incl breakfast from $110; P❄) with an outdoor hot tub and New Orleans–inspired breakfasts.

The town has its share of Western-style saloons, but for something original seek out

SCENIC DRIVES: SAN JUAN MOUNTAIN PASSES

With rugged peaks and deep canyon drops, the scenery of the San Juan mountain range is hard to beat. Suitable for all vehicles, the **Million Dollar Highway** (US 550) takes its name from the valuable ore in the roadbed. But the scenery is also golden – the paved road clings to crumbly mountains, passing old mine-head frames and big alpine scenery.

A demanding but fantastic drive, the 65-mile **Alpine Loop Backcountry Byway** (www.alpineloop.com) begins in **Ouray** and travels east to **Lake City** – a wonderful mountain hamlet worth a visit – before looping back to its starting point. Along the way you'll cross two 12,000ft mountain passes and swap pavement and people for solitude, spectacular views and abandoned mining haunts. You'll need a high-clearance 4WD vehicle and some off-road driving skills to conquer this drive; allow six hours.

Spectacular during autumn for the splendor of its yellow aspens, **Ophir Pass** connects Ouray to Telluride via a former wagon road. The moderate 4WD route passes former mines, with a gradual ascent to 11,789ft. To get there, drive south of Ouray on Hwy 550 for 18.1 miles to the right-hand turnoff for National Forest Access, Ophir Pass.

As with all 4WD routes and mountain passes, check for road closures before going.

Montanya Distillers (www.montanyadistillers.com; 1332 Blair St; mains $8-20; ⏱11:30am-7pm; 👪), a smart and cozy bar with exotic cocktails crafted with homemade syrups and award-winning rum. Organic tamales and other yummy edibles are served.

Silverton is 50 miles north of Durango and 24 miles south of Ouray off US 550.

OURAY

With gorgeous ice falls draping the box canyon and soothing hot springs that dot the valley floor, Ouray is a privileged place for nature, even for Colorado. For ice-climbers it's a world-class destination, but hikers and 4WD fans can also appreciate its rugged (and sometimes stunning) charms. The town is a well-preserved quarter-mile mining village sandwiched between imposing peaks.

Between Silverton and Ouray, US 550 is known as the Million Dollar Hwy because the roadbed fill contains valuable ore. One of the state's most memorable drives, this breathtaking stretch passes old mine-head frames and larger-than-life alpine scenery. Though paved, the road is scary in rain or snow, so take extra care.

Sights & Activities

The visitor center is at the hot-springs pool. Check out their leaflet on an excellent walking tour that takes in two-dozen buildings and houses constructed between 1880 and 1904.

FREE **Ouray Ice Park** ICE CLIMBING
(☎970-325-4061; www.ourayicepark.com; Hwy 361; ⏱7am-5pm mid-Dec-March) Enthusiasts from around the globe come to ice climb at the world's first public ice park, spanning a 2-mile stretch of the Uncompahgre Gorge. The sublime (if chilly) experience offers something for all skill levels.

TOP CHOICE **Chicks with Picks** ROCK, ICE CLIMBING
(☎cell 970-316-1403, office 970-626-4424; www.chickswithpicks.net; 163 County Rd 12, Ridgway; prices vary) Arming women with ice tools and crampons, this group of renowned women athletes gives excellent instruction for all-comers (beginners included) in rock-climbing, bouldering and ice-climbing. Programs are fun and change frequently, with multiday excursions or town-based courses. The climbing clinics also go on the road all over the US.

Ouray Hot Springs SPRING
(☎970-325-7073; www.ourayhotsprings.com; 1220 Main St; adult/child $10/8; ⏱10am-10pm Jun-Aug, noon-9pm Mon-Fri & 11am-9pm Sat & Sun Dec-Feb; 👪) For a healing soak, try the historic Ouray Hot Springs. The crystal-clear natural spring water is free of the sulfur smells plaguing other hot springs around here, and the giant pool features a variety of soaking areas at temperatures ranging from 96° to 106°F (35.5° to 41°C). The complex also offers a gym and massage service.

San Juan Mountain Guides OUTDOORS
(☎970-325-4925, 866-525-4925; www.ourayclimbing.com; 474 Main St) Ouray's own professional guiding and climbing group is certified with the International Federation of Mountain Guides Association (IFMGA). It specializes in ice- and rock-climbing and wilderness backcountry skiing.

Festivals & Events

Ouray Ice Festival ICE CLIMBING
(☎970-325-4288; www.ourayicefestival.com; ⏱Jan; 👪) The Ouray Ice Festival features four days of climbing competitions, dinners, slide shows and clinics in January. There's even a climbing wall set up for kids. You can watch the competitions for free, but to check out the various evening events you will need to make a donation ($15) to the ice park. Once inside you'll get free brews from popular Colorado microbrewer New Belgium.

Sleeping & Eating

TOP CHOICE **Wiesbaden** HOTEL $$
(☎970-325-4347; www.wiesbadenhotsprings.com; 625 5th St; r from $132; 📶🚭) Few hotels can boast their own natural indoor vapor cave (and it's rumored that, long ago, Chief Ouray used this one). This quirky new-age inn charms with quilted bedcovers, free organic coffee and a spacious outdoor hot-spring pool (included). Guests can use the Aveda salon or book a private, clothing-optional soaking tub with a waterfall ($35 per hour).

🌿 **Box Canyon Lodge & Hot Springs** LODGE $$
(☎970-325-4981; www.boxcanyonouray.com; 45 3rd Ave; d $159; 📶👪) With geothermal heat, these pine-board rooms are toasty and spacious. A set of outdoor spring-fed barrel hot tubs are perfect for a romantic stargazing soak. Book well ahead.

Amphitheater Forest Service Campground CAMPGROUND $
(☎877-444-6777; www.ouraycolorado.com/amphitheater; US Hwy 550; tent sites $16; ⊙Jun-Aug) With great tent sites under the trees, this high-altitude campground is a score. On holiday weekends a three-night minimum applies. South of town on Hwy 550, take a signposted left-hand turn.

TOP CHOICE **Buen Tiempo Mexican Restaurant & Cantina** MEXICAN $$
(☎970-325-4544; 515 Main St; mains $7-19; ⊙6-10pm;) From the chili-rubbed sirloin to the posole (hearty hominy soup) served with warm tortillas, Buen Tiempo delivers. Start with one of its signature margaritas, served with chips and spicy homemade salsa.

Information

Visitor center (☎970-325-4746; www.ouraycolorado.com; 1220 Main St; ⊙9am-5pm)

Getting There & Around

Ouray is 24 miles north of Silverton along US 550 and best reached by private vehicle.

TELLURIDE

Surrounded on three sides by mastodon peaks, exclusive Telluride feels cut off from the hubbub of the outside world, and it often is. Once a rough mining town, today it's dirtbag-meets-diva – mixing the few who can afford the real estate with those scratching out a slope-side living for the sport of it. The town center still has palpable old-time charm and the surroundings are simply gorgeous.

Colorado Ave, also known as Main St, is where you'll find most businesses. From downtown you can reach the ski mountain via two lifts and the gondola. The latter also links Telluride with Mountain Village, the true base for the Telluride Ski Area. Located 7 miles from town along Hwy 145, Mountain Village is a 20-minute drive east, but is only 12 minutes away by gondola (free for foot passengers).

WORTH A TRIP

COLORADO HUT TO HUT

An exceptional way to enjoy hundreds of miles of single-track in summer or virgin powder slopes in winter, **San Juan Hut Systems** (☎970-626-3033; www.sanjuan-huts.com; per person $30) continues the European tradition of hut-to-hut adventures with five backcountry mountain huts. Bring just your food, flashlight (torch) and sleeping bag: amenities include padded bunks, propane stoves, wood stoves for heating and firewood.

Mountain-biking routes go from Durango or Telluride to Moab, winding through high alpine and desert regions. Or pick one hut as your base for a few days of backcountry skiing or riding. There's terrain for all levels, though skiers should have knowledge of snow and avalanche conditions. If not, go with a guide.

The website has helpful tips and information on rental skis, bikes and (optional) guides based in Ridgway or Ouray.

Sights & Activities

Telluride Ski Resort SNOW SPORTS
(☎970-728-7533, 888-288-7360; www.tellurideskiresort.com; 565 Mountain Village Blvd; lift tickets adult/child $98/61) Covering three distinct areas, Telluride Ski Resort is served by 16 lifts. Much of the terrain is for advanced and intermediate skiers, but there's still ample choice for beginners.

Paragon Ski & Sport OUTDOORS
(☎970-728-4525; www.paragontelluride.com; 213 W Colorado Ave) Has branches at three locations in town and a huge selection of rental bikes. It's a one-stop shop for outdoor activities in Telluride.

Festivals & Events

Mountainfilm FILM
(www.mountainfilm.org) A four-day screening of outdoor adventure and environmental films on Memorial Day weekend (May).

Telluride Bluegrass Festival MUSIC
(☎800-624-2422; www.planetbluegrass.com; 4-day pass $185) A wild frolic held in June, with all-day and evening music, food stalls and local microbrews. Camping is popular during the festival. Check out the website for info on sites, shuttle services and combo ticket-and-camping packages – it's all very organized!

Telluride Film Festival FILM
(☎603-433-9202; www.telluridefilmfestival.com; tickets $20-650) National and international films are premiered throughout town in early September, and the event attracts big-name stars. For more information on the relatively complicated pricing scheme, visit the film festival website.

DON'T MISS

TELLURIDE'S GREAT OUTDOORS

Sure, the festivals are great, but there's much more to a Telluride summer:

Mountain biking

Follow the River Trail from Town Park to Hwy 145 for 2 miles. Join **Mill Creek Trail** west of the Texaco gas station, it climbs and follows the contour of the mountain and ends at the Jud Wiebe Trail (hikers only).

Hiking

Just over 2 miles, **Bear Creek Trail** ascends 1040ft to a beautiful cascading waterfall. From here you can access the strenuous **Wasatch Trail**, a 12-mile loop that heads west across the mountains to **Bridal Veil Falls** – Telluride's most impressive waterfalls. The Bear Creek trailhead is at the south end of Pine St, across the San Miguel River.

Cycling

A 31-mile (one-way) trip, **Lizard Head Pass** features amazing mountain panoramas.

Sleeping

Telluride's lodgings can fill quickly, and for the best rates it's best to book online. Unless you're planning to camp, however, don't expect budget deals. Telluride's activities and festivals keep it busy year-round. For vacation rentals, the most reputable agency is **Telluride Alpine Lodging** (888-893-0158; www.telluridelodging.com; 324 W Colorado Ave).

TOP CHOICE Hotel Columbia HOTEL $$$
(970-728-0660; www.columbiatelluride.com; 300 W San Juan Ave; d $350;) Locally owned and operated, this stylish hotel pampers guests. The gondola is across the street, so leave your gear in the ski and boot storage and head directly to a room with espresso maker, fireplace and heated tile floors. With shampoo dispensers and recycling, it's also pretty ecofriendly. Other highlights include a rooftop hot tub and fitness room.

Victorian Inn LODGE $$
(970-728-6601; www.tellurideinn.com; 401 W Pacific Ave; r from $159;) The smell of fresh cinnamon rolls greets visitors at one of Telluride's better deals, offering comfortable rooms (some with kitchenettes) and a hot tub and dry sauna in a nice garden area. Staff is friendly and guests get lift-ticket discounts. Kids aged 12 and under stay free, and you can't beat the downtown location.

Telluride Town Park Campground CAMPGROUND $
(970-728-2173; 500 W Colorado Ave; tent sites $20; mid-May–mid-Sep) Right in the center of town, these 20 sites have access to showers, swimming and tennis. It fills up quickly in the high season. For other campgrounds within 10 miles of town, check with the visitor center.

Eating & Drinking

For the best deals, look for a taco stand or hot dog truck on Colorado Ave.

Butcher & the Baker CAFE $$
(970-728-3334; 217 E Colorado Ave; mains $8-14; 7am-7pm Mon-Sat, 8am-2pm Sun;) Two veterans of upscale local catering started this heartbreakingly cute cafe, and no one beats it for breakfast. Organic ingredients and locally sourced meats make it a cut above. The to-go sandwiches are the best bet for a gourmet meal on the trail.

La Cocina de Luz MEXICAN $$
(www.lacocinatelluride.com; 123 E Colorado Ave; mains $9-19; 9am-9pm) As they lovingly serve two Colorado favorites (organic and Mexican), it's no wonder that the lunch line is 10 people deep on a slow day at this healthy taqueria. There are delicious details too, such as handmade tortillas and margaritas with organic lime and agave nectar. Vegan, gluten-free options too.

There TAPAS $
(970-728-1213; www.therebars.com; 627 W Pacific Ave; appetizers from $4; 3pm-late) A hip snack-and-drink alcove featuring yummy East-meets-West inventions. Think soy paper wraps with salmon, steamed pork buns and sashimi tostadas and the Very Special Ramen Soup, with crab, duck or pork. Pair it with an original cocktail – we liked the jalapeño kiss.

New Sheridan Bar BAR
(970-728-3911; www.newsheridan.com; 231 W Colorado Ave) Mixes real local flavor with the see-and-be-seen crowd. Most of this historic bar survived the waning mining fortunes even as the adjoining hotel sold off chandeliers

and fine furnishings to pay the heating bills. Look for the bullet holes in the wall.

Entertainment

Fly Me to the Moon Saloon LIVE MUSIC
(970-728-6666; 132 E Colorado Ave) Let your hair down and kick up your heels to the tunes of live bands at this saloon, the best place in Telluride to groove to live music.

Sheridan Opera House THEATER
(970-728-4539; www.sheridanoperahouse.com; 110 N Oak St) This historic venue has a burlesque charm and is always the center of Telluride's cultural life.

Information

Visitor center (970-728-3041, 888-353-5473; www.telluride.com; 398 W Colorado Ave; 9am-5pm)

Getting There & Around

Commuter aircraft serve the mesa-top **Telluride Airport** (970-778-5051; www.tellurideairport.com; Last Dollar Rd), 5 miles east of town on Hwy 145. If the weather is poor, flights may be diverted to Montrose, 65 miles north. For car rental, National and Budget both have airport locations.

In ski season Montrose Regional Airport, 66 miles north, has direct flights to and from Denver (on United), Houston, Phoenix and limited cities on the East Coast.

Shared shuttles by **Telluride Express** (970-728-6000; www.tellurideexpress.com) go from the Telluride Airport to town or Mountain Village for $15. Shuttles between the Montrose Airport and Telluride cost $48.

MESA VERDE NATIONAL PARK

Shrouded in mystery, Mesa Verde, with its cliff dwellings and verdant valley walls, is a fascinating, if slightly eerie, national park to explore. It is here that a civilization of Ancestral Puebloans appears to have vanished in AD 1300, leaving behind a complex civilization of cliff dwellings, some accessed by sheer climbs. Mesa Verde is unique among parks for its focus on preserving this civilization's cultural relics so that future generations may continue to interpret the puzzling settlement, and subsequent abandonment, of the area.

Mesa Verde rewards travelers who set aside a day or more to take the ranger-led tours of Cliff Palace and Balcony House, explore Wetherill Mesa or participate in one of the campfire programs. But if you only have time for a short visit, check out the Chapin Mesa Museum and walk through the Spruce Tree House, where you can climb down a wooden ladder into the cool chamber of a kiva (ceremonial structure, usually partly underground).

Sights & Activities

FREE **Chapin Mesa Museum** MUSEUM
(970-529-4631; 8am-6:30pm, 8am-5pm winter) A good first stop, with detailed dioramas and exhibits pertaining to the park. When park headquarters are closed on weekends, staff at the museum provide information.

Chapin Mesa ARCHEOLOGICAL SITE
The largest concentration of Ancestral Puebloan sites is at Chapin Mesa, where you'll see the densely clustered **Far View Site** and the large **Spruce Tree House**, the most accessible of sites, with a paved half-mile round-trip path.

If you want to see **Cliff Palace** or **Balcony House**, the only way is through an hour-long ranger-led tour booked in advance at the visitor center ($3). These tours are extremely popular; go early in the morning or a day in advance to book. Balcony House requires climbing a 32ft and 60ft ladder – those with medical problems should skip it.

Wetherill Mesa ARCHEOLOGICAL SITE
This is the second-largest concentration. Visitors may enter stabilized surface sites and two cliff dwellings, including the **Long House**, open from late May through August. South from Park Headquarters, the 6-mile **Mesa Top Road** connects excavated mesa-top sites, accessible cliff dwellings and vantage points to view inaccessible dwellings from the mesa rim.

TOP CHOICE **Aramark Mesa Verde** HIKING
(970-529-4421; www.visitmesaverde.com; adult $20-40) Highly recommended, these backcountry ranger tours are run through the park concessionaire. Backcountry hikes sell out fast, since they provide exclusive access to **Square House** (via an exposed one-mile hike) and **Spring House** (an eight-hour, 8-mile hike), but make very personalized trips to excavated pit homes, cliff dwellings and the **Spruce Tree House** daily from May to mid-October. Tickets available only online.

Sleeping & Eating

The nearby towns of Cortez and Mancos have plenty of midrange places to stay; inside the park there's camping and a lodge.

Morefield Campground CAMPGROUND $

(☎970-529-4465; www.nps.gov/meve; N Rim Rd; tent sites $20, canvas tents from $40; ⏲May–mid-Oct) Deluxe campers will dig the big canvas tents kitted out with two cots and a lantern. The park's camping option, located 4 miles from the entrance gate, also has 445 regular tent sites on grassy grounds conveniently located near Morefield Village. The village has a general store, gas station, restaurant, free showers and laundry.

Free evening campfire programs take place nightly from Memorial Day (May) to Labor Day (September) at the Morefield Campground Amphitheater.

Far View Lodge LODGE $$

(☎970-529-4421; www.visitmesaverde.com; N Rim Rd; r from $119; ⏲mid-Apr–Oct; P❄📶👪) Perched on a mesa top 15 miles inside the park entrance, this tasteful Pueblo-style lodge has 150 rooms, some with kiva fireplaces. Standard rooms don't have air con (or TV) and summer daytimes can be hot. The Southwestern-style kiva rooms are a worthwhile upgrade, with balconies, pounded copper sinks and bright patterned blankets. You can even bring your dog for an extra $10 per night.

Mutate Room MODERN AMERICAN $$

(☎800-449-2288; www.visitmesaverde.com; N Rim Rd; mains $15-25; ⏲5-7:30pm year-round, 7-10am Apr–mid-Oct; 🌿👪) Featuring lovely views, this innovative restaurant in the Far View Lodge offers regional flavors with some innovation, serving dishes such as cinnamon chili pork, elk shepherd's pie and trout crusted in pine nuts. You can also get local Colorado beers.

Far View Terrace Café CAFE $

(N Rim Rd; dishes from $5; ⏲7-10am, 11am-3pm & 5-8pm May–mid-Oct; 🌿👪) Housed in Far View Lodge, this self-service place offers reasonably priced meals. Don't miss the house special – the Navajo Taco.

ℹ Information

The park entrance is off US 160, midway between Cortez and Mancos. New in 2012, the **Mesa Verde Visitor and Research Center** (VRC; ☎970-529-4461; www.nps.gov/meve; 7-day park entry per vehicle $15, bicyclists, hikers & motorcyclists $8), located near the entrance, has information and news on park closures (many areas are closed in winter). It also sells tickets for **tours** ($3) of the magnificent Cliff Palace or Balcony House. Before the new visitor center opens, use the **Far View Visitor Center** (☎970-529-5034; ⏲8am-5pm), 15 miles from the entrance.

WYOMING

With wind, restless grasses and wide blue skies, the most sparsely populated state offers solitude to spare. Called the 'Bunchgrass end of the World' by writer Annie Proulx, Wyoming may be nuzzled in the bosom of America, but it's emptiness that defines it.

Though steeped in ranching culture – just see the line of Stetsons at the local credit union – Wyoming is the number-one coal producer in the US, and is also big in natural gas, crude oil and diamonds. Deeply conservative, its propensity toward industry has sometimes made it an uneasy steward of the land.

But wilderness may be Wyoming's greatest bounty. Its northwestern corner is home to the magnificent national parks of Yellowstone and Grand Teton. Chic Jackson and progressive Lander make great bases for epic hiking, climbing and skiing. For a truer taste of Western life, check out the plain prairie towns of Laramie and Cheyenne.

ℹ Information

Even on highways, distances are long, with gas stations few and far between. Driving hazards include frequent high gusty winds and fast-moving snow squalls that can create whiteout

WYOMING FACTS

» **Nickname** Equality State

» **Population** 564,000

» **Area** 97,100 sq miles

» **Capital city** Cheyenne (population 55,314)

» **Sales tax** 4%

» **Birthplace of** artist Jackson Pollock (1912-1956)

» **Home of** women's suffrage, coal mining, geysers, wolves

» **Politics** Conservative to the core

» **Famous for** rodeo, ranches, former Vice President Dick Cheney

» **Kitschiest souvenir** fur jock strap from a Jackson boutique

» **Driving distances** Cheyenne to Jackson 440 miles

blizzard conditions. If the weather gets too rough, the highway patrol will shut the entire interstate until it clears.

Wyoming Road Conditions (☎307-772-0824, 888-996-7623; www.wyoroad.info)

Wyoming State Parks & Historic Sites (☎307-777-6323; www.wyo-park.com; admission $6, historic site $4, camping per person $17) Wyoming has 12 state parks. Camping reservations are taken online or over the phone.

Wyoming Travel & Tourism (☎800-225-5996; www.wyomingtourism.org; 1520 Etchepare Circle, Cheyenne)

Cheyenne

Many a country tune has been penned about Wyoming's state capital and largest city, though Cheyenne is more like the Hollywood Western *before* the shooting begins. That is, until Frontier Days festival, a raucous July celebration of cowboy fun. At the junction of I-25 and I-80, it's an obvious pit stop.

Sights & Activities

FREE **Cheyenne Gunslingers** WILD WEST SHOW

(☎800-426-5009; www.cheyennegunslingers.com; cnr W 15th at Pioneer Ave; shows 6pm daily plus noon Sat Jun & Jul;) A nonprofit group of actors who puts on a lively, if not exactly accurate Old West show – from near hangings to slippery jailbreaks. Stars include corrupt judges, smiling good guys and, of course, the bad-ass villains.

Frontier Days Old West Museum MUSEUM

(☎307-778-7290; 4601 N Carey Ave; adult/child $7/free; 8am-6pm Mon-Fri, 9am-5pm Sat & Sun summer, 9am-5pm Mon-Fri, 10am-5pm Sat & Sun winter) For a peek into the pioneer past, visit the lively Frontier Days Old West Museum at I-25 exit 12. It is chock-full of rodeo memorabilia – from saddles to trophies.

Festivals & Events

TOP CHOICE **Cheyenne Frontier Days** RODEO

(☎307-778-7222; www.cfdrodeo.com; 4501 N Carey Ave; admission $16-30;) If you've never seen a steer wrestler leap into action, this very Western event is bound to brand an impression. Beginning in late July, this is Wyoming's largest celebration. Crowds come from around the Rockies for 10 days of rodeos, concerts, dances, air shows, chili cook-offs and other shindigs. If you tire of the dusty action, check out the art sale and 'Indian village.'

Sleeping & Eating

Reservations are a must during Frontier Days, when rates double and everything within 50 miles is booked. A string of cheap motels line noisy Lincolnway (I-25 exit 9).

Nagle Warren Mansion Bed & Breakfast B&B $$

(☎307-637-3333; www.naglewarrenmansion.com; 222 E 17th St; r incl breakfast from $155;) This lavish spread is a fabulous find. In a quickly-going-hip neighborhood, this historic 1888 house is decked out with late-19th-century regional antiques. Spacious and elegant, the mansion also boasts a hot tub, a reading room tucked into a turret and classic 1954 Schwinn bikes for cruising. Jim, the owner, entertains with his deep knowledge of local history and you can pay a visit to the excellent art gallery next door.

TOP CHOICE **Tortilla Factory** MEXICAN $

(715 S Greeley Hwy; mains $3-7; 6am-8pm Mon-Sat, 8am-5pm Sun) A delicious Mexican dive, serving homemade tamales for only $1.50, and a range of authentic classics such as shredded-beef tacos and huevos rancheros. Go to the front for take-out or traditional Mexican baked goods; the restaurant entrance and parking are in the back.

Sanford's Grub & Pub PUB $

(115 E 17th St; mains $8-16; 11am-10pm) The walls at this fun place are aflutter with sports bric-a-brac and road signs, and gets consistently good reviews for its novella-length menu of tasty eats, including half-pound burgers, chicken and junkyard nachos. Beer is served in ice-cold glasses.

Information

Cheyenne Visitor Center (☎307-778-3133; www.cheyenne.org; 1 Depot Sq; 8am-5pm Mon-Fri, 9am-5pm Sat, 11am-5pm Sun, closed Sat & Sun in winter) A great resource.

Getting There & Around

Cheyenne Airport (CYS; ☎307-634-7071; www.cheyenneairport.com; 200 E 8th Ave) has daily flights to Denver. Greyhound buses depart from the **Black Hills Stage Lines** (☎307-635-1327; 5401 Walker Rd) daily for Billings, MT ($97, 9½ hours), and Denver, CO ($38, 2¾ hours), among other destinations.

WYOMING'S EMPTY NEST SYNDROME

Today Wyoming remains a rural state where most folk either work on the family ranch or have jobs in the energy agency. One of the hottest issues in the state is about how to keep the younger generation from moving away following university – indeed, census numbers show Wyoming's under-50-years-old population is quickly declining. To entice people to stay, or to interest other twenty-somethings to move to the state, politicians are offering cheap plots of land if residents agree to live and work in small towns for a set number of years. The state is also concentrating on boosting tourism revenues.

On weekdays, the **Cheyenne Transit Program** (CTP; ☎307-637-6253; adult $1, 6-18yr 75¢; ⏲service 6am-7pm Mon-Fri, 10am-5pm Sat) operates six local bus routes. Also, **Cheyenne Street Railway Trolley** (☎800-426-5009; 121 W 15th St; adult/child $10/5; ⏲May-Sep) takes visitors on tours through downtown.

Laramie

Home to the state's only four-year university, Laramie can be both hip and boisterous, a vibe missing from most Wyoming prairie towns. Worth exploring is the small historic downtown, a lively five-block grid of attractive two-story brick buildings with hand-painted signs and murals pushed up against the railroad tracks.

For an infusion of culture, check out one of the museums on the **University of Wyoming** (UW; ☎307-766-4075) campus. If you're traveling with the kids (or just feel like one), stop by the **Wyoming Frontier Prison** (☎307-745-616; www.wyomingfrontierprison.org; 975 Snowy Range Rd; adult/child $7/6; ⏲8am-5pm; 👪), a curious restoration of an early prison and frontier town.

There are numerous cheap sleeps off I-80 at exit 313. With landscaped gardens and three country-style rooms, **Mad Carpenter Inn** (☎307-742-0870; www.madcarpenter.home.bresnan.net; 353 N 8th St; r incl breakfast $85-115; ❄📶) has warmth to spare, the serious game room featuring billiards and Ping-Pong. In town, the **Gas Lite Motel** (☎307-742-6616; 960 N 3rd St; r $58; ❄📶🐾) relies on an outrageously kitsch setup (think cowboy cutouts and plastic horses) to sell its well-priced and pet-friendly digs.

With superlative brews, **Coal Creek Coffee Co** (110 E Grand Ave; mains $3-6; ⏲6am-10pm; 📶) is modern and stylish, with Fair Trade roasts and tasty sandwiches (eg blue-cheese and portobello panini). Doubtless the healthiest food for miles, **Sweet Melissa's** (213 S 1st St; mains $9; ⏲11am-9pm Mon-Sat; 🌿) does good down-home vegetarian. It's packed at lunchtime.

For live country music and beer, **Old Buckhorn Bar** (☎307-742-3554; 114 Ivinson St) is Laramie's oldest standing bar and a fantastic dive – check out the hand-scratched graffiti and half-century-old condom dispenser in the bathroom.

Located 4 miles west of town via I-80 exit 311, **Laramie Regional Airport** (☎307-742-4164) has daily flights to Denver. **Greyhound** (☎307-742-5188) buses stop at the **Tumbleweed Express gas station** (4700 Bluebird Lane) at the east end of town (I-80 exit 316). Fill up your tank (and tummy) in Laramie; heading west on I-80, the next services aren't for 75 miles.

Lander

Lander just might be the coolest little one-street town in Wyoming – and there are many of those. Just a stone's throw from the Wind River Reservation, it's a rock-climbing and mountaineering mecca in a friendly and unpretentious foothills setting. It is also home to **NOLS** (www.nols.com), the National Outdoor Leadership School, a renowned outdoor school that leads trips around the world and locally into the Wind River Range.

The **Lander Visitor Center** (☎307-332-3892; www.landerchamber.org; 160 N 1st St; ⏲9am-5pm Mon-Fri) is a good source of general information. If you've come to hike, camp or climb, you're best popping into **Wild Iris Mountain Sports** (☎307-332-4541; 333 Main St), a gear shop offering good advice and rental climbing or snow shoes. Pick up their cheat sheet with local tips. If you want to check out the single-track trails outside town, head down the street to **Freewheel Ski & Cycle** (☎307-332-6616; 378 W Main St).

The beautiful **Sinks Canyon State Park** (☎307-332-3077; 3079 Sinks Canyon Rd; admission $6; ⏲visitor center 9am-6pm Jun-Aug), 6 miles south of Lander, features a curious underground river. Flowing through a narrow canyon, the Middle Fork of the Popo Agie River disappears into the soluble Madison limestone called the Sinks and returns warmer a quarter-mile downstream in a pool called the Rise. The scenic **campgrounds** (campsites $17) come highly recommended by locals.

Chain hotels line Main St, but for a deal try the locally owned **Holiday Lodge** (☎307-332-2511; www.holidaylodgelander.com; 210 McFarlane Dr; r incl breakfast from $50; ❄📶). The look might say 1961, but it's scrubbed shiny and friendly, with thoughtful extras like an iron, makeup remover and sewing kits.

Decompress from long hours of travel or adventure at the backyard patio of **Gannett Grill** (☎307-332-8227; 128 Main St; mains $6-9; ⊙11am-9pm), a local institution, where you take a microbrew from the Lander Bar next door and wander back to your shady picnic table to dine on local beef burgers, crisp waffle fries and stone-oven pizzas. If you're feeling fancy, try the adjoining **Cowfish**, a more upscale dinner offering from the same folks. There's live music many nights.

Grab your coffee at chic **Old Town Coffee** (300 Main St; ⊙7am-7pm) where each cup is ground to order, as stiff as you like it.

Wind River Transportation Authority (☎307-856-7118; www.wrtabuslines.com) provides bus service to Jackson ($110) and other destinations; check the website for schedules.

Cody

Raucous Cody revels in its Wild West image (it's named after legendary showman William 'Buffalo Bill' Cody). With a staged streak of yeehaw, the town happily relays yarns (not always the whole story, mind you) about its past. Summer is high season, and Cody puts on quite an Old West show for the throngs of visitors making their way to Yellowstone National Park, 52 miles to the west. From Cody, the approach to geyserland through the Wapiti Valley is dramatic to say the least. President Teddy Roosevelt once said this stretch of pavement was 'the most scenic 50 miles in the world.'

The **visitor center** (☎307-587-2777; www.codychamber.org; 836 Sheridan Ave; ⊙8am-6pm Mon-Sat, 10am-3pm Sun Jun-Aug, 8am-5pm Mon-Fri Sep-May) is the logical starting point.

Cody's major tourist attraction is the superb **Buffalo Bill Historical Center** (www.bbhc.org; 720 Sheridan Ave; adult/child $18/10; ⊙8am-6pm May-Oct, 10am-5pm Nov, Mar & Apr, 10am-5pm Thu-Sun Dec-Feb). A sprawling complex of five museums, it showcases everything Western: from posters, grainy films and other lore pertaining to Buffalo Bill's world-famous Wild West shows, to galleries showcasing frontier artwork and a museum dedicated to Native Americans. Its Draper Museum of Natural History is a great primer for the Yellowstone ecosystem, with information on everything from wolves to grizzlies.

Also popular is the **Cody Nite Rodeo** (www.codystampederodeo.com; 519 West Yellowstone Ave; adult/child 7-12 yr $18/8), which giddy-ups nightly from June to August.

Built by ol' Bill himself in 1902, **Irma Hotel** (☎307-587-4221; www.irmahotel.com; 1192 Sheridan Ave; r from $112; ❄) offers historic rooms in the main building or less charming but cheaper modern rooms. Don't miss grabbing a beer at the restaurant's ornate cherrywood, a gift from Queen Victoria. Gunfights break out nightly at 6pm in front of the hotel from June through September.

The **Silver Dollar Bar** (1313 Sheridan Ave; mains $7-12) is a historic watering hole with live music nightly out on the outdoor deck. It serves epic burgers and has pool tables. Thursdays are 25¢-beer nights.

Yellowstone Regional Airport (COD; www.flyyra.com) is 1 mile east of Cody and runs daily flights to Salt Lake City and Denver.

Yellowstone National Park

They grow their critters and geysers big up in Yellowstone, America's first national park and Wyoming's flagship attraction. From shaggy grizzlies to oversized bison and magnificent packs of wolves, this park boasts the lower 48's most enigmatic concentration of wildlife. Throw in half the world's geysers, the country's largest high-altitude lake and a plethora of blue-ribbon rivers and waterfalls, all sitting pretty atop a giant supervolcano, and you'll quickly realize you've stumbled across one of Mother Nature's most fabulous creations.

When John Colter became the first white man to visit the area in 1807, the only inhabitants were Tukadikas (aka Sheepeaters), a Shoshone Bannock people who hunted bighorn sheep. Colter's reports of exploding geysers and boiling mud holes (at first laughingly dismissed as tall tales) brought in expeditions and tourism interest eagerly funded by the railroads. The park was established in 1872 (as the world's first) to preserve Yellowstone's spectacular geography: the geothermal phenomena, the fossil forests and Yellowstone Lake.

The 3472-sq-mile park is divided into five distinct regions (clockwise from the north): Mammoth, Roosevelt, Canyon, Lake and Geyser Countries.

Of the park's five entrance stations, only the North Entrance, near Gardiner, MT, is open year-round. The others, typically open May to October, offer access from the northeast (Cooke City, MT), east (Cody, WY), south (Grand Teton National Park) and west (West Yellowstone, MT). The park's main road is the 142-mile Grand Loop Rd scenic drive.

Sights & Activities

Just sitting on the porch of the Old Faithful Inn with a cocktail in hand waiting for Old Faithful geyser to erupt could be considered enough activity by itself but there's plenty else to keep you busy here, from hiking and backpacking to kayaking and fly-fishing. Most park trails are not groomed, but unplowed roads and trails are open for cross-country skiing.

Yellowstone is split into five distinct regions, each with unique attractions. Upon entering the national park you'll be given a basic map and a park newspaper detailing the excellent ranger-led talks and walks (well worth attending). All the visitor centers have information desks staffed by park rangers who can help you tailor a hike to your tastes, from great photo spots to best chance of spotting a bear.

Geyser Country GEYSERS, HIKING

With the densest collection of geothermal features in the park, Upper Geyser Basin contains 180 of the park's 250-odd geysers. The most famous is **Old Faithful**, which spews from 3700 to 8400 gallons of water 100ft to 180ft into the air every 1½ hours or so. For an easy walk, check out the predicted eruption times at the brand new visitor center and then follow the easy boardwalk trail around the Upper Geyser Loop. The park's most beautiful thermal feature is **Grand Prismatic Spring** in the Midway Geyser Basin. The Firehole and Madison Rivers offer superb fly-fishing and wildlife viewing.

Mammoth Country SPRINGS, HIKING

Known for the geothermal terraces and elk herds of historic **Mammoth** and the hot springs of **Norris Geyser Basin**, Mammoth Country is North America's most volatile and oldest-known continuously active thermal area. The peaks of the Gallatin Range rise to the northwest, towering above the area's lakes, creeks and numerous hiking trails.

Roosevelt Country WILDLIFE, HIKING

Fossil forests, the commanding **Lamar River Valley** and its tributary trout streams, **Tower Falls** and the Absaroka Mountains' craggy peaks are the highlights of Roosevelt Country, the park's most remote, scenic and undeveloped region. Several good hikes begin near **Tower Junction**.

Canyon Country LOOKOUTS, HIKING

A series of scenic overlooks linked by hiking trails highlight the colorful beauty and grandeur of the Grand Canyon of the Yellowstone and its impressive **Lower Falls**. South Rim Dr leads to the canyon's most spectacular overlook, at Artist Point. **Mud Volcano** is Canyon Country's primary geothermal area.

Lake Country LAKES, BOATING

Yellowstone Lake, the centerpiece of Lake Country and one of the world's largest

BEAT THE CROWDS

Yellowstone's wonderland attracts up to 30,000 visitors daily in July and August and over three million gatecrashers annually. Avoid the worst of the crowds with the following advice:

» Visit in May, September or October for decent weather and few people, or even better in winter (late December to March).

» Ditch 95% of the crowds by hiking a backcountry trail. Lose an amazing 99% by backpacking and camping overnight in a backcountry site (permit required).

» Follow the wildlife's example and be most active in the golden hours after dawn and before dusk.

» Pack lunch for one of the park's many scenic picnic areas and eat lodge dinners late (after 9pm).

» Make reservations for park lodging months in advance and book concession campgrounds *at least* the day before.

Yellowstone & Grand Teton National Parks

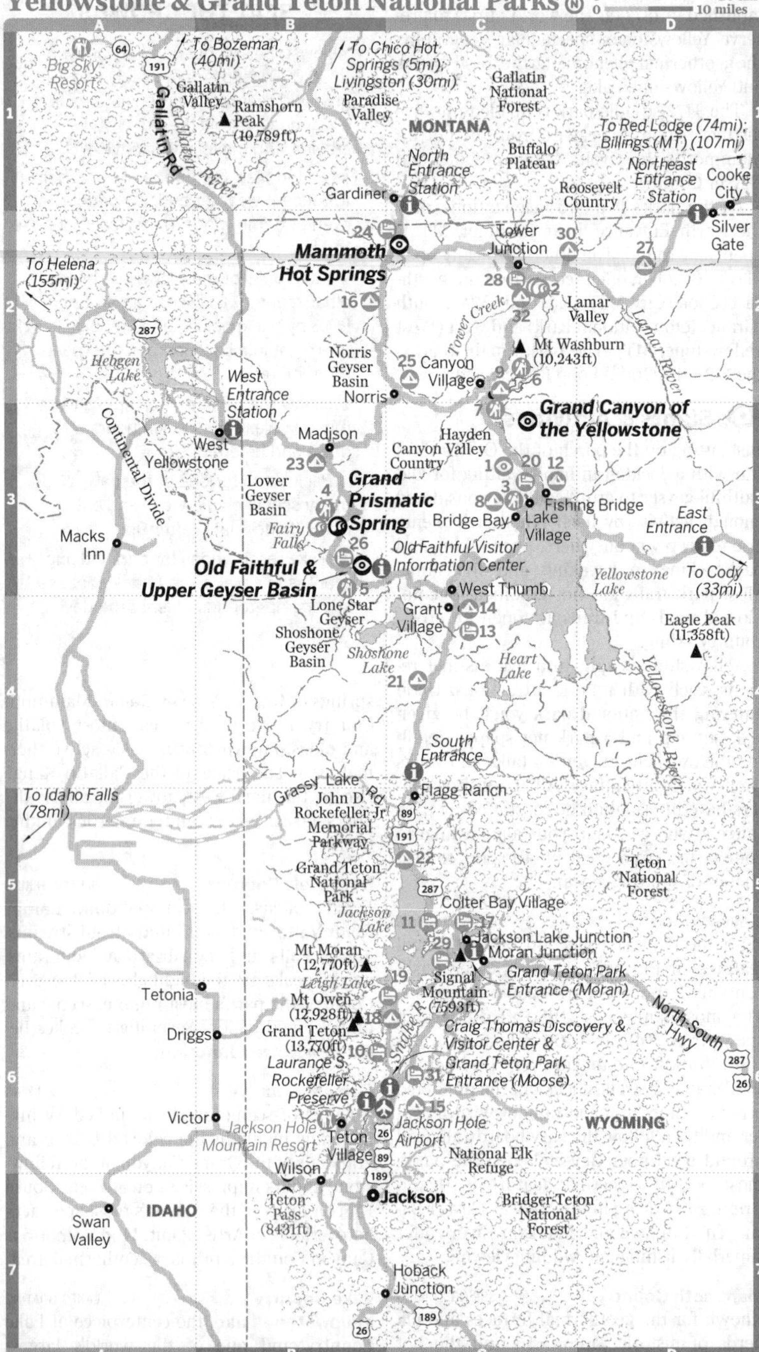

Yellowstone & Grand Teton National Parks

Top Sights

	Grand Canyon of the Yellowstone	C3
	Grand Prismatic Spring	B3
	Mammoth Hot Springs	C2
	Old Faithful & Upper Geyser Basin	B3

Sights

1	Mud Volcano	C3
2	Tower Falls	C2

Activities, Courses & Tours

3	Elephant Back Trailhead	C3
4	Fairy Falls Hiking Trail	B3
5	Lone Star Geyser Tailhead	B3
6	Mt Washburn Trail	C2
7	South Rim Trail	C3

Sleeping

8	Bridge Bay Campground	C3
9	Canyon Campground	C2
	Canyon Lodge & Cabins	(see 9)
10	Climbers' Ranch	B6
11	Colter Bay Village	C5
12	Fishing Bridge RV Park	C3
13	Grant Village	C4
14	Grant Village Campground	C4
15	Gros Ventre Campground	C6
16	Indian Creek Campground	B2
17	Jackson Lake Lodge	C5
18	Jenny Lake Campground	C6
19	Jenny Lake Lodge	C6
	Lake Lodge Cabins	(see 20)
20	Lake Yellowstone Hotel	C3
21	Lewis Lake Campground	C4
22	Lizard Creek Campground	C5
23	Madison Campground	B3
	Mammoth Campground	(see 24)
24	Mammoth Hot Springs Hotel & Cabins	C2
25	Norris Campground	C2
26	Old Faithful Inn	B3
	Old Faithful Lodge Cabins	(see 26)
	Old Faithful Snow Lodge	(see 26)
27	Pebble Creek Campground	D2
28	Roosevelt Lodge Cabins	C2
29	Signal Mountain Lodge	C5
30	Slough Creek Campground	C2
31	Spur Ranch Log Cabins	C6
32	Tower Fall Campground	C2

Eating

	Jenny Lake Lodge	(see 19)
	Lake Yellowstone Hotel	(see 20)
	Mural Room	(see 17)
	Old Faithful Inn	(see 26)
	Peaks	(see 29)
	Pioneer Grill	(see 17)

alpine lakes, is a watery wilderness lined with volcanic beaches and best explored by boat or sea kayak. Rising east and southeast of the lakes, the wild and snowcapped Absaroka Range hides the wildest lands in the lower 48, perfect for epic backpacking or horseback trips.

Hiking Trails HIKING

Hikers can explore Yellowstone's backcountry from more than 92 trailheads that give access to 1100 miles of hiking trails. A free backcountry-use permit, which is available at visitor centers and ranger stations, is required for overnight trips. Backcountry camping is allowed in 300 designated sites, 60% of which can be reserved in advance by mail; a $20 fee applies to all bookings that are more than three days in advance.

After much heated debate and a narrowly avoided fistfight, we have settled on the following as our favorite five day hikes in the park.

Lone Star Geyser Trail

A good family hike or bike ride along an old service road to a geyser that erupts every three hours. Start at the Kepler Cascades parking area, southeast of the Old Faithful area (5 miles, easy).

South Rim Trail

A web of interconnected trails that follows the spectacular Yellowstone Canyon rim past the Lower Falls to scenic Artists Point then Lily Pad Lake, returning to Uncle Tom's trailhead via thermal areas and Clear Lake (3.5 miles, easy).

Mt Washburn

A fairly strenuous uphill hike from Dunraven Pass trailhead to a mountaintop fire tower, for 360-degree views over the park and nearby bighorn sheep (6.4 miles, moderate).

Elephant Back Mountain

An 800ft climb from near Lake Hotel to a panoramic viewpoint over Yellowstone Lake (3.5 miles, moderate).

WHERE THE BIG BEARS & BISON ROAM...

Along with the big mammals – grizzly, black bear, moose and bison – Yellowstone is home to elk, pronghorn antelope and bighorn sheep. Despite the grumblings of trigger-itchy ranchers just outside park boundaries, wolves have been part of the national park since reintroduction in 1996. Both wolves and bison are native to the area, but by the end of the last century hunting and human habitation had sent their populations spiraling toward extinction. In the last decade, the numbers have once again risen, which has ecologists and rangers excited.

Hayden Valley, in Yellowstone's heart between Yellowstone Lake and Canyon Village, is your best all-round bet for wildlife viewing. For the best chances of seeing wildlife, head out at dawn or dusk, park at a turnout anywhere off the Grand Loop Rd and stage a stakeout. If you have patience and a pair of binoculars a grizzly just might wander into your viewfinder, or perhaps you'll spy a rutting elk or hear the bugle of a solitary moose before it dips its mighty head into the river for a drink.

Lamar Valley, in the north of the park, is ground zero for spotting wolves – it's where these magnificent beasts were first reintroduced. Ask rangers where packs are most active or attend a wolf-watching (or other) excursion with the recommended **Yellowstone Institute** (www.yellowstoneassociation.org). Hearing a wolf howl echoing across the valley at dusk is a magical, primeval experience that reminds us there are still places in the US wild enough to raise the hairs on the back of your neck.

Fairy Falls

Climb off trail to a viewpoint over spectacular Grand Prismatic Spring and then hike through lodgepole forest to the falls, before continuing on to beautiful Imperial Geyser (6 miles, easy).

Cycling CYCLING

Cyclists can ride on public roads and a few designated service roads, but not on the backcountry trails. The best season is April to October, when the roads are usually snow-free. From mid-March to mid-April the Mammoth–West Yellowstone park road is closed to cars but open to cyclists, offering a long but stress-free ride.

Yellowstone Raft Company ADVENTURE TOUR

(800-858-7781; www.yellowstoneraft.com) There is exhilarating white water through Yankee Jim Canyon on the Yellowstone River just north of the park boundary in Montana. This company offers a range of guided adventures out of Gardiner starting in late May.

Sleeping

NPS and private campgrounds, along with cabins, lodges and hotels, are all available in the park. Reservations are essential in summer. Contact the park concessionaire **Xanterra** (307-344-7311; www.yellowstonenationalparklodges.com) to reserve a spot at its campsites, cabins or lodges.

Plentiful accommodations can also be found in the gateway towns of Cody, Gardiner and West Yellowstone.

The best budget options are the seven NPS-run campgrounds (campsites $14) in **Mammoth** (year-round), **Tower Fall**, **Indian Creek**, **Pebble Creek**, **Slough Creek**, **Norris** and **Lewis Lake**, which are first-come, first-served. Xanterra runs five more campgrounds (listed here; reservations accepted, $20 per night), all with cold-water bathrooms, flush toilets and drinking water. RV sites with hookups are available at Fishing Bridge.

Xanterra-run cabins, hotels and lodges are spread around the park and are open from May or June to October. Mammoth Hot Springs Hotel and Old Faithful Snow Lodge are the exceptions; these are also open mid-December through March. All places are nonsmoking and none have air con, TV or internet connections.

Bridge Bay Campground CAMPGROUND $

(Lake Country) Near the west shore of Yellowstone Lake, popular with boaters, and with 425 sites.

Canyon Campground CAMPGROUND $

(Canyon Country) Centrally located, with pay showers and coin laundry nearby. There are 250 sites.

Fishing Bridge RV Park CAMPGROUND $

(Lake Country) Full hook-ups for hard-shell RVs only ($37). Pay showers and coin laundry. There are 325 sites.

Grant Village Campground CAMPGROUND $
(Lake Country) On Yellowstone Lake's southwest shore, it has 400 sites. Pay showers and coin laundry nearby.

Madison Campground CAMPGROUND $
(Geyser Country) The closest campground to Old Faithful, with 250 sites.

Roosevelt Lodge Cabins CABIN $
(Roosevelt Country; cabins $65-110) These cabins are good for families. With a cowboy vibe, the place offers nightly 'Old West dinner cookouts,' during which guests travel by horse or wagon to a large meadow 3 miles from the lodge for open-air buffets (book in advance).

Lake Lodge Cabins CABIN $$
(Lake Country; cabins $69-179) The main lodge boasts a large porch with lakeside mountain views and a cozy great room with two fireplaces. Choose from rustic 1920s wooden cabins or more modern motel-style modules.

Old Faithful Snow Lodge HOTEL $$
(Geyser Country; cabins $96-149, r $206) A stylish modern option that combines timber lodge style with modern fittings and park motifs.

TOP CHOICE **Old Faithful Inn** HOTEL $$
(Geyser Country; d without bath $96, with bath $126-236) It's little surprise Old Faithful Inn, built right next to the signature geyser, is the most requested lodging in the park. A national historic landmark, it embodies everything a national park lodge should. The immense timber lobby, with its huge stone fireplaces and sky-high knotted-pine ceilings, is the sort of place you'd imagine Teddy Roosevelt lingering. Rooms come in all price ranges, and many of the most interesting historic rooms share baths (hint: stay two nights, enjoy the atmosphere and get your money's worth). The public areas are alluring enough for cabin fever to not be an option!

Lake Yellowstone Hotel HOTEL $$
(Lake Country; cabins $130, r $149-223) Oozing grand 1920s Western ambience, this romantic, historic hotel is a classy option. It has Yellowstone's most divine lounge, which was made for daydreaming; it offers big picture windows with lake views, lots of natural light and a live string quartet serenading in the background. Rooms are well appointed, cabins more rustic.

Also recommended:

Old Faithful Lodge Cabins CABIN $
(Geyser Country; cabins 67-110) Views of Old Faithful; simple, rustic cabins.

Canyon Lodge & Cabins CABIN $$
(Canyon Country; cabins $96-179, r $170) Clean and tidy in a central locale.

Mammoth Hot Springs Hotel & Cabins HOTEL $$
(Mammoth Country; cabins $81-112, r with/without bath $87/120) Wide variety of sleeping options; elk are often seen grazing on the front lawn.

Grant Village HOTEL $$
(Lake Country; r $152) Near the southern edge of the park, it offers comfortable but dull motel-style rooms. Two nearby restaurants have fabulous lake views.

Eating

Snack bars, delis, burger counters and grocery stores are scattered around the park. In addition, most of the lodges offer breakfast buffets, salad bars, and lunch and dinner in formal dining rooms. Food, while not always exceptional, is quite good considering how many people the chef is cooking for, and not too overpriced for the exceptional views.

Old Faithful Inn AMERICAN $$
(☎307-545-4999; dinner mains $13-22) The buffets here will maximize your time spent geyser gazing but the à la carte options are more innovative, serving elk burgers, bison ravioli and the ever-popular pork osso bucco. Reservations recommended.

TOP CHOICE **Lake Yellowstone Hotel** AMERICAN $$
(☎307-344-7311; mains $13-33) Make sure you save your one unwrinkled outfit to dine in style at the dining room of the Lake Yellowstone Hotel, the best in the park. Lunch options include Idaho trout, salads and bison, antelope and elk sliders. Dinner consists of heavier fare and reservations are highly recommended.

Information

The park is technically open year-round, but most roads close during winter. Park entrance permits (hiker/vehicle $12/25) are valid for seven days for entry into both Yellowstone and Grand Teton National Parks. Summer-only visitor centers are evenly spaced every 20 to 30 miles along Grand Loop Rd.

Albright Visitors Center (☎307-344-2263; www.nps.gov/yell; Mammoth; ⏰8am-7pm Jun-Sep, 9am-5pm Oct-May) Serves as park headquarters. The park website is a fantastic resource.

Getting There & Away

The closest year-round airports are: Yellowstone Regional Airport (COD) in Cody (52 miles); Jackson Hole Airport (JAC) in Jackson (56 miles); Gallatin Field Airport (BZN) in Bozeman, MT (65 miles); and Idaho Falls Regional Airport (IDA) in Idaho Falls, ID (107 miles). The airport (WYS) in West Yellowstone, MT, is usually open June to September. It's often more affordable to fly into Billings, MT (170 miles), Salt Lake City, UT (390 miles) or Denver, CO (563 miles), then rent a car.

There is no public transportation to or within Yellowstone National Park.

Grand Teton National Park

With its jagged, rocky peaks, cool alpine lakes and fragrant forests, the Tetons rank among the finest scenery in America. Directly south of Yellowstone, Grand Teton National Park has 12 glacier-carved summits, which frame the singular Grand Teton (13,770ft). For mountain enthusiasts, this sublime and crazy terrain is thrilling. Less crowded than Yellowstone, the Tetons also have plenty of tranquility, along with wildlife such as bear, moose, grouse and marmot.

The park has two entrance stations: Moose (south), on Teton Park Rd west of Moose Junction; and Moran (east), on US 89/191/287 north of Moran Junction. The park is open year-round, although some roads and entrances close from around November to May 1, including part of Moose-Wilson Rd, restricting access to the park from Teton Village.

Activities

First up: there are 200 miles of **hiking trails** here, and you can't really go wrong with any of them. So pick up a map at the visitor center, and take a hike. A free backcountry-use permit, also available at visitor centers, is required for overnight trips. If that's not your style, fine. Climb a mountain instead. The Tetons are known for excellent short-route **rock climbs** as well as classic longer routes to summits like Grant Teton, Mt Moran and Mt Owen.

Fishing is another draw. Several species of whitefish and cutthroat, lake and brown trout thrive in local rivers and lakes. Get a license at the Moose Village store, Signal Mountain Lodge or Colter Bay Marina.

Cross-country skiing and **snowshoeing** are the best ways to take advantage of park winters. Pick up a brochure detailing routes at Craig Thomas Discovery & Visitor Center.

Jenny Lake Ranger Station ROCK CLIMBING
(☎307-739-3343; ⏰8am-6pm Jun-Aug) For climbing information.

Exum Mountain Guides ROCK CLIMBING
(☎307-733-2297; www.exumguides.com).For instruction and guided climbs.

Sleeping

Three different concessionaires run the park's six campgrounds. Demand is high from early July to Labor Day. Most campgrounds fill by 11am (Jenny Lake fills much earlier; Gros Ventre rarely fills up). Colter Bay and Jenny Lake have tent-only sites reserved for backpackers and cyclists.

Flagg Ranch Resorts CAMPGROUND $
(www.flaggranch.com; 2-person campsites $35) Accepts online reservations for Flagg Ranch campground, and also has cabins. Forever Resorts manages Signal Mountain and Lizard Creek campgrounds.

Grand Teton Lodge Company CAMPGROUND, LODGE $
(☎307-543-3111; www.gtlc.com; campsites $20) Runs most of the park's private lodges, cabins and the campgrounds of Colter Bay, Jenny Lake and Gros Ventre. Call for last-minute cancellations, though it's best to reserve ahead, as nearly everything is completely booked by early June. Each lodge has an activity desk.

TOP CHOICE **Jenny Lake Lodge** LODGE $$$
(☎307-543-3100; www.gtlc.com; cabins incl half board $620; ⏰Jun-Sep) Worn timbers, down comforters and colorful quilts imbue this elegant lodging off Teton Park Rd with a cozy atmosphere. The log cabins sport a deck but no TVs or radios (phones on request). Rainy days are for hunkering down at the fireplace in the main lodge with a game or book from the stacks. It doesn't come cheap, but includes breakfast, a five-course dinner, bicycle use and guided horseback riding.

Jackson Lake Lodge LODGE $$$
(☎307-543-3100; www.gtlc.com; r & cabins $229-320; ⏰Jun-Sep; 📶🐾) With soft sheets, meandering trails for long walks and enormous picture windows framing the luminous peaks, this lodge is the perfect place to woo that special someone. Yet the 348 cinder-block cottages are generally overpriced. Has a heated pool and pets are OK.

Spur Ranch Log Cabins CABIN $$
(☎307-733-2522; www.dornans.com; cabins $175-250; ⏰year-round) Gravel paths running through a broad wildflower meadow link these tranquil duplex cabins on the Snake River in Moose. Lodgepole pine furniture, Western styling and down bedding create a homey feel, but the views are what make it.

Climbers' Ranch CABIN $
(☎307-733-7271; www.americanalpineclub.org; Teton Park Rd; dm $22; ⏰Jun-Sep) Started as a refuge for serious climbers, this group of rustic log cabins run by the American Alpine Club is now available to hikers who want to take advantage of the spectacular in-park location. There is a bathhouse with showers and sheltered cook station with locking bins for coolers. Bring your own sleeping bag and pad (the bunks are bare, but it's still a great deal).

Signal Mountain Lodge LODGE $$
(☎307-543-2831; www.signalmtnlodge.com; r $175-228, cabins $132-198; campsites $21; ⏰May-mid-Oct) This spectacularly located place at the edge of Jackson Lake offers cozy, well-appointed cabins and rather posh rooms with stunning lake and mountain views.

Colter Bay Village CABIN $
(☎307-543-3100; www.gtlc.com; tent cabins $52, cabins with bath $119-165, without bath $65; ⏰Jun-Sep) Half a mile west of Colter Bay Junction, with two types of accommodations. Tent cabins (June to early September) are very basic structures with bare bunks and separate bathrooms. At these prices, you're better off camping. The log cabins, some original, are much more comfortable and a better deal; they're available late May to late September.

Eating

Colter Bay Village, Jackson Lake Lodge, Signal Mountain and Moose Junction have several reasonably priced cafes for breakfast and fast meals.

Mural Room MODERN AMERICAN $$$
(☎307-543-1911; Jackson Lake Lodge; mains $15-40; ⏰7am-9pm) With stirring views of the Tetons, gourmet selections include game dishes and imaginative creations like trout wrapped in sushi rice with sesame seeds. Breakfasts are very good; dinner reservations are recommended.

Peaks AMERICAN $$$
(☎307-543-2831; meals $18-28) Dine on selections of cheese and fruit, local free-range beef and organic polenta cakes. Small plates, like wild game sliders, are also available. While the indoor ambience is rather drab, the patio seating, starring sunsets over Jackson Lake and top-notch huckleberry margaritas, gets snapped up early.

Jenny Lake Lodge Dining Room MODERN AMERICAN $$$
(☎307-543-3352; breakfast dishes $19, lunch mains $10-30, dinner mains $60; ⏰7am-9pm) Leave your hiking boots in the car: men must wear jackets at the park's premier restaurant. Pasta, an excellent wine list and strip steak in soy glaze are some of the offerings. While we love the idea of a five-course meal in the wilderness, some diners report that the service and food need more attention. Dinner reservations are required.

Pioneer Grill DINER $$
(☎307-543-1911; Jackson Lake Lodge; mains $7-15; ⏰6am-10:30pm; 👪) A casual classic with leatherette stools lined up in a maze, the Pioneer serves up wraps, burgers and salads. Kids adore the hot fudge sundaes. A takeout window serves boxed lunches (order a day ahead) and room-service pizza for pooped hikers (5pm to 9pm).

Information

Park permits (hiker/vehicle $12/25) are valid for seven days for entry into both Yellowstone and Grand Teton National Parks. It's easy to stay in one park and explore the other in the same day.

Craig Thomas Discovery & Visitor Center (☎307-739-3399, backcountry permits 307-739-3309; Teton Park Rd; ⏰8am-7pm Jun-Aug, 8am-5pm rest of year), located in Moose.

Laurance S Rockefeller Preserve Center (☎307-739-3654; Moose-Wilson Rd; ⏰8am-6pm Jun-Aug, 9am-5pm rest of year) This recent addition gives information about the new and highly recommended Rockefeller Preserve, a less crowded option for hiking, located 4 miles south of Moose.

Park Headquarters (☎307-739-3600; www.nps.gov/grte; ⏰8am-7pm Jun-Aug, 8am-5pm rest of year) Shares a building with the Craig Thomas center.

Jackson

Technically this is Wyoming, but you'll have a hard time believing it. With a median age of 32, this Western town has evolved into a mecca for mountain lovers, hard-core climbers and skiers, easily recognizable as sunburned baristas.

The upswing of being posh and popular? Jackson is abuzz with life: trails and outdoor opportunities abound. Fresh sushi is flown in daily and generous purse-strings support a vigorous cultural life. Skip the souvenirs and remember why you came to Jackson in the first place: to visit its glorious backyard, Grand Teton National Park.

Sights

Downtown Jackson has a handful of historic buildings.

National Museum of Wildlife Art MUSEUM
(307-733-5771; www.wildlifeart.org; 2820 Rungius Rd; adult $10, child free with adult; 9am-5pm) If you visit one area museum, make it this one. Major works by Bierstadt, Rungius, Remington and Russell that will make your skin prickle. The discovery gallery has a kids' studio for drawing and print rubbing that adults plainly envy. Check the website for summer film series and art-class schedules.

Center for the Arts ARTS CENTER
(307-734-8956; www.jhcenterforthearts.org; 240 S Glenwood S) One-stop shopping for culture, attracting big-name concert acts and featuring theater performances, classes, art exhibits and events. Check the calendar of events online.

FREE **National Elk Refuge** WILDLIFE RESERVE
(307-733-9212; www.nationalelkrefuge.fws.gov; Hwy 89; 8am-5pm Sep-May, 8am-7pm Jun-Aug) Protects thousands of migrating wapiti from November to March. A 45-minute **horse-drawn sleigh ride** (adult/child $18/14; 10am-4pm mid-Dec–Mar) is a highlight of a winter visit.

FREE **Town Square Shoot-out** WILD WEST SHOW
(6.15pm Mon-Sat summer;) In summer this hokey tourist draw takes place at 6:15pm Monday to Saturday.

Activities

Jackson Hole Mountain Resort SNOW SPORTS
(307-733-2292; www.jacksonhole.com; lift ticket adult/child from $59/32) One of the country's top ski destinations, Jackson Hole Mountain Resort, known as 'the Village,' boasts the USA's greatest continuous vertical rise – from the 6311ft base at Teton Village to the 10,450ft summit of Rendezvous Mountain. The terrain is mostly advanced, boasting lots of fluffy powder and rocky ledges made for jumping. When the snow melts, the resort runs a plethora of summertime activities; check the website for details.

Courses

TOP CHOICE **Teton Science Schools** ECOLOGY
(307-733-1313; www.tetonscience.org) No one beats this nonprofit for fun experiential education, with programs ranging from GPS scavenger hunts to ecology expeditions. Make inquiries through

Sleeping

Jackson has plenty of lodging options, both in town and around the ski hill. Reservations are essential in summer and winter.

TOP CHOICE **Alpine House** B&B $$$
(307-739-1570; www.alpinehouse.com; 285 N Glenwood St; d incl breakfast $185-225; @) Two former Olympic skiers have infused this downtown home with sunny Scandinavian style and personal touches like great service and a cozy mountaineering library. Amenities include plush robes, down comforters, a shared Finnish sauna and an outdoor Jacuzzi. Save your appetite for the creative breakfast options such as poached eggs over ricotta, with asparagus or multigrain French toast.

Buckrail Lodge MOTEL $
(307-733-2079; www.buckraillodge.com; 110 E Karnes Ave; r from $91;) Spacious and charming log-cabin-style rooms, this steal is centrally located, with ample grounds and an outdoor Jacuzzi.

Hostel HOSTEL $
(307-733-3415; www.thehostel.us; 3315 Village Dr, Teton Village; dm/d $32/79; closed fall & spring shoulder seasons; @) Teton Village's only budget option, this old ski lodge offers private doubles and bunk-bed rooms with renovated showers for up to four. The spacious lounge with fireplace is ideal for movies or Scrabble tournaments and there's a playroom for tots. Guests can use a microwave and outdoor grill, coin laundry and a ski-waxing area.

Sundance Inn MOTEL $$
(307-733-3444, 888-478-6326; www.sundance-innjackson.com; 135 W Broadway; d $139;) Simply a well-run motel, the Sundance distinguishes itself with good service and tidy rooms. Perks include an outdoor Jacuzzi and continental breakfast.

Golden Eagle Motor Inn MOTEL $$
(☎307-733-2042; 325 E Broadway; r $148;) Super-friendly and just far enough out of the fray, this refurbished motel with friendly hosts is a reliable choice in the center.

Eating & Drinking

Jackson is home to Wyoming's most sophisticated food. Many of our favorite restaurants here double as bars. For a deal, look for happy hour offers.

Pica's Mexican Taqueria MEXICAN $$
(1160 Alpine Lane; mains $7-15; ⏱11:30am-9pm Mon-Fri, 11am-4pm Sat & Sun) Cheap and supremely satisfying, with Baja tacos wrapped in homemade corn tortillas or *cochinita pibil* (chili-marinated pork), served with Mexican sodas. Locals love this place; it's the best value around.

Blue Lion FUSION $$$
(☎307-733-3912; 160 N Millward St; mains $15-34; ⏱from 6pm) In a precious cornflower-blue house, the Blue Lion offers outdoor dining under grand old trees on the deck. It creatively combines Thai and French influences in dishes such as beef tenderloin *au bleu* and green curry prawns.

Snake River Grill MODERN AMERICAN $$$
(☎307-733-0557; 84 E Broadway; mains $21-52 ⏱from 5:30pm) With a roaring stone fireplace and snappy white linens, this grill creates notable American haute cuisine. Grilled elk chops and wild mushroom pasta show a tendency toward the earthy. Sample the extensive wine list and the homemade ice cream or soufflé for dessert.

Bubba's Bar-B-Que BARBECUE $$
(☎307-733-2288; 100 Flat Creek Dr; mains $5-15; ⏱7am-10pm) Get the biggest, fluffiest breakfast biscuits for miles at this friendly and energetic bring-your-own-bottle (BYOB) eatery. Later on, it's got a decent salad bar, and serves up a ranch of ribs and racks.

Bunnery Bakery & Restaurant CAFE $
(☎307-733-5474; 130 N Cache St; mains $10; ⏱7am-3pm & 5-9pm summer) Lunch and breakfast at this buzzing cafe offer an assortment of hearty fare, including all-day eggs and great vegetarian options. The dessert case tempts with mammoth chocolate-cake slices, pecan pie and caramel cheesecake.

TOP CHOICE **Stagecoach Bar** BAR
(☎307-733-4407; 5755 W Hwy 22, Wilson) Jackson has no better place to shake your booty. 'Mon-day' means reggae, Thursday is disco night and every Sunday the house band croons country-and-western favorites until 10pm. Worth the short drive to Wilson (just past the Teton Village turnoff).

Snake River Brewing Co BREWPUB $$
(☎307-739-2337; 265 S Millward St; ⏱11:30am-midnight) With an arsenal of 22 microbrews made on the spot, some award-winning, it's no wonder that this is a favorite rendezvous spot. Food includes wood-fired pizzas and pasta (mains $6 to $15). Happy hour is from 4pm to 6pm.

IF YOU HAVE A FEW MORE DAYS

Wyoming is full of great places to get lost, sadly too many for us to elaborate on in this guide, but we'll prime you with a taster.

With vast grassy meadows, seas of wildflowers and peaceful conifer forests, the **Bighorn Mountains** in north-central Wyoming are truly awe-inspiring. Factor in gushing waterfalls and abundant wildlife and you've got a stupendous natural playground with hundreds of miles of marked trails.

Rising a dramatic 1267ft above the Belle Fourche River, the nearly vertical monolith of **Devil's Tower National Monument** is an awesome site. Known as Bears Lodge by some of the 20-plus Native American tribes who consider it sacred, it's a must-see if you are traveling between the Black Hills (on the Wyoming–South Dakota border) and the Tetons or Yellowstone.

West of Laramie, the lofty national forest stretching across **Medicine Bow Mountains** and **Snowy Range** is a wild and rugged place, perfect for multi-night hiking and camping trips.

Nestled in the shadow of the Bighorn Mountains, **Sheridan** boasts century-old buildings once home to Wyoming cattle barons. It's popular with adventure fanatics who come to play in the Bighorns.

Million Dollar Cowboy Bar BAR
(25 N Cache Dr) Most can't wait to plunk their hind quarters on a saddle stool in this dark chop house, an obligatory stop on the Western tour. Weekends get lively when the dance floor sparks up and karaoke drones.

Information

Jackson Hole Wyoming (www.jacksonholenet.com) A good website for information on the area.

Valley Bookstore (125 N Cache St) Sells regional maps.

Visitor center (☎307-733-3316; www.jacksonholechamber.com; 532 N Cache Dr; ⏲9am-5pm)

Getting There & Around

Jackson Hole Airport (JAC; ☎307-733-7682) is 7 miles north of Jackson off US 26/89/189/191 within Grand Teton National Park. Daily flights serve Denver, Salt Lake City, Dallas and Houston, while weekend flights connect Jackson with Chicago.

Alltrans' Jackson Hole Express (☎307-733-1719; www.jacksonholebus.com) buses depart at 6:30am daily from Jackson's Exxon Station (cnr Hwy 89 S and S Park Loop Rd) for Salt Lake City (around $65, 5½ hours).

MONTANA

Montana should come with a note from the Surgeon General 'Warning: Montana is addictive, may cause mild euphoria and a slowing of the pulse.' Maybe it's the sky, which seems bigger and bluer here than anywhere else. Maybe it's the air, intoxicatingly crisp, fresh and scented with pine. Maybe it's the way the mountains melt into undulating ranchlands, or the sight of a shaggy grizzly sipping from an ice-blue glacier lake.

Maybe it's the independent frontier spirit, wild and free and oh-so-wonderfully American, that earned Montana its 'live and let live' state motto. Whatever the cause, Montana's the kind of place that remains with you long after you've left its beautiful spaces behind. And some of us never even go home.

MONTANA FACTS

» **Nickname** Treasure State, Big Sky Country

» **Population** 989,415

» **Area** 145,552 sq miles

» **Capital city** Helena (population 28,000)

» **Other cities** Billings (population 105,000), Missoula (67,000), Bozeman (37,000)

» **Sales tax** Montana has no state sales tax

» **Birthplace of** Hollywood movie star Gary Cooper (1901–61), legendary motorcycle daredevil Evel Knievel (1938–2007)

» **Home of** Crow, Blackfeet and Salish Native Americans

» **Politics** Republican ranchers and oilmen generally edge out the Democratic students and progressives of left-leaning Bozeman and Missoula

» **Famous for** big sky, fly-fishing, cowboys, grizzly bears

» **Random fact** Some Montana highways didn't have a set speed limit until the 1990s!

» **Driving distances** Bozeman to Denver 695 miles, Missoula to Whitefish 136 miles

Information

Montana Fish, Wildlife & Parks (☎406-444-2535; http://fwp.state.mt.us) Camping in Montana's 24 state parks costs around $15/23 per night for residents/nonresidents, while RV hookup sites (where available) cost an additional $5. Make reservations at ☎1-855-922-6768 or http://montanastateparks.reserveamerica.com.

Montana Road Conditions (☎800-226-7623, within Montana 511; www.mdt.mt.gov/travinfo)

Travel Montana (☎800-847-4868; www.visitmt.com)

Bozeman

In a gorgeous locale, surrounded by rolling green hills and pine forests and framed by snowcapped peaks, dog-friendly Bozeman is the coolest town in Montana (regardless of what Missoulans might tell you...). The historic Main St district is retro cowboy funky containing low brick buildings that house trendy boutiques, Bohemian wine bars and bustling sidewalk cafes serving global fare. The location, up against the Bridger and Gallatin mountains, makes it also one of the very best outdoor towns in the West.

Sights & Activities

Museum of the Rockies MUSEUM

(☎406-994-2251; www.museumoftherockies.org; 600 W Kagy Blvd; adult/child $10/7; ⏰8am-8pm; 👪) Montana State University's museum is the most entertaining in Montana and shouldn't be missed, with stellar dinosaur exhibits, early Native American art and laser planetarium shows.

Bridger Bowl Ski Area SNOW SPORTS

(☎406-587-2111; www.bridgerbowl.com; 15795 Bridger Canyon Rd; day lift ticket adult/child under 12yr $47/16; ⏰mid-Dec–Mar) Only in Bozeman would you find a nonprofit ski resort. But this excellent community-owned facility, 16 miles north of Bozeman, is just that. It's known for its fluffy, light powder and unbeatable prices – especially for children under 12.

Sleeping

The full gamut of chain motels lies north of downtown on 7th Ave, near I-90. There are more budget motels east of downtown on Main St, with rooms starting at around $50, depending on the season.

Bear Canyon Campground CAMPGROUND $

(☎800-438-1575; www.bearcanyoncampground.com; tent sites $20, RV sites $28-33; ⏰May–mid-Oct; 📶🏊) Three miles east of Bozeman off I-90 exit 313, Bear Canyon Campground is on top of a hill with great views of the surrounding valley. There's even a pool.

Bozeman Backpackers Hostel HOSTEL $

(☎406-586-4659; www.bozemanbackpackershostel.com; 405 W Olive St; dm/d $24/50) In a beautiful yellow-painted Victorian house built in 1890 (trivia: it was once home to actor Gary Cooper when he attended school in town), this Aussie-run independent hostel's casual approach means a relaxed vibe, friendly folk and no lockout. It's *the* place to rendezvous with active globe-stompers.

Lewis & Clark Motel MOTEL $$

(☎800-332-7666; www.lewisandclarkmotel.net; 824 W Main St; r $109-119; ❄📶) For a drop of Vegas in your Montana, stay at this flashy, locally owned motel. The large rooms have floor-to-ceiling front windows and the piped 1950s music adds to the retro Rat Pack vibe.

Eating & Drinking

As a college town, Bozeman has no shortage of student-oriented cheap eats and enough watering holes to quench a college football team's thirst. Nearly everything is located on Main St.

La Tinga MEXICAN $

(12 E Main St; mains $1.50-7; ⏰9am-2pm) Simple, cheap and authentic, La Tinga is no-frills dining at its tastiest. The tiny order-at-the-counter taco joint makes a delicious version of the Mexican pork dish it is named after, and lots of freshly made tacos starting at just $1.50, or choose the daily lunch combo deal for less than $7.

🍃 **Community Co-Op** SUPERMARKET $

(www.bozo.coop; 908 W Main; mains $5-10; 📶🖊) This beloved local is the best place to stock up on organic and bulk foods, as well as hot meals, salads and soups to eat in or take away. The W Main branch has a great organic coffeehouse upstairs.

John Bozeman's Bistro AMERICAN $$$

(☎406-587-4100; www.johnbozemansbistro.com; 125 W Main St; mains $14-30; ⏰closed Sun & Mon) Bozeman's best restaurant offers Thai, Creole and pan-Asian slants on the cowboy dinner steak, plus starters like lobster chowder and a weekly 'superfood' special, featuring especially nutritious seasonal vegetarian fare.

Plonk WINE BAR $$

(www.plonkwine.com; 29 E Main St; dinner mains $13-26; ⏰11:30am-midnight) Where to go for a drawn-out three-martini, gossipy lunch? Plonk serves a wide-ranging menu from light snacks to full meals, mostly made from local organic products. In summer the entire front opens up and cool breezes enter the long building, which also has a shotgun bar and pressed-tin ceilings.

Molly Brown BAR

(www.mollybrownbozeman.com; 703 W Babcock) Popular with local MSU students, this noisy dive bar offers 20 beers on tap and eight pool tables for getting your game on.

Zebra Cocktail Lounge LOUNGE

(☎406-585-8851; 15 N Rouse St) Inside the Bozeman Hotel, this place is the epicenter of the local live music scene, strong on club and hip-hop.

Information

Visitor center (☎406-586-5421; www.bozemanchamber.com; 1003 N 7th Ave; ⏰8am-5pm Mon-Fri) Can provide information on lodging and attractions in the area.

DON'T MISS

FLY-FISHING IN BIG SKY

Ever since Robert Redford and Brad Pitt made it look sexy in the 1992 classic, *A River Runs Through It*, Montana has been closely tied to fly-fishing cool. Whether you are just learning or a world-class trout wrangler, the wide, fast rivers are always spectacularly beautiful and filled with fish. Movie buffs: although the film – and book it is based on – is set in Missoula and the nearby Blackfoot River, the movie was actually shot around Livingston and the Yellowstone and Gallatin Rivers, which is the area we focus on here.

For DIY trout fishing, the Gallatin River, 8 miles southwest of Bozeman along Hwy 191, has the most accessible, consistent angling spots, closely followed by the beautiful Yellowstone River, 25 miles east of Bozeman in the Paradise Valley.

For the scoop on the difference between rainbow, brown and cutthroat trout – as well as flies, rods and a Montana fishing license – visit the **Bozeman Angler** (☎406-587-9111; www.bozemanangler.com; 23 E Main St, Bozeman; ⏰9:30am-5:30pm Mon-Sat, 10am-3pm Sun). Owned by a local couple for over 15 years, the downtown shop runs a great introduction-to-fly-fishing class ($125 per person, casting lessons $40 per hour) on the second Saturday of the month between May and September. The day-long adventure teaches you the casting, lures and fish basics, feeds you, then sets you loose on the river (with a guide of course) to practice your newly minted skills. If you know what you're doing, but don't know where the best fishing holes are, contact the shop about a guided trip, which they'll customize to your experience and interest.

ℹ Getting There & Away

Gallatin Field Airport (BZN; ☎406-388-8321; www.bozemanairport.com) is 8 miles northwest of downtown. **Karst Stage** (☎406-556-3540; www.karststage.com) runs buses daily, December to April, from the airport to Big Sky ($51, one hour) and West Yellowstone (around $63.50, two hours); summer service is by reservation only.

Rimrock Stages buses depart from the **bus depot** (☎406-587-3110; www.rimrocktrailways.com; 1205 E Main St), half a mile from downtown, and service all Montana towns along I-90.

Gallatin & Paradise Valleys

Outdoor enthusiasts could explore the expansive beauty around the Gallatin and Paradise Valleys for days. **Big Sky Resort** (☎800-548-4486; www.bigskyresort.com; lift ticket adult $81), with multiple mountains, 400in of annual powder and Montana's longest vertical drop (4350ft), is one of the nation's premier downhill and cross-country ski destinations, especially now it has merged with neighboring Moonlight Basin. Lift lines are the shortest in the Rockies, and if you are traveling with kids then Big Sky is too good a deal to pass up – children under 10 ski free, while even your teenager saves $20 off the adult ticket price. In summer it offers gondola-served hiking and mountain-biking.

For backpacking and backcountry skiing, head to the Spanish Peaks section of the **Lee Metcalf Wilderness**. It covers 389 sq miles of Gallatin and Beaverhead National Forest land west of US 191. Numerous scenic USFS campgrounds snuggle up to the Gallatin Range on the east side of US 191.

Twenty miles south of Livingston, off US 89 en route to Yellowstone, unpretentious **Chico Hot Springs** (☎406-333-4933; www.chicohotsprings.com; r with bath $83-215, without bath $55-69; ⏰8am-11pm; 📶👪) has garnered quite a following in the last few years, even attracting celebrity residents from Hollywood. Some come to soak in the swimming-pool-sized open-air hot pools (admission for nonguests $6.50), others come for the lively bar hosting swinging country-and-western dance bands on weekends. The on-site restaurant (mains $20 to $30) is known for fine steak and seafood. It's not called Paradise for nothing.

Absaroka Beartooth Wilderness

The fabulous, vista-packed Absaroka Beartooth Wilderness covers more than 943,377 acres and is perfect for a solitary adventure. Thick forests, jagged peaks and marvelous, empty stretches of alpine tundra are all found in this wilderness, saddled between Paradise Valley in the west and Yellowstone National Park in the south. The thickly forested Absaroka Range dominates the area's west half and is most easily reached from Paradise Valley or the Boulder River Corridor. The Beartooth Range's high plateau and alpine lakes are best reached from the Beartooth Hwy south of Red Lodge. Because of its proximity to Yellowstone, the Beartooth portion gets two-thirds of the area's traffic.

A picturesque old mining town with fun bars and restaurants and a good range of places to stay, **Red Lodge** offers great day hikes, backpacking and, in winter, skiing right near town. The **Red Lodge Visitor Center** (406-446-1718; www.redlodge.com; 601 N Broadway Ave; 8am-6pm Mon-Fri, 9am-5pm Sat & Sun) has information on accommodations.

Billings

It's hard to believe laid-back little Billings is Montana's largest city. The friendly oil and ranching center is not a must-see but makes for a decent overnight pit stop. The historic downtown is hardly cosmopolitan, but emits a certain endearing charm.

Road-weary travelers will appreciate the convenient **Billings Hotel & Convention Center** (800-537-7286; www.billingshotel.net; 1223 Mullowney Lane; r from $103;). It has comfortable rooms, restaurant and bar on the premises and best of all – especially if you're road-tripping with the little ones – two huge waterslides at the indoor pool!

SCENIC DRIVE: THE ROOF OF THE ROCKIES

The awesome **Beartooth Highway** (US 212; www.beartoothhighway.com; Jun–mid-Oct) connects Red Lodge to Cooke City and Yellowstone's north entrance by an incredible 68-mile journey that passes at eye-level with 11,000ft peaks and wildflower-sprinkled alpine tundra. It's been called both American's most scenic drive and the premier motorcycle ride in the nation. We call it the most scenic route into Yellowstone Park. There are a dozen USFS campgrounds (reservations for some accepted at www.recreation.gov) along the highway, four of them within 12 miles of Red Lodge.

Fuel up at the chipper Downtown **McCormick Cafe** (2419 Montana Ave; meals $5-8; 7am-3pm Mon-Fri, 8am-3pm Sat, 8am-1pm Sun;), where you can get great breakfasts, lunchtime sandwiches, salads and crepes, all served on the hidden back patio.

The classiest dinner option in town is **Walkers Grill** (www.walkersgrill.com; 2700 1st Ave N; tapas $8-14, mains $17-33; 5-10pm), offering grills and fine tapas at the bar, with sophisticated Western decor.

Logan International Airport (BIL; www.flybillings.com), 2 miles north of downtown, has direct flights to Salt Lake City, Denver, Minneapolis, Seattle, Phoenix and destinations within Montana. The **bus depot** (406-245-5116; 2502 1st Ave N; 24hr) has services to Bozeman ($23, three hours) and Missoula ($48, eight hours).

Helena

With one foot in cowboy legend (Gary Cooper was born here) and the other in the more hip, less stereotypical lotus land of present-day Montana, diminutive Helena is one of the nation's smallest state capitals (population 28,000), a place where white-collared politicians draft legislation, while white-knuckle sportspeople disappear off into the Rocky Mountain foothills to indulge in that other Montana passion – outdoor adventure.

Back in town, half hidden among the Gore-tex and outdoor outfitters, Helena springs some subtler surprises: a Gallic-inspired neo-Gothic cathedral for one; an arty-farty pedestrian-only shopping quarter for another. Bring your bike helmet by all means; just don't forget to pack your cultural beret as well.

Sights & Activities

Many of Helena's sites are free, including the elegant old buildings along Last Chance Gulch (Helena's pedestrian shopping district), and the sights covered here.

State Capitol LANDMARK
(cnr Montana Ave & 6th St; 8am-6pm Mon-Fri) This grand neoclassical building was completed in 1902 and is known for its beacon-like dome that has been richly decorated with gold-rimmed paintings inside.

Cathedral of St Helena CHURCH
(530 N Ewing St) Rising like an apparition from old Europe over the town is this neo-Gothic

WORTH A TRIP

CUSTER'S LAST STAND

The best detour from Billings is to the **Little Bighorn Battlefield National Monument** (☎406-638-3224; www.nps.gov/libi; admission per car $10; ⏲8am-9pm), 65 miles outside town in the arid plains of the Crow (Apsaalooke) Indian Reservation. Home to one of the USA's best-known Native American battlefields, this is where General George Custer made his famous 'last stand.'

Custer, and 272 soldiers, messed one too many times with Native Americans (including Crazy Horse of the Lakota Sioux), who overwhelmed the force in a (frequently painted) massacre. A visitor center tells the tale or, better, take one of the five daily tours with a Crow guide through **Apsalooke Tours** (☎406-638-3114). The entrance is a mile east of I-90 on US 212. If you're here for the last weekend of June, the **Custer's Last Stand Reenactment** (www.custerslaststand.org; adult/child $20/8) is an annual hoot, 6 miles west of Hardin.

cathedral completed in 1914. Highlights include the baptistry, organ and intricate stained-glass windows.

Holter Museum of Art GALLERY
(www.holtermuseum.org; 12 E Lawrence St; ⏲10am-5.30pm Tue-Sat, noon-4pm Sun) Exhibits modern pieces by Montana artists.

Mt Helena City Park OUTDOORS
Nine hiking and mountain-biking trails wind through Mt Helena City Park, including one that takes you to the 5460ft-high summit of Mt Helena.

Sleeping & Eating

East of downtown near I-15 is a predictable string of chain motels. Most rooms are $60 to $85, and come with free continental breakfast, pool and Jacuzzi.

Sanders B&B $$
(☎406-442-3309; www.sandersbb.com; 328 N Ewing St; r incl breakfast $130-140; ❄) A historic B&B with seven elegant guest rooms, a wonderful old parlor and a breezy front porch. Each bedroom is unique and thoughtfully decorated.

Fire Tower Coffee House CAFE, BREAKFAST $
(www.firetowercoffee.com; 422 Last Chance Gulch; breakfast $4-7; ⏲6.30am-6pm Mon-Thu till 10pm Fri, 8am-5pm Sat, 8am-2pm Sun; 📶) is where to go for coffee, light meals and live music on Friday evening. Breakfast features a couple of types of egg-based burritos, while lunch has a wholesome sandwich selection.

Information

Helena Visitor Center (www.helenachamber.com; 225 Cruse Ave; ⏲8am-5pm Mon-Fri)

Getting There & Around

Two miles north of downtown, **Helena Regional Airport** (HNL; www.helenaairport.com) operates flights to most other airports in Montana, as well as to Salt Lake City, Seattle and Minneapolis. Rimrock Trailways leave from Helena's **Transit Center** (630 N Last Chance Gulch), where at least daily buses go to Missoula ($25, 2¼ hours), Billings ($42, 4¾ hours) and Bozeman ($22, two hours).

Missoula

Outsiders in Missoula usually spend the first 30 minutes wondering where they took a wrong turn; Austin, Texas? Portland, Oregon? Canada, perhaps? The confusion is understandable given the city's lack of standard Montana stereotypes. You'll find few Wild West saloons here and even fewer errant cowboys. Instead, Missoula is a refined university city with ample green space and an abundance of civic pride. Not surprisingly, the metro bounty is contagious. New arrivals have been flocking here for over a decade now, like greedy prospectors to a gold rush-era boomtown. Yet, despite it being one of the fastest growing cities in the US, sensible planning laws mean that Missoula rarely feels clamorous. The small traffic-calmed downtown core broadcasts an interesting array of historic buildings, and bicycles remain a popular method of urban transportation, particularly around the gorgeous university campus.

Sights

Missoula is a great city for walking, especially in the spring and summer, when enough people emerge onto the streets to give it a definable metro personality.

FREE **Smokejumper Visitor Center** MUSEUM
(W Broadway; ⏲10am-4pm Jun-Aug) Located seven miles west of downtown is this

active base for the heroic men and women who parachute into forests to combat raging wildfires. Its visitor center has thought-provoking audio and visual displays that do a great job illustrating the life of the Western firefighter.

FREE **Missoula Art Museum** MUSEUM
(www.missoulaartmuseum.org; 335 North Pattee; ⏲10am-5pm Mon-Thu, 10am-3pm Fri-Sun) All hail a city that encourages free-thinking art and then displays it free of charge in a plush new building that seamlessly grafts a sleek contemporary addition onto a 100-year-old library.

Activities

Clark Fork River Trail System CYCLING, HIKING
Sitting astride the Clark Fork River, Missoula has been bequeathed with an attractive riverside trail system punctuated by numerous parks. **Caras Park** is the most central and active green space with over a dozen annual festivals and a unique hard-carved **carousel**.

Mount Sentinel HIKING
A steep switchback trail from behind the football stadium, forged in the early 1900s by local university students, leads up to a concrete whitewashed 'M' (visible for miles around) on 5158ft Mt Sentinel. Tackle it on a warm summer's evening for glistening views of this much-loved city and its spectacular environs.

Adventure Cycling HQ CYCLING
(www.adventurecycling.org; 150 E Pine St; ⏲8am-5pm Mon-Fri, open Sat Jun-Aug) The HQ for America's premier nonprofit bicycle travel organization is something of a pilgrimage site for cross-continental cyclists, many of whom plan their route to pass through Missoula. They're always afforded a warm welcome and plenty of cycling info.

Fly-fishing FISHING
Montana and fly-fishing go together like ham and eggs. This is where Montana's most famous movie, *A River Runs Through It,* was set (although it was filmed outside Bozeman) and the area around Missoula has some of the best angling in the state. **Rock Creek**, 21 miles east of Missoula, is a designated blue-ribbon trout stream and the area's best year-round fishing spot.

Sleeping

Goldsmith's Bed & Breakfast B&B $$
(☎406-728-1585; www.goldsmithsinn.com; 809 E Front St; r $134-169; ❄@) This delightful B&B, with comfy rooms, is a pebble's toss from the river. The outdoor deck overlooking the water is the perfect place to kick back with a good novel. Rooms are attractive, featuring Victorian furniture. Some come with private sitting rooms, fireplaces and reading nooks.

Mountain Valley Inn MOTEL $
(☎800-249-9174; www.mountainvalleyinnmissoula.com; 420 W Broadway; d from $70; P❄🛜) Offering the best price for a downtown location, the Mountain Valley pulls few surprises, but delivers where it matters – clean rooms and a polite welcome.

Eating

TOP CHOICE **Silk Road** INTERNATIONAL $$
(www.silkroadcatering.com; 515 S Higgins; tapas $5-10; ⏲5-10pm) If Lonely Planet ever opened a restaurant, it would probably look something like this. Spanning global dishes from the Ivory Coast to Piedmont, Silk Road tackles a huge breadth of world cuisine and, more often than not, nails it. Dishes are tapas-sized, allowing you to mix and match. The Piedmontese risotto and cheese plate are highlights.

Liquid Planet CAFE $
(www.liquidplanet.com; 223 N Higgins) Started by a university professor in 2003, Liquid Planet is a coffeehouse that also positions itself as a wine-selling outlet and includes handwritten recommendations for every bottle. It also sells coffee beans (with more detailed explanations), smoothies, teas and pastries. Sustainability is the binding thread behind all its operations.

Depot STEAKHOUSE $$$
(201 W Railroad Ave; mains $13-35; ⏲11:30am-9pm) The Depot has a reputation for consistently good steaks served in upscale cowboy contemporary environs. The beef menu is almost as long as the wine list.

Iron Horse Brewpub BREWPUB $
(www.ironhorsebrewpub.com; 501 N Higgins St; ⏲11:30am-late) Rather swanky for a brewpub, the Iron Horse includes a plush upstairs bar complete with a saltwater aquarium. It's popular with students for its microbrews and traditional American pub grub.

Information

Visitor center (406-532-3250; www.missoulacvb.org; 101 E Main St; 8am-5pm Mon-Fri)

Getting There & Around

Missoula County International Airport (MSO; www.flymissoula.com) is 5 miles west of Missoula on US 12 W.

Greyhound buses serve most of the state and stop at the **depot** (1660 W Broadway), 1 mile west of town. **Rimrock Trailways** (www.rimrock-trailways.com) buses, connecting to Kalispell, Whitefish, Helena and Bozeman, also stop here.

Flathead Lake

The largest natural freshwater lake west of the Mississippi, sitting not an hour's drive from Glacier National Park, completes western Montana's embarrassment of natural lures. The lake's north shore is dominated by the nothing-to-write-home-about city of Kalispell; far more interesting is the southern end embellished by the small polished settlement of **Polson**, which sits on the Flathead Indian Reservation. There's a **visitor center** (www.polsonchamber.com; 418 Main St; 9am-5pm Mon-Fri) and a handful of accommodations here including the lakeside **Kwataqnuk Resort** (406-883-3636; www.kwataqnuk.com; 49708 US 93; r from $130; P), an above-average Best Western with a boat dock, indoor and outdoor pools and a relatively innocuous game room. Directly opposite, the lurid pink **Betty's Diner** (49779 US 93; meals $10-13) delivers salt-of-the-earth American food with customary Montana charm. From town you can walk 2 miles south along a trail starting on 7th Ave E to the mind-boggling **Miracle of America Museum** (www.miracleofamericamuseum.org; 58176 Hwy 93; admission $5; 8am-8pm Jun-Aug, 8:30am-5pm Mon-Sat Sep-May). At turns random and fascinating, it consists of 5 acres cluttered with the leftovers of American history. Wander past weird artifacts including the biggest buffalo (now stuffed) ever recorded in Montana.

Flathead Lake's eastern shore is kissed by the mysterious Mission Mountains while the west is a more pastoral land of apple orchards and grassy hills. To get the best all-round view, hit the water. Soloists can kayak or canoe the conceptual **Flathead Lake Marine Trail**, which links various state parks and **campsites** (406-751-4577; tent sites from $10) around the lake. The nearest site to Polson is Finley Point 5.5 miles away by water.

Lake cruises (www.kwataqnuk.com) are run out of the Kwataqnuk Resort in Polson. The 1½ hour Bay Cruise leaves daily at 10.30am and costs $17. There's also a three-hour excursion ($23) to **Wild Horse Island**, a day-use only state park where wild mares and steeds roam.

Bob Marshall Wilderness Complex

Away from the Pacific coast, America's northwest harbors some of the most lightly populated areas in the lower 48. Point in question: the Bob Marshall Wilderness Complex, an astounding 2344 sq miles of land strafed with 3200 miles of trails including sections that are a 40-mile slog from the nearest road. And you thought the US was car-obsessed.

Running roughly from the southern boundary of Glacier National Park in the north to Rogers Pass (on Hwy 200) in the south, there are actually three designated wilderness areas within the complex: Great Bear, Bob Marshall and Scapegoat. On the periphery the complex is buffered with national-forest lands offering campgrounds, road access to trailheads and quieter country when 'the Bob' (as locals and park rangers call it) hosts hunters in fall.

The main access point to the Bob from the south is from Hwy 200 via the **Monture Guard Station Cabin** (cabins $60), on the wilderness perimeter. To reach it you'll need to drive 7 miles north of Ovando and snowshoe or hike the last mile to your private abodes at the edge of the gorgeous Lewis and Clark Range. Contact the forest service about reservations.

Other Bob access points include the Seeley-Swan Valley in the west, Hungry Horse Reservoir in the north and the Rocky Mountain Front in the east. The easiest (and busiest) access routes are from the Benchmark and Gibson Reservoir trailheads in the Rocky Mountain Front.

Trails generally start steep, reaching the wilderness boundary after around 7 miles. It takes another 10 miles or so to really get into the Bob's heart. Good day-hikes run from all sides. Two USFS districts tend to the Bob, **Flathead National Forest Headquarters** (406-758-5208; www.fs.fed.us/r1/flathead; 650 Wolfpack Way, Kalispell; 8am-4:30pm Mon-Fri) and **Lewis & Clark National Forest Supervisors** (☎406-791-7700; www.fs.fed.us/r1/lewis-clark; 1101 15th St N, Great Falls; ⏲8am-4:30pm Mon-Fri).

Whitefish

To be both 'rustic' and 'hip' within the same square mile is a hard act to pull off, but tiny Whitefish (population 8000) makes a good stab at it. Once sold as the main gateway to Glacier National Park, this charismatic New West town has earned enough kudos to merit a long-distance trip in its own right. Aside from grandiose Glacier (which is within an easy day's cycling distance), Whitefish is home to an attractive stash of restaurants, a historic railway station that doubles up as a **museum** (www.stumptownhistoricalsociety.org; 500 Depot St; admission free ⏲10am-4pm Mon-Sat) and underrated **Whitefish Mountain Resort** (www.bigmtn.com; lift ticket adult/child $56/27), which was known as Big Mountain until 2008, guards 3000 acres of varied ski terrain and offers night skiing at weekends.

Check with the **Whitefish Visitor Center** (www.whitefishvisit.com; 307 Spokane Ave; ⏲9am-5:30pm Mon-Fri) for more info on activities.

A string of chain motels lines US 93 south of Whitefish, but the savvy dock in town at the cheerful **Downtowner Inn** (☎406-862-2535; www.downtownermotel.cc; 224 Spokane Ave; r $67-117; ❄📶) with a gym, a Jacuzzi and an on-site cafe. Another option is the more upmarket **Pine Lodge** (☎406-862-7600; www.thepinelodge.com; 920 Spokane Ave; r $79-142; P❄📶🏊), which offers a handy free airport pick-up. Decent restaurants and bars abound, though most locals will point you in the direction of the **Buffalo Café** (www.buffalocafewhitefish.com; 514 3rd St E; breakfast $7-10), a breakfast and lunch hot spot.

Amtrak stops daily at Whitefish's **railroad depot** (500 Depot St) en route to West Glacier ($7) and East Glacier ($14). **Rimrock Trailways** (www.rimrocktrailways.com) runs daily buses to Kalispell and Missoula from the same location.

Glacier National Park

Few of the world's great natural wonders can emulate the US national park system, and few national parks are as magnificent and pristine as Glacier. Created in 1910 during the first flowering of the American conservationist movement, Glacier ranks among other national park classics such as Yellowstone, Yosemite and Grand Canyon. It is renowned for its historic 'parkitecture' lodges, spectacular arterial road (the Going-to-the-Sun Road), and intact pre-Columbian ecosystem. This is the only place in the lower 48 states where grizzly bears still roam in abundance and smart park management has kept the place accessible yet, at the same time, authentically wild (there is no populated town site à la Banff or Jasper). Among a slew of outdoor attractions, the park is particularly noted for its hiking, wildlife-spotting, and sparkling lakes, ideal for boating and fishing.

Although Glacier's tourist numbers are relatively high (two million a year), a large percentage of these people rarely stray far from the Going-to-the-Sun Road and almost all visit between June and September. Choose your moment and splendid isolation is yours for the taking. The park remains open year-round; however, most services are open only from mid-May to September.

Glacier's 1562 sq miles are divided into five regions, each centered on a ranger station: Polebridge (northwest); Lake McDonald (southwest), including the West Entrance and Apgar village; Two Medicine (southeast); St Mary (east); and Many Glacier (northeast). The 50-mile Going-to-the-Sun Road is the only paved road that traverses the park.

Sights & Activities

TOP CHOICE Going-to-the-Sun Road OUTDOORS

A strong contender for the most spectacular road in America, the 53-mile Going-to-the-Sun Road is a national historic landmark that skirts near shimmering Lake McDonald before angling sharply to the Garden Wall – the main dividing line between the west and east sides of the park. At Logan Pass you can stroll 1.5 miles to **Hidden Lake Overlook**; heartier hikers can try the 7.5-mile **Highline Trail**. The free shuttle stops on the western side of the road at the trailhead for **Avalanche Lake**, an easy 4-mile return hike to a stunning alpine lake in a cirque beautified with numerous weeping waterfalls.

Many Glacier HIKING

Anchored by the historic 1915 Many Glacier Lodge and sprinkled with more lakes than glaciers, this picturesque valley on the park's east side has some tremendous hikes, some of which link to the Going-to-the-Sun Road.

A favorite is the 9.4-mile (return) **Iceberg Lake Trail**, a steep but rewarding jaunt through flower meadows and pine forest to an iceberg infested lake.

Glacier Park Boat Co BOATING
(☎406-257-2426; www.glacierparkboats.com) Rents out kayaks and canoes, and runs popular guided tours (adult/child $23/11.50) from five locations in Glacier National Park.

Sleeping

There are 13 **NPS campgrounds** (☎406-888-7800; http://reservations.nps.gov; tent & RV sites $10-23) and seven historic lodges in the park, which operate between mid-May and the end of September. Of the sites, only Fish Creek and St Mary can be reserved in advance (up to five months). Sites fill by mid-morning, particularly in July and August.

Glacier also has seven historic lodges dating from the early 1900s.

TOP CHOICE **Many Glacier Hotel** HOTEL $$
(☎406-732-4411; www.glacierparkinc.com; Many Glacier Valley; r $145-189; ⏲mid-Jun–mid-Sep) Modeled after a Swiss chalet, this national historic landmark on Swiftcurrent Lake is the park's largest hotel, with 208 rooms featuring panoramic views. Evening entertainment, a lounge and fine-dining restaurant specializing in fondue all add to the appeal.

Lake McDonald Lodge HOTEL $$
(☎406-888-5431; www.glacierparkinc.com; Lake McDonald Valley; cabin/lodge r $128/182; ⏲May-Sep) Built in 1913, this old hunting lodge is adorned with stuffed-animal trophies and exudes relaxation. The 100 rooms are lodge, chalet or motel style. Nightly park-ranger talks and lake cruises add a rustic ambience. There's a restaurant and pizzeria.

Glacier Park Lodge HOTEL $$
(☎406-226-5600; www.glacierparkinc.com; East Glacier; r from $140; ⏲late May-Sep) The park's flagship lodge is a graceful, elegant place featuring interior balconies supported by Douglas fir timbers and a massive stone fireplace in the lobby. It's an aesthetically appealing, historically charming and very comfortable place to stay. Pluses include nine holes of golf and cozy reading nooks.

Rising Sun Motor Inn MOTEL $$
(☎406-732-5523; www.glacierparkinc.com; r $129-180; ⏲late May-early Sep) One of two classic 1940s-era wooden motels, the Rising Sun lies on the north shore of St Mary Lake in a small complex that includes a store, restaurant and boat launch. The rustic rooms and cabins offer everything an exhausted hiker could hope for.

Eating

In summer there are grocery stores with limited camping supplies in Apgar, Lake McDonald Lodge, Rising Sun and at the Swiftcurrent Motor Inn. Most lodges have on-site restaurants. Dining options in West Glacier and St Mary offer mainly hearty hiking fare.

Park Café AMERCIAN $
(www.parkcafe.us; US 89, St Mary; breakfast $7-12; ⏲7am-10pm Jun-Sep) In St Mary, and recommended for its dessert pies.

Ptarmigan Dining Room INTERNATIONAL $$$
(Many Glacier Lodge; mains $15-30; ⏲mid-Jun–early Sep) With its lakeside views, this is the most refined of the lodge restaurants.

Polebridge Mercantile BAKERY, SUPERMARKET $
(Polebridge Loop Rd; ⏲7am-9pm May-Nov) In the North Fork Valley. Come here for cinnamon buns – known to pump a good couple of hours into tired hiking legs.

Information

Visitor centers and ranger stations in the park sell field guides and hand out hiking maps. Those at Apgar and St Mary are open daily May to October; the visitor center at Logan Pass is open when the Going-to-the-Sun Road is open. The Many Glacier, Two Medicine and Polebridge Ranger Stations close at the end of September. **Park headquarters** (☎406-888-7800; www.nps.gov/glac; ⏲8am-4:30pm Mon-Fri), in West Glacier between US 2 and Apgar, is open year-round.

Entry to the park (hiker/vehicle $12/25) is valid for seven days. Day-hikers don't need permits, but overnight backpackers do (May to October only). Half of the permits are available on a first-come, first-served basis from the **Apgar Backcountry Permit Center** (permits per person per day $4; ⏲May 1-Oct 31), St Mary Visitor Center, and the Many Glacier, Two Medicine and Polebridge ranger stations.

The other half can be reserved at the Apgar Backcountry Permit Center, St Mary and Many Glacier visitor centers and Two Medicine and Polebridge ranger stations.

Getting There & Around

Amtrak's Empire Builder train stops daily at West Glacier (year round) and East Glacier Park (April to October) on its route between Seattle and Chicago. **Glacier National Park** (www.nps.gov/glac) runs free shuttles from Apgar Village to St Mary over Going-to-the-Sun Road from July 1 to Labor Day. **Glacier Park, Inc** (www.glacierparkinc.com) charges for its East Side Shuttle on the eastern side of the park with daily links to Waterton (Canada), Many Glacier, St Mary, Two Medicine and East Glacier.

IDAHO

Ascending Lemhi Pass in August 1805 just west of the headwaters of the Missouri River, American pathfinder, William Clarke of the Corps of Discovery expected to see a vast river plain stretching all the way to the Pacific. Instead he was confronted with range after range of uncharted mountains – the rugged, brutal landscape we now know as Idaho.

Famous for not being particularly famous, the nation's 43rd state is a pristine wilderness of Alaskan proportions that gets rudely ignored by most of the traffic heading west to Seattle or east to the more famous parks of Montana. In truth, much of this lightly trodden land is little changed since the days of Lewis and Clark including a vast 15,000-sq-km 'hole' that's in the middle of the state and bereft of roads, settlements, or any other form of human interference.

Flatter, dryer southern Idaho is dominated by the Snake River, deployed as a transportation artery by early settlers on the Oregon Trail and tracked today by busy Hwy 84. But, outside of this narrow populated strip, the Idaho landscape is refreshingly free of the soulless strip-mall, fast food infestations so ubiquitous elsewhere in the US.

IDAHO FACTS

- **Nickname** Gem State
- **Population** 1,567,582
- **Area** 83,570 sq miles
- **Capital city** Boise (population 205,671)
- **Other cities** Lewiston (population 31,293), Moscow (population 23,800), Idaho Falls (population 56,813).
- **Sales tax** 6%
- **Birthplace of** Lewis and Clark guide Sacagawea (1788–1812); politician and reality TV star Sarah Palin (b 1964); poet Ezra Pound (1885–1972); actress Lana Turner (1921–1995)
- **Home of** Star garnet, Sun Valley ski resort
- **Politics** reliably Republican with small pockets of Democrats, eg Sun Valley
- **Famous for** potatoes, wilderness, clean air, the world's first chairlift
- **State dance** square dance
- **Driving distances** Boise to Idaho Falls 280 miles, Lewiston to Coeur d'Alene 116 miles

Boise

Understated, underrated and underappreciated, Idaho's state capital (and largest city) gets little name recognition from people outside the northwest. But, while rarely San Franciscan in its magnificence, Boise's affable downtown surprises blinkered outsiders with the modest spirit of an underdog. Who knew about the grandiose Idaho capitol building? Who dreamt of well-heeled wine bars and Parisian-style bistros? And what's the story with all that latent Basque culture? The city's highlights include all of the these, plus a salubrious university campus and a 'city of trees' moniker that is far more than just a marketing ploy. The result: Boise leaves a poignant and lasting impression – primarily because it's not supposed to.

Sights & Activities

Delve into the main business district, bounded by State, Grove, 4th and 9th Sts.

TOP CHOICE **Basque Block** NEIGHBORHOOD
(www.thebasqueblock.com) Unbeknownst to many, Boise harbors one of the largest Basque populations outside Spain. The European émigrés first arrived in Idaho in the 1910s to pursue jobs in shepherding and elements of their distinct culture can be glimpsed along Grove St between 6th St and Capitol Blvd. Sandwiched between the ethnic taverns, restaurants and bars is **Basque Museum & Cultural Center** (www.basquemuseum.com; 611 Grove St; adult/senior & student $5/4; 10am-4pm Tue-Fri, 11am-3pm Sat) a commendable effort to unveil the intricacies of Basque culture and how it was transposed 6000 miles west to Idaho. Language lessons in Euskara, Europe's oldest language, are held here, while next door in the **Anduiza Fronton Building** (619 Grove St) there's a Basque handball court

where aficionados play the traditional sport of pelota. The Boise club is affiliated to the US Federation of Pelota.

Idaho State Capitol LANDMARK

The joy of US state capitol buildings is that visitors can wander in spontaneously for free to admire some of the nation's best architecture. The Boise building, constructed from native sandstone, celebrates the neoclassical style in vogue when it was built in 1920. It was extensively refurbished in 2010 and is now heated with geothermal hot water.

Boise River & Greenbelt PARKS, MUSEUMS

Laid out in the 1960s, the tree-lined riverbanks of the Boise River protect 30 miles of vehicle-free trails and, in more recent times, have come to personify Boise's 'city of trees' credentials. In summer, the river is insanely popular for its floating and tubing. The put-in point is **Barber Park** (Eckert Rd; tube rental $12), 6 miles east of downtown from where you can float 5 miles downstream to the take-out point at Ann Morrison Park. There are four rest-stops en route and a shuttle bus ($3) runs from the take-out point.

The most central and action-packed space on the Greenbelt, 90-acre **Julia Davis Park** contains the **Idaho State Historical Museum** (610 N Julia Davis Dr, adult/reduced $5/4; 9am-5pm Tue-Fri, 11am-5pm Sat) with well thought-out exhibits on Lewis and Clark; and the **Boise Art Museum** (www.boiseartmuseum.org; 670 N Julia Davis Dr, adult/senior & student $5/3; 10am-5pm Tue-Sat, noon-5pm Sun) There's also a pretty outdoor **rose garden**.

Ridge to Rivers Trail System HIKING

(www.ridgetorivers.org) More rugged than the greenbelt are the scrub- and brush-covered foothills above town offering 75 miles of scenic, sometimes strenuous hiking and mountain-biking routes. The most immediate access from downtown is via Fort Boise Park on E Fort St, five blocks southeast of the state capitol building.

Sleeping

Here are three true gems.

TOP CHOICE **Modern Hotel** BOUTIQUE MOTEL $$

(208-424-8244; www.themodernhotel.com; 1314 W Grove St; d from $125; P) Making an oxymoron (a boutique motel!?) into a fashion statement, the Modern Hotel offers retro-trendy minimalist rooms and a slavishly hip bar slap-bang in the middle of downtown. The power showers are huge and the service is five-star.

Leku Ona BOUTIQUE HOTEL $

(208-345-6665; 117 S 6th St; www.lekuonaid.com; r $65-85;) A Basque boutique hotel, no less, styled à la 'the old country' and situated next door to a restaurant of the same name that serves delicious *pintxos* (Basque tapas). The operation is run by a Basque-born immigrant and is economical as well as authentic.

Hotel 43 BOUTIQUE HOTEL $$

(800-243-4622; www.hotel43.com; 981 Grove St; r $146-229;) Named after the latitude (Boise sits on the 43rd parallel) and in honor of Idaho being the 43rd state, this is an urban cozy boutique hotel in the heart of downtown. The 112 rooms and suites are artfully laid out and feature views of the state capitol and surrounding foothills. The swanky on-site Chandlers Restaurant and Martini Bar (mains from $15) is one of Boise's most popular watering and eating holes.

Eating & Drinking

Restaurants and nightspots are found downtown in the brick-lined pedestrian plaza of the Grove, and the gentrified former warehouse district between 8th St and Idaho Ave. The overall food scene is what you might call 'a turn up for the books.' Count on some exciting Basque specialties, an abundance of authentic French-style bistros and some exceptional wine bars.

Grape Escape WINE BAR $$

(800 W Idaho St; appetizers $7-11, mains $11-18) Sit alfresco and enjoy your Pinot Noir with light supper fare (bruschetta, salads and highly creative pizzas) logging the ubiquity of downtown cyclists, closet intellectuals and bright young things out for an early evening aperitif. The wine menu is almost as good as the people-watching.

La Vie en Rose BAKERY, BISTRO $

(www.lavieenrosebakery.com; 928 W Main St; mains $7-10; 8am-5pm Tue-Sun) Have a European moment inside the turreted Idanha Hotel building at this authentic French bistro and bakery where the French-imbued menu includes *croque monsieur* (grilled cheese and ham sandwich), homemade *tarte* and Italian Illy coffee.

Bar Gernika PUB $

(www.bargernkia.com; 202 S Capitol Blvd; lunch $8-9; ⏲11am-midnight Mon-Thu till 1am Fri & Sat) *Ongi etorri* (welcome) to the Basque block's most accessible pub-tavern with a menu that leans heavily on old-country favorites such as lamb kabob, chorizo and beef tongue (on Saturdays only). It's a true only-in-Boise kind of place.

Bittercreek Ale House & Red Feather Lounge INTERNATIONAL $$

(www.justeatlocal.com; 246 N 8th St; mains $7-15; ⏲11:30am-late) These adjoining restaurants (owned by the same people) have lively sidewalk patios, intimate environs and lots of personality. They also serve wholesome, usually locally produced food with an emphasis on sustainable growth. The nouveau-American menu at Bittercreek features a good selection of vegetarian options (it does organic Idaho black bean burgers on request). Order one of the whiskey cocktails made using an old-fashioned pre-Prohibition-era recipe. The Red Feather is slightly more upscale, and does delicious wood-oven pizza and a set three-course menu for two ($23 per person).

Bardenay PUB $$

(www.bardenay.com; 610 Grove St; mains $8-18) Bardenay was the USA's very first 'distillery-pub,' and remains a one-of-a-kind watering hole. Today it serves its own home-brewed vodka, rum and gin in casual, airy environs. It gets consistently good reviews.

Information

Visitor center (☎208-344-5338; www.boise.org; 850 Front St; ⏲10am-5pm Mon-Fri, 10am-2pm Sat Jun-Aug, 9am-4pm Mon-Fri Sep-May)

Getting There & Around

Boise Municipal Airport (BOI; I-84 exit 53) has daily flights to Denver, Las Vegas, Phoenix, Portland, Salt Lake City, Seattle and Spokane. Greyhound services depart from the **bus station** (1212 W Bannock St) with routes fanning out to Lewiston and Spokane, Pendleton and Portland, and Twin Falls and Salt Lake City.

Ketchum & Sun Valley

In one of Idaho's most stunning natural locations sits a piece of ski history. Sun Valley was the first purpose-built ski resort in the US, hand-picked by Union Pacific Railroad scion William Averell Harriman (after an exhaustive search) in the 1930s and publicized by numerous members of the then glitterati such as Ernest Hemingway, Clark Gable and Gary Cooper. When Sun Valley opened in 1936 it sported the world's first chairlift and a showcase 'parkitecture' lodge that still acts as its premier resort.

In the years since, Sun Valley has kept its swanky Hollywood clientele and extended its facilities to include the legendary Bald Mountain, yet it remains a refined and pretty place (no fast-food joints or condo sprawl here). Highly rated nationwide, the resort is revered for its reliable high-quality snow, large elevation drop and almost windless weather. Backing it up is adjacent village Ketchum, 1 mile away, which predates Sun Valley and has held onto its authenticity and rustic beauty despite the skiing deluge. Ketchum is prime territory for fishing and hunting in summer, a fact borne out by its famous former resident, Ernest Hemingway.

Activities

Main St between 1st and 5th Sts is where you'll find nearly all the businesses. Sun Valley and its lodge is 1 mile to the north and easily walkable. Twelve miles south of Ketchum, also on Hwy 75, is Hailey, another delightful small town with a bar scene.

Wood River Trail HIKING, CYCLING

There are numerous hiking and mountain biking trails around Ketchum and Sun Valley, as well as excellent fishing spots. The Wood River Trail is the all-connecting artery linking Sun Valley with Ketchum and continuing 32 bucolic miles south down to Bellevue via Hailey. Bikes can be hired from **Pete Lane's** (per day $35) in the mall next to the Sun Valley Lodge.

Sun Valley Resort SNOW SPORTS

(www.sunvalley.com) Famous for its light, fluffy powder and celebrity guests, the dual-sited resort comprises advanced-terrain **Bald Mountain** (lift ticket $55-80) and easier-on-the-nerves **Dollar Mountain** (lift ticket adult $32-38, child $16-30), which also has a **tubing hill** (adult/child $10/5). In summer, take the chairlift to the top of either mountain, and hike or cycle down. Facilities are predictably plush.

Sleeping

Sun Valley Lodge HOTEL $$$

(☎208-622-2001; www.sunvalley.com; 1 Sun Valley Rd; r $229-329; ❄@🛜≋👪) Hemingway

HEMINGWAY: THE FINAL DAYS

Although Sun Valley and Ketchum never featured explicitly in the work of Ernest Miller Hemingway, the globe-trotting author had a deep affection for the area and became a frequent visitor following its development as a ski resort in the late 1930s. Legend has it that he completed his Spanish Civil War masterpiece *For Whom the Bell Tolls* in room 206 of the **Sun Valley Lodge** in between undertaking fishing and hunting excursions with well-heeled friends such as Gary Cooper and Clark Gable.

In the 1940s and '50s, Hemingway's Ketchum trips became more sporadic as he migrated south to Key West and Cuba but, following the Cuban revolution in 1959, and the subsequent expropriation of Hemingway's Havana house, the author moved permanently to Idaho in 1959. Increasingly paranoid and in declining physical and mental health, His final days weren't his happiest and on July 2, 1961, aged 61, he took his favorite gun, walked out onto the porch of his newly acquired home off Warm Springs Rd and blew his brains out.

There is a surprising (and refreshing) lack of hullaballoo surrounding Hemingway in Ketchum and you'll have to look hard to find the small, pretty **cemetery** half a mile north of the center on Hwy 75, where he is buried alongside his granddaughter Margaux. Pennies, cigars and the odd bottle of liquor furnish his simple grave. Hemingway's house is out of bounds to the public but there is a **monument** honoring him near Trail Creek, 1 mile beyond the Sun Valley Lodge. Downtown in Ketchum his favorite drinking holes were the **Casino Club** and the Alpine Club, now known as **Whiskey Jacques**.

completed *For Whom the Bell Tolls* in this swank 1930s-era beauty and the place has lost little of its luxurious pre-war sheen. Old-fashioned elegance is the lure in comfortable rooms that sometimes feel a little small by today's standards. Amenities include a fitness facility, game room, bowling alley and sauna. It also runs a ski shuttle and has a children's program.

Lift Tower Lodge MOTEL **$**
(☎208-726-5163; 703 S Main St; r $65-100; P Wi-Fi) Lifelong members of the hoi polloi can hobnob with the millionaires of Ketchum and decamp afterwards to this friendly and economical small motel on the cusp of the ski village. The building is advertised with a landmark exhibition chairlift (c 1939) that is lit up after dark.

Tamarack Lodge HOTEL **$$**
(☎208-726-3344; www.tamaracksunvalley.com; 500 E Sun Valley Rd; r $109-139; A/C Wi-Fi Pool) Tasteful rooms complete with fireplace, balcony and many amenities are offered at this well-maintained lodge. The Jacuzzi and indoor pool are definite assets. Discounts are often available midweek and off-season.

Eating & Drinking

TOP CHOICE **Roosevelt Grille** STEAKHOUSE, PUB **$$**
(www.rooseveltgrille.com; 280 N Main St; mains $9-19) What use is a classic ski town without the classic ski steakhouse and bar? An imperceptible amalgam of food (beef mostly), beer, sunny rooftop patio and congenial atmosphere make this the most popular vote in town – usually by a mile.

Rickshaw ASIAN **$$**
(www.eat-at-rickshaw.com; 460 Washington Ave N; small plates & mains $5-12; ⏲5:30-10.30pm Tue-Sat, 5:30-9.30pm Sun) Sick of steak? This hippy-ish shack just off Main St does Asian fusion tapas – creative, fresh small plates inspired by the cuisine of Vietnam, Thailand, China and Indonesia, which the chef refers to as 'ethnic street food.'

Desperado's MEXICAN **$**
(☎208-726-3068; 211 4th St; mains $7-10; ⏲11:30am-10pm Mon-Sat) You could eat steak seven nights a week in Ketchum but, to broaden your horizons a little, head metaphorically south to Desperado's for burritos, chimichangas (deep-fried burritos) and tacos washed down with a margarita.

Pioneer Saloon STEAKHOUSE **$$$**
(www.pioneersaloon.com; 320 N Main St; mains $12-25; ⏲5:30pm-10pm) Around since the 1950s and originally an illicit gambling hall, the Pio is an unashamed Rocky Mountain restaurant decorated with deer heads, antique guns, bullet boards and – oh yes – some good food too, as long as you like beef and trout.

Casino Club BAR

(220 N Main St) In a ski resort less than 75 years old, this dive bar is the oldest thing still standing and has witnessed everything from gambling fist fights, to psychedelic hippies, to the rise and fall of Ernest Hemingway (yes, he downed a few in here), to tattooed men on Harleys riding through the front door. A survivor, if nothing else!

Information

Sun Valley/Ketchum Visitors Center (☎208-726-3423; www.visitsunvalley.com; 491 Sun Valley Rd; ⏲9am-6pm)

Getting There & Around

The region's airport, **Friedman Memorial Airport** (www.flyfma.com) in Hailey is 12 miles south of Ketchum. **A-1 Taxi** (☎208-726-9351) offers rides to the airport from Ketchum ($22).

Sun Valley Express (www.sunvalleyexpress.com) operates a daily shuttle between Sun Valley and Boise Airport in both directions ($59 one-way).

Stanley

Tiny Stanley (population 100) might be the most scenic small town in America. Surrounded by protected wilderness and national-forest land, the remote outpost is nestled into the crook of Salmon River, miles from anywhere. It's the kind of place where peaceful high summer twilight stretches on past 10pm and you fall asleep to the river's melodic roar. The aptly named Sawtooth Mountains provide a dramatic backdrop.

Activities

Middle Fork of the Salmon RAFTING

Stanley is the jumping-off point for rafting the legendary Middle Fork of the Salmon. Billed as the 'last wild river' it's part of the longest undammed river system outside Alaska. Full trips last six days and allow you to float for 106 miles through the 300 or so rapids (class I to IV) of the 2.4-million-acre Frank Church–River of No Return Wilderness, miles from any form of civilization.

DON'T MISS

CENTRAL IDAHO'S SCENIC BYWAYS

Goodbye suburban strip malls, hello unblemished wilderness. All three roads into the remote Idahoan outpost of Stanley are designated National Scenic Byways (it's the only place in the US where this happens). Considering there are only 125 such roads in the country, it means 2.4% of American's prettiest pavement runs through bucolic Stanley.

Sawtooth Scenic Byway

Following the Salmon River along Hwy 75 north from Ketchum to Stanley this 60-mile drive is gorgeous, winding through a misty, thick ponderosa pine forest – where the air is crisp and fresh and smells like rain and nuts – before ascending the 8701ft **Galena Summit**. From the overlook at the top, there are views of the glacially carved Sawtooth Mountains.

Ponderosa Pine Scenic Byway

Hwy 21, between Stanley and Boise, is so beautiful it will be hard to reach your destination because you'll want to stop so much. From Stanley the trees increase in density, until you find yourself enveloped in a sweetly scented cloak of pine – an environment that seems more Pacific Northwest than classic Rockies. Fast-moving clouds bring frequent bursts of rain and the roadway can feel dangerous. Even in late May the snowfields stretch right down to the highway. Two of the road's many highlights are **Kikham Creek Hot Springs** (self-pay campsites $16), 6 miles east of Lowman, a primitive campground and natural hot springs boiling out of the creek; and the old restored gold rush town of **Idaho Falls**.

Salmon River Scenic Byway

Northeast of Stanley, Hwy 75 and US 93 make up another scenic road that runs beside the Salmon River for 161 miles to historic **Lost Trail Pass** on the Montana border, the point where Lewis and Clark first crossed the continental divide in 1805. Much of the surrounding scenery has changed little in over 200 years.

Camping is riverside and guides cook excellent food. Book through **Solitude River Trips** (www.rivertrips.com). Trips run June to August and cost approximately $1800 per person with transportation.

Main Fork of the Salmon RAFTING

For more affordable, albeit slightly less dramatic, white-water action than Middle Fork, do a DIY float trip down the Main Fork of the Salmon. There are 8 miles of quiet water, starting in Stanley, with views of the Sawtooth Mountains you can't see from the road. Bring fishing gear. Float trips in inflatable kayaks (single/double $30/40) can be arranged through **Sawtooth Rentals** (www.riversidemotel.biz; Hwy 75) at the Riverside Motel in Stanley.

Silver Creek Outfitters FISHING

(www.silver-creek.com; 1 Sun Valley Rd) There is epic trout fishing on the Salmon and in surrounding mountain lakes from March until November, with late June to early October the best time for dry fly-fishing. Silver Creek, run out of Sun Valley, does custom trips to remote river spots, only accessible via drift boat or float tube. There are no less than eight species of trout in these waters, including the mythical Steelhead. Measuring up to 40in, these fish swim east about 900 miles from the Pacific Ocean at the end of winter, arriving near Stanley in March and April.

Sleeping & Eating

There are about half a dozen hotels in Stanley, all done in traditional pioneer log-cabin style. During the short summer season a couple of restaurants open up.

Sawtooth Hotel HOTEL $

(208-721-2459; www.sawtoothhotel.com; 755 Ace of Diamonds St; d with/without bath $100/70;) This is what happens when the owners of the famous Stanley Baking Co open a hotel. Set in a nostalgic 1931 log motel, the Sawtooth updates the comforts of yesteryear, but keeps the hospitality effusively Stanley-esque. There are six rooms furnished old-country style, two of which have private bathrooms. Don't expect TVs or room phones, but count on home-spun dining that is exquisite.

TOP CHOICE **Stanley Baking Co** BAKERY, BREAKFAST $

(www.stanleybakingco.com; 250 Wall St; breakfast & lunch $6-9; 7am-2pm May-Oct) After having lumbered the world with unhealthy delights of 'junk food,' the US claims culinary penance in more esoteric genres, such as the middle-of-nowhere bakery and brunch spot. Operating for five months of the year out of a small log cabin, Stanley Baking Co is the only place in town where you're likely to see a queue. The reason: off-the-ratings-scale homemade baked goods.

Idaho Panhandle

Borders are arbitrary in the long skinny spoon-handle of northern Idaho that brushes up against Canada. Historically this was never supposed to be Idaho anyway – a land dispute with Montana ended with the state claiming the panhandle in the 1880s – and, in both looks and attitude, the area has more in common with the Pacific Northwest than the Rockies. Tellingly, Spokane, a few miles west in Washington, acts as the regional hub and most of the panhandle observes Pacific Standard Time.

Near the Washington border, fast-growing **Coeur d'Alene** (population 44,000) is an extension of the Spokane metro area and the panhandle's largest town. However, it's overdeveloped with a rather tacky boardwalk waterfront and one of those Anywhere USA–type golf and spa resorts. The adjacent lake is ideal for water-based activities, in particular water-skiing. The **Coeur d'Alene Visitors Bureau** (877-782-9232; www.coeurdalene.org; 105 N 1st; 10am-5pm Tue-Sat) has further information. It's not really worth stopping here unless it's late and you need to sleep, in which case go straight to the quirky pink-door **Flamingo Motel** (208-664-2159; www.flamingomotelidaho.com; 718 Sherman Ave; r $80-100;), a retro 1950s throwback.

Sandpoint, on Lake Pend Oreille, is the nicest of the panhandle's towns. Set in a gorgeous wilderness locale surrounded by mountains, it also sports Idaho's only serviceable Amtrak **train station**, an attractive historic building dating from 1916. The *Empire Builder,* running daily between Seattle/Portland and Chicago, stops here.

You can soak up Idaho's largest lake from the **Pend Oreille Scenic Byway** (US 200), which hugs the north shore. Eleven miles northwest of town is highly rated **Schweitzer Mountain Resort** (www.schweitzer.com), lauded for its tree-skiing.

The best accommodation bargain for miles around is the clean, friendly mom-and-pop-run **Country Inn** (208-263-3333; www.countryinnsandpoint.com; 470700 Hwy 95; s/d $49/59), 3 miles south of Sandpoint.

Southwest

Includes »

Best Places to Eat

» Café Diablo (p368)
» Elote Cafe (p337)
» Joël Robuchon (p313)
» Poco (p353)
» San Marcos Café (p383)

Best Places to Stay

» Cosmopolitan (p307)
» Earthship Rentals (p388)
» El Tovar Hotel (p342)
» Motor Lodge (p338)
» Sundance Resort (p363)

Why Go?

Breathtaking beauty and the allure of adventure merge seamlessly in the Southwest. This captivating mix has drawn dreamers and explorers for centuries. Pioneers staked their claims beside lush riverbanks, prospectors dug into mountains for untold riches, religious refugees built cities across empty deserts, while astronomers and rocket builders peered into star-filled skies. Today, artists and entrepreneurs flock to urban centers and quirky mining towns, energizing the entire region.

For travelers, beauty and adventure still loom large in this land of mountains, deserts and wide-open spaces sprawled across Nevada, Arizona, Utah and New Mexico. You can hike past red rocks, cycle beneath mountain skies, raft through canyons and roll the dice under the mesmerizing lights of Vegas. But remember: beauty and adventure here can also loom small. Study that saguaro up close. Ask a Hopi artist about his craft. Savor some green-chile stew. It's the tap-you-on-the-shoulder moments you may just cherish the most.

When to Go

Las Vegas

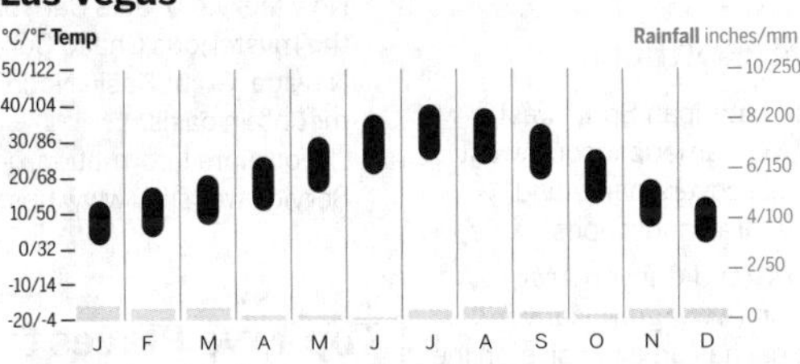

Jan Ski near Taos and Flagstaff. In Park City, hit the slopes and the Sundance Film Festival.

Jun-Aug High season for exploring national parks in New Mexico, Utah and northern Arizona.

Sep-Nov Hike to the bottom of the Grand Canyon or gaze at bright leaves in northern New Mexico.

DON'T MISS

A hike in the desert. Your choices? The Sonoran, Chihuahuan, Great Basin.

Fast Facts

» Hub cities: Las Vegas (population 553,000), Phoenix (population 1.4 million), Salt Lake City (population 181,743)

» Las Vegas to Grand Canyon National Park South Rim: 280 miles

» Los Angeles to Albuquerque: 670 miles

» Time zones: Nevada (Pacific), Arizona (Mountain, does not observe DST), Utah (Mountain), New Mexico (Mountain)

» States covered in this chapter: Nevada, Arizona, Utah, New Mexico

Did You Know?

Flash floods are most common from mid-July to early September. Avoid camping on sandy washes and canyon bottoms; don't drive across flooded roads. If hiking, move quickly to higher ground.

Resources

» American Southwest (www.americansouthwest.net) covers parks and natural landscapes.

» Grand Canyon Association (www.grandcanyon.org) has an extensive online bookstore for the park.

» Recreation.gov (www.recreation.gov) takes reservations for camping and other activities at nationally run outdoor areas.

Getting There & Around

Phoenix' Sky Harbor International Airport and Las Vegas' McCarran International Airport are the region's busiest airports, followed by the airports serving Salt Lake City, Albuquerque and Tucson.

Greyhound stops at major points within the region but doesn't serve all national parks or off-the-beaten-path tourist towns such as Moab. In larger cities, bus terminals can be in less-safe areas of town.

Private vehicles are often the only means to reach out-of-the-way towns, trailheads and swimming spots. For car rentals, see p457.

Amtrak train service is much more limited than the bus system, although it does link many major Southwestern cities and offers bus connections to others (including Santa Fe and Phoenix). The *California Zephyr* crosses Utah and Nevada; the *Southwest Chief* stops in Arizona and New Mexico; and the *Sunset Limited* traverses southern Arizona and New Mexico.

NATIONAL & STATE PARKS

Containing 40 national parks and monuments, the Southwest is a scenic and cultural jackpot. Add some stunning state parks, and, well, you might need to extend your trip.

One of the most deservedly popular national parks is Arizona's Grand Canyon National Park. Other Arizona parks include Monument Valley Navajo Tribal Park, a desert basin with towering sandstone pillars and buttes; Canyon de Chelly National Monument, with ancient cliff dwellings; Petrified Forest National Park, with its odd mix of Painted Desert and fossilized logs; and Saguaro National Park, with pristine desert and giant cacti.

The southern red-rock Canyon Country in Utah includes five national parks: Arches, Canyonlands, Zion, Bryce Canyon and Capitol Reef, which offers exceptional wilderness solitude. Grand Staircase-Escalante National Monument is a mighty region of undeveloped desert. New Mexico boasts Carlsbad Caverns National Park and the mysterious Chaco Culture National Historic Park. In Nevada, Great Basin National Park is a rugged, remote mountain oasis.

For more information, check out the National Park Service website (www.nps.gov).

Top Five Places for Sunset Cocktails

» Asylum Restaurant, Jerome Grand Hotel (p338)

» Bell Tower Bar, La Fonda Hotel (p384)

» Grand Canyon Lodge's veranda (p343)

» Mix, Mandalay Bay (799)

» Parallel 88 (p372)

History

By about AD 100, three dominant cultures had emerged in the Southwest: the Hohokam, the Mogollon and the Ancestral Puebloans (formerly known as the Anasazi).

The Hohokam lived in the Arizona deserts from 300 BC to AD 1450, and created an incredible canal irrigation system, earthen pyramids and a rich heritage of pottery. Archaeological studies suggest that a cataclysmic event in the mid-15th century caused a dramatic decrease in the Hohokam's population, most notably in larger villages. Though it's not entirely clear what happened or where they went, the oral traditions of local tribes suggest that some Hohokam remained in the area and that members of these tribes are their descendants. From 200 BC to AD 1450 the Mogollon lived in the central mountains and valleys of the Southwest, and left behind what are now called the Gila Cliff Dwellings.

The Ancestral Puebloans left the richest heritage of archaeological sites, such as that at Chaco Culture National Historic Park. Today descendants of the Ancestral Puebloans are found in the Pueblo groups throughout New Mexico. The Hopi are descendants, too, and their village Old Oraibi (see the boxed text, p346) may be the oldest continuously inhabited settlement in North America.

In 1540 Francisco Vásquez de Coronado led an expedition from Mexico City to the Southwest. Instead of riches, his party found Native Americans, many of whom were then killed or displaced. More than 50 years later, Juan de Oñate established the first capital of New Mexico at San Gabriel. Great bloodshed resulted from Oñate's attempts to control Native American pueblos, and he left in failure in 1608. Santa Fe was established as the new capital around 1610.

Development in the Southwest expanded rapidly during the 19th century, mainly due to railroad and geological surveys. As the US pushed west, the army forcibly removed whole tribes of Native Americans in often horrifyingly brutal Indian Wars. Gold and silver mines drew fortune seekers, and practically overnight the lawless mining towns of the Wild West mushroomed. Capitalizing on the development, the Santa Fe Railroad lured an ocean of tourists to the West.

Modern settlement is closely linked to water use. Following the Reclamation Act of 1902, huge federally funded dams were built to control rivers, irrigate the desert and encourage development. Rancorous debates and disagreements over water rights are ongoing, especially with the phenomenal boom in residential development. Other big issues today are illegal immigration and fiscal solvency.

SOUTHWEST IN...

One Week

Museums and a burgeoning arts scene set an inspirational tone in **Phoenix**, an optimal springboard for exploring. In the morning, follow Camelback Rd into **Scottsdale** for top-notch shopping and gallery-hopping in Old Town. Drive north to **Sedona** for spiritual recharging before pondering the immensity of the **Grand Canyon**. From here, choose either bling or buttes. For bling, detour onto **Route 66**, cross the new bridge beside **Hoover Dam** then indulge your fantasies in **Las Vegas**. For buttes, drive east from the Grand Canyon into the Navajo country, cruising beneath the giant rock formations in **Monument Valley Navajo Tribal Park** then stepping back in time at stunning **Canyon de Chelly National Monument**.

Two Weeks

Start in glitzy **Las Vegas** before kicking back in funky **Flagstaff** and peering into the abyss at **Grand Canyon National Park**. Check out collegiate **Tucson** or frolic amongst cacti at **Saguaro National Park**. Watch the high-noon gunslinging in **Tombstone** before settling into Victorian **Bisbee**.

Secure your sunglasses for the blinding dunes of **White Sands National Monument** in nearby New Mexico then sink into **Santa Fe**, a magnet for art-lovers. Explore a pueblo in **Taos** and watch the sunrise at awesome **Monument Valley Navajo Tribal Park**. Head into Utah for the red-rock national parks, **Canyonlands** and **Arches**. Do the hoodoos at **Bryce Canyon** then pay your respects at glorious **Zion**.

Southwest Highlights

1. Ponder up to two billion years of geologic history at **Grand Canyon National Park** (p339)
2. Live your own John Wayne Western in northeastern Arizona's **Monument Valley** (p346)
3. Practice your fast draw in dusty **Tombstone** (p353)
4. Gallery-hop and jewelry-shop on the stylish streets of **Santa Fe** (p384)
5. Sled down a shimmering sand dune at **White Sands National Monument** (p394)
6. Wander a wonderland of stalactites at **Carlsbad Caverns National Park** (p397)
7. Live the high life on Las Vegas' **Strip** (p311)
8. Ogle towering spires of clay, silt and ash at **Cathedral Gorge State Park** (p324)
9. Snap a photo of graceful Delicate Arch at **Arches National Park** (p366)
10. Explore a majestic canyon and climb Angels Landing at **Zion National Park** (p371)

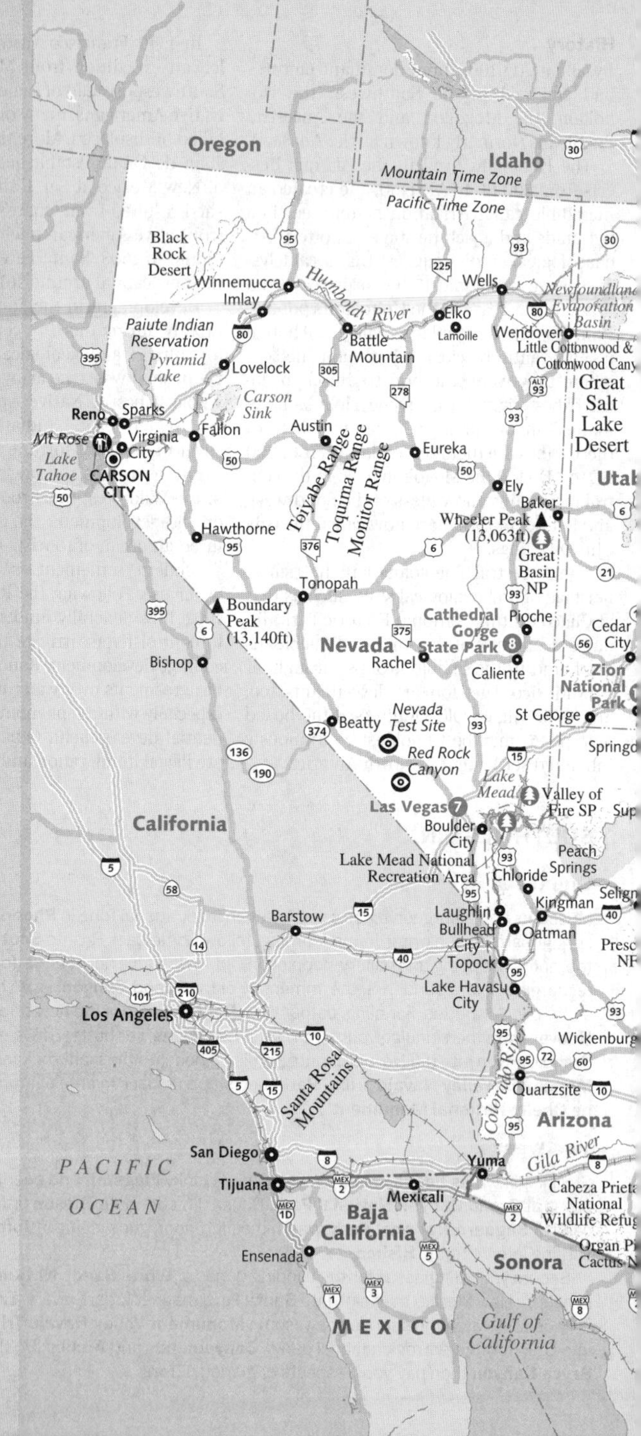

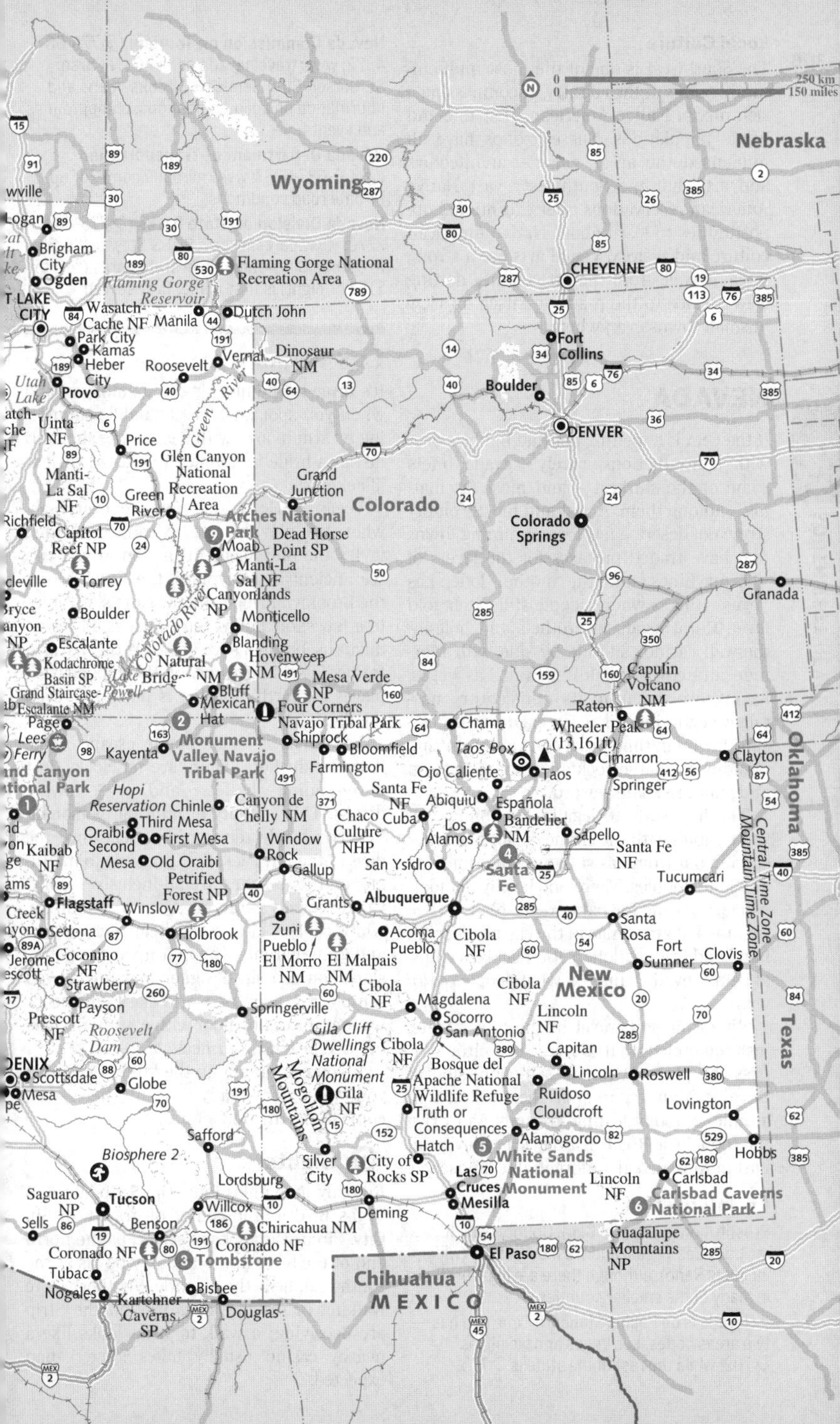

Local Culture

The Southwest is one of the most multicultural regions of the country, encompassing a rich mix of Native American, Hispanic and Anglo populations. These groups have all influenced the area's cuisine, architecture and arts, but the Southwest's vast Native American reservations offer exceptional opportunities to learn about Native American culture and history. Visual arts are a strong force as well, from the art colonies dotting New Mexico to the roadside kitsch on view in small towns everywhere.

NEVADA

If the USA is a melting pot that bubbles over with contradictions, surely Nevada offers some of the starkest – and most fascinating – among them. A vast and mostly empty stretch of desert, a few former mining towns that have traded pickaxes for the levers of slot machines, and the mother lode, Las Vegas – this is where people still catch gold fever. Rural legalized brothels and hole-in-the-wall casinos sit side by side with Mormon and cowboy culture. Even Las Vegas, having evolved from its mid-century nostalgic beginnings, is a far cry from a postcard frozen in time. It's a constantly shifting paradox, a volatile cocktail of sophistication and smut, risk and reward.

The first state to legalize gambling, Nevada is loud with the chime of slot machines singing out from gas stations, supermarkets and hotel lobbies. There's no legally mandated closing time for bars, so get ready to see sequin-clad grandmas in the casino, beers in hand and trading dollars for blackjack chips, at 2am. Nevada banks on what people *really* want.

Wherever you travel in the Silver State, just remember that Nevada is weird. Witness the peaceful riot of self-expression at Burning Man, try to spot alien UFOs, visit atomic-weapons testing grounds and drive the 'Loneliest Road in America': they're all part of this surreal, unforgettable landscape.

Information

Prostitution is illegal in Clark County (which includes Las Vegas) and Washoe County (which includes Reno), although there are legal brothels in many of the smaller counties.

Nevada is on Pacific Standard Time and has two areas codes: Las Vegas and vicinity is ☎702, while the rest of the state is ☎775.

Nevada Commission on Tourism (☎775-687-4322; www.travelnevada.com; 401 N Carson St, Carson City) Sends free books, maps and information on accommodations, campgrounds and events.

Nevada Department of Transportation (☎877-687-6237; www.nvroads.com) For up-to-date road conditions.

Nevada Division of State Parks (☎775-684-2770; www.parks.nv.gov; 901 S Stewart St, 5th fl, Carson City) Camping in state parks ($10 to $15 per night) is first-come, first-served.

Las Vegas

It's three in the morning in a smoky casino when you spot an Elvis look-alike sauntering by arm in arm with a glittering showgirl just as a bride in a long white dress shrieks 'Blackjack!'

Vegas is Hollywood for the everyman, where you play the role instead of watching it. It's the only place in the world you can see ancient hieroglyphics, the Eiffel Tower, the Brooklyn Bridge and the canals of Venice in a few short hours. Sure, they're all reproductions, but in a slice of desert that's transformed itself into one of the most lavish places on earth, nothing is halfway – even the illusions.

Las Vegas is the ultimate escape. Time is irrelevant here. There are no clocks, just never-ending buffets and ever-flowing drinks. This is a city of multiple personalities, constantly reinventing itself since the days of the Rat Pack. Sin City aims to infatuate, and its reaches are all-inclusive. Hollywood bigwigs gyrate at A-list ultralounges, while college kids seek cheap debauchery and grandparents whoop it up at the penny slots. You can sip designer martinis as you sample the apex of world-class cuisine or wander the casino floor with a 3ft-high cocktail tied around your neck.

If you can dream up the kind of vacation you want, it's already a reality here. Welcome to the dream factory.

Sights

Roughly four miles long, the Strip, aka Las Vegas Blvd, is the center of gravity in Sin City. Circus Circus Las Vegas caps the north end of the Strip and Mandalay Bay is at the south end, near the airport. Whether you're walking or driving, distances on the Strip are deceiving; a walk to what looks like a nearby casino usually takes longer than expected.

NEVADA FACTS

» **Nickname** Silver State

» **Population** 2.76 million

» **Area** 109,800 sq miles

» **Capital city** Las Vegas (population 553,000)

» **Other cities** Reno (population 225,000)

» **Sales tax** 6.85%

» **Birthplace of** Patricia Nixon (b 1912), Andre Agassi (b 1970), Greg LeMond (b 1961)

» **Home of** the slot machine, Burning Man

» **Politics** Nevada has six electoral votes – the state swung Democratic in the 2008 presidential election, but it is split about evenly in sending elected officials to Washington; US Senate Majority Leader Harry Reid (D) is Nevada's most well-known politician

» **Famous for** the 1859 Comstock Lode (the country's richest known silver deposit), legalized gambling and prostitution (outlawed in certain counties), and liberal alcohol laws allowing 24-hour bars

» **Weirdest Nevada brothel name** Inez's Dancing and Diddling, Elko

» **Driving distances** Las Vegas to Reno: 452 miles, Great Basin National Park to Las Vegas: 313 miles

Downtown Las Vegas is the original town center and home to the city's oldest hotels and casinos: expect a retro feel, cheaper drinks and lower table limits. Its main drag is fun-loving Fremont St, four blocks of which are a covered pedestrian mall that runs a groovy light show every evening.

Major tourist areas are safe. However, Las Vegas Blvd between downtown and the Strip gets shabby, and Fremont St east of downtown is rather unsavory.

Casinos

TOP CHOICE **Cosmopolitan** CASINO
(www.cosmopolitanlasvegas.com; 3708 Las Vegas Blvd S) Hipsters who have long thought they were too cool for Vegas finally have a place to go where they don't need irony to endure – much less enjoy – the aesthetics. Like the new Hollywood 'It girl,' the Cosmo looks good at all times of the day or night, full of ingenues and entourages, plus regular folks who enjoy contemporary design. With a focus on pure fun, it avoids utter pretension, despite the constant wink-wink, retro moments: the Art-o-Matics (vintage cigarette machines hawking local art rather than nicotine), and possibly the best buffet in town, the **Wicked Spoon**.

TOP CHOICE **Encore** CASINO
(www.encorelasvegas.com; 3121 Las Vegas Blvd S) Steve Wynn has upped the wow factor, and the skyline, yet again with the Encore, a slice of the French Riviera in Las Vegas – and classy enough to entice any of the Riviera's regulars. Filled with indoor flower gardens, a butterfly motif and a dramatically luxe casino, it's an oasis of bright beauty. **Botero**, the restaurant headed by Mark LoRusso, is centered on a large sculpture by Fernando Botero himself. Encore is attached to its sister property, the $2.7-billion **Wynn Las Vegas** (www.wynnlasvegas.com; 3131 Las Vegas Blvd S). The entrance is obscured from the Strip by a $130-million artificial mountain, which rises 7 stories tall in some places. Inside, the Wynn resembles a natural paradise – with mountain views, tumbling waterfalls, fountains and other special effects.

TOP CHOICE **Hard Rock** CASINO
(www.hardrockhotel.com; 4455 Paradise Rd) Beloved by SoCal visitors, this très-hip casino hotel is home to one of the world's most impressive collections of rock and roll memorabilia, including Jim Morrison's handwritten lyrics to one of the Door's greatest hits and leather jackets from a who's who of famous rock stars. The Joint concert hall, Vanity Nightclub and 'Rehab' summer pool parties attract a pimped-out, sex-charged crowd flush with celebrities.

Bellagio CASINO
(www.bellagio.com; 3600 Las Vegas Blvd S) The Bellagio dazzles with Tuscan architecture and an 8-acre artificial lake, complete with don't-miss choreographed dancing fountains. Look up as you enter the lobby: the stunning ceiling adorned with a backlit glass sculpture composed of 2000 handblown flowers by renowned artist Dale Chihuly. The **Bellagio Gallery of Fine Art** (adult/child $13/free; ⌚10am-6pm Sun-Tue & Thu, to 7pm Wed, Fri & Sat) showcases temporary exhibits by

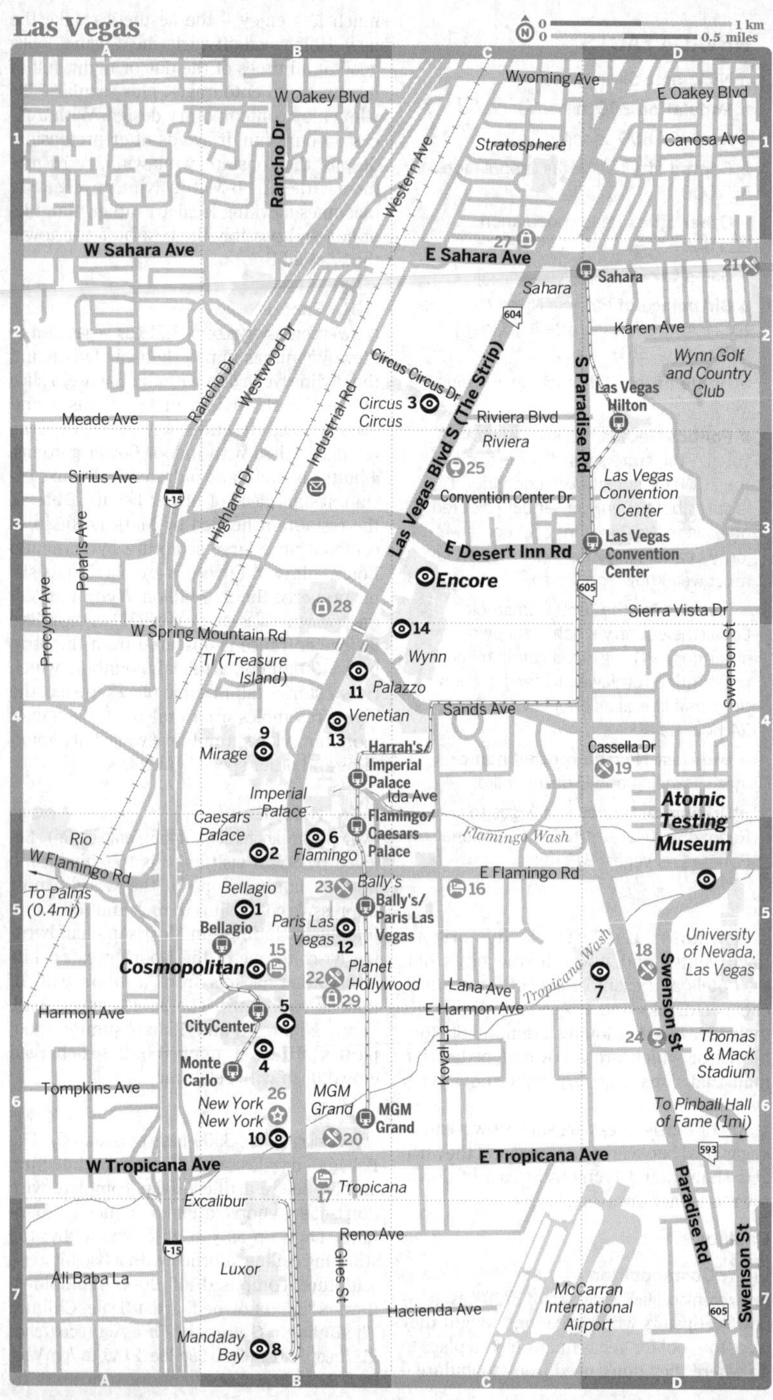
0 1 km
0 0.5 miles
Wyoming Ave
W Oakey Blvd
E Oakey Blvd
Canosa Ave
Stratosphere
Rancho Dr
Western Ave
W Sahara Ave
E Sahara Ave
Sahara
Sahara
Karen Ave
Wynn Golf and Country Club
Rancho Dr
Westwood Dr
Industrial Rd
Circus Circus Dr
Las Vegas Blvd S (The Strip)
S Paradise Rd
Las Vegas Hilton
Circus Circus
Meade Ave
Riviera Blvd
Riviera
Sirius Ave
Highland Dr
Las Vegas Convention Center
Convention Center Dr
Polaris Ave
E Desert Inn Rd
Las Vegas Convention Center
Encore
Procyon Ave
Sierra Vista Dr
W Spring Mountain Rd
Wynn
TI (Treasure Island)
Palazzo
Swenson St
Sands Ave
Venetian
Mirage
Harrah's/ Imperial Palace
Cassella Dr
Imperial Palace
Ida Ave
Atomic Testing Museum
Caesars Palace
Flamingo/ Caesars Palace
Rio
Flamingo Wash
Flamingo
W Flamingo Rd
E Flamingo Rd
To Palms (0.4mi)
Bellagio
Bally's
Bally's/ Paris Las Vegas
Paris Las Vegas
Bellagio
University of Nevada, Las Vegas
Cosmopolitan
Planet Hollywood
Tropicana Wash
Swenson St
Lana Ave
Harmon Ave
E Harmon Ave
CityCenter
Thomas & Mack Stadium
Monte Carlo
Koval La
Tompkins Ave
MGM Grand
MGM Grand
New York New York
To Pinball Hall of Fame (1mi)
W Tropicana Ave
E Tropicana Ave
Tropicana
Excalibur
Paradise Rd
Reno Ave
Giles St
Ali Baba La
Luxor
McCarran International Airport
Hacienda Ave
Swenson St
Mandalay Bay

Las Vegas

Top Sights

Atomic Testing Museum ... D5
Cosmopolitan ... B5
Encore ... C3

Sights

Adventuredome ... (see 3)
Aria ... (see 5)
1 Bellagio ... B5
Bellagio Conservatory & Botanical Gardens ... (see 1)
Bellagio Gallery of Fine Art ... (see 1)
2 Caesars Palace ... B5
3 Circus Circus ... C2
4 CityCenter ... B6
5 Crystals ... B6
6 Flamingo ... B5
7 Hard Rock ... D5
8 Mandalay Bay ... B7
Mandarin Oriental ... (see 4)
Midway ... (see 3)
9 Mirage ... B4
10 New York New York ... B6
11 Palazzo ... B4
12 Paris Las Vegas ... B5
Shark Reef ... (see 8)
Vdara ... (see 4)
13 Venetian ... B4
Wildlife Habitat ... (see 6)
14 Wynn Las Vegas ... C4

Activities, Courses & Tours

Qua Baths & Spa ... (see 2)

Sleeping

Bill's Gamblin' Hall & Saloon ... (see 6)
Caesars Palace ... (see 2)
15 Cosmopolitan ... B5
Encore ... (see 14)
Hard Rock ... (see 7)
Mandalay Bay ... (see 8)
Paris Las Vegas ... (see 12)
16 Platinum Hotel & Spa ... C5
17 Tropicana ... B6

Eating

Buffet Bellagio ... (see 1)
DOCG Enoteca ... (see 15)
18 Ferraro's ... D5
Fiamma ... (see 20)
19 Firefly ... D4
House of Blues ... (see 8)
20 Joël Robuchon ... B6
L'Atelier de Joël Robuchon ... (see 20)
Le Village Buffet ... (see 12)
21 Lotus of Siam ... D2
Olives ... (see 1)
Pink Taco ... (see 7)
RM Seafood ... (see 8)
Sage ... (see 4)
Scarpetta ... (see 15)
Social House ... (see 5)
Society Café ... (see 14)
22 Spice Market Buffet ... B5
23 Sterling Brunch at Bally's ... B5
Sunday Gospel Brunch ... (see 7)
Todd English P.U.B ... (see 4)
Victorian Room ... (see 6)
'wichcraft ... (see 20)
Wicked Spoon Buffet ... (see 15)

Drinking

Chandelier ... (see 15)
24 Double Down Saloon ... D6
25 Fireside Lounge ... C3
Gold Lounge ... (see 5)
LAVO ... (see 11)
Mix ... (see 8)
Parasol Up–Parasol Down ... (see 14)
Red Square ... (see 8)

Entertainment

Drai's ... (see 6)
Gold Lounge ... (see 4)
LOVE ... (see 9)
Marquee ... (see 15)
O ... (see 1)
Tix 4 Tonight ... (see 6)
Tryst ... (see 14)
26 Zumanity ... B6

Shopping

27 Bonanza Gifts ... C2
28 Fashion Show Mall ... B3
Forum Shops ... (see 2)
Grand Canal Shoppes ... (see 13)
29 Miracle Mile Shops ... B5
Shoppes at Palazzo ... (see 11)

top-notch artists. The **Bellagio Conservatory & Botanical Gardens** (admission free; ⊙daily) features changing exhibits throughout the year.

Venetian CASINO

(www.venetian.com; 3355 Las Vegas Blvd S) Hand-painted ceiling frescoes, roaming mimes, gondola rides and full-scale reproductions of famous Venice landmarks are found at the romantic Venetian. Next door, the **Palazzo** (www.palazzo.com; 3325 Las Vegas Blvd S) exploits a variation on the Italian theme to a less interesting effect: despite the caliber of the **Shoppes at the Palazzo** and the star-studded dining – including exhilarating ventures by culinary heavyweights Charlie Trotter, Emeril Legasse and Wolfgang Puck – the luxurious casino floor and common areas somehow exude a lackluster brand of excitement.

Caesars Palace CASINO

(www.caesarspalace.com; 3570 Las Vegas Blvd S) Quintessentially Las Vegas, Caesars Palace is a Greco-Roman fantasyland featuring marble reproductions of classical statuary, including a not-to-be-missed 4-ton Brahma shrine near the front entrance. Towering fountains, goddess-costumed cocktail waitresses and the swanky haute-couture **Forum Shops** all ante up the glitz.

Paris Las Vegas CASINO

(www.parislasvegas.com; 3655 Las Vegas Blvd S) Evoking the gaiety of the City of Light, Paris Las Vegas strives to capture the essence of the grand dame by re-creating her landmarks. Fine likenesses of the Opéra, the Arc de Triomphe, the Champs-Élysées, the soaring Eiffel Tower and even the Seine frame the property.

Mirage CASINO

(www.mirage.com; 3400 Las Vegas Blvd S) With a tropical setting replete with a huge atrium filled with jungle foliage and soothing cascades, the Mirage captures the imagination. Circling the atrium is a vast Polynesian-themed casino, which places gaming areas under separate roofs to evoke intimacy, including a popular high-limit poker room. Don't miss the 20,000-gallon saltwater aquarium, with 60 species of critters hailing from Fiji to the Red Sea. Out front in the lagoon, a fiery faux volcano erupts hourly after dark until midnight.

Flamingo CASINO

(www.flamingolasvegas.com; 3555 Las Vegas Blvd S) The Flamingo is quintessential vintage Vegas. Weave through the slot machines to the **Wildlife Habitat** (admission free; ⊙daily) to see the flock of Chilean flamingos that call these 15 tropical acres home.

New York New York CASINO

(www.nynyhotelcasino.com; 3790 Las Vegas Blvd S) A mini metropolis featuring scaled-down replicas of the Empire State Building, the Statue of Liberty, ringed by a September 11 memorial, and the Brooklyn Bridge.

Mandalay Bay CASINO

(M-Bay; www.mandalaybay.com; 3950 Las Vegas Blvd S) Not trying to be any one fantasy, the tropically themed Mandalay Bay is worth a walkthrough. Standout attractions include the multilevel **Shark Reef** (www.sharkreef.com; adult/child $18/12; ⊙10am-8pm Sun-Thu, 10am-10pm Fri & Sat; ⓕ), an aquarium home for thousands of marine beasties with a shallow pool where you can pet pint-sized sharks.

Palms CASINO

(www.palms.com; 4321 W Flamingo Rd) Equal parts sexy and downright sleazy, the Palms attracts loads of notorious celebrities (think Paris Hilton and Britney Spears) as well as a younger, mostly local crowd. Its restaurants and nightclubs are some of the hottest in town. Other highlights include a 14-screen cinema with IMAX capabilities and a live-music club, the **Pearl**. Just don't take the elevator to the **Playboy Club** expecting debauchery à la Hef's mansion: while a few bunny-eared, surgically enhanced ladies deal blackjack in a stylishly appointed lounge full of mostly men, the sexiest thing about it is the stunning skyline view.

Golden Nugget CASINO

(www.goldennugget.com; 129 E Fremont St) Looking like a million bucks, this casino hotel has set the downtown benchmark for extravagance since opening in 1946. No brass or cut glass was spared inside the swanky casino, known for its nonsmoking poker room; the RUSH Lounge, where live local bands play; the utterly lively casino and some of downtown's best restaurants. Don't miss the gigantic 61lb Hand of Faith, the world's largest gold nugget, around the corner from the hotel lobby.

Other Attractions

TOP CHOICE **Atomic Testing Museum** MUSEUM
(www.atomictestingmuseum.org; 755 E Flamingo Rd; adult/child $14/11; ⏲10am-5pm Mon-Sat, noon-5pm Sun) Recalling an era when the word 'atomic' conjured modernity and mystery, the Smithsonian-run Atomic Testing Museum remains an intriguing testament to the period when the fantastical – and destructive – power of nuclear energy was tested just outside of Las Vegas. Don't skip the deafening Ground Zero Theater, which mimics a concrete test bunker.

TOP CHOICE **Neon Museum** MUSEUM
(☎702-387-6366; www.neonmuseum.org; 821 Las Vegas Blvd N; displays free, guided tours $15; ⏲displays 24hr, guided tours noon & 2pm Tue-Sat) Experience the outdoor displays through a fascinating walking tour ($15) of the newly unveiled Neon Boneyard Park, where irreplaceable vintage neon signs – the original art form of Las Vegas – spend their retirement. At the time of going to print, the museum was expanding its digs and hoped to add a self-guided component in 2012; until then, be sure to reserve your tour at least a few weeks in advance.

Stroll around downtown come evening (when the neon comes out to play) to discover the free, self-guided component of the 'museum.' You'll find delightful al-fresco galleries of restored vintage neon signs, including sparkling genie lamps, glowing martini glasses and 1940s motel marquees. The biggest assemblages are found at the on the 3rd St cul-de-sac just north of Fremont St.

Fremont Street Experience STREET
(www.vegasexperience.com; Fremont St; ⏲hourly 7pm-midnight) A four-block pedestrian mall topped by an arched steel canopy and filled with computer-controlled lights, the Fremont Street Experience, between Main St and Las Vegas Blvd, has brought life back to downtown. Every evening, the canopy is transformed into a six-minute light-and-sound show enhanced by 550,000 watts of wraparound sound.

Downtown Arts District ARTS CENTER
On the **First Friday** (www.firstfriday-lasvegas.org) of each month, a carnival of 10,000 art-lovers, hipsters, indie musicians and hangers-on descend on Las Vegas' downtown arts district. These giant monthly block parties feature gallery openings, performance art, live bands and tattoo artists. The action revolves around the **Arts Factory** (101-109 E Charleston Blvd), **Commerce Street Studios** (1551 S Commerce St) and the **Funk House** (1228 S Casino Center Blvd).

CityCenter SHOPPING CENTER
(www.citycenter.com; 3780 Las Vegas Blvd S) We've seen this symbiotic relationship before (think giant hotel anchored by a mall 'concept') but the way that this futuristic-feeling complex places a small galaxy of hypermodern, chichi hotels in orbit around the glitzy **Crystals** (www.crystalsatcitycenter.com; 3720 Las Vegas Blvd S) shopping center is a first. The uber-upscale spread includes the subdued, stylish **Vdara** (www.vdara.com; 2600 W Harmon Ave), the hush-hush opulent **Mandarin Oriental** (www.mandarinoriental.com; 3752 Las Vegas Blvd) and the dramatic architectural showpiece **Aria** (www.arialasvegas.com; 3730 Las Vegas Blvd S), whose sophisticated casino provides a fitting backdrop to its many drop-dead gorgeous restaurants.

Activities

TOP CHOICE **Qua Baths & Spa** SPA
(☎702-731-7776; www.harrahs.com/qua; Caesars Palace, 3570 Las Vegas Blvd S; ⏲6am-8pm) Social spa going is encouraged in the tea lounge, herbal steam room and arctic ice room, where dry-ice snowflakes fall.

Desert Adventures KAYAKING, HIKING
(☎702-293-5026; www.kayaklasvegas.com; 1647 Nevada Hwy, Suite A, Boulder City; trips from $149) With Lake Mead and Hoover Dam just a few hours' drive away, would-be river rats should check out Desert Adventures for lots of half-, full- and multiday kayaking adventures. Hiking and horseback-riding trips, too.

Escape Adventures MOUNTAIN BIKING
(☎800-596-2953; www.escapeadventures.com; 8221 W Charleston Blvd; trips incl bike from $120) The source for guided mountain-bike tours of Red Rock Canyon State Park.

Sleeping

Rates rise and fall dramatically. Check hotel websites, which usually feature calendars listing day-by-day room rates.

THE STRIP

TOP CHOICE **Mandalay Bay** CASINO HOTEL $$
(☎702-632-7777; www.mandalaybay.com; 3950 Las Vegas Blvd S; r $100-380; ❄@🛜≋) The ornately appointed rooms here have a South Seas theme, and the amenities include

LAS VEGAS FOR CHILDREN

State law prohibits people under 21 years of age from loitering in gaming areas.

The **Circus Circus** (www.circuscircus.com; 2880 Las Vegas Blvd S;) hotel complex is all about the kids, and its **Adventuredome** (adult/child $27/17; 10am-7pm Sun-Thu, 10am-midnight Fri & Sat;) is a 5-acre indoor theme park with fun ranging from laser tag to bumper cars and a roller coaster. The **Midway** (admission free; 11am-midnight;) features animals, acrobats and magicians performing on center stage.

The **Pinball Hall of Fame** (www.pinballmuseum.org; 1610 E Tropicana Ave; admission free, games 25-50¢; 11am-11pm Sun-Thu, to midnight Fri & Sat;) is an interactive museum that's more fun than any slot machine.

floor-to-ceiling windows and luxurious bathrooms. Swimmers will swoon over the pool complex, with a sand-and-surf beach.

TOP CHOICE Tropicana CASINO HOTEL $

(702-739-2222; www.troplv.com; 3801 Las Vegas Blvd S; r/ste from $40/140;) As once-celebrated retro properties go under, the Tropicana – keeping the Strip tropical vibe going since 1953 – just got (surprise!) cool again. The multimillion-dollar renovation shows, from the airy casino to the lush, relaxing gardens with their newly unveiled pool and beach club. The earth-toned, breezy rooms and bi-level suites are bargains

Cosmopolitan CASINO HOTEL $$$

(702-698-7000; www.cosmopolitanlasvegas.com; 3708 Las Vegas Blvd S; r $200-400;) Are the too-cool-for-school, hip rooms worth the price tag? The indie set seems to think so. The rooms are impressive exercises in mod design, but the real delight of staying here is to stumble out of your room at 1am to play some pool in the upper lobbies before going on a mission to find the 'secret' pizza joint.

Bill's Gamblin' Hall & Saloon CASINO HOTEL $

(702-737-2100; www.billslasvegas.com; 3595 Las Vegas Blvd S; r $70-200;) Set slap-bang mid-Strip with affordable rooms nice enough to sport plasma TVs, Bill's is great value, so book far ahead. Rooms feature Victorian-themed decor, and guests can use the pool next door at the Flamingo without charge.

Encore CASINO HOTEL $$$

(702-770-8000; www.encorelasvegas.com; 3121 Las Vegas Blvd S; r $199-850;) Classy and playful rather than overblown and opulent – even people cheering at the roulette table clap with a little more elegance. The rooms are studies in subdued luxury.

Caesars Palace CASINO HOTEL $$

(866-227-5938; www.caesarspalace.com; 3570 Las Vegas Blvd S; r from $99;) Send away the centurions and decamp in style – Caesars' standard rooms are some of the most luxurious you will find in town.

Paris Las Vegas CASINO HOTEL $

(702-946-7000; www.parislasvegas.com; 3655 Las Vegas Blvd S; r from $80;) Nice rooms with a nod to classic French design; the newer Red Rooms are a study in sumptuous class.

DOWNTOWN & OFF THE STRIP

Downtown hotels are generally less expensive than those on the Strip.

TOP CHOICE Hard Rock CASINO HOTEL $$

(702-693-5000; www.hardrockhotel.com; 4455 Paradise Rd; r $69-450;) Everything about this boutique hotel spells stardom. French doors reveal skyline and palm tree views, and brightly colored Euro-minimalist rooms feature souped-up stereos and plasma TVs. While we dig the jukeboxes in the HRH All-Suite Tower, the standard rooms are nearly as cool. The hottest action revolves around the lush Beach Club.

TOP CHOICE Artisan Hotel BOUTIQUE HOTEL $

(800-554-4092; www.artisanhotel.com; 1501 W Sahara Ave; r from $40;) A Gothic baroque fantasy with a decadent dash of rock and roll, each suite is themed around the work of a different artist. Yet with one of Vegas' best after-parties raging on weekend nights downstairs (a fave with the local alternative set), you may not spend much time in your room. The libidinous, mysterious vibe here isn't for everyone, but if you like it, you'll love it. Artisan's sister hotel,

Rumor (☎877-997-8667; www.rumorvegas.com; 455 E Harmon Ave; ste from $69; ❄@📶🏊) is across from the Hard Rock and features a carefree, Miami-cool atmosphere; its airy suites overlook a palm-shaded courtyard pool area dotted with daybeds and hammocks perfect for lounging.

El Cortez Cabana Suites BOUTIQUE HOTEL **$**
(☎800-634-6703; www.eccabana.com; 651 E Ogden Ave; ste $45-150; ❄@📶) You probably won't recognize this sparkling little boutique hotel for its brief movie cameo in Scorcese's *Casino* (hint: Sharon Stone was murdered here) and that's a good thing, because a massive makeover has transformed it into a vintage oasis downtown. Mod suites decked out in mint green include iPod docking stations and retro tiled bathrooms. Plus the coolest vintage casino in town – the El Cortez – is right across the street.

Platinum Hotel BOUTIQUE HOTEL **$$**
(☎702-365-5000; www.theplatinumhotel.com; 211 E Flamingo Rd; r from $120; ❄@📶🏊) Just off the Strip, the coolly modern rooms at this spiffy, non-gaming property are comfortable and full of nice touches – many have fireplaces and they all have kitchens and Jacuzzi tubs.

Red Rock Resort RESORT **$$$**
(☎702-797-7878; www.redrocklasvegas.com; 11011 W Charleston Blvd; r $110-625; ❄@📶🏊) Red Rock touts itself as the first off-Strip billion-dollar gaming resort, and most people who stay here eschew the Strip forever more. There's free transportation between the Strip, and outings to the nearby Red Rocks State Park and beyond. Rooms are well appointed and comfy.

Eating

Sin City is an unmatched eating adventure. Reservations are a must for fancier restaurants; book in advance.

THE STRIP

On the Strip itself, cheap eats beyond fast-food joints are hard to find.

Sage AMERICAN **$$$**
(☎877-230-2742; www.arialasvegas.com; Aria, 3730 Las Vegas Blvd S; mains $25-42; ⏲5pm-11pm Mon-Sat) Acclaimed chef Shawn McClain meditates on the seasonally sublime with global inspiration and artisanal, farm-to-table ingredients in one of Vegas' most drop-dead gorgeous dining rooms. Don't miss the inspired seasonal cocktails doctored with housemade liqueurs, French absinthe, and fruit purees.

TOP CHOICE **Joël Robuchon** FRENCH **$$$**
(☎702-891-7925; MGM Grand, 3799 Las Vegas Blvd S; menus per person $120-420; ⏲5:30-10pm Sun-Thu, to 10:30pm Fri & Sat) A once-in-a-lifetime culinary experience; block off a solid three hours and get ready to eat your way through the multicourse seasonal menu of traditional French fare. **L'Atelier de Joël Robuchon**, next door, is where you can belly up to the counter for a slightly more economical but still delicious meal.

TOP CHOICE **DOCG Enoteca** ITALIAN **$$**
(☎702-698-7920; Cosmopolitan, 3708 Las Vegas Blvd S; mains $13-28; ⏲10am-5pm) Among the

DON'T MISS

COOL POOLS

Hard Rock (p307) Seasonal swim-up blackjack and killer 'Rehab' pool parties at the beautifully landscaped and uberhip Beach Club.

Mirage (p310) The lush tropical pool is a sight to behold, with waterfalls tumbling off cliffs, deep grottoes and palm-tree-studded islands for sunbathing.

Mandalay Bay (p310) Splash around an artificial sand-and-surf beach built from imported California sand and boasting a wave pool, lazy-river ride, casino and DJ-driven topless Moorea Beach Club.

Caesars Palace (p310) Corinthian columns, overflowing fountains, magnificent palms and marble-inlaid pools make the Garden of the Gods Oasis divine. Goddesses proffer frozen grapes in summer, including at the topless Venus pool lounge.

Golden Nugget (p310) Downtown's best pool offers lots of fun and zero attitude. Play poolside blackjack, or sip on a daiquiri in the Jacuzzi and watch the sharks frolic in the adjacent aquarium.

Cosmopolitan's alluring dining options, this is one of the least glitzy – but most authentic – choices. That's not to say it isn't loads of fun. Order up to-die-for fresh pasta or a wood-fired pizza in the stylish *enoteca* (wine shop)–inspired room that feels like you've joined a festive dinner party. Or head next door to sexy **Scarpetta**, which offers a more intimate, upscale experience by the same fantastic chef, Scott Conant.

Social House JAPANESE **$$$**
(☎702-736-1122; www.socialhouselv.com; Crystals at CityCenter, 3720 Las Vegas Blvd S; mains $24-44; ⏰5pm-10pm Mon-Thu, noon-11pm Fri & Sat, noon-10pm Sun) Nibble on creative dishes inspired by Japanese street food in one of the Strip's most serene yet sultry dining rooms. Watermarked scrolls, wooden screens, and loads of dramatic red and black conjure visions of Imperial Japan, while the sushi and steaks are totally contemporary.

RM Seafood SEAFOOD **$$$**
(☎702-632-9300; www.rmseafood.com; Mandalay Place, 3930 Las Vegas Blvd S; lunch $13-36, dinner $20-75; ⏰11:30am-11pm, restaurant 5pm-11pm) From ecoconscious chef Rick Moonen, modern American seafood dishes, such as Cajun popcorn and Maine lobster, come with comfort-food sides (like gourmet mac 'n' cheese), a raw shellfish and sushi bar, and a 'biscuit bar' serving savory salads.

Fiamma ITALIAN **$$$**
(☎702-891-7600; www.mgmgrand.com; MGM Grand, 3799 Las Vegas Blvd S; meals $50-60; ⏰5:30-10pm Sun & Mon, to 10:30pm Tue-Thu, to 11pm Fri & Sat) Fiamma is set in a row of outstanding restaurants at MGM Grand, but what sets it apart is that it's a top-tier dining experience you won't be paying off for the next decade. You haven't had spaghetti until you've had Fiamma's take on it, made with Kobe beef meatballs.

Victorian Room CAFE **$$**
(www.billslasvegas.com; Bill's Gamblin' Hall & Saloon, 3595 Las Vegas Blvd S; mains $8-25; ⏰24hr) A hokey old-fashioned San Francisco theme belies one of the best deals in sit-down restaurants in Las Vegas. The steak and eggs special ($7) is delicious around the clock.

Olives MEDITERRANEAN **$$$**
(☎702-693-8865; www.bellagio.com; Bellagio, 3600 Las Vegas Blvd S; mains $16-52; ⏰lunch & dinner) Bostonian chef Todd English dishes up homage to the life-giving fruit. Flatbread pizzas, housemade pastas and flame-licked meats get top billing, and patio tables overlook Lake Como. Try his rollicking new CityCenter venture, **Todd English PUB** (www.toddenglishpub.com; Crystals at CityCenter, 3720 Las Vegas Blvd S; mains $13-24; ⏰lunch & dinner), a strangely fun cross between a British pub and a frat party, with creative sliders, English pub classics, and an interesting promotion: if you drink your beer in less than seven seconds, it's on the house.

Society Café CAFE **$$**
(www.wynnlasvegas.com; Encore, 3121 Las Vegas Blvd S; mains $14-30; ⏰7am-midnight Sun-Thu, 7am-1am Fri & Sat) A slice of reasonably priced culinary heaven in the midst of Encore's loveliness. The basic cafe here is equal to fine dining at other joints.

'wichcraft SANDWICHES **$**
(www.mgmgrand.com; MGM Grand, 3799 Las Vegas Blvd S; sandwiches $8-11; ⏰10am-5pm) This designy little sandwich shop, the brainchild of celebrity chef Tom Colicchio, is one of the best places to taste gourmet on a budget.

DOWNTOWN & OFF THE STRIP

Traditionally off the culinary radar, downtown's restaurants offers better value than those on the Strip, whether a casino buffet or a retro steakhouse.

Just west of the Strip, the Asian restaurants on Spring Mountain Rd in Chinatown

WORTHY INDULGENCES: BEST BUFFETS

- » **Wicked Spoon Buffet** (www.cosmopolitanlasvegas.com; Cosmopolitan, 3708 Las Vegas Blvd S)
- » **Le Village Buffet** (www.parislasvegas.com; Paris Las Vegas, 3655 Las Vegas Blvd S)
- » **Spice Market Buffet** (Planet Hollywood, 3667 Las Vegas Blvd S)
- » **Sterling Brunch at Bally's** (☎702-967-7999; Bally's, 3645 Las Vegas Blvd S; ⏰Sun)
- » **Buffet Bellagio** (☎702-693-7111; www.bellagio.com; Bellagio, 3600 Las Vegas Blvd S)
- » **Sunday Gospel Brunch** (☎702-632-7600; www.hob.com; House of Blues, Mandalay Bay, 3950 Las Vegas Blvd S)

are also good budget options, with lots of vegetarian choices.

TOP CHOICE **Ferraro's** ITALIAN $$
(www.ferraroslasvegas.com, 4480 Paradise Rd; mains $10-39; ⏲11:30am-2am Mon-Fri, 4pm-2am Sat & Sun) The photos on the wall offer testimony to the fact that locals have been flocking to classy, family-owned Ferraro's for 85 years to devour savory Italian classics. These days, the fireplace patio and the amazing late night happy hour draw an eclectic crowd full of industry and foodie types at the friendly bar. To-die-for housemade pastas compete for attention with legendary osso buco, and a killer antipasti menu served until midnight.

TOP CHOICE **Firefly** TAPAS $$
(www.fireflylv.com; 3900 Paradise Rd; small dishes $4-10, large dishes $11-20; ⏲11:30am-2am Sun-Thu, to 3am Fri & Sat) Locals seem to agree on one thing about the Vegas food scene: a meal at Firefly can be twice as fun as an overdone Strip restaurant, and half the price. Is that why it's always hopping? Nosh on traditional Spanish tapas, while the bartender pours sangria and flavor-infused *mojitos*.

Lotus of Siam THAI $$
(www.saipinchutima.com; 953 E Sahara Ave; mains $9-29; ⏲11:30am-2pm Mon-Fri, 5:30-9:30pm Mon-Thu, 5:30-10pm Fr & Sat) The top Thai restaurant in the US? According to *Gourmet Magazine*, this is it. One bite of simple pad Thai – or any of the exotic northern Thai dishes – nearly proves it.

N9NE STEAKHOUSE $$$
(☎702-933-9900; www.palms.com; Palms, 4321 W Flamingo Rd; mains $26-43; ⏲dinner) At this hip steakhouse heavy with celebs, a dramatic dining room centers on a champagne-and-caviar bar. Chicago-style aged steaks and chops keep coming, along with everything from oysters Rockefeller to Pacific sashimi.

Pink Taco MEXICAN $$
(www.hardrockhotel.com; Hard Rock, 4455 Paradise Rd; mains $8-24; ⏲7am-11am Mon-Thu, to 3am Fri & Sat) Whether it's the 99¢ taco and margarita happy hour, the leafy poolside patio, or the friendly rock and roll clientele, Pink Taco always feels like a worthwhile party.

Golden Gate SEAFOOD $
(www.goldengatecasino.com; 1 E Fremont St; ⏲11am-3am) Famous $1.99 shrimp cocktails (super-size them for $3.99).

EMERGENCY ARTS

A coffee shop, an art gallery, studios, and a de facto community center of sorts, all under one roof and right smack downtown? The **Emergency Arts** (www.emergencyartslv.com; 520 Fremont St) building, also home to **Beat Coffeehouse** (www.thebeatlv.com; sandwiches $6-7; ⏲7am-midnight Mon-Fri, 9am-midnight Sat, 9am-3pm Sun) is a friendly bastion of laid-back cool and strong coffee where vintage vinyl spins on old turntables. If you're aching to meet some savvy locals who know their way around town, this is your hangout spot.

Drinking

For those who want to mingle with the locals and drink for free, check out **SpyOnVegas** (www.spyonvegas.com). It arranges an open bar at a different venue every weeknight.

THE STRIP

TOP CHOICE **Mix** LOUNGE
(www.mandalaybay.com; 64th fl, THEhotel at Mandalay Bay, 3950 Las Vegas Blvd S; cover after 10pm $20-25) THE place to grab sunset cocktails. The glassed-in elevator has amazing views, and that's before you even glimpse the mod interior design and soaring balcony.

TOP CHOICE **Gold Lounge** LOUNGE, CLUB
(www.arialasvegas.com; Aria, 3730 Las Vegas Blvd S; cover after 10pm $20-25) You won't find watered-down Top 40 at this luxurious ultralounge, but you will find gold, gold and more gold. It's a fitting homage to Elvis: make a toast in front of the giant portrait of the King himself.

Chandelier BAR
(www.cosmopolitanlasvegas.com; Cosmopolitan, 3708 Las Vegas Blvd S; ⏲5pm-2am) In a city full of lavish hotel lobby bars, this one pulls out all the stops. Kick back with the Cosmopolitan hipsters and enjoy the curiously thrilling feeling that you're tipsy inside a giant crystal chandelier.

LAVO LOUNGE, CLUB
(www.palazzo.com; Palazzo, 3325 Las Vegas Blvd S) One of the sexiest new restaurant-lounge-nightclub combos for the see-and-be-seen set, Lavo's terrace is the place to be at happy

hour. Sip a Bellini in the dramatically lit bar or stay to dance among reclining Renaissance nudes in the club upstairs.

Parasol Up – Parasol Down BAR, CAFE
(www.wynnlasvegas.com; Wynn Las Vegas, 3131 Las Vegas Blvd S; ⏲11am-4am Sun-Thu, to 5am Fri & Sat) Unwind with a fresh fruit *mojito* by the soothing waterfall at the Wynn to experience one of Vegas' most successful versions of paradise.

Red Square BAR
(www.mandalaybay.com; Mandalay Bay, 3950 Las Vegas Blvd S) Heaps of Russian caviar, a solid ice bar and over 200 frozen vodkas, infusions and cocktails. Don a Russian army coat to sip vodka in the subzero vault.

DOWNTOWN & OFF THE STRIP

Want to chill out with the locals? Head to one of their go-to favorites.

TOP CHOICE **Fireside Lounge** COCKTAIL BAR
(www.peppermilllasvegas.com; Peppermill, 2985 Las Vegas Blvd S; ⏲24hr) The Strip's most unlikely romantic hideaway is inside a retro coffee shop. Courting couples flock here for the low lighting, sunken fire pit and cozy nooks built for supping on multistrawed tiki drinks and for acting out your most inadvisable 'what happens in Vegas, stays in Vegas' moments.

TOP CHOICE **Double Down Saloon** BAR
(www.doubledownsaloon.com; 4640 Paradise Rd; no cover; ⏲24hr) You can't get more punk rock than a dive whose tangy, blood-red house drink is named 'Ass Juice' and where happy hour means everything in the bar is two bucks. (Ass Juice and a Twinkie for $5: one of Vegas' bizarrely badass bargains.) Killer Juke box, cash only.

Beauty Bar COCKTAIL BAR
(www.thebeautybar.com; 517 E Fremont St; cover $5-10) At the salvaged innards of a 1950s New Jersey beauty salon, swill a cocktail while you get a makeover demo or chill out with the hip DJs and live local bands. Then walk around the corner to the **Downtown Cocktail Room**, a speakeasy.

Frankie's Tiki Room THEME BAR
(www.frankiestikiroom.com; 1712 W Charleston Blvd; ⏲24hr) At the only round-the-clock tiki bar in the US, the drinks are rated in strength by skulls and the top tiki sculptors and painters in the world have their work on display.

☆ Entertainment

Las Vegas has no shortage of entertainment on any given night, and **Ticketmaster** (☎702-474-4000; www.ticketmaster.com) sells tickets for pretty much everything.

Tix 4 Tonight BOOKING SERVICE
(☎877-849-4868; www.tix4tonight.com; Bill's Gamblin' Hall & Saloon, 3595 Las Vegas Blvd S; ⏲10am-8pm) Offers half-price tix for a limited lineup of same-day shows and small discounts on 'always sold-out' shows.

Nightclubs & Live Music

Admission prices to nightclubs vary wildly based on the mood of door staff, male-to-female ratio, and how crowded the club is that night.

TOP CHOICE **Marquee** CLUB
(www.cosmopolitanlasvegas.com; Cosmopolitan, 3708 Las Vegas Blvd) When someone asks what the coolest club in Vegas is, Marquee is the undisputed answer. Celebrities (we spotted Macy Gray as we danced through the crowd), an outdoor beach club, hot DJs, and that certain *je ne sais quoi* that makes a club worth waiting in line for.

TOP CHOICE **Tryst** CLUB
(www.trystlasvegas.com; Wynn Las Vegas, 3131 Las Vegas Blvd S) All gimmicks aside, the flowing waterfall makes this place ridiculously (and literally) cool. Blood-red booths and plenty of space to dance ensure that you can have a killer time even without splurging for bottle service.

Drai's CLUB
(www.drais.net; Bill's Gamblin' Hall & Saloon, 3595 Las Vegas Blvd S; ⏲1am-8am Thu-Mon) Feel ready for an after-hours scene straight outta Hollywood? Things don't really get going here until 4am, when DJs spinning progressive discs keep the cool kids content. Dress to kill.

Stoney's Rockin' Country LIVE MUSIC
(www.stoneysrockincountry.com; 9151 Las Vegas Blvd S; cover $5-10; ⏲7pm-late Thu-Sun) An off-Strip place that's worth the trip. Friday and Saturday features all-you-can-drink draft beer specials and free line-dancing lessons. The mechanical bull is a blast.

Moon CLUB
(www.n9negroup.com; Palms, 4321 W Flamingo Rd; cover from $20; ⏲11pm-4am Tue & Thu-Sun) Stylishly outfitted like a nightclub in outer

VEGAS CLUBBING 101

Brave the velvet rope – or skip it altogether – with these nightlife survival tips we culled from the inner circle of Vegas doormen, VIP hosts, and concierges.

» Avoid waiting in that long line by booking ahead with the club VIP host. Most bigger clubs have someone working the door during the late afternoon and early evening hours.

» Ask the concierge of your hotel for clubbing suggestions – he or she will almost always have free passes for clubs, or be able to make you reservations with the VIP host.

» If you hit blackjack at the high-roller table or just want to splurge, think about bottle service. Yes, it's expensive (starting at around $300 to $400 and upwards for a bottle, including mixers, plus tax and tip), but it usually waives cover charge (and waiting in line) for your group, plus you get to chill out at a table – valuable 'real estate' in club speak.

space; the retractable roof opens for dancing to pulsating beats under the stars. Admission includes entry to the only Playboy Club in the world.

Production Shows

There are hundreds of shows to choose from in Vegas. Any Cirque du Soleil show tends to be an unforgettable experience.

TOP CHOICE Steel Panther LIVE MUSIC
(☎702-617-7777; www.greenvalleyranchresort.com; Green Valley Resort, 2300 Paseo Verde Pkwy, Henderson; admission free; ⊙11pm-late Thu) A hair-metal tribute band makes fun of the audience, themselves and the 1980s with sight gags, one-liners and many a drug and sex reference.

TOP CHOICE LOVE PERFORMING ARTS
(☎702-792-7777; www.cirquedusoleil.com; tickets $99-150) This show at the Mirage is a popular addition to the Cirque du Soleil lineup; locals who have seen many Cirque productions come and go say it's the best.

O PERFORMING ARTS
(☎702-796-9999; www.cirquedusoleil.com; tickets $99-200) Still a favorite is Cirque du Soleil's aquatic show, O, performed at the Bellagio.

Zumanity PERFORMING ARTS
(☎702-740-6815; www.cirquedusoleil.com; tickets $69-129) A Sensual and sexy adult-only show at New York New York.

Shopping

Bonanza Gifts GIFTS
(www.worldslargestgiftshop.com; 2440 Las Vegas Blvd S; ⊙11am-midnight) The best place for only-in-Vegas kitsch souvenirs.

The Attic VINTAGE
(www.atticvintage.com; 1018 S Main St; ⊙10am-6pm, closed Sun) Be mesmerized by fabulous hats and wigs, hippie-chic clubwear and lounge-lizard furnishings at Vegas' best vintage store.

Fashion Show Mall MALL
(www.thefashionshow.com; 3200 Las Vegas Blvd S) Nevada's biggest and flashiest mall.

Forum Shops MALL
(www.caesarspalace.com; Caesars Palace, 3570 Las Vegas Blvd S) Upscale stores in an air-conditioned version of Ancient Rome.

Grand Canal Shoppes MALL
(www.thegrandcanalshoppes.com; Venetian, 3355 Las Vegas Blvd S) Italianate indoor luxury mall with gondolas.

Shoppes at Palazzo MALL
(Palazzo, 3327 Las Vegas Blvd S) Sixty international designers, from Tory Burch to Jimmy Choo, flaunt their goodies.

Miracle Mile Shops MALL
(www.miraclemileshopslv.com; Planet Hollywood, 3663 Las Vegas Blvd S) A staggering 1.5 miles long; get a tattoo, a drink and duds.

Information

Emergency & Medical Services

Gamblers Anonymous (☎702-385-7732) Assistance with gambling concerns.

Police (☎702-828-3111)

Sunrise Hospital & Medical Center (☎702-731-8000; 3186 S Maryland Pkwy)

University Medical Center (☎702-383-2000; 1800 W Charleston Blvd)

Internet Access

Wi-fi is available in most hotel rooms (about $10 to $25 per day, sometimes included in the 'resort fee') and there are internet kiosks with attached printers in most hotel lobbies.

Internet Resources & Media

Cheapo Vegas (www.cheapovegas.com) Good for a run-down of casinos with low table limits and their insider's guide to cheap eating.

Las Vegas Review-Journal (www.lvrj.com) Daily paper with a weekend guide, *Neon*, on Friday.

Las Vegas Tourism (www.onlyinvegas.com) Official tourism website.

Las Vegas Weekly (www.lasvegasweekly.com) Free weekly with good entertainment and restaurant listings.

lasvegas.com (www.lasvegas.com) Travel services.

Lasvegaskids.net (www.lasvegaskids.net) The lowdown on what's up for the wee ones.

Vegas.com (www.vegas.com) Travel information with booking service.

Money

Every hotel-casino and bank and most convenience stores have an ATM. The ATM fee at most casinos is around $5. Best to stop at off-Strip banks if possible.

American Express (☎702-739-8474; Fashion Show Mall, 3200 Las Vegas Blvd S; ⊙10am-9pm Mon-Fri, 10am-8pm Sat, noon-6pm Sun) Changes currencies at competitive rates.

Post

Post office (☎702-382-5779; 201 Las Vegas Blvd S) Downtown.

Tourist Information

Las Vegas Visitor Information Center (☎702-847-4858; www.visitlasvegas.com; 3150 Paradise Rd; ⊙8am-5pm) Free local calls, internet access and maps galore.

Getting There & Around

Just south of the major Strip casinos and easily accessible from I-15, **McCarran International Airport** (www.mccarran.com) has direct flights from most US cities, and some from Canada and Europe. **Bell Trans** (☎702-739-7990; www.bell-trans.com) offers a shuttle service ($6.50) between the airport and the Strip. Fares to downtown destinations are slightly higher. At the airport, exit door 9 near baggage claim to find the Bell Trans booth.

All of the attractions in Vegas have free self-parking and valet parking available (tip $2). Fast, fun and fully wheelchair accessible, the **monorail** (☎702-699-8299; www.lvmonorail.com) connects the Sahara to the MGM Grand, stopping at major Strip megaresorts along the way, and operating from 7am to 2am Monday to Thursday and until 3am Friday through Sunday. A single ride is $5, a 24-hour pass is $12, and a three-day pass is $28. The **Deuce** (☎702-228-7433; www.rtcsouthernnevada.com), a local double-decker bus, runs frequently 24 hours daily between the Strip and downtown (two-/24-hour pass $5/7).

Around Las Vegas

Red Rock Canyon CANYON
(www.redrockcanyonlv.org; per car/bicycle $7/5; ⊙6am-dusk) This dramatic park is the perfect antidote to Vegas' artificial brightness. A 20-mile drive west of the Strip, the canyon is actually more like a valley, with the steep, rugged red-rock escarpment rising 3000ft on its western edge. There's a 13-mile scenic loop with access to hiking trails and first-come, first-served **camping** (tent sites $15) 2 miles east of the visitor center.

Lake Mead & Hoover Dam LAKE, HISTORIC SITE
Lake Mead and Hoover Dam are the most-visited sites within the **Lake Mead National Recreation Area** (www.nps.gov/lame), which encompasses 110-mile-long Lake Mead, 67-mile-long Lake Mohave and many miles of desert around the lakes. The excellent **Alan Bible Visitors Center** (☎702-293-8990; ⊙8:30am-4:30pm), on Hwy 93 halfway between Boulder City and Hoover Dam, has information on recreation and desert life. From there, North Shore Rd winds around the lake and makes a great scenic drive.

Straddling the Arizona–Nevada border, the graceful curve and art-deco style of the 726ft **Hoover Dam** (www.usbr.gov/lc/hooverdam) contrasts superbly with the stark landscape. Don't miss a stroll over the new **Mike O'Callaghan-Pat Tillman Memorial Bridge** (www.hooverdambypass.org) which features a pedestrian walkway with perfect

WORTH A TRIP

VALLEY OF FIRE STATE PARK

A masterpiece of desert scenery filled with psychedelically shaped sandstone outcroppings, this **park** (www.parks.nv.gov/vf.htm; admission $10) is a great escape 55 miles from Vegas. Hwy 169 runs right past the **visitor center** (☎702-397-2088; ⊙8:30am-4:30pm), which has hiking and **camping** (tent/RV sites $20/30) information and excellent desert-life exhibits.

views upstream of Hoover Dam. (Not recommended for anyone with vertigo.) Visitors can either take the 30-minute **power plant tour** (adult/child $11/9; ⊙9:15am-5:15pm, to 4:15pm Sep-Mar) or the more in-depth, one-hour **Hoover Dam tour** (no children under 8yr; tours $30).

Tickets for both tours are sold at the **visitor center** (⊙9am-6pm; exhibits adult/child $8/free). Tickets for the power plant tour only can be purchased online.

For a relaxing lunch or dinner break, head to nearby downtown Boulder City, where **Milo's** (538 Nevada Way; dishes $4.50-13; ⊙11am-10pm Sun-Thu, to midnight Fri & Sat) serves fresh sandwiches, salads and gourmet cheese plates at sidewalk tables outside the wine bar.

WORTH A TRIP

PYRAMID LAKE

A piercingly blue expanse in an otherwise barren landscape 25 miles north of Reno on the Paiute Indian Reservation, Pyramid Lake is popular for recreation and fishing. Permits for **camping** (primitive campsites per vehicle per night $9) and **fishing** (per person $9) are available at outdoor suppliers and CVS drugstore locations in Reno, and at the **ranger station** (775-476-1155; www.pyramidlake.us; ⊙8am-6pm) on SR 445 in Sutcliffe.

Western Nevada

A vast and mostly undeveloped sagebrush steppe, the western corner of the state is carved by mountain ranges and parched valleys. The place where modern Nevada began with the discovery of the famous Comstock silver lode in and around Virginia City, these days this part of the state lures visitors with outdoor adventure in the form of hiking, biking, and skiing on the many mountains. Contrasts here are as extreme as the weather: one moment you're driving through a quaint historic town full of grand homes built by silver barons, and the next you spot a tumbleweed blowing by a homely little bar that turns out to be the local (and legal) brothel. And then there's the casino lights and the kitschy mid-century wedding chapels that lure so many toward the gambling mecca of Reno.

For information about the Nevada side of Lake Tahoe, see p172.

RENO

A soothingly schizophrenic city of big-time gambling and top-notch outdoor adventures, Reno (population 225,000) resists pigeonholing. 'The Biggest Little City in the World' has something to raise the pulse of adrenaline junkies, hard-core gamblers and city people craving easy access to wide open spaces.

Sights

National Automobile Museum MUSEUM
(775-333-9300; www.automuseum.org; 10 S Lake St; adult/child/senior $10/4/8; ⊙9:30am-5:30pm Mon-Sat, 10am-4pm Sun;) Stylized street scenes illustrate a century's worth of automobile history at this engaging car museum. The collection is enormous and impressive, with one-of-a-kind vehicles, including James Dean's 1949 Mercury from *Rebel Without a Cause,* a 1938 Phantom Corsair and a 24-karat gold-plated DeLorean, and rotating exhibits bringing in all kinds of souped-up or fabulously retro rides.

Nevada Museum of Art MUSEUM
(775-329-3333; www.nevadaart.org; 160 W Liberty St; adult/child/student & senior $10/1/8; ⊙10am-5pm Wed-Sun, 10am-8pm Thu) In a sparkling building inspired by the geologic formations of the Black Rock Desert north of town, a floating staircase leads to galleries showcasing temporary exhibits and images related to the American West. Great cafe for postcultural refueling.

University of Nevada UNIVERSITY
Pop into the flying saucer-shaped **Fleischmann Planetarium & Science Center** (775-784-4811; http://planetarium.unr.nevada.edu; 1650 N Virginia St; admission free; ⊙noon-5pm Mon & Tue, noon-9pm Fri, 10am-9pm Sat, 10am-5pm Sun) for a window on the universe during star shows and feature **presentations** (adult/child $6/4). Nearby is the **Nevada Historical Society Museum** (775-688-1190; www.museums.nevadaculture.org; 1650 N Virginia St; adult/under 17yr $4/free; ⊙10am-5pm Wed-Sat), which includes permanent exhibits on neon signs, local Native American culture and the presence of the federal government.

VIRGINIA STREET

Wedged between the I-80 and the Truckee River, downtown's N Virginia St is casino central. South of the river it continues as S Virginia St. All of the following hotel-casinos are open 24 hours.

Circus Circus CASINO
(www.circusreno.com; 500 N Sierra St;) The most family-friendly of the bunch, it has free circus acts to entertain kids beneath a giant, candy-striped big top, which also harbors a gazillion carnival and video games that look awfully similar to slot machines.

Silver Legacy CASINO
(www.silverlegacyreno.com; 407 N Virginia St) A Victorian-themed place, it's easily recognized by its white landmark dome, where a giant mock mining rig periodically erupts into a tame sound-and-light show.

Eldorado CASINO
(www.eldoradoreno.com; 345 N Virginia St) The Eldorado has a kitschy Fountain of Fortune that probably has Italian sculptor Bernini spinning in his grave.

Harrah's CASINO
(www.harrahsreno.com; 219 N Center St) Founded by Nevada gambling pioneer William Harrah in 1946, it's still one of the biggest and most popular casinos in town.

About 2 miles south of downtown are two of Reno's biggest casino hotels:

Peppermill CASINO
(www.peppermillreno.com; 2707 S Virginia St) Dazzles with a 17-story Tuscan-style tower.

Atlantis CASINO
(www.atlantiscasino.com; 3800 S Virginia St) Now more classy than zany, with an extensive spa, the remodeled casino retains a few tropical flourishes such as indoor waterfalls and palm trees.

Activities

Reno is a 30- to 60-minute drive from Tahoe ski resorts and many hotels and casinos offer special stay and ski packages.

RENO AREA TRAILS

For extensive information on regional hiking and biking trails, including the Mt Rose summit trail and the Tahoe-Pyramid Bikeway, download the **Truckee Meadows Trails guide** (www.reno.gov/Index.aspx?page=291).

Truckee River Whitewater Park WATER SPORTS
Mere steps from the casinos, the park's Class II and III rapids are gentle enough for kids riding inner tubes, yet sufficiently challenging for professional freestyle kayakers. Two courses wrap around Wingfield Park, a small river island that hosts free concerts in summertime. **Tahoe Whitewater Tours** (775-787-5000; www.gowhitewater.com) and **Wild Sierra Adventures** (866-323-8928; www.wildsierra.com) offer kayak trips and lessons.

Historic Reno Preservation Society WALKING TOUR
(775-747-4478; www.historicreno.org; tours $10) Dig deeper with a walking or cycling tour highlighting subjects including architecture, politics and literary history.

Sleeping

Lodging rates vary widely depending on the day of the week and local events. Sunday through Thursday are generally the best; Friday is more expensive and Saturday can be as much as triple the midweek rate.

In summer, there's gorgeous high-altitude camping at **Mt Rose** (877-444-6777; www.recreation.gov; Hwy 431; tent & RV sites $16).

Peppermill CASINO HOTEL $$
(775-826-2121; www.peppermillreno.com; 2707 S Virginia St; r Sun-Thu $50-140; Fri & Sat $70-200;) Now awash in Vegas-style opulence, the popular Peppermill boasts Tuscan-themed rooms in its newest 600-room tower, and has almost completed a plush remodel of its older rooms. The three sparkling pools (one indoor) are dreamy, with a full spa on hand. Geothermal energy powers the resort's hot water and heat.

Sands Regency CASINO HOTEL $
(775-348-2200; www.sandsregency.com; 345 N Arlington Ave; r Sun-Thu/Fri & Sat from $29/89;) Some of the largest standard digs in town, rooms here are decked out in a cheerful tropical palette of upbeat blues, reds and greens – a visual relief from standard-issue motel decor. The 17th-floor gym and Jacuzzi are perfectly positioned to capture your eyes with drop-dead panoramic mountain views. Empress Tower rooms are best.

Wildflower Village MOTEL $
(775-747-8848; www.wildflowervillage.com; 4395 W 4th St; r $50-75, B&B $100-125;) Perhaps more of a state of mind than a motel,

DON'T MISS

BURNING MAN

For one week at the end of August, **Burning Man** (www.burningman.com; admission $210-320) explodes onto the sunbaked Black Rock Desert, and Nevada sprouts a third major population center – Black Rock City. An experiential art party (and alternative universe) that climaxes in the immolation of a towering stick figure, Burning Man is a whirlwind of outlandish theme camps, dust-caked bicycles, bizarre bartering, costume-enhanced nudity and a general relinquishment of inhibitions.

this artists colony on the west edge of town has a tumbledown yet creative vibe. Murals decorate the facade of each room, and you can hear the freight trains rumble on by.

Eating

Reno's dining scene goes far beyond the casino buffets.

TOP CHOICE Old Granite Street Eatery AMERICAN $$
(☎775-622-3222; 243 S Sierra St; dishes $9-24; ⊙11am-10pm Mon-Thu, 11am-midnight Fri, 10am-midnight Sat, 10am-4pm Sun) A lovely well-lighted place for organic and local comfort food, old-school artisanal cocktails and seasonal craft beers, this antique-strewn hot spot enchants diners with its stately wooden bar, water served in old liquor bottles and its lengthy seasonal menu. Forgot to make a reservation? Check out the iconic rooster and pig murals and wait for seats at a community table fashioned from a barn door.

Pneumatic Diner VEGETARIAN $
(501 W 1st St, 2nd fl; dishes $6-9; ⊙noon-10pm Mon, 11am-10pm Tue-Thu, 11am-11pm Fri & Sat, 8am-10pm Sun;) Consume a garden of vegetarian delights under salvaged neon lights. This groovy little place near the river has meatless and vegan comfort food and desserts to tickle your inner two-year-old, such as the ice-cream-laden Cookie Bomb. It's attached to the Truckee River Terrace apartment complex; use the Ralston St entrance.

Silver Peak Restaurant & Brewery PUB $$
(124 Wonder St; mains lunch $8-10, dinner $9-21; ⊙11am-midnight) Casual and pretense-free, this place hums with the chatter of happy locals settling in for a night of microbrews and great eats, from pizza with roasted chicken to shrimp pasta and filet mignon.

Peg's Glorified Ham & Eggs DINER $
(420 S Sierra St; dishes $7-10; ⊙6:30am-2pm;) Locally regarded as the best breakfast in town, Peg's offers tasty grill food that's not too greasy.

Drinking

Jungle Java & Jungle Vino CAFE, WINE BAR
(www.javajunglevino.com; 246 W 1st St; ⊙6am-midnight;) A side-by-side coffee shop and wine bar with a cool mosaic floor and an internet cafe all rolled into one. The wine bar has weekly tastings, while the cafe serves breakfast bagels and lunchtime sandwiches ($8) and puts on diverse music shows.

Imperial Bar & Lounge BAR
(150 N Arlington Ave; ⊙11am-2am Thu-Sat, to midnight Sun-Wed) A classy bar inhabiting a relic of the past, this building was once an old bank, and in the middle of the wood floor you can see cement where the vault once stood. Sandwiches and pizzas go with 16 beers on tap and a buzzing weekend scene.

St James Infirmary BAR
(445 California Ave) With an eclectic menu of 120 bottled varieties and 18 on tap, beer aficionados will short-circuit with delight. Red lights blush over black-and-white retro banquettes and a wall of movie and music stills, and it hosts sporadic events including jazz and bluegrass performances.

Entertainment

The free weekly *Reno News & Review* (www.newsreview.com) is your best source for listings.

Edge CLUB
(www.edgeofreno.com; Peppermill, 2707 S Virginia St; admission $10-20; ⊙Thu-Sun) The Peppermill reels in the nighthounds with a big glitzy dance club, where go-go dancers, smoke machines and laser lights may cause sensory overload. If so, step outside to the view lounge patio and relax in front of cozy fire pits.

Knitting Factory LIVE MUSIC
(☎775-323-5648; http://re.knittingfactory.com; 211 N Virginia St) This mid-sized venue opened in 2010, filling a gap in Reno's music scene with mainstream and indie favorites.

Information

An **information center** sits near the baggage claim at Reno-Tahoe International Airport, which also has free wi-fi.

Java Jungle (246 W 1st St; per hr $2; 6am-midnight; wi-fi) Great riverfront cafe with a few computers and free wi-fi.

Reno-Sparks Convention & Visitors Authority (800-367-7366; www.visitrenotahoe.com; 2nd fl, Reno Town Mall, 4001 S Virginia St; 8am-5pm Mon-Fri)

Getting There & Away

About 5 miles southeast of downtown, **Reno-Tahoe International Airport** (www.renoairport.com; wi-fi) is served by most major airlines.

The **North Lake Tahoe Express** (866-216-5222; www.northlaketahoeexpress.com) operates a shuttle ($40, six to eight daily, 3:30am to midnight) to and from the airport to multiple North Shore Lake Tahoe locations including Truckee, Squaw Valley and Incline Village. Reserve in advance.

To reach South Lake Tahoe (weekdays only), take the wi-fi-equipped **RTC Intercity bus** (www.rtcwashoe.com) to the Nevada DOT stop in Carson City ($4, one hour, five per weekday) and then the **BlueGo** (www.bluego.org) 21X bus ($2 with RTC Intercity transfer, one hour, seven to eight daily) to the Stateline Transit Center.

Greyhound (775-322-2970; www.greyhound.com; 155 Stevenson St) buses run daily service to Truckee, Sacramento and San Francisco ($34, five to seven hours), as does the once-daily westbound California Zephyr route operated by **Amtrak** (775-329-8638; 280 N Center St). The train is slower and more expensive, but also more scenic and comfortable, with a bus connection from Emeryville for passengers to San Francisco ($46, 7½ hours).

Getting Around

The casino hotels offer frequent free airport shuttles for their guests (and don't ask to see reservations).

The local **RTC Ride buses** (775-348-7433; www.rtcwashoe.com; per ride/all day $2/4) blanket the city, and most routes converge at the RTC 4th St Station downtown. Useful routes include the RTC Rapid line for S Virginia St, 11 for Sparks and 19 for the airport. The free Sierra Spirit bus loops around all major downtown landmarks – including the casinos and the university – every 15 minutes from 7am to 7pm.

CARSON CITY

Is this the most underrated town in Nevada? We're going to double down and say that it is. An easy drive from Reno or Lake Tahoe, it's a perfect stop for lunch and a stroll around the quiet, old-fashioned downtown. Expect pretty historic buildings and pleasant tree-lined streets centered around the **1870 Nevada State Capitol** (cnr Musser & Carson; admission free), where you might spot the governor himself chatting with one of his constituents.

Train buffs shouldn't miss the **Nevada State Railroad Museum** (775-687-6953; 2180 S Carson St; adult/child $5/free; 8:30am-4:30pm), which displays some 30 train cars and engines from the 1800s to the early 1900s.

Skip the sedate casinos and head to one of the worthwhile historical museums, or simply grab lunch at fetching **Comma Coffee** (www.commacoffee.com; 312 S Carson St; dishes $5-9) and eavesdrop on the conversation next to you – they're probably congresspersons or lobbyists discussing a new bill over lattes. Or spend the evening at the town's friendly, locally owned microbrewery, **High Sierra Brewing Company** (www.highsierrabrewco.com; 302 N Carson St; dishes $5-9; 11am-midnight Sun-Thu, to 2am Fri & Sat), for great beer and burgers.

Hwy 395/Carson St is the main drag. The **visitor center** (www.visitcarsoncity.com; 1900 S Carson St; 9am-4pm Mon-Fri, to 3pm Sat & Sun), a mile south of downtown, gives out a local map with interesting historical walking and driving tours. For hiking and camping information in the area, stop by the United States Forest Service (USFS) **Carson Ranger District Office** (775-882-2766; 1536 S Carson St; 8am-4:30pm Mon-Fri).

VIRGINIA CITY

During the 1860s gold rush, Virginia City was a high-flying, rip-roaring Wild West boomtown. Newspaperman Samuel Clemens, alias Mark Twain, spent some time in this raucous place during its heyday; years later his eyewitness descriptions of mining life were published in a book called *Roughing It*.

The high-elevation town is a National Historic Landmark, with a main street of Victorian buildings, wooden sidewalks and some hokey but fun museums. To see how the mining elite lived, stop by the **Mackay Mansion** (D St) and the **Castle** (B St).

Locals agree that the best food in Virginia City is probably at **Cafe del Rio** (www.cafedelriovc.com; 394 S C St; mains $9-15; 4:30-8pm Wed & Thu, 11:30am-8pm Fri & Sat, 10am-2pm Sun), serving a nice blend of *nuevo* Mexican and good cafe food, including breakfast.

LOCAL KNOWLEDGE

WHET THE WHISTLE

Drink like an old-time miner at one of the many Victorian-era watering holes that line Virginia City's C St. We like the longtime family-run **Bucket of Blood Saloon** (www.bucketofbloodsaloonvc.com; 1 S C St; ⌚2-7pm), which serves up beer and 'bar rules' at its antique wooden bar ('If the bartender doesn't laugh, you are not funny') and the **Palace Restaurant & Saloon** (www.palacerestaurant1875.com; 1 S C St; mains $6-10; ⌚vary), which is full of town memorabilia and serves up tasty breakfasts and lunches.

The main drag is C St; check out the **visitor center** (www.virginiacity-nv.org; 86 S C St; ⌚10am-4pm).

Nevada Great Basin

A trip across Nevada's Great Basin is a serene, almost haunting experience. But those on the quest for the 'Great American Road Trip' will relish the fascinating historic towns and quirky diversions tucked away along lonely desert highways.

ALONG I-80

Heading east from Reno, **Winnemucca**, 150 miles to the northeast, is the first worthwhile stop. It boasts a vintage downtown and a number of Basque restaurants, along with a yearly Basque festival. For information, stop by the **Winnemucca Convention & Visitors Authority** (☎775-623-5071; 50 W Winnemucca Blvd; ⌚8am-noon & 1-5pm Mon-Fri, 9am-noon Sat, 11am-4pm Sun). Check out the displays here, like a buckaroo (cowboy) hall of fame and big-game museum. Don't miss a stop at **The Griddle** (www.thegriddlecom; 460 W Winnemucca Blvd; mains $4-12; ⌚breakfast & lunch daily, dinner Thu-Sat), one of Nevada's best retro cafes, serving up fantastic breakfasts, diner classics and homemade desserts since 1948.

The culture of the American West is most diligently cultivated in **Elko**. Aspiring cowboys and cowgirls should visit the **Western Folklife Center** (www.westernfolklife.org; 501 Railroad St; exhibits adult/child $5/1; ⌚10am-5:30pm Tue-Fri, 10:30am-5:30pm Tue, 10am-5pm Sat), which offers art and history exhibits and also hosts the popular **Cowboy Poetry Gathering** each January. There's also a **National Basque Festival**, held every July 4, with games, traditional dancing and a 'Running of the Bulls' event. If you've never sampled Basque food, the best place in town for your inaugural experience is the **Star Hotel** (www.elkostarhotelcom; 246 Silver St; mains $15-32; ⌚lunch Mon-Fri, dinner Mon-Sat), a family-style supper club located in a circa-1910 boardinghouse for Basque sheepherders. The irrepressibly curious will not want to miss a peek behind the restaurant, where Elko's small 'red light' district of legal brothels sits, including 'Inez's Dancing and Diddling,' perhaps the most bizarrely named business – tawdry or not – in the state.

ALONG HIGHWAY 50

As you drive along Hwy 50, you'll soon understand why it's called the 'Loneliest Road in America.' Towns are few and far between, and the only sounds are the hum of the engine or the whisper of wind. Once part of the Lincoln Hwy, lonesome Hwy 50 follows the route of the Overland Stagecoach, the Pony Express and the first transcontinental telegraph line.

A fitting reward for surviving the west-east stretch of Highway 50 is the awesome, uncrowded **Great Basin National Park**. Near the Nevada–Utah border, it encompasses 13,063ft Wheeler Peak, rising abruptly from the desert. Hiking trails near the summit take in superb country with glacial lakes, ancient bristlecone pines and even a permanent ice field. Admission is free; the park **visitor center** (☎775-234-7331; www.nps.gov/grba; ⌚8am-5:30pm), just north of the town of **Baker**, is the place to get oriented.

For a 60- or 90-minute guided tour of the caves here that are richly decorated with rare limestone formations, head to the **Lehman Caves** (www.nps.gov/grba; admission $8-10; ⌚8:30am-4pm) five miles outside of Baker. There are first-come, first-served developed **campgrounds** (tent & RV sites $12) in the park.

ALONG HIGHWAY 95

Hwy 95 runs roughly north–south through the western part of the state; the southern section is starkly scenic as it passes the Nevada Test Site (where more than 720 nuclear weapons were exploded in the 1950s).

Five miles north of Beatty, **Bailey's Hot Springs & RV Park** (☎775-553-2395; tent/RV sites $18/21), a 1906 former railroad depot, has three private hot springs in antique bathhouses, open from 8am to 8pm daily. Overnight guests get complimentary usage, and day-trippers pay $5 per person for a 30-minute soak.

ALONG HIGHWAYS 375 & 93

Hwy 375 is dubbed the 'Extraterrestrial Hwy' because of the huge amount of UFO sightings along this stretch of concrete and because it intersects Hwy 93 near top-secret **Area 51**, part of Nellis Air Force Base and a supposed holding area for captured UFOs. In the tiny town of **Rachel**, on Hwy 375, **Little A'Le'Inn** (☎775-729-2515; www.aleinn.com; r from $45) accommodates earthlings and aliens alike, and sells extraterrestrial souvenirs. Probings not included.

ARIZONA

When it comes to travel, wise men say that you should enjoy the journey, not just the destination. It's ridiculously easy to follow this advice in Arizona. Yes, there's the Grand Canyon. Monument Valley. The red rocks of Sedona. Chiricahua National Monument. But it's the roads between these icons that breathe life and context into a trip. Route 66 was a highway for migrant workers heading west during the Depression. Hwy 89 channels Arizona's mining past as it carves past the sliding buildings of Jerome. Hwy 264 cuts across ancestral Hopi lands, unfurling below a village inhabited for the last 800 years.

Where to begin an Arizona road trip? One good place is Greater Phoenix. The region, ringed by mountains, is one of the biggest metro areas in the Southwest. It has the eating, sights and glorious spas you'd expect in a spot that stakes its claim on rest and renewal. Tucson is the funky, artsy gateway to southern Arizona's astronomical and historical sights. Only 60 miles from the Mexican border, it embraces its cross-border heritage.

Up north is Flagstaff, a cool mountain town where locals seek relief from the searing summer heat and people come to play on the nearby San Francisco Peaks all year long. On the northern edge of the state is the Grand Canyon, Arizona's star attraction. Carved over eons by the mighty Colorado River, the greatest hole on earth draws visitors from around the world.

WORTH A TRIP

CATHEDRAL GORGE STATE PARK

Awe, then *ahhh:* this is one of our favorite state parks not just in Nevada, but in the whole USA. **Cathedral Gorge State Park** (www.parks.nv.gov/cg.htm) really does feel like you've stepped into a magnificent, many-spired cathedral, albeit one whose dome is a view of the sky. Sleep under the stars at the first-come, first-served **tent & RV sites** ($17) set amid badlands-style cliffs.

History

Arizona was the last territory in the Lower 48 to become a state, and it celebrated its centennial in 2012. Why did it take so long for a territory filled with copper and ranchland to join the Union? Arizonans were seen as troublemakers by the federal government, and for years acquiring their riches wasn't worth the potential trouble.

Cynics might say that Arizonans are still making trouble. In 2010, Arizona's legislature passed the most restrictive anti-immigration law in the nation, garnering headlines and controversy. How severe was the illegal immigration problem? In 2009, 250,000 illegal immigrants crossed the state's 350-mile border with Mexico. The legislature wasn't spurred into action, however, until the mysterious shooting of a popular rancher near the border the following year. Today, the hot-button law, known as SB1070, winds through the court system.

The state was shaken in 2011 by the shooting of Democratic Congresswoman Gabrielle Giffords during a public appearance. She was critically injured and six bystanders and staff members were killed.

An ongoing statewide fiscal crisis has forced many state parks to operate on a five-day schedule, closing to visitors on Tuesdays and Wednesdays.

ℹ Information

Arizona is on Mountain Standard Time but is the only western state that does not observe daylight saving time from spring to early fall. The exception is the Navajo Reservation, which *does* observe daylight saving time.

Generally speaking, lodging rates in southern Arizona (including Phoenix, Tucson and Yuma) are

ARIZONA FACTS

- » **Nickname** Grand Canyon State
- » **Population** 6.39 million
- » **Area** 113,637 sq miles
- » **Capital city** Phoenix (population 1.4 million)
- » **Other cities** Tucson (population 520,000), Flagstaff (population 65,800), Sedona (population 10,000)
- » **Sales tax** 6.6%
- » **Birthplace of** Apache chief Geronimo (1829–1909), political activist Cesar Chavez (1927–93), singer Linda Ronstadt (b 1946)
- » **Home of** Sedona New Age movement, mining towns turned art colonies
- » **Politics** majority vote Republican
- » **Famous for** Grand Canyon, saguaro cacti
- » **Best souvenir** pink cactus-shaped neon lamp from roadside stall
- » **Driving distances** Phoenix to Grand Canyon Village: 235 miles, Tucson to Sedona: 230 miles

much higher in winter and spring, which are considered the state's 'high season.' Great deals are to be had in the hot areas in the height of summer.

Arizona Department of Transportation (www.az511.com) Updates on road conditions and traffic statewide with links to weather and safety information.

Arizona Office of Tourism (☎602-364-3700; www.arizonaguide.com) Free state information.

Arizona Public Lands Information Center (☎602-417-9300; www.publiclands.org) Information about USFS, NPS, Bureau of Land Management (BLM) and state lands and parks.

Arizona State Parks (☎602-542-4174; www.azstateparks.com) Fifteen of the state's parks have campgrounds. Online reservations will be available for 14 of them by the end of 2011. Camping in Lyman Lake State Park is first-come, first-served.

Phoenix

Anchoring nearly 2000 square miles of suburbs, strip malls and golf courses, Phoenix is the largest urban area in the Southwest. The beige sprawl does little to inspire travelers upon arrival, but if you look a little closer there's an interesting mix of upscale pampering and sunbaked weirdness.

Several 'towns' make up the region known as Greater Phoenix, which is comparable to a family. The City of Phoenix, with its downtown high-rises and top-notch museums, is the patriarch. Scottsdale is the stylish big sister who married up, Tempe the good-natured but occasionally rowdy college kid, and Mesa is the brother who wants a quiet life in the suburbs. And mom? She left for Flagstaff in June because it's just too darn hot.

How hot? In summer temperatures reach above 110°F (43°C). Resort rates drop dramatically, which is great for travelers on a budget, but the most popular time to visit is winter and spring, when pleasant days prevail.

Sights

Greater Phoenix, also known as the Valley of the Sun, is ringed by mountains that range from 2500ft to more than 7000ft in elevation. Central Ave runs north–south through Phoenix, dividing west addresses from east addresses; Washington St runs west–east, dividing north addresses from south addresses.

Scottsdale, Tempe and Mesa are east of the airport. Scottsdale Rd runs north–south between Scottsdale and Tempe. The airport is 3 miles southeast of downtown.

PHOENIX

TOP CHOICE Heard Museum MUSEUM

(Map p326; www.heard.org; 2301 N Central Ave; adult/6-12yr/student/senior $15/7.50/7.50/13.50; ⌚9:30am-5pm Mon-Sat, 11am-5pm Sun; 👪) This engaging museum houses one of the best Native American collections in the world. Check out the kachina (Hopi spirit doll) collection as well as the 'Boarding School Experience' gallery, a moving look at the controversial federal policy of removing Native American children from their families and sending them to remote boarding schools to Americanize them.

Desert Botanical Garden GARDENS

(Map p326; ☎480-941-1225; www.dbg.org; 1201 N Galvin Pkwy; adult/child/student/senior $18/8/10/15; ⌚8am-8pm Oct-Apr, 7am-8pm May-Sep) This inspirational garden is a refreshing place to reconnect with nature and offers a great introduction to desert plant life. Looping trails lead past an astonishing variety of desert denizens arranged by theme, including

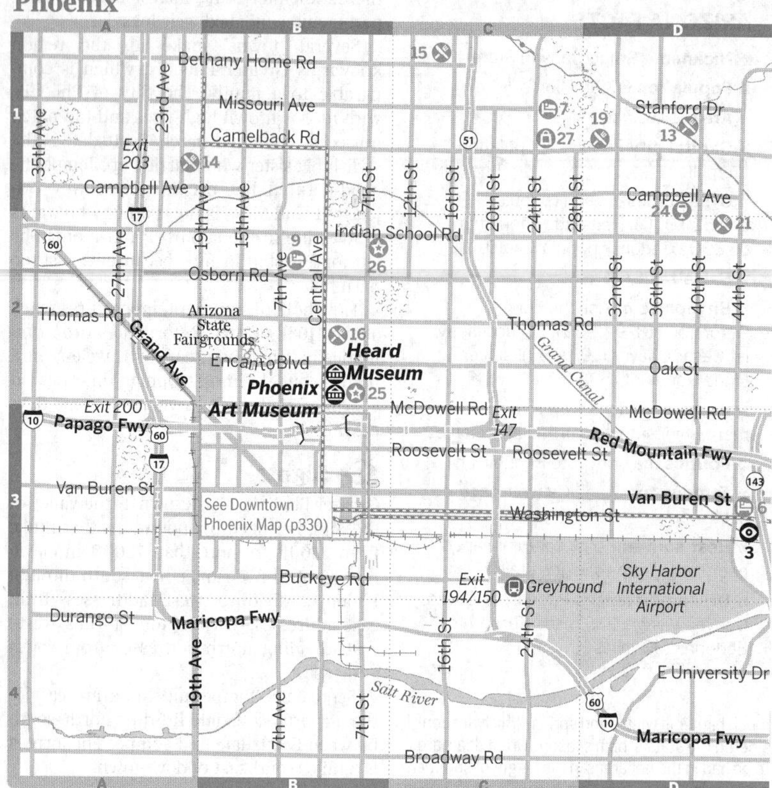

a desert wildflower loop and a Sonoran Desert nature loop. Check for special seasonal events.

Phoenix Art Museum MUSEUM

(Map p326; ☎602-257-1222; www.phxart.org; 1625 N Central Ave; adult/child/student/senior $10/4/8/8, admission free Wed 3-9pm; ⏲10am-9pm Wed, 10am-5pm Thu-Sat, noon-5pm Sun) The Phoenix Art Museum is Arizona's premier repository of fine art. Galleries include works by Claude Monet, Diego Rivera and Georgia O'Keefe. Landscapes in the Western American gallery set the tone for adventure.

Pueblo Grande Museum & Archaeological Park MUSEUM

(Map p326; www.pueblogrande.com; 4619 E Washington St; adult/6-17yr/senior $6/5/3; ⏲9am-4:45pm Mon-Sat, 1-4:45pm Sun) Excavations at this fascinating Hohokam site, which dates back 1500 years, have yielded many clues about the daily lives of these ancient people famous for building a well-engineered 1000-mile network of irrigation canals.

SCOTTSDALE

Scottsdale's main draw is its popular shopping district, known as Old Town for its early-20th-century buildings (and others built to look old). The neighborhood is stuffed chockablock with art galleries, clothing stores for the modern cowgirl, and some of the best eating and drinking in the Valley of the Sun.

TOP CHOICE **Taliesin West** ARCHITECTURE

(☎480-860-2700; www.franklloydwright.org; 12621 Frank Lloyd Wright Blvd; ⏲9am-5pm) Taliesin West was Frank Lloyd Wright's desert home and studio, built between 1938 and 1940. Still home to an architecture school and open to the public for guided tours, it's a prime example of organic ar-

chitecture with buildings incorporating elements and structures found in surrounding nature. The 90-minute **Insights Tour** (adult/4-12yr/student & senior $32/17/28; ⏲half-hourly 9am-4pm Nov–mid-Apr, hourly 9am-4pm mid-Apr–Oct) is both informative and quick-moving.

TEMPE

Founded in 1885 and home to around 58,000 students, **Arizona State University** (ASU) is the heart and soul of Tempe. The **Gammage Auditorium** (cnr Mill Ave & Apache Blvd) was Frank Lloyd Wright's last major building.

Easily accessible by light-rail from downtown Phoenix, **Mill Avenue**, Tempe's main drag, is packed with chain restaurants, themed bars and other collegiate hangouts. While visiting, it's worth checking out **Tempe Town Lake**, an artificial lake with boat rides and paths perfect for strolling or biking its fringes. At **Cox Splash Playground** at the beach park, kids love to frolic under the oversized sprinklers.

FREE Tempe Center for the Arts ARTS CENTER

(Map p326; www.tempe.gov/tca; 700 W Rio Salado Pkwy; ⏲10am-6pm Tue-Fri, 11am-6pm Sat) On the lake, it has a sculpture garden and infinity pool, outside of the curved-steel building. Inside, there's a theater for the performing arts and a 3500-sq-ft gallery.

MESA

Founded by Mormons in 1877, low-key Mesa is one of the fastest-growing cities in the nation and is the third-largest city in Arizona, with a population of around 500,000.

Arizona Museum of Natural History MUSEUM

(off Map p326; ☎480-644-2230; www.azmnh.org; 53 N MacDonald St; adult/3-12yr/student/senior $10/6/8/9; ⏲10am-5pm Tue-Fri, 11am-5pm Sat, 1-5pm Sun; 👪) This captivating museum is worth a trip, especially if your kids are into dinosaurs (aren't they all?). In addition to the multilevel Dinosaur Mountain, there are loads of life-size casts of the giant beasts plus a touchable Apatosaurus thighbone. Other exhibits highlight Arizona's colorful past, from a prehistoric Hohokam village to an eight-cell territorial jail.

Activities

Piestewa Peak/Dreamy Draw Recreation Area HIKING

(☎602-261-8318; http://phoenix.gov/parks/; Squaw Peak Dr, Phoenix; ⏲6am-7pm) Previously known as Squaw Peak, this easy-to-access viewpoint was renamed for local Native

CACTUS LEAGUE SPRING TRAINING

Before the start of the major league baseball season, teams spend March in Arizona (Cactus League) and Florida (Grapefruit League) auditioning new players, practicing and playing games. Tickets are cheaper (from $6 to $8 depending on venue), the seats better, the lines shorter and the games more relaxed. Check www.cactusleague.com for schedules and links to tickets.

Phoenix

Top Sights

Desert Botanical Garden E3
Heard Museum B2
Old Town Scottsdale F2
Phoenix Art Museum B2

Sights

1 Arizona State University F4
Cox Splash Playground .... (see 5)
2 Gammage Auditorium F4
3 Pueblo Grande Museum D3
4 Tempe Center for the Arts E4
5 Tempe Town Lake E4

Activities, Courses & Tours

Tempe Boat Rentals .... (see 5)

Sleeping

6 Aloft Phoenix-Airport D3
7 Arizona Biltmore Resort & Spa C1
8 Best Western Inn of Tempe F3
9 Clarendon Hotel + Suites B2
10 Hotel Indigo Scottsdale F1
11 Hotel Valley Ho F2
12 Royal Palms Resort & Spa E1
Sanctuary on Camelback Mountain .... (see 22)

Eating

13 Chelsea's Kitchen D1
14 Da Vang A1
15 Dick's Hideaway C1
16 Durant's B2
17 Essence E4
18 Herb Box F2
19 Noca D1
20 Sugar Bowl F2
21 Tee Pee Mexican Food D2

Drinking

22 Edge/Jade Bar E1
23 Four Peaks Brewing Co F4
24 Postino Winecafé Arcadia D1

Entertainment

25 Phoenix Theatre B2
26 Rhythm Room B2

Shopping

27 Biltmore Fashion Park C1
28 Scottsdale Fashion Square F1

American soldier Lori Piestewa, killed in Iraq in 2003. The trek to the 2608ft summit is hugely popular and the saguaro-dotted park can get jammed on winter weekends. Dogs are allowed on some trails.

South Mountain Park HIKING, MOUNTAIN BIKING
(☎602-534-6324; http://phoenix.gov/parks/; 10919 Central Ave, Phoenix; ⏰5am-11pm) The 51-mile trail network (leashed dogs allowed) dips through canyons, over grassy hills and past granite walls, offering city views and access to Native American petroglyphs.

Cactus Adventures HIKING, MOUNTAIN BIKING
(☎480-688-9170; www.cactusadventures.com; 4747 Elliot Rd, Suite 21; half-day rentals from $30; ⏰9am-7pm Mon-Sat, 9am-5pm Sun) A quarter-mile pedal from South Mountain Park, Cactus Adventures rents bikes and offers guided hiking and biking tours.

Tempe Boat Rentals BOATING
(Map p326; ☎480-517-4050; http://boats4rent.com; 72 W Rio Salado Pkwy; pedal boats/kayaks/16ft pontoons $25/40/130 for 2hr) Rents watercraft at Tempe Town Lake.

Tours

Arizona Detours SIGHTSEEING
(☎866-438-6877; www.detoursaz.com) Offers day tours to far-flung locations such as Tombstone (adult/child $145/75) and the Grand Canyon (adult/child $155/90), and five-hour city tours (adult/child $80/45).

Arizona Outback Adventures HIKING
(☎480-945-2881; www.aoa-adventures.com; 16447 N 91st St, Scottsdale) Offers day trips for hiking ($95, minimum two people), mountain biking ($125, minimum two people), and other active outings.

Festivals & Events

Tostitos Fiesta Bowl SPORTS
(☎480-350-0911; www.fiestabowl.org) Held in early January at the University of Phoenix Stadium in Glendale, this football game is preceded by massive celebrations and parades.

Sleeping

Greater Phoenix is well stocked with hotels and resorts, but you won't find many B&Bs or cozy inns. Prices plummet in the super-hot summer, a time when Valley residents take advantage of super-low prices at their favorite resorts.

PHOENIX

Royal Palms Resort & Spa RESORT $$$

(Map p326; ☎602-840-3610; www.royalpalmsresortandspa.com; 5200 E Camelback Rd, Phoenix; r $329-429, ste from $366; P❄@🛜🏊) This posh boutique resort at the base of Camelback Mountain is a hushed and elegant place, dotted with Spanish Colonial villas, flower-lined walkways, and palms imported from Egypt. Pets can go Pavlovian for soft beds, personalized biscuits and walking services. There's a $28 daily resort fee.

Arizona Biltmore Resort & Spa RESORT $$$

(Map p326; ☎602-955-6600; www.arizonabiltmore.com; 2400 E Missouri Ave, Phoenix; r $300-459, ste from $489; P❄@🛜🏊👪) With architecture inspired by Frank Lloyd Wright, the Biltmore is perfect for connecting to the magic of yesterday. It boasts more than 700 discerning units, two golf courses, several pools, a spa, a kids club and more such luxe touches. Wi-fi can be spotty beyond the lobby and the main pool. Daily resort fee is $28.

Clarendon Hotel + Suites HOTEL $$

(Map p326; ☎602-252-7363; www.theclarendon.net; 401 W Clarendon Ave, Phoenix; r $160-199; P❄@🛜🏊) The Clarendon's finger-snapping, minimalist cool manages to be both welcoming and hip. In the standard rooms, look for 42-inch flat-screens, artsy prints and dark custom furniture. Ride up to the breezy skydeck for citywide views. The $20 daily fee covers wi-fi, parking and phone calls.

Aloft Phoenix-Airport HOTEL $$

(Map p326; ☎602-275-6300; www.aloftphoenixairport.com; 4450 E Washington St, Phoenix; r $129-160; P❄@🛜🏊) Rooms blend a pop-art sensibility with the cleanest edges of modern design. The hotel is near Tempe and across the street from the Pueblo Grand Museum. No extra fee for pets.

HI Phoenix Hostel HOSTEL $

(☎602-254-9803; www.phxhostel.org; 1026 N 9th St, Phoenix; dm $20-23, d $35-50; ❄@🛜) A veritable UN of half-mad guests, this inviting 14-bed hostel sits in a working-class residential neighborhood and has relaxing garden nooks. The owners are fun, and they know Phoenix. Check-in is from 8am to 10am and 5pm to 10pm. Closed July and August. No credit cards.

Budget Lodge Downtown MOTEL $

(Map p330; ☎602-254-7247; www.blphx.com; 402 W Van Buren St, Phoenix; r incl breakfast $50-55; P❄🛜) This no-nonsense workhorse is a clean, low-cost place to lay your head and provides the most important amenities: a microwave and fridge in every room, and complimentary breakfast.

SCOTTSDALE

TOP CHOICE **Boulders Resort** RESORT $$$

(☎480-488-9009; www.theboulders.com; 34631 N Tom Darlington Dr, Carefree; casitas $350-850, villas from $1050-1250; P❄@🛜🏊) This desert oasis blends nearly imperceptibly into a landscape of natural rock formations – and that's before you've enjoyed a session at the ultraposh on-site Golden Door Spa. Everything here is calculated to take the edge off travel, making it a perfect destination

PHOENIX FOR CHILDREN

Wet 'n Wild Phoenix (off Map p326; ☎623-201-2000; www.wetnwildphoenix.com; 4243 W Pinnacle Peak Rd, Glendale; over/under 48in tall $35/28, senior $28; ⏰10am-6pm Sun-Wed, 10am-10pm Thu-Sat, 11am-7pm Sun Jun-Jul, vary May, Aug & Sep; 👪) water park has pools, tube slides, wave pools, waterfalls and floating rivers. It's in Glendale, 2 miles west of I-17 at exit 217.

At the re-created 1880s frontier town **Rawhide Western Town & Steakhouse** (off Map p326; ☎480-502-5600; www.rawhide.com; 5700 W N Loop Rd, Chandler; admission free, per attraction or show $5, unlimited day pass $15; ⏰5-9pm Wed-Fri, noon-9:30pm Sat, noon-8:30pm Sun; 👪), about 20 miles south of Mesa, kids can enjoy all sorts of hokey-but-fun shenanigans. The steakhouse has rattlesnake for adventurous eaters. Opening hours vary seasonally.

Arizona Science Center (Map p330; ☎602-716-2000; www.azscience.org; 600 E Washington St; adult/3-17yr/senior $14/11/12; ⏰10am-5pm; 👪) is a high-tech temple of discovery, there are more than 300 hands-on exhibits and a planetarium.

Downtown Phoenix

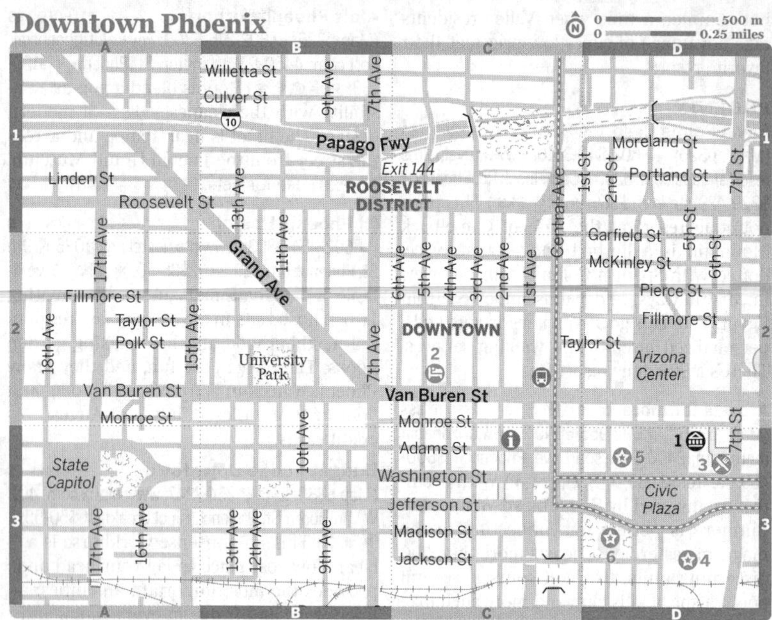

Downtown Phoenix

Sights

1 Arizona Science Center D3

Sleeping

2 Budget Lodge Downtown C2

Eating

3 Pizzeria Bianco D3

Entertainment

4 Chase Field D3
5 Symphony Hall D3
6 US Airways Center D3

for recovering from jet lag or rediscovering your significant other. Daily resort fee is $30. Weekend rates can drop as low as $139 in summer.

TOP CHOICE **Hotel Valley Ho** BOUTIQUE HOTEL **$$$**
(Map p326; ☎480-248-2000; www.hotelvalleyho.com; 6850 E Main St, Scottsdale; r $289-339, ste $399-439; P❄@🛜≋) Everything's swell at the Valley Ho, a jazzy joint that once bedded Bing Crosby, Natalie Wood and Janet Leigh. Today, bebop music, upbeat front staff and the 'ice fireplace' recapture the Rat Pack–era vibe, and the theme travels well to the balconied rooms. Pets stay free, but wi-fi is $10 per day.

Sanctuary on Camelback Mountain RESORT **$$$**
(Map p326; ☎480-948-2100; www.sanctuaryoncamelback.com; 5700 E McDonald Dr, Scottsdale; r $419-629, houses $1800-3500; P❄@🛜≋) Mountain suites, spa casitas, private homes – chic lodgings are decorated with the beautiful warm tones of the desert and outfitted with whatever amenity your heart desires. Enjoy a sunset cocktail on the **Edge**, Sanctuary's swanky outdoor bar. Daily resort fee $18.

Hotel Indigo Scottsdale HOTEL **$$**
(Map p326; ☎480-941-9400; www.scottsdalehiphotel.com; 4415 N Civic Center Plaza; r $174-184, ste $204-224; P❄@🛜≋) Hot-spot trappings include sumptuous bedding, outdoor fire pits, club music in the lobby, fancy toiletries and plasma TVs. Dogs welcome, at no extra charge.

Sleep Inn HOTEL **$$**
(off Map p330; ☎480-998-9211; www.sleepinnscottsdale.com; 16630 N Scottsdale Rd; r incl breakfast $99-114; P❄@🛜) This outpost of the national chain in North Scottsdale wins points for its extensive breakfast,

friendly staff and proximity to Taliesin West.

TEMPE

TOP CHOICE **Sheraton Wild Horse Pass Resort & Spa** RESORT $$$
(602-225-0100; www.wildhorsepassresort.com; 5594 W Wild Horse Pass Blvd, Chandler; r $239-579;) Designed by the Gila River tribe as a luxurious place to soak up the best of Native American healing and wisdom, this oasis has comfortable rooms, spacious common areas, fine dining, two 18-hole golf courses, an equestrian center, tennis courts and a water slide modeled after Hohokam ruins. Wi-fi is available in the lobby.

Best Western Inn of Tempe HOTEL $
(Map p326; 480-784-2233; www.innoftempe.com; 670 N Scottsdale Rd; r incl breakfast $75-90;) This well-kept, helpful hotel is within walking distance of Tempe Town Lake and close to ASU and lively Mill Ave.

Eating

The Phoenix-Scottsdale area has the largest selection of restaurants in the Southwest.

TOP CHOICE **Matt's Big Breakfast** BREAKFAST $
(602-254-1074; www.mattsbigbreakfast.com; 801 N 1st St, at McKinley St; mains $5-8; 6:30am-2:30pm Tue-Sun) Best. Breakfast. Ever. Every regular menu item is great, but daily specials, such as eggs scrambled with peppers and chorizo into fluffy-spicy-ohmygoodness on a bed of mouthwatering crispy homefries are supremely yummy. Sign in on the clipboard and bring quarters for the meter.

TOP CHOICE **Dick's Hideaway** MEXICAN $$
(Map p326; 602-265-5886; www.richardsonsnm.com; 6008 N 16th St; breakfast $8-16, lunch $12-16, dinner $17-37; 7am-midnight) Grab a table beside the bar or join the communal table in the side room and settle in for hearty servings of savory, chile-slathered enchiladas, tamales and other New Mexican cuisine. We especially like the Hideaway for breakfast, when the Bloody Marys arrive with a shot of beer. The unmarked entrance is between the towering shrubs.

Durant's STEAKHOUSE $$$
(Map p326; 602-264-5967; www.durantsaz.com; 2611 N Central Ave; mains $17-34; lunch & dinner) This dark and manly place is a gloriously old-school steakhouse. You will get steak. It will be big and juicy. There will be a potato. The ambience is awesome too: red velvet cozy booths and the sense the Rat Pack is going to waltz in at any minute.

Pizzeria Bianco PIZZERIA $$
(Map p330; www.pizzeriabianco.com; 623 E Adams St; pizzas $12-16; 11am-10pm Tue-Sat) James Beard winner Chris Bianco has stepped back from the ovens at his famous downtown pizza joint (allergies are to blame), but the thin-crust gourmet pies remain as tasty as ever. The tiny restaurant is now open for lunch.

Da Vang VIETNAMESE $
(Map p326; 4538 N 19th Ave; mains $6-13; 8am-8pm) Our favorite Vietnamese in the Valley is served in a Spartan dining room; it's as if the plainness of the location is in direct proportion to the awesomeness of the food. The pho is fantastic, and you'd be remiss not to try some of the lovely 'dry' rice noodle dishes.

Noca AMERICAN $$$
(Map p326; 602-956-6622; www.restaurantnoca.com; 3118 E Camelback Rd; mains $20-33; lunch & dinner Tue-Sun, open Mon Dec-Mar) Short for north of Camelback, Noca serves New American fare using American ingredients in the style of classical innovators such as the French Laundry. Think linguini with Maine lobster with shaved fennel in a spicy tomato broth.

Tee Pee Mexican Food MEXICAN $
(Map p326; www.teepeemexicanfood.com; 4144 E Indian School Rd; mains $8-11; 11am-10pm Mon-Sat, to 9pm Sun) If you like piping-hot plates piled high with cheesy, messy American-style Mexican fare then grab a booth at this 40-year-old fave. George W Bush ate here in 2004 and ordered two enchiladas, rice and beans – now called the Presidential Special.

Chelsea's Kitchen AMERICAN $$
(Map p326; 5040 N 40th St; lunch $10-17, dinner $10-27; lunch & dinner daily, brunch Sun) The Western-inspired cuisine at this chic but casual place includes burgers, salad and tacos, but we're partial to the organic meats tanned to juicy perfection in the hardwood rotisserie. There's a nice patio too.

SCOTTSDALE

Fresh Mint VIETNAMESE, VEGETARIAN $
(off Map p326; www.freshmint.us.com; 13802 N Scottsdale Rd; mains $6-14; 11am-9pm Mon-Sat;) Never had kosher Vietnamese vegan? There's always a first time, and if it tastes like the food at Fresh Mint, you'd want to get

some more. If you're skeptical of soy chicken and tofu, we understand, but we respectfully submit that this stuff is as tasty as any bacon cheeseburger.

Mastro's Ocean Club SEAFOOD **$$$**
(off Map p326; ☎480-443-8555; www.mastrosrestaurants.com; 15045 N Kierland Blvd; mains $30-50; ⊙dinner) Mastro's is gunning for the title of best seafood in the Valley of the Sun, and it may just deserve the crown. It's part of an upscale chain, but don't hold that against it. The entire place screams class and affected atmosphere, but the real draw is incredibly rich decadent takes on everything that swims under the waves.

Herb Box AMERICAN **$$**
(Map p326; www.theherbbox.com; 7134 E Stetson Dr; lunches $10-15, dinners $14-25; ⊙lunch daily, dinner Mon-Sat) It's not just about sparkle and air kisses at this chichi bistro. It's also about fresh, regional ingredients, artful presentation and attentive service.

Sugar Bowl ICE CREAM **$**
(Map p326; 4005 N Scottsdale Rd; ice creams under $5, mains $6-9; ⊙11am-10pm Sun-Thu, 11am-midnight Fri & Sat; 👪) This pink-and-white Valley institution has been working its ice-cream magic since the '50s. For more substantial fare, there's a whole menu of sandwiches and salads.

TEMPE

TOP CHOICE **Kai Restaurant** NATIVE AMERICAN **$$$**
(☎602-225-0100; www.wildhorsepassresort.com; 5594 W Wild Horse Pass Blvd, Chandler; mains $40-49, 8-course tasting menus $200; ⊙dinner Tue-Sat) Simple ingredients from mainly Native American farms and ranches are turned into something extraordinary. Dinners are like fine tapestries with dishes – such as the pecan-crusted Colorado lamb with native seeds mole – striking just the right balance between adventure and comfort. Dress nicely (no shorts or hats). It's at the Sheraton Wild Horse Pass Resort & Spa (p331) on the Gila River Indian Reservation. Kai closes for one month in August.

Essence CAFE **$**
(www.essencebakery.com; 825 W University Dr; breakfasts $5-7, lunches $8-9; ⊙7am-3pm Mon-Fri, 8am-3pm Sat, closed Sun) This breezy box of deliciousness serves egg dishes and French toast at breakfast, and salads, gourmet sandwiches and a few Mediterranean specialties at lunch. The ecominded cafe strives to use organic, locally grown fare.

Drinking

Scottsdale has the greatest concentration of trendy bars and clubs; Tempe attracts the student crowd; and Phoenix has a slew of long-standing dive bars that are in again.

TOP CHOICE **Postino Winecafé Arcadia** WINE BAR
(Map p326; www.postinowinecafe.com; 3939 E Campbell Ave, at 40th St, Phoenix; ⊙11am-11pm Mon-Thu, 11am-midnight Fri & Sat, 11am-10pm Sun) This convivial, indoor-outdoor wine bar is a perfect gathering spot for a few friends ready to enjoy the good life, but solos will do fine too. Highlights include the misting patio, rave-inducing bruschetta and $5 wines by the glass from 11am to 5pm.

Edge/Jade Bar BAR
(Map p326; 5700 E McDonald Dr, Sanctuary on Camelback Mountain, Scottsdale) Enjoy a sunset 'on the edge' at this stylish cocktail bar perched on the side of Camelback Mountain. No room outside? The equally posh, big-windowed Jade Bar should do just fine. Both are within the plush confines of the Sanctuary on Camelback Mountain resort. Complimentary valet.

Four Peaks Brewing Company BREWERY
(Map p326; www.fourpeaks.com; 1340 E 8th St, Tempe; ⊙11am-2am Mon-Sat, 10am-2am Sun) Beer-lovers rejoice: you're in for a treat at this quintessential neighborhood brewpub in a cool Mission Revival–style building.

Greasewood Flat BAR
(☎480-585-9430; www.greasewoodflat.net; 27375 N Alma School Pkwy, Scottsdale; ⊙11am-11pm) Cowboys, bikers and preppy golfers gather around the smoky barbecue and knock back the whiskey at this rustic ex-stagecoach stop, located 21 miles north of downtown Scottsdale. Cash only.

☆ Entertainment

Both the **Arizona Opera** (☎602-266-7464; www.azopera.com) and the **Phoenix Symphony Orchestra** (☎602-495-1999; www.phoenixsymphony.org) perform at **Symphony Hall** (Map p330; 75 N 2nd St, Phoenix).

The men's basketball team, the **Phoenix Suns** (☎602-379-7900; www.nba.com/suns), and the women's team, the **Phoenix Mercury** (☎602-252-9622; www.wnba.com/mercury), play at the US Airways Center. The **Arizona**

Cardinals (☎602-379-0101; www.azcardinals.com) football team plays at the new University of Phoenix Stadium in Glendale. The **Arizona Diamondbacks** (☎602-462-6500; http://arizona.diamondbacks.mlb.com) play baseball at Chase Field (Map p330).

Rhythm Room LIVE MUSIC
(Map p326; ☎602-265-4842; www.rhythmroom.com; 1019 E Indian School Rd, Phoenix) Some of the Valley's best live acts take the stage at this small venue, where you pretty much feel like you're in the front row of every gig. It tends to attract more local and regional talent than the big names, which suits us just fine.

BS West GAY
(☎480-945-9028; www.bswest.com; 7125 E 5th Ave, Scottsdale; ⏲2pm-2am) A high-energy gay video bar and dance club in the Old Town Scottsdale area, this place has pool tables and a small dance floor, and hosts karaoke on Sundays.

Phoenix Theatre PERFORMING ARTS
(Map p326; ☎602-254-2151; www.phoenixtheatre.com; 100 E McDowell Rd) The city's main dramatic group puts on a good mix of mainstream and edgier performances. The attached cookie company does children's shows.

Shopping

The valley has several notable shopping malls. For more upscale shopping, visit the **Scottsdale Fashion Square** (Map p326; cnr Camelback & Scottsdale Rds) and the even more exclusive **Biltmore Fashion Park** (Map p326; cnr Camelback Rd & 24th St). In northern Scottsdale, the new and outdoor **Kierland Commons** (15205 N Kierland Blvd, Scottsdale) is pulling in crowds.

Heard Museum Bookshop ARTS & CRAFTS
(☎602-252-8344; www.heardmuseumshop.com; 2301 N Central Ave, Phoenix) Has the best range of books about Native Americans, and the most reliable and expansive selection of Native American arts and crafts.

Information

Emergency & Medical Services

Banner Good Samaritan Medical Center (☎602-839-2000; www.bannerhealth.com; 1111 E McDowell Rd, Phoenix) Has a 24-hour emergency room.

Police (☎602-262-6151; http://phoenix.gov/police; 620 W Washington St, Phoenix)

Internet Access

Burton Barr Central Library (☎602-262-4636; www.phoenixpubliclibrary.org; 1221 N Central Ave, Phoenix; ⏲9am-5pm Mon, 11am-9pm Tue-Thu, 9am-5pm Fri & Sat, 1-5pm Sun; @ 📶) Free internet access.

Internet Resources & Media

Arizona Republic (www.azcentral.com) Arizona's largest newspaper; publishes a free entertainment guide, *Calendar*, every Thursday.

KJZZ 91.5 fm (http://kjzz.org) National Public Radio (NPR).

Phoenix New Times (www.phoenixnewtimes.com) The major free weekly; lots of event and restaurant listings.

Post

Downtown post office (☎602-253-9648; 522 N Central Ave, Phoenix)

Tourist Information

Downtown Phoenix Visitor Information Center (Map p330; ☎602-254-6500; www.visitphoenix.com; 125 N 2nd St, Suite 120; ⏲8am-5pm Mon-Fri) The Valley's most complete source of tourist information.

Mesa Convention & Visitors Bureau (☎480-827-4700; www.mesacvb.com; 120 N Center St; ⏲8am-5pm Mon-Fri)

Scottsdale Convention & Visitors Bureau (☎480-421-1004; www.scottsdalecvb.com; 4343 N Scottsdale Rd, Suite 170; ⏲8am-5pm Mon-Fri) Inside the Galleria Corporate Center.

Tempe Convention & Visitors Bureau (Map p326; ☎480-894-8158; www.tempecvb.com; 51 W 3rd St, Suite 105; ⏲8:30am-5pm Mon-Fri)

Getting There & Around

Sky Harbor International Airport (www.skyharbor.com; 📶) is 3 miles southeast of downtown Phoenix and served by 17 airlines, including United, American, Delta and British Airways. Its three terminals (Terminals 2, 3 and 4; Terminal 1 was demolished in 1990) and the parking lots are linked by the free 24-hour Airport Shuttle Bus.

Greyhound (Map p326; ☎602-389-4200; www.greyhound.com; 2115 E Buckeye Rd) runs buses to Tucson ($20 to $27, two hours, eight daily), Flagstaff ($32 to $42, three hours, five daily), Albuquerque ($71 to $89, 10 hours, five daily) and Los Angeles ($42 to $54, 7½ hours, 10 daily). Valley Metro's No 13 buses link the airport and the Greyhound station.

Valley Metro (☎602-253-5000; www.valleymetro.org) operates buses all over the Valley and a 20-mile light-rail line linking north Phoenix with downtown Phoenix, Tempe/ASU and downtown

Mesa. Fares for light-rail and bus are $1.75 per ride (no transfers) or $3.50 for a day pass. Buses run daily at intermittent times. **FLASH buses** (www.tempe.gov/tim/bus/flash.htm) operate daily around ASU and downtown Tempe, while the **Scottsdale Trolley** (www.scottsdaleaz.gov/trolley) loops around downtown Scottsdale, both at no charge.

Flagstaff

Flagstaff's laid-back charms are myriad, from its pedestrian-friendly historic downtown crammed with eclectic vernacular architecture and vintage neon to its high-altitude pursuits such as skiing and hiking. Locals are generally a happy, athletic bunch, skewing more toward granola than gunslinger. Northern Arizona University (NAU) gives Flagstaff its college-town flavor, while its railroad history still figures firmly in the town's identity. Throw in a healthy appreciation for craft beer, freshly roasted coffee beans and an all-round good time and you have the makings of a town you want to slow down and savor.

Sights

Museum of Northern Arizona MUSEUM
(www.musnaz.org; 3101 N Fort Valley Rd; adult/student $7/4; ⌚9am-5pm) If you have time for only one sight in Flagstaff, head to the Museum of Northern Arizona. It features exhibits on local Native American archaeology, history and customs, as well as geology, biology and the arts.

Lowell Observatory OBSERVATORY
(☎928-774-3358; www.lowell.edu; 1400 W Mars Hill Rd; adult/child $6/3; ⌚9am-5pm Mar-Oct, noon-5pm Nov-Feb, night hr vary) This observatory witnessed the first sighting of Pluto in 1920. Weather permitting, there's nightly stargazing, helped by the fact that Flagstaff is the first International Dark Sky city in the world. Day tours are offered from 10am to 4pm in summer, with reduced hours in winter.

Walnut Canyon National Monument PARK
(☎928-526-3367; www.nps.gov/waca; admission $5; ⌚8am-5pm May-Oct, 9am-5pm Nov-Apr) Sinagua cliff dwellings are set in the nearly vertical walls of a small limestone butte amid a forested canyon at this worth-a-trip monument. A short hiking trail descends past many cliff-dwelling rooms. The monument is 11 miles southeast of Flagstaff off I-40 exit 204.

Activities

Humphreys Peak HIKING
The state's highest mountain (12,663ft) is a reasonably straightforward, though strenuous, hike in summer. The trail, which begins in the Arizona Snowbowl, winds through forest, eventually coming out above the beautifully barren tree line. The total distance is 4.5 miles one-way; allow six to eight hours round-trip.

Arizona Snowbowl SKIING
(☎928-779-1951; www.arizonasnowbowl.com; Hwy 180 & Snowbowl Rd; lift ticket adult/child $49/26) Four lifts service 30 runs and a snowboarding park at elevations between 9200ft and 11,500ft. You can ride the chairlift (adult/child $12/8) in summer.

Sleeping

Flagstaff provides the widest variety of lodging choices in the region. Unlike in southern Arizona, summer is high season here.

Grand Canyon International Hostel HOSTEL $
(☎928-779-9421; www.grandcanyonhostel.com; 19½ S San Francisco St; dm incl breakfast $18-36, r without bath $43; ❄@🛜) Run by friendly people in a historic building, dorms are clean and small. There's a kitchen, laundry facilities and a host of tours to the Grand Canyon and Sedona. Guests are fetched from the Greyhound bus for free.

Dubeau Hostel HOSTEL $
(☎928-774-6731; www.grandcanyonhostel.com; 19 W Phoenix Ave; dm incl breakfast $21-24, r $46-66; ❄@🛜) Run by the Grand Canyon International Hostel folks. The private rooms are like basic hotel rooms, but at half the price. With a jukebox, things can get a little loud here.

Weatherford Hotel HISTORIC HOTEL $$
(☎928-779-1919; www.weatherfordhotel.com; 23 N Leroux St; r without bath $49-79, r with bath $89-139; ❄🛜) This atmospheric hotel offers 11 charmingly decorated rooms with turn-of-the-20th-century feel. Three rooms also incorporate modern amenities such as TVs, phones and air-conditioning. Since the Weatherford's three bars often feature live music, it can get noisy.

Monte Vista Hotel HISTORIC HOTEL $$
(☎928-779-6971; www.hotelmontevista.com; 100 N San Francisco St; d $65-130, ste $120-175; ❄🛜) Feather lampshades, vintage furniture, bold colors and eclectic decor – things are histori-

cally frisky in the 50 rooms and suites here, which are named for the film stars who slept in them. Ask for a quiet room if you're opposed to live music that may drift up from Monte Vista Lounge.

Eating

Wander around downtown and you'll stumble on plenty of eating options.

Criollo Latin Kitchen FUSION $$
(928-774-0541; www.criollolatinkitchen.com; 16 N San Francisco St; mains $13-30; 11am-10pm Mon-Thu, 11am-11pm Fri, 9am-11pm Sat, 9am-2pm & 4-10pm Sun) This Latin fusion spot has a romantic, industrial setting for cozy cocktail dates and delectable late-night small plates. The blue-corn blueberry pancakes make a strong argument for showing up for Sunday brunch. Food is sourced locally and sustainable when possible.

Beaver Street Brewery PUB $$
(www.beaverstreetbrewery.com; 11 S Beaver St; mains $8-12; 11am-11pm Sun-Thu, 11am-midnight Fri & Sat;) Beaver Street Brewery is a bustling place to go for a bite to eat with a pint of local microbrew. It usually has five handmade beers on tap and some seasonal brews. The menu is typical brewpub fare, with delicious pizzas, burgers and salads. Surprisingly, it's very family friendly.

Mountain Oasis INTERNATIONAL $$
(11 E Aspen; mains $9-19; 11am-9pm;) Vegetarians and vegans will find plenty of options on this internationally spiced menu. Tasty specialties include the TBLT (tempeh bacon, lettuce and tomato) and Thai veggies and tofu with peanut sauce and brown rice. Steak and chicken are also on the menu.

Drinking & Entertainment

TOP CHOICE **Museum Club** ROADHOUSE
(928-526-9434; 3404 E Rte 66; 11am-2am) Yee-haw! Kick up your heels at this honky-tonk roadhouse where the country dancing is nightly. Inside what looks like a huge log cabin you'll find a large wooden dance floor and a sumptuous elixir-filled mahogany bar. See their Facebook page for events.

Charly's Pub & Grill LIVE MUSIC
(928-779-1919; www.weatherfordhotel.com; 23 N Leroux St; 8am-10pm) This restaurant at the Weatherford Hotel has regular live music. Its fireplace and brick walls provide a cozy setting for the blues, jazz and folk played here. Upstairs, stroll the wraparound veranda outside the popular 3rd-floor Zane Grey Ballroom.

Macy's CAFE
(www.macyscoffee.net; 14 S Beaver St; 6am-8pm Mon-Wed, to 10pm Thu-Sun;) Macy's delicious house-roasted coffee has kept Flagstaff buzzing for over 30 years. Tasty vegetarian menu includes many vegan choices, with traditional cafe grub (mains $3 to $7). Cash only.

Cuvee 928 WINE BAR
(www.cuvee928winebar.com; 6 W Aspen Ave, Suite 110; 11:30am-9pm Mon-Tue, to 10pm Wed-Sat) With a central location on Heritage Sq, and patio seating, this wine bar is a pleasant venue for people-watching.

Information

Visitors center (928-774-9541; www.flagstaffarizona.org; 1 E Rte 66; 8am-5pm Mon-Sat, 9am-4pm Sun) Inside the historic Amtrak train station.

Getting There & Around

Flagstaff Pulliam Airport is 4 miles south of town off I-17. **US Airways** (www.usairways.com) offers several daily flights from Phoenix Sky Harbor International Airport. **Greyhound** (928-774-4573; www.greyhound.com; 399 S Malpais Ln) stops in Flagstaff en route to/from Albuquerque, Las Vegas, Los Angeles and Phoenix. **Arizona Shuttle** (928-226-8060; www.arizonashuttle.com) has shuttles that run to the park, Williams and Phoenix Sky Harbor Airport.

Operated by **Amtrak** (928-774-8679; www.amtrak.com; 1 E Route 66; 3am-10:45pm), the Southwest Chief stops at Flagstaff on its daily run between Chicago and Los Angeles.

Central Arizona

This part of Arizona draws people year-round for outdoor fun and is an oasis for summer visitors searching for cooler climes. After Phoenix, the land gains elevation, turning from high rolling desert to jagged hills covered in scrubby trees. Farther north still, mountains punctuate thick stands of pine.

WILLIAMS

Affable Williams, 60 miles south of Grand Canyon Village and 35 miles west of Flagstaff, is a gateway town with character. Classic motels and diners line Route 66, and the old-school homes and train station give a nod to simpler times.

Most tourists visit to ride the turn-of-the-19th-century **Grand Canyon Railway** (800-843-8724; www.thetrain.com; Railway Depot, 233 N

Grand Canyon Blvd; round-trip adult/child from $70/40;) to the South Rim (departs Williams 9:30am). Even if you're not a train buff, a trip is a scenic stress-free way to visit the Grand Canyon. Characters in period costumes provide historical and regional narration, and banjo folk music sets the tone. There's also a wildly popular Polar Express service (adult/child from $30/20) from November through January, ferrying pajama-clad kids to the 'North Pole' to visit Santa.

The **Red Garter Bed & Bakery** (928-635-1484; www.redgarter.com; 137 W Railroad Ave; r incl breakfast $120-145;) is an 1897 bordello turned B&B where the ladies used to hang out the windows to flag down customers. The four rooms have nice period touches and the downstairs bakery has good coffee. The funky little **Grand Canyon Hotel** (928-635-1419; www.thegrandcanyonhotel.com; 145 W Rte 66; dm $28, r without bath $60, r with bath $70-125;) has small themed rooms and a six-bed dorm room.

Route 66 fans will dig the eclectic decor at **Cruiser's Cafe 66** (www.cruisers66.com; 233 W Rte 66; mains $10-20; 3-10pm;). It's a fun place, serving tasty microbrews, BBQ and other American fare inside a 1930s filling station.

SEDONA

Sedona's a stunner, but it's intensely spiritual as well. Nestled amid majestic red sandstone formations at the southern end of Oak Creek Canyon, Sedona attracts spiritual seekers, artists and healers, and day-trippers from Phoenix fleeing the oppressive heat. Many New Age types believe that this area is the center of vortexes that radiate the earth's power, and Sedona's combination of scenic beauty and mysticism draws throngs of tourists year-round. New Age businesses dot downtown, along with galleries and gourmet restaurants, while the surrounding canyons offer excellent hiking and mountain biking.

In the middle of town, the 'Y' is the landmark junction of Hwys 89A and 179. Businesses are spread along both roads.

Sights & Activities

New Agers believe Sedona's rocks, cliffs and rivers radiate Mother Earth's mojo. The world's four best-known vortexes are here, and include **Bell Rock** near Village of Oak Creek east of Hwy 179, **Cathedral Rock** near Red Rock Crossing, **Airport Mesa** along Airport Rd, and **Boynton Canyon**. Airport Rd is also a great location for watching the Technicolor sunsets.

Coconino National Forest PARK
(USFS South Gateway Visitor Center 928-203-7500; www.redrockcountry.org/recreation; 8379 Hwy 179; 8am-5pm) The best way to explore the area is by hiking, biking or horseback riding in the surrounding forest. Most day use and parking areas require a Red Rock Pass ($5/15 per day/week), which can be purchased at most area stores and lodging and at a number of self-serve kiosks at popular sites. The most scenic spots are along Hwy 89A north of Sedona, which snakes alongside Oak Creek through the heavily visited **Oak Creek Canyon**. The USFS visitor center is just south of the Village of Oak Creek.

FREE **Chapel of the Holy Cross** CHURCH
(www.chapeloftheholycross.com; 780 Chapel Rd; 9am-5pm Mon-Sat, 10am-5pm Sun) Situated between spectacular, statuesque red-rock columns 3 miles south of town, this modern, nondenominational chapel was built in 1956 by Marguerite Brunwig Staude in the tradition of Frank Lloyd Wright.

Slide Rock State Park PARK
(928-282-3034; www.azstateparks.com; 6871 N Hwy 89A; per vehicle Jun-Aug $20, Sep-May $10; 8am-7pm Jun-Aug, 8am-5pm Sep-May;) Swoosh down big rocks into cool creek water at Oak Creek Canyon's star attraction, or walk the hiking trails.

Pink Jeep Tours DRIVING TOUR
(928-282-5000; www.pinkjeep.com; 204 N Hwy 89A; tours from $72) Many companies offer 4WD tours, but Pink Jeep Tours has a great reputation and a vast variety of outings.

Fat Tire Bike Shop MOUNTAIN BIKING
(928-284-0210; www.bike-bean.com; 6020 Hwy 179; half-/full day from $30/40) A mountain-bike rental place with hiking, mellow biking and vortex-gazing.

Sleeping

Sedona hosts many beautiful B&Bs, creekside cabins, motels and full-service resorts. Dispersed camping is not permitted in Red Rock Canyon. The **USFS** (928-282-4119; www.recreation.gov) runs campgrounds (none with hookups) along Hwy Alt 89 in Oak Creek Canyon. All are nestled in the woods just off the road. It costs $20 to camp, but you don't need a Red Rock Pass. Reservations are accepted for all campgrounds except Pine Flat East. Six miles north of town, **Manzanita** has 18 sites, open year-round; 11.5 miles north, **Cave Springs** has 82 sites, and showers; **Pine Flat East and Pine Flat West**, 12.5 miles north, has 57 sites.

Cozy Cactus B&B **$$**
(928-284-0082; www.cozycactus.com; 80 Canyon Circle Dr, Village of Oak Creek; r $165-325;) This five-room B&B is particularly well suited for adventure-loving types ready to enjoy the great outdoors. The Southwest-style abode bumps up against a National Forest Trail and is just around the bend from cyclist-friendly Bell Rock Pathway.

Sedona Motel MOTEL **$**
(928-282-7187; www.thesedonamotel.com; 218 Hwy 179; r $79-89;) Directly south of the Y, this friendly little motel offers big value within walking distance of Tlaquepaque and uptown Sedona. Rooms are basic but clean, but the fantastic red-rock views may be all the luxury you need.

Eating & Drinking

TOP CHOICE **Elote Cafe** MEXICAN **$$**
(www.elotecafe.com; King's Ransom Hotel, 771 Hwy 179; mains $17-22; 5pm-late, Tue-Sat) Some of the best, most authentic Mexican food you'll find in the region, with unusual traditional dishes you won't find elsewhere, such as the fire-roasted corn with lime and cotija cheese, or tender, smoky pork cheeks. No reservations.

Dahl & DiLuca Ristorante ITALIAN **$$**
(928-282-5219; www.dahlanddiluca.com; 2321 Hwy Alt 89; mains $13-33; 5-10pm) Though this lovely Italian place fits perfectly into the groove and color scheme of Sedona, at the same time it feels like the kind of place you'd find in a small Italian seaside town. It's a bustling, welcoming spot serving excellent, authentic Italian food.

Coffee Pot Restaurant BREAKFAST **$**
(www.coffeepotsedona.com; 2050 W Hwy Alt 89; mains $4-11; 6am-2pm;) The go-to breakfast and lunch joint for decades, it's always busy. Meals are reasonably priced and the selection is huge – 101 types of omelet, for a start.

Sedona Memories DELI **$**
(928-282-0032; 321 Jordan Rd; mains $7; 10am-2pm Mon-Fri) This tiny local spot assembles gigantic sandwiches on slabs of homemade bread, with several vegetarian options. Cash only.

SCENIC DRIVES: ARIZONA'S BEST

» **Oak Creek Canyon** A thrilling plunge past swimming holes, rockslides and crimson canyon walls on Hwy 89A between Flagstaff and Sedona.

» **Hwy89/89A Wickenburg to Sedona** The Old West meets the New West on this lazy drive past dude ranches, mining towns, art galleries and stylish wineries.

» **Patagonia-Sonoita Scenic Road** This one's for the birds, and those who like to track them, in Arizona's southern wine country on Hwys 82 and 83.

» **Kayenta-Monument Valley** Become the star of your own Western on an iconic loop past cinematic red rocks in Navajo country just off Hwy 163.

» **Vermilion Cliffs Scenic Road** A solitary drive on Hwy 89A through the Arizona Strip linking condor country, the North Rim and Mormon hideaways.

Information

Visitors center (928-282-7722; www.visitsedona.com; 331 Forest Rd; 8:30am-5pm Mon-Sat, 9am-3pm Sun) Has tourist information and last-minute hotel bookings.

Getting There & Around

The **Sedona-Phoenix Shuttle** (928-282-2066; www.sedona-phoenix-shuttle.com) runs between Phoenix Sky Harbor International Airport and Sedona eight times daily (one-way/round-trip $50/90). Try **Bob's Taxi** (928-282-1234) for local cab service.

JEROME

The childhood game Chutes and Ladders comes to mind on a stroll up and down the stairways of Jerome, a historic mining town clinging to the side of Cleopatra Hill – not always successfully as evidenced by the crumbling Sliding Jail. Shabbily chic, this resurrected ghost town has a romantic feel – especially once the weekend day-trippers clear out. It was known as the 'Wickedest Town in the West' during its late-1800s mining heyday, but today its historic buildings have been lovingly restored and turned into galleries, restaurants, B&Bs and, most recently, wine-tasting rooms.

DON'T MISS

VERDE VALLEY WINE TRAIL

Several new vineyards, wineries and tasting rooms have opened their doors along Hwy 89A and I-17, bringing a dash of style and energy to Cottonwood, Jerome and Cornville.

In Cottonwood, you can float to Verde River–adjacent **Alcantara Vineyards** (☎928-649-8463; 3445 S Grapevine Way) then stroll through Old Town where two new tasting rooms, **Arizona Stronghold** (☎928-639-2789; 1023 N Main St) and **Pillsbury Wine Company** (☎928-639-0646; 1012 N Main St), sit across from each other on Main St. Art, views and wine-sipping converge in Jerome, where there's a tasting room on every level of town, starting with **Bitter Creek Winery/Jerome Gallery** (☎928-634-7033; 240 Hull Ave) near the chamber of commerce visitor center. From there, stroll up to **Caduceus Cellars** (☎928-639-9463; www.cadeceus.org) then end with a final climb to **Jerome Winery** (☎928-639-9067; 403 Clark St), with its inviting patio.

Three wineries with tasting rooms hug a short stretch of Page Springs Rd east of Cornville: bistro-housing **Page Springs Cellars** (☎928-639-3004; 1500 N Page Springs Rd), welcoming **Oak Creek Vineyards** (☎928-649-0290; 1555 N Page Springs Rd) and mellow-rock-playing **Javelina Leap Vineyard** (☎928-649-2681; 1565 Page Springs Rd).

A community hospital during the town's mining years, the **Jerome Grand Hotel** (☎928-634-8200; www.jeromegrandhotel.com; 200 Hill St; r $120-205, ste $270-460;) plays up its past with hospital relics in the hallways and an entertaining ghost tour that kids will enjoy. Wi-fi is available in the lobby only. The adjoining **Asylum Restaurant** (www.asylumrestaurant.com), with its valley and red-rock views, is a breathtaking spot for a cocktail. Downtown, the popular **Spirit Room Bar** (☎928-634-5006; 164 Main St; 10am-2am), is the town's liveliest watering hole. For wine drinkers, there are three tasting rooms just a few steps away.

Even the quesadillas have personality at **15.Quince Grill & Cantina** (☎928-634-7087; www.15quincejerome.com; 363 Main St; mains $8-17; 11am-8pm Mon & Wed, 11am-9pm Tue, Thu & Frid, 8am-9pm Sat, 8am-8pm Sun), a small but festive restaurant serving New Mexican–style dishes with a kick – the joint's known for its chile sauces. For a savory gourmet breakfast or lunch, step into the **Flatiron Café** (www.flatironcafejerome.com; 416 Main St; breakfast $7-13, lunch $9-13; 7am-3pm Wed-Mon) at the Y intersection.

The **chamber of commerce** (☎928-634-2900; www.jeromechamber.com; Hull Ave, Hwy 89A north after the Flatiron Café split; 11am-3pm), inside a small trailer, offers tourist information on the local attractions and art scene.

PRESCOTT

With a historic Victorian-era downtown and a colorful Wild West history, Prescott, Arizona's first territorial capital and home of the world's oldest rodeo, feels like the Midwest meets cowboy country. Residents are a diverse mix of retirees, artists and families looking for a taste of yesteryear's wholesomeness. The town boasts more than 500 buildings on the National Register of Historic Places. Along the plaza is **Whiskey Row**, an infamous strip of old saloons that still serve up their fair share of booze.

Just south of downtown, the fun-loving **Motor Lodge** (☎928-717-0157; www.themotorlodge.com; 503 S Montezuma St; r $89-139;) welcomes guests with Fat Tire beers and 12 snazzy bungalows arranged around a central driveway – it's indie lodging at its best.

For breakfast, mosey into the friendly **Lone Spur Café** (106 W Gurley St; mains $7-16; 8am-2pm), where you always order your breakfast with a biscuit and a side of sausage gravy – you can't count calories at a place this good. Portions are huge, and there are three bottles of hot sauce on every table. The cool, loftlike **Raven Café** (www.ravencafe.com; 142 N Cortez St; breakfast $5-9, lunch & dinner $8-18; 7:30am-11pm Mon-Wed, 7:30am-midnight Thu-Sat, 8am-3pm Sun;) offers a mostly organic menu of sandwiches, burgers, salads and a few 'big plates.' And there are 30 beers on tap.

On Whiskey Row, the **Palace** (www.historicpalace.com; 120 S Montezuma St; 11am-11pm) is an atmospheric place to drink; you enter through swinging saloon doors into a big room anchored by a Brunswick bar (saved during a 1900 fire). The divey **Bird Cage Saloon** (www.birdcagesaloon.com; 148 Whiskey Row;

⏲10am-2am) is filled with stuffed birds, and it merits a look-see.

The **chamber of commerce** (☎928-445-2000; www.visit-prescott.com; 117 W Goodwin; ⏲9am-5pm Mon-Fri, 10am-2pm Sat) has tourist information, including a handy walking tour pamphlet ($1) of historical Prescott.

Prescott Transit Authority (☎928-445-5470; www.prescotttransit.com; 820 E Sheldon St) runs buses to/from Phoenix airport (one-way adult/child $28/15, two hours, 16 daily) and Flagstaff ($22, 1½ hours, daily). Also offers a local taxi service.

Grand Canyon National Park

Why do folks become giddy when describing the Grand Canyon? One peek over the edge makes it clear. The canyon captivates travelers because of its sheer immensity; it's a tableau that reveals the earth's history layer by dramatic layer. Mother Nature adds artistic details – rugged plateaus, crumbly spires, shadowed ridges – that flirt and catch your eye as the sun crosses the sky.

Snaking along its floor are 277 miles of the Colorado River, which has carved the canyon over the past six million years and exposed rocks up to two billion years old – half the age of the earth.

The two rims of the Grand Canyon offer quite different experiences; they lie more than 200 miles apart by road and are rarely visited on the same trip. Most visitors choose the South Rim with its easy access, wealth of services and vistas that don't disappoint. The quieter North Rim has its own charms; at 8200ft elevation (1000ft higher than the South Rim), its cooler temperatures support wildflower meadows and tall, thick stands of aspen and spruce.

June is the driest month, July and August the wettest. January has average overnight lows of 13°F (-11°C) to 20°F (-7°C) and daytime highs around 40°F (4°C). Summer temperatures inside the canyon regularly soar above 100°F (38°C). While the South Rim is open year-round, most visitors come between late May and early September. The North Rim is open from mid-May to mid-October.

ℹ Information

The park's most developed area is Grand Canyon Village, 6 miles north of the South Rim Entrance Station. The only entrance to the North Rim lies 30 miles south of Jacob Lake on Hwy 67. The North Rim and South Rim are 215 miles apart by car, 21 miles on foot through the canyon, or 10 miles as the condor flies.

The **park entrance ticket** (vehicles/cyclists & pedestrians $25/12) is valid for seven days and can be used at both rims.

All overnight hikes and backcountry camping in the park require a permit. The **Backcountry Information Center** (☎928-638-7875; fax 928-638-7875; www.nps.gov/grca; Grand Canyon Village; ⏲8am-noon & 1-5pm, phone staffed 1-5pm Mon-Fri) accepts applications for backpacking permits ($10, plus $5 per person per night) for the current month and following four months only. Your chances are decent if you apply early (four months in advance for spring and fall) and provide alternative hiking itineraries. Reservations are accepted in person or by mail or fax. For more information see www.nps.gov/grca/planyourvisit/backcountry.htm.

If you arrive without a permit, head to the office, by Maswik Lodge, to join the waiting list.

SOUTH RIM In addition to the visitor centers listed below, information is available inside the park at Yavapai Observation Station, Verkamp's Visitor Center, El Tovar, Tusayan Ruins & Museum and Desert View Information Center.

Grand Canyon Visitor Center (☎928-638-7644; ⏲8am-5pm) Three hundred yards behind Mather Point, a large plaza encompasses this visitor center and the Books & More Store. On the plaza, bulletin boards display information about ranger programs, the weather, tours and hikes. The center's bright, spacious interior includes a ranger-staffed information desk and a lecture hall, where rangers offer daily talks.

TUSAYAN The **National Geographic Visitor Center** (☎928-638-2468; www.explorethecanyon.com; Hwy 64, Tusayan; adult/child $13/10; ⏲8am-10pm) is in Tusayan, 7 miles south of Grand Canyon Village; pay your $25 vehicle entrance fee here and spare yourself a potentially long wait at the park entrance, especially in summer. The IMAX theater screens the terrific 34-minute film *Grand Canyon – The Hidden Secrets*.

NORTH RIM **North Rim Visitor Center** (☎928-638-7864; www.nps.gov/grca; ⏲8am-6pm, closed mid-Oct–mid-May) Adjacent to the Grand Canyon Lodge, with maps, books, trail guides and current conditions.

SOUTH RIM

To escape the throngs, visit during fall or winter, especially on weekdays. You'll also gain some solitude by walking a short distance away from the viewpoints on the Rim Trail or by heading into the canyon itself.

Grand Canyon Region

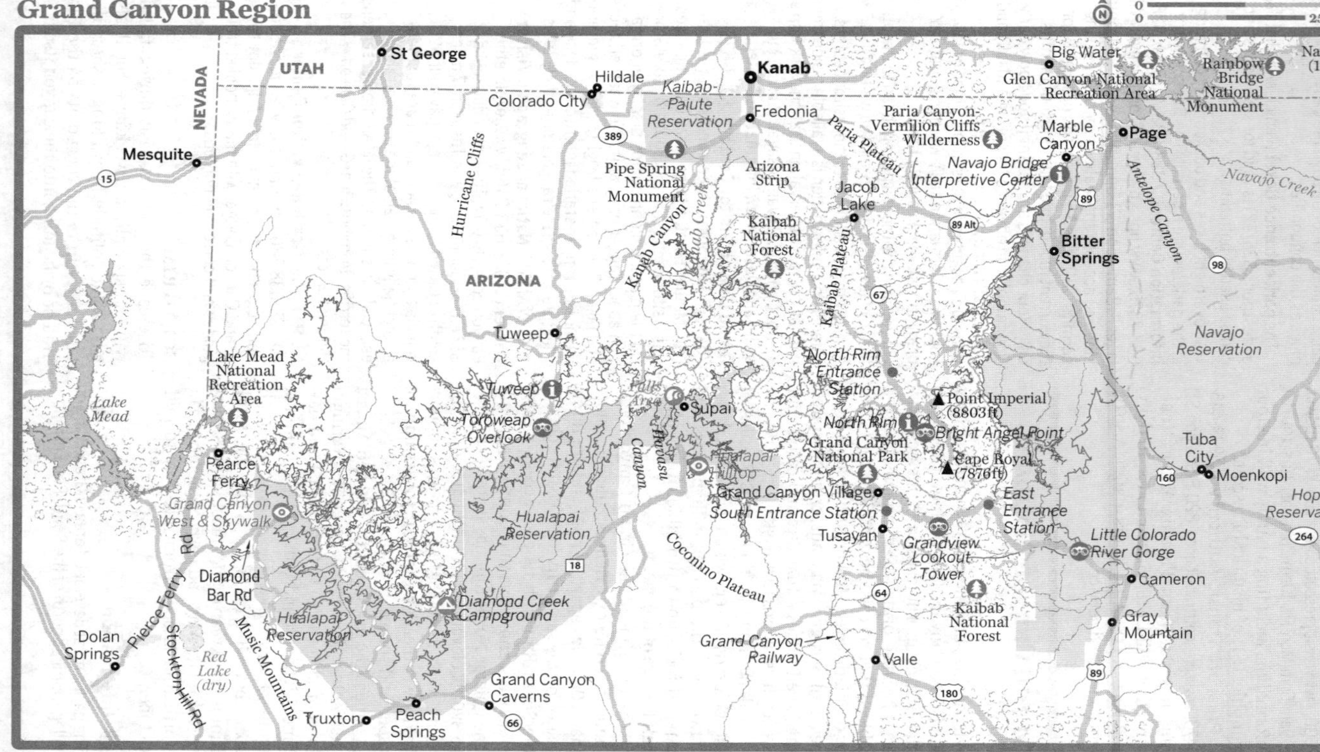

Sights & Activities

DRIVING & HIKING

A **scenic route** follows the rim on the west side of the village along Hermit Rd. Closed to private vehicles March through November, the road is serviced by the free park shuttle bus; cycling is encouraged because of the relatively light traffic. Stops offer spectacular views, and interpretive signs explain canyon features.

Hiking along the South Rim is among park visitors' favorite pastimes, with options for every skill level. The **Rim Trail** is the most popular, and easiest, walk in the park. It dips in and out of the scrubby pines of Kaibab National Forest and connects a series of scenic points and historical sights over 12 miles. Portions are paved, and every viewpoint is accessed by one of the three shuttle routes. The new **Trail of Time** exhibit borders the Rim Trail just west of Yavapai Observation Station. Here, every meter of the trail represents one million years of geologic history, with exhibits providing the details.

Desert View Drive starts to the east of Grand Canyon Village and follows the canyon rim for 26 miles to Desert View, the east entrance of the park. Pullouts offer spectacular views, and interpretive signs explain canyon features and geology.

The most popular of the corridor trails is the beautiful **Bright Angel Trail**. The steep and scenic 8-mile descent to the Colorado River is punctuated with four logical turnaround spots. Summer heat can be crippling; day hikers should either turn around at one of the two resthouses (a 3- to 6-mile round-trip) or hit the trail at dawn to safely make the longer hikes to Indian Garden and Plateau Point (9.2 and 12.2 miles round-trip respectively). Hiking to the river in one day should not be attempted. The trailhead is just wet of Bright Angel Lodge.

The **South Kaibab** is arguably one of the park's prettiest trails, combining stunning scenery and unobstructed 360-degree views with every step. Steep, rough and wholly exposed, summer ascents can be dangerous, and during this season rangers discourage all but the shortest day hikes – otherwise it's a 6-mile, grueling round-trip. Turn around at **Cedar Ridge**, perhaps the park's finest short day hike.

Individuals and groups who prefer a more in-depth experience while still giving something back can apply for various programs with **Grand Canyon Volunteers** (☎928-774-7488; www.gcvolunteers.org). One- and multiday programs include wildlife monitoring, native plant restoration and forest surveying.

CYCLING

Bright Angel Bicycles BICYCLE RENTAL
(☎928-814-8704; www.bikegrandcanyon.com; full day adult/child $35/25; ⏰8am-6pm May-Sep, 10am-4:30pm Mar-Apr & Oct-Nov, weather permitting) Renting 'comfort cruiser' bikes, the friendly folks here custom-fit each bike to the individual. Rates include helmet and bicycle-lock rental.

Tours

Xanterra HORSEBACK RIDING
(☎303-297-2757; www.grandcanyonlodges.com/mule-rides-716.html) Park tours are run by Xanterra, which has information desks at Bright Angel, Maswik and Yavapai Lodges. Various daily bus tours (tickets from $20) are offered.

Due to erosion concerns, the NPS has limited inner-canyon mule rides to those traveling all the way to Phantom Ranch. Rather than going below the rim, three-hour day trips ($119) now take riders along the rim, through the ponderosa, piñon and juniper forest to the Abyss overlook. Overnight trips (one/two people $482/850) and two-night trips (one/two people $701/1170) follow the Bright Angel Trail to the river, travel east on the River Trail and cross the river on the Kaibab Suspension Bridge. Riders spend the night at Phantom Ranch.

If you arrive at the park and want to join a mule trip the following day, ask about availability at the transportation desk at Bright Angel Lodge.

Sleeping

Advance or same-day reservations are required for the South Rim's six lodges, which are operated by **Xanterra** (☎888-297-2757; www.grandcanyonlodges.com). Use this phone number to make advance reservations (highly recommended) at any of the places (including Phantom Ranch) listed here. For same-day reservations or to reach a guest, call the **South Rim switchboard** (☎928-638-2631). If you can't find accommodations in the national park, try Tusayan (at South Rim Entrance Station), Valle (31 miles south), Cameron (53 miles east) or Williams (about 60 miles south).

The **National Park Service** (☎877-444-6777; www.recreation.gov) operates Mather and Desert View Campgrounds. All campgrounds and lodges are open year-round except Desert View, which closes from mid-October to mid-May.

TOP CHOICE **El Tovar Hotel** LODGE $$$
(d $178-273, ste $335-426; ❄📶) Wide, inviting porches wreathe the rambling wooden structure, offering pleasant spots to people-watch and admire canyon views – even if you're not a guest. The public spaces show the lodgelike, genteel elegance of the park's heyday. The standard rooms are small but first-class. Suites are fantastic.

Bright Angel Lodge LODGE $
(d with/without private bath $92/81, cabins $113-178; ❄@📶) Built in 1935, the log-and-stone Bright Angel offers historic charm and refurbished rooms, the cheapest of which have shared bathrooms. Don't expect a TV in these very basic rooms (think university dorm room), but rim cabins have better views than TV.

Phantom Ranch LODGE $
(☎888-297-2757; dm $43; ❄) It ain't the Four Seasons, but this summer-campy complex has its charms. Located at the bottom of the canyon, the ranch has basic cabins sleeping four to 10 people and segregated dorms. The ranch serves family-style meals (breakfast/dinner from $21/27) – reserve well in advance. No sleeping reservation? Show up at the Bright Angel Lodge transportation desk at 6am to snag a canceled bunk.

Mather Campground CAMPGROUND $
(☎877-444-6777; www.recreation.gov; Grand Canyon Village; tent & RV sites $18) Well-dispersed, relatively peaceful sites amid piñon and juniper trees. There are pay showers and laundry facilities nearby, drinking water, toilets, grills and a small general store. First-come, first-served during winter months.

Desert View Campground CAMPGROUND $
(tent & RV sites $12; ⏲mid-May–mid-Oct) Near the East Entrance Station, 26 miles east of Grand Canyon Village, this first-come, first-served campground is a quieter alternative to Mather. A small cafeteria-snack shop serves meals.

Also recommended:

Maswik Lodge LODGE $$
(d South/North $92/173, cabins $92; ❄@📶) Set away from the rim, but with a sports bar and cafeteria.

Kachina Lodge & Thunderbird Lodge LODGE $$
(d streetside/rimside $173/184; ❄) Decent motel-style rooms in a central location. Some rooms have canyon views.

Yavapai Lodge LODGE $$
(d West/East $114/163; ⏲Apr-Oct; ❄📶) Basic lodging amid peaceful piñon and juniper forest.

Trailer Village CAMPGROUND $
(Grand Canyon Village; tent & RV sites $32) Camp here if everywhere else is full. You can reserve well in advance or same day.

Eating & Drinking

El Tovar Dining Room INTERNATIONAL $$$
(☎928-638-2631, ext 6432; El Tovar; mains $18-31; ⏲6:30-11am, 11:30am-2pm & 5-10pm) A stone's throw from the canyon's edge, it has the best views of any restaurant in the state, if not the country. The grand stone and dark-oak dining room warms the soul like an upscale lodge of yore, and the food, especially the steaks, makes the trip worthwhile. If you're not seated near a window, head to the verandah of the El Tovar Lounge afterward for a guaranteed Grand Canyon vista.

Bright Angel Lounge BAR $$
(Bright Angel Lodge; mains $10-26; ⏲11:30am-3pm Mar-Oct & 4:30-10pm Mar-Dec) Perfect for those who want to unwind with a burger and a beer without cleaning up too much; a fun place to relax at night when the lack of windows and dark decor aren't such a big deal. It's beside the charmless Bright Angel Restaurant.

Arizona Room AMERICAN $$
(Bright Angel Lodge; mains $8-28; ⏲11:30am-3pm Mar-Oct & 4:30-10pm Mar-Dec) Antler chandeliers hang from the ceiling and picture windows overlook the canyon. Mains include steak, chicken and fish dishes. No reservations; there's often a wait.

Also recommended:

Maswik Cafeteria CAFETERIA $
(Maswik Lodge; mains $4-10; ⏲6am-10pm) Another cafeteria-style place.

Canyon Cafe at Yavapai Lodge CAFETERIA $
(Yavapai Lodge; mains $4-10; ⏲6am-10pm) Cafeteria food, service and seating.

Canyon Village Marketplace MARKET $
(Market Plaza; ⏲8am-8pm) Stock up on groceries or hit the deli.

Getting There & Around

Most people arrive at the canyon in private vehicles or on a tour. Parking can be a chore in Grand Canyon Village. Under the new Park-n-Ride program, summer visitors can buy a park ticket at the **National Geographic Visitor Center** (p351), park their vehicle at a designated lot, then hop aboard a free park shuttle that follows the **Tusayan Route** (8am-9:30pm mid-May–early Sep) to the Grand Canyon Visitor Center inside the park. Park passes are also okay for this option. The trip takes 20 minutes, and the first bus departs Tusayan at 8am. The last bus from the park leaves at 9:30pm.

Inside the park, free **park shuttles** operate along three routes: around Grand Canyon Village: west along Hermits Rest Route and east along Kaibab Trail Route. Buses typically run at least twice per hour, from one hour before sunset to one hour afterward.

A free shuttle from Bright Angel Lodge during the summer months, the **Hiker's Express** (4am, 5am, 6am Jun-Aug, 5am, 6am, 7am May & Sep) has pickups at the Backcountry Information Center and Grand Canyon Visitor Center, and then heads to the South Kaibab trailhead.

NORTH RIM

Head here for blessed solitude in nature's bountiful bosom; only 10% of park visitors make the trek. Meadows are thick with wildflowers and dense clusters of willowy aspen and spruce trees, and the air is often crisp, the skies big and blue.

Facilities on the North Rim are closed from mid-October to mid-May, although you can drive into the park and stay at the campground until the first snow closes the road from Jacob Lake.

Call the **North Rim Switchboard** (928-638-2612) to reach facilities on the North Rim.

Sights & Activities

The short and easy paved trail (0.5 miles) to **Bright Angel Point** is a canyon must. Beginning from the back porch of Grand Canyon Lodge, it goes to a narrow finger of an overlook with fabulous views.

The **North Kaibab Trail** is the North Rim's only maintained rim-to-river trail and connects with trails to the South Rim. The first 4.7 miles are the steepest, dropping 3050ft to **Roaring Springs** – a popular all-day hike. If you prefer a shorter day hike below the rim, walk just 0.75 miles down to **Coconino Overlook** or 2 miles to the **Supai Tunnel** to get a taste of steep inner-canyon hiking. The 28-mile round-trip to the Colorado River is a multiday affair.

Canyon Trail Rides (435-679-8665; www.canyonrides.com; Grand Canyon Lodge; mid-May–mid-Oct) offers one-hour ($40) and half-day ($75, minimum age 10 years) mule trips. Of the half-day trips, one is along the rim and the other drops into the Canyon on the North Kaibab Trail.

Sleeping

Accommodations are limited to one lodge and one campground. If these are booked, try your luck 80 miles north in Kanab, UT, or 84 miles northeast in Lees Ferry. There are also campgrounds in the Kaibab National Forest north of the park.

North Rim Campground CAMPGROUND $
(928-638-7814; www.recreation.gov; tent sites $6-18, RV sites $8-25) This campground, 1.5 miles north of Grand Canyon Lodge, offers pleasant sites on level ground blanketed in pine needles. There is water, a store, a snack bar and coin-operated showers and laundry facilities, but no hookups. Hikers and cross-country skiers can use the campground during winter months if they have a backcountry permit. Reservations accepted.

Grand Canyon Lodge HISTORIC HOTEL $$
(928-638-2611/12 same-day reservations, 480-337-1320 reservations outside the USA; www.grandcanyonlodgenorth.com; r $116, cabins $121-170; mid-May–mid-Oct;) Made of wood, stone and glass, the lodge is the kind of place you imagine should be perched on the rim. Rustic yet modern cabins make up the majority of accommodations. The most expensive cabins offer two rooms, a porch and beautiful rim views. The canyon views from the Sun Room are stunning, the lobby regal. Reserve far in advance.

Eating & Drinking

The lodge will also prepare sack lunches ($11), ready for pickup at 6:30am, for those wanting to picnic on the trail.

Grand Canyon Lodge Dining Room AMERICAN $$
(928-638-2611; mains $12-24; 6:30am-10am, 11:30am-2:30pm & 4:45-9:45pm mid-May–mid-Oct) The windows are so huge that you can sit anywhere and get a good view. The menu includes several vegetarian options and Western treats such as Utah Ruby trout and bison flank steak. Dinner reservations are required, and it's neighbors with the atmospheric Rough Rider Saloon, full of

memorabilia from the country's most adventurous president.

Grand Canyon Cookout Experience AMERICAN **$$**
(928-638-2611; adult/child $30-35/12-22; 6-7:45pm Jun-Sep;) This chuck-wagon-style cookout featuring barbecue and cornbread is more of an event than a meal. Kids love it. Make arrangements at the Grand Canyon Lodge.

Information

North Rim Visitor Center (928-638-7888; www.nps.gov/grca; 8am-6pm, closed mid-Oct–mid-May) Beside Grand Canyon Lodge, this is the place to get information on the park, and the starting point for ranger-led nature walks and evening programs.

Getting There & Around

The **Transcanyon Shuttle** (928-638-2820; www.trans-canyonshuttle.com; one-way/round-trip $80/150; 7am mid-May–mid-Oct) departs daily from Grand Canyon Lodge for the South Rim (five hours) and is perfect for rim-to-rim hikers. Reserve at least one or two weeks in advance. A complimentary **hikers' shuttle** to the North Kaibab Trail departs at both 5:45am and 7:10am from Grand Canyon Lodge. You must sign up for it at the front desk; if no one signs up the night before, it will not run.

Around the Grand Canyon

HAVASU CANYON

Even after the massive flooding that hit the area in August 2008 and closed it down for 10 months, Havasupai is still one of the most beautiful places in the canyon.

On the Havasupai Indian Reservation, about 195 miles west of the South Rim, the valley around Havasu Canyon has spring-fed waterfalls and sparkling swimming holes. The falls lie 10 miles below the rim, accessed via a moderately challenging hiking trail, and trips require an overnight stay in the nearby village of Supai.

Supai offers two sleeping options and reservations must be secured before starting out. There's a $35 entrance fee for all overnight guests. The **Havasupai Campground** (928-448-2121/2141; per night per person $17), 2 miles north of Supai, has primitive campsites along a creek. In addition, every camper must pay a $5 environmental fee, refunded if you pack out trash. The **Havasupai Lodge** (928-448-2111/2101; www.havasupaitribe.com/lodge.html; r $145;) has motel rooms with canyon views but no phones or TVs. Check in by 5pm, when the lobby closes. A village cafe serves meals and accepts credit cards.

Continue through Havasu Canyon to the waterfalls and blue-green swimming holes. If you don't want to hike to Supai, call the lodge or campground to arrange for a mule or horse (round-trip to lodge/campground $120/187) to carry you there. Rides depart from Hualapai Hilltop, where the hiking trail begins. The road to Hualapai Hilltop is 7 miles east of Peach Springs off Route 66. Look for the marked turnoff and follow the road for 62 miles.

GRAND CANYON WEST

Grand Canyon West is not part of Grand Canyon National Park, which is about 215 driving miles to the east. Run by the Hualapai Nation, the remote site is 70 miles northeast of Kingman, and the last 9 miles are unpaved and unsuitable for RVs.

Grand Canyon Skywalk PARK
(928-769-2636; www.grandcanyonwest.com; per person $71; 7am-7pm Apr-Sep, 8am-5pm Oct-Mar) A slender see-through glass horseshoe levitates over a 4000ft chasm of the Grand Canyon. The only way to visit is to purchase a package tour. A hop-on, hop-off shuttle travels the loop road to scenic points along the rim. Tours can include lunch, horse-drawn wagon rides from an ersatz Western town, and informal Native American performances.

Northeastern Arizona

Between the brooding buttes of Monument Valley, the blue waters of Lake Powell and the fossilized logs of the Petrified Forest National Park are photogenic lands locked in ancient history. Inhabited by Native Americans for centuries, this region is largely made up of reservation land called Navajo Nation, which spills into surrounding states. The Hopi reservation is here as well, completely surrounded by Navajo land.

LAKE POWELL

The country's second-largest artificial reservoir and part of the **Glen Canyon National Recreation Area**, Lake Powell stretches between Utah and Arizona. Set amid striking red-rock formations, sharply cut canyon and dramatic desert scenery, it's water-sports heaven. South of the lake and looking out over a pleasant stretch of the Colorado River is **Lee's Ferry** (tent & RV sites $12), a pleasant stopover with same-day and advance reservations.

The region's central town is **Page**, and Hwy 89 forms the main strip. The **Carl Hayden Visitor Center** (928-608-6404; www.nps.gov/glca; 8am-6pm late May–early Sep, 8am-4:30pm early Sep–late May) is located at Glen Canyon Dam, 2.5 miles north of Page. **Tours** (928-608-6072; adult/child $5/2.50) run by the Glen Canyon Natural History Association take you inside the dam.

To visit photogenic **Antelope Canyon** (www.navajonationparks.org/htm/antelopecanyon.htm), a stunning sandstone slot canyon with two main parts, you must join a tour. **Upper Antelope Canyon** is easier to navigate and more touristed. Several tour companies offer trips into upper Antelope Canyon; try **Roger Ekis's Antelope Canyon Tours** (928-645-9102; www.antelopecanyon.com; 22 S Lake Powell Blvd; adult/child 5-12 $32/20). The more strenuous **Lower Antelope Canyon** sees much smaller crowds.

Chain hotels line Hwy 89 in Page and a number of independent places line 8th Ave. The owner encourages guests to feel right at home at **Debbie's Hide A Way** (928-645-1224; www.debbieshideaway.com; 117 8th Ave; ste $129-199;), where all accommodation is in basic suites. Suites include up to seven people, and there are free laundry facilities.

Six miles north of Page and with a direct view of the lake, **Lake Powell Resort** (928-645-2433; www.lakepowell.com; 100 Lake Shore Dr; RV sites $43, d $160-260, r $170-190, ste $250-280;) offers rooms, camping, houseboat rentals and a dining room with panoramic views. Wi-fi available in lobby only.

For breakfast in Page, the **Ranch House Grille** (819 N Navajo Dr; mains $6-13; 6am-3pm) has good food, huge portions and fast service. A chalkboard menu includes excellent burgers and hot or cold submarines at **Slackers** (www.slackersqualitygrub.com; 810 N Navajo Dr; mains $6-12; 11am-8pm Mon-Sat, vary seasonally), which gets crowded at lunch.

NAVAJO NATION

The wounds are healing but the scars remain on Arizona's Navajo lands, a testament to the uprooting and forced relocation of thousands of Native Americans to reservations.

Amid the isolation is some of North America's most spectacular scenery, including Monument Valley, cultural pride remain strong and many still speak Navajo as their first language. The Navajo rely heavily on tourism; visitors can help keep their heritage alive by staying on reservation land or purchasing their renowned crafts. Stopping at roadside stalls is a nice way to make purchases for personal interaction and making sure money goes straight into the artisan's pocket.

Unlike Arizona, the Navajo Nation observes Mountain daylight saving time. During summer, the reservation is one hour ahead of Arizona.

CAMERON

Cameron is the gateway to the east entrance of the Grand Canyon's South Rim, but the other reason people come here is for **Cameron Trading Post** (www.camerontradingpost.com), just north of the Hwy 64 turnoff to the Grand Canyon. Food, lodging, a gift shop and a post office are in this historic settlement. It's one of the few worthwhile places to stop on Hwy 89 between Flagstaff and Page.

CANYON DE CHELLY NATIONAL MONUMENT

This many-fingered canyon (pronounced *duh-shay*) contains several beautiful Ancestral Puebloan sites important to Navajo history, including ancient cliff dwellings. Families still farm the land, wintering on the rims, then moving to hogans on the canyon floor in spring and summer. The canyon is private Navajo property administered by the NPS. Enter hogans only with a guide and don't photograph people without their permission.

Most of the bottom of the canyon is off-limits to visitors unless you hire a guide. **Thunderbird Lodge** (928-674-5841; www.tbirdlodge.com; d Mar-Oct $115-171, Nov-Feb $66-95;) is the place to book a tour (from $46/35 per adult/child) into the canyon. The lodge also boasts comfortable rooms, an ATM and an inexpensive cafeteria serving tasty Navajo and American meals ($5 to $21).

The Canyon de Chelly **visitor center** (928-674-5500; www.nps.gov/cach; 8am-5pm) is three miles from Rte 191 in the small village of Chinle. Near the visitor center, the **campground** has 96 large sites on a first-come, first-served basis, with water but no showers. At press time, the Navajo Nation was in the process of taking over campground management from the park service and implementing an overnight fee.

WORTH A TRIP

HOPI NATION

Descendants of the Ancestral Puebloans, the Hopi are one of the most untouched tribes in the United States. Their village of Old Oraibi may be the oldest continuously inhabited settlement in North America.

Hopi land is surrounded by the Navajo Nation. Hwy 264 runs past the three mesas (First, Second and Third Mesa) that form the heart of the Hopi reservation. On Second Mesa, some 10 miles west of First Mesa, the **Hopi Cultural Center Restaurant & Inn** (928-734-2401; www.hopiculturalcenter.com; breakfast & lunch $8-12, dinner $8-20; breakfast, lunch & dinner;) is as visitor-oriented as things get on the Hopiland reservation. It provides food and lodging (doubles $85 to $105), and there's the small **Hopi Museum** (928-734-6650; adult/child $3/1; 8am-5pm Mon-Fri, 9am-3pm Sat), filled with historic photographs and introductory cultural exhibits.

Photographs, sketching and recording are not allowed.

FOUR CORNERS NAVAJO TRIBAL PARK

Don't be shy: do a spread eagle at the **four corners marker** (928-871-6647; www.navajonationparks.org; admission $3; 7am-8pm May-Aug, 8am-5pm Sep-Apr), the middle-of-nowhere landmark that's looking spiffy after a 2010 renovation of the central plaza. The only spot in the US where you can straddle four states – Arizona, New Mexico, Colorado, Utah – it makes a good photograph, even if it's not 100% accurate. According to government surveyors, the marker is almost 2000ft east of where it should be (but it is the legally recognized border point, regardless).

MONUMENT VALLEY NAVAJO TRIBAL PARK

With flaming-red buttes and impossibly slender spires bursting to the heavens, the Monument Valley landscape off Hwy 163 has starred in countless Hollywood Westerns and looms large in many a road-trip daydream.

For up-close views of the towering formations, you'll need to visit the **Monument Valley Navajo Tribal Park** (435-727-5874; www.navajonationparks.org; per person $5; 6am-8pm May-Sep, 8am-4:30pm Oct-Apr), where a rough and unpaved scenic driving loop covers 17 miles of stunning valley views. You can drive it in your own vehicle or take a tour ($65, 2½ hours) through one of the kiosks in the parking lot (tours enter areas private vehicles can't).

Inside the tribal park is the **View Hotel at Monument Valley** (435-727-5555; www.monumentvalleyview.com; Hwy 163; r $219-229, ste $299-319;). Built in harmony with the landscape, the sandstone-colored hotel blends naturally with its surroundings, and most of the 96 rooms have private balconies facing the monuments. The Navajo-based specialties at the adjoining restaurant (mains $13 to $23, no alcohol) are mediocre, but the red-rock panorama is stunning. Wi-fi is available in the lobby. A gift shop and small museum are within the hotel complex. Visitors can also overnight in the park's de facto **campground** (per vehicle $10). It's basically just a parking lot, but the awesome sunrise view makes up for the lack of amenities.

The historic **Goulding's Lodge** (435-727-3235; www.gouldings.com; r $185-205, tent sites $25, RV sites $25-44, cabins $79;), just across the border in Utah, offers lodge rooms, camping and small cabins. In Kayenta, 20 miles south, the two-story **Kayenta Monument Valley Inn** (928-697-3221; www.kayentamonumentvalleyinn.com; junction Hwys 160 & 163; r $229-249;) doesn't look like much from the outside, but the rooms flash a little modern style and come with big flat-screen TVs.

WINSLOW

'Standing on a corner in Winslow, Arizona, such a fine sight to see...' Sound familiar? Thanks to the Eagles' twangy 1970s tune 'Take It Easy,' otherwise nondescript Winslow has earned its wings in pop-culture heaven. A small **park** (www.standinonthecorner.com; 2nd St) on Route 66 at Kinsley Ave pays homage to the band.

Just 50 miles east of Petrified Forest National Park, Winslow is a good regional base. Old motels border Route 66, and eateries sprinkle the downtown. The inviting 1929 **La Posada** (928-289-4366; www.laposada.org; 303 E 2nd; r $109-169;) is a restored hacienda designed by star architect du jour Mary Jane Colter. Elaborate tilework, glass-and-tin chandeliers, Navajo rugs and other details accent its palatial Western-style elegance. The on-site restaurant, the much-lauded **Turquoise Room** (928-289-2888; breakfast

$6-11, lunch $9-13, dinner $17-32; ⌚7am-9pm), serves the best meals between Flagstaff and Albuquerque; dishes have a neo-Southwestern flair.

PETRIFIED FOREST NATIONAL PARK

The multicolored Painted Desert here is strewn with fossilized logs predating the dinosaurs. This **national park** (☎928-524-6228; www.nps.gov/pefo; per vehicle $10; ⌚7am-7pm May-Aug, 7am-6pm Mar, Apr & Sep, 8am-5pm Oct-Feb) is an extraordinary site. The hard-to-miss **visitor center** is just half a mile north of I-40 and has maps and information on guided tours and science lectures.

The park straddles I-40 at exit 311, 25 miles east of Holbrook. From this exit, a 28-mile paved park road offers a splendid **scenic drive**. There are no campsites, but a number of short trails, ranging from less than a mile to two miles, pass through the best stands of petrified rock and ancient Native American dwellings in the park. Those prepared for rugged backcountry camping need to pick up a free permit at the visitor center.

Western Arizona

The Colorado River is alive with sun worshippers at Lake Havasu City, while Route 66 offers well-preserved stretches of classic highway near Kingman. South of the I-10, the wild, empty landscape is among the most barren in the West. If you're already here, there are some worthwhile sites, but there's nothing worth planning an itinerary around unless you're a Route 66 or boating fanatic.

KINGMAN & AROUND

Faded motels and gas stations galore grace Kingman's main drag, but several turn-of-the-19th-century buildings remain. If you're following the Route 66 trail (aka Andy Devine Ave here) or looking for cheap lodging, it's worth a stroll.

Pick up maps and brochures at the historic **Powerhouse Visitor Center** (☎928-753-6106; www.kingmantourism.org; 120 W Andy Devine Ave; ⌚8am-5pm), which has an impressive **Route 66 museum** (☎928-753-9889; adult/child/senior $4/free/3; ⌚9am-5pm).

A cool neon sign marks draws road-trippers to the **Hilltop Motel** (☎928-753-2198; www.hilltopmotelaz.com; 1901 E Andy Devine Ave; s/d $42/46; ❄@🛜🏊) on Route 66. Rooms are a bit of a throwback, but are well kept, and the views are superb. Pets (dogs only) stay for $5. Just down the road, the **Dambar Steakhouse** (☎928-753-3523; 1960 E Andy Devine Ave; lunch $6-11, dinner $10-22; ⌚lunch & dinner; 👪) is a local landmark serving giant steaks in Old West bad-boy environs – but kiddies will be just fine at this spit-and-sawdust saloon with cowhide tablecloths.

ROADSIDE KITSCH ON ROUTE 66

Route 66 enthusiasts will find 400 miles of pavement stretching across Arizona, including the longest uninterrupted portion of old road left in the country, between Seligman and Topock. The Mother Road connects the dots between Winslow's windblown streets, Williams' 1940s-vintage downtown, Kingman's mining settlements and gun-slinging Oatman, with plenty of kitschy sights, listed here from west to east, along the way.

» **Wild Burros of Oatman** Mules beg for treats in the middle of the road.

» **Grand Canyon Caverns Tour & Underground Motel Room** A guided tour 21 stories underground loops past mummified bobcats, civil-defense supplies and a $700 motel room.

» **Burma Shave signs** Red-and-white ads from a bygone era between Grand Canyon Caverns and Seligman.

» **Seligman's Snow-Cap Drive In** Prankish burger and ice-cream joint open since 1953.

» **Meteor Crater** A 550ft-deep pockmark that's nearly 1 mile across, near Flagstaff.

» **Holbrook's Wigwam Motel** Concrete wigwams with hickory logpole furniture.

For more information, visit **Historic Route 66 Association of Arizona** (www.azrt66.com).

LAKE HAVASU CITY

When the city of London auctioned off its 1831 bridge in the late 1960s, developer Robert McCulloch bought it, took it apart, shipped it, and then reassembled it at Lake Havasu City, which sits along a dammed-up portion of the Colorado River. The place attracts hordes of young spring-breakers and weekend warriors who come to play in the water and party hard. An 'English Village' of pseudo-British pubs and tourist gift shops surrounds the bridge and houses the **visitor center** (☎928-855-5655; www.golakehavasu.com; 420 English Village; ⏰9am-5pm; @📶) where you can pick up tourist information and access the internet.

The hippest hotel in town is **Heat** (☎928-854-2833; www.heathotel.com; 1420 McCulloch Blvd; r $139-159, ste $191-256; ❄📶), a slick boutique property where the front desk doubles as a bar. Rooms are contemporary and most have private patios with views of London Bridge. For home-cooked Italian, head to **Angelina's Italian Kitchen** (☎928-680-3868; 2137 W Acoma Blvd; mains $8-27; ⏰dinner Tue-Sat), a very busy hole-in-the-wall on an industrial stretch east of downtown. For a hearty, open-air breakfast, rise and shine at the **Red Onion** (2013 N McCulloch Blvd; mains $7-11; ⏰8am-2pm daily, 4-8pm Thu & Fri), a popular eatery where the menu is loaded with omelets and diet-busting fare.

Tucson

Arizona's second-largest city is set in the Sonoran Desert, full of rolling, sandy hills and crowds of cacti. The vibe here is ramshackle-cool and cozy compared with the shiny vastness of Phoenix. A college town, Tucson (the 'c' is silent) is home turf to the 38,000-strong University of Arizona (U of A) and was an artsy, dress-down kind of place before that was the cool thing to be. Eclectic shops and scores of funky restaurants and bars flourish in this arid ground. Tucsonans are proud of the city's geographic and cultural proximity to Mexico (65 highway miles south); more than 35% of the population is of Mexican or Central American descent.

Sights & Activities

Downtown Tucson and the historic district are east of I-10 exit 258. About a mile northeast of downtown is the U of A campus; 4th Ave is the main drag here, packed with cafes, bars and interesting shops.

Saguaro National Park PARK

(www.nps.gov/sagu; 7-day pass per vehicle/bicycle $10/5; ⏰7am-sunset) This prickly canvas of green cacti and desert scrub is split in half by 30 miles of freeway and farms. Both sections sit at the edges of Tucson, but are still officially within the city.

You'll have a nice time exploring in either section, but if you want to make a day of it, head to **Saguaro West** (Tucson Mountain District), where you'll find several fun activities in and around the park. For maps and ranger-led programs, stop at the **Red Hills Visitor Center** (☎520-733-5158; 2700 N Kinney Rd; ⏰9am-5pm), which is also the starting point for the **Cactus Garden Trail**, a short, wheelchair-accessible path with interpretive signs for many of the park's cacti. The **Bajada Loop Drive**, an unpaved 6-mile loop that begins 1.5 miles west of the visitor center, provides fine views of cactus forests, several picnic spots and access to trailheads.

Saguaro East (Rincon Mountain District) is 15 miles east of downtown. The **visitor center** (☎520-733-5153; 3693 S Old Spanish Trail; ⏰9am-5pm) has information on day hikes, horseback riding and backcountry camping. Backcountry camping requires a permit ($6 per site per day) and must be obtained by noon on the day of your hike. This section of the park has about 130 miles of hiking (but only 2.5 miles of mountain-biking) trails. The meandering 8-mile **Cactus Forest Scenic Loop Drive**, a paved road open to cars and bicycles, provides access to picnic areas, trailheads and viewpoints.

TOP CHOICE **Arizona-Sonora Desert Museum** MUSEUM

(☎520-883-1380; www.desertmuseum.org; 2021 N Kinney Rd; adult/child Jun-Aug $12/3, Sep-May $14.50/4.50; ⏰8:30am-5pm Oct-Feb; 👪) This tribute to the Sonoran Desert is one part zoo, one part botanical garden and one part museum – a trifecta that'll keep young and old entertained for easily half a day. All sorts of desert denizens, from precocious coatis to playful prairie dogs, make their home in natural enclosures hemmed in by invisible fences. The grounds are thick with desert plants, and docents are on hand to answer questions and give demonstrations. Strollers and wheelchairs are available, and there's a gift shop, art gallery, restaurant and cafe. Hours vary seasonally.

Old Tucson Studios FILM LOCATION, AMUSEMENT PARK
(☎520-883-0100; www.oldtucson.com; 201 S Kinney Rd; adult/child $17/11; ⏲10am-6pm Oct-May, 10am-6pm Fri-Sun Jun-Sep;) A few miles southeast of the Arizona-Sonora Desert Museum, Old Tucson Studios was an actual Western film set. Today it's a Western theme park with shootouts and stagecoach rides.

Pima Air & Space Museum MUSEUM
(☎520-574-0462; www.pimaair.org; 6000 E Valencia Rd; adult/child/senior & military Jun-Oct $13.75/8/11.75, Nov-May $15.50/9/12.75; ⏲9am-5pm, last admission 4pm) An SR-71 Blackbird spy plane and JFK's Air Force One are among the stars at this private aircraft museum home to more than 300 'birds.' Hardcore plane-spotters should book ahead for the 90-minute bus tour of the nearby 309th **Aerospace Maintenance & Regeneration Center** (adult/child $7/4; ⏲Mon-Fri, departure times vary seasonally) – aka the 'boneyard' – where almost 4000 aircraft are mothballed.

FREE **Center for Creative Photography** MUSEUM
(CCP; ☎520-621-7968; www.creativephotography.org; 1030 N Olive Rd; donations appreciated; ⏲9am-5pm Mon-Fri, 1-4pm Sat & Sun) The CCP is known for its ever-changing, high-caliber exhibits and for administering the archives of landscape photographer Ansel Adams. The museum closes between exhibits, so check the website before visiting.

Festivals & Events

Fiesta de los Vaqueros Rodeo RODEO
(☎520-741-2233; www.tucsonrodeo.com) Held during the last week of February, the huge nonmotorized parade is a locally famous spectacle.

Sleeping

Lodging prices vary considerably, with lower rates in summer and fall.

TOP CHOICE **Catalina Park Inn** B&B $$
(☎520-792-4541; www.catalinaparkinn.com; 309 E 1st St; r $139-149; ; ⏲closed Jul & Aug) Style, hospitality and comfort merge seamlessly at this inviting B&B just west of the University of Arizona. Hosts Mark Hall and Paul Richard have poured their hearts into restoring this 1927 Med-style villa, and their efforts are on display in the six guest rooms, from the oversized and over-the-top peacock-blue-and-gold Catalina Room to the white and uncluttered East Room with an iron canopy bed.

Arizona Inn RESORT $$$
(☎520-325-1541; www.arizonainn.com; 2200 E Elm St; r $259-333, ste $379-449;) The historic feel of this resort provides a sense of being one of the aristocracy. The mature gardens and old Arizona grace provide a respite not only from city life but also from the 21st century. Sip coffee on the porch, take high tea in the library, lounge by the small pool or join in a game of croquet, then retire to rooms furnished with antiques. The on-site spa is our favorite in town.

Hotel Congress HISTORIC HOTEL $$
(☎520-622-8848; www.hotelcongress.com; 311 E Congress St; r $90-120;) A groovy historic hotel with a hip rock-and-roll flavor, the Congress is a nonstop buzz of activity, mostly because of its popular bar, restaurant and nightclub downstairs. Infamous bank robber John Dillinger and his gang were captured here in 1934. Many rooms have period furnishings, rotary phones and wooden radios – but no TV. Ask for a room at the far end of the hotel if you're noise-sensitive. Pets stay for $10 per night.

Flamingo Hotel MOTEL $
(☎520-770-1910; www.flamingohoteltucson.com; 1300 N Stone Ave; r incl breakfast $60-105;) Though recently purchased by Quality Inn, this snazzy motel retains its great 1950s Rat Pack vibe. And the fact that Elvis slept here doesn't hurt. Rooms have stylish striped bedding, comfy beds, flat-screen plasma TVs and a good-sized desk. Pets stay for $20 per day.

Windmill Inn at St Philips Plaza HOTEL $$
(☎520-577-0007; www.windmillinns.com; 4250 N Campbell Ave; r incl breakfast $120-134;) Popular with University of Arizona fans during football season, this modern, friendly place wins kudos for spacious two-room suites (no charge for kids under 18 years of age), free continental breakfast, a lending library, a heated pool and free bike rentals. Pets stay free.

Roadrunner Hostel & Inn HOSTEL $
(☎520-940-7280; www.roadrunnerhostel.com; 346 E 12th St; dm/r incl breakfast $20/40;) This comfortable hostel within walking distance of the arts district has a large kitchen, free coffee and waffles in the morning, and

HOT DIGGETY DOG

Tucson's signature 'dish' is the Sonoran hot dog, a tasty example of what happens when Mexican ingredients meet American processed meat and penchant for excess. The ingredients? A bacon-wrapped hot dog layered with tomatillo salsa, pinto beans, shredded cheese, mayo, ketchup or mustard or both, chopped tomatoes and onions. We like 'em at **El Guero Canelo** (www.elguerocanelo.com; 5201 S 12th Ave, South Tucson).

a big-screen TV for watching movies. Dorms close between noon and 3pm for cleaning. Takes cash and traveler's checks only.

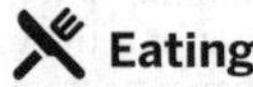

Eating

Your best bet for great food at good prices is 4th Ave; we've listed some of Tucson's standouts.

TOP CHOICE **Café Poca Cosa** SOUTH AMERICAN $$
(☎520-622-6400; www.cafepocacosa.com; 110 E Pennington St; lunch $13-15, dinner $19-26; ⊙lunch & dinner Tue-Sat) At this award-winning Nuevo-Mexican bistro, a Spanish-English chalkboard menu circulates between tables because dishes change twice daily. It's all freshly prepared, innovative and beautifully presented. The undecided can't go wrong by ordering the Plato Poca Cosa and letting chef Suzana D'avila decide. Great margaritas, too.

Pasco Kitchen & Lounge AMERICAN $$
(www.pascokitchen.com; 820 E University Blvd; lunch $9-14; dinner $9-14 ⊙11am-10pm Mon-Wed, 11am-11pm Thu, 11am-1am Fri & Sat, 11am-4pm Sun) The farmers market salad with yard bird is superb at this breezy new eatery near the university. The menu offers fresh, locally sourced homestyle favorites that are prepared with panache and a few tasty twists – think grass-fed all-natural burgers topped with braised pork belly and a fried egg, or grits with catfish and fried okra. The owners call it 'urban farm fare;' we call it delicious.

Mi Nidito MEXICAN $
(www.minidito.net; 1813 S 4th Ave; mains $6-13; ⊙lunch & dinner Wed-Sun) Bill Clinton's order at 'My Little Nest' has become the signature president's plate, a heaping mound of Mexican favorites – tacos, tostadas, burritos, enchiladas etc – groaning under melted cheese. Also give the prickly pear cactus chile or the *birria* (spicy, shredded beef) a whirl.

Lovin' Spoonfuls VEGAN $
(2990 N Campbell Ave; lunch $6-8, dinner $9-11; ⊙9:30am-9pm Mon-Sat, 10am-3pm Sun; ✍) Burgers, country-fried chicken, meatloaf, salads – the menu here reads like those at your typical cafe but there's one big difference: no animal products find their way into this vegan haven.

Hub Restaurant & Creamery AMERICAN $$
(☎520-207-8201; www.hubdowntown.com; 266 E Congress Ave; lunch $9-17, dinner $9-17 ⊙11am-2am) Upscale comfort food is the name of the game here, plus a few sandwiches and salads. If you don't want a meal, pop in for a scoop of flavor-packed gourmet ice cream – bacon scotch anyone?

El Charro Café MEXICAN $$
(☎520-622-1922; 311 N Court Ave; mains $7-18; ⊙lunch & dinner) The Flin family has been making innovative Mexican food at this buzzy hacienda since 1922. It's famous for the *carne seca,* sundried lean beef that's been reconstituted, shredded and grilled with green chile and onions.

Drinking & Entertainment

Downtown 4th Ave, near 6th St, is the happening bar-hop spot, and there are a number of nightclubs on downtown Congress St.

Club Congress LIVE MUSIC
(☎520-622-8848; www.hotelcongress.com; 311 E Congress St; cover $7-13) Live and DJ music are found at this very popular place that's sometimes a rock hangout and sometimes a dance club. The crowd depends on the night, but it's almost always a happening place.

Che's Lounge BAR
(☎520-623-2088; 350 N 4th Ave) A slightly skanky but hugely popular watering hole that rocks with live music Saturday nights. And it never charges a cover.

IBT's GAY CLUB
(☎520-882-3053; 616 N 4th Ave; no cover) Themes change nightly, from drag shows to techno dance mixes to karaoke.

Chocolate Iguana CAFE
(www.chocolateiguanaon4th.com; 500 N 4th Ave; ⊙8am-10pm Mon-Thu, 7am-10pm Fri, 8am-10pm Sat, 9am-6pm Sun) For coffee-lovers and chocoholics, this is the place.

Information

Emergency & Medical Services

Police (☎520-791-4444; http://cms3.tucsonaz.gov/; 270 S Stone Ave)

Tucson Medical Center (☎520-327-5461; www.tmcaz.com/TucsonMedicalCenter; 5301 E Grant Rd) Has 24-hour emergency services.

Internet Access

Joel D Valdez Main Library (☎520-594-5500; 101 N Stone Ave; ⌚9am-8pm Mon-Wed, 9am-6pm Thu, 9am-5pm Fri, 10am-5pm Sat, 1-5pm Sun; @ 📶) Free internet, including wi-fi.

Media

Arizona Daily Star (www.azstarnet.com) The Tucson region's daily newspaper.

Tucson Weekly (www.tucsonweekly.com) A free weekly full of entertainment and restaurant listings.

Money

ATMs are abundant. Foreign exchange is available at most banks; $5 is charged if you don't have an account. Tucson International Airport doesn't exchange currency.

Post

Post office (825 E University Blvd, Suite 111; ⌚8am-5pm Mon-Fri, 9am-12:30pm Sat)

Tourist Information

Tucson Convention & Visitors Bureau (☎520-624-1817; www.visittucson.org; 100 S Church Ave; ⌚9am-5pm Mon-Fri, to 4pm Sat & Sun) Ask for its free *Official Destination Guide*.

Getting There & Around

Tucson International Airport (☎520-573-8000; www.flytucsonairport.com) is 15 miles south of downtown. **Arizona Stagecoach** (☎877-782-4355; www.azstagecoach.com) runs shared van service with fares for about $29 between downtown and the airport. **Greyhound** (☎520-792-3475; www.greyhound.com; 471 W Congress St; ⌚7am-11pm) runs buses to Phoenix (from $21, two hours, daily) and Nogales (from $11, one hour, daily) and other destinations. The station is on the western end of Congress St, three miles from downtown. **Amtrak** (☎520-623-4442; www.amtrak.com; 400 E Toole Ave) is across from Hotel Congress and has train services to Los Angeles (from $38, 10 hours, three weekly) on the Sunset Limited.

The **Ronstadt Transit Center** (cnr Congress St & 6th Ave) is the major downtown transit hub. From here **Sun Tran** (☎520-792-9222; www.suntran.com) buses serve metropolitan Tucson (day pass $3.50).

Around Tucson

The places listed following are less than 1½ hours' drive from town and make great day trips.

NORTH OF TUCSON

About 35 miles away from downtown via backcountry roads, **Biosphere 2** (☎520-896-6200; www.b2science.org; 32540 S Biosphere Rd, Oracle; adult/child/senior $20/13/18; ⌚9am-4pm) is a 3-acre glassed dome housing seven separate microhabitats – a jungle, a desert, a swamp – designed to be self-sustaining. In 1991 eight bionauts entered Biosphere 2 for a two-year tour of duty, during which they were physically cut off from the outside world. They emerged thinner, but in fair shape. Although this experiment could be used as a prototype for future space stations, it was privately funded and controversial. The massive glass structure is now a University of Arizona–run earth science research institute. Visits are by guided tour.

WEST OF TUCSON

From Tucson, Hwy 86 heads west into some of the emptiest parts of the Sonoran Desert – except for the ubiquitous green-and-white border patrol trucks.

The lofty **Kitt Peak National Observatory** (☎520-318-8726; www.noao.edu/kpno; Hwy 86; visitor center admission by donation; ⌚9am-3:45pm) west of Sells features the largest collection of optical telescopes in the world. Guided tours (adult/child $7.75/4 November to May, $5.75/3 June to October, at 10am, 11:30am and 1:30pm) last about an hour. Book two to four weeks in advance for the worthwhile nightly observing program (adult/child $48/44; no programs from mid-July through August because of monsoon season) – clear, dry skies equal an awe-inspiring glimpse of the cosmos. Dress warmly, buy gas in Tucson (the nearest gas station is 30 miles from the observatory) and note that children under eight years of age are not allowed at the evening program for safety reasons. The picnic area draws amateur astronomers at night.

If you truly want to get away from it all, you can't get much further off the grid than the huge and exotic **Organ Pipe Cactus National Monument** (☎520-387-6849; www.nps.gov/orpi; Hwy 85; per vehicle $8) along the Mexican border. It's a gorgeous, forbidding land that supports an astonishing number of animals and plants, including 28 species of cacti, first and foremost its namesake organ-pipe. A giant columnar cactus, it differs from the more prevalent saguaro in that its branches radiate from the base. The 21-mile **Ajo Mountain Drive** takes you through a spectacular landscape of steep-sided, jagged cliffs and rock tinged a faintly hellish red. There are 208 first-come, first-served sites at **Twin Peaks Campground** (tent & RV sites $12) by the visitor center.

SOUTH OF TUCSON

South of Tucson, I-19 is the main route to Nogales and Mexico. Along the way are several interesting stops.

The striking **Mission San Xavier del Bac** (☎520-294-2624; www.sanxaviermission.org; 1950 W San Xavier Rd; donations appreciated; ⏲7am-5pm), nine miles south of downtown Tucson, is Arizona's oldest European building still in use. Dark and moody inside, it's a graceful blend of Moorish, Byzantine and late Mexican Renaissance architecture.

At exit 69, 16 miles south of the mission, the **Titan Missile Museum** (☎520-625-7736; www.titanmissilemuseum.org; 1580 W Duval Mine Rd, Suarita; adult/child/senior $9.50/6/8.50; ⏲8:45am-5:30pm Nov-Apr, 8:45am-5pm May-Oct) features an underground launch site for Cold War–era intercontinental ballistic missiles. Tours are chilling and informative.

If history and/or shopping for crafts interest you, head 48 miles south of Tucson to the small village of **Tubac** (www.tubacaz.com), with more than 100 galleries, studios and shops.

PATAGONIA & THE MOUNTAIN EMPIRE

Sandwiched in between the border, the Santa Rita Mountains and the Patagonia Mountains, this scenic region is one of the shiniest hidden gems in the Arizona jewel box. It's a lovely destination for bird-watching and wine tasting.

Bird-watchers and nature-lovers wander the gentle trails at the **Patagonia-Sonoita Creek Preserve** (☎520-394-2400; www.nature.org/arizona; 150 Blue Heaven Rd; admission $5; ⏲6:30am-4pm Wed-Sun Apr-Sep, from 7:30am Oct-Mar), an enchanting riparian willow forest managed by the Nature Conservancy. The peak migratory season is April through May, and late August to September. For a leisurely afternoon of wine tasting, head to the villages of **Sonoita** and **Elgin** north of Patagonia (see www.arizonavinesandwines.com). The big-sky views are terrific.

If you stick around for dinner, try the gourmet pizzas at **Velvet Elvis** (www.velvetelvispizza.com; 29 Naugle Ave, Patagonia; mains $8-26; ⏲5-9pm Thu, 3-9pm Fri & Sat, 10am-3pm Sun) – they're savory-licious. The photogenic **Duquesne House** (☎520-394-2732; www.theduquesnehouse.com; 357 Duquesne Ave, Patagonia; r $125; @) is an inviting, ranch-style B&B that once served as a boardinghouse for miners.

A small **visitor center** (☎520-394-9186; www.patagoniaaz.com; 307 McKeown Ave; ⏲10am-5pm Mon-Sat, 10am-4pm Sun) is tucked inside Mariposa Books & More in Patagonia.

Southeastern Arizona

Chockablock with places that loom large in the history of the Wild West, southern Arizona is home to the wonderfully preserved mining town of Bisbee, the OK Corral in Tombstone, and wonderland of stone spires at Chiricahua National Monument.

KARTCHNER CAVERNS STATE PARK

The emphasis is on education at **Kartchner Caverns State Park** (☎reservations 520-586-2283, information 520-586-4010; http://azstateparks.com; Hwy 90; park entrance per vehicle/bicycle $6/3, adult/child Rotunda Tour $23/13, Big Room Tour mid-Oct–mid-Apr $23/13; ⏲10am-3pm Mon-Fri Jun-Sep, to 3:40pm Sat & Sun, vary rest of year), a 2.5-mile-long wet limestone fantasia of rocks. Two guided tours explore different areas of the caverns, which were 'discovered' in 1974. The Rotunda/Throne Room Tour is open year-round; the Big Room Tour closes in mid-April for five months to protect the migratory bats that roost here. The park is 9 miles south of Benson, off I-10 at exit 302. The $6 entrance fee is waived for reserved tour tickets.

CHIRICAHUA NATIONAL MONUMENT

The towering rock spires at remote but mesmerizing **Chiricahua National Monument** (☎520-824-3560; www.nps.gov/chir; Hwy 181; adult/child $5/free) in the Chiricahua Mountains sometimes rise hundreds of feet high and often look like they're on the verge of tipping over. The **Bonita Canyon Scenic Drive** takes you 8 miles to Massai Point (6870ft) where you'll see thousands of spires positioned on the slopes like some petrified army. There are numerous hiking trails, but if you're short on time, hike the **Echo Canyon Trail** at least half a mile to the Grottoes, an amazing 'cathedral' of giant boulders where you can lie still and enjoy the wind-caressed silence. The monument is 36 miles southeast of Willcox off Hwy 186/181.

TOMBSTONE

In Tombstone's 19th-century heyday as a booming mining town the whiskey flowed and six-shooters blazed over disputes large and small, most famously at the OK Corral. Now a National Historic Landmark, it attracts hordes of tourists to its old Western buildings, stagecoach rides and nonstop gunfight reenactments.

And yes, you must visit the **OK Corral** (520-457-3456; www.ok-corral.com; Allen St, btwn 3rd & 4th Sts; admission $10, without gunfight $6; 9am-5pm), site of the legendary gunfight between the Earps, Doc Holliday and the McLaurys and Billy Clanton on October 26, 1881. Also make time for the dusty **Bird Cage Theater** (520-457-3421; 517 E Allen St; adult/child/senior $10/7/9; 8am-6pm), a one-time dance hall and saloon now crammed with historic odds and ends. And a merman.

The **Visitor & Information Center** (520-457-3929; www.tombstonechamber.com; cnr 395 E Allen & 4th Sts; 9am-5pm) has walking maps and local recommendations.

BISBEE

Oozing old-fashioned ambience, Bisbee is a former copper-mining town that's now a delightful mix of aging Bohemians, elegant buildings, sumptuous restaurants and charming hotels. Most businesses are found in the Historic District (Old Bisbee), along Subway and Main Sts.

To burrow under the earth in a tour led by the retired miners who worked here, take the **Queen Mine Tour** (520-432-2071; www.queenminetour.com; 478 Dart Rd, off Hwy 80; adult/child $13/5.50; 9am-3:30pm;). Right outside of town, check out the **Lavender Pit**, an ugly yet impressive testament to strip mining.

Rest your head at **Shady Dell RV Park** (520-432-3567; www.theshadydell.com; 1 Douglas Rd; rates $50-145), a kitschy trailer park extraordinaire. Everything's done up with fun, retro furnishings. Swamp coolers provide cold air. **Copper Queen Hotel** (520-432-2216; www.copperqueen.com; 11 Howell; r $122-197;), built in 1902, is still charming as heck and a number of rooms are themed after the famous personalities that stayed in them, including John Wayne. Rooms and hallways are bewitched by lovely copper lamps, and supposedly ghosts.

For good eats, stroll up Main St and pick a restaurant – you can't go wrong. A current hot spot is the fantastic **Poco** (520-432-3733; 15 Main St/Peddlar's Alley; mains $7.50-10; 11am-8pm Wed-Sun;), a courtyard cafe that's earning kudos as far away as Patagonia for Mexican-inspired, mostly organic vegetarian fare. For fine American food continue up Main St to stylish **Cafe Roka** (520-432-5153; www.caferoka.com; 35 Main St; dinner $15-29; dinner Thu-Sat), where four-course dinners include salad, soup, sorbet and a rotating choice of crowd-pleasing mains.

The **visitor center** (520-432-3554; www.discoverbisbee.com; 2 Copper Queen Plaza; 9am-5pm Mon-Fri, 10am-4pm Sat & Sun) is a good place to start.

UTAH

Shhhhh, don't tell. We wouldn't want word to get out that this oft-overlooked state is really one of nature's most perfect playgrounds. Utah's rugged terrain comes ready-made for hiking, biking, rafting, rappelling, rock climbing, skiing, snowboarding, snow riding, horseback riding, four-wheel driving… Need we go on? More than 65% of the state's lands are public, including 12 national parks and monuments – a dazzling display of haunting topography that leaves many awestruck.

Southern Utah red-rock country is defined by soaring Technicolor cliffs, spindles and spires that defy gravity, and seemingly endless expanses of sculpted sandstone desert. Northern Utah is dominated by the 11,000ft-high forest- and snow-covered peaks of the Wasatch Mountains. Interspersed throughout it all you'll find Native American rock-art sites and well-organized little towns with pioneer buildings dating back to the state's founding.

The enticing land was also what drew the first Mormon pioneers to the territory; still today, church members make up more than 50% of the wonderfully polite population. Rural towns can be quiet and conservative, but the rugged beauty has attracted outdoorsy, independent thinkers as well. Salt Lake and Park Cities especially have vibrant nightlife and foodie scenes.

So come wonder at the roadside geographic kaleidoscope, or go hiking where no one (literally) has hiked before. Just don't tell your friends: we'd like to keep this secret to ourselves.

UTAH FACTS

» **Nickname** Beehive State

» **Population** 2.9 million

» **Area** 84,900 sq miles

» **Capital city** Salt Lake City (population 181,743), metro area (1.2 million)

» **Other cities** St George (population 88,001)

» **Sales tax** 4.7%

» **Birthplace of** Entertainers Donny (b 1957) and Marie (b 1959) Osmond, beloved bandit Butch Cassidy (1866–1908)

» **Home of** 2002 Winter Olympic Games

» **Politics** mostly conservative

» **Famous for** Mormons, red-rock canyons, polygamy

» **Best souvenir** Wasatch Brewery T-shirt: 'Polygamy Porter – Why Have Just One?'

» **Driving distances** Salt Lake City to Moab 235 miles, St George to Salt Lake City 304 miles

History

Traces of the Ancestral Puebloan (or Anasazi) and Fremont people, this land's earliest human inhabitants, can today be seen in the rock art and ruins they left behind. But it was the modern Ute, Paiute and Navajo tribes who were living here when European-heritage settlers arrived in large numbers. Led by second church president, Brigham Young, Mormons fled to this territory to escape religious persecution starting in the late 1840s. They set about attempting to settle every inch of their new state, no matter how inhospitable, which resulted in skirmishes with Native Americans – and more than one abandoned ghost town.

For nearly 50 years after the United States acquired the Utah Territory from Mexico, petitions for statehood were rejected as a result of the Mormon practice of polygamy (taking multiple wives), which was illegal in the US. Tension and prosecutions grew until 1890, when Mormon leader Wilford Woodruff had a divine revelation and the church officially discontinued the practice. Utah became the 45th state in 1896. The modern Mormon church, now called the Church of Jesus Christ of Latter-Day Saints (LDS) continues to exert a strong influence here.

Information

Note that it can be difficult to change currency outside Salt Lake City, but ATMs are widespread.

Utah Office of Tourism (☎800-200-1160; www.utah.com) Publishes the free *Utah Travel Guide* and runs several visitor centers statewide. Website has links in six languages.

Utah State Parks & Recreation Department (☎877-887-2757; www.stateparks.utah.gov) Produces comprehensive guide to the 40-plus state parks; available online and at visitor centers.

Reserve America (☎801-322-3770, 800-322-3770; http://utahstateparks.reserveamerica.com) State park camping reservations.

Getting There & Away

Salt Lake City (SLC) has the state's only international airport. The much smaller St George airport has a couple domestic connections, but it's often cheaper to fly into Las Vegas (120 miles south) and rent a car. You will need a private vehicle to reach most places outside SLC and Park City.

Getting Around

Utah towns are typically laid out in a grid with streets aligned north–south or east–west. There's a zero point in the town center at the intersection of two major streets (often called Main St and Center St). Addresses and numerical street names radiate out from this point, rising by 100 with each city block. Thus, 500 South 400 East will be five blocks south and four blocks east of the zero point. The system is complicated to explain, but thankfully it's quite easy to use.

Salt Lake City

Snuggled up against the soaring peaks of the Wasatch Mountains, Salt Lake City is a small town with just enough edge to satisfy city slickers. Yes, it is the Mormon equivalent of Vatican City, but Utah's capital city is quite modern. A redeveloped downtown and local foodie scene balance out the city's charming anachronisms.

Sights

The second Mormon Church president and prophet, Brigham Young, declared 'This is the place!' when he first arrived with settlers in 1847. Salt Lake City remains the LDS church headquarters and most of the town's top sights are church related. The main LDS sights cluster near downtown's zero point for streets and addresses: the corner of S Temple (east–west) and Main St (north–south). Note that the 132ft-wide streets were originally built so that four oxen pulling a wagon could turn around. Just 45 minutes away, world-class hiking, climbing and snow sports await in the Wasatch Mountains.

TEMPLE SQUARE AREA

Temple Square PLAZA
(www.visittemplesquare.com; admission free; ⏲9am-9pm) The city's most famous sight, a 10-acre square filled with LDS buildings, flower gardens and fountains, is certainly awe-inspiring. Disarmingly nice LDS-member 'sister' and 'brother' volunteers answer questions and lead free 30-minute grounds tours from the visitor centers, inside the two entrances (on S and N Temple). Lording over the square, the 210ft-tall **Salt Lake Temple** is at its most ethereal when lit up at night. Atop the tallest spire stands a statue of the angel Moroni, who appeared to first LDS prophet, Joseph Smith, and led him to the Book of Mormon. The Temple and its ceremonies are private, open only to LDS members 'in good standing.' In addition to the noteworthy sights listed below, the square also contains a church history museum, Joseph Smith theatre and restaurants.

Tabernacle RELIGIOUS
(Temple Sq; admission free; ⏲9am-9pm) This domed, 1867 auditorium – with a massive 11,000-pipe organ – has incredible acoustics. A pin dropped in the front can be heard in the back, almost 200ft away. Free daily organ recitals are held at noon Monday through Saturday, 2pm Sunday. For more on choir performances, see Entertainment (p358).

Beehive House HISTORIC SITE
(67 E South Temple; tours free; ⏲9am-9pm Mon-Sat) The Beehive House was Brigham Young's main home during his tenure as governor and church president in Utah. The required tours, which begin on your arrival, vary in the amount of historic house detail provided versus religious education offered, depending on the particular LDS docent.

Family History Library LIBRARY
(www.familysearch.org; 35 N West Temple; admission free; ⏲8am-5pm Mon, 8am-9pm Tue-Sat) Investigating your ancestors? Start here. This incredible library contains more than 3.5 million genealogy-related microfilms, microfiches, books and other records gathered from more than 110 countries.

GREATER DOWNTOWN

State Capitol HISTORIC BUILDING
(www.utahstatecapitol.utah.gov; admission free; ⏲8am-8pm Mon-Fri, 8am-6pm Sat & Sun) The grand, 1916 State Capitol is set among 500 cherry trees on a hill north of Temple Sq. Inside, colorful Works Progress Administration (WPA) murals of pioneers, trappers and missionaries adorn part of the building's dome. Free hourly tours (from 9am to 4pm) start at the 1st-floor visitor center.

Pioneer Memorial Museum MUSEUM
(www.dupinternational.org; 300 N Main St; admission free; ⏲9am-5pm Mon-Sat year-round, 1-5pm Sun Jun-Aug) Vast, four-story treasure trove of pioneer artifacts.

City Creek PLAZA
(Social Hall Ave, btwn Regent & Richards Sts) This LDS-funded, 20-acre pedestrian plaza with fountains, restaurants and retail along City Creek was under construction at the time of research.

CAN I GET A DRINK IN UTAH?

Absolutely. Although there are still a few unusual liquor laws on the books, regulations have relaxed in recent years. Private club memberships are no more: a bar is now a bar (no minors allowed), and you don't have to order food to consume alcohol in one of them. As far as restaurants go, few have full liquor licenses, many more serve just beer and wine.

Remaining rules to remember:

» You must be dining at a full-license restaurant to order any alcoholic drink there. Mixed drinks and wine are available only after noon.

» In bars and restaurants, beer can be served from 10am.

» Packaged liquor can only be sold at state-run liquor stores (closed on Sundays), some beer is sold in convenience stores.

UNIVERSITY-FOOTHILL DISTRICT

This Is the Place Heritage Park HISTORIC SITE
(www.thisistheplace.org; 2601 E Sunnyside Ave; park admission free, village adult/child $10/7 Jun-Aug; 9am-5pm Mon-Fri, 10am-5pm Sat;) A 450-acre park marks the spot where Brigham Young uttered the fateful words, 'This is the place.' The centerpiece is a living-history village where, June through August, costumed docents depict mid-19th-century life. Admission includes a tourist train ride and activities. During other seasons, guests can wander the village at various reduced rates, with varied to no interior-building access.

Utah Museum of Natural History MUSEUM
(http://umnh.utah.edu; Rio Tinto Center, Wakara Way; adult/child $7/5; 10am-5pm Tue-Sun) The museum's prize Huntington Mammoth, one of the most complete of its kind, has a new home near the University of Utah campus. Find out more about area fossils, indigenous peoples and more at this modern center.

Red Butte Gardens GARDENS
(www.redbuttegarden.org; 300 Wakara Way; adult/child $8/6; 9am-9pm May-Aug, 9am-5pm Sep-Apr) Both landscaped and natural gardens cover a lovely 150 acres, all accessible by trail, in the Wasatch foothills. Check online to see who's playing at the popular, outdoor summer concert series also held here.

Activities

Within easy reach on the east side of the Wasatch mountain range, Big and Little Cottonwood Canyons not only have excellent skiing but opportunities for hiking, mountain biking and camping. For more, see p359.

WORTH A TRIP

KENNECOTT'S BINGHAM CANYON COPPER MINE

The view into the century-old **mine** (www.kennecott.com; Hwy 111; per vehicle $5; 8am-8pm Apr-Oct), 20 miles southwest of SLC, is slightly unreal. Massive dump trucks (some more than 12ft tall) look no larger than toys as they wind up and down the world's largest excavation. The 2.5-mile-wide and 0.75-mile-deep gash, which is still growing, is visible from space – and there's a picture from *Apollo* 11 inside the museum to prove it. Overall, it's a fascinating stop.

Church Fork Trail HIKING
(Millcreek Canyon, off Wasatch Blvd; admission $3) Looking for the nearest workout with big views? Hike the 6-mile round-trip, pet-friendly trail up to Grandeur Peak (8299ft). Millcreek Canyon is 13.5 miles southwest of downtown.

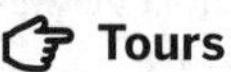

Tours

Brochures for **Utah Heritage Foundation** (www.utahheritagefoundation.com) free self-guided walking tours are available online at the city visitor center.

Sleeping

Downtown rates vary greatly depending on local events and daily occupancy. Outside ski season, prices plunge at Wasatch Mountain resorts, about 45 minutes' from downtown. Cheaper chain motels cluster off I-80 near the airport and south in suburban Midvale.

Parish Place Bed & Breakfast B&B $$
(801-832-0970; www.parrishplace.com; 720 E Ashton Ave; r incl breakfast $99-139;) 'Comfortably antique' well describes SLC's most reasonable, 19th-century mansion B&B. Rooms have both elegant and eclectic details – such as a commode that is behind a decorative screen instead of a door. Continental breakfast arrives in a basket at your door daily. Hot tub and complimentary beverage center on site.

Peery Hotel HOTEL $$
(801-521-4300; www.peeryhotel.com; 110 W 300 South; r $90-130;) This stately historic hotel (1910) stands smack in the center of the Broadway Ave entertainment district. Restaurants, bars and theaters are all within easy strolling distance. Expect upscale conveniences such as Egyptian-cotton robes, iPod docking stations and Tempurpedic mattresses. Parking $10 per day.

Hotel Monaco HOTEL $$
(801-595-0000; www.monaco-saltlakecity.com; 15 W 200 South; r $139-249;) Rich colors, sleek stripes and plush prints create a whimsical mix at this sassy boutique chain. Here pampered guest pets receive special treatment, and the front desk will loan you a goldfish if you need company. Evening wine receptions are free; parking ($15) and internet access ($10), extra.

Anniversary Inn B&B $$$
(801-363-4953; www.anniversaryinn.com; 678 E South Temple St; ste incl breakfast $129-249;

SALT LAKE CITY FOR CHILDREN

Young and old alike appreciate the University-Foothill District attractions, but there are also a couple kid-specific sights to see.

Discovery Gateway (www.discoverygateway.org; 444 W 100 South; admission $8.50; 10am-6pm Mon-Thu, 10am-8pm Fri & Sat, noon-6pm Sun;) is an enthusiastic, hands-on children's museum. The mock network-news desk in the media zone is particularly cool for budding journos.

More than 800 animals inhabit zones like the Asian Highlands on the landscaped 42-acre grounds of **Hogle Zoo** (www.hoglezoo.org; 2600 East Sunnyside Ave; adult/child $9/7; 9am-5pm;). Daily animal encounter programs help kids learn more about their favorite species.

P) Sleep among the tree trunks of an enchanted forest or inside an Egyptian pyramid: these 3-D themed suites are nothing if not over the top. The quiet Avenues location is near a few good restaurants, and not far from Temple Sq.

Grand America HOTEL $$$
(801-258-6000; www.grandamerica.com; 555 S Main St; r $189-289; P) Rooms in SLC's only true luxury hotel are decked out with Italian marble bathrooms, English wool carpeting, tasseled damask draperies and other cushy details. If that's not enough to spoil you, there's always afternoon high tea or the lavish Sunday brunch. Paid parking ($15).

Crystal Inn & Suites MOTEL $
(801-328-4466; www.crystalinnsaltlake.com; 230 W 500 South; r incl breakfast $75-95; P) Utah-owned, multistory motel with a superfriendly staff and loads of free amenities (including a huge, hot breakfast).

Avenues Hostel HOSTEL $
(801-359-3855; www.saltlakehostel.com; 107 F St; dm $18, s/d without bath $30/40, with bath $40/50;) Well-worn hostel; a bit halfway house–like with long-term residents, but a convenient location.

Eating

Many of Salt Lake City's bountiful assortment of ethnic and organically minded restaurants are within the downtown core.

TOP CHOICE **Red Iguana** MEXICAN $$
(736 W North Temple; mains $10-16; 11am-10pm Mon-Thu, 11am-11pm Fri, 10am-11pm Sat, 10am-9pm Sun) Ask for a plate of sample mole if you can't decide which of the seven chile- and chocolate-based sauces sounds best. Really, you can't go wrong with any of the thoughtfully flavored interior Mexican food at this always-packed, family-run restaurant. The incredibly tender *conchinita pibil* (shredded roast pork) tastes like it's been cooking for days.

Squatters Pub Brewery AMERICAN $$
(147 W Broadway; mains $9-15; 11am-midnight Sun-Thu, to 1am Fri & Sat) Come for an Emigration Pale Ale, stay for the blackened tilapia salad. In addition to great microbrews, Squatters does a wide range of American casual dishes well. The lively pub atmosphere is always fun.

Wild Grape AMERICAN $$$
(481 E South Temple; brunch & lunch mains $6-15, dinner mains $18-24; 8am-9:30pm Tue-Thu, 8am-10:30pm Fri, 9am-10:30pm Sat, 9am-9:30pm Sun) Billing itself as a 'new West' bistro, Wild Grape creates modern versions of country classics such as its wood-grilled pork chop with a sweetly sour blueberry sauce. Organic, locally sourced ingredients are a high priority here.

One World Everybody Eats ORGANIC $
(41 S 300 East; 11am-9pm Mon-Sat, 9am-5pm Sun) At this ecoconscious, community-oriented eatery, you get to decide what you pay and what your portion size will be (they'll provide suggestions). Daily changing menus of salads, stir-fries, pastas, Indian dishes and the like include great vegetarian options.

Curryer INDIAN $
(300 South, btwn S State & S Main Sts; dishes $4-6; 11am-2pm) This former hot-dog cart, modified with a tandoori oven, serves up a tasty range of regional Indian food from butter chicken to vegan-friendly *aloo matar* (spiced potatoes and peas).

Takashi JAPANESE **$$$**
(18 W Market St; rolls $8-14, mains $15-25; ⏲11:30am-2pm & 5:30-10pm Mon-Sat) The best of a number of surprisingly good sushi restaurants in landlocked Salt Lake; even LA restaurant snobs rave about the excellent rolls at ever-so-chic Takashi.

Downtown Farmers Market MARKET **$**
(Pioneer Park, cnr 300 South & 300 West; ⏲8am-1pm Sat mid-Jun–late Oct, 4pm-dusk Tue Aug-Sep) The town's summer outdoor market showcases locally grown produce, ready-to-eat baked goodies and local crafts.

Drinking

Pubs and bars that also serve food are mainstays of SLC's nightlife; no one minds if you just drink there.

Gracie's BAR
(326 S West Temple; ⏲11am-2am) Even with two levels and four bars, Gracie's upscale bar-restaurant still gets crowded. The two sprawling patios are the best place to kick back. Live music or DJs most nights.

Green Pig PUB
(31 E 400 South; ⏲11am-2am) Your friendly neighborhood watering hole hosts poker tournaments, has live jam sessions and plays sporting events on big screens. The roof patio is tops.

Café Marmalade GAY
(www.utahpridecenter.com; 361 N 300 West; ⏲7am-9pm Mon-Fri, 8am-9pm Sat, 10am-9pm Sun) The upbeat coffee shop inside the Utah Pride Center has open mike nights, weekend BBQs and concerts, and the largest GLBT library in the state.

Tavernacle Social Club THEME BAR
(201 E Broadway; ⏲5pm-1am Tue-Sat, 8pm-midnight Sun) Dueling pianos or karaoke nightly.

Coffee Garden CAFE
(895 E 900 South; ⏲6am-11pm Sun-Thu, 6am-midnight Fri & Sat; wi-fi) Great, character-filled neighborhood, delicious coffee and baked goods.

☆ Entertainment

Music

A complete list of local music is available online at www.cityweekly.net.

Mormon Tabernacle Choir LIVE MUSIC
(☎435-570-0080 for tickets; www.mormontabernaclechoir.org) Hearing the world-renown Mormon Tabernacle choir is must-do on any SLC visit. A live choir broadcast goes out every Sunday at 9:30am. September through November and January through May, attend in person at the **Tabernacle** (Temple Sq). Free public rehearsals are held there from 8pm to 9pm Thursdays. From June to August and in December, to accommodate larger crowds choir broadcasts and rehearsals are held at the 21,000-seat **LDS Conference Center** (cnr N Temple & Main Sts). Performance times stay the same, except that an extra Monday-to-Saturday organ recital takes place at 2pm.

Theater

The Salt Lake City Arts Council provides a complete cultural events calendar on its website (www.slcgov.com/arts/calendar.pdf). Reserve through **ArtTix** (☎801-355-2787; www.arttix.org).

Local venues include **Abravanel Hall** (123 W South Temple), **Capitol Theater** (50 W 200 South) and the **Rose Wagner Performing Arts Center** (138 W 300 South).

Sports

EnergySolutions Arena BASKETBALL
(www.nba.com/jazz; 301 W South Temple) Utah Jazz, the men's professional basketball team, play downtown.

E Center HOCKEY
(www.utahgrizzlies.com; 3200 S Decker Lake Dr, West Valley City) The International Hockey League's Utah Grizzlies play 8.5 miles outside of town.

Shopping

An interesting array of boutiques, antiques and cafes line up along **Broadway Avenue** (300 South), between 100 and 300 East. A few crafty shops and galleries can be found on in the 300 block of **W Pierpont Avenue**.

Sam Weller Books BOOKS
(☎801-328-2586; 254 S Main; ⏲10am-7pm Mon-Sat) The city's biggest independent bookstore, with a noteworthy local rare book selection. At press time, Weller's was looking for a new location.

ℹ Information

Emergency & Medical Services

Police (☎801-799-3000; 315 E 200 South)

Salt Lake Regional Medical Center (☎801-350-4111; 1050 E South Temple; ⏲24hr emergency)

Internet Access

Main Library (www.slcpl.org; 210 E 400 South; ⏲9am-9pm Mon-Thu, 9am-6pm Fri & Sat, 1-5pm Sun) Free wireless and internet access.

Media

City Weekly (www.cityweekly.net/utah) Free alternative weekly with good restaurant and entertainment listings.

Salt Lake Tribune (www.sltrib.com) Utah's largest-circulation paper.

Money

Wells Fargo (79 S Main St) Limited currency-exchange services.

Post

Downtown post office (200 W 200 South)

Tourist Information

Public Lands Information Center (☎801-466-6411; www.publiclands.org; 3285 E 3300 South; ⏲10:30am-5:30pm Mon-Fri, 9am-1pm Sat) Recreation information for the Wasatch-Cache National Forest; located inside the REI store.

Visitor Information Center (☎801-534-4900; Salt Palace Convention Center, 90 S West Temple; ⏲9am-6pm Mon-Fri, 9am-5pm Sat & Sun) Publishes free guide; on-site gift shop.

Websites

Downtown SLC (www.downtownslc.org) Arts, entertainment and business information about the downtown core.

Salt Lake Convention & Visitors Bureau (www.visitsaltlake.com) SLC's official tourist information website.

 Getting There & Away

Air

Salt Lake City International Airport (www.slcairport.com; 776 N Terminal Dr), 5 miles northwest of downtown, has mostly domestic flights. But you can fly direct to Canada and Mexico. **Delta** (www.delta.com) is the main SLC carrier.

Bus

Greyhound (☎800-231-2222; www.greyhound.com; 300 S 600 West) connects SLC with Southwestern towns including the following:

St George, UT ($55, six hours)

Las Vegas, NV ($62, eight hours)

Denver, CO ($86, 10 hours)

Train

Traveling between Chicago and Oakland/Emeryville, the California Zephyr from **Amtrak** (☎801-322-3510; www.amtrak.com) stops daily at **Union Pacific Rail Depot** (340 S 600 West). Southwest destinations include Denver ($115, 15 hours) and Reno, NV ($64, 10 hours). Schedule delays can be substantial.

CONNECT PASS

Salt Lake City Convention & Visitors Bureau (www.visitsaltlake.com) sells a discount pass (one day, adult/child $24/20). But unless you plan to visit every child-friendly attraction in the town – and some outside of town – it likely isn't worth your while.

 Getting Around

To/From the Airport

Utah Transit Authority (UTA; www.rideuta.com; one-way $2) Bus 550 travels downtown from the parking structure between terminals 1 and 2.

Xpress Shuttle (☎800-397-0773; www.expressshuttleutah.com) Shared van service; $16 to downtown.

Yellow Cab (☎801-521-2100) Private taxi, from $25 to downtown.

Public Transportation

UTA (www.rideuta.com) Trax, UTA's light-rail system, runs east from Central Station (600 W 250 South) to the University of Utah and south past Sandy. The center of downtown SLC is a free-fare zone. During ski season UTA buses serve the local ski resorts (all $7 round-trip).

Park City & the Wasatch Mountains

Utah has awesome skiing, some of the best anywhere in North America. Its fabulous low-density, low-moisture snow – between 300in and 500in annually – and thousands of acres of high-altitude terrain helped earn Utah the honor of hosting the 2002 Winter Olympics. The Wasatch Mountain Range that towers over SLC is home to numerous ski resorts, abundant hiking, camping and mountain biking – not to mention chichi Park City with its upscale amenities and world-class film festival.

SALT LAKE CITY RESORTS

Four world-class resorts in Little Cottonwood and Big Cottonwood Canyons, on the western side of the Wasatch mountain range, lie within 40 minutes' drive of downtown SLC. All have lodging and dining facilities. Day ski passes range from $55 to $75 per adult and $25 to $40 per child. A

Super Pass (www.visitsaltlakecity.com/ski/superpass; 2–6-day pass $114-336) requires reservations at one of the 80-plus area lodgings, but offers discounted ski access to all four resorts plus round-trip transportation from SLC. For a full list of summer hiking and biking trails, see www.utah.com/saltlake/hiking.htm.

BIG COTTONWOOD CANYON

Solitude Mountain Resort SNOW SPORTS
(☎801-534-1400; www.skisolitude.com) Exclusive, European-style village surrounded by excellent terrain. The Nordic Center has cross-country skiing in winter and nature trails in summer.

Brighton Resort SNOW SPORTS
(☎800-873-5512; www.brightonresort.com) Where all of SLC learned to ski; still an old-fashioned, family and first-timer favorite.

LITTLE COTTONWOOD CANYON

Snowbird Ski Area SNOW SPORTS
(☎800-385-2002; www.snowbird.com) The biggest and the busiest of them all, with all-round great snow riding – think steep and deep. Numerous lift-assist summer hiking trails; aerial tramway runs year-round.

Alta Ski Area SKIING
(☎800-258-2716; www.alta.com) A laid-back choice exclusive to skiers. No snowboarders affecting snow cover here.

PARK CITY

A mere 35 miles east of SLC via I-80, Park City (elevation 6900ft) skyrocketed to international fame when it hosted the downhill, jumping and sledding events at the 2002 Winter Olympics. The Southwest's most popular ski destination is still home to the US ski team. Come summer, residents (population 8100) gear up for hiking and mountain biking among the nearby peaks. The town itself – a silver-mining community during the 19th century – has an attractive and well-preserved main street lined with upscale galleries, shops, hotels, restaurants and bars. Despite the spread of prefab condos across the valley, the setting remains relatively charming. Winter (roughly late December through March) is busy season; during other months, businesses may close various days and resorts operate limited facilities.

Activities

In addition to snow sports (day lift tickets from $80/45 per adult/child), each area resort has posh lodging close to the slopes, numerous eateries and various summer activities, including mountain-bike rental and lift-assist hiking. More than 300 miles of hiking/biking trails crisscross area mountains; pick up maps at the visitor centers.

Park City Mountain Resort SNOW SPORTS
(☎435-649-8111; www.parkcitymountain.com) Family-friendly, supercentral Park City Mountain Resort has activities galore: more than 3300 acres of skiable terrain, snowtubing, alpine coaster, year-round in-town lift, summer zip line...

Deer Valley Resort SKIING
(☎435-649-1000; www.deervalley.com) The area's most exclusive resort is known as much for its superb dining and hilltop St Regis Hotel as it is for the meticulously groomed, capacity-controlled slopes and ski valets. No snowboarding.

Canyons SNOW SPORTS
(☎435-649-5400; www.thecanyons.com) The Canyons is busy reinventing itself as part of a multimillion-dollar, multiyear expansion. Already it is the largest Utah resort, with several new lifts – including an enclosed, climate-controlled quad – and year-round gondola.

Utah Olympic Park ADVENTURE SPORTS
(www.olyparks.com/uop; 3419 Olympic Pkwy; admission free, guided tours adult/child $7/5; ⏰9am-

GREAT SALT LAKE

Once part of prehistoric Lake Bonneville, Great Salt Lake today covers 2000 sq miles and is far saltier than the ocean; you can easily float on its surface. The pretty, 15-mile-long **Antelope Island State Park** (www.stateparks.utah.gov; I-15 exit 332; per vehicle $9; ⏰7am-sunset), 40 miles northwest of SLC, has nice hiking and the best beaches for lake swimming (though they're occasionally stinky). It's also home to one of the largest bison herds in the country. A basic **campground** (tent & RV sites $13) operates year-round. Six of the 26 sites are available first-come, first-served, the rest by reservation.

6pm) Tour the 2002 Olympic ski-jumping, bobsledding, skeleton, Nordic combined and luge event facilities, check out the ski museum, and, if you're lucky, watch the pros practice (call for schedules). Paid activities include sports camps, freestyle shows and winter/summer bobsled rides (from $60).

Historic Union Pacific Rail Trail PARK
(http://stateparks.utah.gov; admission free; ⏲24hr) A 28-mile multiuse trail that's also a state park. Pick it up at Bonanza Dr just south of Kearns Blvd.

Festivals & Events

Sundance Film Festival FILM
(www.sundance.org) Independent films and their makers, movie stars and fans fill the town to bursting for 10 days in late January. Passes, ticket packages and the few individual tickets sell out well in advance. Plan ahead.

Sleeping

More than 100 condos, hotels and resorts rent rooms in Park City. For complete listings, check www.visitparkcity.com. High-season winter rates are quoted below (minimum stays may be required); prices drop by half or more out of peak season.

Sky Lodge LUXURY HOTEL $$$
(☎435-658-2500; www.theskylodge.com; 201 Heber Ave; ste $285-495; ❄@📶🏊) The urban-loft-like architecture containing the chic Sky Lodge suites both compliments and contrasts the three historic buildings that house the property's restaurants. You can't be more stylish, or more central, if you stay here.

Washington School House BOUTIQUE HOTEL $$$
(☎435-649-3800, 800-824-1672; http://washingtonschoolhouse.com; 543 Park Ave; ste incl breakfast $700; ❄📶🏊) Architect Trip Bennett oversaw the restoration that turned an 1898 limestone schoolhouse on a hill into a luxurious boutique hotel with 12 suites. How did the children ever concentrate when they could gaze out at the mountains through 9ft-tall windows instead?

🍃 **Treasure Mountain Inn** HOTEL $$$
(☎435-655-4501; www.treasuremountaininn.com; 255 Main St; ste $235-295; ❄📶) Park City's first member of the Green Hotel Association utilizes wind energy and serves organic food in its breakfast restaurant. Some of the upscale condos have fireplaces, all have kitchens and are decorated in earthy tones.

> WORTH A TRIP
>
> ### MIRROR LAKE HIGHWAY
>
> This alpine route, also known as Hwy 150, begins about 12 miles east of Park City in **Kamas** and climbs to elevations of more than 10,000ft as it covers the 65 miles into Wyoming. The highway provides breathtaking mountain vistas, passing by scores of lakes, campgrounds and trailheads in the **Uinta-Wasatch-Cache National Forest** (www.fs.fed.us). Note that sections may be closed to traffic well into spring due to heavy snowfall; check online.

Chateau Après Lodge MOTEL $
(☎435-649-9372; www.chateauapres.com; 1299 Norfolk Ave; dm/d/q $40/105/155; 📶) The only budget-oriented accommodation in town is this basic, 1963 lodge – with a 1st-floor dorm – near the town ski lift. Reserve ahead.

Look for occasional deals at these lodge-like motels:

Best Western Landmark Inn MOTEL $$$
(☎435-649-7300; www.bwlandmarkinn.com; 6560 N Landmark Dr; r incl breakfast $219-239; ❄@📶🏊)

Park City Peaks LODGE $$$
(☎435-649-5000; www.parkcitypeaks.com; 2121 Park Ave; r $189-249; ❄@📶🏊)

Eating

Park City is well known for exceptional upscale eating; a reasonable meal is harder to find. In the spring and summer, look for half-off main-dish coupons in the *Park Record* newspaper. Note that from April through November restaurants reduce open hours variably, and may take extended breaks.

TOP CHOICE **Talisker** MODERN AMERICAN $$$
(☎435-658-5479; 515 Main St; mains $21-42; ⏲5:30-10pm) Talisker elevates superb food to the sublime: lobster hush puppies, anyone? Settle into one of the four individually designed dining rooms and see what longtime resident and chef Jeff Murcko has to offer on his daily changing menu. Reservations required.

Maxwell's PIZZERIA $$
(1456 New Park Blvd; pizza slices $3, mains $10-20; ⏲11am-9pm Sun-Thu, 11am-10pm Fri & Sat) Eat

with the locals at the pizza, pasta and beer joint tucked in a back corner of the stylish outdoor Redstone Mall, north of town. Huge, crispy-crusted 'Fat Boy' pizzas never linger long on the tables.

Zoom AMERICAN **$$$**
(☎435-649-9108; 660 Main St; mains $20-36; ⊙11:30am-2:30pm & 5-10pm) You're guaranteed to see co-owner Robert Redford at this all-American restaurant – if not in person, at least in his big artsy portrait and the Sundance Film Festival photos splashed across the walls of the rehabbed train depot. Reservations recommended.

Good Karma FUSION **$$**
(1782 Prospector Ave; breakfast $7-12, mains $10-20; ⊙7am-10pm) Whenever possible, local and organic ingredients are used in the Indo-Persian meals, with an Asian accent, at Good Karma. You'll recognize the place by the Tibetan prayer flags flapping out front.

Wasatch Brew Pub PUB **$$**
(250 Main St; lunch sandwiches $7-12, dinner mains $10-17; ⊙11am-10pm) Hearty pub grub goes down well with one of Wasatch Brewery's microbrewed drafts... say, First Amendment Lager. Don't forget to pick up a 'Polygamy Porter – Why Have Just One?' T-shirt on the way out.

In addition to any restaurant at Deer Valley Resort (p360), other top-end top picks (reservations advised) include the following:

Jean Louis Restaurant FRENCH **$$$**
(☎435-200-0602; 136 Heber Ave; mains $27-40; ⊙5:30-10pm) Classic French; only slightly snobby.

Wahso FUSION **$$$**
(☎435-615-0300; 577 Main St; mains $25-36; ⊙5-10pm) Sophisticated Indochine fusion.

☆ Entertainment

Main St is where it's at – with half a dozen or more bars, clubs and pubs. In winter, there's action nightly; weekends are most lively outside peak season. For listings, see www.thisweekinparkcity.com.

TOP CHOICE **High West Distillery & Saloon** BAR
(703 Park St; ⊙2pm-1am daily, closed Sun & Mon Apr-Jun & Sep-Dec) A former livery and Model A–era garage is now home to Park City's most happenin' nightspot. You can ski in for homemade rye whiskey at this microdistillery. What could be cooler?

No Name Saloon BAR
(447 Main St; ⊙11am-1am) There's a motorcycle hanging from the ceiling, Johnny Cash's 'Jackson' playing on the stereo and a waitress who might be lying about the history of this memorabilia-filled bar.

O'Shucks PUB
(427 Main St; ⊙10am-2am) A hard-partying dive bar, popular with a young snowboarder crowd, O'Shucks packs 'em in Tuesdays with $3 schooners (32oz beers).

Egyptian Theatre Company THEATER
(www.egyptiantheatrecompany.org; 328 Main St) The restored 1926 theater is a primary venue for Sundance; the rest of the year it hosts plays, musicals and concerts.

ℹ Information

Alpine Internet (638 Main St; internet acces per 15min $2.50; ⊙6:30am-6pm) Cyber coffeehouse.

Main Street Visitor Center (☎435-649-7457; 528 Main St; ⊙11am-6pm Mon-Sat, noon-6pm Sun) Small desk inside the Park City Museum downtown.

Visitor Information Center (☎435-649-6100; www.parkcityinfo.com; cnr Hwy 224 & Olympic Blvd; ⊙9am-7pm Mon-Sat, 11am-4pm Sun Jun-Sep, closes earlier Oct-May) Large office in the northern Kimball Junction area.

ℹ Getting There & Around

Park City Transportation (☎435-649-8567; www.parkcitytransportation.com) and **Powder for the People** (☎435-649-6648; www.powderforthepeople.com) both run shared van service ($39 one-way) and private-charter vans (from $99 for one to three people) from Salt Lake City airport. The latter also has Powder Chaser ski shuttles (from $45 round-trip) that will take you from Park City to Salt Lake City resorts.

The excellent **Park City Transit** (www.parkcity.org/citydepartments/transportation) system covers most of Park City, including the three ski resorts, and makes it easy not to need a car. Free trolleybuses run one to six times an hour from 8am to 11pm (reduced frequency in summer). There's a downloadable route map online.

HEBER CITY & AROUND

About 18 miles southeast of Park City, **Heber Valley** (www.gohebervalley.com) lies below Uinta National Forest in the Wasatch range. Heber City itself is fairly utilitarian, with basic motels and services. From here the 1904 **Heber Valley Historic Railroad** (☎435-654-5601; www.hebervalleyrr.org; 450 S 600 West; adult/child $30/25; ⊙late May–Oct) runs vari-

DON'T MISS

ROBERT REDFORD'S SUNDANCE RESORT

Wind your way up narrow and twisting Hwy 92, for a truly special experience at Robert Redford's **Sundance Resort** (☎801-225-4107; www.sundanceresort.com; 9521 Alpine Loop Rd, Provo; r $225-319; @📶). Even if a night's stay at this elegantly rustic, ecoconscious wilderness getaway is out of reach, you can have a great meal at the Treehouse restaurant or deli, attend an outdoor performance at the amphitheater or watch pottery being made (and sold) at the art shack. Skiing, hiking and spa services on site. The resort is 30 miles south of Park City, and 50 miles southeast of SLC.

ous family-friendly scenic trips through gorgeous **Provo Canyon**.

In nearby Midway, you can swim in **Homestead Crater** (☎435-654-1102; www.homesteadresort.com; Homestead Resort, 700 N Homestead Dr; admission $15; ⊙10am-7pm), a 65ft-deep geothermal pool (90°F) in a tall limestone cone open to the sky. This is way cool.

Northeastern Utah

Most people head northeast to explore Dinosaur National Monument, but this rural, oil-rich area also has some captivating wilderness terrain. All towns are a mile above sea level.

VERNAL

The capital of Utah's dinosaur country, Vernal welcomes visitors with a large pink dino-buddy and plenty of restaurants and motels with themed signs.

The informative film at the **Utah Field House of Natural History State Park Museum** (http://stateparks.utah.gov; 496 E Main St; ⊙9am-5pm Mon-Sat; 👪) is a great all-round introduction to Utah's dinosaurs. Interactive exhibits, video clips and, of course, giant fossils are wonderfully relevant to the area.

Don Hatch River Expeditions (☎435-789-4316; www.donhatchrivertrips.com; 221 N 400 East; ⊙May-Sep) offers rapid-riding and gentler float trips on the Green and Yampa Rivers.

Chain motels are numerous in town. For something different, try the luxe **Landmark Inn & Suites** (☎435-781-1800; Rte 149; r incl breakfast $69-109; 📶). All-American, down-home grub at **Naples Country Café** (1010 E Hwy 40; breakfast & sandwiches $4-8, mains $9-15; ⊙7am-10pm) includes mile-high meringue pies.

Dinosaurland Travel Board (☎800-477-5558; www.dinoland.com; 134 W Main; ⊙8am-5pm Mon-Fri) provides information on the entire region. Pick up driving-tour brochures for area rock art and dino tracks here.

DINOSAUR NATIONAL MONUMENT

One of the largest dinosaur fossil beds in North America was discovered here in 1909. The highlight of this **national monument** (www.nps.gov/dino; per vehicle $10; ⊙9am-5pm) is a dinosaur quarry, which was enclosed with hundreds of bones partially excavated but left in the rock. You can also hike up to touch still-embedded, 150-million-year-old fossils on the trail, and there's a scenic driving tour with Native American rock art. The monument straddles the Utah–Colorado state line. The Utah portion of the park, which contains all the fossils, is about 15 miles east of Vernal via Hwys 40 and 149.

FLAMING GORGE NATIONAL RECREATION AREA

Named for its fiery red sandstone, the **gorge area** (admission per vehicle $5) has boating along 375 miles of reservoir shoreline, fly-fishing and rafting on the Green River, trout-fishing, hiking and cross-country skiing. The lake's 6040ft elevation ensures pleasantly warm but not desperately hot summers – daytime highs average about 80°F. Get general information at www.flaminggorgecountry.com and contact the USFS **Flaming Gorge Headquarters** (☎435-784-3445; www.fs.fed.us/r4/ashley/recreation; 25 W Hwy 43; ⊙8am-5pm Mon-Fri) for the camping lowdown.

Activities at **Red Canyon Lodge** (☎435-889-3759; www.redcanyonlodge.com; 790 Red Canyon Rd, Dutch John; cabins $110; ⊙closed Mon-Thu Nov-Mar) include fishing, rowing, rafting and horseback riding, among others. Its pleasantly rustic cabins have no TVs. **Flaming Gorge Resort** (☎435-889-3773; www.flaminggorgeresort.com; 155 Greendale/Hwy 191, Dutch John; r $110, ste $150) has similar water-based fun, and rents motel rooms and suites. Both have decent restaurants.

Southeastern Utah

Snow-blanketed peaks in the distance provide stark contrast to the red-rock canyons that define this rugged corner of the Colorado Plateau. Over 65 million years, water has carved serpentine, sheer-walled gorges along the course of the Colorado and Green Rivers. Today these define the borders of expansive Canyonlands National Park. At nearby Arches National Park, erosion has sculpted thousands of arches and fin rock formations. Base yourself between the parks in Moab, aka activity central – a town built for mountain biking, river running and four-wheel driving. In the far southeastern corner of the state, Ancestral Puebloan sites are scattered among remote-and-rocky wilderness areas and parks. Most notable is Monument Valley, which extends into Arizona.

LOCAL PASSPORTS

Area national parks sell local passports (per vehicle $25) that are good for a year's entry to Arches and Canyonlands National Parks, plus Hovenweep and Natural Bridges National Monument. **Federal park passes** (www.nps.gov/findapark/passes.htm; per vehicle adult/senior $80/10), available online, allow year-long access to all federal recreation lands and are a great way to support the Southwest's amazing parks.

GREEN RIVER

The 'World's Watermelon Capital,' Green River offers a good base for river running on the Green and Colorado Rivers. The legendary one-armed Civil War veteran, geologist and ethnologist John Wesley Powell first explored these rivers in 1869 and 1871. Learn about his amazing travels at the extensive **John Wesley Powell River History Museum** (☎435-564-3427; www.jwprhm.com; 1765 E Main St; adult/child $4/1; ⊙8am-7pm Sun-Sat), which also has exhibits on the Fremont Native Americans, geology and local history. The museum also serves as the local visitor center.

Local outfitters **Holiday Expeditions** (☎435-564-3273; www.holidayexpeditions.com) and **Moki Mac River Expeditions** (☎435-564-3361; www.mokimac.com) run day-long white-water-rafting trips (adult/child from $80/40), including lunch and transportation; ask about multiday excursions.

Family-owned, clean and cheerful, **Robbers Roost Motel** (☎435-564-3452; www.rrmotel.com; 325 W Main St; s $31-38, d $40-45; ❄📶) is a great little motorcourt budget motel. At the much larger **River Terrace Inn** (☎435-564-3401; www.river-terrace.com; 1880 E Main St; r incl breakfast $110-106; ❄📶🏊), many of the motel rooms overlook the river. Noshing a burger with the post-rafting crowd at **Ray's Tavern** (25 S Broadway; mains $8-26; ⊙11am-10pm) is far and away the best way in town to satisfy your hunger.

In southeastern Utah, Green River is the only stop on the daily *California Zephyr* train run by **Amtrak** (☎800-872-7245; www.amtrak.com; 250 S Broadway) to Denver, CO ($85, 10¾ hours). Green River is 182 miles southeast of Salt Lake City and 52 miles northwest of Moab.

MOAB

Southeastern Utah's largest community (population 5121) bills itself as the state's recreation capital, and… oh man, does it deliver. Scads of rafting and riding outfitters (mountain bike, horse, 4WD…) base here and take forays into surrounding public lands. And you can hike Arches or Canyonlands National Parks during the day, then come back to a comfy bed, a hot tub and your selection of surprisingly good restaurants at night. Do note that this alfresco adventure gateway is not a secret: the town is mobbed, especially during spring and fall festivals. If the traffic irritates you, remember that you can disappear into the vast surrounding desert in no time.

Activities

The Moab visitor center puts out several brochures on near-town rock art, hiking trails, driving tours, etc. Area outfitters offer half-day to multiday adventures (from $50 for four hours) that include transport, the activity, and sometimes, meals. Among the best are the following:

Sheri Griffith Expeditions RAFTING
(☎435-259-8229; www.griffithexp.com; 2231 S Hwy 191) Highly rated rafting outfitter; some multisport adventures.

Canyon Voyages ADVENTURE SPORTS
(☎435-259-6007; www.canyonvoyages.com; 211 N Main St) River running, raft-hike-bike-4WD combos available; kayak and canoe rentals too.

Poison Spider Bicycles CYCLING, MOUNTAIN BIKING
(☎435-259-7882; www.poisonspiderbicycles.com; 497 N Main St) Mountain- and road-bike rentals and tours; superior service.

Farabee's Jeep Rental & Outlaw Tours EXTREME SPORTS
(☎435-259-7494; www.farabeesjeeprentals.com; 1125 S Highway 191) Four-wheel-drive rentals, self-drive and fully guided off-road 4WD tours.

Red Cliffs Lodge HORSEBACK RIDING
(☎435-259-2002; www.redcliffslodge.com/tours-activities; Mile 14, Hwy 128) Half-day trail rides.

Sleeping

Most lodgings in town have bike storage or facilities, plus hot tubs to soothe sore muscles. Despite having an incredible number of motels, the town does book up; reservations are highly recommended March through October.

Individual **BLM campsites** (www.blm.gov/utah/moab; tent & RV sites $8-12; year-round) in the area are first-come, first-served. In peak season, check with the Moab Information Center to see which sites are full.

Cali Cochitta B&B $$
(☎435-259-4961; www.moabdreaminn.com; 110 S 200 East; cottages incl breakfast $125-160;) Make yourself at home in one of the charming brick cottages a short walk from downtown. A long wooden table on the patio provides a welcome setting for community breakfasts.

Sorrel River Ranch LODGE $$$
(☎435-259-4642; www.sorrelriver.com; Mile 17, Hwy 128; r $340-530;) Southeast Utah's only full-service luxury resort and restaurant was originally an 1803 homestead. The lodge and log cabins sit on 240, activity-filled acres along the banks of the Colorado River.

Redstone Inn MOTEL $
(☎435-259-3500; www.moabredstone.com; 535 S Main St; r $79-99;) Great budget digs: simple, pine-paneled rooms have refrigerator, microwave, coffeemakers and free wired internet access. Walls are a bit thin though. Hot tub on-site, pool privileges at sister hotel across street.

Gonzo Inn MOTEL $$
(☎435-259-2515; www.gonzoinn.com; 100 W 200 South; r $159, ste $205-339, incl breakfast Apr-Oct;) Spruced-up standard motel with fun retro splashes of color; favored by cyclists.

Adventure Inn Moab MOTEL $
(☎435-259-6122; www.adventureinnmoab.com; 512 N Main St; s/d incl breakfast $65/80; closed Nov-Feb;) Family-owned and friendly, single-story motel.

Eating

There's no shortage of places to fuel up in Moab, from backpacker coffeehouses to gourmet dining rooms. Pick up the *Moab Menu Guide* (www.moabmenuguide.com) at area lodgings. Some restaurants close earlier, or on variable days, from December through March.

TOP CHOICE **Love Muffin** CAFE $
(139 N Main St; mains $6-8; 7am-2pm;) Early-rising moms and adventure-hunting locals scarf up many of the homemade muffins – like the 'breakfast' with bacon and blueberries – before some people get out of bed. Not to worry; the largely organic menu at this vibrant cafe also includes creative sandwiches, breakfast burritos and inventive egg dishes such as 'Verde,' with brisket and slow-roasted salsa.

Jeffrey's Steakhouse STEAKHOUSE $$$
(☎435-259-3588; 218 N 100 West; mains $22-40; 5pm-10pm) A historic sandstone building serves as home to one of the latest stars of the local dining scene. Jeffrey's is serious about beef, which comes grain-fed, Wagyu-style and in generous cuts. If the night is too good to end, head upstairs to the upscale Ghost Bar. Reservations advised.

Moab Brewery AMERICAN $$
(686 S Main St; mains $8-18; 11:30am-10pm Mon-Thu, 11:30am-11pm Fri & Sat) A good bet for a group with diverse tastes. Choosing among the list of microbrews made in the vats just behind the bar area may be easier than deciding what to eat off the vast and varied menu.

Miguel's Baja Grill MEXICAN $$
(51 N Main St; dishes $12-20; 5-10pm) Dine on Baja fish tacos and margaritas in the sky-lit breezeway patio lined with brightly painted walls. Fajitas, *chile rellenos* (stuffed peppers) and seafood mains are all ample sized.

Buck's Grill House SOUTHWESTERN $$$
(1394 N Hwy 191; mains $15-36; 5:30-9:30pm;) Think upscale-modern Southwest:

duck tamales with adobo, elk stew with horseradish cream...

Milt's BURGERS $
(356 Mill Creek Dr; mains $3-6; ⌚11am-8pm Mon-Sat) A classic 1954 burger stand with fresh-cut fries and oh-so-thick milkshakes.

Shopping

Look for art and photography galleries – along with T-shirt and Native American knickknacks – near the intersection of Center and Main Sts.

Arches Book Company & Back of Beyond BOOKS
(83 N Main St; 🛜) Excellent, adjacent indie bookstores with extensive regional selection. Also has coffee shop.

Information

Most businesses and services, including fuel and ATMs, are along Hwy 191, also called Main St in the center of town.

BLM (☎435-259-2100; www.blm.gov/utah/moab) Phone and internet assistance only.

Grand County Public Library (25 S 100 East; per hr free; ⌚9am-8pm Mon-Fri, to 5pm Sat) Easy 15-minute internet; register for longer access.

Moab Area Travel Council (☎435-259-8825; www.discovermoab.com; ⌚8am-5pm Mon-Fri) Excellent for pre-trip planning

Moab Information Center (cnr Main & Center Sts; ⌚8am-8pm) Excellent source of information on area parks, trails, activities, camping and weather. Extensive bookstore and knowledgeable staff. Walk-in only.

Getting There & Around

Great Lakes Airlines (☎800-554-5111; www.flygreatlakes.com) has regularly scheduled flights from **Canyonlands Airport** (www.moabairport.com), 16 miles north of town via Hwy 191, to Denver, CO, Las Vegas, NV and Page, AZ.

Moab Luxury Coach (☎435-940-4212; www.moabluxurycoach.com) operates a scheduled van service to and from SLC ($149 one-way, 4¾hr) and Green River ($119 one-way, 3¾hr). **Roadrunner Shuttle** (☎435-259-9402; www.roadrunnershuttle.com) and **Coyote Shuttle** (☎435-260-2097; www.coyoteshuttle.com) offer on-demand airport, hiker-biker and river shuttles.

Moab is 235 miles southeast of Salt Lake City, 150 miles northeast of Capital Reef National Park.

ARCHES NATIONAL PARK

One of the Southwest's most gorgeous parks, **Arches** (www.nps.gov/arch; 7-day pass per vehicle $10; ⌚24hr, visitor center 7:30am-6:30pm Apr-Oct, 8am-4:30pm Nov-Mar) boasts the world's greatest concentration of sandstone arches – more than 2000 ranging from 3ft to 300ft wide at last count. Nearly one million visitors make the pilgrimage here, just 5 miles north of Moab on Hwy 191, every year. Many noteworthy arches are easily reached by paved roads and relatively short hiking trails; much of the park can be covered in a day. To avoid crowds, consider a moonlight exploration, when it's cooler and the rocks feel ghostly.

Highlights include **Balanced Rock**, oft-photographed **Delicate Arch** (best captured in the late afternoon), spectacularly elongated **Landscape Arch** and popular **Windows Arches**. Reservations are necessary for the twice-daily ranger-led hikes into the fins of the **Fiery Furnace** (adult/child $10/5; ⌚Apr-Oct). Book in person or online at www.recreation.gov.

Because of water scarcity and heat, few visitors backpack, though it is allowed with free permits (available from the visitor center). The scenic **Devils Garden Campground** (☎518-885-3639; www.recreation.gov; Hwy 191; tent & RV sites $20) is 18 miles from the visitor center and fills up from March to October. Twenty-four sites are available on a first-come, first-served basis, 52 sites by reservation.

CANYONLANDS NATIONAL PARK

Red-rock fins, bridges, needles, spires, craters, mesas, buttes – **Canyonlands** (www.nps.gov/cany; 7-day per vehicle $10; ⌚24hr) is a crumbling, decaying beauty, a vision of ancient earth. Roads and rivers make inroads to this high-desert wilderness stretching 527 sq miles, but much of it is still an untamed environment. You can hike, raft (Cataract Canyon offers some of the wildest white water in the West) and 4WD here but be sure that you have plenty of gas, food and water.

The canyons of the Colorado and Green Rivers divide the park into three districts. **Island in the Sky** (☎435-259-4712; ⌚visitor center 9am-4:30pm Nov-Apr, 9am-6:30pm Mar-Oct) is most easily reached and offers amazing overlooks. Our favorite short hike is the half-mile loop to oft-photographed **Mesa Arch**, a slender, cliff-hugging span framing a picturesque view of Washer Woman Arch and Buck Canyon. Drive a bit further to reach the **Grand View Overlook** trailhead. The path follows the canyon's edge

DON'T MISS

NEWSPAPER ROCK RECREATION AREA

This tiny, free recreation area showcases a single large sandstone rock panel packed with more than 300 **petroglyphs** attributed to Ute and Ancestral Puebloan groups during a 2000-year period. The many red-rock figures etched out of a black 'desert varnish' surface make for great photos (evening sidelight is best). The site, about 12 miles along Hwy 211 from Hwy 191, is usually visited as a short stop on the way to the Needles section of Canyonlands National Park (8 miles further).

and ends at a praise-your-maker precipice. This park section is 32 miles from Moab; head north along Hwy 191 then southwest on Hwy 313.

Needles (435-259-4711; visitor center 9am-4:30pm Nov-Feb, 8am-6pm Mar-May, 8am-5pm Jun-Oct), the second district, is wilder and more far-flung, ideal for backpacking. Follow Hwy 191 south and Hwy 211 west, 40 miles from Moab.

And then there's the **Maze** (no services), a wild and remote area off Hwy 24 that is accessible by 4WD only. The Great Gallery within **Horseshoe Canyon** has superb life-size rock art left by prehistoric Native Americans. But you should not make this trip without adequate preparations in consultation with rangers in other sections.

In addition to normal entrance fees, permits ($5 to $30) are required for overnight backcountry and mountain-biking camping, 4WD trips and river trips. Reserve at least two weeks ahead, by fax or mail only, with the **NPS** (435-259-4351, fax 435-259-4285; www.nps.gov/cany/planyourvisit/backcountry permits.htm). Some same- or next-day spots may be available where you pick up permits at the respective visitor center, but reservations are advised in spring and fall.

DEAD HORSE POINT STATE PARK

A tiny but stunning **state park** (www.stateparks.utah.gov; Hwy 313; admission per vehicle $10; 6am-10pm, visitor center 8am-5pm), Dead Horse Point has been the setting for numerous movies, including the opening scene from *Mission Impossible II* and the finale of *Thelma & Louise*. Located just off Hwy 313 (the road to Canyonlands), the park has mesmerizing views atop red-rock canyons rimmed with white cliffs, of the Colorado River, Canyonlands National Park and the distant La Sal Mountains. The 21-site **Kayenta Campground** (801-322-3770; http://utahstateparks.reserveamerica.com; Hwy 313; tent & RV sites $20) provides limited water (bringing your own is highly recommended) and RV facilities. Four campsites are available, but it's first-come, first-served, the rest by reservation.

BLUFF

Surrounded by red rock, this tiny tot town (population 283) makes a comfortable, laid-back base for exploring the desolately beautiful southeastern corner of Utah. It sits along the San Juan River at the junction of Hwys 191 and 163, 100 miles south of Moab. Bluff was founded by Mormon pioneers in 1880; a few old buildings remain and some settlers' cabins have been reconstructed.

For up-close views of rock art and cliff dwellings, hire Vaughn Hadenfeldt at **Far Out Expeditions** (435-672-2294; www.faroutexpeditions.com; cnr 7th & Mulberry Sts; day trip from $165), to lead a single- or multiday hike into the desert surrounds. A rafting trip with **Wild Rivers Expeditions** (800-422-7654; www.riversandruins.com; 101 Main St; day trip adult/child $165/120; Mar-Oct), a history-and-geology-minded outfitter, also includes ancient sites.

The hospitable **Recapture Lodge** (435-672-2281; www.recapturelodge.com; Hwy 191; r incl breakfast $60-80;) is a rustic, cozy place to stay. Owners know the area inside and out and you can follow trails from here to the river. Also nice are the spacious log rooms at the **Desert Rose Inn** (435-672-2303; www.desertroseinn.com; 701 W Main St; r $99-119;).

Artsy **Comb Ridge Coffee** (Hwy 191; mains $2-6; 7am-3pm Wed-Sun, vary Nov-Feb;) serves espresso, muffins and blue-corn pancakes inside a timber and adobe cafe. For lunch and dinner, the organic-minded **San Juan River Kitchen** (75 E Main St; lunch $8-13, dinner $9-20; 11am-9pm Tue-Sun) offers regionally sourced, inspired Mexican American dishes.

NATURAL BRIDGES NATIONAL MONUMENT

Fifty-five miles northwest of Bluff and 40 miles west of Blanding, this really remote **monument** (www.nps.gov/nabr; Hwy 275; admission per vehicle $6; ⏲24hr, visitor center 8am-6pm Apr-Sep, 8am-5pm Oct-Mar) protects a white sandstone canyon (it's not red) containing three impressive and easily accessible natural bridges. The oldest, the Owachomo Bridge, spans 180ft but is only 9ft thick. The flat 9-mile Scenic Drive loop is ideal for overlooking. Thirteen basic **tent & RV sites** ($10) are available on a first-come, first-served basis; there is overflow camping space but no services (no food, no fuel... no businesses anywhere around).

HOVENWEEP NATIONAL MONUMENT

Beautiful, little-visited **Hovenweep** (Hwy 262; admission per vehicle $6; ⏲dusk-dawn, visitor center 8am-6pm Apr-Sep, 8am-5pm Oct-Mar), meaning 'deserted valley' in the Ute language, contains impressive towers and granaries that are part of prehistoric Ancestral Puebloan sites. The Square Tower Group is accessed near the visitor center, other sites require long hikes. The **campground** (tent & RV sites $10) has 31 basic, first-come, first-served sites (no food or fuel). The main access is east of Hwy 191 on Hwy 262 via Hatch Trading Post, more than 40 miles northeast of Bluff.

MONUMENT VALLEY

Twenty-five miles west from Bluff, after the village of **Mexican Hat** (named for an easy-to-spot sombrero-shaped rock), Hwy 163 winds southwest and enters the Navajo Indian reservation. Thirty miles south, the incredible mesas and buttes of **Monument Valley** rise up. Most of the area, including the tribal park with a 17-mile unpaved driving loop circling the massive formations, is in Arizona. For a complete listing of sights and services, see p346.

Southwestern Utah

Locals call it 'color country,' but the cutesy label hardly does justice to the eye-popping hues that saturate the landscape. The deep-crimson canyons of Zion, the delicate pink-and-orange minarets at Bryce Canyon, the swirling yellow-white domes of Capitol Reef – the land is so spectacular that it encompasses three national parks and the gigantic Grand Staircase-Escalante National Monument (GSENM).

This section is organized roughly northeast to southwest, following the highly scenic Hwy 12 and Hwy 89 from Capitol Reef National Park to Zion National Park and St George.

CAPITOL REEF NATIONAL PARK

Not as crowded as its fellow parks but equally scenic, **Capitol Reef** (www.nps.gov/care; cnr Hwy 24 & Scenic Dr; admission free, scenic drive per vehicle $5; ⏲24hr, visitor center & scenic drive 8am-6pm Apr-Oct, to 4:30pm Nov-Mar) contains much of the 100-mile Waterpocket Fold, created 65 million years ago when the earth's surface buckled up and folded, exposing a cross-section of geologic history that is downright painterly in its colorful intensity. Hwy 24 cuts grandly through the park, but make sure to take the **scenic drive** south, which passes through orchards – a legacy of Mormon settlement. In season, you can freely pick cherries, peaches and apples, as well as stop by the historic **Gifford Farmhouse** to see an old homestead and buy fruit-filled minipies. Grassy, first-come, first-served **tent & RV sites** ($10) fill fast spring through fall.

TORREY

Just 15 miles west of Capital Reef, the small pioneer town of Torrey serves as most visitors' base for sleeping and eating.

Ty Markham has done an exquisite job of bringing the spacious, 1914 **Torrey Schoolhouse** (☎435-633-4643; www.torreyschoolhouse.com; 150 N Center St; r incl breakfast $110-115; ⏲Apr-Oct; ❄📶) back to life as a B&B. Soaring ceilings hang over rooms decked out in dressed-down country elegance and gourmet breakfasts are organic. Western-themed **Austin's Chuck Wagon Lodge** (☎435-425-3335; www.austinschuckwagonmotel.com; 12 W Main St; r $75-85, cabins $135; ⏲mid-Mar–Oct; ❄📶🏊) motel rooms are clean but basic, with sturdy furniture and lots of space. Grab supplies at the on-site general store.

Highly stylized Southwestern food such as turkey *chimole* (a spicy stew), Mayan tamales and fire-roasted pork tenderloin on a cilantro waffle draws visitors to **Café Diablo** (☎435-425-3070; 599 W Main St; mains $22-30; ⏲11:30am-10pm mid-Apr–Oct) from across the state. Be sure to reserve ahead.

Wayne County Travel Council (☎435-425-3365; www.capitolreef.org; cnr Hwys 24 & 12; ⏲noon-7pm Apr-Oct) provides loads of information. Ask about area outfitters.

BOULDER

Though the tiny outpost of **Boulder** (www.boulderutah.com), population 188, is just 32 miles south of Torrey on Hwy 12, you have to cross Boulder Mountain to get there. The area is so rugged and isloated that a paved Hwy 12 didn't connect through until 1985. From here, the attractive **Burr Trail** heads east as a paved road across the northeastern corner of the Grand Staircase-Escalante National Monument, eventually winding up on a gravel road to Capital Reef's Waterpocket Fold and down to Bullfrog Marina on Lake Powell. To explore area canyons and rock art, consider a one-day trek (child-friendly) with knowledgeable **Earth Tours** (☎435-691-1241; www.earth-tours.com; half-/full-day tours $75/100).

The small-but-excellent **Anasazi State Park Museum** (www.stateparks.utah.gov; Main St/Hwy 12; admission $5; ⏲8am-6pm Jun-Aug, 9am-5pm Sep-May) curates artifacts and a Native American site inhabited from AD 1130 to 1175. Get information on area public lands inside the museum, at the GSENM Interagency Desk.

Plush rooms at **Boulder Mountain Lodge** (☎435-335-7460; www.boulder-utah.com; 20 N Hwy 12; r $110-175; ❄@📶) are nice enough, but it's the 15-acre wildlife sanctuary setting that's unsurpassed. An outdoor hot tub with mountain views is a particularly scenic spot to soak off trail-earned aches and bird-watch. The lodge's must-visit **Hell's Backbone Grill** (☎435-335-7464; Boulder Mountain Lodge, 20 N Hwy 12; breakfast $8-10, dinner $16-34; ⏲7-11:30am & 5:30-9:30pm Mar-Oct) serves soulful, earthy preparations of regionally inspired and sourced cuisine. Book ahead.

Organic vegetable tarts, eclectic burgers and scrumptious homemade desserts at **Burr Trail Grill & Outpost** (Hwy 12 & Burr Trail Rd; mains $7-18; ⏲11am-10pm Mar-Oct; 📶) rival dishes at the more famous restaurant next door. There's a coffee shop and gallery too.

GRAND STAIRCASE-ESCALANTE NATIONAL MONUMENT

The 2656-sq-mile **Grand Staircase-Escalante National Monument** (GSENM; www.ut.blm.gov/monument; admission free; ⏲24hr) covers more territory than Delaware and Rhode Island combined. It sprawls between Capitol Reef National Park, Glen Canyon National Recreation Area and Bryce Canyon National Park. The nearest services, and GSENM visitor centers, are in Boulder and Escalante on Hwy 12 in the north, and Kanab on US 89 in the south. Otherwise, infrastructure is minimal, leaving a vast, uninhabited canyonland full of 4WD roads that call to adventurous travelers who have the time and equipment to explore. Be warned: this waterless region was so inhospitable that it was the last to be mapped in the continental US.

A 6-mile, round-trip trail to **Lower Calf Creek Falls** (Mile 75, Hwy 12; admission per vehicle $2), between Boulder and Escalante, is the most accessible, and most used, trail in the park. The 13 creekside **tent & RV sites** ($7) fill fast (no reservations).

ESCALANTE

This gateway town of 750 people is the closest thing to a metropolis for miles and miles. It's a good place to base yourself – or to stock up and map it out – before venturing into the adjacent GSENM. The **Escalante Interagency Office** (☎435-826-5499; www.ut.blm.gov/monument; 775 W Main St; ⏲7:30am-5:30pm mid-Mar–Oct, 8am-4:30pm Nov–mid-Mar) is a superb resource center with complete information on all area monument and forest service lands surrounding. Escalante is 65 miles from Torrey, near Capital Reef National Park, and 30 slow and windy miles from Boulder.

Escalante Outfitters & Cafe (☎435-826-4266; www.escalanteoutfitters.com; 310 W Main St; ⏲8am-9pm; 📶) is a traveler's oasis, selling maps, books, camping supplies, liquor(!), espresso, breakfast and homemade pizza and salads. It also rents out tiny, rustic cabins ($45) and mountain bikes (from $35 per day). Outfitter **Excursions of Escalante** (☎800-839-7567; www.excursionsofescalante.com; 125 E Main St; full day trips from $145) leads area canyoneering, climbing and photo hikes; its cafe was under reconstruction at the time of research.

DON'T MISS

HIGHWAY 12

Arguably Utah's most diverse and stunning route, **Highway 12 Scenic Byway** (http://scenicbyway12.com) winds through rugged canyonland on a 124-mile journey west of Bryce Canyon to near Capitol Reef. The section between Escalante and Torrey traverses a moonscape of sculpted slickrock, crosses narrow ridgebacks and climbs over an 11,000ft-tall mountain.

Recommended lodgings:

Canyons Bed & Breakfast B&B $$ (☎435-826-4747; www.canyonsbnb.com; 120 E Main St; r incl breakfast $125-135; ❄📶) Upscale, cabin-rooms surround a shady terrace.

Circle D Motel MOTEL $ (☎435-826-4297; www.escalantecircledmotel.com; 475 W Main St; r $65-75; ❄📶) Updated, older motel with a friendly proprietor and a full-service restaurant.

Rainbow Country Bed & Breakfast B&B $ (☎435-826-4567; www.bnbescalante.com; 586 E 300 S; r incl breakfast $69-109; ❄📶) Homey and relaxed B&B with a shared TV den.

KODACHROME BASIN STATE PARK

Dozens of red, pink and white sandstone chimneys highlight this colorful **state park** (www.stateparks.utah.gov; Cottonwood Canyon Rd; admission per vehicle $6), named for its photogenic landscape by the National Geographic Society. Twenty-four of the developed sites at the **campground** (☎801-322-3770; http://utahstateparks.reserveamerica.com; tent/RV sites with hookups $16/20) are available by reservation.

BRYCE CANYON NATIONAL PARK

The Grand Staircase, a series of steplike uplifted rock layers elevating north from the Grand Canyon, culminates at this rightly popular **national park** (www.nps.gov/brca; Hwy 63; 7-day pass per vehicle $25; ⏲24hr, visitor center 8am-8pm May-Sep, 8am-4:30pm Nov-Mar, 8am-6pm Oct & Apr) in the Pink Cliffs formation. It's full of wondrous sorbet-colored pinnacles and points, steeples and spires, and totem-pole-shaped 'hoodoo' formations. The canyon is actually an amphitheater eroded from the cliffs. From Hwy 12, turn south on Hwy 63; the park is 50 miles southwest of Escalante.

Rim Road Scenic Drive (8000ft) travels 18 miles one-way, roughly following the canyon rim past the visitor center, the lodge, incredible overlooks (don't miss **Inspiration Point**) and trailheads, ending at **Rainbow Point** (9115ft). From May through September, a free **shuttle bus** (⏲8am-6pm) runs from a staging area just north of the park to as far south as **Bryce Amphitheater**.

The two campgrounds, **North Campground** (☎877-444-6777; www.recreation.gov; tent & RV sites $15) and **Sunset Campground** (tent & RV sites $15; ⏲late spring–fall), both have toilets and water. Sunset is more wooded, but has fewer amenities and doesn't accept reservations. For laundry, showers and groceries, visit North Campground. During summer, sites fill before noon.

The 1920s **Bryce Canyon Lodge** (☎435-834-8700; www.brycecanyonforever.com; Hwy 63; r $135-180; ⏲Apr-Oct; @) exudes rustic mountain charm. Rooms are in modern hotel-style units, with up-to-date furnishings, and thin-walled duplex cabins with gas fireplaces and front porches. No TVs. The lodge **restaurant** (breakfast $6-10, lunch & dinner $12-40; ⏲6:30-10:30am, 11:30am-3pm & 5-10pm Apr-Oct) is excellent, if expensive.

Just north of the park boundaries, **Ruby's Inn** (☎435-834-5341; www.rubysinn.com; 1000 S Hwy 63; campsites $25-40, r $89-199; ❄@📶🏊) is a town as much as it is a motel complex. Choose from several Best Western lodging options, plus a campground, before you take a helicopter ride, watch a rodeo, admire Western art, wash laundry, shop for groceries, fill up with gas, dine at one of several restaurants and then post a letter about it all.

Eleven miles east on Hwy 12, the small town of Tropic has additional food and lodging.

> WORTH A TRIP
>
> ### CEDAR CITY & BREAKS
>
> At 10,000ft, the summer-only road to **Cedar Breaks National Monument** (www.nps.gov/cebr; admission $3; ⏲24hr Jun-Sep, visitor center 8am-6pm Jun-Sep) is one of the last to open after winter snow. But it's worth the wait the amazing amphitheater overlooks rival those of Bryce Canyon. Nearby **Cedar City** (www.scenicsouthernutah.com) is known for its four-month-long Shakespeare Festival and an abundance of adorable B&Bs. The town is on I-15, 52 miles north of St George and 90 miles west of Bryce Canyon; the national monument is 22 miles northeast of the town.

KANAB

At the southern edge of Grand Staircase-Escalante National Monument, vast expanses of rugged desert surround remote Kanab (population 3564). Western filmmakers made dozens of films here from the 1920s to the 1970s, and the town still has an Old West movie set feel to it.

The **Kanab GSENM Visitor Center** (www.ut.blm.gov/monument; 745 E Hwy 89; ⏲8am-5pm)

ELEVATION MATTERS

As elsewhere, southern Utah is generally warmer than northern Utah. But before you go making any assumptions about weather, check the elevation of your destination. Places less than an hour apart may have several thousand feet of elevation – and 20°F temperature – difference.

» St George (3000ft)

» Zion National Park – Springdale entrance (3900ft)

» Cedar Breaks National Monument (10,000ft)

» Bryce National Park Lodge (8100ft)

» Moab (4026ft)

» Salt Lake City (4226ft)

» Park City (7100ft)

provides monument information; **Kane County Office of Tourism** (☎435-644-5033; www.kaneutah.com; 78 S 100 E; ⏰10am-5pm, closed Sun Nov-May) focuses on town and movie sites.

John Wayne, Maureen O'Hara and Gregory Peck are a few Hollywood notables who slumbered at the somewhat-dated **Parry Lodge** (☎435-644-2601; 89 E Center St; r $60-80; ❄📶🏊). An old, brickfront building houses **Rocking V Cafe** (97 W Center St; mains 10-20; ⏰5-10pm), where fresh ingredients star in dishes such as buffalo tenderloin and curried quinoa.

ZION NATIONAL PARK

Entering **Zion** (www.nps.gov/zion; Hwy 9; 7-day pass per vehicle $25; ⏰24hr, Zion Canyon Visitor Center 8am-7pm May-Sep, 8am-6pm Apr & Oct, 8am-5pm Nov-Mar) from the east along Hwy 9, the route rolls past yellow sandstone and **Checkerboard Mesa** before reaching an impressive gallery-dotted tunnel and 3.5 miles of switchbacks going down in red-rock splendor. More than 100 miles of park trails here offer everything from leisurely strolls to wilderness backpacking and camping.

If you've time for only one activity, the 6-mile **Scenic Drive**, which pierces the heart of Zion Canyon, is it. From April through October, taking a free **shuttle** (⏰6:45am-10pm) from the visitor center is required, but you can hop off and on at any of the scenic stops and trailheads along the way. The famous **Angels Landing Trail** is a strenuous, 5.4-mile vertigo-inducer (1400ft elevation gain, with sheer drop-offs), but the views of Zion Canyon are phenomenal. Allow four hours round-trip.

For the 16-mile backpacking trip down through the **Narrows** (June to September only), you need a hiker shuttle and a backcountry permit from the visitor center, which usually requires advance reservation on the website. But you can get part of the experience by walking up from **Riverside Walk** 5 miles to **Big Springs**, where the canyon walls narrow and day trips end. Remember, in either direction, you're hiking *in* the Virgin River for most of the time.

Reserve far ahead and request a riverside site in the cottonwood-shaded **Watchman Campground** (☎800-365-2267; http://reservations.nps.gov; Hwy 9; tent sites $16, RV sites with hookups $18-30) by the canyon. Adjacent **South Campground** (tent & RV sites $16) is first-come, first-served only. Together these two campgrounds have almost 300 sites.

Smack in the middle of the scenic drive, rustic **Zion Lodge** (☎435-772-7700; www.zionlodge.com; r & cabins $160-180; ❄@📶) has 81 well-appointed motel rooms and 40 cabins with gas fireplaces. All have wooden porches with stellar red-rock cliff views, but no TVs. The lodge's full-service dining room, **Red Rock Grill** (breakfast $10-15, lunch $8-20, dinner $15-30; ⏰7am-10pm, hr vary Dec-Mar) has similarly amazing views. Just outside the park, the town of Springdale offers many more services.

Note that you must pay an entrance fee to drive on Hwy 9 through the park, even if you are just passing through. Motorhome drivers are also required to pay a $15 escort fee to cross through the 1.1-mile Zion-Mt Carmel tunnel at the east entrance.

SPRINGDALE

Positioned at the main south, entrance to Zion National Park, Springdale is a perfect little park town. Stunning red cliffs form the backdrop to eclectic cafes, restaurants are big on organic ingredients, and artist galleries are interspersed with indie motels and B&Bs. Many of the outdoorsy folk who live here moved from somewhere less beautiful, but you will occasionally run into a lifelong local.

In addition to hiking trails in the national park, you can take outfitter-led **climbing** and **canyoneering** trips (from $150 per half-day) on adjacent BLM lands. All the classes and trips with terrific **Zion Rock & Mountain Guides** (☎435-772-3303; www.zionrockguides.com; 1458 Zion Park Blvd) are private. Solo travelers can save money by joining an existing group with **Zion Adventure Company** (☎435-772-1001; www.zionadventures.com; 36 Lion Blvd). The latter also offers river tubing in summer; both have hiker/biker shuttles.

Springdale has an abundance of good restaurants and nice lodging options. The updated motorcourt rooms at **Canyon Ranch Motel** (☎435-772-3357; www.canyonranchmotel.com; 668 Zion Park Blvd; s $84-94, d $94-99, r with kitchenette $114-125;) ring a shady lawn with picnic tables and swings.

From colorful tractor reflectors to angel art, the owners' collections enliven every corner of the 1930s bungalow that is **Under-the-Eaves Bed & Breakfast** (☎435-772-3457; www.under-the-eaves.com; 980 Zion Park Blvd; r incl breakfast $95-185;). Five flower-filled acres spill down to the Virgin River bank at **Cliffrose Lodge** (☎435-772-3234; www.cliffroselodge.com; 281 Zion Park Blvd; r $129-259;).

Grab a coffee, breakfast burrito or turkey panini at **Mean Bean** (932 Zion Park Blvd; mains $4-10; 7am-5pm Jun-Aug, 7am-2pm Sep-May;), a hiker-and-cyclist haven with a roof deck. Top-notch, seasonal meals at **Parallel 88** (☎435-772-3588; Driftwood Lodge, 1515 Zion Park Blvd; breakfasts $10-14, dinner mains $28-40; 7:30-10:30am & 5-10pm) may include impossibly tender green-apple pork loin or a mile-high quiche. Gorgeous red-rock views are best appreciated at sunset; make a reservation.

POLYGAMY TODAY

Though the Mormon church eschewed plural marriage in 1890, there are those that still believe it is a divinely decreed practice. Most of the roughly 7000 residents in Hilldale-Colorado City on the Utah–Arizona border are polygamy-practicing members of the Fundamentalist Church of Jesus Christ of Latter-day Saints (FLDS). Walk into a Wal-Mart in Washington or Hurricane and the shoppers you see in pastel-colored, prairie-style dresses – with lengthy braids or elaborate up-dos – are likely sister wives. Other, less-conspicuous sects are active in the state as well.

The Mexican-tiled patio with twinkly lights at **Oscar's Café** (948 Zion Park Blvd; breakfast & sandwiches $5-10, mains $12-20; 7:30am-10pm) and the **Bit & Spur Restaurant & Saloon** (1212 Zion Park Blvd; mains $13-18; 5-10pm) are local-favored places to hang out, eat and drink at.

The **regional visitors bureau** (☎888-518-7070; www.zionpark.com) does not have a physical office. Request a travel planner by mail or check online. A Springdale menu guide, available at local lodgings, comes out every spring.

ST GEORGE

Nicknamed 'Dixie' for its warm weather and southern location, St George (population 88,001) is popular with retirees. This spacious Mormon town, with an eye-catching temple and pioneer buildings, makes a good stop between Las Vegas and Salt Lake City – or en route to Zion National Park.

St George's first residents weren't snowbirds from Idaho, but Jurassic-era dinosaurs. Entry to the **Dinosaur Discovery Site** (www.dinotrax.com; 2200 E Riverside Dr; adult/child $6/3; 10am-6pm Mon-Sat) gets you an interpretive tour of a 15,000-sq-ft collection of in-situ dino tracks, beginning with a video. At 7400-acre **Snow Canyon State Park** (www.stateparks.utah.gov; Hwy 18; admission per vehicle $5), 9 miles north of town, short easy trails lead to tiny slot canyons, cinder cones, lava tubes and vast fields of undulating red slickrock.

Nearly every chain hotel known to humanity is represented somewhere in St George. When events aren't going on, lodging is plentiful and affordable; when they are, prices skyrocket. **Best Western Coral Hills** (☎435-673-4844; www.coralhills.com; 125 E St George Blvd; r incl breakfast $80-129; @) is walking distance from downtown restaurants and historic buildings. Two lovely, late-1800 houses contain **Seven Wives Inn** (☎800-600-3737; www.sevenwivesinn.com; 217 N 100 West; r incl breakfast $99-185; @), a charming B&B with manicured gardens and a small swimming pool.

Homemade cupcakes are not all **Twenty-five on Main** (25 N Main St; mains $6-14; 8am-9pm Mon-Thu, to 10pm Fri & Sat) bakery-cafe does well. We also like the breakfast panini, a warm salmon salad and the veggie-filled pasta primavera. For something fancier, try the creative modern American mains at **Painted Pony** (2 W St George Blvd, Ancestor Sq;

lunch $12-20, dinner $21-38; ⌚11:30am-10pm Mon-Sat, 4-10pm Sun).

The **Chamber of Commerce** (☎435-628-1658; www.stgeorgechamber.com; 97 E St George Blvd; ⌚9am-5pm Mon-Fri) is the primary source for town info. **Utah Welcome Center** (☎435-673-4542; http://travel.utah.gov; Dixie Convention Center, 1835 Convention Center Dr; ⌚8:30am-5:30pm), off I-15, addresses statewide queries.

SGU Municipal Airport (www.flysgu.com; 4550 S Airport Parkway) has expanded service in recent years, with more to come. **Delta** (☎800-221-1212; www.delta.com) shuttles between Salt Lake City and St George several times daily; **United Express** (☎800-864-8331; www.united.com) has four weekly flights to-and-from Los Angeles. Taxis (downtown $15) and all the standard chain car rentals are available. Note that Las Vegas' McCarran International Airport, 120 miles south, often has better flight and car rental deals than Utah airports.

Greyhound (☎435-673-2933; www.greyhound.com; 1235 S Bluff St) departs from the local McDonald's, with buses to SLC ($65, 5½ hours) and Las Vegas, NV ($29, two hours). **St George Express** (☎435-652-1100; www.stgeorgeexpress.com; 1040 S Main St) has shuttle service to Las Vegas ($35, two hours) and Zion National Park ($25, 40 minutes).

NEW MEXICO

It's called the Land of Enchantment for a reason. The play of sunlight on juniper-speckled hills that roll to infinity; the traditional Hispanic mountain villages with pitched tin roofs atop old adobe homes; the gentle magnificence of the 13,000-foot Sangre de Cristo Mountains; plus volcanoes, river canyons and vast high desert plains beneath an even vaster sky – the beauty sneaks up on you, then casts a powerful spell. The culture, too, is alluring, with silhouetted crosses topping historic mud-brick missions, ancient and living Indian pueblos, chile-smothered enchiladas, real-life cowboys and a vibe of otherness that makes the state feel like it might be a foreign country.

The legend of Billy the Kid lurks around every corner. Miracle healings bring flocks of faithful pilgrims to Chimayo. Bats plumb the ethereal corners of Carlsbad Caverns. Something crashed near Roswell...

NEW MEXICO FACTS

» **Nickname** Land of Enchantment

» **Population** 2 million

» **Area** 121,599 sq miles

» **Capital city** Santa Fe (population 68,00)

» **Other cities** Albuquerque (population 545,800), Las Cruces (population 97,600)

» **Sales tax** 5% to 8%

» **Birthplace of** John Denver (1943–97), Smokey Bear (1950–76)

» **Home of** International UFO Museum & Research Center (Roswell), Julia Roberts

» **Politics** a 'purple' state, with a more liberal north and conservative south

» **Famous for** ancient pueblos, the first atomic bomb (1945), where Bugs Bunny should have turned left

» **State question** 'red or green?' (chile sauce, that is)

» **Driving distances** Albuquerque to Carlsbad 275 miles, Santa Fe to Taos 71 miles

Maybe New Mexico's indescribable charm is best expressed in the captivating paintings of Georgia O'Keeffe, the state's patron artist. She herself exclaimed, on her very first visit: 'Well! Well! Well!...This is wonderful! No one told me it was like this.'

But seriously, how could they?

History

People roamed the land here as far back as 10,500 BC, but by Coronado's arrival in the 16th century, Pueblos were the dominant communities. Santa Fe was crowned as the colonial capital in 1610, after which Spanish settlers and farmers fanned out across northern New Mexico and missionaries began their often violent efforts to convert the area's Puebloans to Catholicism. Following a successful revolt in 1680, Native Americans occupied Santa Fe until 1692, when Diego de Vargas recaptured the city.

In 1851 New Mexico became US territory. Native American wars, settlement by cowboys and miners and trade along the Santa Fe Trail further transformed the region, and the arrival of the railroad in the 1870s created an economic boom.

Painters and writers set up art colonies in Santa Fe and Taos in the early 20th century. In 1943 a scientific community descended on Los Alamos and developed the atomic bomb. Big issues include water rights (whoever owns the water has the power) and immigration.

Information

Where opening hours are listed by season (not month), readers should call first, as hours can fluctuate based on weather, budgets or for no reason at all.

New Mexico CultureNet (www.nmcn.org) A great overview of the state's contemporary cultural legacy.

New Mexico Magazine (www.nmmagazine.com) Good guide to the state with sections on destinations, diversions and comforts.

New Mexico Route 66 Association (www.rt66nm.org) Information on the famous path through the state.

New Mexico State Parks Division (www.emnrd.state.nm.us/prd; 1220 South St Francis Dr, Santa Fe) Info on state parks, with a link to camping reservations.

New Mexico Tourism Department (505-827-7400; www.newmexico.org) Order a free *Vacation Guide,* download a Scenic Byways map or research activities and accommodations.

Public Lands Information Center (877-851-8946; www.publiclands.org) Camping and recreation information.

Albuquerque

This bustling crossroads has a sneaky charm, one based more on its locals than big-city sparkle. The citizens here are proud of their city, and folks are more than happy to share history, highlights and must-try restaurants – which makes the state's most populous city much more than a dot on the Route 66 map.

Centuries-old adobes line the lively Old Town area, and the shops, restaurants and bars in the hip Nob Hill zone are all within easy walking distance of each other. Ancient petroglyphs cover rocks just outside town while modern museums explore space and nuclear energy. There's a distinctive and vibrant mix of university students, Native Americans, Hispanics, gays and lesbians. You'll find square dances and yoga classes flyered with equal enthusiasm, and ranch hands and real-estate brokers chow down at hole-in-the-wall taquerias and retro cafes.

Albuquerque's major boundaries are Paseo del Norte Dr to the north, Central Ave to the south, Rio Grande Blvd to the west and Tramway Blvd to the east. Central Ave is the main artery (aka old Route 66) – it passes through Old Town, downtown, the university and Nob Hill. The city is divided into four quadrants (NW, NE, SW and SE), and the intersection of Central Ave and the railroad tracks just east of downtown serves as the center point of the city.

Sights

OLD TOWN

From its foundation in 1706 until the arrival of the railroad in 1880, the plaza was the hub of Albuquerque; today Old Town is the city's most popular tourist area.

American International Rattlesnake Museum MUSEUM

(www.rattlesnakes.com; 202 San Felipe St NW; adult/child/senior $5/3/4; 11:30am-5:30pm Mon-Fri, 10am-6pm Sat, 1-5pm Sun) From eastern diamondback to rare tiger rattlers, you won't find more types of live rattlesnakes anywhere else in the world. Once you get over the freak-out factor, you'll be amazed not just by the variety of vipers but by the intricate beauty of their colors and patterns. Hopefully you'll never see them this close in the wild! Weekday hours are a little longer in summer.

Albuquerque Museum of Art & History MUSEUM

(www.cabq.gov/museum; 2000 Mountain Rd NW; adult/4-12yr/senior $4/1/2, admission free 1st Wed of month & 9am-1pm Sun; 9am-5pm Tue-Sun) Conquistador armor and weaponry are highlights at the Albuquerque Museum of Art & History, where visitors can study the city's tricultural Native American, Hispanic and Anglo past. Works by New Mexico artists also featured.

Also in the Old Town are **San Felipe de Neri Church** (built in 1793), **¡Explora! Children's Museum** (p376) and the **New Mexico Museum of Natural History & Science** (p376).

AROUND TOWN

The University of New Mexico (UNM) area has loads of good restaurants, casual bars, offbeat shops and hip college hangouts. The main drag is Central Ave between University and Carlisle Blvds. Just east is trendy Nob Hill, a pedestrian-friendly neighborhood

SCENIC DRIVES: NEW MEXICO'S BEST

» **Billy the Kid Scenic Byway** (www.billybyway.com) This mountain-and-valley loop in southeastern New Mexico swoops past Billy the Kid's stomping grounds, Smokey Bear's gravesite and the orchard-lined Hondo Valley. From Roswell, take Hwy 380 west.

» **High Road to Taos** The back road between Santa Fe and Taos passes through sculpted sandstone desert, fresh pine forests and rural villages with historic adobe churches and horse-filled pastures. The 13,000ft Truchas Peaks soar above. From Santa Fe, take Hwy 84/285 to Hwy 513 then follow the signs.

» **NM Highway 96** From Abiquiu to Cuba, this little road wends through the heart of Georgia O'Keeffe country, beneath the distinct profile of Cerro Pedernal, then passing Martian-red buttes and sandstone cliffs striped purple, yellow and ivory.

» **NM Highway 52** Head west from Truth or Consequences into the dramatic foothills of the Black Range, past the old mining towns of Winston and Chloride. Continue north, emerging onto the sweeping Plains of San Augustin before reaching the bizarre Very Large Array.

lined with indie coffee shops, stylish boutiques and patio-wrapped restaurants.

Indian Pueblo Cultural Center MUSEUM
(www.indianpueblo.org; 2401 12th St NW; adult/child & student/under 5yr $6/3/free; ⏲9am-5pm) Operated by New Mexico's 19 pueblos, the Indian Pueblo Cultural Center is a must for contextualizing the history of northern New Mexico. Appealing displays trace the development of Pueblo cultures, exhibit customs and crafts, and feature changing exhibits.

National Museum of Nuclear Science & History MUSEUM
(www.nuclearmuseum.org; 601 Eubank Blvd SE; adult/child & senior $8/7; ⏲9am-5pm) Exhibits examine the Manhattan Project, the history of arms control and the use of nuclear energy as an alternative energy source. Docents here are retired military, and they're very knowledgeable.

Petroglyph National Monument ARCHAEOLOGICAL SITE
(www.nps.gov/petr) More than 20,000 rock etchings are found inside the Petroglyph National Monument northwest of town. Stop by the visitor center (on Western Trail at Unser Blvd) to determine which of three viewing trails – in different sections of the park – best suits your interests. For a hike with great views but no rock art, hit the Volcanoes trail. Note: smash-and-grab thefts have been reported at some trailhead parking lots, so don't leave valuables in your vehicle. Head west on I-40 across the Rio Grande and take exit 154 north.

Sandia Peak Tramway CABLE CAR
(www.sandiapeak.com; Tramway Blvd; vehicle entrance fee $1, adult/13-20yr & senior/child/under 5yr $20/17/12/free; ⏲9am-8pm Wed-Mon, 5-8pm Tue Sep-May, 9am-9pm Jun-Aug) The 2.7-mile Sandia Peak Tramway starts in the desert realm of cholla cactus and soars to the pines atop 10,378ft Sandia Peak in about 15 minutes. The views are huge and that's what you're paying for at the restaurant at the top.

Activities

The omnipresent Sandia Mountains and the less crowded Manzano Mountains offer outdoor activities, including hiking, skiing (downhill and cross-country), mountain biking, rock climbing and camping. For information and maps, head to the **Cibola National Forest office** (☎505-346-3900; 2133 Osuna Rd NE, Albuquerque; ⏲8am-4:30pm Mon-Fri) or the **Sandia Ranger Station** (☎505-281-3304; 11776 Hwy 337, Tijeras; ⏲8am-4:30pm Mon-Fri), off I-40 exit 175 south, about 15 miles east of Albuquerque.

Sandia Crest National Scenic Byway DRIVING, HIKING
Reach the top of the Sandias via the eastern slope along the lovely Sandia Crest National Scenic Byway (I-40 exit 175 north), which passes numerous hiking trailheads. Alternatively, take the Sandia Peak Tramway or Hwy 165 from Placitas (I-25 exit 242), a dirt road through Las Huertas Canyon that passes the prehistoric dwelling of **Sandia Man Cave**.

ALBUQUERQUE FOR CHILDREN

The gung-ho **¡Explora! Children's Museum** (www.explora.us; 1701 Mountain Rd NW; adult/under 12yr $8/4; ⏲10am-6pm Mon-Sat, noon-6pm Sun; 👪) will captivate your kiddies for hours. From the lofty high-wire bike to the leaping waters to the arts-and-crafts workshop, there's a hands-on exhibit for every type of child (don't miss the elevator). Not traveling with kids? Check the website to see if you're in town for the popular 'Adult Night.' Typically hosted by an acclaimed local scientist, it's become one of the hottest tickets in town.

The teen-friendly **New Mexico Museum of Natural History & Science** (www.nmnaturalhistory.org; 1801 Mountain Rd NW; adult/under 13yr $7/4; ⏲9am-5pm; 👪) features an Evolator (evolution elevator), which transports visitors through 38 million years of New Mexico's geologic and evolutionary history. The new Space Frontiers exhibit highlights the state's contribution to space exploration, from ancient Chaco observatories to an impressive, full-scale replica of the Mars Rover. The museum also contains a **Planetarium** (adult/child $7/4) and the newly 3-D IMAX-screened **DynaTheater** (adult/child $7/4).

Sandia Peak Ski Area SKIING, CYCLING
(☎505-242-9052; www.sandiapeak.com; half-/full-day lift tickets adult $35/50, teen, child & senior $30/40) Sometimes the snow here is great, other times it's lame, so check before heading up. The ski area opens on summer weekends and holidays (June to September) for mountain bikers. You can rent a bike at the base facility ($48 with $650 deposit) or ride the chairlift to the top of the peak with your own bike ($10). Drive here via Scenic Byway 536, or take the Sandia Peak Tramway (skis are allowed on the tram, but not bikes).

Discover Balloons BALLOONING
(☎505-842-1111; www.discoverballoons.com; 205c San Felipe NW; adult/under 12yr $160/125) Several companies will float you over the city and the Rio Grande, including Discover Balloons. Flights last about an hour, and many are offered early in the morning to catch optimal winds and the sunrise.

Tours

From mid-March to mid-December, the Albuquerque Museum of Art & History offers informative, guided **Old Town walking tours** (⏲11am Tue-Sun). They last 45 minutes to an hour and are free with museum admission.

Festivals & Events

Gathering of Nations CULTURAL
(www.gatheringofnations.com) The biggest Native American powwow in the world, with traditional music, dance, food, crafts and the crowning of Miss Indian World. Held each April.

Zia Regional Rodeo RODEO
The **New Mexico Gay Rodeo Association** (www.nmgra.com) hosts this event during the second weekend of August.

International Balloon Fiesta BALLOONING
(☎888-422-7277; www.balloonfiesta.com) In early October, some 800,000 spectators are drawn to this weeklong event. The highlight is the mass ascension, when more than 500 hot-air balloons launch nearly simultaneously.

Sleeping

Route 66 Hostel HOSTEL $
(☎505-247-1813; www.rt66hostel.com; 1012 Central Ave SW; dm $20, r from $25; P❄📶) Clean, fun and inexpensive, this place is simple and has a good travelers' vibe. A kitchen, library and outdoor patio are available for its guests to use.

TOP CHOICE **Andaluz** BOUTIQUE HOTEL $$
(☎505-242-9090; www.hotelandaluz.com; 125 2nd St NW; r $140-240; P❄@📶) Albuquerque's best hotel will wow you with style and attention to detail, from the dazzling lobby – where six arched nooks with tables and couches offer alluring spaces to talk and drink in public-privacy, to the Italian-made hypoallergenic bedding. The restaurant is one of the best in town, and there's a beautiful guest library and a rooftop bar. The hotel is so 'green' you can tour its solar water-heating system – the largest in the state. You'll get big discounts if you book online.

Mauger Estate B&B B&B $$
(☎505-242-8755; www.maugerbb.com; 701 Roma Ave NW; r incl breakfast $99-195, ste $160-205; P 📶) This restored Queen Anne mansion (Mauger is pronounced 'major') has comfortable rooms with down comforters, stocked fridges and freshly cut flowers. Kids are welcome and there's one dog-friendly room complete with Wild West decor and a small yard ($20 extra).

Böttger Mansion B&B $$
(☎505-243-3639; www.bottger.com; 110 San Felipe St NW; r incl breakfast $104-179; P ❄ @ 📶) A friendly and informative proprietor gives this well-appointed Victorian-era B&B an edge over some tough competition. The eight-bedroom mansion, built in 1912, is close to Old Town Plaza, top-notch museums and several in-the-know New Mexican restaurants such as **Duran's Central Pharmacy** (1815 Central Ave; cash only). The honeysuckle-lined courtyard is a favorite with bird-watchers. Famous past guests include Elvis, Janis Joplin and Machine Gun Kelly.

Hotel Blue HOTEL $
(☎877-878-4868; www.thehotelblue.com; 717 Central Ave NW; r incl breakfast $60-99; P ❄ @ 📶 🏊) Well positioned beside a park and downtown, the art-deco 134-room Hotel Blue has Tempurpedic beds and a free airport shuttle. Bonus points awarded for the good-sized pool and 40in flat-screen TVs.

Eating

TOP CHOICE **Golden Crown Panaderia** BAKERY $
(☎505-243-2424; www.goldencrown.biz; 1103 Mountain Rd NW; mains $5-20; ⊙7am-8pm Tue-Sat, 10am-8pm Sun) Who doesn't love a friendly neighborhood bakery? Especially one with gracious staff, fresh-from-the-oven bread and pizza, fruit-filled empanadas, smooth coffee and the frequent free cookie. Call ahead to reserve a loaf of quick-selling green-chile bread. Go to the website to check out the 'bread cam.'

Frontier CAFETERIA $
(2400 Central Ave SE; dishes $3-10; ⊙5am-1pm; 👪) An Albuquerque tradition, the Frontier boasts enormous cinnamon rolls, addictive green-chile stew, and the best huevos rancheros ever. The food and people-watching are outstanding, and students love the low prices on the breakfast, burgers and Mexican food.

Annapurna INDIAN $$
(www.chaishoppe.com; 2201 Silver Ave SE; mains $7-12; ⊙7am-9pm Mon-Sat, 10am-8pm Sun; 📶 🌿) For some of the freshest, tastiest health food in town, grab a seat within the bright, mural-covered walls of Annapurna. The delicately spiced ayurvedic dishes are all vegetarian or vegan, but they're so delicious that even carnivores will find something to love.

Flying Star Café DINER $
(www.flyingstarcafe.com; mains $8-11) Central Ave (3416 Central Ave SE; ⊙6am-11pm Sun-Thu, 6am-midnight Fri & Sat) Juan Tabo Blvd (4501 Juan Tabo Blvd NE; ⊙6am-10pm Sun-Thu, 6am-11pm Fri & Sat; 📶) With seven constantly packed locations, this is the place to go for creative diner food made with regional ingredients, including homemade soups, main dishes from sandwiches to stir-fry, and yummy desserts. There's something here for everyone.

Artichoke Café MODERN AMERICAN $$$
(☎505-243-0200; www.artichokecafe.com; 424 Central Ave SE; lunch mains $8-16, dinner mains $19-30; ⊙11am-2:30pm Mon-Fri, 5-9pm Mon & Sun, 5:30-10pm Tue-Sat) Voted an Albuquerque favorite many times over, this place takes the best from Italian, French and American cuisine and serves it with a touch of class.

Drinking & Entertainment

Popejoy Hall (www.popejoyhall.com; cnr Central Ave & Cornell St SE) and the historic **KiMo Theatre** (www.cabq.gov/kimo; 423 Central Ave NW) are the primary venues for big-name national acts, local opera, symphony and theater. To find out what's happening in town, grab a free copy of the weekly *Alibi* or visit www.alibi.com.

Satellite Coffee CAFE
(2300 Central Ave NE) Don't be put off by the hip, space-age appearance. The staff is welcoming and seats are filled with all manner of laptop-viewing, java-swilling locals. There are eight locations scattered across town; also try the one in Nob Hill (3513 Central Ave NE).

Copper Lounge LOUNGE
(1504 Central Ave SE, 2nd fl) If a parking lot filled with pickup trucks spells the word 'fun' in your party dictionary, then pull over for the red-brick Copper Lounge, where baseball caps and cowboy hats sip beer, play pool and scope the ladies.

Kelly's Brewery BREWERY
(3226 Central Ave SE) Grab a seat at a communal table then settle in for a convivial night of people-watching and beer-drinking at this former Ford dealership and gas station. On warm spring nights, it seems everyone in town is chilling on the sprawling patio.

Launch Pad LIVE MUSIC
(www.launchpadrocks.com; 618 Central Ave SW) Indie, reggae, punk and country bands rock the house most nights (though not at the same time). Look for the spaceship on Central Ave. Right next door is the **El Rey Theater** (www.elreytheater.com; 620 Central Ave SW), another longtime favorite for live music.

Shopping

For eclectic gifts, head to Nob Hill, east of the university. Park on Central Ave SE or one of the college-named side streets, then take a stroll past the inviting boutiques and specialty stores.

Palms Trading Post HANDICRAFTS
(1504 Lomas Blvd NW; 9am-5:30pm Mon-Sat) If you're looking for Native American crafts and informed salespeople who can give you advice, stop by the Palms Trading Post.

Silver Sun JEWELRY
(116 San Felipe St NW; 9am-4:30pm) Just south of the plaza, Silver Sun is a reputable spot for turquoise.

Mariposa Gallery ARTWORK
(www.mariposa-gallery.com; 3500 Central Ave SE) Beautiful and funky arts, crafts and jewelry, mostly by regional artists.

IMEC JEWELRY
(www.imecjewelry.net; 101 Amherst SE) Around the corner from Mariposa, you'll find more artistic fine jewelry at IMEC.

Information

Emergency & Medical Services

Police (505-764-1600; 400 Roma Ave NW)

Presbyterian Hospital (505-841-1234; 1100 Central Ave SE; 24hr emergency)

UNM Hospital (505-272-2411; 2211 Lomas Blvd NE; 24hr emergency) Head here if you don't have insurance.

Internet Access

Lots of restaurants and cafes have wi-fi.

Main Library (505-768-5141; 501 Copper Ave NW; 10am-6pm Mon & Thu-Sat, 10am-7pm Tue & Wed) Free internet access after purchasing a $3 SmartCard. Wi-fi available for free but must obtain access card.

Internet Resources

Albuquerque.com (www.albuquerque.com) Attractions, hotels and restaurants.

City of Albuquerque (www.cabq.gov) Information on public transportation, area attractions and more.

Post

Post office (505-346-1256; 201 5th St SW)

Tourist Information

The **Albuquerque Convention & Visitors Bureau** (www.itsatrip.org) has three visitor centers:

Downtown (505-842-9918; 20 First Plaza NW, cnr 2nd St & Copper Ave; 9am-4pm Mon- Fri)

Old Town (505-243-3215; 303 Romero St NW; 10am-5pm Oct-May, 10am-6pm Jun-Sep)

Sunport (Albuquerque International Airport) At the lower-level baggage claim.

Getting There & Around

Air

Albuquerque International Sunport (www.cabq.gov/airport; 2200 Sunport Blvd SE) is New Mexico's main airport and most major US airlines fly here. Cabs to downtown cost $20 to $25; try **Albuquerque Cab** (505-883-4888).

Bus

The **Alvarado Transportation Center** (100 1st St SW, cnr Central Ave) houses **ABQ RIDE** (505-243-4435; www.cabq.gov/transit; 8am-5pm), the public bus system. It covers most of Albuquerque from Monday to Friday and hits the major tourist spots daily (adult/child $1/35¢; one-day pass $2). Most lines run until 6pm. ABQ RIDE Route 50 connects the airport with downtown (last bus at 8pm Monday to Friday; limited service Saturday). Check the website for maps and exact schedules. Route 36 stops near Old Town and the Indian Pueblo Cultural Center.

Greyhound (505-243-4435; www.greyhound.com, 320 1st St SW) serves destinations throughout New Mexico.

Sandia Shuttle (888-775-5696; www.sandiashuttle.com) runs daily shuttles from Albuquerque to many Santa Fe hotels between 9am and 11pm (one-way/round-trip $25/45).

Twin Hearts Express (800-654-9456) runs a shuttle service from the airport to northern New Mexico destinations, including Santa Fe and Taos.

Train

The Southwest Chief stops daily at Albuquerque's **Amtrak station** (☎505-842-9650; www.amtrak.com; cnr 1st St & Central Ave), heading east to Chicago ($194, 26 hours) or west through Flagstaff, AZ ($90, five hours), to Los Angeles, CA (from $101, 16½ hours).

A commuter line, the **New Mexico Rail Runner Express** (www.nmrailrunner.com), shares the station, with eight departures for Santa Fe weekdays (one-way/day pass $7/8), four on Saturday and two on Sunday, though weekend service will likely be discontinued. The trip takes about 1½ hours.

Along I-40

Although you can zip between Albuquerque and Flagstaff, AZ, in less than five hours, the national monuments and pueblos along the way are well worth a visit. For a scenic loop, take Hwy 53 southwest from Grants, which leads to all the following sights, except Acoma. Hwy 602 brings you north to Gallup.

ACOMA PUEBLO

The dramatic mesa-top 'Sky City' sits 7000ft above sea level and 367ft above the surrounding plateau. One of the oldest continuously inhabited settlements in North America, this place has been home to pottery-making people since the later part of the 11th century. Guided **tours** (adult/senior/child $20/15/12; ⏲hourly 10am-3pm Fri-Sun mid-Oct–mid-Apr, 9am-3:30pm daily mid-Apr–mid-Oct) leave from the **visitor center** (☎800-747-0181; http://sccc.acomaskycity.org) at the bottom of the mesa and take two hours, or one hour just to tour the historic mission. From I-40, take exit 102, which is about 60 miles west of Albuquerque, then drive 12 miles south.

EL MORRO NATIONAL MONUMENT

The 200ft sandstone outcropping at this **monument** (www.nps.gov/elmo; adult/child $3/free; ⏲9am-6pm Jun-Aug, 9am-5pm Sep-Oct, 9am-4pm Nov-May), also known as 'Inscription Rock,' has been a travelers' oasis for millennia. Thousands of carvings – from petroglyphs in the pueblo at the top (c 1275) to elaborate inscriptions by the Spanish conquistadors and the Anglo pioneers – offer a unique means of tracing history. It's about 38 miles southwest of Grants via Hwy 53.

ZUNI PUEBLO

The Zuni are known worldwide for their delicately inlaid silverwork, which is sold in stores lining Hwy 53. Check in at the visitor center for information, photo permits and tours of the **pueblo** (☎505-782-7238; www.zunitourism.com; 1239 Hwy 53; tours $10; ⏲8:30am-5:30pm Mon-Fri, 10:30am-4pm Sat, noon-4pm Sun), which lead you among stone houses and beehive-shaped adobe ovens to the massive **Our Lady of Guadalupe Mission**, featuring impressive kachina murals. The **A:shiwi A:wan Museum & Heritage Center** (☎505-782-4403; www.ashiwi-museum.org; Ojo Caliente Rd; admission by donation; ⏲9am-5pm Mon-Fri) displays early photos and other tribal artifacts.

The friendly, eight-room **Inn at Halona** (☎505-782-4547; www.halona.com; Halona Plaza; r incl breakfast $79; ❄📶), decorated with local Zuni arts and crafts, is the only place to stay on the pueblo.

GALLUP

Because Gallup serves as the Navajo and Zuni peoples' major trading center, you'll find many trading posts, pawnshops, jewelry stores and crafts galleries in the historic district. It's arguably the best place in New Mexico for top-quality goods at fair prices. Gallup is another classic Route 66 town, with loads of vintage motels and businesses.

The town's lodging jewel is **El Rancho** (☎505-863-9311; www.elranchohotel.com; 1000 E Hwy 66; r from $76; P❄📶🏊). Many of the great actors of the 1940s and '50s stayed here. El Rancho features a superb Southwestern lobby, a restaurant, a bar and an eclectic selection of simple rooms. There's wi-fi in the lobby.

Visit the **chamber of commerce** (☎800-380-4989; www.thegallupchamber.com; 103 W Hwy 66; ⏲8:30am-5pm Mon-Fri) for details and events listings.

Santa Fe

Walking among the historic adobe neighborhoods or even around the tourist-filled plaza, there's no denying that Santa Fe has a timeless, earthy soul. Founded around 1610, Santa Fe is the second-oldest city and oldest state capital in the USA. It's got the oldest public building and throws the oldest party in the country (Fiesta). Yet the city is synonymous with contemporary chic, and boasts the second-largest art market in the nation, gourmet restaurants, great museums, spas and a world-class opera.

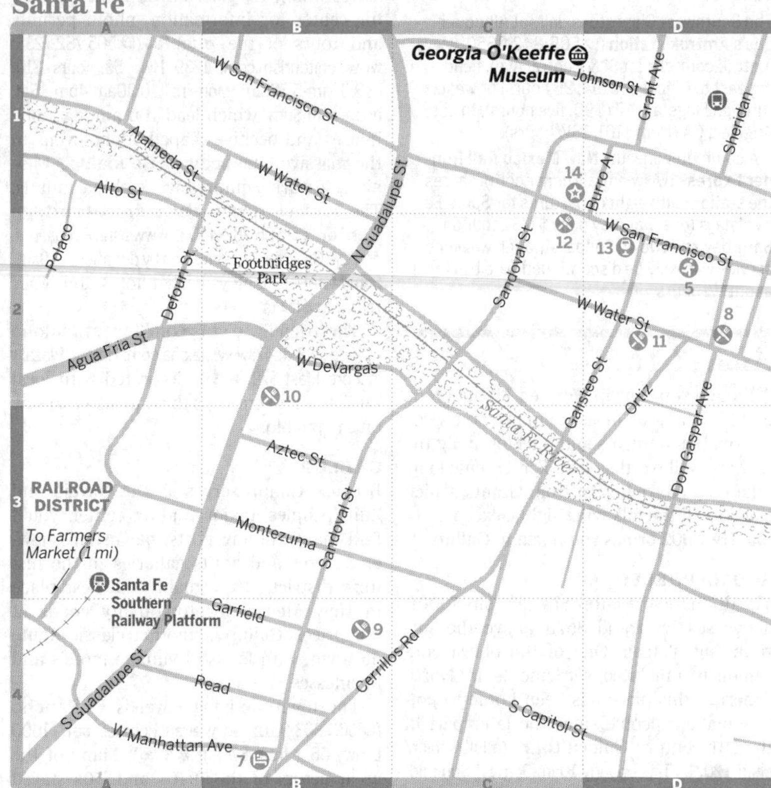

At 7000ft, it's also the highest state capital in the US, sitting at the base of the Sangre de Cristo range, a conveniently fantastic place to hike, mountain bike, backpack and ski.

Cerrillos Rd (I-25 exit 278), a 6-mile strip of hotels and fast-food restaurants, enters town from the south; Paseo de Peralta circles the center of town; St Francis Dr (I-25 exit 282) forms the western border of downtown and turns into Hwy 285, which heads north toward Los Alamos and Taos. Most downtown restaurants, galleries, museums and sights are within walking distance from the plaza, the historic center of town.

Sights

Art enthusiasts coming for the weekend may want to arrive early on Friday to take advantage of the evening's free admission policies at many museums.

Georgia O'Keeffe Museum MUSEUM
(☎505-946-1000; www.okeeffemuseum.org; 217 Johnson St; adult/senior/child $10/8/free; ⊙10am-5pm, to 8pm Fri) Possessing the world's largest collection of her work, the Georgia O'Keeffe Museum features the artist's paintings of flowers, bleached skulls and adobe architecture. Tours of O'Keeffe's house in Abiquiu (p386) require advance reservations.

Canyon Road NEIGHBORHOOD
(www.canyonroadarts.com) The epicenter of the city's upscale art scene. More than 100 galleries, studios, shops and restaurants line the narrow historic road. Look for Santa Fe School masterpieces, rare Native American antiquities and wild contemporary work. The area positively buzzes with activity during the early-evening art openings on Fridays, and especially on Christmas Eve.

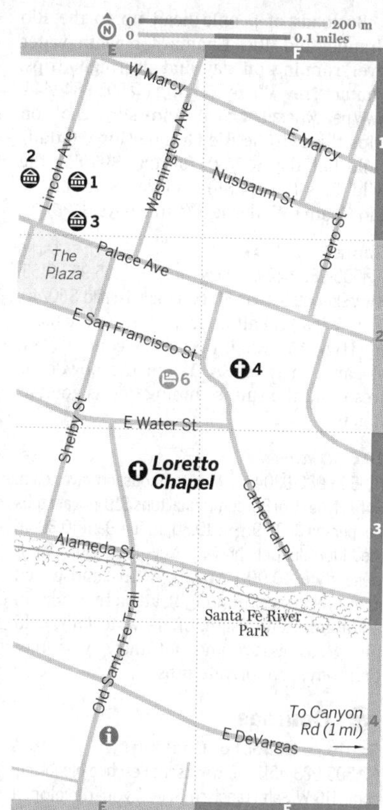

Santa Fe

Top Sights

Georgia O'Keeffe Museum C1
Loretto Chapel E3

Sights

1 New Mexico History Museum E1
2 New Mexico Museum of Art E1
3 Palace of the Governors E1
4 St Francis Cathedral F2

Activities, Courses & Tours

5 Santa Fe School of Cooking D2

Sleeping

6 La Fonda E2
7 Santa Fe Motel & Inn B4

Eating

8 Cafe Pasqual's D2
9 Cleopatra Café B4
10 Cowgirl Hall of Fame B2
11 Coyote Café D2
12 Tia Sophia's C2

Drinking

Bell Tower Bar ..... (see 6)
13 Evangelo's D2

Entertainment

14 Lensic Performing Arts Center C1

FREE **Wheelwright Museum of the American Indian** MUSEUM
(www.wheelwright.org; 704 Camino Lejo; ⏲10am-5pm Mon-Sat, 1-5pm Sun) In 1937, Mary Cabot established the Wheelwright Museum of the American Indian, part of Museum Hill, to showcase Navajo ceremonial art. While its strength continues to be Navajo exhibits, it now includes contemporary Native American art and historical artifacts as well.

Museum of New Mexico MUSEUM
(www.museumofnewmexico.org; 1 museum $9, 4-day pass to all 4 museums $20, under 16yr free; ⏲10am-5pm Sat-Thu, 10am-8pm Fri, closed Mon winter) The Museum of New Mexico celebrated its centennial in 2009. It administers four museums around town:

Palace of the Governors HISTORIC BUILDING
(www.nmhistorymuseum.org; 105 W Palace Ave) On the plaza, this 400-year-old abode was once the seat of the Spanish colonial government. It displays a handful of regional relics, but most of its holdings are now shown in an adjacent exhibit space called the **New Mexico History Museum** (113 Lincoln Ave), a glossy, 96,000-sq-ft expansion that opened in 2009.

New Mexico Museum of Art MUSEUM
(www.nmartmuseum.org; 107 W Palace Ave) Just off the plaza, there are more than 20,000 piece of fine art here, mostly by Southwestern artists.

Museum of Indian Arts & Culture MUSEUM
(www.indianartsandculture.org; 710 Camino Lejo) On Museum Hill, this is one of the most complete collections of Native American arts and crafts – and a perfect companion to the nearby Wheelwright Museum.

Museum of International Folk Art MUSEUM
(www.internationalfolkart.org; 706 Camino Lejo; 👪) Also on Museum Hill, the galleries here are at once whimsical and mind-blowing – featuring the world's largest collection of traditional folk art. Try to hit the incredible folk art market, held each June.

SANTA FE FOR CHILDREN

The newly expanded **Santa Fe Children's Museum** (www.santafechildrensmuseum.org; 1050 Old Pecos Trail; admission $9, $5 Sun; ⏲10am-6pm Tue-Sat, noon-5pm Sun; 👪) features hands-on exhibits on science and art for young children. There are daily programs tackling subjects such as solar energy and printmaking.

Santa Fe Southern Railway (☎505-989-8600; www.thetraininsantafe.com; 410 S Guadalupe St; 👪) runs excursions on restored railcars. Its four-hour trips (adult/child from $32/18), departing Saturdays at noon (with extra summer-only trains on Friday at 11am), venture through the high desert and are pulled by working freight trains. Shorter rides are offered on Sundays (year-round) and Wednesdays (summer). Reservations are recommended.

Also don't miss:

St Francis Cathedral CHURCH
(131 Cathedral Pl; ⏲8:30am-5pm) Houses the oldest Madonna statue in North America.

Shidoni Foundry GALLERY
(www.shidoni.com; 1508 Bishops Lodge Rd, Tesuque; ⏲10am-5pm Mon-Sat; 👪) Five miles north of the plaza; outdoor sculpture garden, indoor gallery and on-site glass-blowing studio. On Saturdays, watch the artisans do huge bronze pours in the workshop ($2).

Loretto Chapel CHURCH
(207 Old Santa Fe Trail; admission $3; ⏲9am-5pm Mon-Sat, 10:30am-5pm Sun) Famous for its 'miraculous' spiral staircase that appears to be supported by thin air.

Activities

The **Pecos Wilderness** and **Santa Fe National Forest**, east of town, have more than 1000 miles of hiking trails, several of which lead to 12,000ft peaks. Summer storms are frequent, so prepare for hikes by checking weather reports. For maps and details, contact the Public Lands Information Center (p385). If mountain biking is your thing, drop into **Mellow Velo** (☎505-995-8356; www.mellowvelo.com; 621 Old Santa Fe Trail), which rents bikes and has loads of information about regional trails.

Busloads of people head up to the Rio Grande and Rio Chama for white-water river running on day and overnight trips. Contact **New Wave Rafting** (☎505-984-1444; www.newwaverafting.com) and stay cool on trips through the Rio Grande Gorge (adult/child half-day $57/50, full day $95/85), the wild Taos Box (p388) (full day $116) or the Rio Chama Wilderness (three days $525).

Santa Fe Ski Area SKIING
(☎505-982-4429, snow report 505-983-9155; www.skisantafe.com; lift ticket adult/child $60/40; ⏲9am-4pm) A half-hour drive from the plaza up Hwy 475, you'll find the second-highest ski area in the USA. When the powder is fresh and the sun is shining, it's as good as it gets.

10,000 Waves SPA
(☎505-982-9304; www.tenthousandwaves.com; 3451 Hyde Park Rd; communal tubs $19, private tubs per person $29-49; ⏲2-10:30pm Tue, 9am-10:30pm Wed-Mon Jul-Oct, hr vary Nov-Jun) The Japanese-style 10,000 Waves, with landscaped grounds concealing eight attractive tubs in a smooth Zen design, offers waterfalls, cold plunges, massage and hot and dry saunas. Call to reserve private tubs.

Courses

Santa Fe School of Cooking COOKING
(☎505-983-4511; www.santafeschoolofcooking.com; 116 W San Francisco St) If you develop a love for New Mexican cuisine, try cooking lessons here. Classes, including traditional New Mexican and Southwestern breakfast, are typically between 1½ and three hours long and cost $70 to $98. The family course is fun for kids.

Festivals & Events

Santa Fe's biggest festivals:

Spanish Market CULTURAL
(www.spanishmarket.org) In late July, traditional Spanish colonial arts, from *retablos* (paintings on wooden panels) and *bultos* (wooden carvings of religious figures), to handcrafted furniture and metalwork, make this juried show an artistic extravaganza.

Santa Fe Indian Market CULTURAL
(www.swaia.org) Typically held the weekend after the third Thursday in August, this event draws the country's finest Native American artisans to the plaza – and tens of thousands of visitors.

Santa Fe Fiesta CULTURAL
(www.santafefiesta.org) Two weeks of events in early September, including concerts, dances, parades and the burning of Zozobra (Old Man Gloom).

Sleeping

Cerrillos Rd is lined with chains and independent motels. There's camping in developed sites in Santa Fe National Forest and Hyde State Park on Hwy 475, the road to the ski basin.

Santa Fe Motel & Inn HOTEL $$
(505-982-1039; www.santafemotel.com; 510 Cerrillos Rd; r $89-155, casitas $119-169; P❄@) It's the aesthetic and technological attention to detail that make this downtown-adjacent motel a great pick. Bright tiles, clay sunbursts, LCD TVs and a welcoming chile pepper carefully placed atop your towels are just a few memorable pluses. Savor hot breakfasts on the kiva-anchored patio.

Silver Saddle Motel MOTEL $
(505-471-7663; www.silversaddlemotelllc.com; 2810 Cerrillos Rd; r incl continental breakfast from $45; P❄@) Shady wooden arcades outside and rustic cowboy-inspired decor inside, including some rooms with attractively tiled kitchenettes. For a bit of kitsch, request the Kenny Rogers or Wyatt Earp room. Probably the best value in town.

TOP CHOICE **La Fonda** HISTORIC HOTEL $$$
(505-982-5511; www.lafondasantafe.com; 100 E San Francisco St; r $210-400, ste $430-800; P❄@) Claiming to be the original 'Inn at the end of the Santa Fe Trail,' here since 1610, La Fonda has always offered some of the best lodging in town. The hotel today seamlessly blends modern luxury with folk-art touches; it's authentic, top-shelf Santa Fe style.

El Rey Inn HISTORIC HOTEL $$
(505-982-1931; www.elreyinnsantafe.com; 1862 Cerrillos Rd; r incl breakfast $99-165, ste from $150; P❄@) A highly recommended classic courtyard hotel, with super rooms, a great pool and hot tub, and even a kids' playground scattered around 5 acres of greenery. The inn recycles and takes a lot of green-friendly steps to conserve resources. Most rooms have air con.

Rancheros de Santa Fe Campground CAMPGROUND $
(505-466-3482; www.rancheros.com; 736 Old Las Vegas Hwy; tent/RV sites $23/39, cabins $48; mid-Mar–Oct;) Superfriendly, this wooded campground is seven miles southeast of town. Enjoy hot showers, cheap morning coffee and evening movies.

Eating

TOP CHOICE **San Marcos Café** NEW MEXICAN, AMERICAN $
(505-471-9298; www.sanmarcosfeed.com; 3877 Hwy 14; mains $7-10; 8am-2pm) About 10 minutes' drive south on Hwy 14, this spot is well worth the trip. Aside from the down-home feeling and the best red chile you'll ever taste, turkeys and peacocks strut and squabble outside and the whole place is connected to a feed store, giving it some genuine Western soul. The pastries and desserts – especially the bourbon apple pie – sate any sweet tooth. Make reservations on weekends.

Tune-Up Café INTERNATIONAL $$
(505-983-7060; www.tuneupcafe.com; 1115 Hickox St; mains $7-14; 7am-10pm Mon-Fri, 8am-10pm Sat & Sun) Santa Fe's newest favorite restaurant is casual, busy and does food right. The chef, from El Salvador, adds a few twists to classic New Mexican and American dishes, while also serving Salvadoran *pupusas* (stuffed corn tortillas), huevos and other specialties. The fish tacos and the *mole colorado enchiladas* (flavored with a red chile and a hint of chocolate) are especially tasty.

Horseman's Haven NEW MEXICAN $
(4354 Cerrillos Rd; mains $6-12; 8am-8pm Mon-Sat, 8:30am-2pm Sun) Hands down the hottest green chile in town! (The timid should order it on the side). Service is friendly and fast, and the enormous 3-D burrito might be the only thing you need to eat all day.

Cowgirl Hall of Fame BARBECUE $$
(www.cowgirlsantafe.com; 319 S Guadalupe St; mains $8-18; 11am-midnight Mon-Fri, 10am-midnight Sat, 10am-11pm Sun, bar open later) Two-step up to the cobblestoned courtyard and try the salmon tacos, butternut-squash casserole or the BBQ platter – all served with Western-style feminist flair. Youngsters are welcomed, with an outdoor play yard and buckets of coloring crayons to draw on the lengthy kids' menu. It also has a perennially popular bar with live music.

TOP CHOICE **Geronimo** MODERN AMERICAN $$$
(505-982-1500; 724 Canyon Rd; dishes $28-44; 5:45-10pm Mon-Thu, 5:45-11pm Fri & Sat)

Housed in a 1756 adobe, Geronimo is among the finest and most romantic restaurants in town. The short but diverse menu includes fiery sweet chile and honey-grilled prawns and peppery elk tenderloin with applewood-smoked bacon.

Other good choices:

Tia Sophia's NEW MEXICAN $
(210 W San Francisco St; mains $7-10; 7am-2pm Mon-Sat) Arguably the best New Mexican food around the plaza.

Café Pasqual's INTERNATIONAL $$$
(505-983-9340; www.pasquals.com; 121 Don Gaspar Ave; breakfast & lunch $9-17, dinner $20-30; 8am-3pm, 5:30-9pm) Sante Fe's most famous breakfast, for good reason.

Cleopatra Café MIDDLE EASTERN $
(418 Cerrillos Rd; mains $5-12; 6am-8pm Mon-Sat, 6am-6pm Sun;) Makes up for lack of ambience with taste and value – big platters of delicious kebabs, hummus, falafel and other Middle Eastern favorites. It's inside the Design Center.

Coyote Café MODERN AMERICAN $$$
(505-983-1615; www.coyotecafe.com; 132 W Water St; mains $28-56; 5:30-9:30pm) Simply legendary for its innovative cuisine and all-star kitchen.

Drinking & Entertainment

You'll also find live music and good drinking most nights at the Cowgirl Hall of Fame (p383).

Santa Fe Brewing Company BREWERY, LIVE MUSIC
(www.santafebrewing.com; 35 Fire Pl) Santa Fe's original microbrewery covers the full beer spectrum, from pilsner to porter to stout. Big-name bands perform here surprisingly often.

Evangelo's BAR, LIVE MUSIC
(200 W San Francisco St) There's foot-stompin' live music nightly at Evangelo's and the sounds of rock, blues, jazz and Latin combos spill into the street.

Lensic Performing Arts Center PERFORMING ARTS
(505-988-1234; www.lensic.org; 211 W San Francisco St) For live performances and movies, see what's doing at the Lensic Performing Arts Center. This beautifully renovated 1930s movie house is the city's premier venue for performing arts. Continuing its film history, it also holds $5 classic-movie screenings.

Santa Fe Opera OPERA
(800-280-4654; www.santafeopera.org; tickets $26-188; Jul & Aug) You can be a decked-out socialite or show up in cowboy boots and jeans; it doesn't matter. Opera fans (and those who've never attended an opera in their lives) come to Santa Fe for this alone: an architectural marvel, with views of wind-carved sandstone wilderness crowned with sunsets and moonrises, and at center stage internationally renowned vocal talent performing masterworks of aria and romance.

Bell Tower Bar BAR
(100 E San Francisco St) At La Fonda hotel, ascend five floors to the Bell Tower and watch one of those patented New Mexico sunsets.

El Farol BAR, LIVE MUSIC
(www.elfarolsf.com; 808 Canyon Rd) As much a restaurant as a bar; the specialties are tapas ($8), live music and the ambience of Santa Fe's oldest cantina.

Shopping

Offering carved howling coyotes, turquoise jewelry and fine art, Santa Fe attracts shoppers of all budgets. Head to the sidewalk outside the Palace of the Governors to buy Indian jewelry direct from the craftspeople who make it.

TOP CHOICE **Santa Fe Farmers Market** MARKET
(www.santafefarmersmarket; 1607 Paseo de Peralta; 7am-noon Sat mid-Apr–Oct, 9am-1pm Sat Nov–mid-Apr, 7am-noon Tue mid-May–Oct) Don't miss this market at the redeveloped rail yard. Free samples and a festive mood make for a very pleasant morning.

Pueblo of Tesuque Flea Market MARKET
(Hwy 84/285; 8am-4pm Fri-Sun Mar-Nov) This outdoor market a few minutes' drive north of Santa Fe at Tesuque Pueblo offers deals on high-quality rugs, jewelry, art and clothing.

Travel Bug MAPS, BOOKS
(www.mapsofnewmexico.com; 839 Paseo de Peralta; 7:30am-5:30pm Mon-Sat, 11am-4pm Sun;) A huge selection of guidebooks, maps and travel gear, plus travel slide shows on Saturdays.

Information

Emergency & Medical Services

Police (505-428-3700; 2515 Camino Entrada)

St Vincent's Hospital (☎505-983-3361; 455 St Michael's Dr; ⏲24hr emergency)

Internet Access

Santa Fe Public Library (☎505-955-6781; 145 Washington Ave) Reserve up to an hour of free access.

Travel Bug (☎505-992-0418; www.mapsofnewmexico.com; 839 Paseo de Peralta; @📶) Free wi-fi and internet access from on-site terminals.

Internet Resources

New Mexican (www.santafenewmexican.com) Daily paper with breaking news.

SantaFe.com (www.santafe.com) Listings for upcoming concerts, readings and openings in northern New Mexico.

Santa Fe Information (www.santafe.org) Official online visitors guide.

Santa Fe Reporter (www.sfreporter.com) Free alternative weekly; culture section has thorough listings of what's going on.

Post

Post office (120 S Federal Pl)

Tourist Information

New Mexico Tourism Department (☎505-827-7400; www.newmexico.org; 491 Old Santa Fe Trail; ⏲8:30am-5:30pm; 📶) Has brochures, a hotel reservation line, free coffee and free internet access.

Public Lands Information Center (☎505-438-7542; www.publiclands.org; 301 Dinosaur Trail; ⏲8:30am-4:30pm Mon-Fri) Tons of maps and information. Just south of the intersection of Cerillos Rd and I-25.

ℹ Getting There & Around

American Eagle (☎800-433-7300; www.aa.com) flies in and out of **Santa Fe Municipal Airport** (wwwsantafenm.gov; 121 Aviation Dr) with three daily flights to/from Dallas (DFW) and one daily flight to/from Los Angeles (LAX).

Sandia Shuttle Express (☎505-242-0302; www.sandiashuttle.com) runs between Santa Fe and the Albuquerque Sunport ($27). **North Central Regional Transit** (www.ncrtd.org) provides free shuttle bus service to Espanola, where you can transfer to shuttles to Taos, Los Alamos, Ojo Caliente and other northern destinations. Downtown pickup/drop-off is on Sheridan St, a block northwest of the plaza.

The **Rail Runner** (www.nmrailrunner.com) commuter train has multiple daily departures for Albuquerque – with connections to the airport and the zoo. The trip takes about 1½ hours. Weekend service may be discontinued. **Amtrak** (☎800-872-7245; www.amtrak.com) stops at Lamy; buses continue 17 miles to Santa Fe.

Santa Fe Trails (☎505-955-2001; www.santafenm.gov) provides local bus service (adult/senior & child $1/50¢ per ride, day pass $2/1). If you need a taxi, call **Capital City Cab** (☎505-438-0000).

If driving between Santa Fe and Albuquerque, try to take Hwy 14 – the **Turquoise Trail** – which passes through the old mining town (now art gallery town) of **Madrid**, 28 miles south of Santa Fe.

Around Santa Fe

Don't get too comfy in Santa Fe, because there's lots to see nearby.

PUEBLOS

North of Santa Fe is the heart of Puebloan lands. **Eight Northern Pueblos** (www.enipc.org) publishes the excellent and free *Eight Northern Indian Pueblos Visitors Guide,* available at area visitor centers. Its annual arts-and-crafts show is held in July; check the ENIPC website for exact dates and location.

Eight miles west of Pojoaque along Hwy 502, the ancient **San Ildefonso Pueblo** (☎505-455-3549; per vehicle $7, camera/video/sketching permits $10/20/25; ⏲8am-5pm daily, visitor center closed Sat & Sun winter) was the home of Maria Martinez, who in 1919 revived a distinctive traditional black-on-black pottery style. Several exceptional potters (including Maria's direct descendants) work in the pueblo; stop at the **Maria Poveka Martinez Museum** (admission free; ⏲8am-4pm Mon-Fri), which sells the pueblo's pottery.

Just north of San Ildefonso, on Hwy 30, **Santa Clara Pueblo** is home to the **Puye Cliff Dwellings** (☎888-320-5008; www.puyecliffs.com; tours adult/child $20/18; ⏲hourly 9am-5pm Apr-Sep, 10am-2pm Oct-Apr) where you can visit Ancestral Puebloan cliffside and mesa-top ruins.

LAS VEGAS

Not to be confused with the glittery city to the west in Nevada, this Vegas is one of the loveliest towns in New Mexico and one of the largest and oldest towns east of the Sangre de Cristo Mountains. Its eminently strollable downtown has a pretty Old Town Plaza and some 900 historic buildings listed in the National Register of Historic Places. Its architecture is a mix of Southwestern and Victorian.

Built in 1882 and carefully remodeled a century later, the recently expanded **Plaza Hotel** (☎505-425-3591, 800-328-1882; www.plazahotel-nm.com; 230 Plaza; r/ste incl breakfast

DON'T MISS

CHIMAYO

Twenty-eight miles north of Santa Fe is the so-called 'Lourdes of America' – **El Santuario de Chimayo** (www.elsantuariodechimayo.us; ⌚9am-5pm Oct-Apr, 9am-6pm May-Sep), one of the most important cultural sites in New Mexico. In 1816, this two-towered adobe chapel was built where the earth was said to have miraculous healing properties – even today, the faithful come to rub the *tierra bendita* – holy dirt – from a small pit inside the church on whatever hurts; some mix it with water and drink it. During holy week, about 30,000 pilgrims walk to Chimayo from Santa Fe, Albuquerque and beyond, in the largest Catholic pilgrimage in the USA. The artwork in the *santuario* is worth a trip on its own. Stop at **Rancho de Chimayo** (☎505-984-2100; www.ranchodechimayo.com; County Rd 98; mains $7-15; ⌚11:30am-9pm daily, 8:30am-10:30am Sat & Sun, closed Mon Nov-Apr) afterward for lunch or dinner.

from $79/139; ❄@📶) is Las Vegas' most celebrated and historic lodging. The elegant building now offers 72 comfortable accommodations. Choose between Victorian-style, antique-filled rooms in the original building or bright, monochromatic rooms in the new adjoining wing.

Indulge in a good New Mexican meal at **Estella's Café** (148 Bridge St; mains $6-12; ⌚11am-3pm Mon-Wed, 11am-8pm Thu & Fri, 10am-3pm Sat). Estella's devoted patrons treasure the homemade red chile, *menudo* (tripe and grits) and scrumptious enchiladas.

From the plaza, Hot Springs Blvd leads 5 miles north to Gallinas Canyon and the massive **Montezuma Castle**; once a hotel, it's now the United World College of the West. Along the road there, you can soak in a series of natural **hot-spring pools**. Bring a swimsuit and test the water – some are scalding hot! Don't miss the **Dwan Light Sanctuary** (admission free; ⌚6am-10pm) on the school campus, a meditation chamber where prisms in the walls cast rainbows inside.

Ask for a walking-tour brochure from the **visitor center** (☎800-832-5947; www.lasvegasnewmexico.com; 500 Railroad Ave; ⌚10am-5pm Mon-Fri, 11am-4pm Sat & Sun Oct 15–Apr, longer hours May–Oct 14).

LOS ALAMOS

The top-secret Manhattan Project sprang to life in Los Alamos in 1943, turning a sleepy mesa-top village into a busy laboratory of secluded brainiacs. Here, in the 'town that didn't exist,' the first atomic bomb was developed in almost total secrecy. Today you'll encounter a fascinating dynamic in which souvenir T-shirts emblazoned with atomic explosions and 'La Bomba' wine are sold next to books on pueblo history and wilderness hiking.

You can't actually visit the **Los Alamos National Laboratory**, where lots of classified cutting-edge research still takes place, but you can visit the well-designed, interactive **Bradbury Science Museum** (www.lanl.gov/museum; cnr Central Ave & 15th; admission free; ⌚10am-5pm Tue-Sat, 1-5pm Sun & Mon; 👪), which covers atomic history. A short film traces the community's wartime history and reveals a few fascinating secrets. The small but interesting **Los Alamos Historical Museum** (www.losalamoshistory.org; 1050 Bathtub Row; admission free; ⌚10am-4pm Mon-Fri, 11am-4pm Sat, 1-4pm Sun) is on the nearby grounds of the former Los Alamos Ranch School – an outdoorsy school for boys that closed when the scientists arrived.

BANDELIER NATIONAL MONUMENT

Ancestral Puebloans dwelt in the cliffsides of beautiful Frijoles Canyon, now preserved within **Bandelier** (www.nps.gov/band; admission per vehicle $12; ⌚8am-6pm summer, 9am-5:30pm spring & fall, 9am-4:30pm winter). The adventurous can climb four ladders to reach ancient caves and kivas used until the mid-1500s. There are also almost 50 sq miles of canyon and mesalands offering scenic backpacking trails, plus camping at **Juniper Campground** (tent & RV sites $12), set among the pines near the monument entrance.

ABIQUIU

The tiny community of Abiquiu (sounds like 'barbecue'), on Hwy 84 about 45 minutes' drive northwest of Santa Fe, is famous because the renowned artist Georgia O'Keeffe lived and painted here from 1949 until her death in 1986. With the Chama River flowing through farmland and spectacular rock landscape, the ethereal setting continues to attract artists, and many live and work in Abiquiu. O'Keeffe's adobe house is open for limited visits, and the Georgia O'Keeffe Museum (p380) offers one-hour **tours** (☎505-685-4539; www.okeeffemuseum.org) on Tuesday, Thursday and Friday from March to November ($35), and also on Saturdays from June to October ($45), often booked months in advance.

A retreat center on 21,000 Technicolor acres that obviously inspired O'Keeffe's work (and was a shooting location for the movie *City Slickers*), **Ghost Ranch** (☎505-685-4333; www.ghostranch.org) has free hiking trails, a **dinosaur museum** (⊙9am-5pm Mon-Sat, 1-5pm Sun) and offers horseback rides (from $40), including instruction for kids as young as four years ($20). Basic **lodging** (tent sites $19, RV sites $22-29, dm incl breakfast $50, r without/with bath incl breakfast from $50/80) is available, too.

The lovely **Abiquiú Inn** (☎505-685-4378; www.abiquiuinn.com; Hwy 84; RV sites $18, r $140-200, ste $170, 4-person casitas $190; ❄📶) is a sprawling collection of shaded faux-adobes; spacious casitas have kitchenettes. Wi-fi is available in the lobby and the on-site restaurant, **Cafe Abiquiú** (breakfast mains $5-9, lunch & dinner mains $10-20; ⊙7am-9pm). The lunch and dinner menu includes numerous fish dishes, from chipotle honey-glazed salmon to trout tacos.

OJO CALIENTE

At 140 years old, **Ojo Caliente Mineral Springs Resort & Spa** (☎505-583-2233; www.ojospa.com; 50 Los Baños Rd; r $139-169, cottages $179-209, ste $229-349; 📶) is one of the country's oldest health resorts – and Pueblo Indians were using the springs long before then! Fifty miles north of Santa Fe on Hwy 285, the newly renovated resort offers 10 soaking pools with several combinations of minerals (shared/private pools from $18/40). In addition to the pleasant, if nothing special, historic hotel rooms, the resort has added 12 plush, boldly colored suites with kiva fireplaces and private soaking tubs, and 11 New Mexican–style cottages. Wi-fi is available in the lobby. The on-site **Artesian Restaurant** (breakfast mains $5-10, lunch $9-12, dinner $11-28; ⊙7:30am-10:30am, 11:30am-2:30pm & 5-9pm Sun-Thu, 5-9:30pm Fri & Sat) prepares organic and local ingredients with aplomb.

Taos

Taos is a place undeniably dominated by the power of its landscape: 12,300ft snow-capped peaks rise behind town; a sage-speckled plateau unrolls to the west before plunging 800ft straight down into the Rio Grande Gorge; the sky can be a searing sapphire blue or an ominous parade of rumbling thunderheads so big they dwarf the mountains. And then there are the sunsets…

Taos Pueblo, believed to be the oldest continuously inhabited community in the United States, roots the town in a long history with a rich cultural legacy – including conquistadors, Catholicism and cowboys. In the 20th century it became a magnet for artists, writers and creative thinkers, from DH Lawrence to Dennis Hopper. It remains a relaxed and eccentric place, with classic adobe architecture, fine-art galleries, quirky cafes and excellent restaurants. Its 5000 residents include Bohemians, alternative-energy aficionados and old-time Hispanic families. It's rural and worldly, and a little bit otherworldly.

Sights

The Museum Association of Taos offers a five-museum pass for $25 to the four museums listed below.

Harwood Museum of Art MUSEUM
(www.harwoodmuseum.org; 238 Ledoux St; adult/senior & student $8/7; ⊙10am-5pm Tue-Sat, noon-5pm Sun) Housed in a historic mid-19th-century adobe compound, the Harwood Museum of Art features paintings, drawings, prints, sculpture and photography by northern New Mexico artists, both historical and contemporary.

Taos Historic Museums MUSEUM
(www.taoshistoricmuseums.com; adult/child individual museums $8/4, both museums $12; ⊙10am-5pm Mon-Sat, noon-5pm Sun) Taos Historic Museum runs two houses: **Blumenschein Home** (222 Ledoux St), a trove of art from the 1920s by the Taos Society of Artists, and **Martínez Hacienda** (708 Lower Ranchitos Rd), a 21-room colonial trader's former home from 1804.

Millicent Rogers Museum MUSEUM
(www.millicentrogers.org; 1504 Millicent Rogers Museum Rd; adult/child $10/6; ⊙10am-5pm, closed Mon Nov-Mar) Filled with pottery, jewelry, baskets and textiles, this has one of the best collections of Native American and Spanish Colonial art in the US.

DON'T MISS

TAOS PUEBLO

Built around AD 1450 and continuously inhabited ever since, the streamside **Taos Pueblo** (☎575-758-1028; www.taospueblo.com; Taos Pueblo Rd; adult/child/under 11yr $10/5/free, photography or video permit $6; ⏰8am-4pm, closed for 6 weeks around Feb & Mar) is the largest existing multistoried pueblo structure in the US and one of the best surviving examples of traditional adobe construction.

Taos Art Museum & Fechin Institute MUSEUM
(www.fechin.com; 227 Paseo del Pueblo Norte; admission $8; ⏰10am-5pm Tue-Sun) The longtime home of Russian-born artist Nicolai Fechin, the house itself is worth just as much of a look as the collection of paintings, drawings and sculptures.

San Francisco de Asís Church CHURCH
(St Francis Plaza; ⏰9am-4pm Mon-Fri) Four miles south of Taos in Ranchos de Taos, the San Francisco de Asís Church, famed for the angles and curves of its adobe walls, was built in the mid-18th century but didn't open until 1815. It's been memorialized in Georgia O'Keeffe paintings and Ansel Adams photographs.

Rio Grande Gorge Bridge BRIDGE, CANYON
At 650ft above the Rio Grande, the steel Rio Grande Gorge Bridge is the second-highest suspension bridge in the US; the view down is eye-popping. For the best pictures of the bridge itself, park at the rest area on the western end of the span.

Earthships NEIGHBORHOOD
(www.earthship.net; Hwy 64; adult/under 12yr $5/free; ⏰10am-4pm) Just 1.5 miles west of the bridge is the fascinating community of Earthships, with self-sustaining, environmentally savvy houses built with recycled materials that are completely off the grid. You can also stay overnight in one.

Activities

During summer, **white-water rafting** is popular in the **Taos Box**, the steep-sided cliffs that frame the Rio Grande. Day-long trips begin at around $100 per person; contact the visitor center for local outfitters, where there's also good info about **hiking** and **mountain-biking** trails.

Taos Ski Valley SKIING
(☎866-968-7386; www.skitaos.org; lift ticket adult/teen 13-17 & senior/child $71/60/42) With a peak elevation of 11,819ft and a 2612ft vertical drop, Taos Ski Valley offers some of the most challenging skiing in the US and yet remains low-key and relaxed. The resort now allows snowboarders on its slopes.

Sleeping

TOP CHOICE **Earthship Rentals** BUNGALOW $$
(☎575-751-0462; www.earthship.net; Hwy 64; r $120-160) Experience an off-grid overnight in a boutique-chic, solar-powered dwelling. A cross between organic Gaudí architecture and space-age fantasy, these sustainable dwellings are put together using recycled tires, aluminum cans and sand, with rain catchment and gray-water systems to minimize their footprint. Half-buried in a valley surrounded by mountains, they *could* be hastily camouflaged alien vessels – you never know.

Historic Taos Inn HISTORIC HOTEL $$
(☎575-758-2233; www.taosinn.com; 125 Paseo del Pueblo Norte; r $75-275; P 📶) Even though it's not the plushest place in town, it's still fabulous, with a cozy lobby, a garden for the restaurant, heavy wooden furniture, a sunken fireplace and lots of live local music at its famed Adobe Bar. Parts of this landmark date to the 1800s – the older rooms are actually the nicest.

Abominable Snowmansion HOSTEL $
(☎575-776-8298; www.snowmansion.com; 476 State Hwy 150, Arroyo Seco; tent sites $15, dm $20, tipis $35, cabins $37, r with/without bath $59/45; P @ 📶) About 9 miles northeast of Taos, this well-worn and welcoming hostel is a cozy mountainside alternative to central Taos. A big, round fireplace warms guests in winter, and kitschy tipis are available in summer. There's a $3 discount on dorms and private rooms for Hostelling International (HI) members.

Sun God Lodge MOTEL $
(☎575-758-3162; www.sungodlodge.com; 919 Paseo del Pueblo Sur; r from $55; P ❄ 📶) The hospitable folks at this well-run two-story motel can fill you in on local history as well as the craziest bar in town. Rooms are clean – if a bit dark – and decorated with low-key

Southwestern flair. The highlight is the lush green courtyard dappled with twinkling lights, a scenic spot for a picnic or enjoying the sunset. Pets can stay for $20. Located 1.5 miles south of the plaza, the Sun God is a great budget choice.

Eating

TOP CHOICE Trading Post Cafe INTERNATIONAL $$$
(☎575-758-5089; www.tradingpostcafe.com; Hwy 68, Ranchos de Taos; lunch $8-14, dinner $16-32; ⏰11:30am-9:30pm Tue-Sat, 5-9pm Sun) A longtime favorite, the Trading Post is a perfect blend of relaxed and refined. The food, from paella to pork chops, is always great. Portions of some dishes are so big, think about splitting a main course – or if you want to eat cheap but well, get a small salad and small soup. It'll be plenty!

TOP CHOICE Love Apple ORGANIC $$
(☎575-751-0050; www.theloveapple.net; 803 Paseo del Pueblo Norte; mains $13-18; ⏰5-9pm Tue-Sun) Housed in the 19th century adobe Placitas Chapel, the understated rustic-sacred atmosphere is as much a part of this only-in-New-Mexico restaurant as the food is. From the posole with shepherd's lamb sausage to the grilled trout with chipotle cream, every dish is made from organic or free-range regional foods. Make reservations!

Taos Pizza Out Back PIZZERIA $$
(712 Paseo del Pueblo Norte; slices $3.50-7, whole pies $13-27; ⏰11am-10pm daily May-Sep, 11am-9pm Sun-Thu, 11am-10pm Fri & Sat Oct-Apr) Warning: these pizza pies may be cruelly habit-forming. Located behind another business, this place uses organic ingredients and serves epicurean combos such as a Portabella Pie with sun-dried tomatoes and camembert. Slices are the size of a small country.

Taos Diner DINER $
(908 Paseo del Pueblo Norte; mains $4-12; ⏰7am-2:30pm) It's with some reluctance that we share the existence of this marvelous place, a mountain-town diner with wood-paneled walls, tattooed waitresses, fresh-baked biscuits and coffee cups that are never less than half-full. This is diner grub at its finest, prepared with a Southwestern, organic spin. Mountain men, scruffy jocks, solo diners and happy tourists – everyone's welcome here. We like the Copper John's eggs with a side of green chile sauce.

Michael's Kitchen NEW MEXICAN $
(304 Paseo del Pueblo Norte; mains $7-16; ⏰7am-2:30pm) Great breakfasts, freshly made pastries and tasty New Mexican fare.

El Gamal MIDDLE EASTERN $
(12 Dona Luz St; mains $6-10; ⏰9am-5pm;) Vegetarians rejoice! Here's a great meatless Middle Eastern menu. There's a big kids' playroom in back, plus a pool table and free wi-fi.

Drinking & Entertainment

Adobe Bar BAR, LIVE MUSIC
(Historic Taos Inn, 125 Paseo del Pueblo Norte) Everybody's welcome in 'the living room of Taos.' And there's something about it: the chairs, the Taos Inn's history, the casualness, the tequila. The packed streetside patio has some of the state's finest margaritas, along with an eclectic lineup of great live music and never a cover.

KTAO Solar Center BAR, LIVE MUSIC
(www.ktao.com; 9 Ski Valley Rd; ⏰from 4pm) Watch the DJs at the 'world's most powerful solar radio station' while hitting happy hour at the solar center bar. It's also the home of the best live-music venue in town; you could catch a grooving local or big-name band.

Alley Cantina BAR, LIVE MUSIC
(121 Teresina Lane) It's a bit-cooler-than-thou, but maybe 'tude happens when you inhabit the oldest building in town. Catch live rock, blues, hip-hop or jazz almost nightly.

Shopping

Taos has historically been a mecca for artists, demonstrated by the huge number of galleries and studios in and around town. Indie stores and galleries line the **John Dunn Shops** (www.johndunnshops.com) pedestrian walkway linking Bent St to Taos Plaza. Here you'll find the well-stocked **Moby Dickens Bookshop** and the tiny but intriguing **G Robinson Old Prints & Maps** – a treat for cartography geeks.

Just east of the Plaza, pop into **El Rincón Trading Post** (114 Kit Carson Rd) and **Horse Feathers** (109 Kit Carson Rd) for classic Western memorabilia.

Information

Taos Vacation Guide (www.taosvacationguide.org) Great resource with lots of easy-to-navigate links.

Visitor center (☎575-758-3873; 1139 Paseo del Pueblo Sur; ⏲9am-5pm; @📶)

Wired? (705 Felicidad Lane; ⏲8am-6pm Mon-Fri, 8:30am-6pm Sat & Sun) Funky coffee shop with computers ($7 per hour). Free wi-fi for customers.

ℹ Getting There & Away

From Santa Fe, take either the scenic 'high road' along Hwys 76 and 518, with galleries, villages and sites worth exploring, or follow the lovely unfolding Rio Grande landscape on Hwy 68.

North Central Regional Transit (www.ncrtd.org) provides free shuttle-bus service to Espanola, where you can transfer to Santa Fe and other destinations. **Twin Hearts Express** (☎800-654-9456) will get you to Santa Fe ($40) and the Albuquerque airport ($50).

Northwestern New Mexico

Dubbed 'Indian Country' for good reason – huge swaths of land fall under the aegis of the Navajo, Pueblo, Zuni, Apache and Laguna tribes – this quadrant of New Mexico showcases remarkable ancient Indian sites alongside modern, solitary Native American settlements.

FARMINGTON & AROUND

The largest town in New Mexico's northwestern region, Farmington makes a convenient base from which to explore the Four Corners area. The **visitors bureau** (☎505-326-7602; www.farmingtonnm.org; Gateway Park, 3041 E Main St; ⏲8am-5pm Mon-Sat) has more information.

Shiprock, a 1700ft-high volcanic plug that rises eerily over the landscape to the west, was a landmark for the Anglo pioneers and is a sacred site to the Navajo.

An ancient pueblo, **Salmon Ruin & Heritage Park** (adult/child $3/1; ⏲8am-5pm Mon-Fri, 9am-5pm Sat & Sun) features a large village built by the Chaco people in the early 1100s. Abandoned, resettled by people from Mesa Verde and again abandoned before 1300, the site also includes the remains of a homestead, petroglyphs, a Navajo hogan and a wickiup (a rough brushwood shelter). Take Hwy 64 east 11 miles toward Bloomfield.

Fourteen miles northeast of Farmington, the 27-acre **Aztec Ruins National Monument** (www.nps.gov/azru; adult/under 16yr $5/free; ⏲8am-5pm Sep-May, 8am-6pm Jun-Aug) features the largest reconstructed kiva in the country, with an internal diameter of almost 50ft. A few steps away, let your imagination wander as you stoop through low doorways and dark rooms inside the West Ruin. In summer, rangers give early-afternoon talks at the c-1100 site about ancient architecture, trade routes and astronomy.

About 35 miles south of Farmington along Hwy 371, the undeveloped **Bisti Badlands & De-Na-Zin Wilderness** is a trippy, surreal landscape of strange, colorful rock formations, especially spectacular in the hours before sunset; desert enthusiasts shouldn't miss it. The Farmington **BLM office** (☎505-599-8900; www.nm.blm.gov; 1235 La Plata Hwy; ⏲8am-4:30pm Mon-Fri) has information.

The lovely, three-room **Silver River Adobe Inn B&B** (☎505-325-8219; www.silveradobe.com; 3151 W Main St, Farmington; r incl breakfast $115-175; 📶) offers a peaceful respite among the trees along the San Juan River.

Managing to be both trendy *and* kid-friendly, the hippish **Three Rivers Eatery & Brewhouse** (101 E Main St, Farmington; mains $8-26; ⏲11am-10pm; 👪) has good steaks and pub grub and its own microbrews.

CHACO CULTURE NATIONAL HISTORIC PARK

Featuring massive Ancestral Puebloan buildings set in an isolated high-desert environment, intriguing **Chaco** (www.nps.gov/chcu; admission per vehicle $8; ⏲7am-sunset, visitor center 8am-5pm) contains evidence of 5000 years of human occupation. In its prime, the community at Chaco Canyon was a major trading and ceremonial hub for the region – and the city the Puebloan people created here was masterly in its layout and design. Pueblo Bonito is four stories tall and may have had 600 to 800 rooms and kivas. As well as taking the self-guided loop tour, you can hike various **backcountry trails**. For stargazers, there's the **Night Skies** program offered Tuesday, Friday and Saturday evenings April through October.

The park is in a remote area approximately 80 miles south of Farmington. **Gallo Campground** (tent sites $10) is 1 mile east of the visitor center; no RV sites.

CHAMA

Nine miles south of the Colorado border, Chama's **Cumbres & Toltec Scenic Railway** (☎575-756-2151; www.cumbrestoltec.com; adult/child $91/50; ⏲late May–mid-Oct) is the longest (64 miles) and highest (over the 10,015ft-high Cumbres Pass) authentic narrow-gauge steam railroad in the US. It's a beautiful trip, particularly in September and October during the fall foliage, through mountains, canyons and high desert.

Northeastern New Mexico

East of Santa Fe, the lush Sangre de Cristo Mountains give way to vast rolling plains. Dusty grasslands stretch to infinity and further – to Texas. Cattle and dinosaur prints dot a landscape punctuated with volcanic cones. Ranching is an economic mainstay, and on many roads you'll see more cows than cars.

The Santa Fe Trail, along which pioneer settlers rolled in wagon trains, ran from New Mexico to Missouri. You can still see the wagon ruts in some places off I-25 between Santa Fe and Raton. For a bit of the Old West without a patina of consumer hype, this is the place.

CIMARRON

Cimarron once ranked among the rowdiest of Wild West towns; it's name even means 'wild' in Spanish. According to local lore, murder was such an everyday occurrence in the 1870s that peace-and-quiet was newsworthy, one paper going so far as to report: 'Everything is quiet in Cimarron. Nobody has been killed in three days.'

Today, the town is indeed quiet, luring nature-minded travelers who want to enjoy the great outdoors. Driving here to or from Taos, you'll pass through gorgeous **Cimarron Canyon State Park**, a steep-walled canyon with several hiking trails, excellent trout fishing and camping.

You can stay or dine (restaurant mains $5 to $20) at what's reputed to be one of the most haunted hotels in the USA, the 1872 **St James** (☎888-376-2664; www.exstjames.com; 617 S Collison St; r $70-120; ⊙7am-9pm) – one room is so spook-filled that it's never rented out! Many legends of the West stayed here, including Buffalo Bill, Annie Oakley, Wyatt Earp and Jesse James, and the front desk has a long list of who shot whom in the now-renovated hotel bar. The authentic period rooms make this one of the most historic-feeling hotels in New Mexico.

CAPULIN VOLCANO NATIONAL MONUMENT

Rising 1300ft above the surrounding plains, **Capulin** (www.nps.gov/cavo; admission per vehicle $5; ⊙8am-4pm) is the most accessible of several volcanoes in the area. From the visitor center, a 2-mile road spirals up the mountain to a parking lot at the crater rim (8182ft), where trails lead around and into the crater. The entrance is 3 miles north of Capulin village, which itself is 30 miles east of Raton on Hwy 87.

Southwestern New Mexico

The Rio Grande Valley unfurls from Albuquerque down to the bubbling hot springs of funky Truth or Consequences and beyond. Before the river hits the Texas line, it feeds one of New Mexico's agricultural treasures: Hatch, the so-called 'chile capital of the world.' The first atomic device was detonated at the Trinity Site, in the bone-dry desert east of the Rio known since Spanish times as the Jornada del Muerto – Journey of Death.

To the west, the rugged Gila National Forest is wild with backpacking and fishing adventures. The mountains' southern slopes descend into the Chihuahuan Desert that surrounds Las Cruces, the state's second-largest city.

TRUTH OR CONSEQUENCES & AROUND

An offbeat joie de vivre permeates the funky little town of Truth or Consequences, which was built on the site of natural hot springs in the 1880s. A bit of the quirkiness stems from the fact that the town changed its name from Hot Springs to Truth or Consequences (or 'T or C') in 1950, after a popular radio game show of the same name. Publicity these days comes courtesy of Virgin Galactic CEO Richard Branson and other space-travel visionaries driving the development of nearby **Spaceport America**, where wealthy tourists will launch into orbit sometime soon.

Spaceport tours (☎505-897-2886; www.ftstours.com; adult/under 12yr $59/29; ⊙9am & 1pm Fri-Sun) include a look at the launch site and mission control.

In T or C, wander around the hole-in-the-wall cafes, pop into a gallery, check out the engaging mishmash of exhibits at the **Geronimo Springs Museum** (www.geronimospringsmuseum.com; 211 Main St; adult/child $5/2.50; ⊙9am-5pm Mon-Sat, noon-5pm Sun) and definitely enjoy a soak in a hot-spring spa. The **visitor center** (☎575-894-1968; www.truthorconsequenceschamberofcommerce.org; 211 Main St; ⊙9am-4:30pm Mon-Fri, 9am-5pm Sat, noon-5pm Sun) has local listings.

About 60 miles north of town, sandhill cranes and Arctic geese winter in the 90 sq miles of fields and marshes at **Bosque del Apache National Wildlife Refuge** (www.fws.gov/southwest/refuges/newmex/bosque; admission per vehicle $5; State Hwy 1; ⏲refuge sunrise-sunset, visitor center 7:30am-4pm Mon-Fri, 8am-4:30pm Sat & Sun). There's a visitor center and driving tour. The Festival of the Cranes is held in mid-November.

Sleeping & Eating

Many local motels double as spas.

Riverbend Hot Springs BOUTIQUE HOTEL **$**
(☎575-894-7625; www.riverbendhotsprings.com; 100 Austin St; r from $70; ❄📶) Former hostel Riverbend Hot Springs now offers more traditional motel-style accommodations – no more tipis – from its fantastic perch beside the Rio Grande. Rooms exude a bright, quirky charm, and several units work well for groups. Private hot-spring tubs are available by the hour (guest/nonguest $10/15 for the first hour then $5/10 per additional hour), as is a public hot-spring pool (guest/nonguest free all day/$10 for the first hour then $5 per hour or $25 per day).

TOP CHOICE **Blackstone Hotsprings** BOUTIQUE HOTEL **$**
(☎575-894-0894; www.blackstonehotsprings.com; 410 Austin St; r $75-125; ❄📶) Blackstone embraces the T or C spirit with an upscale wink, decorating each of its seven rooms in the style of a classic TV show, from the *Jetsons* to the *Golden Girls* to *I Love Lucy*. Best part? Each room comes with its own hot-spring tub or waterfall. Worst part? If you like sleeping in darkness, quite a bit of courtyard light seeps into some rooms at night.

Happy Belly Deli DELI **$**
(313 N Broadway; mains $2-8; ⏲7am-3pm Mon-Fri, 8am-3pm Sat, 8am-noon Sun) Draws the morning crowd with fresh breakfast burritos.

Café BellaLuca ITALIAN **$$**
(www.cafebellaluca.com; 303 Jones St; lunch $6-15, dinner $10-34; ⏲11am-9pm Sun-Thu, 11am-10pm Fri & Sat) Earns raves for its Italian specialties; pizzas are amazing.

LAS CRUCES & AROUND

The second-largest city in New Mexico, Las Cruces is home to New Mexico State University (NMSU), but there's surprisingly little of real interest for visitors.

> **IF YOU HAVE A FEW MORE DAYS**
>
> Past the town of Magdalena on Hwy 60 is the **Very Large Array** (VLA; www.vla.nrao.edu; admission free; ⏲8:30am-dusk) radio telescope facility, a complex of 27 huge antenna dishes sprouting like giant mushrooms in the high plains. At the visitor center, watch a short film about the facility and take a self-guided walking tour with a window peek into the control building. It's 4 miles south of Hwy 60 off Hwy 52.

Sights

For many, a visit to neighboring **Mesilla** (aka Old Mesilla) is the highlight of their time in Las Cruces. Wander a few blocks off Old Mesilla's plaza in to gather the essence of a mid-19th-century Southwestern town of Hispanic heritage.

New Mexico Farm & Ranch Heritage Museum MUSEUM
(www.nmfarmandranchmuseum.org; 4100 Dripping Springs Rd, Las Cruces; adult/child $5/2; ⏲9am-5pm Mon-Sat, noon-5pm Sun) This terrific museum in Las Cruces has more than just engaging displays about the agricultural history of the state – it's got livestock! There are daily milking demonstrations and an occasional 'parade of breeds' of beef cattle, along with stalls of horses, donkeys, sheep and goats. Other demonstrations include blacksmithing (Friday to Sunday), spinning and weaving (Wednesday), and heritage cooking (call for schedule).

FREE **White Sands Missile Test Center Museum** MUSEUM
(www.wsmr-history.org; ⏲8am-4pm Mon-Fri, 10am-3pm Sat & Sun) About 25 miles east of Las Cruces along Hwy 70 (look for the White Sands Missile Range Headquarters sign), has been a major military testing site since 1945, and it still serves as an alternative landing site for the space shuttle. Look for the crazy outdoor missile park. Since it's on an army base, everyone entering over the age of 18 years must show ID, and the driver must present car registration and proof of insurance.

Sleeping

Lundeen Inn of the Arts B&B **$$**
(☎575-526-3326; www.innofthearts.com; 618 S Alameda Blvd, Las Cruces; r incl breakfast $79-125,

ste $99-155; ❄📶) In Las Cruces, Lundeen Inn of the Arts, a large turn-of-the-19th-century Mexican territorial-style inn, has seven guest rooms (all wildly different), genteel hosts, an airy living room with soaring ceilings (made of pressed tin) and a 300-piece fine-art gallery.

Eating

La Posta NEW MEXICAN $$
(www.laposta-de-mesilla.com; 2410 Calle de San Albino, Old Mesilla; mains $9-15; ⏲11am-9pm Sun-Thu, 11am-9:30pm Fri & Sat) The most famous restaurant in Old Mesilla, in a 200-year-old adobe, may at first raise your doubts with its fiesta-like decor and touristy feel. But the New Mexican dishes are consistently good, portions are huge, and service is prompt.

Nellie's Cafe NEW MEXICAN $
(1226 W Hadley Ave, Las Cruces; mains $6-10; ⏲8am-2pm) A favored local New Mexican restaurant, great for breakfast and lunch. Cash only.

Information

Las Cruces Visitors Bureau (☎575-541-2444; www.lascrucescvb.org; 211 N Water St, Las Cruces; ⏲8am-5pm Mon-Fri)

Getting There & Away

Greyhound (☎575-524-8518; www.greyhound.com; 390 S Valley Dr) has buses traversing the two interstate corridors (I-10 and I-25), as well as daily trips to Albuquerque ($27, 3½ hours), Roswell ($49, four hours) and El Paso ($11.25, one hour).

SILVER CITY & AROUND

The spirit of the Wild West still hangs in the air here, as if Billy the Kid himself – a former resident – might amble past at any moment. But things are changing, as the mountain-man/cowboy vibe succumbs to the charms of art galleries, coffeehouses and gelato. (One word of caution when strolling through downtown Silver City – look carefully before you step off the sidewalk. Because of monsoonal summer rains, curbs are higher than average, built to keep the Victorian and the brick and cast-iron buildings safe from quick-rising waters.)

Silver City is also the gateway to outdoor activities in the **Gila National Forest**, which is rugged country suitable for remote cross-country skiing, backpacking, camping, fishing and other activities.

Two hours north of Silver City, up a winding 42-mile road, is **Gila Cliff Dwellings National Monument** (www.nps.gov/gicl; admission $3; ⏲8:30am-5pm Jun-Aug, 9am-4pm Sep-May), occupied in the 13th century by Mogollons. Mysterious and relatively isolated, these remarkable cliff dwellings are easily accessed from a 1-mile loop trail and look very much as they would have at the turn of the first millennium. For **pictographs**, stop by the Lower Scorpion Campground and walk a short distance along the marked trail.

Weird rounded monoliths make the **City of Rocks State Park** (www.emnrd.state.nm.us/prd/cityrocks.htm; Hwy 61; day use $5, tent/RV sites $8/10) an intriguing playground, with great camping among the formations; there are tables and fire pits. For a rock-lined gem of a spot, check out campsite 43, the Lynx. Head 24 miles northwest of Deming along Hwy 180, then 3 miles northeast on Hwy 61.

For a smattering of Silver City's architectural history, overnight in the 22-room **Palace Hotel** (☎575-388-1811; www.silvercitypalacehotel.com; 106 W Broadway; r incl breakfast from $51; 📶). Exuding a low-key, turn-of-the-19th-century charm (no air con, older fixtures), the Palace is a great choice for those tired of cookie-cutter chains. On the corner, the lofty **Javalina** (201 N Bullard St; pastries $2-4; ⏲6am-9pm Mon-Thu, to 10pm Fri & Sat, to 7pm Sun; 📶) offers coffee, snacks and wi-fi in a comfy, come-as-you-are space.

Downtown offers a variey of restaurants, including the gourmet Mediterranean-themed **Shevek & Co Restaurant** (☎575-534-9168; www.silver-eats.com; 602 N Bullard St; mains $20-30; ⏲5-8:30pm Sun-Tue & Thu, 5-9pm Fri & Sat) and the vegetarian sandwich-and-salad shop **Peace Meal Cooperative** (601 N Bullard St; mains $5-8; ⏲9am-3pm Mon-Sat). For a real taste of local culture, head 7 miles north to Pinos Altos and the **Buckhorn Saloon** (☎575-538-9911; Main St, Pinos Altos; mains $10-35; ⏲4pm-10pm Mon-Sat), where the specialty is steak and there's live music most nights. Call for reservations.

Information

The **visitor center** (☎575-538-3785, www.silvercity.org; 201 N Hudson St; ⏲9am-5pm Mon-Fri, 10am-2pm Sat & Sun) and the **Gila National Forest Ranger Station** (☎575-388-8201; www.fs.fed.us/r3/gila; 3005 E Camino Del Bosque; ⏲8am-4:30pm Mon-Fri) have area information. To learn about the town's contentious mining history, watch the blacklisted 1954 movie *Salt of the Earth*.

Southeastern New Mexico

Two of New Mexico's greatest natural wonders are tucked down here in the arid southeast – mesmerizing White Sands National Monument and magnificent Carlsbad Caverns National Park. This region is also home to some of the state's most enduring legends: aliens in Roswell, Billy the Kid in Lincoln and Smokey Bear in Capitan. Most of the lowlands are covered by hot, rugged Chihuahuan Desert, but you can escape to cooler climes by driving up to higher altitudes around the popular forested resort towns such as Cloudcroft and Ruidoso.

WHITE SANDS NATIONAL MONUMENT

Slide, roll and slither through brilliant, towering sand hills. Sixteen miles southwest of Alamogordo (15 miles southwest of Hwy 82/70), gypsum covers 275 sq miles to create a dazzling white landscape at this crisp, stark **monument** (www.nps.gov/whsa; adult/under 16yr $3/free; ⏲7am-9pm Jun-Aug, 7am-sunset Sep-May). These captivating windswept dunes are a highlight of any trip to New Mexico. Don't forget your sunglasses – the sand is as bright as snow!

Spring for a $15 plastic saucer at the visitor center gift store then sled one of the back dunes. It's fun, and you can sell the disc back for $5 at day's end (no rentals to avoid liability). Check the park calendar for sunset strolls and occasional moonlight bicycle rides (adult/child under 16 years $5/2.50), the latter best reserved far in advance. Backcountry campsites, with no water or toilet facilities, are a mile from the scenic drive. Pick up one of the limited permits ($3, issued first-come, first-served) in person at the visitor center at least one hour before sunset.

ALAMOGORDO & AROUND

Alamogordo is the center of one of the most historically important space- and atomic-research programs in the country. The four-story **New Mexico Museum of Space History** (☎877-333-6589; www.nmspacemuseum.org; Hwy 2001; adult/senior/4-12yr $6/5/4; ⏲9am-5pm) has excellent exhibits on space research and flight. Its **Tombaugh IMAX Theater & Planetarium** (adult/senior/child $6/5.50/4.50) shows outstanding science-themed films on a huge wraparound screen.

Numerous motels stretch along White Sands Blvd, including **Best Western Desert Aire Motor Inn** (☎575-437-2110; www.bestwestern.com; 1021 S White Sands Blvd; r from $78; P❄@☎⛆), with standard-issue rooms and suites (some with kitchenettes), along with a sauna. If you'd rather camp, hit **Oliver Lee State Park** (www.enmrd.state.nm.us/prd/oliverlee.htm; 409 Dog Canyon Rd; tent/RV sites $8/14), 12 miles south of Alamogordo. Grab some grub at the friendly **Pizza Patio & Pub** (2203 E 1st St; mains $7-15; ⏲11am-8pm Mon-Thu & Sat, to 9pm Fri) with pizzas, pastas, big salads and pitchers or pints of beer on tap.

CLOUDCROFT

Pleasant Cloudcroft, with turn-of-the-19th-century buildings, offers lots of outdoor recreation, a good base for exploration and a low-key feel. Situated high in the mountains, it provides welcome relief from the lowlands heat to the east. For good information on hiking trails, free maps of forest roads, and topo maps for sale, go to the **Lincoln National Forest Ranger Station** (4 Lost Lodge Rd; ⏲7:30am-4:30pm Mon-Fri). **High Altitude** (310 Burro St; rentals per day from $30; ⏲10am-5:30pm Mon-Thu, 10am-6pm Fri & Sat, 10am-5pm Sun) rents mountain bikes and has maps of local fat-tire routes.

The **Lodge Resort & Spa** (☎800-395-6343; www.thelodgeresort.com; 1 Corona Pl; r from $79; ❄@☎⛆) is one of the Southwest's best historic hotels. Rooms in the main Bavarian-style hotel are furnished with period and Victorian pieces. Within the lodge, **Rebecca's** (☎575-682-3131; breakfast & lunch $8-15, dinner $28-36; ⏲7-10:30am Mon-Sat, 7-10am Sun, 11:30am-2pm & 5:30-9pm, slightly longer hr summer), named after the resident ghost, offers by far the best food in town.

RUIDOSO

Downright bustling in summer and big with racetrack bettors, resorty Ruidoso (it means 'noisy' in Spanish) has an utterly pleasant climate thanks to its lofty and forested perch near Sierra Blanca (12,000ft). It's spread out along Hwy 48 (known as Mechem Dr or Sudderth Dr), the main drag.

Sights & Activities

To stretch your legs, try the easily accessible **forest trails** on Cedar Creek Rd just west of **Smokey Bear Ranger Station** (901 Mechem Dr; ⏲7:30am-4:30pm Mon-Fri & Sat summer). Choose from the USFS Fitness Trail or the meandering paths at the Cedar Creek Picnic Area. Longer day hikes and backpacking routes abound in the White Mountain Wilderness, north of town. Always check fire restrictions around here – it's not unusual for the forest to close during dry spells.

Ski Apache SKIING

(575-464-3600, snow report 575-257-9001; www.skiapache.com; all-day lift ticket adult/child $39/25; 9am-4pm) The best ski area south of Albuquerque, 18 miles northwest of Ruidoso on the slopes of beautiful Sierra Blanca Peak (about 12,000ft). To get there, take exit 532 off Hwy 48.

Flying J Ranch WILD WEST SHOW

(575-336-4330; www.flyingjranch.com; Hwy 48 N; adult/child $24/14; from 5:30pm Mon-Sat late May–early Sep, plus Sat Sep & early Oct;) Circle the wagons and ride over about 1.5 miles north of Alto, for a meal. This 'Western village' stages gunfights and offers pony rides with its cowboy-style chuckwagon.

Ruidoso Downs Racetrack HORSE RACING

(575-378-4431; www.ruidownsracing.com; Hwy 70; grandstand seats free, boxes $35-55; races Fri-Mon late May–early Sep, casino 10am-midnight year-round) Serious horse racing happens here.

Hubbard Museum of the American West MUSEUM

(www.hubbardmuseum.org; 841 Hwy 70 W; adult/senior/child $6/5/2; 9am-5pm;) Displays Western-related items, with an emphasis on Old West stagecoaches, Native American artifacts and, well, all things horse.

Sleeping & Eating

Numerous motels, hotels and cute little cabin complexes line the streets. There's plenty of primitive camping along forest roads on the way to the ski area.

Sitzmark Chalet HOTEL $

(800-658-9694; www.sitzmark-chalet.com; 627 Sudderth Dr; r from $60;) This ski-themed chalet offers 17 simple but nice rooms. Picnic tables, grills and an eight-person hot tub are welcome perks.

Upper Canyon Inn LODGE $$

(575-257-3005; www.uppercanyoninn.com; 215 Main Rd; r/cabins from $79/119;) Rooms and cabins range from simple good values to rustic-chic luxury.

TOP CHOICE **Rickshaw** ASIAN $$

(575-257-2828; 601 Mechem Dr; www.rickshawnewmexico.com; lunch $7-9, dinner $11-22; 11am-9pm Thu-Tue) The best Asian food south of Albuquerque, with selections inspired by but not slavish to the cuisines of Thailand, China and India. Finish with the gingerpear crumble over homemade cinnamon ice cream.

Cornerstone Bakery BREAKFAST $

(359 Sudderth Dr; mains under $10; 7:30am-2pm Mon-Sat, 7:30am-1pm Sun) Stay around long enough and this eatery may become your touchstone. Everything on the menu, from the omelets to croissant sandwiches, is worthy, and the piñon-flavored coffee is wonderful.

Café Rio PIZZERIA $$

(2547 Sudderth Dr; mains $5-25; 11am-9pm) Friendly service isn't the first description that leaps to mind at this scruffy pizza joint, but oh…take one bite of a pillowy slice and all will be forgiven.

Information

The **chamber of commerce** (575-257-7395; www.ruidosonow.com; 720 Sudderth Dr; 8am-4:30pm Mon-Fri, 9am-3pm Sat) has visitor information.

LINCOLN & CAPITAN

Fans of Western history won't want to miss little Lincoln. Twelve miles east of Capitan along the **Billy the Kid National Scenic Byway** (www.billybyway.com), this is where the gun battle that turned Billy the Kid into a legend took place. The whole town is beautifully preserved in close to original form and the main street has been designated the **Lincoln Town Monument**; modern influences (such as neon-lit motel signs, souvenir stands, fast-food joints) are not allowed.

Buy tickets to the most historic buildings at the **Anderson Freeman Visitors Center & Museum** (Hwy 380; admission to 5 sites adult/child $5/free; 8:30am-4:30pm), where you'll also find exhibits on Buffalo soldiers, Apaches and the Lincoln County War. Make the fascinating **Courthouse Museum** your last stop; this is the well-marked site of Billy's most daring – and violent – escape. There's a plaque where one of his bullets slammed into the wall.

For overnighters, the **Ellis Store Country Inn** (575-653-4609; www.ellisstore.com; Mile 98, Hwy 380; r incl breakfast $89-119) offers three antique-filled rooms (complete with wood stove) in the main house; five additional rooms are located in a historic mill on the property. From Wednesday to Saturday the host offers an amazing six-course dinner ($75 per person), served in the lovely dining room. Perfect for special occasions; reservations recommended.

A few miles west on the road to Capitan, **Laughing Sheep Farm and Ranch** (575-653-4041; www.laughingsheepfarm.com; mains $11-36; 11am-3pm Wed-Sun, 5-8pm Fri & Sat) raises sheep, cows and bison – along with vegetables and fruits – then serves them for lunch and dinner. The dining room is comfortable and casual, with a play-dough table and an easel for kids and live fiddle music on weekend nights.

Like Lincoln, cozy Capitan is surrounded by the beautiful mountains of **Lincoln National Forest**. The main reason to come is so the kids can visit **Smokey Bear Historical State Park** (www.smokeybearpark.com; adult/7-12yr $2/1; 9am-5pm;), where Smokey (yes, there actually was a real Smokey Bear) is buried.

ROSWELL

If you believe 'The Truth Is Out There', then the Roswell Incident is already filed away in your memory banks. In 1947 a mysterious object crashed at a nearby ranch. No one would have skipped any sleep over it, but the military made a big to-do of hushing it up, and for a lot of folks, that sealed it: the aliens had landed! International curiosity and local ingenuity have transformed the city into a quirky extraterrestrial-wannabe zone. Bulbous white heads glow atop the downtown streetlamps and busloads of tourists come to find good souvenirs.

Believers and kitsch-seekers must check out the **International UFO Museum & Research Center** (www.roswellufomuseum.com; 114 N Main St; adult/child $5/2; 9am-5pm), displaying documents supporting the cover-up as well as lots of far-out art and exhibitions. The annual **Roswell UFO Festival** (www.roswellufofestival.com) beams down over the July 4 weekend, with an otherworldly costume parade, guest speakers, workshops and concerts.

Ho-hum chain motels line N Main St. About 36 miles south of Roswell, the **Heritage Inn** (575-748-2552; www.artesiaheritageinn.com; 209 W Main St, Artesia; r incl breakfast $104;) in Artesia offers 11 Old West-style rooms and is the nicest lodging in the area.

Superhero-themed **Farley's** (1315 N Main St; mains $7-13; 11am-11pm Sun-Thu, to 1am Fri & Sat) has 29 beers on tap as well as pub food and pizza in a huge industrial space. For simple, dependable Mexican fare downtown, try **Martin's Capitol Café** (110 W 4th St; mains $7-15; 6am-8:30pm Mon-Sat).

Pick up local information and have your picture snapped with an alien at the **visitors bureau** (575-624-0889; www.roswellmysteries.com; 912 N Main St; 8:30am-5:30pm Mon-Fri, 10am-3pm Sat & Sun;).

The **Greyhound Bus Depot** (575-622-2510; www.greyhound.com; 1100 N Virginia Ave) has buses to Carlsbad ($28, 1½ hours) and El Paso, TX, via Las Cruces ($54, five hours).

CARLSBAD

Travelers use Carlsbad as a base for visits to nearby Carlsbad Caverns National Park and the Guadalupe Mountains. The **Park Service office** (575-885-8884; 3225 National Parks Hwy; 8am-4:30pm Mon-Fri) on the south edge of town has information on both.

On the northwestern outskirts of town, off Hwy 285, **Living Desert State Park** (1504 Miehls Dr; adult/7-12yr $5/3; 8am-8pm late Jun–Aug, 9am-5pm Sep-May;) is a great place to see and learn about desert plants and wildlife. There's a good 1.3-mile trail that showcases different habitats of the Chihuahuan Desert, with live antelopes, wolves, roadrunners and more.

Most Carlsbad lodging consists of chain motels on S Canal St or National Parks Hwy. The top value is the **Stagecoach Inn** (575-887-1148; 1819 S Canal St; r from $40;), with clean rooms, a pool, and a good on-site playground for kids. The best accommodation in town is the new, luxurious **Trinity Hotel** (575-234-9891; www.thetrinityhotel.com; 201 S Canal St; r $129-199;), a historic building that was originally the First National Bank; the sitting room of one suite is inside the old vault! The restaurant here is Carlsbad's classiest.

The perky **Blue House Bakery & Cafe** (609 N Canyon St; mains under $10; breakfast 6am-noon Mon & Sat, breakfast & lunch 6am-2pm Tue-Fri) brews the best coffee in this quadrant of New Mexico. Get there before 10am for the full selection of pastries. Locals and visitors crowd **Lucy's** (701 S Canal St; mains $7-16; 11am-9pm Mon-Thu, 11am-9:30pm Fri & Sat), where you can scarf down cheap New Mexican meals.

For other in-the-know advice, visit the **chamber of commerce** (575-887-6516; www.carlsbadchamber.com; 302 S Canal St; 9am-5pm Mon, 8am-5pm Tue-Fri year-round, 9am-3pm Sat May-Sep).

Greyhound (575-628-0768; www.greyhound.com; 3102 National Parks Hwy) buses depart from the Shamrock gas station inside Food Jet South. Destinations include El Paso, TX ($49, three hours), and Albuquerque ($49, 4½ hours).

CARLSBAD CAVERNS NATIONAL PARK

Scores of wondrous caves hide under the hills at this unique **national park** (☎575-785-2232, bat info 505-785-3012; www.nps.gov/cave; 3225 National Parks Hwy; adult/child $6/free; ⏲caves 8:30am-4pm late May–early Sep, 8:30am-3:30pm early Sep–late May), which covers 73 sq miles. The cavern formations are an ethereal wonderland of stalactites and fantastical geological features. You can ride an elevator from the visitor center (which descends the length of the Empire State Building in under a minute) or take a 2-mile subterranean walk from the cave mouth to the Big Room, an underground chamber 1800ft long, 255ft high and more than 800ft below the surface. If you've got kids (or are just feeling goofy), plastic caving helmets with headlamps are sold in the gift shop.

Guided tours of additional caves are available (adult $7 to $20, child $3.50 to $10), and should be reserved well in advance (call ☎877-444-6777 or visit www.recreation.gov). Bring long sleeves and closed shoes; it gets chilly.

The cave's other claim to fame is the 300,000-plus Mexican free-tailed bat colony that roosts here from mid-May to mid-October. Be here by sunset, when they cyclone out for an all-evening insect feast.

Understand Western USA

population per sq/mile

WYOMING | USA | CALIFORNIA

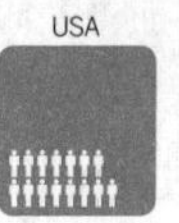

≈ 6 people

Western USA Today

It's All About Money...

Fiscal woes are affecting states across the West, and legislatures are slashing their budgets. In Arizona, California and Utah, state parks have been especially hard hit. In Arizona, many state parks are now operating on a five-day schedule, while the number of law-enforcement rangers has been significantly cut in Utah. In California, 70 of the state's 278 parks are scheduled for closure, although Governor Jerry Brown has signed a bill to allow them to explore partnerships with nonprofit organizations to remain open. Nevada's unemployment rate hit 12% in the spring of 2011, which was higher than the national average. And real estate? Luxury condominiums in Vegas sit empty and mountain resort properties in Colorado are experiencing declines.

Natural Wonders

Highest Point: Mt Whitney, CA 14,497ft

Lowest Point: Death Valley, CA -282ft

The Grand Canyon is 277 miles long.

...Politics...

Illegal immigration remains a hot-button issue even though the number of arrests for illegal border crossings dropped from 1.6 million in 2000 to 448,000 in 2010. The number of border patrol agents jumped from 10,000 in 2004 to more than 20,700 in 2010, with agents having a very visible presence in southern Arizona, where their green-and-white SUVs are a common sight on rural roads. Arizona has also passed a stringent anti-immigration law, requiring police officers to ask for ID from anyone they suspect of being in the country illegally.

In California the most divisive issue has been same-sex marriage and the constitutional amendment to ban it, which is tied up in legal battles. Colorado remains the West's most visible swing state. The state went Republican in all but three of the last 12 presidential elections, but during the 2010 mid-term elections Democrats won a senate seat and the governorship, the latter by a razor-thin margin.

Dos and Don'ts

» Do leave a 15% to 20% tip for your server at a restaurant (unless service is appalling).

» Don't assume you can smoke, even if outside. Most Americans have little tolerance for smokers and have even banned smoking from many parks and beaches.

» Don't be overly physical when you greet someone. Some Americans will hug; urbanites may exchange cheek kisses, but most folks – especially men – will just shake hands.

How to Blend In

» If the ground shakes a little, don't freak out. Locals are used to low-level earthquakes.

» Glide up to that gas pump in Oregon and...sit tight. No self-pumping allowed.

USA belief systems
(% of population)

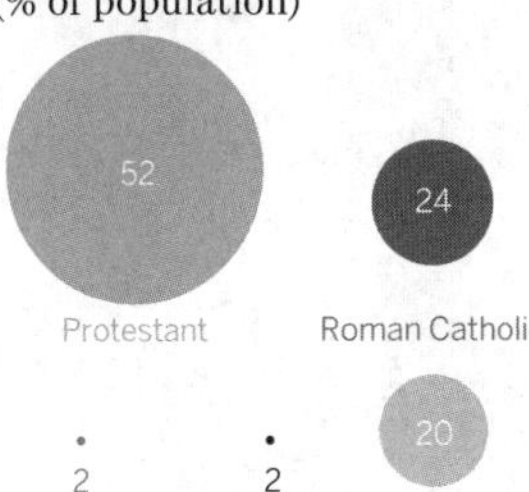

if USA were 100 people

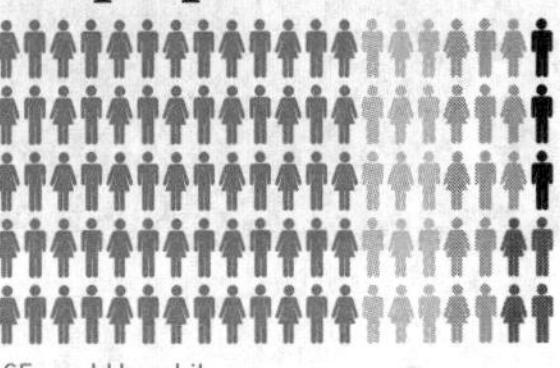

65 would be white
15 would be Hispanic
13 would be African American
4 would be Asian American
3 would be other

...or Fire and Water

Although the exact causes are unclear – climate change, residential development, government policy – the West has been hard hit by forest fires. The 2011 Wallow Wildfire was the worst in Arizona's history, burning about 538,000 acres. At about the same time, the Las Conchas Fire burned more than 244 square miles near Los Alamos, New Mexico. The good news? A record snowpack in western mountain ranges in 2011 spells w-a-t-e-r (after melting) for Nevada and Arizona, where water levels have been dropping the last 10 years. Lake Mead might swell by 40ft.

Moving Forward

The recession marches on but so does technological development, and the tributes describing the accomplishments of Apple co-founder and California native Steve Jobs show just how far and how quickly. California's innovations are myriad: PCs, iPods, Google, the internet. But Northern California holds more than Silicon Valley – it's also the site of a burgeoning biotech industry. In the Pacific Northwest, the Seattle area is headquarters for Microsoft, Nintendo and Amazon.com. Branches of Intel, Tektronix and Google support Oregon's 'Silicon Forest.'

In the Southwest, Richard Branson's Virgin Galactic plans to send civilian 'astronauts' into space from the new Spaceport in central New Mexico. At the Grand Canyon, an impressive new South Rim visitor center has opened, and eco-friendly initiatives there are gaining traction, including a park-and-ride shuttle from Tusayan and a bicycle rental service. Environmentally, Colorado leads the way with progressive clean-energy standards, legislated incentives for residents to use clean energy and significant growth in solar energy jobs.

Sprinting speed of a roadrunner: 15 mph

Percentage of land that is public in Utah: 70%

Cost of marriage license in Nevada: $60

Top Films

» **Stagecoach** (1939)
» **Sunset Boulevard** (1950)
» **Butch Cassidy & The Sundance Kid** (1969)
» **Chinatown** (1974)
» **One Flew Over the Cuckoo's Nest** (1975)
» **The Shining** (1980)
» **Boyz n the Hood** (1991)
» **Thelma & Louise** (1991)
» **Sideways** (2004)
» **The Hangover** (2009)
» **127 Hours** (2010)

Top Books

» **The Grapes of Wrath** (1939) John Steinbeck
» **Desert Solitaire** (1968) Edward Abbey
» **Bean Trees** (1988) Barbara Kingsolver
» **Into the Wild** (1996) Jon Krakauer

History

The first inhabitants of this region actually arrived from the west, crossing the Bering Strait about 20,000 years ago. These hardy souls flowed south, splitting into diverse communities that adapted as required by the weather and surrounding landscape. The Spanish arrived in the Southwest in the 1540s, looking for the Seven Cities of Gold. Missions and missionaries followed in the 1700s as the Spanish staked their claim along the California coast.

The Spanish, as well as the British and Americans, were soon searching for the Northwest Passage, an east–west water route, but President Thomas Jefferson eventually scooped this endeavor with the Louisiana Purchase in 1803. His emissaries, Meriwether Lewis and William Clark, marched west from St Louis to explore America's newest holding, opening the door for a wave of pioneers.

Those Who Came Before, by Robert H and Florence C Lister, is an excellent source about the prehistory of the Southwest and the archaeological sites of its national parks and monuments.

An estimated 400,000 people trekked west across America between 1840 and 1860, lured by tales of gold, promises of religious freedom and visions of fertile farmland. The 'Wild West' years soon followed with ranchers, cowboys, miners and entrepreneurs staking claims and raising hell. Law, order and civilization arrived, hastened by the telegraph, the transcontinental railroad and a continual flow of new arrivals who just wanted to settle down and enjoy their piece of the American pie.

This goal became harder to accomplish in the arid West because lack of water limited expansion. The great dam projects of the early 1900s tempered the water problem and allowed for the development of cities – Los Angeles, Las Vegas, Phoenix – in places where cities didn't necessarily belong.

The West took on a more important economic and technological role during WWII. Scientists developed the atomic bomb in the secret city of Los Alamos. War-related industries, such as timber production and work at naval yards and airplane factories, thrived in the Pacific Northwest and California. After the war, industry took on new forms, with Silicon

TIMELINE

20,000–40,000 BC

The first peoples to the Americas arrive from Central Asia by migrating over a wide land bridge between Siberia and Alaska (when sea levels were lower than today).

8000 BC

Widespread extinction of ice-age mammals including the woolly mammoth, due to cooperative hunting by humans and a warming climate. People begin hunting smaller game and gathering native plants.

7000 BC–AD 100

'Archaic period' marked by nomadic hunter-gatherer lifestyle. By the end of this period, corn, beans and squash and permanent settlements are well established.

Valley's dot-com industry drawing talented entrepreneurs to the Bay area in the 1990s. The film industry still holds strong in Los Angeles, but tax incentives have drawn filmmakers to other western enclaves, particularly New Mexico.

Today, the West has been forced to take a closer look at the effects of rapid growth. Immigration, traffic, dropping water levels and environmental concerns all grab headlines and affect people's way of life. The continuing allure of the West will depend on how these issues are tackled.

The First Americans

Western America's earliest inhabitants crossed the Bering Strait more than 20,000 years ago. When Europeans arrived, approximately two to 18 million Native American people lived north of present-day Mexico and spoke more than 300 languages.

Pacific Northwest

In the Pacific Northwest, early coastal inhabitants went out to sea in pursuit of whales or sea lions, or depended on catching salmon and cod and collecting shellfish. On land they hunted deer and elk while gathering berries and roots. Food was stored for the long winters, when free time could be spent on artistic, religious and cultural pursuits. The construction of ornately carved cedar canoes led to extensive trading networks that stretched along the coast.

Inland, a regional culture based on seasonal migration – between rivers and temperate uplands – developed among tribes. During salmon runs, tribes gathered at rapids and waterfalls to net or harpoon fish. In the harsh landscapes of Oregon's southern desert, tribes were nomadic peoples who hunted and scavenged in the northern reaches of the Great Basin desert.

California

By 1500 AD more than 300,000 Native Americans spoke some 100 distinct languages in the California region. Central-coast fishing communities built subterranean roundhouses and saunas, where they held ceremonies, told stories and gambled for fun. Northwest hunting communities constructed big houses and redwood dugout canoes, while the inhabitants of southwest California created sophisticated pottery and developed irrigation systems that made farming in the desert possible. Native Americans in California had no written language but observed oral contracts and zoning laws.

Within a century of the arrival of Spanish colonists in 1769, California's Native population would be decimated to 20,000 by European diseases, conscripted labor regimes and famine.

Cliff Dwellings

- » Mesa Verde National Park, NM
- » Bandelier National Monument, NM
- » Gila Cliff Dwellings National Monument, NM
- » Montezuma Castle National Monument, AZ
- » Walnut Canyon National Monument, AZ

1300–1400

One of history's most enduring unsolved mysteries occurs when the entire civilization of Ancestral Puebloans living in Mesa Verde, CO, abandons the area, leaving behind a sophisticated city of cliff dwellings.

1492

Italian explorer Christopher Columbus 'discovers' America, eventually making three voyages throughout the Caribbean. He names the indigenous inhabitants 'Indians,' mistakenly thinking he'd reached the Indies.

1598

A large force of Spanish explorers, led by Don Juan de Onate, stops near present-day El Paso, TX, and declares the land to the north New Mexico for Spain.

c 1600

Santa Fe, America's oldest capital city, is founded. The Palace of Governors is the only remaining 17th-century structure; the rest of Santa Fe was destroyed by a 1914 fire.

The Southwest & Southern Colorado

Archaeologists believe that the Southwest's first inhabitants were hunters. The population grew, however, and wild game became extinct, forcing hunters to augment their diets with berries, seeds, roots and fruits. After 3000 BC, contacts with farmers in what is now central Mexico led to the beginnings of agriculture in the Southwest.

In 1680, during the Pueblo Revolt, the northern New Mexico pueblos banded together to drive out the Spanish after the latter's bloody campaign to destroy Puebloan ceremonial objects. The Spanish were pushed south of the Rio Grande and the Pueblo people held Santa Fe until 1682.

By about AD 100, three dominant cultures were emerging in the Southwest: the Hohokam of the desert, the Mogollon of the central mountains and valleys, and the Ancestral Puebloans – formerly known as the Anasazi.

The Hohokam lived in the deserts of Arizona, adapting to desert life by creating an incredible river-fed irrigation system. They also developed low earthen pyramids and sunken ball courts with earthen walls. By about 1400, the Hohokam had abandoned their villages. There are many theories on this tribe's disappearance, but the most likely involves a combination of factors including drought, overhunting, conflict among groups and disease.

The Mogollon culture settled near the Mexican border from 200 BC to AD 1400. They lived in small communities, often elevated on isolated mesas or ridge tops, and built simple pit dwellings. Although they farmed, they depended more on hunting and foraging for food. Around the 13th or 14th century, the Mogollon had probably been peacefully incorporated by the Ancestral Puebloan groups from the north.

The Ancestral Puebloans inhabited the Colorado Plateau, also called the Four Corners area. This culture left the richest archaeological sites and ancient settlements that are still inhabited in the Southwest. Their descendants live in Pueblo Indian communities in New Mexico. The oldest links with the Ancestral Puebloans are found among the Hopi tribe of northern Arizona. The mesa-top village of Old Oraibi (see the boxed text, p346) has been inhabited since the 1100s, making it the oldest continuously inhabited settlement in North America.

Anasazi, a Navajo word meaning 'enemy ancestors,' is a term to which many modern Pueblo Indians object; it's no longer used.

The Europeans Arrive

Spain's Mission Impossible

Francisco Vasquez de Coronado led the first major expedition into North America in 1540. It included 300 soldiers, hundreds of Native American guides and herds of livestock. It also marked the first major violence between Spanish explorers and the native people.

The expedition's goal was the fabled, immensely rich Seven Cities of Cibola. For two years, they traveled through what is now Arizona, New Mexico and as far east as Kansas. Instead of gold and precious gems, the

1787–91

The Constitutional Convention in Philadelphia draws up the US Constitution. The Bill of Rights is later adopted as constitutional amendments articulating citizens' rights.

1803

Napoleon sells the Louisiana Territory to the US for $15 million, thereby extending the boundaries of the new nation from the Mississippi River to the Rocky Mountains.

STEPHEN SAKS / LONELY PLANET IMAGES ©

» Rocky Mountain National Park (p254), Colorado

expedition found adobe pueblos, which they violently commandeered. During the Spaniards' first few years in northern New Mexico, they tried to subdue the pueblos, with much bloodshed. The Spanish established Santa Fe as the capital around 1610. The city remains the capital of New Mexico today, the oldest capital in what is now the USA.

When 18th-century Russian and English trappers began trading valuable otter pelts from Alta California, Spain concocted a plan for colonization. For the glory of God and the tax coffers of Spain, missions would be built across the state, and within 10 years these would be going concerns run by local converts.

Spain's missionizing plan was approved in 1769, and Franciscan Padre Junípero Serra secured support to set up *presidios* (military posts) alongside several missions in northern and central California in the 1770s and '80s. Clergy relied on soldiers to round up conscripts to build missions. In exchange for their labor, Native Americans were allowed one meal a day (when available) and a place in God's kingdom – which came much sooner than expected due to the smallpox the Spanish brought with them. In the Southwest, more than half of the Pueblo populations were decimated by smallpox, measles and typhus.

Lewis & Clark

After President Thomas Jefferson bought the Louisiana Territory from Napoleon in 1803 for $15 million, he sent his personal secretary, Meriwether Lewis, west to chart North America's western regions. The goal was to find a waterway to the Pacific while exploring the newly acquired Louisiana Purchase and establishing a foothold for American interests. Lewis, who had no training for exploration, convinced his good friend William Clark, an experienced frontiersman and army veteran, to tag along. In 1804, the 40-member party, called the Corps of Discovery, left St Louis.

The expedition fared relatively well, in part because of the presence of Sacagawea, a young Shoshone woman married to a French-Canadian trapper who was part of the entourage. Sacagawea proved invaluable as a guide, translator and ambassador to the area's Native Americans. York, Clark's African American servant, also softened tensions between the group and the Native Americans.

The party traveled some 8000 miles in about two years, documenting everything they came across in their journals. Meticulous notes were made on 122 animals and 178 plants, with some new discoveries being made along the way. In 1805 the party finally reached the mouth of the Columbia River and the Pacific Ocean at Cape Disappointment and bedded down for the winter nearby, thus establishing Fort Clatsop.

Lewis and Clark returned to a hero's welcome in St Louis in 1806.

EXPEDITION

You can follow the Lewis and Clark expedition on its extraordinary journey west to the Pacific and back again online at www.pbs.org/lewisandclark, featuring historical maps, photo albums and journal excerpts.

1803–06

President Jefferson sends Meriwether Lewis and William Clark west. Guided by Shoshone tribeswoman Sacagawea, they trailblaze from St Louis, Missouri, to the Pacific Ocean and back.

1811

Pacific Fur Company mogul John Jacob Astor establishes Fort Astoria, the first permanent US settlement on the Pacific Coast. He later becomes the country's first millionaire.

1841

Wagon trains follow the Oregon Trail, and by 1847 over 6500 emigrants a year are heading West, to Oregon, California and Mormon-dominated Utah.

1844

First telegraph line is inaugurated with the phrase 'What hath God wrought?' In 1845, Congress approves a transcontinental railroad, completed in 1869. Together, telegraph and train open the frontier.

Eureka!

Real estate speculator, lapsed Mormon and tabloid publisher Sam Brannan was looking to unload some California swampland in 1848 when he heard rumors of gold flakes found near Sutter's Mill, 120 miles from San Francisco. Figuring this news should sell some newspapers and raise real estate values, Brannan published the rumor as fact. Initially the story didn't generate excitement. So Brannan ran another story, this time verified by Mormon employees at Sutter's Mill who had sworn him to secrecy. Brannan reportedly kept his word by running through the San Francisco streets, brandishing gold entrusted to him as tithes for the Mormon church, shouting, 'Gold on the American River!'

Chinatown (1974) is the fictionalized yet surprisingly accurate account of the brutal water wars that were waged to build both Los Angeles and San Francisco.

Other newspapers hastily published stories of 'gold mountains' near San Francisco. By 1850, the year California was fast-tracked for admission as the 31st state, its non-native population had ballooned from 15,000 to 93,000. Most arrivals weren't Americans, but Peruvians, Australians, Chileans and Mexicans, with some Chinese, Irish, native Hawaiian and French prospectors.

Early arrivals panned for gold side by side, slept in close quarters, drank firewater with Chinese takeout and splurged on French food and Australian wines. But with each wave of arrivals, profits dropped and gold became harder to find. In 1848 each prospector earned an average of about $300,000 in today's terms; by 1849, earnings were $95,000 to $145,000, but by 1865 they had dipped to $35,000. When surface gold became harder to find, miners picked, shoveled and dynamited through mountains. The work was grueling and dangerous, and with few doctors, injuries often proved lethal.

Westward, Ho!

As the 19th century dawned on the young nation, optimism was the mood of the day. With the invention of the cotton gin in 1793 – followed by threshers, reapers, mowers and later combines – agriculture was industrialized, and US commerce surged. The 1803 Louisiana Purchase doubled US territory, and expansion west of the Appalachian Mountains began in earnest.

Exploiting the West's vast resources became a patriotic duty in the 1840s – a key aspect of America's belief in its Manifest Destiny. New York editor John Sullivan, echoing the expansionist credo of President James Polk, urged Americans to 'overspread the continent allotted by providence for the free development of your yearly multiplying millions.' During the early territorial days, movement of goods and people from the East to the West was very slow. Horses, mule trains and stagecoaches represented state-of-the-art transportation at the time.

1846–48
The battle for the West is waged with the Mexican-American War. War ends with the 1848 Guadalupe-Hidalgo treaty that gives most of present-day Arizona and New Mexico to the USA.

1847
Mormons fleeing religious persecution in Illinois start arriving in Salt Lake City; over the next 20 years more than 70,000 Mormons will head to Utah via the Mormon Pioneer Trail.

1849
After the 1848 discovery of gold near Sacramento, an epic cross-country gold rush sees 60,000 'forty-niners' flock to California's Mother Lode. San Francisco's population explodes to 25,000.

1859
The richest vein of silver ever discovered in the USA, the Comstock Lode, is struck in Virginia City, NV, which quickly becomes the most notorious mining town in the Wild West.

One of the major routes was the Oregon Trail. Spanning six states, it sorely tested the families who embarked on this perilous trip. Their belongings were squirreled away under canvas-topped wagons, which often trailed livestock. The journey could take up to eight months, and by the time the settlers reached eastern Oregon their food supplies were running on fumes. Other major routes included the Santa Fe Trail and the Old Spanish Trail, which ran from Santa Fe into central Utah and across Nevada to Los Angeles in California. Regular stagecoach services along the Santa Fe Trail began in 1849; the Mormon Trail reached Salt Lake City in 1847.

The arrival of more people and resources via the railroad led to further land exploration and the frequent discovery of mineral deposits. Many Western mining towns were founded in the 1870s and 1880s; some are now ghost towns like Santa Rita while others like Tombstone and Silver City remain active.

Riders and swift horses were the backbone of the Pony Express (1860–61). They carried letters between Missouri and California in an astounding 10 days!

The Long Walk & Apache Conflicts

For decades, US forces pushed west across the continent, killing or forcibly moving whole tribes of Native Americans who were in their way. The most widely known incident is the forceful relocation of many Navajo in 1864. US forces, led by Kit Carson, destroyed Navajo fields, orchards and houses, and forced the people into surrendering or withdrawing into remote parts of Canyon de Chelly. Eventually, they were starved out. About 9000 Navajo were rounded up and marched 400 miles east to a camp at Bosque Redondo, near Fort Sumner in New Mexico. Hundreds of Native Americans died from sickness, starvation or gunshot wounds along the way. The Navajo call this 'The Long Walk,' and it remains an important part of their history.

The last serious conflicts were between US troops and the Apache. This was partly because raiding was the essential path to manhood for the Apache. As US forces and settlers moved into Apache land, they became obvious targets for the raids that were part of the Apache way of life. These continued under the leadership of Mangas Coloradas, Cochise, Victorio and, finally, Geronimo, who surrendered in 1886 after being promised that he and the Apache would be imprisoned for two years and then allowed to return to their homeland. As with many promises made during these years, this one, too, was broken.

Even after the wars were over, Native Americans were treated like second-class citizens for many decades. Non-Native Americans used legal loopholes and technicalities to take over reservation land. Many children were removed from reservations and shipped off to boarding schools where they were taught in English and punished for speaking

Among the provisions recommended for those traveling the Oregon Trail were coffee (15lb per person), bacon (25lb per person), 1lb of castile soap, citric acid to prevent scurvy and a live cow for milk and emergency meat.

1861–65
American Civil War erupts between North and South. The war's end on April 9, 1865, is marred by President Lincoln's assassination five days later.

1864
Kit Carson forces 9000 Navajo to walk 400 miles to a camp near Fort Sumner. Hundreds of Native Americans die from sickness, starvation and gunshot wounds along 'The Long Walk.'

1881
In 1881, Wyatt Earp, his brothers Virgil and Morgan, and Doc Holliday, kill Billy Clanton and the McLaury brothers in a blazing gunfight at the OK Corral in Tombstone, AZ.

1882
Racist sentiment, particularly in California (where over 50,000 Chinese immigrants have arrived since 1848) leads to the Chinese Exclusion Act, the only US immigration law to exclude a specific race.

their own languages or behaving 'like Indians' – this practice continued into the 1930s.

The Wild West

Romanticized tales of gunslingers, cattle rustlers, outlaws and train robbers fuel Wild West legends. Good and bad guys were designations in flux – a tough outlaw in one state became a popular sheriff in another. Gunfights were more frequently the result of mundane political struggles in emerging towns than storied blood feuds. New mining towns mushroomed overnight, playing host to rowdy saloons and bordellos where miners would come to brawl, drink and gamble.

On November 7, 1893, Colorado became the first US state – and one of the first places in the world – to grant women the right to vote.

Legendary figures Billy the Kid and Sheriff Pat Garrett, both involved in the infamous Lincoln County War, were active in the late 1870s. Billy the Kid reputedly shot and killed more than 20 men in a brief career as a gunslinger – he himself was shot and killed by Garrett at the age of 21. In 1881, Wyatt Earp, along with his brothers Virgil and Morgan, and Doc Holliday, shot dead Billy Clanton and the McLaury brothers in a blazing gunfight at the OK Corral in Tombstone – the showdown took less than a minute. Both sides accused the other of cattle rustling, but the real story will never be known.

Butch Cassidy and the Sundance Kid once roamed much of Utah. Cassidy, a Mormon, robbed banks and trains with his Wild Bunch gang during the 1890s but never killed anyone.

Water & Western Development

Americans began to think about occupying the area between the coasts. The lingering image of the Great American Desert, a myth propagated by early explorers, had deterred agricultural settlers and urban development. Though the western interior was not a desert, water was a limiting factor as cities such as Denver began to spring up at the base of the Front Range.

The Denver Mint struck and minted its first gold and silver coins on February 1, 1906. It is the largest producer of coins in the world. The mint was robbed of $200,000 in broad daylight on 18 December, 1922.

The struggle for an adequate supply of water for the growing desert population marked the early years of the 20th century, resulting in federally funded dam projects such as the 1936 Hoover Dam and, in 1963, the Glen Canyon Dam and Lake Powell. Water supply continues to be a key challenge in this region.

Reforming the Wild West

When the great earthquake and fire hit San Francisco in 1906, it signaled change for California. With public funds for citywide water mains and fire hydrants siphoned off by corrupt bosses, there was only one functioning water source in San Francisco. When the smoke lifted, one thing was clear: it was time for the Wild West to change.

1913

William Mulholland, Director of Los Angeles Water & Power, presides over the opening of the 233-mile Owens Valley-Los Angeles Aqueduct. As water gushed forth he proclaimed, 'There it is. Take it.'

1919

The Grand Canyon becomes the USA's 15th national park, and a dirt road to the North Rim is built from Kanab. The park was visited by 4.4 million in 2007.

1938

Route 66 becomes the first cross-country highway to be completely paved, including more than 750 miles across Arizona and New Mexico. The Mother Road is officially decommissioned in 1984.

1945

The first atomic bomb is detonated in the ironically named Jornada del Norte (Journey of Death) Valley in southern New Mexico that is now part of the White Sands Missile Range.

While San Francisco was rebuilt at a rate of 15 buildings per day, California's reformers set to work on city, state and national politics, one plank at a time. Californians concerned about public health and trafficking in women pushed for passage of the 1914 statewide Red Light Abatement Act. Mexico's revolution from 1910 to 1921 brought a new wave of migrants and revolutionary ideas, including ethnic pride and worker solidarity. As California's ports grew, longshoremen's unions coordinated a historic 83-day strike in 1934 along the entire West Coast that forced concessions for safer working conditions and fair pay.

At the height of the Depression in 1935, some 200,000 farming families fleeing the drought-struck Dust Bowl in Texas and Oklahoma arrived in California, where they found scant pay and deplorable working conditions at major farming concerns. California's artists alerted middle America to the migrants' plight, and the nation rallied around Dorothea Lange's haunting documentary photos of famine-struck families and John Steinbeck's harrowing fictionalized account in his 1939 novel *The Grapes of Wrath*.

The Oscar-winning *There Will Be Blood* (2007), adapted from Upton Sinclair's book *Oil!*, depicts a Californian oil magnate and was based on real-life SoCal tycoon Edward Doheny.

WWII & The Atomic Age

Los Alamos

In 1943, Los Alamos, New Mexico, then a boys school perched on a 7400ft mesa, was chosen as the top-secret headquarters of the Manhattan Project, the code name for the research and development of the atomic bomb. The 772-acre site, accessed by two dirt roads, had no gas or oil lines and only one wire service, and it was surrounded by forest.

Isolation and security marked every aspect of life on 'the hill.' Not only was resident movement restricted and mail censored, there was no outside contact by radio or telephone. Perhaps even more unsettling, most residents had no idea why they were living in Los Alamos. Knowledge was on a 'need to know' basis; everyone knew only as much as their job required.

In just under two years, Los Alamos scientists successfully detonated the first atomic bomb at the Trinity site, now White Sands Missile Range.

After the US detonated the atomic bomb in Japan, the secret city of Los Alamos was exposed to the public. The city continued to be cloaked in secrecy, however, until 1957 when restrictions on visiting were lifted.

John Steinbeck's *The Grapes of Wrath* (1939) tells the saga of Depression-era farmers from the Great Plains desperately trying to escape the Dust Bowl by heading for the promised land of California.

Changing Workforce & New Industries

California's workforce permanently changed in WWII, when women and African Americans were recruited for wartime industries and Mexican workers were brought in to fill labor shortages. Contracts in military communications and aviation attracted an international elite

1946

The opening of the glitzy Flamingo casino in Las Vegas sparks a mob-backed building spree. By the fabulous '50s, Sin City has reached its first golden peak.

RICHARD CUMMINS / LONELY PLANET IMAGES ©

» Flamingo, Las Vegas

1947

An unidentified object falls in the desert near Roswell. The government first calls it a crashed disk, then a day later a weather balloon and mysteriously closes off the area.

1963

The controversial Glen Canyon Dam is finished and Lake Powell begins, eventually covering up ancestral Indian sites and stunning rock formations but creating 1960 miles of shoreline and a boater fantasyland.

of engineers, who would launch California's high-tech industry. Within a decade after the war, California's population had grown by 40%, reaching almost 13 million.

The war also brought economic fortune to the Pacific Northwest, when the area became the nation's largest lumber producer and both Oregon's and Washington's naval yards bustled, along with William Boeing's airplane factory. The region continued to prosper through the second half of the 20th century, attracting new migrations of educated, progressively minded settlers from the nation's east and south.

Hollywood & Counterculture

In 1908, California became a convenient movie location for its consistent sunlight and versatile locations, although its role was limited to doubling for more exotic locales and providing backdrops for period-piece productions. But gradually, California began stealing the scene in movies and iconic TV shows with waving palms and sunny beaches.

Not all Californians saw themselves as extras in *Beach Blanket Bingo,* however. WWII sailors discharged for insubordination and homosexuality in San Francisco found themselves at home in North Beach's bebop jazz clubs, bohemian coffeehouses and City Lights Bookstore. San Francisco became the home of free speech and free spirits, and soon everyone who was anyone was getting arrested: Beat poet Lawrence Ferlinghetti for publishing Allen Ginsberg's epic poem *Howl,* comedian Lenny Bruce for uttering the F-word onstage and Carol Doda for going topless. When Flower Power faded, other Bay Area rebellions grew in its place: Black Power, Gay Pride and medical marijuana clubs.

But while Northern California had the more attention-grabbing counterculture in the 1940s to '60s, nonconformity in sunny Southern California shook America to the core. In 1947, when Senator Joseph McCarthy attempted to root out suspected communists in the movie industry, 10 writers and directors who refused to admit communist alliances or to name names were charged with contempt of Congress and barred from working in Hollywood. The Hollywood Ten's impassioned defenses of the Constitution were heard nationwide, and major Hollywood players boldly voiced dissent and hired blacklisted talent until California lawsuits put a legal end to McCarthyism in 1962.

On January 28, 1969, an oil rig dumped 200,000 gallons of oil into Santa Barbara Channel, killing dolphins, seals and some 3600 shore birds. The beach community organized a highly effective protest, spurring the establishment of the Environmental Protection Agency.

GERONIMO!

The cry 'Geronimo!' became popular for skydivers after a group of US Army paratroopers training in 1940 saw the movie *Geronimo* (1939) one night, then began shouting the great warrior's name for courage during their jumps.

1973

The debut of the MGM Grand in 1973 signals the dawn of the corporate-owned 'megaresort,' and sparks a building bonanza along Vegas' Strip that's still going strong.

1980

Mt St Helens blows her top, killing 57 people and destroying 250 homes. Her elevation is cut from 9677ft to 8365ft, and where a peak once stood, a mile-wide crater is born.

1995

Amazon, one of the first major companies to sell products online, is launched in Seattle. Originally started as a bookseller, it will not become annually profitable until 2003.

2000

Coloradans vote for Amendment 20 in the state election, which provides for dispensing cannabis to registered patients. A proliferation of medical marijuana clinics ensues over the next decade.

CALIFORNIA'S CIVIL RIGHTS MOVEMENT

When 110,000 Japanese Americans along the West Coast were ordered into internment camps by President Roosevelt in 1942, the San Francisco-based Japanese American Citizen's League immediately filed suits that advanced all the way to the Supreme Court. These lawsuits established groundbreaking civil rights legal precedents, and in 1992 internees received reparations and an official letter of apology for internment signed by George HW Bush.

Adopting the nonviolent resistance practices of Mahatma Gandhi and Martin Luther King Jr, labor leaders César Chávez and Dolores Huerta formed United Farm Workers in 1962 to champion the rights of underrepresented immigrant laborers. While civil rights leaders marched on Washington, Chávez and Californian grape pickers marched on Sacramento, bringing the issue of fair wages and the health risks of pesticides to the nation's attention. When Bobby Kennedy was sent to investigate, he sided with Chávez, bringing Latinos into the US political fold.

Geeking Out

When California's Silicon Valley introduced the first personal computer in 1968, advertisements breathlessly gushed that Hewlett-Packard's 'light' (40lb) machine could 'take on roots of a fifth-degree polynomial, Bessel functions, elliptic integrals and regression analysis' – all for just $4900 (about $29,000 today). Hoping to bring computer power to the people, 21-year-old Steve Jobs and Steve Wozniak introduced the Apple II at the 1977 West Coast Computer Faire with unfathomable memory (4KB of RAM) and microprocessor speed (1MHz).

By the mid-1990s, an entire dot-com industry boomed in Silicon Valley with online start-ups, and suddenly people were getting their mail, news, politics, pet food and, yes, sex online. But when dot-com profits weren't forthcoming, venture funding dried up, and fortunes in stock-options disappeared on one nasty Nasdaq-plummeting day: March 10, 2000. Overnight, 26-year-old vice-presidents and Bay Area service-sector employees alike found themselves jobless. But as online users continued to look for useful information and one another in those billions of web pages, search engines and social media boomed.

Meanwhile, California biotech has been making strides. In 1976, an upstart company called Genentech cloned human insulin and introduced the hepatitis B vaccine. California voters approved a $3 billion bond measure in 2004 for stem cell research, and by 2008 California had become the biggest funder of stem cell research and the focus of Nasdaq's new Biotech Index.

From gunslingers and prospectors to Native Americans ancient and contemporary, www.desertusa.com deals the goods on people and places that call (and have called) the Southwestern desert home.

2002

Salt Lake City hosts the Winter Olympics, becoming the most populated place to ever hold the games. Women also compete in bobsled racing for the first time.

2008

California voters pass Proposition 8, defining legal marriage as between a man and a woman. Courts rule the law unconstitutional, given California's civil rights protections; appeals are pending.

2010

Arizona passes controversial legislation requiring police officers to ask for identification from anyone they suspect of being in the US illegally. Immigration rights activists call for a boycott of the state.

2012

New Mexico and Arizona, the 47th and 48th states to join the Union, celebrate their Centennials.

The People

Who lives in the West? If you believe the headlines, it's angry Arizonans up-in-arms (literally) about illegal immigration, gay couples rushing to marry in San Francisco, hair-pulling housewives in Orange County and pot-smoking invalids in Colorado. And, if the *Twilight* novels are to be believed, the damp and foggy state of Washington is a favorite of stylish vampires and shirtless werewolves. Are these headlines accurate depictions of Westerners? Yes and no. The actions of the headline grabbers may reflect some regional attitudes, but most folks are just trying to go about their daily lives with as little drama as possible.

Key Sports Websites

- » **Baseball** www.mlb.com
- » **Basketball** www.nba.com
- » **Football** www.nfl.com
- » **Hockey** www.nhl.com
- » **Nascar** www.nascar.com
- » **Soccer** www.mlssoccer.com

Regional Identity

The cowboy has long been a symbol of the West. Brave. Self-reliant. A solitary seeker of truth, justice and a straight shot of whiskey. The truth behind the myth? Those who settled the West were indeed self-reliant and brave. But they had to be. In that harsh and unforgiving landscape, danger was always a few steps behind opportunity. As the dangers dissipated, however, and settlers put down roots, the cowboy stereotype became less accurate. Like the red-rock mesas that have weathered into new and varying forms over the years, the character of the populace has also evolved. Stereotypes today, accurate or not, are regionally based, and the residents of Portland, San Diego, Santa Fe and Phoenix are perceived very differently from one another.

California

Californians are stereotyped as laid-back, self-absorbed, health-conscious, open-minded and eco-aware. The stats behind the stereotypes? Some 80% of Californians live near the coast. The state's southern beaches are sunniest and most swimmable, thus Southern California's inescapable associations with surf, sun and prime-time TV soaps like *Baywatch* and *The OC*. And there's truth in another outdoorsy stereotype: more than 60% of Californians admit to having hugged a tree. Self-help, fitness and body modification are major industries throughout California, successfully marketed since the 1970s. Exercise and good food help keep Californians among the fittest in the nation. Yet almost 250,000 Californians are apparently ill enough to merit prescriptions for medical marijuana. Environmentally, Golden Staters have zoomed ahead of the national energy-use curve in their smog-checked cars, buying more hybrid and fuel-efficient cars than any other state.

Since 1988, California's prison population has increased by over 200%, mostly for drug-related crimes. More than four out of every 1000 Californians are currently in jail.

Pacific Northwest

And what about those folks living in Washington and Oregon? Tree-hugging hipsters with activist tendencies and a penchant for latte? That's pretty accurate, actually. Many locals are proud of their independent spirit, profess a love for nature and, yes, will separate their plastics when it's time to recycle. They're a friendly lot and, despite the common tendency

THE SPORTING LIFE

» Westerners cherish their sports, whether they're players themselves or just watching their favorite teams. Here's a breakdown of the West's professional teams by sport.

» **National Football League** AFC West: Denver Broncos, Oakland Raiders, San Diego Chargers; NFC West: Arizona Cardinals, San Francisco 49ers, Seattle Seahawks

» **National Basketball Association** Pacific: Golden State Warriors, LA Clippers, LA Lakers, Phoenix Suns, Sacramento Kings; Northwest: Denver Nuggets, Portland Trailblazers, Utah Jazz

» **Women's National Basketball Association** LA Sparks, Phoenix Mercury, Seattle Storm

» **Major League Baseball** American League: LA Angels, Oakland Athletics, Seattle Mariners; National League: Arizona Diamondbacks, Colorado Rockies, LA Dodgers, San Diego Padres, San Francisco Giants

to denigrate Californians, most are transplants themselves. Why did they all come here? Among other things, for the lush scenery, the good quality of life and the lack of pretension that often afflicts bigger, more popular places. Primping up and putting on airs is not a part of Northwestern everyday life, and wearing Gore-Tex outerwear to restaurants, concerts or social functions will rarely raise an eyebrow.

The Rocky Mountain States

Still looking for that Western cowboy? Start here. Ranching is big business in these parts, and the solitary cowboy – seen riding a bucking bronco on the Wyoming license plate – is an appropriate symbol for the region. It takes a rugged individualist to scratch out a living on the lonely, windswept plains – plains that tend to leave big-city travelers feeling slightly unmoored.

Politically, the northern Rockies – Wyoming, Montana and Idaho – skew to the conservative, although you will find pockets of liberalism in the college and resort towns. Wyoming may have been the first state to give women the right to vote, but this nod to liberal thinking has been overshadowed by Wyoming's association with former vice-president Dick Cheney, the divisive Republican who was a six-term congressman from the state. In addition to ranching, the other big industry in Wyoming is energy.

Colorado is the West's most recognizable swing state. For every bastion of liberalism like Boulder there's an equally entrenched conservative counterpart like Colorado Springs. It's a state where people as disparate as Hunter S Thompson and Ken Buck can make a run for public office; where escaped slaves and beat-down Confederates picked up the pieces after the Civil War; where right-wing militias gather and where eco-terrorists plot.

It's no myth. Colorado really does average 300 days of sun annually, and 300,000 people float down Colorado rivers every year.

Southwest

The Southwest has long drawn stout-hearted settlers pursuing slightly different agendas – Mormons, cattle barons, prospectors – than those of the average American. A new generation of idealistic entrepreneurs has transformed former mining towns into New Age art enclaves and Old West tourist attractions. Scientists flocked to the empty spaces to develop and test atomic bombs and soaring rockets. Astronomers built observatories on lonely hills and mountains, making the most of the dark skies and unobstructed views. And there are still a few mainstream outcasts coming to the Southwest to 'turn on, tune in and drop out.'

For years, these disparate individuals managed to get along with little strife. In recent years, however, high-profile governmental efforts to stop illegal immigration have destroyed the kumbaya vibe, at least in the southern reaches of Arizona. The anti-immigration rhetoric isn't common

In September 2011, more than 53,700 euphoric souls descended upon the Nevada desert for Burning Man, a camping extravaganza, art festival and rave where freedom of expression, costume and libido are all encouraged; see the boxed text, p321.

MARRIAGE: EQUAL RIGHTS FOR ALL

Forty thousand Californians were already registered as domestic partners when, in 2004, San Francisco Mayor Gavin Newsom issued marriage licenses to same-sex couples in defiance of a California same-sex marriage ban. Four thousand same-sex couples promptly got hitched. The state ban was nixed by California courts in June 2008, but then a proposition passed in November 2008 to amend the state's constitution to prohibit same-sex marriage. Civil-rights activists are challenging the constitutionality of the proposition, but meanwhile California's reputation for tolerance is lagging behind other states that have already legalized same-sex marriage.

in day-to-day conversation, but heightened press coverage of the most vitriolic comments, coupled with a heavy Border Patrol presence, does cast a pall over the otherwise sunny landscape. Other regions of the Southwest, for the most part, have retained a live-and-let-live philosophy.

Population & Multiculturalism

California, with 37 million residents, is the most populous state in the entire US. More than 30% of the USA's Asian American population currently lives in California, and the state's Latino population, currently 14 million, is expected to become California's majority ethnic group by 2020. Today, California has an estimated two million undocumented immigrants. Latino culture is deeply enmeshed with California's culture and most residents see the state as an easygoing multicultural society that gives everyone a chance to live the American Dream.

Colorado, Arizona and New Mexico all have large Native American and Hispanic populations. These residents take pride in maintaining their cultural identities through preserved traditions and oral history lessons. Generally, Southwestern states have developed and retained a live-and-let-live philosophy. One exception is Arizona, particularly the southern region, which shares a 350-mile border with Mexico. Relations have been strained since the legislature passed a controversial law in 2010 requiring police officers to ask identification from anyone they suspect of being in the country illegally.

IMMIGRATION

The Phoenix Suns protested Arizona's new immigration law in 2010 by changing the team's name on their jerseys to 'Los Suns' (that's Spanglish) for one game.

Religion

Although Californians are less churchgoing than the American mainstream, and one in five Californians professes no religion at all, it remains one of the most religiously diverse states. About a third of Californians are Catholic, due in part to the state's large Latino population, while another third are Protestants. But there are also more than one million Muslims statewide, and LA has the second-largest Jewish community in North America. California also has the largest number of Buddhists anywhere outside Asia.

Only a quarter of Pacific Northwesterners have a religious affiliation, and a good portion of those adhere to Christianity, Judaism or the Mormon Church. Asian Americans have brought Buddhism, Hinduism, Sikhism and Islam, and New Age spirituality isn't a stranger here.

The Southwest has its own anomalies. In Utah, 58% of the state's population identifies as Mormon. The church stresses traditional family values, and drinking, smoking and premarital sex are frowned upon. You won't see much fast fashion or hear much cursing. Family and religion are also core values for Native Americans and Hispanics throughout the Southwest. For the Hopi, tribal dances are such sacred events they are mostly closed to outsiders. And although many Native Americans and Hispanics are now living in urban areas, working as professionals, large family gatherings and traditional customs are still important facets of daily life.

Native Americans

'A lot of people look at us as a real downtrodden and poor people. But to the Navajo people, you're not poor if you have the things that are sacred to you, which for us are the six sacred mountains, our homeland. To have lots and lots of money, sure that's great, but if you don't have your language, if you don't have your culture or spirituality, if you don't know your clan, then you are the poor man.'
Dan Mose, Navajo

More than 3 million Native Americans (full and part-Indian) from 500 tribes reside in every region of the US and speak 175 languages. California has the largest Native American population in the country, with Arizona and New Mexico ranking third and fifth respectively. The Navajo tribe is the largest western tribe, second only to the Cherokee nationwide.

The indigenous people of the West are extremely diverse, with unique customs and beliefs molded in part by the landscapes they inhabit. Native Americans follow equally diverse paths, as they inherit a legacy left by both their ancestors and the cultures that invaded from outside. Some may be weavers who live on reservations, others may be web designers living in Phoenix. Some plant corn and squash, others seek to harvest the sun in solar-energy farms. Some are medicine men, others are alcoholics.

Culturally, tribes today grapple with questions about how to prosper in contemporary America while protecting their traditions from erosion and their lands from further exploitation, and how to lift their people from poverty while maintaining their sense of identity and the sacred.

One of the best museums devoted to Southwest Native American life and culture is Phoenix's Heard Museum (p325).

The Tribes

Most of the major western tribes are located in the Southwest. Well-known tribes with large reservations in Arizona include the Navajo, the Hopi and the Apache. Two smaller Arizona tribes, the Hualapai and the Havasupai, live on reservations beside the Grand Canyon. New Mexico's tribes are clustered in 19 pueblos located in the north-central region of the state.

Apache

The Southwest has three major Apache reservations: New Mexico's Jicarilla Apache Reservation and Arizona's San Carlos Apache Reservation and Fort Apache Reservation, home to the White Mountain Apache tribe. All the Apache tribes descend from Athabascans who migrated from Canada around 1400. They were nomadic hunter-gatherers who became warlike raiders, particularly of Pueblo tribes and European settlements, and they fiercely resisted relocation to reservations.

The most famous Apache is Geronimo, a Chiricahua Apache who resisted the American takeover of Indian lands until he was finally subdued by the US Army with the help of White Mountain Apache scouts.

Havasupai

The Havasupai Reservation abuts Arizona's Grand Canyon National Park beneath the canyon's south rim. The tribe's one village, Supai, can only be reached by an 8-mile hike or a mule or helicopter ride from road's end at Hualapai Hilltop.

Havasupai (hah-vah-*soo*-pie) means 'people of the blue-green water,' and tribal life has always been dominated by the Havasu Creek tributary of the Colorado River. Reliable water meant the ability to irrigate fields, which led to a season-based village lifestyle. The deep Havasu Canyon also protected them from others; this extremely peaceful people basically avoided Western contact until the 1800s. Today, the tribe relies on tourism, and Havasu Canyon's gorgeous waterfalls draw a steady stream of visitors. The tribe is related to the Hualapai.

The People by Stephen Trimble is a comprehensive and intimate portrait of Southwest native peoples, filled with Native American voices and beautiful photos.

Hopi

The Hopi Reservation occupies more than 1.5 million acres in the Navajo Reservation. Most Hopi live in 11 villages at the base and on top of three mesas jutting from the main Black Mesa; Old Oraibi, on Third Mesa, is considered (along with Acoma Pueblo) the continent's oldest continuously inhabited settlement. Like all Pueblo peoples, the Hopi are descended from the Ancestral Puebloans (formerly known as Anasazi).

Hopi (*ho*-pee) translates as 'peaceful ones' or 'peaceful person,' and perhaps no tribe is more renowned for leading such a humble, traditional and deeply spiritual lifestyle. The Hopi practice an unusual, near-miraculous technique of 'dry farming'; they don't plow, but plant seeds in 'wind breaks' and natural water catchments. Their main crop has always been corn (which is central to their creation story).

Hopi ceremonial life is complex and intensely private, and extends into all aspects of daily living. Following the 'Hopi Way' is considered essential to bringing the life-giving rains, but the Hopi also believe it fosters the wellbeing of the entire human race. Each person's role is determined by their clan, which is matrilineal. Even among themselves, the Hopi keep certain traditions of their individual clans private.

The Hopi are skilled artisans; they are famous for pottery, coiled baskets and silverwork, as well as for their ceremonial kachina (spirit) dolls.

For decades, traditional Navajo and Hopi have thwarted US industry efforts to strip mine sacred Big Mountain. Black Mesa Indigenous Support (www.blackmesais.org) tells their story.

Hualapai

The Hualapai Reservation occupies around 1 million acres along 108 miles of the Grand Canyon's south rim. Hualapai (*wah*-lah-pie) means 'people of the tall pines.' Because this section of the Grand Canyon was not readily farmable, the Hualapai were originally seminomadic, gathering wild plants and hunting small game.

Today, forestry, cattle ranching, farming and tourism are the economic mainstays. The tribal headquarters are in Peach Springs, AZ, which was the inspiration for 'Radiator Springs' in the animated movie *Cars*. Hunting, fishing and rafting are the reservation's prime draws, but the Hualapai have recently added a unique tourist attraction, Skywalk (p344).

In *From Sand Creek*, Acoma poet Simon Ortiz creates a riveting amalgam of poetry and history, sorrow and hope. It's a politically engaged, spiritually centered vision of Indian America.

Navajo

The Navajo Reservation (www.discovernavajo.com) is by far the largest and most populous in the US. Also called the Navajo Nation and Navajoland, it covers 17.5 million acres (over 27,000 sq miles) in Arizona and parts of New Mexico and Utah.

The Navajo were feared nomads and warriors who both traded with and raided the Pueblos and who fought settlers and the US military. They also borrowed generously from other traditions: they acquired sheep and horses from the Spanish, learned pottery and weaving from the Pueblos, and picked up silversmithing from Mexico. Today, the Navajo are renowned for their woven rugs, pottery and inlaid silver jewelry, as well as for their intricate sandpainting, which is used in healing ceremonies.

Pueblo

New Mexico contains 19 Pueblo reservations. Four reservations lead west from Albuquerque: Isleta, Laguna, Acoma and Zuni. Fifteen pueblos fill the Rio Grande Valley between Albuquerque and Taos: Sandia, San Felipe, Santa Ana, Zia, Jemez, Santo Domingo, Cochiti, San Ildefonso, Pojoaque, Nambé, Tesuque, Santa Clara, Ohkay Owingeh (or San Juan), Picuris and Taos.

These tribes are as different as they are alike. Nevertheless, the term 'pueblo' (Spanish for 'village') is a convenient shorthand for what these tribes share: all are believed to be descended from the Ancestral Puebloans and to have inherited their architectural style and their agrarian, village-based life – often atop mesas.

Pueblos are unique among American Indians. These adobe structures can have up to five levels, connected by ladders, and are built with varying combinations of mud bricks, stones, logs and plaster. In the central plaza of each pueblo is a kiva, an underground ceremonial chamber that connects to the spirit world. A legacy of missionaries, Catholic churches are prominent in the pueblos, and many Pueblo Indians now hold both Christian and native religious beliefs.

The Navajo's Athabascan tongue is the most spoken Native American language, despite its notorious complexity. In the Pacific Theater during WWII, Navajo 'code talkers' sent and received military messages in Navajo; Japan never broke the code, and the code talkers were considered essential to US victory.

Arts

Native American art nearly always contains ceremonial purpose and religious significance; the patterns and symbols are woven with

ETIQUETTE

When visiting a reservation, ask about and follow any specific rules. Almost all tribes ban alcohol, and some ban pets and restrict cameras. All require permits for camping, fishing and other activities. Tribal rules may be posted at the reservation entrance, or visit the tribal office or the reservation's website (most are listed in this book).

When you visit a reservation, you are visiting a unique culture with perhaps unfamiliar customs. Be courteous, respectful and open-minded, and don't expect locals to share every detail of their lives.

Ask First, Document Later

Some tribes restrict cameras and sketching entirely; others may charge a fee, or restrict them at ceremonies or in certain areas. *Always ask before taking pictures or drawing.* If you want to photograph a person, ask permission first; a tip is polite and often expected.

Pueblos Are Not Museums

The incredible adobe structures are homes. Public buildings will be signed; if a building isn't signed, assume it's private. Don't climb around. Kivas are nearly always off limits.

Ceremonies Are Not Performances

Treat ceremonies like church services; watch silently and respectfully, without talking, clapping or taking pictures, and wear modest clothing. Powwows are more informal, but remember: unless they're billed as theater, they are for the tribe, not you.

Privacy and Communication

Many Native Americans are happy to describe their tribe's general religious beliefs, but not always or to the same degree, and details about rituals and ceremonies are often considered private. Always ask before discussing religion and respect each person's boundaries. Also, Native Americans consider it polite to listen without comment; silent listening, given and received, is another sign of respect.

spiritual meaning that provides an intimate window into the heart of the people.

In addition to preserving their culture, contemporary Native American artists have used sculpture, painting, textiles, film, literature and performance art to reflect and critique modernity since the mid-20th century, especially after the civil rights activism of the 1960s and cultural renaissance of the '70s. *Native North American Art* by Janet Berlo and Ruth Phillips offers a superb introduction to North America's varied indigenous art – from pre-contact to postmodernism.

Not all pueblos have websites, but available links and introductions to all are provided by the Indian Pueblo Cultural Center (www.indianpueblo.org; p375).

By purchasing arts from Native Americans themselves, visitors have a direct, positive impact on tribal economies, which depend in part on tourist dollars. Many tribes run craft outlets and galleries, usually in the main towns of reservations. The **Indian Arts & Crafts Board** (IACB; www.iacb.doi.gov) lists Native American–owned galleries and shops state-by-state online – click on 'Source Directory of Businesses.'

Pottery & Basketry

Pretty much every Southwest tribe has pottery and/or basketry traditions. Originally, each tribe and even individual families maintained distinct styles, but modern potters and basket makers readily mix, borrow and reinterpret classic designs and methods.

N Scott Momaday's Pulitzer Prize–winning *House Made of Dawn* (1968), about a Pueblo youth, launched a wave of Native American literature.

Pueblo pottery is perhaps most acclaimed of all. Initially, local clay determined color, so that Zia pottery was red, Acoma white, Hopi yellow, Cochiti black and so on. Santa Clara is famous for its carved relief designs, and San Ildefonso for its black-on-black style, which was revived by world-famous potter Maria Martinez. The Navajo and Ute Mountain Utes also produce well-regarded pottery.

Pottery is nearly always synonymous with village life, while more portable baskets were often preferred by nomadic peoples. Among the tribes who stand out for their exquisite basketry are the Jicarilla Apache (whose name means basket maker), the Kaibab-Paiute, the Hualapai and the Tohono O'odham. Hopi coiled baskets, with their vivid patterns and kachina iconography, are also notable.

Navajo Weaving

Navajo legend says that Spider Woman taught humans how to weave, and she seems embodied today in the iconic sight of Navajo women patiently shuttling handspun wool on weblike looms, creating the Navajo's legendary rugs (originally blankets), so tight they hold water. Preparation of the wool and sometimes the dyes is still done by hand, and finishing a rug takes months (occasionally years).

To donate to a cause, consider Black Mesa Weavers for Life & Land (see www.culturalsurvival.org or www.migrations.com), which aids traditional Dine women on the Navajo Reservation to sell and market their handmade weavings.

Authentic Navajo rugs are expensive, and justifiably so, ranging from hundreds to thousands of dollars. They are not average souvenirs but artworks that will last a lifetime, whether displayed on the wall or the floor. Take time to research, even a little, so you recognize when quality matches price. (To start learning about Navajo rugs, visit www.gonavajo.com.)

Silver & Turquoise Jewelry

Jewelry using stones and shells has always been a native tradition; silverwork did not arrive until the 1800s, along with Anglo and Mexican contact. In particular, Navajo, Hopi and Zuni became renowned for combining these materials with inlaid-turquoise silver jewelry. In addition to turquoise, jewelry often features lapis, onyx, coral, carnelian and shells.

Authentic jewelry is often stamped or marked by the artisan, and items may come with an Indian Arts & Crafts Board certificate; always ask. Price may also be an indicator: a high tab doesn't guarantee authenticity, but an absurdly low one probably signals trickery. A crash course can be had at the August Santa Fe Indian Market (p382).

Western Cuisine

Western cuisine? What's that? A chuckwa gon dinner served on a fancy plate? Mmm, not really. The term western cuisine is a misnomer because food served in the western part of the United States can't be slotted into one neat category. Regional specialties abound, and half the fun of any trip is digging into a dish that has cultural and agricultural ties to a region, from hearty steaks in southern Arizona to green chile enchiladas in New Mexico to grilled salmon in the Pacific Northwest. And let's not forget San Diego's messy but delicious fish tacos.

Staples & Specialties

Breakfast

Morning meals in the West, as in the rest of the country, are big business. From a hearty serving of biscuits and gravy at a cowboy diner to a quick Egg McMuffin at the McDonald's drive-thru window and lavish Sunday brunches, Americans love their eggs and bacon, their waffles and hash browns, and their big glasses of orange juice. Most of all, they love that seemingly inalienable American right: a steaming cup of morning coffee with unlimited refills.

Lunch

Usually after a midmorning coffee break, an American worker's lunch hour affords only a sandwich, quick burger or hearty salad. The formal 'business lunch' is more common in big cities like Los Angeles, where food is not necessarily as important as the conversation.

Dinner

Usually early in the evening, Americans settle in to a more substantial weeknight dinner, which, given the workload of so many two-career families, might be takeout (eg pizza or Chinese food) or prepackaged meals cooked in a microwave. Desserts tend toward ice cream, pies and cakes. Some families still cook a traditional Sunday night dinner, when relatives and friends gather for a big feast, or grill outside and go picnicking on weekends.

TRUCKS

The hottest dining craze on wheels has hit America: food trucks. From crab cake tacos to red velvet cupcakes, there's no telling what kind of creative, healthy, gourmet, decadent or downright bizarre twist on 'fast food' you'll find. To chase down the best trucks, visit Portland, Los Angeles and Las Vegas.

LA'S MOVEABLE FEASTS

In 2009, Korean-born, LA-raised chef Roy Choi began roving the streets of LA in a food truck, selling Korean grilled beef inside Mexican tacos and tweeting the locations, and a trend was born. His Kogi truck spawned some of LA's most creative mobile kitchens – Brazilian to Singaporean, southern BBQ, Vietnamese *banh mi* sandwiches and grilled cheese sandwiches topped with short ribs and mac'n'cheese. Now hundreds of gourmet food trucks plough the city streets (standouts include Kogi, the Grilled Cheese Truck and the Dim Sum Truck). Check out www.trucktweets.com for each day's locations.

BREAKFAST BURRITOS

There is one Mexican-inspired meal mastered far and wide in the West: the breakfast burrito. It's served in diners and delis in Colorado, in coffee shops in Arizona and beach-bum breakfast joints in California. In many ways, it is the perfect breakfast – cheap (usually under $6), packed with protein (eggs, cheese, beans), fresh veggies (or is avocado a fruit?), hot salsa (is that a vegetable?) and rolled to go in paper and foil. Peel it open like a banana and let the savory steam rise into your olfactories.

Dos and Don'ts

» Do tip: 15% of the total bill is standard; tip 20% (or more) for excellent service.

» It's customary to place your napkin on your lap.

» Avoid putting your elbows on the table.

» Wait until everyone is served to begin eating.

» In formal situations, diners customarily wait to eat until the host(ess) has lifted their fork.

Quick Eats

Fast-food restaurants with drive-thru windows are ubiquitous across the West, and you'll usually find at least one beside a major highway exit. Eating a hot dog from a street cart or a taco from a roadside truck – delightfully referred to as a 'roach coach' – is a convenient option in downtown business districts. Despite the nickname, health risks are small. These vendors are usually supervised by the local health department. At festivals and county fairs, pick from cotton candy, corn dogs, candy apples, funnel cakes, chocolate-covered frozen bananas and plenty of tasty regional specialties. Farmers markets often have more wholesome, affordable prepared foods.

California

Owing to its vastness and variety of microclimates, California is truly America's cornucopia for fruits and vegetables, and a gateway to myriad Asian markets. The state's natural resources are overwhelming, with wild salmon, Dungeness crab and oysters from the ocean; robust produce year-round; and artisanal products such as cheese, bread, olive oil, wine and chocolate.

Starting in the 1970s and '80s, star chefs such as Alice Waters and Wolfgang Puck pioneered 'California cuisine' by incorporating the best local ingredients into simple yet delectable preparations. The influx of Asian immigrants, especially after the Vietnam War, enriched the state's urban food cultures with Chinatowns, Koreatowns and Japantowns, along with huge enclaves of Mexican Americans who maintain their own culinary traditions across the state. Global fusion restaurants are another hallmark of California's cuisine scene.

North Coast & the Sierras

San Francisco hippies headed back to the land in the 1970s for a more self-sufficient lifestyle, reviving traditions of making breads and cheeses from scratch and growing their own *everything* (note: farms from Mendocino to Humboldt are serious about No Trespassing signs). Hippie-homesteaders were early adopters of pesticide-free farming, and innovated hearty, organic cuisine that was health-minded yet satisfied the munchies.

On the North Coast, you can taste the influence of wild-crafted Ohlone and Miwok cuisine. In addition to fishing, hunting game and making bread from acorn flour, these Native Northern Californians also tended orchards and carefully cultivated foods along the coast. With such attentive stewardship, nature has been kind to this landscape, yielding bonanzas of wildflower honey and blackberries. Alongside traditional shellfish collection, sustainable caviar and oyster farms have sprung up along the coast. Fearless foragers have identified every edible plant from Sierras wood sorrel to Mendocino sea vegetables, though key spots for wild mushrooms remain closely guarded local secrets.

San Francisco Bay Area

San Francisco's adventurous eaters support the most award-winning chefs and restaurants per capita of any US city – five times more restaurants than New York, if anyone's keeping score – and 25 farmers markets in San Francisco alone.

Some SF novelties have had extraordinary staying power, including ever-popular *cioppino* (Dungeness crab stew), chocolate bars invented by the Ghirardelli family, and sourdough bread, with original gold rush–era mother dough still yielding local loaves with that distinctive tang. Dim sum is Cantonese for what's known in Mandarin as *xiao che* (small eats) or *yum cha* (drink tea), and there are dozens of places in San Francisco where you'll call it lunch.

Mexican, French and Italian food remain perennial local favorites, along with more recent SF ethnic food crazes: *izakaya* (Japanese bars serving small plates), Korean tacos, *banh mi* (Vietnamese sandwiches featuring marinated meats and pickled vegetables on French baguettes) and *alfajores* (Arabic-Argentine crème-filled shortbread cookies).

Favorite Vegetarian Eateries

» Poco, Bisbee, AZ

» Fresh Mint, Scottsdale, AZ

» Veggie Grill, West Hollywood, CA

» Andy Nguyen's, Sacramento, CA

» Ubuntu, Napa Valley, CA

SoCal

Los Angeles has long been known for its big-name chefs and celebrity restaurant owners. Robert H Cobb, owner of Hollywood's Brown Derby Restaurant, is remembered as the namesake of the Cobb salad (lettuce, tomato, egg, chicken, bacon and Roquefort). Wolfgang Puck launched the celebrity-chef trend with the Sunset Strip's star-spangled Spago in 1982.

For authentic ethnic food in Los Angeles, head to Koreatown for flavor-bursting *kalbi* (marinated barbecued beef short ribs), East LA for tacos *al pastor* (marinated, fried pork) and Little Tokyo for ramen noodles made fresh daily.

Further south, surfers cruise Hwy 1 beach towns from Laguna Beach to La Jolla in search of the ultimate wave and quick-but-hearty eats like breakfast burritos and fish tacos. And everybody stops for a date shake at Ruby's Crystal Cove Shake Shack south of Newport Beach.

For LA's most brutally honest foodie opinions, check www.laweekly.com and www.eater.com.

Pacific Northwest

The late James Beard (1903–85), an American chef, food writer and Oregon native, believed foods prepared simply, without too many ingredients or complicated cooking techniques, allowed their natural flavors to shine. This philosophy has greatly influenced modern Northwest cuisine. Pacific Northwesterners don't like to think of their food as trendy or fussy, but at the same time, they love to be considered innovative, especially when it comes to 'green,' hyperconscious eating.

Farmland, Wild Foods & Fish

The diverse geography and climate – a mild, damp coastal region with sunny summers and arid farmland in the east – foster all types of farm-grown produce. Farmers grow plenty of fruit, from melons, grapes, apples and pears to strawberries, cherries and blueberries. Veggies thrive

SLOW, LOCAL, ORGANIC

The 'Slow Food' movement, along with renewed enthusiasm for eating local, organically grown fare, is a leading trend in American restaurants. The movement was arguably started in 1971 by chef Alice Waters at Berkeley's Chez Panisse (p148). Recently, farmers markets have been popping up all across the country and they're great places to meet locals and take a big bite out of America's cornucopia of foods, from heritage fruit and vegetables to fresh, savory and sweet regional delicacies.

here too: potatoes, lentils, corn, asparagus and Walla Walla sweet onions, all of which feed local and overseas populations.

Many wild foods thrive, especially in the damper regions, such as the Coast Range. Foragers seek the same foods once gathered by local Native American tribes – year-round wild mushrooms, as well as summertime fruits and berries.

With hundreds of miles of coastline and an impressive system of rivers, Northwesterners have access to plenty of fresh seafood. Depending on the season, specialties include razor clams, mussels, prawns, albacore tuna, Dungeness crab and sturgeon. Salmon remains one of the region's most recognized foods, whether it's smoked, grilled, or in salads, quiches and sushi.

Must-Try Regional Specialties

- Fish tacos (San Diego, CA)
- Frito pie (New Mexico)
- Green chile cheeseburgers (New Mexico)
- Navajo tacos (northeastern Arizona)
- Sonoran dogs (Tucson, Arizona)
- Rocky Mountain oysters (Colorado)

The Southwest

Diners, grab your steak knives and unbutton your fat pants because the food in Arizona, New Mexico, Utah, southern Colorado and Las Vegas doesn't have time for the timid. Sonoran hot dogs, green chile cheeseburgers, huevos rancheros, juicy steaks and endless buffets – moderation is not a virtue.

Two ethnic groups define Southwestern food culture: the Spanish and the Mexicans, who controlled territories from Texas to California until well into the 19th century. While there is little actual Spanish food today, the Spanish brought cattle to Mexico, which the Mexicans adapted to their own corn-and-chile-based gastronomy to make tacos, tortillas, enchiladas, burritos, chimichangas and other dishes made of corn or flour pancakes filled with everything from chopped meat and poultry to beans. In Arizona and New Mexico, a few Native American dishes are served on reservations and at tribal festivals. Steaks and barbecue are always favorites on Southwestern menus, and beer is the drink of choice for dinner and a night out.

For a cosmopolitan foodie scene, visit Las Vegas, where top chefs from New York City, LA and even Paris are sprouting satellite restaurants.

Steak & Potatoes

Have a deep hankerin' for a juicy slab of beef with a salad, baked potato and beans? Look no further than the ranch-filled Southwest, where there's a steakhouse for every type of traveler. In Phoenix alone the choices range from the old-school Durant's (p331) and the outdoor Greasewood Flat (p332) to the family-friendly Rawhide Western Town & Steakhouse (see the boxed text, p329). In Utah, the large Mormon population influences culinary options. Here, good, old-fashioned American food like chicken, steak, potatoes, vegetables, homemade pies and ice cream prevail.

Some Pacific species have been overfished to near-extinction, disrupting local aquaculture. For best options, good choices, and items to avoid on local seafood menus, reference Monterey Bay Aquarium's Seafood Watch (www.montereybayaquarium.org/cr/seafoodwatch.aspx).

Mexican & New Mexican Food

Mexican food is often hot and spicy. If you're sensitive, test the heat of your salsa before dousing your meal. In Arizona, Mexican food is of the Sonoran type, with specialties such as *carne seca* (dried beef). Meals are usually served with refried beans, rice and flour or corn tortillas; chiles are relatively mild. Tucsonans refer to their city as the 'Mexican food capital of the universe,' which, although hotly contested by a few other places, carries a ring of truth. Colorado restaurants serve Mexican food, but they don't insist on any accolades for it.

New Mexico's food is different from, but reminiscent of, Mexican food. Pinto beans are served whole instead of refried; *posole* (a corn stew) may replace rice. Chiles aren't used so much as a condiment (like salsa) but more as an essential ingredient in almost every dish. *Carne adobada* (marinated pork chunks) is a specialty.

If a menu includes red or green chile dishes and sauces, it probably serves New Mexican style dishes. The state is famous for its chile-enhanced Mexican standards. The town of Hatch, New Mexico, is particularly known for its green chiles.

Native American Food

Modern Native American cuisine bears little resemblance to that eaten before the Spanish conquest, but it is distinct from Southwestern cuisine. Navajo and Indian tacos – fried bread usually topped with beans, meat, tomatoes, chile and lettuce – are the most readily available. Chewy *horno* bread is baked in the beehive-shaped outdoor adobe ovens *(hornos)* using remnant heat from a fire built inside the oven, then cleared out before cooking.

Most other Native American cooking is game-based and usually involves squash and locally harvested ingredients like berries and piñon nuts. Though becoming better known, it can be difficult to find. Your best bets are festival food stands, powwows, rodeos, Pueblo feast days and casino restaurants.

Not all chiles are picked – those left on the plant are allowed to mature to a deep ruby red, then strung on the *ristras* which adorn walls and doorways throughout the Southwest.

Drinks

Work-hard, play-hard Americans are far from teetotalers. About 67% of Americans drink alcohol, with the majority preferring beer to wine.

Beer

Beer is about as American as Chevrolet, football and apple pie. While alcohol sales in the USA have soared to record highs in recent years, only about 20% of Americans drink wine on a regular basis; beer is far more popular. American lager is by far the most popular beer, with a relatively low alcohol content between 3% and 5%.

Craft & Local Beer

Today, beer aficionados sip and savor beer as they would wine, and some urban restaurants even have beer 'programs,' 'sommeliers' and cellars. Microbrewery and craft beer production is rising meteorically, accounting for 11% of the domestic market in 2010. In recent years it's become possible to 'drink local' all over the West as microbreweries pop up in urban centers, small towns, and unexpected places. They're particularly popular in gateway communities outside national parks, including Moab, Flagstaff and Durango.

A microbrewery sells most of its beer off site. A brewpub sells most of its beer on site, and typically there's a restaurant attached.

Wine

According to the *LA Times,* 2010 marked the first year that the US actually consumed more wine than France. To the raised eyebrows of European winemakers, who used to regard even California wines as second class, many American wines are now even (gulp!) winning prestigious international awards. In fact, the nation is the world's fourth-largest producer of wine, behind Italy, France and Spain.

Wine isn't cheap in the US, but it's possible to procure a perfectly drinkable bottle of American wine at a liquor or wine shop for around US$10 to US$12.

Wine Regions

Today almost 90% of US wine comes from California, and Oregon and Washington wines have achieved international status.

Without a doubt, the country's hotbed of wine tourism is in Northern California, just outside of the Bay Area in Napa and Sonoma Valleys. As other areas – Oregon's Willamette Valley, California's Central Coast

California's latest and greatest wines and wine-making trends are covered by *Wine Enthusiast's* West Coast editor, Steve Heimoff, on his blog: http://steveheimoff.com.

BEER GOES LOCAL

In outdoorsy communities across the west, the neighborhood microbrewery is the unofficial community center – the place to unwind, swap trail stories, commune with friends and savor seasonal brews. Here are a few of our favorites:

» Beaver Street Brewery, Flagstaff, AZ (p335)

» Four Peaks Brewing Company, Tempe, AZ (p332)

» Kelly's Brewery, Albuquerque, NM (p378)

» Great Divide Brewing Co, Denver, CO (p246)

» Steamworks Brewing, Durango, CO (p268)

» Snake River Brewing, Jackson, WY (p285)

» North Coast Brewing Co, Fort Bragg, CA (p155)

» Bridgeport Brewpub, Portland, OR (p216)

» Pike Pub & Brewery, Seattle, WA (p191)

San Diego has so many good ones that we've prepared a separate list (see the box, p99).

and Arizona's Patagonia region – have evolved as wine destinations, they have spawned an entire industry of bed-and-breakfast tourism that goes hand in hand with the quest to find the perfect Pinot Noir.

There are many excellent 'New World' wines that have flourished in the rich American soil. The most popular white varietals made in the US are Chardonnay and Sauvignon Blanc; best-selling reds include Cabernet Sauvignon, Merlot, Pinot Noir and Zinfandel.

Margaritas

In the Southwest it's all about the tequila. Margaritas are the alcoholic drink of choice, and synonymous with this region, especially in heavily Hispanic New Mexico, Arizona and southwestern Colorado. Margaritas vary in taste depending on the quality of the ingredients used, but all are made from tequila, a citrus liquor (Grand Marnier, Triple Sec or Cointreau) and either fresh squeezed lime or premixed Sweet & Sour.

Margaritas are either served frozen, on the rocks (over ice) or straight up. Most people order them with salt. Traditional margaritas are lime flavored, but the popular drink comes in a rainbow of flavors – best ordered frozen.

WHISKEY

In all the glory of Colorado microbrews, don't overlook the whiskey. Based in Denver, Stranahan's is a small batch distiller that makes its whiskey from only 12 barrels per week out of locally grown barley.

Coffee

America runs on caffeine, and the coffee craze has only intensified in the last 25 years. Blame it on Starbucks. The world's biggest coffee chain was born amid the Northwest's progressive coffee culture in 1971, when Starbucks opened its first location across from Pike Place Market in Seattle. The idea, to offer a variety of roasted beans from around the world in a comfortable cafe, helped start filling the American coffee mug with more refined, complicated (and expensive) drinks compared to the ubiquitous Folgers and diner cups of joe. By the early 1990s, specialty coffeehouses were springing up across the country.

Independent coffee shops support a coffeehouse culture that encourages lingering; think free wi-fi and comfortable seating. That said, when using free cafe wi-fi, remember: order something every hour, don't leave laptops unattended and deal with interruptions graciously.

Arts & Architecture

Western art is marked by a unique merging of personality, attitude and landscape: the take-it-or-leave-it cow skulls in Georgia O'Keeffe paintings; the prominent shadows in an Ansel Adams' photograph of Half Dome; the gonzo journalism of Hunter S Thompson in the sun-baked Southwest; even Nirvana's grunge seems inseparable from its rainy Seattle roots. The landscape is a presence, beautiful yet unforgiving.

Literature

The state with the largest market for books in the US is California, whose citizens also read more than the national average. But why should we be surprised? California is the most populous state in a region that has long inspired novelists, poets and storytellers.

Social Realism

Arguably the most influential author ever to emerge from California was John Steinbeck, who was born in Salinas in 1902. His masterpiece of social realism, *The Grapes of Wrath,* tells of the struggles of migrant farm workers.

Playwright Eugene O'Neill took his 1936 Nobel Prize money and transplanted himself to near San Francisco, where he wrote the autographical play *Long Day's Journey into Night.*

Upton Sinclair's *Oil!,* which inspired Paul Thomas Anderson's movie *There Will Be Blood,* was a muckraking work of historical fiction with socialist overtones.

FICTION

In Northern California, professional hell-raiser Jack London grew up and cut his teeth in Oakland. He turned out a massive volume of influential fiction, including tales of the late-19th-century Klondike Gold Rush.

Pulp Noir & Mysteries

In the 1930s, San Francisco and Los Angeles became the capitals of the pulp detective novel. Dashiell Hammett *(The Maltese Falcon)* made San Francisco's fog a sinister character. The king of hard-boiled crime writers was Raymond Chandler, who thinly disguised his hometown of Santa Monica as Bay City.

Since the 1990s, a renaissance of California crime fiction has been masterminded by James Ellroy *(LA Confidential),* Elmore Leonard *(Jackie Brown)* and Walter Mosley *(Devil in a Blue Dress),* whose Easy Rawlins detective novels are set in South Central LA's impoverished neighborhoods.

But not all detectives work in the cities. Tony Hillerman, an enormously popular author from Albuquerque, wrote *Skinwalkers, People of Darkness, Skeleton Man* and *The Sinister Pig.* His award-winning mystery novels take place on the Navajo, Hopi and Zuni Reservations.

Movers & Shakers

After the chaos of WWII, the Beat Generation brought about a provocative new style of writing: short, sharp, spontaneous and alive. Based in San Francisco, the scene revolved around Jack Kerouac *(On the Road),* Allen Ginsberg *(Howl)* and Lawrence Ferlinghetti, the Beats' patron and publisher.

Joan Didion nailed contemporary California culture in *Slouching Towards Bethlehem,* a collection of essays that takes a caustic look at 1960s flower power and the Haight-Ashbury district. Tom Wolfe also put '60s San Francisco in perspective with *The Electric Kool-Aid Acid Test,* which follows Ken Kesey's band of Merry Pranksters.

The National Cowboy Poetry Gathering (www.westernfolklife.org) – the bronco of cowboy poetry events – is held in January in Elko, Nevada. Ropers and wranglers have waxed lyrical here for more than 25 years.

In the 1970s, Charles Bukowski's semi-autobiographical novel *Post Office* captured down-and-out downtown LA, while Richard Vasquez's *Chicano* took a dramatic look at LA's Latino barrio.

Hunter S Thompson, who committed suicide in early 2005, wrote *Fear and Loathing in Las Vegas,* set in the temple of American excess in the desert; it's the ultimate road-trip novel, in every sense of the word.

Eco-Warriors & Social Commentators

Edward Abbey, noted for his strong environmental and political views, created the thought-provoking and seminal works of *Desert Solitaire* and *The Journey Home: Some Words in Defense of the American West.* His classic *Monkey Wrench Gang* is a comic fictional account of real people who plan to blow up Glen Canyon Dam before it floods Glen Canyon.

Wallace Stegner's western-set novel *Angle of Repose* won the Pulitzer Prize in 1972. His book of essays *Where the Bluebird Sings to the Lemonade Springs* discusses the harmful consequences of the mythologizing of the West. Former Tucsonian Barbara Kingsolver published two novels with Southwestern settings, *The Bean Trees* and *Animal Dreams*. She shares her thoughts about day-to-day life in the Southwest in a series of essays in *High Tide in Tucson*.

Music

Much of the American recording industry is based in Los Angeles, and SoCal's film and TV industries have proven powerful talent incubators. Indeed, today's troubled pop princesses and *American Idol* winners are only here thanks to the tuneful revolutions of all the decades of innovation that came before, from country folk to urban rap.

Wanna hear the next break-out indie band before they make it big? Tune into the 'Morning Becomes Eclectic' show on Southern California's KCRW radio station for live in-studio performances and musician interviews. Listen online (www.kcrw.com), download KCRW's free podcasts or buy the mobile app.

Rockin' Out

The first homegrown rock-and-roll talent to make it big in the 1950s was Richie Valens, whose 'La Bamba' was a rockified version of a Mexican folk song. When Joan Baez and Bob Dylan had their Northern California fling in the early 1960s, Dylan plugged in his guitar and played folk rock. When Janis Joplin and Big Brother & the Holding Company developed their shambling musical stylings in San Francisco, folk rock splintered into psychedelia. Meanwhile, Jim Morrison and The Doors and the Byrds blew minds on LA's famous Sunset Strip. The epicenter of LA's psychedelic rock scene was the Laurel Canyon neighborhood, just uphill from the Sunset Strip and the legendary Whisky a Go-Go nightclub.

Rap & Hip-Hop Rhythms

Since the 1980s, LA has been a hotbed for West Coast rap and hip-hop. Eazy E, Ice Cube and Dr Dre released the seminal NWA (Niggaz With Attitude) album, *Straight Outta Compton,* in 1989. Death Row Records, cofounded by Dr Dre, has launched megawatt rap talents including Long Beach bad-boy Snoop Dog and the late Tupac Shakur, who launched his rap career in Marin County and was fatally shot in 1996 in Las Vegas in a suspected East Coast/West Coast rap feud.

Throughout the 1980s and '90s, California maintained a grassroots hip-hop scene closer to the streets in LA and in the heart of the black power movement in Oakland. In the late 1990s, the Bay Area birthed underground artists like E-40 and the 'hyphy movement,' a reaction against the increasing commercialization of hip-hop. Also from Oakland, Michael Franti & Spearhead blend hip-hop with funk, reggae, folk, jazz and rock stylings into messages for social justice and peace in 2010's *The Sound of Sunshine*. Meanwhile, Korn from Bakersfield and Linkin Park from LA County have combined hip-hop with rap and metal to popularize 'nu metal.'

Stephenie Meyers' popular *Twilight* series, about a high school vampire and the mortal who loves him, is set in Forks, WA. The Forks Chamber of Commerce cheerfully embraces its newfound fame and features *Twilight*-related attractions on its website (www.forkswa.com/twilight).

Grunge & Indie Rock

Grunge started in the mid-1980s and was heavily influenced by a cult group called the Melvins. Distorted guitars, strong riffs, heavy drumming and gritty styles defined the unpolished musical style. Grunge didn't explode until the record label Sub Pop released Nirvana's *Nevermind* in 1991, skyrocketing the 'Seattle Sound' into mainstream music. True purists, however, shunned Nirvana for what they considered selling out to commercialism while overshadowing equally worthy bands like Soundgarden and Alice in Chains. The general popularity of grunge continued through the early 1990s, but the very culture of the genre took part in its downfall. Bands lived hard and fast, never really taking themselves seriously. Many eventually succumbed to internal strife and drug abuse. The final blow was in 1994, when Kurt Cobain – the heart of Nirvana – committed suicide.

A few western cities are especially connected with indie music. Seattle was the original stomping grounds for Modest Mouse, Death Cab for Cutie and The Postal Service. Olympia, WA, has been a hotbed of indie rock and riot grrls. British Columbia meanwhile claims popular indie bands like The New Pornographers, Black Mountain and Hot Hot Heat. Portland, OR, has boasted such diverse groups as folktronic hip-hop band Talkdemonic, alt-band The Decemberists and multi-genre Pink Martini, not to mention The Shins, The Dandy Warhols, Blind Pilot and Elliot Smith.

Film

From the moment movies – and later TV – became a dominant entertainment medium, California took center stage in the world of popular culture. In any given year some 40 TV shows and scores of movies use California locations, not including all of those shot on SoCal studio backlots.

You can see the handwritten lyrics of Nirvana singer/songwriter Kurt Cobain (born in Aberdeen, WA) at the Experience Music Project in the Seattle Center.

The Industry

The movie-making industry grew out of the humble orchards of Hollywoodland, a residential neighborhood of Los Angeles, where entrepreneurial moviemakers, many of whom were European immigrants, established studios in the early 1900s. German-born Carl Laemmle built Universal Studios in 1915, selling lunch to curious guests coming to watch the magic of moviemaking; Polish immigrant Samuel Goldwyn joined with Cecil B DeMille to form Paramount Studios; and Jack Warner and his brothers, born to Polish parents, arrived a few years later from Canada.

LA's perpetually balmy weather meant that most outdoor scenes could be easily shot there. Fans loved early silent-film stars like Charlie Chaplin and Harold Lloyd, and the first big Hollywood wedding occurred in 1920 when Douglas Fairbanks wed Mary Pickford, becoming Hollywood's first de facto royal couple. The silent-movie era gave way to 'talkies' after

1927's *The Jazz Singer,* a Warner Bros musical starring Al Jolson, premiered in downtown LA, ushering in Hollywood's glamorous Golden Age.

Hollywood & Beyond

From the 1920s, Hollywood became the industry's social and financial hub, but only one major studio, Paramount Pictures, stood in Hollywood proper. Most movies have been shot elsewhere around LA, from Culver City (at MGM, now Sony Pictures), to Studio City (at Universal Studios) and Burbank (at Warner Bros and later at Disney).

Today's high cost of filming has sent location scouts outside the state. During his two terms as governor of New Mexico (2002–2010), Bill Richardson wooed production teams to the state by offering a 25% tax rebate on expenditures. His efforts helped inject more than $3 billion into the economy. Film and TV crews have also moved north to Canada, often shooting in Vancouver, Toronto and Montréal.

Top Film Festivals

- AFI Fest (www.afi.com)
- Outfest (www.outfest.org)
- San Francisco International Film Festival (www.sffs.org)
- Sundance Film Festival (www.sundance.org)
- Telluride Film Festival (www.telluridefilmfestival.org)
- Seattle International Film Festival (www.siff.net)

Westerns

Though many westerns have been shot in SoCal, a few places in Utah and Arizona have doubled as film and TV sets so often that they have come to define the American West. In addition to Utah's Monument Valley, first popularized by director John Ford in *The Stagecoach,* movie-worthy destinations include Moab (p364) for *Thelma and Louise* (1991), Dead Horse Point State Park (p367) for *Mission Impossible: 2* (2000), Lake Powell (p344) for *Planet of the Apes* (1968) and Tombstone (p353) for the eponymous *Tombstone* (1993). Scenes in *127 Hours,* the film version of Aron Ralston's harrowing time trapped in Blue John Canyon in Canyonlands National Park, were shot in and around the canyon.

The Small Screen

The first TV station began broadcasting in Los Angeles in 1931. Through the following decades, iconic images of LA were beamed into living rooms across America in shows such as *Dragnet* (1950s), *The Beverly Hillbillies* (1960s), *The Brady Bunch* (1970s), *LA Law* (1980s), *Baywatch, Melrose Place* and *The Fresh Prince of Bel-Air* (1990s), through to teen 'dramedies' *Beverly Hills 90210* (1990s) and *The OC* (2000s) set in Newport Beach, Orange County. If you're a fan of reality TV, you'll spot Southern California starring in everything from *Top Chef* to the *Real Housewives of Orange County.*

Southern California is also a versatile backdrop for edgy cable-TV dramas, from Showtime's *Weeds* about a pot-growing SoCal widow to TNT's cop show *The Closer* about homicide detectives in LA and FX's *The Shield,* which fictionalized the City of Angels' police corruption. But SoCal isn't the only TV backdrop. Albuquerque is the setting for *Breaking Bad,* an Emmy-winning series about a science teacher turned meth dealer. Some exterior shots for David Lynch's quirky *Twin Peaks* were shot in Snoqualmie and North Bend, WA. Because of tax incentives, Vancouver, BC has long been a popular shooting location for television production companies. Many of their shows, from the *X-Files* to *Battlestar Galactica* to *Fringe,* are actually set somewhere else.

Jim Heimann's *California Crazy & Beyond: Roadside Vernacular Architecture* is a romp through the zany, whimsical world of California, where lemonade stands look like giant lemons and motels are shaped like tepees.

Architecture

Westerners have adapted imported styles to the climate and available materials, building cool, adobe-inspired houses in Tucson and fog-resistant redwood-shingle houses in Mendocino.

Spanish Missions & Victorian Queens

The first Spanish missions were built around courtyards, using materials that Native Americans and colonists found on hand: adobe, limestone and grass. Many missions crumbled into disrepair as the church's influence waned, but the style remained practical for the climate. Early California settlers later adapted it into the rancho adobe style, as seen at El Pueblo de Los Angeles and in San Diego's Old Town.

Once the mid-19th-century Gold Rush was on, California's nouveau riche imported materials to construct grand mansions matching European fashions, and raised the stakes with ornamental excess. Many millionaires favored the gilded Queen Anne style. Outrageous examples of Victorian architecture, including 'Painted Ladies' and 'gingerbread' houses, can be found in such Northern California towns as San Francisco, Ferndale and Eureka.

Many architects rejected frilly Victorian styles in favor of the simple, classical lines of Spanish colonial architecture. Mission revival details are restrained and functional: arched doors and windows, long covered porches, fountains, courtyards, solid walls and red-tiled roofs.

Arts & Crafts and Art Deco

Simplicity was the hallmark of the Arts and Crafts style. Influenced by both Japanese design principles and England's Arts and Crafts movement, its woodwork and handmade touches marked a deliberate departure from the Industrial Revolution. SoCal architects Charles and Henry Greene and Bernard Maybeck in Northern California popularized the versatile one-story bungalow, which became trendy at the turn of the 20th century. Today you'll spot them in Pasadena and Berkeley with their overhanging eaves, terraces and sleeping porches harmonizing indoors and outdoors.

In the 1920s, the international art-deco style took elements from the ancient world – Mayan glyphs, Egyptian pillars, Babylonian ziggurats – and flattened them into modern motifs to cap stark facades and outline streamlined skyscrapers, notably in LA and downtown Oakland. Streamline moderne kept decoration to a minimum and mimicked the aerodynamic look of ocean liners and airplanes, as seen at LA's Union Station.

A few years later master architect Frank Lloyd Wright was designing homes in the Romanza style – for every indoor space there's an outdoor space – and this flowing design is best exhibited in LA's Hollyhock House, constructed for heiress Alice Barnsdale. His part-time home and studio in Scottsdale, Arizona, Taliesin West (p326), complements and showcases the surrounding desert landscape.

Postmodern Evolutions

Architectural styles have veered away from strict high modernism and unlikely postmodern shapes have been added to the landscape. Richard Meier made his mark on West LA with the Getty Center, a cresting white wave of a building atop a sunburned hilltop. Canadian-born Frank Gehry relocated to Santa Monica. His billowing, sculptural style for LA's Walt Disney Concert Hall winks cheekily at shipshape Californian streamline moderne. Renzo Piano's signature inside-out industrial style can be glimpsed in the saw-tooth roof and red-steel veins on the Broad Contemporary Art Museum extension of the Los Angeles County Museum of Art.

San Francisco has lately championed a brand of postmodernism by Pritzker Prize–winning architects that magnifies and mimics California's great outdoors, especially in Golden Gate Park. Swiss architects Herzog & de Meuron clad the MH de Young Memorial Museum in copper, which will eventually oxidize green to match its park setting. Nearby, Renzo Piano literally raised the roof on sustainable design at the LEED platinum-certified California Academy of Sciences, capped by a living garden.

In 1915, newspaper magnate William Randolph Hearst commissioned California's first licensed female architect Julia Morgan to build his Hearst Castle – a mixed blessing, since the commission would take Morgan decades, careful diplomacy through constant changes and a delicate balancing act among Hearst's preferred Spanish, Gothic and Greek styles.

HEARST CASTLE

ART IN NEW MEXICO

Both Taos (p387) and Santa Fe (p379) have large and active artist communities considered seminal to the development of Southwestern art. Santa Fe is a particularly good stop for those looking to browse and buy art and native crafts. More than 100 of Santa Fe's 300-plus galleries line the city's Canyon Rd. Native American vendors sell high-quality jewelry and crafts beside the plaza. Friday art walks begin at 5pm. Serious collectors can also take a studio tour or drive the bucolic High Rd, a low-key scenic byway between Santa Fe and Taos that swings by galleries, historic buildings and an art market (p37).

Visual Arts

Although the earliest European artists were trained cartographers accompanying Western explorers, their images of California as an island show more imagination than scientific rigor. This mythologizing tendency continued throughout the Gold Rush era, as Western artists alternated between caricatures of Wild West debauchery and manifest-destiny propaganda urging pioneers to settle the golden west. The completion of the Transcontinental Railroad in 1869 brought an influx of romantic painters, who produced epic California wilderness landscapes.

Art in Out-of-the-Way Places

- Bisbee, AZ
- Jerome, AZ
- Aspen, CO
- Park City, UT
- Bellingham, WA

In the early 1900s, homegrown colonies of California Impressionist plein-air painters emerged, particularly at Laguna Beach and Carmel-by-the-Sea. In the Southwest, Georgia O'Keeffe (1887–1986) painted stark Southwestern landscapes that are seen in museums throughout the world.

Photographer Pirkle Jones saw expressive potential in California landscape photography after WWII, while San Francisco native Ansel Adams' sublime photographs had already started doing justice to Yosemite. Adams founded Group f/64 with Edward Weston from Carmel and Imogen Cunningham in San Francisco. Berkeley-based Dorothea Lange turned her unflinching lens on the plight of Californian migrant workers in the Great Depression and Japanese Americans forced to enter internment camps in WWII.

As the postwar American West became crisscrossed with freeways and divided into planned communities, Californian painters captured the abstract forms of manufactured landscapes. In San Francisco, Richard Diebenkorn and David Park became leading proponents of Bay Area Figurative Art, while San Francisco sculptor Richard Serra captured urban aesthetics in massive, rusting monoliths resembling ship prows and industrial Stonehenges. Pop artists captured the ethos of conspicuous consumerism, through Wayne Thiebaud's gumball machines, British émigré David Hockney's LA pools and, above all, Ed Ruscha's studies of SoCal pop culture. In San Francisco, artists showed their love for rough-and-readymade 1950s Beat collage, 1960s psychedelic Fillmore posters, earthy '70s funk and beautiful-mess punk, and '80s graffiti and skate culture.

Photography buffs can plan their California trip around the top-notch SFMOMA, whose superb collection runs from early Western daguerreotypes to experimental postwar Japanese photography, and LA's Getty Center, which has become California's Louvre of photography with over 31,000 images.

Today's contemporary art scene brings all these influences together with muralist-led social commentary, an obsessive dedication to craft and a new-media milieu that embraces cutting-edge technology. LA's Museum of Contemporary Art puts on provocative and avant-garde shows, as does LACMA's Broad Contemporary Art Museum and the Museum of Contemporary Art San Diego, which specializes in post-1950s pop and conceptual art. To see California-made art at its most experimental, browse the SoCal gallery scenes in downtown LA and Culver City, then check out independent NorCal art spaces in San Francisco's Mission District and the laboratory-like galleries of SOMA's Yerba Buena Arts District.

The Land & Wildlife

Crashing tectonic plates, mighty floods, spewing volcanoes, frigid ice fields: for millions and millions of years, the American West was an altogether unpleasant place. But from this fire and ice sprang a kaleidoscopic array of stunning landscapes bound by a common modern trait: an undeniable ability to attract and inspire explorers, naturalists, artists and outdoor adventurers.

The Land

As Western novelist and essayist Wallace Stegner noted in his book *Where the Bluebird Sings to the Lemonade Springs* the West 'is actually half a dozen subregions as different from one another as the Olympic rainforest is from Utah's slickrock country, or Seattle from Santa Fe.' The one commonality in Stegner's view? The aridity of the region. Aridity, he writes, sharpens the brilliance of the light and heightens the clarity of the air in most of the West. It also leads to fights over water rights, an historic and ongoing concern.

California

The third-largest state after Alaska and Texas, California covers more than 155,000 sq miles, making it larger than 85 of the world's smallest nations.

Geology & Earthquakes

California is a complex geologic landscape formed from fragments of rock and earth crust scraped together as the North American continent drifted westward over hundreds of millions of years. Crumpled coast ranges, the downward-bowing Central Valley and the still-rising Sierra Nevada are evidence of gigantic forces exerted as the continental and ocean plates crush together.

About 25 million years ago the ocean plates stopped colliding and instead started sliding against each other, creating the massive San Andreas Fault. Because this contact zone doesn't slide smoothly, but catches and slips irregularly, it rattles California with an ongoing succession of tremors and earthquakes.

The state's most famous earthquake in 1906 measured 7.8 on the Richter scale and demolished San Francisco, leaving more than 3000 people dead. The Bay Area made headlines again in 1989 when the Loma Prieta earthquake (7.1) caused a section of the Bridge to collapse. Los Angeles' last 'big one' was in 1994, when the Northridge quake (6.7) caused parts of the Santa Monica Fwy to fall down, making it the most costly quake in US history – so far.

EARTHQUAKES

According to the US Geological Survey, the odds of a magnitude 6.7 or greater earthquake hitting California in the next 30 years is 99.7%.

The Coast to the Central Valley

Much of California's coast is fronted by rugged coastal mountains that capture winter's water-laden storms. San Francisco divides the Coast Ranges roughly in half, with the foggy North Coast remaining sparsely populated, while the Central and Southern California coasts have a balmier climate and many more people.

California claims both the highest point in the contiguous US (Mt Whitney, 14,505ft) and the lowest elevation in North America (Badwater, Death Valley, 282ft below sea level) – plus they're only 90 miles apart, as the condor flies.

In the northernmost reaches of the Coast Ranges, nutrient-rich soils and abundant moisture foster forests of giant trees. On their eastern flanks, the Coast Ranges subside into gently rolling hills that give way to the 450-mile long Central Valley, an agricultural powerhouse producing about half of America's fruits, nuts and vegetables valued at over $14 billion a year.

Mountain Highs

On the eastern side of the Central Valley looms the world-famous Sierra Nevada. At 400 miles long and 50 miles wide, it's one of the largest mountain ranges in the world and is home to 13 peaks over 14,000ft. The vast wilderness of the High Sierra (lying mostly above 9000ft) presents an astounding landscape of glaciers, sculpted granite peaks and remote canyons. The soaring Sierra Nevada captures storm systems and drains them of their water, with most of the precipitation over 3000ft falling as snow. These waters eventually flow into half a dozen major river systems that provide the vast majority of water for San Francisco and LA as well as farms in the Central Valley.

The Deserts & Beyond

With the west slope of the Sierra Nevada capturing the lion's share of water, all lands east of the Sierra crest are dry and desertlike, receiving less than 10in of rain a year. Surprisingly, some valleys at the eastern foot of the Sierra Nevada are well-watered by creeks and support a vigorous economy of livestock and agriculture.

Areas in the northern half of California, especially on the elevated Modoc Plateau of northeastern California, are a cold desert at the western edge of the Great Basin, blanketed with hardy sagebrush shrubs and pockets of juniper trees. Temperatures increase as you head south, with a prominent transition as you descend from Mono Lake into the Owens Valley east of the Sierra Nevada. This southern hot desert (part of the Mojave Desert) includes Death Valley, one of the hottest places on earth.

On the evening of July 5, 2011, a mile-high dust storm with an estimated 100-mile width enveloped Phoenix after reaching speeds of between 50mph and 60mph. Visibility dropped to between zero and one-quarter of a mile. There were power outages and Phoenix International Airport temporarily closed.

The Southwest

Extremely ancient rocks (among the oldest on the planet) exposed in the deep heart of the Grand Canyon show that the region was underwater two billion years ago. Younger layers of rocks in southern Utah reveal that this region was continuously or periodically underwater. At the end of the Paleozoic era (about 286 million years ago), a collision of continents into a massive landmass known as Pangaea deformed the earth's crust and produced pressures that uplifted the ancestral Rocky Mountains. Though this early mountain range lay to the east, it formed rivers and sediment deposits that began to shape the Southwest.

The sequence of oceans and sand ended around 60 million years ago as North America underwent a dramatic separation from Europe, sliding westward over a piece of the earth's crust known as the East Pacific Plate and leaving behind an ever-widening gulf that became the Atlantic Ocean. The East Pacific Plate collided with the North American Plate. This collision, named the Laramide Orogeny, resulted in the birth of the modern Rocky Mountains and uplifted an old basin into a highland known today as the Colorado Plateau. Fragments of the East Pacific Plate also attached themselves to the leading edge of the North American Plate, transforming the Southwest from a coastal area to an interior region increasingly detached from the ocean.

In contrast to the compression and collision that characterized earlier events, the earth's crust began stretching in an east-west direction about 30 million years ago. The thinner, stretched crust of New Mexico and Texas cracked along zones of weakness called faults, resulting in a rift valley where New Mexico's Rio Grande now flows. These same forces created the stepped plateaus of northern Arizona and southern Utah.

During the Pleistocene glacial period, large bodies of water accumulated throughout the Southwest. Utah's Great Salt Lake is the most famous remnant of these mighty ice-age lakes. Basins with now completely dry, salt-crusted lakebeds are especially conspicuous on a drive across Nevada.

For the past several million years the dominant force has probably been erosion. Not only do torrential rainstorms readily tear through soft sedimentary rocks, but also the rise of the Rocky Mountains generates large, powerful rivers that wind throughout the Southwest, carving mighty canyons in their wake. Nearly all of the contemporary features in the Southwest, from arches (Arches National Park has more than 2500 sandstone arches) to hoodoos, are the result of weathering and erosion.

Edward Abbey shares his desert philosophy and insights in his classic *Desert Solitaire: A Season in the Wilderness*, a must-read for desert enthusiasts and conservationists.

Geographic Makeup of the Land

The Colorado Plateau is an impressive and nearly impenetrable 130,000-sq-mile tableland lurking in the corner where Colorado, Utah, Arizona and New Mexico join. Formed in an ancient basin as a remarkably coherent body of neatly layered sedimentary rocks, the plateau has remained relatively unchanged even as the lands around it were compressed, stretched and deformed by powerful forces.

Perhaps the most powerful testament to the plateau's long-term stability is the precise layers of sedimentary rock stretching back two billion years. In fact, the science of stratigraphy – the reading of earth history through its rock layers – stemmed from work at the Grand Canyon, where an astonishing set of layers have been laid bare by the Colorado River cutting across them. Throughout the Southwest, and on the Colorado Plateau in particular, layers of sedimentary rock detail a rich history of ancient oceans, coastal mudflats and arid dunes.

Landscape Features

The Southwest is jam-packed with remarkable rock formations. One reason for this is that the region's many sedimentary layers are so soft that rain and erosion readily carve them into fantastic shapes. But not any old rain. It has to be hard rain that is fairly sporadic, because frequent rain would wash the formations away. Between rains there have to be long arid spells that keep the eroding landmarks intact. The range of colors derives from the unique mineral composition of each rock type.

Visit www.publiclands.org for a one-stop summary of recreational opportunities on government-owned land in the Southwest, regardless of managing agency. The site also has maps, a book index, links to relevant agencies and updates on current restrictions and conditions.

Geology of the Grand Canyon

Arizona's Grand Canyon (p339) is the best-known geologic feature in the Southwest and for good reason: not only is it on a scale so massive it dwarfs the human imagination, but it also records two billion years of geologic history – a huge amount of time considering the earth is just 4.6 billion years old. The canyon itself, however, is young, a mere five to six million years old. Carved by the powerful Colorado River as

Geology of the Grand Canyon

Kaibab Limestone
Toroweap Formation
Coconino Sandstone
Hermit Shale
Supai Group
Redwall Limestone
Muav Limestone
Bright Angel Shale
Tapeats Sandstone
Vishnu Schist
Zoroaster Granite

the land bulged upward, the 277-mile-long canyon reflects the differing hardness of the 10-plus layers of rocks in its walls. Shales, for instance, crumble easily and form slopes, while resistant limestones and sandstones form distinctive cliffs.

The layers making up the bulk of the canyon walls were laid during the Paleozoic era, 570 to 245 million years ago. These formations perch atop a group of one- to two-billion-year-old rocks lying at the bottom of the inner gorge of the canyon. Between these two distinct sets of rock is the Great Unconformity, a several-hundred-million-year gap in the geologic record where erosion erased 12,000ft of rock and left a huge mystery.

Pages of Stone: Geology of the Grand Canyon & Plateau Country National Parks & Monuments by Halka and Lucy Chronic provides an excellent introduction to the Southwest's diverse landscape.

Pacific Northwest

From 16 to 13 million years ago, eastern Oregon and Washington witnessed one of the premier episodes of volcanic activity in earth's history. Due to shifting stresses in the earth's crust, much of interior western North America began cracking along thousands of lines and releasing enormous amounts of lava that flooded over the landscape. On multiple occasions, so much lava was produced that it filled the Columbia River channel and reached the Oregon coast, forming prominent headlands like Cape Lookout. Today, the hardened lava flows of eastern Oregon and Washington are easily seen in spectacular rimrock cliffs and flat-top mesas.

Not to be outdone, the ice ages of the past two million years created a massive ice field from Washington to British Columbia – and virtually every mountain range in the rest of the region was blanketed by glaciers.

Wildlife

Although the staggering numbers of animals that greeted the first European settlers are now a thing of the past, it is still possible to see wildlife thriving in the West in the right places and at the right times of year.

Read Marc Reisner's *Cadillac Desert: The American West and Its Disappearing Water* for a thorough account of how exploding populations in the West have utilized every drop of available water.

Animals

Reptiles & Amphibians

On a spring evening, canyons in the Southwest may fairly reverberate with the calls of canyon tree frogs or red-spotted toads. With the rising sun, these are replaced by several dozen species of lizards and snakes that roam among rocks and shrubs. Blue-bellied fence lizards are particularly abundant in the region's parks, but visitors can always hope to encounter a rarity such as the strange and venomous Gila monster. Equally fascinating are the Southwest's many colorful rattlesnakes. Quick to anger and able to deliver a painful or toxic bite, rattlesnakes are placid and retiring if left alone.

Birds

MIGRATIONS

There are so many interesting birds in the Southwest - home to 400 species - that it's the foremost reason many people travel to the region. Springtime is a particularly rewarding time for bird-watching here as songbirds arrive from their southern wintering grounds and begin singing from every nook and cranny. In the fall, sandhill cranes and snow geese travel in long skeins down the Rio Grande Valley to winter at the Bosque del Apache National Wildlife Refuge (p392). The Great Salt Lake in Utah is one of North America's premier sites for migrating birds, including millions of ducks and grebes stopping each fall to feed before continuing south.

California lies on major migratory routes for more than 350 species of birds, which either pass through the state or linger through the winter. This is one of the top birding destinations in North America. Witness, for example, the congregation of one million ducks, geese and swans at the Klamath Basin National Wildlife Refuges (p163) every November. During winter, these waterbirds head south into the refuges of the Central Valley, another area to observe huge numbers of native and migratory species.

Many of the Southwest's common flowers can be found in *Canyon Country Wildflowers* by Damian Fagan.

UNIQUE LANDSCAPE FEATURES IN THE SOUTHWEST

» **Badlands** Crumbling, mineral-filled soft rock; found in the Painted Desert at Petrified Forest National Park (p347), at Capitol Reef National Park (p368) or in the Bisti Badlands (p390).

» **Hoodoos** Sculptured spires of rock weathered into towering pillars; showcased at Bryce Canyon National Park (p370) and Arches National Park (p366).

» **Natural Bridges** Formed when streams cut through sandstone layers; three bridges can be seen at Natural Bridges National Monument (p367).

» **Goosenecks** Early-stage natural bridges formed when a stream U-turns across a landscape; visible from Goosenecks Overlook at Capitol Reef National Park (p368).

» **Mesas** Hulking formations of layered sandstone where the surrounding landscape has been stripped away; classic examples at Monument Valley (p346 and p368) on the Arizona–Utah border.

CALIFORNIA CONDORS & BALD EAGLES

With a 9ft wingspan, the California condor looks more like a prehistoric pterodactyl than any bird you've ever seen. Pushed to the brink of extinction, these unusual birds – which fed on the carcasses of mastodons and saber-toothed cats in prehistoric days – are staging a minor comeback at the Grand Canyon. After several decades in which no condors lived in the wild, a few pairs are now nesting on the canyon rim. Best bets for spotting them are Arizona's Vermilion Cliffs. In California, look skyward as you drive along the Big Sur coast or at Pinnacles National Monument.

The Pacific Northwest is a stronghold for bald eagles, which feast on the annual salmon runs and nest in old-growth forests. With a 7.5ft wingspan, these impressive birds gather in huge numbers in places like Washington's Upper Skagit Bald Eagle Area and Oregon's Klamath Basin National Wildlife Refuges (p163). In California, bald eagles have regained a foothold on the Channel Islands, and they sometimes winter at Big Bear Lake near LA. At their low point, only two or three breeding pairs nested in Colorado, but that number has increased by eight or nine each year, and at last count there were 51 breeding pairs and a stable population of over 800 eagles in the state.

An estimated nine million free-tailed bats once roosted in Carlsbad Caverns (p397). Though reduced in recent years, the evening flight is still one of the premier wildlife spectacles in North America.

Mammals

Many of the West's most charismatic wildlife species – grizzlies, buffalo, prairie dogs – were largely exterminated by the early 1900s. Fortunately, there are plenty of other mammals still wandering the forests and deserts. At the very least, if you keep your eyes open, you'll see some mule deer or a coyote.

California's mountain forests are home to an estimated 25,000 to 35,000 black bears, whose fur actually ranges in color from black to dark brown, cinnamon and even blond.

BEARS

The black bear is probably the most notorious animal in the Rockies. Adult males weigh from 275lb to 450lb; females weigh about 175lb to 250lb. They measure 3ft high on all fours and can be over 5ft when standing on their hind legs.

Black bears also roam the Pacific Northwest, the Southwest and California. They feed on berries, nuts, roots, grasses, insects, eggs, small mammals and fish, but can become a nuisance around campgrounds and mountain cabins where food is not stored properly.

The grizzly bear, which can be seen on California's state flag, once roamed California's beaches and grasslands in large numbers, eating everything from whale carcasses to acorns. Grizzlies were particularly abundant in the Central Valley. The grizzly was extirpated in the early 1900s after relentless persecution. Grizzlies are classified as an endangered species in Colorado, but they are almost certainly gone from the state. The last documented grizzly in Colorado was killed in 1979.

Salmon conservation includes protecting populations around the entire Pacific Rim from the Russian Far East to northern California. Learn more at www.wildsalmoncenter.org.

ELK

About 2000 elk winter in the Rocky Mountain National Park's lower elevations, while more than 3000 inhabit the park's lofty terrain during summer months. Mature elk bulls may reach 1100lb, cows weigh up to 600lb. Both have dark necks with light tan bodies. Like bighorn sheep, elk were virtually extinct around Estes Park by 1890, wiped out by hunters. In 1913 and 1914, before the establishment of the park, people from Estes Park brought in 49 elk from Yellowstone. The population increase since the establishment of Rocky Mountain National Park is one of the National Park Service's great successes.

Among the Pacific Northwest's signature animals is the Roosevelt elk, whose eerie bugling courtship calls can be heard each September and

PLANTS OF THE WEST

The presence of many large mountain ranges in the West creates a remarkable diversity of niches for plants. One way to understand the plants of this region is to understand life zones and the ways each plant thrives in its favored zone.

In the Southwest, at the lowest elevations, generally below 4000ft, high temperatures and a lack of water create a desert zone where drought-tolerant plants such as cacti, sagebrush and agave survive. Many of these species have small leaves or minimal leaf surface area to reduce water loss, or hold water like a cactus to survive long hot spells.

At mid-elevations, from 4000ft to 7000ft, conditions cool a bit and more moisture is available for woody shrubs and small trees. In much of Nevada, Utah, northern Arizona and New Mexico, piñon pines and junipers blanket vast areas of low mountain slopes and hills. Both trees are short and stout to help conserve water.

Nearly pure stands of stately, fragrant ponderosa pine are the dominant tree at 7000ft on many of the West's mountain ranges. In fact, this single tree best defines the Western landscape and many animals rely on it for food and shelter; timber companies also consider it their most profitable tree. High mountain, or boreal, forests composed of spruce, fir, quaking aspen and a few other conifers are found on the highest peaks in the Southwest. This is a land of cool, moist forests and lush meadows with brilliant wildflower displays.

Incredibly diverse flowers appear each year in the deserts and mountains of the Southwest. These include desert flowers that start blooming in February, and late summer flowers that fill mountain meadows after the snow melts or pop out after summer thunderstorms wet the soil. Some of the largest and grandest flowers belong to the Southwest's 100 or so species of cacti.

Southern California's desert areas begin their peak blooming in March, with other lowland areas of the state producing abundant wildflowers in April. As snows melt later at higher elevations in the Sierra Nevada, Yosemite National Park's Tuolumne Meadows is another prime spot for wildflower walks and photography, with peak blooms usually in late June or early July.

In the Pacific Northwest, the wet and wild west side of the Cascade Range captures most rain clouds coming in from the ocean, relieving them of their moisture and creating humid forests full of green life jostling for space. The dry, deserty east side – robbed of rains by the tall Cascades – is mostly the stomping grounds for sagebrush and other semi-arid-loving vegetation, although there are lush pockets here and there, especially along the mountain foothills.

When it comes to trees, California is a land of superlatives: the tallest (coast redwoods approaching 380ft), the largest (giant sequoias of the Sierra Nevada over 36ft across at the base) and the oldest (bristlecone pines of the White Mountains that are almost 5000 years old). The giant sequoia, which is unique to California, survives in isolated groves scattered on the Sierra Nevada's western slopes, including in Yosemite, Sequoia and Kings Canyon National Parks.

October in forested areas throughout the region. Full-grown males may reach 1100lb and carry 5ft racks of antlers. During winter, large groups gather in lowland valleys and can be observed at Jewell Meadows Wildlife Area (about 65 miles northwest of Portland), Dean Creek Elk Viewing Area and along the Spirit Lake Memorial Highway in Mt St Helens National Volcanic Monument (p206). Olympic National Park (p196) is home to the world's largest unmanaged herd of Roosevelt elk.

A fully hydrated giant saguaro can store more than a ton of water.

BIGHORN SHEEP

Rocky Mountain National Park is a special place: 'Bighorn Crossing Zone' is a sign you're unlikely to encounter anywhere else. From late spring through summer, groups of up to 60 sheep – typically only ewes and lambs – move from the moraine ridge north of the highway across the road to Sheep Lakes in Horseshoe Park. Unlike the big under-curving horns on mature rams, ewes grow swept-back crescent-shaped horns that reach only about 10in in length. The Sheep Lakes are evaporative ponds ringed with tasty salt deposits that attract the ewes in the morning and early afternoon after lambing in May and June. In August they rejoin the rams in the Mummy Range.

PRONGHORN ANTELOPE

The open plains of eastern Oregon and Washington are the playing grounds of pronghorn antelope, curious-looking deer-like animals with two single black horns instead of antlers. Pronghorns belong to a unique antelope family and are only found in the American West, but they are more famous for being able to run up to 60mph for long stretches – they're the second-fastest land animal in the world.

In 1990, the northern spotted owl was declared a threatened species, barring timber industries from clear-cutting certain old-growth forests. The controversy sparked debate all across the Pacific Northwest, pitting loggers against environmentalists.

FORESTS

Environmental Issues

Growth in the West has come with costs. In the Pacific Northwest, the production of cheap hydroelectricity and massive irrigation projects along the Columbia have led to the near-irreversible destruction of the river's ecosystem. Dams have all but eliminated most runs of native salmon and have further disrupted the lives of remaining Native Americans who depend on the river. Logging of old-growth forests has left ugly scars. Washington's Puget Sound area and Portland's extensive suburbs are groaning under the weight of rapidly growing population centers.

Ongoing controversies in the Southwest include arguments about the locations of nuclear power plants and the transport and disposal of nuclear waste, notably at Yucca Mountain, 90 miles from Las Vegas. Water distribution and availability continue to be concerns throughout the region.

Still, the inhabitants of many regions of the West – Colorado, Utah, the Pacific Northwest – generally manage to find a reasonable balance between their natural resources and continued popularity, and the region continues to be one of the USA's most beautiful places to visit.

Survival Guide

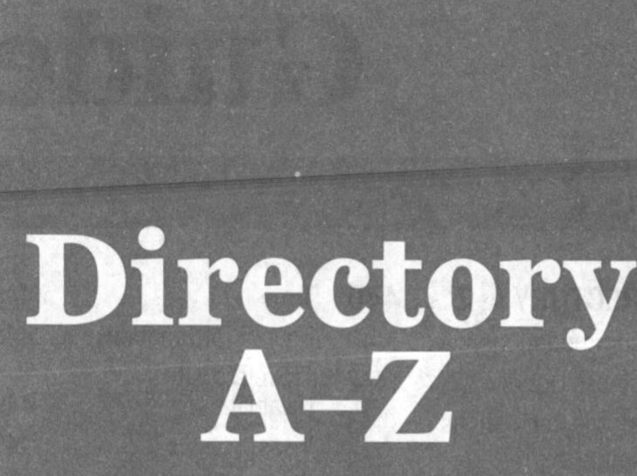

Directory A–Z

Accommodations

Exceptional picks in this book are marked with a TOP CHOICE icon, but every property recommended meets a certain baseline standard for quality within its class. Accommodations are listed in order of author recommendation.

Rates

» Rates are categorized as **$** (under $100), **$$** ($100 to $200) or **$$$** (over $200). Unless noted, rates do not include taxes, averaging more than 10%.

» Generally, midweek rates are lower except in hotels geared toward weekday business travelers, which then lure leisure travelers with weekend deals.

» Rates quoted in this book are for high season: June to August everywhere, except the deserts and mountain ski areas, where December through April are the busiest months.

» Demand and prices spike even higher around major holidays (p448) and for festivals (p24), when some properties may impose multiday minimum stays.

Discounts

» Discount cards (p443) and auto-club membership (p457) may get you 10% or more off standard rates at participating hotels and motels.

» Look for freebie ad magazines packed with hotel and motel discount coupons at gas stations, travel centers, highway rest areas, tourist offices and online at **Roomsaver.com** (www.roomsaver.com).

» You might get a better deal by booking through discount-travel websites like **Priceline** (www.priceline.com), **Hotwire** (www.hotwire.com) or **Hotels.com** (www.hotels.com).

» Bargaining may be possible for walk-in guests without reservations, especially during off-peak times.

B&Bs

In the USA, many B&Bs are high-end romantic retreats in restored historic homes that are run by personable, independent innkeepers who serve gourmet breakfasts. These B&Bs often take pains to evoke a theme – Victorian, rustic, Cape Cod – and amenities range from merely comfortable to indulgent. Rates normally top $100, and the best run $200 to $300. Some B&Bs have minimum-stay requirements, some exclude young children and many exclude pets.

Still, European-style B&Bs exist: these may be rooms in someone's home, with plainer furnishings, simpler breakfasts, shared baths and cheaper rates. These often welcome families.

B&Bs can close out of season and reservations are essential, especially for top-end places. To avoid surprises, always ask about bathrooms (whether shared or private). B&B agencies are sprinkled throughout this guide. Also check listings online:

Bed & Breakfast Inns Online (www.bbonline.com)

BedandBreakfast.com (www.bedandbreakfast.com)

BnB Finder (www.bnbfinder.com)

Camping

Most federally managed public lands and many state parks offer camping. First-come, first-served 'primitive' campsites offer no facilities; overnight fees range from free to under $10. 'Basic' sites usually provide toilets (flush or pit), drinking water, fire pits and picnic tables; they cost $5 to $15 a night, and some or all may be reserved in advance. 'Developed' campsites, usually in national or state parks,

> **BOOK YOUR STAY ONLINE**
>
> For more accommodations reviews by Lonely Planet authors, check out hotels.lonelyplanet.com/USA. You'll find independent reviews, as well as recommendations on the best places to stay. Best of all, you can book online.

have nicer facilities and more amenities: showers, barbecue grills, RV sites with hookups etc. These run $13 to $40 a night, and many can be reserved in advance.

Camping on most federal lands – including national parks, national forests, Bureau of Land Management (BLM; see box, p442) and and so on – can be reserved through **Recreation.gov** (☎518-885-3639, 877-444-6777; www.recreation.gov). Camping is usually limited to 14 days and can be reserved up to six months in advance. For some state park campgrounds, you can make bookings through **ReserveAmerica** (www.reserveamerica.com). Both websites let you search for campground locations and amenities, check availability and reserve a site, view maps and get driving directions online.

Private campgrounds tend to cater to RVs and families (tent sites may be few and lack atmosphere). Facilities may include playgrounds, convenience stores, wi-fi access, swimming pools and other activities. Some rent camping cabins, ranging from canvas-sided wooden platforms to log-frame structures with real beds, heating and private baths. **Kampgrounds of America** (KOA; http://koa.com) is a national network of private campgrounds with a full range of facilities. You can order KOA's free annual directory (shipping fees apply) or browse its comprehensive campground listings and make bookings online.

Dude Ranches

Most visitors to dude ranches today are city-slickers looking for an escape from a fast-paced, high-tech world. These days you can find anything from a working-ranch experience (smelly chores and 5am wake-up calls included) to a Western Club Med. Typical week-long visits start at over $100 per person per day, including accommodations, meals, activities and equipment.

While the centerpiece of dude-ranch vacations is horseback riding, many ranches feature swimming pools and have expanded their activity lists to include fly-fishing, hiking, mountain biking, tennis, golf, skeet-shooting and cross-country skiing. Accommodations range from rustic log cabins to cushy suites with Jacuzzis and cable TV. Meals range from family-style spaghetti dinners to four-course gourmet feasts.

Arizona Dude Ranch Association (☎520-823-4277; www.azdra.com)

Colorado Dude & Guest Ranch Association (☎866-942-3472; www.coloradoranch.com)

Dude Ranchers' Association (☎307-587-2339, 866-399-2339; www.duderanch.org)

Hostels

In the West, hostels are mainly found in urban areas in the Pacific Northwest, California and the Southwest.

Hostelling International USA (HI-USA; ☎301-495-1240; www.hiusa.org; annual membership adult/child/senior $28/free/$18) runs 26 hostels in the US; 19 of them are in California. Most have gender-segregated dorms, a few private rooms, shared baths and a communal kitchen. Overnight fees for dorm beds range from $21 to $45. HI-USA members are entitled to small discounts. Reservations are accepted (you can book online) and advised during high season, when

PRACTICALITIES

Newspapers & Magazines

National newspapers *New York Times* (www.nytimes.com), *Wall Street Journal* (http://online.wsj.com/home-page), *USA Today* (www.usatoday.com)

Western newspapers *Arizona Republic* (www.azcentral.com), *Denver Post* (www.denverpost.com), *Seattle Times* (www.seattletimes.com), *Los Angeles Times* (www.latimes.com), *San Francisco Chronicle* (www.sfgate.com)

Mainstream news magazines *Time*, *Newsweek*, *US News and World Report*

Radio & TV

Radio news National Public Radio (NPR), lower end of FM dial

Broadcast TV ABC, CBS, NBC, FOX, PBS (public broadcasting)

Major cable channels CNN (news), ESPN (sports), HBO (movies), Weather Channel

Video Systems

» NTSC standard (incompatible with PAL or SECAM)

» DVDs coded for Region 1 (US and Canada only)

Weights & Measures

Weight ounces (oz), pounds (lb), tons

Liquid ounces (oz), pints, quarts, gallons

Distance feet (ft), yards (yd), miles (mi)

WHAT'S THE BLM?

The Bureau of Land Management (www.blm.gov) is a Department of Energy agency that oversees more than 245 million surface acres of public land, much of it in the West. It manages its resources for a variety of uses, from energy production to cattle grazing to overseeing recreational opportunities. What does that mean for you? Outdoor fun, as well as both developed camping and dispersed camping (meaning you can camp almost anywhere). Generally, when it comes to dispersed camping on BLM land, you can camp where you want as long as your campsite is at least 900ft from a water source used by wildlife or livestock. You cannot camp in one spot longer than 14 days. Pack out what you pack in and don't leave campfires unattended. Some regions may have more specific rules, so check the state's camping requirements on the BLM website and call the appropriate district office for specifics. For developed campground information, you can also visit www.recreation.gov.

there may be a three-night maximum stay.

The USA has many independent hostels not affiliated with HI-USA, particularly in the Southwest. For online listings, check:

Hostels.com (www.hostels.com)

Hostelworld.com (www.hostelworld.com).

Hostelz.com (www.hostelz.com)

Hotels

Hotels in all categories typically include in-room phones, cable TV, alarm clocks, private baths and a simple continental breakfast. Many midrange properties provide minibars, microwaves, hairdryers, internet access, air-conditioning and/or heating, swimming pools and writing desks, while top-end hotels add concierge services, fitness and business centers, spas, restaurants, bars and higher-end furnishings.

Even if hotels advertise that children 'sleep free,' cots or rollaway beds may cost extra. Always ask about the hotel's policy for telephone calls; all charge an exorbitant amount for long-distance and international calls, but some also charge for dialing local and toll-free numbers.

Lodges

Normally situated within national parks, lodges are often rustic looking but are usually quite comfy inside. Rooms generally start at $100, but can easily be double that in high season. Since they represent the only option if you want to stay inside the park without camping, many are fully booked well in advance. Want a room today? Call anyway – you might be lucky and hit on a cancellation. In addition to on-site restaurants, they also offer touring services.

Motels

Motels – distinguishable from hotels by having rooms that open onto a parking lot – tend to cluster around interstate exits and along main routes into town. Some remain smaller, less-expensive 'mom and pop' operations; a light continental breakfast is sometimes included; and amenities might top out at a phone and a TV (maybe with cable). However, motels often have a few rooms with simple kitchenettes.

Although many motels are of the bland, cookie-cutter variety, these can be good for discount lodging or when other options fall through. For deals, pick up free coupon books at visitor centers, rest areas and travel centers. At an independent motel, if the lot isn't full and you're not afraid to move on, try negotiating your rate at the counter.

Don't judge a motel solely on looks. Facades may be faded and tired, but the proprietor may keep rooms spotlessly clean. Of course, the reverse could also be true. Try to see your room before you commit.

Resorts

Luxury resorts really require a stay of several days to be appreciated and are often destinations in themselves. Start the day with a round of golf or a tennis match, then luxuriate with a massage, swimming, sunbathing and drinking. Many are now kid friendly, with extensive children's programs.

Business Hours

Reviews won't list operating hours unless they deviate from the following normal opening times:

Banks	8:30am-4:30pm Mon-Thu, to 5:30pm Fri (and possibly 9am-noon Sat)
Bars	5pm-midnight Sun-Thu, to 2am Fri & Sat
Nightclubs	10pm-2am Thu-Sat
Post offices	9am-5pm Mon-Fri
Shopping malls	9am-9pm
Stores	10am-6pm Mon-Sat, noon-5pm Sun
Supermarkets	8am-8pm, some open 24hr

Customs Regulations

For a complete list of US customs regulations, visit the official portal for **US Customs and Border Protection** (www.cbp.gov).

Duty-free allowance per person is as follows:

» 1L of liquor (provided you are at least 21 years old)

» 100 cigars and 200 cigarettes (if you are at least 18)

» $100 worth of gifts and purchases ($800 if a returning US citizen)

» If you arrive with $10,000 or more in US or foreign currency, it must be declared.

There are heavy penalties for attempting to import illegal drugs. Other forbidden items include drug paraphernalia, lottery tickets, items with fake brand names, and most goods made in Cuba, Iran, North Korea, Myanmar (Burma), Angola and Sudan. Any fruit, vegetables or other food or plant material must be declared (whereby you'll undergo a time-consuming search) or left in the bins in the arrival area.

Discount Cards

America the Beautiful Interagency Annual Pass (http://store.usgs.gov/pass; $80) Admits four adults and all children under 16 years old for free to all national parks and federal recreational lands (eg USFS, BLM) for one year. It can be purchased online or at any national park entrance station. US citizens and permanent residents 62 years and older are eligible for a lifetime **Senior Pass** ($10) that grants free entry and 50% off some recreational-use fees like camping, as does the lifetime Access Pass (free to US citizens or permanent residents with a permanent disability). These passes are available in person or by mail.

American Association of Retired Persons (AARP; ☎888-687-2277; www.aarp.org; annual membership $16) Advocacy group for Americans 50 years and older offers member discounts (usually 10%) on hotels, car rentals and more.

American Automobile Association (AAA; ☎877-428-2277; www.aaa.com; annual membership from $48) Members of AAA and its foreign affiliates (eg CAA, AA) qualify for small discounts (usually 10%) on Amtrak trains, car rentals, motels and hotels, chain restaurants, shopping, tours and theme parks.

Seniors People over the age of 65 (sometimes 55, 60 or 62) often qualify for the same discounts as students; any ID showing your birth date should suffice as proof of age.

International Student Identity Card (ISIC; www.isic.org; $22) Offers savings on airline fares, travel insurance and local attractions for full-time students. For nonstudents under 26 years of age, an **International Youth Travel Card** (IYTC; $22) grants similar benefits. Cards are issued by student unions, hostelling organizations and travel agencies.

Student Advantage Card (☎877-256-4672; www.studentadvantage.com; $23) For international and US students, offers 15% savings on Amtrak and Greyhound, plus discounts of 10% to 20% on some airlines and chain shops, hotels and motels.

Electricity

AC 110/120V is standard; buy adapters to run most non-US electronics.

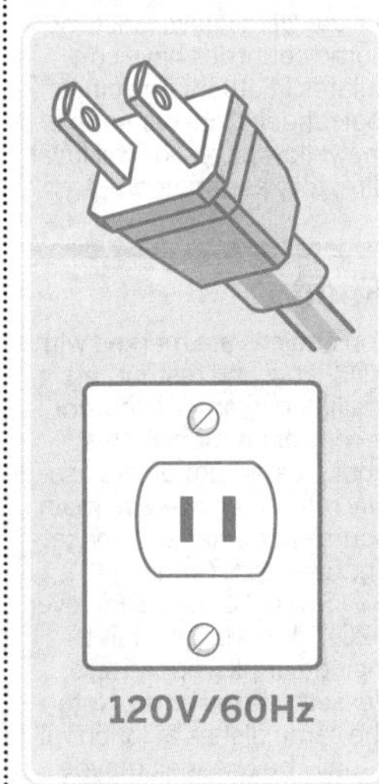

Embassies & Consulates

International travelers who want to contact their home country's embassy while in the US should visit **Embassy.org** (www.embassy.org), which lists contact information for all foreign embassies in Washington, DC. Most countries have an embassy for the UN in New York City. Some countries have consulates in other large cities; look under 'Consulates' in the yellow pages, or call local directory assistance.

Food

Top choices are marked with a TOP CHOICE icon, and restaurants are listed in order of author recommendation. In this book, restaurant prices usually refer to an average main course at dinner and are categorized as $ (under $10), $$ ($10 to $20) or $$$ (over $20). These prices don't include drinks, appetizers, desserts, taxes or tip. Note the same dishes at lunch will usually be cheaper, maybe even half-price. Many Utah restaurants are closed on Sunday. Also see the Western Cuisine chapter, p419.

Gay & Lesbian Travelers

GLBT travelers will find lots of places where they can be themselves without thinking twice. Naturally, beaches and big cities typically are the most gay-friendly destinations.

Hot Spots

You will have heard of San Francisco, the happiest gay city in America, and what can gays and lesbians do in Los Angeles and Las Vegas? Hmmm, just about anything. In fact, when LA or Vegas gets to be too much, flee to the desert resorts of Palm Springs.

Attitudes

Most major US cities have a visible and open GLBT community. In this guide, many cities include a boxed text or section that describes the city's best GLBT offerings.

The level of acceptance varies across the West. In some places, there is absolutely no tolerance whatsoever, and in others acceptance is predicated on GLBT people not 'flaunting' their sexual preference or identity. In rural areas and extremely conservative enclaves, it's unwise to be openly out, as violence and verbal abuse can sometimes occur. When in doubt, assume locals follow a 'don't ask, don't tell' policy. Same-sex marriage, a hotly debated topic, is now legal in a handful of states.

Resources

Advocate (www.advocate.com) Gay-oriented news website reports on business, politics, arts, entertainment and travel.

Damron (www.damron.com) Publishes the classic gay travel guides, but they're advertiser-driven and sometimes outdated.

Gay Travel (www.gaytravel.com) Has online guides to dozens of US destinations.

Gay Yellow Network (www.gayyellow.com) Yellow-page listings for over 30 US cities. Also available as smartphone app (GLYP).

GLBT National Help Center (☎888-843-4564; www.glbtnationalhelpcenter.org; ⌚1-9pm PST Mon-Fri, 9am-2pm PST Sat) A national hotline for counseling, information and referrals.

National Gay and Lesbian Task Force (www.thetaskforce.org) National activist group's website covers news, politics and current issues.

OutTraveler (www.outtraveler.com) Has useful online city guides and travel articles to various US and foreign destinations.

Purple Roofs (www.purpleroofs.com) Lists gay-owned and gay-friendly B&Bs and hotels nationwide.

The Queerest Places: A Guide to Gay and Lesbian Historic Sites by Paula Martinac is full of juicy details and history, and covers the country.

Health

Healthcare & Insurance

» Medical treatment in the USA is of the highest caliber, but the expense could kill you. Many health-care professionals demand payment at the time of service, especially from out-of-towners or international visitors.

» Except for medical emergencies (call ☎911 or go to the nearest 24-hour hospital emergency room or ER), phone around to find a doctor who will accept your insurance.

» Keep all receipts and documentation for billing and insurance claims and reimbursement purposes.

» Some health-insurance policies require you to get pre-authorization for medical treatment before seeking help.

» Overseas visitors with travel health-insurance policies may need to contact a call center for an assessment by phone before getting medical treatment.

» Carry any medications you may need in their original containers, clearly labeled. Bring a signed, dated letter from your doctor describing all medical conditions and medications (including generic names).

Environmental Hazards

ALTITUDE SICKNESS

» Visitors from lower elevations undergo rather dramatic physiological changes as they adapt to high altitudes.

» Symptoms, which tend to manifest during the first day after reaching altitude, may include headache, fatigue, loss of appetite, nausea, sleeplessness, increased urination and hyperventilation due to overexertion.

» Symptoms normally resolve within 24 to 48 hours.

» The rule of thumb is, don't ascend until the symptoms descend.

» More severe cases may display extreme disorientation, ataxia (loss of coordination and balance), breathing problems (especially a persistent cough) and vomiting. These folks should descend immediately and get to a hospital.

» To avoid the discomfort characterizing the milder symptoms, drink plenty of water and take it easy – at 7000ft, a pleasant walk around Santa Fe can wear you out faster than a steep hike at sea level.

DEHYDRATION, HEAT EXHAUSTION & HEATSTROKE

» Take it easy as you acclimatize, especially on hot summer days and in Southern California's deserts.

» Drink plenty of water. One gallon per person per day minimum is recommended when you're active outdoors.

» Dehydration (lack of water) or salt deficiency can cause heat exhaustion, often characterized by heavy sweating, pale skin, fatigue, lethargy, headaches, nausea, vomiting, dizziness, muscle cramps and rapid, shallow breathing.

» Long, continuous exposure to high temperatures can lead to possibly fatal heatstroke. Warning signs include altered mental status, hyperventilation and flushed, hot and dry skin (ie sweating stops).

» Hospitalization is essential. Meanwhile, get out of the sun, remove clothing that retains heat (cotton is OK), douse the body with water and fan continuously; ice packs can be applied to the neck, armpits and groin.

HYPOTHERMIA

» Skiers and hikers will find that temperatures in the mountains and desert can quickly drop below freezing, especially during winter. Even a sudden spring shower or high winds can lower your body temperature dangerously fast.

» Instead of cotton, wear synthetic or woolen clothing that retains warmth even when wet. Carry waterproof layers (eg Gore-Tex jacket, plastic poncho, rain pants) and high-energy, easily digestible snacks like chocolate, nuts and dried fruit.

» Symptoms of hypothermia include exhaustion, numbness, shivering, stumbling, slurred speech, dizzy spells, muscle cramps and irrational or even violent behavior.

» To treat hypothermia, get out of bad weather and change into dry, warm clothing. Drink hot liquids (no caffeine or alcohol) and snack on high-calorie food.

» In advanced stages, carefully put hypothermia sufferers in a warm sleeping bag cocooned inside a wind- and water-proof outer wrapping. Do not rub victims, who must be handled gently.

Insurance

See p444 for health insurance and p457 for car insurance.

Getting travel insurance to cover theft, loss and medical problems is highly recommended. Some policies do not cover 'risky' activities such as scuba diving, motorcycling and skiing, so read the fine print. Make sure the policy at least covers hospital stays and an emergency flight home.

Paying for your airline ticket or rental car with a credit card may provide limited travel accident insurance. If you already have private health insurance or a homeowners or renters policy, find out what those policies cover and only get supplemental insurance. If you have prepaid a large portion of your vacation, trip cancellation insurance may be a worthwhile expense.

Worldwide travel insurance is available at www.lonelyplanet.com/travel_services. You can buy, extend and claim online anytime – even if you're already on the road.

Internet Access

This guide uses an internet icon @ when a place has a net-connected computer for public use and a wi-fi icon when it offers wireless internet access, whether free or fee-based.

» Internet cafes listed throughout this guide typically charge $6 to $12 per hour for online access.

» With branches in most cities and towns, **FedEx Office** (800-463-3339; www.fedex.com) offers internet access at self-service computer workstations (20¢ to 30¢ per minute) and sometimes free wi-fi, plus digital-photo printing and CD-burning stations.

» Wi-fi hot spots (free or fee-based) can be found at major airports; many hotels, motels and coffee shops (eg Starbucks); and some tourist information centers, RV parks (eg KOA), museums, bars, restaurants (including chains such as McDonalds and Panera Bread) and stores (eg Apple).

» Free public wi-fi is proliferating and even some state parks are now wi-fi enabled.

» Public libraries have internet terminals, but online time may be limited, advance sign-up required and a nominal fee charged for out-of-network visitors. Increasingly libraries offer free wi-fi access.

» If you're not from the US, remember that you will need an AC adapter for your laptop, plus a plug adapter for US sockets; both are available at larger electronics shops, such as **Best Buy** (☎888-237-8289; www.bestbuy.com).

Legal Matters

In everyday matters, if you are stopped by the police, remember that there is no system of paying traffic or other fines on the spot. Attempting to pay a fine to an officer is frowned upon at best and may result in a charge of bribery. For traffic offenses, the police officer or highway patroller will explain the options to you. There is usually a 30-day period to pay a fine. Most matters can be handled by mail.

If you are arrested, you have a legal right to an attorney, and you are allowed to remain silent. There is no legal reason to speak to a police officer if you don't wish, but never walk away from an officer until given permission to do so. Anyone who is arrested is legally allowed to make one phone call. If you can't afford a lawyer, a public defender will be appointed to you free of charge. Foreign visitors who don't have a lawyer, friend or family member to help should call their embassy; the police will provide the number upon request.

As a matter of principle, the US legal system presumes a person innocent until proven guilty. Each state has its own civil and criminal laws, and what is legal in one state may be illegal in others.

Driving

In all states, driving under the influence of alcohol or drugs is a serious offense, subject to stiff fines and even imprisonment. For more information on driving in the USA and road rules, see p458.

Drugs

Recreational drugs are prohibited by federal and state laws. Some states, such as California and Alaska, treat possession of small quantities of marijuana as a misdemeanor, though it is still punishable with fines and/or imprisonment.

Possession of any illicit drug, including cocaine, ecstasy, LSD, heroin, hashish or more than an ounce of pot, is a felony potentially punishable by lengthy jail sentences. For foreigners, conviction of any drug offense is grounds for deportation.

Money

For US dollar exchange rates and setting your trip budget, see p18.

ATMs

» ATMs are available at most banks, shopping malls, airports and grocery and convenience stores.

» Expect a minimum surcharge of $2 to $3 per transaction, in addition to any fees charged by your home bank. Some ATMs in Las Vegas may charge $5 to withdraw cash.

» Most ATMs are connected to international networks and offer decent foreign-exchange rates.

» Withdrawing cash from an ATM using a credit card usually incurs a hefty fee and high interest rates; check with your credit-card company for a PIN number.

Cash

» Most people do not carry large amounts of cash for everyday use, relying instead on credit cards, debit cards and ATMs. Some businesses refuse to accept bills over $20.

Credit Cards

Major credit cards are almost universally accepted. In fact, it's almost impossible to rent a car, book a room or buy tickets over the phone without one. A credit card may also be vital in emergencies. Visa, MasterCard and American Express are the most widely accepted.

Moneychangers

» You can exchange money at major airports, some banks and all currency-exchange offices such as **American Express** (www.americanexpress.com) or **Travelex** (www.travelex.com). Always inquire about rates and fees.

» Outside big cities, exchanging money may be a problem, so make sure you have a credit card and sufficient cash on hand.

Taxes

» Sales tax varies by state and county.

» Hotel taxes vary by city.

Tipping

Tipping is *not* optional. Only withhold tips in cases of outrageously bad service.

Airport skycaps and hotel bellhops $2 per bag, minimum $5 per cart

Bartenders 10% to 15% per round, minimum $1 per drink

Concierges Nothing for simple information, up to $20 for securing last-minute restaurant reservations, sold-out show tickets etc

Housekeeping staff $2 to $4 daily, left under the card provided; more if you're messy

Parking valets At least $2 when handed back your car keys

Restaurant staff and room service 15% to 20%, unless a gratuity is already charged

Taxi drivers 10% to 15% of metered fare, rounded up to the next dollar

Traveler's Checks

» Traveler's checks have pretty much fallen out of use.

» Larger restaurants, hotels and department stores will often accept traveler's checks (in US dollars only), but small businesses, markets and fast-food chains may refuse them.

» Visa and American Express are the most widely accepted issuers of traveler's checks.

National & State Parks

Before visiting any national park check out its website, using the navigation search tool on the NPS home page (www.nps.gov). On the Grand Canyon's website (www.nps.gov/grca), you can download the seasonal newspaper, *The Guide*, for the latest information on prices, hours and ranger talks. There is a separate edition for both the north and south rims.

At the entrance of a national or state park, be ready to hand over cash (credit cards may not always be accepted). Costs range from nothing at all to $25 per vehicle for a seven-day pass. If you're visiting several parks in the Southwest, you may save money by purchasing the America the Beautiful annual pass (see p443).

Due to ongoing fiscal woes, many state governments across the West and Southwest are slashing their budgets for state parks. State parks in Arizona, California and Utah have been particularly hard hit, and it's not yet clear which ones will ultimately survive. In California, 70 of the state's 278 state parks were scheduled to close by the middle of 2012. In Utah, funding has been cut from $12.2 million to $6.8 million in the last few years. Some state parks in Arizona are operating on a five-day schedule, closed Tuesdays and Wednesdays. Before traveling to a state park, visit its website to confirm its current status.

Photography & Video

Print film can be found in drugstores and at specialty camera shops. Digital camera memory cards are widely available at chain retailers such as Best Buy and Target.

Some Native American tribal lands prohibit photography and video completely; when it's allowed, you may be required to purchase a permit. Always ask permission if you want to photograph someone close up; anyone who then agrees to be photographed may expect a small tip.

For more advice on picture-taking, consult Lonely Planet's *Travel Photography* guide.

Post

For 24-hour postal information, including post office locations and hours, contact the **US Postal Service** (USPS; ☎800-275-8777; www.usps.com), which is reliable and inexpensive.

For sending urgent or important letters and packages either domestically or overseas, **Federal Express** (FedEx; ☎800-463-3339; www.fedex.com) and **United Parcel Service** (UPS; ☎800-742-5877; www.ups.com) offer more expensive door-to-door delivery services.

Postal Rates

At the time of writing, the postal rates for 1st-class mail within the USA were 44¢ for letters weighing up to 1oz (20¢ for each additional ounce) and 29¢ for postcards. First-class mail goes up to 13oz, and then priority-mail rates apply.

International airmail rates (except to Canada and Mexico) are 98¢ for a 1oz letter or a postcard; to Canada and Mexico it's 80¢.

TIPS FOR SHUTTERBUGS

» If you have a digital camera, bring extra batteries and a charger.

» For print film, use 100 ASA film for all but the lowest light situations; it's the slowest film, and will enhance resolution.

» A zoom lens is extremely useful; most SLR cameras have one. Use it to isolate the central subject of your photos. A common composition mistake is to include too much landscape around the person or feature that's your main focus.

» Morning and evening are the best times to shoot. The same sandstone bluff can turn four or five different hues throughout the day, and the warmest hues will be at sunset. Underexposing the shot slightly (by a half-stop or more) can bring out richer details in red tones.

» When shooting red rocks, a warming filter added to an SLR lens can enhance the colors of the rocks and reduce the blues of overcast or flat-light days. Achieve the same effect on any digital camera by adjusting the white balance to the automatic 'cloudy' setting (or by reducing the color temperature).

» Don't shoot into the sun or include it in the frame; shoot what the sunlight is hitting. On bright days, move your subjects into shade for close-up portraits.

Sending & Receiving Mail

If you have the correct postage, you can drop mail weighing less than 13oz into any blue mailbox. To send a package weighing 13oz or more, go to a post office.

Poste restante mail can usually be sent to you c/o General Delivery at any post office that has its own zip code. Domestic mail is usually held for 10 days and international mail for 30 days before it's returned to the sender; you might ask the sender to write 'Hold for Arrival' on the envelope. You'll need photo ID to collect mail. In some big cities, general-delivery mail is not held at the main post office but at a postal facility away from downtown.

Public Holidays

On the following national public holidays, banks, schools and government offices (including post offices) are closed, and transportation, museums and other services operate on a Sunday schedule. Holidays falling on a weekend are usually observed the following Monday.

New Year's Day January 1

Martin Luther King Jr Day Third Monday in January

Presidents' Day Third Monday in February

Memorial Day Last Monday in May

Independence Day July 4

Labor Day First Monday in September

Columbus Day Second Monday in October

Veterans' Day November 11

Thanksgiving Fourth Thursday in November

Christmas Day December 25

During spring break, high school and college students get a week off from school so they can overrun beach towns and resorts. These occur throughout March and April. For students of all ages, summer vacation runs from June to August.

Telephone

Cell Phones

» You'll need a multiband GSM phone in order to make calls in the US. Popping in a US prepaid rechargeable SIM card is usually cheaper than using your network.

» SIM cards are sold at telecommunications and electronics stores. These stores also sell inexpensive prepaid phones, including some airtime.

Dialing Codes

» US phone numbers consist of a three-letter area code followed by a seven-digit local number.

» When dialing a number within the same area code, use the seven-digit number; however, some places now require you to dial the entire 10-digit number even for a local call.

» If you are calling long distance, dial ☎1 plus the area code plus the phone number.

» Toll-free numbers begin with ☎800, ☎866, ☎877 or ☎888 and must be preceded by ☎1.

» For direct international calls, dial ☎011 plus the country code plus the area code (usually without the initial '0') plus the local phone number.

» For international call assistance, dial ☎00.

» If you're calling from abroad, the country code for the US is ☎1 (the same as Canada, but international rates apply between the two countries).

Payphones & Phonecards

» Where payphones still exist, they are usually coin-operated, although some may only accept credit cards (eg in national parks).

» Local calls usually cost 50¢ minimum.

» For long-distance calls, you're usually better off buying a prepaid phonecard, sold at convenience stores, supermarkets, newsstands and electronics stores.

Time

» For more information about western Time Zones and Daylight Saving Time (DST), see p19.

» The US date system is written as month/day/year. Thus, the 8th of June, 2008, becomes 6/8/08.

Tourist Information

In this book, state tourism offices are listed in the Information section at the start of each regional chapter, while city and county visitor information centers are listed throughout the regional chapters.

Any tourist office worth contacting has a website, where you can download free travel e-guides. They also field phone calls; some local offices maintain daily lists of hotel room availability, but few offer reservation services. All tourist offices have self-service racks of brochures and discount coupons; some also sell maps and books.

State-run 'welcome centers,' usually placed along interstate highways, tend to have materials that cover wider territories, and offices are usually open longer hours, including weekends and holidays.

Many cities have an official convention and visitor bureau (CVB); these sometimes double as tourist bureaus, but since their main focus is drawing the business trade, CVBs can be less useful for independent travelers.

Keep in mind that, in smaller towns, when the local

chamber of commerce runs the tourist bureau, their lists of hotels, restaurants and services usually mention only chamber members; the town's cheapest options may be missing.

Similarly, in prime tourist destinations, some private 'tourist bureaus' are really agents who book hotel rooms and tours on commission. They may offer excellent service and deals, but you'll get what they're selling and nothing else.

Travelers with Disabilities

If you have a physical disability, the USA can be an accommodating place. The Americans with Disabilities Act (ADA) requires that all public buildings, private buildings built after 1993 (including hotels, restaurants, theaters and museums) and public transit be wheelchair accessible. However, call ahead to confirm what is available. Some local tourist offices publish detailed accessibility guides.

Telephone companies offer relay operators, available via teletypewriter (TTY) numbers, for the hearing impaired. Most banks provide ATM instructions in Braille and via earphone jacks for hearing-impaired customers. All major airlines, Greyhound buses and Amtrak trains will assist travelers with disabilities; just describe your needs when making reservations at least 48 hours in advance. Service animals (guide dogs) are allowed to accompany passengers, but bring documentation.

Some car rental agencies – such as Budget and Hertz – offer hand-controlled vehicles and vans with wheelchair lifts at no extra charge, but you must reserve them well in advance. **Wheelchair Getaways** (☎800-642-2042; www.wheelchairgetaways.com) rents accessible vans throughout the USA. In many cities and towns, public buses are accessible to wheelchair riders and will 'kneel' if you are unable to use the steps; just let the driver know that you need the lift or ramp.

Many national and some state parks and recreation areas have wheelchair-accessible paved, graded dirt or boardwalk trails. A relatively new website for accessible trails in the US is www.greatwheelchairaccessiblehikes.com; check out its 'other resources' link for more websites.

US citizens and permanent residents with permanent disabilities are entitled to a free 'America the Beautiful' Access Pass (p443), which gives free entry to all federal recreation lands (eg national parks).

Some helpful resources for travelers with disabilities:

Access-Able Travel Source (☎www.access-able.com) General travel website with useful tips and links.

Accessing Arizona (www.accessingarizona.com) Up-to-date information about wheelchair-accessible activities in Arizona.

Access Northern California (www.accessnca.com) Extensive links to accessible-travel resources, publications, tours and transportation, including outdoor recreation opportunities and car and van rentals, plus a searchable lodgings database and an events calendar.

Access San Francisco (www.onlyinsanfrancisco.com/plan_your_trip/access_guide.asp) Free downloadable accessible travel info (somewhat dated, but still useful).

Disabled Sports USA (☎301-217-0960; www.dsusa.org) Offers sports and recreation programs for those with disabilities and publishes *Challenge* magazine.

Flying Wheels Travel (☎507-451-5005, 877-451-5006; www.flyingwheelstravel.com) A full-service travel agency.

Mobility International USA (☎541-343-1284; www.miusa.org) Advises disabled travelers on mobility issues and runs educational international-exchange programs.

Moss Rehabilitation Hospital (☎215-663-6000; www.mossresourcenet.org/travel.htm) Extensive links and tips for accessible travel.

Society for Accessible Travel & Hospitality (SATH; ☎212-447-7284; www.sath.org) Advocacy group provides general information for travelers with disabilities.

Splore (☎801-484-4128; www.splore.org) Offers accessible outdoor adventure trips in Utah.

Visas

Warning: all of the following information is highly subject to change. US entry requirements keep evolving as national security regulations change. All travelers should double-check current visa and passport regulations *before* coming to the USA.

The **US State Department** (www.travel.state.gov/visa) maintains the most comprehensive visa information, providing downloadable forms, lists of US consulates abroad and even visa wait times calculated by country.

For information about Passports, see p452

Visa Applications

Apart from most Canadian citizens and those entering under the Visa Waiver Program (see p450), all foreign visitors will need to obtain a visa from a US consulate or embassy abroad. Most applicants must schedule a personal interview, to which you must bring all your documentation and proof of fee payment. Wait times for interviews vary, but afterward, barring problems, visa issuance takes from a few days to a few weeks.

Your passport must be valid for at least six months after the end of your intended stay in the USA. You'll need a recent photo (2in by 2in), and you must pay a non-refundable $140 processing fee, plus in a few cases an additional visa issuance reciprocity fee. You'll also need to fill out the online DS-160 non-immigrant visa electronic application.

Visa applicants are required to show documents of financial stability (or evidence that a US resident will provide financial support), a round-trip or onward ticket and 'binding obligations' that will ensure their return home, such as family ties, a home or a job. Because of these requirements, those planning to travel through other countries before arriving in the USA are generally better off applying for a US visa while they are still in their home country, rather than while on the road.

VISA WAIVER PROGRAM

Currently under the Visa Waiver Program (VWP), citizens of the following countries may enter the USA without a visa for stays of 90 days or fewer: Andorra, Australia, Austria, Belgium, Brunei, Czech Republic, Denmark, Estonia, Finland, France, Germany, Greece, Hungary, Iceland, Ireland, Italy, Japan, Latvia, Liechtenstein, Lithuania, Luxembourg, Malta, Monaco, the Netherlands, New Zealand, Norway, Portugal, San Marino, Singapore, Slovakia, Slovenia, South Korea, Spain, Sweden, Switzerland and the UK.

If you are a citizen of a VWP country, you do not need a visa *only if* you have a passport that meets current US standards (see p452) *and* you have gotten approval from the Electronic System for Travel Authorization (ESTA) in advance. Register online with the Department of Homeland Security at https://esta.cbp.dhs.gov at least 72 hours before arrival; once travel authorization is approved, your registration is valid for two years. The fee, payable online, is $14.

Visitors from VWP countries must still produce at the port of entry all the same evidence as for a non-immigrant visa application. They must demonstrate that their trip is for 90 days or less, and that they have a round-trip or onward ticket, adequate funds to cover the trip and binding obligations abroad.

Entering the USA

If you have a non-US passport, you must complete an arrival/departure record (form I-94) before you reach the immigration desk. It's usually handed out on the plane along with the customs declaration. For the question, 'Address While in the United States,' give the address where you will spend the first night (a hotel address is fine).

No matter what your visa says, US immigration officers have an absolute authority to refuse admission to the USA or to impose conditions on admission. They will ask about your plans and whether you have sufficient funds; it's a good idea to list an itinerary, produce an onward or round-trip ticket and have at least one major credit card. Showing that you have over $400 per week of your stay should be enough. Don't make too much of having friends, relatives or business contacts in the USA; the immigration official may decide that this will make you more likely to overstay. It also helps to be neatly dressed and polite.

The Department of Homeland Security's registration program, called **US-VISIT** (www.dhs.gov/us-visit), includes every port of entry and nearly every foreign visitor to the USA. For most visitors (excluding, for now, most Canadian and some Mexican citizens), registration consists of having a digital photo and electronic (inkless) fingerprints taken; the process takes less than a minute.

The National Security Entry/Exit Registration System (NSEERS) applies to certain citizens of countries that have been deemed particular risks; however, US officials can require this registration of any traveler. Currently, the countries included are Iran, Iraq, Libya, Sudan and Syria, but be sure to visit www.ice.gov for updates. Registration in these cases also includes a short interview in a separate room and computer verification of all personal information supplied on travel documents.

Short-Term Departures & Reentry

It's temptingly easy to make trips across the border to Canada or Mexico, but upon return to the USA, non-Americans will be subject to the full immigration procedure. Always take your passport when you cross the border. If your immigration card still has plenty of time on it, you will probably be able to reenter using the same one, but if it has nearly expired, you will have to apply for a new card, and border control may want to see your onward air ticket, sufficient funds and so on.

Citizens of most Western countries will not need a visa to visit Canada, so it's really not a problem at all to cross to the Canadian side of Niagara Falls, detour up to Québec or pass through on the way to Alaska. Travelers entering the USA by bus from Canada may be closely scrutinized. A round-trip ticket that takes you back to Canada will most likely make US immigration feel less suspicious. Mexico has a visa-free zone along most of its border with the USA, including the Baja Peninsula and most of the border towns, such as Tijuana and Ciudad Juárez. You'll need a Mexican visa or tourist card if you want to go beyond the border zone. See Border Crossings, p453.

Women Travelers

Women traveling alone or in groups should not expect to encounter any particular problems in the USA. In terms of safety issues, single women just need to practice commonsense street smarts. When first meeting someone, don't advertise where you are staying, or even that you are traveling alone. Americans can be eager to help and even take in solo travelers. However, don't take all offers of help at face value. If someone who seems trustworthy invites you to his or her home, let someone (eg hostel or hotel manager) know where you're going. This advice also applies if you go for a hike by yourself. If something happens and you don't return as expected, you want to know that someone will notice and know where to begin looking for you.

Some women carry a whistle, mace or cayenne-pepper spray in case of assault. If you purchase a spray, contact a police station to find out about local regulations. Laws regarding sprays vary from state to state; federal law prohibits them being carried on planes.

If you are assaulted, consider calling a rape-crisis hotline before calling the police, unless you are in immediate danger, in which case you should call ☎911. But be aware that not all police have as much sensitivity training or experience assisting sexual assault survivors, whereas rape-crisis-center staff will tirelessly advocate on your behalf and act as a link to other community services, including hospitals and the police. Telephone books have listings of local rape-crisis centers, or contact the 24-hour **National Sexual Assault Hotline** (☎800-656-4673; www.rainn.org). Alternatively, go straight to a hospital emergency room.

Transportation

GETTING THERE & AWAY

Flights and tours can be booked online at www.lonelyplanet.com/bookings.

Entering the USA

International visitors flying into the US must register with the US-VISIT program. Your fingerprints will be scanned and a digital photo taken. For more information on visa requirements for visiting the USA, including the Electronic System for Travel Authorization (ESTA) now required before arrival for citizens of Visa Waiver Program (VWP) countries, see p449.

Passports

» Under the Western Hemisphere Travel Initiative (WHTI), all travelers must have a valid machine-readable (MRP) passport when entering the USA by air, land or sea.

» The only exceptions are for most US citizens and some Canadian and Mexican citizens traveling by *land* who can present other WHTI-compliant documents (eg pre-approved 'trusted traveler' cards). For details, check www.getyouhome.gov.

» All foreign passports must meet current US standards and be valid for at least six months longer than your intended stay.

» MRP passports issued or renewed after October 26, 2006 must be e-passports (ie have a digital photo and integrated chip with biometric data). If your passport was issued before October 26, 2005, it must be 'machine readable' (with two lines of letters, numbers and <<< at the bottom); if it was issued between October 26, 2005, and October 25, 2006, it must be machine readable and include a digital photo.

» For more information, consult www.cbp.gov/travel.

Air

Airports

The western USA's primary international airports:

Los Angeles International Airport (LAX; www.lawa.org/lax) California's largest and busiest airport, 20 miles southwest of downtown LA, near the coast.

San Francisco International Airport (SFO; www.flysfo.com) Northern California's major hub, 14 miles south of downtown, on San Francisco Bay.

Seattle-Tacoma International (SEA; www.portseattle.org/seatac) Known locally as 'Sea-Tac'.

Major regional airports with limited international service (most have wi-fi access – check the website):

Albuquerque International Sunport (ABQ; ☎505-244-7700; www.cabq.gov/airport; wi-fi) Serving Albuquerque and all of New Mexico.

CLIMATE CHANGE & TRAVEL

Every form of transport that relies on carbon-based fuel generates CO^2, the main cause of human-induced climate change. Modern travel is dependent on aeroplanes, which might use less fuel per kilometer per person than most cars but travel much greater distances. The altitude at which aircraft emit gases (including CO^2) and particles also contributes to their climate change impact. Many websites offer 'carbon calculators' that allow people to estimate the carbon emissions generated by their journey and, for those who wish to do so, to offset the impact of the greenhouse gases emitted with contributions to portfolios of climate-friendly initiatives throughout the world. Lonely Planet offsets the carbon footprint of all staff and author travel.

Denver International Airport (DEN; ☎303-342-2000; www.flydenver.com) Serving southern Colorado; if you rent a car in Denver, you can be in northeastern New Mexico in four hours.

LA/Ontario International Airport (ONT; www.lawa.org/ont) In Riverside County, east of LA.

McCarran International Airport (LAS; ☎702-261-5211; www.mccarran.com) Serves Las Vegas, NV, and southern Utah. Las Vegas is 290 miles from the South Rim of Grand Canyon National Park and 277 miles from the North Rim.

Mineta San José International Airport (SJC; www.flysanjose.com) In San Francisco's South Bay.

Oakland International Airport (OAK; www.flyoakland.com) In San Francisco's East Bay.

Palm Springs International Airport (PSP; www.palmspringsairport.com) In the desert, east of LA.

Portland International Airport (PDX; www.flypdx.com) About 12 miles from downtown Portland, OR.

Salt Lake City International Airport (SLC; ☎801-575-2400; www.slcairport.com) Serving Salt Lake City and northern Utah; a good choice if you're headed to the North Rim and the Arizona Strip.

San Diego International Airport (SAN; www.san.org) Four miles northwest of downtown.

Sky Harbor International Airport (PHX; ☎602-273-3300; www.skyharbor.com) Serving Phoenix and the Grand Canyon, it's one of the 10 busiest airports in the country. Phoenix is 220 miles from the South Rim of Grand Canyon National Park and 335 miles from the North Rim.

Tucson International Airport (TUS; ☎520-573-8100; www.tucsonairport.org) Serving Tucson and southern Arizona.

Vancouver International Airport (YVR; www.yvr.ca) Located six miles south of Vancouver, on Sea Island; between Vancouver and the municipality of Richmond.

Security

» To get through airport security checkpoints (30-minute wait times are standard), you'll need a boarding pass and photo ID.

» Some travelers may be required to undergo a secondary screening, involving hand pat-downs and carry-on luggage searches.

» Airport security measures restrict many common items (eg pocket knives) from being carried on planes. Check current restrictions with the **Transportation Security Administration** (TSA; ☎866-289-9673; www.tsa.gov).

» Currently, TSA requires that all carry-on liquids and gels be stored in 3oz or smaller bottles placed inside a quart-sized clear plastic zip-top bag. Exceptions, which must be declared to checkpoint security officers, include medications.

» All checked luggage is screened for explosives. TSA may open your suitcase for visual confirmation, breaking the lock if necessary. Leave your bags unlocked or use a TSA-approved lock like **Travel Sentry** (www.travelsentry.org).

Land

Border Crossings

It is relatively easy crossing from the USA into Canada or Mexico; it's crossing back into the USA that can pose problems if you haven't brought your required documents. Check the ever-changing passport (p452) and visa (p449) requirements with the **US Department of State** (http://travel.state.gov) beforehand. **US Customs and Border Protection** (http://apps.cbp.gov/bwt/) tracks current wait times at every Mexico border crossing.

Some borders are open 24 hours, but most are not.

Have your papers in order, act polite and don't make jokes or casual conversation with US border officials.

At research time, drug cartel violence and crime were serious dangers along the US–Mexico border. See p454 for more details.

Bus

» US-based **Greyhound** (☎800-231-2222, international customer service 214-849-8100; www.greyhound.com) and **Greyhound Mexico** (☎01-800-010-0600; www.greyhound.com.mx) have cooperative service, with direct buses between main towns in Mexico and the US.

» Northbound buses from Mexico can take some time to cross the US border, since US immigration may insist on checking every person on board.

» **Greyhound Canada** (☎800-661-8747; www.greyhound.ca) routes between Canada and the US usually require transferring buses at the border.

» Greyhound's Discovery Pass (p456) allows unlimited travel in both the USA and Canada.

Car & Motorcycle

» If you're driving into the USA from Canada or Mexico, bring your vehicle's registration papers, liability insurance and driver's license; an international driving permit (IDP) is a good supplement, but not required.

» If you're renting a car or motorcycle, ask if the agency allows its vehicles to be taken across the Mexican or Canadian border; chances are it doesn't.

TO/FROM CANADA

» Canadian auto insurance is typically valid in the USA, and vice-versa.

» If your papers are in order, taking your own car across the US–Canada border is usually quick and easy.

CROSSING THE MEXICAN BORDER

At the time of research, the issue of crime-related violence in Mexico was front and center in the international press. Nogales, Arizona, for example, is safe for travelers, but Nogales, Mexico was a major locus for the drug trade and its associated violence. Travelers should also exercise extreme caution in Tijuana. We cannot safely recommend crossing the border for an extended period until the security situation changes. You're fine for day trips, but anything past that may be risky.

The State Department recommends that travelers visit its **website** (http://travel.state.gov/travel/cis_pa_tw/cis/cis_970.html) before traveling to Mexico. Here you can check for travel updates and warnings and confirm the latest border-crossing requirements. Before leaving, US Citizens can sign up for the **Smart Traveler Enrollment Program** (STEP; http://travel.state.gov/travel/tips/registration/registration_4789.html) to receive email updates prior to departure.

US and Canadian citizens returning from Mexico must present a US Passport or Passport Card and Enhanced Driver's License or a Trusted Traveler Card (either NEXUS, SENTRI or FAST cards). US and Canadian children under age 16 can also enter using their birth certificate, a Consular Report of Birth Abroad, Naturalization Certificate or Canadian Citizenship Card. All other nationals must carry their passport and, if needed, visas for entering Mexico and reentering the US. Regulations change frequently, so get the latest scoop at www.cbp.gov.

» On weekends and holidays, especially in summer, border-crossing traffic can be heavy and waits long.

» Occasionally the authorities of either country decide to search a car *thoroughly*. Remain calm and be polite.

TO/FROM MEXICO

» Very few car-rental companies will let you take a car from the US into Mexico.

» US auto insurance is not valid in Mexico, so even a short trip into Mexico's border region requires you to buy Mexican car insurance, available for around $25 per day at most border crossings, as well as from **AAA** (☎800-874-7532; www.aaa.com).

» For a longer driving trip into Mexico beyond the border zone or Baja California, you'll need a Mexican *permiso de importación temporal de vehículos* (temporary vehicle import permit).

» Unless you're planning an extended stay in Tijuana, taking a car across the Mexican border is more trouble than it's worth. Instead take the trolley from San Diego or leave your car on the US side and walk across.

» Expect long border-crossing waits, as security has tightened in recent years.

» See Lonely Planet's *Mexico* guide for details, or call Mexico's **tourist information number** (☎800-446-3942) in the USA.

Train

» **Amtrak** (☎800-872-7245; www.amtrakcascades.com) operates daily Cascades rail service with thruway bus service between Vancouver, BC, in Canada and Seattle, WA.

» **VIA Rail** (☎888-842-7245; www.viarail.ca) also serves the Pacific Northwest and Canada.

» US/Canadian customs and immigration inspections happen at the border, not upon boarding.

» From Seattle, Amtrak's *Coast Starlight* (p460) connects south to several destinations in California en route to LA.

» For more details about Amtrak trains, including costs, reservations, and passes, see p460.

» Currently, no train service connects Arizona or California with Mexico.

GETTING AROUND

Air

The domestic air system is extensive and reliable, with dozens of competing airlines, hundreds of airports and thousands of flights daily. Flying is usually more expensive than traveling by bus, train or car, but it's the best option if you're in a hurry.

Airlines in the Western USA

Overall, air travel in the USA is very safe (much safer than driving on the nation's highways); for comprehensive details by carrier, check out **Airsafe.com** (www.airsafe.com).

The main domestic carriers in the West:

Alaska Airlines/Horizon Air (☎800-252-7522/547-9308; www.alaskaair.com) Serves Alaska and the western US, with flights to the East Coast and Hawaii.

American Airlines (☎800-433-7300; www.aa.com) Nationwide service.

Continental Airlines (☎800-523-3273; www.continental.com) Nationwide service.

Delta Air Lines (☎800-221-1212; www.delta.com) Nationwide service.

Frontier Airlines (☎800-432-1359; www.frontierairlines.com) Denver-based airline with nationwide service, including to Alaska.

Hawaiian Airlines (☎800-367-5320; www.hawaiianair.com) Serves the Hawaiian Islands and the West Coast, plus Las Vegas and Phoenix.

JetBlue Airways (☎800-538-2583; www.jetblue.com) Nonstop connections between eastern and western US cities, plus Florida, New Orleans and Texas.

Southwest Airlines (☎800-435-9792; www.southwest.com) Service across the continental USA.

Spirit Airlines (☎800-772-7117; www.spiritair.com) Florida-based airline; serves many US gateway cities.

United Airlines (☎800-864-8331; www.united.com) Nationwide service.

US Airways (☎800-428-4322; www.usairways.com) Nationwide service.

Virgin America (☎877-359-8474; www.virginamerica.com) Flights between East and West Coast cities and Las Vegas.

Bicycle

Regional bicycle touring is popular. It means coasting over winding back roads (because bicycles are often not permitted on freeways), and calculating progress in miles per day, not miles per hour. Cyclists must follow the same rules of the road as automobiles, but don't expect drivers to respect your right of way. Wearing a helmet is mandatory for riders under 18 years of age.

Some helpful resources for cyclists:

Adventure Cycling Association (www.adventurecycling.org) Excellent online resource for purchasing bicycle-friendly maps, long-distance route guides and gadgets.

Better World Club (☎866-238-1137; www.betterworldclub.com) Annual membership ($40, plus $12 enrollment fee) entitles you to two 24-hour emergency roadside pickups with transportation to the nearest bike repair shop within a 30-mile radius.

Rental & Purchase

» You can rent bikes by the hour, the day or the week in most cities and major towns.

» Rentals start from around $10 per day for beach cruisers up to $45 or more for mountain bikes; ask about multiday and weekly discounts.

» Most rental companies require a credit card security deposit of $200 or more.

» Buy new models from specialty bike shops, sporting-goods stores and discount-warehouse stores, or used from notice boards at hostels, cafes and universities.

» To buy or sell used bikes, check online bulletin boards like **Craigslist** (www.craigslist.org).

Transporting Bicycles

» If you tire of pedaling, some local buses and trains are equipped with bicycle racks.

» Greyhound transports bicycles as luggage (surcharge $30 to $40), provided the bicycle is disassembled and placed in a box ($10, available at some terminals).

» Most of Amtrak's *Cascades, Pacific Surfliner, Capital Corridor* and *San Joaquin* trains feature onboard racks where you can secure your bike unboxed; try to reserve a spot when making your ticket reservation (surcharge $5 to $10).

» On Amtrak trains without racks, bikes must be put in a box ($15) and checked as luggage (fee $5). Not all stations or trains offer checked-baggage service.

» Before flying, you'll need to disassemble your bike and box it as checked baggage; contact the airline directly for details, including applicable surcharges (typically $50 to $100, sometimes more).

Boat

There is no river or canal public transportation system in the West, but there are many smaller, often state-run, coastal ferry services. Most larger ferries will transport private cars, motorcycles and bicycles. For details, see the regional chapters.

Off the coast of Washington, ferries reach the scenic San Juan Islands (p201). Several of California's Channel Islands (p111) are accessible by boat, as is Catalina Island, offshore from Los Angeles. On San Francisco Bay, regular ferries operate between San Francisco and Sausalito, Larkspur, Tiburon, Angel Island, Oakland, Alameda and Vallejo.

Bus

Greyhound (☎800-231-2222; www.greyhound.com) is the major long-distance bus company, with routes throughout the USA and Canada. To improve efficiency and profitability, Greyhound has recently stopped service to many small towns; routes generally trace major highways and stop at larger population centers. To reach country towns on rural roads, you may need to transfer to local or county bus systems; Greyhound can usually provide their contact information.

Most baggage has to be checked in; label it loudly and clearly to avoid it getting lost. Larger items, including skis, surfboards and bicycles, can be transported, but there may be an extra charge. Call to check.

TRAVELING TO ALASKA AND HAWAII

Alaska

At the northwest tip of North America lies the USA's 49th state, Alaska. It's the biggest state by far, and home to stupendous mountains, massive glaciers and amazing wildlife. Mt McKinley (the continent's highest peak) is here, as are huge numbers of humpback whales and bald eagles. See Lonely Planet's *Alaska* guide for details.

The majority of visitors to Alaska fly into **Ted Stevens Anchorage International Airport** (ANC; http://dot.alaska.gov/anc;). **Alaska Airlines** (800-252-7522; www.alaskaair.com) has direct flights to Anchorage from Seattle, Chicago, Los Angeles and Denver. It also flies between many towns within Alaska, including daily north-/southbound flights year-round through southeast Alaska, with stops at all main towns including Ketchikan and Juneau. **Delta** (800-221-1212; www.delta.com) offers direct flights from Minneapolis, Phoenix and Salt Lake City, while **Continental** (800-525-0280; www.continental.com) flies nonstop from Houston, Chicago, Denver and San Francisco. There are also daily flights from Seattle to Juneau.

By ferry it takes almost a week on the **Alaska Marine Highway** (800-642-0066; www.dot.state.ak.us/amhs/pubs), which connects Bellingham, WA, with 14 towns in southeast Alaska. The complete trip (Bellingham to Haines; $353, 3½ days) stops at ports along the way and should be scheduled in advance. Alaska Marine Highway ferries are equipped to handle cars ($462), but space must be reserved months ahead.

The Alaska–Canada Military Hwy is today the Alcan (the Alaska Hwy). This 1390-mile road starts at Dawson Creek in British Columbia, ends at Delta Junction (northeast of Anchorage) and in-between it winds through the vast wilderness of northwest Canada and Alaska. The driving distance between Seattle and Anchorage is about 2250 miles.

Hawaii

Floating all by itself more than 2500 miles off the California coast, Hawaii enjoys a unique sense of self, separate from the US mainland. On its islands you can hike across ancient lava flows, learn to surf and paddleboard, snorkel with green turtles or kayak to your own deserted island. The primary islands are O'ahu, Hawaii the Big Island, Maui, Lana'i, Moloka'i and Kaua'i. No matter the adventure or the island, encounters with nature are infused with the Hawaiian sensibilities of *aloha 'aina* and *malama 'aina* – love and care for the land. See Lonely Planet's *Hawaii* guide for details.

About 99% of visitors to Hawaii arrive by air, and the majority of flights – both international and domestic – arrive at **Honolulu International Airport** (HNL; http://hawaii.gov/hnl) on O'ahu. In Maui, the **Kahului Airport** (OGG; http://hawaii.gov/ogg) is about 25 minutes from Kihei and 45 minutes from Lahaina.

Most cruises to Hawaii include stopovers in Honolulu and on Maui, Kaua'i and the Big Island. Cruises usually last two weeks, with fares starting at around $100 per person per day. Popular cruise lines include **Holland America** (www.hollandamerica.com), **Princess** (www.princess.com) and **Royal Caribbean** (www.royalcaribbean.com).

The frequency of bus services varies widely. Despite the elimination of many tiny destinations, nonexpress Greyhound buses still stop every 50 to 100 miles to pick up passengers. Long-distance buses stop for meal breaks and driver changes.

Greyhound buses are usually clean, comfortable and reliable. The best seats are typically near the front away from the bathroom. Limited onboard amenities include freezing air-con (bring a sweater) and slightly reclining seats; select buses have electrical outlets and wi-fi. Smoking on board is prohibited.

Many bus stations are clean and safe, but some are in dodgy areas. Some towns have just a flag stop. If you are boarding at one of these, pay the driver with exact change.

Bus Passes

Greyhound's **Discovery Pass** (www.discoverypass.com), which is available to both domestic and international travelers, allows unlimited, unrestricted travel for periods of seven ($246), 15 ($356), 30 ($456) or 60 ($556) consecutive days in both the USA and Canada. This pass is also accepted by a few dozen regional bus companies; check with Greyhound for a list.

You can buy passes at select Greyhound terminals up to two hours before departure, or purchase them online at least 14 days in advance, then pick them up using the same credit card, with photo ID, at least an hour before boarding.

Costs

For lower fares, purchase tickets seven to 14 days in advance. Round trips and Monday through Thursday travel may be cheaper.

Discounts (on unrestricted fares only) are available for seniors over 62 (5%), students (20%) with a Student Advantage Card (p443) and children aged two to 11 (25%).

Special promotional discounts, such as 50% off companion fares, are often available on the Greyhound website, though they may come with restrictions or blackout periods.

Reservations

Greyhound bus tickets can be bought over the phone or online. You can print tickets at home or pick them up at the terminal using 'Will Call' service (bring photo ID).

Seating is normally first-come, first-served. Greyhound recommends arriving an hour before departure to get a seat. Travelers with disabilities who need special assistance should call ☎800-752-4841 (TDD/TTY ☎800-345-3109) at least 48 hours before traveling. Wheelchairs are accepted as checked baggage and service animals are allowed on board.

Car & Motorcycle

A car allows maximum flexibility and convenience, and it's particularly helpful if you want to explore rural America and its wide-open spaces.

For recommended driving routes, turn to the road trips chapter (p32) and Scenic Drive boxed texts throughout the regional chapters.

Automobile Associations

For 24-hour emergency roadside assistance, free maps and discounts on lodging, attractions, entertainment, car rentals and more:

American Automobile Association (AAA; ☎800-874-7532; www.aaa.com) Add-on coverage for RVs and motorcycles, and reciprocal agreements with some international auto clubs (eg CAA in Canada, AA in the UK) – bring your membership card from home.

Better World Club (☎866-238-1137; www.betterworldclub.com) Ecofriendly alternative supports environmental causes and also offers cyclists' emergency roadside assistance (see p455).

Driver's License

Foreign visitors can legally drive a car in the USA for up to 12 months using their home driver's license. However, an international driving permit (IDP) will have more credibility with US traffic police, especially if your home license doesn't have a photo or isn't in English. Your automobile association at home can issue an IDP, valid for one year, for a small fee. Always carry your home license together with the IDP.

To drive a motorcycle in the USA, you will need either a valid US state motorcycle license or an IDP specially endorsed for motorcycles.

Insurance

When renting a car, check your auto-insurance policy from home or your travel insurance policy to see if you're already covered. If not, expect to pay about $20 per day.

Insurance against damage to the car itself, called Collision Damage Waiver (CDW) or Loss Damage Waiver (LDW), costs another $20 per day; the deductible may require you to pay the first $100 to $500 for any repairs. Some credit cards cover this, provided you charge the entire cost of the car rental to the card. If there's an accident you may have to pay the rental-car company first and then seek reimbursement from the credit-card company. Check your credit card's policy carefully before renting.

Rental

CAR

To rent your own wheels, you'll typically need to be at least 25 years old, hold a valid driver's license and have a major credit card, *not* a check or debit card. A few companies may rent to drivers under 25 but over 21 for a surcharge (around $25 per day). If you don't have a credit card, you may occasionally be able to make a large cash deposit instead.

With advance reservations, you can often get an economy-size vehicle with unlimited mileage from around $30 per day, plus insurance, taxes and fees. Weekend and weekly rates are usually more economical. Airport

USEFUL BUS ROUTES

SERVICE	PRICE ($)	DURATION (HR)
Las Vegas–Los Angeles	42-68	6
Los Angeles–San Francisco	45-71	8
Phoenix–Tucson	21-28	2
Seattle–Portland	30-44	4
Denver–Salt Lake City	76-106	10-12¼

locations may have cheaper rates but higher fees; if you get a fly-drive package, local taxes may be extra when you pick up the car. City-center branches may offer free pick-ups and drop-offs.

Rates generally include unlimited mileage, but expect surcharges for additional drivers and one-way rentals. Some rental companies let you pay for your last tank of gas upfront; this is rarely a good deal.

Major international car-rental companies:

Alamo (877-222-9075; www.alamo.com)

Avis (800-331-1212; www.avis.com)

Budget (800-527-0700; www.budget.com)

Dollar (800-800-3665; www.dollar.com)

Enterprise (800-261-7331; www.enterprise.com)

Hertz (800-654-3131; www.hertz.com)

National (877-222-9058; www.nationalcar.com)

Thrifty (800-847-4389; www.thrifty.com)

You might get a better deal by booking through discount-travel websites like **Priceline** (www.priceline.com) or **Hotwire** (www.hotwire.com), or by using online travel-booking sites, such as **Expedia** (www.expedia.com), **Orbitz** (www.orbitz.com) or **Travelocity** (www.travelocity.com).

A few major car-rental companies (including Avis, Budget, Enterprise, Hertz and Thrifty) offer 'green' fleets of hybrid or biofueled rental cars, but they're in short supply. Reserve well in advance and expect to pay significantly more for these models. Also try:

Simply Hybrid (323-653-0011, 888-359-0055; www.simplyhybrid.com) In Los Angeles. Free delivery and pick-up from some locations with a three-day minimum rental.

Zipcar (866-494-7227; www.zipcar.com) Available in 22 California cities (mostly along the coast), this car-sharing club charges usage fees (per hour or daily), including free gas, insurance (damage fee of up to $500 may apply) and limited mileage. Apply online (foreign drivers OK); annual membership $50, application fee $25. Also available in larger cities in Colorado, New Mexico, Oregon and Washington.

To compare independent car-rental companies, try **Car Rental Express** (www.carrentalexpress.com), which is especially useful for finding cheaper long-term rentals. Independent companies that may rent to drivers under 25:

Rent-a-Wreck (877-877-0700; www.rentawreck.com) Minimum rental age and surcharges vary by location.

Super Cheap Car Rental (www.supercheapcar.com) Normally surcharge for drivers aged 21 to 24; daily fee applies for drivers aged 18 to 21.

For wheelchair-accessible van rentals, see p449.

MOTORCYCLE & RECREATIONAL VEHICLE (RV)

If you dream of cruising across America on a Harley, **EagleRider** (888-900-9901; www.eaglerider.com) has offices in major cities nationwide and rents other kinds of adventure vehicles, too. Motorcycle rental and insurance are expensive.

Companies specializing in RV and camper rentals:

Adventures on Wheels (866-787-3682; www.wheels9.com)

Cruise America (800-671-8042; www.cruiseamerica.com)

Happy Travel Campers (800-370-1262; www.camperusa.com)

Road Conditions & Hazards

Road hazards include potholes, city commuter traffic, wandering wildlife and distracted and enraged drivers.

Where winter driving is an issue, many cars are fitted with steel-studded snow tires; snow chains are sometimes required in mountain areas. Driving off-road, or on dirt roads, is often forbidden by rental-car companies, and it can be very dangerous in wet weather.

In deserts and range country, livestock sometimes graze next to unfenced roads. These areas are signed as 'Open Range' or with the silhouette of a steer. Where deer and other wild animals frequently appear roadside, you'll see signs with the silhouette of a leaping deer. Take these signs seriously, particularly at night.

For nationwide traffic and road-closure information, visit www.fhwa.dot.gov/trafficinfo/index.htm.

For current road conditions within a state, call 511. From outside a state, try:

Arizona (888-411-7623; www.az511.com)

California (800-427-7623; www.dot.ca.gov)

Colorado (303-639-1111; www.cotrip.org)

Idaho (888-432-7623; http://511.idaho.gov/)

Montana (800-226-7623; www.mdt.mt.gov/travinfo/)

Nevada (877-687-6237; www.safetravelusa.com/nv)

New Mexico (800-432-4269; http://m.nmroads.com)

Oregon (503-588-2941; www.tripcheck.com)

Utah (866-511-8824; www.commuterlink.utah.gov)

Washington (800-695-7623; www.wsdot.wa.gov/traffic/)

Wyoming (888-996-7623; www.wyoroad.info)

Road Rules

» Cars drive on the right-hand side of the road.

» The use of seat belts and child safety seats is required in every state. Most car rental agencies rent child safety

ROAD DISTANCES (MILES)

	Denver	Grand Canyon National Park (South Rim)	Las Vegas	Los Angeles	Phoenix	Portland	San Francisco	Santa Fe	Seattle
Grand Canyon National Park (South Rim)	68								
Las Vegas	750	270							
Los Angeles	1020	485	270						
Phoenix	825	215	285	375					
Portland	1260	1330	1020	965	1335				
San Francisco	1270	790	570	380	750	635			
Santa Fe	395	455	635	850	530	1450	1145		
Seattle	1330	1365	1165	1135	1500	175	810	1545	
Yellowstone National Park	530	810	670	950	920	795	1000	820	875

seats for around $12 per day, but you must reserve them when booking.

» In some states, motorcyclists are required to wear helmets.

» On interstate highways, the speed limit is sometimes raised to 75mph. Unless otherwise posted, the speed limit is generally 55mph or 65mph on highways, 25mph to 35mph in cities and towns and as low as 15mph in school zones (strictly enforced during school hours). It's forbidden to pass a school bus when its lights are flashing.

» When emergency vehicles (ie police, fire or ambulance) approach from either direction, pull over safely and get out of the way.

» In an increasing number of states, it is illegal to talk on a handheld cell (mobile) phone while driving; use a hands-free device or pull over to take your call.

» The maximum legal blood-alcohol concentration for drivers is 0.08%. Penalties are very severe for 'DUI' – driving under the influence of alcohol and/or drugs. Police can give roadside sobriety checks to assess if you've been drinking or using drugs. If you fail, they'll require you take a breath test, urine test or blood test to determine the level of alcohol or drugs in your body. Refusing to be tested is treated the same as if you'd taken the test and failed.

» In some states it is illegal to carry 'open containers' of alcohol in a vehicle, even if they are empty.

Local Transportation

Except in cities, public transport is rarely the most convenient option, and coverage to outlying towns and suburbs can be sparse. However, it is usually cheap, safe and reliable. See the regional chapters for details.

Airport Shuttles

Shuttle buses provide inexpensive and convenient transport to/from airports in most cities. Most are 12-seat vans; some have regular routes and stops (which include the main hotels) and some pick up and deliver passengers 'door to door' in their service area. Costs average $15 to $30 per person.

Bicycle

Some cities are more amenable to bicycles than others, but most have at least a few dedicated bike lanes and paths, and bikes can usually be carried on public transportation. See p455 for more on cycling in the USA.

Bus

Most cities and larger towns have dependable local bus systems, though they are often designed for commuters and provide limited service in the evening and on weekends. Costs range from free to between $1 and $3 per ride.

Subway & Train

The largest systems are in Los Angeles and the San Francisco Bay Area. Other cities may have small, one- or two-line rail systems that mainly serve downtown.

Taxi

» Taxis are metered, with flag-fall fees of $2.50 to $3.50, plus $2 to $3 per mile. Credit cards may be accepted.

» Taxis may charge extra for baggage and/or airport pick-ups.

» Drivers expect a 10% to 15% tip, rounded up to the next dollar.

» Taxis cruise the busiest areas in large cities, but elsewhere you may need to call a cab company.

Train

Amtrak (☎800-872-7245; www.amtrak.com) operates a fairly extensive rail system throughout the USA. Fares vary according to the type of train and seating (eg reserved or unreserved coach seats, business class, sleeping compartments). Trains are comfortable, if a bit slow, and are equipped with dining and lounge cars on long-distance routes.

Amtrak routes in the West:

California Zephyr Daily service between Chicago and Emeryville (from $149, 52 hours), near San Francisco, via Denver, Salt Lake City, Reno and Sacramento.

Coast Starlight Travels the West Coast daily from Seattle to LA (from $104, 35 hours) via Portland, Sacramento, Oakland and Santa Barbara; wi-fi may be available.

Southwest Chief Daily departures between Chicago and LA (from $149, 44 hours) via Kansas City, Albuquerque, Flagstaff and Barstow.

Sunset Limited Thrice-weekly service between New Orleans and LA (from $138, 47 hours) via Houston, San Antonio, El Paso, Tucson and Palm Springs.

USEFUL TRAIN ROUTES

SERVICE	PRICE ($)	DURATION (HR)
Los Angeles–Flagstaff	148	11
Los Angeles–Oakland/San Francisco	54	12
San Francisco/Emeryville–Salt Lake City	180	18
Seattle–Oakland/San Francisco	154	23

Costs

Purchase tickets at train stations, by phone or online. Fares depend on the day of travel, the route, the type of seating, etc. Fares may be slightly higher during peak travel times (eg summer). Round-trip tickets cost the same as two one-way tickets.

Usually seniors over 62 and students with an ISIC or Student Advantage Card (p443) receive a 15% discount, while up to two children aged two to 15 who are accompanied by an adult get 50% off. AAA members save 10%. Special promotions can become available anytime, so check the website or ask.

Reservations

Reservations can be made any time from 11 months in advance up to the day of departure. Space on most trains is limited, and certain routes can be crowded, especially during summer and holiday periods, so it's a good idea to book as far in advance as you can; this also gives you the best chance of fare discounts.

Train Passes

» Amtrak's **USA Rail Pass** (www.amtrak.com) is valid for coach-class travel for 15 ($389), 30 ($579) or 45 ($749) days; children aged two to 15 pay half-price.

» Actual travel is limited to eight, 12 or 18 one-way 'segments,' respectively. A segment is *not* the same as a one-way trip; if reaching your destination requires riding more than one train, you'll use multiple pass segments.

» Purchase rail passes online and make advance reservations for each travel segment.

» For travel within California, consider the seven-day California Rail Pass (adult/child $159/$80).

Scenic Routes

» **Cumbres & Toltec Scenic Railroad** Living, moving museum from Chama, NM, into Colorado's Rocky Mountains (p390).

» **Durango & Silverton Narrow Gauge Railroad** Ends at historic mining town Silverton in Colorado's Rocky Mountains (p266).

» **Mount Hood Railroad** Winds through the scenic Columbia River Gorge outside Portland, OR (p223).

» **Skunk Train** Runs between Fort Bragg, CA, on the coast and Willits further inland, passing through redwoods (p155).

» **Grand Canyon Railway** Vintage steam and diesel locomotives with family-oriented entertainment runs between Williams, AZ, and Grand Canyon National Park (p335).

Also worth riding is Pikes Peak Cog Railway (p248), an 8.9-mile track outside Colorado Springs that climbs from a canyon to above the timberline.

behind the scenes

SEND US YOUR FEEDBACK

We love to hear from travelers – your comments keep us on our toes and help make our books better. Our well-traveled team reads every word on what you loved or loathed about this book. Although we cannot reply individually to postal submissions, we always guarantee that your feedback goes straight to the appropriate authors, in time for the next edition. Each person who sends us information is thanked in the next edition – and the most useful submissions are rewarded with a free book.

Visit **lonelyplanet.com/contact** to submit your updates and suggestions or to ask for help. Our award-winning website also features inspirational travel stories, news and discussions.

Note: We may edit, reproduce and incorporate your comments in Lonely Planet products such as guidebooks, websites and digital products, so let us know if you don't want your comments reproduced or your name acknowledged. For a copy of our privacy policy visit lonelyplanet.com/privacy.

AUTHOR THANKS

Amy C Balfour

Thank you Suki and the West team for top-notch editing and mapping. Big cheers to my intrepid co-authors. Many thanks to Deb Corcoran, Tucson's greatest docent, and Judy Hellmich-Bryan, who provided the latest news for Grand Canyon National Park. A special shout-out to Lucy, Michael, Madeline, Claire and Clay Gordon for their hospitality and Phoenix insights. Thanks also Rob Hill, Mark Baker and numerous guides and tipsters along the way.

Michael Benanav

Thank you, Whitney George in Ruidoso, for a great story about one Mike the Midget and a mysterious village beneath Bonita Lake. I owe the biggest thanks to Kelly and Luke, who always let me go and always welcome me back.

Andrew Bender

Suki Gear, Sam Benson, Regis St Louis and Justin Flynn, for the opportunity and their good cheer and advice.

Sara Benson

Thanks to Suki Gear, Regis St Louis, my talented USA co-authors and everyone at Lonely Planet for making this book happen. I'm grateful to all those I met on the road who shared their local expertise and tips, from park rangers to brewpub barflies, and also to my friends and family who live in the Golden State, especially the Picketts for their Lake Tahoe hospitality. PS to MSC Jr: Whew! Glad that avalanche didn't kill us.

Alison Bing

Many thanks and crushing California bear hugs to editor Suki Gear, San Francisco city guide co-author John Vlahides, co-authors Regis St Louis and Sam Benson, editors Anna Metcalfe and Sasha Baskett, but above all Marco Flavio Marinucci, who made waiting for a Muni bus the adventure of a lifetime.

Nate Cavalieri

Thanks to my partner Florence Chien for joining my research travels through Northern California. (Sorry about the speeding tickets.) Thanks also to the lovely people at Lonely Planet and particularly for the enthusiasm of commissioning editor and mentor Suki Gear.

Sarah Chandler

Suki Gear, thanks for trusting me to get into enough (but not too much) trouble in Sin City. My trusty co-pilot, the intrepid Jennifer Christensen, deserves serious props for remaining calm during flat tires, blizzards, and a losing streak in the smokey blackjack room of the Hotel Nevada. Finally, to Jack and everyone at the Hard Rock, thanks for showing me how the locals rock Vegas nightlife (fearlessly, of course).

Lisa Dunford
I always meet so many kindred spirits on the Utah road. Thanks go to Nan Johnson, Peggy Egan, Trista Rayner, Nicole Muraro, David Belz, Jessica Kunzer, Lisa Varga and Ty Markham, among others. I very much enjoyed talking to you all. Thanks, too, to the many park rangers I met, for the ever-helpful job they do.

Bridget Gleeson
I'm grateful to my sister Molly, my brother-in-law Germán Parra, and my dear friend Starla Silver for their hospitality in southern California – and to all their friends for their dining recommendations (and willingness to go to Disneyland). Thanks to my mother, as always, for joining me on the road.

Beth Kohn
All the usual suspects get thanks again, especially the fabulous multitasking Suki Gear and the dynamo known as Sam Benson. California cohorts and experts this time around included Agent 'Pedal-to-the-metal' Moller, Felix 'Hella Loves Oakland' Thomson, Jenny 'Stink' G, Dillon 'The Scientist' Dutton and Julia 'Wawona' Brashares, plus all the helpful and patient rangers at Yosemite National Park. Kudos to Regis St Louis, Alison Lyall and Anna Metcalfe for all their crucial work.

Bradley Mayhew
Thanks to all the Yellowstone Park rangers who took time to answer my many questions and to my wife Kelli who gave me her opinion on the best mussels from Billings to Bozeman.

Carolyn B McCarthy
Sincere thanks goes out to all those who helped me, especially the park rangers who are so committed to preserving our great wilderness. Richard Carrier proved adept at attacking the snowy passes of southern Colorado. Thanks also to Louise, Conan, Anne and the Cameron Johns family for their thoughtful hospitality. Virtual beers go out to ace authors Bradley Mayhew, Brendan Sainsbury and Regis St Louis for their collaboration.

Brendan Sainsbury
Thanks to all the untold bus drivers, tourist info volunteers, restaurateurs, national park rangers, weather forecasters, oenologists and innocent bystanders who helped me during my research. Special thanks to Andy McKee, for his hiking company in the Glacier National Park; and Scott Davies, for his intriguing insights into Pike Place Market in Seattle. Thanks also to my wife Liz and five-year-old son Kieran for their company on the road.

Andrea Schulte-Peevers
Big thanks to Suki Gear for letting me have another shot at California. A heartfelt thank you also to my husband David for being such good company while tooling around the desert. Big kudos to all the good folks who shared their local insights, steered me in the right direction and made helpful introductions, including Hillary Angel, Mark Graves, Cheryl Chipman and Christopher Vonloudermilk.

John A Vlahides
I owe heartfelt thanks to my commissioning editor, Suki Gear, and co-authors, Sam Benson and Regis St Louis, for their stellar assistance and always-sunny dispositions. And to you, the readers, thank you for letting me be your guide to California Wine Country. Have fun. I know you will.

ACKNOWLEDGMENTS

Climate map data adapted from Peel MC, Finlayson BL & McMahon TA (2007) 'Updated World Map of the Köppen-Geiger Climate Classification', *Hydrology and Earth System Sciences*, 11, 163344.

Cover photograph: View of a barn, Montana; Carol Polich, LPI. Many of the images in this guide are available for licensing from Lonely Planet Images: www.lonelyplanetimages.com.

THIS BOOK

This 1st edition of *Western USA* was written by Amy C Balfour. The content was researched and written by Amy, along with Michael Benanav, Andrew Bender, Sara Benson, Alison Bing, Nate Cavalieri, Sarah Chandler, Lisa Dunford, Bridget Gleeson, Beth Kohn, Bradley Mayhew, Carolyn B McCarthy, Brendan Sainsbury, Andrea Schulte-Peevers and John A Vlahides. This guidebook was commissioned in Lonely Planet's Oakland office, and produced by the following:

Commissioning Editor Suki Gear
Coordinating Editors Pete Cruttenden, Gina Tsarouhas
Coordinating Cartographer Mark Griffiths
Coordinating Layout Designer Lauren Egan
Managing Editors Annelies Mertens, Anna Metcalfe, Angela Tinson
Managing Cartographer Alison Lyall
Managing Layout Designer Chris Girdler
Assisting Editors Anne Mulvaney, Saralinda Turner
Assisting Cartographers Andras Bogdanovits, Xavier Di Toro, Brendan Streager
Assisting Layout Designers Frank Deim, Carlos Solarte
Cover Research Naomi Parker
Internal Image Research Sabrina Dalbesio
Thanks to Ryan Evans, Justin Flynn, Victoria Harrison, Yvonne Kirk, Alison Ridgway, Gerard Walker

ABBREVIATIONS

AZ Arizona
CA California
CO Colorado
ID Idaho
MT Montana
NM New Mexico
NV Nevada
OR Oregon
UT Utah
WA Washington
WY Wyoming

A

B

000 Map pages
000 Photo pages

000 Map pages
000 Photo pages

000 Map pages
000 Photo pages

N

O

000 Map pages
000 Photo pages

P

Q

R

S

000 Map pages
000 Photo pages

000 Map pages
000 Photo pages

how to use this book

These symbols will help you find the listings you want:

- Sights
- Beaches
- Activities
- Courses
- Tours
- Festivals & Events
- Sleeping
- Eating
- Drinking
- Entertainment
- Shopping
- Information/ Transport

These symbols give you the vital information for each listing:

- Telephone Numbers
- Opening Hours
- Parking
- Nonsmoking
- Air-Conditioning
- Internet Access
- Wi-Fi Access
- Swimming Pool
- Vegetarian Selection
- English-Language Menu
- Family-Friendly
- Pet-Friendly
- Bus
- Ferry
- Metro
- Subway
- Tram
- Train

Reviews are organised by author preference.

Look out for these icons:

TOP CHOICE Our author's recommendation

FREE No payment required

A green or sustainable option

Our authors have nominated these places as demonstrating a strong commitment to sustainability – for example by supporting local communities and producers, operating in an environmentally friendly way, or supporting conservation projects.

Map Legend

Sights
- Beach
- Buddhist
- Castle
- Christian
- Hindu
- Islamic
- Jewish
- Monument
- Museum/Gallery
- Ruin
- Winery/Vineyard
- Zoo
- Other Sight

Activities, Courses & Tours
- Diving/Snorkelling
- Canoeing/Kayaking
- Skiing
- Surfing
- Swimming/Pool
- Walking
- Windsurfing
- Other Activity/ Course/Tour

Sleeping
- Sleeping
- Camping

Eating
- Eating

Drinking
- Drinking
- Cafe

Entertainment
- Entertainment

Shopping
- Shopping

Information
- Post Office
- Tourist Information

Transport
- Airport
- Border Crossing
- Bus
- Cable Car/ Funicular
- Cycling
- Ferry
- Metro
- Monorail
- Parking
- S-Bahn
- Taxi
- Train/Railway
- Tram
- Tube Station
- U-Bahn
- Other Transport

Routes
- Tollway
- Freeway
- Primary
- Secondary
- Tertiary
- Lane
- Unsealed Road
- Plaza/Mall
- Steps
- Tunnel
- Pedestrian Overpass
- Walking Tour
- Walking Tour Detour
- Path

Boundaries
- International
- State/Province
- Disputed
- Regional/Suburb
- Marine Park
- Cliff
- Wall

Population
- Capital (National)
- Capital (State/Province)
- City/Large Town
- Town/Village

Geographic
- Hut/Shelter
- Lighthouse
- Lookout
- Mountain/Volcano
- Oasis
- Park
- Pass
- Picnic Area
- Waterfall

Hydrography
- River/Creek
- Intermittent River
- Swamp/Mangrove
- Reef
- Canal
- Water
- Dry/Salt/ Intermittent Lake
- Glacier

Areas
- Beach/Desert
- Cemetery (Christian)
- Cemetery (Other)
- Park/Forest
- Sportsground
- Sight (Building)
- Top Sight (Building)

Carolyn B McCarthy

Rocky Mountains Carolyn became enamored of the Rockies as an undergraduate at Colorado College. She studied, skied and hiked her way through the region, even working as a boot fitter. In the last seven years she has contributed to over a dozen Lonely Planet titles and has written for *National Geographic*, *Outside*, *Lonely Planet Magazine* and other publications. You can follow her Americas blog at www.carolynswildblueyonder.blogspot.com.

Brendan Sainsbury

Rocky Mountains, Pacific Northwest UK-born Brendan lives in White Rock in Canada within baseball-pitching distance (well, almost) of the USA and the Pacific Northwest. He has been researching the area for Lonely Planet since 2007 and his forays across the border have included fine-dining in the San Juan Islands, hitchhiking in western Montana and running 100 miles unassisted across the Cascade Mountains in a so-called endurance race. Brendan is also a co-author of Lonely Planet's current *Washington, Oregon & the Pacific Northwest* guidebook.

Read more about Brendan at:
lonelyplanet.com/members/brendansainsbury

Andrea Schulte-Peevers

California Andrea fell in love with California – its pizzazz, people and sunshine – almost the instant she landed in the Golden State. She grew up in Germany, lived in London and traveled the world before getting a degree from UCLA and embarking on a career in travel writing. Andrea has written or contributed to some 60 Lonely Planet books, including several editions of this one as well as the guides to *California* and *Los Angeles & Southern California*.

John A Vlahides

California John A Vlahides co-hosts the TV series *Lonely Planet: Roads Less Travelled*, screening on National Geographic Channels International. John studied cooking in Paris, with the same chefs who trained Julia Child, and is a former luxury-hotel concierge and member of *Les Clefs d'Or*, the international union of the world's elite concierges. He lives in San Francisco, where he sings tenor with the San Francisco Symphony, and spends free time skiing the Sierra Nevada. Read more about John at JohnVlahides.com, Twitter.com/JohnVlahides.

Read more about John at:
lonelyplanet.com/members/johnvlahides

Alison Bing

California After 18 years in San Francisco, Alison has done everything you're supposed to do in the city and some things you're definitely not, including falling in love on the Haight St bus and eating a Mission burrito in one sitting. Alison contributes to Lonely Planet's Venice, USA, San Francisco and Morocco guides from home bases in San Francisco and Central Italy. Alison holds degrees in art history and international relations – respectable diplomatic credentials she regularly undermines with opinionated culture commentary for newspapers, magazines, TV, radio and books, including Lonely Planet's *USA Trips*, *California*, *San Francisco* and *San Francisco Encounter* guides.

Nate Cavalieri

California A native of central Michigan, Nate Cavalieri lives in Northern California and has crisscrossed the region's back roads by bicycle, bus and rental car on a tireless search for the biggest trees, the best camping and the hoppiest pints of craft beer. In addition to authoring guides on California and Latin America for Lonely Planet, he writes about jazz and pop music and is the Jazz Editor at Rhapsody Music Service. His website is www.natecavalieri.com.

Sarah Chandler

Southwest Long enamored of Sin City's gritty enchantments, Sarah jumped at the chance to sharpen her blackjack skills while delving into the atomic and alien mysteries of rural Nevada. In Vegas, Sarah learned the secret art of bypassing velvet ropes, bounced from buffets to pool parties, and explored the seedy vintage glamour of downtown. Sarah is currently based between the US and Amsterdam, where she works as a writer, actress, and lecturer at Amsterdam University College. When in doubt, she always doubles down.

Lisa Dunford

Southwest As one of the possibly thousands of great, great grand-daughters of Brigham Young, ancestry first drew Lisa to Utah. But it's the incredible red rocks that keep her coming back. Driving the remote backroads outside Bluff, she was once again reminded how here the earth seems at its most elemental. Before becoming a freelance Lonely Planet author 10 years ago, Lisa was a newspaper editor and writer in South Texas. Lisa co-authored Lonely Planet's *Zion & Bryce Canyon National Parks*.

Bridget Gleeson

California A journalist who divides her time between California and Argentina, Bridget has written about food, wine, hotels and adventure travel for Budget Travel, Afar, Delta Sky, Jetsetter, Continental, Tablet Hotels and Mr & Mrs Smith. Follow her travels at www.bridgetgleeson.com.

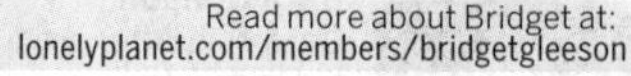

Read more about Bridget at:
lonelyplanet.com/members/bridgetgleeson

Beth Kohn

California A lucky long-time resident of San Francisco, Beth lives to be playing outside or splashing in big puddles of water. For this guide, she hiked and biked Bay Area byways, lugged a bear canister along the John Muir Trail and selflessly soaked in hot springs – for research purposes, of course. An author of Lonely Planet's *Yosemite, Sequoia & Kings Canyon National Parks* and *California* guides. You can see more of Beth's work at www.bethkohn.com.

Bradley Mayhew

Rocky Mountains An expat Brit, Bradley currently calls southeastern Montana home. Half a lifetime of travels through Central Asia, Tibet and Mongolia has made him feel quite at home in Big Sky country. He is the coordinating author of a dozen Lonely Planet guides, including *Tibet*, *Bhutan*, *Nepal*, *Central Asia* and *Yellowstone & Grand Teton National Parks* and he hikes nearby Yellowstone Park and the Beartooth Mountains every chance he gets. Read more about Bradley at www.bradleymayhew.blogspot.com.

OUR STORY

A beat-up old car, a few dollars in the pocket and a sense of adventure. In 1972 that's all Tony and Maureen Wheeler needed for the trip of a lifetime – across Europe and Asia overland to Australia. It took several months, and at the end – broke but inspired – they sat at their kitchen table writing and stapling together their first travel guide, *Across Asia on the Cheap*. Within a week they'd sold 1500 copies. Lonely Planet was born.

Today, Lonely Planet has offices in Melbourne, London and Oakland, with more than 600 staff and writers. We share Tony's belief that 'a great guidebook should do three things: inform, educate and amuse'.

OUR WRITERS

Amy C Balfour

Coordinating Author, Southwest Amy has hiked, biked, skied and gambled her way across the Southwest, finding herself returning again and again to Flagstaff, Monument Valley and, always, the Grand Canyon. On this trip she fell hard for Bisbee and Chiricahua National Monument. When she's not daydreaming about red rocks and green chile hamburgers, she's writing about food, travel and the outdoors. Amy has authored or co-authored 11 guidebooks for Lonely Planet, including *Los Angeles Encounter*, *California*, *Hawaii* and *Arizona*.

Read more about Amy at:
lonelyplanet.com/members/amycbalfour

Michael Benanav

Southwest Michael came to New Mexico in 1992 and quickly fell under its spell; soon after, he moved to a rural village in the Sangre de Cristo foothills, where he still lives. A veteran international traveler, he can't imagine a better place to come home to after a trip. Aside from his work for Lonely Planet, he's authored two nonfiction books and writes and photographs for magazines and newspapers. Read more about Michael at www.michaelbenanav.com.

Andrew Bender

California Andy is a true Angeleno, not because he was born in Los Angeles but because he's made it his own. Two decades ago, this native New Englander packed up the car and drove cross-country to work in film production, and eventually realized that the joy was in the journey (and writing about it). His work has since appeared in the *Los Angeles Times*, *Forbes* and over two dozen Lonely Planet titles. Current obsessions: discovering LA's next great ethnic enclave, and winter sunsets over the bike path in Santa Monica. Read more about Andy at www.wheres-andy-now.com.

Sara Benson

California After graduating from college in Chicago, Sara jumped on a plane to California with just one suitcase and $100 in her pocket. She has bounced around the Golden State ever since, in between stints living in Asia and Hawaii and working as a national park ranger. The author of 50 travel and nonfiction books, Sara dodged avalanches in Lake Tahoe and rockslides along Big Sur's splendid coast while writing this guide. Follow her adventures online at www.indietraveler.blogspot.com and www.twitter.com/indie_traveler.

Read more about Sara at:
lonelyplanet.com/members/Sara_Benson

OVER PAGE MORE WRITERS

Published by Lonely Planet Publications Pty Ltd
ABN 36 005 607 983
1st edition – April 2012
ISBN 978 1 74220 591 5

10 9 8 7 6 5 4 3 2 1
Printed in Singapore